A

GLOSSARY

OF

JUDICIAL AND REVENUE TERMS

A

GLOSSARY

OF

JUDICIAL AND REVENUE TERMS,

AND OF
USEFUL WORDS OCCURRING IN OFFICIAL DOCUMENTS
RELATING TO THE ADMINISTRATION OF THE
GOVERNMENT
OF

BRITISH INDIA,

FROM THE
ARABIC, PERSIAN, HINDUSTÁNÍ, SANSKRIT, HINDÍ,
BENGÁLÍ, URIYA, MARÁTHI, GUZARÁTHÍ, TELUGU,
KARNÁTA, TAMIL, MALAYÁLAM,
AND OTHER LANGUAGES.

BY
H. H. WILSON, M. A., F. R. S.

GYAN

Published by

Gyan Publishing House
5, Ansari Road
Daryaganj, New Delhi-110002
Phone: 011-47034999, 9811692060
E-mail: books@gyanbooks.com

Distribution Network
gyanbooks.com
India, USA, Canada, UK, Australia

ISBN: 978-81-212-7015-1 (PB)
First Published, 1855

2nd Impression 2024

Printed at: Gyan Press, Delhi.

A GLOSSARY OF JUDICIAL AND REVENUE TERMS
Author: H. H. WILSON

A

GLOSSARY

OF

JUDICIAL AND REVENUE TERMS,

AND OF

USEFUL WORDS OCCURRING IN OFFICIAL DOCUMENTS

RELATING TO THE ADMINISTRATION OF THE GOVERNMENT

OF

BRITISH INDIA,

FROM THE

ARABIC, PERSIAN, HINDUSTÁNÍ, SANSKRIT, HINDÍ, BENGÁLÍ, UṚIYA, MARÁṬHI, GUZARÁTHÍ, TELUGU, KARNÁTA, TAMIḺ, MALAYÁLAM, AND OTHER LANGUAGES.

COMPILED AND PUBLISHED UNDER THE AUTHORITY OF THE HONORABLE THE COURT OF DIRECTORS OF THE EAST-INDIA COMPANY.

BY

H. H. WILSON, M.A. F.R.S.

LIBRARIAN TO THE EAST-INDIA COMPANY, AND BODEN PROFESSOR OF SANSKRIT IN THE UNIVERSITY OF OXFORD, &c. &c. &c.

LONDON:

Wm. H. ALLEN AND CO.

BOOKSELLERS TO THE HONORABLE EAST-INDIA COMPANY.

MDCCCLV.

PREFACE.

THE numerous documents relating to the administration of the government of India by the East-India Company which have been printed, and the still more voluminous correspondence which remains in manuscript, have, from the earliest to the most recent dates, been thickly studded with terms adopted from the vernacular languages of the country, and commonly inserted without any explanation of their purport. Various reasons may be assigned for a practice which, to say the least of it, is attended with considerable perplexity to those who have not studied the languages of India at all, and is not free from embarrassment even to many by whom those languages have been in part only, or imperfectly acquired. In many cases, no doubt, it might be difficult or impossible to discover exact equivalents for the native words in English, and the use of the original term most expressively conveys its meaning to those to whom the occasion of its employment is familiar, although they be not Oriental scholars: *Ryot* and *Ryotwár,* for instance, suggest more precise and positive notions in connexion with the subject of the land revenue in the south of India, than would be conveyed by cultivator, or peasant, or agriculturist, or by an agreement for rent or revenue with the individual members of the agricultural classes: in this and similar instances the employment of the original native term is recommended by the advantages of conciseness and precision.

In the far greater number of cases, however, the practice cannot be vindicated by an equally cogent plea, and must be ascribed to other considerations. It may sometimes, perhaps, be assigned to a pedantic affectation of conversancy with the native languages, but it may more frequently be attributed to indolence—to a reluctance to take the trouble of ascertaining the proper sense of the word, and of seeking for a suitable equivalent, even where such an equivalent is at hand, and where the original term denotes nothing peculiar or technical. It is scarcely necessary, for example, to introduce the word *Midde* in its native dress, when it signifies only "an Upper-storied house;" and "Widow" is quite as much to the purpose as *Avírá,* especially when the latter is barbarously transmuted to *Obeera.* It is very obvious, however, that whatever may be the familiarity acquired in some instances with the spoken language of the Courts of Justice and Revenue, that familiarity is restricted to a few of the dialects, and that a critical acquaintance, even with those that are understood, is far from common. This is very evident when, as is sometimes the case, an attempt has been made by officers of unquestioned efficiency in other respects, to analyse etymologically the terms they employ, particularly in regard to the languages of the south of India. Thus it is said by a functionary of more than ordinary merit, and one who was specially selected for his knowledge of the languages, that the last syllable of *Dessaye* is a Canarese term for "mother," when it is nothing more than the abridgment of *adhi,* "over—one who is placed in authority over a district." The same functionary explains *Desmukh,* literally the head or chief (*mukhya*) of a country (*des*), as meaning "ten blows," confounding evidently the Sanscrit *des,* "a country," with the Hindí *das,* "ten," and *mukha,* "face," with the Hindustani *muth,* "a fist."—East-India Selections, iv. 798. In fact, the whole linguistic stock of the major portion of the Civil Service was for many years a little Hindustani and less Persian; and it is only recently that attempts have been made to extend the range of attainment, and place it upon a sound and comprehensive basis.

Whatever the acquirements, however, of those with whom Indian official documents originate, it is undeniable that many of those to whom they are addressed, or for whose information they are designed, members of the Court of Proprietors, of the Court of Directors, of the Board of Controul, the Houses of

Parliament, the British public, pretend to no acquaintance with the languages of India, and to them an interpretation of the native words which come before them is indispensable. A few may have become almost naturalized by repetition, but by far the greater number remain unintelligible. Even of the meaning of those however which have been longest and most extensively current, precise ideas are not always entertained; and it may be doubted if there are many persons, of those who have not been in India, or who have no knowledge of Hindustani, who possess a ready and correct conception of the purport of such frequently recurring terms, as *Ádálat* and *Zamindár*.

But besides the great proportion of those who may feel it their duty to consult the records of the Indian governments for information, without pretending to any conversancy with the Indian languages, many even of those who have been educated for the service of the Company will be occasionally perplexed by the appearance of native terms with which they are unacquainted. The Company's servants at the different Presidencies are not expected to be proficients in the languages spoken in the territories of other Presidencies than their own, and yet they must find it of material benefit to be able to consult their records; while even in their own branch of the service, they will not unfrequently be crossed by unusual designations. The Persian or Hindustani scholar will not, therefore, always be competent to appreciate the value of the Sanskrit and Arabic vocables which constitute the language of Hindu and Mohammadan law. Those languages will but imperfectly prepare the Bengal civilian for Hindí, Bengalí, and Panjabí: they will be of equally little avail in the peninsula for the interpretation of terms pertaining to Tamil, Telugu, Karnáta, and Malayalim; and they will but lamely help the Bombay servant over the intricacies of Maraṭhí and Guzeraṭhí, to say nothing of Sindhí and Marwárí. Even with the scale of acquirements extended as far as may be reasonably expected, the great variety of the prevailing forms of speech in India renders it impossible, perhaps, that even all those which would be of service may be so mastered, that words derived from them will always convey the meanings they bear independently of such explanation as is to be looked for from a Glossary or a Lexicon.

Supposing, indeed, that a much more comprehensive and critical acquaintance with the languages of India existed than that which usually prevails, such knowledge will still not be always sufficient to enable its possessor to recognise a native word, however familiar to him in its original characters, in the unusual and often preposterous form in which it appears when represented by the English alphabet. Of course, English documents cannot admit Oriental letters; and Indian words, when transferred from their native garb to an English dress, are often so strangely disguised, that it is always difficult, sometimes impossible, to identify them. The causes of their transfiguration are easily understood: they may have been written down by the European functionary from native enunciation, agreeably to his conception of the sound, without advertence to the original characters, the only guides entitled to reliance: the ear is far from accurate, particularly the English ear, which is unaccustomed to a definite system of pronunciation in its own alphabet, especially as regards the vowel sounds. The consequences are, an entire misrepresentation of the original spelling, and a total want of consistency, the very same word being written in every possible variety of orthography. Another source of error is the employment of a native amanuensis, who knows a little English, to write the word, and in all likelihood, he will diverge still farther from accuracy than his European superior. The term thus incorrectly and blunderingly set down has to be transcribed repeatedly by native copyists for transmission to higher authority, and eventually, perhaps, to England; and every time that it is re-written there is a renewed probability of error. In this state it comes home, and is here re-copied by English clerks, who are, of course, unable to correct the most palpable mistakes, and are fully qualified to commit more. In the last place, it has to be transferred to the press, the correction of which is entrusted to incompetent revision, and by which fresh blunders are copiously grafted on the already abundant crop. Many printed documents, of the first importance as to their subjects, and upon which very great expense has been incurred by the Company, have been rendered almost useless by the innumerable inaccuracies which disfigure almost every page. The collection, for example, known as Selections from the Judicial and Revenue Records, in four folio volumes, containing many most important and valuable documents, is all but spoiled by the perpetual recurrence of such errors as *Lokar* and *Sokar* for *Lohar; Sale* for *Lal; Derk* and *Desh* for *Derh; Pottar* for *Pot-dár; Swinjammy* for *Sarinjami; Kadarnaibh* for *Kadárambam.* Such as these admit of correction: others are more puzzling, but may be corrected conjecturally: *Bazar-heetick,* is no doubt intended for *Bazar-baithak; Mohcuddum Quaz* appears from the context to be designed for *Mukaddam-ḳarz;*

and *Ooleim kaley* and *Muddum kaley* are intended for *Uttama káli* and *Madhyama káli*. Others, again, baffle conjecture. It passes my ingenuity to propose probable substitutes for *Barhee Mutputti, Herymut desa*, or *Quaeem seodi jumma*. The Selections are not singular in this respect, and strange perversions find their way into official reports, even when printed in India, where competent revision is more plentiful than it should be in this country. In the reports of the judicial proceedings in the Zila Courts we have *Jummee*, and even *Jemmy* for *Janmí*, "one who holds a birthright;" and *Halfan*, "by or upon oath," is metamorphosed to *Hul Fun*. Documents emanating from the highest authority are not exempt from such disfigurement. In the Instructions to the Settlement Officers from the Governor of the North-west Provinces we have *Dhurkast* for *Durkhast;* and in the Decisions of the *Sadr Âdálat* we find *Tun-khaw* for *Tankhwáh*, and *Joonmoohoostee* for *Junum-moohoortee*, "the hour of nativity." Now, whether these be blunders of transcription or typography, they are calculated to perplex even Oriental scholars, and are grave blemishes in documents emanating from authority, and intended to communicate information on which implicit reliance may be placed.

The deficiencies in this respect, of the published and unpublished documents relating to India, as well as the want of a more comprehensive key to the numerous native terms employed than any previously compiled, having been brought to the attention of the Court of Directors in August 1842, it was resolved to adopt measures for forming a Glossary of words in current use in various parts of India, relating to the administration of public business in every department, the want of which had long been found a source of much inconvenience. Under an impression that this could not be effected without the co-operation of the Company's servants locally employed in all parts of India, instructions were given to the Supreme Government of India to call upon the functionaries at the several Presidencies for their assistance. In order to serve as a guide for their proceedings, a rough Glossary, alphabetically arranged, was compiled in the India-House, taken chiefly from a list of words collected by the late Mr. Warden during his residence at Bombay, and from sundry printed collections; and a sufficient number of printed copies were transmitted to India for distribution to the several officers. In this Glossary the words were inserted purposely as they were met with, without any attempt to correct them, or to reduce their spelling to a uniform system; as, in the absence of the native characters, any attempt to represent the words in those of Europe might only have multiplied the obvious inaccuracies of the original collection: their correction was left to the Indian authorities, by whom the proper native orthography could be most readily ascertained, and they were instructed to return the lists in an accurate form, and accompanied by the native characters of the district in which the words were current. The authorities were also directed to add to the collection the many words that were known to be wanting, and to subjoin full, careful, and accurate explanations of their meaning. The copies were printed in such a shape as to admit of the insertion of the requisite additions and emendations, and several hundreds were sent out from time to time, with an expectation expressed that they would be returned in six months from the time of their distribution. The final arrangement of the whole work was to be committed to the compiler of the present publication.

After a much more protracted interval than that of six months, the rough Glossaries found their way back from Bengal and partially from Madras: from Bombay none returned. The latter default was not much to be regretted, for however judicious the design, its execution at the other Presidencies proved almost an entire failure. Many of the lists came back blank; of several the leaves had not been cut; in the far greater number, a mere pretence of doing something was displayed by the insertion of a few terms neither novel nor important; a few afforded some serviceable materials, especially when, as was frequently the case, the task had been transferred to the subordinate officers, Munsiffs, Amíns, Sadr-amíns, and Deputy-collectors, the uncovenanted servants of the Company. Some of these did furnish lists of native terms, of a useful description, written in both the English and native characters. Several of the native officers, however, misapprehended the object of the collection, and admitted a copious infusion of words which had no peculiarly official significations. More than one, indeed, in Upper India, turned to Shakespear's Hindustani Dictionary, and deliberately covered the blank pages of the Glossary with words taken at random from the Lexicon. The practice was too glaringly obvious to be doubted; but it was confessed to me by one of the perpetrators, Mir Shahamat Ali, whom I taxed with it when in England. He was an individual eminently qualified to have responded to the intentions of the Court as an efficient public officer, a scholar, and a man of ability; but so little interest was felt in India in the subject, such was the unwillingness to devote any time or trouble to the task, that even he evaded its performance. The same feelings pervaded the service in Bengal. At Madras, matters were not much better. The returns were collected by the Persian and Telugu translator to the Government, Mr. C. P. Brown, and embodied in one compilation. The character which he gives of those returns shews that they were equally meagre and insufficient as those of Bengal. He has since printed them, enlarged with additions of his own, under the denomination of a *Zillah Dictionary*, the utility of which is somewhat impaired by the erroneous explanations derived from the documents with which he had been furnished. From his aggregate collection in manuscript, some useful terms, however, have been obtained, although their accuracy has been rendered occasionally questionable by the observations of the Board of Revenue on the printed form which was not received in time to be made much use of. From Madras, also, came two serviceable lists supplied by the Residents at Mysore and Hyderabad, Generals Cubbon and Fraser. From Bombay, as already observed, not a single list has been returned. The fate which has attended a measure so judiciously conceived, and so well calculated to have brought together a large body of valuable information of the most authentic character, is far from creditable to the public zeal and philological proficiency of the East-India Company's Civil Service.

One honourable exception must, however, be acknowledged. "Observing with regret that the call for information had not been responded to, except to a very limited extent, by any of the officers under the control of the Board of Revenue of the North-western Provinces," of which he was then a member, the late Sir Henry Elliot—whose early death has deprived the Bengal Civil Service of a most zealous and accomplished Oriental scholar, and an enlightened and efficient public officer—undertook to supply the deficiency, and to put together the information he had collected respecting the tribes, the customs, and the fiscal and agricultural terms current in Upper India. The collection was printed under the modest designation of a Supplement to the Glossary, and contains a number of local terms of the most useful and authentic description, arranged alphabetically according to the order of the English alphabet, but accompanied by the native characters, both Arabic and Sanksrit, and expressed according to the modified system of spelling devised by Dr. Gilchrist, as well as that of Sir William Jones. The greater portion of the contents of this collection are embodied in the present, but some, especially the articles relating to the different Hindu clans and tribes, have been necessarily abbreviated or omitted, as assuming a higher character than that of the mere items of a Glossary, being, in fact, memoirs subservient to the History of India. The north-west provinces of Hindustan limit the extent of the compilation of course to Hindí and Urdu terms, and unfortunately, also, the compilation stops with the letter J. As far, however, as the Supplement goes, it is a contribution to the compilation contemplated by the Court, of which the value and merit cannot be too highly estimated.

The first returns of the blank Glossaries from India having proved that little aid was to be expected from that quarter, it became necessary to look round for other sources of information; and in the first instance, at least, to make use of such as were in print. Of this class were Gladwin's Dictionary of Mohammadan Law and Revenue Terms, Rousseau's Vocabulary of Persian Words in common use in India, and the Indian Vocabulary of Lieutenant Robertson. For the south of India there were the technical terms attached to Morris's Telugu Selections, Brown's Gentoo Vocabulary, and Robertson's Glossary in Tamil and English of words used chiefly in the business of the Courts. There were also, for general reference, the Indices of the Regulations, whether attached to them separately, or as collectively formed by Dale, Fenwick, and Small, the Glossary of the Fifth Report, and, above all, the Dictionaries of all the principal languages, in which a great number of technical terms are necessarily comprised, although the explanations are not always as full and particular as could be wished. The most comprehensive of them in this respect are Major Molesworth's Maraṭhí Dictionary, Reeves's Karnáta Dictionary, and Mohammad Kasim's Dictionary of Guzaraṭhí. The Bengalí Dictionaries of Carey and Houghton are singularly defective in technical and colloquial words. Steele's Summary of the law and custom of Hindu castes in the Presidency of Bombay affords a mass of very valuable information respecting the west of India, although sadly disfigured by an uncouth and unsystematic representation of the original words. These were, in the first instance, available: manuscript materials were at first less abundant, and the only collections in the India House were a Glossary of Maraṭhí terms of some extent and authenticity, compiled for the use of the Bombay Government, and a collection of Malayalim words compiled by the late Mr. Græme. The stock of manuscript materials was, however, speedily and importantly augmented.

A collection of Indian technical terms had been for some time in progress, made by my friend Richard Clarke, Esq., whose connexion with the Privy Council in the matter of Indian appeals had impressed him with the necessity of a general compilation of this description, and whose high position when in India as a judicial servant of the Madras Government, and whose attainments as a Tamil scholar, fully qualified him to supply the want. He had accordingly been diligently engaged in the collection and arrangement of materials for such a work, and had accumulated a large quantity of the most useful words selected from the Regulations, from the Reports of the Committees of Parliament at different dates, from the Selections from the Records, from the early Reports of cases decided in the Ṣadr Âdálat of Calcutta, from Harington's Analysis of the Regulations, Ellis's Mirasi Tenures, Malcolm's Central India, Buchanan's Travels and Eastern India, and various other standard authorities. He had also formed lists of Mohammadan law terms, extracted from the Hidáya, Macnaghten's Mohammadan Law, and Baillie's Digest, and of Hindu law terms from Colebrooke's Digest and Law of Inheritance, Macnaghten's Hindu Law, and my Sanskrit Dictionary. There were also MS. collections of words in the languages of the south of India, accompanied, in some instances, by the native characters. These materials had been classed and arranged alphabetically, and constituted an aggregate of about six or seven thousand terms. They were written according to the system of Sir William Jones, but not accompanied by the native characters. The whole of these materials were most liberally placed at my disposal by Mr. Clarke, when he learned that I was occupied in a similar task; and the greater portion of them, all those which came within the plan of the present compilation, have been incorporated with it, after verifying them by reference to the authorities whence they were taken, and supplying, wherever practicable, the original native letters.

Copious as were the materials furnished by these different sources, it was very soon evident that the supply was far from exhausted, and that a great number of words employed in official documents still remained to be collected and explained. Public documents respecting the judicial and revenue and other departments of the administration of India have of late years been communicated to the public through the press with a liberality which, although no doubt in many respects of great public utility, might perhaps be now curtailed with advantage, as the voluminous extent of the publications may appal some who would wish to consult them, and deter them from availing themselves of the information. Thus we have in print Monthly Reports of Cases decided in the Ṣadr Courts of Appeal at Calcutta, Agra, Madras, and Bombay; Monthly Reports of the Cases decided in the Zila and subordinate Courts of Bengal, the North-west Provinces, and Madras, which have come latterly to average about 500 pages each, or 6000 pages per annum, or, altogether, 18,000 octavo pages annually. Besides these, the Settlement Reports of the Revenue Officers of the North-west Provinces have been printed, and, at all the Presidencies, Extracts from the Records for many years past have been published, or are in course of publication. All these documents abound more or less with native terms, which, if not in all instances strictly technical, are treated as officially current, and are therefore in need of interpretation. All these have been gone over for several years past, from 1846 to 1853, and such words as were not previously included have been added to the compilation.

Still, these, however ample, are not the only authorities which it has been thought advisable to refer to. Various other public documents are in print, calculated to supply additional materials, such as the Circular Orders of the Ṣadr Diwání Âdálat; Instructions to Settlement Officers emanating from the Government of the North-west Provinces; the particulars of the Settlement Miṣl, or Collection of Official Forms; and other similar Documents. Others, originating with private intelligence, have been also found of service, such as Smyth's Bengal Zamíndárí Accounts; the clever Tract in Urdu and Hindi, termed *Khet-karm*, or Field Business; the amusing and instructive "Revelations of an Orderly;" and a host of contributions to the Asiatic Researches, the Transactions of the Bombay Literary Society, the Transactions and Journal of the Royal Asiatic Society, and the Journals of the Asiatic Society and Agricultural Society of Bengal, of the Literary Society of Madras, and of the Branch Asiatic Society of Bombay. The great extent of these several authorities renders it impossible to have bestowed upon them more than a cursory examination, and there are, no doubt, still abundant materials to be gathered from them; but they have been consulted with more or less care, and from these and other works incidentally referred to, the collection has been carried far beyond the limit which was anticipated when the task was undertaken. The Index of the Glossary exhibits an aggregate of more than 26,000 words; and although many of them are mere varieties of spelling, yet the far greater proportion are leading terms, in their correct orthography, agreeably to the system which has been followed in representing Indian words by the letters of the Roman alphabet.

The only trustworthy representation of an Indian word is its native costume: it can never be thoroughly nationalised in any other: but as it has to take a place in English documents, and is addressed to those to whom it would otherwise be illegible, it is the especial object of the present compilation to give it as faithful an equivalent as the difference in the values of letters and the peculiarities of national enunciation will permit, attaching to it at the same time, as a check upon the copy, the original delineation of the word in the letters of its own alphabet, wherever verifiable, for the use of those who are qualified to make the comparison. To be able to appreciate, however, the intention of the copy, and to make use of it with advantage, it is necessary that the principles upon which it has been developed should be properly understood.

The extreme and contradictory variety which prevails in the spelling of Oriental words has been often made the subject of remark, and not unfrequently of censure. The latter may not be always undeserved; yet those who condemn are not always qualified to judge, and they often exhibit in themselves a most perverse determination not to be set right. Above a century ago the most unexceptionable authorities established by their example how *Mohammed* should be spelled, or nearly so, but to so little purpose that it still is most common to write it *Mahommed*, and even *Mahomet* is still far from unfrequent. As long as this disregard of exactitude is so universal it little imports what animadversions may be passed upon the want of it by incompetent judges; but those who should know better, those who are acquainted with the original languages, are inexcusable when they write the native words without reference to their proper form, and without any consistent or systematic mode of expressing them, each individual writing it as he hears, or thinks he hears it articulated, and without paying any attention to its original alphabetical structure. It is undoubtedly true that many of those who are in the habit of hearing and uttering native words in the course of official duty are unfamiliar with their written forms, and will not take the trouble to acquire a knowledge of their alphabet. Even, however, when acquainted with the characters, they will not be at the pains of acquiring a systematic plan of representing them, but write them according to the fancy of the moment, and with a total indifference to consistency which produces the most needless and incompatible misrepresentations of one and the same word, to an extent that would scarcely be thought possible if it were not substantiated by daily experience, even in the most ordinary and simple words. It would, for instance, be thought impossible to represent *Lakhiraj* (from *la*, "without," and *khiraj*, "tax,") by any other letters, and the disciples of the two chief propounders of schemes of Oriental orthography, Sir William Jones and Dr. Gilchrist, would unhesitatingly concur in the representation; yet notwithstanding the concurrence of the two systems, and the simplicity of the original word, we meet with *Lakhiraj* under the monstrous disguises of *Lakerage, Lackeradge, Lackiraz, Lackerage, Laqueerauz,* and *Leeakeerazee.* It is high time that such monstrosities should no longer be perpetrated or tolerated, and that the only remedy of which it admits should be applied—the authoritative enforcement of a uniform system for the representation of the original letters by those of the English alphabet. For this purpose a system must be devised, and then it must be learned. The cause of the confusion is, chiefly, neglect of the latter. We have systems, good enough in their respective ways, but few or none will take the trouble to study and apply them.

The representation of Oriental words by Roman characters has not now for the first time to be considered: the question was most ably discussed nearly seventy years ago by Sir William Jones, and was placed upon its right footing in his Memoir, which judiciously prefaces the Researches of the Asiatic Society of Bengal, and commences the first volume, printed in 1788. There are but two principles involved in the adaptation of one alphabet to another: 1. an analogous classification of the *letters themselves*, according to their original arrangement; or, 2. the representation of *their sounds* in equivalents of similar enunciation; in other words, the one principle is analogy, the other, pronunciation. Sir William Jones adopts the former as the more simple, universal, consistent, and scientific, and as exempt from the anomalies and contradictions which the English alphabet presents, in which, as he ingeniously pointed out, every vowel and a diphthong may be used to articulate one and the same sound, as in the sentence "a mother bird flutters over her young," in which every vowel of the alphabet and the combination *ou* has the sound of *u* in *but.* He also instances, in the quotation from Maleherbe, the absurd results that would follow an attempt to transcribe the original French passage according to even its French pronunciation,—an absurdity which we commonly, though not invariably, avoid in ordinary life by writing foreign names, not according to their pronunciation, but their original spelling. No one would think of writing *Paris* "Paree," *Rousseau* "Roosso;" nor, except in a conundrum, *Toulon* and *Toulouse,* "Too long" and "Too loose;" and it would be a sorry jest that should convert *Grisi* into "Greasy." We do not, therefore, follow sound alone in the Anglicising of European foreign words; and the principle is, if possible, still less applicable to the languages of the East.

Not very long, however, after the system of Sir William Jones had been adopted by the Asiatic Society of Bengal, the principle of pronunciation was taken up by Dr. Gilchrist, with relation especially to the

Hindustani language as written in the Arabic and Persian alphabet; and with great ingenuity he devised a scheme for expressing the letters of one alphabet by the other, according to their prevailing sounds. This plan he advocated with an earnestness which savoured something of extravagance; but his scheme, as finally developed as his Hindee-Roman Orthoepical Ultimatum, was, with one or two exceptions, exceedingly well adapted to its object, that of expressing with uniformity and consistency the Oriental characters in English letters, in such a manner that English readers, unacquainted with the former, would be enabled to articulate the words with a very near approach to their correct pronunciation. Here, then, is all that is wanted—two ingenious systems, one based on analogy, one on pronunciation; and it is only requisite that a person proposing to write Oriental words in Roman letters should make himself familiar with one or the other. It has been more congenial, however, to the natural indolence and self-sufficiency of writers on Indian subjects to study neither, but to blunder on without any previous preparation, to put down words at random, and mystify the public with all sorts of incongruous creations.

Although fully adequate to the determination of the principles on which the mutual adjustment of the Oriental and Roman alphabets ought to be grounded, yet some of the details of the two systems have been thought to admit of improvement, and different modifications of both have been from time to time proposed. The system of Sir William Jones was scrupulously adhered to by Mr. Colebrooke, and prevails in the Asiatic Researches, and in the Journals of the Asiatic Society of Bengal and of the Royal Asiatic Society; it was used, somewhat modified, by Sir Charles Wilkins, in his edition of Richardson's Persian Dictionary, and in Shakespear's Hindustani Dictionary; nearly unaltered in Rottler's Tamil, Campbell's Telugu, and Bailey's Malayalam Dictionaries; and, in a mixed form, in Reeves's Karnáta Dictionary. Major Molesworth, in his Maráṭhí Dictionary, follows generally Dr. Gilchrist's system. The public authorities in Bengal also usually observe a modification of Gilchrist's spelling, when they follow any system at all; but there is little uniformity in this respect. In 1834, a vigorous effort was made in Bengal to establish what was termed the Romanizing system, or the substitution of the Roman letters for the characters of the country, in all printed books, and the project is still in operation to a limited extent. Competent scholars from different Missions, Dr. Duff, and Messrs. Pearce, Yates, and Thomas; and distinguished Members of the Company's Service, Mr. H. T. Prinsep, the late Mr. J. Prinsep, Mr. John Tytler, and Mr., now Sir Charles Trevelyan, took part in the discussion, and their several communications were collected and printed at Serampore. The different modes of writing the Oriental words in Roman letters were then fully and fairly considered, and a system nearly identical with that of Sir William Jones was adopted. Again, in 1845, an intelligent and ingenious treatise on the mode of writing Oriental words, having especial reference to the present Glossary, by Mr. Crow, Deputy Collector, was published in Calcutta, who was wrong only in supposing that the crude spelling of the Draft Glossary was final. Still more recently, the subject has been taken up by the Missionaries of England and America, and some eminent German Oriental scholars and philologers; and several conferences were held, under the auspices of Chevalier Bunsen, for the purpose of fixing a standard in Roman characters for the expression of foreign forms of speech, whether possessed of alphabets or without them. Proposals for a Missionary alphabet founded on these discussions, have been published by my friend Maximilian Müller, Professor of Modern Languages in the University of Oxford. There is no lack, therefore, of careful and competent investigation of the subject; and although uniformity of practice has not been, and probably will not be, the result, yet an approximation has been made to it, and the principle of analogy, where alphabets exist, is recognised as preferable to that of pronunciation. Where the language is unwritten, sound must be more or less the guide; but with such forms of speech we have no concern, all the languages of the civilised races of India being provided with alphabets.

In the following pages the principle of analogy has been preferred, and the system of Sir William Jones has been pursued, with some modifications of detail, which will be particularised in the remarks on the table of equivalents, which will presently be given. Their object will be rendered more obvious by prefacing a few general rules for the conversion of one set of characters into another, and the observations which they suggest. The rules are in general harmony with those acknowledged as the basis of the Missionary alphabet. The observations have also reference to the propositions for its development.

I. The same letter should be invariably used to represent the same letter or the same sound: if *a* be chosen as the representative of the short vowel, it should never be allowed to alternate with *e* or *u*, *o* or *œ*.

II. The same letter should never be used to express two different letters or sounds.

On this account I object to the proposal to represent both *k* and *ch* by *k*, although etymologically there may be an affinity between them, as pointed out half a century ago by Dr. Gilchrist, in his recognition of the identity of *kirk* and *church*. Etymology, however, is admitted to be a somewhat unsafe guide; and I would restrict *k* to its guttural duties, on the same principle as, inconsistent with this rule, I conceive it objectionable to give a double office to *g*, although it has such a duality in English, as in *gin* and *gun*. It is proposed, indeed, to distinguish both the *k* and the *g* by printing them in italics when palatals, but the distinction is insufficient, as it is one of form, not of value, and is both uncouth and likely to be overlooked. My friend Müller's "*G*agatai *K*ingis khan" will be much more consistently and correctly written "Jagatai Chingis khan," *i. e. ch* and *k* each having but one power.

III. Simple letters should, as far as possible, be used for simple letters.

On this ground, objections may be taken to the use of *ch*; but although written as two letters, it has in English the power of but one: and although the nations of the Continent express it by combinations of a rather uncouth appearance, yet, as symbols have to be devised for sounds which are foreign to an individual alphabet, there is no good reason why one should not borrow of another. *Ch*, as a novelty, is not more novel than *k* as *ch*; and the one has an existence, which the other has not. On this, and on the use of aspirates as simple letters, we shall have further occasion to animadvert.

It is sufficiently obvious, that if an alphabet of twenty-four letters is to express one of fifty or more, some contrivance must be had recourse to, to extend the elasticity of the former. If the sounds are wholly and radically strange, new symbols must be invented; but if, as is most usual, they are only qualifications of sounds, of which, in the unmodified form, symbols exist, the latter may be adapted to these expressions conformably to the following:—

IV. Diacritical signs, lines, accents, or dots, are to be attached to the Roman letters, in order to enable them to represent modifications of the symbols or sounds which they themselves express.

The choice of these diacritical or distinguishing marks is matter of taste, or, more correctly speaking, of convenience. Sir William Jones objected to the ordinary modes of characterising long and short vowels as properly belonging to prosodial distinctions; and as the use of accents was familiar to some of the European languages, he preferred their employment, and distinguished the long vowels by the acute accent in the middle of words, and by the grave accent in the last syllable: he also characterised the cerebral consonants by the accent. Dr. Gilchrist's representation of the vowels proceeded on a different plan altogether, and he expressed them by special equivalents. In his earliest scheme he distinguished peculiar consonants by small circles above them, as *t̊*, *d̊*, &c.; but in his final alphabet he substituted dots underneath *ṭ*, *ḍ*, *ṣ*, *ẓ*, *z̤*, and the like. Mr. Shakespear, in his Hindustani Dictionary, uses both, lines above or below, and dots underneath, as *ā*, *ī*, *k͟h*, *ṣ*, *s̤*, &c.; and Mr. Crow proposes, in various instances, a line, or a line and dot, below the letter, as *a̱*, *i̱*, *ḵ*, *ḵ̣*. It seems inexpedient, however, to diversify the diacritical marks beyond the distinction of vowels and consonants, and the acute accent may be reserved for the long vowel, and dots underneath for the peculiar consonants: the latter have the advantage of being typographically more convenient, of being unobtrusive to the eye, and of being easily multiplied with any number of modifications of the original sound, as will be hereafter shewn.

V. The vowels are to have the powers which they enjoy in most languages except English, and especially in Italian; and, as in Latin, quantity is not to be represented by a difference in the letter, the long and short vowel being held to be one and the same letter, the former being distinguished by the acute accent in whatever part of the word it may occur, as *a*, *á*, *i*, *í*, *u*, *ú*.

It is in this respect that Dr. Gilchrist's system differs radically from that of Sir William Jones, and violates the rule with which we set out, as well as the preceding, in representing one vowel, varying only in the accident of quantity, by two or more, as the short *a* by *u*, the long by *a*, the short *i* by *i*, the long by *ee*, the short *u* by a new character, which he proposed to be *ω*, and the long *u* by *oo*. There is no doubt that these equivalents represent to an English eye and ear the sounds of the original vowels more readily than the unaccented *a* or the accented *í* and *ú*; but they do not represent the original letters, and destroy all alphabetical identity. A vowel is the same letter, whether it be long or short, and in most languages, except our own, is so written. To represent the long vowel by one symbol and the short by another is to create a distinction where none exists, and to disjoin words which are closely connected. To change the short *a* to *u*, and leave *a* to represent the long, divides words which are essentially identical, and places one at the head and the other at the tail of a dictionary. *Dabee*, for instance, and *dubea*, are radically the same word: the latter occurs in Sir Henry Elliot's Supplement at an interval of forty pages from the former; in the present compilation, as *Dábi* and *Dabiá,* they come as they should do together. However accommodating, therefore, to national peculiarities, the Gilchrist vowel system will never be universally adopted; and accordingly it does not form an element in any of the schemes proposed for the Missionary alphabet. We shall have further occasion to advert to this part of the subject.

VI. Consonants of the same elementary sound, modified only by pronunciation, but expressed by different symbols, are to be expressed by one and the same symbol, distinguishing it as the equivalent of the original sign by dots underneath the letter, multiplying them according to the multiplied variety of the original sounds.

The multiplied modifications of sounds may be expressed by separate signs in the same alphabet, or they may occur in different alphabets with their respective representations. Thus we have five or six nasals in the Hindu alphabets, and five modifications of *z* in the Semitic alphabets, each of which it is necessary to represent separately, both with regard to the appropriation of the word to the language to which it belongs, and to discriminate between words of very different significations, although very nearly similar forms. Thus, in Arabic, *kul* means "all;" in Karnáta, *kuḷ* is a payer of government revenue: they are not the same word, however, even in form: the final *l* of the Karnáta word being peculiar to its alphabet in figure, and slightly, perhaps, in pronunciation: it is therefore distinguished from the ordinary *l* which the same alphabet also possesses by a dot underneath. *Pát,* in Hindi, is "a leaf;" *Páṭ,* in Maráṭhí, is "a plank:" the difference is in the *t,* which, in the latter, is the cerebral, in the former, the dental letter: the cerebral then is to be distinguished by the dot. *Tár,* Persian, is "a wire;" *Táṛ,* Hindi, "a palm-tree:" the hard *ṛ* indicated by the dot marks an essential difference. In the mouth of a native there is no doubt a different enunication of these apparently identical words, but the distinction is not easily caught by the European ear; and as the general articulation is the same, it does not require to be represented by any other than a modified symbol. In proportion as these varieties increase, the diacritical dots may be multiplied to any required extent without becoming obtrusive or uncouth, as would be the case with accents; *n̤,* for instance, is typographically less offensive than *n̈̃.* In some cases the marks may be dispensed with, as in that of the nasals, the value of which is commonly determined by the following letter, and *n* before *k* or *g* would be necessarily the guttural nasal, and *n* before *ch* and *j* the palatal letter; and, except for the sake of systematic consistency, would not need to be distinguished as *n̤, n̤.* It has been proposed in the scheme for the Missionary alphabet to represent peculiar consonantal symbols by italics, or the cerebrals of the Nágarí alphabet for instance, t, d, by *t, d*; but, besides that the presence of an oblique italic letter amongst the upright broad-faced Roman letters were offensive to the eye, the contrivance would be able to represent only a single modification. It could not, in the case of *t* be extended to the Arabic *to* (ط), and it could not be possible to repeat an italic *z* three times over to represent the Semitic letter *zo* (ظ), although that may be easily typographed as *z̤.* The argument in favour of the italic letter is, that all founts are already provided with *them,* and not with dotted letters: the latter can, however, be provided with equal facility, if required.

VII. The aspirates of the original letters must be represented in European alphabets by a double letter, or the proper equivalents with the addition of *h,* as *kh, gh,* &c., considering the composite as representing a single sound.

We have here some slight difficulty as regards the English alphabet in the forms and powers of *ch, th, sh:* these, to be consistent, should be treated as aspirates, which they are not; and they therefore constitute exceptions to the rule, that a single consonant with *h* added is to be regarded as a single aspirated letter. In order to avoid the dilemma, Sir William Jones proposed to distinguish the aspirates by an apostrophe, separating the aspiration above, as in *aswatt'ha;* Dr. Gilchrist, by a comma below, as *b,h, k,h,* &c.; but these distinctions are inconvenient and scarcely necessary. There can be no misconception as to *ch* and *sh,* which in English and in Russian, as well as in the Indian alphabets, are simple sounds. *Th* with the sound of *theta* is not of frequent occurrence, and, if it be thought expedient, may be distinguished by a diacritical mark as a line underneath it, *t͟h,* or even the Greek letter Θ might be borrowed, as it would harmonise well enough with the Latin characters. So, if it be considered indispensable that a single symbol should be always employed for a single unaspirated sound, the Russian *ch* (ч) and *sh* (ш) might be pressed into the service.

VII. When it is necessary, as it is in the monosyllabic languages, and in some of those of barbarous nations, to express intonations, these may be designated by conventional marks or figures placed above or below the letters, as has been proposed in the Journal of the American Oriental Society, Vol. IV. No. 2, by the Hon. C.W. Bradley, late Consul at Amoy; but we have no concern with these at present in the languages of the people subject to the government of British India.

In conformity to the tenor of the rules thus laid down, I have adopted for the representation of the Oriental words that occur in the subsequent pages the system of equivalents described in the following Table, in which it will be observed that the characters of the English alphabet have been enabled to represent letters, in nine alphabets of thirteen Indian languages, without the introduction of a single new character. I may not be found invariably to have adhered to the scheme as it appears in the Table, partly from my not having definitively determined all the equivalents when the compilation was commenced, partly from occasional inattention or forgetfulness, and partly for special considerations strongly recommending a departure from uniformity. These deviations are, however, only occasional, and the Table may be accepted as embodying the plan which I have conclusively adopted, and which I think will be found to provide for the representation of all the alphabetical symbols hitherto known in India. The progress of events may bring other alphabets within the range of similar representation, and to them the principles of the scheme will admit, it may be expected, of its adaptation.

ENGLISH.		ARABIC. PERSIAN. ÚRDU.	SANSKRIT. HINDI. MARÁṬHÍ.	GUZARÁTHÍ.	BENGÁLÍ.	URIYA.	TELUGU.	KARNÁTA.	TAMIḶ.	MALAYÁLAM.
A	a	ـَ ا	अ . .	અ . .	অ . . .	ଅ . . .	అ ్ .	ಅ ್ .	அ . . .	അ
Á	á	ا آ	आ ा .	આ ા .	আ া .	ଆ ା .	ఆ ా .	ಆ ಾ .	ஆ ா .	ആ ാ
Â	â	ع ـٰ	—	—	—	—	—	—	—	—
Ai	ai	اَي ـَي	ऐ ै .	ઐ ૈ .	ঐ ৈ .	ଐ ୈ .	ఐ ై	ಐ ೈ .	ஐ ை	ഐ ൈ
Au	au	اَو ـَو	औ ौ .	ઔ ૌ .	ঔ ৌ	ଔ ୌ	ఔ ౌ	ಔ ೌ	ஔ ௌ	ഔ . ൌ
B	b	ب بـ	ब . . .	બ . . .	ব . . .	ବ . . .	బ . . .	ಬ . . .	ப . . .	ബ
Bh	bh	بھ	भ . . .	ભ . . .	ভ . . .	ଭ . . .	భ . . .	ಭ . . .	—	ഭ
Ch	ch	چ چـ	च . . .	ચ . . .	চ . . .	ଚ . . .	చ . . .	ಚ . . .	ச . . .	ച
Chh	chh	چھ . . .	छ . . .	છ . . .	ছ . . .	ଛ . . .	ఛ . . .	ಛ . . .	—	ഛ
D	d	د . . .	द . . .	દ . . .	দ . . .	ଦ . . .	ద . . .	ದ . . .	த . . .	ദ
Dh	dh	دھ . . .	ध . . .	ધ . . .	ধ . . .	ଧ . . .	ధ . . .	ಧ . . .	—	ധ
Ḍ	ḍ	ڈ . . .	ड . . .	ડ . . .	ড . . .	ଡ . . .	డ . . .	ಡ . . .	ட . . .	ഡ
Ḍh	ḍh	ڈھ . . .	ढ . . .	ઢ . . .	ঢ . . .	ଢ . . .	ఢ . . .	ಢ . .	—	ഢ
E	e	ي يـ	ए े	એ ે	এ ে .	ଏ େ .	ఎ ె .	ಎ ೆ .	எ ெ .	എ െ
É	é	—	—	—	—	—	ఏ ే .	ಏ . ೇ	ஏ ே .	—
F	f	ف فـ	—	—	—	—	—	—	—	—
G	g	گ گـ	ग . . .	ગ . . .	গ . . .	ଗ . . .	గ . . .	ಗ . . .	க . . .	ഗ
Gh	gh	گھ . . .	घ . . .	ઘ . . .	ঘ . . .	ଘ . . .	ఘ . .	ಘ . .	—	ഘ
Ġh	ġh	غ غـ	—	—	—	—	—	—	—	—
H	h	ح حـ	ह . . .	હ . . .	হ . . .	ହ . . .	హ . .	ಹ . . .	—	ഹ
Ḥ	ḥ	ه ﻫ	—	—	—	—	—	—	—	—
Ḥ̤	ḥ̤	—	ः . . .	ઃ . . .	ঃ . . .	ଃ . . .	ః . . .	ಃ . . .	—	ഃ
I	i	ي يـ	इ ि .	ઇ િ .	ই ি .	ଇ ି .	ఇ ి .	ಇ ಿ .	இ ி .	ഇ ി
Í	í	ي يـ	ई ी .	—	ঈ ী .	ଈ ୀ .	ఈ ీ .	ಈ ೀ .	ஈ ீ .	ഈ ീ
J	j	ج جـ	ज . . .	જ . . .	জ . . .	ଜ . . .	జ . . .	ಜ . . .	—	ജ
Jh	jh	—	झ . . .	ઝ . . .	ঝ . . .	ଝ . . .	ఝ . .	ಝ . .	—	ഝ
K	k	ك كـ	क . . .	ક . . .	ক . . .	କ . . .	క . . .	ಕ . . .	க . . .	ക
Ḳ	ḳ	ق قـ	—	—	—	—	—	—	—	—

ENGLISH.		ARABIC. PERSIAN. ÚRDU.	SANSKRIT. HINDI. MARÁṬHÍ.	GUZARÁTHÍ.	BENGÁḶÍ.	URIYA.	TELUGU.	KARNÁTA.	TAMIḺ.	MALAYÁLAM.
Kh	kh	خ خ	ख . . .	ખ . . .	খ . . .	ଖ . . .	ఖ . .	ಖ . . .	—	ഖ
Kh̤		کھ	—	—	—	—	—	—	—	—
L	l	ل ل	ल . . .	લ . . .	ল . . .	ଲ . . .	ల . . .	ಲ . . .	ல . . .	ല
Ḷ	ḷ	—	ळ . . .	—	—	—	ళ . . .	ಳ . . .	ள . . .	ള
Ḷ̤	ḷ̤	—	—	—	—	—	—	—	ழ . . .	—
M	m	م م	म . . .	મ . . .	ম . . .	ମ . . .	మ . . .	ಮ	ம . . .	മ
N	n	ن ن	न . . .	ન . . .	ন . . .	ନ . . .	న . . .	ನ . . .	ந . . .	ന
N̥	n̥	—	ं . . .	ં . . .	ং . . .	—	—	—	—	—
Ṇ	ṇ	—	ण . . .	ણ . . .	ণ . . .	ଣ . . .	ణ . . .	ಣ . . .	ண . .	ണ
N̤	n̤	—	—	—	—	—	—	—	ன . . .	—
Ṅ	ṅ	—	ङ . . .	—	ঙ . . .	ଙ . .	ఙ . . .	ಙ . . .	ங . .	ങ
N̈	n̈	—	ञ . . .	—	ঞ . . .	ଞ . .	ఞ . .	ಞ . .	ஞ . . .	ഞ
O	o	و او	ओ ो .	ઓ ો	ও ো	ଓ ୋ	ఒ ొ	ಒ ೊ	ஒ ொ	ഒ ൊ
Ó	ó	—	—	—	—	—	ఓ ో	ಓ ೋ	ஓ ோ	—
P	p	پ پ	प . . .	પ . . .	প . . .	ପ . . .	ప . . .	ಪ . . .	ப . . .	പ
Ph	ph	پھ . .	फ . . .	ફ . . .	ফ . . .	ଫ . . .	ఫ . . .	ಫ . . .	—	ഫ
R	r	ر . .	र . . .	ર . . .	র . . .	ର . . .	ర ్ర	ರ ್ರ	ர . . .	ര
Ṛ	ṛ	ڑ . .	—	—	—	—	ఱ . .	ఱ . . .	ற . . .	റ
R̤	r̤	—	—	—	—	—	—	—	—	ം
Ṛi	ṛi	—	ऋ ृ .	—	ঋ ৃ	ଋ . . .	ఋ ృ	ಋ ೃ	—	ഋ ൃ
Ṛí	ṛí	—	ॠ ॄ .	—	ৠ ৄ	ୠ .	ౠ ౄ	ೠ ೄ	—	ൠ ൄ
S	s	س س	स . . .	સ . . .	স . . .	ସ . . .	స . . .	ಸ . . .	ச . . .	സ
Ṣ	ṣ	—	श . . .	શ . . .	শ . . .	ଶ . . .	శ . . .	ಶ . . .	—	ശ
S̤	s̤	ص ص	—	—	—	—	—	—	—	—
S̥	s̥	ث ث	—	—	—	—	—	—	—	—
Sh	sh	ش ش	ष . . .	ષ . .	ষ . . .	ଷ . . .	ష . . .	ಷ . . .	—	ഷ
T	t	ت ت	त . . .	ત . . .	ত . . .	ତ . . .	త . . .	ತ . . .	த . . .	ത
Th	th	تھ . .	थ . . .	થ . . .	থ . . .	ଥ . . .	థ . . .	ಥ . . .	—	ഥ
Ṭ	ṭ	ٹ ٹ	ट . . ,	ટ . . .	ট . . .	ଟ . . .	ట . . .	ಟ . . .	ட . . .	ട
Ṭh	ṭh	ٹھ . .	ठ . . .	ઠ . . .	ঠ . . .	ଠ . . .	ఠ . . .	ಠ . . .	—	ഠ
Ṭ̤	ṭ̤	ط ط	—	—	—	—	—	—	—	—
U	u	و و	उ ु .	ઉ ુ	উ ু	ଉ . .	ఉ ు	ಉ ು	உ ு	ഉ ു
Ú	ú	—	ऊ ू .	ઊ ૂ	ঊ ূ	ଊ . .	ఊ ూ	ಊ ೂ	ஊ ூ	ഊ ൂ
V	v	و . .	व . . .	વ . . .	—	—	వ . . .	ವ . . .	வ . . .	വ
W	w									
X	ksh	—	क्ष . . .	—	ক্ষ . . .	କ୍ଷ . . .	క్ష . . .	ಕ್ಷ . . .	—	—
Y	y	ي . .	य . . .	ય . . .	য . . .	ଯ . . .	య ్య	ಯ . . .	ய . . .	യ
Z	z	ز . .	—	—	—	—	—	—	—	—
Zh	zh	ژ . .	—	—	—	—	—	—	—	—
Ẓ	ẓ	ذ . .	—	—	—	—	—	—	—	—
Z̤	z̤	ض ض	—	—	—	—	—	—	—	—
Z̦	z̦	ظ ظ	—	—	—	—	—	—	—	—

REMARKS.

A a represents the short *A* of the Indian alphabets; it is found in English plentifully as an initial, as in "adore, amend, above." It occurs also as a medial in "woman," and as initial and final in "America," in all which it has the dull sound of the common English *u* in "bud, but." It is the equivalent proposed by Sir William Jones, although he allows its alternating with *E*, a licence incompatible with our Rule I. The *A* has had the concurrence of Sir Charles Trevelyan, of the Calcutta Missionaries, Mr. Shakespear, Mr. Crow, and has been most usually adopted in the Transactions and Journals of the several Asiatic Societies. The proposed Missionary alphabet suggests for the short vowel *œ, ĕ*, or *ŏ*; but these are not necessary, and would be inconsistent with Rule I. The same objection applies to Dr. Gilchrist's representation of *a* short, by *u*, however more congenial that may be to the practice of our own language, and although the *a* as representing the short vowel, constitutes a stumbling block in the way of English articulation, which, it must be admitted, it is almost impossible to overcome. It is very difficult, almost impossible, to induce an English reader to pronounce *Man* as *Mun*, *Pan* as *Pun*, *Sab, Sub, Thag, Thug*, and the like; but the difficulty may be surmounted with a little perseverance, and the spelling must be adhered to if consistency is to be observed. In conformity, however, to the prevailing prejudice, I have frequently inserted, in leading Hindustani words especially, the Gilchrist reading, as in *Man, Mun, Thal, Thul*, as parallel with the more correct form. Since, in the Index the letter *U*, either as an initial or medial, occurs twice over, the words that first come being identical with those having an initial or medial *A*, those that succeed having the proper vowel or Italian *U*, they are separated by a short line, thus, *Bhuda, Bhudahur*, equivalent to *Bhada, Bhadahar*, and the like, precede and are distinct from *Bhu, Bhuband;* and *Bubool, Buboor*, precede and are distinct from *Bú, Buá, Bubu*, and the like. Leading words commencing with *U* as *A*, or as the vowel proper, are also separately classed.

The short *A* of the other Indian alphabets is pronounced commonly in Bengálí as *O*, but it is not so written, the Bengálí being essentially the same as the Nágarí alphabet, and the value thus given to the vowel is merely provincial, and, in some degree, a vulgarism. I have not, therefore, altered the spelling, as the object of all the above equivalents is not the sound but the symbol, the letter as it stands in its own alphabet, and not as it may happen to be enunciated.

Á á is our letter in "far, car," expanded sometimes, in the pronunciation of Arabic and Persian words into a broader sound, as in "ball, fall, water." It is admitted by all the systems as representing the long vowel. In the table it is distinguished, after Sir William Jones, by the acute accent. Dr. Gilchrist uses it unaccented, as he does not need to distinguish it from the short *A;* Mr. Shakespear marks it by the prosodial mark, a line above the letter; Mr. Crow would designate it by a similar line underneath; but there does not seem to be any reasonable objection to the accent.

The Arabic letter ع has always constituted a difficulty, owing not only to its peculiar articulation, but to its combining with the different vowel-sounds of *a, i* and *u*. Hence Meninski proposed to retain it unaltered, in which he has been followed by Richardson, Sir Charles Wilkins, and Mr. Johnson, and, in an abbreviated form, by Mr. Shakespear. Sir William Jones adopted this modification in his Grammar, but proposed in his Memoir to distinguish it by a circumflex, as *â, î, û*, which plan has been here adopted; the appearance of the character itself in the midst of English letters being anomalous, and, to persons not acquainted with the Arabic alphabet, unintelligible, as for *Duâát, Du*ع*át*, or for *Âhd,* ع*ahd*, for *Rabâ, Rab*ع, for *Khilât, Khil*ع*t:* Sir Charles Trevelyan agrees with Dr. Gilchrist in expressing it by a dot under the vowels: Mr. Crow would employ two dots; but as the letter is a peculiar one, it is perhaps best distinguished by a peculiar diacritical mark of its own. Its representation by *'h* in the proposed Missionary alphabet would be wholly inadequate to its verification, as in *Âmlah, Îlm, Ûmr*, and the like.

The diphthong *Ai* occurs in the word "aisle." For *Au* we have only, in English, the representative sound of *ou*, as in "hour," but the compound is $a + u$, not $o + u$; and the above therefore follows Sir William Jones's plan, which is generally concurred in. Dr. Gilchrist proposed to express them by *ue* and *uo*, but few even of his disciples have followed him. Mr. Elliot generally writes them *ei* and *ou*, as in *Beis* for *Bais, Gour* for *Gaur*.

B is uniformly rendered, as in "beat, bad." The aspirate *Bh*, as Gilchrist observes, may be represented in "abhor" dropping the initial; but it may be doubted if we have any exact equivalents in English for these aspirated letters other than by the addition of the *h*, which, with the unaspirated letter, is to be regarded, as it is in the Oriental alphabets, a simple sound.

The scantiness of the Tamil alphabet, comprising but eighteen consonants, has compelled the assignment of multiplied powers to certain of the letters, to enable them to express the Sanskrit words with which the language is copiously infused: hence the equivalent of *B* ப is also that of *Bh*, and is more especially the representative of *P* and *Ph*: the differences of value depend, in this case and in the analogous instances of *K* and *T*, upon the position of the letter. As an initial, the ப represents *P*, and so it does when double in the middle of the word; but when single as a medial it represents either *B* or *Bh*. Thus, *Mahábhárata* is written in Tamil letters *Makápárata*, but it is pronounced by native scholars correctly according to its Nágarí valuation. Some difficulty occasionally occurs with regard to the reduplication of these letters as medials. According to Beschi, the reduplication has only the effect of preserving for the letter its proper sound, as *pagaippán* is nothing more than *pagaipán*. Rhenius, however, says that both are to be pronounced hard, as in *iruppu*, not as Beschi would make it, merely *irupu*. The preservation or rejection of the duplicate can only be determined by practice, the only essential point being the retainment of what may be considered the especial value of *P*, *K*, and *T*, as a medial when repeated.

C, except in the combination *Ch*, does not occur in the above scheme. Sir William Jones employed it to represent the *K* of the Nágarí alphabet, retaining the *K* for the harsher Arabic guttural; but in that case we employ two letters to represent but one, for the Arabic is only a modification of the guttural, not a distinct power. *C*, in English also, is an inconsistent letter, having, in fact, no power of its own but that of *K* before *a* and *o*, and of *S* before *e* and *i*: its use is therefore apt to mislead. It took me some time to read Sir William Jones's *Cocila*, not as *Kosila*, but *Kokila*, as it should be: so in a word in common use, *Circar*, we have one letter for two sounds, and two sounds for one letter, a breach of all system. *C* is therefore altogether discarded, except in the form of *Ch*, which, although written with two letters, is as much a simple sound in English as it is in Sanskrit. Mr. Crow proposes to represent it by *C*, but all other English orientalists retain the combination. The sound is peculiar in some degree to English and Russian, although the Italians have it in *ce* and *cio*; and its representation as *tch* or *tsch* in French and German is no doubt somewhat uncouth. For this reason, as well as to distinguish it from the guttural *ch*, as in *macht*, *nicht*, the German orientalists have latterly represented it by K with an asterisk, as K', and in the proposed Missionary alphabet the italic *K* is suggested. To this I have already objected, as employing one letter to represent two different letters, and therefore a violation of an important principle. There seems no reason for the non-adoption of the English form: in either case the equivalent is conventional: K' or *K*, with the sound of *Ch*, is quite as much an innovation as would be the graft of *Ch* itself on the German alphabet. The power it possesses must be explained and agreed upon in either case equally, and its being confounded with the guttural *ch* might be obviated by a diacritical point or *c̣h*. If, however, a single symbol that could not be mistaken for any thing else were thought indispensable, it would be preferable to borrow the Russian ч. For English uses, however, it will be far the most convenient to preserve the combination. The aspirate of *Ch* or *Chh* is to be considered as a single sound.

Here, again, we have a case of the assignment of more than one power to one symbol in the Tamil alphabet, and *Ch* can only be expressed by ச, which has to do duty also for *J*, for *S*, and for *Sh*. It has the power of *Ch* when double, as a medial following certain letters or *ḷ*, or when single following *ṭ*, as in *kániyáṭchi*. In Telugu, *Ch* before certain vowels has the sound of *Ts*, as *J* has that of *Dz*, but these are dialectical peculiarities, and do not alter the identity of the letter.

D and *Dh*, as dentals, require no comment: they are the same in all systems. But we have another *D* and *Dh* which are cerebrals, and are pronounced harder than the dentals, the *d* especially often becoming in pronunciation like a rough *r*, as *ghoḍa* is pronounced *ghoṛa*. The letters, however, are the same. We have only to deal with modifications of sound, and these may be distinguished in all the consonants by a dot or dots underneath. Sir William Jones distinguished them by accents; but besides the advantage of confining the accent to the vowels, the form of the *d* renders an accent over it, as *d̆*, typographically inconvenient. Dr. Gilchrist's final use of the dot, concurred in by Mr. Shakespear and Sir C. Trevelyan, has been adopted.

The representation of *D* in the English alphabet by the same letter in the Oriental alphabets has one exception, and we have nothing for it in Tamil, as observed above, but *T*, which has the power of *T*, *Th*, *D*, or *Dh*, according to its position: it is *T* as an initial, or as a medial when double; it is *Th* or *D* when medial and single.

E has the power of the vowel in French or Italian rather than in English, but we have it in the word "there." In Sanskrit, it is always a long vowel, but in some of the languages of the south of India a more prolonged sound is sometimes given to it, and different symbols are employed for it. Sir William Jones and Dr. Gilchrist both represent it by one symbol, *E:* the former accents it, as in *Véda;* but I have thought it better to retain the accent for the more prolonged sound. The proposed Missionary alphabet suggests the italic *E* for the long letter.

F occurs with the same power in the Semitic alphabets. In the Indian dialects it has no representative, but the aspirated *P* or *Ph* takes its place, as *Faisala, Phaisala.*

G is the English letter in "go, gun," *Gh* in "ghost." In the two leading systems *Gh* is written *g'h* and *g,h,* but Mr. Shakespear and Sir Charles Trevelyan are satisfied with *gh.* The harsh Arabic guttural is a mere modification of the same sound, and is therefore indicated by *Ġh.* Jones and Gilchrist rendered it simply by *gh.* Shakespear underlines it *g͟h.*

For reasons already urged—the inconsistency of representing two different symbols by one, although in this case sanctioned by the practice of our own alphabet—I must object to the use of *G* with the power of *J,* as in "gin, general," as adopted by the German orientalists in the form of G', or as in the proposed Missionary alphabet in that of the italic letter *G.*

H occurs in varions modifications in the Oriental alphabets, but they are mere modifications of the simple breathing, and may therefore be easily discriminated by dots: the two that are derived from the Arabic alphabet are not very nicely distinguished in Indian pronunciation. One may be something harsher than the other, and so far agrees with the strong Sanskrit aspirate, whilst the softer breathing of the Nágarí alphabet, the Visarga, or sign of the nominative case, may be regarded as peculiar. Sir William Jones distinguishes the harsher forms by an accent, as *Aḱmed.* Gilchrist and Shakespear distinguish it by a dot underneath it. I have transferred the dot to the softer Arabic aspirate, as otherwise it would have been applied to two letters instead of one, which would be typographically less convenient. I am afraid, however, I have not always observed or rightly applied the diacritical mark, having for some time hesitated as to its preferable application. The representation of the unmodified flatus by an apostrophe, in the proposed Missionary alphabet, as *ve'ement* for "vehement," is too uncongenial to European habits to be readily concurred in.

I short is as familiar to English as to the Continental languages, as in "kin, king." *Í* long is less familiar, but we have it in "police, pique, ravine." The accent is according to Sir William Jones. Gilchrist, as observed above, represents it by *ee,* which is objectionable on principle.

J in English, as in "just, join," corresponds exactly with the same letter in the Oriental alphabets. Foreign alphabets have it not, and, as has been observed, German writers propose to render it by G' or by the italic *G;* but this has been already objected to, as using one letter to represent two sounds; and, as of *Ch,* it may be said there seems no good reason why so convenient a symbol should not be borrowed from the English alphabet. The objection as relates to German is its present power in that language of *Y;* but as G' for *J* is equally strange to that alphabet, there is no ground for preferring one conventional sign to another, especially when the one is a fact as regards English, the other a fiction as regards both English and German. The aspirate *Jh* will follow the general analogy.

K is generally employed with its simple guttural power, as in "keep, king." The strong choking guttural of the Arabic alphabet is only a modified sound, which may be expressed by a dot underneath, as *Ḳ.* Sir William Jones, as above stated, reserved the *K* for the Arabic letter, and employed *C* for the simpler guttural. Gilchrist employed for the former, *Q,* without its usual qualification *Qu,* as in *Qazi,* in which he is followed by Sir C. Trevelyan. Shakespear marks it, as here proposed, by a dot underneath, which seems the simplest and most consistent mode of distinguishing it. To the use of K' or the italic *K* as the representative of *Ch,* I have already objected. The aspirate *Kh* is analogous to the preceding aspirates, and is to be regarded as a simple sound. There is also a minor aspiration as a final in Hindustání, arising from the omission of the following short vowel in the original, as *Bhukh* for *Bhukha.* This may be distinguished by a dot under the *h,* as *ḥ Bhukḥ;* but it is not perhaps material. Mr. Shakespear distinguishes it by a double dotunder the *h,* as *kẖ.*

L, as in "Lord," needs no remark; but there are two other modifications of this semivowel which require to be distinguished. One of them, the *L* of the Vedas, is used in Maráṭhí, and in several of the languages of the south, being a rather harsher sound: this I have denoted as *Ḷ.* The other is peculiar to Tamil. Beschi says it is an *L* "quod crassiori sono reflexa omnino ad interiorem palati partem linguâ pronunciatur. Anderson calls it a cerebral *r* when medial, a cerebral *l* when final. Rhenius directs it to be pronounced as *lr;* but the late Mr. Ellis represented it by *zh*, and he is followed by Mr. Clarke. As, however, there is sufficient authority for its being a modification of *L*, I have preferred adhering to that letter, marking it by two dots, as *ḷ*. The enunciation is singularly obscure, and cannot be precisely represented by any written characters.

M, as in "mouth, mother," is the same labial in the Oriental languages as in English. In Hindustani it is often represented before a labial by *n*, as in *Bambu*, sometimes written *Banbu*.

N offers a greater variety of symbols. There are four in the Nágari alphabet, all which exist in English, although not distinguished by separate letters, the distinction not being in the letter itself so much as in the influence exercised upon it by the letter that follows it, as a guttural, palatal, cerebral, or dental, as in the words "sink, change, ant, end," as I have shewn in my Sanskrit Grammar, p. 5. Hence it is, perhaps, scarcely necessary to provide the symbols severally with diacritical points, but they are added for the sake of consistency, as *n, ṅ, ṇ, ṇ̤*. There is another *n* which is peculiar to the Tamil alphabet, although little different from the dental nasal in sound: this I have marked as *ṉ*. Again, in Hindustání, and still more in Guzeráṭhí and Maráṭhí, there is a nasal, usually a final, though sometimes a medial, which is scarcely sounded, although it gives a sort of nasality to a preceding vowel, like the *n* in the French *bon, soins:* this it is proposed to denote by a small circle below the letter *n̥*. These marks, however, have not been very rigorously retained in the following pages.

O, like *E*, is in Sanskrit always long, but in the southern dialects there is a still more prolated quantity of it, which has been therefore marked by the accent. Perhaps it were more correct to treat the former letter as a short *e* or short *o;* but they are scarcely as short as our *e* and *o* in "bed" or "gone." They hold more of a middle place, and are as often as not of Sanskrit derivation.

P requires no remark: it is the English letter in "parent, pair." *Ph* is to be treated as a simple aspirate, as in "up-hill," not as an *F*, although, as there is no equivalent for it in the Indian languages, *Ph* is always used for such Arabic words as begin with *F*, as *Fakír, Phakír* The use of the Tamil *P* (ப) to represent *ph* as well as *b* and *bh* has already been pointed out.

Q is discarded from our system. Its employment for the Arabic *K*, as proposed by Dr. Gilchrist, has been noticed.

R offers various modifications. The usual semivowel has the sound of the letter in our "round, ruin." We have next a rougher *ṛ*, and its aspirate *ṛh*, which, in Hindustani, alternate with the cerebral letters *ḍ, ḍh*. Gilchrist, considering it as a nominal deviation from *ḍ*, did not think it necessary to assign it a separate symbol; but Mr. Shakespear discriminates it as here done, by a dot underneath. The alphabets of the south, Telugu, Karnáta, and Tamil, have a second and harsher *r*, which is similarly distinguished as *ṛ*. As, however, it is not, like the Hindustání letter, an alternation of *ḍ;* and as it offers some peculiar changes, it would have been better to have given it its peculiar mark, and written it with two dots, or *r̤*. In that case the third *r* of the Malayálam alphabet should be distinguished by three dots, not by two, as has been done in the following pages. The *r̤* of the Tamil and the *r̤* of the Malayálam are also, in some respects, identical, as, when doubled, they have the power of a double *ṭṭ;* thus *Ar̤r̤i* becomes *Aṭṭi*, in which form it appears in the Glossary, this being one of the cases in which a departure from systematic uniformity could scarcely be avoided.

In connexion with *R* we have further to provide for the vowel-sounds of Sanskrit *ri* and *rí*, modified in the southern dialects as *ru* and *rú*. A dot under the *r*, as proposed by Dr. Gilchrist, is a sufficient distinction, *ṛi, ṛí, ṛu, ṛú*.

The modifications of the sibilant, as occurring in the same, or in different alphabets, require diacritical designations. The simple sibilant of the European and Indian alphabets, whether of Arabic or Sanskrit origin, is expressed by *S*, as in "sun, sound." The palatal *S* of the Nágarí alphabet has no exact equivalent in English, but may be indicated by *ṣ*, as by Shakespear: it is the *ś* of Sir William Jones. In the dialects it is commonly pronounced, in words of Sanskrit origin, as *sh* somewhat softened, and it is so represented by Molesworth, Stevenson, Reeve, and others. The main objection to this is its being confounded with the more genuine representation of *sh* in the Sanskrit cerebral, and in our "shore, shun;" and it is not exactly *sh*, although a thickened sound of the *s*. However, in conformity to a practice so general, I have given, in many instances of leading words, both forms, as *ṣ* and *sh*. The Arabic alphabet has another form of *s*, that called *ṣád* or *ṣwád*, which, in India at least, is a simple sibilant, although among the Arabs it may have a modified sound; by Erpenius it is called *Dad*, and by De Sacy, *Dhad*, making it a dental, but this is not observed in India: to distinguish it from the Persian *sin* and Sanskrit *s* and *ṣ*, two dots are subjoined, as *s̤*. A third modification of *S*, agreeably to Indian pronunciation, occurs in what is more properly the English lisping sound of *th*, as "thin, then;" so that *thulth* becomes in India undistinguishable from *suls*. In order to denote the difference it is written in the scheme with three dots below, as *s*. In the Niskh alphabet it is termed *thai muthalatha*, or the trebly doted *th*, the dots being above, as ث. The *sh* of the Nágarí alphabet finds an exact representation in the English *sh*, which is not to be considered as an aspirate. It is a continental difficulty; but there seems no great reason why it should not be borrowed from the English alphabet, unless the Russian form be preferred, which has the advantage of being a single symbol.

T, the simple dental, has the same power in both families of languages as in English "tune, time." It occurs also as the cerebral letter in the English "ten, trumpet," and the Italian *tutto*. Its representation of *d* in Tamil has been explained above. In some of the dialects of the west and south, the dental *T* is pronounced almost like the English *th* in "thin;" but this is provincial, and the alphabetical character is merely *T*. *Th* and *Ṭh*, dental or cerebral, are to be regarded as simple aspirates, and never as the English *Th* in "think." If ever necessary to represent this sound, it might be done by placing the dot under *h*, as *Tḥ*, or by the use of the Greek Theta. The Arabic *to* (ط) has, in that language, its peculiar articulation, but it is still only a modified *T*, and in India no difference is made. It is sufficient to distinguish it by a double dot as *T̤*, as is done by Mr. Shakespear.

Although, as a principle, the representation of pronunciation is not attempted in the present scheme, yet occasional departure from the rule is not always to be avoided, as has been instanced in the case of the double *ṛ* of the Tamil and Malayálam becoming double *tt*. So, in the latter language, the cerebral *ṭ*, although correctly written, is with a singular perversity, so constantly pronounced as a cerebral *ḍ*, and that in words of constant recurrence, that to have adhered to the proper form would have tended to produce greater perplexity than a breach of the rule; thus *kuḍi*, and its derivatives *kuḍián*, &c., are properly written *kuṭi*, and *náḍ* is written *náṭ;* but they would not be recognisable under the correct spelling, and in these cases *ḍ* has been substituted for *ṭ*.

The vowels *U* and *Ú* have the Italian sounds proposed by Sir William Jones, and concurred in by Sir Charles Trevelyan, Mr. Shakespear, and the majority of authorities: we have the sounds as well as symbols in "full" and "rule." Shakespear marks the long vowel by the prosodial mark *ū;* Mr. Crow by the same under the letter *u̱*. Dr. Gilchrist adopts *oo* for the long *u*, and suggested a new combination, *ꝏ*, for the short. His disciples, however, have abandoned this form, and are content to write both the vowels in the same manner, as in the English words, "foot, fool." The proposed Missionary alphabet distinguishes the long vowel by the italic letter *u*

V has the same sound in Sanskrit as in English; but in Bengálí and Uriya it is always changed to *B*, in symbol as well as in sound; as *bári* for *vári, barsha* for *varsha*. The same change is not unfrequent in Hindí, as *baras* for *varsha, sambat* for *samvat*, whilst, in Guzaráthí, if we may trust the Dictionary, there is a curious propensity to reverse this arrangement, and write *v* for *b*, as *víghu* for *bíghá, vímo* for *bímá*. In all the dialects, also, there is a perpetual tendency to approximate the sound of *v* to that of *w*, or to substitute the latter altogether. Even in Tamil, in which the pure pronunciation of *v* is preserved according to Anderson and Rhenius, the change is not uncommon, and *váram* is most frequently written *wáram*. According to Mirza Ibrahim, the *wau* of Persian should be pronounced *vau*, yet in Hindustání words derived from Arabic and Persian it is quite as often *w* as *v*, as *wakíl, vakíl, wazír, vazír*. In Maráthí, according to Stevenson, we have both sounds, but for the same letter, व, the one exactly *w*, the other more like *v*, especially when before *i, í*, and *e*, and combined with *ṛi* or *r*. In Malayálam, Spring says it is *v*, and only *w* in composition, as *Swarga*. Peel and Bailey make it *w*; but the fact is that which is intimated by Mr. Clarkson, in his Guzaráṭhí Grammar, the uneducated approximate the sound to *w*, the educated to *v*. The use of *w* for *v* is, in fact, a sort of Indian Cockneyism, but as it is very prevalent, I have admitted the *w* to be the representative in various words of the Sanskrit *v*. As a final letter, *v* in the dialects often assumes the power of *u*, as in Guz. *pav* is pronounced *pau*.

It has been sometimes the practice to represent the Sanskrit *ksh* by the letter *x*, and there is no great objection to the equivalent; but *ksh* is an acknowedged compound of *k* and *sh*, and its representation, therefore, by a single letter would be unsystematic, neither is it necessary; and I have therefore, in the Glossary, always retained the compound form.

The semivowel *Y* finds unequivocal representatives in both classes of alphabets, as in "yoke, young." In Bengálí, when uncompounded, its power is that of *j*, a curious contrast to the German, which gives to *j* the power of *y*. The proposed Missionary alphabet retains *y*.

It is quite a characteristic distinction between the Sanskritic and Semitic dialects of India, that the former are utterly destitute of the symbol and the sound of *Z*, whilst in the latter we have no fewer than five modifications. In the original Arabic these letters have individual powers, but with the exception of *zh*, the sound which were best represented by the French *j* in "jour," no difference of pronunciation is made in India. As it is, nevertheless, necessary to preserve the distinctions of the form, for the sake of identifying the Roman with the Arabic orthography, this is effected by the same method that is followed in the case of other multiplied modifications by the number of dots, and the several symbols occur, as *z*, *ẓ*, *z̤*, *z̤̣*; *zh* requires no mark, but it is to be regarded as representing a single letter.

By these simple arrangements, then, which do not pretend to the merit of originality, but are derived from the practice of those Orientalists who have devoted the most careful consideration to the subject, the various characters of nine alphabets current in India, amounting to sixty-four, have been, without any difficulty, represented by the twenty-four letters of the English or Roman alphabet. It is no part of the present inquiry to extend the application of the scheme more widely, but the principle could no doubt admit of its extension to all the modifications of those sounds which the similar conformation of the organs of speech in all the races of man establishes in all spoken and written languages. There may be occasional novelties, but the greater portion of articulate sounds must be the same in all languages, and their modifications do not change their identity. The Tamil *l̤* or *lr* is still an *l*, and the Arabic *ḳáf* is a *k*; and they may, therefore be expressed by those letters, indicating their modified enunciation and use by diacritical signs. Of course, for the purpose of expressing such signs, special characters must be added to the types now employed in English alone; but the use once established, there would be no more difficulty in furnishing the Roman type intended for printing any foreign tongue, than there is now in equipping a fount with italic letters and the marks of punctuation.

This supposes a systematic plan for the representation of foreign tongues and Roman letters, but without insisting upon a very rigorous observance of the laws of such a system, it is obvious that it is very possible to introduce a scheme of equivalents which will advantageously displace the arbitrary, unphilosophical, and conflicting modes of writing Oriental terms, by which most publications regarding British India have hitherto been disfigured.

Any representation of the words of a language by other than its own characters will, however, be more or less unsatisfactory, and will fail to inspire implicit reliance, unless checked by a comparison with the original letters. I have therefore endeavoured to ascertain the original forms of the words in their respective characters, and place them in contiguity with their English representatives. As the Oriental characters are not given in the official documents, their verification has been effected only by a laborious search through Dictionaries and original authorities. In a very few cases I have been unable to verify the original spelling, and in that case, if the authority was questionable, have omitted the word: when, however, there was reason to believe it genuine, I have inserted the term with a mark of interrogation, as "Máö-Mawása (?) H." In some cases, the doubt has extended to the language, as in the case of "Hari, Haria," where the interrogation takes the place of the initial representing the language. In the case of the slang of the Thags, the words are taken from Colonel Sleeman's Vocabularies, which do not contain the native characters, and rest entirely upon his authority, the English spelling which, in his lists, follows the system of Dr. Gilchrist, having been adapted to that used in the Glossary. The names of the servile tribes, as given in the various public reports on the subject, are also unaccompanied by native characters; and, in general, sad havoc has been made with their orthography. In some cases they have been traced to their originals, and the names of others have been verified, by which, also, a source of much misapprehension, occasioned by looseness of language, has been corrected; as where it is said, in the Bengal Reports, that the slaves are termed *kaits, kumars, chasas, kaibartts*, and the like. They are no such thing: these are the names of castes who, for the greater part, are free and independent, but who furnish domestic or prædial slaves, their children being sometimes sold to slavery, or they become bond slaves themselves. There are, no doubt, slaves of these castes, but not by virtue of the caste, which is not necessarily servile.

The original alphabets amount to nine, the Arabic or Niskh character being applicable to Arabic, Persian, and Hindustání, and the Devanágarí to Sanskrit, Hindí, and Maráṭhí; the others have their respective individual alphabets. The preparation of so many unusual characters has been a matter of much cost, time, and trouble; but it is due to Mr. Watts, the printer of the Glossary, to acknowledge the invariable readiness with which he has supplied the requisite founts, constituting, with other Oriental types in his possession, a richness of Oriental typography which no other press in this country can boast, and which is rivalled only by the Imperial Press of Vienna.

Composition in such diversified and uncommon characters has unavoidably led to some inaccuracies, to the correction of which I have not been myself always sufficiently attentive. My friend, Professor Johnson, has supplied me with some errata, chiefly in Arabic and Persian, and it is probable that other Oriental scholars will discover more. In Tamil I have had the benefit, for the most part, of the revision of Mr. Clarke. But when all the circumstances are considered, the comparative infrequency of Oriental printing in this country, and the impossibility of obtaining qualified assistance in the correction of the press, it will not be thought, perhaps, that the errors are very serious, or exceed a limit that might reasonably be expected.

Some mistakes will, no doubt, be observable, which may be ascribed to an imperfect knowledge of the several languages from which the terms are taken, amounting to thirteen—Sanskrit, Hindí, Bengálí, Uriya, Maráṭhí, Guzaráṭhí, Tamil, Telugu, Karnáta, Malayálam, Arabic, Persian, and Hindustání, besides a few from other dialects. Of course I do not pretend to be conversant with all these tongues. Of some of them I may have acquired more or less knowledge, but of the greater number I have little more than the letters and the most elementary rudiments, sufficient to enable me to consult a grammar and a dictionary. The interpretation of the terms collected, however, it must be remembered, does not usually rest upon my responsibility. Their application, and, in some instances, their explanation also, lies with the authors of the documents whence they have been extracted; and there is evidence that the words are not always consistently used or accurately defined. In general, however, the sense of the words may be made out from the context, and their use is not so much characterised by the want of correctness as by insufficiency of detail and absence of precision. Errors of explanation, however, do occur, as in one report, where *Be-dánistagi* is explained "knowingly," when it implies exactly the reverse: it is possibly, however, a typographical error for *bá-dánistagí*, which would have the meaning of "with knowledge." Difference of interpretation, however, may occur, without any mistakes being committed, as the word possibly bears a different sense in different places. *Ahar*, for instance, usually implies a small pond, but in some places it means a continuous embankment. *Chatwar* is explained in one place "the land between the houses of a village and its arable land," and in another, "the homestead or ground adjacent to a house." Perhaps this is rather want of exactitude than a different meaning. In a recent document, *Foras* is explained "waste land adjacent to cultivated land, and granted to the cultivators of the latter at a quit rent:" this is not wrong; but a subsequently printed report on the *Foras* lands of Bombay shews that it is not sufficiently comprehensive, the *Foras* lands forming an extensive part of the Island of Bombay reclaimed from the sea, which the inhabitants were encouraged to bring into cultivation by a low rate of rent. These are imperfections which the multiplication of authentic documents will gradually amend.

Even variations of spelling are not always to be regarded as originating in error: they may be local, arising from dialectic peculiarities, and the inability of one alphabet to express the letters of another. *Jamín* for *Zamín*, *Jamíndár*, or even *Jamídár*, for *Zamíndár*, are not wrong: they are the necessary forms which the Arabic words must take in the Hindí, Bengálí, and other Hindu characters, &c.; *Taắlluka* necessarily becomes *Táluk* in its Hindu version; and *Máphi* and *Mámlá* represent what are originally *Muắáfi* and *Muắámlat*.

In the arrangement of the contents of the Glossary I have thought it advisable to bring compound and derivative forms under their general parent, as likely to give a more definite notion of their purport. This classification has recommended the occasional introduction of words that may be regarded as not at all technical. *Áb*, "water," for example, is an ordinary Dictionary term, but I have inserted it at the head of its compounds, such as *Ábdár, Ábi, Ábistání*, which have a special or technical application, the force of which will be better appreciated when the meaning of *Áb* is referred to. I have, however, been chary of this extension, and many such general words will not be met with.

As a consequence of arranging compounds and derivatives under their respective primitives and radicals, a strictly alphabetical order has been departed from, and this has imposed the necessity of adding an

Alphabetical Index. Such an addition was also indispensable, for another reason, constituting the main usefulness of the compilation. The forms under which native words occur in public documents are much more frequently wrong than right—corrupt and blundering misrepresentations of the original. Yet it is of them especially that the uninitiated reader requires to know the signification; and in order to provide him with this assistance, whatever corruptions have been met with have been inserted. There are probably still more to be found, for it is impossible to affix limits to carelessness and ignorance; but most of those which are most frequent have been, it is believed, included. In order to avoid repetition, as well as to shew what the words ought to be, the corruptions are grouped round the correct form; as, *Kabúlíyat*, corruptly *Cabooleat, Kabooleat, Cubalyt, Quobooleut, Cooboolеat, Kubooleeat, Kaboolet, Caboolyat*; and the reader meeting with either of these has to turn to *Kabúlíyat* only, for its signification; but of course, without a previous knowledge of the correct form, he will be unable to recur to it, and the Glossary would be an instrument of which he could only imperfectly avail himself. This difficulty is obviated by the Index, which is invariably alphabetical, and in which, it is hoped, will be found whatever term may be desiderated, whether correct or corrupt. The references to page and column will not be attended with any material embarrassment: that which is made to the line of each column may be less readily effected from the omission of the figures which should have been inserted at least in fives or tens in the margin; but the advantage of such addition did not occur to me until far advanced in the work; a little practice, however, will soon render this reference also sufficiently easy, especially as every column contains the same number of lines, or forty-five. The preparation of this Index, the work of my own hand alone, has been attended with some labour and still greater delay, and has retarded the publication. It is, however, at last completed, and will, it is hoped, be found of use to the servants of the Company, and to all who, in England or in India, may wish to understand the objects and implements of the civil administration of the latter country.

Although these preliminary observations have perhaps rather exceeded the limits of an Introduction, it will probably be expected that some account should be given of the several languages from which the words of the following compilation are derived, especially for the benefit of those by whom the diversity of tongues that prevails in the territories of British India may be imperfectly appreciated. This unacquaintance with the polyglot nature of the current speech of India is not confined to individuals who have had no opportunity of personal observation, but may sometimes be evinced by those from whom more accurate information might be anticipated. A distinguished public character, for instance, a member of the late Committee of the Commons for the affairs of India, and long known to be conversant with its interests, observed to me, when I had occasion to mention Malayálam, that it was a language he had never heard of before; yet it is an ancient and cultivated form of speech current through an extensive and well-known tract of country, and the vernacular language of numerous suitors in several of the Judicial Courts and Revenue Collectorates under the Madras Presidency.

The languages of British India resolve themselves into two classes, although in somewhat unequal proportions; the speech that has grown up from an admixture of the original languages of the Mohammadan conquerors with those of the Hindus, Urdú or Hindustání, constituting one class, the other being formed of the different dialects of the Hindus. The former may be considered as perhaps more than equal in extent to any single form of the latter, but it is loosely spread, and at considerable intervals, over the surface. It is concentrated only at the still subsisting Mohammadan courts, as Delhi, Lucknow, Hyderabad. It is elsewhere restricted, in a great measure, to the Mohammadans, by whom, in many parts of India, especially in Bengal, it is greatly corrupted. It is very commonly in use among the native officers of our courts, especially in communication with their European superiors; and it is extensively, although not always accurately, understood by the commercial and trading classes. It is understood, after a fashion, by the Sipáhís of the Gangetic provinces, but the agricultural population are little, or not at all, acquainted with it, even in Upper India. In the South it is, of course, wholly unknown to them, and is very little understood by the other classes. When the College of Fort William was first organised, liberal encouragement was held out to native Hindustání scholars to become instructors, and many of the early teachers were men of high literary distinction among their countrymen. Several of them, under the guidance of Dr. Gilchrist, composed useful books, which were printed, and are still in use. Well-known Grammars and Dictionaries have also been compiled by different European scholars, and ample materials, therefore, are provided for facilitating the acquirement of the language. The Bengal civilian is required to master it as one condition of his employment in the

Lower Provinces; for although Bengálí be the language of the people in most of the districts, yet, besides the use of the Hindustání in the Sadr Courts and in Calcutta, it prevails, in greater or lesser approximation to Hindí in the Zilas of Bahár, Purnea, Tirhut, Sáran, Bhágalpur, and Sháhábád, and is therefore indispensable even in the Presidency of Bengal.

Under the Mohammadan Government the language of judicial and revenue proceedings was Persian, borrowing lavishly from Arabic, in which the principal legal authorities are written; and until within a comparatively recent period, the English Courts followed the example of their Mohammadan predecessors, and all the proceedings were recorded in Persian. Although this is no longer the case, yet the employment of that language, and of terms derived through it from Arabic for centuries, could not fail to influence the spoken languages of the country; and Hindustání comprises a large proportion, perhaps a third, of Arabic and Persian words. They are not wanting in Hindí; and even the purer Hindu dialects of the South, Tamil and Telugu, are copiously interlarded with technical terms borrowed from this source, and more or less modified to suit the vernacular pronunciation.

As, besides the extensive use of official terms of Persian and Arabic origin, the latter is the language of the authorities of Mohammadan law, it has of course been necessary to comprehend it as well as Persian in a vocabulary of the judicial and fiscal nomenclature of India, as far as it owes its origin to them. A full and authentic description of the principal authorities on Mohammadan law, accessible in India by Mohammadans and Europeans, is to be found in the Introduction to Morley's Analytical Digest.

Although the Sanskrit has not supplied the administration of India with technicalities to the same extent as Arabic, yet, being the language of the laws of the Hindus, it furnishes, in its unadulterated form, a copious vocabulary of words relating to caste, to contracts, to inheritance, to marriage, and to a variety of the incidents of Hindu life; and it still more abundantly pervades the different Indian dialects, supplying them with the ordinary designations of trades and occupations, the terms of agriculture, the names of plants and animals, the affinities of relationship, and an infinity of words connected with the social circumstances of the people in all parts of India which come within the scope of the present compilation. Combined with Arabic, therefore, it forms the great groundwork of the official language of law, of revenue, and of manners and customs throughout British India. The absence of a competent knowledge of it is painfully displayed in most of the official documents, although the works of Colebrooke, Ellis, Sutherland, and Macnaghten, besides sufficient elementary works, render a conversancy with its technology at least of comparatively easy attainment. A like copious and learned account of Sanskrit authorities on Hindu law as that of the authorities of Mohammadan law is given in the same valuable work.

As the most direct offset from Sanskrit, we may begin, amongst the vernacular tongues, with the Hindí, although the term is rather indefinite, being scarcely applicable to any single modification of the language spoken by the thirty millions of the Hindus of Hindustan. Each province may be said to have its own form of Hindí; and in Bahar, Bhojpur, Benares, Bindraban, Delhi, various shades of it are known under the appellations of Mágadhí, the dialect of Magadha or South Behar; Maithilí, that of North Bahar or Purnea and Tirhut; Bhojpurí, that of Bhojpur; Púrbí, Eastern, Braj Bhákhá, or the speech of Braj, and others.

There is, however, a sufficient concordance to render any one form of comparatively easy acquirement to one who, in addition to a competent knowledge of Hindustání, possesses a stock of Sanskrit vocables; for the grammar of Hindí is, in the main, the same as that of Hindustání, whilst nine-tenths of its words are Sanskrit. There is, however, a great want of the necessary helps to its acquirement. The peculiarities of the Hindí dialects have never been investigated, and we have a grammar of only one of them, the Braj, which is somewhat meagre. There is nothing that deserves the name of a Dictionary. The books usually read, the Baítál Pachísi and Sinhásan Battísí, are little else than Hindustání disguised in Nágarí letters; and the Premságar is the only work that is an authority of any value. There is, however, a Hindí Literature of some extent, from which serviceable extracts might be made, particularly from the Rámáyana of Tulsi Dás, and the Mahábhárata of Gokulnáth, both of which have been printed, although little known in Europe. From these and other available sources, and from personal investigation, it would be very possible to analyse the specialties of each provincial dialect of Hindí, and thus render an important service to the philology of Gangetic India.

The next immediate offset from the Sanskrit is the language of those provinces of the Bengal Presidency in which Bengálí is current. The Presidency, as already observed, includes districts to which that language is foreign, and in those in which it prevails, there are, no doubt, important local modifications. The Bengálí of Midnapur is probably somewhat different from that of Chittagong; I say probably, for, if possible, we know less of the dialects of Bengálí than of Hindí. Little was known of the language when the College of Fort William was founded. According to my late friend, Ram Komol Sen, in the Introduction to his English and Bengálí Dictionary, there were no adequate means of knowing much about it from the almost total absence of any literature. With the College came into existence the books at present in use: they were necessarily the work of Pandits, and they were consequently little else than Sanskrit compositions with a Bengálí grammatical structure. Of late years, elementary as well as other works have rapidly multiplied; and a list compiled by the Rev. Mr. Long shews a series of fifteen hundred publications in Bengálí from the presses of Calcutta alone. It is doubtful, however, if sufficient use is made of this opportunity of selection, and the publications in question are liable, for the most part, to the original defect: they are not the language of the people. This character applies especially to the best dictionaries yet published, those of Dr. Carey and Professor Haughton, both learned and laborious works, but works in which one may look in vain for a large proportion, perhaps the largest, of the spoken Bengálí. Here, again, is an ample field for investigation, the successful exploring of which would be not only of philological but administrative benefit. A real knowledge of the speech of another thirty millions of people should not be an object of indifference to their rulers; nor should the materials for its acquirement be suffered to remain imperfect, even if no loftier aim were entertained than that proficiency in Bengálí, which is required as a condition of public employment from the junior civilian.

Conterminous with Bengálí on the south-west is the province of Cuttak, in which the Uriya language, or that of Orisa, is current. It is framed from the Sanskrit stem, and of near affinity to Bengálí; but it has its own alphabet, grammar, and vocabulary. We have a useful grammar and dictionary of Uriya by Mr. Sutton, but the latter is scarcely sufficiently comprehensive. Of the languages of the barbarous tribes inhabiting the hills and forests of the western portion of the district, the Khonds and Gonds, very little is yet known: the population of the province is estimated at four millions and a half.

Of the direct descendants of Sanskrit, which are current in Central and Western India, Bundelkhand, Malwa, and the Rajput States, nothing is known beyond their general connection with the Hindí family: no attempt has ever been made, except in the Serampur translations of the Scriptures, to obtain any conversancy with them, or convey a knowledge of them to others; yet it is evident, from the quotations made by the late Colonel Tod from the great record of Rájputána, the Prithí Raï Raisa, that the dialects have national peculiarities, which must be acquired before a free intercourse can be maintained with the people. The same may be said of Panjábí, of which, at present, little or nothing is known, except as to its being one of the great Sanskrit family. Since, however, the province has been "annexed," we may hope to become acquainted with its speech, and elementary works are beginning to make their appearance, although on a limited and inadequate scale. A well-digested and comprehensive dictionary should be set about without delay, especially as in the Sikh books there are copious materials for such a compilation, not forgetting, however, as has been too often the case, the spoken language of the people.

Proceeding westward and to the south, we come to two important languages, which are those of the Courts and Collectorates of the Presidency of Bombay—Guzaráthí and Maráthí, both members of the Sanskrit stock. Little has yet been done for the first of these, and for many years we had nothing to apply to but the very elementary work of Drummond, the Rudiments of Guzeráthí and Maráthí, published in 1808. In 1829 a more copious grammar, by Mr. Forbes, of the Civil Service, was lithographed at Bombay, and a second edition was printed in 1845: since then other useful grammars have been published. We have also a dictionary by Mirza Mohammad Kasim, which, although of limited extent, is very serviceable as far as it goes. The population of the country is somewhat uncertain, but it is estimated at about three millions. The Zila Courts in which the language is chiefly required are those of Ahmadabad, Baroch, and Surat.

The language of the Maráthas is still more important, as spoken by a still more numerous body of people, and more diligently cultivated both by natives and Europeans. It has a copious literature of its own, and this has been enriched by translations from English works of literature and science, as Duff's History and De Morgan's Algebra. The Missionaries have also published a great number of tracts and translations. We have several useful grammars and the very best dictionaries of any native tongue in Molesworth's Maráthí and English Dictionary, an improved edition of which is in progress, and Molesworth and Candy's Dictionary, English and Maráthí. In these works we have what is so much missed in other similar compilations—the language of the people as well as the language of the books. Still, however, something has to be effected, particularly with respect to the dialects of the Maráthí. That spoken in the Konkan, for instance, differs so much from that which is current on the east of the Ghats, that the Serampur Missionaries translated the New Testament into it as if it had been a distinct form of speech, which brought upon them the scarcely deserved severity of the late Colonel Vans Kennedy's criticism. Very possibly there are other modifications of which a knowledge would be of service. The population by whom, in one or other form, Maráthí is spoken, is rated at about eight millions. The Zila Courts in which it is principally current are Ahmadnagar, Ratnagiri, Khandesh, Puna, Konkan, and Sholapur. At Dharwar it is mixed with Karnáta. Formerly, a knowledge of either Maráthí or Guzeráthí was required as a condition of public service by the Bombay Government, but either was made secondary to proficiency in Hindustání; and as it was the practice to attach the young civilian to the Court of a Judge or Collector before his proficiency had been tested, it commonly happened that no test was ever applied, especially with regard to a second language, and the latter was left to independent and voluntary exertion: of course the acquirement was rare. Very recently, however, more stringent measures have been announced, and the Bombay civilian is expected to qualify, in either Maráthí or Guzeráthí, in nine months at furthest, under penalty of removal from the service: the term allowed is something of the shortest.

The Presidency of Madras embraces a greater variety of distinct divisions and of languages than that of Bombay; and here we also lose that direct descent of the native languages from the Sanskrit which is so unmistakeably evident in the Hindu languages of Central and Northern India. Modern philology traces those of the South of India to the Ugrian, Tatar, or Mongolian stock, difficult as it is to comprehend how or when the population of the Dakhin immigrated from the steppes of Central Asia. Whatever the origin, however, of these languages, they are dependent upon Sanskrit, in a greater or less degree, for their literature, and for the language of their religion, their institutions, and their government. Although they are all nearly connected, yet there are obviously two main divisions, one comprehending Telugu and Karnáta, the other Tamil and Malayálam; and we shall proceed to offer a few notices of them in that order, derived especially from the remarks of the late Mr. Ellis, the most accomplished oriental scholar that has done credit to the civil service of Madras.

The Telugu, as stated in Mr. Ellis's memoir, forming part of the Introduction to Campbell's Telugu Grammar, is the vernacular language of the Hindus on the coast of Coromandel, extending from the Dutch settlement of Pulicat on the south, just above Madras, northwards through the Northern Sarkárs to Chikakol, and spreading westwards from the coast to the frontiers of Maisur on the south, and on the north through part of Berar and the territories of the Nizam; meeting on the north with Uriya, on the west with Maráthí and Karnáta, and on the south with Tamil. It is consequently the language of the Zila Courts and Collectorates of Belari, Gantur, Nellur, Rajamahendrí, Chikakol, Kadapa and Masulipatam, as well as the non-regulation districts of Ganjam and Vizagapatam, and is current, according to estimate, amongst nine millions of people. There are good practical grammars of the language by Messrs. Campbell and Brown, of the Madras Civil Service; and to the former we owe a dictionary, Telugu and English, of which the only defect is its want of comprehensiveness. Reversed dictionaries of English and Telugu have been published by Messrs Morris and Brown, and the same gentlemen have supplied very useful selections for study. There is a considerable body of literature in Telugu, principally consisting of translations from Sanskrit, which enters extensively into the body of the language. A knowledge of Telugu is required of the civil servant of Madras before he is capable of public employment.

The Karnáta, or, less accurately, the Canarese language, has an alphabet scarcely differing from that in which Telugu is written, and the radicals of the two languages are essentially the same: a large proportion of the words are also the same, whether indigenous or Sanskrit, modified by slight variations of inflexion and peculiarities of pronunciation. There is a literature partly original, but, in a still greater degree, translated from Sanskrit; but no Karnáta works had been printed until lately, when encouragement has been given to the publication of lithographed copies of some popular compositions. We have, however, long had a serviceable grammar and dictionary of Karnáta, the former by Mr. M'Kerrell, a Madras civilian, published in 1820, and the latter, both Karnáta and English, and English and Karnáta, in four volumes quarto, by Mr. Reeves, of the London Missionary Society. The former follows Captain Wilks in his description of the limits through which the language is in use—from Bedar, north-west of Haidarabad, passing by Adoni and through Nandidrug to the Eastern Ghats, the course of which it follows until it passes by Koimbatur, and, running to the north-west, ascends to the sources of the Krishna, whence it returns to Bedar. It is used also, but with other dialects, on the sea coast in the interval between the Principality of Kurg and the Portuguese territory of Goa, to which tract the designation of Canara is, with questionable propriety, restricted. The Zila Courts where it is chiefly employed are those of Honawar, Mangalur, and Dhárwár; but it is in use generally throughout Maisur. The population of whom it is the vernacular are estimated at about two millions. Encouragement is held out, in the shape of pecuniary rewards to the junior civilians of the Madras Presidency, to acquire some knowledge of Karnáta in addition to those languages which are indispensable, or Tamil and Telugu.

The Tamil language is one of those of which a knowledge is highly essential in the provinces subject to the Presidency of Madras, and it is accordingly one of the two of which the study is now imperative on the Madras civilian. It is the language of the country termed, in Sanskrit, Drávira, comprising the provinces of the Coromandel coast, from a short distance north of Madras to Cape Komorin, and extending inland to the limits of the Karnáta language. It comprises, therefore, the Presidency Courts, and those of Arcot, Salem, Koimbatur, Kumbhakonam, Trichinapallí, Madura, Tinivelli, and is spoken, it has been estimated, by five millions of people. There are two dialects, or, perhaps, rather styles of it—Shen and Kodun, or high and low Tamil—in both of which there is a copious literature, Tamil having been highly cultivated at as early a date as the ninth century, when a college, established at Madura for its especial encouragement, was in a flourishing condition. Ample means for the acquirement of its structure exists, as the Missionaries of both the Roman and Protestant Churches have long ago contributed ably to its illustration. Beschi's grammar of the common dialect was published in 1728, and that of the higher Tamil has been translated by Mr. Babington. A grammar of the current language, by Ziegenbalg, was printed in 1716. The originals of these were in Latin, but more recently an excellent grammar has been published by Rhenius, in English. We have also an English Grammar by Mr. Anderson. We are indebted to the Missionaries also for Tamil dictionaries, but the first published is printed in an uncouth type and on bad paper, and is now scarce. A much more comprehensive dictionary, Tamil and English, was undertaken by the late Dr. Rottler, and has been printed in four parts. Unfortunately it was left by the compiler unfinished, and it has been printed in a defective state, long lists of Tamil words being inserted without any English interpretation. The portions which are translated form much the larger share, and the manner in which what has been done is effected enhances the regret that some competent scholars should not have been employed to render the work entire. The language is difficult of acquirement, but with these helps it is to be mastered. It is no doubt, in its origin, independent of Sanskrit, but, to judge from the dictionary, admits of Sanskrit insertions as freely as any other of the southern dialects. It is also peculiar in its dealings with Sanskrit words, so that, without a previous knowledge of the latter, it is scarcely possible to recognise them in their Tamil form. It has, as shewn above, a scanty alphabet. It has no aspirates, and abhors compounds; and therefore substitutes unaspirated letters for the former, and resolves the latter into syllables; *Bhárata,* therefore, becomes *Párada,* and *Grámam, Kirámam;* for *Siva-prakása* we have *Siven-pirikasan,* and for *Tattwam, Tattuvan.* It is evident that Tamil scholars who are not Sanskrit scholars also must be continually embarrassed by these equivocal expressions.

Radically related to Tamil, but employing a different alphabet modelled on the Devanágarí, and differing very frequently in its grammatical structure, is the Malayálam or Malayálma language, which is spoken along the southern portion of the Malabar coast from Quilon to Cape Kumarí. North of Quilon, as far as to Goa, the Tuluva, which is a distinct dialect, although of the same derivation as the Malayálam, is the provincial form of speech, though much intermixed with other dialects, especially Karnáta; and, according to Mr. Ellis, the Koduga or Kurg language is a modification of Tuluva. The Kurg Raja, however, when in England, wrote in the Karnáta character, and declared that to be his native tongue. Besides the relation of the order of the alphabet, the Malayálam abounds, more perhaps than either of the other dialects of the south, in Sanskrit derivations, in a proportion exceeding a half, equal perhaps to three-fifths of the whole under the two heads which Mr. Ellis specifies as common to the dialects of Southern India, *Tat-samam,* pure Sanskrit words, or *Tad-bhavam,* derived from Sanskrit. The *Desya,* or native words of the country, may also be divided into Tamil *Tatsamam,* or pure Tamil, and Tamil *Tadbhavam,* derivatives from Tamil.

There are several serviceable grammars of the language. One was published by Mr. Drummond, of the Bombay Medical Service, soon after the province was subject to British authority, or in 1799;—but this is now superseded by the grammars of Mr. Spring, of the Madras Civil Service, and the Rev. Mr. Peet, of the Church Mission Society. There are also good dictionaries, Malayálam and English, and English and Malayálam, by the Rev. Mr. Bailey, of the same Society. There is a dearth of printed books, but something has been lately done to provide students with the means of study. Malayálam is the language of the Zila Court of Kalikat, or Calicut, and it mixes with Karnáta in the Courts of Honawar and Mangalur. It is spoken by about two millions and a half of people, inclusive of North and South Canara.

These are the principal languages of British India, but there are others which are of growing importance, although not yet forming objects of official requisition. In the north, the Bhot dialects, which spread through the Himálaya districts, are of Tibetan origin, and terms from the latter find their way into the language of administration. The grammar and dictionary of Csoma Körösi are the only means of becoming conversant with the language; and no English scholar has yet trodden in his steps, although Petersburgh and Paris can boast of cultivators of Tibetan. The Panjábí, of course, becomes of primary importance; and our intercourse with our neighbours, the Affghans, renders Pushtu a valuable acquisition; but nothing has yet been effected towards facilitating the acquirement of the latter beyond the very circumscribed grammar and vocabularies of Lieutenant Leech, or of the former, except the similar publications of the same intelligent officer, and a grammar, vocabulary, and dialogues, by Captain Sterling. On the west, a knowledge of the language of Sindh has become essential; and here, also, the means are yet limited, although they begin to be supplied in a grammar and short dictionary by Captain Stack. Of the dialects of the Hill tribes on the east, from Asam to Arakan, all that is yet known is from the comparative vocabularies of the Rev. Mr. Brown and of Mr. Hodgson, the object of which is rather comparative than practical. When we get to Arakan we come upon the Burma language, a knowledge of which, since the annexation of the provinces along the coast from Arakan to Tenaserim, is indispensable to the government of an extensive tract of country and a numerous population. There are grammars of the language, sufficient to enable the European to acquire it, by the late Missionaries Judson and Hough, and by Captain Latter. There is also a good English and Burma dictionary, by Mr. Lane; but a comprehensive Burma and English dictionary is still a desideratum. There is a want, also, of printed books, which might easily be multiplied from the copious stores of Burma literature, both historical and Buddhist.

To give liberal encouragement to the preparation and publication of these and similar works in all the languages current in the wide provinces and among the many millions of people subject to its authority is the positive duty and the obvious interest of the Government of British India. Much has, no doubt, been accomplished; but it may be questioned if the encouragement that has been given has been always judiciously bestowed. The efforts of individuals must always be desultory, and will often be ineffective. There wants a systematic course of proceeding, and the selection of competent agents; and it might be worth while to adopt official arrangements for ascertaining what has been done, and what remains to be done, towards providing the civil and military servants of the Company with ample and adequate means of acquiring a command of all the languages through which they may have to minister to the necessities and claims of the different races amongst whom the course of service may call them. In the meanwhile the following pages will, it is hoped, contribute to facilitate their acquirement of the qualifications which are indispensably necessary for the due performance of their important functions—knowledge of the languages, and knowledge of the people, of India.

H. H. WILSON.

LONDON, *January* 1855.

ERRATA.

PAGE	COL.	LINE		
2	1	80	For	আবেদন্ব read আবেদন.
8	1	31	..	Diwani, read Díwání.
9	1	17		كاغز read كاغذ.
.	..	..	..	Kághaz, read Kághaẓ.
10	2	7	..	प्रमाखं read प्रमाणं.
11	2	31	..	Agwasi, read Agwási.
13	1	5	.	Mahmud, read Mahmúd.
.	.	20	.	دقتر read دفتر.
..	..	30	.	Jaigir, read Jaigír.
18	1	5	..	آسامي read اسامي.
15	1	7		واحيد read واحد.
18	1	20	..	వాబు read వాంబు.
20	2	42	.	گزار read گذار.
..	..	..	..	Guzár, read Guẓár.
21	1	31	..	دقتر read دفتر.
..	..	45	..	నష్ట్ర read నష్ట.
..	2	28	..	அமீ read அம.
22	1	3	..	Amaváluḍana, read Amuváludana.
..	..	15	..	Dáhale, read Ḍábaḷe.
..	2	11	..	दहले read डाहळे.
..	..	6	..	Ambarakkadai, read Ambárakkaḍai.
23	2	38	..	Múmanín, read Múminín.
25	2	19	..	౦ read ఠ.
26	2	36	..	ஆநி read ஆணி.
27	1	39	..	Das, read Dár.
..	..	42	..	Kar read Kár.
29	2	33	..	আপিলাৎ read আপিলাং.
31	2	3	..	Ârázi, read Aráẓí.
..	..	.	.	عرض read ارض.
..	..	..	..	عراض read اراض.
33	1	37	..	Pála, read Pala.
36	2	31	..	Asoea, read Asoca.
37	1	1	..	Váṇa, read Vána.
..	1	24	..	Ṣinchana, read Sinchana.
..	..	..	..	शिञ्चन read सिञ्चन.

PAGE	COL.	LINE		
37	1	28	For	వాశ్ఠి read వాంశ్ఠి.
..	..	32	..	ఆశ్ఠి read ఆస్ఠి.
43	2	7	..	వా read వాం.
..	..	34	..	possesson, read possession.
44	1	11	..	mâash, read mâásh.
..	..	..	..	معش read معاش.
46	1	30	..	চালাণ read চালান.
50	1	24	.	বেকযা read বকেযা.
..	..	28	..	توجيه read توجيح.
..	..	..	..	Tauji, read Taujíh.
51	1	26	..	Baladasti, read Báládastí.
..	..	..		بلدستي read بالادستي.
56	2	10	..	মাতি read মাটি.
59	2	42	..	Banijaga, read Banijiga.
61	1	4	..	Bánsphor, read Bánsphoṛ.
..	.	..	..	پهور read پهوڑ.
..	.	10	.	বংচ, বাংচ read বংট বাংট.
	..	12	..	বাংচা read বাংটা.
..	..	16	..	বংচক read বংটক.
..	..	18	..	বংচন, বাংধন read বংটন, বাংটন.
63	1	43	..	Ârázi, read Aráẓí.
..	..	..		عراضي read اراضي.
67	2	3	..	বচ read বট.
..	..	17	.	বাচ read বাট.
68	1	17	..	বাচ্চা read বাট্টা.
63	2	15	.	Bhauli, read Bhaoli.
69	2	5	..	Bâzi, read Bâẓí.
..	..	..	..	بعذي read بعضي.
75	1	33	..	ফোচ read ফোট.
84	1	39	..	ভুচ read ভুট.
87	1	28	..	انام read انعام.
..	..	..	..	Inám, read Inâám.
93	2	5	..	T, read Tam.
97	1	24	..	Ârázi read Aráẓí.
..	..	..	..	عراضي read اراضي.

ERRATA.

PAGE	COL.	LINE	
101	2	9	.. Chándla, read Chándlá.
102	1	15	.. Chánwál, read Chánwal.
110	1	37	.. Chhaṛ, read Chháṛ.
110	2	15	.. ছচাক read ছটাক.
111	2	7	. ছিচ read ছিট.
.	..	20	.. ছোচা read ছোটা.
114	1	3	. চিচা read চিটা.
120	2	44	.. Phareolus, read Phaseolus.
129	1	23	. Ḳaz̤â, read Ḳaz̤í.
.	..	.	.. قضع read قضي.
..	2	35	.. Ḍáulu read Ḍaúlu.
130	1	24	.. تشخيس read تشخيص.
131	1	23	.. Ḍehrí, read Dehrí.
135	1	11	.. Dhálbhol, read Dhálbol.
136	2	15	.. Dhárat, read Dharaṭ.
138	1	15	.. ङपाध्याय read उपाध्याय.
154	2	44	.. فلكال read فلك ال.
159	2	21	.. الاة read الاه.
168	2	33	مهال read محال.
180	1	35	.. Goshṭashthami, read Goshṭháshṭamí.
197	2	37	.. همال read حمّال.
205	1	7	.. حازر read حاضر.
..	2	6	.. Huzur, read Huz̤úr.
.	..	..	.. Guz̤ár, read Guz̤ár.
..	..	..	.. گزار read گذار.
207	1	29	.. حجره read هجره.
215	1	27	.. Iḳráh, read Ikráh.
..	..	..	.. اقراه read اكراه.
218	2	12	.. Kánungo, read Ḳánungo.
..	..	..	.. كانونگو read قانونگو.
220	1	31	.. Ishhád, read Ishḥád.
..	..	..	.. اشحاد read اشهاد.
..	2	4	.. Ishrák, read Ishráḳ.
..	..	..	.. اشراك read اشراق.
221	1	10	.. బస్తుతాం read ఇస్తుతాం.
..	..	27	.. استقاق read استحقاق.
.	..	34	After lawful, insert استهلاه.
..	..	..	.. .. Istiḥláh.
..	2	39	For گزاري read گذاري.
222	1	5	.. Istihshád read Istishḥád.
..	..	..	.. استهشاد read استشهاد.
..	1	27	.. Itíḳáf, read Îtikáf.
..	..	..	.. اتقاف read اعتكاف.
..	..	29	.. Ramaz̤án, read Ramz̤án.

PAGE	COL.	LINE	
225	1	39	For تهاته read تهانه.
..	2	14	.. جهيم read جحيم.
227	1	39	.. كاغز read كاغذ.
..	..	..	.. Kághaz, read Kághaẕ.
229	1	31	.. بهر read بحر.
..	2	22	.. Tashkhís, read Tashkhíṣ.
..	..	.	.. تشخيس read تشخيص.
..	..	42	. Sadr, read Ṣadr.
..	..	..	.. سدر read صدر.
230	1	44	.. زامن read ضامن.
231	2	24	.. جاناب read جانب.
232	1	1	.. "but," read "as it is."
..	2	31	.. यन्त्री read यंत्री.
233	1	17	.. जारी read जारी.
..	2	16	.. كشين read كشيدن.
..	..	39	.. Kafífa, read Khafífa
..	..	..	.. كفيفه read خفيفه.
235	2	15	.. جانه read خانه.
236	1	18	.. كاغز read كاغذ.
..	2	25	.. Jazar, read Jaẕar.
..	..	..	.. جزر read جذر.
240	1	37	.. حسات read حساب.
..	2	35	.. जिताष्ठमी read जिताष्टमी.
245	2	4	.. "second," read "last."
249	2	33	Dele "probably the same word."
251	2	36	for भुमी read भूमि.
260	1	26	.. تعالقدار read تعلقدار.
..	2	6	.. قنض read كنض.
..	..	..	.. Ḳanz, read Kanz̤.
264	2	29	.. كرار read قرار.
..	..	..	.. Karár, read Ḳarár.
267	2	34	.. Ḳatâ al ṭaríḳ, read Ḳâṭâ al ṭaríḳ.
..	..	..	.. قطع الطاريق read قاطع الطريق.
268	2	19	.. Kaṭakina, read Kaṭkina.
271	2	8	.. Kávál, read Kával.
273	1	25	.. Kessiriya, read *Kessiriya.*
274	1	28	.. খাজর read খাজুর.
279	2	30	.. Sadr, read Ṣadr.
..	..	..	.. سدر read صدر.
..	..	36	.. Kad, read Bad.
280	1	12	.. گزار read گذار.
..	..	..	.. Guzár, read Guz̤ár.
..	2	10	.. تعلك read تعلق.
285	1	26	.. Khaïn, read Kháïn.

ERRATA.

PAGE	COL.	LINE	
285	1	26	For خين read خاين.
286	1	9	.. Khém, read Khéni.
289	2	33	Insert, H. (كرانا).
290	1	29	For قرّات read قرّاط.
297	1	13	. Krushikudu, read Kṛushikuḍu.
..	.	..	.. కృషికుదు read కృషికుడు.
..		..	.. Krushivaludu, read Krushivalaḍu.
.	..	..	.. కృషీవలుదు read కృషీవలుడు.
..	2	10	.. Kṛiya, and the same in the following compounds, read Kriyá.
299	2	43	.. كانون read قانون.
300	1	37	.. लेखर्ण read लेखनं.
303	1	32	.. అంచన read అంచనా.
..	..	..	.. Anchana, read Anchaná.
304	1	35	.. Kuri, read Kuṛi.
308	1	19	.. Miráj, read Mîráj.
..	..	..	.. مراج read معراج.
.	2	4	.. Lakít, read Laḳíṭ.
..	..	..	.. لقيت read لقيط.
310	2	33	.. لاوارشي read لاوارثي.
312	1	44	.. శిఖి read లిఖి.
316	1	8	.. Vádu, read Váḍu.
..	..	..	.. వాదు read వాడు.
320	1	39	.. مهانره read مهرانه.
..	2	27	.. محصلاني read محصلانه.
323	1	13	Sadr, read Ṣadr.
..	.	..	.. سدر read صدر.
..	..	41	.. پيشكلر read پيشكار.
..	2	9	.. ماجب read واجب.
330	1	26	.. منصبزات read منصبذات.
..	..	..	.. Manṣabzát, read Manṣabẕát.
332	1	18	.. مرحون read مرهون.
333	2	24	.. مشرك read مشرق.
335	2	11	.. متول read مطول.
337	2	21	.. تعالق read تعلق.
..	..	24	.. مزر read مزرع.
..	..	35	.. Mâzúlí, read Mâzúli.
..	..	40	.. Mazún, read Mauzún.
..	..	..	.. مزون read موزون.
342	1	21	.. آتشت read آتش.
..	..	28	.. مر read مير.
344	1	25	.. مزاح read مزاج.
346	1	9	.. محسل read محصل.
346	1	44	.. Mṛigarṣírsha, read Mṛigaṣirsha.

PAGE	COL.	LINE	
349	2	29	For كانونگو read قانونگو.
354	2	5	.. Mulḳ, read Mulk.
..	.	..	.. ملق read ملك.
..	..	8	.. Mulḳí, and in the following, read Mulkí, &c.
..	..	..	.. ملقي read ملكي.
356	2	37	.. ரூறை read ரூறை.
357	2	29	.. مشعا read مشاع.
.	.	..	. Mushâá, read Mushâa.
358	2	44	.. تارخ read تاريخ.
..	..	..	.. Tarikh, read Tárikh.
359	1	2	.. متغرق read متفرق.
361	1	36	.. داوع read دعوا.
364	1	4	.. چيتتها read چتّها.
..	..	13	.. مضكورات read مذكورات.
..	..	..	.. Maẓkúrát, read Maẕkúrát.
374	1	18	.. نزانه read نذرانه.
378	1	36	.. Níránambam, read Níràrambam.
..	..	..	.. நீராநம்பம் read நீராரம்பம்.
386			.. 286, read 386.
408	2	9	.. పత్రుదు read పత్రుడు.
..	..	..	.. Patrudu, read Patruḍu.
410	1	22	.. Paṭṭan, read Pattan.
..	2	27	. Pattaní, read Pattani.
411	1	9	.. നൈ read പൈ.
416	2	21	.. Pharnivasi, read Pharnivísi.
419	2	38	. Pod, read Poḍ.
421	2	2	.. Porombadom, read Poromkadom.
423	1	8	.. Absolute, read absentee.
..	2	21	.. كاغض read كاغذ.
429	2	17	.. پرسلش read پرسش.
..	..	26	.. पुरष read पुरुष.
430	1	12	.. تشت read پشت.
431	1	30	.. العرض read الارض.
432	1	8	.. فوگر read رفوگر.
..	2	5	.. رهاي read رهائي.
439	2	42	.. نضارت read نظارت.
..	..	..	.. Naẓárat, read Naẕárat.
At bottom,			.. 339, read 439.
444	1	37	.. رشة read رشته.
445	2	6	.. Roja, read Roju.
446	1	18	.. روربكاي read روبكاري.
..	2	1	.. اسشهادت read الشهادت.
446	2	37	.. اس سرقة read السرقة.

ERRATA.

PAGE	COL.	LINE		
447	2	19	For	بانوس read مانوس.
451	1	44	..	کانونگو read قانونگو.
458	2	42	..	Samba, read Sam̀bá.
462	1	1	..	کلنتا read کانتا.
466	1	42	..	Sarafrázi, read Sarfarázi.
468	1	40	..	سغره read صغره.
..	..	..	..	Sughra, read Ṣughra.
475	2	43	..	శేవకుదు read శేవకుడు.
..	..	..	..	Ṣevakudu, read Ṣévakuḍu.
481	1	31	..	کاغص read کاغذ.
..	..	36	..	خابه read خانه.
482	2	30	..	Síhaṣâï, read Siháṣáhí.
491	2	38	..	Ṣúchaka, read Súchaka.
..	..	..	.	शूचक read सूचक.
492	2	5	..	शूचि read सूचि.
496	2	20	..	स्वमित्वं read स्वामित्वं,
497	1	1	..	Swaist, read Swastí.
..	..	29	.	श्वेतामवर read श्वेताम्बर.
..	..	31	.	उयार्जित read उपार्जित.
498	1	42	..	زامني read ضامني.
501	1	33	..	تعيات read تعينات.
503	2	19	..	نقسيم read تقسيم.
509	1	31	..	ننصف read تنصف.
512	1	24	..	تزاوي read تراوي.
518	1	10	For	Taṣadaḳ, read Taṣadduḳ.
..	..	..	..	تصدق read تصدّق.
514	1	28	..	تعتيل read تعطيل.
515	1	39	..	توجع read توجيع.
516	2	39	..	Tengalay, read Tengalai.
520	1	17	..	Selection, read Selections.
522	2	26	..	جمبندي read جمعبندي.
524	2	4	..	টোলী read টোলা.
530	2	7	..	عزر read عذر.
538	1	34	.	प्रदि read प्रति.
546	2	7	..	Vetkanam, read Vettukánam.
549	2	34	..	ضابته read ضابطه.
553	1	24	..	گذاشه read گذاشته.
584	2	6	..	تکسيم read تقسيم.
557	1	11	Should be	وسيل بالنكاح.
..	..	19	For	واصطه read واسطه.
..	..	32	..	वतबंधु read वतनबंधु.
561	2	31	..	ذابيح *zábíh* read ذابح *zábih*.
569	1	14	..	ذاده read زاده.
575	1	4	..	దాసుసు read దాసును.
582	2	39	..	کراري read قراري.
590	1	3	..	مذّن read مؤذن.
592	1	1	..	يبيري read پيري.

GLOSSARY.

Áb, H. (آب, contracted from the A. ابو *Abu*) A father.

Ábái, H. (اباي) Patrimonial, descending from paternal ancestors (land, property).

Áb, H. (P. آب, S. आपः) Water.

Ábdár, H. (آبدار) A servant whose office it is to prepare water for domestic use, or for drinking.

Ábdár khána, H. (آبدارخانه) The room where such water is kept in suitable earthen vessels.

Áb-páshi, H. (آبپاشي) Irrigating fields, watering fields; *lit.* water-sprinkling.

Áb-rawán, H. (آبروان) Running water; *metaphor.* Fine muslin.

Ábí, H. (آبي, *lit.* Relating to water, watered). In the north-west provinces it is applied to land watered from ponds, tanks, lakes, or water-courses, in distinction to that which is watered from wells; as the supply from the former is liable to fail in the hot season, *Ábí* land is assessed at a lower rate; in some cases at less than a half of that watered from wells.

Ábistáni, H. (آبستاني) Land artificially irrigated.

Áb-khez, H. (آبخيز) A soil impregnated with water, moist or wet soil.

Ábkár, H. (آبكار) A manufacturer or retailer of spirituous liquors; *lit.* a maker of (strong) waters.

Ábkári, also written Abkaree, Abkary, Abkarry, Aubkaury, H. &c. (آبكاري), or in Telugu, Ábukári, (ఆబుకారి) Revenue derived from duties levied on the manufacture and sale of inebriating liquors, as *tári* or *toddy*, *pachwai*, *arrach*, &c., and on intoxicating drugs, whether in substance, infusion, or extract, as *opium*, *bhang*, *chiras*, &c. It is levied on certain licenced distilleries, or in fees for licences granted by the collector to retailers. In some parts of the south of India the *Ábkári* included duties on eating-shops, gaming-houses, itinerant tumblers, jugglers, and the like. [In the Report of the House of Commons, 1832, p. 95, it is said to comprehend duties on pepper and betel; but this is a mis-statement, as no such duties are levied; although, in Mysore, the areka-nut was sometimes included in the Ábkári farm.] The principal Regulations in Bengal for the Ábkári duties are xxvii. 1793, x. 1813, xiii. 1816, and vii. 1824

Ábkári Dárogha, H. (آبكاري داروغه) The head native officer appointed to superintend distilleries, spirit-shops, and the like.

Ábkári Mahál, H. (آبكاري محال) The department or office of *Ábkári*, the excise.

Abáb, Mar. (अबाब, from A. *Abwáb*, q.v.) A particular item in revenue accounts: the grain falling to the share of the Government after deducting the portions of the several sharers.

Ábád, H. (P. آباد). The word is very generally adopted; as Hindi and Mar. (आबाद), Beng. (আবাদ), Telugu (ఆబాదు), Populous, cultivated, as a village or tract of country; the reverse of *Wirán*, (ويران), waste, deserted. A village or tract which is designated in revenue phrase as *Ábád* is one from which revenue may be levied: in military topography it denotes a place where supplies may be expected. It occurs also, though less commonly, as *Ábádán* (آبادان). *Ábád karna* means, to introduce or extend cultivation or population, to settle, to people; whence may arise a claim to property through descent from the *Ábád-kár*, the originator or founder. As the second member of a compound *Ábád* often denotes a city, as *Akbar-ábád*, the city of *Akbar*, or Agra, which he made his capital; *Aurang-ábád*, the city of *Aurang-zeb*; *Murshid-ábád*, the city of *Murshid Kuli Khan*, Governor of Bengal, by whom it was enlarged and embellished; *Sháhjahán-ábád*, the city of *Sháhjahán*, or Delhi; with many others of Mohammedan origin and improvement. From the attributives *Ábád* and *Ábádán* come the substantives *Ábádi*, *Ábádáni*, Populousness, cultivation: in Bengali the meanings have been transposed, *Ábád* (আবাদ) signifying cultivation, populousness, and *Ábádi* (আবাদী), cultivated, peopled.

Ábád-beshi, H. (آباد بيشي, from P. *béshi* بيشي, Excess). First assessment of newly-settled or cultivated land.

Abarátam, Tam. (அபராதம், from S. *Aparádha* अपराध, Fault, offence, in which sense it also occurs in most dialects). Fine, amercement, forfeiture.

Âbd, Ûbd, H. (A. عبد, plur. *Âbíd* عبيد) A slave, two descriptions of whom are alone recognised in Mohammedan law—infidels made captives in war, and their descendants. In practice much greater latitude is allowed, although not strictly legal; and a title to slaves may be acquired by purchase, donation, or inheritance. The term enters largely into the formation of Mohammedan proper names, as *Âbd-ullah*, slave of God; *Âbd-âli*, slave of Ali; *Âbd-ul-málik*, the slave of the Lord (God). It is also frequently prefixed in affectation of humility to the official signatures of native officers, whether Hindus or Mohammedans; and in law papers it is sometimes prefixed to the name of each subscribing witness.

Ábdá, Ben. (আবদা, S. अब्द, a year). The period during which a party who reclaims waste land is allowed to hold it rent-free. The rent remitted. The land so held. [The term in this sense is confined to Eastern Bengal and Chittagong.]

Abdhút, Ubdhoot, H. (S. *Avadhúta* अवधूतः) A religious mendicant of the Hindus, one who professes to have "shaken off" the infirmities of humanity. In Hindustan the *Abdhút* is generally of the *Vaishṇava* sect. In the south it is said he is usually a *Ṣaiva* mendicant.

Ábédak, Beng. (S. আবেদক *ávedaka*) A complainant or suitor, a petitioner.

Ábedan, Beng. (S. আবেদন) A petition, a plaint, an affidavit.

Ábedan patra, or *Ábedan lipi*, (S. আবেদন পত্র, or লিপি) A written plaint or petition, a representation in writing.

Abhar, Ubhur, Mar. (अभर) The collections from a village in the Maráṭha country. *Kacha Abhar*, The gross collections, without any deduction.

Abhaya, Ubhuyu, Mar. (S. अभय, from अ neg., and भय, fear), An assurance of safety or immunity.

Abhayaḍinḍima, Mar. (S. अभयडिंडिम) A proclamation by beat of drum (*ḍinḍima*) of general security to all who submit in the case of a captured town or conquered country.

Abhaya patra, S. &c. (अभयपत्र) A written document in assurance of safety, a safe conduct.

Abhichár, H. (S. अभिचारः) Employment of charms or spells for the destruction of an enemy.

Abhipaṭṭi, Ubhipuṭṭee, Mar. (अभिपट्टी) Any extra cess or assessment [under the Peshwa's Government.]

Abhír, Ubheer, H. &c. (ابهير, S. अभीरः, also, with the initial long Ábhíra आभीरः) A shepherd, a cowherd. According to *Menu* (B. x. 15) the *Ábhira* is of mixed origin, the offspring of a Brahman father, and a mother of the *Ambashṭha*, or medical caste; but the *Abhíras* were a people, a pastoral tribe, settled, about the beginning of the Christian era, on or near the lower course of the Indus, on a tract known to classical geographers, as the *Abiria* of Ptolemy, lying north of the Sahyadri mountain, and of Syrastrene. The *Abhírs* of *Saurashtra* are mentioned in the *Mahábhárata*. From their pastoral habits the name came to be generally applied to the cowherds of Hindustan. In the spoken dialects of upper India the word is corrupted to *Ahír*, *Uheer*, q.v. In Bengálí and Maráṭhí it is unchanged, occurring as *Abhír*.

Abhijog, Beng. (অভিজোগ, S. *Abhiyoga* अभियोगः) Plaint, complaint, beginning of a suit.

Abhijogi, Beng. (অভিজোগী, S. अभियोगी) A plaintiff, a complainant.

Abhijog-patra, Beng. (অভিজোগপত্র, S. अभियोगपत्र) A petition, or writing of complaint.

Abhyudayaka-ṣráddha, S. (अभ्युदयकश्राद्ध) Offering to deceased progenitors, or to the manes collectively, on some prosperous event, as the birth of a son, or the like.

Abhyupetya Ṣuṣrúshá, S. (अभ्युपेत्यशुश्रूषा) Contracted service, a title of Hindu law, treating of disputes between master and servant.

Abíḳ-Ubeek, H. (A. ابيق) A runaway slave, in Mohammedan law.

Âbír-Ûbeer, H. (from A. عبير, Saffron), A powder of a red or yellow colour, composed of various vegetable and mineral ingredients, as turmeric, safflower, saffron, red or yellow orpiment, talc, ground to a fine powder, and used by the natives to throw over one another and stain their faces and clothes with at the vernal festival of the *Holi*, as typical of the buds and blossoms of the season of spring.

Abwáb, H. (A. ابواب, plur. of *báb* باب, a door, a section, a chapter, a title,) Heads or subjects of taxation, or the taxes which were imposed under the Mohammedan Governments in addition to the regular assessment on the land. Miscellaneous cesses, imposts, and charges, levied by Zemindars and public officers. These cesses were either abolished or consolidated with the land revenue, and are no longer payable to the British Government; but such as existed before the perpetual settlement, and were not specially abrogated or not consolidated, are still claimed sometimes by the Zemindars, (Reg. viii. 1793, xxx. 1803, v. 1812). They were variously designated, as, 1. after the princes by whom they were ordered, as *Abwáb Kásim Âli Khán*, taxes of *Kásim* (Cossim) *Âli*, Nawab of Bengal; or, 2. from the pretext on which they were raised, as *Abwáb-Faujdári,* taxes on the Zemindars, in commutation of fees which had been payable to the office of *Faujdar*, or chief military and police magistrate, and *Abwáb Thánadári,* fees exacted by *Shujâ Khán* from retailers of spirituous liquors and other articles in bazars attached to police or military stations, and payable to the *Kotwál; Abwáb Khamsi* (from *khamsa*, five, for *several*), different taxes levied by the Governor of Dacca when the *Diwáni* was granted to the Company, on pretence of presenting the proceeds to the Emperor in acknowledgment of the grant (*Fifth Rep. and Gloss.*); also *Abwáb mehmáni,* a cess levied on the inhabitants of a village to defray the expenses of the Zemindar on his paying it an occasional visit; *Abwáb ráhdári,* rates charged on the people of a town or district for the repair of the public roads; *Abwáb Pátakí,* a cess apparently peculiar to Orissa, literally, "taxes on the wicked or fallen," applying the term to eight inferior or degraded castes or occupations, namely, *Tántís,* weavers, *Támbúlis,* venders of betel and *pân*, *Guṛiyas,* confectioners, or makers of sweetmeats with *Guṛ* or molasses, *Sonárs,* goldsmiths, and *Kaiwartts, Kibárats* and *Gokas,* different tribes of fishermen.

ACHALIT-UCHULIT, H. (S. अचलितः *lit.* What has not moved, or is immoveable), Real or landed property.

ÁCHANDRÁRGAM, Tam. (ஆசந்திரார்க்கம், from the S. आ *á,* as long as, चन्द्र *chandra,* the moon, and अर्क *arka,* the sun, *i.e.* as long as the sun and moon endure). In Tanjore and Kanara, any village, of which the lands are permanently apportioned among the hereditary proprietors. The term, slightly modified according to dialect, appears to be in common currency in the south of the Peninsula to denote perpetuity.

ÁCHAMANA, S. (आचमन) Rinsing the mouth, sipping a little water and ejecting it before and after meals, and before and after various ceremonies, one of the permanent and daily practices of the Hindus.

Áchamaníya, S. (आचमनीय) Water fit for sipping, also for offering it to an idol.

ÁCHÁR, H. &c., (آچار, S. आचारः *Áchára,* whence it is introduced into all the dialects, sometimes slightly modified). Institute, established and essential observance, as daily ablutions and personal purification, daily worship, tonsure, investiture, marriage, obsequial rites, or *Ṣráddhas.* Performance of appropriate duties in different stages of life, &c. It is also used in composition with terms limiting its application, as *Kuláchár,* family usage; *Déṣáchár,* custom of the country; *Matáchár,* practice of any particular sect; *Nityáchár,* invariable observance; *Ṣuddháchár,* ceremonial purity; *Vṛíddháchár,* old established custom.

ÁCHÁRJ, ÁCHÁRI, ÁCHÁRYA, H. &c. (اچارج, आचारी, from the S. *Áchárya* आचार्यः) A religious teacher; properly, the Brahman who instructs the religious student of the two next castes—the *Kshatriya* and the *Vaiṣya*—as well as the Brahman, in the Vedas. In modern use it is applied to any religious instructor, or to any Brahman or religious mendicant professing to be qualified to give spiritual instruction. In the south of India it especially denotes the head of a religious society—the *Mahant* of Hindustan, or the *Paṇḍa,* or head Priest of a temple. Among the Maráṭhas it was given to Brahmans employed by respectable families as cooks. In the Tamil provinces it is assumed by carpenters and other artisans.

ACHCHAKA, Karn. (ಅಚ್ಚಕ) Assessment, taxes. One who pays taxes.

Achchavaḍi, or *Achchuaḍi,* Karn. (ಅಚ್ಚುವಡಿ) Assessment, tax.

Achchavaḷiga, Karn. (ಅಚ್ಚವಳಿಗ) One who pays taxes.

ACHCHAḌI, Mal. (അച്ചടി) Printing, stamping.

Achchaḍikáran, Mal. (അച്ചടികാരൻ) A printer, a coiner.

ACHCHAḶÁYATARU, Karn. (ಅಚ್ಚಳಾಯತರು) Police officers, peons.

ACHCHHAṆ, Mal. (അച്ഛൻ, Tam. அச்சன்) A father; used also as a title of respect, and in Malabar applied especially to the males of the royal family who have no office nor official rank in the state.

ACHCHÁRAM, Mal. (അച്ചാരം) Earnest-money, money advanced.

ACHCHU, Karn. (ಅಚ್ಚು), *Achcha,* Mal. (അച്ച) A mould, a type, a form for casting or taking impressions, a printing-press, the pivot of a hand-mill.

Achchugár, or *Achchuḷi,* Karn. (ಅಚ್ಚುಗಾರ—ಅಚ್ಚುಳಿ) A printer, a cotton-printer, a pressman.

ACHCHUKAṬṬU, corruptly ACHKAT and ATCHKUTT, Tam. (அச்சுக்கட்டு) ACHUKAṬṬU, Tel. (అచుకట్టు) Land divided into beds to admit and retain the water let in for irrigation. Lands prepared for the cultivation of rice.

ÁCHU-KÁVALI, Tel. (అచుకావలి). In the south of India, grants of revenue and perquisites in grain, formerly received by the Poligar for protecting the crops, and engaging to make good any depredations on the lands under protection.

ACHÉ, Tel. (అచే) The principal harvest, the heavy crop (used in Vizagapatam).

ÁCHIDAIYAN, Tam. (ஆசிதையன்) A barber.

ÁCHITA, Karn. (ಅಚಿತ, Mal. (ആചിതം) A weight of ten khandakas, or bharas (each being ten tulams); a cart-load.

ÁCHHRA, Ben. (আছরা) The straw of paddy.

AḌ, ÁḌ, Mar. &c. (अड, आड), in Hindustan pronounced, and usually written, with the hard *r*, as *Aṛ* or *Áṛ* (آڑ, اڑ) *q. v.* (It also occurs in other dialects, modified by the substitution of the soft *d* for the hard *ḍ*, or by duplication of one or other, of which examples will be given.) A syllable used as a prefix, implying obstructing, screening, barring; also inferiority, irregularity, or deviation.

Aḍ-al-hukm. Uriya. Disobedience of orders, resistance of process.

Áḍ-gaon, Mar. (आडगाचों) A small or inferior village.

Áḍgír, Hindi (आडगीर) A strip of sward encompassing a field.

Áḍ-ját, Mar. (आडजात) People of the inferior or mixed castes.

Áḍ-márg, Mar. (आडमार्ग) A bye-way, a cross-road; also cross or internal traffic, and duty levied on such-traffic. (This occurs, incorrectly written, *Udh marwa* and *Urdh margh*).

Áḍmúṭh, Mar. (आडमूठ) Sowing seed carefully on hilly or broken ground (so as to close the hand or fist (*múṭh*) readily.)

Aḍ nav, Mar. (अडनाव) Family or surname.

Aḍ saṭṭá, Mar. (अडसट्टा) Estimate, rough calculation. See *Aḍasattá* and *Aṛsatha*.

Áḍwan, Mar. (आडवण) The space between the top and foot of a hill, the slope.

AḌWEPÁṆÍ, Mar. (अडवेपाणी) Water of irrigation derived from tanks, &c.; artificial water, not rain-water.

ÁḌ, Mar. (आड्) A well without steps.

ADÁ, H. (A. ادا) Fulfilment of an agreement, performance of a contract, payment of a debt. This is sometimes confounded, but incorrectly, with *Ahda*, q. v.

Adá-bandi, or *bundee*, H. (ادا بندي) Fixing a term for the payment of a debt or the performance of a contract.

Adá karná, H. (ادا كرنا) To pay a debt, to make an agreement.

Adá hona, H. (ادا هونا) To be settled, paid or fulfilled, as a debt or contract.

Adá-i-málguzárí, H. (ادا مالگزاري) Payment of revenue.

ADÁ, Mar. (अदा) Gain, profit, fund, stock, income.

AḌAGU-UḌUGOO, Tam. (அடகு), Tel. (అడగు) A pawn, a pledge.

AḌA, or AḌAI MÁNAM, Tam. (அடமானம்—அடைமானம்) A mortgage, a simple mortgage, in which the mortgager retains possession of the property pledged, paying interest on the loan.

Aḍaiyolai, Tam. (அடையோலை) The palm-leaves on which a mortgage, deed, or lease, or other engagement, is written.

AḌAVU, also AḌARVU, Karn. (ಅಡವು-ಅಡರ್ವು) A pledge; a mortgage, a simple mortgage, in which the mortgager retains the property, paying interest on the loan.

Aḍavu chíṭu, *Aḍavu-sáthana*, or *Aḍavu-patra*, Karn. (ಅಡವುಚೀಟು, &c.) A mortgage-deed, or bond.

Aḍavu-kár, Karn. (ಅಡವುಕಾರ) A mortgagee, one who holds a pledge or mortgage.

ADAHÁRÍ, Hindi (अदहारी) A bullock not broken in for work.

AḌAKAM, Tam. (அடக்கம்) An enclosure.

AḌÁṆI, Karn. (ಅಡಾಣಿ) Unrewarded or compulsory labour.

Aḍáṇijana, Karn. (ಅಡಾಣಿಜನ) An unpaid labourer, a slave, a serf.

AḌAṄGAL, Tam. (அடங்கல்), Mal. (അടങ്കൽ) An estimate, an appraisement, a valuation; the whole contents, or whole quantity of any thing; a contract; examining the cultivation of village lands.

AḌAR-UḌUR, or AḌARA-UḌURU, Hindi (अडर) A ditch, and the mound of earth thrown up from it, forming the boundary of a field.

AḌASAṬṬÁ-UḌUSUṬṬA, Tel. (అడసట్టా) Estimate, computation, an account by estimate. (The *ḍ* being pronounced and written *ṛ*, the word occurs more usually in Hindustan as *Aṛsath*, q.v.)

AḌAT-UḌUT, Mar. (अडत) Mercantile correspondence, agency, brokerage; charge or fee for commission or brokerage. This word also occurs in other dialects differently spelled, as *Aḍhat* (अढत), or the hard *ḍ*, *ḍh* being pronounced like *r*, *Aṛat*, *Aṛhat*, or *Uṛhut*; or, again, with the soft *t* and the aspiration transposed, as *Arthí*, or *Urthee*.

Aḍatyá, *Uḍutyá*, or *Uḍutiya*; also, very corruptly, *Adut-*

teeyo, Mar. (अडत्या) A mercantile correspondent, a broker, an agent; also *Arhatiya* and *Arthiya*.

Ádat, or Árat, Beng. (আড়ৎ) A warehouse, a store occupied by a wholesale dealer, or a monopolist; a place from which all must purchase what they want.

Ádat dár, Beng. (from P. دار, who has). A store-keeper, a monopolist.

Adatta, S. (अ, neg. &c. दत्तः given, ungiven). In Hindu law, illegal, or void and resumable donation.

Adavi, or Adivi-kottuta, Tel. (అడవికొట్టుట, S. अटवि, *Atavi*, a forest). Clearing away jungle, and bringing the land into cultivation.

Adavá, or Adaví-pálki, Mar. (अडवा, अडवी, athwart, and पालकी). The privilege of being carried in a palankin sideways; that is, with the poles across the road, or at a right angle with it, a distinction enjoyed by the head of the Brahmans of *Sringagiri*, the spiritual descendants of *Sankara Áchárya*; latterly also claimed by the head of the *Lingayits*, and the subject of litigation in the Company's Courts of the Bombay Presidency.

Ádáya, Tel. Karn. (ఆదాయ, from the S. आदायः) Gain, profit, receipt.

Ádáya vichha, Karn. (ಆದಾಯವಿಛ) Profit and loss, receipt and disbursement; [the last term is possibly from the S. *Vyaya* व्यय, expenditure.]

Adda, Uddu, Karn. (ಅಡ್ಡ) A half; but in this sense more correctly *arddha*, q. v. In composition it also implies hindrance, obstruction, going transversely, diverging, &c., corresponding in these respects to the Maráthí *Ad* and Hindi *Ar*, but doubling the cerebral *d*.

Addadandige, Karn. (ಅಡ್ಡದಂಡಿಗೆ) A palankin carried transversely. See *Adavá-pálki*.

Adda káluvé, Karn. (ಅಡ್ಡ-ಕಾಲುವೆ) A subordinate channel, one cut from a main water-course for irrigation.

Adda kasibi, kasibe, kasabu, kasibi, or *kasubu*, Karn. (ಅಡ್ಡಕಸಿಬಿ, ಕಸಿಬೆ, ಕಸಬು, &c.) A trade, a profession not hereditary, an employment to which the person was not born or bred.

Adda kattu, or *katte*, Karn. (ಅಡ್ಡಕಟ್ಟು-ಕಟ್ಟೆ) A dam for the purpose of confining water.

Adda márga, Karn. (ಅಡ್ಡಮಾರ್ಗ) A cross or bye road.

Adda mátu, Karn. (ಅಡ್ಡಮಾತು) Evasive answer, prevarication.

Adda-náma, Karn. (ಅಡ್ಡನಾಮ) A family or surname.

Addanálige, Karn. (ಅಡ್ಡನಾಲಿಗೆ) A stone put across the mouth of a well.

Addani, Karn. (ಅಡ್ಡಣಿ) The woof or cross threads.

Addasálu, Karn. (ಅಡ್ಡಸಾಲು) A transverse furrow in ploughing.

Adda-sunka, Karn. (ಅಡ್ಡಸುಂಕ) Duty on sheep collected from those only who sell them, not from the ryots.

Adde, Karn. (ಅಡ್ಡೆ) A bambu across the shoulder, by which two burthens are carried.

Addéhkalu, Karn. (ಅಡ್ಡೆಕ್ಕಲು) A new comer, a settler in a village.

Adda, Tel. (అద్ధ) Half; more properly *Ardha* (అర్ధ, from S. अर्द्ध).

Adda, Tel. (అడ్డ) A measure equal to two *Mánikas*.

Addavu-dosili, Tel. (అద్దవుదోసిలి) An allowance of grain made to the village barber.

Áddá, Dekhini, H. (اڈّا, आड्डा). This differs from the Telugu and Karn. *Adda, Adda*, as above, in beginning and ending with a long, in place of a short vowel. It is sometimes written with a short initial and final, as *Adda*, or *Uddu*, Mar. (अड्ड), but never with a dental *d*; the word occurs, with some modifications of meaning, in Tel., Mar., Uriya, and perhaps other dialects. A stand, a station or place where porters, bearers, or labourers attend to be hired; a place where people assemble, a stall, a booth, a shop, a post or dawk station or office; a company or association of persons engaged in the same business; any business constantly going on, especially on a large scale; the place where it is transacted, or any place where people congregate, whether for business or idleness; a salt-heap (in Ganjam); the perch of a bird-cage.

Áddá-dár, H. (اڈّا دار) A palankin bearer, or dawk-runner; a postman, a courier; a shop or stall-keeper.

Addana, Karn. (ಅದ್ದಣ) A measure equal to about half-a-pint.

Adde, Tel. (అద్దె) Hire, rent.

Áddi, Beng. (আঢ্ডি) A title or cognomen given to persons who are, or whose ancestors were, money weighers and changers.

Addika, or Addiga; also Addakadár and Addakadava, Karn. (ಅದ್ದಿಕ, ಅದ್ದಿಗ, ಅದ್ದಕದಾರ, from the S. *Adhyaksha* अध्यक्षः, an overseer). A village officer, whose duty it is to keep the cultivators to their work, and to prevent the clandestine removal of any part of the common crop.

Addiseyuta, Tel. (అద్దెసేయుట) A contract, by which a

cultivator pledges the whole or a portion of his crop to a banker as security for money borrowed.

Adeya, Udeyu, S. (अ neg., and देयं, to be given), What may not be legally alienated or given away.

Ádh, Ádhá, Ádhí, or Adhee, H. (آدھ ,آدھا ,آدھي, from the S. *arddha* अर्द्धः, half, or a part), A half. (The word occurs in most dialects, modified according to their peculiarities of enunciation, as in the *Adda* of Tel. and Karn., as above. It is also used extensively in composition, with the initial most usually made short, as,

Ádh-baṭáï, or *buṭaee*, H. (آدھ بٹّائي) Division of produce in equal shares.

Adhela, Udhela, H. (ادھيلا) Half a pice, or copper coin so called.

Adhelí, Udhelee, H. (ادھيلي) Half a silver rupee, or eight anas. A half share. In Ságar, a measure of corn, half a *chautiya*. (In Garwhal) a small fractional measure of land.

Adheliya, H. (ادھيليا) Proprietor of a half share.

Adhiár, H. (ادھيار). A man who spends half his time in one village, half in another, cultivating lands in both, is said *Adhïár-karna*, or, in Rohilkhand, *Adh-bár*.

Adhiári, H. (ادھياري) A half share.

Adhiá, H. (ادھيا) Division of produce between two parties in equal proportions; one furnishing the land and seed, and the other the labour. The payment of half the annual assessment by the cultivators to the person who is responsible to the Government for the revenue at the vernal and autumnal harvests.

Adh-kachcha, H. (ادھ کچّا) A soil lying between the land named Pahára and the Taraï in the district of Saharanpur.

Adh-karí, or *kuree*, H. (अधकरी) An instalment of eight anas in the rupee, or half the Government revenue, (from the S. *kara* कर, tax).

Addhak, Uddhuk, H. (अद्धक) A half, a part: less in use than *Ádhá*.

Áḍhak, Aḍhuk, or Áṛhak, H. (S. आढकः) A measure of capacity, used as a dry measure; a vessel 18 inches in depth, containing 4 prasthas, the 16th part of a *khári*. In the Dekhin nearly 7lb. 11oz. avoirdupois. In Mysore the *Áḍak*, or *Áḍhak* is a measure of grain, equal to 7lb. avoirdupois, or a measure of capacity, containing about 750 cubic inches: also called a *Markál*.

Ádháram, Mal. (ആധാരം, S. आधारं) A prop, or support; that on which any thing lit. or fig. rests; also a canal, a dyke; a document, a voucher or title-deed, by which a right to property is established. Karn. (ಆಧಾರಂ) A canal, or water-course for irrigation. It is used in Karnáta in composition, to denote various modes of irrigation, as,

Ámej-ádháram, (from P. *ámez*, mixing) Irrigation from more than one source, or from tanks, wells, water-courses, &c. The land so irrigated.

Bhávi, or *Bhávádi ádháram*, Tel. Karn. (ಭಾವಿ, S. *Bápi*, or *vápi*, a well) Irrigation from wells. The land so watered.

Nala, or *Nálá ádháram*, (from S. नालः *nála*, a pipe). Irrigation from natural water-courses, or *nalas*. The fields so watered.

Taṭákádháram, Tel. (from the S. *taḍága* तडाग) A pond, a tank; irrigation from a tank or pond, or the fields so supplied.

Ádharshan, Beng. (S. আধর্ষণ) Conviction of a criminal.

Adhi, or Udhi, less correctly, Udhee; also corruptly, Ad, Adh, Adi, Audi, H. (S. अधि) Over, above, in place, office, or possession. It is used chiefly in composition.

Adhikár, H. &c. (S. अधिकारः) Office, duty; superintendence, government; right, rightful claim or property.

Adhikár-patra, or *patrika*, Beng. (অধিকারপত্র) A power of attorney, a letter of credit.

Adhikárí, corruptly, *Adhkár, Adkári, Adikari, Audicarei*; hence also the *Adigar* of Ceylon, H. &c. (S. अधिकारी) One who holds a superior office or authority; a superintendant, a ruler, a governor; as,

Grámádhikárí, The headman of a village.

Deśádhikárí, The head of a district or province; abbreviated in the south of India to *Desaï*, corruptly *Deysaee*, or *Desaye*: also one who claims a right; as, *Uttarádhikárí*, Subsequent claimant, *i.e.* Successor, heir, especially as applicable to landed property: it may also denote one who, although a member of a village community, occupies his land in his own right, or in severalty. See *Arudikárai*.

Adhikarma, H. (S. अधिकर्म्म) Superintendence, supervision, government.

Adhikarma-kṛit, H. (S. अधिकर्म्मकृत्) A supervisor, a superior, a governor.

Adhipati, or *Udhiputee*, corruptly *Adhiput*, H. (S. अधिपतिः) A superintendant, a headman. It is used like *Adhikárí* in composition, as *Grámádhipati*, Head of a village; *Deśádhipati*, Head of a district.

Adhiráj, or *Udhiraj*, H. (S. अधिराजा) A paramount prince or sovereign, but also commonly used as a title to persons of inferior pretensions, although of consequence. It is sometimes abbreviated to *Dhíraj*, as *Maháráj, Dhíráj, Jay Sinh*, the great king, the supreme Jay Sinh.

Adhi-vinná, S. (अधिविन्ना) In Hindu law, a superseded wife, one who has been succeeded by other wives.

Adhi-vedanika, S. (अधिवेदनिक) In Hindu law, Dowry or settlement given to a first wife on her supercession by a second marriage.

Adhyagni, S. (अध्यग्नि) Property given to the wife at the time of marriage, or over the (nuptial) fire. One of the items of *Strí-dhan*, or female property, in Hindu law.

Adhyáváhanika, S. (अध्यावाहनिक) An item of woman's property; property that has descended to her lineally.

ADHIK, or UDHIK, H. (S. अधिकः) More, any thing in addition or excess. It occurs in most of the dialects, singly or in composition.

Adhika-váram, Tam. (அதிகவாரம்) In South India, a division of the crop in which a larger share is assigned to Brahmans or other privileged persons.

ÁDHI, S. (आधिः) A pledge, or deposit, which may be of two kinds—*Gopya*, to be preserved entire and perfect, or *Bhogya*, to be used or enjoyed; also *Bandhaka*, q. v.

Ádhi bhoga, S. (आधिभोग) Use of a thing pledged, either as the equivalent of a partial or entire remission of interest.

ADHORÍA, or UDHOREEA, Thug. A person who has separated from a party, and has thereby escaped their fate of being waylaid and murdered.

ÁḌI, or ÁḌHI, Beng. (আডি, আঢি) A measure of capacity, equal, in the neighbourhood of Calcutta, to two maunds.

AḌI, corruptly ADDY, Tam. (அடி) A foot; also a measure of length, a short foot = 10.46 inches: 57,600 square *adis* are equal to a *káṇi*, *q.v.*

Aḍikol, Tam. (அடிக்கோல்) A measuring rod.

AḌI CHERI, Tam. (அடிச்சேரி) Near the town; a village near a town, a suburb; that part of the village in which the hereditary proprietors reside.

ÁDIDÁDI, (In Chingleput) Breach of the peace.

ADIKÁSU, Karn. (ಅಡಿಕಾಸು) A daily tax levied on shops, especially in regimental bazars, varying from one to four *kás*, or *cash*.

AḌIKI, AḌIKÉ, Karn. (ಅಡಿಕಿ, ಅಡಿಕೆ) Betel or *Areka*-nut.

Aḍiké-gonikár, Karn. A tax on the hire of the *Gonikars*, a low caste of Hindus employed to gather the areka-nut from the gardens of the Ryots in Mysore.

Aḍiké-hriyávási, Karn. A tax on betel-nut tree groves in Mysore.

AḌIMA, UḌIMA, Mal. (അടിമ); *Aḍimai*, Tam. (அடிமை); *Aḍime*, Tel. (అడిమె) Slavery, bondage in general. A bondman, a slave. In Tam., especially a predial slave attached hereditarily to the land, and only transferable with it. In Malabar it also implies the feudal dependency of a Nair upon some chief whom he selects for his protector or patron.

Aḍimaichittu, Tam. (அடிமைச்சீட்டு) Bill of sale for a slave.

Aḍima, or *Uḍima janm*, Mal. (ജന്മ, S. जन्म, birth, birthright). Mortgage of land for a sum inferior to its value by a superior to a person of a low caste; hence sometimes applied to a grant of land by a superior to an inferior, either rent-free, or at a quit-rent: the land, in either case, reverting to the granter on failure of heirs of the grantee. [This is evidently the same as the *Adoni-janm* of the Glossary, Fifth Report. See R. p. 801.]

Aḍima-janm kár, or *Adima-janm-kolunavan*, Mal. (കൊലുനവൻ) The person who holds an Adima grant.

Aḍima-janm paṇam, Mal. (പണം, price). Price or fee paid for receiving land by *Aḍima* tenure.

Aḍimapaṇi, Mal. (അടിമപ്പണി) The duty of a slave, servitude.

Aḍima-paramba, Mal. (പറമ്പ, a garden), A plantation or garden held by an *Aḍima* grant.

Aḍimayávan, Mal. (അടിമയാവന) Immunities granted to slaves by their masters, as land, gardens, &c.

ÁDIMÁN, corruptly, *Adehmaun*, Mar. (आदिमान, from the S. आदि, first, and मान, respect). The first rights or privileges enjoyed by a village officer; certain claims or rights of precedence, &c.

ÁDÍNAM, Tam, (S. ஆதீனம்) Government. Property.

Ádínattukudaiyavan, or *Ádinakartan*, Tam. (ஆதீனத்துக்குடையவன் ஆதீனகர்த்தன்) A proprietor, an owner, a landlord, an heir or inheritor.

AḌI-PAṬṬADENELLU, Tam. (அடிப்பட்டதெநெல்லு) Waste or sweepings at the foot (*adi*) or bottom of a stack of straw; a band of straw tied round a stack of grain to prevent the clandestine removal of any part of it.

Aḍippukkúli, Tam. (அடிப்புக்கூலி) Wages for thrashing corn.

Aḍittumutalánatu, Tam. (அடித்துமுதலானது) Quantity of grain thrashed.

ADIRÁSU, Karn. (ಅದಿರಾಸು) Remains of a heap of corn; gleanings.

ADI ṢÚDRA, Tam. (அடிசூத்திரான்) A man of a low caste; one of a caste inferior to (adi), even the Súdra.

ADITI, or ADITIYA, H. (अडित) A mercantile correspondent or agent; but the word is a corruption of *Aḍat, Aṛhat*, or *Aṛhatiya*, q. v.

ÁDITYA, H. (S. आदित्यः) The sun.

Âdítya-vár, or *Âditya-bár*, abridged to *A-it-war*, or more commonly, *Etwar* (H. ايتوار) Sunday.

ADIYÁṆ, plur. ADIYÁR, Mal. (അടിയാൻ) A slave, a serf, a vassal; a man of low caste in Malabar, who lives under the protection of a Raja or religious establishment. Tam. (அடியான்) A man-servant; *Adiyáḷ*, Tam. (அடியாள்) a woman-servant.

ÂDL, ÛDL, H. &c. (A. عدل) Justice, equity. Equality, equipoise. The word occurs in most dialects, with slight modifications, and in some places denotes an official seal or stamp for documents, parcels, &c.; also, in Orissa and the northern Cirkars, a wooden stamp for blocks of salt.

Âdl-dár, H. (عدل دار) A sealer; an officer whose duty it is to apply seals or stamps.

Addala-váḍu, Tel. (అడ్డలవాడు) An officer who stamps blocks of salt; also a manufacturer of salt, or hired labourer employed in the manufacture.

Âádil, H. (A. عادل) A just or upright person; one in whom trust may be placed.

Âádil al Rahn, A. (عادل الرهن). In Mohammadan law, a third party, to whose keeping a pledge or security given by a borrower to a lender is entrusted.

ÂDÁLAT, ÛDALUT, corruptly, ADAWLUT, H. (A. عدالت) Court of justice; justice, equity. Under the Mohammedan Government the *Âdálats*, or Courts of Justice, were four:

1. *Niẓámat Âdálat*, (نظامت عدالت) The Supreme Court of Criminal Justice, nominally presided over by the *Názim*, or Viceroy of the province. This was subdivided into the *Roz-âdálat*, or Court held on a Sunday by the *Názim* for the trial of capital offenders, and the *Âdálat ul Âáliyat* (from عالي), The High Court, in which affrays, quarrels, and cases regarding personal property were tried: this was usually presided over by the *Nizam's* deputy, or *Dárógha*.
2. *Diwani Âdálat* (ديواني عدالت) The Civil Court of the Diwan, the chief officer in charge of the revenue of the principality.
3. *Faujdári Âdálat* (فوجداري عدالت) The Court of the Faujdar, or chief of the magistracy and police of a district; the Subordinate, or District Criminal Court.
4. *Âdálat ul Ḳázi* (عدالت القاضي) The Court of the *Ḳázi*, the chief judge of a town or district in civil causes and questions regarding the Mohammedan religion. Under him the *Muhtasib* held a Court for the adjudication of offences against morals—as drunkenness, gambling, &c. Under the British Government these Courts were continued, with some modifications, until 1793, when the judicial and revenue departments were separated, and Zila and Provincial Courts were established, subordinate to one Supreme *Âdálat* at the Presidency, distinguished as the ṢADR, or SUDDER ÂDÁLAT (A. صدر عدالت) High Court of Justice, or Court of Final Decision, subdivided into,

Ṣadr-Diwáni Âdálat, or, corruptly, *Sudder Dewanny Adawlut*, High Court of Civil Jurisdiction.

Ṣadr Niẓámat, or *Faujdári Âdálat*, High Court of Criminal Justice. Beng. Reg. iii. ix. xii. xiii. 1793, ii. 1795, ii. 1801, viii. 1803, v. 1809, &c.

Âdálat Akbar, H. (A. اكبر, greatest), A superior Court of Justice; a Court of Appeal.

Âdálat Asghar, H. (A. اصغر, smallest), An inferior, or subordinate Court of Justice.

ÂDM, ÛDM, H. (A. عدم) Cessation, discontinuance. In *Urdu* it is chiefly used to form technical compounds; as,

Âdm-i-jaidád, H. (P. جايداد, a grant), Loss or forfeiture of a grant; loss of subsistence.

Âdm-nishán, H. (P. نشان, sign or trace), Unclaimed or untraceable property, &c.

Âdm-i-ṣabút, P. (A. ثبوت, confirmation), Wanting proof, defective in evidence.

Âdm-i-tandehi, H., Remissness or neglect in pursuing a cause, suffering it to go by default, (*lit.* want of bodily exertion; or P. *tan*, and S. *ḍeh*, both meaning body).

ADMARJÁI, Hindi (अदमरजाई) A term used in leases, signifying failure from drought.

ADONI-JANM, Mal. Lands held by individuals of low caste and artisans under grants from persons of rank and property. See *Adima-janm*, for which it is no doubt an error.

ÁḌU, Tam. (ஆடு), ÁṬA, Mal. (ആട) A sheep, a goat.

Áṭṭukáraṇ, Mal. (ആട്ടുകാരൻ) A shepherd, a goatherd.

Áṭṭukhiḍai, Tam. (ஆட்டுக்கிடை) A field, cote, or place where goats or sheep are penned, for the sake of their manure.

Áṭṭumari-kúli (?) Tam. The hire paid to the owner of a flock of sheep or goats for their detention in a field for the purpose of manuring it.

Áṭṭu-vari, Tam. (வரி, tax), A tax on sheep or goats.

Aḍukkuvata, Mal. (അടുക്കുവത) Any right retained by the original proprietor from the purchaser or mortgagee.

Aḍutti, Tam. (அடுத்தி), Usury.

Ádya-śráddha, S. (आद्यश्राद्ध) The first Śráddha, or obsequial ceremony after a person's decease.

Aentha, Thug. Silver money.

Áfat, Afut, vernacularly, Áphat, H. (A. آفت, आफत्, S. आपत्) Misfortune, calamity.

Áfat ásmáni, H. (P. آسمان, heaven), Misfortune from heaven, as bad seasons, storm, drought, &c.

Áfat farmáni, or *sulṭáni*, H. (A. سلطاني - فرماني) Misfortune from the tyranny or exactions of the Government or its officers.

Afím, Ufeem, or Upheem, H. (A. افيم, अफीम); also Afiun, (A. افيون) Opium.

Afsháni-káġhaz, H. (P. افشاني كاغز) Paper studded or spangled with gold-leaf, used in writing to persons of distinction.

Áftábá, H. (P. آفتابا) A ewer.

Áftáb-gír, H. (P. *áftáb* آفتاب, the sun, and *gír* گير, what receives), A large flat semicircular parasol.

Áftáb-gíri, H. The servant who carries the parasol.

Áftábi, H. (from the P. آفتاب, the sun), A large flat circular or semicircular parasol carried by the side of the person or palankin shaded by it. Under the Mogul Government it was one of the insignia of high rank, and could be carried only by special permission or grant of the Emperor.

Aphtada, for Aftáda, Hindi (अफतादा, from P. افتاده, fallen), Lands of which possession has been transferred to another; also, neglected land, or that which has fallen out of cultivation.

Âfu, Ûfoo, A. (عفو, *lit.* pardon), Balance or residue of an estate. Exemption from, or remission of surplus charge.

Afzún, Afzoon, H. (P. افزون) Increase; increased revenue. Addition (in account); an account in which a certain number of items are added together, and their totals are then progressively added, until the final sum is obtained.

Ágaira, corruptly, Augayra, H. (آگيَره, from S. *agra* अग्र, and H. *áge* آگي, before, at first), The first sheaves of the crop presented to the Zemindar.

Agaiyá, Ugaiya, H. (اگيا, from *ág*, from S. अग्नि, Fire, abridged to आग) A disease affecting rice, in which the plant seems burnt up.

Agam, Tam. (அகம்) The earth. Grain.

Agamuḍaiyán, Tam. (அகமுடையான்) A landholder; also, the name of a caste.

Agavilai, Tam. (அகவிலை) Market-price of grain.

Ágama, S. (आगमः) A work on sacred science; a scripture. In law, a voucher, a document, a title; also, descent of property.

Ágámi, Beng. (S. আগামি), Future, what is to come; whence *Ágám*, an advance of payment; also used in deeds and leases, to indicate all future possible privileges or profits.

Agan, Ugun, or Ág, H. (آگ S. *Agni* अग्निः, fire), Fire, or its personified divinity.

Aganhotri, more correctly, *Agnihotṛi*, H. (S. अग्निहोतृ) A Brahman who maintains a perpetual fire in his house. See *Agni-hotri.*

Ágar, Agur, H. (آگر, probably from S. आकर, a mine), A salt-pit.

Ágari, *Aguree*, H. (آگري) A manufacturer of salt.

Ágar, Mar. (आगर) A plantation of fruit-trees, especially of betel-nut and cocoa-nut trees. A place on the sea-shore having salt-pits.

Ágar-gaon, Mar. (आगरगावं) A village having plantations or orchards attached.

Agaram, Tam. (அகரம்) A corruption of *Agrahâram*, q.v.

Ágárí, Agaree, H. (آگاري, from the S. *agra* अग्र, before), Money, &c., paid in advance. There are various dialectical modifications of the same, as, *Agáï* or *Agaee*, *Agúri* or *Agooree*, *Agáu*, *Agávu*, &c., all derived from *Agra*, meaning, Before, either in place or time, through the vernacular form *Áge.*

Agari (?). Said to be the name of a low caste of Hindus in Cuttack: according to one authority, bullock-drivers; to another, domestic slaves.

Agaríya, Agureeya, Thug. Descendants of the original Thugs, who, after being expelled from Delhi, settled for a time at Agra.

Agarwál, Ugurwal, or Agarwálá, H. (اگروالا) An important sub-division of the mercantile caste, comprising many of the wealthiest traders and bankers in Hindustan. According to Mr. Elliot they derive their name from *Agroha* in *Hariana*, whence they originally migrated to other provinces after the capture of that place by *Shaháb-ad-Din Gori.* Common tradition refers their name and origin to *Agra*. The *Agarwal* is one of the *Gachhas*, or families of the Jains; and most of its members profess the Jain religion.

AGASA or AGASI, UGUSU, UGUSEE; also AGUSA, Karn. (ಅಗಸ, ಅಗುಸ) A washerman.

Agasara-terige, Karn. (ತೆರಿಗೆ, a tax), A tax on washermen.

AGÁSI, UGÁSEE, H. (اگاسي) A turban, in which sense it is also used by the Thugs; but they apply the term likewise to the cry of the kite. If heard between the first watch of the night and day-break it is unlucky; in the day it is immaterial.

ÁGÁSI- (probably for *Ákási*, skiey)-BIRAR, Thug. (but used in the Dekhin), Thunder.

AGASTWAR, H. (اگستوار) A small clan of Rajputs in Haveli-Benares.

AGÁŬ, H. (اگاو), *Agavu*, Tel. (అగవు, from S. अग्र) An advance of money. In the northern Circars the same as *Takávi*, or money-advance to the cultivators; also collection of revenue before it is due.

AGAYADI, UGUYUDEE, Karn. (ಅಗಯಡಿ) Small spots of land on which rice is sown for transplanting, and which the ryots claim free of rent.

ÁGḌÁ, or ÁGṚÁ, H. (آگڑا) An ear of corn or rice which has been blighted and contains no grain.

AGHAM, Mar. (?). In the Dekhin, an extra assessment imposed upon the hereditary proprietors of a village to cover charges for unusual expenses or default of any of the community.—*E. I. Sel.* iv. 541.

A'GHAN, UGHUN, corruptly, AUGUN, H. (اگهن, S. अग्रहायण) One of the months of the luni-solar year—the eighth, corresponding with November—December.

AGHANI, UGHUNEE, H. (اگهني) Produce of that portion of the *Kharif*, or cold weather crop, which is gathered in the month *Aghan*. It is also applied to the harvest of the cold season.

Aghani-fasl, Ughunee-fusl, H. (اگهني فصل; also, vernacularly, but incorrectly, in Hindi, *Aghani-phasil* अघनीफशील) The cold-weather harvest, reaped in Nov.—Dec.

AGHÁT, UGHAT, corruptly, AGHAUT, H. (اگهات, S. अघात, from S. *a* अ, neg., and *ghâta* घात, struck), Land held in perpetuity, and inalienable.

AGHORA, H. Mar. (S. अघोरः, dreadful), A name of SIVA. A religious mendicant, of an order of which the practices are most filthy and disgusting, the food being ordure and carrion, and, it is said, human flesh; but much of this is imposture, the object of which is to excite the wonder of the beholders, and make them believe in the utter indifference of the Aghora to worldly enjoyments.

Aghora-pantha, or *márga*, H. Mar. (S. पंथ, मार्ग, a road), The path or practices of the Aghoras.

Aghora-panthi, H. Mar. One following the Aghora path.

Aghora-pramánam, S. (प्रमाणं, authority), A peculiarly solemn form of oath used in the south of India, wherein the person to be sworn, after fasting and bathing, sits down, decorated with flowers, in a temple; and having made his asseveration in front of the idol, puts out a lamp burning before it, and wishes he may be similarly extinguished if he has uttered an untruth.

AGNI, UGNI, S. (अग्निः, written also, but incorrectly, *Ugnee*, and abbreviated in several dialects to *Áy* آگ) Fire. Either the element, or domestic or sacred fire, or the element personified as the god of fire, to whom oblations of clarified butter are offered at most domestic rites.

Agni-astra, S. Fire-arms, a weapon of fire; a fabulous weapon so called; a rocket.

Agni-bráhmaṇa, S. A Brahman who officiates as priest at the burning of dead bodies.

Agni-dagdha, S. Ben. A Hindu, who having died without issue, is burnt at once, without the previous ceremony of having fire put into the mouth of the corpse.

Agni-dáha, S. The ceremony of burning a dead body; *lit.* burning with fire.

Agni-dik, S. The south-east quarter, of which Agni is the regent.

Agni-hotra, S. Performance of daily or occasional worship with fire lighted from a perpetual fire preserved in the dwellings of a particular class of Brahmans.

Agni-hotṛi, S. A Brahman who maintains a perpetual household fire.

Agni-homa, S. Performance of worship with fire; offering oblations to fire. The ceremony is denominated also simply, *Homa*.

Agni-kriyá, S. Any ceremony with fire, but especially the burning of the dead.

Agni paríkshá, S. (from परीक्षा, trial), Ordeal by fire, as formerly practised by walking through it, or as subsequently practised, dipping the hand into boiling oil, &c.

Agni pratishṭhá, S. Consecration of fire; fire lighted from the perpetual fire for any particular ceremony, as that of marriage.

Agni-sanskára, S. The sacrament of fire; the burning of the dead body as an essential rite of the Hindu religion. The completion of any essential rite by worship with fire.

Agni-shoma, or *Agnishomíya-yága*, S. A ceremony performed at the new moon, when oblations of milk are offered to Indra through fire.

Agnishṭoma, S. A sacrifice, in which the juice of the Soma or asclepias is offered in oblation.

Agni-sútra, S., *lit.* A thread of fire, but in Mysore applied to a girdle of sacrificial grass placed round the waist of a young Brahman when he is invested with the sacred string of his caste.

AGOṬ, Mar. (अगोट) The period shortly before or after the setting in of the rainy season.

AGOR, UGOR, or AGORYA, H. (اگور اگوریا) A man appointed to watch the crops (used chiefly in the Benares district). A division of the crop.

AGOR-BAṬAÏ, UGOR-BUṬAEE, corruptly, AGORE-BETAY, H. (اگور بتّاي) Division of the crop immediately after reaping between the cultivator and the Government, the latter taking half the produce in kind. A division of the crop in predetermined proportions between landlord and tenant; *lit.* a watching and sharing, each party keeping a watch over the fields, that none of the crop may be fraudulently made away with. Reg. ii. 1795.

AGORA, UGORA, H. (اگورا) Daily hire.

AGOUND, UGOUND, H. (اگوند) The top of the sugar-cane cut up for seed, in distinction to *Bel-ká-bíj*, in which the cane itself is cut into five or six pieces. In some parts of the north-west provinces the different portions of the cane have different names. *Pát* implies the leaves of the top; *Ag, Agao, Agoura, Agin*, or *Gaundi*, are applied to the cane a few inches below the top; *Káncha, Gulla, Palwa*, or *Phungi*, about a foot lower, and is the part generally used for seed. The rest of the plant is termed *Gande, Gunda*, or *Gunna* (perhaps for the S. *Khaṅḍa* खण्डः).—*Elliot.*

AGOUR, H. (اگور, from H. *Áge* آگے, S. *agra* अग्र) An advance of rent paid by the cultivator to the Zemindars in the months of *Jeth* and *Áshárh* (Oude).

AGRADÁNA, Ben. (অগ্রদান) A Brahman of an inferior order, who conducts funeral obsequies, or Śráddhas, for hire; also called *Mahápátra, Mahábráhmana*, Great Brahman, ironically.

AGRAHÁRAM, UGRUHARUM, or, with the inflective sign, AGRAHÁRAMAH, AGRAHÁRAMU; also abbreviated as AGARAM, AGRÁRAM, and corruptly, AGRAGHRAH; also, but superfluously, AGRAHÁRAVÁDAI. Tel., Karn., Tam., Mar. (S. अग्रहारः, from *agra* अग्र, first, and *hára* हार, what receives), A village, or a part of one, occupied by Brahmans, and held either rent-free under special grants, or at a reduced rate of assessment. The precise nature of the tenure is usually denoted by a term prefixed, as *Sarvágraháram*, free from all (*sarva*) tax; *Bil-makt agraháram*, a village at a stipulated (A. بالمقطع) rent; and *Kattubadi agraharam*, a village held at a rent which fluctuates with the produce (from the Tel. *Kattubadi*, a favourable or quit rent). The same is termed, in Karnata *Jodí-agrahára* (ಜೋಡಿ ಅಗ್ರಹಾರ).

Agraháravádai, Tam. (அக்கிரகாரவாடை), *Agrahára vádike*, Karn. (ಅಗ್ರಹಾರವಾಡಿಕೆ) One of the former divisions of the villages in the Drávira countries; those exempt from revenue, usually occupied by Brahmans, but sometimes by other classes.

Agrahárika, Ugruharika, Tel. Karn. (ಅಗ್ರಹಾರಿಕ) A Brahman inhabiting an Agrahára village. In Bengal, a Brahman who conducts Śráddhas, or obsequial ceremonies.

AGULA, Uriya (ଅଗୁଳ) In the northern Circars, a dam to divert the course of a stream, and turn it over the fields for irrigation.

ÁGURÍ, Beng. (আগুরী) A low caste; mostly cultivators.

AGWÁ, H. (اگوا) A village servant, who acts as a guide to travellers.

AGWÁR, H. (اگوار) The portion of corn set apart for the village servants (from *Áge*, first; the first part to be taken from the heap). In the eastern provinces it implies the perquisite of the ploughmen in kind.

AGWASI, H. (اگواسي) The body of the plough-share.

ÁGYÁ, H. &c. (آگیا, from the S. *Ájná* आज्ञा) An order, an edict, award, decree.

Ágyá-patra, H. A written order, a warrant or commission, an edict.

Abágya, Uriya (for S. अव, against, and आज्ञा) Disregard of orders; resistance to process.

ÂHAD, ÛHUD, H. (A. عهد) An agreement, an engagement, a compact.

Ahad-dár, H. One who makes an agreement; an officer of the Mogul Government who, for a per-centage on the collection, engaged for the revenue of a district.

Ahad-náma, H. A written engagement.

AHÁDIS, H. (A. احاديث, plur. of حديث) Traditions; especially the traditionally transmitted sayings and doings of

Mohammed, as constituting the basis of the *Sunnat*, or traditional law.

ÁHAK, AHUK, H. (P. آهك) Quick-lime; an *abwáb*, or cess upon lime.

ÁHAL, Hindi (आहल) Freshness of soil.

ÁHAN, AHUN, H. (P. آهن) Iron.

Áhani-kolimi, Tel. (from *áhan*, iron, and Tel. *kolimi* కొలిమి, a forge), A tax on blacksmiths.

ÁHAR, AHUR, or ÁHARA, AHURU, or AHARI, AHUREE, H. (آهر, اهري, from S. *ádhára* आधार) A small pond; a reservoir for collecting water for irrigation; a drain or ditch for the same purpose; a trough for watering cattle.

ÁHAR, AHUR, H. (آهر) A salt-pit.

AHAR, AHUR, H. (اهر) The name of a tribe or caste extensively spread through Rohilkhand and other districts in the north-west provinces, following pastoral occupations, and claiming to be descended from the *Yadu*-race of *Rajaputs*, but not so recognised by other castes. The tracts they occupy are known collectively as the *Ahárát*.

ÁHAVANÍYA, S. (आहवनीयः) The consecrated fire taken from the household fire for the purpose of receiving oblations.

ÂHDAH, UHDUH, or more correctly, OHDUH, *q.v.* H. (A. عهده) An office, whether civil or military.

Ahdah-dár, H. (P. دار, who has), An officer, a functionary, whether military or civil.

AHERA, Mar. (अहेर) Presents made to a person by his relations on occasion of a marriage in his family.

AHERIYA, H. (اهيريا) A sportsman, a fowler.

AHEVA, Mar. (अहेव, from S. *a* अ, not, and *vidhavá* विधवा, widow), A woman whose husband is living.

Aheva-navamí, Mar. The ninth of the dark fortnight of Bhádra (Aug.—Sept.), when offerings are made to the manes of women who have died before their husbands.

AHÍR, UHEER, H. (اهير, from the S. ABHÍR, q.v.), A caste of Hindus following the occupation of shepherds; originally a pastoral tribe in the west of India, but now spread universally, and especially numerous in the north-west provinces, where they are distinguished as three races, acknowledging no other connection than the name of *Ahír*. These are of the *Nand-bansa* (race), *Jad* or *Yadu-bansa*, and *Gwál* (*Go-wála*, cowherd) *bansa*. The first are most numerous in the Central Doab; the second in the Upper Doab, and on the west of the Jumna; and the last in the Lower Doab and the province of Benares. The two first are numerously sub-divided, bearing distinctive appellations, taken usually from the place where they reside. Some of the *Jad-bansís* have been converted to Mohammedanism, and are known as *Rángars* in common with some other tribes. Tribes of Ahírs are numerous also in Rajputána and the Panjáb. In the Delhi territory the Ahírs eat, drink, and smoke with Játs and Gújars, and in some cases with Rajputs. The several sub-divisions intermarry, avoiding only the four families nearest in affinity; and where they are much intermixed, as in the Delhi district, with Gújars and Játs, they conform to their usage of the marriage of the widow of an elder brother by the next in seniority.

AHÍṬA, UHEETU, H. (اهيٹه) A person appointed to watch the grain when it is ripe, and see that none is carried away before the demands on it are liquidated.

ÁHITÁGNI, S. (आहिताग्निः) A Brahman householder who maintains a perpetual family-fire.

AHKÁM, H. (A. احكام, plur. of حكم) Orders, commands.

Ahkám-náma, corruptly, *Ahám-nama*, or *Akám náma*, H. Written orders; the title given, in the Karnatic, to the assessment of the land-revenue made under Tipu.

Ahkámi-zamindár, H. A Zamindar appointed by the ruling power.

AHL, UHL, H. (A. اهل) People belonging to either person, place, or practice; family dependants; the women and children of the head of a family. It is commonly used in composition, as,

Ahl-ul-Ijtihád, A. (اهل الاجتهاد) In Mohammedan law, People capable of legal investigation; qualified jurists.

Ahl-i-kár, H. (اهل كار) People of business; officers of a court.

Ahl-i-kalam, H. (اهل قلم) Civil officers; people of the pen. This is also used in Mysore, as Karn. (ಅರಲಿಕಲಂ).

Ahl-i-kitab, H. (A. كتاب, a book), People of the Book—Mohammedans, Jews, and Christians.

Ahl-i-mâásh, H. (A. معاش) Possessor of a means of subsistence; holder of a rent-free tenure.

Ahl-ul-maṣárif, A. (from مصارف) In Mohammedan law, A proprietor; one who has the right of appropriation, or disbursing.

Ahl-i-naṣrat, A. (from نصرة) In Mohammedan law, Coadjutors, colleagues; persons fit or able to assist or restrain their associates, and who are therefore amenable to punishment if they suffer or aid them to commit any offence.

Ahl-i-sunnat, A. (from سنت) The followers of the traditional, as well as the written law. The Sunnis, as opposed to the Shí-as.

Ahlá, H. (اهلا) Inundation, overflow.

Ahmaḳána, H. (احمقانه, from the A. احمق, a fool, *lit.* foolishly), A fine paid by a collector or farmer of the revenue on account of deficiency or default.

Ahmed-Mahmud, H. (A. محمود, احمد, *lit.* the praised, but used as proper names), A term applied in the Courts to two persons who have combined to defraud a third.

Ahmedi, H. (A. (احمدي) A gold coin of Tipu Sultan, equal to 5 pagodas, Marsden. miii. miv. It is also applicable to the coins of Ahmed Shah of Delhi.

Áhnika, S. (आह्निक, from अहन्, a day, diurnal), The daily observances of the Hindus; a diary, a journal.

Ahoratra, S. (अहोरात्र:) A day and night, from sunrise to sunrise.

Ahshám, corruptly, Ashám, (H. احشام, A. plur. of حشم) Karn. (ಅಶಾಂ), Hasham, or Hashám, Mar. (हशम, हशाम), Attendants, followers, retinue. In the Dekhin and Carnatic, A kind of irregular troops or militia, employed chiefly as garrisons, and as an armed police.

Ahshám, or *Hashám-daftar*, H. Mar. (P. دفتر, an office), The muster-roll or return of the local militia, and their expense.

Ahshám, or *Hashám daftardár*, H. Mar. (P. دار) An officer in the Maraṭha state who made out the annual accounts of the expenses and dues of the irregular troops from the rough accounts.

Hasham, or *Hashám-farnavis*, Mar. (फडनवीश) An officer who made out the muster and pay-rolls of the irregular troops; also *Ahshám* or *Hashám-navís*.

Ahshám, or *Hashám-jáigir*, H. Mar. (جايگير) Assignments of revenue for the support of the irregular troops.

Ahshám, or *Hashám-sibandi*, or *Ahshám*, or *Hashám Sipáhi*, H. Mar. (शिबन्दी, शिपाही) Local militia, or irregular troops, employed in garrisons, or as an armed police, in the Maraṭha countries.

Ahwál, H. (A., plur. of حال) Circumstances, condition, events; a report or record of the particulars of an affair, or of the condition of a thing or person.

Ahya al-Mawát (A. احيا الموات, *lit.* revival of the dead), Cultivation of waste lands.

Al Ahyái bâd al-Mawát, Mar. (ال احياي بعد الموات) Surviving heirs after others' death (Mohammedam law).

Á-ígalu, or Áyígalu, Karn. (ಅಯಿಗಲು) The box in which the portable emblem of the Lingaits is carried hung round the neck.

Á-ídene, Karn. (ಅಯಿದೆನೆ) Ears of corn selected for seed. First crop.

Ailá, or Ilá, A. (ايلا) A vow; but in Mohammedan law, especially a vow to abstain from carnal knowledge of a wife for four months, the fulfilment of which is equivalent to a divorce.

Á-íl, A-eel, Ben. (আইল) A bank or mound of earth forming a division between fields, a boundary mark, an embankment.

Aima, less correctly, Ayma, H. (A. ايمه) Land granted by the Mogul Government, either rent-free or subject to a small quit-rent, to learned and religious persons of the Mohammedan faith, or for religious and charitable uses in relation to Mohammedanism. Such tenures were recognised by the British Government as hereditary and transferable. Beng. Regulations before 1793, p. 24. Reg. viii. 1793, &c.

Aima-báz-yáft, H. (P. بازيافت) Lapsed *Aima* grants, or such grants subsequently assessed.

Aima-báẓi-zamín, H. (A. باضي زمين) Land held rent-free, or at a quit-rent, under an *Aima* grant.

Aima-dár, H. (P. دار, who has), Holder of land granted for religious or charitable uses, or to religious or learned Mohammedans.

Aima-mauzâ, H. (A. موضع) A village given as a charitable endowment to learned or religious persons.

Ain, A. (the Arabic letter ع). The official counter-mark of the Vazir upon a royal mandate for an assignment of revenue under the Mohammedan Governments.

Á-ín, Aeen, Áyín, Ayeen, *q. v.* H. (P. آئين) Laws, statutes, rules, regulations; the laws enacted by secular authority in distinction to those of the Korán or sacred tradition.

Áïn-dán, H. (P. دان) Literally, One who knows the law, but applied especially to one who, by his knowledge of Government regulations, takes advantage of those who are unfamiliar with them.

Áïn-wartan, or *wurtun*, (?) (S. वर्त्तन) A special allowance in some parts of the south of India to the Zemindar from the resources of the village.

Áïn-i-sharkat, H. (A. شركت) Terms or rules of partnership.

Âin, A. (عين) Property actually existing, specific sum or value, the most precious or substantial part of property. As adopted in Maraṭha finance, *Ain* (ऐन), incorrectly written sometimes *Ayen*, implies either the original fixed or standard assessment of the revenue or the lands bearing such assessment. It occurs also in various com-

E

binations in the revenue language of the Maraṭha provinces and some other parts of India, chiefly in the South, in the sense of actual, original, or originally fixed or standard.

Ainbábati, Mar. (ऐनबाबती) The original *Bábati*, or portion, of the fourth of the Maraṭha tribute set apart for the prince.

Ainberij, Tam. (அய்ன்பேரீஜ்) Actual or standard assessment.

Aindasta, Mar. (ऐनदस्त) The regular cess upon fields, &c., as opposed to any incidental or extra charge.

Ainjamâ, corruptly, *Ayen-jumma*, H. (from the A. *ain* عين, special, and *jamâ* جمع, collection) Mar. (ऐनजमा) Tam. (அய்ன்ஜமா) The regular or standard collections or revenue, fixed exclusive of extra cesses, the same as the *Asal jamâ* of Bengal.

Ainjamábandi, Mar. (P. بندي) The settlement or account of the assessment upon any given tract.

Ainjinnas, Mar. (ऐनजिन्नस, from the A. جنس) The produce of the soil as assessed in kind, not in money.

Ainkamávisjamá, Mar. (ऐनकमावीशजमा) The original articles of the extra revenue not included in the land revenue; cesses or fees of some standing.

Ain-mohásá, Mar. (ऐनमोकासा, from the A. *mukassar*, مقصر, diminished, or *mukhassas*, مخصص, appropriated ?) The original amount of assignment of lands, or of a portion of the Government claim of the fourth of the revenue, to the Maraṭha Sirdars, on condition of their keeping up troops, &c., for the service of the State; also the fixed share of the Government in the property of a village, and the revenue derived from it, or the village originally paying part revenue to the State.

Ainâti, corruptly *Ayanatee* and *Einatee*, Mar. (ऐनाती) The original standard assessment of the revenue.

Ain-mulki, Mar. (A. ملك, a kingdom) The original land revenue.

Ain-sibandi, Mar. (शिबंदी) The original establishment of militia.

Ain-taram, Tam. (A. عين, original, and T. *taram* தரம், kind, species), The original classification of lands in the Madras provinces at the time of the survey, according to their kinds or qualities; also the assessment thus fixed, exclusive of sums imposed on account of subsequent improvement.

Ain-tankhá Dekh. (P. تنخواه) The original and fixed assignment of the revenue of lands; a particular settlement of the revenue in the Dekhin. See *Tanhhá*.

ÂINAT (A. عينة), Delivery of goods on credit at an enhanced price, instead of a loan of money at interest.

ÂISH-MAHAL, H. (from A. عيش, pleasure, and محل, a chamber), The inner or female apartments of the house of a person of wealth or rank.

AIVAJU, Tel .Kar. (ఐవజు, corruption of the A. عوض, *iwaz*), Substitute, equivalent; one thing substituted for another. Money.

Aivaj-ákaram, Tel. (?) Gross product.

AIWÁRA, H. (ايوارة) A cow-shed in the middle of a jungle.

AIYAṆ, Tam. (ஐயன்) A father, also more reverentially *Aiyangar*, and, in the South of India, a title added to the names of Brahmans, especially those of the *Śrívaishṅava* or *Rámánujíya* order.

AJA, UJU, or ADJA, UDJU, Tel. (అజ) Amount, total, whole, the gross produce of the land, including the shares of the Government and of the Ryots.

AJA, Mar. (अज) The line drawn over the items of a paper of accounts; also of the columns and several lines across it.

ÁJALU, Tuluva, but current in Karnáta, (?). Hereditary fees and perquisites of the village officers and servants.

AJAMÁN, Tel. (corruption of S. *yajamána*, यजमानः) Householder, manager, master: it properly means the householder at whose expense, and on whose behalf, a religious ceremony is performed.

AJAN, Hindi (अजन) The length of a field.

AJÁRA, UJARU, more correctly IJÁRA, q. v. A farm, a contract.

AJÁTA-PUTRA, S. (from अजात, unborn, and पुत्र, a son), A man to whom no son has been born, (and who has, therefore, power to adopt one).

AJAURI, UJOUREE, H. (اجَوري) Advances, particularly to agricultural labourers.—East Oude. *Agrourhi* is the term used in some other places.—*Elliot.*

AJAULI, UJOULEE, H. (اجَولي) Perquisite of the lower castes from the threshing floor: *Benares*. It is derived from the S. *Anjali*, the two hands joined, being as much as may be so taken away.—*Elliot.*

AJIL, A. (اجل) Procrastination in law. Suffering such an interval to elapse as does not preclude complaint.

AJINA, S. &c. (अजिनं) The hide of an antelope or tiger used as a seat by the religious student, also in the South of India at weddings.

AJÍR, UJEER, H. (A. اجير) A hired servant or labourer,

a bondsman, a bond-slave, one who has entered into an engagement for a stipulated sum to serve another for a specific term, or until he repay the sum advanced; also, a hirer: a lessee.

Ajir mushtarik, A. (اجير مشترك) A common hireling, one whose services are not confined to a single employer.

Ajir wáhid, A. (اجير واحيد) A hireling who takes service with one master only for a given term.

ÁJNÁ, in some dialects but corruptly, *Ágyá*, q. v. H. Ben. (S. आज्ञा) Order, command, decree, award. In Tam. it is transmuted in writing to *Ákkiṇai* (ஆக்கினை).

Ájná patra, H. Ben. (S. पत्र, a leaf), A written order or decree.

AJNAGDI, Hindi (अजनगदी) Taken at a fixed money rate.

AJR, UJR, H. (A. اجر) Hire, wages.

AJÚRÁ, UJOORA, Mar. (अजूरा, from the A. اجر) Hire, wages, especially to one employed by the job. In commercial transactions the fee or per-centage charged on a dishonoured bill, for the expence of returning it to the drawer when residing at a distance.

Ajúrá dar, Mar. (P. دار) A hired labourer.

Ajúrá dári, Mar. (P. داري) Hire, wages, pay by the job.

ÁJYA, S. (आज्यं) Butter that has been clarified by boiling, more commonly called Ghee, and peculiarly fit for oblations at sacrifices with fire: it is also drank at meals.

Ájya bhága, or *Ajya-bhása*, S. The portion of a ceremony when the oblation of butter is presented.

ÁK, H. (اك, from the S. अर्क) Gigantic swallow-wort. A sprout of sugar-cane.

ÁKÁ, Ben. (आका) A sack, a bag, a furnace.

ÁKABATI-ṬOKRI, Uriya. A basket for heaving salt overboard from salt-sloops.

AKÁL, H. (S. *a* अ neg., *kála*, कालः, time), Famine, drought, any unseasonable occurrence.

Akál-vrishṭi, Hindi (S. वृष्टि, rain), Untimely or unseasonable rain.

AḲÁLA, A. (اقالة) Cancelling or revocation of sale.

AKÁLÍ, S. (अकाली) A class of armed devotees among the Sikhs, worshippers of "Him who is without time, eternal."

ÁKAN, AKUN, H. (آكن) Grass and weeds collected from a ploughed field.

ÁKÁR, less correctly, AKUR, Mar. (S. आकारः lit. form, shape), The assessed rent or revenue of a village or district. Estimate in general.

Ákár band, or *bund*, Mar. (आकारबंद) A statement prepared at the time of the annual settlement, shewing the highest amount of revenue derivable from a village, the quantity of land paying rent, or rent free, the sum assessed, and land cultivated during preceding years; the balances due, and instalments by which they are to be discharged; the sums payable to the village officers, and the shares in which the assessment is to be distributed among the occupants of the lands.

Ákár patra or *patrak*, Mar. (S. पत्र, a leaf), Account of rules of assessment, and amount of revenue kept by the *Kulkarní*.

AKARMÁHI, Mar. (अकरमाही, from अकरा, eleven, and माह, a month) Employment, &c., in which only eleven months' pay is received for twelve months' service.

AKÁRAṆ, H. &c. (S. अ neg., and कारणं, cause), Causeless, groundless.

Akáraṇa-vyájya, Karn. (ಅಕಾರಣವ್ಯಾಜ್ಯ) An idle or groundless suit.

AKARÁYÁ, Hindi (अकराया) Ground not properly cleaned for receiving the seed.

ÁKÁṢ, H. (from the S. आकाशः) Ether, the fifth element of the Hindus; but, in common use, atmosphere, sky.

Ákáṣ-birt, H. (S. आकाशवृत्तिः) One who has no ostensible means of subsistence: *lit.* one whose subsistence is the air.

Ákáṣ-diä, H. (from S. आकाशदीपः) A lamp or lanthorn raised on a pole, a signal or watch light, a light raised at the Diwáli festival.

Ákáṣ-mukhi, H. (S. आकाश and मुख, the face), A devotee of the Ṣaiva order, who keeps his face turned up to the sky, so that sometimes he cannot, without difficulty, restore his head to its natural position.

AKAṢÁLIGA, or AGUṢÁLIGA, Karn. (ಅಕ್ಕಸಾಲಿಗ, ಅಗಸಾಲಿಗ) A goldsmith.

AKBARI-RÁI, or AKBAR-AR-RÁI, A. (اكبري راي or اكبر الراي) Strong presumptive evidence; sufficient to convict.

ÂKD, ÛKD, H. (A. عقد) A knot, a tie; an agreement, a compact, a contract of marriage.

Âkdána, H. (عقدانه) Marriage fee paid to the Ḳaẓi.

Âkd-kitábat, A. (A. كتابت) A contract of Kitábat or conditional ransom granted by a master to his slave.

Âkd-náma, H. (P. نامه, writing) A written contract, a marriage settlement.

ÁKHÁ, H. (آكها) A pair of grain bags used as a pannier.

Ákhen, Mar. (आखें) One of the pair of grain or water bags forming a horse or bullock load.

Ákhá, Ben. (আথা) A sack or bag; a furnace. See *Áká.*

Akháḍá, Ukháḍá, or Ákhaḍá, Akhuḍá, pronounced also, Akháṛá, H. &c. (अखाडा, आखडा) A place where people are assembled either temporarily or permanently; a wrestling ground, a place for bodily exercises and games, a stand or place of resort for low people and hired labourers. The residence of a society of religious mendicants, a monastery. In Bengal it also means a band of singers.

Akharwar. A division of the Kurmi tribe (?).

Akharját, corruption of Ikhráját, q. v. Expenses.

Ákhat, Hindi (आखत) A portion of the crop per each plough paid to the village artisans, or the smith, carpenter, &c. —North-West Provinces.

Akhbár, H. (A. plur. of خبر) News, intelligence, a newspaper; especially the written intelligence of the proceedings of Native Courts and Princes circulated to other Courts and Princes by their appointed agents—a regular practice under the Native administration.

Akhbár-navís, A. (P. نویس) A news-writer, an appointed communicator of intelligence—'our own' correspondent.

Ákhir, H. (A. آخِر) Akher, Mar. (अखेर) Final, last, end. In the Dekhin, the last assessment, the rate at which the revenue was last fixed.

Ákhiri, A. (آخري) Last, final.

Ákhiri-hisab-kharch, H. (A. حساب خرچ) Adjustment of the cultivators at the end of the year, shewing the amount of revenue assessed, paid, and in arrears, with the items of deduction for expenses.

Ákhir-jamâ ṭumári, H. (جمع طوماري) Improved revenue from that fixed originally; applied especially to the revenues of Bengal, Behar, Orissa, Allahabad, &c., in the time of Mohammed Shah, as contrasted with those fixed in the time of Akbar.

Akhiri-jamâ-wáṣil-báḳi, H. (A. واصل باقي) Final settlement of the accounts of a Zemindari, or a village, crediting profits and receipts; debiting all disbursements and payments of revenue, and adjusting the balance.

Ákhir-i-nikás, H. (نكاس, S. निःकास) Final settlement of an account, final adjustment of demand for revenue to be levied on a village or an estate; annual account of collections duly balanced, furnished by an assistant collector or subordinate revenue officer. *Nikás* implies, properly, the settlement of an account or payment of rent by the cultivating Ryots to the Zemindar.

Ákhir-patraka, H. (S. पत्रक) In the Dekhin, account of the last preceding assessment kept by the village accountant.

Ákhir-i-sál, H. (P. سال) The end of the 'revenue' year.

Akher-sálpaṭṭi, Mar. (अखेरसालपट्टी) The last instalment and final settlement of the revenue at the end of the official year.

Akhtíj, Ukhteej, H. (اكهتيج, from S. *ashta* अष्ट, in the North-West pronounced *akhtá,* and *daṣa* दश, ten, eighteen), The 18th of the month *Baiṣákh* (April—May), on which it is customary for the cultivators to settle their accounts for the expenses of the *Rabi,* or spring crop, and repayment of advances. It is proper on this day also to begin the manufacture of agricultural implements, to feed Brahmans, and to eat a small quantity of the new grain. A plough is also slightly passed over the fallow fields for good luck, but it is forbidden to sow seed on this day, except under particular circumstances.

Akhtíj ká bhao, H. (بهاو) The rate or price of corn prevailing on the day of *Akhtíj,* at which rate the cultivator agrees to repay, in kind, the amount of any money advanced, together with the interest.

Akhu, Uriya (S. इक्षु) Sugar-cane.

Ákhun, or Ákhund, H. (P. آخوند آخون) A Mohammedan teacher or schoolmaster. In the Mohammedan villages of the South he is one of the village officers, and is paid by fees or perquisites by the community.

Âákila, A. (عاقله, from *âkl,* عقل, having for one sense, restraint; but applied especially to the fine for bloodshed; as, a restraint upon the commission of violence), In Mohammedan law, an individual connected with one who, whether intentionally or unintentionally, perpetrates homicide, and who is held jointly responsible for the fine to be paid by the perpetrator.

Akkaḍi, Ukkuḍee, Karn. (ಅಕ್ಕಡಿ) Pulse, or leguminous plants with a bivalve pericarp, having the seeds fixed to one only of the sutures.

Akkaḍi-pairu, Karn. (ಅಕ್ಕಡಿಪೈರು) Sowing different kinds of pulse at the fit season.

Âkkár, A. (عقّار) Real property.

Akkasari, Ukkusuree, Tel. (అక్కసరి) Neighbouring, contiguous.

Akkasari grámamu, Tel. (గ్రామము) A neighbouring village.

Akki, Karn. (ಅಕ್ಕಿ) Rice deprived of its husk before boiling.

Akkuṣai, Ukkoosaee, Tel. (అక్కుశాయి) Commission on goods, brokerage.

Aklif, Uklif, H. (A. اكلف) A Mohammedan, who, from

adequate cause, has omitted circumcision, but is not thereby disqualified from giving evidence.

AKOR, UKOR, H. (اكور) A bribe. Used also in the North-West Provinces to signify the coaxing of a cow or she-buffalo which has lost its calf, and inducing it to eat. *Akor*, or *Kor*, as sometimes pronounced, also denotes the food which a labourer eats at intervals of work in the open field.—*Elliot.*

Akori, H. One who takes a bribe.

ÂḲR, A. (عقر) In Mohammedan law, a marriage portion or dower; also one to be settled on the female slave, termed Mukatiba, with whom the owner has cohabited; also, price paid for the violation of a maiden.

AKRÁ, H. (اكرا) A grass or vetch which grows in fields under the spring crop, twining round the young corn and checking its growth (Vicia sativa). It is also termed *Ankri* (انكري), and is used as fodder.

AḲRIBÁ, A. (plur. of قريب) Kinsmen; relations within the degrees recognised by law.

AḲSÁT, UKSAT, H. (A. plur. of قسط, *kist*), Instalments of the annual revenue.

AKSHATA, read in some dialects, *Achchata*, Mar. &c. (from S. *Akshata*, अक्षत, unbroken) Grains of rice, coloured with saffron or vermilion, placed on the forehead of an idol, or on those of the bride and bridegroom at their marriage; also presented to persons invited to a feast, who place them on their foreheads if they accept the invitation. The sectarial mark worn by Hindus on the forehead, or the pigment with which it is made.

AKSHAYA, S. &c. (अक्षय, imperishable) The sixtieth year of the cycle of sixty years.

Akshaya-pátra, Tel. (S. अक्षय, unwasting, and पात्र, a vessel) A charitable allowance to Brahmans from the gross crop. A beggar's dish or platter.

Akshaya tritíyá, S. (अक्षय, imperishable, and तृतीया, third) The third lunation of the light half of Vaiṣákhá—April, May—when offerings are made to the manes, also to Krishṇa. It is the supposed anniversary of the creation.

Akshaya lalitá, S. (अक्षय, and ललिता, agreeable (day) The 7th of Bhadra (August, September), when a festival is celebrated by women in honour of Ṣiva and Durgá.

AḲṬÁÂ, corruptly, ATKÁ, and more correctly, IḲṬÁÂ, H. (A. اقطاع) An assignment of land for the maintenance of a body of troops, a jagir.

AKTA, also, AKTI, corruptly, AKHTY, OCKHTAY, Mar. (अक्ता, from the A. *ḳaṭá*, قطع, cut off, separated; whence also Mar. *Maktá* and *Makti*, &c.) Land held at a fixed rate, which is lower than it is capable of paying: it is of two descriptions, *Makti gatkul mirási*, land belonging to the village community, let for a specified term for a fixed sum, less than the probable demand of the Government; and *Khand-mukti mirási*, land similarly let, but in perpetuity, and held in absolute property by the occupant: (such are the explanations given by the collector of Poona, Rev. Selections, 4, 543, but *Akti* and *Makti* are clearly only the epithets of *Mirási*, hereditary property, implying, set apart, let on lease, either for a term or for ever.)

ÁKU, Tel. (ఆకు) A leaf, the betel leaf; the young rice plant ready for transplanting.

Áku-toṭa, Tel. (ఆకుతోట) A betel plantation or garden.

ÂḲÚBAT, ÛḲOOBUT, H. (A. عقوبت, from عقبت, behind, subsequent), Punishment, torture.

ÁL, corruptly, AUL, H. (آل) A plant (Morinda citrifolia), from the roots of which a red dye is prepared. The best kind in the North-West Provinces comes from Bundelkhand. In the same Provinces *Âl* sometimes denotes a *Paṅa*, or division of a village.

Ál kárí, H. (S. कारी, who makes) A class of Rajput cultivators in Nagpur, from their especial cultivation of the *Ál* tree.

ÂL, or ÂÁL, H. (A. عال) Boundary of a field.

ÁḶ, Tam. (ஆள்), ÁḶ or ÁḶA, Mal. (ആൾ, ആള), ÁḶU, Karn. (ಆಳು), A man, a person, an individual, an adult, or one equal to take care of himself, a servant, a labourer, a messenger, a slave (perhaps from the A. آل, progeny, dependants).

Áḷkúli, Mal. (ആൾക്കൂലി) Wages of a labourer.

Áloṭṭi, Tam. (ஆளொட்டி) An overseer, one who superintends and urges on labourers.

Álpáṭṭam, Mal. (ആൾപാട്ടം) Hire or rent of a slave lent out to another person.

Áḷusunka, Karn. (ಆಳುಸುಂಕ) A tax levied on cultivators in Mysore, who employ labourers or slaves, at so much per head.

ALÁ, H. (الا) Wet, moist, as land saturated with water, especially rain-water: the word occurs in the dialects as *Ál*, *Áhal*, *Ali*, and *Aïl*.

AL-ÂBD, H. (A. ال, the, عبد, slave) Form of countersignature by a subordinate clerk or officer, *lit.* the slave or servant.

Alag, Ulug, corruptly, Alagá, Uluga, or Alga, Ulgu, H. (الگ, from the S. *a* अ, neg., and *lagna* लग्न, connected; disjoined, unconnected) Separate, several, detached: the word, modified, occurs in most dialects.

Alagá-ásámilu, Tel. (A. آسامي) Loose folks, wanderers, vagrants, temporary occupants, persons not reckoned among the inhabitants of a village.

Alagá bhúmi, Tel. (S. भूमि) Waste land, land set apart for pasture.

Alagá pullari, Tel. (పుల్లరి) Grazing tax or fine levied on stray cattle.

Alakh námi, H. (from S. *alakshya*, अलक्ष्य, the indefinable God; and *náma*, a name), A mendicant of the Saiva sect.

Aḷakkiṛa-kol, Tam. (அளக்கிறகோல்) A measuring rod or pole. See *Alavu*.

Aḷakkiravaṉ, Tam. (அளக்கிரவன்) A measurer.

Aḷavaṉ, Tam. (அளவன்) A measurer, a guager.

Aḷakkugai, Tam. (அளக்குகை) Measurement.

Alalhisábu, Tel. Karn. (అలలహిసాబు, from the Ar. *l'il-hisábu*, (للحساب, according to the account) Pay given before hand, money paid in advance or on account.

Áḷ-amaṉji, Tam. (ஆள்-அமஞ்சி, from *Ál*, a labourer, and *amaṉji*, compulsory service) Compulsory service which the villagers in the Dravira provinces were formerly compelled to render to Government officers or persons travelling on public duty.

Âlam, H. (علم) A banner; the banner of Hasan and Hosain carried in procession at the Muharram.

Aḷam, Uḷum, Tam. (அளம்) A salt pan, a place where salt is made.

Aḷavan, Tam. (அளவன்) A salt maker.

Aḷattu nilam, Tam. (அளத்துநிலம் also, in some lists, *Alava-nilam*, or *Alava-podal*) Land impregnated with salt, and therefore unfit for cultivation.

Alam, Hindi (अलम) Sticks set up for creeping plants to grow upon.

Alandadey? A class of slaves in the Tamil countries.—*Chingleput*.

Aḷata, or Aḷati-gára, Karn. (ಅಳತೆ, ಅಳತಿ, a measure, and ಗಾರ, from S. कार, who makes) A person employed in Mysore to measure corn or land, sometimes included among the village officers.

Âlámat, H. (A. علامت) *Lit.* A sign. It is usually written before the signature of a female. It is also used to signify a discoverable trace or vestige of a robbery or murder on the spot where committed.

Âlámat-i-dastkhat, H. (P. دستخط) A mark in place of signature; usually the mark of one unable to write.

Alasandi, Karn. (ಅಲಸಂದಿ) A species of pulse (Dolichos catjang).

Aḷavi, Karn. (ಅಳವಿ) A lease or agreement given to the Ryot in writing; one stipulating a progressive assessment: also termed *Alavi Geni*.

Alavi-sair, Karn. (A. ساير) Sea-customs. Extra revenue let on lease or in farm.

Aḷavu, or Aḷavái, Tam. (அளவு, அளவை) Measure, measurement, especially of grain. Portion of produce set apart as payment for the measurement of the crop.

Aḷavu-káraṉ, Tam. (அளவுக்காரன்) A measurer, the village officer who measures the threshed grain and regulates the proportionate distribution of water for irrigation.

Aḷavu-paimaish, Tam. (from *Aḷavu* and P. *paimaish*, measurement), Survey or measurement of fields, especially the name of a particular survey and valuation of the lands in Malabar, made for the purpose of assessing the revenue in 1807-8.

Alavogulu, Tam. (?) An account specifying the measurement of each field in a farm or hamlet.

Aláwa, H. &c. (P. الاوه, अलावा) A fire-place; applied in Hindustan especially to a hole in front of the shed where the paraphernalia of the Muharram are deposited, and in which a fire is lighted every evening during the festival.

Alchaliku, (?) The mouldering away of the banks between the corn fields.

Áḷdhola, Karn. (ಆಳ್ಧೊಲ) A field in one's own possession.

Ále, Karn. (ಅಲೆ), Alai, Tam. (ஆலை) A press for extracting the juice from the sugar-cane; a sugar-mill; the juice of the cane; also a forge.

Áléguṇi, Karn. (ಆಲೆಗುಣಿ) A hole for receiving the juice of the cane.

Álé hogé, Karn. (?) A tax on sugar-mills in Mysore.

Álemanésunka, Karn. (ಆಲೆಮನೇಸುಂಕ) A duty levied on sugar works.

Alekal, more correctly, Anaikal, q. v. Tam. Stone embankment of a reservoir.

Áli, Alee, H. (آلي) A land measure of four Bísis. Nine *Ális* go to one Júla.—*Gerwhal*.

Aḷidava, or Aḷdava, or Aḷidodeya, Karn. (ಅಳಿದವ, ಅಳ್ದವ, ಅಳಿದೊಡೆಯ) A ruler, a master, a king.

Alíya, H. (الیا) A branch of the Turkia subdivision of the travelling grain dealers, called Banjáras.

Âḷiya, Karn. (ಅಳಿಯ) A son-in-law.

Aliya santána, Karn. (S. संतान, offspring) Succession or descent by the female line in Malabar.

Âli-gol, H. (علیگول, from the A. *Âli*, علي, lofty, excellent, and the S. *gola*, गोल, a ball, a troop), Irregular foot in the Maratha service, without discipline or regular arms. According to some they are so named from charging in a dense mass, or *Gol,* and invoking Âli, the son-in-law of Mohammed, being chiefly Mohammedans.

Alḳáb, Ulḳab, H. (A. plur. of لقب, a title) Titles, honours, part of a form of address to persons of high rank; as to the Governor-General, who is commonly styled Nawab Mâli-alkáb Bahádur, the noble, the Nawab, of lofty titles.

Allu, Ulloo, Guz. (?). In Kattiwar a kind of ordeal in cases of disputed boundaries in which the claimant walks over the contested limits with a raw hide or a cloth on his shoulders, previously dedicated to one of the fearful forms of Durgá, from whose vengeance he will receive some calamity if his claim is unjust.

Aḷḷu, Uḷḷoo, Tam. (அள்ளு) A handful of grain given to the village servant by whom a quantity has been measured; or a small quantity of any article sold in the bazar taken as a cess or tax.

Alledukiṛavaṉ, Tam. (அளளெடுக்கிறவன்) The measurer who is paid by a handful from each quantity measured.

Álma, Karn. (ಆಳ್ಮ) A king, a ruler.

Álmaga, Karn. (ಆಳ್ಮಗ) A servant.

Almâra, or Almâri, H. (الماري, Port. Ulmaria) A cabinet, a wardrobe, a cupboard, a chest of drawers.

Almara-koneru, Tel. (?) A well with steps down one side.

Alo, H. (الو) A portion of unripe corn.—Province of Benares.

Áltá, H. (آلتا) Balls of cotton impregnated with lac dye; hence also the dye itself.

Altamghá or Áltamghá, Altumgha or Ultumgha, H. (from the Turkish *ál* ال, red, and *tamghá* تمغا, a stamp or impression; Bianchi, Dict. Turc-francais) A royal grant under the seal of some of the former native princes of Hindustan, and recognised by the British Government as conferring a title to rent-free land in perpetuity, hereditary and transferable. Although probably originally bearing a red or purple stamp, the colour of the imperial seal or signature became in Indian practice indifferent.—*Elliot.*

Alu, H. &c. (S. آلو, आलु) An esculent root, a kind of arum, and applied to any similar root, as to the potato, also called Bilaiti-álu, and the yám, called Phul-álu.

Aluku, Tel. (అలుకు) Sowing seed in ground prepared for its reception.

Alugu, Tel. (అలుగు) A channel, a sluice to carry off the overflowing water of a reservoir or tank.

Aluté, corruptly, Ulootay, Allootie, Allooty, Alowtay, Mar. (अलुते, plur. of अलुता, possibly a mere alliterative term derived from *Balute*, q. v. as *Baluté-aluté*) The collective designation of the persons whom it is customary in some of the provinces of the Dekhin, to retain as village servants, in addition to the *Baluté*, or regular village servants, such as superannuated members of the Baluté, or their widows, religious mendicants, and the helpless and lazy in general. Besides these, twelve classes of the Aluté, as well as of the Baluté, are specified, viz. 1. The *Jangam,* or priest of the Lingayits, who is employed to blow the conch shell in the temples; 2. The *Koli,* or water-carrier, who supplies travellers and government functionaries travelling on public duty with drinking-water, also the cultivators with water to wash their threshing floors, and the village at large with water on public festivals; 3. The *Bhâṭ,* or village bard, who chants hymns in the temples, and is employed when children are betrothed to ascertain that there are no physical impediments to the marriage; 4. The *Rámúsi,* or village watchman, by caste and practice a thief. In different parts of the South-West of India his place is taken by the *Bhíl* or the *Koli,* both wild and lawless tribes, residing chiefly in the thickets of the Satpura hills, but taking service in the plains; 5. The *Máli, Bághbán,* or gardener, who grows flowers to decorate the temples with, and prepares nosegays to present to Government officers or men of rank passing through the village; 6. The *Turáḷ* or *Yeskar,* who is considered the same as the *Mher,* except that the latter is usually ranked among the Baluté receiving only a different scale of compensation. All the *Mhers* in the village take the office of Tarâl for a year in rotation, and, besides the fixed allowance of land or grain, each receives annually a pair of shoes and a blanket. The Tarál is to be always resident and at the call of the *Patíl,* and is especially assigned to attendance on strangers, whom he furnishes with local information, and for whom he procures the necessary supplies; 7. The *Gondhali,* beater of a double kettle-drum; 8. The *Ḍaurí Gosain,* who beats a sort of small drum; 9. The *Garsi*, (?) or piper; 10. The *Sempi*, *Darjí*, *Súti*, or *Suï*, the village tailor; 11. The *Telí*, or oil presser and vender; 12. The *Támbúli*, or preparer of the *Pán*, or betel-leaf, &c. Few of these hold land, but are mostly paid by an allowance of grain. There are some varieties in their specification; as, for instance, in Duff's History of the Marathas the twelve *Alutas* are called, 1. The *Sonar*, goldsmith; 2. The *Jangam*; 3. The tailor; 4. The water-carrier; 5. The *Tarál*; 6. The *Máli*; 7. The drummer; 8. The piper; 9. The *Rámúsi* or *Bhíl*; 10. The *Taili*; 11. The *Támbúli*, and 12. The *Gondali*. But the whole number of twelve are rarely found in any village establishment. On the other hand, there are occasional additions to the list, as, *Bájantris*, musicians and comedians; *Kalávantins*, dancing girls; a *Vaidya*, or village physician; a *Ghota-khor*, a diver, one who plunges into the water to recover lost articles; and a *Gárpagári*, a village conjuror and fortune teller.

Áḻvár, Tam. (*pl.* ஆழ்வார்) Álwáru, Tel. (*pl.* ఆళ్వారు), Rulers, persons of authority, the collective title of twelve reputed saints of the Southern Vaishnavas, who are said to have each written a portion of the *Drávida Prabandha*, or *Tamil Veda*, chiefly designed for *Súdras* and women. Rámánuja, the founder of the Srí Vaishnava sect, which is one of the three great sects of the Peninsula, is sometimes considered the same as Yembiru-mánáru, the last of the Álvár.

Âám, or Âm, corruptly, Aum, H. (A. عام) The general people, the commonalty, as opposed to the *Khás*, the nobility, or the select.

Diwan-i-Âám, H. The public hall of audience, that to which all persons may be admitted; in distinction to the Diwan-i-khás, the hall of the select, the privy council.

Ámad, Amud, H. (from the P. *ámdan* آمدن, to come), Income, revenue.

Ámad-o-raft, H. (from the P. آمدن, and رفتن, to go, *literally*, coming and going), Income and expenditure. Imports and exports. (In Guzerat) Town duties: also applied to Safe-conduct, permission to come and go without harm.

Ámad-o-raft bhandári, H. Surety for safe conduct; guarantee for coming and going with impunity.

Ámad- or *Amda-wála*, H. A merchant who purchases imported goods wholesale for retail to petty dealers.

Am-i-walad, or, more correctly, Um-al-walad, A. (from ام, a mother, and *walad* ولد, offspring) A female slave who has borne a son to her master, and is therefore, by the law, to be emancipated at his death.

Âmal, Ûmul, H., used in most dialects, with the import sometimes slightly modified, (A. عمل, अमल) Business, affairs, an office, collection of revenue, administration of justice, management of any land or business on behalf of another, deputation, authority, government. In Maratha finance an item or head of collection, the share or portion of the revenue after the expenses and extra charges have been defrayed. In the Tamil countries commonly, Confiscation, seizure.

Âmal-dár, H. &c. (عملدار) A manager, an agent, a governor of a district, a collector of revenue. An officer appointed to collect the revenue of an estate which has been attached by Government. In the South it is applied especially to the native revenue collector acting under the authority of the European collector. Any person holding a post or office. The title is also given to the native head of the police in a district, usually also the head revenue officer, whose duties are defined by Bombay Regulations, xii. of 1827, and iv. of 1830, and Act xx. of 1835. Under the Maratha Government, Amaldars or Aumildars were of three kinds; those holding the office of collector on a lease from the Government; those who were appointed by the Sarsubahdárs; and Bankers or Sáhukars, who, having advanced money to the Government or its revenue officers, were appointed to collect the revenue of a district until they had paid themselves.

Âmal-dári, H. &c. (عملداری) Management, administration, collection of revenue. The office of *Amaldár*. Possession, occupancy.

Âmal-dastak, *Umul-dustuk*, H. (عملدستك) Deed of conveyance; any document giving possession of property. Warrant or authority to collect the rents of an estate; a written order from the proper authority to enable the purchaser of an estate at a public sale to obtain possession of it.

Âmal farmáish, Mar. (P. فرمایش, order) An item in the deductions from the net revenue, fees paid to revenue officers (?)

Âmal-guzár, H. (عملگزار) A collector of revenue.

Âmal-náma, H. (P. عملنامه) Authority to manage or administer property, an order for possession, a warrant from a competent public functionary to an individual, authorising his taking possession and management of landed or other property, an order from a Zemindar to his cultivators to give possession to a renter.

Âmal-paṭṭa, H. (عملپتّه) A deed appointing an agent or manager, a warrant authorising a person to collect the rents of an estate.

Âmal-sanad, H. (عمل سند) A deed or warrant empowering a person to collect rents or manage an estate.

ÂMALI, AMLI, UMULEE, or UMLEE, H. (عملي) Payment of the revenue by a division of the crop or in kind; applied also to a village where the revenue is paid in kind: any thing related to, or connected with, managements, collections, and the like. The title of the revenue year in Bengal and Orissa, the same as Faṣli, q. v.

AMAL-I-JINS, H. (from H. امل *amal*, intoxication, and A. *jins* جنس, sort, kind) Intoxicating liquors or drugs. Among the Marathas the revenue levied upon their sale, the same as *Ábkári.*

ÂMAL, AMUL, Hindi (आमल, perhaps an error for ÂÂMIL) Being in charge or possession of.

AMAN, UMUN, also, AMÁN, UMAN, H. (A. امان, امن) Safety, security, protection: protection granted to an infidel during the first year of his residence in a Mohammedan country.

Amánat, Umanut, H. (امانت, from *aman* امن) occuring, slightly modified, in most dialects, or sometimes corrupted, as in Tel. to *Anámat* or *Anámatu*, (అనామతు), as well as *Amánatu* అమానతు. Deposit, charge, any thing held in trust, money deposited in court. Among the Maraṭhas, profit derived from deposits and temporary sequestration of estates.

Amánat daftar, H. (P. دفتر, office) An office under the Mohammedan Government for deposits, or for a register of trusts. The superintendant was invested sometimes with judicial powers in civil suits. Reg. xxii. 1795, preamble.

Amánat dár, H. (P. دار, who has) The holder of a deposit or charge, a trustee, a guardian.

Amánát-dári, H. (P. داري, having) Guardianship, agency, trust.

Amánat-jari, H. (A. جاري, proceeding) (In the South of India) Assignments of revenue resumed or held temporarily in charge of a Government officer.

Amánat-mahál, H. (P. محال) An estate.

Amánat-náma, H. (P. نامه) A deed of trust or deposit, a document conveying any thing in trust.

Amánat-nashṭa, Karn. (ನಷ್ಟ) A tax on ground first cultivated for the Piper Betel, and afterwards for rice, in which the difference of the revenue from dry and wet lands is charged to the Ryots.

AMÁNI, UMANEE, corruptly, UMAUNEE, AUMANY, AMAUNY, H. (اماني) Held in trust or deposit; applied especially to the collection of the revenue direct from the cultivators by the officers of Government upon the removal or suspension of an intermediate claimant or Zemindar, the same as the *khás* collection: it is also applied to Ryotwari settlements, or settlements with each cultivator individually, where no renter or proprietor has been acknowledged; also to lands in the possession of the collector's officers for arrears of revenue, or which, on any other account, are not held by individual tenants.

Amáni-bâẕi-báb, H. (بعضي باب) Miscellaneous heads of receipt or revenuè held in trust or deposit, or collected direct by the officers of government.

Amáni-táláo, H. (اماني تالاو) Karn. *Amánikere*, (ಅಮಾನಿ-ಕೆರೆ) In Mysore, an unrented tank or reservoir of water, not belonging exclusively to any one village, but subservient to the watering of the lands of several, under the superintendence of the officers of the Government.

ÁMAN, ÁMUN, Hindi, Ben. (आमन, আমণ) Rice grown on low wet grounds, the rice that is sown in July and August, and reaped in December, winter rice.

Ámaniya, H. Ben. (आमनिया) Land on which the winter crop of rice is sown.

AMAṈJI, or AMIṈJI, Tam. (அமஞ்சி, அமிஞ்சி) Compulsory service without payment; the gratuitous employment of the villagers in the transport of baggage, &c., for public officers; also the general levy of men inhabiting irrigable villages for the purpose of clearing out the channels or tanks, and for repairing breaches or constructing dams.

AMÁNTA GÁḌU, Tel. (అమాంతగాడు) A pedlar, a hawker.

AMARAM, Tam. (அமரம், *lit.* command of a thousand foot.) A grant of revenue by the Prince or a Poligar, on condition of service generally, military or police; such grants were resumable when the *Amarakár*, or grantee, failed to perform the stipulated service.

ÂMÁRÍ, UMAREE, H. (A. عماري) A canopied seat on an elephant.

AMÁTYA, Mar. (S. अमात्य, a minister), One of the eight principal officers of the Maratha state.

AMAVÁLUJINDAGI, Karn. (ಅಮವಾಲುಜಿಂದಗಿ, the latter word is a corruption of the P. *zindagi*, life) In Mysore, the property of a person dying without heirs and escheating therefore to the Government.

Amavál̤udana, Karn. (ಅಮವಾಲುದನ) Cattle without owners, claimable by the Government.

Amávasi, Umavusee, H. (اماوسي, from the S. अमावसी or अमावास्या) Day of conjunction, day of new moon, when it rises invisible. The term is current throughout India, sometimes slightly modified, as, *Amavási, Amási, Amavasé, Amamási*, and, as corruptly spelled, *Amaubasee, Amauvasy, Amawus*, &c.

Ámb, or Ám, H. (آنب or آم, from S. *Amra* or *Ámra* अम्रः, आम्रः) A mango, the mango-tree; occurring in most dialects, sometimes slightly modified, as, *Amb, Ambá*, or *Ambí*.

Ambá, or *Ambi-dáhale*, Mar. (अंबा, अंबी दहले) A branch of a mango-tree; an extra cess paid in commutation of presents of mangoes formerly required. Rev. Sel. iv. 652.

Ambarái, or *Ámrái*, Mar. (अंबराई, आमराई) A grove of mango-trees, or any garden. Revenue derived from gardens and groves. Rev. Sel. i. 693, and iv. 167.

Ambarái-guttigé, Karn. (ಗುತ್ತಿಗೆ, assessment) Rent or revenue from mango groves or orchards.

Ambá or *Ambí-taka*, Mar. (अंबाटका) Revenue from a tax on mango groves.

Ambadi-kovilakam, Mal. (?) The chief palace, the residence of the eldest and principal wife of the Samúri or Zamorin.

Ambalam, Tam. (அம்பலம்) A place where public affairs are discussed. (Mal. അമ്പലം) In Malabar, a temple of the first class.

Ambala-káran̤, or *Ambalagár*, Tam. (அம்பலக்காரன்) The patel, or head of a village, particularly of villages inhabited by Ṣúdras. The person who presides in the meeting-house of a village. An officer who publishes the decrees of an assembly. R. Sel. ii. 530.

Ambala-mán̤yam, Tam. (அம்பலமாணியம்) A portion of land held free of revenue by the headman of a village, as a perquisite of office.

Ambala-paṭi, Mal. (from പടി, a step) In Malabar the hereditary dignity of an elevated seat or step in a temple, giving to the person who enjoys it the right of directing the ceremonies: the dignity commonly devolves on the headman of a village, but it is saleable.

Ambala-vási, Tam. Mal. (அம்பலவாசி) A caste in Travancore who are makers of garlands: they are attendants in temples, and rank between Brahmans and Nairs.

Ambár, H. &c. (P. انبار, S. अंबार) A store, a heap, a granary, a heap of any thing.

Ambáram, Tel. Karn. Tam. (అంబారము, அம்பாரம், from the P. انبار) A heap, a pile, a stack of corn; grain on the threshing floor; Government share of the crop.

Ambarakkadai, Tam. (அம்பாரக்கடை) A store, a granary, a place where any thing is stored.

Ambára khána or *-khané*, Karn. (ಖಾನೆ, P. خانه) A magazine of grain, a granary.

Ambara-rási, Karn. (ರಾಶಿ, S. राशी, a heap) The Government share of the crop collected in a heap.

Ambár-sári, Mar. (अंबारसारी) A tax on houses, except those of Brahman village-officers. Rev. Sel. iv. 166.

Aṭṭambár, Karn. (ಅಟ್ಟಂಬಾರ) The whole heap, or the shares of the Government and cultivator before the crop is divided.

Âmbári, also Âmári, H. (A. عماري) A canopied seat on on elephant. A litter borne by a camel. (P. انبار) A granary.

Ambári paṭṭi, Mar. (अंबाडी पट्टी) A tax on the cultivation of hemp or making of rope from it.

Ambashṭha, vernacularly, Ambashth, S. &c. (अम्बष्ठः) A man of a mixed tribe, the offspring of a Brahman father and a Vaisya mother; by occupation a physician.

Ambattan̤, Tam. Mal. (அம்பட்டன) A barber, the barber of the village.

Ambuváchí, S. (अम्बुवाची) Four days in Ásharh (June—July), the 10th to the 13th, inclusive of the dark half of the month, or moon's wane, when the earth is regarded as unclean, and agriculture is prohibited.

Ambuváchí pradá, S. (प्रद, what gives) The first of the four days.

Ambuváchí tyága, S. (त्याग, leaving) The last of the four days.

Âmd, Ûmd, A. (عمد) Wilful; as, *Ḳatal-âmd*, Wilful murder. *Shabih-âmd*, Apparently wilful, *i. e.* manslaughter.

Ámdani, Amdunee, corruptly, Aumdany, or Amdauny, still more so, Amdenny, and Amdehny, H. (P. آمدني, *lit.* a coming, from آمدن, to come) Income, receipts: as a Government term, receipt of revenue or customs.

Amdáni, Mar. (आमदानी, vernacular for the preceding) Products of the earth, articles of merchandize generally arriving at market in their fit season, also that particular season. Profits, perquisites; sway, rule.

Améthiya, H. (اميٿهيا) A tribe of Chouhan Rajputs, originally from *Âmethi*, in Oude, some of whom are settled in Gorakhpur.

ÂMEZ ÁDHÁRAM, H., but current in the Dekhin, (from P. آميز, mixing, and S. *âdhára* आधार, support, receptacle) Land having mixed resources, *i. e.* being irrigated both naturally and artificially; also with *bhúmi*, land, *Ámez-ádhár bhúmi*.

ÂMIL, or ÂÁMIL, corruptly, AUMIL, H., but used in most dialects, sometimes slightly modified, and frequently confounded with AMAL, (A. عامل, *n.* of agency, from *âmal* عمل, he performed a task, he transacted an affair) An officer of Government in the financial department, especially a collector of revenue on the part of the Government, or of the farmer of the revenue, also himself a farmer of, or contractor for, the revenue under the native system, and invested with supreme authority, both civil and military, in the districts which he farmed, as is still the case in several native states, especially Oude and Hyderabad. In the early settlement of Benares by the Government of Bengal the *Âmil* was intrusted with the joint power of Hákim or magistrate, and Tehsildar or collector, and was responsible for the realization of a fixed amount of revenue, being precluded from levying any excess on the Government demand. Reg. ii. 1795.

Âmil-dár, H. (عامل دار) A collector of, or contractor for, the revenue: (used as synonymous with *Âmil*, but no doubt an inaccuracy for *Âmal-dár*, q. v.)

Âmil-dári, corruptly, *Aumil-darrei*, H. (عاملداري) The district or estate for the revenue of which the *Âmil* was responsible: (probably an error for *Amal-dári*.)

Âmil-daul, H. (عامل دول) The estimated amount of revenue to be realized by the native collector or contractor.

Âmil-náma, *Aumil-namah*, H. (عاملنامه) A written order or warrant to an *Âmil*, a commission to take possession of land in the name of the Government; preferably, *Âmal-náma*.

Âmili, *Aumily*, H. (عاملي) The harvest year, more correctly, *Amali*; also the same as *Fasli*.

ÂMLA, ÛMLA, corruptly, OMLAH, H. (A. عمله, plur. of ÂAMIL, عامل) The collective head native officers of a judicial or revenue court under the European judge or collector.

Âmla-i-ahshám, H. The collective officers of the irregular militia under the native Government. In Bengal a jagir was assigned for their support.

Âmla-i-nawárá, H. Under the Mohammedan Governments the collective officers of the fleet of boats maintained for the defence of the sea-coast; the assignments of revenue for their maintenance and that of the flotilla.

AMÍN, UMEEN, corruptly, AUMIN, AUMEEN, H., but occurring, slightly modified sometimes, in most of the dialects, (A. امين, from امن, to trust, Hindi, अमीन) A confidential agent, a trustee, a commissioner; applied in Upper India especially to a native officer of Government, employed either in the revenue department to take charge of an estate and collect the revenues on account of Government, or to investigate and report their amount; or in the judicial department, as a judge and arbitrator in civil causes. In the Presidency of Bengal, in particular, two classes of native judicial functionaries are now so named, or the *Ṣadar Amín* صدرامين, empowered to try causes to the extent of 1000 rupees, and the *Ṣadar Amín Âálí* (صدرامين عالي), or *Principal Ṣadar Amín*, to whom lies an appeal from the decisions of the *Amín*, and who decides suits to an unlimited amount. Beng. Reg. iv. xlv. 1793; vii. 1822; xxiii. 1814; iv. 1827; v. 1831; Act ix. 1844.

Amín-daftar, H. (امين دفتر) An office in which the accounts of the Amíns were audited; the recorded or registered accounts.

Amín-patel, Guz. Superintendant over the village Patels of a district, appointed to adjust boundary disputes, and furnish local information for the assessment of the revenue to the collector. This officer has come, in some instances, to supersede the Desaï, or former chief district officer: in some places the office is hereditary.

AMÍR, corruptly EMIR, H. (A. امير, from امر, to command) A nobleman, a Mohammedan of high rank.

Amrá, or *Umrá*, corruptly, *Omrah*, H. (A. امرا, plur. of امير) The nobles of a native Mohammedan court collectively.

Amír-ul-Umrá, H. A. Chief of the nobles, a title conferred by the sovereign at his pleasure, sometimes designating the Commander-in-Chief.

Jágír-i-Amír-ul-Umrá, H. Assignment of lands or their revenue to the Commander-in-Chief for his personal remuneration.

Amír-al-Múmanín, H. A. (اميرالمومنين) Prince of the faithful, a title of the Khalifs especially, but often assumed by Mohammedan princes.

AMJI, Dekh. (امجي) Compulsory service. (See *Amanji*).

AMR-BA-YAD, A. (امربيد) In Mohammedan law, a form of divorce. If a man say to his wife, "Your business is in your own hands" (*Amruki-ba-yadiki*), and the woman assents, an irreversible divorce takes place.—*Hed.*

Ámisham, Ámesham, or **Ámusham** (?) Tam. (ஆமிஷம்) The produce of a piece of land, the crop. An estimate especially of the value or yield of a standing crop.

Aḍangal-ámisham, or *Ámisham dáppu,* Tam. (டாப்பு, an account) Estimate of the produce of a piece of land for a whole year.

Amlák, A. (plur of ملك) Landed possessions, real property.

Amma, (Tel. &c. అమ్మ, S. *Ambá* अम्बा) In all the languages of Southern India except Tuluva, Mother, and affixed, as a respectful term of address to females in general, to their names; as, *Sitamma, Vangamma.* It forms, also, a designation of various popular goddesses unknown to the general system; as, *Mariyammá,* and *Agathammá,* tutelary goddesses of Madras. The latter is usually called *Yágatha,* and both are, no doubt, adopted from the Roman Catholics, being, in fact, the Virgin *Mary,* and *Sta Agatha,* although now especially worshipped by shopkeepers and Pareyar. In Tuluva the word means father.

Ammat, (آمة) One of the ten kinds of wounds compensated by fine, a wound of the head not penetrating the dura-mater.

Âmri, or **Umreé,** H. (from A. عمر, Life) A grant or the like for life, interest for life.

Amṛit, corruptly, **Amreeta,** H. &c. (S. *Amṛita* अमृतं, from *a* अ neg. and *mṛita,* dead) Ambrosia, nectar, the beverage of immortality; applied in common use to various items.

Amṛit-mahál, H. (A. محال) A term used in Mysore to designate a public establishment for rearing cattle for military uses.

Amṛit-manodhri, erroneously, *Amrit-maṇdhara,* and *Amrit-mandhi,* Uriya (ଅମୃତମନୋଧି) Funds for the support of the temple of Jagannátha, allowance to the Brahmans to provide sweetmeats for the idol *Jagannáth,* which, after presentation to him, are distributed among all who are present.

Amumat, A. (امومت, from ام, a mother) In Mohammedan law, the condition of being a mother, maternity.

Amwál, H. (A. plur. of *mál* مال) Property, goods, chattels, personal property.

Amwál-rabwi, A. Property that may be lent at a usurious interest.

Ána, H. (آنا, S. आना, B. আনা, Mar. आणा or अणा) The sixteenth part of a rupee, commonly, but incorrectly, written *Anna*; it is used either singly or in its multiples to denote proportional fractions of any article; thus, one *ána* of any thing—of land or chattels—is one-sixteenth; four *ánas,* a quarter; eight *ánas* a half, &c. In central Hindustan it is applied also to land measure. One *ána* of land is equal to sixteen rúsís, and sixteen *ánas* to one kanchu. It also expresses the divisions of village lands, the minor portions of each share being subdivided into ánas or sixteenths; thus, one share and eight ánas is equivalent to $1\frac{1}{2}$, &c. In Western India it is also applied to land measure, one *ána* being the sixteenth part of a *gonta,* or 7.5625 square yards; or it denotes one link of a measuring chain containing sixteen links.

Áná-kara or *kuru,* corruptly, *Annah-khureh,* H. (from S. *kara,* कर, tax) A fee of one ána on each rupee of revenue levied by the headmen in Asam to cover local charges.

Áná paṭṭi, Mar. An extra cess at the rate of one Aná on each rupee of the assessment, or a like charge per plough or per head, &c.

Anád banjar or **bunjur,** corruptly, **Anod bunger,** H. (اناد بنجر) Land that has been waste from time immemorial (from S. *anádi* अनादि, without beginning, and H. *banjar,* waste land).

Anádi bhúmi, H., used in Mysore. Land transferred by mortgage (from S. अनादि, and भूमि, land.)

Anádi-biḍú, Tel. Tam. (అనాదిబీడు, அனாதிபீடு) A piece of ground that has never been cultivated; also similar terms as, *Anádi karambu, Anádi tarisu.*

Anáj, H. (اناج, अनाज) Grain, commonly, but incorrectly, pronounced **Náj.**

Anákálabhrita, (S. अनाकालभृतः) One of the fifteen kinds of slaves in Hindu law, a man who has become a slave voluntarily, for the sake of sustenance at a season of famine.

Ânán, incorrectly, **Ainán,** A. (عنان) Traffic in partnership, in Mohammedan law.

Anakaṇ, Mal. (അണകൻ) A low or inferior person.

Ánanda, Karn., &c. (S. आनन्दः, felicity) The 48th year of the cycle of sixty years which will fall in the year 1854.

Ananta, S. &c. (अनन्तः) Without end, eternal. A cord with fourteen knots in it, which the Hindus tie round the arm at the festival of *Ananta-chaturdaṣí.*

Ananta-chaturdaṣí, S. The fourteenth of Bhádra (August, September), when a festival is held in honour of 'the eternal' Vishnu.

Anantaravan, less correctly, **Anandravan,** Mal. (അനന്തരവൻ, from S. अनन्तरं, without an interval) An heir, the heir apparent or next of kin, the heir of the acting head of the family.

Anantaravan-naṭu-káṇam, Anandravannadu, &c. (from നടു, middle, and കാണം, fee).

Anantarasthánam, Mal. (സ്ഥാനം, S. स्थानं, place) Succession, right of inheritance.

ANANYÁṢRITA, (S. (अन् not, *anya* अन्य, another, and *ásrita* आश्रित, dependent) Independent, not supported by or dependent on another. In Hindu law, unencumbered property.

ANAṢANA, S. (अन् neg., अशनं, eating) Fasting. In law, fasting of a creditor or of a Brahman employed by him to enforce payment of a debt, the debtor incurring the guilt of Brahmanicide if the person should die of inanition.

ANÁTHA, S. (अ neg. and नाथः, a master) Having no protector or owner. An orphan.

Anáthi-banjar, S. and H. Waste, or rather unclaimed land. Uncultivated land without an owner. See *Anádi-banjar.*

ANAVANTU POLAM, Tel. Land of which the ownership is disputed.

ANÁVRUSHTI, Karn. Tel. (S. *an* अन् neg. and *ávrishti* आवृष्टिः, rain) Drought; want of rain.

ÁNAYA, (S. आनयः) The ceremony of tying on the girdle of Munja grass preparatory to investiture with the sacrificial string. The rite of investiture.

ÁNÁYAN, Mal. (ആനായൻ) A cowherd, a shepherd.

ANBHANTA, UNBHUNTA, (?) Undivided, applied to lands. *Garhwal.*

ÁNCHA, ANCHU, Tel. (అంచు), ÁNCHÉ, Karn. (ಅಂಚೆ), ANCHAL, Mal. (അഞ്ചൽ) Tam. (அஞ்சல்) Public conveyance, post, posting, a post-stage, a relay of palankin bearers or post-runners.

Anchalpura, Mal. (അഞ്ചൽപ്പുര) A post-office.

Ánche-kacheri, Karn. (ಅಂಚೆಕಚೇರಿ) The post-office.

Ánché-mané, Karn. (ಅಂಚೆಮನೆ) A station for post-runners.

ANCHANÁ, UNCHUNA, or, ANTSANÁ, UNTSUNA, corruptly, ANCHINA, ANCHINNA, ANCHUMNA, ANCHUMMA, Tel. (అంచనా, from S. *ánṣana* अंशन, dividing, apportioning) An estimate or appraisement of the probable amount and value of the crops on a field; salt in a pile; hay in a stack, and the like. Grant derives it from two Persian adverbs, *án,* there is, *chanán,* so much! App. v. Rep. 642.

Níluvu-anchaná, Tel. (నిలువు) Estimate of the produce of a field before the crop is cut.

Kuppa-anchaná, Tel. (కుప్ప) Estimate of the produce of a field after the crop is gathered, but before it is measured.

Anchaná-dár or *-dárudu,* Tel. An officer employed to survey the standing crops and estimate their probable value; an estimator, an appraiser.

Anchaná-jábitá, Tel. (జాబితా) Estimate of each Ryot's share of the value of the crop. An account of the estimated crop kept by the village accountant.

ÁṆDAI, Tam. (ஆண்டை) Master of a family, owner of slaves.

AṆDÁDI, Mal. (അങ്ങാടി) A shop, a market-place, a bazaar.

Andádivánibham, Mal. (അങ്ങാടിവാണിഭം) Merchandise, goods, wares, articles for sale.

ÁNDANA, Mar. (आन्दन) Presents made by the bride's father to the bridegroom after the celebration of the marriage.

ANDÁRU (?). A Mobed, or officiating priest of the Parsis.

ANDÁZ, H. (P. انداز) Estimate, valuation, guess.

Andáz-paṭṭi, Mar. Estimate of the value of a growing crop.

ANDHÁ-DARBÁRU, Karn. (ಅಂಧಾದರಬಾರು, from S. *andha* अन्ध, blind, and P. *darbár* دربار, a court) A public office notoriously ill conducted, a bad government.

ÁNDHÍ, ANDHEE, H. (آندهي, from S. अन्ध, blind, dark) A hurricane, a tempest; a darkening of the day.

ANDHRA, or, ÁNDHRA, S. (अन्ध्रः, आन्ध्रः) The country now known as Telingana. *Ándhra* more properly denotes a native of that country, also a caste of Brahmans in Mysore, or a Brahman of Telingana, who is known by the name of *Ándhra* Brahman in most parts of India. The name was known to the ancients, and Pliny speaks of the Rex Andrarum as a powerful Indian prince.

ÁṆDI, Tam. (ஆண்டி) Karn. (ಆಂಡಿ) A religious mendicant of the Saiva sect in the South.

ÁNDI, Karn. (ಆಂದಿ) Bail, bond, security.

ÁṆDA, Mal. (ആണ്ട,) ÁṆDU, Tam. (ஆண்டு) A year.

ÁṆE, Karn. (ಆಣೆ) ÁṆAI, Tam. (ஆணை) An oath, an adjuration, a protestation, a citation on the part of Government; also Karn. *Ánebhashe,* or *Anebase* (from S. *bháshá,* speech).

ÁNE, Karn. (ಆನೆ) An elephant (differing from the preceding in the '*n,*' which, in the first word, is the cerebral, in the second, the dental letter).

AṆE, corruptly, ANI, and ANAY, Karn. (ಅಣೆ), AṆAI, Tam. (அணை), AṆA, Mal. (അണ) A dam, a dyke, a bank, a bridge. *Kallané,* Karn. (ಕಲ್ಲಣೆ) A dam or embankment of stone.

AṆEKAṬṬU, AṆEKAṬṬE, corruptly, ANICUT, Karn. (ಅಣೆಕಟ್ಟು)

H

A dam, a dyke, an embankment, a channel to direct water into different streams for purposes of irrigation.

Aṇaihál, Tam. (அணைக்கால்) An embankment of stone.

Allaṇai, Tam. (அல்லணை) A dam or bridge of stone.

ANEKAGOTRA, S. (अनेकगोत्र) One who is a member of more than one Gotra or family.

ÁNEYÁR, Hindi (आनेयार) The time of agricultural labour in the hot weather, from sunrise till noon.

ÁNG, H. (آنگ, from S. अङ्ग, a particle of assent) Demand on each head of cattle for right of pasture by the proprietor of the ground. Mode of computing a tax on cattle in Hariána, two bullocks making one Áng.

ANGA, UNGU, S. (अङ्गः) The body, or a part of it; a limb, a member. Whence, figuratively, a branch of literature, a supplemental portion of the Vedas, &c.

Anganyása, S. Touching different parts of the body as a religious exercise.

Angaprâyaşchitta, S. Expiation of personal impurity, especially the expiatory offering made by the next of kin of a person recently deceased, at the first Şráddha after his death.

ANGÁ, or ANGARKHÁ, H. (انگا, انگرکھا) A long tunic, a coat worn both by Hindus and Mohammedans: the former tie it on the left, the latter on the right breast.

ANGA, UNGU, Tel. (అంగ) A stride or pace of about three feet.

Angakála, Tel. (అంగకాల) Measurement by paces.

ANGAḌI, Karn. (ಅಂಗಡಿ), ANGÁḌI, Tam. (அங்காடி) A stall or shop in a market where provisions are sold. A betel stall. A tax on shops or stalls, a village in which there is a market.

Angaḍikár or *gár*, &c. Karn. (ಅಂಗಡಿಗಾರ) A shopkeeper.

Angáḍikáran, Tam. (அங்காடிக்காரன்) A vender of provisions.

Angaḍi-pasike, or *pasige*, Karn. (ಪಸಿಕೆ, ಪಸಿಗೆ) A fee or cess upon booths or stalls.

Angáḍi-paṭṭi, or *paṭṭaḍai*, Tam. (பட்டி, பட்டடை) A tax upon moveable shops or stalls.

ÁNGADÍÁ, or ÁNGARÍYÁ, Guz. (આંગડીઆ) A person employed in the West of India to carry money and jewels, which he conceals in his garments.

ANGAN, H. (انگن, from S. अङ्गणः) A court-yard, an inclosed area within or without the house; also pronounced *Ángna*.

ANGAUNGÁ, ANGOUNGA, H. (انگونگا) Perquisites of grain from the threshing-floor distributed to the Brahman, Purohit, Guru, grazier, and god of the village.

ANGAURIA, H. (انگوریا) A ploughman. In some places, as Benares, the practice of allowing the use of the plough as part of the wages of labour.

ANGDENA, (?) A tax formerly levied by the Portuguese at Bombay on fishermen and their boats, and on other occupations.

ÁNGIRASA, S. &c. (आङ्गिरसं) The sixth year of the cycle. A Gotra or family of Brahmans: both are derived from the name of the ancient Ṛishi or Sage ANGIRAS.

ANGJHAP, Thug. (from H. or S. *Ang*, body, and H. *chhipána*, to hide) Temporary burial of their victims until a convenient opportunity of effectually concealing them is found (used in the Dekhin).

ANGLÍS, (corruption of 'English') An invalided soldier, or lands granted to him under Ben. Reg. xliii. 1793; i. 1804.

ANGULA, vernacularly, ANGUL, S. &c. (from अंगुलि, a finger) A linear measure; eight barleycorns make an Angula, and twelve Angulas a span; a finger's breadth.

ANGULI-TORAṆA, S. (from *anguli*, a finger, and *toraṇa*, an ornamental archway) Three semicircular lines drawn across the forehead, made with sandal or ashes of burnt cow-dung, denoting a worshipper of Siva; more commonly termed *Tripunḍra*.

ANGWÁRA, H. (from S. अङ्ग, a limb, a part) The proprietor of a small share of a village in the Benares district, where it also implies mutual help in tillage.

ANGWÁTÁ, Mar. (अंगवाटा) The share of the actual cultivator in the produce of a field divided between him and the landlord and the owner of the bullocks for ploughing.

ANHAR, Thug. Any metallic utensil for eating, drinking, or cooking.

AṆI, Karn. (ಅಣಿ) The comb or reed of a loom, or a weaver's *lam*, or the threads of the woof wound in the form of the figure 8.

ÁNI, Tam. (ஆநி) The month of June.

ANITYA-DATTA, S. (अनित्य, not for ever, and दत्त, given) Temporarily given, as a son adopted for a term; also *Anitya dattaka*, and *Anitya dattrima*.

ANIYA-UTTA, or UTTHA, Mal. (?) Daily meals given to Brahmans at the temples in Malabar.

ÁNIYAM, Tam. (ஆநியம்) A day.

ANIYUKTA, S. (अ neg. and नियुक्त, appointed) Not duly appointed. In Hindu law, a Brahman who attends a court without having been appointed a member of it.

Anjal, Unjul, or Anjali, Unjulee, H. (انجل, انجلي, from S. अञ्जलिः, the two hands placed together and carried to the forehead as a reverential mode of salutation) A respectful mode of salutation. As much grain as can be held by the two hands put together. A handful of corn given from the threshing-floor; the same as *Angaunga*, q. v.

Anjal, Tel. (corruption of Anchal, q. v.) The post, the mail.

Anjaman, Unjumun, (P. انجمن) An assembly. Among the Parsis, a constituted council or assembly to which all questions regarding their peculiar customs are referred.

Anjan, Unjun, H. (انجن) A grass which grows in the North-West Provinces abundantly, and is used as fodder. Commonly, the word (from the S. अञ्जनं) denotes a collyrium, or any application, whether solid or fluid, to the eyes, to give them strength and brilliancy.

Anjaná, Unjana, H. (انجنا) An inferior sort of rice.

Anje, Karn. (ಅಂಜೆ) Clean or dressed cotton ready for spinning.

Ank, or Ánk, corruptly, **Auk**, H. &c. (انك, from the S. *anka* अंक, a mark, a cypher) A mark, a number, an arithmetical figure, a share. Figures on coins, &c., shewing the date of a Raja's accession. In Karnáta, *Anka* or *Anke* is also applied in compounds to the tables or statements of relative measures; as, *Khandugadanke*, dry measure; *Varaháda-anke*, money accounts; *Manuvisa-anke*, troy and avoirdupois measure, &c. In Cuttack, an era commencing with the accession of each Raja, and, counting by the year of his Ráj, all deeds commence with the year of the *Ank* in which they were executed.

Ankana, S. (अंकन) Marking, making a number or cypher, especially branding or cauterising the limbs with the symbols or names of a divinity.

Ánk-bandi, or *bundee*, H. (P. بندي, binding) An adjustment of the rents to be paid by the individual collector through the person held liable for the realisation of the Government demand.

Ánk-dar, corruptly, *Aukdar*, (P. دار, who has) The holder of a share in village lands. The person who is responsible for a portion of the revenue.

Ánk-kar, H. (S. كار, who makes) An assayer, a stamper, a money changer.

Ankam, Mal. (S. അങ്കം) In Malabar, A duel, a single combat: these were formerly frequent among the Nairs, and were a source of revenue to the Raja, each combatant paying for the privilege of fighting. The combat was sometimes fought by hired champions.

Ánkhen-wálá, H. (from آنکھ, from S. अक्षि, the eye) A term used in Mysore to denote a class of police employed by Hyder Ali; a spy, an inspector.

Ánkháu, H. (آنكهاو, from S. अक्षि, the eye) Valuation by the eye of growing crops.

Ánkaṛo, Guz. (આંકડો), A bill an account. Discount. See *Ant*.

Ankura, Thug. A thousand; the word in S. (अङ्कुरः) signifies a shoot, a sprout, a bud or blossom; also, sometimes, 'water.'

Ankurárpaṇa, S. (अर्पण) Offering of water, a preliminary offering of water at the beginning of a ceremony.

Anna, S. (अन्नं) Food, boiled rice.

Anna-kúṭa yátrá, S. (The festival (*yátrá*) of the mountain (*kúṭa*) of boiled rice). A festival of the Hindus in the month of November, when they make a pile of rice as a type of the hill *Govarddhana* in *Vraj*, near Mathurá, observed especially by cowherds.

Anna-práṣana, vernacularly, *Annprásan*, S. &c. (अन्नप्राशनं) Putting a little food into the mouth of an infant between five and eight months old, accompanied with a religious ceremony.

Anna-vyavákara, S. (व्यवहार, law) Law or custom relating to food, that is, to the practice of eating together or not, as followed by different castes.

Anolá, commonly pronounced *Aoṅlá*, H. (انولا, from the S. अमलः) The myrobalan tree, which is worshipped by agriculturists in the West of India on the 11th of Phalgun (Feb., March): libations are poured at the root of the tree, a yellow or red thread is tied round the trunk, and prayers and songs are recited in honour of the plant.

Anṣ, or Anṣa, pronounced **Angsha**, or **Ungshu**, also written **Amsha**, H. &c. (انس, from the S. अंशः) A part, a share, a portion.

Anṣánṣa, S. (अंशांश) A subdivision, a share of a share.

Anansa, S. (अनंश) Having no share; excluded from a share, as of inheritance, on account of some physical or legal defect.

Anṣapatra, S. (अंशपत्र) A deed setting forth the shares or portions of a property. A deed of partition between the members of a Hindu family.

Anṣakara, S. (अंशहर) A co-parcener, a co-heir; one who takes a share of an estate or property.

Anṣwánsa, H. (انسوانسه) A measure of land in Hindustan, twenty of which are equal to one Pilwánṣa.

ANṢÁRI, H. (A. انصاري) A tribe of Sheikhs in the North-west Provinces who pretend to be descended from the original *Anṣár*, or auxiliaries of Mohammed, who adopted his faith at Medina. They appear to have come into India from Herat at the time of Firoz Shah.

ÁNSU-TORE, Thug. (from the H. آنسو *ánsu*, a tear) Any shower of rain that falls before the usual rainy season: it is regarded as of evil omen, and if it occur during the first day or night of an expedition the party must return and start again.

ÁNṬ, Guz. (આંટ) Credit, transfer. In Guzerat it implies a fictitious currency or book-credit, in which bills of exchange and dealings in articles of trade may be paid at the option of the holder, varying according to the exchange of the day and the value of the coin in which the amount is computed. The difference on cashing a bill in *Ánt* is termed *Ánkaṛa*, discount.

ANTAH-PAṬA, Mar. (S. अन्तर्, between, and पट, a cloth) A screen of silk or cloth held up between the bride and bridegroom, or between the student who is to receive the sacred cord and the spiritual teacher, until the proper moment arrives for the parties to see each other.

ANTAH-PURA, S. (अन्तः, inner, and पुरं, city) The inner or female apartments.

ANTARBED, UNTURBED, H. (انتربيد, from S. अन्तर्, between, and वेदि, an altar, or ground raised to serve for one) The old name of the lower portion of the Doab, from Etawa to Allahabad: it was sometimes applied to the Doab throughout.

ANTARAPAR or -PARA, UNTURPUR or -PURU, B. (S. अन्तर, an interval, and पर, after) Applied in the Upper Provinces of Bengal, to lands allowed to lie fallow for one year.—E. I. Records, iii. 173.

ANTASSTHA, less correctly, ANTASTA, or ANTASTHI, Mar. (S. अन्तःस्थः, what is or stays within, secret, hidden) Secret expenditure. Sums expended in presents or bribes to official persons. An item in the *Darbar kharch*, or Court-charges of the Peshwa.

Antasstha-ki-yádi, Mar. (P. ياد, memory) Account of secret service expenditure.

ANTEVÁSÍ, very corruptly, ANTYBASHY, and ANTWÁSÍ, H. (S. अन्तेवासिन्) A disciple, a pupil residing with his teacher.

ANTU, UNTOO, Tel. Karn. (అంతు) Total amount, aggregate (from the S. *anta*, end, final sum).

ANTYESHTI, S. (अन्त्येष्टि) The final sacrifice or funeral obsequies.

ANUÁ, or ANWÁ, H. (انوا) The place where the men stand who throw up water from a lower to a higher level. See *Daurí*.

ANUBHAVAM, Mal. (അനുഭവം, from S. अनु, after, according to, and भव, being) Enjoyment: a grant of hereditary land in Malabar, either rent-free or at a pepper-corn-rent, in reward of service; also a present of betel, or a cocoa-nut, from the proprietor at the time of executing a deed of transfer of a garden or plantation to the person to whom the transfer is made, as symbolical of the character of the land made over; also *Anubhogam*.

ANUBHOGAM, Mal. (അനുഭോഗം, S अनुभोगं) Enjoyment; usufruct; a grant of land, &c.; the same as *Anubhavam*, as above.

ANUGAMAN, UNOOGUMUN, H. (انوگمن, from the S. अनु, after, and गमन, going) The burning of a widow after hearing of the death of an absent husband; also *Anu-maraṇam*, subsequently-dying.

ANUKSHETRA, corrupted vernacularly to ANUCHHATR, or ANOOCHUTTREE, or ANNAKSHATTRA, or, in *Uriya*, to ANRACHUTTUR, S. (*Anu* अनु, according to, *kshetra* क्षेत्र, a sacred shrine or place of pilgrimage) A charitable allowance made to the native servants of certain temples in Orissa, by the Marathas, and continued by the British Government. Ben. Reg. xii. 1815, sec. 30.

ANULOMAJA, S. (from अनु, according to, *loma*, लोम, the hair of the body, and *ja* जः, born, born *with* the hair or grain, *i. e.* in due order) The offspring of two persons of different classes, of whom the father is of the superior class in the regular succession, as of a Brahman father and Kshatriya mother. If the woman were of the Brahman and the man of the Kshitriya class, the order is inverted, and the progeny is termed *Pratilomaja*, born against the hair.

ANUPÁTAK, or ANOOPATUK, H. (S. अनुपातकं) A heinous offence short of a capital crime.

ANUMATIPATRA, S. (from *anumati*, अनुमति, assent, and *patra* पत्र, a leaf) A deed expressive of assent or concurrence; especially a deed executed by a husband about to die, authorising his widow to adopt a son.

ANUPÚRVAJA, S. (अनु, after, पूर्व्व, before, *ja*, born) Offspring born of parents in the regular sequence of the castes. See *Anulomaja*.

Anwádheya, or -dheyika, S. (अनु, after, आधेय, to be received) A class of woman's property (in law); what has been given to her by her husband or relations after marriage.

Anwáhárya-śráddha, S. (अन्वाहार्य्यश्राद्धं) Funeral obsequies in honour of deceased ancestors performed monthly on the day of new moon.

Anwáhita, S. (अन्वाहितं), also Anwádhi, S. (from अनु, after, and आधि, a pledge) A pledge or deposit placed with a third party.

Ánwaṇ, Mar. (आंवण) The first field of rice, that in which the plants have grown from seed.

Ánwaṇú, Mar. (आंवणू) Transplanted, as rice plants, from the first field.

Anwashṭaká, S. (अन्वष्टका) Funeral obsequies performed on the ninth day of the months *Paush*, *Mágh*, *Phálgun*, and *Aświn*.

Anyagotra, S. (from *anya* अन्य, other, and *gotra* गोत्र, family) Of a different lineage.

Anyakudi, Tam. (அன்னியக்குடி, from S. *anya*, other, and *kudí*, house; corruptly, Anícoody, Gl. 5th Rep.) A cultivator or other person who is an inhabitant of a different village from that in which he labours or trades.

Anyapurvá, S. (अन्य and पूर्ब्व, before) A woman who has been previously married.

Anyáyam, S., but used in the dialects (अ neg., न्याय, judicial inquiry) Injustice. A complaint of injustice.; a plaint in a civil suit.

Aodi, or Aoodi, H. (اودي) A tribe of Játs in the divisions of Soneput and Paniput.

Aodiya, H. (probably for *Ayodhia*, or native of *Ayodh* or *Oude*) A thief of a tribe of thieves inhabiting villages in the Cawnpore and Fattehpur districts. They make remote excursions at particular seasons, in different disguises, and sometimes plunder on a large scale.

Aogáhi, H. (اوگاهي) Collection of rent or revenue from a village.

Aokán, H. (اوكان) Straw and grain heaped up (Benares).

Aokhal, Aokhul, H. (اوكهل) Land reclaimed from waste and brought under cultivation.

Aolánia, H. (اولانيه) A tribe of Jats residing in the Paniput district. Although Hindus, they claim the appellation of *Malik* or *King* conferred upon them, they affirm, by some ancient prince, to denote their sovereignty over other *Ját* tribes.

Áoli, Aolee, H. (آولي) Mode of estimating the produce of a larger extent of land by the ascertained produce of a smaller quantity.

Áont, H. (?) Accommodation bills (the term is used in Central India, and is probably the *Ánt* of Guzerat, q. v.

Aori, or Áwari, H. (اوري) Bank of a pond or rivulet to the water's edge; a piece of dry land left uncultivated.

Aosat, or Aosut, H. (no doubt a corruption for *Ársat*, q. v.) An average.

Apá, or Ápá, Mar. (अपा, आपा) A term of respectful address to a senior; also of affection to a son or junior. It is often affixed to a proper name; as, *Govind-pant-ápá*. See also Appa.

Apapátrita, also Apayátrita, S. (अपपात्रितः, or अपयात्रितः) One who has lost caste, and with whom his kindred will not eat and drink: he is thereby incapacitated from inheritance (from *Apa*, particle implying severance, off, from, and *pátra*, a dish, or *yátrá*, intercourse).

Aparádha, Aparadhi, Karn. Aparádhamu, Tel. It occurs in most dialects (S. अपराधं) Fault, offence. The punishment of offence, fine, penalty. This latter meaning is peculiar to the South of India.

Aparádha kshame, Karn. (from S. क्षमा) Pardoning an offence, remitting a fine.

Aparálu, Tel. (అపరాలు) All kinds of pulse or grain in pods, also Aparajinsulu.

Apaviddha putra, S. (अपविद्ध, rejected, and पुत्र, a son) A son deserted by his parents and adopted by strangers. One of the kinds of affiliation formerly permitted by the Hindu law.

Apharia, H. (اپهريا) A subdivision of the Ahír or cowherd tribe.

Ápíl, Beng. (আপিল) The English word Appeal. So also *Ápilant*, (আপিলাণ্ট) Appellant.

Appa, Uppu, Tel. Karn. (అప్ప) A father, a term commonly added to proper names as a mark of respect; as, *Ranga-appa*, or *Rangappa*. The word in Mar. is Apá, or Ápá, q. v.: it also occurs in Tel. as Appaya, and in Tamil, Appañ. In Tuluva, Appá, means mother.

Appanam, Uppanum, Tel. (అప్పనము) Tax, tribute. Rent revenue. Rack-rent. Any taxed lands, especially lands highly assessed, which are required to be held by cultivators who, as an equivalent, hold other lands on favourable terms, or rent-free. Usufruct.

Appasam, Tel. (In the northern Circars) A cut or channel for water.

Apratibandha, S. (अ neg., and प्रतिबन्धः, obstruction) Undisputed inheritance.

Ápta-punjan, Mar. (आप्तपुंजण, from S. *ápta*, fit, and *punja*, a heap) Presents made at the Dasahara festival to the Patel or head of a village.

Aptá-kanakku, Tam. (அப்தாக்கணக்கு) A weekly account (from P. *Haftah*).

Áptí, Mar. (आप्ती, from S. *apat*, calamity) Distress from failure of the harvest, from either excess or deficiency of rain.

Aputra, S. (अ neg., and पुत्र, a son) A man who has no son, who has never had, or who has lost an only son, and may therefore adopt one.

Aṛ, H. (آڑ, the final being the hard *ḍ* or *ṛ*) Stop, hindrance, whence, fig., a mound or bank forming the boundary of a field; a well: also an abbreviation of *Aṛára*, the bank of a river. In composition it denotes also inferiority or deviation, being the same, essentially, as the Maratha particle *Aḍ*, or *Áḍ* (अड, आड), q. v.

Aṛ-gir, H. A strip of sward encompassing a field.

Áṛ, H. (آڑ) A ladle used in the sugar factories (Oudh): it more usually signifies a sharp spike, a goad.

Áṛá, H. (آڑا) A saw, a large saw, a shoemaker's knife. **Áṛí**, (آڑی) a small saw.

Áṛa, Mal. (ആറ) A river.

Áṛṛukál, Mal. (ആറ്റുകാൽ) A channel from a river.

Ara, (?) A ford or ferry. Gl. 5th Rep.

Árá, (with a soft *r*) Total, aggregate.

Arába, H. (P. ارابه) A cart.

Árad, H. (آرد) Flour-meal.

Árádhya, S. (आराध्यः, venerable) In the South of India the term is applied especially to a Brahman who professes the Jangama worship of Ṣiva, but is not acknowleged by other members of the sect, from his retaining the distinction of caste. Among the Marathas, a tutelary divinity.

Aragu, Karn., **Arakku**, Tel. (అరక్కు, from the S. *laksha*, लक्ष) The resin of the nest of the Lac insect; *Shel-lac*.

Âraḳ, **Ûruḳ**, H. (A. عرق) Spirit, juice, essence.

Araku, or **Arukí**, Tam. (அரக்கு, அருக்கி) A fermented liquor from the juice of the palm: *Tári*, or *Arrack*, which is probably derived from the Tamil, which again may be a dialectical modification of the Arabic **Âraḳ**, as above.

Araka, Tel. (అరక) A plough, with oxen and implements of husbandry complete.

Arakala-jábitá, Tel. Per. An account shewing the number of ploughs belonging to each Ryot (northern Circars).

Arakattaraka, Tel. A plough with a pair of bullocks.

Arakál-palisha, Mal. (from *ara*, half, *kál*, quarter, and *palisha*, interest) Interest at $1\frac{1}{4}$ per cent., or one-eighth of the highest legal rate in Malabar, or 10 per cent. per annum.

Araḷe, Karn. (ಅರಳೆ) Cotton.

Aráḷu, Karn. (ಅರಾಳು) Half a day's labour.

Aráḷuhúli, Karn. (ಅರಾಳುಹೂಲಿ) Half a day's hire.

Aramaïshi paramaïshi, Karn. (ಅರಮಾಯಿಷಿ, ಪರಮಾಯಿಷಿ, dialective derivatives from the P. *arám* and *firmán*) Gratuitous assistance given by the Government to a respectable person in the cultivation of rent-free lands. —Mysore.

Aramane, Karn. (ಅರಮನೆ) A royal palace. Government.

Áramane sambala, Karn. Dependant upon Government, in Government pay.

Aramaneyavaru, Karn. (ಅರಮನೆಯವರು) The officers of Government, or the Government collectively.

Áramba, or **Árambha**, **Arumbu**, **Arumbhu**, Karn. (ಅರಂಬ, ಅರಂಭ, S. आरम्भः, beginning, undertaking) Agriculture, farming, cultivating land.

Káḍ-áramba, Karn. (ಕಾಡಾರಂಬ) Dry cultivation.

Nír-áramba, Karn. (ನೀರಾರಂಬ) Wet cultivation.

Áramba-gár, Karn. (ಆರಂಬಗಾರ, from S. *kára* कार, who makes) A farmer, a cultivator.

Árambada-sámánu, Karn. (ಆರಂಬದಸಾಮಾನು) Implements of husbandry.

Áramvaṭhá, Mar. (आरंवठा) A rice field after clearing, ready for the next year's crop.

Ara, or **Arai-nir**, Tam. (அறைநீர்) Water for irrigation which may be drawn freely from the public reservoir during a certain period of the year.

Ara-palisha, Mal. Half interest, or 5 per cent in Malabar; also interest that absorbs half the rent of mortgaged lands.

Arapaḷh, Tam. (?) A crop entirely blighted and withered before the time of reaping.

Aráṛ, **Uṛar**, or **Aḍáḍ**, **Uḍaḍ**, H. (اراڑ, or अडाड) Outhouses for cattle. Harvest floor for the blossoms of the Máhwa.

Aráṛa, or **Aḍáḍa**, **Uṛaṛu**, or **Uḍaḍu**, H. (اراڑا, अडाड) The steep bank of a pond or river.

Aráṛí, or **Aḍáḍi**, or **Uṛaree**, or **Uḍaḍee**, H. (اراڑی, or अडाडी) The old established measure of a field to which the occupant appeals, in preference to actual measurement.

Áranya, S. (आरण्य) A forest.

Aranya-sabhá, S. A court for a community of hermits; a forest-court.

Aranya-shashṭhi, S. A Hindu festival on the 6th (*shashthi*) of Jyeshth (May, June), observed by women in the hope of obtaining handsome children: part of the ceremonial is walking in a wood.

Arasa, or **Arasu**, **Urusu**, **Urusoo**, corruptly **Ursoo**, Karn. (అరసు), **Arachan**, Mal. (അരചൻ). **Arasu**, or **Arasan**, Tam. (அரசு, அரசன், from S. *Rájá*, or, as pronounced sometimes in the Southern dialects, *Rátsu*) A king, a ruler; so, **Arasí**, or **Arasati**, Karn., A queen; also, governing, ruling; also, privileges allowed for watching.

Arasukáran, Tam. (அரசுக்காரன்) A person holding certain privileges for performing police duty.

Arasu, Tam. The Pípal, or sacred fig-tree.

Arasáni, or *Arasáni-stambha*, Tam. A branch of the Pípal tree placed in the middle, under the canopy erected for a marriage, as a type of Vishnu, round which all the parties walk, worshipping and performing ceremonies.

Arasinage-inám, Karn. (from Karn. *Arasina*, turmeric, and A. *Inám*, grant of land) Land granted in dower, or as pin-money; *literally*, for turmeric, which enters largely into the materials of a Hindu lady's toilet in the South of India, being applied to stain her forehead, finger-nails, soles of her feet, &c.

Árati, or **Ártí**, H. (ارتي, आरती, occurring in most dialects, from the S. आरात्रिकं, nocturnal ceremony) Waving lights circularly in front of an idol or object of worship, part of the usual evening ceremonial. In the South of India it is performed in honour of individuals at marriages and festivals.

Araituki, Tam. (அரைத்துக்கி, A Madras phrase) The pillory, *lit.* half-hanging.

Arava, **Aravi**, or **Aravu**, Tel. Karn. People and language of Drávira, or the country from the North of Madras to Cape Comorin, along the Coromandel Coast.

Aravár, Karn. (అరవార) In Canara, a mortgage in which the mortgagee retains possession of the property, in lieu of interest, until the debt is paid; also called *Iláravár* and *Iládáravár*, from the S. *Ilá*, the earth.

Avadhi-aravár, Karn. (from S. *avadhi*, limit) Usufruct, as before, with a stipulation that the mortgagee shall not be dispossessed before a given term.

Ara-vári, Tam. (from அரை *arai*, half) Half revenue, applied to a village or lands assessed at half the usual rate.

Árázi, **Ûrazee**, H. (A. from the plur. of عرض, or عراض, lands) Applied especially to detached portions of land which are either rent-free or have been recovered from the retrocession of rivers.

Arbáb, H. (A. ارباب, plur. of رب) Masters, lords, possessors.

Arbab-ul-mál, H. Officers of the treasury. Extra allowance to the officers of account.—Gl. 5th Rep.

Arbáb-i-shara, H. A. (شرع) Law officers.

Ardal, Thug. A person who has separated from his party, and has, in consequence, escaped the fate of his companions.

Ardáwa, H. (اردادة) Ground meal, coarse flour; ground pulse. The term more commonly denotes a mixture of the meal of chick-pea and barley, which is given to the horses of Europeans, or barley parched and ground, and similarly employed.

Arddha, S. &c. (अर्द्ध, a moiety) Half, or a part in general.

Arddha-khil, Ben. (অর্দ্ধখিল) Land only partially in cultivation (from S. *arddha*, part, and *khil*, B. fallow land).

Ardhal, or *Ardhola*, Mar. (from S. अर्द्ध, half) A half share, either of the produce of land or profits of trade.

Ardheli, or *Ardheliya*, Mar. (S. अर्द्ध, a half) In the Konkan, a temporary cultivator, one who undertakes the cultivation of the land for a share, generally a half, of the produce.

Ardda-mániyam, Tam. (அர்த்தமானியம்) Land partly or half rent-free, being assessed at half the usual rate; also a grant of the Government share of the rent to one who does not enjoy the share of the hereditary proprietor.

Arddha-siri, Beng. (from শীর, ploughing) Cultivating the land on condition of receiving half the crop.

Arddháya, Karn. (అర్ధాయు) An incomplete heap of corn.

Artole, or *Arthole*, Karn. (అర్తోలి) A weight of half a rupee.

Aré, Karn. The Karnátaka name of a Maraṭha.

Ârfa, A. (عرفه) The eve of a festival on which preliminary religious rites are practised, especially on the days preceding the two great Mohammedan festivals, the *Shab-i-Barát*, and the *Bakr-íd*.

Argh, **Argha**, or **Arghya**, H. (ارگهه, from the S. अर्घः) A respectful offering, chiefly of fruit and flowers, or water, or milk and honey, to an idol, a Brahman, any venerable person, or a bridegroom at the marriage ceremony. A libation of water between the threshold and the spot where the first bundle of corn is deposited after it is brought home from the threshing-floor; or, the ceremony of placing on the threshold, at seed time, cowdung, dried and formed into a cup, filling it with seed, and pouring water upon it: both these ceremonies are intended to secure prosperity. *Argha*, or *Arghya*, also signifies the boat-shaped earthen or metallic vessel in which the offering or libation is presented.

Arhar, Hindi, &c. (अरहर, S. आढकी) A kind of pulse very generally cultivated throughout India (Cytisus cajan).

Arhat, Urhut, or Ârhut, H. (अड़हत, अढत, आढत) Agency, brokerage, commission.

Arhatiya, H. An agent, a broker, a correspondent. See *Arthiya*.

Arhat, Urhut, H. (ارهٹ) A revolving wheel for raising water when the water is near the surface, or from a river; also *Rahat*, and *Rahát*.

Arhwal, H. (ارهول) A day labourer.—Benares.

Ari, Tam. (அரி, S. हरि and हरित, green) A bunch or bundle, a bundle of corn, a cornstack, a heap of grain before the straw is separated from it, a handful; also raw rice.

Aridála, or *Aridarán*, Tam. (அரிதால, அரிதராளர்) Stubble.

Aridaluku, or *Ariyedupu*, Tam. (அரிதலுக்கு, அரியெடுப்பு) A handful of corn, or as much as can be held by both hands put together, as the perquisite or fee of certain village servants.

Aridála-billi, Tam. An estimate of the produce of a field from the appearance of the stubble.

Arikattu, Tam. (அரிகட்டு) A sheaf of corn.

Árina-pattí, or patté, Karn. (ಆರಿನಪಟ್ಟಿ, from *áru* ಆರು, a plough) An account of the number of ploughs belonging to each cultivator in a village.

Árindi, H. (P. آرنده, *lit.* a bringer) An agent, a broker.

Arini kattu, Tel. (అరినికట్టు) Dams in a salt pan.—Vizagapatam.

Ârish, A. (عرش) Damages, fine for injury done to person or property, particularly for bloodshed not causing loss of life.—Mohammedan Law.

Arisi, Tam. (அரிசி) Any kind of grain, but especially rice freed from chaff.

Âríyat, H. (A. عاريت) Loan of any thing which is itself to be returned. Land or orchards of which the owner allows others to have the use, under certain stipulations. —Mohammedan Law.

Aríyat, H. (अरीयत) Land recently recovered from jungle.

Arjanna, H. A tribe of Kunbís, or cultivators, in Western India.

Árjá, H. (S. आर्या, fem of आर्य, respectable, venerable) A female mendicant, so termed in central Hindustan.

Arju, or Ardzu, Urdzoo, or Urjoo, Tel. (అర్జు, corruption of P. ارز) Price, value.

Arju-bájári dhárá, Tel. Price-current, or market price.

Arju, Urjoo, Tel. (అర్జు, corruption of A. عرض, breadth) The measurement of a heap of grain from the bottom to the top, as opposed to Tula, a measurement of the circumference.

Árola, Hindi (आरोल) A sweet grass growing in short tufts, the seeds of which, when ripe, are often used as food by the poorer classes.

Arolat, (?) In the Dekhin, land held at a quit-rent by the *Mehr*, who acts as the village watchman and messenger, in compensation of his services.

Áropanam, Mal. (S. ആരോപണം) An accusation, a false charge.

Arru, Urroo, Tel. (అర్రు) Sore on a bullock's neck, made by the yoke of the plough.

Arsál, Ursal, or more correctly, Irsál, H. (A. ارسال) Sending, mission, despatch, especially of treasure or of revenue-collections to the treasury.

Arz-i-Irsál, H. Invoice. Particulars of the despatch of treasure.

Arsath, Ursuth, H. (ارستة) A monthly account of receipts and disbursements.

Arsattá, or Adsattá, Ursutta, or Udsutta, also, corruptly, Arsotta, and Átosatta, possibly also a modification of the preceding, or Arsuth, H. Mar., but it occurs in other dialects also (ارستا, अडसट्टा) Estimate, guess, a rough calculation; a monthly treasury account of receipts and disbursements made up from the daily entries.

Arsattá navís, H. Per. The clerk or accountant who keeps the monthly account.

Ársha, S. (आर्षः, from ऋषि, an inspired sage) One of the modes of marriage according to Hindu law: the gift of a girl, by her father, on receiving one or two pairs of oxen from the bridegroom. Scriptural, any thing for which a Rishi is an authority.

Artha, S. (अर्थः) Object, purpose, meaning, wealth.

Arthí, H. (S. अर्थिन्, one who has an object, &c.) A suppliant, a plaintiff, a prosecutor, a petitioner.

Arthyávedana, S. The complaint of a plaintiff taken verbally by the officers of a Court before the filing of the written plaint recorded by them in writing.

Vidyárthi, or *Bidyárthí*, S. Ben. (from *vidyá*, knowledge, and *arthí*, who seeks for) A student, a pupil, a schoolboy or collegian.

Arṭhi, Arṭhiyá, Urṭhee, Urṭhiya, H. (ارتهي, ارتهيا) A broker, a commissioner, an agent, a salesman, a commercial correspondent, one who conducts business on commission for a principal at a distance; a banker who grants and accepts bills on other bankers or correspondents. See also *Aḍat*, *Aṛhat*, *Aḍatya*, and *Aṛhatiya*, as spelled with the hard *ḍ* ड, or hard *ṛ* ड़, and with a soft or hard *t*, त or ट, also with or without the aspirate.

Áru, or **Árukáru**, Karn. (ಆರು, ಆರುಕಾರು) A plough with oxen and implements of husbandry complete.

Áru bhatta, Karn. A tax on grain at so much per plough, afterwards commuted to a fixed money rate.

Árugidgával, Karn. A tax on the Ryots for leave to cut timber from the jungle, for the fabric of their ploughs.

Áru-káṇike, Karn. A tax on ploughs.

Áṛu, Tam. (ஆறு) **Áṛa**, Mal. (ആറ) A river, a rivulet, a watercourse. See *Áttukal*.

Aṛudi-karai, Tam. (அறுதிக்கரை, from *aṛuthi*, or *aṛudi*, fixed or final, and *karai*, boundary) One of the three kinds of tenures under which land is held in the Tamil provinces; that in which the distribution is final or absolute, that is to say, the occupant holds a defined portion of the village lands, of which he has the entire disposal, and may let or sell them: his other rights and privileges, which he holds in common with the other proprietors, are transferable along with his share of the land. This is corrupted to *Ard-karry*, and *Audi-carei*, in the Fifth Report, and as the *Adhihári*, of the more recent returns. It is also called *Pála-bhogam*, q. v. Selections from the Records, i. 904, 905.

Aṛudi-hraya, corruptly, *Urdi*, or *Urdee-krayum*, Tam. (அறுதிக்கிரயம், S. क्रय, sale) A final or permanent sale; sale of a share held under the Aṛudi-karai tenure.

Arudi paṇgu, Tam. (அறுதிப்பங்கு) Final settlement or allotment. What is given in full of all demands

Aṛugu, Tam. (அறுகு) A raised platform or terrace covered over and forming a veranda or porch on the outside of a native house; also termed a Piäl, a screen to shade persons of respectability from the sun.

Arulu, or **Arlu**, Karn. (ಅರುಲು, ಅಲು) Mud, clay, or miry soil.

Aṛumbu, Tam. (அறும்பு) Scarcity, dearth.

Aṛuppu, Tam. (அறுப்பு) Cutting, harvest, cutting the crop, the act of reaping.

Aṛuppu-chíṭṭu, Tam. (அறுப்புச்சீட்டு) An order or permission to cut the standing crop.

Aṛuppu-kálam, Tam. (அறுப்புக்காலம்) Season of harvest.

Aṛuppu-kuli, Tam. (அறுப்புக்குலி) Wages of reaping.

Aruwá, Uriya. (ଅରୁଆ) Rice cleaned from unboiled paddy.

Aṛuvari, Tam. (அறுவரி) Á tax paid at fixed times.

Ârúẕ, Ûrooẕ, A. (عروض) In Mohammedan law, Personal property, exclusive of money, goods and chattels.

Arvela, Karn. (ಅವೇಲ) A caste of Smártha Brahmans in Mysore.

Arwádiya-ghareniya, Guz. In Guzerat, Lands mortgaged by the village authorities for a definite period.

Arwan, Arwun, H. (ارون) The first cuttings of the harvest, not taken to the threshing-floor, but brought home to be eaten by the family and presented to the household gods and to Brahmans. The corn is taken out of the ear and eaten with milk and sugar: the term is chiefly current in Rohilkhand and the Upper Doab. The more usual and intelligible term is *Nawán*, from the S. *nava*, new, and *anna*, rice or food.

Arwar, Karn. (?) A kind of mortgage, in Mysore, in which the land is made over to the lender until the produce has discharged the debt.

Arz, Urz, H. (P. ارز) Price, value. *Arz-i-bazar*, Current or market rate.

Arẕ, Urẕ, H. (A. ارض) Land, earth, landed property.

Ârẕ, Urẕ, vernacularly **Arj, Urj, Arji, Urjee**, H. &c. (A. عرض, अरज, अर्ज़) Petition, representation. In Mohammedan law, personal property except money. See *Âruẕ*.

Arẕi, *Urẕee*, H. &c. (عرضي, अर्ज़ी, ಅರ್ಜಿ) A petition, an address, a memorial, a respectful statement or representation, whether oral or written.

Ârẕ-begi, H. (T. بيگ, a lord) An officer who, under the Mogul Government, was appointed to receive and present petitions, &c.

Ârẕi-dâwá, H. (A. دعوي) A petition of complaint, the plaint, the first pleading in a suit.

Arẕ-dásht, H. (P. داشت, what contains) A written petition or memorial.

Ârẕ-i-marammat, H. (from A. *marammat*, مرمت, repairing) A petition to amend or amplify a preceding petition or complaint.

Ârẕ-i-mújibát, H. (from A. *mujibát* موجبات, reasons) A representation of reasons or pleas, a petition of appeal setting forth the grounds of it.

Ârẕ-i-muḳarrar, H. (from *muḳarrar* مقرّر, established) A petition or memorial representing the circumstances of a case, a representation to the royal authority of the proceedings taken in respect of a grant of revenue or a Zemindari.—Har. Anal. iii. 407.

Âráychi, Tam. (ஆர்ாய்ச்சி, perhaps from A. *Ârẕ*) An officer under the magistrates, head of the police, a sheriff.

Arzál, H. (A. ارزال, for ارذل, plur. of رذل, vile) Low castes located on the estates of Zemindars, in some parts of Hindustan, as tenants at will, partly paying rent and partly rendering personal services, considered, in some measure, as adscripti glebæ, and not entitled to remove off the lands except by the landlord's pleasure; dependent also upon him for support in unfavourable seasons.

Arẕámini, or Aḍẕámini, H. (from *aṛ*, *aḍ*, H. M. اڑ, اڈ, आड, or आड़, q. v., implying protection or screening, and *ẕámini*, A. ضامني, security) Counter security. Surety for a surety, mutual surety or responsibility.

Arzíz, Urzeez, A. (ارزيز, *lit.* tin) Base or light money.

Âṣá, H. (A. عصا) A staff, a stick, a long stick or mace, usually coated with a thin plate of silver, carried by a personal attendant as a mark of rank.

Âṣá-bardár, H. A staff or mace bearer.

Âṣab, A. (عصب) Incidental or indirect heir. Residuary heir (in Mohammedan law).

Âṣúbat, *Asoobut*, A. Inheritance in the male line from incidental contingencies.

Asádhárana, S. (from अ, neg., and साधारण, common, special, individual) In Hindu law applied to property held by one person without the participation of another, as opposed to co-heirship or co-parcenary.

Asaga, Karn. (ಅಗಸ) The washerman of the village, one of the village servants.

Asagotra, S. (from अ, neg., and सगोत्र, of kin) In Hindu law, A kinsman by the female line only, one not of the same lineage or descent.

Aṣal, Usul, corruptly, Asil, Asool, Assil, Azil, Ausil, Awsil, H., but occurring in all the dialects, sometimes slightly modified, as Tel. Asulu, and the like (A. اصل) Root, origin, foundation. Principal, capital, original property or estate, also the original of a document. As a revenue term it is applied especially to the original or established rate of assessment without any extra cess. In Mohammedan law, a principle or ground of decision.

Aṣal-beríz, H. In the Northern Circars and the Carnatic, the standard or original assessment of the land revenue, without any extra cess. Also *Aṣal-jamâ*.

Aṣal-chiṭṭu, Tam. (அசல்சீட்டு) The original or first copy of a bond.

Aṣal dastáwez, H. An original document or record, in contradistinction to a copy.

Aṣal-jamâ, H. (A. جمع, total) The original rent or revenue charged upon the lands of an estate, or village, or district, without any *Abwáb* or extra cesses; also the amount taken as the basis of a revenue settlement.

Aṣal-mukaddama, H. The original suit, in distinction to one appealed.

Aṣal-tan, H. (from Pers. *tan* تن, a person) A party pleading his own cause, the principal party in a suit.

Aṣálatan, H. (A. اصالتً) In person, personally (appearing or pleading), in antithesis to *Wakálatan*, pleading by a Vakíl. These are both adverbs from the substantives *Aṣálat* and *Wakálat*, with the Arabic syllable *an* added.

Aṣal-tumar-jamâ, H. The original rent-roll of the assessment of the land revenue in the Mogul provinces according to the register of Raja Todar Mal, in the reign of Akbar. Also the same as subsequently modified.

Aṣli, Uṣlee, or Aṣali, Uṣulee, H. (formed from *aṣal*, denominative) Primary, original, applied to a registered village under the Mohammedan system, in opposition to the Dákhili one subsequently occupied. In the directions to Settlement officers in the N. W. provinces, 1844, par. 45, the application of these terms was modified, and thenceforward those *Mauẕâs* only which were numbered in the Settlement lists were to be called *Âṣali*, while *Dákhili* was to be confined to such smaller *mauẕâs* as might be afterwards formed.

Aṣli-gaon, H. A principal or original village, one from which others have branched out, that on which the revenue was originally assessed.

Aṣli-mauẕâ, H. An original village. See the preceding.

Aṣli-zamín, H. Original land, that forming part of the

originally assessed estate, exclusive of subsequent additions, as from alluvial deposits, &c.

Aṣíl, Uṣeel, H. A female servant among Mohammedans who is a free woman, and therefore superior to the *Laundí*, or purchased slave. It is sometimes, but incorrectly, applied to any female slave.

ASÁMI, corruptly, ASSAMEE, ASSAMIE, ASSAUMY, H. &c. (A. اسامي, असामी, plur. of *ism*, a name, sometimes derived from *iṣám* اثام, a criminal) A cultivator, a tenant, a renter, a non-proprietary cultivator; also a dependant; also a debtor, a culprit, a criminal, a defendant in a suit. Mr. Elliot (Supplement to the Glossary) conjectures, with every appearance of probability, that *Asámi* has come to signify 'an individual,' from the heading of the register in which the appellations of the villagers, &c. were recorded, as, *Asám*, 'names,' each item then becoming an *Asám-i*, or one of the names, or an individual person. The term is adopted in most of the dialects.

Asámi-ch'happer band, H. A resident cultivator, one who occupies his own *ch'happer band*, or thatched cottage; one who holds at a fixed rent.

Asámi-jái-báki kágaj, Ben. A record kept by a Zamindar in which the names of the tenants, and the balances due by them, are registered.

Ásámi maurúṣi, H. An hereditary cultivator, one who, although not a proprietor, cannot be dispossessed as long as he pays a stipulated rent.

Asámi-paikásht, H. A man who cultivates land in a village without any hereditary right, a tenant at will.

Asámi-shikami, H. One who cultivates the land of another person and pays him a fixed rent: a sub-tenant; one who labours for his support (*shikam*, *lit.* belly).

Asámi-wár, H. Individually, personally, according to name; applied to a revenue settlement with each individual cultivator, the same as Ryot-war.

Asámiwár-gutta, Tel. (from *gutta* (గుత్త, rent) The rent or revenue to be levied from each cultivator. A Ryot-war settlement.

Asámiwár-hisáb, H., *-hissébu*, Tel. (from P. *hisáb*, an account), An account, kept in the Madras provinces, shewing the particulars of each Ryot's produce, assessment, payments and balance as it stands at the end of the year.

Asámiwári, Tel. Individually, according to name. A settlement or assessment made on each.

Asámiwár or *-wári makta*, H. Mar. Tel. (from the A. *muhaṭa* مقطع, divided) The rent or revenue payable by each individual cultivator. An account shewing the distribution.

Asámiwár or *-wári mufrid*, (from A. *mufrid* مفرد, single) In the northern Circars, an account shewing the amount of each cultivator's produce, both by estimate and measurement.

ASAPIṆḌA, S. (from अ, neg. and सपिण्ड) One not connected by offerings of the funeral cake to the same ancestors; a distant kinsman.

ASAPUTRA, S. (from अ, neg., स, with, and पुत्र, a son) In Hindu law, A son adopted from a different family, not descended from a common ancestor.

ÁSÁṚH, ÁSÁḌH, more correctly, ÁSHÁḌH, H. (اساڑھ, from S. आषाढः), also vernacularly, ÁKHÁṚ, Mar. &c. (आखाड) The fourth month of the Hindu solar year (June—July), considered the first of the rainy season, and beginning of the rice cultivation.

Ásárhi, Ásárhee, H. (اساڑھي) The harvest of Ásárh, but differently applied to the harvest that springs from ploughing or from sowing in that month. In the former case it denotes the spring harvest, and is so used in the North-west. In the Benares district and Eastern Oude it is applied to the latter, and then imports the autumnal harvest.

ÁSARÁ, H. (?) In the northern Circars, Lands of which the revenues are paid in kind, also lands which are not dependent on the rains, but may be irrigated from a tank or river.

ÁSARÁ, or ÁSRÁ, H. (آسرا, from S. आश्रयः) A place of protection, a shelter, a home, a sanctuary.

ÁṢARÁ-SISTU, Tel. Fixed, unfluctuating amount.

ÁṢÁRI, Mal. (ആശാരി) A carpenter.

AṢÁṢ, H. (A. اثاث) Property, wealth, effects.

Aṣáṣ ul bait, H. Household furniture.

AṢAUCH, AṢAUCHA, H. Ben. (اسوچ, from the S. अशौचः) Social or legal uncleanness, as from the death of a relation or the like.

ASBÁB, H. (A. plur. of سبب) Goods, effects, materials, implements, &c.

ÁSEDHA, S. (आसेधः) Legal arrest, restraint; which may be of four kinds, *Kálásedha*, confinement for a time, by the end of which the affair must be settled; *Karmásédha*, restraint from any particular act, restriction from religious rites; *Praváśásedha*, prohibition of removal, a writ of 'ne exeat;' *Sthánásedha*, confinement in any given place.

ASHHÁD, H. (A. plur. of *shahíd*) Witnesses, eyewitnesses. In Mohammedan law.

ÂSHAR, ÛSHUR, A. (from عشرة, ten) A tenth, tithe. In Mohammedan law, the tithe assessed on lands occupied by Mohammedans, or which have been divided amongst a victorious army from the possessions of infidels.

Âshari, H. Subject to tithe.

Âshir, A. An officer appointed to collect the tithes.

Âshara, also *Âáshúra*, or *Ûshoora*, H. (A. عشرة , عاشورة) The first ten days of the month Moharram, which, by the Shías, are dedicated to the commemoration of the death of Âli and his sons.

Âshúr-khána, H. A building in which the bier, the banners, and isignia used at the ceremonies of the Moharram are set up.

ASHRÁBAT, A. (plur. of شراب, drink) Drinks, but in law applied especially to wines or spirituous liquors produced from the fermentation of grapes, raisins, or dates, the drinking of which is prohibited.

AṢ-HÁR, A. (اصهار, plur. of صهر) Relations by marriage within the degree in which marriage is prohibited.

ASHRÁF, corruptly, ASHROF, H. (A. اشراف, plur. of شريف, noble) Noblemen, persons of rank. In Behar and other provinces of Hindustan, the designation is assumed by the more respectable classes of both Mohammedans and Hindus, most of whom rent and cultivate lands, although they consider themselves soldiers and gentlemen and as degraded by personal labour, to which, nevertheless, they are frequently reduced, performing all kinds of agricultural work except driving the plough. In some places they hold their lands under more favourable terms than other cultivators: "the Government Revenue (in Aligerh), when settled by a division of the crop, was one-third from Zemindars, one-fourth from Ashrofs, and one-half from ordinary cultivators." App. Revenue Report.

ASHRAFI, USHRUFEE, corruptly, USHURFEE, H. (from the A. شريف, noble) A gold coin; a mohur, rated at sixteen rupees silver.

ASHṬA, S. (अष्टन्) Eight.

Ashṭa bhága mányam, S. An estate, in the south of India, held on favourable terms, paying only an eighth of a share of the produce as revenue.

Ashṭa-bhogam, S. Enjoyment of the whole, or the eight products of an estate; or the land cultivated, *Siddhi*; the produce of such land, *Sádhya*; uncultivable or rocky land and its products, as minerals, &c., *Páshána*; property deposited on the land, *Nikshepa*: treasure-trove, *Nidhi*; waters and their produce, *Jalámṛitam*; actual privileges, *Akshiní*; prospective rights and privileges, *Ágámi*.

Ashṭaká, S. Eighth; the 8th day of the moon in certain months, when progenitors are to be worshipped.

Ashṭamí, S. The eighth day of the lunar fortnight.

Ashṭa-pradhána, S. The eight chief ministers of the Maratha principality.—See Duff. i. 236, 265.

ASÍCHÁ, USEECHA, H. (اسيچا, from S. अ, neg., and सिच, to sprinkle) Unwatered, unirrigated, as land.

ÁSÍN, corruptly, ASSIN, more correctly, ÁSWIN, H. (اسن, from S. आश्विनी *aswini*, the constellation in which the moon is full) The seventh month of the Hindu luni-solar year (September—October).

ÁṢÍR, or, in the crude form, ÁṢÍS, S. (आशीस्) A blessing.

Ásír-bád, H., but used in most dialects (from *ásír* and *bád*, or *váda*, speech) The benedictive address of a Brahman or religious teacher.

ÁSIYA, H. (P. آسيا) A mill, a water-mill.

ÁSIYÁNA, H. (آسيانه) A whetstone.

ASMÁNI-FARMÁNI, H. (P. اسمان, heaven, and فرمان, command) A term used formerly in deeds and leases, providing for any incidents or injuries arising from calamitous seasons or unjust exactions of the Government, which, if affecting the Zemindar, the Ryots engaged to make good. In Garwhal, estimated fines and forfeitures, as part of the revenue.

ASNÁN, H. (اسنان, corruption of S. *snána* स्नानं) Bathing, ablution.

ASON, H. (اسون) The current year.

AṢOKÁSHṬAMÍ, S. (from *Aṣoka* अशोकः, the tree so called, *Jonesia asoea*, and *ashtamí*, eighth) The eighth of the light fortnight of Chaitra (April—May), when a festival in honour of Vishnu is observed, part of the ceremonial of which consists in drinking water with the buds of the Asoka in it.

ÂṢR, ÛṢR, H. (A. عصر) The afternoon.

Âṣr-namáz, The afternoon prayer of the Mohammedans, to be repeated at any time from half-past four until sunset.

ÁṢR, plur. AṢÁR, A. (اثار, آثر) Signs, marks, traditions; the traditional law of the Mohammedans based on the sayings and doings of Mohammed.

ÁṢRAMA, S. (आश्रमः) A condition or order of life of which four should be passed through in succession by Hindus of the three superior castes, viz. that of the *Brahmachárí*, or religious student; of the *Gṛihastha*, or householder;

of the *Vánaprastha,* or hermit; and *Bhikshuka,* or *Sanyási,* religious mendicant. Also a hermitage, the abode of persons leading a religious or contemplative life. A name borne in addition to their own proper name by one of the orders of *Dandi Gosains.*

Áṣrita, S. (आश्रितः lit., protected, supported) A dependant. A Brahman maintained by an opulent householder.

Ast, H. (است, S. अस्तः) Setting of the sun. Place of sunset. West.

Astáchal, H. (S. अस्त and अचलः, a mountain) The mountains of the west, behind which the sun is supposed to set.

Asthal, Usthul, H. &c., (استهل, from S. स्थल, place) Place of residence or abiding, especially the kind of free monastery in which communities of religious mendicants reside together under a *Mahant,* a chief or abbot.

Asthán, Usthan, inaccurately, Astán, H. &c., (استهان, from S. स्थान, a place) Abode, place of abiding, a hall of audience, a king's court or palace. The residence of a Mohammedan fakir. The shrine of a Mohammedan saint.

Ásthanakáran, Tam. (ஆஸ்தானகாரன்) A speaker in court, a pleader, an advocate

Asthi-ṣinchana, S. from *asthi* अस्थि, a bone, and *ṣinchana* शिञ्चन, sprinkling) The ceremony of sprinkling the remaining bones of a corpse that has been burnt, a few days afterwards.

Asti, Tel. (అస్తి, from the S. अस्ति, what is), Ásti or Áste, or Ástipásti, Karn. (ಆಸ್ತಿ, ಆಸ್ತೆ, ಆಸ್ತಿಪಾಸ್ತಿ), also Tam. (ஆஸ்தி, ஆஸ்திபாஸ்தி) Real or personal goods, riches. Estate. Property, possessions. That which is of, or belongs to, an individual.

Ástikár or *-gár,* Karn. (ಆಸ್ತಿಕಾರ), *Ástikáraṇ,* Tam. (ஆஸ்திகாரன்) A rich man, a man of property.

Ástigevaḍeya, Karn. (ಆಸ್ತಿಗೆವಡೆಯ) The proprietor of an estate.

Ásti-viparam, or *-vivaram,* Tam. (ஆஸ்திவிபரம்) An account or detailed statement of assets.

Asur, Usoor, H. &c., (اسر, from the S. असुरः) An evil spirit, a demon, an enemy of the gods.

Ásura, or *Ásuri,* S. Demoniacal, applied especially to one form of marriage formerly recognised by Hindu law; that in which the bridegroom gives as much wealth as he can afford to the bride, her parents, and relations.

Aswádhyáya, S. (अ neg., and स्वाध्यायः, sacred study) Days or seasons on which it is prohibited to read the Vedas. A Brahman who has not gone through his study of the Vedas.

Aswamedha, S. (अश्व, a horse, and *médha,* sacrifice) The actual or typical sacrifice of a horse. If performed a hundred times, the sacrificer obtains the rank of *Indra,* or king of Swarga.

Aswámi-bábat, H. (from S. *aswámi* अस्वामिन्, and *bábat* بابت, account) A term used in Kattiwar to signify extra and unauthorized charges levied by the revenue officers for their own emolument—not the demand of the *Swámi,* the lord, or Government.

Aswámi-bikri, or *-vikri,* H. (S. अ neg., स्वामी, a master, and *vikraya* विक्रयः, sale) Sale without ownership, one form of illegal sale.

Aswánsí, H. (اسوانسي) A land measure, one twelfth of a Kachwánsi.

Aṣwapati, S. (अश्व, a horse, and पति, lord) A title borne by some of the ancient Rajas of the South of India.

Aswari, Karn. An extra levy on a village.

Aṣwattha, S. current in most dialects, (अश्वत्थः) The Pípal-tree—Ficus religiosa.

Aṣwatthodyápana, or *A-pratishṭhá,* (S. *Aṣwattha* and *Udyápana,* setting up; or *pratishṭhá,* consecrating) The setting up of an Aṣwattha-tree, or a branch of it, as a part of various religious ceremonies.

Áṭá, corruptly, Otta, H. (آٹا) Flour, meal.

Átá, A. (آتي, lit., giving) In law, an appointed allowance or gratuity to soldiers and ministers of law or religion.

Aṭá, or Aṭári, H. (اٹا, اٹاري, from S. अट्टाली) An upper-roomed house, an upper story.

Aṭa-gorru, Tel. (అటగొఱ్ఱు) A kind of rake used in husbandry.

Atai, Uriya, A cattle pound.

Âtáḳ, or Âtáḳat, A. (عتاق, عتاقة) Manumission of slaves—in Mohammedan law.

Âtíḳ, A. (عتيق) Emancipated, manumitted (a slave).

Aṭál, H. (اٹال) A stack, a rick, a heap, or pile of anything.

Aṭamánam, Mal. (അടമാനം) A pledge, a mortgage, a security.

Atarpál, Uturpal, H. (اترپال) Land which has been formerly cultivated, but has been subsequently abandoned (more correctly, *Antar-pál,* from S. *antar,* an interval, and *pála,* cherishing. The word is current in the central and lower Doab.—Elliot.

Átatáyí, S. (आततायी) In Hindu law, one guilty of a heinous offence.

Áṭchi, Tam. (ஆட்சி) A heritage, inheritance. It is most usually compounded as *Kániyáṭchi*, q. v. A domain or lordship obtained by inheritance. A right, a privilege. *Árasáṭchi*, Royalty. See *Arasa*.

Athal, (?) Land farmed or rented (perhaps for *Asthal*). Gl. 5th Rep.

Aṭhavani or **Aṭhavané**, also **Aththavane**, or, with the unaspirated *t* doubled, **Attavane**, or **Attavani**, q. v. Karn., (అఠవణి, అఠవణೆ, అట్టవణೆ) Revenue. An armed messenger or peon employed in revenue affairs.

Aṭhavani-kacheri, Karn. (ಕಚೇರಿ) Office for revenue accounts. A Collector's kacheri.

Aṭhavaneïlákhé, Karn. (ಅಠವಣೆಯಿಲಾಖೆ) Revenue department.

Aṭhavaneyalekhkha, Karn (ಅಠವಣೆಯಲೆಖ್ಖ) A revenue account.

Áṭhmás, H. (آتهماس, from آٹھ, the vernacular form of S. अष्ट *ashṭa*, eight, and *mása*, a month) Lands constantly ploughed for eight months for sugar-cane; or, from *Áshárh* to *Mágh*, both inclusive.

Áṭhmaná, H. (آتهمنا, from S. अस्त:) The west, in opposition to *Agmaná*, the east. **Athaye** (अथये) is used in the same sense, but more commonly to signify 'evening.'

Áṭh-pahari, **Áṭh-puhuree**, H. (آٹھ پہری) One who is always on duty (lit., an eight-watch man), applied especially to a servant employed to collect rents; or, in Bengal, to one who is set to watch the crop, and acts as a messenger for the rest of the villagers.

Áṭhwára, corruptly, *Athvyára*, H. (آٹھوارا, from अष्ट, eight) A money-lender who advances money on condition that the borrower shall pay by weekly instalments a larger sum than he receives. A cultivator who, for the use of agricultural implements on his own account for eight days, works the rest of the month for the benefit of the lender.

Áṭí, Hindi (आटी) A sheaf, a handful of stalks of any kind corn given to the reapers for cutting a *bojha*, or load, usually about one-sixteenth.

Atipátak, H. (from S. अति, implying much, exceeding, and पातक, crime) Heinous or capital offence.

Atít, **Uteet**, H. (from the S. अतीत, passed away, by whom worldly interests are discarded) A religious mendicant of the Hindus, usually a Vaishṇava.

AT

Atith, **Atithi**, H. but used in most dialects, (S. अतिथि:) A guest, any stranger entitled to hospitality.

Atithi-pújá, S. (पूजा, worship) Hospitality, reverence of guests.

Átithyam, S. (आतिथ्यं) Hospitality.

Átash-behrám, Pers. (from *Atash* آتش, fire) A chief temple of the Parsis, the sacred fire in which is said to be composed of 1001 kinds. Six such temples exist in India.

Átash-kada, or *-khána*, P. (کده, خانه) A fire-temple.

Ativása, S. (अतिवास:) The fast observed on the day preceding a *Sráddha*, or obsequial ceremony.

Aṭkáo, H. (اٹکاو) Arrest. Sequestration.

Átkári, H. (آتکاري) A caste of silk weavers in the Dekhin.

Átmá, S. (आत्मा) The soul, the self. **Paramátmá**, The Supreme Soul—God.

Átma-bandhu, S. (आत्मबंधु:) A person's own or cognate kinsman.

Átmaja, S. (आत्मज:) A son.

Atmaghátah, Ben. (from S. आत्मघात:, a self-destroyer) One who commits suicide.

Atmavikrayi, S. (आत्मविक्रयी) One who sells himself as a slave.

Âṭr, **Ûṭr**, or, more correctly, **Iṭr**, corruptly *Ottar* and *Otto*, A. (عطر) Fragrance, perfume, essence, especially of roses.

Âṭr-dán, H. (P. دان, holding) An ornamental box or phial containing essence of roses.

Âṭár, H. (A. عطار) A perfumer, a maker of perfumes and essences, a druggist, a chemist.

Aṭráf, **Uṭráf**, H. (A. اطراف, plur. of طرف) Limits, boundaries.

Atráfi-rawana, H. (P. روانه) A pass for the transit of goods beyond the limits of the custom-stations.

Attáṭchi, Tam. (அத்தாட்சி) Proof, evidence, attestation.

Atta-tarisu, Tam. (?) Land which has laid waste for a long time.

Aṭṭavaṇai, Tam. (அட்டவணை) An index, a register. A cash-book, a statement in figures; also an accountant or writer. When prefixed to any official designation, it implies that the person is duly registered as holding the office.—In Mysore, Revenue, &c. See **Athavani**.

Áṭṭavanai-kanakan, Tam. (அட்டவணைக்கணக்கன்) An accountant, a book-keeper, a registrar.

Aṭṭiper, Mal. (അട്ടിപേറ്) Freehold property. (*Aṭṭi* is here a various and apparently less accurate reading of Otti, q. v.).

Aṭṭiperṛola, pronounced **Aṭṭipeṭṭola** Mal. (അട്ടി-പെരൊാല) Title deeds of freehold property. See the last.

Attu, Tam. (அத்து, from A. حد) A boundary a limit.

Aṭṭu, Karn. (ಅಟ್ಟು) A shelf, a platform in corn-fields on which persons are stationed to watch the crop.

Áṭṭu-kál, Tam. (ஆற்றுக்கால், from ஆறு, a river, and *kál*, a channel, the double ற pronounced as *tt*) A rivulet. A channel for conducting water from a river for the purpose of irrigation.

Áṭṭukál-éri, Tam. (ஏரி, a tank) A pond or tank filled from a river by a water-course.

Áṭṭu-páchal, or *-páyachal*, Tam. (ஆற்றுப்பாய்ச்சல்) In S. India, River irrigation, lands watered from a river.

Áṭṭu-veppa, Mal. (ആറുവെപ്പ്) New land left by the retiring of a river, or gained from the sea. Plantations by the sea-shore.

Atuku bádi, or **-ábadi**, Tel. (?) Giving waste or unoccupied land to a cultivator at a low rate of assessment on condition of his bringing it into cultivation.

Aṭṭupu, Tam. (அட்டுப்பு) Boiled salt. Earth-salt.

Aukáṣ, A. (plur. of *Wakaṣ* وقص) In Mohammedan law, any number of cattle intermediate between two numbers which are liable to Zakát, and on which additional payment is not levied; thus, the numbers from 40 to 50 are *Aukáṣ*, being charged as 40, from 50 to 60 as 50, and so on.

Âul, or **Âol**, A. (عول) Increase. In Mohammedan law, The distribution of a fractional proportion of inherited property more than the amount of the legal shares of the respective heirs: thus, if a woman deceased have left a husband and two sisters, the first is entitled by law to a half or $\frac{3}{6}$ths of her wealth, and the two last to $\frac{2}{6}$ths each; making, therefore, $\frac{7}{6}$ths, or one more than the whole. In such case the denominator of the fraction is made equal to that of all the shares, or to seven, and the numerator remains unaltered, forming the fractions $\frac{3}{7}$, $\frac{2}{7}$, $\frac{2}{7}$, or giving to the husband $\frac{3}{7}$ths, and to the sisters $\frac{2}{7}$ths each.

Aulád, H. (A. اولاد, plur. of ولد) Children, progeny, descendants.

Aulaï, Thug. A person who is a Thug, as opposed to one who is not.

Aulia, A. (plur. of ولی) In law, The nearest of kin, and therefore entitled to demand the fine of blood, or commutation for murder. In ordinary use, holy men, reputed prophets.

Aurasa, S., but adopted in most dialects, (औरसः) Uterine, as a son by a wife. A maternal brother, or son of the same mother.

Aurang, **Aurung**, H. (اورنگ) A place where any article of trade is manufactured and collected for wholesale disposal or export. During the Company's commerce, it was applied to the factories for piece goods, &c.

Áüs, more correctly **Ásu**, corruptly, **Ouse**, Beng. (আউশ, or আশু) Rice ripening early, being sown in Chaitra or Vaiṣákh (February, March), and ripening in Srávana or Bhádra (August, September), growing rapidly through the rainy season. The same word *Áṣu* occurs in other dialects, as in Mal. *Áṣu*, (ആശു) Rice ripening in the rainy season; being from the S. *Áṣu*, (आशु) Quick, quickly.

Áút, **Áoot**, Mar. (आउत, from S. आयुध, a weapon) An implement, a tool, especially one used in agriculture, as a plough. As much land as may be ploughed by a pair of bullocks, usually considered equal to 80 bighas.

Áüt-bandi, *Áoot-bundee*, corruptly, *Out-bundee*, Mar. (आउतबंदी) Assessment of revenue calculated at a fixed rate per plough. Engagement to pay a fixed charge for the use of a plough and pair of bullocks.

Áut-paṭṭi, *Áoot-puṭṭee*, Mar. (आउतपट्टी) The tax on ploughs; also any extra cess, whether authorised or unauthorised, upon each owner of a plough.

Avadhi, S. (अवधिः) Limit, term, period.

Avadhi-aravár, Karn. (ಅರವಾರ) In Kanara, A kind of mortgage, in which the land is held for a term in lieu of interest. See *Aravár*.

Avadi-kraya, or *Avadirana-kraye*, Tam. (from S. अवधि, and क्रय, sale) In Southern India, a conditional sale, to become absolute if the purchase-money be not repaid within a stipulated time.

Avadhuta, S. (अवधूतः, liberated) A religious mendicant in the South of India, of the Ṣaiva and Ṣákta sects, one who is exempt from ceremonial observances and worldly restraints. See *Abdhút*. Among the Ṣáktas there are two classes of such devotees.

Vyaktávadhúta, (from S. *vyakta*, manifested) One who openly professes religious emancipation.

Guptávadhúta, (from S. *gupta*, hidden) One who throws off the usual restrictions of caste, &c., unavowedly and in private.

Avakáșam, Mal. (അവകാശം, from S. अवकाशं, opportunity) Right, title, privilege. Inheritance.

Avakásam-muṛi, Mal. (മുറി, a written agreement) A deed of partition, a deed declaring the several rights and privileges of persons having a joint interest in property.

Avakási, Mal. (അവകാശി) An heir, a rightful owner.

Avalakki, Karn. (ಅವಲಕ್ಕಿ) Rice bruised or flattened by beating the paddy after being scaled in the husk, sometimes eaten without being boiled.

Avanejana, S. (अवनेजन) Washing, ablution. A ceremony prior to offering the funeral cake, pouring water in which white flowers and sandal paste are immersed upon the bed of kușa grass placed to receive the cake.

Avatára, S. (अवतारः, a descent) The descent or incarnation of a deity, his appearance or birth upon earth for some important purpose. The principal Avatárs of Vishṇu are ten: 1. the *Matsya*, or fish; 2. *Kúrma*, or tortoise; 3. *Varáha*, boar; 4. *Nṛisinha*, or man-lion; 5. *Vámana*, dwarf; 6. *Parașuráma*; 7. *Rámachandra*, or *Ráma*; 8. *Balaráma*; 9. *Buddha*; and 10. yet to come, *Kalki*. *Krishṇa* is usually considered not as a mere *avatár*, but as Vishṇu himself. A number of other descents or incarnations, both of Vishṇu and Șiva, are specified by modern sectaries.

Avati, or **Aüti**, Mahr. (अवटी) A goldsmith's stamp. The officer of a town who has charge of the standard measures, and measures all the grain that is brought to market.

Ávibhájya, S. (अ neg., विभाज्य, to be divided) Indivisible, as property.

Avibhakta, S. अ neg., विभक्त, divided, partitioned) Undivided, as property held in common, or as joint property. One who is unseparated from his family, a co-parcener.

Avírá, S. (अ neg., and वीर, *vir*, a man) A childless widow, a woman who has neither husband nor son.

Ávro or **Ávaro**, Guz. (આવરો) In Surat, One of the account-books kept by merchants—a waste book.

Awá, H. (اوا) A potter's kiln or furnace.

Awái, H. (اواي) A pick-axe

Áwak, H. (آوك, आवक) Insurance. In Western India, Respondentia, an advance of money to a merchant upon the goods or merchandise in a ship before sailing, under the condition that if the voyage be profitable the loan is to be repaid with an extra rate of interest or per centage.

Áwak-vyáju, or *-biájú*, H. (from व्याजू, principal) A transaction in which a person who has made a respondentia advance enters into an engagement with some third person, who, for a bonus or stipulated interest, insures him against loss.

Awár, Mar. (S. अवार) A fence, &c., enclosing a yard round a house.

Awál, Hind. (S. अवाल) An enclosed space formed by a cluster of Ryots' houses.

Áwan, or, more correctly, **Ánwan**, q. v., the nasal being blended with the vowel, Mar. (आंवण) The first field of rice, that in which it has been raised from seed.

Áṇwanú, Mar. (आंवणू) The part of the field into which the young shoots of rice are transplanted from the *Áṇwan*. Transplanted, applied to the young rice-stalks from the first growth.

Awangilli, H. (?) A mode of torture, compelling a man to stand with each foot upon an inverted earthen vessel, the shape and position of which endanger his falling; a Chaprási stands by to flog him if he loses footing.

Áwardah-navís, H. (from P. *awardah* آورده, what is brought, and *navis* نويس, a writer) A writer or registrar of accounts as delivered, applied to a class of accountants in the ceded districts.

Awárija, **Uwariju**, or **Awarija**, **Uwuriju**, corruptly, **Awerja**, H. &c. (P. اوارجه, अवारिज, supposed to be derived from *Awárá* اوارا, scattered, and occurring in Persian also, as *Ábár*, *Ábára*, and *Áwára*) A diary, a day-book, a ledger, a rough note-book, an abstract account of receipts and disbursements. The word occurs in most dialects, somewhat modified occasionally in spelling and in meaning, as in Cuttack, it denotes a revenue account, specifying, first, the unproductive lands of a village, and then those paying revenue, field by field, arranged under the names of the occupants, with a specification in separate columns of the number of each field in the Bhauriya or field-book, the quantity of land and kind of cultivation; the total rent by each occupant being also summed up. Mar. **Awaṛjá**, corruptly, **Awuzza**, (अवरजा) A particular and distinct head of account abstracted from the day-book, or a separate account of each cultivator's land revenue and charges upon it. Tel. **Awarjá**, (అవర్జా) A distribution of items of account under appropriate heads. Posting an account.

Awárijá-jamâ kharch, H. An account of receipts and disbursements.

Awásí, **Uwásee**, H. (اواسي, S. अवासी) Unripe corn cut from time to time, and brought home to be eaten without being threshed.—Benares. See DADRI.

AWASTÁ, corruptly, AVESTA, Pehlevi. Literally, 'word;' but used by the Parsis to denote a mystical prayer or incantation. Wilson, Religion of the Parsis, pp. 14. 167.

AWÁSTHI, H. One of the subdivisions of the Kanauj Brahmans.

AWKHAR, Thug. Dakhini. Any person maimed or deprived of the use of his limbs.

ÁYA, S. (आय:) Income, profit.

ÁYA, or ÁYAM, Karn. Tam. (ಆಯ , ஆயம், S. आय:, income, profit) Toll, tax, tribute, custom, measurement. In the Dakhin, the portion of the crop formerly paid to the hereditary village officers and servants.

Áyanáya or *Áyanámya*, Tam. (?) Fees in kind paid to the village officer: perhaps an error for *Áyasáya*, q. v.

Áyakár, or *Ayagár*, Karn. (ಆಯಕಾರ, ಆಯಗಾರ) A village servant or officer, one entitled to the Áya, or proportion of the crop, for his services to the community. (Plur. *Áyagárru*, or *Áyengandlu*, also written, but either locally or incorrectly, *Áyengade*, *Áyengadlu*, and *Áyengandea*.) The officers and servants of a village, the whole establishment, the *Baluté* of the Maraṭha countries, q. v.

Áyakaṭṭu, or *Ayukuṭṭoo*, corruptly, *Ayacut*, Karn. Tam. (ಆಯಕಟ್ಟು, ஆயக்கட்டு) Regulation, settlement. Measurement of lands, determining the boundaries of a village. An account of the total land belonging to a village, including houses, wells, &c., and particulars of its distribution and condition, to be kept by the village accountant,

Áyaketta, Mal. (ആയകെട്ട) Register of assessed land. Land prepared for cultivation. (In Malabar) the same also as *Áyakaṭṭu*, q. v.

Áyakrit, (?) (probably an error for *Áyakaṭṭu*, or *Ayacut*) Total cultivable land. Gl. 5th Rep.

Áyakallu, (?) Mar. Rent on Government lands in cultivation.

Áyasáya, also *Áyasámya*, Karn. (ಆಯಸಾಯ, ಆಯಸಾಮ್ಯ) The share of the crop paid to village servants.

Áyapásaké, Karn. (ಆಯಪಾಸಕೇ) Fees in kind paid to the village servants.

Áyati, or *Áyoti*, (?) Karn. An officer in towns in the Dakhin, whose duty it is to examine, adjust, and mark the weights and measures, charging a fee for so doing.

Áyatturai, Tam. (ஆயத்துறை) A custom-house, a place where tolls and taxes are collected.

Áyavyáya, H. S. (आयव्याय) Income and expenditure, receipts and disbursements, profit and loss.

ÁYA, or ÁYYA, (from S. आर्य, respectable) A common adjunct in the south of India to the names of Brahmans or spiritual guides, especially to the religious teachers of the Lingayits.

ÁYAṆ, Tam. Mal. (ஆயன்) A shepherd.

Áyarpáḍi, Tam. (ஆயர்பாடி) A village of shepherds.

ÁYAṆ, Tam. (ஆயன்) A general term for the revenue collected on six kinds of produce. See *Áin*.

ÂYÁN-I-MAZMUN, A. (عيان مضمون) Things lent or pledged, to be restored, when redeemed, in the same condition as when deposited.

AYIN, or AYEEN, H., but current in most dialects, See *Áïn*, Rule, statute, ordinance.

ÁYATNIRGAT, Mar. (from H. *áyá* ایا, what has come, and S. *nirgata* निर्गत:, what is gone out) Customs levied on imports and exports.

AZÁD, H. (P. ازاد) Free, liberated. A Mohammedan devotee who shaves his beard and eyelashes, and takes a vow of continence, but considers himself exempt from the usual observances of religion.

AZAN, H. (A. اذان) The cry or summons to prayer.

AZHI, or AZHIVA, also written ÁṞI, Mal. (?) Expense, the expense of improving and cultivating land.

Azhi-kuzhi-kánam, Tam. (ஆழிக்குழிக்காணம்) A kind of mortgage, in Malabar, in which the proprietor transfers the lands to the mortgagee on condition of his bringing them into cultivation or improving them, engaging to reimburse him all expenses incurred for that purpose when the mortgage is redeemed.

ÁZHIYA-PADAM, ÁḺIYA-PÁDAM, Mal. Tam. (from *ázham* or *álam*, depth, and *pádam*, place, ஆழியப்பதம், അഴിയപാടം) Land in a low situation, capable of irrigation, and especially favourable for rice cultivation.

AZMAÏSH, H. (P. ازمایش, literally, trial, examination) Estimate of the crop while standing made by the subordinate revenue officer. Re-measurement or repetition of survey. Among the Maraṭhas, an anticipatory statement or estimate of the receipts, expenses, and nett balance of a district made up at the beginning of the revenue year.

Azmaïsh gomashta, H. A revenue officer, one who computes the crop. A native surveyor, a measurer. Also *Azmaïsh mutasaddi*.

AZUBAG, (?) Abstract of an account (Ganjam). MSS.

B

Báb, corruptly, Baub, H. (A. باب), Bábu, Tel. Karn. (ಬಾಬು) A section, a chapter, a title, a head of accounts. A tax, a cess. See Abwáb.

Báb-wár, H. (بابوار) Arranged, classified, as fields or items of account; whence *Báb-wári*, classification.

Báb-yáft, H. (P. يافت, found) Classified, entered under its proper head.

Bábá H. (Turkish, بابا) A father, but addressed as a term of kindness to young as well as to old persons.

Bábat, Babut, corruptly, Baubut, H., but used in most dialects, (A. بابت) Account, statement. Head of an account. Article or item of an account. Matter, business affair; also adverbially in some places, as in *Puraniya*, to signify, from the account of, or by the relinquishment of.

Bábatán, (P. plur. of بابت) Sundries, miscellaneous items of an account.

Bábat-wár, H. (بابت وار) According to entry, agreeably to the particulars of any account or statement.

Bábat-wári, H. (بابت واري, बाबतवारी) Any thing which is registered or entered in a general statement or account, as lands belonging to a village not actually cultivated, but entered in the village accounts, or as land held by a tenant at a registered rate. In *Puraniya* the term is applied to lands which have fallen into the renter's hands when taken up by another Ryot, and held at rates fixed by the renter.

Babat-wári jámâ, H. (A. جمع) The revenue of an estate according to a registered amount.

Babat-wári zamín, H. (P. زمين) Lands registered in the statements of a village or Zamíndári. In *Puraniya* this and the preceding are also applied to two columns in the general account shewing the quantity of land which had been relinquished, retaken, and the rent derived from them.

Bábat-yáft, H. (P. يافت, what has found entry) The particular items of any charge, applied especially to a statement of fees and perquisites under the government of the Nawab of Bengal. The fees and perquisites so registered.

Bábatí, corruptly, *Babtí*, *Babtee*, or *Baubtee*, Mar. (बाबती, that which is according to the *bábat*, or account) The shares of the public revenue, especially those arising from the *Chauth*, which were appropriated to the chief officers of the Maratha State. H. (بابتي) Any cess or item of revenue, particularly when imposed in addition to the ordinary revenue.

Babbaliyá, Babbuliya, Beng. (বব্লিয়া) A hanger-on about courts of law, ready to give false testimony, or to bring false and malicious charges against a person for hire.

Babu, Baboo, Beng., &c. (বাবু, S. बाबू) A title of respect attached to a name, as "Mr.," or "Esq." In Bengal it has lost something of its respectability, and is commonly given to natives who manage the pecuniary concerns of the English, and to native clerks who write English. In Gorakhpur, it is applied to any man of family or influence. In Benares it was formerly assigned to younger brothers or near relatives of a Raja. In Beng. Reg. viii. of 1795 Baboos are defined "persons of the blood and family of the Raja of Benares." *Bábu*, in Karn. (ಬಾಬು) is a synonym of "father."

Babúl, Bubool, also Babúr, Buboor, H. (ببول) The name of a tree (Acacia arabica), the wood of which is much used in making agricultural implements; the bark is employed in tanning leather, and, in the north-west, in the manufacture of a spirituous liquor.

Bach, Buch, H. (بچ, बच) An inferior tribe of Rájputs in the district of Jonpur.

Bach-goti, Buch-gotee, H. (بچگوتي, बचगोती) A tribe of Rájputs, said to be a branch of the great family of Chauhans, chiefly settled on the borders of Jonpur, Gorakhpur, and Oudh.

Bách'h, Baach, Batch, and, corruptly, Buch, H. (باچھ, बाछ, lit., selection, from S. वाञ्छा, wish, desire) The proportionate rate or division either of lands or liabilities attached to them. The apportionment of a village or estate, or of the produce in separate portions among associated or coparceny occupants, especially in the case of mixed *Paṭṭidari* tenures: where part is held in common, and part in severalty, the Government rent and village expenses are paid from the land held in common, and any overplus is distributed, or any deficit made good, by a *bách'h*, or rate levied on the several holdings. The rate is sometimes levied according to the number of ploughs employed by the cultivators. In some parts of India the term implies, a share of the village lands, which consists, in general, of as much as may be ploughed with one plough.

Bách'h-barár, H. (باچھ برار) A tenure, common in *Bundelkhand*, in which the shares of the revenue payable by the joint proprietors of a village are liable to occasional re-adjustment and alteration; also, *Bhej-barár*, q. v.

Bad-bách'h, Bud-bach'h, H. (P. بد *bad*) A fraudulent division or apportionment of the assessment.

Bach'hontá, Buch'honta, H. (بچهونٹا, S. बछौंटा) Distribution of an aggregate sum among several individuals (Upper Doab).

BÁCHHAL, BÁCHHUL, H. (باچھل, बाछल) A tribe of Rájputs who claim a descent from the Lunar race, formerly Zamindárs of Farida and Shah-jehan-pur, now settled in Aligerh, and in different parts of Badaon, Mathurá, and Shah-jehan-pur.

BÁCHṚÁ, (বাচড়া) Land formerly cultivated, but now neglected.

BÁD, H. (P. باد) Remission of revenue on account of deficient crops. (North-West provinces. Mr. Elliot derives the term from the P. *Bád*, which, in the *Burhán-i-káṭi*, has, for one meaning, *Ná-bud* (نابود), not existing).

BÁD, corruptly, BUDH, Mar. (बाद) Deducted. Excluded from a number, a list, or collection.

BADA, Karn. (ಬದ) A ridge.

Gaddebada, Karn. (ಗದ್ದೆಬದ) A ridge between rice-beds.

BAḌAGALEYAVARU, Karn. (ಬಡಗಲೆಯವರು, from ಬಡಗ, north) Brahmans, followers of Vishṇu, wearing a mark of three perpendicular lines. (Mysore).

BADAGE, (?) A tribe of slaves in Kurg.

BAḌAGI, or BAḌIGA, Karn. (ಬಡಗಿ, ಬಡಿಗ) A carpenter. A man who supplies travellers with water.

BADAHAND, H. P. (3d pers. plur. imp. of the Persian verb *dádan*, to give; بدهند, lit., let them give) A superscription of assent by the Emperor on a petition for an assignment of revenue.

BADAL, BUDUL, or BUDL, H. (A. بدل, बदल), Tel. Karn. BADALU, BADULU, (ಬದಲು, ಬದುಲು) Exchange, substistution, equivalent. Change of money. Pledge, loan. Rejoinder.

Badalá, or *Badali*, or *Badlá*, *Badli*, or *Budla*, *Budlee*, H., and in other dialects, (بدلي, बदला, बदली) A substitute, a person or thing taken in representation or exchange of some other person or thing.

Badal-musháhara, less correctly, *Budul-mooshara*, H. (A. مشاهره) Stipend given in money or kind to public or private servants.

BADAR-NAWÍSI, H. (P. بدر, lit., to the door, نويسي, writing) Writing off items of an account which are objectionable or excessive. Audit of an account.

BÁDÁR, Hindi (बादार) A large house-granary raised on piles, *Puraniya*.

BAḌAVÁ-HṚITA, S. (बडवा, lit., a mare, a female slave, हृत, taken) One of the fifteen kinds of slaves. In Hindu law, A man who becomes a slave that he may marry a female slave in the family.

BÁḌAVA-POLAMU, Tel. (బాడవపొలము) Low, swampy ground, a bog, a marsh.

BAḌḌI, Karn. (ಬಡ್ಡಿ, S. वृद्धि) Interest of money.

Baḍḍigantu, Karn. (ಬಡ್ಡಿಗಂಟು) Interest and principal.

Múrbaḍḍi, Karn. (ಮೂರ್ಬಡ್ಡಿ) Compound interest.

BADEGACHI, Tam. (?) A low caste in Travancore, but superior to the Pariahs.

BÁDH, H. (बाध) A lesser division of an estate. A plain, a desert.

BADHA, S. (बधः) Killing, slaughter; also, striking, wounding. In law, Corporal punishment, which may be of three kinds: 1. *Tárana*, Beating, caning, flogging; 2. *Chheddana*, Cutting, mutilation; 3. *Múraṇa*, Putting to death: the second is abolished by the British Government.

Badhak, Budhuk, corruptly, *Badhik, Budduck, Buddich*, H. (بدهك, बधक, from the S. बध) A killer, a murderer. A robber of a particular tribe associated with Thugs, and, like them, murdering those they rob, residing chiefly on the borders of Oudh, but carrying on their depredations usually at a distance.

Badhya, S. (बध्य) One who ought to be punished or put to death; fit for, or deserving death.

BADHÁWÁ, Hindi (बधावा) Presents to a woman after lying in.

BAḌHIA, BUḌHIÁ, H. (بڈهيا) A disease affecting *Jawar*, *Bájrá*, Indian corn, and sugar-cane, which prevents the head from shooting.

BÁDHYA, Karn. (ಬಾಧ್ಯ) Relationship. An obligatory duty. A right or claim of possessson.

Bádhyanu, Bádhyasta, Karn. (ಬಾಧ್ಯನು, ಬಾಧ್ಯಸ್ತ) An heir.

BÁDÍ, more correctly, VÁDI, S., but adopted in most dialects, (वादी, from *Báda* or *Váda*, a dispute, a discourse) A plaintiff, a complainant, a suitor. An advocate, one who states a plaint, whether for himself or another.

Pratibádí, or *Prativádí*, S. &c. (प्रतिवादी) Defendant, respondent. Opponent or replicant.

BÁDI-CHOR, H. (بادي چور) A determined thief.

BADI, BUDEE, H. (بدي, S. बदी) The dark fortnight, that of the moon's wane from full to new moon.

BÁDIGA, Tel. (బాడిగ), BÁDIGE, Karn. (ಬಾಡಿಗೆ) Rent, hire, quit-rent, or a low rent on lands granted in *Inam*.

BÁDIGE, or BÁDIGI, Karn. (ಬಾಡಿಗೆ) A carpenter.

BADI-KAṬṬU, Tel. (బడికట్టు) Ascertainment, measurement.

Badi-váradi, Tel. (బడివారడి) Classification of land as of first, second, or third class, &c. Collections of contributions for extra expenses of the village rated on each *Káti* of the village lands.

BAḌIYA, or BAṚIYÁ BHÚM, Hindi (बड़िया भूम) A rich and fat soil. *Puraníya*.

BAD-MÂASH, BUD-MÂASH, H. (P. *bad* بد, bad, and A. معش, means of living) A disreputable person, one following evil courses.

BAD-NÁMI, BUD-NAMI, H. (بدنامي, from بد, bad, and نام, *nám*, a name) Disrepute, ignominy; but in *Tel.*, corrupted to *Bad-lámi*, it implies, also, responsibility.

BADNI, BUDNEE, H. (بدني) A contract by which a borrower gives a bond at high interest, in satisfaction of which he assigns his crops at a rate below the market value (from بدنا, *badná*, to wager, to agree).

BADRAKA, or BADRIKA, BUDRAKA, BUDRIKA, H., also occurring in other dialects, and read BADARAKA, and BADARKE, also, corruptly, BADRUCKA, (A. بدرقة) A guide, a guard, an escort. Safe conduct. Also a charge for convoy formerly levied on merchandise at the rate of 1 per cent., as the expense of keeping the highways and rivers safe from robbers.

Badraká-hisáb, H. (A. حساب, an account) An account sent with a guard of goods or treasure under its charge. An invoice; also, transit duty.

BÁDSHÁH, H. (P. بادشاه) A king, a sovereign.

Bádsháhí, *Badshahee*, H. (P. بادشاهي, royal, from بادشاه, king) As applied to tenures, it denotes land, &c. held under a royal grant, or, in the language of the Regulations, a *Bádsháhee* grant extended to all grants made by the ruling authority for the time being, and comprehended royal grants properly so termed, grants by the Subáhdar of Oudh, and by the British Government. Ben. Reg. xiii., 1795.

Bádsháhí Sanad, corruptly, *Sunnud*, H. (A. سند, a grant) A royal grant, a written document conveying lands or titles from the ruling power.

BÁDU, Tel. (బాడు) Fees in grain paid to the village servants before the division of the crop.

BÁ-FARZANDÁN, or -FURZUNDAN, less correctly, BÁ-FARZAND, vernacularly, BÁ-FARJAND, H. (from the P. با, with, فرزند, offspring, in the plur. 'with children') A term inserted in a grant which is made to the grantee and his posterity; also, BÁ-AULÁD (با اولاد), having the same meaning. It has been ruled that both apply to heirs and descendants generally, although, in strictness, they denote only the children of the grantee, or his heirs, in a direct line of descent.

BAFT, H. (P. بافت, from بافتن, to weave) Weaving, web.

Báfta, H. (P. بافته) Woven. A kind of cotton cloth.

Báf, H. (P. باف) Weaver, woven, used chiefly in composition; as, *Zar-báf*, (from زر, gold) Gold-tissue, cloth of gold. A gold lace or brocade weaver.

BÁG, Beng. Uriya, Mar. (বাগ, बाग) A garden; more correctly, BÁGH, q. v., but in the dialects noted, and perhaps in others, both in this word and its derivatives the unaspirated Sanscrit *g* is substituted for the Arabic final.

BAGALYA, corruptly, BAGLAH, Mar. (बगल्या) An assistant, a mate; sometimes applied to the *Chaughala* of a village.

BÁGANDEN, or BÁGHI, Tam. (?) The caste of Palankin-bearers. *Tinnevelly*.

BÁGAR, BAGUR, H. (باگر) A hedge of thorns or twigs (*Malwa*).

BAGÁR, BUGAR, H. (بگار) Pasture-ground (*Bundelkhand*).

BAGÁṚ, Mar. (बगाड) Swinging from a pole with iron hooks fastened to the back. See *Charkh*.

BAGARI, BUGUREE, H. (بگري) A species of rice cultivated chiefly in the province of Benares.

BAGARIA, Thug. A class of Thugs who reside chiefly in the Gwalior country.

BÁGDI, or BHÁGDI, (?) A low and servile caste of Hindus following unclean and out-of-door avocations. *Bengal* and *Cuttack*.

BÁGH, dialectically, BÁG, corruptly, BAUGH, H. (P. باغ, plur. BÁGHÁT बाग, बाघ) A garden, an orchard, a plantation.

Bágháyat, *Bágáyat*, *Bagaït*, *Bágáyati*, corruptly, *Bagáhat*, *Baugáyut*, *Baughayhir*, H. (P. باغايت, from the plur. of *Bágh* or *Bághát*) Mar. (बागाईत), Karn. (ಬಾಗಾಯತಿ) Land which, being well supplied with water, and adapted to the cultivation of various useful and edible vegetable substances, is appropriated to their growth, or to that of betel, hemp, sugar-cane, plantains, saffron, ginger, pepper, tobacco, onions, garlic, chilis, and other vegetables; also to that of fruit-trees, and the areka, cocoa-nut, and other palms. It is assessed at a higher rate than arable lands, according to the value of the produce. In Birbhum the term was formerly applied also to garden lands held free of revenue.—Parl. Papers, 1813, p. 293.

Bágháyati, *Bághaiti*, or *Bágaíti*, corruptly, *Baggaite*, &c., H. (باغايتي), Mar. (बागाईति) Fit for, or relating to, garden cultivation (land, &c.). Having much garden ground (a town or village). Raised on garden ground (fruit, &c.). Assessed or levied on gardens (revenue, tax).

Bágáyat-kachéri, Karn. (ಕಚೇರಿ, from H. كچهري, an office) Department or office in Mysore for the superintendence of the revenue levied on garden cultivation in the time of the Mohammedan Government.

Bágáyat-jásti-biráḍ, Karn. (ಜಾಸ್ತಿ ಬಿರಾಡ) An extra cess charged on garden cultivation in Mysore.

Bághícha, *Bágícha*, *Bageechu*, H. &c., (باغيچه) A garden, a little garden.

Bágbagíchá, Mar. (बागबगीचा) Gardens; comprehensively, orchards, plantations, cocoa-nut or areka groves, &c.

Bághbán, *Bághwán*, or *Bágwan*, H. &c. (باغبان, बागवान) A gardener, one who cultivates garden produce; also, in the west of India, a vender of vegetables, fruits, and flowers.

Bagh-kárí, H. (P. كاري) Garden cultivation, the business of a gardener.

BÁGH, H. (باگه, S. व्याघ्रः) A tiger.

Bágh-márí-ináám, H. (from S. मारण, killing, and A. انعام, a gift) A grant of land made to one who kills tigers.

BAGHEL, BUGHEL, H. (بگهيل) A branch of the *Sisodhiya* Rájputs of Guzarat, who migrated to the East, and gave their name to *Baghel-khanḍ*, or *Rewa*, the Raja of which is a *Baghel*. Subdivisions of the tribe, under different denominations, are extensively spread through the Company's provinces of Bundelkhand, Allahabad, Benares, Gorakhpur, Kanpúr, and Farakhábád.

BAGHI, BUGHEE, H. (A. بغي) Tyranny, oppression. Insurrection, rebellion, turbulence, infraction of the laws.

Bághi, H. (A. باغي, plur. *Baghát* بغات, or, with a Pers. plur., *Bághián* باغيان) An insurgent, a robber, a rebel, one who disobeys the *Imam*, or civil and religious head of the State.

Bagháwat, H. (A. بغاوت) Insurrection, rebellion, opposition to, and defection from, the rightful *Imam*. Violence, plunder, breach of law.

BAGINI, Karn. (ಬಗಿನಿ) A species of palm from which *Táṛi* is extracted.

BÁGRI, H. (باگري) Name of a tribe inhabiting the district of *Bágar*, between the south-west borders of Hariana and the Setlej. They seem to have been originally *Rájputs*, but are now looked upon as a branch of the *Játs*. The term is also applied to other tribes, and there is one tribe of *Bágri Brahmans*. *Bágar* is also the name of a tract on the south-west of Malwa; and *Bágri* denotes a native of the province. *Bágris* are also described as Hindus of the lowest caste, robbers by profession, who came from the west of India, and settled in considerable numbers in the eastern parts of Malwa.—*Malcolm, Central India*. *Tod* considers them as one of the aboriginal races.

BAGSARIA, BUGSUREA, H. (بگسريا) Name of a small clan of Rájputs in the Moradábád district; also of a branch of *Kanauj* Brahmans.

BÁHÁ, H. (باها, S. वाह, प्रवाह) A water-course, usually an artificial one; but in the Delhi district applied to a natural one also.

BAHÁ, BUHÁ, H. (P. بها) Price, cost, value.

Bahá-i-khilát, H. (A. خلعت, a dress of honour) A cess or tax added at so much per cent. to the ordinary revenue to defray the cost of complimentary dresses or robes of honour granted by the Mohammedan rulers or governors to persons whom they thought proper so to distinguish.

Bahá-i-kághaz, H. (كاغذ, paper) Price or expense of office paper.

BÁHÁCHINA, Uriya, (ବାହାଚିନ) A fee or cess levied by a Zamindar on his tenants on occasion of a marriage.

BA-HÁL, BU-HÁL, H. (بحال, from the P. *ba* به, according to, and A. *hál* حال, condition) Re-instated, re-established, restored to, or replaced in, a former condition, restored to a situation or appointment. (It occurs in different dialects, as in Tel., *Bahálu* (బహాలు), &c.

Ba-háli-sanad, H. (بحالي سند) A grant restoring to a person possessions or privileges of which he had been deprived, or confirming him in their enjoyment.

BÁHAN, BAHUN, H. (باهن, बाहन, from *báhná*, to plough) Fallow land, land ready for sowing. Ploughing (Hariana). Land that has been ploughed and left unsown (*Khetharm*).

BAHANGI, corruptly, BANGY, H. (بهنگي, बहंगी) A pole with slings at either end supporting portable boxes or baskets for baggage, carried over one shoulder.

Bahangi-bardár, H. (P. بردار, who bears) A bangy, or baggage-bearer or porter.

BAHÁṚ, Mar. (बहाड) Ground liable to be overflowed. The tide. A salt marsh or meadow.

BÁHARA, BAHURA, H. (باهره) A man who stands by the mouth of a well to turn over the bucket when drawn up. Dehli.

BÁHAR, or BÁHIR-BHÚM, or -BHOOM, H. (from S. *bahir* बहिर्, out, and भूमि, land) Lands lying beyond the village boundaries.

Báhar-, or *Bahir-vási*, corruptly, *Barwasee*, H. (from S. *bahir* बहिर्, out, and वासी, who abides) A Hindu of low caste and dirty avocations who is not permitted to dwell in a village or town.

BAHERIÁ, H. (بهيريا) A clan of Rájputs in Jonpur and Chunar.

BAHÍ, BUHEE, H. &c., (بهي, वही) An account-book, a journal, a diary, a ledger.

Bahí-khasra, H. (P. بهي كهسرا) A day-book.

Bahí-khátá, H. (بهي كهاتا) A day-book kept by merchants.

Bahí-mahájan, H. (S. महाजन) A merchant's or banker's book.

Bahí-patwári, H. (پٿواري) Register kept by the village accountant.

BAHÍN, Mar. (बहीण, S. भगिनी) A sister. A female cousin.

BAHIṚ, BUHEEṚ, H. (بهيڙ) A camp-follower of any kind. The baggage and incumbrances of an army: (not to be confounded with *Bhíṛ*, H. بهيڙ, a crowd).

BAHIRANGA-KÁGADA, Karn. (ಬಹಿರಂಗಕಾಗದ, from the S. *bahir* बहिर and *anga* अंग, body, and A. *kághaẓ* كاغذ, paper) A public advertisement, a public edict or proclamation.

BÁHIR CHÁLÁN, Beng. (বাহির চালান) An open pass or despatch. A summons issued by the Police Darogah to witnesses to attend the Court in a criminal case.

BAHIYÁR, H. (بهيار, from the S. बहिर्, out) Lands at a distance from the village. (Bhagalpur).

BAHLÍM, BUHLEEM, H. (بهليم) A tribe of Mohammedans in the neighbourhood of Dasna and Meerut: they assume the name of *Sheikh*, but have no right to it. The name is also applied to some divisions of the Rohilkhand Banjáras. In the *Thug* jargon the name denotes one of their seven original clans or gangs, scarcely any of whom are to be found north of the Nerbudda.

BAHONḌÁ, or BAHAUNḌÁ, Hindi, (बहोंडा, बहौंडा) Land given rent free to the village watchman, or Chaukidar.

BAHORÁ, BUHORÁ, H. (بهورا, बहोरा) A shopkeeper, or monied man in a village who makes advances to, or on account of, the cultivators. The word is a vernacular corruption of the S. *Byabahára*, or *Vyavahára*, business, or it may be a corruption of *Bohra*, q. v.

BAHORO, BUHORO, H. (بهورو) The sloping pathway for bullocks drawing water from a well, especially that by which they return to the well. (Central Doab, from *baharná*, to return, probably from the S. *bhrama*, to turn round).

BAHRA, Thug. Four travellers or victims in the hands of the gang.

BAHURÚPÍÁ, BUHROOPEEA, H. (بهروپيا, from S. *bahu* बहु, many, and *rúpa* रूप, form) A mime, an actor, a person assuming various characters and disguises.

BAHU, S. (बहु) Much, many. Large, great.

Bahúdaka, S. A mendicant who lives in a strange town, and begs his food from house to house. One class of the fourth order, or Bhikshu (from *bahu*, many, and *udaka*, water, drinking water from various sources).

Bahudhánya, S. &c., (from *Bahu*, much, and *dhánya* धान्य, corn) The 12th year of the cycle, supposed to be particularly fertile.

Bahuputra, or *-putraka*, S. (from बहु, many, and पुत्रः, a son) A man who has many sons.

BAHU, BUHOO, H. (بهو, from S. वधू) A wife, especially a son's wife.

BÁHU, H. and other dialects, (S. बाहु) The arm; also a measure of two cubits.

Báhu-band, Mar. (?) Association or joint interest in the property of a village, or the persons so associated, usually kinsmen of the *Patíl*.

Báhuband-mirási, Mar. (?) Occupancy of land in coparcenership, especially by members of the same family.

BAHULA, (S. of India) The dark fortnight. S., Much, many.

Bahulapádya, Karn. (ಬಹುಳಪಾಡ್ಯ) The first lunar day of the fortnight.

BÁI, BÁEE, corruptly, BYE, BHYE, Mar. (बाई) A lady, a mistress, a respectful adjunct to the name or address of a woman in general. H. Beng., (باي, বাই) A dancing girl, a prostitute.

BAIÂ, commonly, BAI, BYE, BAYA, BEEA, or BUYA, A. (بَيع) Sale.

Baê for *Baî-bát*, Uriya, (ବଏବାତ) Foreclosure of a mortgage.

Baî bil wafá, H. (A. بيع بالوفا, lit., sale with faith) In Mohammedan law, Conditional sale, sale depending for its completion on the consent of the seller. Also the nominal sale of an article, in lieu of a debt, to be returned when the debt is paid, or upon condition that the debt shall be paid by a given term, in default of which, the article becomes definitely the property of the purchaser. A contract of pawn or of usufruct.

Baí bil wafadár, H. (P. دار, who has) A person having the use of an article conditionally sold to him in acquittance of a debt.

Baí lá kalámi, A. (lit., sale without (*lá*, لا) words (كلام), Absolute sale.

Baî miâádi, H. (A. بيع ميعادي) Conditional or eventual sale.

Baî mukáṣa, also *Baï mukáyaẕa*, A. (بيع, and مقاصه, balancing accounts, or مقايضه, proposing an exchange) Sale or exchange of one article for another, sale of goods for goods, barter. Sale or transfer of property by a husband in liquidation of dower due to the wife.

Baî náma, H. A. (P. نامه, a document) A deed of sale.

Baî paṭṭá, H. &c., (پٿا, lease) A lease or sub-lease obtained by purchase.

Baî sulṭáni, H. (A. سلطان) Sale of lands or other property by order of Government.

Baî taljih, H. (A. تلجيع) A fictitious or temporary sale.

Báiâ, *Báyâ*, or *Báyî*, *Bayêe*, H. (A. بايع) A seller.

Baî dár, H. A. (بيع دار) A purchaser, a possessor by purchase.

Baîâná, or **Bayâna**, corruptly, **Baina**, or **Byna**, H. (A. بيعانا) **Bayáṇá**, Mar. बयाणा) Earnest money.

Bái, **Baee**, Thug. A frequented road.

Baiáli, **Byali**, Mar. (?) An indefinite land measure, $\frac{1}{8}$th of a *hún*,

Baid, **Baidya**, corruptly, **Bayd**, H. Beng. (from S. वैद्यः) A physician, a man of the medical caste.

Baigár, **Bygár**, H. (بيگار) A name of the *Kharwar* tribe.

Baiharia, Thug. A scout, a spy (used by the river Thugs).

Baikhat, H. (بيكهت) Sale. (East Oudh and Benares: it may perhaps be derived from the H. *bíkna*, to sell, rather than from the A. *baî* بيع).

Baikunth, corruptly, **Bykont**, **Bykontah**, H. (S. वैकुण्ठः) The heaven of Vishṇu. Pits in which, in the time of *Jaffir Khan*, revenue defaulters were confined until they paid the demands against them.

Bail, or **Beyl**, Thug. A spot chosen for burying those who have been strangled.

Bailha, Thug. The person who selects the spot where the murder is to be committed.

Bailhai, Thug. The office of selecting the spot where the crime is to be perpetrated

Bail, **Byl**, H. Beng. Mar. (بَيل, बैल, S. बलिवर्द्दः) A bullock.

Bail-begáṛi, Mar. (बैलबेगारी) Bullocks impressed for public service, or a tax in commutation.

Bail-dám, Mar. (बैलदाम) A duty or tax formerly levied on the sale of bullocks.

Bailu, Karn. (ಬೈಲು) A plain, an open field, especially such a field as is best fitted for rice cultivation, lying low, and having abundance of water. The first sort of rice-land, producing in general two crops of rice and one of dry grain or vegetables, or sometimes even three crops of rice in the year. It also means waste, uncultivated.

Bailuṣíme, Karn. (ಬೈಲುಶೀಮೆ) Open or champaign country, in opposition to hilly.

Bailukammár, Karn. (ಬೈಲುಕಂಮಾರ) A class of blacksmiths who work in the open air. Mysore.

Baimátra, or **Baimatreya**, Beng. (S. বৈমাত্র, বৈমাত্রেয) A brother by a different mother (also *Bai-* or *Vai-mátura*).

Bain, Beng. (বহিন, S. भगिनी) A sister.

Bainjhi, Beng. (বহিনঝি) A sister's daughter.

Bainpo, Beng. (বহিনপো) A sister's son.

Bainsi, **Bynsee**, H. (بَينسي) A subdivision of the *Gujar* tribe.

Baindí, H. (بينڐي, बैंडी) Throwing up water from a pond or reservoir with a basket for irrigation.

Baipitra, Beng. (বৈপিত্র, S. वैपित्रः) A brother by a different father.

Bairágí, **Byragee**, corruptly, **Bairaggie**, **Byraghee**, H. but occuring in most dialects, (بَيراگي, S. *Vairági* वैरागी, lit., one devoid of passion) A Hindu religious mendicant, most correctly, one attached to the worship of *Vishṇu*, but the term is indiscriminately applied to different classes of vagrants professing a religious life.

Bais, corruptly, **Bice**, **Byse**, or **Bhyce**, H. &c., (بَيس, S. वैस, S. *Vaiṣya* वैश्यः) The Hindu of the third order, whose especial duties are agriculture and trade.

Bais, **Beis**, H. (بَيس, बैस) A numerous tribe of Rájputs found in Oudh, in which they give name to the district. They are also numerous in the Company's territories in the north-west provinces of *Baiswára*. Their traditions are very remarkable. They refer their origin to *Munji-Paithan* in the Dakhin, and assert that the 360 clans into which they are said to be subdivided are the descendants of *Ṣálivâhana*, king of that city A. D. 78, giving name to the *Sáka* era, by as many of his wives. They are included amongst the thirty-six royal races, and may intermarry with *Chouháns, Kachwáhas,* and other eminent Rájput tribes. The branch of them named *Tilak-Chandra* (*i. e.* having the moon for their 'tilaka,' or frontal mark), residing at *Dundia-khera*, and their nearest of kin, hold themselves superior to the other divisions, and profess to give their daughters to none but the very purest races. There is reason to suspect that, in the Oudh territory at least, they practice female infanticide.

BAISAK, BYSUK, H. (بَیسك) A spot in a *Jangal* where cattle are sent to graze (Dehli). The term is also applied to old and worn out animals.

BAIṢÁKH, BYSAKH, corruptly, BESAK, and BEISAK, H. &c., (بَیساکھ, S. वैशाख:) The first month of the luni-solar year of the Hindus (April, May).

BAISHNAV, BYSHNAV, H. &c., in Beng. and Uriya pronounced BOISHNOB, (بیشنو, বৈষ্ণব, S. *vaishnava* वैष्णव:, from *Vishṇu* विष्णु:) Any Hindu professing the preferential worship of Vishṇu, of whom there are many sects. The term is commonly applied to vagrant mendicants bearing the marks and insignia of *Vishṇu*, and repeating hymns in honour of his *Avatárs*, especially *Ráma* and *Krishṇa*.

Baishnavottar, or *Boishnobottar*, most corruptly, *Bastomittur*, H. &c., (بیشنوتر, বৈষ্ণবোত্তর) Lands granted rent-free to the worshippers of *Vishṇu*, epecially of the mendicant orders.

BAIT, BYT, corruptly, BEIT, BIET, H. (A. بَیت) A residence in general, a place of abode, a house or office. In Mohammedan law, the simplest kind of residence, or any roofed chamber surrounded by walls, and having an entrance or door.

BAIT-UL-MÁL, H. (A. بَیت, place or office, ال مال *al-mál*, the treasure or revenue) The public treasury or exchequer, into which payments on various accounts are made, and, according to the sources whence they are derived, applicable to the support of different classes of persons. The principal sources are, 1. Duties on merchandise which, after paying the officers employed in the collection, should be applied to the support of the poor and destitute; 2. The fifth of the spoil taken in war, and the produce of mines and of treasure trove, to be applied to the support of orphans, paupers, and travellers; 3. The amount of the tax and tribute levied from unbelievers, from which the salaries of magistrates, the pay of teachers, students, and soldiers, and the expense of public works are to be defrayed; and 4. Property escheated, or for which there is no owner, and also the fines for manslaughter and murder, which is to be expended on the maintenance of the sick, the poor, and foundling children. The Sultan may take from the *Bait-ul-mál* the necessary expenses of the State, but not for his personal use. "The *Bait-ul-mál* is not the property of the ruling power, but that of all Mohammedans, for whose benefit it should be administered." The term is sometimes erroneously confounded with *Betan-mál*, q. v., and rendered an escheat, or the escheat and place of deposit are confounded. One or other has misled the Maráṭhas, as the term occurs in Mr. Elphinstone's Report, *Bait-ul-mál*, Escheats.—Sel. iv. 166.

BÁÏṬH, H. &c., (بائٹھ) Value of the Government share of the produce of land.

BAIṬHAK, BYṬHUK, H. (بیٹھك, S. बैठक) A place where people sit together, a solemn assembly, the customary public seat of a religious mendicant.

BAIṬHÁPAGÁR, Mar. (बैठापगार) Pay without exaction of service.

BAIṬHÁROJGÁR, Mar. (बैठारोजगार, from *baitha*, sitting, abiding, and the vernacular form of the Pers. *rozgár* روزگار, service) Service or occupation that does not require departure from home.

BAIYÁ, BYÁ, H. (بَیا) A person appointed in bazars to measure grain. (Lower Doab and Bundelkhand).

Baiyáï, H. (بَیاي) The perquisite of the Baiya, or fee for measuring grain.

BAIẒ, H. (A. بیض) A sort of cypher or monogram formerly affixed to a written paper in place of a signature by Mohammedan functionaries and persons of rank.

Baiẓána, H. (بیضانہ) Fee to a magistrate or public officer for affixing his cypher to a deed or document.

BÁJ, H. (P. باج) Tax, toll, tribute.

Bájgír, H. (P. باجگیر) A tax-gatherer, a collector of tribute or revenue.

BAJÁNI, Thug. A gun.

BÁJANTARI, BAJUNTUREE, also BÁJA-WÁLA, H. (from *bájá* باجا, a musical instrument, S. *vádya* वाद्य) A musician, a village musician.

Bájantarí-mahál, H. (باجنتري محال) A tax under the Mohammedan Government imposed upon all professional singers, dancers, and musicians.

BÁJÁR, Beng. Mar. (बाजार) Tel. Karn. BÁDZÁRU, (బాజారు) A market (vernacular corruption of the Pers. *bázár*).

Báje, Mar. Beng. Uriya, (**बाजे**), Tel. Karn., **Bájá**, or **Báji**, (ಬಾಜಾ, ಬಾಜಿ) Some, several, miscellaneous vernacular) corruption of *Bâzi*, q. v.

Báje-áráji, Uriya, (ବାଜେଆରାଜି) An estate or Taluk, the lands belonging to which are scattered over a number of villages.

Báje báb, or *bábu*, Karn. (ಬಾಜೆಬಾಬು) Miscellaneous items. Revenue derived from various small farms and licences in Mysore, but allowable in all Mohammedan States (vernacular for *bazi abwáb*).

Báje fasl, Uriya, (ବାଜେଫସଲ) Miscellaneous and extra crops, as sugar-cane, tobacco, wheat, &c.

Báje kharch, Mar. Ben. (**बाजे खर्च**), Tel. *Bájá kharchu*, (బాజాఖర్చు) Extra expenses, miscellaneous charges, such as are not included in the regular account. Miscellaneous expenses incurred by a village. See *Bâzi-kharch*.

Bajhá, H. (بجها, **बझा**) Marshy soil.

Bajhárat, H. (بجهارت.) Adjustment of accounts.

Bajhwaṭ, **Bujhwuṭ**, H. (بجهوت.) Stalk without ear. (East Oudh).

Bajíd, Thug. A term implying that the road is clear of danger, and that the victims may be murdered.

Bajidár, **Bujeedár**, H. (بجيدار.) An agricultural servant who is paid with grain, not money. (Rohilkhand).

Bájnamá, Hindi, (**बाजनामा**) A deed of surrender by a Ryot for lands which he gives up to a farmer of the revenue, acknowledging what he has done. *Puraniya*.

Bájpai, H. (باجپاي, corruption of S. *vájapeyí* **वाजपेयी**) A branch of the Kanauj Brahmans.

Bájra, **Bájri**, or **Bájrá**, H. &c., (باجره or باجري, **बाजरा**) A grain much cultivated throughout India, a species of Panic or millet (Panicum spicatum). *Bájri* properly denotes a smaller kind which ripens earlier. It is also applied to the stalk of either sort used as fodder.

Bajra, **Bujra**, H. &c., (بجره., S. **वज्र**) The thunderbolt.

Bajrághát, H. S. (lit., struck by a thunderbolt) Any sudden calamity, especially if considered a judgment.

Bajrá, H. (بجرا., Beng. **বজরা**) A large boat used in travelling, round bottomed, and without keel.

Báju, **Bájoo**, Karn. (ಬಾಜು) An open file of retainers preceding a man of rank.

Bák, H. (باك, from S. **वाक्**, a speech) An estimate of the crop without measuring the field.

Bákal, Karn. (ಬಾಕಲ) A low caste of labourers from Kánara.

Bákand, H. (باكند) Proportion of two-fifths of the crop which is sometimes paid by cultivators to Zemindars as rent.

Bakár, **Bukar**, H. (بكار) Value of a crop fixed by the appraiser.

Bakárá, **Bukara**, H. (بكارا) Intelligence by word of mouth.

Bakh, **Bukh**, Thug. The word used by the Thugs in calling to each other to assemble after having been dispersed by accident or design.

Bakhá, **Bukhá**, H. (بكها) Grass kept for pasturage (Rohilkhand).

Bakhaḷ, **Bukhuḷ**, Mar. (**बखळ**) An open or clear space in a town or village, one not built on or cultivated.

Bakhal, **Bukhul**, Mar. (**बखल**) Low ground. A bottom, a hollow.

Bakhár, **Bakhári**, **Bukhar**, **Bukharee**, H. (بكهار, بكهاري) A granary, a store-house.

Bakhar, **Bákhar**, **Bukhur**, **Bakhur**, also **Bákhal**, (بكهر, باكهل, باكهر, S. **बाखर**, **बाखल**) A house, an inclosure, dwellings within an inclosure. In Dehli, a cattle shed. In Bundelkhand and Malwa, a sort of cattle hoe, a rough sort of plough usually employed instead of the ordinary plough for first breaking up the black soil of those provinces.

Bakhar, **Bukhur**, Mar. (**बखर**) A history, a narrative, memoirs, &c.

Bakharí, Hindi, (**बखरी**) A round granary of grass, reeds, and mud, raised on piles. *Puraniya*.

Bakhéḍá, Karn. (ಬಖೇಡಾ) Loss by bad debts.

Bakheḍiyavanu, Karn. (ಬಖೆಡಿಯವನು) A bankrupt, an insolvent.

Bakhrá, H. (P. بخرا.) A share, a portion.

Bakhri, H. (بخري.) A sharer.

Bakhsh, **Bukhsh**, H. (بخش., from the Pers. *bakhshiden* بخشيدن., to give, to forgive) One who gives, a donor. Gift, donation. Pay. Pardon, forgiveness; used also in the composition of names, as *Khoda-bakhsh*, Gift of God—a proper name.

Bakhsh náma, H. (بخش نامه.) A deed of gift.

Bahshayimpu, Tel. (?) Pardon, forgiveness. (Ganjam).

Bakhshi, *Bukhshee*, corruptly, *Buxy*, *Buxey*, H. (بخشي.) A paymaster, an officer whose especial duty it was also to keep an account of all disbursements connected with military tenures, as those of *Mansabdars* and *Jagirdars*. Paymaster of the forces. Under the Mogul system, frequently one with the Commander-in Chief.

Bahshi, Karn. (ಬಕ್ಷಿ) A superior magistrate. A superintendant of revenue officers. Mysore.

Bakhshiát, H. (بخشيات) A pargana in the Jonpur Sirkár mentioned in Beng. Reg. ii. 1795. The term appears to have been originally restricted to villages assigned to provide funds for the *Bakhshi*, the paymaster or commandant of the province. It is now merged in later subdivisions.

Bakhshían-i-Áázem, corruptly, *Bakhsian Azam*, H. (A. and Pers., lit., the most eminent (اعظم) of commanders) A title given to four *Bakhshis* in immediate attendance on the Emperor. Assignment of a Jagír for the maintenance of the commanders of the forces in Bengal.

Bakhshish, H. (P. بخشش) Gift, donation, reward. Forgiveness. In the *Dakhin* the term was applied under the *Marátha* Government to land, especially garden land, held rent and tax free during the pleasure of the Government, although rarely resumed during the life-time of the occupant.

Bakhshish náma, H. P. A deed of gift.

BÁḲI, BAQEE, corruptly, BAKY, H. (A. باقي, from بقا, what is perpetuated or remains; plur. Pers. باقيات, Hindi, बाकी) Remaining, continual. *Subs.*, Remainder, balance, arrears, especially of revenue, in which sense the term is current in most parts of India. Also balance of an account.

Baḳáia, H. (بقايا, A. plur. of بقية *bakíya*, B. বকেয়া) Balance of revenue arrears. In Bengal, a tax levied before the permanent settlement to make up for deficiencies in the revenue payments.

Baḳáia-tauji, corruptly, *towjee*, H. (بقاياتوجيه) Account of arrears of revenue for any given period past.

Baḳáia-báki, H. (بقايا باقي, S. बकैया बाकी) Arrear on arrear, the arrears of the revenue of the preceding as well as of the current year.

Báḳi-dár, H. (P. دار, who has) A revenue defaulter, one who is in arrears.

Báḳi-jáï, H. (P. جاي, a place) An account shewing a deficit or balance of revenue.

Báḳi-jamâ, H. (A. جمع) Statement of revenue after deducting the balances of former years.

Báḳi-kaifiyat, corruptly, *Baḳy keffyet*, H. (A. P. باقي كيفيت) Statement or account of outstanding balances. Statement of surplus or improvement in any branch of the revenue. As formerly applied to the accounts of the salt lands of Bengal, the profit on the salt sales.

Báḳi khwáh, H. (from خواه, who requires) A landlord, or the Government in that capacity.

Báḳi lekha, Karn. (ಬಾಕಿಲೆಖ, from A. باقي, and S. लेख *lekha*, writing) Written statement of arrears.

Baḳi málguzári, H. (P. مالگذاري) Arrears of revenue.

Báki patrak sanwát, Mar. (?) An annual account of the balance due from each cultivator.

Báḳi-zamín, or *-jamín*, H. (P. زمين) The balance of the land revenue after deducting any deficit from the preceding year.

BAKIRU or BAKILU, BUKIROO, -LOO, Tel. (బకీరు) A statement, return, or report.

BAKKÁL, H. (A. بقال, Mar. बकाल) A grocer, a chandler, a grain merchant. A cloth dealer. A shopkeeper in general. In Mar. it is more usually *Bakálbáni* (बकालबाणी).

BAKOLI, BUKOLEE, H. (بكولي) A small caterpillar destructive of rice crops.

BAKOT, BUKOTE, Thug. The strangler, the person whose office it is to throw the noose or turban round the neck of the victim.

BAKR-ÎD, BUQR-EED, H. (A. بكر عيد) A festival observed by the Mohammedans on the 10th of the month *Zulhaja*—the feast of the ox—in commemoration of the offering of *Ishmaïl* (according to Mohammedan tradition) by *Abraham*. Sheep, oxen, and camels are sacrificed on this occasion. It is also termed the *Îd az-zoha*.

BÁKUL-ASWARI, Karn. (?) A tax levied upon each house in a village for the expense of peons sent to expedite the collection of the revenue by the Government of Mysore, consolidated by Tipu with the general collections.

BÁLA, and BÁLAKA, S. &c., (बाल, बालक) A child. In law, a minor, who is distinguished as, 1. *Kumára*, a boy under five years of age; 2. *Śiśu*, under eight; 3. *Poganda*, a boy from the 5th to the end of the 9th year; or, where the next distinction is omitted, till the 16th year; 4. *Kiśora*, a boy from the 10th to the 16th year: to the end of it is apparently the most correct limit, but some make it the commencement. (Each of these terms is used also in the general sense of a child, a boy, a youth). After the close of his minority the youth is termed *Vyavahárí*, or *Játa*, or *prápta-vyavahára*, one by whom affairs (*vyavahára*) may be conducted. Some authorities maintain that these epithets do not apply to him, and that he is not to be trusted with the management of his own interests till the end of his 20th year, although minority expires at the close of the 16th. The British Government has extended the completion of minority to the end of the 18th year.—Beng. Reg. xxvi. 1793.

Bálahatyá, S. (हत्या, killing) Infanticide. (Or with *Bálá*, fem. of *Bála*), Female infanticide.

Baḷgopál, Mar. (बाळगोपाळ) A collective term for all the people of a place as uniting in a petition to some great man, &c. Lit., boy-cowherd, in which sense *Bálagopála*, S. vern. *Bálgopál*, is universally current as a name of the juvenile *Krishṇa*.

Bálparweṣi, or *-parwaṛashi*, Mar. (बाळपरवेशी, -परवरशी, from P. پرورش, cherishing) A pension granted by the Government to the family of a soldier or servant who has died in its service.

Báḷsantosh, Mar. (बाळसंतोष्) A particular class of beggars, or an individual of it. They generally ask for clothes, crying out "*Báḷsantosh*," child-satisfaction.

Bálá, H. (بالا, बाला) A grub that eats young plants of wheat or barley when about six inches high.

Bala, S. (बल) Strength, force.

Balát-kára, vernacularly, *Balátkár*, S. &c., (بلاتکار, from बलात्, by force, and कार, doing) Violence, oppression. Any act of violence, as robbery, rape, &c. In Karnata and Malabar, Detention of the person of a debtor, and infliction by the creditor of personal punishment to compel payment.

Balátkár-nebar, Uriya, (ନେବାର, taking) Exaction, extortion.

Baladastí, or *-dustee*, corruptly, *Baladusty*, H, (بلدستي) Unauthorised or oppressive exactions.

Balbhog, H. (بلبهوگ) Taking forcible possession of another's right.

Bál, H. (بال) An ear of corn.

Balad, or Bald, Bulud, Buld, H. &c., (بلد, from S. बलीवर्द्द) A drove of cattle.

Baldana, H. (بلدانه) A tax on laden oxen.

Bal-dev, H. (بلديو, बलदेव) A cow-herd.

Baldiyá, H. (بلديا) A herdsman, a drover.

Baldihaï, H. (بلدهاي) Compensation for pasture ground, also termed *Bardaihi* to the eastward.

Baladur, (?) Averting an omen, waving a lamp to avert a spell or unlucky omen.

Bálágashti, also, in some dialects, Bálágastí, and, incorrectly, Bhálagashti, H. (بالاگشتي, from *Bálá*, above, and *gashtí*, walking about) A superintendant of watchmen, an inspector of police. A watchman, a patrol.

BA

Balagye-játi, Karn. (ಬಲಗೈಜಾತಿ) The right-hand castes.

Baláhar, Bulahur, also, Baládhar, incorrectly Bilahur, H. (بلاهر, बलाहर) A low-caste servant, a village guide or messenger, a village watchman, inferior to the ordinary Chaukidar: he is also employed as a sweeper.

Baláhi, H. (بلاهي) A man of low caste—a *Chamár*, or worker in hides and leather, sometimes employed to measure land.

Bálái, corruptly, Ballae, and Bullaee, H. (بالاي, from Pers. بالا, above (?)) Any extra cess or tax, especially such as were formerly levied by the Peshwa and Gaekwar at Cambay and Surat, of undetermined amount and varying application. Payment of revenue in kind, or a village where it is so paid.

Báláïyapht, Mar. (बाळाईयाफत, from P. يافت) Fees, perquisites.

Balaji, or Balajiváḍu, Tel. (బలిజ, బలిజవాడు) A caste, or individual of it, engaged in trade, a dealer, a shopkeeper, a merchant; sometimes occupied in agriculture, and usually of the Lingamite sect.

Bálám, Beng. (বালাম) An excellent sort of rice grown in Bengal, especially about *Bákharganj*.

Báland, H. (بالند) Name of a tribe who were expelled by the *Chandels* from the southern parts of Mirzapur, and settled at Manwai, where they formed a Ráj in subordination to the Raja of *Rewá*.

Baḷasu, Karn. (ಬಳಸು) Husbandry.

Baḷasiga, Karn. (ಬಳಸಿಗ) A husbandman, a cultivator.

Bálaṭ, Bálanṭ, or Báláṭ, Bálánṭ, Mar. (बाळट, बाळंट, बाळाट, बाळांट) A false charge, a calumnious accusation.

Balawa, Mar. (?) Tax on travellers in Kandesh to defray the expense of keeping up guards in dangerous places.

Bálband, Balbund, Mar. (बाळबंद) The alphabetical character peculiar to the Maráṭha language.

Bálbodh, Mar. (बाळबोध) The Devanágarí alphabet, also in common use among the Maráṭhas.

Baḷegár, Karn. (ಬಳೆಗಾರ) A maker of the *Bale*, or glass rings worn by women on the fore-arm.

Balesar, H. (बलेसर्) A sub-division of the Gujar tribe.

Báli, Bálí, Balee, Beng. (বালি, বালী) Sand (also, in this and other dialects, *Bálu*, q. v.).

Bali, Bulee, S., but adopted in most dialects, (बलि) Any offering to an idol, flowers and other articles for worship. Presentation of food to all created beings, that is, small quantities of grain, &c., thrown up into the air for that purpose. Animals offered in sacrifices, or the sacrifice of animals, as goats, &c., to Durgá; more correctly, *Bali-dán.*

Bali-akki, Karn. (from ಅಕ್ಕಿ, rice) Rice placed on a stone outside of a temple in Kanara, having been previously offered to the idol. Eating it by women separates them from their caste and families, and converts them into courtesans, not necessarily servants of the temple, but connected with it by occasional offerings.

Bali-dán, Mar. Beng. &c., (बलिदान, বলিদান, S. *Bali*, and दानं *dánam*, gift) Presentation of an offering to a deity. When presented by the worshippers of Vishṇu to any of his forms, the *Bali* usually consists of rice, milk, curds, fruits, and flowers; when offered to the terrific forms of *Ṣiva*, and more especially of *Durgá*, it consists of living victims, as sheep, goats, buffaloes, and the like, the heads of which, after decapitation in presence of the idol, are given to the priests, the carcases are carried away and eaten by low castes. Presentation of grain and the like to all creatures.

Balikallu, Karn. (ಬಲಿಕಲ್ಲು) A large stone slab outside of a temple on which rice offered to the idol is placed.

Bali-kul, or *-kool*, Karn. (?) The rice so placed. See *Bali-akki*.

BALICHATA, Tel. (?) An allowance of grain made to the persons who are employed to measure the crop.

BALIJEVÁRU, or BALJEVÁRU, Tel. (బలిజెవారు, బల్జెవారు) A numerous tribe of *Súdras* in Telingana (probably the same as the *Balajiváḍu*, q. v.).

BÁLIGH, BÁLIGHA, H. (A. بالغ, fem. بالغة) Adult, mature. Of years of legal maturity.

Bulúgh, H. (A. بلوغ) Maturity. Legal maturity, being of age.

BÁLISHT, H. (بالشت) A span from the tip of the thumb to that of the little finger both extended.

BAḶIVAḶI, Karn. (ಬಳಿವಳಿ) A wife's dowry.

BÁLKÁ, H. (from S. बालक, a boy) A young follower of a religious Hindu mendicant.

BALKAṬ, BULKUṬ, H. (بلكت) Rent taken in advance. (Lower Doab, Bundelkhand, and Benares) Cutting of ears of corn without regularly reaping (from *Bál*, an ear of corn, and *háṭná*, to cut).

Balkaṭi, H. (بلكتي) A tax formerly levied on the commencement of reaping.

BAḶḶA, BUḶḶA, Karn. (ಬಳ್ಳ) A measure of capacity, containing 48 double handfuls, or two *Sers*. A large land measure in Coimbatore, equal to 3.83 acres. Beng. (বল্ল) A weight of two *Ratis*.

BALLABA, Beng. (বল্লব) A cook. A cowherd.

BAḶḶÁLA, or VAḶḶÁLA, Karn. (ಬಳ್ಳಾಲ, or ವಳ್ಳಾಲ) The title of an officer under the Government of Bidnur who engaged to collect and pay the revenue of a village or district for certain fees or perquisites, and exercised the civil and criminal jurisdiction. He had no power to alter the assessment, or to interfere with the proprietary rights of the villagers. In many respects he corresponded to the Zamindar of Hindustán.

Balláyi, or *Balláí*, (?) (In central India) The village servant who is employed to preserve the village boundaries, also wood-cutter to the village.

BALRAKH, H. (?) A person put in charge of property under distraint for arrears of revenue.

BÁLRAKHÁ, H. (بالرکها) Wages of persons employed to watch ripe crops at night (from *bál*, an ear of corn, and *rakhná*, to protect.

BALSUNDAR, BULSOONDUR, H. (بلسندر) A kind of soil, clay much mixed with sand.

BÁLU, BALOO, H. &c., (بالو, बालु, from the S. बालुका) Sand.

Báluä, H. (بالوا, बालुआ) Sandy.

Bálubard, *Baloo-burd*, H. (from P. بردن, to bear, to take away) also, vernacularly, *Bálu-búrd* (बालुबूरद्), Arable land destroyed by a deposit of sand from inundation. An item of remission of revenue on this account.

Bálu-char, or *chur*, H. &c., (from *Bálu* and *Char* چر, a shoal, a bank) Land covered by a deposit of sand. A sand-bank formed by a deposit of sand from the waters of a river. The name of a village near Murshidabad, perhaps originally so formed from the river; whence *Báluchari*, a kind of silk manufactured at *Bálu-char*.

BALUCH, corruptly, BULOOTCH, or BULOTCH, (?) A bundle of corn, to which, in the northern Sirkars, the village artificers are entitled. A portion of corn paid at harvest-time as a moiety of their wages to the village peons by the peasantry. (Although repeated in the Glossary from the Fifth Report, and found there p. 681, the word is most probably a typographical error for *Bulooteh*, corrupt reading of *Balute*, or *Bulooté*, q. v.).

BALUTÁ BULOOTA, Mar. (बलुता) or, as the persons so named are usually spoken of collectively, plur., BALUTE, BULOOTE (बलुते), or, with BÁRÁ, twelve, prefixed, BÁRÁ-BALUTE (बाराबलुते), The twelve BALUTÁS, from their being twelve in number, or, according to some, from the amount set apart for them being divided into twelve parts. The word is also spelled **Balote**, **Balutyá**, and **Balotyá**, and is corruptly written in a variety of forms, as, **Bulootee**, **Balootee**, **Bullooteh**, **Ballutay**, **Bullotee**, **Bulowteh**, **Balowtay**, &c. A village officer or servant. The popular enumeration is twelve, but the whole number, by including three who may be regarded as the heads of the village, and the twelve inferior classes, or *Alute*, q. v., extends to twenty-seven. The actual number, however, varies in different parts of India, as do the respective appellations: there is less variety, although some, in the duties. According to *Molesworth* (Mar. Dict.), the twelve *Balutas* of the Maraṭha villages in which the system is preserved most entire, are, 1. The *Páṭíl* (पाटील), or Head-man; 2. *Kulkarṇí* (कुलकरणी), Accountant; 3. *Chaudhari* (चौधरी), Head of the trades; 4. *Potadár* (पोतदार), Assayer, money-changer, and silversmith; 5. *Deṣ-páṇḍyá* (देशपाण्ड्या), District accountant; 6. *Nhávi* (न्हावी) Barber; 7. *Paríṭ*, (परीट), Washerman; 8. *Gurav* (गुरव), Attendant on a temple; 9. *Sutár* (सुतार), Carpenter; 10. *Kumbhár* (कुंभार), Potter; 11. *Vésahar* (वेसकर), Gate-keeper, usually a *Mahár* by caste; and, 12. *Joṣi* (जोशी), Astrologer. Most enumerators, however, exclude the principal officers or administrators of the village affairs. Thus, *Grant Duff* specifies the village officers; the *Páṭíl*, the *Kulkarṇi*, and *Chaugala*, assistant or deputy of the *Páṭíl*, as distinct from the *Bárá Balute*, and *Bárá Alute*. For the latter, see the word *Alute*. The twelve village servants he terms, 1. The Carpenter; 2. Blacksmith; 3. Shoemaker; 4. *Mahár*, or watchman; 5. *Máng*, worker in leather; 6. Potter; 7. Barber; 8. Washerman; 9. *Gurav* or *Ṣúdra*, attendant on a temple; 10. The astrologer; 11. The *Bháṭ*, or bard; and, 12. The *Mauláná* or *Mulla*, or Mohammedan priest. In some places the *Balute* are fourteen, divided into three classes, severally denominated the *Thoralá-khás* (थोरलाखास), Elder or principal division; *Madhalá-khás* (मधलाखास) The middle; and *Dhákaṭá-khás* (धाकटाखास) Younger or inferior; the first comprising the Carpenter, Blacksmith, Shoemaker, and *Mahár*; the second, The Washerman, Potter, Barber, and *Máng*; and the third, The Goldsmith, *Mauláná*, *Gurav*, *Joṣi*, Waterman, and the *Rámúsi* or *Bhíl*. In the Kanara countries these village servants and officers are termed *Ayakárru*, or *Ayagárru*, or *Ayangáṇḍlu* (అయకార్రు, అయగార్రు, and అయంగాండ్లు), q. v., and are enumerated by Reeve as, 1. The *Gauḍa*, head-man; 2. *Ṣánabhóga* (శానభోగ), accountant; 3. *Joïsa* (జోయిస), astrologer; 4. *Pattárí* (పత్తారి); corn-measurer, or money-changer; 5. *Kammáranu* (కంమారను), blacksmith; 6. *Baḍiga* (బడిగ), carpenter; 7. *Kumbhára* (కుంబార), potter; 8. *Naïda* (నాయిద), barber; 9. *Agasa* (అగస), washerman; 10. *Bárika* (బారికి), One who affixes the public seal to public papers; 11. *Taḷawára* (తళవార), watchman; 12. *Níraganṭí* or *Koḷavára* (నీరగంటి, కొళవార), waterman; 13. *Konikárachakra* (కొనికారచక్ర), betel-nut gatherers. In the Telugu villages we have the 1. *Pedda kápu* (పెద్దకాపు), head-man; 2. *Karanam* (కరణము), accountant; 3. *Vaḍla-vaḍu* (వడ్లవాడు), carpenter; 4. *Kammari* (కమ్మరి), smith; 5. *Kummari* (కుమ్మరి), potter; 6. *Chákáli*, (చాకలి), washerman; 7. *Mangali* (మంగలి), barber; 8. *Madiga-váḍu* (మదిగవాడు), A *Chandála*, and *Vetti-váḍu* (వెట్టివాడు), a sweeper. In Guzerat, the *Desaï* and *Majmudár*, properly district officers, sometimes exercise the functions of *Pátél*; at other times, the *Pátél* is the head-man of the village, under whom are the *Taláti*, accountant; *Sutár*, carpenter; *Lohár*, ironsmith; *Kumbhár*, potter; *Ḍarji* or *Suï*, tailor; *Dhobi*, washerman; *Hajám*, barber; *Mochi*, shoemaker; *Khálpá*, leather-dresser; *Bhangi*, sweeper; *Dheṛ*, watchman; *Kosia*, water-drawer; *Sonar*, goldsmith; *Bhát* or *Bhárat*, bard; besides the *Akhun*, Mohammedan teacher; *Baid*, Hindu doctor; *Joṣi*, astrologer; Gosains, Fakirs, &c. In the Dehli district they are known collectively as the *Kamín* (کمین), the inferiors of the village, and are, the *Lohár*, smith; *Barhaï*, carpenter; *Kumhár*, potter; *Dhobí*, washerman; *Náï*, barber; *Kahár*, bearer; *Sagga*, water-carrier; *Darzi*, tailor; *Dóm*, musician; *Dhúniya*, cotton-stuffer; *Chipi*, cloth-stamper; *Rangrezi*, dyer; *Brahman*; *Balahar*, or *Dhanuk*, messenger; *Khákrob*, sweeper; *Dauráha*, guide, intelligencer; and *Chamár*, shoemaker. In Bengal, and those parts of Hindustan where the village organization has been greatly disturbed by the long period of Mohammedan rule, the establishment of village officers and servants is less complete, but the head-man and accountant are almost universally retained, and more or fewer of the rest are to be found. In most instances the offices are hereditary, are capable of being mortgaged or sold, and are paid by recognised fees and perquisites, by allotments of corn at the time of harvest or sometimes, by small portions of land held rent-free, or at a low quit-rent. The following is a further specification of their synonymes and functions:

1. Mar. *Páṭíl*, Guz. *Páṭel*, H. A. *Mukaddam*, *Kadím*, H. *Chaudhari*, *Mahto*, *Mahájan*, *Thákur*, *Jethráyat*, Ben. *Mandal*, S. *Grámádhipati*, *Pradhán*, Tam. *Grámáttan*, *Ambalagár*, *Ijamán* (S. *Yajamána*), *Máṇiya káraṇ*, *Monigar*, *Pravarttika*, Karn. *Gauḍa*, Mal. *Náttár*, *Náttári-káre*, Tel. *Naidu*, *Náyadu*, *Pedda-kápu*, *Pedda-kár* or *Pedda Reddi*, *Reddi-váḍu*. (These, and the synonymous appellations of the other village servants, are not always exclusively applied to them, and many are so applicable only in virtue of their general purport; as, S. *Pradhána*, vern. *Padhán*, the principal; A. *Muhaddam*, one who precedes or takes the lead, or *Kadím*, elder, senior; Tam. *Ijámán*, lit., the institutor of an act of worship; and Tel. *Pedda-kápu*, the old or chief man, &c.).

The head-man, the *Páṭíl* (Mar.), or *Páṭél*, (of other dialects), has the general controul of the affairs of the village, usually assisted by a sort of village council of the most respectable of the community, but not exclusively, as any discussions that may occur are mostly held in an open space in the village, where all have access, and do not hesitate to give their opinions. With their concurrence, the head-man superintends the cultivation, apportions the assessment, collects the revenue, either in money or kind, and pays it to the Government district-collector, regulates the village expenses, distributes the quotas for defraying them, and collects the money and pays the charges. He examines and checks the accounts. In some places, especially in the south, he has charge of the police, and is entrusted with limited magisterial powers. — Madras Reg. xi. 1816, Bomb. Reg. xii. 1827, sec. vi. xlix. And as village Munsiffs, the heads of villages are also entrusted with powers to decide civil causes of small value.—Madras Reg. iv. 1816. The *Páṭél* also usually settles petty disputes in the village either by his own authority or through the agency of a Panchayat, or court of arbitration. He is the chief organ of Government in its dealings with the village. In some places the office is hereditary; in others the head-man is appointed by the Zamindar, or contractor for the revenue; in others he is elected by the villages. In some villages, especially those held by coparcenary tenure, their affairs are usually managed by several of the principal inhabitants, not by one head-man; and even where such a functionary is recognised, there are sometimes more than one individual regarded in the same light, in which case the eldest, or more respectable of the number, takes the lead in transacting public business. Such a head-man is distinguished among the Marathas by the Hindustani or Arabic term *Muhaddim*: his fellows retain the national term of *Páṭíl*. Where the office is hereditary, as it commonly is among the Marathas, its fees, perquisites, and privileges may be pledged for a loan, or may be sold. The office of *Páṭíl* is regarded as extremely respectable, and Hindus of the highest rank have not disdained the title. *Daulut Rao Sindhia* particularly affected the title of *Páṭíl*, and in some villages of the Dakhin exercised the office by deputy, and claimed the perquisites and rights; and *Bhairi Sál*, the first noble of the Court of Jaypur, boasted of the title of hereditary *Páṭíl* of the principality. In Maratha villages the *Páṭíl* is commonly assisted by a deputy, the *Chaughalá* (चौघला), who, on his part, or in his absence, conducts the affairs of the community. He is not known elsewhere by any specific designation.

Mar. *Kulkarṇi*, *Bhoï*, H. A. *Kanun-go*, H. *Patwári*, S. *Gráma-harana*, or *Káyastha*, Tam. *Kanakapilli*, B. *Kayeth*, *Moharir*, Karn. *Ṣánabhoga*, Tel. *Karanam* or *Karnam*, Guz. *Taláti*, *Rígal*, Mal. *Menava*, *Menon*. The accountant's business is to keep accurate accounts of the lands of the village, their extent, quality, produce, and proprietary distribution, whether held singly or in common, of changes of possession or property of the lands, of the village expenses, and assessment and payment of the revenue. He acts as clerk and notary, and often as the scribe, or letter-writer and accountant of the villagers.

The village servants, properly so called, are,

1. S. *Sútradhára* or *Varddhaki*, Mar. Guz. H. *Sutár*, H. *Barháï*, Karn. *Badige*, Tel. *Vardhaki*, *Vaḍla-váḍu*. The carpenter and wheelwright, who makes and repairs all the wood-work and agricultural implements of the villagers.

2. S. *Lohakára*, H. Mar. Guz. Beng. *Lohár*, Karn. *Kammár* (S. *Karmakára*), Tam. *Karumári*, Tel. *Kammari*, blacksmith or ironsmith, who makes and repairs all iron-work for the village.

3. S. *Charmakára*, H. Beng. *Chamár*, Mar. *Chámhár*, Tam. *Chakkili* or *Shakkili*, Tel. *Cheppulu-kutta-váḍu*, H. Beng. Guz. *Mochi*, Guz. *Khálpá*. A man of

low caste, who works in hides and leather, and makes the leather bags for drawing water, and any other leather article for public use. He makes shoes, whips, thongs, &c., for the villagers, but for hire when for individual use. He also dresses and tans skins, and sometimes skins dead animals.

4. Mar. *Mahár* or *Mhár, Dheṛ, Balláyi, Mhau,* &c. These are local names current in the Maraṭha and Guzerat provinces for particular tribes of outcasts, members of which are usually found in the villages. The Mahár is the guardian of the village boundaries and land-marks, and is the public servant of the head-man. He summons the villagers to public meetings, carries the collected revenue to the Government office, and acts as public letter-carrier and messenger. He cuts wood and grass, and serves as scout, guide, baggage-porter, and general attendant on travellers. He assists the head-man in his police duties, and traces and apprehends thieves. He officiates also, sometimes, as watchman, especially of the crops, and is the sweeper of the roads through the village. Some of these functions are wholly or in part discharged by other servants, as the *Máng* and *Yeshar*. The office of village *Mahár* is generally held by one or more families; so that, although there is nominally one officer, the duties are commonly performed by several individuals. The functions of the *Mahár*, are, in part at least, also discharged in different places by other low tribes or castes, especially those of protecting the village boundaries, and acting as guides, messengers, and watchmen, who are frequently *Bhils*, *Kolis*, or *Rámusis*. The persons employed to protect the roads and boundaries are also termed *Rakh-wálas* and *Varttaniyas*, whilst the village watchman is designated by a variety of terms in different parts of India, as H. Mar. Beng. *Chaukidar*, *Kotwar*, Uriya. *Chokiá*, H. *Dosád*, *Dhanuk*, *Goret*, *Hári*, &c., Tel. *Payik*, *Pásbán*, Tam. *Kávali* or *Kával-háran*, Tel. Karn. *Talári*, Karn. *Talávára*, also Mar. *Jagla*.

5. Mar. *Máng*, Tel. *Bárikudu, Mádiga-váḍu, Vetti-váḍu*, Tam. *Veṭṭiyáṇ*, H. *Bhangi*, *Khakrob*, *Mehtar*, *Halál-khor*, Karn. *Totí*. A man of very low caste who is the scavenger and sweeper of the village. He is also employed as skinner, and as executioner, and occasionally as a watchman.

6. H. *Dhobi*, Mar. *Paríṭ*, Karn. *Ayási*, Tel. *Cháhali* or *Cháhala-váḍu*, Tam. *Vaṇṇun* (வண்ணான்). The washerman, who washes the clothes of the villagers.

7. S. *Kumbhakára*, H. *Kumhár*, Mar. *Kumbhár*, Tel. *Kummári*, Karn. *Kumbhára*, Tam. *Kuyavan*. The potter, who makes pots and tiles for the village, and has sometimes to supply travellers with water.

8. S. *Nápita*, H. *Naï*, Mar. *Nháwi*, Karn. *Náïda*, Tel. *Mangali* (S. *Mangala*), Tam. *Ambaṭṭan*, Guz. *Nári*, also from the A. *Hajám*, which is also used in other dialects, as Hin. and Beng. The barber, who has to shave the inhabitants, more especially their heads: he also bleeds, and acts as surgeon. His wife is the general midwife. He is occasionally called upon to carry a torch before travellers at night.

9. S. *Jyotishi*, H., and in most dialects, *Joshi* or *Joṣi*. The village astronomer, who prepares the almanack, announces lucky and unlucky days, and the days appropriated to public festivals, and casts nativities. The name applies to the office, which is filled most commonly by a Brahman, who in that character conducts the village ceremonies and religious observances, and is known by the terms *Bhaṭ* or *Bhuṭ*, *Parsái*, *Purohiṭ*, and others.

10. S. *Swarnakára*, whence the *Sonár* of most of the dialects, also H. Mar. Beng. *Potadár* or *Potdár*, Karn. *Pattári*, and H., from the A., *Saráf*, vulgarly, *Shroff*. Goldsmith, silversmith, assayer, and money-changer, weigher of coin and bullion. He declares the value of coins tendered in payment of the revenue, and makes the silver ornaments worn by the villagers.

11. Mar., from S., *Guru*, *Gurav*, or *Pujári*, A Ṣudra whose especial duty it is to clean the village temple and deck the idol. He acts also as a servant to the more respectable villagers, and attends their wives when they go out. He has also to assist in the carriage of travellers' baggage, and sometimes acts as trumpeter.

12. Mar. (S.) *Bhát*, A bard, or genealogist, who keeps a record of family descents, and arranges marriages. He composes and recites poems or songs on particular festive occasions. He is sometimes reckoned one of the *Alute*, q. v.

13. H. Mar., from A., *Mauláná*, *Mulla*, *Akhund*, The Mohammedan priest who conducts the ceremonies of the Mohammedans of the village, and acts as schoolmaster. In some places he has degenerated into the butcher, killing animals for such of the villagers as eat meat. Where there are no Mohammedans, the place of the Mulla is filled up by the *Koli*, or waterman, who supplies water to the villagers and travellers, but who is

more usually enumerated amongst the *Alute*. In Karnáta, the waterman, *Niraganti* or *Kolaváru*, has charge of the supplies of water for irrigation, superintending its distribution, and preventing waste. The Karnáta establishment, also, includes officers not recognised elsewhere; as the *Alatigára* or *Pattári*, Corn-measurer, who apportions the shares of Government and the cultivators where the revenue is paid in kind; and the *Addiha* or *Addiga*, who superintends the cultivation, q. v.: also the *Konikára-chakra*, who gathers betel-nuts for the villagers from the public plantations. For the other classes of village servants, see *Alute* and *Nárú-kárú*.

BALUTEN, BALOTEN, BULOOTEN, BULOTEN, Mar. (बलुतें, बलोतें, the final *n* is scarcely sounded), also read BALUTEH, BALOTEH. The portion of the crop assigned to the village servants for their maintenance, also their fees, perquisites, or other rights.

Balute-dár, Mar. (बलुतेदार) A village officer or servant receiving a share of the crop, &c.

Balute-patti, corruptly, *Bullooty-puttee*, Mar. (बलुतेपट्टी) A cess or tax upon the shares or claims of village servants.

BÁLUTTARAM, Karn. (ಬಾಳುತ್ತರ) Land in Kanara with which temples were endowed, but remaining in the hands of the original proprietors. They were not at first included in the assessment, being considered religious property; but subsequently they were assessed, such share of the produce as the temples had formerly received being continued to them. Land claimed as the special endowment of an officer of the temple.

BAM, BUM, H. (بم, बम) An exclamation of salutation in passing, interchanged especially with *Saiva* mendicants carrying the water of sacred rivers to a distance, who call out as they go along to those they meet, *Bam-bam Mahádeo*, and receive the same words in reply.

BAM, or BÁM, H. (بام, بم) A measure of three cubits and a-half. A measuring-rod.

BAMÁL, H. (بمال, from با, with, and مال, property) Found in the possession of the thief (stolen property).

BAMB, BUMB, (?) A revenue defaulter, one who owes a balance to the State.

BAMBETÍYÁ, Beng. (বম্বেটিয়া, from Bombardier (?)) A pirate, a river pirate or robber.

BÁMBHÁ, BAMBHEE, H. (بانبهي), An ant-hill.

BAMHAN, BUMHUN, H. corruption of Brahman (بمهن), A Brahman.

BAMHANGAUR, H. (بمهنگور), A class of the Gaur Rájputs.

BAMHANIA, BUMHUNEA, H. (بمهنيا), A subdivision of the *Káchhi* tribe, a class of cultivators.

BAMHNÍ, H. (بمهني), Light red soil. (East Oudh).

BAMÍTHÁ, BUMEETHA, H. (بميٹها), An ant-hill. A snake's hole (Lower Doab).

BAMLÁ, Hindi (बमला) A spring, a hole from which water left by the inundations springs up after the waters have retired.

BÁM-MÁTI, Asam. (বামমাটি) Land not subject to inundation.

BAM-TELE, H. (بمتيلي) A Rájput tribe in the eastern parts of the central Doab, not in much consideration.

BAN, BUN, H. (بن, S. वन:) A wood, a forest.

Bánaprasth, corruptly, *Banperust*, H., from the S., वान, a solitude in the (वन) wood, and प्रस्थ, who proceeds to) The Hindu of the third order, who has discharged the duty of a householder, and has become a hermit.

Ban-char, *Banchur*, H. (S. بنچر) A forester, a woodman. A wild animal, one who goes or dwells in a wood.

Banchari, *Bunchuree*, H. (بنچري) A high jangli grass, also called Baro.

Bangaunthá, *Bungounṭha*, H. (بن گونٹها) Cow-dung found in forests.

Bankandá, *Bunkundá*, H. (بن كندا) Cow-dung found in forests and dried for fuel.

Bankar, *Bunkur*, H. (بنكر) Spontaneous produce of jangal or forest-land, timber, brushwood, gums, wild honey, &c. This is considered as distinct property from the general estate or Zamindari, and as not conveyed by the sale of the estate unless so specified. The *Bankar* may be sold separately. The term is also sometimes applied to pasture lands, Beng. Reg. i. 1804, and to revenue derived from forest lands.—Elliot.

Bankatti, *Bunhutti*, H. (بن كٹي) A fee paid for cutting timber. The title obtained by cutting away jangal or thicket, and bringing the land into cultivation.

Banotsarga, H. (from S. *ban*, a wood, and *utsarga* उत्सर्ग, abandoning) Consecration of a wood or orchard newly planted by going through the forms of marrying the *Sálágram* stone or ammonite, a type of *Vishnu*, to a branch of the *Tulasi* tree (Ocymum sanctum), the type of a nymph beloved by *Vishnu or Krishna*: one man, carrying the stone, represents the bridegroom; another, holding the plant, the bride. The usual ceremony, somewhat modified, takes place, and on the completion of the ceremonial the fruit which the orchard is to bear may be eaten.

Ban-salámi, H. (from *Salám* سلام, salutation) A fee formerly exacted by the Zamindar from the Ryot for permission to gather the juice of the date-tree for the purpose of making a fermented liquor.

Bantariá, *Buntariá*, H. (بنتریا, बनतरिया) A class of wood-rangers formerly holding rent-free lands in quittance of police duties in the northern Parganas of Gorakhpur. The duties having ceased, revenue has been levied on the occupants (Bantarias) at an easy rate.

Ban, Bun, H. (بن, बन) Cotton.

Bankhará, *Bunkhura*, H. (بنکھرا) Land on which cotton has grown during the past season (Central Doab), and is succeeded by a crop of grain.

Ban, Bun, (?) A division of a Pátílship.

Bán, Beng. (বান) An inundation within the influence of the tide; also the rapid influx of the flood-tide, commonly termed the Bore.

Báṇ, Mar. &c., (S. बाण) An arrow. A fire-work or rocket.

Báṇdár, Mar. (बाणदार) An archer. A rocket-bearer. Guz., A village watchman.

Báná, H. (بانا) A vat, a large jar without feet. An iron bucket used for raising water for irrigation.

Báṇá, Mar. (बाणा) The woof of cloth.

Báṇátáná, Mar. (बाणाताणा) The woof and warp.

Baná, Hindi, (बना, from बनाना, to make) Land dressed and ready for seed. Made up.

Baṇabe, Baṇave, Karn. (ಬಣಬೆ, ಬಣವೆ) A stack.

Banáfar, H. (بنافر) A tribe of *Yadubansi* Rájputs, chiefly settled in Oudh, but also in Allahabad, Benares, and Bundelkhand.

Baṇajiga, Baṇanjiga, Banjiga, Karn. (ಬಣಜಿಗ, ಬಣಂಜಿಗ, ಬಂಜಿಗ) A sect of dissentients from the Hindu system, Lingayits, or, according to some authorities, a tribe of Súdras engaged in trade or business: (the same, apparently, as the Tel. *Balajiváru*). Also *Baṇijaga*, q. v.

Banár, Thug. Bad news. A road become unsafe.

Bánasiga, Karn. (ಬಾಣಸಿಗ, from ಬಾಣಸ, cooking) A cook.

Banaulá, Bunoula, H. (بنَولا) The seed of the cotton plant.

Banbu, or Bambu, Bunboo, Bumboo, Karn. (ಬಂಬು) A bambu (Arundo bambusa).

Band, Bund, H. &c., (بند, बंद, from the imp. بند *band* or *bund* of the Pers. verb بستن, to bind, to confine; when derived from the S. बन्ध *bandh*, also signifying to bind, to tie, the word and its derivatives preserve the final aspirate, and are properly written *Bandh* or *Bundh*, &c., q. v.) A band, a binding, literally or figuratively, as imprisonment, fetters, a tie, a cord. A bundle of papers tied together. A written contract, an account, a pledge, a bond, an agreement, an arrangement, stipulated allowance, deduction, &c. In Mar., also, a law, a regulation.

Bandá, *Bundá*, H. &c., (बंदा, from the Pers. participle بنده, bound, tied, and thence, in H., more usually *Bandah*) A servant, a slave.

Bandah, *Bunduh*, H. (P. بنده) A slave, a bondman, a servant. A term of humility in speaking of one's self to a superior.

Bandagi, *Bundugee*, H. (بندگی) Service, slavery. A term used as a complimentary salutation.

Bandah-wálá-i-Bárgáh, (lit., the slave of the exalted Court) A nobleman under the Mogul system charged with the Diwani or revenue administration of a province, and holding a Jagír for his personal and official expenses.

Bandi, or *Bándí*, *Bundee*, (باندی, بندی) A slave girl.

Bandi, Karn. (ಬಂದಿ) Imprisonment. A prisoner.

Bandiwán, *Bundeewan*, H. (بندیوان) *Bandiyán*, Beng. (বন্দিযাণ), A prisoner, a convict; *Bandivánanu*, Karn. (ಬಂದಿವಾನನು) One in custody under suspicion.

Band- or *Bund-khána*, *Bandi-* or *Bundee-khána*, (بندخانه) A prison, a jail.

Bandi poṭu, Tel. (బందిపోటు) Gang-robbery.

Band- or *Bund-behri*, H. (بندبیهری) Statement of the amount of each share of the money instalment of the revenue assessed on a village.

Band- or *Bund-bardásht*, H. (بند برداشت) Account of a share or portion of an instalment to be paid by each member of a village.

Band-baṭai, H. (بند بٹای) Account of each share of the assessment paid in grain.

Band-hisáb, H. (بند حساب) An abstract account.

Bandi, *Bundee*, H. (بندی) Agreement, arrangement. Distribution. Stipulated allowance. Deduction or charge, as *Behri-bandi*, *Bét-bandi*, &c., q. v.

Band-i-jamá, H. (A. جمع) Distribution of the assessed lands among the cultivators so as to allot to each an equal proportion of good and bad lands, and to make him responsible for a fixed proportion of both.

Band-i-mudat, H. (بند مدّت), Mar. (बन्दीमुदत्) A stated term for the settlement of an account.

Band-i-Sale or *-Seal*, H. (a compound of *Band* with the English word *Sale* or *Seal*) A contract of sale, a document executed immediately after the sale of a Zamindárí, specifying the lands sold, the amount of assessment, and the price.

Band-navís, H. (*Band*, and P. *navís* نویس, a writer) A clerk, an accountant.

Band-o-bast, *Bund-o-bust*, or sometimes inverted as *Bast-o-band*, H. (P. بندوبست or بستوبند), Beng. (বন্দোবস্ত), Mar. (बन्दोबस्त), lit., tying and binding, both words being derived from the same P. verb بستن, to bind) Agreement, settlement, bargain, adjustment, arrangement. Settlement of revenue to be paid by the Zamindar, renter, or farmer to the Government, or by the tenant to the Zamindar.

Band-o-bast dawámi, H. (from A. دوام, perpetuity) Perpetual or permanent settlement.

Band-o-bast miâdi, H. (from A. میعاد, fixed time) Temporary settlement, one for a prescribed time.

Band-o-bast-i-mulk, H. (A. ملك) The sum total of the revenue of a kingdom or province as settled and engaged for.

Band-o-bast-i-parwána, H. (پروانة) Patent or deed of settlement. A warrant given by the Government to the person with whom a revenue settlement had been agreed upon, empowering him to make the collections from the cultivators or land-holders.

Band-o-bast-i-sanad, H. (A. سنّد) Warrant or patent of settlement. See the last.

Band-o-bast sarsari, H. (سرسري) Summary and temporary settlement.

Ḍaul-band-o-bast, H. (डौल, ڈول, manner) Particular statement of the manner in which the rental of an estate or district is subdivided.

Band-o-bast-i-Sarrishtadár, (P. سررشتةدار) A revenue officer attached to some of the Government offices in Bengal to assist in making and revising revenue settlements, and to keep and record all documents relating to them.

Band-phánta, *Bundphanta*, H. (بندپهانتة) An account of the shares of the liabilities of a village.

BAND, BUND, H., and in most dialects: (the same as the preceding in its literal sense, but having a specific application) A dam, a dyke, a causeway, a raised bank or mound of earth constructed to confine the waters of a river or reservoir, or to preserve a road-way across plains inundated in the rainy season; also *Bandh*, *Bundh*, or *Bándh*.

Band-ṭál, H. (بندتّال) Damming a watercourse for the purpose of irrigation.

BÁNḌ, Mar. (बांड) A field of grain blighted before coming into ear, or of which the heads have been eaten by cattle. The stalks of such corn.

BANḌ, BUNḌ, Mar. (बंड) Insurrection, sedition. A band or body of insurgents.

BANDÁ, BUNDÁ, H. (بندا) A grain magazine above ground.

BANDÁ, BUNDÁ, Mar. (बंदा) Whole, unbroken, unexchanged for smaller coin.

BANDAR, BUNDUR, H. (P. بندر) A port, a harbour, an emporium. In Bengal, also, a market, a mart.

Shah-bandar, Harbour or custom-master.

BANḌAWALA, BANḌAWÁḶA, Karn. (ಬಂಡವಲ, ಬಂಡವಾಳ) Stock in trade, capital.

BANDE, BUNDE, Tel. (బంది) A fine for trespass by cattle.

BANDH, BUNDH, occurring in most dialects, (from S. बन्ध, binding, confining, literally or figuratively) Confining, fastening. A cord, a fetter, a tie, a ligature, a bond, a deed, an agreement, a pledge. A rule, a regulation, &c. See *Band*, also *Bandhan* or *Bundhun*.

Bandh, *Bundh*, or, preferably, *Bándh*, H. Mar. &c., (बंध, बांध) A bank, a dyke, a mound for confining water, or forming a roadway over inundated fields. Boundary of a field or village.

Bandhak, *Bundhuk*, in most dialects, (बन्धक), Tam. *Bandagam* (பந்தகம்) A pledge, a pawn, a mortgage.

Bandhak-dátá, Beng. Uriya, &c., (S. दाता, a giver) A mortgager, a pawner.

Bandhahgráhí, Beng. (বংধকগ্রাহী) A pawnbroker, one who lends upon pledges.

Bandhak-grahítá, Beng. Uriya, &c., (from S. ग्रहीता, who takes) A mortgagee.

Bandhak-lewá-byahti, Beng. Uriya, &c., (বংধকলেবা ব্যক্তি, from H. لينا, to take, and S. व्यक्ति, a person) A pawnbroker, one who takes a pledge, a mortgagee.

Bandhak-náma or *-patra*, Beng. Uriya, &c., (নামা, পত্র) A mortgage-deed.

Bandhan, *Bundhun*, H. &c., (S. बन्धन) Binding, the act or implement of binding, &c. See *Bandh*.

Bándhan, *Bandhun*, Mar. (बांधण) Ground formed into

rice-fields by damming a stream, and laying the soil under water. A dam, an embankment. A mound raised across a field to prevent the soil from being washed away.

Bandhárá, Bundhara, Mar. (बंधारा) A bank, a dyke.

Bándhárá, Mar. (बांधारा) The ground adjoining and along the course of a field-dyke or embankment.

Bandhára, Bundhara, Mar. (? perhaps for *Bhandára*, q. v.) An assembly of religious mendicants convened to celebrate the funeral obsequies of a deceased Mahant, or principal of an establishment of the order, and confirm the nomination by him of his successor.

Bándhíl, Mar. (बांधील) Tying up rice in sheaves.

Bandhiyá, H. (بندهيا) Raised embankment for confining water and flooding fields.

Bándhṇe, Mar. (बांधणे) A gap made in the bed of a stream to let the water through: the rubbish with which it is occasionally stopped.

Bandhwás, Bundhwas, H. (بندهواس) Land embanked all round so as to admit of being flooded.

BANDHÁN, BUNDHAN, H. &c., (بندهان) A pension, a stipend.

BANDHÁN, BUNDHAN, H. (بندهان), also BANDHÚR, BUNDHOOR, (بندهور) Purchase of grain in advance of the harvest.

BÁNDHAL-GOTI, BANDHUL-GOTEE, H. (باندهلگوتي) A tribe of Rájputs of Chauhan descent, occupying part of Bundelkhand and Benaudhia. Sometimes pronounced *Bádhil-* or *Banjil-goti*.

BANDHU, S. (बन्धु) A relation, a kinsman in general. In law, a cognate kinsman in a remote degree. Three kinds are enumerated, personal, paternal, and maternal. The first are the sons of the deceased's father's sister, of his mother's sister, and of his maternal uncle. The second are the sons of his father's paternal aunt, of his father's maternal aunt, and of his father's maternal uncle. The third are the sons of his mother's paternal aunt, of his mother's maternal aunt, and of his mother's maternal uncle. These succeed after the *Gotrajas* or Gentiles.

Bándhava, S. (बान्धवः) A kinsman in general. A cognate kinsman. See the preceding.

BANDI, BUNDEE, corruptly, BANDY, H. (بندي) Name of a dry measure. Tel. Karn. (ಬಂಡಿ) A cart, a carriage, a gig, any wheeled conveyance.

BANDLI, BUNDLEE, H. (بندلي) A sort of rice grown in Bundelkhand.

BANDRÍ, H. (بندري) A kind of grass growing in rice-fields, and used as fodder.

BÁNGÁ, H. (بانگا) Raw cotton. The cotton plant. *Banaula*, q. v., is, properly, the seed of the plant; *Rui* or *Rooee*, the cotton itself; and *Kapás*, the seed and cotton in the pod.

BANGÁ, BUNGA, H. (بنگا) Soil impregnated with oily well-water, and cultivable at either the spring or autumn harvest (Agra). Well water slightly brackish (Central Doab).

BANGALIYÁ, H. (بنگليا) A sort of rice grown in the eastern parts of the north-west provinces.

BÁNGAR, BANGUR, H. (بانگر) High ground. Uplands. Upper; as *Panipat bángar*, Upper Panipat, in opposition to *Panipat-kádir*, Lower Panipat.

BANGÁRA, Karn. (ಬಂಗಾರ) Gold; golden.

BANGÍ, Tam. (பங்கி) A species of village tenure in Tinnevelly by which the fields are divided once in every six years among the villagers by lot.

Bangáli, Tam. (பங்காளி) A shareholder of village lands under the preceding tenure.

BANGKÁ, H. (بنگکا) A sort of water-beetle that feeds upon rice plants.

BANG-KAṬÍA, H. (بنگ کٹیا) A species of Solanum resembling a thistle—not of any use.

BANGKI, H. (بنگکي) A sort of rice cultivated in the Benares district.

BÁNGLÁ, corruptly, BUNGALOW, Beng. (বাংলা, probably from *Banga*, Bengal) A thatched cottage, such as is usually occupied by Europeans in the provinces or in military cantonments.

BANGṚI, BUNGṚEE, H. (بنگڑي) A bracelet, an ornament for the wrist; corruptly, 'a bangle.'

BANGU, Thug. The river Thug of Bengal. These inveigle people into their boats, and, after strangling, cast them into the water,

BÁNI, H. (باني) A weight equal to eighty rupees. A yellow earth with which potters sometimes decorate their pottery. The thread with which cloth is woven. Price paid for a work. Thug., Blood.

BAṆIJ, BUNIJ, H. (بنيج, from S. वणिज्) Trade, traffic. Thug., A traveller.

Baṇik, Buṇik, H. (بنيك, S. वणिज्, nom. वणिक्) A merchant, a trader. In Bengal it most commonly denotes a money-changer, or banker.

BAṆIJAGA, BANIJAGA, plur. BANIJAGÁRU, Karn. Tel (ಬಣಿಜಗ, ಬಣಿಜಗ, ಬಣಿಜಗಾರು) The name of a class or sect, including several divisions, generally followers of the Lingayit sect. See *Baṇajiga*.

Panchama baṇajiga, Karn. (పంచమ బణజిగ) Merchants and traders of the Lingayit sect.

Tenugu baṇajiga, Karn. (తెలుగు బణజిగ) Persons following the business of tailors, bracelet-makers, and speaking *Telugu.*

Baniwál, H. A subdivision of the Bahangi sect.

Banjar or Bánjar, Bunjur or Bánjur, H. (بانجر, بنجر, बंजर, बांजर, from S. बन्ध्या *bandhyá,* barren), also Bánjh, H. (بانجه), Banjaru, and Banje, Karn. (బంజరు, బంజె) Waste or fallow-land.

Banjar-jadíd, H. (A. جديد, new) Land again brought into cultivation after lying fallow for some years.

Banjar-ḳadím, H. (A. قديم, ancient) Land left fallow from a remote period.

Banjar-kami, H. (from P. *kam* کم, less, little, deficient) Abatement of revenue on account of land left uncultivated (South of India).

Banjar-kandáyam, Karn. (బంజర కందాయం) Tax in Mysore levied on waste lands.

Banjar-khárij-i-jamá, H. (A. خارج جمع) Waste lands excluded from the rental. In Cuttack, lands which, being waste, and therefore not yielding revenue, were sold by the district and village officers clandestinely as rent-free lands. They were subsequently subjected to a light quit-rent.

Banjárá, Banjári, Bunjaree, corruptly, Bunjary, Benjary, Brinjaree, &c., H. (بنجارا, from S. वणिज्, a trader). The term is most usually applied to a grain and cattle merchant, who, with a more or less numerous party of the same calling, moves about to different markets, and especially accompanies bodies of troops to supply them with corn. It is especially applicable, also, to a numerous tribe spread along the foot of the mountains from Haridwar to Gorakhpur, and forming various subdivisions, many of whom are stationary, and follow agriculture. They comprise both Hindus and Mohammedans, acknowledging a common origin and affinity. The most migratory are the *Bahurúpa Banjárás*, of whom there are five branches, four of whom assume the well-known appellations of the chief Rájput tribes, or *Rahtore, Chauhán, Powar,* and *Tumár*. The fifth, called *Barha*, is said to be descended from a Gaur Brahman. Each of these is infinitely subdivided. The *Rahtore* branch, for instance, splits into four families, and these comprehend 138 sub-branches. Some of these *Banjárás* have the privileges of the *Cháran* and *Bhát*, q. v., their persons being sacred, and accepted in guarantee of engagements. The origin of these people is obscure: if they were primarily a distinct race, they are now much intermixed.

Banjin, Bunjin, H. (بانجن) Lands close to a village. A weed which springs up with the *kharif* crop to the height of about three feet. It is much prized by mendicants professing alchemy.

Bánk, H. &c., (بانك, बांक, S. वक्र, crooked) A bend or reach of a river.

Bánká, H. (بانكا) An idle, dissolute fellow. A bully. A bravo.

Bankṣál, Beng. (बंकशाल, from S. वणिक्, a trader, and शाला, a hall) The office of the chief officer of the marine, or harbour-master.

Bankṭa, Hindi, (बंकटा) The crop on the field irrecoverably spoiled.

Bannan, Tam. (?) The washerman caste. *Travancore.*

Bannan-adiga, (?) Tam. A smaller grain measure used in giving grain to slaves and labourers. *Tinnivelly.*

Banni, Bunnee, H. (بني) A portion of grain given to a labourer in requital of his services.

Banni- or *Bani-hár*, H. (بنهار, بني) A ploughman or labourer whose services are paid in kind.

Banṣ, Bunṣ, H. &c., (بنس S. वंश:) A race, a family.

Banṣávalí, H. (بنساولي, S. वंशावली) A genealogy, a family record.

Banṣ or Bánṣ, Bunṣ or Baṇṣ, H. &c., (بانس, بنس, S. वंश:) A bambu, a measure of length. A rod or bambu about ten feet long used to measure excavations.

Bánṣá, H. (بانسا, probably from *Bans,* a bambu) The hollow tube or bambu through which the seed descends in a drill-machine, usually, but not always, attached to a plough.

Bánṣái, Beng. (बाँशाइ) A frame of bambu-work like a ladder, used as a harrow for breaking the clods after ploughing.

Bánsgáṛí, Beng. (बाँशगाडी) Planting a bambu in the ground as a monument of any transaction.

Bansá, Bunsa, H. (بنسا) A grass growing amongst rice, and used as fodder.

Bánsari, Bansuree, H. (بانسري) A weed found in parts of the Doab near the Jumna, injurious to the crops, and difficult to be eradicated.

Banslochan, H. (بنس لوچان, S. वंशलोचन) Bambu-manna, a sort of white flinty substance found in the joints of the Bambu.

Bánsphor, H. (بانس پهور) A caste who work with bambu-canes. A basket-maker.

BANSI, BUNSEE, H. (بنسي) A sort of wheat with blackish ears.—North-west Provinces.

BANT or BANTAR, BUNT or BUNTUR. Karn. (ಬಂಟ, ಬಂಟರ) A cultivator, a Ryot.

BÁNṬ, H. &c., (بانٹ, from S. वण्टन), BANT, BUNT, or BÁNT, Beng. (বঁট, বাঁট) A share, a portion, division of property.

Bántá, Beng. (বাঁটা) A partition, an allotment; also Hindi, (बांटा) Tying up the crop into sheaves or trusses. *Puraníya.*

Bantak, Beng. S. (বন্টক) A share, a portion. A sharer.

Bánṭ-chont, H. (بانٹ چونٹ) Share, portion, distribution.

Bantaṇ or *Bántaṇ*, Beng. (S. বঁটন, বাঁটন) Sharing, dividing, partitioning.

Bant-patra, Uriya, (S. पत्र, a leaf) Record of division of property.

BANṬROTU, BUNṬROTOO, Tel. (బంట్రోతు) A peon, a footman, a courier usually wearing a badge. A policeman.

BANUĪ, Beng. (বনুই) A sister's husband.

BANVIKRI, corruptly, BUNVICKREE, H. (from the S. वन, a wood, and *vikraya* विक्रयः, sale) The sale of an adult of one of the agricultural classes as a slave in his absence (in the woods or elsewhere), the purchaser taking the risk of finding and securing him (formerly practised in Behar).

BANYA, BUNYA, corruptly, BANIAN, BANYAN, H. (بنيا), BÁṆIYÁ, BÁṆYA, BÉṆYA, Beng. (বানিয়া, বানে, বেনে), from S. वणिक्) A Hindu trader, shopkeeper, or money-changer. In Bengal it is commonly applied to the native cashier or man of business in the service of Europeans. In the West of India it ordinarily denotes Hindu merchants settled either as agents or principals at the chief places of traffic in the Persian Gulf or Red Sea.

BAOLI, or sometimes BAORÁ or BAORI, corruptly, BOWLEY or BOWREE, H. (باولي, باوري), Mar. (बावडी) A deep well, the descent to the brink of which is by long flights of steps leading far down below the surface of the ground, relieved by landing-places and covered chambers where travellers may rest and take refreshment during the heat of the day. Some *Baolis* are constructed with much architectural embellishment, particularly in the west of India.

BAOLIEN, BAOLIER, Mal. (?) Outcast slaves who reside in the jungle.

BÁONI, BAONEE, H. (باوني) Seed-time. Sowing.

BÁOṚI, H. (باوڑي) A vagrant tribe in the Bhattí country and west of Dehli, who subsist chiefly by stealing. A low caste in the Jangal Mahals, cultivators and palankin-bearers.

BAPANS, H, (بپنس, from *báp*, a father, or S. *vapra*, a field, and *anṣ* अंश, a part, a share) Patrimony, patrimonial inheritance.

BAPOTí, erroneously, BAPROTTEE, H. (بپوتي) Patrimony.

BÁṚ, H. Hindi, Mar. (باڑ, बाड) A fence, a hedge, an inclosure. The boundary of a field. The outer screen of a tent.

Báṛí, *Báṛee*, H. Beng. (باڑي, বাড়ী) An inclosed piece of ground, a plot for sugar-cane or other garden produce, also cotton.

Báṛí, H. Beng. (বাড়ী, from S. वाटी) A house, a dwelling.

BÁR, more correctly, VÁRA, H. &c., (بار, S. वार) A day of the week, used chiefly in composition, as, *Som-bár*, Monday; *Buddh-báṛ*, Tuesday; *Mangal-bár*, Wednesday; *Bṛihaspati-bár*, Thursday; *Sukra-bár*, Friday; *Sani-bár*, Saturday; *Áditya-bár*, corrupted to *Etwar*, Sunday: also, A time, a turn.

Bár-bár, H. Repeatedly, time after time, turn after turn,

Bárí, H. (باري) A mode of keeping up the village watch in some places, in which the villagers watch by turns; also, in the season of grinding the sugar-cane, the working of the mill by turns, so that there shall be no intermission night and day until the whole is ground, the villagers uniting for this purpose.

BÁR, BÁRA, H. (بار, بارہ) A perquisite of the *Ahír*, or cow-herd, in milk, generally the milk of every eighth day.

BÁR, H. (P. بار) A load, a burthen.

Bár-bardár, H. (P. بردار, who takes up) A porter, a carrier, a burthen-bearer.

Bár-bardári, H. P. (برداري, bearing) Carriage hire, cost of conveyance, charge of porterage, and the like.

Bár-baṭáï, H. (باربٹاي) Division of the crop by sheaves (or loads) before the corn is trodden out.

Bár-gír, *Bargeer*, corruptly, *Bageer*, H. &c., (P. بارگير, बारगीर, lit., one who takes a load) A trooper who is mounted on a horse which is supplied by the State or the chief he serves.

Bár, H. (P. بار) A court, a tribunal, a place of audience.

Bár-i-áám, H. P. (بارعام) Public hall of audience.

Bár-gáh, H. (P. بارگاه) Place of audience, a royal court. The court of the Mogul.

Bár-i-khás, H. (P. بار خاص) Private audience or council chamber.

Bár-yábi, H. (P. بار يابي) Admission at court, presentation.

Bárnís, Mar. (बारनीश) An officer whose duty is to affix the word बार *bár*, to notes, bills, &c., implying that they are to be entered on the account-book.

Bár, H, P. (بار) Fruit.

Báramba, Barumba, H. (بارنبه) Revenue derived from the lease of a mango-orchard.

Bár, H. (بار, S. वारि) Water.

Bárán, H. (باران) Rain.

Báráni, H. (باراني, lit., rainy) Applied to land, it signifies that which is watered by rain, not by irrigation. It is also the name of a cloak for keeping off rain, commonly corrupted by Europeans to *Brandy*, as *Brandy-koortee* for *Báráni-kurtah*.

Bar, Bur, Beng. (বড) A band of straw to secure a thatch, or to bind down a stack of salt.

Bar, Bur, Bargat, H. (بڑ, or بڑگت, from S. वटः) The Indian fig-tree, commonly, the Banian-tree.

Bára or **Báru**, Karn. (ಬಾರ, ಬಾರು) Troops, a line of troops. The infantry of the Mysore State.

Bára kachéri, Karn. (ಬಾರಕಚೇರಿ) The head-quarters or office of the infantry.

Bárigátu kachéri, Karn. (ಬಾರಿಗಾಟುಕಚೇರಿ) The cavalry office. In *Tipu's* time, the office of the body-guard. The 'horse-guards.' It seems to be confounded with *Bárgir*, as it is also written *Bárigíra kachéri* (ಬಾರಿಗೀರಕಚೇರಿ).

Bárá, corruptly, **Barah, Burra**, H. (باڑا, बाडा) Land next to, or surrounding, a village; (perhaps from *Bár*, an inclosure). Land of the first quality, although containing a portion of sand.

Bárá-zamín, H. (from P. زمين, land) Land adjacent to a village, also land of the first class.

Bára, or **Bárah**, H. (باره), Mar. **Bárá**, (बारा) Twelve.

Bára-dari, H. (from *Barah*, twelve, and P. *dar* در, a door) A summer-house, a summer palace (having twelve, *i. e.* many, doors and windows).

Bárah gáon, corruptly, *gaum*, H. (S. گانو) Any tract containing twelve villages (or more), with their dependent lands. In this and similar compounds, however, very commonly only one village is meant, as, *Tín-gáon*, three villages; *Pánch-gáon*, five villages; *Sáth-gáon*, seven ditto, &c.; each being the appellation now borne by a single village.

Bárah-thákuraï, H. (from ठाकुर, a chief) The twelve lordships. Twelve petty hill States between the Jumna and the Setlej.

Bárah-wafát, H. A. (from وفات, death) The twelfth of the month *Rábi-ul ával*, on which day Mohammad died. It is observed by the Mohammadans as a religious festival.

Bárotra, Mar. (बारोत्रा) Interest at the rate of 12 per cent. per annum. The twelfth part of the interest due on any sum.

Bárulá, Mar. &c., (बाहला) A measure of 12 *pailis*. A *man*, or *mun*, or *maund*.

Bará, Bura, corruptly, **Burra**, (بڑا) Great, large, much.

Bará-bháv, H. (بڑا بهاو, lit., great price) Premium or money borrowed by the cultivators at a rate per cent. to be reckoned according to the highest rate during the season.

Bará-brahman, H. (بڑا براهمن) A great Brahman, used ironically to denote an inferior class of Brahmans who conduct funeral ceremonies, and are thereby held impure; also *Mahá-bráhman*.

Bará-mián, H. (بڑا ميان) Term of address to an elderly and respectable or venerable person, also to the head of a village.

Bará nagar takávi, H. (A. تقاوي, advance) Fee or allowance granted to the cultivator who uses the '*bará nagar*,' or large plough used for breaking up new land.

Bara-Thákur, corruptly, *Barra-Thahoor*, H. Great chief. A title given in Típera to the person who stands next but one to the succession to the Raj. *Puraniya*.

Bara, Karn. (ಬರ) Famine.

Baragála, Karn. (ಬರಗಾಲ) A season of famine.

Barad, Burud, corruptly, **Burrud**, Mar. (बरद) Inferior soil. Stony and sandy land. In the Dakhin it is distinguished as *Lál-barad*, red gravelly soil; *Piüla-barad*, yellow; and *Mál-barad*, hilly and stony.

Bárad, Hindi (बारड) Division, parcel or portion of land in a village distinguished by some epithet, as, *Purwári-bárad*, eastern parcel; *Matiári-bárad*, clay-soil division, &c.

Bárad salámi, Hindi, (from A. سلام, compliment) A consideration taken by the proprietor from the *Rakhwála*, or watchman of a *Bárad* for granting him permission to be employed. *Puraníya*.

BARÁHI, BURAHEE, H. (براهي) A small kind of sugar-cane.

BÁRÁHI, H. (باراهي) Land, or, more properly, the earth, from its having been raised from the deep by the *Baráha* or *Varáha*, the boar-avatar of *Vishṇu*.

BARÁI KHOR O POSH, H. (P. براي خور و پوش, lit., for the sake of feeding and clothing) Designation of an assignment of real or personal property to a person for maintenance for life, not conveying a right of transfer.

BARAKA, Karn. (ಬರಕ) A double sack with which manure is carried on land with buffaloes.

BARÁL, Thug. Omen from the howling or appearance of wolves, bad or good according to circumstances, but always of great weight.

BARÁMAD, Mar. (बरामद, from P. بر, and آمد, what comes) Export duty.

BÁRA-MÁRG, also BÁRÁ-BHÁṬÍ, Karn. (ಬಾರಮಾರ್ಗ, ಬಾರಾಭಾಟಿ) The high or royal road. Transit duty or toll.

BARAMÁTTÍ, Thug. Cry of the lizard, always a good omen.

BARÁMDAH, BURAMDUH, H. (برامده, from the Pers. بر, off, and آمده, what has come) Issue, expenditure, disbursements.

BARAN, BURUN, corruptly, BURRUN, H. &c., (برن, बरण, S. *varṇa* वर्णः) A caste, a class, a colour.

Baraṇ-Sankar, corruptly, *Burrun-Shunkur*, H. Beng. (S. *Varna-Sankara* वर्णसंकर) The mixed castes, the classes of the Hindus other than the four first pure castes.

BARAN, Hindi, (बरन) Alluvial. Fresh earth thrown into hollows by water.

BARAN, Beng. (বরণ) Betrothing of a female, making a promise of marriage.

BARÁR, BURAR, H. (برار, बरार) Tax in general, as, *Hal-barár*, a tax on ploughs. Land-tax or rent. Apportionment of revenue payments according to agreement with the village community. See *Bhej-barár*. Any division of shares. See *Báchh*.

Barárí, H. (براري, बरारी) A shareholder, a co-parcener. One paying his portion of the assessment.

Árázi barárí, H. (A. عراضي, lands) Land in a village retained by the proprietary cultivators, not let to strangers, and paying the rent or revenue. Bundelkhand.

BARAS, BURUS, H. (برس, from the S. वर्षः) A year. Rain, raining. An intoxicating preparation of opium.

Barasáliá, *Barasoliá*, or *Barasodiá*, shortened in pronunciation to *Barsáliá*, &c., H. (برسوديا , برسوليا , برساليا) An agricultural labourer or servant who is hired for a year.

Barasauṛi, H. (برسَوڑي) An annual rent or tax.

Baras-gánth, H. (برسگانٹھ) The custom of tying a knot on a thread on the anniversary of a child's birth. Birth-day observance.

Baraspaḍi or *-paṛi*, Uriya (?), An annuity.

BARAT, BURUT, H. (برت) A disease affecting rice crops. A leather girth or rope for drawing up a bucket from a well. (In the Dehli district) Government revenue, or a part of it.

BARÁT, BURÁT, corruptly, BERAUT, H. (A. برات) A record, a register. A diploma, a warrant, a commission. An assignment or order on the revenue. In this last sense it is adopted in Mar. (बरात), Tel. (బరాతము), and Karn. (ಬರಾತ್): in the latter it also implies a peremptory demand, or dunning for payment.

Barátakár or *gár*, Karn. (ಬರಾತಗಾರ) One who holds a written order or assignment. One who presses for payment.

Barát, *Burat*, or, more correctly, *Shab-i-barát*, or *Shub-i-burat*, H. (A. P. شب برات, lit., the night of record, or that on which men's deeds during the coming year are said to be registered in heaven) A Mohammadan festival, held on the 14th, or rather on the eve of the 14th of *Shabán*, on which a vigil is observed with prayers, fasting, and illuminations. In Hindustan, lamps are lighted and prayers repeated in honour of deceased ancestors, a practice no doubt borrowed from the Hindus.

BARÁT, BURAT, H. (برات, probably from the S. *vara* वर, a bridegroom, and *rátrí* रात्रि, night, at which season the principal ceremonies take place) A bridal procession.

BARATHA, H. (برتها) Land situated amidst jangal.

BARAUNDHÁ, H. (برَوندها) Cotton soil.

BARÁWARDA, BURAWURDU, or BARÁWARD, BURAWURD, corruptly, BURRAWURD, and BIRAWIRD, H. &c., (P. بر, on, and *awardah* آورده, brought, brought up or forward) An estimate, a calculation. What is summed up. In the west of India, a monthly statement sent to the Government of the revenue and village establishments of the sums payable to each person, and the increase or decrease as compared with preceding months. A statement of district disbursement.

BARDA, BURDU, H. (P. بردہ) A slave, a captive.

Barda or *Burdu farosh*, H. (P. فروش, a seller) A slave-dealer.

BARḌÁ or BARḌI, H. (برڈا, برڈي) Light stony and sandy soil.

BARDÁSHT, H. (from P. بر, on, and داشت, what has) Stores, supplies.

Bardásht-khána, H. (P. خانه) A temporary store-house, or houses for preserving supplies for travellers or troops. North-west Provinces.

BAREHṬÁ, H. (بريهٹا) Land of the third quality on which sugar-cane has been lately grown.

BAREJ, BAREJÁ, H. (بريج, بريجا), Ben. BARAJA or BARJA, (বরজ) A betel garden.

BARESIRI, H. (بريسري) A tribe of inferior Rájputs in the Agra district.

BARETHA, H. (بريتھ) A washerman.

BARGÁ, Beng. (বরগা) An agreement by which the cultivator engages to pay the landlord half the produce, the latter providing half the seed, and paying the whole revenue.

Bargá-ít, Beng. (বরগাইৎ) One who cultivates the land on the above terms; also *Barga-jot-dár*.

Bargá-patta, Beng. (পট্টা) Deed or lease by which land is rented on the above terms.

BARGAN, BURGUN, H. (برگن) Partition, share. Hoshangabad.

BARHÁ, BURHA, H. (برها, बरहा) A narrow channel for the passage of water from a well to a field, or from one field to another. A field in which cows are fed. A rope or string, especially one by which a harrow is drawn, or one thrown over a loaded cart to secure the load. In some places in the Central or Upper Doab, *Barhá*, corruptly, *Burreh* (बरहा), and *Barheta* (बरहेता), is the land of a township or village farthest from the inhabited portion, constituting the third class of land. *Bárá* (बाड़ा) is that immediately adjacent, and *Manjhá* (मंझा), middle or intermediate. *Barhá*, corruptly, *Burreh*, in Etawa is applied to the uplands.

BARHÁI, BURHAEE, H. (برهاي, S. वर्द्धकि), BADÁÍ, Karn. (ಬಡಾಯಿ) A carpenter. As the name of a caste following the occupation of carpentry, it comprehends several subdivisions.

BÁRHAH-SÁDAT, H. (بارهه سادت) A powerful tribe of Saiads still numerous in *Muzzeffar-nagar*. The Saiads of *Bárh* furnished many persons of note to the Court of Dehli from the reign of Akbar to that of Farokhsír.

BAṚHÁWAN, BUṚHAWUN, H. (بڑهاون) A cake of cow-dung placed on the top of a heap of corn to protect it against an evil eye, and to secure it good luck.

BAṚHI, BUṚHEE, H. (بڑهي, S. *vriddhi* वृद्धि) Profit, increase, interest.

Báṛhi, *Baṛhee*, H. (باڑهي) Interest in kind upon seed-grain.

BARHIÁ, BUṚHIYA, H. (برهيا) A sugar-mill stone. A species of pulse (Eastern Oudh). A grain measure of one *seer*, or, in some places, one and a-half. A small clan of Rájputs.

BAṚHNI, BUṚHNEE, H. (بڑهني) Advance on a contract for goods or grain.

BAṚHOLIÁ, H. (بڑهوليا) A branch of the Bhrigu-bansi Rájputs, chief proprietors of the town of Barhoul.

BAṚHOTARÍ, H. (بڑهوتري) Profit, interest.

BAṚHTI, spelled most correctly, BADHTI, but pronounced as the first, H. (بڈهتي, from S. वृद्धि, lit., increase), BÁḌTI, (বাড়তি) Mercantile profit, gain on stock, surplus, excess.

BÁRI, Beng. (বারি, S. वारि) Water.

Bári-ganḍi, Beng. (বারিগন্ডী) An extra cess formerly levied on the Ryots in Bengal, abolished by the British Government (perhaps for irrigation (?)).

BÁRÍ, BAREE, Mar. (बारी) A hollow way, a passage through hills. One infested by tigers, robbers, &c.

BÁRI, Karn. (ಬಾರಿ) An inclined plane sloping from the edge of a well, down which the bullocks employed to raise the water descend as they drag up the bucket. A time, a turn. See *Bár*.

BARI, BUREE, corruptly, BURREE, H. (بري) Wedding gifts carried in procession. The marriage procession, and the day of its performance. See *Barát*,

BÁRI, BAREE, H. (باري) A caste of men employed to make and bear torches. They also act as barbers, and, in the Oudh service, have the character of good soldiers.

BARI, BUREE, H. (بري, probably from the P. بر, off) Release. Released, exempted, acquitted; applied to a defendant who is released by the plaintiff from the demand against him.

BARIÁR, H. (بريار) Strong; applied in the Purania district to land, to denote fertile, rich, productive.

Bárik, H. (بارك, corruption of *Bárish* بارش, from S. वर्ष) Rain.

Barik paṭṭi, H. (پتّي) A statement shewing the quantity of rain fallen.

Bárika, or **Bárike**, Karn. (ಬಾರಿಕ, ಬಾರಿಕೆ) A village officer who affixes the public seal to official papers. Any one who applies a public seal or stamp.

Báriki váḍu, Tel. (బారికి వాడు) A person employed to watch the standing crops.

Bárikudu, Tel. (బారికుడు), also **Báriyá váḍu**, Tel. (బారియావాడు, and, less correctly, **Bárki**, perhaps for **Báriki**) The low-caste man who discharges the lowest menial offices in a village, the sweeper, or scavenger, employed also as a messenger, watchman, &c.

Báriz, H. (بارز) A term in accounts. The half of the left-hand page in which the balance is entered. Account of the assessment of the land revenue on any estate, formerly entered in the middle of the paper prepared by the Zamindar as an application for investiture in the Zamindárí. See *Berij*.

Bárjá, Beng. (?, perhaps for বর্জা, abandoning, from S. वृज) also **Bárjái** and **Bárját**, corruptly, **Barjoy**, **Bárjaut** (?). Forcing people to purchase goods at more than the market price. *Bárjáñ* is said also to mean a grant of land rent-free by a Zamindar to one of his retainers, and an enhancement of the rents of the other Ryots so as to cover the loss arising from the grant. (Gladwin, Revenue Terms).

Barká, **Burká**, Thug. A leader of Thugs, one qualified to organize as well as head a gang.

Barkala, **Burkulu**, H. (بركله) An inferior tribe of Rájputs found in Bulandshahar.

Barkandáz, **Burkundaz**, subject to most extraordinary corruptions, as, **Burkendoss**, **Burkondoss**, **Burgundass**, &c., H. (P. *Bark* برق, lightning, and *andáz* انداز, who casts) A matchlock man, but commonly applied to a native of Hindustan, armed with a sword and shield, who acts as doorkeeper, watchman, guard, or escort.

Bar-, **Bur-kúyán**, H. (بركويان) A well not lined with brick (Oudh).

Bar-, **Bur-khwást**, pron., **Khást**, H. (from P. بر, up, and خواستن, to will, or wish) A rising up. A breaking up of a court of justice.

Barmhotar, more correctly, **Brahmottar**, q. v., H. (برمهوتر) A grant of rent-free land to Brahmans for charitable or religious purposes.

Barṇak-bráhman, Beng. (বর্ণকব্রাহ্মণ) A Brahman who performs ceremonies for the lower classes.

Barṇár-maṭṭi, H. (برنار مٿّي, वर्णारमट्टी) Coloured soil of two kinds, one tinged with yellow, the other yellow and white.

Barni, **Burnee**, H. (برني) An advance made for cultivation or manufacture.

Bárnís, **Bárnees**, Mar. (बारनीस, from *Bár*, and *nís*, abbrev. of Pers. *nawis* نويس, a writer) An officer under the Maratha Government whose duty it was to write the word *Bár* upon original documents, to intimate that they had been entered in the public register.

Bár-nísí, Mar. (नीसी, for P. نويسي) The making or registering of copies of public documents, and marking upon them the word *Bár*.

Baro, H. (برو) Name of a high jangal grass.

Baronkhá, H. (برونكها) A kind of sugar-cane with long thin joints.

Barothi, H. (بروتهي) A tribe of Ahirs in the Mynpuri district.

Barrá, **Burra**, H. (برا) A rope, especially one pulled on the 14th of the light half of the month *Küár*, by two opposing villages. The party that breaks it, or drags it out of the hands of the other is regarded as victor, and retains the character for a year, when the contest is repeated.

Barroh, **Burroh**, H. (برّوه) Uplands on the right bank of the Jamná in the zilla of Etáwa.

Barsát, **Bursat**, corruptly, **Bursaut**, H. (برسات, from the S. वर्ष) Rains, the rainy season.

Barsáti, H. (برساتي) A disease in the heels of horses. Relating to the rains or rainy season.

Barsáti faṣl, H. (برساتي فصل) The rainy-season crop. The various kinds of grain and pulse sown during the rains.

Bart, H. (برت, बरत) The rope attached to the bucket of a well.

Bart, **Burt**, H. (برت, S. वृत्ति) Maintenance, support, means of livelihood.

Bartan, **Burtun**, H. (برتن) A vessel, a bason. In Cuttack, a salt-sloop.

Bartanio, Guz. (વરતનીઓ) A village watchman; a police peon: a guard armed with sword and shield, or with bow and arrows, never with fire-arms.

BARṬARAF, BUR-ṬURUF, H. (P. بر, off, and *ṭaraf* طرف, part, or side) Set aside, dismissed, as a plaint; also, sub., Discharge, dismissal (from office). It is adopted in other dialects, as, Tel. BARTARAVU (బరతరవు).

Bar-ṭarafi, H. (برطرفي) Dismissal, discharge.

BARTUSH, BURTOOSH, H. (برتش) Land sown with sugar-cane after rice. (Rohilkhand.)

BARU, Thug. A Thug who is considered by his tribe as a respectable person.

BARUÁ, BUROOA, less correctly, BARWÁ, H. (بروا, बरुआ) Sandy soil of inferior quality, a mixture of sand and clay, the same as *Bhúḍ* or *Bhúṛ*.

BARUI, BUROEE, Thug. An omen from the cry of the jackal.

BÁRULI, Mar. (?) A measure by which the grain was measured in villages paying their revenue in kind. *Dakhin.*

BÁRUṆÍ, Thug. An old and venerable Thug female: (properly, S., the wife of Varuṇa, the god of the waters).

BÁRUṆÍ, H. (باروني, S. वारुणी) A Hindu festival in honour of Varuṇa on the 13th of the dark half of *Chait.*

BARWÁIK, H. (بروايك) A class of hereditary Chaukidars, or watchmen, introduced into the south-east extremity of the forest tract under the Sewalik hills.

BARWÁR, H. (بروار, बरवार) A class of people in the north-west employed in cleaning and selling rice. A tribe of Rájputs in Gorakhpur and the adjacent zillas.

BARWÁṬIYÁ, Hindi (बरवाटिया) An outlaw, a vagrant. See *Bhárwatiya.*

BÁS, H. (باس, S. वासः) Scent, odour.

Bás-banya, H. (بنيا, a dealer) A dealer in fragrant articles, a perfumer.

Bás-matí, H. (باسمتي) A fragrant kind of rice and of millet.

BÁS or VÁSA, H. (باس, S. वासः) A house, a dwelling.

Básí or *Vásí*, H. S. (باسي, वासी) An inhabitant, a dweller. A native; as *Braj básí* or *vásí*, a native of Braj.

BAṢ, BUṢ, H. (बश्) Letting lands newly cleared of thicket (Rangpur).

Baṣinia, Businia, less correctly, *Basunia*, H. (बशिनिया) The head-man of a village (Rangpur).

BASÁIMPU, (?) Money advanced to a cultivator. (Ganjam).

BASAK, BASAKÍ, or BASKÍ, Mar. (बसक, बसकी) Tax or toll for holding a stall in a market.

BASANT, BUSUNT, H. (بسنت, S. वसन्त) The season of spring, also (in Bengal), the small-pox.

Basantí, H. (بسنتي, बसन्ती) Yellow, as the colour of spring, applied especially to the yellow garment worn by the Rájputs when about to sacrifice themselves in a hopeless conflict.

Basant-panchamí, H. (*Basant* or *Vasanta*, and *panchamí*, the fifth, from the S. पञ्चमी) The vernal festival of the Hindus on the fifth lunar day of *Mágh*; formerly observed as the beginning of the spring.

BÁSAT or BASAT, H. (باست, بست, from S. वस, to dwell) Inhabited, land occupied and cultivated.

BASÁURÍ, H. (بساوري, बसावरी) Ground-rent, rent paid for the ground on which the huts of a village are erected by such of the inhabitants as do not cultivate the village lands.

BASAVÁ, Mar. (बसवा), BASAVAḌU or BASAVANNA, Tel. (బసవడు, బసవన్న), Karn. (ಬಸವ) The sacred bull—the vehicle of *Siva*; also a proper name, that of the first teacher of the Lingayit sect.

BASAVI, Mar. (बसवी), BASIVI, Tel. Karn. (ಬಸವಿ) A prostitute, but especially one who has been married or dedicated to the deity *Ṣiva*, and waits upon the idol. They are also called *Linga basavis, Garuḍa basavis*, &c., according to the deity to whose service they are dedicated.

BASGAT, H. (بسگت, बसगत्) Homestead. The site of a village, the extent of which is to be deducted from the lands paying revenue.

BÁṢGIYÁ, Hindi (बाशगिया) Crops being choked and destroyed by weeds.

BÁSIÁN, H. (باسيان) A branch of the Gaur-taga tribe, q. v.

BASÍKAT, BUSEEKUT, H. (بسيكت, from S. वस, to dwell) Inhabited, peopled.

BÁṢINGÁ, Mar. (बाशिंगा or बासिंगा) An ornament of gilded paper, silk, or other material in the form of a diadem, placed upon the heads of the bride and bridegroom on the second day of the marriage ceremony: it is supposed to counteract the effects of the evil eye.

BASÍT, BUSEET, inaccurately, BURSEET, H. (بسيت, बसीत्) The head-man of a village, the Mukaddam, or Pátíl.

BASTA, BUSTA, H. (بسته, the past part. of the P. verb بستن, to bind) A parcel, a bundle, a bale. A cloth in which papers or other articles are wrapped up.

BASTÍ, BUSTEE, sometimes written BASATI, BUSUTEE, H. (بستي, बसती, from the S. वस, to dwell) A village, a town, any inhabited place. In the South of India also, a Jain temple.

Bástu or **Vástu**, H. (باستو, S. वास्तु) Site or foundation of a house.

Bástu-pújá, H. (S. पूजा, worship) Ceremony observed on laying the foundation of a building.

Basu, Beng. (বসু, S. वसु) An adjunct to names borne by families of the *Káyath*, or writer caste in Bengal, commonly pronounced *Bose*.

Basur or **Baswárí**, H. (بسور, بسواري, from S. वंश) A bambu grove.

Baṭ, **Buṭ**, H. (بٹ, from S. वट, to divide) A partition, a division, a share.

Baṭái, *Buṭace*, corruptly, *Betay*, *Buttaee*, *Buttai*, *Buttei*, *Buttaye*, *Bhuttye*, &c., H. (بٹاي, बटाई, also, बतैई) Division of the crop between the cultivator and the landlord, or the Government in that capacity. The proportions vary: in some poor lands the share of the landholder may not exceed a sixth; in the Konkan it is a half: the more usual proportion was a third. *Baṭái-noasia* was a divison which, in the Benares district, assigned nine-sixteenths to the cultivator, seven-sixteenths to the landlord. The portion in kind was early commuted in Bengal for a money payment. Beng. Reg. ii. 1795, defines "Betay lands as those of the produce of which Government or the collector of its dues is entitled to a certain proportion, the value of which, estimated at the current market price, is paid in money by the cultivator of the land." The proportion in kind is still receivable in some parts of the south. The word is also applied to a kind of joint interest in land, in which one party pays the Government assessment, and the other furnishes the labour: the seed and implements are provided jointly, and the nett produce or profit is equally divided. In Mar. *Baṭái* means also difference of exchange. See *Baṭṭa*.

Baṭái-dár, H. (P. دار, who has) A cultivator who shares the crop with the proprietor.

Hisáb-i-Baṭái, H. (حساب, an account) Accounts kept by the village accountants, in which the partitioning system prevails, of the particulars of the settlement between the village and the Government.

Batenth, H. (بٹینتھ) Proprietor or holder of a share.

Baṭwárá, *Buṭwara*, corruptly, *Butwarra*, H. (بٹوارا, बटवारा, less correctly, *Báṭwárá* باٹوارا, बाटवारा) A share, a portion. Division of a crop in shares. The partition of an estate by co-heirs (Act xx. 1836). Distribution of the lands of a village in allotments as originally made or agreed upon. The allotment so held which the occupant may let in subdivisions.

Baṭ, **Buṭ**, Beng. (বট) Fallow-land, in Eastern Bengal. In common use, the *Bar*, or Indian fig, or banyan-tree.

Báṭ, H. (باٹ, बाट) A weight. A measure of weight whether of stone or metal.

Báṭ-chháp, H. (باٹچھاپ) Stamping weights and measures. The stamp upon them to warrant their accuracy.

Báṭ-chhápi, *Báṭ-chhápái*, or *Báṭ-chhápni*: the first and second vowels are also sometimes made short, as, *Baṭ-chhapi*, *Buṭ-chhupee*, &c., the word is also grossly corrupted, as, *Baad-chhuppy*, *But-chhuppaee*, *But-chappanee*, &c., H. (باٹچھاپي) Stamping weights and measures. A fee charged for applying the stamp.

Baṭ-kara or *Baṭ-khará*, *Buṭ-kuru* or *Buṭ-khura*, H. (بٹکرہ, بٹکھرا) A stone used as a weight. A weight in general.

Báṭ, H. Beng. (باٹ, বাট) A road, a highway.

Baṭ or *Báṭpár*, H. (پار or پار, باٹ, بٹ), *Báṭpáṛa*, Beng. (বাটপাড়) A robber, a highwayman.

Báṭ-páṛá or *-paṛi*, Beng. (বাটপাড়া, -পাড়ী) Robbery, highway robbery. Gang-robbery or Dakaiti. A robber, a thief; also, in this sense, *Báṭpáṛiya*.

Batán, Hindi (बतान) Place of assemblage of cattle at night in an open field. *Puraníya*.

Batar, **Butur**, H. (بتر) Land in a state fit for the plough.

Batáwaní, Mar. (बतावणी, from H. بتانا, to exhibit or explain) A rough account of a tradesman framed from the day-book.

Batelá, Mar. (बतेला) A boat from 50 to 500 kandis burden.

Baṭes, **Buṭes**, H. (بٹیس, बटेस) A passage, a pathway.

Bathán, **Buṭhán**, H. (بتھان, बठान्) Pasture grounds.

Bathia, H. (بتھیا) A heap of dried cow-dung (Rohilkhand).

Bathúá, H. (بتھوا) A kind of weed which springs up with the *Rabi* crops and in the vicinity of water; also a pot-herb (Chenopodium album).

Báṭí or **Baṛi**, Beng. (বাটী, বাড়ী) A house, a dwelling.

Báṭi, Uriya (ବାଟି) A measure of land equal to 20 mánas.

Báṭi-ṭankí, Uriya (ବାଟିଟଙ୍କି) Land paying a quit-rent of one rupee per Báṭi, equal to 20 mánas or bighás.

Baṭía, **Buṭeea**, H. (بٹیا) A passage, a pathway.

Bátin, H. (باتن) A tract of land in Etáwa between the Jamná and the Ghár.

Báṭin, H. (A. باطن, lit., interior, internal) Private, domestic. In law, Property of a domestic nature. The concealed or internal meaning of a passage in a book of law or religion.

BÁṬKE, Beng. (বাটকে) A labourer in the salt-works. An under-Malangi.

BÁTMÍ or BÁTNÍ, Mar. (बातमी or बातनी) Intelligence, news.

Bátmí or *Bátní-dár*, Mar. (دار, who has) An intelligencer, a scout, a spy.

BAṮNAN-BÂD BAṮNAN, BUṮNUN-BAD BUṮNUN, H. (بطناً بعد بطناً) Generation after generation: a term inserted in a grant to denote its descent in the direct male line: at present it is understood to imply the right of perpetual descent to heirs general without restriction.

BAṬOHI, BUṬOHEE, H. (بٹوهي) A wayfarer, a traveller.

BAṬORAN or BAṬOLAN, BUṬORUN, BUṬOLUN, H. (بٹورن, بٹولن) Gathering or heaping grain in one place at the time of harvest.

BAṬṬA, BUṬṬA, H. (بٹّہ, बट्टा), BÁṬṬÁ, Beng. (বাট্টা), BAṬṬÁ, Mar. (बट्टा) Difference or rate of exchange. In revenue matters it applies to the amount added to, or deducted from, any payment according to the currency in which it is paid as compared with a fixed standard coin. Discount on uncurrent or short-weight rupees. A cess or charge imposed to make up for any probable deficiency in the value of the coin. (It is often confounded, but incorrectly, with *Bhatta*, q. v.).

Báher-baṭṭá, Mar. (बाहेरबट्टा) Difference of value added, in opposition to *Ántabaṭṭá* (आंतबट्टा), difference of value deducted, in exchanging various currencies.

Bájár-batta, Mar. Rate at which various coins are current in the bazar with reference to a standard currency.

BATTA, Karn. (ಬತ್ತ) Rice before it is deprived of the chaff, *Paddy*, which is probably derived from this word. Corn in general.

BAṬṬA-VARTTI, Tam. (பட்டவர்த்தி) Property held in severalty, in contrast to that which is held in joint shares.

BATTEMU, more correctly, BHATYAMU, q. v., Tel. (బత్తెము) Daily allowance of food or money for subsistence.

BATTENA-SETHI, Tam. (?) An arbitrator among the right-hand castes.

BATTNAUL-KAI, Tam. (?) A tribe of weavers in the Madura and Tinnivelly districts who have a peculiar slang dialect.

BATTI, H. (بتّي) A still for distilling spirits. A candle.

BAṬWÁR or BAṬWÁL, BUṬWAR, BUṬWAL, H. (بٹوال بٹوار) A custom or police-officer stationed on the road to collect transit duties.

BATWADE-PATRAK, (?) A tabular statement of pay due for a given term to every person on the establishment of a *Kamavisdár* or *Mahalkarni*, except the peons.

BATWON, Hindi (बतवोन) Finish, the preparation of land for the reception of seed. *Puraniya.*

BAU, BOU, H. (بَو, बाउ) The fee or perquisite of a Zamindar when a daughter of one of his tenants is married.

BAÜ, Beng. (বউ) A wife. A son's wife.

BÁÚ or BÁV, BÁVÍ, Mar. (बाव, बावी) A large-mouthed well.

Báükhol, Mar. (बावखोल) A dry well, or one partly choked with rubbish.

BAUCHHÁR, H. (بوچهار) Wind and driving rain.

BÁÚL, Mar. (बाउळ) Moist soil over rock favourable for rice. Ground on the bank of a river, &c.

BAULÍ, more correctly, BHAULÍ, q. v., corruptly, BOWLEY, H. (بَولي, बौली) Settlement direct with the Ryots; a *khás* or Ryotwar assessment.

BÁÜNI, Beng. (বাউনী) Hansel, the first money taken by a dealer.

BAUTÍ JAMÍN, Hindi (बौती जमीन) Lands held by the owner of a village to give out to the Ryots for cultivation, sharing the crop. *Puraniya.*

BÁÜRI, Beng. (বাউরি) A Hindu of a low caste, commonly, by avocation, a swine-herd.

BÁVA, Karn. (ಬಾವ) The son of a mother's brother, or of a father's sister if older than one's self; also a man's brother-in-law if he is the elder, and a woman's brother-in-law if older than her husband.

Bávamaiduna, Karn. (ಬಾವಮೈದುನ) A man's brother-in-law.

BÁWAG, BAWUG, H. (باوگ) Seed-time (Benares).

BÁWARI, H. (باوري) A robber by profession, one belonging to a numerous tribe dispersed through India, and known in different places by different appellations, but called by themselves BÁWARI. They are all Hindus, and use a peculiar dialect, which is said to be spoken in some parts of Guzerat.

BAWERA, H. (بويره) Sowing seed. See BOARA.

BAYÁ, BYÁ, H. (بَيا) A person appointed in bazars to measure grain.

Bayái, *Byaee*, H. (بيائي) The weighman's fee or perquisites.

BAYALU, Karn. (ಬಯಲು) A field, a plain, an open space.

BÁYANÁ, Beng. (বায়না) Earnest-money, money given to bind a bargain.

BÁYANÁKKÁ, Beng. (বায়নাক্কা, from P. بيان, relation, and واقع, event) A report or recital of particulars.

BAYÁT, BYAT, H. A. (?) Inauguration. The ceremony of admitting a person as a disciple.

BÁZ, vernacularly, BÁJ, H. (P. باز, बाज) Again, back.

Báz-ámad, H. (P. باز, again, and آمد, what comes) Returned, reported, resumed.

Báz-ámad ahkám, H. A (احکام, orders) Return to the orders of the Court by the head criminal officer or Názar.

Báz-dári, H. (P. داري, having) Relinquishment of a claim of action, or withdrawal of a suit.

Báz-giri, H. (P. باز, again, and *giri*, from گرفتن, to take) Taking back, resuming; resumption of alienated revenue on lands.

Báz-náma, also *Báz-i-náma*, H. P. (نازنامه) A deed of relinquishment; one abandoning or renouncing a claim, whether valid or not.

Báz-yáft, H., &c., sometimes dialectically modified, as in Uriya, *Bájiáft*; or *Báj-yáfta*, (from the P. باز, again, and يافتن, to find, to obtain) Resuming, recovering; especially resumption, either wholly or in part, of alienated lands, and again subjecting them to a revenue assessment. Money refunded when in excess of the authorised collection. Any escheat or lapsed property falling to the Government.

Báz yáfti, H. (P. يافتي, a finding) The article recovered or resumed; a grant of revenue, or a land-free tenure resumed.

BÁZÁR, H. (P. بازار) in the dialects which have not a *z*, BÁJÁR, Hindi and Mar. (बाजार), Ben. (বাজার), Tel. (బాజారు), &c. A market, a daily market. A market-place. As opposed to a *Bázár*, a *Hát* is held only on certain days; a *Ganj* is where grain and the necessaries of life are principally sold, and generally wholesale. *Bázárs* and *Háts* are sometimes included in *Ganjes*.

Bázár-baṭṭa, H. The market rate of exchange for different coins.

Bázár- or *Bájár-baiṭhak*, blunderingly, *Bazar-heetick*, H. (بيٹھك, बैठक, a place of sitting) A fee or tax for setting up a shop or stall, or for trading at a Bázár.

Bájár-chalan, Mar. (बाजारचलन) Current in the market, as coin.

Bázár-kharch, H. (P. خرچ) Expenses incurred for market purchases; daily or domestic disbursements.

Bázár-nirakh, H. (P. بازار نرخ) Mar. (बाजारनिरख) Market rate of prices. Price-current.

Bázár or *Bájár-phasgi*, Karn. (ಬಾಜಾರಫಸಗಿ) Tax or toll on articles brought to market.

Bájárwáḍá, Mar. (बाजारवाडा) Market-place.

BAẒÁÂT, H. A. Agency, commission. See *Biẓáât*.

BÂẒÍ, H. (A. بعضي) Some, several, miscellaneous. (In the Hindu dialects it always becomes *Báji* or *Báje*, बाजी, बाजे).

Bâẓí- or *Bâjí-báb*, H. (A. باب) Various or miscellaneous items. Head of a revenue account, comprehending various petty taxes and cesses. Also *Bâẓí-bábat* and *Bâẓí-dafâ*.

Bâẓí- or *Bâjí-jamâ*, H. (A. جمع) Miscellaneous revenue. Aggregate of revenue derived from other sources than the Mál and Sair or land revenue and customs and excise; as from fines for petty offences, fees, cesses, &c., most of which are now abolished.

Bâẓí- or *Bâjí-kharch*, H. (A. خرچ) *Báje-kharch*, Mar., *Bája-kharchu*, Tel., also corruptly, *Bázi-curtch* or *kurch*, Miscellaneous expenses. An item in revenue accounts for sundry charges not included in the fixed regular disbursement. A deduction in revenue accounts formerly allowed to Zamindars to cover their claims to compensation for expenses incurred in the collection of the revenue, the repair of roads and bridges, including something additional by way of remuneration for their public services.

Bâẓí-zamín or *zumeen*, H. (P. زمين, land) Miscellaneous lands: applied especially to Lá-kharáj lands, or lands exempted from assessment, and paying no revenue, or a light quit-rent only, to the Government, held under different tenures: according to some authorities, not inclusive of Chákarán lands, or those held in lieu of pay for public services.

Bâẓí-zamín daftar, H. P. (دفتر) Before the permanent settlement, an office in Bengal for the investigation and registry of miscellaneous rent-free tenures.

BÁZÍGAR, H., or, in some dialects, BÁJÍGAR, BAJEEGUR, (from P. باز, sport, play) A juggler, a tumbler; a low caste, living by sleight of hand and bodily tricks.

BÁZIK, A. (بازك) A kind of spirituous liquor made from grapes boiled down to about a third, whether before or after fermentation, prohibited by Mohammedan law.

BAZZÁZ, H. (A. بزّاز) A cloth merchant, a draper.

BÁZU, H. (بازو) A document bearing the seal or signature of a competent officer of the Mogul government authenticating a royal grant.

Bázu-i-farmán, H. A document giving effect to a royal grant.

Be, H. (P. بي) A particle prefixed to words to imply absence or privation; as *Be-báḳ*, H. P. Without arrears, paid up in full.

Be-chhápar, Ben. (বেছাপর) Without a roof. Applied to the site of a village on which no huts longer remain, having been abandoned by the inhabitants.

Be-chirágh. H. (P. بي and چراغ, a lamp; without a light) Ruined, deserted, desolate (as a village).

Be-dákhil, H. (from دخل, entering) Dismissed, set aside, not admitted; also, ejected, dispossessed (of land).

Be-dákhilí, H. (داخلي, entering) Ejection, dispossession.

Be-dâwá, H. (from the A. دعوي, a plaint) Relinquishment of a claim or suit.

Be-dâwá-patra, H. A. S. An acquittance, a release, a paper acknowledging the abandonment of a suit.

Be-já, H. (P. جا, a place) Improper, out of place, unseasonable.

Be-já-ḳurḳi, H. (قرقي, distraint) Illegal distraint, a suit for replevin.

Be-kár, H. (P. كار, business) Unemployed, without work.

Bekári, H. (P. بيكاري) An unemployed labourer. Incorrectly confounded with *Begári*, q. v.

Be-ḳasur or *Be-taḳṣír*, H. (A. قصور, تقصير) Without blame, innocent, acquitted.

Be-námí, H. P. (from نام, a name) Nameless, fictitious, fraudulent; as a purchase under a false name, or land held in another name than that of the real proprietor.

Be-wáriṣ, H. (A. وارث, an heir) *Bewáraṣí*, Mar. (बेवारशी) Without heirs; lands, property, &c.

Bewáriṣ-mál, H. A. Property that escheats to the Government in default of heirs.

(There are many other such compounds, as they may be formed at pleasure.)

Beb, H. (بيب) A grass from which a twine is made; also called Bábar.

Bebartta, Beburttu, Uriya. Head officer of a tributary Rájá.

Beḍá or Beṛá, Hindi (बेड़ा) Ben. (বেড from S. वेष्टन) A fence or hedge, an inclosure.

Beḍi or Beṛi, Ben. (বেড়ী) A fetter.

Béḍa, Béḍanu, plur. *Bedaru*, whence commonly *Beder* or *Vedar*, Karn. (ಬೇಡ, ಬೇಡನು, ಬೇಡರು) The name of a caste, or of members of it, who are considered as outcastes, or Chanḍálas, and live by the chase; hunters, fowlers: they are considered in Mysore as coming originally from Telingana.

Béḍara-halli, Karn. (ಬೇಡರಹಳ್ಳಿ) A village of Béḍars, or outcastes, living as hunters and fowlers.

Beddalu, Karn. (ಬಿದ್ದಲು) Tax upon the straw of the dry grain, the whole of which is taken by the Ryots.

Beḍḍa-ṣistu, Tel. (బెడ్డశిస్తు) The summer crop.

Béḍiga, Tel. (బెడిగ) Quit rent.

Begár, Begári, also Bigar, Bigári, corruptly, Beegar, Beegarah, Bagárah, H. (بيگار, بيگاري, from P. بي, and گار, for كار, who works, S. कार) A forced labourer, one pressed to carry burthens for individuals or the public. Under the old system, when pressed for public service, no pay was given. The *Begári*, though still liable to be pressed for public objects, now receives pay. Forced labour for private service is prohibited.

Begári, H. Ben. (بيگاري, বেগারী) The act of pressing labourers or servants. In Mar., *Bigár* or *Begár* (बिगार, बेगार) is the forced labour, *Bigári* or *Begári* (बिगारी, बेगारी) the labourer. In Karnáta, *Begári* (ಬೇಗಾರಿ) is the performance of the lowest village offices without pay, but requited by fees in grain, or rent-free land.

Behára, Ben. (বেহারা, S. व्यवहार:) A domestic servant, 'a bearer,' a palanquin-bearer.

Behḍá, pronounceable Behṛá, also Beharḍ and Beheṛá, incorrectly Baheṛa, Mar. (बेहडा, बेहेडा) A document under the Mahratta Government, shewing the amount of all the fixed receipts and disbursements of the state, all establishments, grants, and endowments, and all particular transactions during the past year. It formed the basis of the collections of the ensuing year. A budget. A statement of ways and means.

Behjar, (?) Cultivation of barley and grain mixed.—*Doab*.

Behnaur or Behan, H. (بيهن, بيهنور) Nursery for rice plants. (Eastern Oudh.)

Behrá, H. (بيهرا) Grass kept for pasturage.

Behrí, Behree, incorrectly, Bheri, Bheree, Behry, Bihri, H. (بيهري, P. بهره, a share, a quota) A proportionate rate or subscription: assessment on a share: instalments paid by under-tenants to the landlord: distribution of an aggregate sum among a number of individuals, or a monthly collection from them according to circumstances. A subdivision of a *Paṭṭidári* or *Bhayachári* estate, being an unequal fractional part of a Thók; that is, a Thók of three Biṣwas may be divided into three Behris; one containing two Biṣwas, one $\frac{3}{4}$ths, and one $\frac{1}{4}$th of a Biṣwa. The share or interest of one of the coparceners in such estate. Beng. Reg. vii. 1822, s. 12.

Behrí-bandi, corruptly, *Bhery-bundy*, *Bery-bundy*, or *Behry-bundy*, H. (بيهري بندي) One of the items formerly allowed in the revenue accounts as abatements of the collection. An allowance for keeping causeways and embankments in repair, also for digging and repairing wells and other public works, the charge of which was borne in common by the Zamindars of a district, in proportion to their estates.

Behrí-barár, H. (برار, tax) Collection on shares of the revenue in kind.

Behrí-dár, corruptly, *Beyrydar*, H. (P. دار, who has) The holder of a share in the lands of a village. One bearing his quota in the assessment and charges.

BEJHARÁ, BEJHURA, H. (بيجهرا) A mixed crop, generally of rice and barley.

BEJOT, H. (P. بي, without, and H. جوت, tillage) Untilled, as land: applied also to a Ryot who has ceased to cultivate, and has thrown up his land.

Bejot-jamá, H. (A. جمع) A statement in the public account of the revenue leviable on the land left untilled.

Bejot-zamín, H. (A. زمين) Land abandoned or untilled, as registered in the village accounts.

BEJWÁR or BÍJWÁR, H. (بيجوار, from *Bíj*, بيج, seed) Perquisite of the lower classes, consisting of a portion of the seed-corn brought away daily from the fields. (Rohilkhand.)

BEL or BÍL, H. (P. بيل) A sort of spade or hoe, a pick-axe.

Belcha, or *Belchak*, or *Belak*, *Belchu*, *Belchuk*, *Beluk*, (بيلچك, بيلچه, بيلك) A small spade or hoe.

Beldár, or *Bíldár*, H. (بيلدار) A digger, a delver, one who works with a *Bél*, a pick-axe, or a spade; a pioneer, a sapper, a miner.

BEL, H. (بيل, S. बिल्व) A creeping plant, a sort of jasmine. A fruit-tree (*Ægle marmelos*). A spot on which the receiving-pans of a sugar-factory are placed. A line marked out on a road, or in a garden, to shew the direction of any proposed work.

Bel-bhaṇḍár, corruptly, *Belbundar*, Mar. (बेलभंडार) The leaves of the *Bél* tree and turmeric placed upon an idol. A form of oath. Taking such leaves from off the idol, and swearing by them. An agreement or promise satisfied by this oath.

BELÁ, also BEHLÁ, H. (P. *Bíla*, بيلا, بيهلا) Mar. BELEṈ, (बेलें) Money, or a bag of money, carried by a person of rank and wealth as he travels, for the purpose of distributing or throwing among the poor.

Belá-bardár, H. (P. بردار) An officer who distributes or scatters money among the poor on the part of a superior, a purse-bearer, an almoner.

Belá-hharch, H. Expenditure of a man of rank or wealth in almsgiving.

BEḶASU, BEḶAVI, BEḶE, &c., Karn. (ಬೆಳಸು, ಬೆಳವಿ, ಬೆಳೆ, and other deriv. from ಬೆಳೆ, to grow) Growing corn, a standing crop.

Beḷasáda-hola, Karn. (ಬೆಳಸಾದಹೊಲ) A field of grown corn.

BELBÚTA, H. (بيلبوته) A bush.

BÉḶE, Karn. (ಬೇಳೆ) One-eighth of a rupee; also split pulse.

BELHA, or BEYLHA, Thug. The person who selects the spot where the murder is to be committed.

Belhaï, Thug. Selection of the spot where travellers are to be strangled.

BELKÍ, BELKEE, H. (بيلكي) A cattle-breeder, a grazier.

BELLA, Karn. (ಬೆಲ್ಲ) A coarse kind of sugar, commonly called Jágari.

Bella-dále, Karn. (ಬೆಲ್ಲದಾಲೆ) A sugar-mill or press, sugar-baking.

Bella-dagáṇa, Karn. (ಬೆಲ್ಲದಗಾಣ) A coarse sugar-mill.

BELWA, Karn. (ಬೆಲ್ವ) A man whose business it is to gather the juice of the Tál tree, speaking Máláyalim, though settled in Mysore.

BELWAL, Mar. (?) High land.

BENÁP, Hindi (बेनाप, from P. بي, without, and S. माप, measuring, corruptly changing *m* to *n*) Unmeasured, unsurveyed.

Benáp-ka-paṭṭá, Hindi (बेनाप का पट्टा) A lease in which it is agreed between the renter and the cultivator that the original measurement and average rates shall remain unaltered as long as the cultivator pays the stipulated rent.

BENAUDHÁ, H. (بينودها) A name commonly given to the country between Allahabad and the further side of the Sarju river, also called Benáwat.

Beṇḍe, Karn. (ಬೆಂಡೆ) A kind of hemp made from the fibres of the *Hibiscus esculentus.*

Bengat, Bengut, H. (بینگت, बेंगत) Seed: especially when lent for sowing to an indigent Ryot, who is to repay the same at harvest, with such addition as may be agreed upon.—Benares.

Benṭ, H. (بینٹ, बेंट) The handle of a hoe, axe, or similar implement. Pronounced Bít in Rohilkhand, and Binta in Dehli.

Bentagam, Tam. (possibly an error for *Bandagam,* q. v.) Mortgaged plough-land. (Travancore.)

Beohár, H., &c. (بیوهار, बेओहार, S. व्यवहार) **Béhára**, Karn (ಬೇಹಾರ) Business, calling, trade, traffic, money-lending. A loan. 'In law,' legal proceedings. At Jabalpur, a *Kánungo.*

Beoharā, Beohárá, Beohâriyá, and less correctly, *Bahorá,* H., &c. (بیوهرا, بیوهارا, بیوهاریا, बेओहरा, बहोरा, S. व्यवहारी, व्यवहारिक,) *Béhári,* Karn. (ಬೇಹಾರಿ) A trader, a man of business, a merchant, a money-lender, a creditor. A litigant, one who engages, or may engage, in legal proceedings.

Bepár, H. (بیپار, बेपार, S. व्यापारः) Trade, traffic.

Bepárí, H., Ben., Mar., also pronounced *Baipárí* or *Byopárí,* and written *Bayparee, Beopáree,* &c. (بیپاري, بیوپاري, বেপারী, বৈপারী, बेपारी, S. व्यापारी) A trader, a dealer, a shopkeeper, a travelling trader or pedlar. A merchant, a grain merchant.

Ber, Mar. (बेर) Second or transverse ploughing of a field.

Béra, Karn. (ಬೇರ) Trade, merchandise.

Beṛá, H. (بیڑا) A raft, a float, especially one on which a sort of paper and tinsel boat, with the face of a female and crest and breast of a peacock at the prow, is set afloat by the Mohammadans on the rivers of Bengal, with lights and music, in honour of *Khaja Khizr,* on the evenings of the Thursdays, especially of the last Thursday, of *Bhádon* (Aug.—Sept.). Opulent persons amuse themselves with being rowed up and down the river during part of the night in illuminated boats, having musicians and singers on board. The *Beṛá* is usually presented in consequence of a vow made during the previous year, in acknowledgment of some benefit, as the birth of a child, supposed to have been obtained through the intercession of the saint.

Beraḍ, Mar. (बेरड) A low tribe in the South Maraṭha country, inhabiting the hills and thickets, and subsisting by the chase, and by plunder. They are sometimes employed in police duties, and in garrisoning forts, and are also called *Rámosí.*

Beragáḍu, Tel. (బేరగాడు) A purchaser.

Berájee-ká paṭṭá, Hindi, (बेराजी का पट्टा) A lease of certain rates to be paid by the Ryot for ploughing the soil, levied upon the crop raised by actual measurement. The amount paid is never to be less than that of the preceding year, and increases with additional cultivation, according to the usual rates (Puraniya). (The word is of doubtful origin, and may be a corruption of *Beríj,* q. v.; or of the P. *be,* without, and *rázi,* assent.)

Beramu, Tel, (బేరము) Traffic, trade, a bargain.

Berár, H. (بیرار) In Baitul and the Dakhin the same as the *Kánungo* of Hindustan, the village registrar and accountant.

Beṛha, H. (بیڑها, S. वेष्टनं) A paling, an inclosure. **Berhná**, (بیڑهنا, from the same S. root, वेष्ट, to surround) means also to drive off cattle by force, to foray.

Beṛí, Beṛee, H. (بیڑي, बेडी, from S. वेष्ट, to surround) **Biṛí**, or **Beṛí**, Mar. (बिडी, बेडी) Iron fetters, or a chain for man or animals. A sort of basket with two ropes, by which water is thrown up from a pond or well to a higher elevation, when it irrigates a garden or field.

Beri, Tel. (బేరి) The name of a caste in the south of India, following trade, and claiming to belong to the original *Vaiṣya* caste. They also call themselves *Chitti,* or, more correctly, *Sheti,* from the S. *Ṣreshṭhí,* a merchant; but, as belonging to the left-hand castes, they are distinct from the *Komatis* or *Chittis* of the right-hand division.

Beríj, also written **Barij**, and **Beriz**, or **Bariz**, Mar. (बेरीज) **Béríju**, Tel. (బేరిజు) Karn. (ಬೇರೀಜು) all from the P. بریج, an account) The total sum or aggregate of an account. The total amount of a revenue assessment, the same as *Jamâ;* the total assessment of a district. The items of the assessment on a *Zamindárí,* usually inserted, in former times, in the middle of the grant, and thence identified with that part of the document in which the entry was made, or 'the middle' of the paper; also the nett revenue assessment, after allowing for village and other fixed charges. In Karnáta the original *Bidnur* assessment was termed the *Shist;* the additions made by Hyder and Tipu, the *Shámil.* The two together constituted the *Karim* (? *Ḳadím*) *Beríj,* or old or original assessment. The assessment of 1819-20 is termed the *Tarao Beríj:* the *Ṣáswata* (S. perpetual) *Beríj* is the permanent settlement. The term is more usually employed in the south than in the north of India to express the sense of a settlement of the Revenue. In Hindustan it more commonly referred to the entry of the *Jamâ* in the *Zamindárí* grant.

BÉSÁYA, more correctly, VYAVASÁYA, Karn. (ಬೇಸಾಯ, from S. व्यवसाय) Cultivation, agriculture, farming.

Bésáyadava, Karn. (ಬೇಸಾಯದವ) A farmer, a cultivator.

Bésáyadabhúmi, Karn. (ಬೇಸಾಯದಭೂಮಿ Land under tillage.

BESHI, H. (P. بيشي) Increase, surplus. Increased assessment, either on the general account, or any particular item of the revenue; as corrupted, *Beeshy* and *Beeshy-mamooli* occur to express the additional duty formerly levied on the cultivator of opium.

Beshi-jamâ, H. (A. جمع) Increase of revenue or assessment upon that of the preceding year.

Beshi-zamín, H. (A. زمين) Increase in the lands cultivated, either by addition, or by more accurate measurement. Separate columns are kept for this and the preceding in the books of the village.

BESTA, Tel. Karn. (బెస్త) The name of the caste of fishermen in the Madras and Mysore provinces, to which the palankeen-bearers usually belong.

Bestarava, Bestaru, Karn. (ಬೆಸ್ತರವ, plur. ಬೆಸ್ತರು) The name of a caste in Mysore, comprising fishermen, lime-burners, and palankeen-bearers. (Probably the same as the preceding Telugu word.)

BEṬÁ, H. &c. (بيتا) A son, BEṬÍ (بيتي) A daughter.

BE-TAN-MÁL, H. (P. بي, without, تن, *tan,* a body or person, and *mál,* مال, property) An escheat, property devolving to the State in default of legal claimants. (This has evidently been confounded with *Bait ul-mál,* q. v., which has thence been incorrectly interpreted an escheat.

BET- or BETRA-BANDI, H. (بيت, بيتر بندي, from S. *vetra,* वेत्र, a cane or willow) A Pargana or Zamindárí charge formerly allowed to be set off from the assessment as being incurred for mats or wicker work in which goods or treasure were packed for transmission to the *Ṣubadár* of the province, or to the court of Dehli. (Misprinted in the fifth Report, and so copied into the Glossary, *Bedrh-cundy.*)

BEṬH, H. (بيته) Sandy, unproductive soil. (Rohilkhand.)

BEṬHIÁ, Uriya (ବେଠିଆ) An impressed labourer, a *Begárí.*

BEṬṬA, or BEṬṬ, Karn. (ಬೆಟ್ಟ) High land, a hill, a mountain. The third and worst kind of land for rice, situated on high ground, and imperfectly irrigated, yielding but one crop a-year; also called BORU-BEṬṬ.

BEWÁRÁ, Mar. (बेवारा) Discharge of business, settlement of a debt, &c. See *Beohár.*

BHÁBAR, BHABUR, H. (بهابر) The forest under the Sewalik hills. The name of a light black soil in the neighbourhood of Baitul.

BHABHÚT, H. (بهبهوت, S. विभूति) The ashes of burnt cow-dung, with which mendicants, of the *Ṣaiva* orders chiefly, besmear their bodies.

BHÁCHÁ, also BHÁCHRÚ, Mar. (भाचा, भाचरू) A nephew: BHÁCHÍ, (भाची) A niece: the son or daughter of a man's sister, of a woman's brother or sister, or of a husband's sister.

Bháchejáṇwái, Mar. (भाचेजांवाई) The husband of such a niece.

Bháchesún, Mar. (भाचेसून) The wife of such a nephew.

BHAḌÁ, BHUḌA, H. (بهڈا) A kind of grass growing in a poor soil to the height of little more than a foot, making excellent fodder.

BHADÁHAR, BHUDAHUR, H. (بهداهر, भदाहर) Cutting grain when it is only half ripe.

BHADAÍ, BHUDUYEE, H. (بهدئي, भदई) The produce of the month Bhádoṉ; the grain, &c., gathered in that month—Aug.—Sept.

BHAḌARÍÁ, BHUḌUREEA, H. (بهڈريا, भडरीआ) A tribe of mendicants of Brahmanical descent, professors of astrology. (Probably from *Bhadra,* S., auspiciousness.)

BHADAURÍÁ, BHADOURIA, corruptly, BHUDOREA, H. (بهدوريا, भदौरीआ) A branch of the Chauhan Rájputs, residing chiefly in the provinces of Agra and Etáwa, and in other places along the Jumna, whence the tract is termed Bhadáwar. The Raja of the district pretends to be descended from an ancient family, the members of which enjoyed high consideration at the court of Delhi from the reign of Akbar, and his pretensions are admitted by the surrounding Rajas, who yield him precedence, and accept from him the Tilaka or frontal mark on their accession.

BHADBHADÁNÁ, BHUDBHUDANA, H. (بهدبهدانا, भदभदाना) Cutting grain when half ripe. Stealing fruit from a tree.

BHÁḌE, Mar. (भाडे) BHÁḌÁ, or BHÁṚÁ, Ben. (ভাডা) BHÁṬAK, Karn. (ಭಾಟಕ) Hire, rent, price, recompence.

Bháḍatakíyá, Ben. (ভাডতকীযা) A renter, a tenant.

Bháḍekarí, Mar. (भाडेकरी) One who lets out any thing for rent or hire, one who works for hire, a hireling.

BHADOṆ, corruptly, BAUDOON, H. (بهادوں, भादों, S. भाद्रः) The fifth month of the luni-solar year (Aug.—Sept.).

Bhádoṇwí, or *Bháduí*, corruptly, *Bhádovey*, Hindi,(भादोंवी, भादुई) *Bhádaví*, Mar. (भादवी) Relating to the month Bhádoṇ, or the harvest gathered in Aug.—Sept. : autumnal.

BHÁDRA, S., &c. (भाद्र) The fifth month of the luni-solar year (Aug.—Sept.)

BHÁDRABAU, Ben. (ভাদ্রবৌ) A younger brother's wife.

BHÁG, BHÁGAM, corruptly, BAUG, BAUGAUM, BAUGOM, H., but in most other dialects also, (بهاگ, S. भागं) A share, a part, a portion, a share in kind : tax, duty, the share of the Government. Share or portion of inheritance. In Hindu law, partition may be regulated amongst the sons according to the number of their mothers, or the wives of the deceased, which is termed *Patní bhága;* but this is allowable only where the usage has been long established as the custom of the family. The more regular distribution is according to the number of sons (*putra*), thence denominated *Putra-bhága*. See *Vibhága*.

Bhág-baṭáí corruptly, *Bhugwuttee*, H. (بهاگ بٹائي, भागबटाई) Apportionment of shares of the crop in kind between the cultivator and the Government.

Bhág-batti (?) *Bhágavatí*, (from S. *Bhága*, share, and the possessive particle *vatí*, belonging to, or possessed of). In Guzerat, division of the crop in kind, the Government taking one-half of the crop in the rainy season, and from one-third to one-fifth of that in the dry season, if the land be irrigated; (probably an error for the preceding).

Bhágdár, corruptly, *Baugdar*, H. (بهاگدار, भागदार) *Bhágidár*, Guz. (ભાગીદાર) A sharer, a partner; also, in Cuttack, an accomplice.

Bhágdárí, H. (بهاگداري, भागदारी) Holding a share; the same as *Paṭṭidárí*, in the Dakhin.

Bhágí, H. (भागी) A sharer, a partner; also, a share, a portion.

Bhágí-dár, Mar. (भागीदार) A sharer, a partner. It also occurs *Bhágil* and *Bhágelí*.

Bhág-joṭ, Ben. (ভাগজোট) Cultivation by the Ryot on the terms of sharing the crop with the Zamindar.

Bhág-khamár, Ben. (ভাগখামার) The transfer of land, held on the condition last named, from one Ryot to another Ryot, the latter engaging to give to the former a half share of the produce.

Bhágwár, H. (بهاگوار, भागवार) Held upon a joint or sharing tenure (land, &c.)

BHAGAT, H. (بهگت, corruption of *Bhakt*) A religious mendicant, a worshipper of *Vishṇu*.

BHÁGNAR, H. (بهاگنر, भागनर) A name given to the rich alluvial lands under the banks of the Jumná.

BHAGTÁ, H. (بهگتا) A tribe of Ahírs.

BHÁÍ, BHAEE, also BHAIYÁ, less correctly, BHAYA and BHYE, H., &c. (بهاي, بهيا, भाई, भैया, S. भातृ) Ben. (ভাই) A brother, a natural brother; also, a friend and companion; metaphorically, a brother. It is especially applied also to individuals connected by community of origin and joint interest in a common ancestral property, proprietors of shares, either actually or conventionally, in the same village lands. (The derivatives and compounds may follow either form of the primitive, but those which take the second form, *Bhaiyá* or *Bhaya*, are most frequent.

Bháí-ans, *Bhaiyánṣ*, H. (بهاي انس, भैयांश, from अंश, a share) The share or portion of a brother or a co-parcener.

Bhaiyánṣí-bíghá, H. (भैयांशीबीघा) An arbitrary measure of land, used by the brotherhood of a co-parcenary village, for apportioning the revenue upon the lands they cultivate. It is larger than that in common use upon which the revenue is assessed at so much per Bigha.

Bháí-band, *Bhaee-bund*, H. (بهاي بند) A brother, one by lineal affinity, or one by community of origin and interest, or only by friendship and association.

Bháí-bandí, H. (بهاي بندي, भाईबंदी) Brotherhood, fraternity, actual or incidental.

Bháí-bat, *Bhaeebut*, or *Bháíwad*, *Bhaeewud*, or *Bhybut*, *Bhywud*, H. (بهايبت, भाईबत, from *bat* or *wad* affix implying like to) As a brother or co-parcener, brother or partner-like (acting, engaging, sharing, &c.)

Bháíbau, Ben. (ভাইবৌ) A brother's wife.

Bhaiyá-bánṭ, H. (भैयाबांट) Held in common, as a village. See the next.

Bhaiyáchárá, or *Bhaiyáchárí*, less correctly, *Bhayachára*, &c., H. (بهياچارا, بهياچاري, भैयाचारा, भैयाचारी, either from the S. *chara*, चर, going, or *áchára*, institute, fraternal establishment) Lands, or villages, or certain rights and privileges held in common property, either entirely or in part, as in the perfect, or imperfect *Paṭṭidári* tenure by a number of families forming a brotherhood, originally perhaps descended from a common ancestor, but now not always connected by sameness of descent. Their several claims and liabilities are sometimes regulated by established custom, but they sometimes rest upon ancestral rights, the nature and extent of which are not always easy of determination and adjustment, and require careful investigation. In all such fraternities the Government revenue is most usually paid through one of the number representing the whole. Any one of the co-parceners may let or mortgage his share to a non-proprietor; in some places, subject to the concurrence of the rest of the fraternity. In such case, the original shareholder may retain his privileges of administering and voting, in regard to the interests of the community, as well as his share in the manorial rights of the whole to waste lands, water-courses and reservoirs, ground-rents on land let to strangers, taxes on trades, fees on occasional fairs, and a variety of other emoluments which are shared in common.

Bhái-hiṣṣi, H. (from the P. حصہ, a part) The shares of a brotherhood.

Bháijhi, Ben. (ভাইঝী) A brother's daughter.

Bhái- or *Bhaiyá-jamâ*, H. (भाई- भैयाजमा) A fee paid to the head or heads of the village on settling the assessment of the revenue.

Bhái, or *Bhaiyá-pansi*, H. (بهاي پنسي, भाई- भैयापंसी) The shares of a co-parcenary or brotherhood.

Bhái-dwitíyá, H., &c. (from the S. भातृद्वितीया) A Hindu festival. See *Bhrátṛi-dwitíyá*.

Bhái-phoṭ, Ben. (ভাইফোট) Marking the foreheads of brothers with sandal, on the preceding festival.

Bhái-puä, Uriya, (ଭାଇପୁଅ) Lit., A brother's son, applied to a relation holding lands in a village on easier terms than others not related to the Zamindar, on paying a proportion of the revenue and village charges.

Bhaimí, S. (भैमी, from *Bhíma*, भीम) The eleventh of Mágha, on which day offerings are presented to the manes, in honour of Bhíma.

Bhais, Thug. One of the seven original clans.

Bhaitá, Hin. (भैता) A stunted crop.

Bhajanappura, Mal. (ഭജനപ്പുര) The palace of the Elia Raja of Travancore. A private residence in a temple.

Bhájawal, Mar. (भाजावळ) Burning the weeds off the ground before sowing the seed. Ground so burned.

Bhájídast, Mar. (from भाजी, vegetables, and P. *dast*, دست, the hand) A tax levied in kind, either by the Government or the village officers, on fruit and vegetables brought to market.

Bhákar, Mar. (भाकर) A plain cake of bread; most usually applied to bread made from inferior grains, as holcus, millet, &c.

Bhaksi, H. (بهكسي, भकसी) A dungeon, a chamber in which revenue defaulters in native states are confined.

Bhakshya, S. (भक्ष्यः) Eatable, what may be legally eaten; in opposition to *Abhakshya*, what is not to be eaten, what is prohibited.

Bhakt, Bhukt, also read Bhakat, Bhakta, and Bhagat, H. (بهكت, S. *bhakta*, भक्तः) A follower, a worshipper, one devoted to, as to a divinity, as *Śiva-bhakt*, a follower of Śiva; *Vishṇu-bhakt*, an adorer of Vishṇu.

Bhákta, S. (deriv. of भक्तः) A follower, a dependant, a pensioner, a religious sect or school, as those of *Śaivas*, or of *Vaishṇavas*. The right-hand worshippers of *Śaktí* are also called *Bháktas*.

Bhakti, S. (भक्तिः) Faith, devotion, service, hire of labour.

Bhál, H. (भाल) A tribe of Rajputs, proprietors of lands in the districts of Bulandshahar and Aligarh.

Bhálṣultán, H. (بهالسلطان) A clan of Rajputs, same as the Bhál, but freer from intermixture.

Bhaláwan, Bhulawun, Mar. (भलावण) A letter of credit, one of introduction or recommendation.

Bhále, or Bhálu, Thug. The cry of the jackall—an unlucky omen.

Bhámaṭyá, or Bhánwaṭyá, Mar. (भामट्या, भांवट्या) A sly thief, a pickpocket, a shoplifter, &c.

Bhánḍ, commonly pronounced *Bhánṛ*, H. (भाण्ड, from the S. भाण्डः, buffoonery) A native actor, mime, and jester, of a particular tribe, now usually Mohammadans, but sprung from the Hindu Bahrupiyas.

Bhánḍ, H., &c. (S. بهانڈ, भाण्ड) A vessel. Stock, capital.

Bhanḍár, or *Bhánḍár*, or *Bhanḍára*, also *Bhánḍár-hhána*, H., Mar. (भण्डार, भाण्डार, भण्डारा, from the S. भाण्डागारः) *Bandára*, or *Bhanḍára*, Karn. (ಬಂಡಾರ, ಭಂಡಾರ) A treasury, a store, a room where household supplies are kept. Villages managed by the Raja or Zamindar himself, his own peculiar estate, not rented or farmed to others. In Cuttack, also, a reservoir.

Bhánḍárí, H., Mar. (भाण्डारी) A treasury, a store. See the last. In Guzerat, a kind of guarantee-assurance to a creditor that a loan made by him shall be repaid by the borrower, without the surety's becoming personally liable. Also, guarantee or assurance to any person of the undisturbed enjoyment of recognised office or property, granted on many occasions by the British Government to the creditors and officers of the *Gaíkwar*.

Bhánḍárí, H., Mar., &c. (from *Bhanḍára*) A treasurer, a storekeeper. In Sylhet, a servant, an out-door servant. In other parts of Bengal, a steward. In Cuttack, also, a barber.

Bhanḍárá, Bhundara, Mar. (भंडारा) A feast given to a number of religious mendicants or Gosains. (Perhaps the same as *Bandhára*, q. v.)

Bhanḍárí, Bhundaree, Mar. (भंडारी) A man of a low caste, whose especial employment it is to draw the sap from the cocoa-nut tree, and convert it, by fermentation, into a strong spirituous liquor.

Bhanḍár-már, Mar. (भंडारमाड) A cocoa-nut tree reserved for the preparation of spirit, and not allowed to bear fruit.

Bhang, Bháng, Bhung, Bhang, corruptly, **Bang**, H. (بهنگ, بهانگ, P. بنگ, *bang*) Mar. (भंग, भांग) Ben. (ভাং) Tam. (பங்கு) &c. An intoxicating preparation of hemp (*Cannabis sativa*), either an infusion of the leaves and capsules, or the leaves and stalks bruised and pounded, and chewed or smoked like tobacco. According to Mr. Elliot, the natives of Hindustan distinguish the Bhang from the Ganja plant; the former bearing female flowers only, the latter male. From Dr. O'Shaughnessy's description, the term Bhang properly applies to the larger leaves and capsules, and Ganja to the dried plant with the stalks. From the Bhang is prepared the infusion bearing the same name. The Ganja is used for smoking.—Bengal Dispensatory.

Bhangí, H. (بهنگي, भंगी) One addicted to the use of Bhang.

Bhángrá, H. (بهانگرا, भांगरा) One who is addicted to the use of Bhang.

Bhángera, H. (بهانگيره, भांगेरा) A seller of Bhang.

Bhangela, H. (بهنگيلا) Hempen cloth for wear, or for sacks, also sacks made of it.

Bhángá, Mar. (भांगा) A field, a division of a field.

Bhangí, Bhungee, corruptly, **Bangy**, or **Bahangy**, H. (بهنگي, भंगी) The name of a low caste, employed as sweepers, and in the most inferior menial offices. They are said to be of mixed origin, having sprung from the union of a Brahman woman and a Sudra man. They extend throughout Hindustan, where they are known by different appellations, as *Mehtar*, *Halál-khor*, &c. They profess to be Hindus, observing some Hindu usages, but in others they follow the practices of the Mohammadans, and can scarcely be considered as members of either faith. The name is probably derived from Bhang, for the Bhangis are generally addicted to the use of intoxicating drugs and liquors.

Bhangá, Uriya, (ଭଙ୍ଗା) Correct weighment of salt.

Bhangá-moharir, Uriya, (A. a clerk, محرر) An officer who superintends the weighment of salt.

Bhanguni, Tel. (?) Settlement of a dispute among Ryots by arbitration. (Ganjam.)

Bhanguriá, H. (بهنگوريا) A branch of the *Gaur-taga* tribe in Bulandshahar.

Bhánjá, H. (بهانجا, भांजा, S. भञ्ज, to divide) An arrangement by which three or four Ryots engage to assist each other in turn, either in preparing the crop or getting in the harvest. When it is the turn, or *Bhánjá*, of the one to be assisted, the others contribute ploughs, bullocks, and labourers.

Bháṉs, Mar. (भांस) Heap of husks and grains of rice produced from grinding in order to husk.

Bháṉsaḷ, Mar. (भांसळ) Husked rice.

Bhansara, H. (بهنسره) A branch of the Ahír tribe.

Bhans-lena, Thug. To defraud one another in the partition of the spoil.

Bhanṭá, Bhunṭa, H. (بهنٹا, भंटा) A ploughman's wages in kind. (Rohilkhand. Elsewhere the word is *Bhaṭṭa*.)

Bhanwag, Bhunwug, H. (بهنوگ) A small clan of Rajputs.

Bháo, Ben. (ভাও) Mar. (भाव) Price of any thing, value of an article, market price or rate; interest on money or seed advanced.

Bháolí, Bhaolee, or **Bhávalí**, corruptly, **Bhowley, Bhaweley, Behavilley**, H. (بهاولي, भावली) Distribution of the products of the harvest, in previously stipulated proportions between the landlord and tenant. Rent paid in kind, instead of money. It is also possibly the correct form of *Baoli*, q. v.

Bháoli-khil, H. (بهاولي كهيل) Land recently brought

into cultivation, and of which the cultivator is allowed a larger share of the produce.

Bháoli-pá, H., corruptly, *Bhowley-pah*, (بهاولي پا) Land long cultivated, in which the proportional share of the cultivator is less than in land of recent cultivation.

Bhar, Bhur, H. (بهر, S. भर) Full, complete (used chiefly in composition).

Bhar-kas, Mar. (?) Land paying full rent. (*Dakhin.*)

Bharpái, or *paee*, H. (بهرپاي) Mar. (भरपाई) A release in full endorsed on the back of a receipt (being properly the two last words of the phrase, *main ne kauri bharpái*, the kauris have been received in full by me).

Bharwaṣúl, Mar. (भरवसूल, from A. وصول) Full revenue received.

Bharwasulí, Mar. (भरवसुली) A village, &c., from which full revenue is realized.

Bhar, Bhur, H. (بهر) One of the aboriginal races of Hindustan, called also *Rájbhar*, *Bharat*, and *Bharpatwa*. Tradition assigns for their original seat the whole country from Gorakhpur to Bundelkhand, and the Pargana of Bhadoï, properly *Bhar-doï*, in Benares, is named from them. Many old stone forts, embankments, and excavations in Gorakhpur, Azimgarh, Jonpur, Mirzapur, and Allahabad, are ascribed to them. Amongst others, the celebrated fortress of *Vijayagarh*, or *Bijaygarh*, is still called, after them, a *Bharáwati* fort. When met with they are found following the meanest vocations. They are especially swineherds; and are considered as knowing where treasure is hidden. In the hills eastward of Mirzapur there are some *Bhar* Rájas. The name may be possibly an abbreviation of *Bhárata*, a native of *Bhárata* or India; especially as it is retained unaltered as one of their synonymes.

Bháṛá, H. (بهاڑا, भाड़ा) Ben. (ভাড়া) Mar. *Bháreṇ*, (भाडें) Hire, wages, rent, recompense. In Bengal it is especially the hire of any inanimate thing, and therefore does not imply wages.

Bháṛáṭiya, Ben. (ভাড়াটিয়া) A tenant, a renter.

Bhárekarí, Mar. (भाडेकरी) One who lets out houses, cattle, &c. One who hires them. A labourer, a hireling.

Bháreṇtoreṇ, Mar. (भाडेंतोडें) A loose term for rent, hire, fare, &c.

Bhár, or **Bhárá**, H. &c. (بهار, بهارا, S. भार, P. بار) A load, a burthen. A rupee weight. A weight of gold equal to twenty tolas.

Bhárí, H. (بهاري) Heavy, weighty, a load.

Bhárá, Mar. (भारा) A bundle of grass, a sheaf of corn.

Bhárebhát, Mar. (भारेभात) Threshed rice, usually yielding half a maund per *bhárá*, or bundle.

Bháṛá, (?) A charge made to the Ryot who pays his rent in kind for the carriage of the grain to the place where it is sold. (This may be derived from *Bhár*, a load, or from *Bháṛá*, hire; in the latter case it should be written with the hard ṛ, (بهاڑا.)

Bhárá, Thug. The dead bodies of the victims (Dakhini).

Bharahar, Thug. A pitcher full of water. A lucky omen.

Bharaí, corruptly, **Bhurrye, Bhuray, Burry**, H. (بهرئي, भरई) An allowance formerly made to the Government revenue officers in the provinces of Bareilly and Benares, to cover the cost of remitting the collections to the Government treasury, and of exchanging the different sorts of rupees received in payment into standard currency. A cess or tax raised on pretext of providing for such deductions and allowances, which was originally divided between the Raja and the *Amil*. *Bharaí* was finally abolished by Reg. xiv. 1807, cl. 14.

Bharaki, Thug. A gun.

Bharan, Bharana, or **Bharna**, H., Mar., &c. (بهرن, S. भरण) Completing, filling, rearing. Paying in full. (In the south) A row of betel-nut trees.

Bharana, Uriya, (ଭରଣ) A measure of rice in the husk, equal to eighty *gaunis*.

Bharantu-dibba, Tel, (భరంతుదిబ్బ) A platform or mound on which a salt-heap is raised. (From *bharantu*, a floor, and *dibba*, a heap.)

Bharat, Bhurut, also pronounced **Bharit** and **Barat**, H. (بهرت) Amount of rent paid by an individual, or a party (Dehli).

Bharata, Guz. (ભરત) Measurement. An account opened by the debtor in his own handwriting in his creditor's book.

Bhárat, corruptly, **Bharote**, Guz. (ભારત) A bard. See *Bhát*.

Bhárata, or **Bharata-varsha**, S. (भारत, भरतवर्षः) India; the country or kingdom of Bharata, the son of Dushyanta.

Bharauná, H. (بهرونا) A load of wool.

Bharauti, H. (بهروتي) A release in full.

Bhar-bhunjá, Bhur-bhoonja, corruptly, **Bhadbhooja, Burboonja**, H. (بهربهونجا, from S. भाष्ट्र, a frying-pan, and भर्जक, who fries) Mar. (भडभुंजा) also **Bhujárí**, or **Bhuṇjárí** (भुजारी, भुंजारी) Grain-parcher or fryer. The name of a caste employed in parching and frying different sorts of grain, pulse, &c. They are said to spring from a Kahár father and Ṣúdra mother, and pretend to be distinguished into seven tribes, which do not intermarry. There is also a tribe of Kayeths distinct from these, who follow the same business.

BHARE, H. (بهري) A kind of grass growing to the height of about nine feet, and used for thatching and making screens.

BHAREKARÍ, Mar. (भरेकरी) A travelling cloth merchant, who buys it from the manufacturer, and retails it to the shopkeepers.

BHARGAT, BHURGUT, Mar. (भरगत, from S. भर, full, and गति, condition) Full complement of any thing, load, lading, cargo.

BHARI, BHUREE, H. (بهري) A weight, that of the old Sicca rupee. In Cuttack, a weight of gold equal to ten máshas.

BHARIPPUKÁRAN, Mal. (ഭരിപ്പുകാരൻ) A superintendant or overseer of a kitchen.

BHARIYÁ, H. (بهريا, भरिया) Land watered by irrigation.

BHARKI, BHURKEE, H. (بهركي) A kind of land in Behar, superficially of a dark colour, but lighter when turned up by the plough. It is suited to both spring and autumn crops, but requires abundant watering.

BHARNÁ, BHURNÁ, H. (بهرنا) Filling, completing, nourishing. Giving up property in payment of a debt.

BHARNÁ, H. (بهرنا, भरना) The vessel that receives the expressed juice of the sugar-cane.

BHARPATWÁ, H. (بهرپتوا) A branch of the Bhar tribe.

BHARTKUL, H. (بهرتكول) One of the branches of the Gaur-Brahmans (for *Bharata-kul*, of the race of Bharata).

BHARTOT, BHURTOTE, Thug. The strangler, the person who applies the noose.

Bhartoti, Thug. The office of strangler.

BHARTRI, S. (भर्तृ) A protector, a master, a husband.

BHARTRI-HARI-JOGÍ, H. (جوگي, योगी) An order of Hindu mendicants, who profess to have been instituted by Bhartrihari, the brother of Vikramáditya, in the century before Christ.

BHÁRUTHÁL, Mar. (?) A tax for liberty to graze cattle.

BHARWÁṚ, BHURWAR, Guz. (ભરવાડ) A shepherd, leading a nomadic life, pasturing sheep, goats, and camels, and living on or by their produce in milk and wool.

BHÁRWATIA, or BHARWUTTIA, (?) A feudal dependant or chief in a state of open insurrection against his liege lord, or against the State, committing robbery and depredation on the country, and assuming the character of an outlaw. (Captain McMurdo, Bombay Trans. i. 271, derives it from *Bhar*, out, and *wut*, country; but in that case it would more correctly be *Báherwatanía;* for the words in Guz., as in other dialects, are *Báhar* or *Báher*, from the S. *bahír*, out, and *watan*, from the Arabic, country. Perhaps the aspirate is altogether incorrect, and the word should be *Barwáṭia*, q. v.)

BHÁRYÁ, pronounced also BHÁRJÁ, H., Ben., &c. (S. भार्या) also BHÁJ, Mar. (भाज) A wife, one wedded according to the ritual of the Vedas. It sometimes denotes a second or inferior wife, as distinct from the *Patní*, the wife first married. It also applies to the female of the Nairs in Malabar.

BHÁSÁN, Ben. (ভাসান) The name of a class of Sirdars in the Kasiya hills.

BHASÁWAN, H. (भसावन) A tax on boats carrying grain.

BHÁSHÁ, S. &c. (भाषा) Speech, a speech, a form of speech, a dialect or language, commonly applied to Hindi. The plaint in a law-suit; (also *Bháshá-páda*).

BHÁSKARA-SAPTAMÍ, S. &c. (भास्कर, the sun, and सप्तमी, seventh day) A festival in honour of the sun, held on the seventh of Mágha.

BHASMA, or BHASM, H. (بهسم, S. भस्मन) Ashes.

Bhasma-snána, S. (भस्मस्नान) Rubbing or smearing the body with the ashes of burnt cow-dung, a common practice of the Ṣaiva mendicants.

Bhasmi, Thug, (from S. भस्म, ashes) Fine earth or sand, such as is best suited for the interment of those who have been murdered. Also, Flour.

BHAṬ, BHUṬ, also written BHAṬṬ, BHUṬṬ, H. &c. (بهت, S. भट्टः) A title or cognomen of learned Brahmans, as *Kumaril Bhaṭ*, and others. Also, the name of a particular tribe of Brahmans in the province of Benares, said to have sprung from a Maraṭha father and a mother of the *Sarwaria* tribe of Brahmans. A common title or appellation of Maraṭha Brahmans, especially of such as live by begging.

BHÁṬ, also BHÁRATA, H. &c. (بهات, S. भाटः, भारतः) BAṬṬU, BHAṬṬU, and BHAṬRÁJU, Tel. (బట్టు, భట్టు, భట్రాజు) The bard, herald, genealogist, and chronicler of ancient days, sprung from a Kshatriya father and Vaiṣya mother. The modern Bháṭ is sometimes said to have been born of a Brahman widow by a Kshatriya father. He fulfils the same office as his prototype, though with inferior dignity;

although in the west of India, where he is identified with the *Cháran*, his personal security is held sufficient for the payment of a debt, or fulfilment of an engagement; its violation being followed by the voluntary death either of the Bháṭ himself, or of some member of his family, the retribution of which falls upon the defaulter. In some parts of India the *Bháṭs* are distinguished as *Birm-bháṭ* and *Jaga-bháṭ*; the former being hired on particular occasions to recite the traditions of a family; the latter being the chroniclers of the family by hereditary descent, and visiting the members periodically, to take note of all occurrences regarding them. Both classes are as much dreaded for their rapacity, as respected for their reputed sanctity. In some places in Upper India the *Bháṭs* are found forming village communities, and branching into various subdivisions. Some have become converts to Mohammadanism. The *Bháṭ* of the village establishment appears to be of an inferior class.

Bhát, H. (بهات) Advances to cultivators without interest. The name of a particular soil north of the Ganges, containing much nitre. In the Lower Doab and Bundelkhand the word means, Uneven ground. The more universal sense of *Bhát* is, Boiled rice, from the S. *Bhakta.* In Maraṭha, and in other places in the south of India, it is applied also to rice in the husk.

Bhátan, *Bháten*, Mar. (भातण, भातेण, for भात-तृण, S.) Rice-straw.

Bhát-ṣet, Mar. (भातशेत) A rice-field, land fit for rice cultivation.

Bháṭ, Mar. (भाट) An elevated spot of land, dry and fit only for the cultivation of inferior grain; also a shoal, a sand-bank.

Bháṭí, Mar. (भाटी) Rich soil along the banks of rivers, creeks, &c.

Bháṭ, Tel. (భాట) Karn. *Bháṭe*, (భాటె) A road. In Upper India the word is always given with the initial unaspirated, *Báṭ*.

Bháṭsari, Tel. (భాటసరి) A traveller.

Bhata, Bhutu, or Bhátá, incorrectly, Batta, H. (بهتّه, بهاتا) Bhattá, Bhateṉ, Mar. (भत्ता, भातें) Bhatyamu, Tel. (భత్యము) Additional allowance. Extra pay or allowances to public servants or soldiers. Subsistence money, or additional allowances to officers employed on special duties, or in distant places. Often confounded erroneously with Baṭṭa, exchange, q. v.

Bhat gaur, H. A sub-division of the Gaur Rájputs.

Bháṭha, H. (بهاٹها) The current of a river, the ebb-tide.

Bhaṭí, Bhuṭee, Bhaṭhá, Bhuṭha, Bhaṭhí, Bhuṭhee, H. (بهٹّي, بهٹّها, or بهٹهي, from the S. भ्राष्ट्र), A furnace, a kiln, a still, a distillery, a liquor-shop. (In Cuttack) also a fire-place for evaporating brine for salt.

Bhaṭhi dár, H. (P. دار, who has) One who manufactures or sells spirituous liquors.

Bhaṭia, H. (بهٹّيه) The poorest land in Ságar and Bundelkhand. In the latter it is also termed more usually *Bhaṭṭi* and *Bhaṭuä.*

Bhaṭiárá, or Bhaṭiyárá, fem. Bhatiárí, H. (بهٹّيارا, بهٹّياري) A man or woman who cooks victuals for travellers in a Serai.

Bhatkaria, H. A class of inferior Bais-Rájputs in Jonpur.

Bhatnagar, H. A large tribe of Kayeths who derive their name from Bhatnir.

Bhaṭolar, H. (بهٹّولر) Land granted to Brahmans bearing the designation of *Bhaṭ*.

Bhatt, or Bhatta, Bhuṭṭ, Bhuṭṭa, H. S. (بهٹّ, भट्टः) A learned Brahman. In some parts of the south of India it especially designates a Brahman who professes a knowledge of the Védas, or belongs to a family in which they have been taught.

Bhaṭṭáchárj, H. (بهٹّاچارج), Ben. (ভট্টাচার্জ), both from the S. *Bhaṭṭáchárya* (भट्टाचार्य्यः) A learned Brahman; one who teaches any branch of Sanscrit literature. In Bengal it is also applied to any respectable Brahman.

Bhaṭṭa-mányam, Tel. Karn. (భట్టమాన్యం) Land granted either rent-free, or at a low rate, to Brahmans.

Bhaṭṭa-vritti, also *Bhaṭṭa-vartulu* and *Bhaṭṭvartti*, Tel. Tam. (from S. वृत्तिः, maintenance) An assignment of revenue or lands granted to Brahmans at a low rent, or rent-free, for their subsistence; the lands in such case being mostly held in severalty. The term sometimes designates a village, the lands of which are permanently distributed among hereditary sharers.

Bhatta, Bhuttu, Karn. (భత్త) Rice in the husk, commonly called by Europeans in the south of India *Batty*, in the North, *Paddy*, both derived apparently from this term, which again is derived from the Sanskrit *Bhakta*, properly, not raw, but boiled rice.

Bhaṭṭa, H. (بهٹّا) Ploughman's wages in kind.

Bhatta-gutta, Bhuttu-goottu, Karn. (భత్తగుత్త)

An addition to the revenue assessment in Mysore, according to the productiveness of the soil, originally fixed by Sivapá naik, one of the petty chiefs of Mysore.

BHAṬṬI, BHUṬṬEE, H. (بهتّي) A Rájput tribe of the Yadubansi race, ruling in Jesalmer, and giving their name to the *Bhaṭṭi* country between Hisar and the Garhi.

Bhaṭṭiána, H. (بهتّيانه) The tract occupied chiefly by the Bhatti tribe.

BHATTI-KÁRI, Mar. (?) An extra peon employed to collect outstanding revenue.

BHATTI-KUMBHÁR, Mar. (?) A tax in kind or money levied formerly upon potters in the Dakhin.

BHÁTUÁ, BHÁTUḌIYÁ, Beng. (ভাতুআ ভাতুড়িযা, from *Bhát* ভাত, boiled rice) A servant who serves for his food.

BHAṬULA, H. (بهٹُله) Bread made from the flour of the Arher and other sorts of pulse.

BHAṬUVÁ, H. (भटुवा) Light dry soil, yielding only an autumn crop.

BHÁÜ, corruptly, BHOW, Mar. (भाऊ) A brother, a cousin. It is affixed respectfully to the names of persons, as Hari-bhaü.

Bháügardi, Mar. (भाऊगर्दी) Any terrible defeat; *lit.* the defeat of Parasuram Bhaü at-Pánipat.

Bháüi, Beng. (ভাওই) A younger brother's wife.

Bhaüj, (ভাওজ) An elder brother's wife.

BHAÜNRI, Uriya (ଭଉଂରୀ) A salt village; a place in which salt-works are set up.

BHAÜNRIÁ, Uriya (ଭଉଂରୀଆ) An account of all the lands of a village, specifying the fields according to their numbers, with the name of the cultivator, the length, breadth, square contents and species of land and cultivation.

BHÁVÁ, S. &c. (भावा) The eighth year of the cycle.

BHAVANTI, H. (?) A house built after the customary Indian fashion, having externally four dead walls, in one of which is the entrance to an external quadrangle, surrounded by chambers, or sometimes with one chamber only at each angle, connected by an open viranda or roofed passage.

BHAVÁYA or BHAVAIÁ, Guz. (ભવઈઆ) An itinerant actor, dancer, and musician.

BHÁWÁ, Mar. (भावा, from भाऊ) A husband's elder brother.

BHEDÁ, Tel. (భేడా) Levying a contribution from the other Ryots, to enable one who has been unfortunate, to pay his rent.

BHEDÍ, or BHERÍ, Beng. (ভেডী) A dyke, an embankment.

Bheḍíbandhí, Beng. (ভেডীবন্ধী) An embankment.

BHEDIYÁ, H. (بهيديا, भेदिया) Soil in which various kinds of crops are grown (from S. भेद, difference),

BHEJ, H. (بهيج, भेज, Rent, a proportionate share of it, an instalment.

Bhej-barár, corruptly, *Bhej-barrar*, H. (بهيجبرار, भेजबरार) A tenure frequent in Bundelkhand, in which the proportions of the revenue or tax (Barár) payable by the common proprietors of a village are subject to periodical or occasional adjustment, and in which balances of the revenue and of village charges arising from the fraud or dishonesty of a sharer are made good by rateable contributions from the other sharers. Strangers are sometimes introduced into over-assessed estates on condition of paying the Barár; but their admission is not a necessary incident of the tenure, the essential feature of which is the re-adjustment of the shares. The term is also applied to a village in which this tenure prevails: it is said to be a *Bhej-barár gáon*.

BHELI, H. (بهيلي) A lump of coarse sugar, usually consisting of four or five Sers (8 to 10 pounds).

BHEṬ, or BHENṬ, corruptly, BHETE, BHAINT, H. (بهيٹ بهينٹ), *Bheṭá*, Ben. (ভেটা) Interview, introduction; but more commonly the presentation of a gift made to a superior on occasion of being presented or introduced to him; a complimentary gift, a *Nazar*. A present made by the cultivator to the collector or farmer on settling his assessment. In the south of India, the offering of a small present, as of one rupee, to the European collector by the Patel, or head of the village, on the settlement of the revenue for the year.

Bheṭ-bahrá, H. &c. (بهيٹ بكرا, भेटबक्रा) A present made by the villagers to the governor of a district on his coming to the village; *lit.* the present of a goat, which is the original usual offering.

Bheṭí, Ben. (ভেটী) A present at a visit or meeting made by the mother of the bride to the mother of the bridegroom to propitiate her good will to her daughter-in-law.

Bheṭ-patra, H. A deed of gift made on being introduced to a superior or public officer.

BHIÁṆ, Uriya (ଭୀଆଣ) A statement of the particulars of an estate; the value of produce, amount of revenue, and distribution among the cultivators, with their names and numbers; the basis of the settlement. See BHAÜNRIÁ.

BHÍHAR, H. (بهيهر) A tribe which, according to tradition, was one of the primitive tribes of the Upper Doab. They were expelled from Nirauli and the neighbouring districts by the Bir-gujar Rájputs. In the Doab they are commonly called *Beimhar*, and in Rohilkhand, *Bíhar*.

Bhikh, H. &c. (بهیک, S. भिक्षा) Alms, asking for alms, begging, giving alms. An item in the allowances formerly made as abatements from the revenue; a small sum so deducted on account of charity or alms-giving by the village or the Zamindar. The term occurs in most dialects, with or without modification, as *Bhikshá* and *Bhík* (भिक्षा, भीक) Marathi.

Bhikhu, H. (بهیکهو, from S. *Bhikshu*, भिक्षु, or *Bhikshuka*, भिक्षुकः) A beggar, a mendicant; especially the Hindu of the fourth order. In the present day, in the south of India the *Bhikshuh* may have a wife and family; or the term may be applied to a *Gṛihastha*, or householder, subsisting upon alms, being used, in fact, in its general acceptation.

Bhikhári, Beng. (ভিখারী, from भिक्षा) A mendicant, a beggar.

Bhíl, Bheel, H. (بهیل, S. भिल्लः) The name of a wild race inhabiting the mountains and forests of Malwa, Mewar, and Kandesh, and in the Dakhin to the north of Poona. They subsist partly by agriculture, and partly by the chase, and in former times were notorious for their depredations. They are also found settled in the villages of the low lands, and are employed as the village watchmen, as guides to travellers, and in various menial offices, for which they are remunerated by fees and perquisites; sometimes by small grants of land. The Bhíls of the Company's territories are much improved, and follow agriculture steadily: a number are incorporated as a local militia under European officers.

Bhímarátrí, S. (भीमरात्री) The seventh night of the seventh month of the seventy-seventh year of a man's age, after which a person is exempt from all instituted observances, it being considered the end of his natural life.

Bhímjodha, Thug. A small bird, a sort of cuckoo.

Bhinnagotra, S. (*bhinna*, भिन्न, different, and *gotra*, गोत्र, family) One not belonging to the same general family.

Bhinnodara, S. (*bhinna*, different, and *udara*, उदर, womb) A brother by a different mother, a half-brother.

Bhír, H. (بهیر) A crowd, a mob.

Bhis, H. (بهیس, S. बिशः) The edible root of the lotus, or, more correctly, the fibres of the stem; also called *Basend*, *Bhisenda*, *Bhasínr*.

Bhíshmáshṭamí, S. (भीष्माष्टमी) The eighth day of the month Mágha, when libations are offered to *Bhíshma*, the son of *Gangá*.

Bhít, H. (بهیت, S. भित्ति) The wall of a house.

Bhíṭ, Bhiṭí, or Bhíṭí, H. (بهیٹ, بهٹی, بهیٹی) Ground either naturally or artificially raised, and fit for various purposes, as for the site of a house, or of a village. Mounds confining a tank or piece of water. Raised ground near a tank for planting the Piper betel upon. Vestiges of an old house. The old or main land of a village, that which has been always cultivated, in opposition to that which is gained from the river, or by alluvial deposit; also, but apparently erroneously, *Bíta*, *Beeta*. Although somewhat differently spelled, especially with regard to the last consonant, which is the hard *ṭ* instead of the soft, the word has probably the same origin as the preceding one, or S. *Bhitti*, a wall.

Bhitauri, H. (بهیتَوری) Ground-rent, rent paid for the site of a house by one not a cultivator of the village lands.

Bhitariá, H. (بهیتریا, from بهیتر, within, S. अभ्यन्तर) A domestic, male or female, one admitted to the inner apartments of a dwelling, a guest at a marriage-feast who is admitted to eat with the relatives of the bride.

Bhitri, Thug. A pair of travellers.

Bhog, Bhoga, or Bhogam, corruptly, *Bogum*, H., but occurring in most, or perhaps all the dialects, sometimes slightly modified, (بهوگ, S. भोग) Enjoyment, fruition, use: possession, of two kinds, *savedha* or *savádha*, with obstruction, and *nirvedha* or *nirvádha*, unobstructed, undisputed; corruptly, *savedhbhogy* and *nirwedhbhogy*.

Bhogya, H. S. (भोग्यं) Any thing that may be used or possessed. (Tel. *Bhógyamu*, భోగ్యము)

Bhogádhi, or *Bhogyádhi*, H. S. (from *bhoga*, or *bhogya*, and *ádhi*, आधिः, a pledge) A pledge or deposit which may be used until redeemed.

Bhoga-bandhak, or *-bundhuk*, or *Bhogya-bandhak*, H., &c. (भोगबन्धक, S. *Bhogabandhaka*) Tel. *Bhóg-bandá*, (భోగబండా) A kind of bond or mortgage in which the article pledged or mortgaged may be converted to use, as land, houses, cattle, trees, &c., the profits of which are to be appropriated by the lender or mortgagee in lieu of interest.

Bhogabandá-sanadu, Tel. (సనదు) The document by which a usufruct bond or mortgage is settled.

Bhoga, or *Bhog-dár*, H. &c. (P. دار, who has) One in the possession or enjoyment of any property.

Bhogádhikár, or *Bhogyádhikár*, H. S. (from *bhoga* or

bhogya and अधिकार, a right) The possessor of the usufruct of pledged or mortgaged property.

Bhoga-lábha, or *-labdhi*, the latter very corruptly *Book-labby*, H. &c. (भोगलाभः, भोगलब्धिः, from *lábha* or *labdhi*, S. acquiring) Usufruct in lieu of interest.

Bhogotra, or *Bhogottar*, corruptly, *Bhoguevottur*, H., &c. (بهوگوتر, from S. भोग and उत्तर, subsequent, or त्र, what preserves) A grant of revenue for the enjoyment or use of an individual, especially of a Brahman or religious character.

Bhogí, H. &c. (S. भोगी) The person who enjoys or possesses any thing.

BHOGA, H. S. (भोग, enjoyment, as before) The food offered to an idol.

Bhoga-maṇḍapa, H. S. (from *maṇḍapa*, a temple, *lit.*, pleasure-temple or chamber) That part of the temple of Jagannáth where the food to be presented to the idol is cooked.

Bhoga-múrtti, Mar. (from S. मूर्त्तिः, a form) An idol carried about in processions, representing the principal idol, which is never taken from the shrine; also, fig., The head of a concern, one who has only the benefit of it; also, the active manager under a nominal head.

BHOGHIYÁ, Hindi (भोघिया) A small basket in which the sower carries his seed.

BHOÏ, BHOEE, incorrectly, BHOYEE, H. Mar. (بهوی, भोई) An individual of a caste whose business it is to carry palankins, and who is at other times a fisherman. Also read *Boï*, q. v.

BHOJAN, H. (بهوجن, S. भोजन) Food. Eating or taking food, feeding, entertaining.

Bhojan-kharch, H. (A. خرچ, expense) Table expenses.

Bráhman-bhojan, Ben., Feeding Brahmans.

BHOJPATRA, H. S. (भोजपत्रः) The birch tree, or rather its bark.

BHOPÍ, BHOPYÁ, Mar. (भोपी, भोप्या) The priest of a village temple, generally a *Ṣúdra*.

BHOTÍ, H. (भोती) Labour.

Bhotíhár, H. (भोतीहार) A labourer.

BHRÁTṚI, S. (भ्रातृ) A brother.

Bhrátṛi-datta, S. (दत्त, given) What is given by a brother to a sister on her marriage; one sort of *Strí-dhan*, or woman's wealth.

Bhrátṛi-dwitíya, S. (द्वितीय) A Hindu festival on the second of Kártik, on which sisters give entertainments to brothers, in commemoration of *Yamuná's* entertaining her brother *Yama*.

BHRIGU-BANSI, H. A tribe of Rájputs deriving their origin from Parasuráma, the stem of the Barhoulia clan.

BHRITA, S. (भृतः) Hired, a hired servant or labourer.

BHRITI, S. (भृतिः) Hire, wages.

Bhriti-rúpa, S. (from रूप, form, nature) A reward given to a person in lieu of wages for the performance of a duty for which stipulated payment or hire is improper, as for the performance of a Ṣráddha on behalf of another person.

BHÚ, or BHÚMI, S., but current in most or all the dialects, occasionally modified, as, BHÚM or BHOOM, BHU-IN or BHOO-EEN, or BHÚN, BHOON, &c., H. (بهو, بهومي, بهوم, بهوئيں, بهون, S. भूः, भुई, भूमिः) Earth, land, ground, soil. (*Bhúm*, as derived from the P. *Búm*, بوم, is said to be applied to uncultivated land only, but the Persian word was no doubt originally the same as the S. *bhûmi* abbreviated, signifying land in general, earth, *the* earth).

Bhú-bandu, Tel. (భూబందు) Boundary of a field or an estate, particulars relating to it.

Bhú-bandu-jábitá, Tel. (జాబితా, from the A. ضابطه) The ground statement, shewing the total extent of the lands of a village, and their distribution as arable, garden, and unproductive, and distinguishing those held free of assessment. Particulars of the boundaries of an estate. Also, *Bhú-band-likhá*, *Bhu-band-hissebu*, and similar compounds.

Bhú-dánam, or *Bhúmi-dánam*, S. (from दानं, *donum*) A grant of land, or of the revenue assessed upon it.

Bhú-dána patra, H. &c. (पत्र, a leaf) A deed of grant of land.

Bhuí bháṛeṇ, Mar. (भुईभाडें) Ground-rent.

Bhúpati, S. (from पतिः, a lord) A prince, a sovereign, a landholder, a Zamindar. Also *Bhumipati*, *Bhúmipa*, and *Bhúpa*.

Bhú-swámi, S. (from स्वामिन्, master) Landholder, proprietor, prince, sovereign.

Bhúmi, H. (from S. भूमिः) Earth, land. (In Rájputána) Hereditary landed estate held free of assessment.

Bhúmiá, H. (بهوميا, from भूमिः) A landlord, a proprietor of the soil. Descendant of the founder of a village. The head of a village or Patél. Among the Bhíls, a guide.

Bhumyá, Mar. (भुम्या, from S. भूमिः) An old inhabitant of a place, one whose family has been settled there for several generations.

Bhúmak, Mar. (भूमक) In Nagpur, a village officer who

performs the worship of the boundary deity, and attends upon the Government revenue officers when they visit the village.

Bhúmká, Mar. (भूमका) The tutelary divinity of a village, or of its boundaries, or of the soil, or any particular spot.

Bhúmiáwat, *Bhoomiawut*, H. (بہومیاوت) A general plundering, especially the depredations of petty chiefs holding lands of which an attempt has been made to dispossess them, or from which a revenue not heretofore paid is demanded.

Bhúmiáwatí, H. (بہومیاوتي) A discontented and insurgent chief.

Bhúmi dáhá, H. (بہومي داها) Being burnt (as a corpse), being reduced to earth.

Bhúmi dár, H. (P. دار, who has) A landholder, a proprietor. A head-man. A chief.

Bhúmij, H. (from भूमि, and ज, born, Earth-born) A caste of low Hindus numerous in *Ghatṣilá*.

Bhúmika, H. &c., (भूमिक) A landholder, a proprietor. A head-man. A military chief.

Bhoi, Uriya (ଭୋଇ, probably a vernacular corruption of *Bhuĩ*, from भूमि, earth, land) A village accountant.

Bhoi-múl, Uriya (ଭୋଇମୂଲ) A district accountant: also the salary or perquisites of the village accountant.

Bhúĩn dagdhá, H. (بہوئین دگدها, from *Bhuin*, and दग्ध, burnt) Gifts at marriages and funerals, some earth being burned before their presentation. (Eastern Oudh.)

Bhúĩn-hár or *Bhún-hár*, *Bhooeen-har* or *Bhoonhar*, H. (بہونہار , بہوئینہار, from the S. भूमि, and हार, who takes; in the vernacular terms the *n* is of very nasal enunciation) A tribe of Hindus settled in great numbers in the districts of Gorakhpur, Azimgarh, and Benares, the Raja of which last is a member of the clan. They claim to have been originally Brahmans; and although they admit that the distinction is impaired by their having become cultivators, which pure Brahmans should not be, they do not wholly abandon their pretensions, and style themselves Thákurs, a title common to both Brahman and Rájput tribes. Many of their subdivisions have names which are common to them and the Sarwaria Brahmans, as Sandal Gautam, Díkshit, Upádhyáya, and Pande; and those which have not identical appellations, have titles connecting them with the same stock; thus, the Sankar-wár take the title of Misr, the Donwár that of Tewari, &c. This renders their account of themselves credible, and they are probably Brahmans degraded by being cultivators, their usual avocation. The term may also designate a landholder in general.

Bhúĩhárí, H. (भूईहारी) Land let at a low rent to tenants liable to be called out for military service.

Bhúĩn málí, H. (بہوئین مالي) A Hindu of a low caste engaged in the lowest menial offices.

Bhún-bhái, *Bhoon-bhaee*, H. (بہونبهاي, from S. भूमि, and भ्रातृ, a brother) A man invited by a proprietor to reside in a village upon a portion of land assigned to him to cultivate for his own benefit, but which he may not dispose of: a land or estate-brother.

Bhúndari, *Bhoonduree*, H. (بہوندري, from S. भूमि) A small patch of cultivation. Land let rent-free to the village servants, or to indigent relations, or paupers, temporary occupants. The term also occurs, *Bhúnḍá*, *Baunḍá*, and *Bhaunḍári*.

Bhúniyá, H. (भूनिया) The head of a village. In Cuttack, one of the former petty chiefs holding lands by tenure of military service.

Bhún-jari, (?) A term of the south-west provinces. Lands held by those who first brought them into cultivation, or by their direct heirs: they cannot be alienated or transferred, and, in default of direct heirs, escheat to the Government.

Bhúyán or *Bhúyí*, H. (from S. भूमि) A landholder. A chief holding by military service. A head of a village.

Bhúda, H. (بہوڈا) Soil of a light inferior quality. (North-west Provinces) Sandy soil. See Bhúṛ.

Bhudki, Bhoodkee, H. (?) A well sunk for purposes of irrigation, either in the bed or immediate vicinity of a river or watercourse: if near them, a channel is cut for a supply of water from the main stream to the well.

Bhúngáí, Bhoongaee, H. (بہونگاي) The name of a tax levied by the Raja of Bijpur on part of the forest-produce of Tappa Sattísgarh, in Mirzapur. In the official report of the Settlement of the Tappa, the term is said to be derived from *Bhunga*, an axe.

Bhuksá, H. (بہکسا) Name of a tribe inhabiting the forests from Sabna on the Sarda to Chandpur on the Ganges, claiming to descend from the Powar Rájputs, having been expelled from Dhár, and taken refuge, first in Oudh, and finally in the hills bordering on Kamaon. They are divided into fifteen clans, twelve superior, three inferior.

Buktan, Beng. (ভুক্তন) Making additions to stock. Adding new sums to what is paid off.

Bhuṇḍiá, H. (بهونڈیا) One who cultivates with a borrowed plough.

Bhunjá, H. (भंजा) Parched grain.

Bhúṛ, Bhúḍ, Bhuḍá, Bhooṛ, Bhooḍa, corruptly, **Budah** and **Booda**, also **Bhuḍa, Bhuduh**, H. (بهوڑ, بهوڈ, properly written with the cerebral *ḍ*, as भूड) An unproductive soil, consisting for the most part of seven-tenths of sand and the rest of clay, with very little vegetable fertility, being the third in common enumeration. Varieties of it are termed *Bhúḍ-hháki* and *Bhúḍ-páráni*. It is also described as land not retentive of moisture.

Bhúrá, H. (بهورا, भूरा) Land belonging to a village lying farthest from the inhabitants.

Bhurari, Bhoorurее, H. (بهوری) Corn remaining in the ear after it has been trodden down, especially applicable to the grains of the Rabi crop.

Bhúrdaṇḍ, Mar. (भूरदंड) Money paid, or a fine imposed, to counterbalance a profit unjustly suspected of having been improperly made. A fine, a forfeit. Money oppressively exacted or carelessly lost.

Bhúrí, Bhurbhurí, Hindi (بهوری, भूरी, بهربهری, भुरभुरी) Light sandy soil.

Bhurṣí, Bhurí, Mar. (भुरशी, भुरी) Mould. See **Burá**.

Bhús, Bhúsá, Bhoos, Bhoosa, also with the vowel short, **Bhus**, &c., H. (بهوس, بهوسا), Mar. (भुसा, भुंसा, भुंस, भूस), S. (बुसः) The husk or chaff of corn. The straw.

Bhúsá- or *Bhúnsá-jins*, (بهونساجنس) All kinds of grain in husk.

Bhusár or *Bhunsár*, corruptly, *Bhursar*, Mar. (from भूसा) A generic term used chiefly in marketing, for grains, grasses, and esculent culms.

Bhusári, Mar. (भुसारी) A grain-dealer, a corn-chandler. A petty shopkeeper or chandler; also one who husks or cleans grain.

Bhúsaurí, also *Bhúsehrá* and *Bhúsaula*, H. (بهوسوری, بهوسیهرا, بهوسولا) Room in a house where straw is kept.

Bhúsáwan, H. (بهوساون) A tax on boats carrying grain.

Bhúsrá, *Bhoosra*, H. (بهوسرا) An inferior kind of wheat.

Bhuṭ, Beng. (ভুট) Rescission of an order. Reversing any thing.

Bhút, Bhoot, also **Bhúta**, H. &c. (from S. भूत, been, become, past part. of भू, to be) A ghost, an evil spirit. Any living being. A material element. (In law) Matter of fact, the real state of the case.

Bhút- or *Bhúta-bali*, H. &c. (S. वलि, a sacrifice) Offerings to malignant spirits, or to ghosts and goblins. Offerings to demons or spirits at funerals. Offerings to all creatures.

Bhúta chaturdaṣí, S. &c., (चतुर्दशी) The 14th of the dark half of Áṣwin, when offerings are made to malignant spirits.

Bhúta-devatá, H. &c. (S. देवता) A spirit worshipped as a divinity.

Bhút-hundá, Mar. (?) A tax on witches or persons professing to exorcise evil spirits.

Bhút-khet, H. (from S. भूत, and क्षेत्र, a field) A field or land granted to the Páhan for the cost of sacrifices to propitiate the evil spirits (South-west frontier).

Bhúta-yajna, S. (यज्ञ, sacrifice) Worship of all creatures; also, offerings to evil spirits.

Bhuṭyá, Mar. (भुट्या) A mendicant devotee of the goddess Bhavání.

Bhúṭ, H. (بهوٹ, भूट, but it is probably only a various spelling of *Bhúṛ* भूड़, q. v.) Land irretentive of moisture.

Bhuṭṭá, H. (بهٹّا) Indian corn, maize. Mar. (भुटा, भुट्टा) An ear of Indian corn.

Bhuṭe- or *Bhuṭṭe-chor*, Mar. (भुटे-, भुट्टेचोर) A petty thief.

Bhyns, H. (بهَینس) A buffalo.

Bhynssonda, H. (?) A tax or cess for the privilege of grazing buffaloes.

Biáj, also **Biáz**, H. (بیاج, बीआज), **Vyáj**, q. v., Mar (व्याज) Interest on money or grain. In the north-western provinces, the interest paid by the cultivators on the advances made to them by the shopkeepers for their subsistence and repair of agricultural implements, for seed, and for the Government revenue. What is borrowed between Áshárh and Kártik they repay after the autumn harvest, with 2 anas per rupee, or about 12 per cent., addition. What they borrow between Ághan and Phálgun they repay with the same addition after the Rabi. *Khet karm*.

Biáju, H. (بیاجو) Capital put out at interest.

Biáj-khaibár, Uriya (ବିଆଜଖାଇବାର) Usury.

Biaṛ, H. (بیاڑ) Seed-bed (Delhi). Evening (Sagar). Waste land fit for cultivation (Lower Doab). Subdivision of a village, synonymous with *Paṭṭí*, q. v.

Biás, H. (بیاس) Land prepared for sowing in the following year. Land under preparation for rice.

Bibád, Ben., but also in most dialects, (বিবাদ, more correctly, S. *vivâda* विवादः) Dispute, argument, controversy; a suit at law.

Bibhág, Ben. &c. (বিভাগ, more correctly, S. *vibhága*

BI

विभागः) Portion, partition, division. Share of inheritance.

Bichár, Ben. &c. (**বিচার**, more correctly, S. **Vichára**, **विचारः**) Discussion, consideration, investigation, trial.

Bichár-karttá, Ben. &c. (**বিচারকর্ত্তা**) A judge.

Bichárak, Ben. &c. (**বিচারক**) An investigator, a commissioner, a judge.

Bichháítí, corruptly, **Bechaití** and **Bedchaití**, Mar. (**बिछाइती**, from **बिछाना**, a mat, a bed, &c.) A petty dealer who does not keep a shop, but carries his goods to a fair or market, or exhibits them in a street, or on the steps of a door, on a mat or cloth spread on the ground.

Bíchwaí, **Bíchwání**, H. (from بيچ, intermediate, بيچوي, بيچواني) An umpire, an arbitrator, a middleman.

Bíchrá, Hindi (**बीचरा**) Seeds sown for the purpose of raising plants to be transplanted, especially rice seedlings.

Bíḍá, H. (بيڏا) Mounds, raised ground (Oudh). Perhaps a corruption of *Bihar*, q. v.

Bidá, H. (بدا, from the A. وداع) **Bidáy**, Ben. (**বিদায়**) Taking leave, granting leave, dismissal.

Bidâat, H. (A. بديعت) Novelty or change in religion, heresy, schism; also, oppression.

Bidániyá, Ben. (**বিডানিয়া**) An umpire.

Bídar, Hindi (**बीदर**) A sort of rake or harrow worked by oxen to loosen the soil and extricate weeds from among the standing crops of young rice.

Bídar-parotá, Hindi (**बीदरपरोता**) Dressing the rice crops, first by raking, and then passing a roller over the field.

Bidaru, **Biduru**, Karn. (ಬಿದರು, ಬಿದುರು) A bambu.

Bidáru, Tel. (బిదారు) **Bidára**, Karn. (ಬಿದಾರ) A troop of grain carriers, or Banjáras: their camps: a herd of loaded cattle, a number of bullocks carrying grain, grain in a heap. In Karnata, also, a load of any other articles, as *Aralíbidára*, a piled heap of cotton packs; *Kobarībidára*, a heap of cocoa-nuts in bags, &c.

Bidhi, H., and in most dialects, (بدهي, S. *vidhi*, **विधिः**) Rule, precept, prescribed rule or ceremony, statute law.

Bidhibat, H. &c. (**विधिवत्**, more correctly, *Vidhivat*) Conformably to rule, precept, or law.

Bíḍíkeyavaru, Karn. (ಬೀಡಿಕೆಯವರು) Persons carrying corn, cotton, &c., from one part of the country to another.

Bidige, Tel. (బిడిగె) A favourable or quit-rent.

Bíḍike, Karn. (ಬೀಡಿಕೆ) A herd of loaded cattle, the pile of their loads.

Bidri, H. (بدري) A kind of mixed metal of copper and tin, of which vessels and hukka bottoms are made; so called from its being originally made at Bídar.

Bíḍu, Tel. (బీడు), **Bíḍukáḍu**, Karn. (ಬೀಡುಕಾಡು) Waste, uncultivated land.

Bíga, or **Bíganu**, Karn. (ಬೀಗ, ಬೀಗನು) The father of a son's wife or daughter's husband; a person related by marriage.

Bígati, Karn. (ಬೀಗತಿ) A sister-in-law, the mother of a son's wife or daughter's husband.

Bigár, corruptly, **Beegah**, Mar. (**बिगार**) Forced labour, compulsory and uncompensated service. See *Begár*.

Bigári, also, *Begari*, Mar. (**बिगारी**) A forced or pressed labourer.

Bíghá, **Beegha**, corruptly, **Beega**, **Beegah**, **Begah**, &c., H. (بيگها) **Bighá**, Mar. (**बिघा**) A measure of land, varying in extent in different parts of India. The standard Bíghá of the revenue surveys of the north-west provinces is equal to 3025 square yards, or $\frac{5}{8}$ths of an acre. In Bengal, the Bíghá contained only 1600 square yards, or little less than $\frac{1}{3}$d of an acre. In Benares it was, at the time of the settlement, determined at 3136 square yards. In other parganas it was equal to 2025, to 3600, or to 3925 square yards. A Kachha (an immature or crude) Bíghá is in some places a third, in others only a fourth of a full or standard Bíghá. Akbar's Bíghá contained 3600 Ilahi-gaz, which have been considered as equal to the 3025 square yards of the Bíghá of Hindustan. Mr. Elliot specifies the following as some of the variations found in the Upper Provinces:—

		Bíghás.	Biswas.	Kattas.
Farakhabad - - - - - -	100 acres	=175	12	0
East and South Gorakhpur - -	,,	=192	19	7
Allahabad & part of Azimgerh,	,,	=177	5	6
Part of Azimgerh & Ghazipur,	,,	=154	6	8
Bijnur - - - - - - - -	,,	=187	19	15
In the Upper Doab (Kachha) -	,,	=582	3	0

In Cuttack the Bíghá is now considered to be an English acre. The Maraṭha *Bíghá* is called twenty *Páṇḍs*, or 400 square Káṭhis or rods, each five cubits and five hand-breadths: as the rod varies, so does the Bíghá: under the Âadil Shahi dynasty it was equal to 4383 square yards, or only 457 square yards less than an English acre. The Guzerat Bíghá contains only $284\frac{2}{9}$ square yards.

Bighaṭí, or *Bigháoṭí*, corruptly, *Begehree*, *Beegotee*, *Beeghari*, *Bighari*, *Bigharni*, H. (بيگهتي, بيگهاوتي) According to measurement by *Bíghás;* as revenue assessed at so much per *Bíghá;* also, division of lands by Bíghás among coparceners. Settlement of the revenue per Bíghá, with reference also to the quality and produce of the lands, generally made at a money rate, but sometimes in kind. A coparcenary village, in which the lands are distributed among the sharers in Bíghás and their fractional parts.

Bíghá-dám, H. (from *dám,* دام, price) Settlement of the revenue at so much per Bíghá, especially in villages held in common, in which the lands are apportioned in Bíghás, and the assessment proportionably rated.

Bigha-dán, H. (?) Rate levied on the sharers of an imperfect Paṭṭídárí village, to make good any deficiency of revenue left by the produce of the land held in common. (? If this and the preceding are not essentially the same.)

Bíghá-daftari, corruptly, *Beghah-duftery,* H. (from the P. دفتر, a record) Official record of the measurement of the lands of a district in Bíghás in the time of Akbar.

Bighávaṇí, corruptly, *Begownee,* Mar. (बिघावणी) Assessment of villages at a stipulated rate per *Bíghá.* Reduction into *Bíghás* of measurements by a different standard.

BIGHA, BEEGHA, Thug. A term used by the Thugs of Behar and Bengal to express a share of the spoil.

BÍHAN, Hindi, (बीहन) Seed. *Puraniya.*

BIHAṆḌ, BEEHUND, H. (بہنڈ) Land cut up by torrents, broken land abounding with ravines.

BIHAṚ, BEEHUṚ, H. (بیہڑ) Sterile land, land uneven and broken into ruts and ravines. (No doubt the same as the preceding, differently pronounced).

BIHNOṚ, BIHNOṆḌ, H. (بیہنوڑ, विहनोड) Land on which the plants of rice or other grain are sown for transplanting.

BIHRI, H. (بیہری, P. بہرہ, a share) A subscription, a contribution, an extra cess or assessment. In Benares, a ward or street rate, or a contribution from each house for cleaning and repairing the drains. (See *Behri:* the words are no doubt the same, slightly varied in pronunciation).

BÍJ, BEEJ, H., and in most dialects, (بیج, S. *víja,* बीज) Seed, lit. or fig., as origin, cause, commencement, &c.

Bijái, H. (بجاي, बिजाई) A portion of seed corn which the poorer classes are allowed to take from the field; see *Bejwar:* also the portions of corn given to the village smith, carpenter, barber, and washerman, by each cultivator.

Bíjávarí, Karn. (ಬೀಜಾವರಿ) Extent of land computed according to the quantity of seed required to be sown in it (Mysore). Allowance for such corn (Madras). Read also *Bíjwari.*

Bíjkhád, H. (بیج کھاد) Advance of seed and food to agriculturists (Rohilkhand).

Bíjmár, H. (بیج مار, from *máraṇa,* destroying) Failure of germination of the seed.

Bíj-parava, Tel. Land actually sown (Bellary).

Bíj-parmia, (? prameya) *chi paṭṭí,* Mar. (?) An account kept by the village accountant of the quantity of land sown, and the amount of revenue due upon it.

Abíj, or *Nirbíj,* H. (from S. *bíj* or *víj,* with the privative *a* or *nir* prefixed) Seed that does not germinate.

BÍJAK, H., and in most dialects, (بیجک) A note of grain when stored; thence, a note or memorandum attached to any article of trade or transport, as a ticket, a label, a list, an invoice.

BÍJAR, BIJUR, H. (بیجر) A sort of soil in which the cerealia are generally sown (Lower Doab).

BIJHERIYÁ, H. (بیجھیریا) A tribe of Rájputs in the district of Gorakhpur.

BÍJHONIÁ, H. (بیجھونیا) A tribe of Rájputs in the Zilla of Jonpur.

BIHISHTÍ, H. (بہشتی, from the P. بہشت, paradise) A water-bearer.

BIKRI, H. &c. (بکری, from the S. विक्रयः) BIKRAY, BIKRÍ, Ben. (विक्रय, विक्री) Sale, selling.

Bikrí-gola, Ben. Uriya, (विक्रीगोला) A salt store where Government salt is sold by retail.

BIKWÁN, H. (بکوان) A branch of the *Gaur-tagá* tribe (North-west Provinces).

BIL, Ben. (बिल, S. बिल, a hole) A lake, a pond, a swamp, low marshy ground.

BÍL, H. (بیل) A spade, a hoe. See *Bel.*

Bíldár, H. (بیلدار) A digger, a miner, a pioneer. See *Beldar.*

BILABANDÍ, BILABUNDEE, or BILAHBANDI, corruptly, BEELABUNDY, H. Ben. (بلہ بندي, विलाबन्दी, possibly from विल, to arrange, to allot, or a vernacular variety of *Behri* and *Behri-bandi,* q. v.) An account of the revenue settlement of a district, specifying the name of each Mahal, the farmer of it, and the amount of the rent. In the north-west provinces, *Bila-bandi* usually means an arrangement for securing the payment of the revenue. In Behar it is said to imply the annual distribution of the portions of the lands among the Ryots for their respective cultivation.

Bila-dár, H. (بله دار) A collector of the revenue (Central India).

Bil, H. A. (a contraction of the Arabic preposition ب, *bi*, and article *al*, ال, prefixed to many words, forming compounds in daily use, several of which are employed technically as well as generally) In, with, by, &c.

Bil-ijmál, H. (A. بالجمال) In the whole (as an estate without co-parceners.

Bi-l-âks, H. A. (بالعكس) On the contrary.

Bi-l-fail, H. A. (بالفعل) In fact, indeed, actually.

Bi-l-kul, H. A. (بالكل) Universally, entirely.

Bi-l-maḳtâ, *Bil muqtâ*, corruptly, *Bilmookta*, *Bilmohta*, *Bilmugta*, H., but adopted in various dialects, (A. بالمقطع) According to agreement, stipulated, fixed, consolidated; applied especially to a tenure by which a Ryot holds his land at a fixed rate per plough or per Bíghá, or to the engagement by which his rent is fixed for a given term, without liability to enhancement. In Benares it was applied to the fixed or consolidated revenue, including in one aggregate the Mál, or land-tax, and Abwáb, or miscellaneous cesses. In the Northern Circars, *Bíl-makhtá*, Tel. (బల్మక్తా) was applied to a fixed quit-rent or revenue assessed at a rate below the usual standard. In the South it implies land or a village held at a fixed rate. See *Agraháram*.

Bil-maktâ Inám, H. A. (A. انام) A grant of land at a low fixed rent.

Bil-maktâ jamâ, H. A. (جمع) Consolidated revenue, stipulated assessment.

Bil-maktâ-mukhása, H. (A. مخاصه) A village held either rent-free, or at a low stipulated quit-rent.

Bil-maktâ paṭṭá, H. A. (H. पट्टा) A lease for a gross aggregate rent, one in which the land-tax and all other cesses or Abwábs were consolidated.

Bil-maktâ Râï, H. M. (رعي) Consolidated rent or assessment, aggregate rate per Bíghá.

Bilá, H. A. (بلا) Without; a preposition and prefix to many terms in common use.

Bilá bandi, H. (P. بندي, a binding) Doing any thing, as cultivating land, pending the final adjustment of the conditions.

Bilá sharaṭ, or *Bilá mashrúṭ*, H. (from A. شرط, an agreement, or مشروط, agreed) Unconditional, absolute: a grant of land or the like without any condition, as of service, &c., being attached to it.

Bílá, Beelá, see *Bela*, H. &c. (P. بيلا) Money distributed to the poor from the private funds or privy purse of a man of rank. According to Gladwin (Vocabulary), Funds appropriated to the support of the ladies or other members of the family of a Nawáb.

Bilgárí, Thug. An extensive jangal or waste, a convenient spot for murder.

Bílha, Thug. A great enemy of the Thugs. A leper. A man deprived of his nose and ears. One much emaciated by sickness.

Bilía, Thug. A brass cup; technically, a place for murdering or burying the victims. *Bilía marjana* (? for *márjana*), to clean the cup, *i. e.* to choose a spot where to commit murder.

Bilkharia, H. (بلكهريه) A tribe of Rájputs of the *Bachgotí Chauhan* stock, so named from Bilkhar in Oudh.

Billadugu, Tel. (?) An allowance of grain made to the person appointed to measure it.

Bílu, Karn. (ಬೀಳು) Waste, uncultivated land.

Bíládahola, Karn. (ಬೀಳಾದಹೊಲ) A field lying waste.

Bílu bitti, Karn. (ಬೀಳು ಬಿತ್ತಿ) The quantity of seed required to sow a given extent of land.

Bímá, Beema, also Bímán, Beeman, H. (بيمان بيما) Insurance.

Bíṇ, Mar. (बीं, from S. बीज) Seed, especially as kept for sowing.

Biṇbiṇwaḷá, Mar. (बींबिंवळा) Seeds, slips, roots, or any thing of the kind for sowing or setting.

Bíná, Beena, H. (بينا) A sort of long grass.

Binaha, Binnaha, Binnapa, Karn. (ಬಿನಹ, ಬಿನ್ನಹ, ಬಿನ್ನಪ, from S. *vijnapti*, विज्ञप्ति) Petition, respectful statement or request.

Binahar, Binuhur, H. (بنهر) A gatherer of cotton (from بنّا, *binná*, to pick). Benares. Elsewhere termed *Paihár*, *Paihara*, or *Puï*.

Binái, Binávat, H. (بناوت ,بناي) Weaving.

Binaula, H. (بنولا) Cotton seed: it is used as fodder for cattle.

Binauria, H. (بنوريه) A weed which grows in fields sown for the kharif crops: it is used as fodder.

Bínd, Beend, H. (بيند) A reed, a rush, a landmark.

Binḍá, Mar. (बिंडा) A mass of cotton or cordage rolled together, a small load or bundle (of sticks, grass, &c.).

Bíndá, **Beenda**, H. (بيندا) A kind of rope made of grass or of the fibres of the Arher plant.

Binderi, Thug. A sword.

Bindu, Thug. A Hindu.

Bipakh, Ben. (S. বিপক্ষ, S. विपक्ष) An opponent (in a suit).

Bipal, H. (بپل, S. विपल) A measure of time, either the same as a *Pal* or second, or $\frac{1}{6}$th of a second.

Biphai, H. (بپهي) also, **Bhiphai**, (بهپهئي) S. (*Vrihaspati*, वृहस्पतिः) Thursday.

Bír, **Beer**, H. (بير) Pasturage, grass land.

Bírá, **Beera**, H. (بيرا, बीरा) Rate of rent of lands according to the quality of the soil and value of the crops.

Bírá beshi, H. (P. بيشي, surplus) Increase of rent with increased value of produce.

Bíṛa, **Bíṛá**, or **Bíṛí**, corruptly, **Beree** or **Beedee**, Anglicised **Betel**, H. (بيڑا بيڑہ, बीड़ा, बीड़ी, S. वीटिका) A Pán or Paun, or small pieces of areka-nut, spice, catechu, and sometimes a little quick-lime, rolled up in a leaf of the piper-betel, to be slowly masticated, answering the purpose of an aromatic, astringent, and alkalescent condiment. It is much used by the natives of all parts of India, and is commonly presented from one to another, in token of civility or affection. It is also given in confirmation of an assurance of a pledge or promise, and among the Rájputs is sometimes exchanged as a pledge of defiance.

Birana, or, vernacularly, **Bírná-khar**, Hindi, (बीरनाखर, from S. वीरण) A tough coarse grass spreading over uncultivated lands which are inundated yearly, and removable only by digging.

Biṛár, Dakh. (بڑار) A drove of bullocks laden with grain, cotton, &c.; also **Biṛki**, (بڑکي).

Birár, Thug. The fighting of cats, or their cries when fighting.

Bírbání, **Beerbanee**, H. (بيرباني, from *vír* or *bír* (Lat. *vir*) a man, and *báni*, a form of the possessive affix, having a man, or husband) A term used among the Játs, and in the north-west provinces, to designate a man's own wife.

Bíṛgújar, **Biṛgoojur**, also **Bargújar**, **Burgoojur**, H. (بڑگوجر) One of the thirty-six royal races of Rájputs, settled chiefly along the Jumna, from Rohilkhand to Mathurá. Their chief town was Anupsheher, the rulers of which, as well as the branch of Katehr Bírgújars, are Hindus, but the other tribes are Mohammadans, although adopting the Hindu title of Thákur along with the Mohammadan appellation, as, Thákur Akbar Ali Khán. The Mohammedan tribes retain many Hindu customs, so that, as Mr. Elliot remarks, it is almost doubtful which religion they prefer. According to some of their traditions, they migrated into the Doab from Dajore, in the Macheri country; to others, from Deosar, in Jaypur, whence they were expelled by the Kachwahas. Rathor tradition places them in the vicinity of the hills bordering Rohilkhand in the fifth century.

Birháḍ, or **Birhaṛ**, Mar. (बिऱ्हाड) Lodging, residence in a lodging for a time.

Birháḍ bájálen, Mar. (बिऱ्हाडबाजालें) A traveller's bag and baggage; lit., Lodging and bedstead.

Birháḍ karí, Mar. (बिऱ्हाडकरी) A lodger.

Birháná, H. (برهانا) Lands in which culinary herbs are grown.

Birheriá, H. (برهيريا) A branch of the Chumár tribe.

Birinj, H. P. (برنج) Rice.

Birinjári, H. (P. آر, who brings) A dealer in rice following camps; more correctly, *Banjári*, q. v.

Birinjphal, H. A sort of rice.

Birjiá, H. (برجيا) A division of the *Ahír* tribe.

Birká, H. (برکا) A pond, a small well.

Birmbháṭ, H. (برمبهاٹ) A branch of the Bháṭ tribe, whose office is the recitation of ancestral exploits at family festivals. They are hired for the occasion. They reside permanently in villages and towns, and do not lead a migratory life, like some of the other Bháṭs. See *Bháṭ*.

Birodh, Ben. &c. (বিরোধ, from the S. *virodha*) Litigation, opposition.

Birra, H. (برّہ) Gram and barley sown in the same field. In the Delhi district, chana or gram injured by wet. In East Oudh, a ceremony connected with the building of a house.

Birra, H. (برّہ, but more correctly, بيورہ, detail) Entry of the different crops of the village lands under separate heads in the Patwári's account.

Birrá-barár, H. (برّابرار, but apparently either a various reading, or an error for *Behri-barár*, q. v.) Collection in kind (Central Doab). Mr. Elliot suggests its derivation from '*Birat*,' separation on account of the crops being divided before appropriation, or from the *Birra* of the *Patwári*.

Birt, or **Brit**, H. (برت, from S. *vritti*, वृत्तिः, maintenance, support, means of livelihood) Grant or endowment to any person for his maintenance, or for religious and charitable objects. Proprietary right, whether acquired by purchase, inheritance, or grant, heritable and transferable, subject to payment of revenue, either to Government, or to the Raja or Zamindar, when not specially exempt. A right, custom, or privilege derived from the performance of offices, whether secular or religious. A right to perform certain offices claimed by different castes. Fees to family priests. *Birt*, as used in Gorakhpur, has been supposed to indicate a peculiar tenure; but it does not seem to have any especial sense, or to be more than a local term, equivalent to other terms indicating a grant of land, either rent-free or at a stipulated rent, being merely a gránt of land made originally by the Rajas of Gorakhpur and Benares, and held in absolute and hereditary right upon payment of a stipulated rent or revenue to the representatives of the original granter. The rent is liable to occasional adjustment, and to increase, if the Government demand on the Raja be increased. Although not liable to be dispossessed as long as the rent is paid, yet the occupant may be ousted, for a time at least, during which he is entitled to Málikána. He is also considered as at all times entitled to the Jalkar aud Bankar, or products of the waters and the woods.—Revenue Report, Commons, App. iii. 81, par. 380. Various kinds of Birt are specified as recognised in Gorakhpur: as—

Jivan Birt, H. (جيون برت, lit., maintenance for living;) An assignment by the Raja to a younger son and his descendants of villages in perpetuity, granting them by Paṭṭa, or deed of lease, and receiving a fixed sum as rent. An allowance to the family of an old servant deceased.

Marwat Birt, H. (مروت برت, from *Marná*, to die) Compensation in land to the family of a man killed in the service of the Raja, chargeable with half the rent of a village held as Birt on the usual terms.

Sanhalp Birt, H. (سنكلپ برت, from S. *Sankalpa*, संकल्पः, a vow) A religious grant to a Brahman, and held at first rent-free, but latterly subject to a small payment.

Birta, H. (in Nepal) Grant of land rent-free in absolute property and for ever.

Birtiá, H. (برتيا) One holding a *Birt*, or subsistence grant of any description, upon the terms of the grant. In Gorakhpur, the Birtias, according to Mr. Elliot, pay a fixed yearly sum, equivalent to 20 per cent. of the Government revenue, on account of the Raja or superior landholder; but they are the owners of the soil, and exercise the entire management of their villages, not liable to be ousted, holding an hereditary and transferable tenure, and subject to enhancement of rent only when the Government revenue is increased. (They do not appear, therefore, to differ essentially from Ryots holding hereditary property under a Zamindar, and not liable to dispossession as long as paying their rent; except that they are analogous to village Zamindars in excluding the district Zamindar from interference in the management of the villages.)

Birwá, H. (بروا) A tree. In East Oudh, The labourer employed to raise water with the Beri, q. v.

Birwáhi, H. (برواهي) An orchard. (From *Birwá*, a tree).

Bisáh, H. (بساه) Purchase, buying.

Bisahru, H. (بسهرو) A purchaser.

Bisal, Thug. A person intended to be killed, but who has clothes round his neck, or some hindrance to strangulation. A victim awkwardly handled. A Thug with traces of his crime ou his dress.

Bísanam, Mal. (?) A second or lighter crop (Travancore).

Bisandhi, Thug. Fetters, any metal utensil.

Bisár, H. (بسار) Loan of seed, to be repaid with increase after harvest.

Bisát, H. (بسات, less correctly, بساط) Mar. (बिशात) Stock, capital, goods, means.

Bisátí (A. بساتي, بساطي, from the A. بسط, a bed, a carpet) A pedlar, a hawker; a trader not keeping a shop, but exposing his wares on a carpet or mat spread on the ground. (The notion is the same as is expressed by *Bichháíti*, q. v., and the terms are probably confounded.)

Bisen, H. (بسين) A powerful tribe of Rajputs in the eastern parts of the north-west provinces, the head of whom is the Raja of Salempur Majjhauli.

Bish, corruptly, Beesh and Beeshy, H. &c. (بش, also written and pronounced Bikh, بکھ, S. विषः, *visha*) Poison in general, but usually applied to a root used sometimes in medicine (aconitum ferox). The fibrous stalk of the lotus (from S. विश).

Bishá, Uriya (ବିଶା) A brass weight equal to 20 palas.

Bishkapra, H. (بشکپره) A kind of spreading grass used in medicine (trianthema pentandra).

Bishnprít or preet, corruptly, Bishunpereet, H. &c. (بشنپريت, S. विष्णु, *vishnu* and *príta*, प्रीत, grateful to, beloved by) whence also, *Bishnuprít*, Ben. (বিষ্ণুপ্রীত)

Lands held rent-free by Brahmans, or religious persons, professing the especial service of the deity *Vishṇu.*

Bishnprít-dár, H. (P. دار, who has) A Brahman holding lands granted in honour of Vishṇu.

BISHNOTTAR, corruptly, BISHNOWATTUR, H. &c. (بشنوتّر, S. विष्णोत्तर) Land held rent-free by Brahmans professing the worship of *Vishṇu*, or granted in honour of that divinity: hence also, *Baishnavottar* (from *Baishnav*, a follower of *Vishṇu*).

BISHNOWI, H. (بشنوي) A tribe of growing importance in some parts of the north-west provinces, combining Hindu and Mohammedan practices and belief, generally terming themselves Sheikhs, but adding the title to a Hindu name.

BISHT, H. (بشت) A provincial term in Kamaon for a kind of *Tálukdár*, appointed by Government.

BÍSÍ, BEESEE, H. (بيسي) A measure of weight, commonly a *Vis* or *Vísí*, equal to five *Sers.* In Garwhal and Kamaon, a dry measure; also a measure of land equal to 20 nalís, and 4800 square yards. In Rangpur, a land measure equal to 16 *dhans.*

BISÍ, BISEE, Uriya, (ବିଷୀ) A fiscal division of the county a province or district paying revenue under the Hindu Government of Orissa: also termed *Bishe* (from S. *vishaya*, विषयः, a country).

Bissoï, or *Bishayi*, read also, *Bisaye*, (?) Uriya, The chief of a district in Orissa, collecting the Government revenue, and exercising police and judicial authority. The Desmukh of the Maraṭhas.

BISNI, Thug. A Thug, a thief, any one living by plunder.

BIṢODHAN, Ben., Uriya, &c. (বিশোধন, S. विशोधनं, lit., making clean or pure) Acquitting, discharging, as a debt.

Bisodhan patra, Ben. &c. (পত্র, a document) An acquittance, a receipt, a written discharge or release.

BIṢWA, H. (بسوه, विश्व, from *bís* بيس, S. *vinṣati* विंशति twenty) Lit., a twentieth, but applied especially to the twentieth part of a *Bígha.* It is also used to express a proportionate share of proprietary right in a village which is conventionally taken as a *Bígha*, divisible into twenty parts distributed among the sharers; as, a holder of five *Biṣwas* is proprietor of one-fourth; of ten *Biṣwas*, of a-half; of one *Biṣwa*, of one-twentieth; of half a *Biṣwa*, of one-fortieth, &c.

Biṣwa-barár, H. (برار, बरार, tax) Assessment or collection of the revenue upon the *Biṣwas* or shares of the land.

Biṣwadár, H. (P. دار, who has) The holder of a share or shares in a coparcenary village.

Biswadári, H. (P. داري, having) Proprietary tenure in *Biṣwas*, or shares so designated. Also the tenure of independent village communities holding under a superior Tálukdar, as in Aligarh, Mynpuri, and Gorakhpur. In some places, as in the Delhi district, the term is equivalent to *Paṭṭidári* or *Zamindari.* (In that case the derivation is probably different, and it may come from the S. *viṣwa* विश्व, all, whole).

Bíswak, Mar. (बीस्वक, from S. विंशति, twenty) The twentieth part of a *Pád*, which is the twentieth of a *Bígha.* The *Bíswak* is one square *Káti*, or rod, which, however, varies in length.

Biswáli, Uriya (ବିସ୍ୱାଲି) Land assigned to the *Khandáyat*, or head of a division called a *Khanda* (or, more probably, the land assigned to the *Bissoï*, the H. *Khand* and U. *Bishé* meaning the same).

Biswánsa, or *Bíswansí*, H. (بسوانسه, from *Bisva*, and S. अंश *anṣa*, portion) The fraction of a *Biṣwa*, usually the twentieth.

BIṢWÍ, H. (بسوي, विश्वी) The holder of a *Biṣwa*, or share, in which character the person may be appointed by a collector of revenue to collect the dues of the other sharers. Alienation of lands on a low quit-rent or payment of a fine (East Oudh). In the north-west provinces it sometimes implies a deduction of two Biṣwas per each Bíghá cultivated by under-tenants, claimed as his right by the landlord or lessor.

BÍTÁ, BEETA, H. (बीता, more correctly, perhaps, BHITÍ, q. v.) Lands of a village that have existed from time immemorial, in opposition to lands recently acquired by alluvial deposit.

BITA or BHÍTA, Thug. A hundred.

BITAURÁ, H. (بتورا) A heap of dried cow-dung.

BÍṬAURÍ, Hindi (बीटौरी) A tax upon artificers and shopkeepers for permission to work or trade in a village. Puraniya.

BIṬHAK, H. (بٹهك) Ant-hills (East Oudh and Benares); also a seat or platform where people meet to converse. See *Baithak.*

BIT KHÉT, H. (بيت كهيت) Lands on which forced or unrequited labour is demanded from the Ryots by the owner of the village.

BIṬ- or BID LAVAṆ, corruptly, BITNOBEN, Hindi (बिट or

बिड लवण) A kind of medicinal salt, commonly known as black salt, formed by fusing common salt with Emblic myrobalan.

Bitrá-bandi, H. (بترا بندي) Arrangements for securing the revenue (Sagar). See Bila-bandi.

Bittadahola, Karn. (ಬಿತ್ತದಹೊಲ) A field left fallow.

Biṭṭe, Karn. (ಬಿಟ್ಟೆ) Performance of inferior offices in a village, as porterage, &c., for fees in grain, or lands exempt from revenue.

Biṭṭé-khádi, Karn. (ಬಿಟ್ಟೆಖಾದಿ) A cess levied in lieu of a piece of cloth formerly exacted annually from each loom.

Biṭṭiyava, Bíṭṭiyáḷu, Karn. (ಬಿಟ್ಟಿಯವ, ಬಿಟ್ಟಿಯಾಳು) A free porter.

Biṭṭe yettu, Karn. (ಬಿಟ್ಟೆಯೆತ್ತು) A tax levied in Mysore in lieu of bullocks formerly required from the villages for the conveyance of grain to the Paligars.

Bittuvadu, (బిత్తువడు) Sowing seed.

Bitu, Beetoo, Thug. Any person not a Thug.

Biyutát, H. (بيوتات, pl. of *bait*, a house, lit., house expenses) A term applied to lands in the neighbourhood of Agra that were assigned originally to members of the royal family, but had come under general cultivation.

Bizáât or Bazaât, A. (بضاعت) Agency, commission, in which the profit on the sale accrues to the proprietor of the article sold, and is not divided between the owner and the agent. Capital. Stock in trade.

Bo, H. (بو, root of *Bo-ná*, to sow) Cultivation. Sowing seed.

Boái or *Boárá*, (بوارا, بواي) Sowing seed. Time for sowing.

Boyar, H. (بوير, बोयर) Land that never lies fallow.

Bob, H. (بوب) Sowing grain by the drill (Bundelkhand).

Boï báchh, H. (بوي باچھ) Assessment to be realised on actual cultivation (Delhi).

Boni, H. (بوني) Sowing. Seed-time.

Bobháṭá, Mar. (बोभाटा) Notoriety. Publicity of what ought to be kept quiet. General outcry. A clamorous complaint or accusation.

Bodá, H. (بودا) A buffalo.

Bodar, Bodur, H. (بودر) A place to stand on whilst throwing up water with the Dauri, or basket, from a lower to a higher level.

Boddhá, Ben. (বোদ্ধা) A security, a bondsman, a bail.

Bogami, Tel. (?) The chief of the left-hand caste in Dindigul.—Gl. 5th Rep.

Bógamu, Tel. (బోగము, from S. भोग, enjoyment) The dancing-girl caste.

Bógamu-vádu, Tel. (బోగమువాడు) A dancing girl.

Bógamudi or *Bhógandi*, Tel. (బోగముది, బోగంది) A dancing girl.

Bogase, Karn. (ಬೊಗಸೆ) The two hands joined so as to hold any thing; whence it comes to imply the small perquisites granted to the village servants measured by handfuls.

Bohaudiá, H. (بوهوديا) A cultivator who has not a plough, and either works with a hoe or a borrowed plough.

Bohni, H. (بوهني) Baüni, Ben. (বউনি), Bóni, Tel. Karn. (బోణి), Mar. (बोहनी) The first money received during the day, or the first ready-money sale by shopkeepers and hucksters. Handsel. No credit is given for the article first sold.

Bohrá, incorrectly, Borah, H. (بوهرا, S. *vyavahárí* व्यवहारी, a trader, a man of affairs), also Bohárá, Boharí, or Bohárí, Mar. (बोहारा, बोहरी, बोहारी) A banker. A money-lender, or merchant of a particular tribe so called, usually receiving any article of marketable value in payment of money advanced. The Bohras appear to have originated in Guzerat, where they became converts to Mohammadanism, but they are settled in many parts of central and western India and in the north-west provinces.

Bóí, Boee, Tel. (బోయీ) A man of the fisherman-caste, but whose usual avocation is also the carrying of litters and palankins, and who is employed as a domestic servant at Madras, where the word is pronounced like, and confounded with, the English "boy:" also written and pronounced "Bhoï," q. v.

Bóídu, Tel. (బోయీడు) A man of the cow-herd or shepherd-caste.

Bojh, H. (بوجھ), Ben. Bojá or Bojhá, (বোজা, বোঝা, Hindi (बोझा) A sheaf or bundle of grain or grass; also, a load, a burthen. A load of corn equal to five Dhokas, but the measure varies in different districts, and also according to the crops. The first of the pans placed for receiving sugar from the boiler.

Bojh-baṭái, H. (بوجھ بٹاي) Division or shares by stocks or bundles of mowed corn (Rohilkhand).

Boká, H. (بوكا, बोका) A basket, pail, or leather bag for throwing up water; possibly connected with the Anglo-Saxon term *Buk*, *Bouk*, *Bucket*.

Bokkasa, Karn. (ಬೊಕ್ಕಸ) Treasure.

Bokkasadamane, Karn. (ಬೊಕ್ಕಸದಮನೆ) A treasury.

Bókkena, Tel. (బొక్కెన, from the H. *boka*) A bucket

for drawing water from a well. A leather bag for baling out water. A grain or corn bag.

Bolá, H. (بولا, from بولنا, to speak) Verbal agreement between two parties. (In the Delhi district) agreement between the village lessees and cultivators as under-tenants.

Bolans, H. (بولنس) Making over one's share to another.

Bolansi, H. (بولنسي) The holder of a share properly belonging to another. An adopted heir. (This and the preceding are current in Benares and East Oudh, from *bolná*, to speak, and *anṣ* अंश, a share).

Bolkhat or Bolekhut, elsewhere written Bholkat, (?) Mar. One of the accounts kept by the Kulkaraní, a debit and credit account, shewing the amount received from the cultivators, and how it has been disposed of.

Boḷwaṇ, Mar. (बोळवण) Ceremony of conducting a bride to her husband's house; also, dismissal of the bridegroom's friends and attendants. Ceremony of propitiating Bhútas or evil spirits, who have entered a village, to induce them to leave it, and conducting them with music and in procession to the confines.

Bombyá, Mar. (बोंब्या) A person in office at Gaya, who, when a party of pilgrims arrives, precedes them, making a noise by beating his mouth.

Bomkar, Mar. (?) A class of weavers in Kandesh.

Boṇḍa or Boṇḍa koyya, Tel. (బొండ, బొండకొయ్య) Stocks for confining petty offenders.

Bondu, Tel. (బొందు) A field or crop dried up for want of rain.

Bondu-powadam, Tel. (?) Parched or dried-up crops, yielding no grain.

Bontalu-ráṣí, Tel. (?) Ears of *Jawári* retaining the grain after threshing.

Bora, H, Ben. (بوره) A sack for holding rice.

Boro, H. Ben. (বোরো) A sort of rice sown in January and reaped in April: it is sown in low swampy ground, or near the banks of a river where irrigation is not required.

Boro faṣl, H. Ben. (فصل) The season of spring, or that in which the Boro rice is reaped.

Boṭṭu, Tel. Karn. (బొట్టు) A drop. A spot. An ornament or spot-mark on the forehead of a bride at the time of marriage. Sectarial mark with paint or ashes on the forehead. Also $\frac{1}{64}$th of a pagoda.

Bottu, Tel. (బొత్తు) The husk or chaff of grain after threshing.

Brahmá, S. (masc. *Brahmá*, ब्रह्मा) One of the chief Hindu deities. The agent in creation. The creator.

Brahma, with the final vowel short (ब्रह्म) The first cause of all things. The Supreme Being. Also, the Vedas collectively.

Bráhman, Brahmun, dialectically, Bahman or Bohman, or, in Tamil, Párappan or Pirramanan, corruptly, Braman, Bramin, &c., H. (براهمن, S. ब्राह्मन्) A man of the first order or caste of Hindus, properly charged with the duty of expounding the Vedas, and conducting the ceremonies they enjoin: in modern times, engaged not only in such duties, but in most of the occupations of secular life. The Bráhmans of the present day are distinguished into a variety of divisions and subdivisions, between most of which no social relations exist. The first distinction is between those who maintain a sacred fire—and are thence termed Agnihotras—and those who do not, by far the larger proportion. A more universal distinction is that of the five *Gauṛa* and five *Dráviṛa* races. The first are the *Kányahubja*, or Bráhmans of Kanuj; *Sáraswat*, or north-west of India; *Gauṛ*, or Bengal; *Maithila*, or north Bahar; *Utkala*, or Orissa. The second are the *Dráviṛa*, *Tailanga*, *Karnáta*, *Maharáshtra*, and *Gurjar*, or Guzerat Bráhmans. Each of these has various subdivisions. According to a *Játi Málá*, or list of castes current in Hindustan, the principal are thus enumerated: 1. Kányakubja, four: *Sarjupári*, *Sarwaria*, *Jijhaulia*, and *Sanaudhiya*. 2. Sáraswat, ten: *Bháradwájí*, *Sípoli*, *Chaini*, *Súdhani*, *Bháratí*, *Khukaṭí*, *Ranhhaṭi*, *Bolí*, *Málí*, *Grahaṇi*. 3. Gauṛ, six: *Gauṛ*, *Párihh*, *Báhimí*, *Khandelwál*, *Sáraswat*, *Suhhwál*. 4. 5. The Maithila and Utkala Bráhmans have but one order. Of the five *Dráviṛas*, the Dráviṛa properly so termed has three divisions: *Bádam*, *Brihatcharan*, *Ashṭasahasra*. 2. Tailanga has six: *Telghánya*, *Belnáḍ*, *Begináḍ*, *Karnákammala*, *Munganáḍ*, *Kásalnáḍ*. 3. Karnáṭa, two: *Badgalnáḍ-Ṣilnáḍ*. 4. Maharáshṭra, eight: *Karáḍe*, *Chitpáwan*, *Deṣastha*, *Yajurvedi*, *Ápastambha*, *Abhír*, *Serabaï*, *Kayasthíprabhu*. 5. The Gurjara Bráhmans are of eighty-four tribes; the principal of which are the *Nágara*, *Moṛa*, *Audíah*, *Mewára*, *Srí-gaur*, *Khedewal*, and *Bhúïnhár*: (some of these names are very possibly inaccurate.) There are also two classes considered additional to the whole, *Ṣákadwípí*, who came latterly, it is said, from *Ṣákadwípa*, and *Gayáli*, said to have been made *Bráhmans* by *Vyása.* Each of the above has an infinite number of subdivisions. The Kanouj Bráhmans, from whom the Bráhmans of Bengal are reputed to spring, are said to have been divided, after their settling in Bengal, into a hundred and fifty-six families. Of these, one hundred are to be found in the portion of Bengal termed *Várendra*, and fifty-six in that termed *Ráṛh*. Of the former, eight, and of the latter, six are considered *Kulína*, or of good family, or noble; a classification ascribed to *Balál Sen*, a Raja of Bengal in the twelfth century. The first are named *Maitra, Bhíma, Rudra, Vágísí, Santámani or Sandyál, Láhuri, Bháduri, Sudhu-vágísí*, and *Bhadara*. The fourth and fifth names are not unfrequently met with, the rest seldom. Those of the *Ráṛh* Bráhmans are more common: they are *Mukhuti* or *Mukharji, Gánguli, Kanjláha, Goshála, Bandygati* or *Banarji, Chatati* or *Chatoji.*

BRÁHMAṆÍ, corruptly, BRAMINEE and BAHMANEE, H. S. (ब्राह्मणी) A female of the Bráhmanical caste, the wife of a Bráhman.

Brahmacharya, H. (ब्रह्म, from *Bráhmana*, and *Charya*, चर्य्य, practice) The condition of the religious student. Leading a similar life, or one of continency and self-denial. Mendicancy.

Brahmachárí, H. I. (ब्रह्म, for ब्राह्मण and चारी, who follows or practises) A youth of either of the three first pure classes during his pupillage, and while studying the Vedas. A mendicant who professes to have prolonged the period of studentship, and to observe through life the practice of study, poverty, and continence. In general, however, an ignorant vagrant.

Brahmáduya, corruptly, *Bremhaday, Bramadayum, Bramandoyan, Bumadya*, H. S. (ब्रह्म, for ब्राह्मण, and *ádáya*, आदाय, what is received) Any grant or perquisite appropriated to Bráhmans. In the Carnatic, a twentieth of the Government revenue was formerly considered as payable to the Bráhmans for religious purposes.

Brahmahatyá, S. (ब्रह्महत्या) The murder of a Bráhman. Any crime of like enormity.

Brahma, or *Brahman-jái* or *-jaee*, Mar. (ब्रह्मजाई) A man of a mixed race, sprung from a Bráhman father and woman of inferior caste. He is usually engaged in service, agriculture, or trade.

Bráhmanabhojaná, S. &c. (ब्राह्मणभोजना) Distribution of food to Bráhmans.

Bráhmanadivya, S. Mar. (ब्राह्मणदिव्य) A form of oath: making oath while holding the feet of a holy Bráhman.

Bráhmanjan, Mar. (from S. जन, a person) A Bráhman entertained in a Bráhman family as a menial.

Brahmavásittí, T. (பிரமவாஸித்தீ, spelled *Piramavásittí*) A Bráhman village.

Brahmottara, corruptly, *Burmhotur, Bruhmutter, Bromutter, Barmautar, Burmuter, Bermertur*, &c., Ben. Uriya (ବ୍ରହ୍ମୋତ୍ତର, S. ब्रह्म, A Brahman, and उत्तर, *uttara*, what comes after or belongs to, but the derivation and form of this compound, notwithstanding its very general use, are not quite certain. It is sometimes written *Brahmatrá*, as if derived from S. *trá*, what preserves, from the root त्रा, *trá*, to preserve or protect, but the correctness of this is doubtful) Land granted rent-free to Bráhmans, for their support and that of their descendants; properly as a reward for their sanctity or learning, or to enable them to devote themselves to religious duties and education. Such lands have not unfrequently fallen into the possession of lay proprietors.

Bráhmanvád, Karn. (?) A term used in the Nagar district of Mysore for the *garden* country.

BRAJ, or BRUJ, incorrectly, BRIJ, H. (برج, from the S. *vraja*, व्रज, a cow-pen or pasture) The tract about Mathura and Brindaban, the residence of the juvenile Kṛishṇa, and the scene of his boyish gambols with the Gopas and Gopís, or cowherds and milkmaids.

Brajbásí, Brujbasee, corruptly, *Brijbasi, Birjebassy, Birjebussie*, and *Birjebaussie*, H. S. (lit., an inhabitant *Vásí* or *Básí* of the district of *Braj*) An armed attendant, one carrying arms, as a sword and shield, or sometimes a matchlock, and employed as a doorkeeper, a guard, or an escort. He is always a native of Western or North-Western India, and is thence identified with a Hindu of *Braj*.

Braj-bháshá, or *-bhákhá*, H. S. (from S. भाषा, speech) The dialect of *Braj*, the form of Hindi spoken in the neighbourhood of Mathura and other parts of the north-western provinces, and in which the most popular poems of the Hindus are written; as, the Rámáyaṇa, by Tulaṣí Dás.

BRAT, or BRUT, corruptly, BURT, H. (برت, S. *vrata*, व्रत) A vow, a fast, any self-imposed religious obligation. (The word is improperly confounded with *Birt* and *Brit*. See the next.)

BRIT, H. (برت, S. *vritti*, वृत्तिः, means of subsistence) A grant of land or other means of support to any one. (In the spoken dialect the word is most usually pronounced *Birt*, q. v.)

Brittánt, H. (برتّانت, S. वृत्तान्त, *vrittánta*) Information, news, intelligence of a transaction or occurrence.

Brittánt-patra, H. (*patra*, a leaf) Record of a decision pronounced by a *Pancháyat*.

Bu, Buá, Bubu, H. (بو, بوا, بوبو) A sister. *Buá* is also an aunt by the father's side. *Bubu* in the west of India is a lady.

Búd, Bood, H. (from the P. بود, third person preter. of بودن, to be) Being, state or condition of being, especially with reference to the past. It is used in Hindi chiefly in composition; as, *Búd-básh*, a residence, *Búd-ná-búd* or *Hast-ná-búd*, remission of rent on failure of crops.

Budh-Gangá, Boodh-Gunga, H. (بڈّھگنگا, from *Budh*, pronounced *Búṛh*, or *Búṛha*, old) The old bed of the Ganges, traceable below Hastinapur, and also below Soron and Kampil.

Budhavára, vernacularly, *Budhwár*, or *Budhbár*, S. &c. (बुधवार, from *Budha*, the planet Mars, and *vára*, a day) Wednesday.

Budibudaki, Karn. (ಬುಡಿಬುದಕಿ) A class of religious mendicants in Mysore.

Búḍide pannu, Tel. (బూడిదెపన్ను, from *budide*, ashes) A fee for permission to burn a corpse.

Buḍít, Booḍeet, Mar. (बुडीत) A loss, a sum of money given up as lost. Money imprudently invested.

Buḍítkúl, Mar. (बुडीतकूल) A bad debtor, one not likely to pay.

Buḍít khat, Mar. (from *hhat*, खत, P. a writing) A bond not expected to be discharged.

Buḍít kharch, Mar. (खर्च, from خرچ) Expenditure without return. Head of an account specifying losses.

Buḍít kháteṇ, Mar. (बुडीतखातें) An account or register of bad debts.

Buḍkí, Buṛkí, Mar. (बुडकी) A hole or pit dug by the side of a stream to collect water for distribution in irrigation.

Budrúkh, Mar. (बुद्रूख, dialectic corruption of P. *Buzúrg*, بزرگ, great) Venerable, dignified. Greater or upper, as fields or towns opposed to lesser or lower: also, senior as opposed to junior, or major to minor.

Bugára ráṣí, Tel. (?) A heap of unwinnowed grain.

Bujhárat, H. (بجهارت., from بوجهانا, to explain or cause to understand) An audit or adjustment of accounts.

Bujhonta, H. (بجهونتا., from بوجهنا, to understand) An abstract account of a village proprietary, made out annually by the Patwárí, shewing the profit on each share.

Búk, Book, H. (بوك) Land recovered through the recession of a river (Rohilkhand).

Búkára, Bookara, H. (بوكاره) Land left by a river, but rendered useless by a deposit of sand (Rohilkhand).

Bulandi, Boolundu, H. (from the P. *buland*, بلند, lofty) High land.

Bun, Hindi (बुन) The quantity of grain given to a labourer for a day's work in weeding, from two-and-a-half to three *Sers* of rough grain (Puraniya).

Bun, Boon, H. (بُن) Coffee in seed, before it is ground.

Bundela, Boondela, H. (بونديله) A spurious tribe of Rájputs, who give name to the province of Bundelkhand, corruptly, Bundlecund. They are descended from the Garhwárs of Kantit and Khairagarh, and first settled in Bundelkhand in the thirteenth or fourteenth century. There are few genuine Bundelas in the British portion of the province, except in the Pargana of Panwári.

Búndu, Karn. (ಬೂಂದು) The coffee plant (Mysore).

Búndu bíj, Karn. (from S. *víja*, seed) The coffee berry.

Bunga, or Bonga, H. (بونگه) A stack of straw.

Bungáh, corruptly, **Bounga**, H. (P. بنگاه), Mar. **Buṇugeṇ**, (बुणुगें) Followers, suttlers, and baggage of an army.

Búnṭ, Boonṭ, H. (بونت) Unripe grain or pulse (Cicer arietinum).

Bunyád, H. (P. بنياد), Mar. (बुन्याद) Lit., foundation, but applied to offices or appointments which have existed from time immemorial.

Bunyádí, Mar. (बुन्यादी) Original, fundamental.

Bunyádí thalkarí, Mar. (थलकरी, landholder) The original landlord or proprietor of an estate.

Burá, Burhá, Mar. (बुरा, बुऱ्हा) Mould.

Búra, Boora, H. (بوره) Redeemable mortgage (East Oudh).

Buranṭ, Buránṭ, Mar. (बुरंट, बुरांट) A place overgrown with grass and bushes. A thicket of low bushes.

Búṛa-ṭukra, Boora-tokra, Ben. (?) An account of village receipts and disbursements made up for six or eight months by the Patwárí, and balanced. The balance is carried to the demands of the rest of the year.

Buṛi, Ben. (বুড়ি) An inundation, immersion of a tract under water. A measure of value equal to five Gaṇḍas, or twenty Kauṛris.

Burída, Booreedu, H. (P. بريده, lit., cut) Fields cut by stealth (Rohilkhand),

Búrká, Mar. (?) A subdivision or share of the lands of a village, varying from ten to fifty, each comprising a certain number of fields, but not a defined quantity of land.

Búrká chi húl, Mar. (?) The managing Ryot who apportions the Burkas and the revenue among the other cultivators. *Dakhin.*

Búrki, Mar. (?) A structure of masonry for drawing water from rivers and nalas.

Burṛi, Booṛree, H. (بڙي) Sowing seed by dropping it from the hand into the furrow, instead of sowing broadcast or by drill; also read Gurri and Gulli.

Buruḍ or **Buraḍ**, Mar. (बुरूड, बुरड) The name of a caste, or individual of it, whose occupation is mat-making. He is sometimes enumerated among the village servants.

Butádu, Tel. (బుతాడు) Household expenses.

Butárad, Hindi (बुतारद) A name given to extra cesses upon the cultivator. *Purańiya.*

Bút-faroshi or **-paroshi**, Tel. (from P. *bút*, an idol, and *parwarish*, cherishing) A tax levied on different trades in a town or village to defray the cost of celebrating the worship of the tutelary divinity. A tax levied on the festivals of the inferior castes and the drums beaten on such occasions. In former times, also, a fine imposed by a Guru, or spiritual guide, to expiate certain breaches of the laws of caste.

Buttáwal, (?) Tamil. Land newly cleared for cultivation. In the first year it is exempt from rent, in the succeeding years it pays the Government revenue in progressive fourths, until, in the fifth year, it is fully assessed. Travancore.

Byabasáy, for S. Vyavasáya, Ben. (ব্যবসায), S. (व्यवसाय:) Trade, business affairs.

Byabasáyí, Ben. A tradesman, any one engaged in affairs or business.

Byabasthá, for S. Vyavasthá, Ben. (ব্যবস্থা) A statute, a law. A written opinion or dictum on a point of Hindu law drawn up by Pandits.

Byabahár, Ben. (ব্যবহার), S. (व्यवहार) Custom, usage. Business, profession, affairs in general. A suit at law; whence, also, *Byabahárik*, one engaged in affairs, in a suit, &c.

Byáh, H. (بياه, S. विवाह) Marriage.

Byáj, H. (بياج) Interest. See *Biáj*.

Byáju, H. (بياجو) Principal bearing interest. See *Biáju*.

Byáṇa, Byára, Karn. (ಬ್ಯಾಣ, ಬ್ಯಾರ) A piece of pasture-ground attached to a village, and assigned as a perquisite to the head-man, who lets it out for the grazing of cattle at a charge per head.

Byápár, H. Ben. (بياپار, व्यापार) Business, affairs.

Byápárí, H. (بياپاري, S. व्यापारी) One who transacts business of any kind, a merchant, a dealer, a trader. (It occurs in most dialects, slightly modified, as, *Beparí, Baipárí, Beopárí, Byopárí, Byaupárí*, &c.

Byaurá, H. (بيَورا, S. व्यवहार:) Detail, narration, statement of circumstances.

Byay or **Byayhár**, (بيُي, بييهار, S. व्यय) Expense, expenditure.

Byohár or **Byauhár**, properly, **Byabahár**, as above, or **Vyavahára**, H. (بيوهار) Business, affairs, trade, calling.

Byohar, H. (بيوهر, from the S. व्यवहार) A loan.

Byohará or *Byohárí*, H. (بيوهرا, بيوهاري, S. व्यवहारिक:) A creditor, a lender.

C

Caste, Eng. A word applied to the distinctions of birth, tribe, and occupation, which separate the people of India of the Hindu religion, and preclude their eating, drinking, and smoking together; their using the same vessels; their intermarrying; and other relations of social life. The lower orders of Indian Mohammadans pretend to similar distinctions; caste being in all cases matter of pride, not of humiliation. The word is derived from the Portuguese *Casta*, race, species.

Chabená, Chabeni, H. (چبينا, چبيني, S. चबै, to chew) Parched grain.

Chabutarah, Chubootura, Chabutrá, Chubootra, H. (چبوتره, चबुतरा -चा) A raised bank or terrace detached from the residence, sometimes covered over, on which persons sit and converse. A kind of summer-house or pavilion. A place where the head of the police is usually stationed. A police-office or station, or the magistrates' court. A room or hall used for public meetings of the villagers. A custom-house or station. A guard-house. A market-place. A stone platform erected as a boundary mark.

Chábuk, corruptly, **Chawbuck**, H. (چابك) A whip.

Chábuk-suwár, corruptly, *Chawbuck-swaar*, H. (P. سوار, a rider) A rough rider, a groom, a jockey.

CHACHÁ, CHÁCHÁ, H. &c. (چچا, چاچا, चचा, चाचा) A paternal uncle, a father's brother.

Chachí, or *Cháchí*, H. &c. (چچي, چاچي) A father's brother's wife.

Chacherá, H. &c. (چچيرا) Connected through a paternal uncle; as, *Chacherá-bhái*, A first cousin, the son of a paternal uncle.

CHACHAR, also CHANCHAR, CHUCHUR, or CHUNCHUR, H. (چچر, چنچر, चंचर) Land that has lain fallow for a year or more, but not a very long time: on being taken under cultivation the produce was divisible for the first year in the proportion of one share to Government and three to the cultivator: after a year of cultivation it was placed on the footing of fully cultivated land of the same description.

CHÁCHAR, H. (چاچر) A Hindu festival held after the Holi.

CHÁCHAR, Ben. (চাচর) Land on the banks or in the bed of a river, from which the water has lately been dried. Inferior fallow land.

CHADAR, CHUDUR, H. (P. چدر) A sheet or cloth.

Chadar andázi, H. (P. اندازي, throwing) A ceremony among the Sikhs: when a man marries a widow a sheet is thrown over the parties.

CHADARÚ-GUDDI, (?) Karn. Boundaries of an estate or of village lands, including waste.

CHAḌÁVU, Karn. (ಚಡಾವು) Increase of price or rent. See *Charhai*.

Darchaḍávu, Karn. (ದರಚಡಾವು) Disposing of the Government share of the crop to farmers at an advanced rate.

CHAḌH, pronounced also CHAṚH, Mar. (चढ) Increase, advance (as of assessment or price, &c.)

Chaḍhpaṭṭí, Mar. (चढपट्टी) An extra cess.

CHÁḌI, Tel. Karn. (ಚಾಡಿ) An accusation, slander, defamation.

CHÁH, H. (P. چاه) A well.

Cháhi, or *Cháhi-zamin*, H. (زمين, land) Land irrigated from wells.

Mahíṭi Cháh, H. (from A. محيط, surrounding) Land watered by wells in alternate years.

CHAH, CHUH, H. (چه) A platform, a pier-head.

CHAHÁR-SHAMBA, H. (P. چهار شمبه) Thursday.

CHAHÁR-SU, H. (P. چهار, four, and سو, a side) A square, a quadrangle, a market-place.

CHAHAL, H. (چهل) A strong soil, ranking between those termed *Rauslí* and *Ḍánkar* (Dehli).

CHAHAL SITÚN, H. (P. چهل, forty, ستون, a pillar) A pavilion, a chamber, a summer-house supported by forty, *i. e.* many pillars. (Also with the H. numeral, *Chálís*, forty, *Chálís-sitún*).

CHAHALDÁ, Mar. (चहलदा) A tax formerly levied on Banjáras in the Dakhin.

CHÁHIL, or CHÁHIRÁ, H. (چاهل, چاهرا) A tribe of Rájputs in Hisar, mostly converts to Mohammadanism. They nevertheless retain charge of the tomb of *Goga Chauhán*, a Hindu prince now esteemed a saint.

CHAHLI, CHUHLEE, H, (چهلي) The wheel on which the rope revolves at the top of the well.

CHAHORÁ, H. (چهورا) Rice dibbled in a field after being sown in a separate bed. A fine sort of rice.

CHAHOTRÁ, or CHAHUTRÁ, Mar. (चहोत्रा, चहुत्रा, from चहुं, four, and उत्तर, subsequent) Interest at four per cent. per month.

CHÁHÚR, Mar. (चाहूर) A long measure of land. According to one statement, equal to 120 square *Bíghás*, to another, to 150 *Bíghás*.

CHÁHVARÍ, Mar. (चाह्वरी) The drag rope of a plough or of the bucket of a well, to which the head pair of oxen are yoked.

Cháhvarí moṭ, Mar. (चाह्वरी मोट) The bucket of a draw-well worked by bullocks.

CHAIL, H. (چيل) Land twice tilled (Rohilkhand).

CHAIN, H. (چين) Cultivated land.

CHAÍN, H. (چئين) A low caste of Hindus.

CHAINA, H. (چينه) An inferior kind of grain. A sort of millet (Panicum pilosum), also called *Chena* and *Chína*.

Cháiṇkhaṭi, Ben. (চাঁইখটি) A spot in the salt-works where the drainage of the baskets is collected.

Cháiṇ laban, Ben. (চাঁইলবণ) Basket salt.

CHAIT, or CHYT, properly, CHAITRA, H. &c. (چيت, S. चैत्र) A month so called (March—April) beginning with the sun's entrance into Pisces.

Chaití, H. (चैती) Relating to or produced in *Chait*, as, the spring harvest. In Bundelkhand it is usually so applied, denoting the *Rabí*, or spring crops.

CHAITYA, S. (चैत्य) Any large tree in a village, held in peculiar sanctity: an altar, a monument. A Buddhist temple or monument.

CHAK, CHUK, corruptly, CHUCK, H. &c. (چك, चक, S.

चक्र, a circle or district) CHAKU, or CHEKU, Tel. (చకు, చెకు) A portion of land divided off; as, the detached fields of a village, or a patch of rent-free land, or any separate estate or farm. In old revenue accounts the term was applied to lands taken from the residents of a village, and given to a stranger to cultivate. In the north-west provinces the subdivision of a Pargana formed under cl. 88, Settlement Circular of 1839. In the Dakhin survey the term is used to designate a field within a field, when it is necessary to subdivide a field without changing the number or series of the larger portion of the land into which a village is divided.

Chak-bandí, *Chukbundee*, H. (چکبندي, चकबंदी) Determining the limits or boundaries of a detached piece of land, an estate, or *Chak*. The limits of a police or revenue jurisdiction.

Chak barár, *Chuk burár*, H. (برار a tax) Collecting the rents of a *Chah* according to its size or productiveness.

Chak náma, *Chuk námu*, H., or *Chekunámá*, Tel. (P. نامه a document) A register of the extent and boundaries of a detached or separate piece of land, or of a separate village. A grant authorising individuals to hold alienated lands, and specifying their limits.

Chak náma árázi, H. (A. عراضي, See *Árázi*) A document given to a Zamindar from whom a portion of land has been taken by the Government for public or other purposes, defining the extent, boundaries, and quality of the land.

Chak ṭukra, H. (چك and تكره, a piece) A plot or parcel of a landed estate.

CHAK, Ben. (চক) A square; also, a market-place enclosed by building. It has also the sense of the preceding.

Chak bandí, Ben. (চকবংদী) Building a square, connecting the buildings round it.

CHAK, Thug. Suspicion.

Chak-bele, Thug. A dangerous or suspicious place.

CHÁK, H. Ben. (چاك, চাক, S. चक्र) A wheel; especially applied to the pulley through which the rope attached to the bucket of a well passes. Also a mill. Also the rings of baked clay used in sinking a well, and a vessel in which sugar is manufactured.

Cháká, Ben. (চাকা) A wheel, a discus. The upper portion of the salt-boiling furnace.

CHÁKALAVÁḌU, Tel. (చాకలవాడు) A washerman.

CHAKAR, CHUKUR. H. &c. (چكر, S. CHAKRA, चक्र, in which form it occurs in most dialects) A wheel, a circle, or any thing revolving in a circle.

Chakar-bardeshi, (?) H. Compound interest.

CHÁKAR, CHAKUR, H. (P. چاكر, चाकर) A servant.

Cháhará, Ben. (চাকরা) Land given in reward of past services.

Chákarán, H. (properly the plural of چاكر, servants) Allowances of land, or the revenue derived from it, professedly appropriated in Bengal to the pay and support of the public officers and servants of a village or Zamindári, including the Zamindar, Kánungo, Mokaddem, Patwárí, and the Peons and Chaukidárs. Under the ancient system the lands so appropriated were exempted from the Government assessment in favour of the Zamindar, but this was disallowed on the formation of the decennial settlement. Ben. Reg. viii. 1793; ix. 1825.

Chákarán-zamín, corruptly, *Chakeram-zemeen*, *Chakeran-jemmy*, H. (*chákarán*, as above, and P. *zamín*, زمين, land) Lands exempted from revenue on the plea of being appropriated to maintain the public officers and servants.

Chákari, H. (چاكري) Service. Allowance of land, &c., for public officers and servants. Service land.

Chákariá, incorrectly, *Chákriá*, Mar. (चाकरीया) Applied to land held revenue-free, on condition of performing some office, or discharging some obligation. Service land.

CHAKI, CHUKEE, (?) Karn. An extra assessment in Kanara.

CHÁKÍ, Ben. (চাকী, from S. चक्र) A mill, a grinding stone, an apparatus for spinning twine suspended from the hand.

CHAKIRI, Mal. (ചകിരി) The fibres of the husk of the cocoa-nut, of which rope, or kayar, is made.

CHÁKIYÁRA, Mal. (ചാക്കിയാര) A class of out-caste Brahmans.

CHAKKÁ, CHUKKA, H. (چكّا, from *chakra*, a wheel) A circular lump of clay, used to press down the smaller arm of the lever employed in raising water from a well. A wheel.

CHÁKHAṆḌ, Uriya (ଚାଖଣ୍ଡ) A measure of length, half a cubit.

CHAKKALU, Tel. (చక్కలు) Small bubbles of salt that rise upon the first ebullition of the brine.

CHAKKAN, CHAKKÁLA, Mal. (ചക്കൻ, ചക്കാല) An oil presser.

CHAKKARA, Mal. (ചക്കര) Coarse sugar, made from the juice of the cocoa-nut and other palms.

Chakkarakhaḷḷa, Mal. (ചക്കരക്കള്ള്) The *tárí*, or juice of the cocoa-nut, from which coarse sugar is made.

Chakkat, Chukkut, H. (چکّت) The loss of a *chak*, or plot of ground, by inundation.

Chakki, H. (چکّي) A handmill, a grindstone.

Chakki náma, H. (نامہ) A song sung by women at weddings, while grinding a perfumed powder.

Chakki náuri, H. (ناوري) Presentation of perfumed powder to the bride and bridegroom, and the female assistants by whom it has been prepared.

Chakkili, Tam. Mal. (சக்கிலி) A low-caste man, working in hides and leather; a currier, a shoemaker, the village shoemaker. Apparently corrupted to *Chuckler*, the word in common use among Europeans.

Chakku, Karn. (ಚಕ್ಕು) A pack or bale of raw cotton.

Chakkubandhi, Karn. (ಚಕ್ಕುಬಂಧಿ) Land measure.

Chaklá, Chukla, corruptly, Chuckla, H. (چکلا) Chaklá, or Cháklá, Ben. (চকলা, চাকলা, from the S. चक्र) A large division of a country, comprehending a number of Parganas; first introduced as a recognised local division in the reign of *Shahjehan*. Bengal was divided by Jaffir Khan, about 1772, into thirteen *Chaklas*, each under a separate superintendant of finance. At different times, and in different parts of the country, the *Chakla* seems to have varied in extent, and in its subdivisions. In modern times it is applied to the part of a town chiefly inhabited by prostitutes. In Mar., besides a division of country, it also means the court or office of the magistrate of a ward.

Chaklá bandi, corruptly, *Chucklabundy*, H. (چکلا بندي) The distribution of a Zamindári or of a province into *Chaklas*, especially for financial convenience.

Chakle dár, H. (چکلي دار) The superintendant or proprietor, or renter of a *Chahla*.

Chakle dári, H. (چکلي داري) Superintendence or possession of a *Chakla*. The right of occupancy as admitted payer of the Government assessment, with such fees or privileges as usage may have attached to the office or possession.

Chakle kharch, H. (چکلي خرچ) Expenses of the whole *Chakla* or district, charged in proportion to each Ryot, under the old revenue system of Bengal.

Chaklá nawís, H. (چکلا نويس) The accountant of the revenues and charges of a *Chaklu*.

Chaklí, Mar. (चकली) A division of a village in some places.

Chakalyá, Mar. (चकल्या) An officer of police, a magistrate.

Chakra, S., but it occurs in all dialects, most commonly unchanged, but sometimes slightly modified, as, *Chakar*, *Chakí*, *Chák*, (चक्र) A wheel, a discus, a quoit, any thing circular or revolving, lit. or fig., as a potter's wheel, an oil-mill, a period of time, a district, a province, a region. An ancient small gold coin in Mysore, usually 10 fanams. In *Mar.* also, a rule, a regulation, an extra cess or tax. In *Karnáta*, the extra assessment of 1720, which was to cover the interest of money advanced by the Raja to pay off the demands of the *Śáhukárs* or Bankers on the Ryots. (The word is incorrectly printed in the 5th Report, p. 804, *Chuckes*, for *Chucker*, whence it has been entered in the Glossary *Chuckees*, as a separate word.)

Chakramu, Tel. (చక్రము) A wheel, &c., (being, in fact, the same with *Chakra*.) An ancient coin current formerly in the south of India, equal to $\frac{1}{16}$th of a Pagoda.

Chakráwal, *Chakráwalí*, Mar. (S. चक्रावळ, चक्रावली) Compound interest, (from *chakra*, revolving, and *ávalí*, a range or series).

Chakravartti, H. S. (चक्रवर्त्ती) A prince, a ruler, an emperor. A name borne by some families of Bráhmans in Bengal, corrupted commonly into *Chuckerbutty*.

Chakra-vriddhi, S. (*chakra*, and *vriddhi*, वृद्धि, increase) Compound interest.

Chakra-vantige, Tel. (చక్రవంతిగె) An extra assessment of $\frac{1}{16}$th under the Mohammadan Government.

Chakatí, or Chuktee, Mar. (चकती) A scrap of writing paper, a note, a passport, an English letter.

Chakrí, Ben. (S. চক্রী) An oilman.

Chákríkuḍu, Tel. (చాక్రీకుడు) An oilmaker.

Chakwáen, H. (چکواين) A small class of Rajputs in Ghazipur.

Chakwand, H. (چکوند) A common weed, bearing a long legume, growing from eight inches to two feet high, used by the poor as a potherb.

Chál, H. (چال) Habit, practice, course of life; as, *Bad-chál*, a man of bad habits; *Su-chál*, one of good habits, of respectable conduct.

Chálá, (?) Mal. The hut of a slave in Malabar. (Possibly *Śálá*, q. v.)

Chalab, Thug. Early part of the evening, between sunset and dark.

Chalán, Chulan, also Chálán, corruptly, Chellaun, Chillaun, Chullaun, H. &c. (چلان, چالان, from چل, S. चल, to go, sending off, despatching, [goods, &c.])

A document sent with goods, treasure, or individuals; an invoice, a voucher, a pass, a passport. The post-office list of letters forwarded, &c. Ben. Reg. x. 1819.

Chalán-dár, H. (P. دار, who has) A person who accompanies a despatch or remittance, and has charge of the invoice.

Chalaní, Chaláoní, or *Chalní*, H. (چلني ,چلاوني ,چلني, from the v. چلنا, to go) Current, circulating (as coin).

Chalantá, (from چلنا, to go) Passing, moveable, vendible, saleable. Duties formerly levied by Zamindars on goods passing through their jurisdiction. Ben. Reg. xxvii. 1793.

Chalantí-jáëdad, Uriya (ଚଲନ୍ତିଯାଏଦାଦ) Moveable or personal property.

CHÁLAN, Ben. (চালন) Sifting any thing, passing it through a sieve.

Chálaní, Ben. (চালনী) A sieve.

CHALAVÁDI, Karn. (ಚಲವಾದಿ) A low caste. (In Mysore) The servant of a *Linga* merchant carrying a large ladle with chain and bell on his shoulders. (In Telingana) A Śúdra who goes from house to house to give notice of a death.

Chalavádi ayu joti, Karn. (ಚಲವಾದಿ ಅಯು ಜೋತಿ) Tax levied on the preceding in a village.

CHALÁWAN AMDÁNÍ, Hindi (चलावन अमदानी) Statement of collections sent with the collections to the Zamindar by the Patwárí (*Puraniya*).

CHÁLÍ, erroneously, CHOWLEE and CHOOLEE, Mar. (चाली) Land that bears the highest rate of assessment, cultivated by permanent inhabitants of the village agreeably to allotment, by which each cultivator has a fixed proportion of the lands of highest, medium, and lowest assessment. Hereditary land held at a fixed rate, which, after being brought into cultivation from waste, may be assessed at a rate proportioned to its quality, and to custom. It is sometimes said that a Ryot cannot throw up his *Chálí* land.

CHÁLI, Ben. (चालि) A thatch, a shelf, a gang or separate station of convicts engaged on public work.

CHALIGARAVU, Tel. (చలిగరవు) Soil sandy on the surface with black earth underneath.

CHALIPANDILI, Tel. (చలిపందిలి) A shed where cool water, &c., is distributed to passengers.

CHÁLI GAINI, corruptly, CHAUL GAINEE, CHALLY, CHALLI, or CHALIE GUENY, Karn. &c. (ಚಾಲಿ ಗೈಣಿ, probably from the S. चल, *chala*, moving, going) Tenancy-at-will, or occupation on paying rent for a short or indefinite term.

Cháli gaini-chíṭu, Karn. (ಚೀಟು) An agreement or lease for a short time, usually for a year.

Cháli gaini-gár, Karn. (ಗೈಣಿಗಾರ) A tenant-at-will.

CHÁLÍSÍ, H. &c. (P. چاليسي, forty) CHÁḶSÍ, CHÁḶISÁ, Mar. (चाळसी, चाळिसा) An aggregate of forty, as of forty sers, forty cubits, &c. Also a period of forty days of impurity from the birth of a child, or death of a relative. A period of quarantine. The great famine in Hindustan of 1783 is known by this name, from its occurring *Samvat* 1840.

CHAḶI SIDAKKA, Karn. (ಚಳಿಸಿದಕ್ಕ) Rice husked.

CHALIT, H. (چلت, S. चलित, lit., gone) Moveable or personal property.

CHÁLIYAN, Mal. (ചാലിയൻ) A weaver.

CHALKI, (?) H. A crop raised by irrigation.

CHALLANIDORA, Tel. (చల్లనిదొర) A cold gentleman, a European functionary of a calm and gentle temperament, a highly complimentary designation.

CHALTÍ, H. Mar. (چلتي, चलती) Passing, moving, current. In Dehli, Cultivated lands. In Masulipatam, Gross measurement of the grain after gathering.

Chalti daftar, H. (P. دفتر, an office) Under the Maraṭha Government, the records required for current business. That portion of the Peshwa's register which was always in the hands of the *Farnavis*, or Secretary of State.

CHALTÚ, Hindi (चलतू) Land in cultivation.

CHÁLU, Tel. (చాలు) A furrow. Ben. (চালু) Rice cleaned fit for cooking.

CHÁMA, Mal. (ചാമ) A kind of grain, a sort of millet (Panicum miliaceum). S. *Śyámá*, (श्यामा).

CHAMAN, Thug. A Brahman.

CHAMÁR, CHUMAR, H., but in most dialects also, (چمار) Ben. CHÁMÁR (চামার) Mar. CHÁMHÁR (चाम्हार) from the S. *Charma-kára*, or worker in skins, चर्म्मकार) A man of a low caste, whose business is working in hides and leather, a currier, a tanner, a shoemaker, a harness-maker, and the like. *Chamárs* are said to be descended from a Bráhman father and *Chandál* mother, according to some authorities: in the north-western provinces the *Chamárs* are considered as divided into seven classes, who do not eat together or intermarry: they are known by the names, *Jatúä, Kaean, Kúril, Jaiswara, Jhusia, Azimgerhia* or *Birheria*, and *Kori* or *Korchamri.* The last are most commonly weavers. Different tribes of *Chamárs* are also known in the Dakhin, as *Sultangerh, Maraṭhí, Paradosh, Pardesí, Haralbhakt, Dabáli, Woj,* and *Chaur.*

Chamar-gaur, Chumur-gour, H. (چمر گور) A division of the Gaur Rajputs. The highest class, although from their name liable to the suspicion of intercourse with *Chamárs.* They affect to call themselves *Chaunhar-gaur,* from a Raja named *Chaunhar;* or sometimes *Chiman-gaur,* from a Muni called *Chiman.*

Chamráwat, H. (چمراوت) Perquisites or privileges of Chamárs.

CHÁMARA, Ben. Mar. (চামর, S. चामरः) The bushy tail of the Tibetan ox set in a handle, and used to drive away flies. In H. *Chaunri,* (چونري).

CHAMÁYEN, CHUMAYEN, H. (چماين) A small class of the Gujar tribe in Panipat Bangar.

CHAMBAL, CHUMBUL, H. (چمبل) A log of wood with grooves, fixed on the banks of canals, and used in drawing water for irrigation.

CHÁMCHORÍ, H. (چام چوري, lit., skin stealing) Adulterous connexion with the wife of another,

CHAMÍA, Thug. Those of the gang who assist in seizing and holding down the victim.

CHAMOSÍA, Thug. The person who holds the hands of the victim (Dakhini).

CHAMPAKA CHATURDAṢÍ, S. (चम्पक, a yellow flower, and चतुर्दशी, fourteenth lunation) A Hindu festival on the fourteenth of *Jyeshṭh,* when the flowers of the Michelia Champaka are offered to idols.

CHÁṆ, Mal. (ചാണ) A span, a span measure.

CHANÁ, CHUNA, corruptly, CHENNA, CHUNNA, H. (چنا, चना) A kind of pulse commonly known as gram (Cicer arietinum). Three kinds are usually reckoned in the north-west provinces, *Píla, Pachmil,* and *Kasa.* The last is an inferior sort, also called *Rakswa, Chaptái,* and *Kasárí. Pachmil* is a mere mixture of the first and last sorts. There is also a small kind called *Chaní* and *Batorí. Chaná,* to the eastward of the upper provinces, is frequently called *Rehla* and *Lona,* but in general *Lona* is applied to an acidulous salt which forms upon the leaves, and is collected for chemical purposes. *Chaná* also implies a species of plant, of which the seeds are often mixed with corn, giving it a disagreeable taste. (*Vicia* of one or two undescribed species).

CHANAMBU PARATÍ, (?) Mar. The name of a servile caste in Anjengo, employed apparently as domestic servants.

CHANAMIÁ, H. (چنميا) A tribe of Chandrabansi Rájputs in Jonpur, Azimgerh, and Gorakhpur.

CHANÁN, commonly from the plural SHÁNÁR, Mal. (ചാ-ന്നാൻ) A man of a tribe whose business it is to extract the sap from the palmyra tree, a *táṛí* drawer.

CHANAPPAN, Tam. Mal. (சணப்பன்) A weaver of coarse cloth for sacks, of hempen cords, &c. (From *Chaṇa* or *Sana,* hemp.) See *Ṣanappan.*

CHAṆÁTTAM, Mal. (ചണാട്ടം) Favourable or privileged rent of land granted to persons liable to be called out for occasional work or service.

CHANCHAR, CHUNCHUR, H. (چنچر, चंचर) Land left untilled for a year or more, but not for a very long interval. See CHACHAR.

CHÁNCHARÍ, H. (چانچري) Inferior grain, as Mung or Jawár, remaining in the ear after being trodden out.

CHANCHARU, Karn. (ಚಂಚರು) A tribe of savage people tenanting the forests in the south of India.

CHÁNCHÍo, Guz. (ચાંચીઓ) The name of a tribe, or of an individual of it, inhabiting Guzerat, Kach, and Sind, and wearing a large long-pointed turban. A pirate, a sea-robber.

CHÁND, H. &c. (چاند, S. चन्द्रः) The moon.

Chándí, H. (چاندي) Silver. (From *Chánd,* the moon). A tax formerly levied by the Zamindars of Bengal.

Chándní, H. &c. (چاندني) Moonlight, an awning.

Chándní Chauk, H. (چاندني چوك) The principal market-place of any considerable city.

Chánḍní karan, Hin. (चांदनी करण) The practice of *Bráhmans, Chárans,* and others, of wounding themselves, in order to extort alms or payment of a debt.

CHANDÁ, CHUNDA, H. (چندا, from the P. *Chand,* چند, how much) Subscription, quota, assessment.

Chandá aogáhi, H. &c. (چندا اوگاهي) Levy of rent or revenue from the Ryots, according to their shares or proportions. See *Aogáhi.*

CHÁNDÁ, Ben. (চাদা) A subscription, a collection of money.

CHÁNDA, H. (چانده) A common station of the revenue survey.

CHÁNDA, Thug. Cloth.

CHANDAI, Tam. (சந்தை) A fair, one held annually, the melá of Hindustan.

CHANḌAL, CHANḌÁL, H., and most dialects, (چندال ,چندل,

S. चण्डाल) A man of a low mixed caste, sprung from a *Súdra* father and *Brahman* mother. In common use it is indiscriminately applied to all low-caste or out-caste tribes.

Chanḍáliá, H. (چنڈالیا) A tribe of the *Bhangis*, who might be also termed *Chanḍálas*.

CHÁNDAM, H. (چاندم) A small tribe of Rajputs in Allahabad and Jonpur.

CHANDANAYÁTRA, also CHANDANOTSAVA, S. (from *chandana*, चन्दन, sandal, and *yátrá*, यात्रा, or *utsava*, उत्सवः, a festival) The ceremony of offering sandal paste or other perfume to an idol. A festival held at Puri in honour of Jagannáth.

CHANDÁNA, or CHANDÍNAH, CHUNDANA, CHUNDEENU, H. (P. چندانه, چندینه, from *chand*, چند, some, how many) Sundry or miscellaneous, applied to a division of the *Sair*, or a variety of petty taxes, under the Mogul Government; as,

Chandína Álamganj, H. A tax on all persons engaged in trade at Dacca, from one to two rupees per annum.

Chandína bajantri, H. (باجنتری) A tax on musicians.

Chándiná, Uriya (ଚାନ୍ଦିନା) Ground-rent, rent of land on which a house is erected. Tenure derived from such payment. (It is probably from the P. چندانه, like the preceding).

Chándinadár, Uriya (ଚାନ୍ଦିନାଦାର) A person paying ground-rent, and holding his house and garden by that payment.

Chandína damdhárí, H. (دمدهاری) A tax on exhibitors of snakes, monkeys, and bears, or fakirs, jugglers, &c.

Chandan-khuri mahal, (?) H. A tax formerly levied in Rangpur upon the sale of hogs, abolished since the decennial settlement.

CHANḌAVÁ, Hindi (चंडवा) Shaft of the share of a plough.

CHANDEL, H. (چندیل, चंदेल, perhaps from *Chandra*, the moon) A numerous tribe of Rajputs, originally from Mahoba in Bundelkhand, but now scattered over the north-western provinces: they claim to be of the *Somabansí*, or lunar race, and gave their name to the district of *Chanderi* or *Chandeli*. In the lower Doab they are divided into four tribes, bearing the several Hindu designations of a ruler or king: as, *Rája*, *Ráo*, *Rána*, and *Ráwat*.

CHANDELÍ, H. (چندیلی) A very fine sort of cotton cloth, originally fabricated at *Chanderi*, on the left bank of the Betwa, from a kind of cotton grown at *Amaráwati* in Berar. The thread, when of fine quality, is sold for its weight in silver; and the cloth is of so costly a description, as to be worn only by persons of the highest rank in native courts.

CHANḌIVAḶA, Karn. (ಚಂಡಿವಳ) Earnest money, hansel, also what is given to dissolve a bargain.

CHANDIYÁ, H. (چندیا) Deep places (East Oudh).

CHÁNDLA, H. from *Chánd*, the moon, (چاندلا) A small wafer-like ornament of gold or other metal worn on the forehead between the eyes. The ceremony of affixing the ornament on the foreheads of persons present at the drawing up of a marriage contract, as the ratification of the agreement.

CHANDRA, S. (चन्द्रः) The moon.

Chandra Grahaṇa, S. (from ग्रहण, seizing) An eclipse.

Chandraseni Kayastha, S. Mar. (चन्द्रसेनी कायस्थ) A caste of writers in Puna, who pretend to be descended from a Raja named *Chandrasena*, and therefore claim to be regarded in some degree as *Kshatriyas*, and to be entitled to perform the ceremonies of the Vedas; a claim not recognised by the Bráhmans. There are two divisions: the *Pataní Prabhu*, and the *Dawani Prabhu*. The former are found at Bombay and other towns, the latter at Goa.

CHANEṬH, H. (چنیٹھ) Drugs for cattle.

CHANGÁR, Thug. A thief of any kind.

CHANGEL, H. (چنگیل) A herb growing among ruined buildings. The seed, used in medicine, is termed *Khabáji*.

CHANGÚLÍ, Karn. (ಚಂಗೂಲಿ) Daily hire.

CHÁNK, or CHÁNKÁ, H. (چانک, چانکا) A stamp fixed on the side of a stack or heap of grain, when the heaps are to be divided; or when, after division, they are left in charge of one of the sharers. A piece or pieces of cow-dung placed on a heap of grain, to protect it from the evil eye. A ceremony observed in the threshing-floor, when the winnowed corn is gathered into a heap. It is variously observed in different places, but the essence consists in reverentially and silently circumambulating the heap, finishing the process with a short prayer.

CHANK, CHUNK, or more correctly, ṢANKH, H. (چنک, سنکھ, S. शंख) A conch shell. When entire, with the greater end cut off, it is used as a kind of horn formerly blown in war, but now at the worship of idols. Cut in segments of circles, it forms ornaments for the fore-arms and wrists of women. The chief supply of these shells is from Ceylon, and when the volutes turn to the right the shell is held in peculiar estimation.

CHANNANGI-NELLU, Karn. (ಚೆಂನಂಗಿನೆಲ್ಲು) A kind of rice grown in Mysore.

CHANNEL-MÁRA, or CHANNEL-VARI, (?) Names of a small additional money tax on the cultivators of Karnáta under the old system: (apparently, *Channel* is the English word connected with the local terms for cess or tax, being a charge for keeping up the water-courses necessary for irrigation, or a tax on fields so watered, as being more productive; also denominated *Channel fees.*—5th Rep. p. 966.)

CHÁNṬÍ, H. (چانٿي) Cesses levied from artisans and others (from *Chánṭná*, to squeeze).

CHÁNWÁL, or CHÁWAL, or CHÁOL, or CHÁUL, (چاول, چانول) Undressed rice, but cleaned of the husk.

CHANTA, Mal. (ചന്ത) A fair, a market.

Chanta nagaram, Mal. (ചന്തനഗരം) A market town.

Chantavila, Mal. (ചന്തവില) Market price.

CHANTRAM, Mal. (ചന്ത്രം) The office of a petty district treasurer.

Chantrakkáran, Mal. (ചന്ത്രക്കാരൻ) The petty treasurer in a district.

CHANWÁN, CHUNWÁN, H. (چنوان) A small sort of millet.

CHÁP, Beng. (চাপ) Mar. (चाप) A weight or block used to press down any thing, a press, a screw press; an impression, a seal (but in this sense the original word is more correctly *Chháp*, the initial being aspirated. The substitution of the unaspirated *Ch* has probably arisen from confounding the two words.

Chápá, Beng. (চাপা) A weight, a cover, any thing laid upon another to press it down; treading down clay or salt to press it together, pressing salt together for weighment.

Chápá dar, Uriya (ଚାପାଦାର) The officer who puts the salt into the scales.

Chápa gaṭṭu, Tel. (చాపగట్టు) A bank or mound on which salt is placed immediately after it is taken out of the pans.

CHÁPANI, (?) Asam. Islands formed in rivers, or any alluvial deposit.

CHAPÁTÁ, or CHAPÁTÍ, H. (چپاتا , چپاتي) A thin cake of flour and water, without leaven, slightly baked or toasted over an open fire.

CHÁPÁVANI, Karn. (ಚಾಪಾವಣಿ, from H. *Chhapna*, to be hid) Concealment of lands in order to defraud the revenue.

CHÁP-JARÍB, H. (چاپ جريب) Gross measurement of the lands of an estate: (perhaps from *Cháp*, in one sense, a bow, and *jaríb*, a land measure, a bow-shot, or bird's-eye measurement).

CHAPOLALU, (?) Tel. Watering by hand.

CHAPPÁ, Tel. Karn. (చప్పా, a dialectical form of *Chhápá*) An impression, a stamp, a custom-house stamp; the straw of an inferior kind of grain.

Chappekaṭṭe, Karn. (ಚಪ್ಪೆಕಟ್ಟೆ) The office of a custom-house where goods are stamped.

CHAPPAR, CHAPRA, Karn. (ಚಪ್ಪರ, ಚಪ್ರ) A thatched roof, a shed; any temporary thatched structure, as for the celebration of a marriage, giving water to travellers, a mat, a screen, &c. The *Chhappar*, of Hindustan and Bengal, q. v. has not such a range of meaning.

CHAPRÁS, H. (چپراس) A badge, a plate worn on a belt as a mark of office.

Chaprásí, H. (چپراس) A messenger or courier wearing a *chaprás*, most usually a public servant.

CHÁPRE, H. (چاپري) Cakes of cow-dung after drying, used as fuel.

CHAPRI, CHUPREE, H. (چپري) A puddle: a small kind of pulse somewhat resembling millet.

CHAR, CHUR, H. (چر) A sand-bank or island in the current of a river, deposited by the water, claims to which were regulated by Ben. Reg. xi. 1825. Pasturage, fodder.

CHÁRA, H. (چارہ) Grass, food for beasts and birds; fodder, pasturage.

Charágáh, H. (چراگاہ) Grazing ground, a field, a meadow.

Charáí, or *Charáu*, H. (چراو , چراي) Pasture lands, fields appropriated to the grazing of cattle. Sending out cattle to graze. Rent derived from pasturage.

CHÁR, Thug. A strangler, peculiar to certain classes.

Chárai, Thug. The office of strangler.

CHÁRA-PAIR, or CHAR-PAIR, Karn. (ಚಾರಪೈರು, ಚರಪೈರು) Duties on grain levied from the peasantry, whether it be of their own growing or purchased for re-sale. A tax on villages of various items.

CHARAGI, Thug. A Bairagi.

CHARAK, Ben. (চরক, also written চড়ক, from the S. चक्र, a wheel) CHARKH, H. (P. چرخ, a wheel) A wheel or lathe for turners' work, cleaning cotton, &c.; a sugar-mill. The ceremony of swinging suspended by hooks passed through the skin, above each bladebone, and connected by ropes with one end of a lever traversing an upright post with a circular motion. The apparatus for swinging.

Charakgáchh, Ben. (চরকগাছ) The upright pole or mast supporting the horizontal lever on which the swinging is performed.

Charak-pújá, Ben. (S. পূজা, worship) The swinging festival held on the Sun entering Aries. As a religious observance it is confined to Bengal, but the swinging is practised in other parts of India as a feat of dexterity for obtaining money.

Charaki, Ben. (চরকি) A small wheel, a reel, a machine for separating seeds from cotton.

CHARAKKA, Mal. (ചരക്ക) Goods, merchandise.

CHARÁN, H. (چران), CHARÁNÍ, Ben. (চরানী) A meadow, fallow land, grazing ground.

Charán, Ben. (চরান) Pasturing or attending cattle.

Charáramná, Hindi (चरारमना) Lands appropriated for grazing, in consequence of being left unploughed for more than a year.—Puraniya.

CHÁRAN, H. (چارن, चारण) The name of a caste analogous to, or identical with, the *Bháṭ*, following the profession of bards, heralds, and genealogists; and held in like estimation, so that their personal security is considered sufficient for engagements of the most important description, the breach of which involves the death of the surety, or of some of his family. They also subsist by carrying grain, salt, groceries, and the like. The latter, in Central India, are styled *Kachili Chárans*; those who are not engaged in trade are the *Maru Chárans*, or *Chárans* of the desert, or the sandy tract east of the Indus.

CHARANÁMṚIT, H. (S. चरण, foot, and अमृतं, ambrosia) Water in which the feet of a Bráhman has been washed; also with *Udaka*, water, *Charanodaka*.

CHARAS, incorrectly, CHURRUS, and CHERRUS, H. (چرس, चरस) The resinous exudation of the hemp plant, possessing strong intoxicating powers, and the basis of all the inebriating preparations of hemp: see *Bhang* and *Ganja*. Also, a large leather bag or bucket used for drawing water from wells.

CHÁRÁYAM, Mal. (ചാരായം) Spirituous liquor; *rum*, *árak*, any intoxicating beverage.

Cháráya kaṭa, Mal. (ചാരായകട) An árak or spirit shop.

Cháráya káran, Mal. (ചാരായകാരൻ) A distiller or vender of spirituous liquor.

Cháráya kuttumata, Mal. (ചാരായക്കുത്തുമത) Contract with Government for the sale of spirituous liquors. Spirit or árak farm.

CHÁRDEHAT, H. (from *chár*, four, and A. *dehát*, دهات, villages) An estate formed of the lands of four villages, or a subdivision of four villages set apart from the Pargana.

CHARGAN, CHURGUN, Mar. (चरगण) Grazing ground, pasturage.

CHARH, corruptly, CHUR, H. (چڑہ) Rise; lit. or fig., Increase, augmentation of revenue or rent. An item of the public revenue in Bombay.

Charháí, or *Charháú*, H. (چڑھاي, چڑھاو, from چڑھنا, to mount, to rise; or چڑھانا, to raise) Mounting, ascending. Raising, as price or rent.

Charháit, H. (چڑھایت, from چڑھنا, to mount) A trooper mounted at the expense of the State. Also *Charhwáya*, &c.

Charhandár, incorrectly, *Churundár*, (چڑھندار) A servant accompanying a cargo of goods, a supercargo, a passenger by a boat or vessel.

Charháwá, H. (چڑھاوا) Offerings made to idols. Raising in price, &c.

Charhtá, or *Charhtí*, H. (چڑھتا, چڑھتي) Increase of price, making additional profit, settlement of revenue at a progressively increasing rate.

Charhtá-paṭṭa, (پٿا) H. A lease for a term of years at a progressively increasing rent.

Charhwí, H. (چڑھوي) Raising, as rent or price.

CHARI, CHUREE, corruptly, CHURREE, H. (چري) Jawár sown close and not suffered to run to seed, but cut unripe, and used as fodder for cattle. In the Lower Doab, a small portion of rent-free land.

CHÁRI-KÁGAJA, Uriya (ଚାରିକାଗଜ) Paper of pleadings.

CHARHLI-PHOLLU, Thug. Time between sunrise and noon.

CHARKHI, H. (چرخي, from the P. چرخ, a wheel, S. चक्र) The pulley, or rather spindle, by which water is raised from a well by two water pots tied to the ends of a rope that passes over the cylinder, and are raised alternately. A spinning-wheel.

CHARMAJODA, Mar. (from S. चर्म्म, leather) A pair of shoes exacted periodically by the head village officer from the village shoemaker, or a money cess in lieu of it.

CHARMAK, CHARMAKÁRA, Mar. (S. चर्म्मक, चर्म्मकार) A currier, a shoemaker, a worker in leather.

CHARNI, H. (چرني) A feeding trough.

CHÁRSHAMBA, H. (from چار, four and P. *shambah*, شنبه, a day) Wednesday, the fourth day of the week.

CHÁRSU, H. (P. چارسو, from *chár*, four, and *sú*, a quarter) A square, a market-place, a place where four roads meet.

CHÁRTTA, Mal. (ചാൎത്ത) A writing, a document, a title-deed, a register, a catalogue. (Probably adopted from the Portuguese.)

Chárttumuri, Mal. (ചാൎത്തുമുറി) A document, title-deeds, writings of land, &c.

CHARUTÁR, H. (چروتار) A life-rent grant.

CHARWÁHA, H. (چرواها) A herdsman, a grazier.

Charwáhi, H. (چرواهي) The wages of a herdsman in grain.

Charwái, H. (چرواي) Price paid for grazing.

CHÁR-YÁR, H. (چاريار, from *chár*, four, and *yár*, a friend, P. *Chahár*) A Mohammadan of the Suni sect, one who maintains the rightful succession of the first four Khalifs, *Abubakr*, *Omar*, *Oṣmán*, and *Âli*.

CHÁS, or CHÁSA, H. and other dialects (چاس) CHÁSH, Ben. (চাষ) Cultivation, tillage.

Chashá, *Chashán*, Ben. (চষা, চষান) Ploughing a field, causing it to be ploughed.

Chásá, H. (چاسا) *Chásha*, Ben. (চাষা) A cultivator, a ploughman, a husbandman.

Cháshbásh, Ben. (চাষবাষ) Cultivation, tillage.

Chásh-sanad, Uriya (from A. سند, a grant) Grant of rent-free lands (Cuttack).

Chásí, H. (چاسي) *Cháshí*, Ben. (চাষী) Cultivation, tillage, a cultivator.

Chásháchási, H. Land prepared for cultivation by repeated ploughings (Cuttack).

CHÁSHT, also CHÁSHT-GÁH, H. (P. چاشت, چاشت گاه) The middle hour between sunrise and noon. Refreshments taken at that season.

Chásht-namáz, H. Morning prayer.

CHÁSNI, H. (چاسني) A pan in which the sugar juice is boiled.

CHÁṬÁ, Hindi (चाटा) The vessel that receives the juice of the sugar-cane as it drops from the mill.

CHAṬÁN, H. (چٹان) Rocky soil.

CHAṬÁNÁ, H. (چٹانا, caus. of چاٹنا, to lick) The ceremony of feeding a child for the first time.

CHATÁO, or CHATÁI, Thug A share of the booty.

CHÁTÁNULU, Tel. (చాతానులు) A class of Ṣúdras who worship Vishnu exclusively, and whose occupation is the sale of flowers.

CHÁTAR, Uriya (ଚାତର) The place in the salt works where the saline earth is collected and prepared for filtration.

CHATARÁ (?) Ben. Land of an inferior quality. Indifferent fallow land (Jessore).

CHÁṬÍ, Uriya (ଚାଟି) A salt manufactory.

Cháṭipáik, Uriya (ଚାଟିପାଇକ) A peon attached to a salt work. An assistant to a native collector.

Cháṭia malangí, Uriya (ଚାଟିଆମଲଙ୍ଗି) Head salt manufacturer. (More correctly *Chuliámalangi*, q. v.)

CHAṬṬAMU, Tel. (చట్టము) CHAṬṬAM, Mal. (ചട്ടം) A regulation, a rule, a law.

CHAṬṬIGA, Karn. (ಚಟ್ಟಿಗ) The head man of a drove of cattle for exporting corn.

CHATTIRAM, or SHATTIRAM, pronounced CHATTRAM, Tam. (சத்திரம், vernacular representative of S. सत्रं) A place where refreshment is given gratuitously, especially to Bráhmans; funds set apart for such purpose: also, an umbrella.

CHATTIRIYAṆ, or SHATTIRIYAṆ, Tam. (சத்திரியன், S. क्षत्रियः) A man of the military caste.

CHATTU BÁVALI, Tel. (చత్తుబావలి) A well sunk in a rock (from చత్తు, hard, solid.)

CHATUKULU, Tel. (చతుకులు) A weight of four Dabs.

CHATUR BHÁGAMU, Tel. Karn. (చతుర్భాగము, S. चतुर्, four, and भाग, a part) The fourth part of the annual crop received by Government from the holders of certain alienated lands. According to the definitions of the term as applied in the Tamil provinces, it is the grant or alienation of the Government fourth in favour of the holders of the land.

CHATURDAṢÍ, H. (چتردسي, S. चतुर्दशी, fourteenth) The fourteenth; as the fourteenth lunar day.

CHÁTURMÁSYA, S. (from चतुर्, four, and मास, a month) Relating to four months. Applied to four kinds of sacrifices, the *Vaiṣwadeva*, *Váruṇa praghása*, *Sákamedha*, *Sunásiríya*, to be offered in four consecutive months, or every four months, or, according to some, in the months *Ásháṛh*, *Kártik*, and *Phálguna*, consisting of roasted cakes of rice flour, offered in the first to the *Viṣwadevas*, in the second to *Varuṇa*, with two figures of sheep made also of flour, in the third with vegetables to *Agni* (?), and in the fourth to *Indra*.

Chaturvedi, S. (चतुर्, four, and वेद, the Vedas) A Bráhman professing to have studied the four Vedas. In common speech, *Chaubí*.

Chatussímá, H. (चतुस्सीमा) The four boundaries of a field or village.

Chatushpatha, S. (चतुष्पथ) A place where four roads meet, an open place or square.

Chaturupádhyáya, S. (चतुर्, four, the four Vedas, and उपाध्यायः, a teacher) The name of a family of Bráhmans in Bengal: in common pronounced *Chaturjia* or *Chaturjee*.

Chaturtha, S. (चतुर्थः) A fourth, the fourth day, &c.

Chaturtha-kriyá, S. (from क्रिया, act, rite) Offering funeral cakes on the fourth day after a person's decease; also *Chaturtha-piṇda*, (from पिण्डः, the funeral cake.)

Chaturthí, S. (चतुर्थी) The fourth day of the lunar fortnight.

CHATWATTA, (?) Mar. A place where four roads meet. See *Chawátha*.

CHAU, H. (چَو) A ploughshare.

CHAU, H. (چَو, abbreviation of S. *Chatur*, four; used chiefly in composition) Four.

Chaubáchha, H. (چوباچھہ) A mode of apportioning the assessment formerly practised in the Delhi territory or the levying of a revenue upon four things; viz. 1. A fixed rate per plough; 2. The same per head on each male above twelve years old; 3. A rate per family, hearth money; 4. and one on each head of cattle. Instead of the plough tax, some statements separate the poll tax into two, one on adults and one on children. Thus arranged, the four heads of taxation are denominated, *Pág*, from *pagri*, a turban; *Tág*, the cloth worn round a child's waist; *Kúḍí*, or *Korí*, a hearth; and *Púnchhí*, a tail.

Chau-bandí, Mar. (चौबन्दी) Made up of four, or containing four, as a sheet of paper of four leaves. Any connexion of four. Fourfold state or quality.

Chaubár, or *Chaubárá*, H. (چوبارا, چوبار) A summer-house, a place where villagers assemble, a shed, a police station, especially that of the principal officer or Kotwal.

Chaubáṛí, or *Chaupári*, Ben. (চৌবাড়ী, চৌপারী) A school a college, especially one in which Sanskrit is taught by a Pandit.

Chaubí, H. (چَوبي, abbreviated from *Chatur-bedi* or *-vedi*) A Bráhman learned in the four Vedas; now applied to a class of Bráhmans who are not always men of literary habits. In the upper provinces they are usually boxers, wrestlers, and the like.

Chau-bísa, H. (چَوبيسہ, from S. चतुर्विंशति, twenty-four) A tract of country containing twenty-four villages occupied by a particular tribe: they are frequent in the north-west provinces.

Chaudharí, or *Choudhuree*, sometimes, but incorrectly, *Chaudhri*, corruptly, *Chowdrah*, *Chowdry*, H. (چودھري, lit., a holder of four, perhaps shares or profits) The head man of a profession or trade in towns. The head man of a village. A holder of landed property classed with the Zamindar and Talukdar. In Cuttack the *Chaudharí* was the revenue officer of a district corresponding with the *Desmukh*: the *Chaudharí Taluhdar*, or head revenue officer, was there treated under the British Government as a proprietor or Zamindar.

Chaudharáí, corruptly *Chowdrawy*, H. (چودھراي) The office, jurisdiction, or privileges of a *Chaudharí*.

Chaudharáyet, H. (چودھرايت) The fees of a *Chaudharí's* office.

Chaugaḍḍa, *Chouguḍḍu*, H. (چَوگڈّہ) The place where the boundaries of four villages meet.

Chaugháchár, Mar. (चौघाचार) Ownership by many, common property.

Chaughalá, *Chaugulá*, or *Chaughulá*, corruptly, *Chougulla*, Mar. (चौघला, चौगुला, चौघुला) The second officer of a Maraṭha village, an assistant of the headman or *Pátíl*: he holds his office by hereditary tenure.

Chauhadda, or *Chauhaddi*, H. (چَوحدّي, چوحدّا, from *chau*, four, and A. *hadd*, a boundary) A place where the boundaries of four villages meet.

CHAUḌU, Tel. (చౌడు) Salt soil.

CHAUHÁN, CHOUHAN, H. (چَوهان) One of the principal Rajput races, numerous and powerful branches of whom are found in every part of the north-west provinces, as well as in Malwa and Rájasthan. The most distinguished families in Central India are the *Khíchi*, *Hára*, *Bhadauria*, *Rájkumár*, and others: in the Company's territories, *Rajor*, *Pratapnír*, *Chakarnagar*, and *Manchana*; the head of which last is usually known as the Raja of Mainpuri: they trace their descent from the celebrated *Prithí Raï*.

CHAUK, CHOUK, corruptly, CHOWKE, H. (چوك, चौक) A square, an open place in a city where the market is held, and the chief police office is commonly stationed.

Chauk-nikás, H. (निकास) A tax or duty levied on all articles sold in a market-place in Bengal under the Mogul Government.

Chauk-mārá, H., or Ben. *márú* (from مارن, or مارنا, to kill, to strike) Smuggling.

CHAUKÁ, H. Ben. (چوكا, চৌকা) A cleared space in which a Hindu cooks and eats his food, or performs any religious ceremony.

CHAUKAṚÁ, H. (چوكڑا) Division of the crop, in which the cultivator gives up only one-fourth.

CHAUKARA-BHÚMI, (?) Karn. Indifferent land.

CHAUKARI, H. (چوكري) A measure of grain, a quarter of a Chauthia, q. v.

CHAUKASÍ, corruptly, CHOKUSSEE, H. (چوكسي) Vigilance. An examiner, an assayer. Mar. (चौकसी) Careful inquiry or investigation.

Chaukasnís, Mar. (चौकसनीश) An inspector, an overseer, a visitor; a registrar or record keeper.

CHAUKALṢÁ, Mar. (चौकलशा) A class of Ṣúdras, or an individual of it, from their having four (*chau*) ornaments (*kalaṣis*) to the bridegroom's litter in a marriage procession.

CHAUK-BHARNA, H. Filling a square space with coloured meal, perfumes, sweetmeats, &c., on occasions of rejoicing, a Mohammadan custom.

CHAUKHÁ, H. (چوكها) A station where four boundaries meet.

CHAUKÍ, CHOUKEE, corruptly, CHOWKY, CHOKY, CHOKEE, H. &c. (جوكي، चौकी) The act of watching or guarding property, &c. Station of police or of customs, a guard, a watch, or the post where they are placed.—Ben. Reg. iv. 1795. ix. x. 1810. xvii. 1816, &c.

Chaukidár, corruptly, *Chowkeydar*, *Choheedar*, &c., H. (چوكيدار) A watchman, a police or custom peon, a village watchman.—Ben. Reg. xiv. 1807. xxii. 1816. vii. 1817, &c.

Chaukidárí, H. (چوكيداري) The office of watchman. A tax levied to defray the cost of a town or village watch. The fees or wages paid to the town or village watchman.—Ben. Reg. xxii. 1816.

CHÁÜL, Ben. (চাউল) Rice freed from the husk. See *Cháuwal*.

CHAULÁ, H. (چولا) A kind of bean much cultivated in Hindustan (Dolichos sinensis).

CHAULA, S. (चौल) The ceremony of tonsure. See *Chúdá*.

CHAULÍ, Mar. (चौली) A small silver coin, equal to two anas.

CHAUMÁSA, H. (چوماسه) A period of four months, the rainy season.

Chaumás, corruptly *Chowmass*, H. (چوماس). Land tilled during the four months of the rainy season, or from *Ashárh* to *Kuär*. A rate in a Ryot's lease for those lands which he sows after the rains, not having had a crop previously raised on them in the same year.

Chaumasiá, H. (چومسيا) A ploughman hired for the four months.

CHAUNDHÍ, Thug. A turban.

CHAUNRÁ, CHOUNRÁ, H. (چونرا) A subterranean apartment for grain.

CHÁÚNRI, H. (چاونري) A police-station, usually the *Kotwali*, (Sagar).

CHAUNTÁLI, CHOUNTÁLEE, H. (چونتالي) Cotton pods in which the fibre is equal to one-fourth of the whole produce.

CHAUPÁL, CHAUPÁR, or CHAUPÁṚ, H. (چوپال، چوپار، چوپاڑ) A shed in which the village community assemble for public business (generally erected by the head man of a village, and used by him as an office). A raised platform near a house, a Chabutara, q. v.

CHAUPAN, (?) Mar. Stiff, clayey soil.

CHAUPANI, (?) Uriya. A tax formerly levied by petty chiefs in Cuttack, to cover the expense of maintaining police, commuted for a money payment. Ben. Reg. xii. 1805, cl. 4.

CHAUR, H. (چور) A large open space in a forest (Rohilkhand). An extensive tract of low land (East Oudh).

CHAURÁHA, H. (چوراها) The meeting of the boundaries of four villages, or junction of four roads.

CHAURÁSI, H. (چوراسي, lit. eighty-four) A subdivision of a district or Pargana comprising originally eighty-four villages, although now reduced to a smaller number. The division was very common in Hindustan, and numerous traces of *Chaurásis* have been detected by the industry of Mr. Elliot, who has added to the fact some highly valuable observations on the selection of this particular numeral.—Supplement to the Glossary, p. 151.

CHAURKANÍ, Mar. (चौरकानी, used with रेखा, &c.) A line drawn across a sheet of country paper through the four columns into which it is folded, a form used in letters to sons, pupils, &c.

CHAURSI, CHOURSI, H. (چَورسي) A granary above ground (Rohilkhand).

CHAUS, CHOUS, H. (چوس) Land four times tilled (Rohilkhand).

CHAUSINGHÁ, H. (چوسنگها) A raised mound indicating where the boundaries of four villages meet.

CHAUTH, CHOUTH, corruptly, CHOT, and CHOUT, H. (چوته)

Mar. (चौथ, for CHAUTHÁÏ, from the S. चतुर्थ, fourth) An assessment equal to one-fourth of the original standard assessment, or generally to one-fourth of the actual Government collections demanded by the Marathas from the Mohammadan and Hindu princes of Hindustan, as the price of forbearing to ravage their countries. The *Chauth* was collected by the Marathas through their own agents, and was divided into four parts: 1. *Ráj bábti*, a fourth allotted to the head of the State; 2. From the other three parts, denominated collectively *Mukhása*, six per cent. of the whole *Chauth*, termed *Sahotra*, was set apart for the *Pant Suchu*; 3. and *Nargunda*, or three per cent. was given away at the pleasure of the Raja or Peshwa; 4. The remainder, or *Ain Mukhása*, sixty-six per cent., was distributed among different *Jagírdárs*, to assist them in maintaining the troops they were bound to furnish for the use of the State. Even when a country came into the actual possession of the Marathas, the collections were made under the same titles as before, and appropriated in like manner. Under the British Government the *Sahotra* portion, or six per cent. on a fourth of the Government collections, is still enjoyed by the *Pant Suchu*; and some of the grants made from the *Ain Muhkása*, or nett surplus of the fourth, are still held by individuals. In Hindustan, under the Mogul Government, a *Chauth* was levied from the successful party in a law-suit or arbitration: the precise proportion is not stated, but it was probably a fourth of a rupee, or four anas per cent. on the value of the litigated property. Also, a fourth of the pay of hired servants taken by the head officer who hires them. A fourth of the fee paid to a peon for serving a process taken by the *Názir*, or head native executive officer of a Court.

Chauthái, H. (چوتهاي) A fourth, a fine equal to a fourth of the revenue.

Chauthará, Mar. (चौथरा) A condition of letting land, in which the landlord takes one-fourth of the produce. A fourth of the produce of a field, &c.

CHAUTHÍ, H. (चौथी) The fourth lunar day. The ceremony of untying the wedding bracelet on the fourth day after consummation.

CHAUTHIÁ, CHOUTHEA, H. (چوتهيا) A measure of grain in general use in the north-west provinces, about equal to a *Sér* of wheat: five *Chauthias* make one *Panseri*.

ÇHAUTKÍ KAIÁLÍ, Hindi (चौकी कैआली) An annual sum paid to the farmer or Zamindar, for the privilege of weighing the grain of the Ryots, either to determine the quantity, or for sale, for which the weighman has a fee of about half a ser per maund; the deficiency, when the grain is sold, falls upon the purchaser (Puraniya).

CHAUTRÁ, H. (چوترا) A court, corrupted perhaps from *Chabutara*.

CHAVALAMU, Tel. (చవలము) One-eighth of a pagoda.

CHAVAḶAN, Mal. (ചവളൻ) The name of a low caste of Nairs, or of a member of it, a fisherman.

CHAVATU-BHÚMI, Tel. Karn. (చవతుభూమి) Brackish ground.

CHÁVEṚṚUVUTTÍ, Mal. (ചാവെറുവൃത്തി) Lands, &c., granted to the family of a person who has conquered, or who has fallen in battle, a military pension or reward for service.

CHAVIKA, Karn. (చవికె) A house with four pillars. A guard-house.

CHAVILE, Tel. (చవిలె) Four *dabs* of twenty *kás* each.

CHAVU, or CHAU, corruptly, CHOW, Tel. (చవు) The weight by which pearls are valued.

CHAVUDÁI, Tel. (చవుదాయి, dialectic form of H. *Chauthâyi*, or S. *Chaturthi*, a fourth) Land held on payment of one-fourth of the nett produce to the State.

CHAVUKA, or CHAUKA, Karn. (చవుకె) A square. The box containing the Linga.

CHAVUKÁLU, Tel. (చవుకాలు) A measure of seven cubits and a quarter.

CHAVUḶU, CHAUḶU, or CHAUḌU, Karn. (ಚೌಳು, ಚಾಳು, ಚಾಡು) Sterile land. Saline soil, in which corn will not grow, unless much watered. Fullers' earth.

Chavuḷu or *Chauḷu gaḍḍe*, Karn. (ಚೌಳುಗಡ್ಡೆ) Sterile wet cultivation.

Chavuḷu or *Chauḷu gadde*, Karn. (ಚೌಳುಗದ್ದೆ) Barren dry cultivation. (It differs from the last in the dental *dd*.)

Chavuḷu nela, Karn. (ಚೌಳುನೆಲ) Barren unproductive land.

Chavuḷuppu, Karn. (చవుళుప్పు) Earth-salt. Also *Chauṭuppu*, *Chauḍuppu*.

CHAVUṬU, or CHAUṬU, Karn. (చవుటు) Saline, as soil.

CHAWAL, Mar. (चवल) Two anas, or an eighth of a rupee.

CHAWALÍ, Mar. (चवली) A silver coin worth two anas.

CHÁWAL, (?) Guz. A small share in a co-parcenary village. (Perhaps the same as the preceding, implying a two-ana or one-eighth share).

CHÁWAR, Mar. (चावर) A measure of land, 120 square *bighás*.

Chawáṭhá, Mar. (चवाठा) A place where four roads meet. Any place where gossips meet, as a barber's shop, the village tree, &c.

Cháwaṭí, or **Chauṭí**, corruptly, **Choltry** or **Choultry**, Mal. (ചാവടി) **Cháwaḍi**, Tel. (చావడి) A public lodging place, a shelter for travellers.

Ánchecháwaḍi, Karn. (ಅಂಚೆಚಾವಡಿ) The post office.

Chestaracháwaḍi, Karn. (ಚೆಸ್ತರಚಾವಡಿ) A station for palankin bearers.

Kandácháradacháwaḍí, Karn. (ಕಂದಾಚಾರದಚಾವಡಿ) Station of armed peons or militia.

Kottawálachávaḍi, Karn.. (ಕೊತ್ತವಾಲಚಾವಡಿ) The office of the chief police magistrate, or Kotwal, &c.

Cháwaḍiyava, Karn. (ಚಾವಡಿಯವ) The keeper of a choultry or karavansarai.

Cháwarí, Mar. (चावडी) Any place of resort, the magistrates' court, a police office, a custom station, an inn.

Cháwarí-kharch, Mar. (A. خرچ, expenses) Cost of keeping up a public lodging-place.

Cháhwarí, Mar. (चाह्वरी) The drag rope of a plough, a well, &c., to which the bullocks are yoked.

Cháhwarímoṭ, Mar. (चाह्वरीमोट) The bucket of a draw-well.

Cháhwaryábail, Mar. (चाह्वर्याबैल) One of the bullocks yoked to the rope of a plough or well.

Cháwupula, or **Chaupula**, Mal. (ചാവുപുല) Mourning for a relative. Period of impurity arising from such a death.

Chaya, Tam. (சாய) A root from which a red dye is extracted (Oldenlandia umbellata).

Cheḍávu, Tel. (చెడావు) Increase.

Dhar-cheḍávu, Tel. (from ధర, price) An extra assessment, by relinquishing the Government share of the crop to the Ryot at a higher than the market price.

Cheduru, Tel. (చెడురు) An allowance of grain made to the Ryots in compensation of the right of gleaning.

Chehar, Thug. Jungle, forest.

Chehra, H. (P. چهره, a countenance) Descriptive roll of a servant; also, *Chehra-bandi.*

Chékavan, or **Chegavan**, Mal. (ചേകവൻ) A man of a low caste, commonly a Tair: one whose occupation is drawing the Tárí juice.

Cheku, Tel. (చెకు) A separate portion of land. See *Chak.*

Chekku, Tel. (చెక్కు) Grain derived from extra measure, Karn. (ಚೆಕ್ಕು) Half a bullock load.

Chela, H. (چيلا, S. चेटः) A servant, a slave, a pupil, a disciple, especially one brought up by a religious mendicant, to become a member of his order. In Mysore, a Hindu boy seized in early life and forcibly made a Mohammadan, by order of Tipu: these boys, as they grew up, were incorporated in a military corps, retaining the name of *Chelas.*

Chelávaṇi, or **Chelauṇi**, Tel. (చెలావణి) Current, as coin.

Chelike, Tel. (చెలికె) A field left fallow, a field after the crop has been cut and cleared.

Chellam, Mal. (ചെല്ലം) Royal treasure, hidden treasure.

Chellu chíṭí, Tel. Karn. (చెల్లుచీటీ) A receipt.

Chellubákilu, Tel. (చెల్లుబాకీలు) Collections and balances.

Chembaḍiváḍu, Tel. (చెంబడివాడు) A fisherman.

Chemmán, Mal, (ചെമ്മാൻ) A currier, a shoemaker, a worker in leather. See *Chamar.*

Chena, H. (چينه) A kind of millet (Panicum miliaceum).

Chench, H. (چينچ) A herb which springs up in uncultivated places in the rainy season.

Chenchuváḍu, Tel. (చెంచువాడు) A tribe of half-savage Hindus dwelling in the hills and forests; also Karn. plur. *Chenchukuladavaru.*

Chendi, Tel. (చెంది) The fermented juice of the date tree.

Chengavarusa, Tel. (చెంగవరుస) A land roll, a list of farmers and fields.

Cheṇgoli, Mar. (चंगोलि) Work done for hire.

Chenu, Tel. (చేను) A field of dry grain, a crop.

Chenvukoṭṭí, Mal. (ചെമ്പുകൊട്ടി, from *chenva*, copper) A brazier or coppersmith.

Cheota, Thug. Rupees.

Cheṛa, Cheḷi, Mal. (ചെറ, ചെളി) Soft or wet soil, mud, mire, soil in general, or such as is fit for rice cultivation.

Cher-lápam or *-lábham*, Mal. (from *cheṛ*, and S. लाभ, gain) The profit of cultivation, the cultivator's share of the profit.

Chérṛuvita, Mal. (ചെറുവിത) Cultivation of wet lands.

Cheṛuman, plur. *Cheṛumar*, whence corruptly, *Chermers, Charmas, Churmars*, also plur. *Cheṛumahkal*, corruptly, *Chermakhal*, and *Shurrumukhul*, Mal. (ചെറുമൻ, plur. ചെറുമക്കൾ) A slave or slaves, prædial slaves; the term designating them as "children of the soil."

Cherádáya. Karn. (ಚೇರಾದಾಯ) Profits to Government

from the sale of unchaste women. Assessment on cattle graziers.

CHERÁI, Karn. (ಚೆರಾಯಿ) Pasturage among the hills.

CHÉRI, Tam. (சேரி) Mal. (ചെരി) A town, a village, a hamlet.

Paraicheri, Tam. (பறைச்சேரி) A village of Pariars.

Puducheri, Tam. (புதுச்சேரி) A new village or town, the original form of *Pondicherry*.

CHÉRIKKAL, Mal. (ചെരിക്കൽ) Threshing-floor and farm attached to Government lands. Jungle or hilly tracts sometimes cultivated.

CHERNADÁR, Tam. (சேர்ந்தார்) Relations, dependants.

CHERRÁ, Mal. (ചെററാ) An artificial reservoir, constructed for irrigating lands.

CHERU, H. (چيرو) The name of a wild tribe inhabiting the hills and woods in the southern parts of the province of Benares, in Mirzapur and Behar, sometimes called a branch of the *Bhars*, and sometimes identified with the *Koles*. Mr. Elliot considers them to be the aboriginal inhabitants of the provinces, on the skirts of which they are now found, driven from their proper seats by Rajput races.

CHERUKU, Tel. (చెఱుకు) Sugar cane.

CHERUJANMAM, Mal. (ചെറുജന്മം, from *cheru*, little) The rights or perquisites of the inferior members of the village community.

CHÉRUMÁNAM, Mal. (ചെരുമാനം) Collection of revenue, the duty of an inferior collector.

Chérumánakáran, Mal. (ചെരുമാനകാരൻ) An inferior revenue officer.

CHERUVU, Tel. (చెరువు) An artificial pond or tank.

Panta-cheruvu, Tel. (from పంట, crop) A tank for the irrigation of various crops.

Úru-cheruvu, (from ఊరు, a village) A tank for the common use of the inhabitants of a village.

CHET, Thug. A traveller who has discovered the designs of the Thugs. A gold coin.

CHÉTA, Tel. (చేట) A cribble: an allowance of grain made to the head of the village. *Maila-chéta*, A similar allowance to the village washerman (from మయిల, H. *maila*, dirty).

CHETAN, Mal. (ചെടൻ) A man servant, a slave, a weaver of a particular caste.

CHETRAM, or SHETRAM, Mal. (ക്ഷെത്രം) A temple of the first order, one dedicated to the *Trimurtti*. See *Kshetra*.

CHETTE, Karn. (ಚೆಟ್ಟೆ) Half a bullock load.

CHETTI, Mal. (ചെട്ടി) A foreign or Karnata Śúdra, a tradesman, a weaver by caste and occupation.

CHETTUKÁRAN, Mal. (ചെത്തുകാരൻ) A *Tári* drawer: a grass cutter.

Chettupáttam, Mal. (ചെത്തുപാട്ടം) Rent of cocoanuts or other palms for extracting *Tári*.

CHÉTUKUDU, Tel. (చేటుకుడు) A male servant or slave.

CHEWARA, or CHEWARRA, (?) Lands situated at the extreme boundaries of a village.

CHHADÁM, corruptly, CHUDAM and CHHEDUM, H. (چهدام) A coin of very small value, one of six, or properly six and a quarter *dáms*, or two *damris*, a quarter of a *paisa* valued at twenty-five *dáms*. The word is used to imply any thing of no worth or value.

CHHAHEL, Hindi (छहेल) Land.

CHHAHKÚR, CH'HUH-KOOR, H. (چهکر, from چهه, six) Division of crops in which the Zamindar gets only one-sixth.

CHHAI, H. (چهئي) A pad to prevent laden bullocks from being galled.

CHHÁJ, or CHHÁCH, H. (چهاج, چهاچه, छाज) A winnowing basket.

CHHAKRÁ, H. (چهکڑا, S. शकट) A cart.

CHHAL, CHHUL, H. (چهل, S. छल:) Deceit, fraud. In law, a misdemeanor; also, a legal quirk or deceit.

CHHÁLÁ, Ben. (छाला) A pair of sacks or panniers, or any other article, so placed on a bullock as to hang on either side.

CHHALAVÁDI, Karn. (ಛಲವಾದಿ) A menial under the head merchant of a village.

CHHÁLNÁ, Ben. (छालना) An awning under which a father or guardian presents the bride to the bridegroom on the day of marriage.

CHHÁMUCHITÁÜ, Uriya (ଛାମୁଚିଟାଉ) Grant of land by the Raja of Khurda.

Chhámukáran, Uriya (ଛାମୁକରଣ) The accountant of a Raja.

CHHÁNTÁ, H. (چهانٹا) Throwing additional seed among a growing crop of rice (Delhi). Land in which seed has been sown after a single ploughing, especially at the extremities of a village, to secure possession.

CHHANPÁT, Uriya (ଛଣପାଟ) Grass lands. Hemp.

CHHÁONI, H. (چهاوني) Cantonments, station of troops.

CHHÁP, incorrectly *Cháp*, corruptly *Chop*, H. (چهاپ) A stamp, a seal. The impression of a stamp or seal. The Government stamp on papers or on coins. A mark on weights and measures to shew their accuracy. The custom-house stamp on goods having paid duty, &c. In

Delhi the word is also applied to a small bundle of thorns about a foot high.

Chhápa, H. (چهاپه) The village seal used to impress grain with any stamp or impression. A fee on stamps. In recent times the word has come to signify printing; as *Chhápa kághaz*, a printed paper, a newspaper; *Chhápa khána*, a printing-house or office; *Chhápa karṇa*, to print. Also adj. Sealed, under seal, distrained, attached.

Chhápa haṣil, H. (چهاپه حاصل) A tax on stamping cloth.

Chhápi, H. (چهاپي) Bearing a stamp, stamped, authenticated, printed.

Chhápikari, H. (کري, who makes) An officer whose duty it is to apply a stamp or seal, a printer.

Chhápi rupaiya, H. (روپيه) Rupees which have been defaced by private marks punched on them, and somewhat depreciated in value on that account.

Chhápti, corruptly, *Shaptee*, H. (چهاپتي) A coarse seal of cow-dung and mud affixed to the pile of grain on the threshing-ground, to prevent its removal until the Government or proprietor's dues are paid.

CHHÁPA, H. (چهاپه) A heap of refuse corn formed in winnowing, a small heap of grain appropriated to purposes of charity. In some places, the name of the basket used for throwing up water out of a pond.

CHHAPPAR, CHHUPPUR, corruptly, CHOPPER, CHUPPUR, CHUPPRA, CHAPROW, H. (چهپّر) CHHÁPAR, Ben. (ছাপর) A thatch, a thatched roof.

Chhappar-band, *Chhuppur-bund*, H. (P. بند, a binding) A thatcher, forming in the Dakhin a subdivision of the Kumbi caste. A resident cultivator, in contradistinction to one who takes part in the cultivation of the lands of a village in which he is not a permanent inhabitant.

Chhappar-bandi, H. (بندي, binding) Thatching. Expense of thatching. Cultivating with permanent residence in a village.

CHHÁṚ, H. (چهاڑ, छाड़) The bank of a river, alluvium, land gained from rivers.

CHHAR, written CHHÁḌ, but pronounced as if with a final *r*, Ben. Uriya (ছাড) Letting go, relinquishing, allowing to pass, &c.

Chháṛá, Ben., Uriya (ছাড়া) Letting go, relinquishing. Relinquished, deserted, as lands out of cultivation.

Chháṛá-báḳi, Ben., Uriya (A. باقي) Balance due for lands deserted.

Chháṛi, Ben., Uriya (ছাড়ি) Remission of revenue: lowering or letting off rent: acquittal of a prisoner, release: laches, not prosecuting a suit, and other uses implying abandonment.

Chháṛ-chiṭṭhi, H., Ben., Uriya, &c. (چهاڑچٹّهي, ছাড়চিঠী) A pass, a permit, a passport on sale of salt, to the extent of twenty *mans* within a given jurisdiction; also an order for its release. (Shakespeare derives the compound from *Chháṛ*, a bank of a river, but it is probably a modification of *Chháṛ*, letting go: or, as applied in the salt agencies, it may be referred to *Chhár*, vernacular form of S. *Kshár*, salt. As derived from the Hindustani *Chhorṇa*, to let go: the compound is *Chhoṛ-chiṭṭhi*). Ben. Reg. x. 1819.

CHHARÍDÁR, or BARDÁR, Mar. (छडीदार, बरदार) A cane-bearer, an usher.

CHHAT, CHHUT, H. (چهت) CHHÁT, Ben. (ছাত) The roof of a house.

CHHAṬÁK, Ben. (ছটাক) CHHAṬÁNK, or CHHAṬÁNKÍ, Mar. (छटांक, छटांकी), also Uriya, CHHATÁNKI, (S. षट, six, and अंक, a mark) One-sixteenth part of a *Sér* measure, either of weight or capacity.

CHHAṬÁO, H. (چهٹاو) Cleaning rice from the husk.

CHHAṬHÍ, H. (چهٹهي, from S. षट्, six) Sixth. A ceremony performed a few days, from six to nine, after the birth of a child, by women among the Mohammadans. The sixth day of the month.

CHHATR, CHHÁTRA, or CHHATAR, CHHUTR, CHHUTRA, or CHHUTUR, H. &c. (چهتر, S. छत्र) also CHHÁTÁ, H. (چهاتا) An umbrella. (S. छत्र) A place of shelter for travellers, especially for Bráhmans (Mysore), a serai.

Chhatri, *Chhutree*, corruptly, *Chitree* and *Chiteree*, H. &c. (چهتري, from S. छत्री, a small umbrella) A monumental structure or pavilion erected in honour of some person of rank. In Mal., One who carries an umbrella; also a barber.

Chhatra-pati, H. S. A prince or Raja, one over whom a parasol is carried as a mark of dignity.

Chhatra-dhár, B., lit. an umbrella-bearer—A mixed caste, formerly known in the Dakhin, whose function it was to hold the umbrella over persons of rank, and fetch water for the four pure castes.

Chhatra-varttana, Karn. (ಛತ್ರವರ್ತನ) A tax formerly levied for feeding the Bráhmans of the Chaultris.

CHHATRÍ, or CHHETRÍ, H. (چهتري, چهيتري, S. क्षत्रिय:) A man of the second, or regal and military caste.

CHHATTÚR, CHHUTTOOR, H. (چهتّور, from छत्र, an umbrella) An article placed upon the top of a heap of winnowed corn; a cake of dried cow-dung, or a shoot of grass, or bundle of twigs, or a spear placed by the side of it, or a flower near the bottom, to protect the corn from the effects of the evil eye.

Chhatrapati-paisá, Mar. (पैसा) The copper coin of Puna, &c., established originally by Sivaji, stamped with the word *Chhatrapati*.

CHHAUR, CHHOUR, H. (چھور) A large stack of Jawár collected for fodder, comprising several smaller stacks (Delhi). Also, walking a boundary with a raw cow-skin on the head, under a solemn oath to decide correctly: five sticks are held in the hand, to imply that the arbitrator is the representative of the Panchayat (In the north-west).

CHHEDÁ, H. (چھیدا, from S. छेद, cutting) An insect injurious to corn; the disease occasioned by it.

CHHEDANA, S. (छेदनं) lit. cutting, In criminal law, mutilation, cutting off a member or limb.

CHHELA, Uriya (ଛେଲ) A weight of metal equal to 40 *bishas*.

CHHENKWÁU, or CHHENKWÁIÁ, H. (چھینکواو, چھینکوایا) Sequestration, distraint.

CHHENCHAN, Ben. (ছেঁচন) Throwing up water from a pond or any reservoir.

CHHETR, or CHHETRA, H. (چھیتر, S. क्षेत्रं) A field. A place of reputed sanctity, as, *Kuru-chhetra* or *Kuru-khet*, at Panipat. A geometrical figure: whence the Sanskrit translation of Euclid is known as the *Cshetra-* or *Kshetra-sanhitá*.

Chhetra-phal, H. (چھیترپھل) The superficial contents of a field or any geometrical figure.

CHHÍDÁ, H. (چھیدا) Thin, not close, as a crop of corn or grove of trees, &c.

CHHIKÁI, H. (چھکائی) A fee on granting a release or acquittance of rent or revenue (Rohilkhand).

CHHÍMÍ, H. (چھیمي, S. शिंबी) A pod or legume.

CHHIND, Ben. (ছিঁড) A water-course.

CHHÍNKÁ, H. (چھینکا, छींका, S. शिक्य) A sort of bag of rope fastened on the mouth of an ox with straw for him to eat while ploughing. A net or loop for hanging pots or boxes in.

CHHÍNṬ, H. (چھینت, S. चित्र, variegated) Chintz, spotted cottons.

CHHÍNṬÁ, H. (چھینٹا) A field in which peas and linseed have been sown broad-cast while the rice crop is standing, and left to grow after the rice is reaped.

Chhíntab, H. (چھینتب) Sowing broad-cast (Bundelkhand).

CHHÍPÍ, incorrectly CHIPI, corruptly CHEEPA and CHEAPARA, H. (چھیپي, from the v. چھیپنا) A printer of cottons, a chintz-stamper. Also *Chhípi-gar*.

CHHÍR, H. (چھیر, S. क्षीर, milk) The land cultivated by the proprietor of a village, or the lessee himself on his own account. See *Sír*.

CHHIṬ, Ben. (ছিট) Chintz, (also from S. शिष्ट) Balance, remainder.

CHHIṬUA, H. (چھٹوا) Sowing broad-cast (Benares).

CHHOLA, H. (چھولا) Gram, (Cicer arietinum) The man who cuts the standing sugar-cane, and pares off the leaves and tops, which are in part payment of his labour.

CHHÓṚ, H. (چھوڑ, from چھوڑنا, to let go) Letting go, dismissal, remission, acquittance. Also *Chhoṛán* and *Chhoṛáwa*.

Chhoṛ-chiṭṭhi, H. (چھوڑ چٹھي) A deed of release, a pass, a permit: a deed of divorce, or abandonment of a wife, a document giving up claim to a girl betrothed to the repudiator, but married in his absence to another man.

CHHOṬÁ THÁKUR, Ben. (ছোটা, H. چھوٹا, little, ঠাকুর, a lord) The youngest brother of a husband's father, to be used only by the wife of an elder brother's son. A wife's father's younger brother, to be used by an elder brother.

Choṭá thákurání, Ben. (ছোটাঠাকুরানী) The wife of a husband's father's younger brother, or of a wife's father's younger brother.

Choṭábaú, Ben. (ছোটাবউ) A younger brother's wife. The youngest of a man's wives, or the one last married.

CHHÚRIKABANDHA, Mar. (छुरिका, a knife, and बंध, binding) A ceremony formerly in use of formally investing a Súdra with a billhook, in imitation of the investiture of the Bráhman with the cord.

CHHÚṬ, H. (چھوت, from the v. چھوٹنا, to let go) Remission, acquittance, letting go or relinquishing. Remission of revenue either on the *bíghá* or in rupees.

Chhúṭ, *Chhúṭ-máfi* or *mujrái*, are terms especially applied to the reductions made in the assessment of the Fasli year 1197 (A. D. 1789). Some have been authorised by Government, but most have been granted without any such authority.

Chhúṭaúti, H. (چھوٹاوتي) Remission of rent or revenue.

Chhúṭṭi, H. (چھٹي) Leave, leave of absence, discharge, dismissal, leisure, opportunity.

CHÍBHAR, H. (چیبھر) Land which long remains moist (Ságar).

CHIGARAVANTIGE, Karn. (ಚಿಗರವಂತಿಗೆ) A tenure of

land in Mysore by shares, in which the whole village was parcelled out in lots of equal value, each containing a due proportion of wet, dry, and garden land.

CHIHÁÍ, CHIHÁNÁ, CHIHÁRÁ, H. (چهانا چهاي) A place where dead bodies are burned.

CHIHEL, H. (چهيل) Wet oozy land. From CHIHLÁ, (چهلا) mud.

CHÍHE, H. (چيهي) A division of the Gujar tribe.

CHIHNA, S. &c. (चिह्न) A mark, a sign, a badge, any distinguishing mark or sign.

Chihnit, H. (چهنت, S. चिह्न, a mark) Known, ascertained, measured, identified. *Uriya*. Identity.

Chihnit náma, H. (P. نامه) A specification of land with its boundaries.

CHIḲ, H. &c. (चिक, چق) A kind of screen, usually made of split bambus loosely fastened together in parallel lines by perpendicular strings, and painted.

CHÍK, CHÍKAR, CHEEK, CHEEKUR, H. (چيك, چيكر) CHIKHAL, Mar. (चिखल, S. चिकिल) Mud, slime. The bundle of rushes or turf on which the bucket rests when brought to the top of the well. Land that has been recently irrigated.

Chikhalwat, Mar. (चिखलवत) Miry, muddy, land rendered so by irrigation.

CHÍK, Thug. A gold Mohur.

CHÍKA, Thug. A timid or cowardly Thug.

CHIKAL, (?) Planting surplus parcels of rice-plants on unoccupied village lands, for the use of which the transplanters agree to pay a portion of the produce.

CHIKAN, H. (چكن) Working flowers on muslin, or embroidering.

Chikan-doz, H. (P. دوز, a sewer) An embroiderer, a worker of flowers in muslin.

CHÍKAṬ, CHIKṬÍ, CHEEKUT, CHIKTEE, H. (چيكت, چكتي) Clayey soil (Ságar).

CHIKÁÚṬ, H. (چكاوت) Clayey soil of a black colour.

CHIKHAR, H. (چكهر) The husk of Chana.

CHIKHARWÁI, H. (چكهرواي) Wages for weeding (Oudh).

CHIKKAN, CHIKNÁ, corruptly, CHICKUM, H. (چكن, چكنا) Mar. (चिकण) S. (चिक्कण:) Greasy, fat, unctuous. Thick, loamy, as soil. Pure clay, incapable of cultivation.

Chikanwat, Mar. (चिकणवत) Greasy or fat, especially as soil; loamy or clayey soil.

Chikankhadu, (?) Mar. A particular kind of rich soil (Western India).

Chiknáwat or *Chiknoṭ*, H. چكناوت, चिकनोट) A clayey or loamy soil, a fat soil.

CHIKLI, corruptly, CHICKLEE, (?) A ryot cultivating in one village and residing in another.

CHILIKI, Tel. (చిలికి) A field left fallow.

CHIKSÁ, H. (چكسا) A fragrant powder made up of a great variety of ingredients; the principal of which are sandal, andropagon, minnakun, benzoin, and camphor.

CHILAM, corruptly, CHILLUM, H. &c. (چلم) The part of the *hukka* which contains the tobacco and charcoal balls, whence it is sometimes loosely used for the pipe itself, or the act of smoking it.

CHILAVA, Mal. (ചിലവ) Expense, disbursement, money allowed for expenses, *batta*, or extra allowance.

CHILLA, H. (چله, from the P. چهل, forty) A forty days' fast, a similar period of religious seclusion, or the place where it is observed. The period of forty days after childbirth during which a woman is unclean. Ceremony of purification. The shrine or residence of a saint.

CHILLAGINJE, Karn. (ಚಿಲ್ಲಗಿಂಜೆ) The nut of the Strychnos potatorum, which is rubbed on the inside of water jugs to purify the water.

CHILLAR, CHILLARU, CHILLARE, CHILRE, corruptly, CHILLER or CHILTA, Tel. (చిల్లరు) Karn. (ಚಿಲ್ಲರೆ, ಚಿಲ್ರೆ) Mal. (ചില്ലറ) Trifling, petty, sundry, an odd sum of money, a small grant or allowance.

Chillar-báb, Karn. Sundry items or cesses in revenue.

Chillar-kharchu, Tel. (చిల్లరఖర్చు) vernacularly or incorrectly, *Chilhar khurch*, Mar. (?) Sundry or petty expenses, deductions from the revenue allowed for village expenses and for the contingent expenses of the native revenue servants (Dakhin).

Chillaṛ-káraṇ, Mal. (ചില്ലറക്കാരൻ) A petty shopkeeper.

Chillaṛ-vari, Mal. (വരി, a tax) The minor or petty payments made to the inferior village servants.

Chillari-mányam, corruptly, *Chillary-mannium*, Tel. (చిల్లరిమాన్యం) Small grants of land for village charges, the pay of revenue officers, or support of temples, &c.

CHILṬÁ, Karn. (ಚಿಲಟಾ) Sandal chips (Mysore).

CHILWÁÍ, H. (چلوائي) The turf or rushes on which the bucket, when drawn up from the well, rests; and which therefore becomes sloppy and muddy.

CHIMAMA, Thug. The cry of the wolf, a bad omen.

CHIMOTA, Thug. A boy. *Chimotí*, a girl.

CHIMPIGA, Karn. (ಚಿಂಪಿಗ) A tailor.

Chín, H. (چين) A kind of sugar (Upper Doab and Rohilkhand).

Chíni, H. (چيني) Coarse sugar.

Chindá, Guz. (ચીંડા) Allowance made by Grásias to village Pátíls for collecting their dues.

Chíng, Thug. A sword.

Chingana, Thug. A boy.

Chingarí, Thug. A clan of Muttarí Thugs of the Mohammadan religion, following ostensibly the business of Banjáras, or travelling grain and cattle dealers.

Chingoria, Thug. One of the sects of the Thug clans.

Chínhá, Thug. A boy.

Chinkalu, Tel. (చింకలు) The inferior grains of millet separated by winnowing from the better.

Chinkalu-rásí, Tel. (రాశి, S. राशी) A heap of such grain.

Chintal-makta, or Chintal- lana guti, (?) Mar. A tax levied on large scales.

Chinwal, (?) Mar. Tax payable from the customs revenue.

Chippala, Karn. (ಚಿಪ್ಪಳ) An instrument of torture—two sticks tied together at one end, between which the hand is placed, and the loose ends are forcibly pressed together.

Chippevádu, Tel. (చిప్పెవాడు) Chippiga, Karn. (ಚಿಪ್ಪಿಗ) A tailor, said to have sprung from a Shakili female by a Bráhman.

Chipten, Mar. (चिपतें) A measure of capacity, one-fourth of a *ser*.

Chir, Mal. (ചിറ) A bank, a dam, an embankment, a mound across rivers, or dividing fields, serving as a causeway in the rains; the *Band* or *Bund* of Bengal. A large pond.

Chira, S. (चिर) Long, in time.

Chiranjív, B. S. (চিরংজীব) Long-lived, said as a benediction.

Chiráyu, S. (चिरायुः) Long-lived.

Chira, Thug. Call of the Ruparíl, or the bird itself.

Chíra, S. (चीर) Cloth, clothes, bark. An effigy placed upon the funeral pile when a woman burnt herself after her husband's decease in a distant place.

Chirághi, H. (چراغي, P. چراغ, a lamp) An allowance, either public or private, for keeping a lamp or lamps constantly burning at the tomb of a Mohammadan saint, or for illuminating a mosque. Presents of money for like purposes.

Chiravara-pádu, Tel. (చిరవరపాడు) Land recovered from the waste, and prepared for the cultivation of the Chiravara or *Chái*, a plant yielding a red dye.

Chirchera, Thug. Cry of the lizard.

Chirchitta, H. (چرچٿّا) A kind of grass bearing a small seed which may be eaten.

Chireta, Thug. A Maratha, a Pandit.

Chireya, Thug. Chirping of the small owl, an unlucky omen.

Chiriyá-már, Ben. (চিড়িযামার) A low caste, by profession bird catchers.

Chírppa, Mal. (ചീർപ്പ) A flood-gate, a piece of wood or a door to shut up a sluice.

Chísa, Thug. Any good or blessing, especially a wealthy traveller.

Chit, abbreviation of *Chitthi*, q.v. Mar. (चिट्) A note, a letter.

Chitnavís, or *Chitnís*, (नवीस्, or नीस, from *Chit*, and P. *nawís*, writer) Under the Maratha Government, an under secretary of state, who wrote and answered despatches. Any clerk or registrar. The same as the *Sarrishtadár* of the Company's Courts, in the Dakhin.

Chit, H. &c. (چت, S. चित्) Mind, understanding, the intellectual faculty, the soul.

Chitá, H. &c. (چتا, S. चिता) A funeral pile, a heap of sticks on which a dead body is burned.

Chitákha, H. (چتاکه) A funeral pile.

Chitápinda, S. (चितापिण्ड) Offerings of cakes to the manes at the funeral pile at the time of burning the corpse.

Chitárohana, S. (चितारोहण) Ascending the funeral pile, burning with the dead body of a husband.

Chitká, Hindi (चिटका) A place where dead bodies are burned.

Chitá-khandá, Ben. (চিতাখংডা) Spring-harvest.

Chitári, corruptly, Cheetaro, H. (چتاري, S. चित्रकारी) A painter.

Chitra, S. &c. (चित्र) Variegated, spotted: a picture, chintz.

Chitrabhánu, S. (चित्रभानुः) The sixteenth year of the cycle of sixty.

Chitragupt, Mar. (चित्रगुप्त) A skilful writer, both as regards his style and handwriting. (From the mythological Chitragupta, S. the registrar of the dead.)

Chítpekalárá, Arakan. A class of slaves, those who are taken in battle.

Chitt, H., and other dialects, (چتّ, S. चित्तं) Mind, heart, the intellectual faculty, or its supposed seat.

Chittpáwan, Mar. (चित्तपावन) A Bráhman of a particular tribe; also termed *Konkanastha*, or Konkan Bráhman.

CHITTAṚI, Tam. (சித்தரி) A small tank.

CHIṬṬÉ, Tel. (చిట్టె) An incomplete heap of salt.

CHIṬṬHÁ, H. (چٿها) CHIṬÁ, Ben. (চিটা) CHIṬṬHÁ, Tel. (చిఠ్ఠా) A memorandum, a rough note or account, rough journal or day-book. Pay of public servants. Particular statement of the measurement of a Zamindar's estate founded on actual measurement. It also applies to an account of all the lands in a village, divided numerically into *dághs* or shares, shewing the quantity of land in each, the sort of cultivation, and the name of the cultivator. Also a field book, more usually termed *khasra*, an account of all the lands of a village, according to their allotment, in the order in which they have been measured.

Chiṭṭhá-ámaldári, H. (چٿها عملداري) A deed conveying a proprietary right.

CHIṬṬHI, H. (چٿهي) CHIṬÍ, Ben. (চিটী) CHIṬÍ, CHIṬṬÍ, CHIṬHÍ, or CHIṬHṬHÍ, Mar. (चिटी, चिट्टी, चिठी, चिट्ठी, CHÍṬI, Karn. (ಚೀಟಿ) corruptly CHITEE, abbreviated CHIT. A note, a short letter, any letter, a note conveying an order or demand.

Chiṭṭhi talab, or *Talab chiṭṭhi*, (from the A. طلب, inquiry) A process, a precept, a summons to a defaulter to appear and pay his arrears.

Chíṭihuṇḍi, Karn. (ಚೀಟಿಹುಂಡಿ) A bill of exchange.

Chíttu, Karn. (ಚೀಟ್ಟು) A rough copy or draft.

Chíṭu, or *Chíṭé*, Karn. (ಚೀಟು, ಚೀಟೆ) *Chiṭṭu*, Tam, (சிட்டு) A bill, a bond, a deed: the Hindi *Chiṭṭhí*.

CHIṬṬI, or CHEṬṬI, more correctly, SEṬHI, corruptly, CHITTY, Tel. (చిట్టి, or చెట్టి, from S. *Sreshthí*, श्रेष्ठी) All members of the trading castes in the Madras provinces, either shopkeepers or merchants.

CHÍVÁṬI, Mal. (ചീവാടി) A small vessel, a kind of Pattamar.

CHIVUKA, Tel. (చివుక) A coin of the value of a quarter rupee.

CHIWÁNÁ, H. (چوانا) A place where dead bodies are burned.

CHOB, H. (چوب) CHOP or CHOB, Mar. (चोप, चोब) A stick, a staff, a staff of office.

Chobdár, corruptly *Chubdár*, H. (چوبدار) An attendant carrying a short staff or mace.

CHOHÁ, H. (چوها) A small well.

CHOHÁṚ, less correctly, CHOÄṚ, Ben. (চোহাড়) A tribe of mountaineers in the hills of Ramgarh, &c.

CHOÍL, Hindi (चोईल) Land lying low, and always moist.

CHOIYÁ, H. (چويا) A hole dug in the dry bed of a river. A rivulet.

CHOKÁ, H. (چوکا) Rice (Ságar).

CHOKÁBÁG, H. (चोकाबाग) Seeds sown immediately after a fall of rain.

CHÓḶḶU, Tel. (pl. చొల్లు) A kind of grain (Cynosurus corocanus).

CHONḌÁ, Mar. (चोंडा) A clump of rice plants.

CHONḌÁ, H. (چونڈا) A well not faced with masonry, where water is near the surface.

CHONḌHÁ, Mar. (चोंढा) A small bed or banked-up portion of a rice field.

CHONTA, Ben. (চোংতা) A rough copy, a rough draft (of a writing).

CHONṬÍ, or CHOṬÍ, H. (چونٿي, چوٿي, from S. चूडा) A tuft of hair left at the top of the head when the rest is shaved off, in the case of boys at an early age. Among the Mohammadans it is sometimes dedicated to a particular saint.

CHOPḌÍ, pronounced CHOPṚÍ, corruptly, CHOPEDDI, Mar. (चोपडी) A stitched or bound book for accounts.

CHOPPA, Tel. (చొప్ప) Straw.

CHOP-SANAD, (?) Uriya. Grant of rent-free lands in perpetuity.

CHOR, H. &c. (چور, S. चोर) A thief.

Chorank or *ánk*, Mar. (चोरअंक -आंक, from S. अङ्क, a cypher) An extremely small figure on the leaves of a MS., or on a bale of cloth or piece of goods, to mark its price. A secret or furtive mark.

Chordarwáza, (from P. دروازه, a door) A back door, a private way.

Chorgalí, H. (गली, a lane) A bye street or lane.

Chorgast, Mar. (चोरगस्त) Secret rounds, going privily round streets, &c.

Chorsirhi, H. (سرهي) Back stairs.

Chorugasti, (?) Tel. A spy, a secret watcher.

Chorwáḍá, Mar. (चोरवाडा) A haunt of thieves.

Chorzamin, H. (چورزمين) A quagmire.

Chora-nimah, H. (چورنمك) but used in Cuttack, Contraband salt.

Choránna-lútle, (?) Karn. An item of revenue; remission on account of plunder by thieves or robbers.

Chorí, H. &c. (چوري, चोरी) Theft, robbery; also, doing any thing furtively or clandestinely.

Chorímárí, Mar. (चोरीमारी) A collective term for illegal and violent practices, robbery, battery, murder.

Chori-sarakula-phāramu, (?) Tel. A statement of smuggled goods.

CHOṬ, H. (چوٹ) Folding a blanket or sheet as a covering for the head and shoulders, so as to keep out rain: practised by shepherds and herdsmen.

CHOṬÁ, H. (چوٹا) Discount or premium.

CHOTANA, Mal. (ചൊതന, S. शोधन) A liquid measure, varying in different places. Searching, determining.

Chotanakáran, Mal. (ചൊതനകാരൻ) A custom officer, a searcher, one who examines goods in transit to verify their having paid the proper duty.

CHUÃ, H. (چوا) A plant used as a potherb in some places, but in Garwal and Kamaon the small grains of it are largely used as food (Amaranthus oleaceus).

CHÚḌÁ, Ben. Mar. (S. चूडा) A tuft of hair left on the top of a boy's head at the time of tonsure. (It is also pronounced *Chúṛá* and *Chúlá,* whence come the derivatives *Chauṛa* and *Chaula,* signifying the ceremony of tonsure.)

Chúḍá-karanam, -karma, or *-kriyá,* (from S. करणं, &c., act, ceremony) The ceremony of tonsure performed on Hindu boys, which should properly take place between the third and fifth year of their age, but sometimes later, when a single lock of hair is left on the top of the head. See *Chauṛa* or *Chaula, Chauṛa-karaṇa, Chaula-karaṇa,* &c.

Chaul-otsava, S. A festival held on occasion of the ceremony of tonsure.

CHUGÁI, CHOOGÁEE, H. (چگاي) Pasturage.

CHUGHAL, or CHUGHLI, H. (P. چغل, چغلي) Tale-telling, backbiting, informing.

Chughalkhor, H. (خور, who eats) A tale-bearer, an informer.

CHÚHRÁ, H. (چوهڑا) The lowest description of village servants, the same as the *Bhangi, Halálkhor, Mehtar,* &c.

CHUK, Ben. (চুক) CHÚK, but often short in derivatives and compounds, Mar. (चूक) A mistake, an error, especially in figures.

Chuhí, Mar. (चुकी) A small mistake.

Chukbhúl, Mar. (चुकभूल) All kinds of errors or inadvertencies.

CHUKÁDO, Guz. (ચુકાદો) Decision, adjustment, settlement of a dispute, &c.

CHUKÁNÍ, Ben. (চুকানী) An under-tenant (Rangpur).

CHUKÁRÁ, CHOOKARA, H. (چکارا) Customs, duty (Sagar).

CHUKAT, H. (چکت, from چکنا, to be finished or settled) Agreement, a contract.

CHUKAUTA, CHOOKOUTA, H. (چکوتا) Fixed rates of rent, money rate.

CHUKKÁN, Mal. (ചുക്കാൻ) A helm, a rudder.

Chuhkánkáran, Mal. (ചുക്കാൻകാരൻ) A steersman. See *Seacunny.*

CHUKRI, CHOOKREE, H. (چکري) A fractional division of land (Kamaon and Garhwal).

CHUKTÁ, Mar. (चुक्ता) Settled, cleared, as a debt.

Chukti, Ben. (চুকতী) or *Chukoti,* (चुकोती) *Chuknvati,* Mar. (चुकवती) Settlement of a debt or bargain.

CHULA, or CHULAH, H. (چوله) A tribe of Tagas in Baghpat.

CHULAT, Mar. (चुलत) A term expressing collateral relationship, used in composition; as, *Chulat-ájá,* a grandfather's brother; *Chulat-bháü,* son of a paternal uncle.

CHULHÁ, or CHULHÍ, H. (چولها, چولهي) CHÚLA, Mar. (चूल) in other dialects, CHULA, CHULLI, from the S. (चूलि) A fire-place, a temporary and moveable receptacle for fire, made of dried clay.

CHULIÁ, (?) A name given to the Mohammadans in Malabar. In Cuttack (ଚୁଲିଆ) A salt-boiler.

Chuliá-malangi, Uriya (ଚୁଲିଆମଲଙ୍ଗି) The head salt-maker, the one who makes engagements with the Government.

CHULLÍ, CHOOLLEE, H. (چلّي) Supports placed beneath stacks of straw or stores of grain. A fire-place. See *Chulha.*

CHULLU, CHOOLLOO, H. (چلو) The palm of the hand hollowed for holding liquids. A handful of any thing fluid.

CHULTÁ, Mar. (चुलता) A paternal uncle.

CHUMAṬA, Mal. (ചുമട) A load, a burthen.

Chumaṭṭál, Chumaṭṭukáran, Mal. (ചുമട്ടാൾ, ചുമട്ടുകാരൻ) A porter.

CHUMBAK, Ben. (চুম্বক) Substance or abstract of a document.

CHUMWA, (?) Asamese. Name of a tribe in Asam exempt from manual labour.

CHÚN, or CHÚNI, CHOON, CHOONEE, H. (چون, چوني, S. चूर्ण) Pease-meal, pulse coarsely ground.

CHÚNÁ, H. (چونا, S. चूर्ण) CHUNNAM, whence the current word CHUNAM, Tam. (சுண்ணம்) Lime.

Chunáru, or *Chunárí,* H. (چونارو, چوناري) Lime-burners, or workers in lime, as plasterers.

CHUNDIGAR, Guz. (ચુંડીગાર) A bracelet-maker, one who makes armlets of glass or ivory for married women.

CHUNGADI, Karn. (ಚುಂಗಡಿ) Interest of money, odds.

CHUNGAL, CHOONGUL, H. (چنگل) A handful of any thing dry.

CHUNGÍ, H. (چنگی) A handful of grain levied as a tax or fee for weighing, or as a compensation for the use of market conveniences, as bags, booths, &c. Similar contributions to religious mendicants, or allowance to Zamindars for establishing a new market or permitting a fair to be held. This is also sometimes called CHUṬKÍ, (چٹکی) lit. a pinch.

Chungi-penth, H. (from *Penth*, پینٹھ, a market) A market or fair held on the tenure of giving a small portion of each saleable article to the Zamindar.

CHUNGUḌU, Tel. (చుంగుడు) A small or trifling arrear.

CHUNKAM, Mal. (ചുങ്കം) Duty, customs. See *Sunka*.

CHUNKIPPA, Mal. (ചുങ്കിപ്പ) Petty theft, pilfering, fraud.

CHÚṆNI, Mal. (ചൂണ്ണി) A sum of a hundred *kaunris*.

CHÚNTRU, CHOONTROO, H. (چونترو) Head man of a district in Dehra Dún.

CHÚṚ, CHÚṚÁ, or CHÚṚÍ, H. (چوڑ, S. चूडा) A crest, a topknot, a ring, an armlet, the bracelet put on a bride's arm at the time of marriage, and which she is entitled to wear only while her husband lives: hence, metaphorically, the married, as opposed to the widowed state. See also *Chúḍá*.

Chúṛá bhandára, H. An allowance or portion of land granted as means of maintenance to the junior members of a Zamindar's family.

CHÚRA, Karn. (ಚೂರು, from the S. चूर्ण) The smallest pieces of sandal assorted for sale.

CHUTHÁCHÚTH, Mar. (चुथाचूथ, lit. deranging) Applied to writing which has been or is being spoiled by numerous corrections, erasures, interlineations, &c.

CHUṬI, Karn. (ಚುಟ್ಟಿ) A roll of tobacco, a cigar.

CHUTUL, Mal. (ചുരുൾ) A roll, a scroll, a roll of tobacco, a cigar.

CHUYÁṚ, Ben. (চুয়াড়) The name of a tribe of mountaineers inhabiting the mountains bordering Bengal on the west, in Ramgarh and the neighbouring districts.

D

DÁ, Ben. (দা) DÁU, H. (داو) A sickle, a billhook, a sort of hatchet with the point curved. (From the S. *Dá*, or *Do*, to cut.)

DÁÁÍ, H. (A. داعي) A claimant, a plaintiff.

Dáâia, H. (A. داعیه) A plaint, a claim, a petition. See *Dâwá*.

ḌÁB, H. (ڈاب, *Darbha*, दर्भ) A kind of grass (Poa cynosuroides) with sharp points; whence a sharp-witted man is said to be *Darbh-ágra*, keen-pointed as *Dáb* grass. It is not much used for ordinary purposes, but is held sacred by the Hindus, and is strewed upon the floor or on the altar at offerings with fire: it is also considered desirable that a dying person should expire upon a bed of this grass. It is also called *Kuṣa*.

ḌÁBÁ, Ben. (ডাবা) A large vessel to receive the juice of the sugar-cane from the mill.

ḌÁBA, Uriya (ଡାବ) Memorandum, inventory, list.

ḌÁBAK, or ḌABKA, ḌABUK, ḌUBKA, H. (ڈابك, ڈبکا) Fresh well water.

ḌÁBÁLIYA, Ben. (ডাবালিয়া) Low land.

ḌÁBAR, ḌÁBUR, H. (ڈابر) Low ground where water lies. A small tank.

ḌABBÍ, DUBBEE, Tel. Mar. (డబ్బి) A small box, a cash-box, one kept in temples to receive contributions. The contributions so received. The treasury of a temple.

ḌABARO, Guz. (ડબરો) A vessel of leather for holding oil, ghee, &c., commonly called a *Dubber*.

ḌABBU, Tel. &c. (డబ్బు) A *Dab* or *Dub*, a small copper coin of the value of twenty *kas*; whence it comes to signify money in general.

DABEHRÁ, DUBEHRÁ, H. (دبیهرا) A large ploughshare (East Oudh).

Dabehri, *Dubehree*, H. (دبیهری) A light kind of plough in the west of Oudh and Rohilkhand.

DÁBI, H. (دابي) Ten handfuls of the autumn crop. See the next.

Dabiá, *Dubea*, H. (دبیا, from دبنا, to press) A measure of grain: when applied to the autumn crops it usually designates about ten handfuls; when to the spring crops, sixteen; but it varies in different places.

DABÍR, DUBEER, H. (P. دبیر) A writer, a secretary.

ḌABRÁ, ḌUBRÁ, H. (ڈبرا) A marsh, a puddle. In the Upper Doab, a small field.

ḌABRI, DUBREE, H. (ڈبري) Division of profit among a village community according to their respective shares.

ḌABULEṆ, or ḌABOLEṆ, also ḌABULKEṆ, &c. Mar. (डबुलें, डबोलें, डबुलकें) A hidden or reserved treasure.

DACH, DUCH, H. (دچ) Homestead (East Oudh).

DÁD, H. (P. داد) Justice, complaint, representation. (In

some dialects, as in Maraṭhí, the latter appears to be the more common use of the word, although the former is its more legitimate meaning).

Dádí, H. (دادي) A plaintiff, a complainant.

Dádi-fariádi, H. (P. دادي فريادي) Hindi, *Dádu-phiriádu*, (दादुफिरियादु) A complainant, an appellant for justice.

Dád-khwáh, H. P. (خواه) A plaintiff, a suitor, an appellant for justice.

Dád-khwáhi, H. P. (خواهي, desiring) Applying for justice, instituting a suit.

DÁD, H. (P. داد, from دادن, to give) A gift. Giving.

Dád-o sitad, H. (P. ستد, taking) Giving and taking, exchange, barter, traffic.

Dádai, Hindi (दादै) A term used in leases, meaning that the lessor 'gives,' or 'has given.'

Dádaní, or, abbreviated, *Dádní*, H. &c. (دادني, दादनी) Paying in advance, advancing pay to labourers or manufacturers: any additional grant or allowance.

Dádani malangián, H. (ملنگي, salt maker) An additional allowance to the makers of salt, an item in the former revenue accounts of Bengal.

DÁDÁ, H. &c. (دادا) Paternal grandfather, an elder brother, any elder or venerable person.

Dádí, fem. (دادي) A paternal grandmother, any venerable old woman.

DÁḌH, incorrectly, DÁT, Mar. (दाढ) Ground prepared by burning for being planted; the weeds and grass strewed over it to be burned. Grain growing on ground so prepared. Ground in which rice, &c. is grown from seed for the purpose of transplanting.

DADH, DUDH, Thug. A man who is not a Thug.

DAḌEYA, Karn. (ದಡೆಯ) A measure of weight, the fourth of a *man*, or ten *sers*.

DADRI, DUDREE, H. (ددري) Unripe corn, chiefly barley, which is cut occasionally, and brought home to be eaten, without being taken to the threshing-floor.

DÁDUPANTHÍ, H. (دادوپنتهي) A follower of the religious sect of Dádu, a cotton cleaner of Ahmedabad, in the beginning of the seventeenth century, who endeavoured to establish a sort of monotheistical worship.

DÁEN, H. (داين) Tying a number of bullocks abreast, that they may tread the corn under their feet and force out the ear. Also DÁON.

DÁER, Uriya (ଦାଏର) Pending, as a suit.

DAERD, (a probable error for ḌHER, q. v.) A class of agricultural slaves, said to be numerous in Kanara.

DAFÂ-DÁR, corruptly DUFFADAR, H. &c. (P. دفعه دار) In the Hindu dialects which have no *f*, the *ph* is substituted; as, DAPHEDÁR, Mar. (दफेदार) DAPHEDÁRUDU, Tel. (దఫేదారుడు) Commandant of a body of horse, head of a party of police, a police officer. In Bengal, a person at the head of a number of persons, whether labourers or soldiers.

DAFTAR, DUFTUR, H. (P. دفتر) or, *ph* being substituted for *f*, Ben. (দফতর) DAPHTARAMU, Tel. (దఫ్తరము) DAPHTAR, Mar. (दफ्तर) A record, a register, an account, an official statement or report, especially of the public revenue, roll, archives, &c. An office in which public records are kept; more correctly, *Daftar-khána*.

Daftar-band, or *-bund*, H. (P. بند) A record or office-keeper. Allowance paid to such an officer.

Daftardár, *Daphtardár*, H., also in Mar. *Daphtarnís*, (دفتردار, दफ्तरनीस) A record keeper, a registrar, an accountant. The head native revenue officer on the collector's and sub-collector's establishments of the Bombay Presidency. Under the Maraṭha Government, a district officer whose duty it was to collect and enter together in the ledger the accounts of the waste-book as prepared by the *Pharnís*, and to transmit monthly and yearly abstracts to the head of the State. Under the English administration his duties are still more multifarious and responsible; and he takes an active part, not only in the record, but in the settlement of the revenues with the Ryots.

Daftardárí, or *Daftarnísí*, (دفترداري) The office of the *Daftardár*.

Daftarí, *Dufturee*, H., M. (دفتري, दफ्तरी) A record-keeper, a registrar. In Hindustan it more usually denotes an inferior office servant, who prepares writing materials, and arranges the books of the establishment.

Daftar-khána, H. (دفترخانه) An office in general, a counting-house, an office of public records.

Daftar-kharch, (دفترخرچ) Office charges.

Daftar-saranjámi, H. (سرنجامي, effects) Office charges an article of disbursement formerly deducted from the revenue payable by the Zamindar.

DÁG, Ben. (দাগ) A spot, a stain, a brand. See *Dágh*. A lot or portion of an estate which has been measured, and of which the measurement is recorded in the order of time at which it was made.

Dág bháura, Ben. (ভাউরা, awry) A lot or parcel of land

out of its place, not following a preceding one in numerical succession.

Ḍagar, Ḍagrá, Ḍugur, Ḍugra, H. (ڐگر ,ڐگرا) A path. Mar. (डगर, डग्रा) A steep slope, as of the bank of a river. A small hill.

Dagdha, S. (दग्धः, lit., burned) Applied to a day on which an inauspicious aspect of the planets may occur, and on which, therefore, no religious ceremony should be performed.

Dágḍugí, Dágḍují, Dágḍúg, or Dágḍojí, Mar. (डागडुगी, -जी, -डागडूग, -डोजी) Repairing tanks, buildings, &c.

Dágh, H. (P. داغ) the Hindu dialects commonly drop the aspirate, as Dág, Ben. (দাগ) and with the initial optionally changed, Dág or Ḍág, Mar. (दाग, डाग) A spot, a stain, a mark made with a hot iron, a brand, especially such a mark stamped on the necks of horses belonging to the Emperor of Hindustan, or maintained for his service.

Dágh-i-tashiha, H. The office where the public horses of the state are mustered and branded.

Dárogha-i-dághi-tashiha, H., A. The officer who superintended the branding of the horses for public service.

Daghá, Dugha, H. (A. دغا) *Dagá* in most dialects, Ben. (দগা) Deceit, fraud, cheating, treachery.

Daghábáz, H. (دغاباز) in other dialects, Ben., Mar., &c., *Dagábáj*, A cheat, a deceiver, a swindler, a rogue.

Dagábájire-chaláibár, Uriya. Issuing fraudulently.

Dah, Duh, commonly written Deh, H. (ده, from the Pers. ده, and S. दश) also with the vowels long, Dáhá, or, less correctly, Dahá, Duha, Mar. (दाहा, दहा) The number ten, forming various derivatives and compounds.

Dáhá, H. (داها) The ten days of the Moharram, during which public mourning for *Áli* and his sons is observed by the *Shiáh* Mohammadans.

Dahak-patti, corruptly, *Dehug-puttee*, Mar. (दहकपट्टी) A tax upon hereditary offices, the whole receipts of which, except the revenues of the rent-free lands attached to them, might be stopped once in ten years, and carried to public account, under the Maratha Government.

Dahmardá, *Duhmurdá*, H. (دهمردا, from ده, ten, and مرد, a man) A cart of a moderate size, one capable of holding ten men.

Dahnímí, *Duhneemee*, H. (P. دهنيمي, from نيم, a half) Five per cent (Delhi).

Dahotará, *Duhotura*, H. (دهوترا, from ده, and S. *Uttará*, اترا, over) Tythes, an allowance of ten per cent. Dáhotara, or Dáhotrá, Mar. (दाहोतर, दाहोत्रा, from दाहा, ten) Rate of interest at ten per cent.: allowance on articles sold of ten on the hundred.

Dahsaní, *Duhsunee*, or *Dehsunnee*, corruptly, *Duhsemee*, H. (دهسني, from ده, ten, and سن, a year) Relating to ten years. The title of a book comprising the revenue accounts of ten years. Such a record, called *Dahsaní kitáb* was compiled for the Bareilly district in 1802, under the directions of the collector, showing the occupancy of the lands for the previous period of ten years, so as to verify the title of the holder as *Málik kadím* and *Málik hál*, the ancient proprietor known in the Kanungo records, and the more recent or actual occupant.

Dah-sála, H. (دهساله) Decennial, for ten years. The decennial, as introductory to the perpetual settlement of the revenues of Bengal, and therefore applied commonly to the latter.

Dahyek, *Dehyeh*, corruptly, *Deyek*, H. (دهيك, from *dah*, ten, and *ék*, ايك, one) An allowance of ten per cent., which used to be assigned to the farmer or collector of the revenue as his profit, and for charges of management, and to the native collectors or Zamindars for police charges: abolished by Reg. xiv. 1807.

Dáh, or Dáha, H., and in most dialects, (S. दाहः) Burning, lit., as with fever or disease: also the burning of dead bodies.

Dáha-karma, or *-karaṇa*, or *-kriyá*, S. (कर्म्म, &c., act) The act or ceremony of burning a dead body.

Dahá, Duha, Ben. (দহা) Brine obtained from saline earth.

Dahá-bulán, Ben. (দহাবুলান) Placing the brine in the boiler.

Dahal, Duhul, H. (دهل) A quicksand, a quagmire.

Dahan, Duhun, H. (دهن) A gold coin, in value six rupees.

Dahand, Duhund, H. (from the P. participle *Dahanda*, دهنده, giving) A good payer, one willing to pay or give.

Ḍahar, Ḍuhur, less correctly, Ḍehar, or Ḍehur, H. (ڐهر, डहर) Low lands flooded during the rains, and yielding, after their drying up, good crops. A road. Ben. (ডহর) A lane.

Dahiá, Duhia, H. (دهيا) A field, land near a village (Benares, Sagar). A tribe of Jats in the Dehli district, more properly *Ḍahiá*, (ڐهيا).

Dahia, Thug. Cry of the hare, an ill omen.

Dahlán, Duhlan, H. (دهلان) A tribe of Tugas, in the Upper Doab.

Dahliz-khandalná, H. (دهليز كهندلنا, lit., to tread the threshold) Invitation of the bridegroom to an entertainment at the house of the bride's parents, when a delay intervenes between the betrothment and the marriage, a custom of the Mohammadans.

Dahr, Dahrí, Duhr, Duhree, H. (دهر, دهري) Stiff clay soil in low grounds. A marsh or inundated land (Delhi).

Dái, Daee, H. (داي, Pers., or from S. धात्री, when it is more correctly written Dhái) A nurse, a wet-nurse, a midwife, a female commissioner employed under early Regulations to interrogate and swear native women of condition, who could not appear to give evidence in Court.

Dai, Thug. The road.

Dáibá, Ben. (দাইবা) Reaping corn.

Dáij, Mar. (दाईज, from S. दायादः) An heir, a kinsman, one entitled to inherit.

Daijá, Dyjá, H. (دئجا) A dowry or portion which a wife brings to her husband in marriage, or presents made to the bridegroom by the parents of the bride, the object of which in the present day is usually to obtain a husband for the daughter of higher rank or tribe.

Dáími, H. (دايمي, from دائم, perpetual) Relating to what is perpetual; the perpetual settlement of the revenue: a criminal sentenced to imprisonment for life: also *Dáím-ul-habs*.

Dáín, corruptly, *Deeyne*, H. (A. دين) Debt, either one actually incurred by borrowing, or, in matters of sale, by purchasing on credit.

Daïn-dár, H. (P. دار, who has) A debtor.

Daïn muájjal, A. (دين معجّل) A debt payable on demand.

Daïn-muwajjal, A. (دين موجّل) A debt of which payment is deferred.

Dáïn, H. (دائِن, दायं) A threshing-floor.

Dáïn, H. (داين) A hamlet or estate, the lands of which are intermixed with those of another. Dehra Dhún.

Dáïn, Ben. &c. (ডাইন, S. डाकिनी) A witch, a female malignant being.

Dáir o Sáir, H. (A. دايروساير, going about) Proceeding on circuit (judges, &c.).

Dáïrah, H. (A. دايره) A circle, a circular inclosure, &c. A monastery.

Dáirah-dár, H. (P. دار, who has) The head of an establishment of Mohammadan ascetics.

Daitya, S. (दैत्य) A demon, a goblin,

Daiva, S. (दैवः, from देवः, a deity) Divine, relating to a divinity. A form of marriage, the gift of the maiden to the officiating priest. Fate, destiny.

Daivaka, or *Daivajna*, S. &c. (दैवक, दैवज्ञ) An astrologer, a calculator of nativities, and announcer of lucky and unlucky days, an almanac maker: he is usually a Bráhman; but there is also a caste professing the same functions.

Ḍák, corruptly, **Dawk**, H. &c. (ڈاك, डाक) Mar., also **Ḍáṅk**, (डांक) Post, post-office, or establishment for the conveyance of letters and of travellers. Relays of men or cattle along the road for these purposes.

Ḍák-chaukí, H. (چوكي) A stage or station where a relay is posted.

Ḍák-ghar, H. &c. (ڈاك گهر) A post-office.

Ḍáká, H., Ben., Mar. (ڈاكا, डाका) An attack by robbers especially armed and in a gang. (This and its derivatives are also written with the dental *d*, as দাকা, &c., but perhaps incorrectly).

Ḍákáït, corruptly, *Dakoit*, *Decoit*, H. &c. (ڈاكيت, डाकाइत) A robber, one of a gang of robbers.

Ḍakáití, or *Ḍákátí*, corruptly, *Decoity*, H., Ben., &c. (डाकाईती, डाकाती) Gang robbery.

Ḍáku, H., Ben., &c. (ডাকু) A robber, a burglar, a gang-robber or Dákáït.

Ḍákará, also **Dákar**, **Ḍáṅkrá**, **Ḍhákar**, H. (ڈاكرا, ڈانكرا, ڈهاكر, डाकरा, ढाकर) The best or second best quality of soil in the Upper Doab and Dehli. In many places it is considered inferior to the soil termed *Rauslí*, whilst in others it is regarded as the same.

Dakhal, Dukhul, H., but used, as well as its derivatives, in most dialects, with the meanings occasionally modified, although bearing a relation to the original (A. دخل, entrance, as into a house) Taking possession, occupancy, engaging or meddling in an affair, entering in an account, and the like. In Mar., Known, familiar to.

Dakhal náma, H. (P. نامه) A deed of possession or occupancy, a document giving right of occupancy.

Dákhalá, incorrectly, *Dakhlá*, H., Mar. (दाखला) Proof, evidence, a receipt, a bond, a certificate.

Dákhalu, Tel. Karn. (దాఖలు) Examination or comparison of accounts, records, &c. Entry in a book. Delivery of money or other article due.

Dákhil, H. (A. داخل) Entrance, taking possession, entry of an item in a deed or register, a receipt for money, annexation of lands, inclusion of a minor in a major parcel of land.

Dákhil daftar, H. (داخل دفتر) Entered upon the record, which is equivalent to being laid on the table, or postponed indefinitely; struck off the judge's or magistrate's file.

Dákhil-dár, or *Dákhil-kár*, H. &c. (كار, who makes) An occupant, either in his own right, or as a manager or trustee.

Dákhil-khárij, or *Dákhil-mukhárij*, H. (خارج, ejecting) Entering and ejecting, erasure of an entry. In Bengal, especially, the removal of the name of one proprietor and insertion of that of another, on occasion of a transfer of the property. Receipts and disbursements, *Dákhil-mukhárij* is also applied to fees on the registry of estates.

Dáhhil-náma, H. Warrant or deed of possession, a conveyance.

Dakhíl, *Dukheel*, H. (دخيل) An occupant.

Dákhilá, H. (داخلا) A receipt for money or goods, payment of revenue, or rent.

Dákhilábitam, Ben. (দাখিলাবিত°) Transfer of revenue or land from one Ryot to another.

Dákhalápalli, Tel. (దాఖలాపల్లి) A small village within the lands of a larger.

Dákhilí, sometimes *Dakhlá*, corruptly, *Dakhlee* and *Dáklee*, incorrectly, *Dukhilee*, H. (داخلي) Included, comprehended: applied especially to villages which have become included in the revenue list of villages paying revenue, having branched off from, and being dependent upon, those on which the assessment was originally levied; and which are therefore termed *Asalí*, original, in opposition to *Dákhilí*, the subordinate or included.

Dákhilí mauzá, H. (موضع) A village supplementary or additional. See the last.

Dákhhilí naklá, H. (A. نقلا) An additional or supplementary subordinate village, or subdivision of a *Mauzá*.

ḌÁKINÍ, H., S. (डाकिनी) A female goblin, a witch, or an old woman so reputed.

DÁKOCHÁ, or DÁKOTÁ, Mar. (दाकोचा or -ता) A man of mixed caste, professing to descend from a Bráhman father by a cowherd mother: they follow the avocations of fortune-tellers, almanac-makers, &c.

ḌAKAUT, ḌUKOUT, H. (ڈكوت, डकौत) A tribe of mendicants of Bráhman descent, practising astrology, fortune-telling, and the like. (The word is no doubt the same as the preceding, vernacularly modified).

DAKSHIṆA, S. vernacularly, DAKHIN, or DUKHIN, or sometimes DAKKAN, and DACHHIN, corruptly, DECCAN, DECKHAN, DEKHIN, &c., H. &c. (دكهن, S. दक्षिण) The south, the south of India, the right-hand, opposed to the left, whence the vernacular terms, *Dáhna*, *Dáhná*, *Dá-en*, &c.

Dakshiṇáchárí, S. (दक्षिणाचारी) One who follows the observances (ácháras) of the right-hand tribe or caste, practicers of the purer forms of the ritual, as opposed to the *Vámácharí*.

Dakshiṇáyana, S. (दक्षिणायन) The sun's southern declination, the six months of his progress from the northern to the southern limit of the tropics.

DAKSHINÁ, also vernacularly, DAKHINÁ, DAXINÁ and DACHHINÁ, or DACHHNÁ, corruptly, DUCKNEH, S. (दक्षिणा) A present, especially one made to a Bráhman on the conclusion of any public ceremonial. Presents to other persons are also sometimes so termed. Presents made annually by the Peshwa to the Bráhmans at Puná, and continued as a definite allowance applied partly to them and partly to the maintenance of the Puná college by the British Government.

DÁL, H. The letter of the Persian alphabet *d*, د, formerly affixed to Zamindárí and other grants by the head native revenue officer under the early British administration of Bengal.

DAL, DUL, H. (دل) Wild rice.

DAL, DUL, H. &c. (دل, from S. दल, to divide) A portion, a part, a body of troops. In Bengal it commonly designates a club or association of artificers, or, among the higher classes, a faction, a coterie, into many of which native society in large towns is split.

Daláí, *Dulaee*, Uriya (ଦଲାଈ, from ଦଲ, a troop) A subordinate officer in command of Paiks.

Dalbeherá, Uriya (ଦଲବେହେରା) The chief or head of the Gwala and other castes. An officer in command of Paiks, the hereditary militia and police of Cuttack. Under the former system, a military or feudal chief holding lands, most usually in the hills, on the tenure of military service.

Dalwárí, Mar. (दलवारी) The officer in command of the local militia, or *Sersanradis*.

DAL, DUL, Thug. A weight.

DÁL, corruptly, DOL, H. &c. (دال, from S. दल, to divide) A kind of pulse (Phareolus aureus), but applied to other kinds, the pea of which, especially when converted into a sort of coarse pease soup, enters largely into the food of the natives.

ḌÁL, H. &c. (ڈال, डाल, from H. *ḍálná*, to throw) A bough: a basket used to throw up water from a pond or canal for irrigation.

DÁLA, H. (داله) A particular tenure in the Doab. See *Dhála*.

DALÁL, H. (دلال) A tribe of Jats in the Rohtak Zila. A broker, but in this sense more correctly *Dallál*, q. v.

DAḶAMBU, Tam. (தளம்பு) A flood-gate, a sluice.

DALAR, or DALAR KHAN, Thug. A name pronounced to put the party on their guard, or uttered by the leader as a signal for the stranglers to be ready.

DAḶAWÁ, Mal. (ദളവാ) One of the ministers of state in Travancore.

DAḶAWÁI, Karn. (ದಳವಾಯಿ, from ದಳ, an army) The commander-in-chief, and hence, also, the prime minister under the Hindu rulers of Mysore.

DAḶDAL, or DALDALI, DULDUL, DULDULEE, H. (دلدل) A quagmire, a quicksand, a sandy swamp, a marshy soil.

DALGANJANÁ, H. (دلگنجنا) A kind of rice.

DALHÁRÁ, H. (دلهارا) A grain seller.

ḌÁLÍ, H. &c. (ڈالي, डाली) A tray, or a couple of trays, fastened by slings to each end of a pole, carried over the shoulders. Such an apparatus is used especially to carry complimentary presents of fruit, sugar, spices, fish, &c., on festive occasions, whence it has come to specify the presents so offered. Such complimentary envoys from natives to Europeans were formerly frequent, but those in the Company's service are now forbidden to accept them.

DALIÁ, H. (دليا) Any sort of split pulse ground finer than *Dál*.

ḌALIÁJHÁR, H. (ڈلیاجھار) The conclusion of the sowing season: lit., the brushing out of the sowing basket.

DALÍL, H. (A. دليل, plur. دلايل) Argument in pleading, proof, evidence. Precedent, example. A voucher.

Dalálat, H. (A. دلالت) Proof, evidence. Argument.

DALÍMÁ, H. (دليما) A class of Tugas in Moradabad.

DALKAR, DULKUR, Uriya (ଦଲକର) Rent for pasturage.

DALLÁL, DULLAL, sometimes with one *l*, DALÁL, corruptly, DELLOL, H. (دلال, from the A. دلّ, to point out) DÁLÁL, Ben. (দালাল) An agent between buyer and seller, a broker, a salesman.

Dalláli, or Daláli, H. (دلالي) Brokerage, agency, commission. A tax upon brokers.

Dalláli-paradeṣi, H. (پرديسي, a stranger) Brokerage or agency for strangers or pilgrims (paradeṣís) at Benares: for permission to act in which capacity a fee was formerly paid to Government.

DALLAR, DULLUR, Thug. The head.

DÁḶŪÁ, Uriya, DÁḶUVÁ, or DÁḶWÁ, Tel. (దాళువా) Light crops of rice grown in the dry hot weather in moist situations, commonly called the black crop (Northern Circars and Cuttack).

DÁM, corruptly DAUM, H. (دام) A coin, originally a copper coin, but adopted as money of account. In the reign of Akbar, 40 *dáms* were reckoned to a rupee; in that of Alemgir, $46\frac{1}{3}$d; at later periods, 80 and 90 are the proportionate rates, which appear to have been liable to great fluctuation. By the common people in the upper provinces 25 *dáms* are calculated to a *paisa*.—Elliot.

DÁM, H. (P. دام) Price; Mar. (दाम) Money, cash.

DÁMÁD, H. &c. (S. داماد) A daughter's husband.

DAMÁÏ, DUMAEE, H. (دمئي) Amount of assessment. (From *dám*, the money of account.

DÁMANGÍR, H. (دامن, lit., a skirt of a garment, and *gír*, گير, who holds) A complainant, a plaintiff, one who sues for justice.

ḌÁMAR, incorrectly, DAMMAR, H. (ڈامر) Resin, pitch, especially the resinous extract of the Sál tree used as pitch.

DÁMÁSÁHÍ, H. (داماساهي) DÁMÁṢÁÍ, Mar. (दामाशाई) DÁMÁSHAÏ, Tel. (దామాషాయి) Equitable partition of the effects of an insolvent amongst his creditors: hence, any just proportionate distribution. (The word is said to be derived from a proper name, one *Dámasáh*, who, becoming insolvent, distributed all his property in just proportions amongst those to whom he was indebted).

DÁMCHA, H. (دامچه) A platform on which a person is stationed to protect crops: a boundary mark.

DÁMDUPAṬ, Mar. (दामदुपट, from दाम, and *dupat*, doubled) Principal of a debt doubled by accumulated interest.

DÁMI, H. (دامي, from *dám*, price) An assessment.

Dámí bighá, H. (بيگها) The assessment of the lands of a village per bíghá

Dami-wáṣilát, H. (A. واصلات) Gross assets of a village.

DAMÍAT, A. (دمعت) A slight wound, a scratch causing blood to appear, but not to flow: in Mohammadan law.

Dámíat, A. (دامية) In Mohammadan law, A slight wound, a scratch, but causing blood to flow.

DAMKÁ, DUMKA, H. (دمکا) A hillock (East Oudh).

DAM-MADÁR, DUM-MUDAR, H. (دممدار) A ceremony observed by the peasantry of Upper India in honour of a Mohammadan saint named Madár, who is believed to have lived four centuries, having the faculty of retaining his breath (*dam* or *dum*). The ceremony consists in jumping into a fire of wood and treading it out, exclaiming, Dam-madár—by the breath of Madár. It is supposed to be a preservative against the effects of snake or scorpion bites.

DAMMIDHI, Tel. (దమ్మిధి) A quarter of a *dab*—five *kás*.

DAMMU, Tel. (దమ్ము) Mud, miry ground, land prepared for receiving young rice plants.

Dampakarṛu, Tel. (దంపకర్రు) The ploughshare used in the tillage of wet ground.

DAMPATÍ, S. (दम्पती) Husband and wife.

Dampatí tambula, Karn. Betel-leaf and areka-nut presented at marriages by the bride and bridegroom to each married couple present.

DAMṚÍ, DUMREE, H. (دمڑی) A nominal coin, of the value of $3\frac{1}{8}$ or $3\frac{1}{4}$ *dáms*, or from 8 to 12 *kaunris*. Any money of very small value. It is also applied in the Dehli territory to subdivisions of land, one *damṛí* being equal to 25 Kacha *bíghás*.

DÁMṚÍ, Ben. (দামড়ী) In retail dealing, five *gandas* of *kaunris*.

DAMWAST, DUMWUST, H. (دموست) An inferior tribe of Rájputs in the Benares district.

DÁNA, vernacularly, DÁN, S. &c. (دان, S. *dánam*, Lat. *donum*, दानं) Gift, giving a gift, a gift by will, a bequest.

Dánadharma, S. (दानधर्म्मः) The virtue of liberality. Giving for pious and charitable purposes, alms-giving, building or endowing temples, digging tanks, &c.

Dánamávasyaka, S. (from अवश्यं, certainty) An imperative gift, as gifts to Bráhmans on certain days, as full moon, &c.

Dánpatr, H., or *Dánapatra*, S. (दानपत्रं, from *patra*, पत्र, a leaf) A deed of gift, a grant, an assignment of land, especially to Bráhmans.

Dánapátra, S. (from पात्रं, a vessel) One deserving of, or fit for, a gift: one to whom by law property may be conveyed.

Danpatrdár, or *Dánapatradár*, H. One who holds a grant, or deed of gift: a grantee of the Bráhman caste to whom lands have been assigned for religious purposes.

Dání, H. S. (दानी) A giver, a donor: applied also to a gratuity to the village accountant, at the rate of six paisas on each rupee of the revenue (Etawa).

DÁNA, H. (دانه) Grain, corn.

Dánabandí, *Dánubundee*, H. (دانهبندی) Cursory survey or a partial measurement of a field, or weighment of the crop, to ascertain the value of the crop, and the amount of the assessment.

Dánabandí-kankúti, H. (کنکوتی) Assessment of the revenue without measurement, upon a partial valuation of the standing crops.

Dánadár, H. (دانهدار) Apportionment of revenue, or any other contributions, according to the actual produce (Benares).

DANA, DUNU, Karn. (ದನ, S. *dhana*, धनं, wealth) Cattle, domestic cattle: also wealth. A corruption of *Dhan*, q. v.

Danaga, Karn. (ದನಗ) A shepherd, a cowherd.

Danagávi, Karn. (ದನಗಾವಿ) A herdsman.

Danadahaṭṭi, Karn. (ದನದಹಟ್ಟಿ) A cattle-fold.

Danamár, Karn. (ದನಮಾರ) A tax on the transfer of cattle from one Ryot to another.

DAṆD, or DAṆDA, DUṆD, DUṆDA, S. (दण्डः) and in most dialects, as Ben. (দণ্ড) Mar. (दण्डः) Tel. (దండము) &c. In Hindustani, and occasionally in other dialects also, the initial is written either with the dental or cerebral *d*, and the following vowel is optionally made long, DÁṆD, or ḌÁṆD, (ڈانڈ, ڈانڈ) also Ben. (ডাংড) Punishment, of two kinds—personal, *Sarírа-daṇḍa*; or pecuniary, *Artha-daṇḍa*: also a fine, a mulct: and, in Ajmer, a proportionate share of the revenue formerly levied on the wealthier cultivators to make good any deficit in that due from the poorer.

Daṇḍa dása, S. (from दास, a slave) A slave, one who is condemned to servitude as a punishment.

Daṇḍa pálaka, S. (from पालकः, who protects) A magistrate, the head of the police.

Daṇḍa párushya, S. (दण्डपारुष्य, from *daṇḍa*, punishment, and *párushyam*, violence) Assault and battery.

Danḍiga, or *Danḍuga*, Tel. (దండిగ, దండుగ) A fine, an exorbitant assessment, any extortionate demand.

DAṆDA, DAṆD, or ḌÁṆḌ, S. &c. (दण्ड) H. (ڈنڈ, or ڈانڈ, the final sometimes pronounced like *r*, as DÁṆṚ) A stick, a staff, a rod, a cane carried by certain mendicants, an oar: a measure of length, a rod or pole of four or six cubits: a measure of time—twenty-four minutes.

Daṇḍa grahaṇa, S. &c. (दण्डग्रहण) Taking the staff, entering upon a religious or mendicant course of life.

Daṇḍa-zani, H. (from P. *zan*, زن, striking) A mode of torture—fastening a man's hands behind him with a cord, which is twisted round by means of a stick until the tension produces excessive pain.

Daṇḍáwat, H. (S. دنڈاوت, दण्डावत्) Prostration, lying flat like a stick on the ground.

Daṇḍi, S. &c, (दण्डी) Any one who bears a staff, applied especially to a numerous order of religious mendicants, founded by Sankara Áchárya, many of whom have been eminent as writers on various subjects, especially on the Vedánta philosophy. They are divided into ten classes, each of which is distinguished by a peculiar name; as, *Tírtha, Áṣrama, Vana, Áranya, Saraswatí, Purí, Bhá-ratí, Girí* or *Gir, Párvata*, and *Sagara*, which is added to the proper name of the individual, as *Purushottama Gir*, or *Bodhendra Saraswatí*. They are hence known collectively as the *Daṣ-námí*, or ten-name Gosains. Of these, only the classes named *Tírtha, Áṣrama, Saraswatí*, and part of *Bhárati*, are now considered as pure *Daṇḍis*: the others are of a more secular character, and are more usually termed *Atíts*.

Ḍáṇdi, H. &c. (ڈانڈي, डांडी) A boatman, a rower.

Daṇḍidár, H. (دنڈيدار) An inferior servant or officer in an opium agency.

Daṇḍiyá, Mar. (दंडिया) A petty officer in a bazar, a beadle.

Dandyá, Tel. (దండ్యా) A police officer, a peon.

Ḍándio, Guz. (ડાંડીઓ) A watchman who goes the rounds at night beating a drum.

ḌÁṆD, DÁṆD, or ḌÁṆDÁ, H. (ڈانڈ, دانڈ, ڈانڈا, डांड, दांड, डांडा) High ground, opposed to DÁBAR, q.v. Sterile land, of the kind called *Bhúr*, land in which sand predominates. Elevated land of the sort called *Dumat*.

DAṆD, or DAṆDA, H. &c. (دنڈا) Raised ground forming a ridge or causeway, a path for cattle, or a boundary between fields, also a landmark; from analogy, perhaps, to a straight line or stick.

Daṇḍá-meṇḍá, H. (دنڈا مينڈا) The boundary between two estates, or the lands of two villages. (Either from *daṇd*, a stick or pole set up as a landmark, or a boundary or raised bank, and *meṇd*, a limit.

Daṇḍá-meṇḍá takrár, H. (تكرار, a quarrel) A boundary quarrel.

Daṇḍásulu, Tel. (దండాసులు) Village watchers. (? from *daṇḍá*, a boundary).

Daṇḍuási, Uriya (ଦଣ୍ଡୁଆସି) A watchman.

DAṆḌÁ, DUṆDA, DAṆḌI, or DÁṆḌI, DUNDEE, DANDEE, H. (ڈنڈا, ڈنڈي, ڈانڈي) DÁṆḌÍ, Ben. (ডাণ্ডী) The beam of a balance. (From S. *daṇda*, a stick).

Daṇḍá, or, *Daṇḍia*, H. (ڈنڈا, ڈنڈيا) A collector of market dues.

Daṇḍi, or, *Daṇḍia*, H. (ڈنڈي) A weighman.

Ḍáṇḍídár, Ben. (ডাংডীদার) A weighman.

DAṆDA, DUṆDA, H. &c. (S. दण्डः) A measure of time, equal to twenty-four minutes: a sixteenth part of the day and night.

N.B.—In this, and all the preceding forms of what is originally but one word, viz. S. *Danda* or *Duṇda*, great confusion has been made in the vernacular languages by the irregular and arbitrary alteration of the first syllable; in the optional substitution of the cerebral for the dental *d*, ड for द, and the elongation of the vowel: so that we have in some instances four different forms, or द, *da*; दा, *dá*; ड, *ḍa*; and डा, *ḍá*.

DAṆDAKAṬṬU, Tel. (దండకట్టు) A wisp of straw bound round the bottom of a heap of grain. Area within which the corn is threshed.

DÁṆḌÍ, Hindi (دانڈي, दांडी) A dry, hard soil that does not retain moisture, and dries quickly when irrigated: a gravelly soil on high ground.

DANDÚ, Thug. Braying of an ass (Dakhini).

DAṆḌIKÁLA, Karn. (ದಂಡಿಕಾಲ, from ದಂಡಿ, abundant) Harvest time.

Daṇḍibele, Karn. (ದಂಡಿಬೆಳೆ) A plentiful crop.

DAṆḌWÁRA, H. (ڈنڈوارہ) A south wind.

ḌANG, DUNG, Mar. (डंग) A thicket, a place overrun with bushes.

DÁNG, H. (دانگ) A hill, a precipice, the top of a mountain, the high bank of a river. Corrupted provincially into *Dháng* and *Dháyang*.

ḌÁNG, Mar. (डांग) An ascent, or rising part of a road. A name given in the Dakhin to a tract of country along, near to, or below, the Ghats; and which, although not mountainous, is so much interspersed with hills as to have no extent of level ground: it is generally overrun with low thicket. Also forest or jangal land.

Ḍángí, Mar. A forester, an inhabitant of a low, hilly, and jangali tract. In the Dakhin a tribe of Rájputs inhabiting the woody districts of Eastern Malwa.

Ḍángi-gaon, Mar. (गांव) A village in the *Ḍáng*, or low hills at the foot of the Ghats.

Dáng, H. (P. دانگ) A weight, the fourth part of a dram.

Ḍángá, Ben. (ডাংগা) Dry land, upland, ascent.

Ḍangá, H. &c. (دنگا) **Dángá**, Ben. (দাংগা) A riot, a disturbance, a tumult, an affray.

Ḍangá, Karn. (ದಂಗೆ) Dunning for payment, sitting *Dharna*, q. v.

Ḍangar, Ḍángar, Ḍungur, Ḍangur, H. (ڈنگر, ڈانگر, डंगर) Horned cattle, especially those belonging to a village. Sometimes applied only to such as are worn out.

Dangast, Dungust, H. (دنگست) A class of Rájputs in Ghazipur.

Dáṇgi, H. (دانگي) A name given to the Bundelas (Ságar).

Ḍangí, Mar. (डंगी) A basket or baskets slung to a pole carried over the shoulders: the *Bahangi*, q. v., of Hindustan.

Ḍángorá, Mar. (डांगोरा) A proclamation, notice by the public crier. **Ḍangara**, Karn. (ಡಂಗರ) Proclamation by beat of drum.

Ḍangwára, Ḍungwara, H. (ڈنگوارہ) Reciprocal assistance in tillage (Dehli).

Ḍanka, Tel. (డొంక) A path between two fields for cattle.

Dánt, Hindi (दांत) Hard, dry soil, not retaining moisture.

Dánt. H. &c. (دانت) S. दन्तः) A tooth.

Dánt-ghunghni, H. (from घुंघनी, a preparation of wheat and pulse with sugar) or, *Dánt-nikalna*, H. (from نکلنا, to go forth, to appear) A ceremony observed by the Mohammadans on the appearance of the child's first tooth.

Dante, or **Dantí**, Tel. (దంతె, దంతి) A kind of rake or hoe. (Probably from *danta*, a tooth).

Ḍánṭan, Ben. (ডাংটন) Threatening a person, putting him in bodily fear.

Dantáoli, H. (دنتاولي) A harrow or rake. (From दन्त, a tooth).

Dánte, H. (دانتي) A sickle.

Dánt-tinká, H. (دانت تنکا) Taking a straw or blade of grass in the mouth to deprecate anger or express submission.

Ḍánṭh, H. (ڈانٹھ) Refuse of harvest-floors, especially of the kharíf produce.

Danthal, Dunthul, or *Danthlá, Dunthla*, H. (دنتھل, دنتھلا) The bare stalks or stubble of bájra, jawár, and Indian corn: either the stems after the heads have been cut off, or the roots left in the ground after reaping. The refuse of harvest-floors, especially of the kharíf crops.

Danthi, Thug. Noise of jackals fighting—a bad omen.

Dánwán, H. (دانوان, from S. दाव) Burning stubble, or fire in a forest.

Dánwarí, H. (دانوري) The rope by which the bullocks are tied together when treading out the corn. See **Dáuri**.

Dáo, H. (داو) A hatchet or cleaver with a bent point.

Dapání, Uriya (ଦପାଣି) Brine.

Daphaet, Dafât, Uriya (ଦଫାଏତ, from the A. دفعه, a turn or time) Pay in addition to the rent for privileges attaching to the land, as right of fishing, &c.

Dapháte-jamá, Karn. (ದಫಾತೆಜಮಾ, from the A. دفعه, and *jamâ*, collection) Extra or miscellaneous collections (Mysore).

Dapháte kharchu, Karn. (ದಫಾತೆಖರ್ಚು, from the A. as before) Extra or sundry disbursements (Mysore).

Daphedar, Uriya (ଦଫେଦାର) Land of second quality.

Daphe raphe, Mar. (दफेरफे, A. دفع and رفع) Clearance of a debt, settlement of any business.

Dápita, S. &c. (दापित) Fined, sentenced to pay a fine or compensation.

Dápya, S. &c. Punishable by fine, liable to pay compensation.

Dápní, Dahkini Thug. A dagger.

Ḍáppu, Tam. (டாப்பு) A list, a schedule, an inventory.

Dar, Dur, H. (P. در) In, within.

Dar-ámad, Duramud, H. (درامد) An account of fees paid for serving a process, the return of a process: lit., coming in.

Darbandí, H. (دربندي) An item in the village accounts, statement of proportionate rates of revenue payment.

Dar-bast, or, *Dar-o-bast, Dur-bust, Dur-o-bust*, H. (P. دروبست) Entire, whole. The whole of a district or estate, as opposed to a kismat, or portion of it.

Dar-bast-i-aima, H. Grant of the whole of the lands, constituting a rent-free estate.

Dar- (Dur-) hawála, H. (from در, in or sub, and A. حواله, charge) Sub-tenure, holding a farm on lease from a farmer or lessee.

Dar-ijára, H. (P. A. در اجاره) A sub-lease or farm.

Dar-ín-willá, H. (P. A. دراين ولا, lit., in this proximity) A phrase heading official papers in some of the Courts in the south of India, implying, In this case, or, At this time, By these presents.

Dar-mustájar, H. (P. درمستاجر, from *mustájar*, a tenant) A sub-lessee, or tenant holding of a farmer, not of the *Zamindár*.

Daróbastu lekkalu, Tel. (దరోబస్తు లెక్కలు, plur.) All the accounts of a district, &c.

Dar-pattani, or commonly, *Durputnee*, Ben. (দরপত্তনি) A subordinate or sub-leasehold tenure.

Dar-pattani-dár, Ben. (দরপত্তনিদার) The holder of a lease from a leaseholder, a sub-lessee.

Dar-pattani-táluk, Ben. (দরপত্তনিতালুক) An estate held under a sub-lease. See *Patni* or *Pattani*.

DAR, DUR, H. &c. (در, दर) Rate, price, a number or quantity fixed as a standard, an allowance.

Darbandí, *Durbundee*, H. (دربندي) A statement of the different rates of a village. Assessing the price or value of crops or produce. Fixing the value or price of any thing according to a standard.

Darjásti, Karn. (ದರಜಾಸ್ತಿ) An extra assessment, by making the cultivators buy the Government share of the crop at a rate above the market price.

Darterrot, (?) Mar. Fixing of rates, revision of assessment.

DÁR, H. (P. دار, from داشتن, to have or hold) One who has, holds, possesses, &c.: used in compounds with the object held or possessed, as, *Chob-dár*, a mace-bearer; *Zamindár*, a landholder; and the like. Also in Maraṭhí, Solvent, having funds, as opposed to *Nádár*, having nothing, insolvent.

Dárí, H. (P. داري) The act or function of a possessor or holder, as Zamindári, the condition of a Zamindár, an estate.

Dármadár, H. (دارمدار) An agreement, a stipulation. Adjustment of a dispute (holding or not holding).

DAR, DUR, H. (P. در) A door.

Darwán, H. (P. دروان) *Darbán*, Ben. (দরবান) A doorkeeper, a porter.

DÁR, H. (A. دار) A house, a mansion, one with various rooms or tenements and an open court. Used in composition, it implies a place where any public work is carried on, as, *Dár-ul-zarab*, the house of striking 'coin,' the mint; *Dar-ul-inshá*, the secretary's office, or house of letters; *Dár-us-shefâ*, the house of healing, an hospital; or the residence of a prince, as, *Dár-al-khiláfat*, the residence of the khalif; *Dár-us-sultanat*, the dwelling of the Sultan—titles given to any royal capital or metropolis.

Dár-ul-harb, A. (دارالحرب) A country under a Government that is not Mohammadan: lit., the seat of hostility or war, infidels at all times being legitimate objects of attack.

DAṚÁ, or, DAḌA, incorrectly, DURRAH, Mar. (दडा) A body or company of Pindáris.

DARAḌ, Mar. (दरड) A steep slope, a high bank.

DARAK or DARK, DURUK or DURK, Mar. (दर्क, दरक) A hereditary public office, as that of *Pharnavís*, *Chiṭnís*, &c.

Darak-dár, Mar. (दरकदार) A hereditary public officer, or functionary. The term was applied under the Maraṭha government especially to eight offices:—1. The *Kárbári*, *Mukhtiyár*, or *Diwán*, the chief financial minister. 2. *Majmûdár*, auditor and accountant. 3. *Pharnavís*, his deputy. 4. *Sabnís* or *Daftardár*, clerk. 5. *Karkánís*, (?) Commissary. 6. *Chiṭnís*, secretary. 7. *Jamâdár*, an officer in charge of all valuables, except cash. 8. *Potnís*, cashier. The term was also applied to all the *Kárkuns*, or officers of account, who were paid by fees from the villagers, in addition to their salaries, but who were appointed and removed only by the supreme government, not by the district officers.

Darak-paṭṭí, Mar. (दरकपट्टी) A tax upon public functionaries: a fee levied from them, especially a tax of one year's revenue in ten on the lands of the *Deșmukh* and *Despáṇḍe*.

DARAṆAMU, OR DHARAṆAMU, Tel. (దరణము, ధరణము) An imaginary coin, of the value of two fanams.

DARBÁR, DURBAR, H. &c. (دربار) A court, a royal court, an audience or levee.

Darbár-charaṇiyá, Ben. (দরবার চড়নিযা) A plaintiff, or complainant.

Darbar-kharch, H. &c. (دربار خرچ) Political and diplomatic expenditure, court charges, charge for presents and gratuities made to princes and public functionaries, bribes, &c. In many places under the old *régime*, an addition made to the assessment by government officers or the Zamindars, on the plea of providing for gratuities exacted by their superiors or the State on their payment of the revenue.

DARES, H. (دريس, दरेस) A road. Margin. Any line very straight. (Supposed to have been adopted from the English military term "dress.")

DARGÁH, DURGAH, H. (P. درگاه) A royal court. In India it is more usually applied to a Mohammadan shrine, or the tomb of some reputed holy person, and the object of worship and pilgrimage.

DARHOT, H. (درحوت) Advance.

DARÍ, Hindi, &c. (दरी) A cave, a cavern, a natural or artificial excavation, a dell, a hollow.

Dariá-bar-ámad, H. (P. دريا, a river, and برآمد, what comes up) Alluvial soil, land gained from a river.

Dariá-burd, or *-shikast*, *Durya-boord*, or *-shikust*, H. (from P. دريا, and *burdan*, بردن, to bear, or *shikastan*, شكست, to break) Lands carried away by the encroachments of a river.

Darı́bá, Hindi (दरीबा) A stall in a market where betel is sold.

Dáridr-khedná, H. (دارِدر كهيدنا, from S. दारिद्र्, poverty, and *khedná*, to chase, from S. आखेट) Driving out poverty: a custom observed on the morning of the *Diwálí*, when a sieve or winnowing basket is beaten in each corner of the house, or the dirt in each place is swept with a brush, and carried away in a basket, with the exclamation, *Íśwar paithau*, *Dáridr niklo*, 'May God be present! Poverty depart!' or some equivalent prayer. —Elliot.

Dark, or, allowably, Darak, incorrectly, Dirk, A. (دَرْك, or دَرَك) Consequence of any act or thing. In law, a contingency, a possible event.

Kafíl-bil-dark, A. (كفيل بلدرك) A surety or bail against what may happen, liability for contingencies.

Darkhál, H. (دركهال) A cattle enclosure (Benares).

Darkhást, corruptly, Dhurkast, H. (P. درخواست) Tel. and Karn. (ದರಖಾಸ್ತು) Darkhás, Guz. (દરખાસ્ત) Darakhása, Mal. (ദരഖാസ്ത) A contract, a tender: a representation, an application, a petition. In judicial proceedings, an application which is required to be made for the admission of each exhibit in a suit, and for the summoning of each witness. In revenue matters, the representation of the proprietor of an estate as to the amount of revenue he is able to pay; or a proposal for renting or farming an estate, or any branch of the public revenue; or the engagement entered into by the Lambardárs to be responsible for a stipulated amount of revenue payment for a given time.

Darkhást-i-khárij, H. (خارج, exclusion) A petition of exclusion. In Bengal, a petition to the collector for the exclusion of the name of a proprietor, whose interest has lapsed by death or sale, and the insertion of that of another in the public books.

Darkhás-karaví, Guz. (દરખાસ્તકરવી) Making a motion in a court of law.

Darmá, Ben. &c. S. (दरमा) A sort of long grass, much used for making mats (Arundo bengalensis). A mat, four or five feet long by three or four wide, much used in Bengal to make fences and walls to native huts.

Darmáhá, Durmaha, or -máhi, H. &c. (درماها, or درماهي, from P. در, in, and ماه, a month) Monthly pay or wages.

Dárogha, H. (داروغه) in some of the Hindu dialects it is written with the simple *g*, and with either a long or short vowel in the first syllable, as, Dárogá, Tel. దారోగా) Mar. Darogá, or Dárogá, (दरोगा, दारोगा) The chief native officer in various departments under the native Government, a superintendant, a manager; but in later times he is especially the head of a police, custom, or excise station. In the Dakhin, also, the officer employed to prevent the removal of the crops before the payment or assessment of the Government demand. A tax originally imposed to meet the expense of employing a Dárogha, and afterwards brought to credit as an item of public revenue.

Dárogha-i-Ádálat, H. Under the native system, a judge or deputy presiding over a court in the absence of a superior of high rank; as, the *Dárogha-i-Ádálat-al Álía*, the deputy of the Názim in the Supreme Criminal Court of Bengal; *Dárogha-i-Ádálat-Diwáni*, the deputy of the Diwan in the Civil Court.

Dárogha-i-árz-mukarrar, H. (عرض مكرر) An officer under the Mohammadan Government, whose office it was to draw up an abstract of papers which required the royal assent, and present them for confirmation and signature. He was especially charged with the superintendence of the assignments to the *Mansabdars*, for the horse they maintained.

Dároghagi, H. (داروغگي) The function, charge, or jurisdiction of a *Dárogha*.

Dároghána, H. (داروغانه) The pay or fees of a Dárogha. Taxes levied for the payment of Dároghas under the Mohammadan Government.

Darogagiri, Karn. (ದರೊಗಗಿರಿ) Office of a Dárogha, superintendence, headship.

Darogatana, Karn. (ದರೊಗತನ) Superintendence, inspectorship, duty of a Dárogha.

Darogh, or, more correctly, Darúgh, H. (P. دروغ) A lie.

Darogh, or Darúgh-halfi, H. (دروغ حلفي, from A., *half* an oath) Perjury, false swearing.

Dará, Durá, corruptly, Durrah, Mar. (दडा, properly Daḍa, but the cerebral *ḍ* is sounded like *r*) A body of Pindárís.

Darra, Durra, H. (درّه) Dará, Dura, Mar. (दरा) A hollow among hills, a ravine, a defile, a pass.

Darṣa, S. (दर्शः) Sight, seeing. The day of new moon, when it rises invisible. A sacrifice with fire on that day, performed by householders, who maintain a perpetual fire. Also *Darṣa-yága*, from *yága*, a sacrifice.

Darṣapaurṇamása, S. (दर्शपौर्णमासं) Sacrifices or oblations with fire, performed at the new and full moon by householders, who maintain a perpetual fire.

Darṣana, vernacularly, *Darṣan*, H. (درسن, S. दर्शनं) Seeing: especially visiting temples, and seeing or reverencing idols. A school or system of speculative doctrine, of which six are recognised by the Hindus:—1. *Púrvá mímánsá*, treating of the purport of the ceremonies of the Vedas. 2. *Uttara mímánsá*, or *Vedánta*, inculcating unity of spirit and matter. 3. *Sánkhya*, dualistic, teaching the distinctness of soul and matter. 4. *Pátanjala*, teaching the practice of abstraction, or *Yoga*. 5. and 6. Logic or dialectics in two parts: the *Nyáya*, as taught by *Gotama*, and *Vaiṣeshika*, founded by *Kanáda*.

Darṣana-pratibhú, S. (दर्शनप्रतिभूः) Bail or security for appearance.

Darsar, (?) H. Distribution of the Government revenue amongst the several Mauzâs of a Pargana (Garhwal). Corrupted strangely to *Dírroa*.

Dáru, H. &c. (دارو) Spirituous liquor. Gunpowder.

Dáru-kalálí, Mar. (दारुकलाली, from *kalál*, a distiller) A tax or excise upon distilleries and liquor-shops.

Dáru-sísá, H. &c. (دارو سیسا) Military stores, ammunition; lit., powder and lead.

Daruvu, Tel. (దరువు) An embankment for irrigation. A mound on the bank of a river from which to raise water in buckets. A well.

Darwadá, incorrectly, Daroḍá, Mar. (दरवडा) A gang of robbers. An attack on a village by such a gang.

Darwesh, or Darvesh, corruptly, Dirvesh, and Dervise, H. (P. درویش) A Mohammadan religious mendicant; in many instances a mere vagabond and stroller, occasionally leading about bears and monkeys, but in some cases persons leading a religious life, either independently, or enrolled in different orders.

Daryáft, H. (P. دریافت) Dariyáphat, or Dariyáphtí, Mar. (दरियाफत, दरियाफ्ती, also दर्याफ्त, &c.) Dariyáptu, Tel. (దరియాప్తు) Inquiry, investigation, detection.

Darzi, Durzee, vernacularly, Darji, Durjee, H. (P. درزي) A tailor.

Daṣ, Duṣ, H. Daṣa, S. (दश् or दश, Lat. *decem*) Ten.

Daṣabhandamu, Tel. (దశబంధము) A deduction of one-tenth of the revenue, on account of compensation for some public work, as the construction of a tank, &c.

Daṣáha, Mar. &c. (S. दशाह) A period of ten days. The period of impurity from the death of a relative.

Daṣahará, or vernacularly, *Dashará*, written incorrectly, *Dasará*, and corruptly, *Dusrah*, *Dasehra*, *Daserru*, *Dussarat*, *Dusserat*, *Dussora*, &c. H. (دسہرا) Mar. (दसरा) S. (दशहरा, from दश, ten, *i. e.* sins, and हर, what removes or expiates) A popular festival in honour of the goddess Durgá. In Bengal it is exclusively appropriated to her worship, and is celebrated for nine days in Aṣwin—September, October. In the west and south of India it is a military festival held at the same season, which, being the close of the rains, is the commencement of the period for military operations. It is said to have originated with *Ráma's* worship of *Durgá*, on his invasion of *Lanká*, by which he secured victory; hence the tenth of Aṣwin is also called the *Vijaya daṣamí*, or tenth of victory. The original festival, however, appears to have had no relation whatever to *Durgá*, being held on the tenth of *Jyeshṭha*, in honour of *Gangá's* descent from heaven.

Daṣamí, H. S. (दशमी) The tenth lunar day of the fortnight.

Dashará-bakra, H. (A. بکرہ) Goats or sheep levied from a village in some parts of India as an offering to Durgá at the Dashará.

Dashará kharch, H. (A. خرچ) Expenses of the Dashará festival. A cess levied on that pretext by a Zamindar.

Dashará jhandá paṭṭi, Mar. (झंडा, a flag, and पट्टी, a tax) Tax upon hoisting flags at the Dashará.

Dashará paṭṭi, Mar. (पट्टी, a tax) The instalment of the public revenue, which is levied at the Dashará. A portion of the allowance granted to temples under the Maraṭha Government, set apart for the Dashará festival.

Dasṇámi, H. S. (नाम, a name) One of the ten-named order of ascetics. See *Danḍí*.

Dasotara, *Dasotra*, H. (دسوترہ) Ten per cent.

Dasrát-panchrát, Mar. (रात, for रात्रि, night, with दश, ten, and पंच, five) An ordeal or, test of evidence: if a person's children or cattle should die within a few days after preferring a plaint, or giving evidence, it shewed that his case was bad, or testimony false.

Daṣ-ṣála, H. (دسّالہ) Decennial, decennial settlement.

Daṣatrá, H. (दशत्रा) Ten per cent. A tenth part. The

tenth of the value of property litigated exacted from the successful parties under the Mohammadan system.

Daswáná, H. (دسوانا) A tenth. Addition of a tenth to the revenue, as made in Bidnur in 1723.

DÁSA, vernacularly, DÁS, corruptly, Doss, H. S. (दासः, fem. DÁSÍ, दासी) A slave. Fifteen kinds of slaves are recognised by Hindu law:—1. *Gṛihajáta*, one born in the house of the owner by a female slave. 2. *Kríta*, one purchased. 3. *Labdha*, one acquired, as by gift. 4. *Dáyádupágata*, inherited. 5. *Anakálabhṛita*, taken as a slave in a time of famine, for support. 6. *Áhita*, taken as a pledge. 7. *Ṛiṇadása*, one becoming a slave in payment of a debt. 8. *Yuddhaprápta*, acquired in war. 9. *Panejita*, won in a wager. 10. *Taváham*, one who voluntarily makes himself a slave, saying, 'I am thine.' 11. *Pravrajyávasita*, an apostate—one who, having entered a religious order, forsakes it, and thereby becomes a slave of the Raja. 12. *Kṛita*, made, one who makes himself a slave for a definite term. 13. *Bhahta dása*, one who is a slave for his food. 14. *Vaṛavákṛita*, one who becomes a slave by marrying a female slave. 15. *Átmavikrayí*, one who sells himself. DÁSA also means, in some places, A fisherman. It is a suitable agnomen also for a man of the Ṣúdra caste, as *Chandra-dása*; but it is also borne with that of a divinity, in token of devotion by other superior castes, as *Vishṇu-dás*, *Siva-dás*, *Kṛishṇa-dás*, *Náráyan-dás*—the slave of *Vishṇu*, *Ṣiva*, *Kṛishṇa*, *Náráyan*, &c. In the days of Akbar it was borne by Rájputs, as *Raja Bhagwán Dás*, of the *Kachwáha* tribe. It is now seldom used by them, except for illegitimate offspring.

Dása, also *Dásari*, and *Dásayya*, Tel. Karn. (దాస, దాసరి, దాసయ్య) A mendicant of a class in the south of India, a worshipper of *Vishṇu*.

Dásiputra, S. (दासीपुत्रः) A son by a female slave.

Dásira, Karn. (ದಾಸಿರ) Son of a female slave.

DÁSA, H. (داسه) A reaping-hook.

DASSA, (?) H. Stones for building, from the Chunar quarries. —Ben. Reg. xxii. 1795, cl. 82.

DAST, DUST, H. (P. دست) lit., The hand; also, technically, money in hand, Tel. (దస్తు) The portion of revenue actually realised by some head-man, but not paid to government. Mar. (दस्त) Tax or assessment of the revenue.

Dastak, *Dustuk*, corruptly, *Dustuck*, H. (دستک, from P. *dast*, the hand, the signature) A passport, a permit. In the early days of the British government, a document authorizing the free transit of certain goods, and their exemption from custom dues, in favour of English traders. In later times, it applies more generally to a summons, a writ, or warrant; especially to a process served on a revenue defaulter, to compel him to pay any balance that may be due.

Dastakána, H. (دستکانه) Fee or remuneration to the officer who serves a writ or summons.

Dastak-i-ṯalb-i-zar, H. P. (دستک طلب زر) Warrant issued against defaulters of revenue, demanding payment, and subjecting them to the expense of maintaining the officer who serves it until the amount is paid.

Dastáwez, *Dustawez*, vernacularly, *Dastáwej* H. (P. دستاویز) *Dastáveju*, Tel. (దస్తావేజు) *Dasta-aiwaj*, Mar. (दस्तऐवज) A voucher, a document, any legal paper, a note of hand, a bond, a title-deed, and the like. Any thing in writing producible in evidence, or by which a person may be bound in law. A certificate of any kind.

Dastáwez-i-hibba, H. (from A. حبّه, a gift) A deed of gift or bequest.

Dastáwez-i-hiṣṣa, H. (from A. حصه, a share) A deed of partition.

Dast-ba-dast, H. (lit., hand with hand) Ready-money transaction.

Dast-báḳi, or *Dastu-báḳi*, H., Mar., Tel., Karn. (A. باقي, remainder) Balance in hand, money collected but not brought to account, whether referring to balances in the hands of the native collectors, or to collections made and embezzled by them.

Dast-bardárí, H. (from P. برداشتن, to lift up or off) Withdrawal of a suit from a court.

Dast-farosh, H. (from P. فروش, who sells) A pedlar, a hawker.

Dast-gardán, H. (from P. گردان, turning) A loan without any voucher.

Dastí, Mar. (from दस्त, a tax) Assessable, taxable, (land, &c.) H. (دستي) A present to native officials at the Dashará.

Dastíbád, Mar. (दस्तीबाद) Exempt from taxation.

Dast-jamá-kharch, H. Debit and credit account of collections. Account current.

Dast-kardan-i-daftar, corruptly, *Duskerdon-dufter*, H. Account of money in hand. Cash account of collections.

(From *dast*, as above, *kardan*, P., to make, and *daftar*, account).

Dastkhaṭ, sometimes abridged to *Daskhaṭ*, H. (P. دستخط, دسخط) Handwriting, signature.

Dast-láf, H. (from P. لاف, boasting) Handsel, first money received in the day.

Dast-muzd, H. (دستمزد) Wages, recompense. Revenue assessed upon the land.

DÁSTÁN, Mar. (दास्तान) A store, a granary.

DASTRAM, Tel. (దస్త్రం) The public document or record of a district or office. (? an error for *Daphtaramu*.)

DASTÚR, DUSTOOR, H. &c. (P. دستور, plur. دستورات, DASTURÁT) Custom, usage, regulation. A customary fee or perquisite. A commission or per-centage on the collections, allowed by the Mohammadan government to the Zamindars. A subdivision of a Sirkár, or aggregate of several adjacent Parganas (a sense in which it is now rarely, if ever, used). A high priest of the *Pársis*.

Dastúrí, H. &c. (دستوري) *Dasturí*, Ben. (দস্তুরী) A fee, a perquisite, a commission; especially a fee claimed by cashiers and servants on articles purchased, or on payments made.

Dastúr-i-ḳazá, H. (دستور قضع) Fees paid to a Ḳázi for putting his seal to a document.

Dastúr-al-âmal, *Dustoor-ool-umul*, H. (دستورالعمل, from A. عمل, business) Rule, regulation, rules of practice, prescriptive mode of carrying on public business. The orders and rules of government. A body of regulations agreed upon by any number of persons for their future guidance. A body of instructions and tables for the use of native revenue officers, under the Mohammadan Government. (Although professing to be copied from the original of *Akbar*, no two copies of the *Dastur-al-âmal* agree; owing in part, Mr. Elliot conjectures, to their having been made up, in various degrees of completeness, from another account left by the Kanungos, the *Âmal-dastúr*, in which orders superseding those of the *Dastúr-al-âmal* were registered).

Dastúr-paradeṣí, H. (from S. परदेशी, a foreigner) Fees formerly levied at Benares from pilgrims from countries beyond Hindustan.

DASTÚR, DUSTOOR, Mar. (दस्तूर) Handwriting, signature, the signature of a clerk or amanuensis. The form of an official paper; (besides the ordinary meanings as above).

Dastúr-khud, Mar. (from P. خود, self) Written with one's hand, in opposition to a paper written or signed by an amanuensis.

DÁTAN, Thug. A police guard. Any person found unexpectedly on a place selected for a murder.

DATTA, DUTTA, S. (past part. of दा, to give, *datus*) Given, (or used as a noun substantive) A son given in adoption; also, Gift, donation. (It is sometimes vernacularly changed to *Dat*, *Dut*).

Dattá, S. (fem. of दत्तः) Given (a girl) in marriage, betrothed.

Dattaka, or *Dattrima*, S. (from दत्त, given) An adopted son, one given by his parents to a person who legally adopts him. (Also with *Putra*, a son, as *Dattaputra*, *Dattakaputra*).

Dattátma, S. (from आत्मन्, self) The son self-given, one who offers himself of his own accord to be adopted.

Datta-homam, S. (from होम, burnt-offering) Oblations of clarified butter to fire, a ceremony performed at the adoption of a son, and by some held to be essential to the validity of the adoption.

Dattola, Mal. (ദത്തോല) A deed of adoption.

Dattápradániham, S. (from अप्रदानिक, not like a gift) Retraction or resumption of gifts, a head of Hindu law. (Also called *Dattasya-anapakarma*, The non-taking back of what has been given).

Dat-patra, Uriya. A deed of gift.

Datta, commonly *Dutt*, Ben. (দত্ত, from the S. दत्त) A subdivision of the writer caste. A name commonly borne by members of the caste, as, *Jaykrishn-Dutt*.

DATUÄ, Thug. Cry of the hare: if on the right, a bad omen, and travellers must be spared.

ḌAUL, DOUL, corruptly, DOWLE, H. (A. دول, state, condition) ḌAUL, Ben. and Mar. (ডৌল, डौल, the initial being changed to the cerebral *d*) also ḌAVULU, or ḌÁULU, Karn. (ಡವುಲು) Mode, manner, shape, appearance, form, estimate, valuation, a statement of the particulars of the gross revenue levied from an estate or district. An estimate of the amount of revenue which a district or estate may be expected to yield. In the west of India it is also used to signify a blank form ready to be filled up, and sometimes signed and sealed; or a blank return, of crimes when none have been committed, or of revenue when no collections have been made.

Daul-band-o-bast, H. (P. بند و بست, agreement) Statement or particulars of the arrangement made for the amount of revenue realizable from a district. Although applicable to the settlement between the revenue payers and the Government, it was formerly used in Bengal and the northern Sirkars to signify especially the rent-roll of estates, the gross receipts demanded by the Zamindars from their tenants or farmers, or the agreement made with them with reference to the amount payable to the government after making certain authorized allowances and deductions.

Daul-izáfat, H. (A. اضافت) Statement or estimate of additional sources of revenue.

Daul-jamá, H. (دول جمع) Particulars of the total revenue assessed upon a district or a village.

Daul-khazána, H. (خزانه, a treasury) A memorandum given to the Ryot by the native revenue-officer, specifying the sum due by him for the current instalments.

Daul-kistbandi, H. (كست بندي) Engagement to hold land upon payment of the revenue by fixed instalments.

Daul-náma, H. (P. نامه, a document) Extract from the general particulars of an estimated assessment, for the information of the person paying, supplied to him as a Paṭṭa, or lease: also termed *Daul-paṭṭa*.

Daul-patra, Mar. (S. पत्र, a leaf) A blank form, a blank return.

Daul-tashkhiṣ-i-band-o-bast, H. (from A. تشخيص, assessment) Particulars of the assessment of a village: one of the accounts formerly kept by the Kanungo.

Daul-wáṣil-báḳi, H. (واصل باقي) Statement of collections and balances.

Ḍavuludár, or *Ḍavuldár*, Karn. (ಡವುಲುದಾರ, ಡವುಲ್ದಾರ) An appraiser, one who estimates the amount and value of the crop.

Ḍavulu-hutturaḷi, Karn. (ಡವುಲುಹುಟ್ಟುವಳಿ) Estimate of the probable produce.

Ḍavulu-jamá-bandi, Karn. (ಡವುಲುಜಮಾಬಂದಿ) Estimated assessment of the revenue of a village.

Ḍavulupatti, Karn. (ಡವುಲುಪಟ್ಟಿ) An account of the estimate of each farmer's produce.

Ḍaul, or Ḍaula, H. (ڈول, ڈولا, डौल) The boundary of a field, a boundary mark, or mound of earth for that purpose.

Daundi, (?) Mar. A small drum beat by a public crier. A proclamation.

Daur, H. (ڈور) The strings attached to a basket to throw up water for irrigation.

Daurí, H. (ڈوري) The basket so used.

Ḍaur, Mar. (डौर) A small drum, shaped like an hour-glass.

Ḍaurí, Mar. (डौरी) A player on the *Ḍaur*.

Ḍaurí-gosávi, Mar. (डौरीगोसावी) The Gosain who beats the *Ḍaur*: he is one of the inferior village officers, or *Áluté*.

Daurá, Uriya (ଦଉରା, probably from H. *Dauṛ-ná*, to go about) Sessions, circuit.

Dauṛápa, H. (from ڈوڑنا, to run) A village runner or messenger.

Daurí, or Ḍaurí, H. (دوري, ڈوري) The rope that ties the bullocks together when treading out corn.

Davasa, Karn. (ದವಸ) Produce of the fields. Grain in general.

Davasadavanu, Karn. (ದವಸದವನು) A corn factor.

Dâwá, or Dâwí, H. (A. دعوي) as there is no equivalent for the A. ع in the Hindu dialects, this word and its derivatives are written with the simple long vowel, followed by *u* or *v*, व, pronounced as *w*, Ben. (দাওয়া) Mar. (दावा) Tel. (దావా) Karn. (ದಾವಾ, ದಾವೆ) A claim, a demand, a complaint, a suit, a prosecution. In the west of India it has come to signify a right, a just claim.

Dâwá, or *Dâwí-dár*, H. &c. (دعويدار) A complainant, a plaintiff, one who has a just claim or right.

Dâwí-ghalaṭ, A. (دعوي غلط) Plea of error; in Mohammadan law.

Dâwí-hinṣ, A. (دعوي حنث) Claim of penalty; in Mohammadan law.

Dâwat, H. (A. دعوت) Invitation, benediction, a feast, a banquet.

Dawám-band-o-bast, H. (دوام بند و بست, from دوام, perpetuity) Perpetual settlement.

Dáwan, Dawun, H. (داون) Threshing the corn by bullocks, attaching some six or eight in a row, and driving them round a central pivot over the corn strewed upon the floor.

Dáwaṇ, or Dáweṇ, Mar. (दावण, दावें) A rope fastened at both ends to which cattle are tied.

Ḍawará, Ḍaürá, or Ḍahwará, corruptly, Dowra, Mar. (डवरा or डव्हरा) A hole dug for water (in the dry bed of a river, or the like).

Dáya, S., but adopted in most dialects, at least in its legal sense, (दायं) Gift, donation. In Hindu law, Portion, inheritance, which may be of two kinds; without hindrance or impediment, absolute, direct, *Apratibandha*; and *Sapratibandha*, with obstruction, indirect, contingent, or presumptive.

Dayabhága, or *Dayavibhága*, S. (from भाग, a share, or विभाग, partition) Partition of inheritance. Title of law-books relating to the apportionment of heritable property amongst heirs.

Dáyáda, S. (from आदा, to take) An heir, whether direct, collateral, or contingent. A claimant.

Dayádopágata, S. (from उपागत, come or descended to) A slave received as inheritance.

Dáyají, Mar. (दायजी) An heir, a kinsman.

Dáya, Ben. (S. दाय) Charge, plaint, law-suit (besides the preceding senses).

Dáyak, Ben. (দায়ক) An accuser. Also, a donor, &c.

Deb, Ben., Uriya, &c. (দেব, the vernacular pronunciation of *Dev*, q. v.) A divinity, a deity, an idol, a king, a title of respect in addressing a person of rank, a cognomen appropriate to Bráhmans, as *Chandradeb*. (There being no *v* in Bengali, the *b* is substituted for it in this and all similar words).

Deb-díhí, Uriya. Enumeration of estates and villages.

Debhi-ásámi, or *Debhi-raiyat*, (?) In Behar and western Bengal said to mean, a resident cultivator, one having a right of property in the ground he cultivates.

Ḍehrí, H. (ڈیہری) A marshy soil. See *Ḍahr*.

Dejá, H. (دیجا, from S. देय, to be given) A portion, a dowry. Deja, or Dej, Mar. (देज) Money given at Ṣúdra marriages: given by the bridegroom to the father of the bride.

Dejú, H. (دیجو) Part of a dowry.

Ḍel, H. (ڈیل) Land ploughed and ready for the *Rabi* crop (Bundelkhand). Land prepared for cotton after being cropped for gram (Sagar).

Dená, H. &c. (from the v. دینا, to give, that which should be given, देना) Deṇe, Mar. (देणे) Money due, a debt.

Dená, or *Dene-dár*, or *Dendár*, H. &c. (دیندار, देनेदार, দেনদার) A debtor.

Dená-páná, H. (from دینا, and پانا, to obtain) Profit and loss, settlement of affairs.

Deṇeghene, Mar. (देणेघेणे) Money transactions, paying and receiving, lending and borrowing.

Den-hákimí, H. (حاکمی) The share of the government or Zamindar of the produce.

Deṇekarí, Mar. (देणेकरी) A debtor.

Den-len, H. (abbreviated from دینا and لینا, to take) Money dealings, paying and receiving, borrowing and lending, buying and selling, &c.

Den-mahr, H. &c. (from A. مہر, a portion) A dowry, a wife's portion.

Detághetá, Mar. (देताघेता) A regular dealer, one who is punctual in money transactions.

Ḍenda pronounced Ḍendo, Ḍendú, also Ḍenpa pronounced Ḍenpo, Ḍenpú, Ben. (ডেংদ, ডেংদূ, ডেংপ, ডেংপূ) Technical terms used in the measurement of land, implying relative position or bearing—thus, *Ḍenda* imports that there is a parcel of land between the lots last named and the next lot, lying a little to the south of the land which is immediately to the south. *Ḍendú* imports that which is a little to the north of the land immediately north. *Ḍenpa* is that which is a little to the west of the land immediately west. *Ḍenpú* is that which is a little to the west of that lying west. (The *o* of *Ḍendo* and *Ḍenpo* is only the common Bengali articulation of the short *a*).

Deo, H. &c. (دیو, for S. देव, Deva) A god, a divinity. See देव and its compounds.

Deo, or Deo Link, Thug. An exclamation from the look-out confederates, to signify that all is safe and the murder may be committed.

Ḍeola, H. (ڈیولہ) Mounds, high ground (East Oudh).

Ḍeoṛhá, H. (ڈیوڑھا) One-and-a-half: used to express interest in kind on grain at the rate of fifty per cent.

Ḍeoṛhi, H. (ڈیوڑھی) A threshold, a porch.

Ḍeorhi-dár, H. A porter.

Ḍerá, H. (ڈیرا, डेरा) A tent, any temporary dwelling, a Ryot's hut

Ḍeṛh, (ڈیڑھ) One-and-a-half.

Ḍeṛh-páo, H. A quarter-and-a-half, three-eighths.

Ḍeṛhpawá, A weight equal to three-eighths of a *sér*.

Deṛi, Ben. (দেড়ী) Ill-prepared; applied to rice when only half cleaned, or husked once and-a-half, it being usual to make the most ordinary kinds pass through the mortar three times.

Déṣa, S. (देश) vernacularly, Dés, H. (دیس) H. Mar. (देश) Ben. (দেশ) Tel. (దేశము) Karn. (ದೇಶ) Tam. (தேசம்) Mal. (ദേശം) as the palatal *s*, which is used by all, except the Hindustani, is slightly aspirated in Sanskrit, the aspiration is exaggerated in some of the dialects, and the word and its compounds are pronounced, as in Marathi, *Desh*: in that language, however, it also occurs, less correctly, but optionally, *Des*, with the dental sibilant (देस) Country, district, place, region. In different parts of India it is emphatically applied to particular districts, as constituting '*the*' county. In Rohilkhand it denotes the cleared villages on the borders of the *Tarái*. In the Himalayan regions it signifies the plains of Hindustan. With the Maraṭhas it especially designates the country between the Sahyádri and Bálaghát hills, the Karnatik and the Godaveri river. It also applies to any plain, open, or champaign country. In Malabar it likewise signifies, the proprietary possession of a village, and the rank derived from it.

Deṣáchár, H. S. (देशाचार) Local observance, custom of the country.

Deṣádhikárí, incorrectly, *Deṣadikár*, S. (देशाधिकारी) Chief, or governor, or superintendant of a given tract of country.

Deṣádhipati, S. (देशाधिपति) Chief or head ruler of a district or country. The representative of the Raja.

Deṣádhipatyam, S. &c. Office of governor, government of a district.

Deṣahásilu, or *Deṣ-háṣil*, Tel. (దేశహాశిలు) Inland or transit duties.

Deṣáí, corruptly, *Desae*, and *Dessye*, Mar. (देशाई, from S. देशाधिपति) The superintendant or ruler of a Pargana or province, the principal revenue officer of a district, under the native government: the office was hereditary, and frequently recompensed by grants of land, so that the *Deṣáí* often became a kind of petty chief in the south of India.

Deṣáí, Karn. (ದೇಶಾಯಿ) A chief man among the merchants of the Lingam sect.

Deṣáí-giri, Mar. (देशाईगिरि) Office of *Deṣáí*, emoluments or fees attached to it.

Deṣa-lehhaka, S. (लेखक, a writer) The accountant of a district.

Deṣánt, H. (from S. अन्त, end) The boundaries of a country or district.

Deṣántar, H. (from S. अन्तर, different) A foreign country, belonging to a different country, a foreigner.

Deṣastha, or *Deṣasth*, less correctly, *Deṣhasth*, Mar. (देशस्थ, from S. स्थ, who is, or belongs to) One of a tribe of Maraṭha Bráhmans, who consider themselves superior to the rest. In other parts of the South, a Maraṭha Bráhman in general.

Deṣáwar, H. (دیساور) A foreign or different country.

Deṣáwarí, H. (دیساوری) Goods, the manufacture of another country.

Deṣ-chaughalá, Mar. (देशचौघला) The assistant to the chief native revenue officer of a district.

Deṣ-hetá, Uriya (ଦେଶହେତା) Service lands of a village officer.

Deṣí, H. &c. (S. देशी) Belonging to, born or produced in a country, a native of a country.

Deṣiya, H. &c. (S. देशिय) Belonging to a country, native, local.

Deṣ-kávali, Tel. (దేశకావలి) Black mail, fees paid to prevent a village from being pillaged, expenses of guarding a district.

Deṣ-kuḷkaraṇí, Mar. (देशकुळकरणी) The district accountant, one who prepares a general account from the several statements of the village accountants.

Deṣ-kulkaraní-varttana, Karn. (S. वर्त्तन, subsistence) A per-centage formerly allowed to the district accountants on the collections of the revenue.

Deṣmukh, *Deṣmookh*, or *Deshmookh*, corruptly, *Desmook*, Mar. (देश, and S. मुख, chief) A hereditary native officer under the former governments, exercising chief police and revenue authority over a district, containing a certain number of villages, and responsible for the revenue: holding for compensation lands rent-free, and being entitled to the various fees and allowances, corresponding generally to the Zamindars of Bengal. Under the present administration the Deṣmukh is a district revenue officer who is expected to superintend the cultivation, and report on the state of the crops, to assist in the settlement of the annual revenue, and to give general aid to the collector and his establishment in the discharge of revenue duties.

Deṣmukhí, Mar. (देशमुखी) The office or duty of Deṣmukh. The fees or perquisites levied by him, or on his account.

Deṣ-nikálá, H. (دیس نکالا, from نکالنا, to send out) Exile, banishment.

Deṣpáṇḍe, or *Deṣpáṇḍyá*, corruptly, *Deṣpandeah*, *Despondeah*, *Despondee*, *Daispaundee*, Tel. (దేశపాండ్యా) Mar. (देशपांडे, देशपांड्या) The hereditary revenue accountant of a district or certain number of villages, holding office by hereditary tenure, and paid by lands. Under the British administration this officer is expected to keep a duplicate set of the public accounts, to superintend and cheek those of the village accountants, keep note of the collections, and see that they are regularly paid, to assist in the annual settlements, and give general information and aid to the collector and his subordinates. In some parts of Telingana the Deṣpaṇḍyá acts independently of the *Deṣmukh*, discharges the same duties, and enjoys the same privileges and emoluments.

Deṣapramáṇi, Mal. (ദേശപ്രമാണി) Head of a village: also, *Deṣamukhyasthan.*

Deṣ-tyág, H. (from the S. त्याग, abandoning) Emigration.

Deswál, H. (دیسوال) A tribe of Tagas, holding a few villages in Bhagpur.

Deṣwálá, or *Deṣwálí*, Mar., H. (देशवाला) A native of any country. In Bengal it is applied to a native of the north-west provinces.

Desawáḷi, Mal. (ദേശവാഴി) The head or ruler of a district. The same as *Desaï*, q. v.

Deswár, H. (دیسوار) Relating to a district or districts, a statement, assessment, &c.

DEULA, Ben Uriya (দেউলা, from the S. *Devala*) A temple.

Deula-karan, Uriya. Accountant of a temple.

DEVA, S., vernacularly pronounced whether singly or in many of its compounds, DEWA, DEV, DEB, or DEO, (देव, *Deus*) A god, a divinity, an idol. A man of high rank, a sovereign. A Bráhman. A cognomen suited to Bráhmans.

Devadána, S. (देवदानं) A gift or offering to a divinity.

Devadarṣana, S. (दर्शन, seeing) Visiting or paying reverence to an idol: particularly, in the south of India, such a visit paid by the bride and bridegroom, with their friends, at a particular period after their marriage.

Devadásí, H. &c. (from S. दासी, a female slave) A dancing girl attached to a temple.

Dévadáya, *Devadáyamu*, corruptly, *Devadow*, *Devadyen*, and *Devadoyam*, Karn. (ದೇವದಾಯ) Tel. (దేవదాయము, from S. दायं, a donation) Lands or allowances for the support of a temple, an endowment.

Devadevhárá, Mar. (देवदेव्हारा) Running about from idol to idol, importunate in prayers and supplications.

Devadharma, S. Religious offices, acts of supererogation in honour of a divinity.

Devadigár, Karn. (ದೇವಡಿಗಾರ) A man of a low caste, who performs menial offices in temples in the south of India.

Devaka, Mar. (from S. देवक, a deity, or a minor deity) The deities worshipped at marriages, and other essential ceremonies,

Devaha-gondala, Karn. &c. Decorating the household or other deities who are worshipped at the Sanskáras or essential ceremonies.

Devala, (from S. *Devaláya*) vernacularly in Ben., &c. *Deval* or *Dewal*, *Deul*, &c. (देवलं) A temple.

Devala, S. and Mar. (देवळ) *Devalan*, Karn. (ದೇವಲಣ) A Bráhman of an inferior order, who attends upon idols, and lives upon the offerings made to them.

Deválaya, S. (from आलय, an asylum) A temple, a shrine.

Devala-prajá, corruptly, *Dewul purchá*, Ben. (দেবলপ্রজা) One of three officers, so named, managing the temple of Jagannáth, under the Raja of Khurda, but appointed formerly by the collector.

Devala, or *Deválaya-divya*, (from S. *Divya*. दिव्य, an oath) Making an oath in a temple, or before an idol.

Devaḷí, Mar. (देवळी) A small building made for an idol only, not admitting worshippers. A frame or shrine within a temple.

Devamátrika, Mar. *Devamátruka*, Tel. (S. देवमातृक) Watered by rain; fields, lands, &c., as opposed to those dependent upon artificial irrigation.

Deváng, Karn. (from S. अङ्ग, the body) A Lingáyat, one who carries the emblem of Ṣiva on his person.

Devánga, Tel. (దేవాంగ) *Devángada*, Karn. (ದೇವಾಂಗದ) The title assumed by the caste of weavers in the Karnatic.

Devaráya-vaṭṭa, Karn. (ದೇವಾರಾಯವಟ್ಟ) A tax formerly levied in Mysore on the lands of rebellious subjects, rated at so much for each temple on them.

Devaskí, Mar. (देवस्की) Annual ceremonies in honour of village divinities.

Devasthala S. (देवस्थलं) Any sacred place or temple. In Malabar, a temple of the first order, dedicated to Ṣiva, as Trimurtti.

Devasthána, corruptly, *Deostan*, S. &c. (from S. स्थानं, a place) A temple. Revenue applied to the support of a temple.

Devasthápana, S. (देवस्थापनं) Setting up an idol in a temple, or in a room in a dwelling.

Devasthána-pudi-vaṭṭa, Karn. (ದೇವಸ್ಥಾನಪುದಿವಟ್ಟ) A tax of two-and-a-half fanams per *kándi* of land, levied upon the Ryots, on behalf of the temple or temples of a district (Mysore).

Devaswa, Mar. (देवस्व) Karn. (ದೇವಸ್ವ, from the S. स्वं, own) Property belonging to a temple. An endowment.

Devaṭhike, Mar. (देवठिके) A spot of land held rent-free in some villages by the Mukaddam or Mhar, in reward of his having established by ordeal the disputed boundaries of the village.

Devotthána, S., vernacularly, *Deotthán*, (from उत्थानं, rising) The eleventh day of the light half of Kártík, when Vishṇu is supposed to rise up from his four months' sleep.

The end of the rainy season. It is also the period at which the sugar-cane is first cut. See *Dithwan*.

Devhárá, Mar. (देव्हारा) The niche or shrine in which an idol is placed.

Deví, S., adopted in all the dialects, (देवी) Any goddess, but especially a name of Durgá, the wife of Ṣiva, *the* goddess.

Devotthápana, or *Deotthápan*, (from S. उत्थापनं, raising up) The ceremony of removing or dismissing deities at the end of the rite at which they were supposed to be present.

Devatá, S. (देवता) A divinity. a deity, an idol.

Devátara, Mal. (ദേവാതര) A temple dedicated to an inferior divinity.

Devatávuttára, Karn. (ದೇವತಾವುತ್ತಾರ) Lands allotted rent-free for the support of a temple.

Devatrá, or *Devottara*, S., vernacularly, *Deotar*, *Deotara*, Ben. and Uriya, *Debottar*, Karn. *Devatávuttára*, corruptly, *Deowuttur* and *Dewitter*, (S. देव, and त्र, what preserves, or उत्तर, what belongs to) Land rent-free, granted for the support of a temple or an idol.

Devatotthápana, Mar. (from S. उत्थापनं, raising up) Dismissing the deities who have been invited to a ceremony, upon its termination.

Dhabbu, Dhubboo, Mar. (धब्बु) A double pice.

Dhabdhabí, Mar. (धबधबी) A waterfall, the noise of falling water.

Dháḍ, Mar. (धाड, pronounced Dháṛ) An onset, an overwhelming multitude or crowd, whether of robbers and the like, or of locusts or other destructive creatures.

Dháḍá, pronounced Dháṛá, Hindi (धाडा) A robbery.

Dháḍá, H. (دھاڑا, S. धारा, a stream) Water falling from above, a waterfall (Rohilkhand).

Dhaḍá, Mar. (धडा) A weight of ten *sérs*, an accumulation of weight in a balance.

Ḍhaḍá, or Ḍhaḍḍi, Ḍhuḍḍa, Ḍhuḍḍee, H. (ڈھڈا, ڈھڈي) A term applied to low ground (Rohilkhand).

Dhágá, Thug. Eliciting the intentions of travellers. Negociation with persons in authority for protection or release from arrest.

Dhágal, Thug. Papers.

Dhagsa, Thug. Hilly or woody country.

Dháhima, H. (دھاهمه, धाहिमा) A tribe of Rájputs, formerly lords of Biana, one of the thirty-six royal races. There are also Dháhima Játs and Ahírs

Dhai-giyá, Hindi (धैगिया, from गिया, gone) Washed away by inundation (Puraniya).

Dhajá, Dhujá, H. (دھجا, S. ध्वज:) A flag. A pole with a strip of cloth tied to the end of it, and erected sometimes near a place of worship, in satisfaction of a vow. Also, a flag hoisted on some lofty situation on the last day of *Ásharh*, called the *Pawan-paríkshá*, trial of the wind; as, from the direction of the wind on the sunset of that day, as shewn by the flag, the people draw their auguries of the quantity of rain likely to fall in the ensuing rainy season. If the wind blows from the west, it is said that there will be *Banya ká páni*, grain-dealers' water—the season will be dry: if a little more round, it is *Kumhár ká páni*, potter's water, as they do not like much wet: if from the north, moderate weather may be expected, and it is called *Málí ká páni*, gardener's water: and if from the east, copious rains are expected, called *Dhobí ká páni*, washerman's water, *i. e.* abundant rain.

Ḍhak, Ḍhuk, Ben. (ঢক) A weight.

Ḍhák, Ḍháká, or Ḍhákhá, corruptly, Dawk, H. (ڈھاک, ڈھاکا, ڈھاکھا) A tree common in India (Butea frondosa), also called Palása, the products of which are very useful. The bark yields an astringent exudation, called *Palásgond*, or Bengal kino; a strong rope, called Bukel, is made from the root; the wood is used for coating wells, and is valued as fuel for sacrificial fire; the flowers are of a bright red colour, and yield a yellow or orange dye. In Bengal, and in and along the hills, it is a good-sized tree; but in the plains of the north-west it is of stunted growth, and comes to signify any dwarf shrubs or brushwood. *Dhák-jangal*, is any wilderness of bushes.

Dhák, Hindi (धाक) Arable land in a ravine (Puraniya).

Dhákara, H. (دھاکره) A tribe of Rájputs, scattered over the country, from the south bank of the Jumna about Agra and Mathura, across the Doab to Rohilkhand.

Dhákatá, or Dhákuṭá-paṇa, corruptly, Dháktepuna, Mar. (धाकटापण, धाकुटापण) Inferiority in stature, age, &c., lesserness. Claim to inheritance, or other rights of the junior branches of a family.

Dhakata, or *Dháhatí*, incorrectly, *Dhaktí*, *-khás*, Mar. The third or inferior class of village officers. See *Baluta*.

Ḍhákí, Ben. (ঢাকী) A deduction of rent allowed to tenants by the Zamindar.

Dhal, Hindi (दल) An influx of water coming down a river from the hills (Puraniya).

Dhála, H. (ڈھالہ) Collections from the individual villagers, to cover village expenses in Rohilkhand, usually at the rate of one *ana* in a rupee, or one *sér* of grain per maund. In the Central and Lower Doab it is generally used with *Jamâ*, as *Jamâ-dhála*, and signifies a particular tenure. See *Dhár-báchh*. In this sense it occurs also *Dála*, with the initial unaspirated.

Ḍhalaït, H. &c. (ڈھلایت, probably from *Ḍhál*, a shield) An armed attendant or peon.

Dhalál, Thug. Spirit vender.

Dhálbhol, H. (ڈھالبول) Complete transfer by sale (Kamaon).

Dhalphor, (?) H. A class of the *Kúrmí*, or great agricultural tribe in Hindustan (clod piercers).

Ḍhalwáṇ, Hindi (ढलवां) The slope of the inclined plane down which the oxen descend from a well.

Dhamán, H. (?) Payment of rent in kind: applied also to lands or a village when the revenue is so paid.

Dhámí, H. (دھامي, plur. *Dhámián*) A follower of Prán-náth, a Hindu reformer, who flourished in the seventeenth century in Bundelkhand.

Dhamkaï, H. &c. (from H. دھمکانا, or Ben. धमका, to threaten) Reprimand, reproof, threatening.

Dhamháibá, Ben. Uriya (ଧମକାଇବା) Intimidation.

Dhamoni-ki-manj, Thug. Fighting of cats, a bad omen.

Dhámri, Thug. Metal utensils.

Dhamuká, Tel. (ధముకా) A road made with gravel. A ridge or bank passing across water.

Dhán, corruptly, **Daun**, H. &c. (دھان, from the S. धान्य) Grain in general, but especially applied to the rice plant, or to rice in the husk, of which there are a great number of varieties, bearing different names. Sixty-six different appellations are enumerated by Mr. Elliot as known in the western provinces; and he states that the variety is still greater in Bengal and Bahar. In what respects they differ, except in name, does not appear.

Dhán, or *Dhána-bandi*, corruptly, *Danabundy*, H. (دھانہ بندي) Estimate of the extent of the crops of rice or other grain.

Dhanhá, *Dhunha*, H. (دھنہا, from धान) A rice cultivator; rice-bearing, as a field, &c.

Dhání, H. (دھاني) A good soil, fit for grain.

Dhanhar, *Dhunkur*, H. (دھنکر, abridged from دھان, धंकड) A stiff soil, bearing rice if rain has fallen plentifully. A field cropped with rice in the previous season.

Dhán-káti, H. The season for cutting rice.

Dhán-madi, Tel. (ధానమడి) A rice field.

Dhant'hiá, *Dhunteá*, (دھنتھیا) A field which has been reaped for rice (Rohilkhand).

Dhánwáiyá, H. (دھانوایا) A thresher or a seller of rice.

Dhan, **Dhun**, H. &c. (دھن, S. धनं) Wealth, property. A loan. The cattle of a village.

Dhaní, and *Dhanik*, H. &c. (S. धनी, धनिक) One having property, a master, an owner: also, a lender, a creditor.

Dhaní-jog, Mar. (धनीजोग, from S. *Yogya*, योग्य, fit, proper) Payable to the purchaser, a bill, &c., as distinguishable from that which is payable to some other, *Ṣahájog* (शहाजोग).

Dhanteras, Mar. (धनतेरस) The thirteenth of the dark half of Aswin, when the bankers worship money.

Dhána, Mal. (ധാന) Fried barley or rice.

Dhána, H. (دھانہ) The Gond portion of a village, which is always separate from the rest (Ságar).

Dhána, Uriya (ଧାନ, probably vernacular corruption of **Dána**, a grain, a seed) A measure of weight for the precious metals, four *dhánas* (grains) equal to one *ratti*.

Dhának, Ben. (धानक) A copper coin, about the value of two-pence.

Dhandhol, Thug. Any man employed in the pursuit of Thugs.

Ḍhanḍhoï, **Ḍhunḍhoee**, H. (ڈھنڈھوي) The scum of the sugar-cane juice when boiling (Dehli).

Ḍhanḍhorá, **Ḍhunḍhorá**, corruptly, **Dhandero**, H. (ڈھنڈھورا, from S. ढुण्ढ, to search) Proclamation by beat of drum.

Ḍhandhoria, H. A crier.

Dhanga, (?) Any hiding-place of robbers and marauders; three such were especially notorious in Katiwar—one in the neighbourhood of Chutíla, one about twenty *kos* to the southward, and the third in the forest of Chachai.

Dhángar or **Dhangar**, **Dhungur**, H. &c. (دھانگر, دھنگر) A tribe of people inhabiting the hill country in Rámgarh and Chota-nagpur: some of them come periodically into the plains for employment, and are engaged as labourers and scavengers. In the south of India, **Dhangar** is generally applied to the caste of shepherds and weavers of wool. In Telingana, they are also cultivators, and are divided into twelve tribes, who do not eat together, nor intermarry.

Dhangar-mág, Mar. (from माग, a loom) The loom of a woollen weaver.

Dhangar-mániyam, Karn. (ధంగరమాణియం) Taxes on shepherds. Charge for pasturage.

Dhangi, Thug. A brass pot.

Dhantera, Thug. An ass, whose braying is an omen highly esteemed, whether for good or evil.

Dhánya, H., but in all the dialects also: (S. धान्यं) Grain in general, especially rice, but nine principal kinds are enumerated under this title; small quantities of each of which are sometimes given to Bráhmans at festivals: the donation is called the *Nava-dhánya-dánam*.

Dhányádáyam, Tam. (S. தானியாதாயம்) Receipt of revenue, &c., in grain.

Dhányadulu, Tel. (plur. of ధాన్యదులు) All sorts of grain.

Dhánya-sáramu, Tel. &c. (ధాన్యసారము) Grain after threshing (from S. सार, substance).

Dhányavarddhanam, Mal. (ധാന്യവൎദ്ധനം, from S. धान्य, and वर्द्धनं, increasing) Lending grain at interest, receiving a usurious return for seed corn supplied to the cultivators.

Dhánya-vruddhi, Mal. (ധാന്യവൃദ്ധി, from S. वृद्धि, increase) First-fruits, or the first sheaf reaped.

Dhánuk, H. (دهانوك, from S. *Dhanush*, a bow) The name of a low tribe in the upper provinces, but most numerous in Bahar: they follow the practice of fowlers and archers, and feed upon their booty: they are also employed as house guards, and in various menial offices, and sometimes become slaves. The females are in request as midwives. They are said to be divided into seven branches, between whom there is no social intercourse.—Elliot. According to Buchanan, however, the Dhánuks of Bahar, Bhagalpur, and Puraniya are a pure agricultural tribe, perhaps not essentially different from Kurmis: many of them, however, are agricultural slaves. —Western India, i. 167.

Dhanus, or Dhanush, vernacularly, Dhanu and Dhanuk, S. (धनुस, धनुष) A bow, a bow used for cleaning cotton. A land measure of four cubits.

Dhanur-vidyá, S. (धनुष, the final being changed to *r* before certain consonants, and विद्या, knowledge) The science of archery, literally, but comprehending the whole of military science, the art of war: also *Dhanu-veda* and *Dhanur-sástram*.

Dháp, H. (دهاپ) One-fourth of a *kos*: a pass, a ghat: an expanse of low ground.

Dhapia, *Dhupea*, H. (دهپيا, from S. *Dháva*, running) A short kos, a distance which a man may run without stopping to take breath.

Ḍhár, H. (ڈهار) A heap of corn (Benares).

Dhár, H. (دهار) A hollow tree inserted in the mouth of wells in the Taráí, to prevent their falling in.

Dhár, or Dhárá, H. &c. (دهار, دهارا) A stream, a channel, a flow of water.

Dhár, Hindi (धार) A ravine with or without water.

Dhár, or Dhárá, H. &c. (دهار, دهارا) Settled assessment, fixed or customary rate, a proportionate share or charge. The same tenure as *Dhárbachh*, q. v. Also, Mar. Dháre (धारे).

Dhár, Ben. (ধার) A loan, a debt: an edge, a limit, a boundary.

Dharáṭ, or *Dhartta*, (?) Ben. (ধরট) A loan, a sum deducted from the amount lent, by the lender, as a bonus.

Dharttá, Ben. (ধর্ত্তা) A debtor.

Dhárá, Thug. Vessels of metal.

Dhará, Dhura, Ben. Uriya (ধরা, from S. धर, having, holding) Personal restraint, arrest, apprehension of a criminal.

Dhárá, incorrectly, Dhur, Ben. Mar. (ধারা, धारा) Usage, practice, custom, customary or current price, rate, or assessment, tax on gardens and plantations.

Dhárá-chadáo, Tel. (?) The former custom of making the cultivators pay a premium on the market price for the share of the crop relinquished by the government.

Dhárá-kari, or *Dháre-kari*, Mar. (from S. कर, who makes) A tenant, one who pays the government assessment, one who is possessed of fixed rates or fees. The permanent occupant of a farm, one who cannot be dispossessed as long as he pays his revenue, and who may abandon his farm for a time without losing the right of resumption on paying a compensation to the temporary occupier.

Dhárá-pramáṇ, Uriya. According to custom.

Dharauki, Dhuroukee, H. (دهروكي) Ascertaining by guess.

Dharáuná, H. (دهراونا) A woman married a second time. In case of a dispute, the quantity of land in cultivation (East Oudh).

Dharáwaṭ, H. (دهراوت) Land ascertained and apportioned by estimate, not measured (Benares).

Dharáwatu, Tel. (ధరావతు) A deposit, an instalment of revenue in advance; also read *Dharávati*, and, incorrectly, *Dharotí*.

Dhaṛá, Mar. (धडा) A weight of ten *sérs*, the quantity weighed by it, a peculiar mode of multiplying weights.

Dharai, Thug. Share assigned to the leaders of an expedition, usually one article in ten, or one ana in the rupee on the value.

Ḍharakhá, or **Ḍharalá**, H. (ڈھرکھا, ڈھرلا) A scarecrow.

Dháraṇ, Mar. (धारण) Rate, current or market price.

Dharaṇ, Mar. (धरण, from the S. धरणं, holding, confining) A dam, a bank across a river: a weight of twenty-four gunja seeds: a sum of nine anas.

Dharband, Mar. (धरबंद) A law, a rule, a regulation.

Dhárbáchh, H. (دھارباچھ) Any even or general distribution of charge or rate, &c., especially that which is levied from the individual holders of a coparcenary estate, to make good any deficiency in the produce of land held in common, or let to cultivators. In the central part of the north-west provinces the term denotes an imperfect Paṭṭidárí tenure, in which part of the village land is held in common and part in severalty. The profits of the former are first applied to the payment of the government assessment and the village charges; and any deficit is made good by the proprietors of the latter, in proportion to their holdings.

Dharbigár, Mar. (from S. धर, seizing, and *bigár*, forced labourer) Pressing people for carrying burthens.

Dhardho, Thug. A river.

Dhár-dhúra, H. (دھاردھورہ) The boundary formed by a stream. (From *dhár* or *dhárá*, a stream, and *dhura*, a boundary).

Dháre-bandi, Mar. (धारेबन्दि) (Land) held on condition of paying a part of the produce: settling the portion to be given.

Dháre-ehsán, Mar. (धारेएहसान, from P. احسان, easy, light) A mitigated assessment, a stipulation favourable to the cultivators.

Dháre-ehsání, Mar. (धारेएहसानी) Land lightly assessed.

Dháre-máp, Mar. (from माप, measure) The measure by which the government share is received in kind.

Dhaṛí, **Dhuṛee**, H. (دھڑی) A measure of five *sérs*.

Dharíchá, H. (دھریچا) The second husband of a widow, among the lower classes of the Hindus.

Dharingá, H. (دھرنگا) A kind of rice (Rohilkhand).

Dharma, more correctly, **Dharmma**, but in practice commonly dropping the second *m*, S., used in all dialects, but commonly corrupted to **Dharm** or **Dharam**, **Dhurm**, **Dhurum**, incorrectly, **Durum**, (S. धर्म्म, from धृ, to hold, that which keeps man in the right path) Law, virtue, legal or moral duty.

Dharmádhikár, or *kárí*, S. &c. (from अधिकार, who presides over) A judge, a magistrate: a superior over Bráhmans invested with power to investigate and chastise breaches of custom, violations of caste, and the like.

Dharmádhikaraṇa, S. (from अधिकरण, superintendence) A court of justice. The duty of a magistrate or judge.

Dharma-dána, or *Dharmadáyam*, S. &c., vernacularly, *Dharmadáo*, corruptly, *Dhurmadow*, (from दान or दाय, donation) An endowment, grant of food, or lands, or funds, for religious or charitable purposes.

Dharma, or *Dharm-dás*, S. &c. (from दास, a slave) An attendant upon a temple.

Dharma-karttá, S. &c. (from कर्त्ता, who makes) A judge, a magistrate. In the south of India, the manager of a temple, and appropriator of the benefits derived from it.

Dharma-kárya, S. &c. (from कार्य्य, an act) Any good or pious work, building a temple, digging a tank, &c.

Dharma-khátenַ, Mar. (धर्म्मखातें, from P. خط, a writing) The head of accounts under which pious or charitable gifts are entered.

Dharmma-kílam, Mal. (ധര്മ്മകിലം) A jurisdiction, a district under the same legal administration.

Dharma-patní, S. &c. (from पत्नी, a wife) A wife who has been married according to the legal forms, and is of the same caste as her husband.

Dharma-patra, or *Dharm-patra*, S. (from पत्र, a leaf) A deed of gift or endowment for religious or pious purposes.

Dharma-poï, or *-povaï*, Mar. (धर्म्मपोई, -पोवई) Giving water and food to wayfarers or paupers. A booth or shed where they are given.

Dharma-putra, S. &c. (from पुत्र, a son) A legitimate or adopted son, a person appointed by a widow or by the caste of one deceased to act as a son in performing the obsequial ceremonies: as applied to Europeans, it signifies god-son; as *Dharm-pitá*, or *Dharm-báp*, or *Dharm-má*, signify godfather or godmother.

Dharmárth, S. &c. (from अर्थ, object) Any thing given for charitable or pious purposes.

Dharma, or *Dharm-ṣálá*, S. &c. (from शाला, a hall) A building for any legal or pious purpose, as a court of justice, a place where religious persons assemble, a place of accommodation for travellers and pilgrims, or for the poor and sick, a *Serái*, an hospital, a monastery, a temple.

Dharma-sabhá, S. &c. (from सभा, an assembly) The word has much the same meanings as the preceding; but in Bengal it applies to an association of influential Hindus, to uphold their religion.

Dharma-śástra, S. (from शास्त्र, a scripture) A work on the whole body, or on particular subjects of Hindu law. The collective writings of the Hindus on their laws and institutions. The Hindu code.

Dharmátar, more properly, perhaps, *Dharmottar*, H. (دهرماتر) A charitable grant, an endowment.

Dharmávatár, S. &c. (from अवतार, descent from heaven, incarnation) A term addressed by Hindus to a respectable person, sometimes in the way of flattery to Europeans.

Dharmopádhyáya, or *Dharmopádhyáyika*, S. (from उपाध्यायः, a teacher) A Bráhman supposed to be acquainted with the law, and exercising in some places in the Maraṭha country the functions of censor and judge of offences against the laws, especially of caste, and receiving perquisites and fees in that capacity.

DHARNÁ, or DHARṆÉ, H., Ben., Mar., &c. (دهرنا, धरना, धरणे, from the S. धरणं) Sitting at the door of a house or tent, to compel payment of a debt due by a debtor, or of arrears owing by a public officer or prince. The person so sitting observes a strict fast, and as long as he so sits the person from whom he demands payment is obliged to fast also, and abstain from his usual occupations and amusements; as, if the suitor were to perish, the consequences of the sin would fall upon him. Originally the person sitting in Dharná was necessarily a Bráhman, either on his own behalf or that of another, and the sin of Bráhmanicide would be incurred by his death. The practice is not restricted to Bráhmans; but is altogether obsolete in the Company's provinces, having been made a punishable offence by Ben. Reg. vii. 1820. In some parts of the south of India a similar practice is observed, to extort a boon, or the promise of one, from an idol, by sitting permanently at the door of a temple until the attendant priests assure the person his desire will be granted. *Dharne*, in Mar., also means an armed party sent to seize an offender.

DHAROHAR, H. (دهروهر, from *Dharná*, to place) A deposit, an instalment.

DHAROHAR, Thug. Strangling.

DHARTA, H. (دهرتا) Discount and commission. Increase of demand upon land: also, an item of account usual with bankers, in addition to a sum actually lent, generally about three per cent. (Ságar).

DHARTÍ, H. (دهرتي, from S. धरित्री) The earth, land, soil.

DHAṚWÁI, H. (دهڑواي) The village officer or accountant who weighs grain. (From *Dhaṛi*, a weight of five *sérs*, which is considered his perquisite at the harvest).

ḌHASÁNI, Ben. (ঢসানি) Falling in of the banks of a pond or river.

DHASÁN, DHUSAN, DHASÁO, DHASAM, H. (دهسان, &c.) A swamp, a quagmire. (From *Dhasná*, دهسنا, to sink).

DHATÚRÁ, H. &c. (دهتورا, S. धुस्तुर) A plant (Datura fastuosa), the seeds of which have strong narcotic properties, and are often given with sweetmeats, to stupify previous to robbery.

DHÁTÁ, S. &c. (धाता) The tenth year of the cycle.

DHÁTKAR, Hindi (धातकर) A pound or pen for cattle, or the rails of it (Puraniya).

DHAUL, or DHAUR, H. (دهول, دهور) A kind of sugar-cane (Rohilkhand).

DHAULÁNI, Thug. One of the sects of the Thugs.

ḌHAUḶ, Mar. (ढौळ) An official paper, sealed and signed ready to have the blanks in it filled up when required.

DHAURÍ, H. (دهوري, for *Adhauri*, a half) A bull's hide cut in two pieces (Dehli).

DHAVÁ, Hindi (धवा) The best kind of grass for thatching.

DHÁWAṚ, Mar. (धावड) Name of a tribe, smelters of iron.

ḌHE, H. (ڈهي, ढे) A chief but recent subdivision of the Jat tribe in the north-west provinces.

ḌHELÁ, or ḌELÁ, H. (ڈهيلا, ढेल, डेला) A clod of earth: also a small piece of clay made into a pellet, and cast at birds from a sling, by a person stationed to protect the crop.

DHEN, H. &c. (دهين, S. धेनुः) A milch cow.

ḌHENKÁ, or ḌHENKÍ, H., Ben. (ڈهينكا, ڈهينكي, ঢেঁকী) A kind of pestle or pedal projecting from the end of a lever, one end of which being pressed down by a weight, or by the foot, the other falls of its own weight when the pressure is withdrawn. It is used to clean rice or tobacco, to pound brick-dust, &c.

DHENKAYÁ, Ben. (ধেঁকযা) A debtor, a creditor.

ḌHENKLÍ, H. (ڈهينكلي, ढेंकली) A machine for raising water, a horizontal lever resting on an upright, having a weight at one end and a string pulled by a man with a bucket or water-jar attached to it at the other. The word is provincially corrupted into ḌHEKLI, ḌHUKLI, ḌHIKLÍ, and ḌHEOKAL.

Ḍhelí, Mar. (ढेली) Having the impression worn; a coin.

Ḍheṇri, H. (ڈهینري) A seed vessel, a capsule.

Ḍhepá, Hindi (ढेपा) **Ḍhep**, or **Ḍheṇp**, Mar. (ढेप, ढेंप) A clod of earth, any large lump. Arable land. A piece of ground assessed in the lump, or according to the quantity of grain it is estimated to yield, without reference to its area.

Ḍheṇppáhaṇi, Mar. (ढेंपपाहणी) Inspection or survey of arable land.

Ḍhepálí, Mar. (ढेपाली) A hole in the ground into which the boiled juice of the sugar-cane is poured to harden and form into lumps.

Ḍheṛ, or **Ḍheḍ**, corruptly, **Dhair**, **Dheyr**, Mar. (धेड) **Ḍheṛh**, H. (ढेढ) **Dheda**, **Dheḍ**, or **Dher**, Guz. (ઢેડ, ઢેર) A man of a low caste, employed as a watchman and messenger in the village establishments. In the Dahkin especially, commonly but incorrectly identified with the Mahár, and properly a worker in leather and hides. In some places he performs the duty of scavenger. In the Ságar territory the *Ḍheṛs* eat dead animals, clean the skins, and sell them to the *Chamárs*. In Kanara, they are labourers on the soil, and in a very large proportion are slaves, the property of individuals, saleable with or without the land on which they work: they are very numerous, and are distinguished into twelve subdivisions, who do not intermarry. They are rare in the north-west provinces.

Ḍherwáṛo, Guz. (ઢેડવાડો) A place set apart for the huts of the *Ḍheṛs*.

Ḍher, or **Ḍherí**, H. (ڈهیر, ڈهیري) A heap, a parcel. In the upper provinces, a piece or share of landed property in a joint-tenancy village, a subdivision of a Pattí, or a Taraf. In the Upper Doab, *Ḍherí* is applied to a sharer, especially in landed property, one who has a lot or heap.

Ḍheridár, H. The holder of a *Ḍheri*, or subdivision of joint-tenancy lands.

Ḍherá, Ben. (ঢেরা) A mark made by a person who cannot write.

Dheri, Thug. A sarai, a village.

Dhí, or **Dhíh**, Hindi (धी, धीह) The site of a village, whether occupied or deserted (Puraniya).

Dhíaurí, Hindi (धीऔरी) Ground-rent for the land on which the houses stand of those who do not cultivate village lands.

Dhíṣáa, Hindi (धीशाख) Lands on the site of a deserted village; much valued.

Ḍhí, **Ḍhee**, H. (ڈهي) The high bank of a river (Ságar).

Ḍhíhá, *Ḍheehá*, H. (ڈهیہا) Rising ground, mounds. Also *Díha*.

Ḍhíkadi, Guz. (ઢીકડી) A contrivance for drawing water from the bed of a river.

Dhilka, Thug. A *paisa*.

Dhima, Thug. The belly. Dahkini Thug. Goats or sheep.

Dhímar, H. (دهیمر, S. *Dhívara*, धीवर:) A fisherman by caste and occupation. They are, properly speaking, a branch of the Kahár or Bearer caste, but are sometimes considered offshoots of the Mallas or Boatmen.

Dhimatu, Tel. (ధిమతు) A notice, a memorandum, a document given before a lease is finally granted, a private agreement. (Probably a vernacular form and local use of *Dimmat*, q. v.)

Dhingá, or **Dhinká**, H. (دهنگا, دهنکا) A small kind of rake or pitchfork with curved prongs.

Dhingar, (?) Ben. An agricultural slave (Puraniya).

Dhínkhar, H. (دهینکهر) A bundle of thorns tied together and drawn by bullocks, either as a harrow, or to beat out ears of corn.

Ḍhirhor, H. (ڈهرهور) A tribe of inferior Ahírs in Benares and Gorakhpur.

Dhírná, Thug. The belly.

Dhoáṭ, Ben. (ধোআট) Alluvial soil: what has been washed down by the rains.

Dhobí, H. (دهوبي) A washerman in general. The washerman of a village. As forming a caste, various subdivisions are recognised, which do not eat, drink, or marry together. There are seven such in the north-west provinces, but they differ, or are at least differently named in different provinces.

Dhobi-hardi, (perhaps for *har*, every, *din*, a day) Mar. (?) A right of having a garment washed daily by the village washerman claimed by the *Pátíl*.

Dhoï, H. (دهوي, from دهونا, to wash) lit. Washings, applied in the opium department to refuse opium. Soaked pulse, a mash. In Cuttack, (ଧୋଇ) Inundation.

Dhoka, H. (دهوکا) A grain measure, equal to five *dabiás* of the khárif crop. Ten *dhokas* make a *bojh*, or load.

Ḍhoka, or **Ḍhúka**, **Ḍhooka**, H. (ڈهوکا) Small stones, of irregular shape and inferior quality, allowed to be extracted from the Chunar quarries by poor people for sale—Ben. Reg. xxii. 1795, cl. 82.

Dhokar, Thug. A dog. A man who seizes Thugs.

Dhokhá, H. (ڈھوکھا) A scarecrow.

Ḍholáï, or **Ḍholán**, Ben. Uriya (ঢোলাই, ঢোলান, but vernacular corruption of H. ڈولا, S. दोलन, swinging) Transport of goods, transit; or the charge for conveyance from one place to another.

Dholia, Thug. An old woman.

Dhonchá, H. (ڈھونچا) Four-and-a-half: a term used in tables of the multiplication of fractions used by the native surveyors in reducing their linear measurements to *bíghas*. The several terms are thus specified by Mr. Elliot:— *Deoṛhá*, (डेवढा) $=1\frac{1}{2}$; *Dhamá*, (धमा) $=2\frac{1}{2}$; *Hontá*, (होंटा) $=3\frac{1}{2}$; *Dhonchá*, $=4\frac{1}{2}$; *Ponchá*, (पोंचा) $=5\frac{1}{2}$; *Khonchá*, (खोंचा) $=6\frac{1}{2}$; *Satonchá*, (सतोंचा) $=7\frac{1}{2}$. The size of the fields seldom requires the specification to proceed further.

Dhonḍáḷ, Mar. (धोंडाळ, from धोंडा, a stone) Stony, abounding with stones: applied to one kind of black soil, that which has stones in it, and which is therefore more retentive of water, and is the most esteemed for crops depending on the rains for irrigation.

Dhondá, **Dhondí**, H. (ڈھونڈا, ڈھونڈي) A grass that grows in rice fields, and sometimes chokes the crop.

Ḍhondh, H. (ڈھونڈھ) A capsule, a seed vessel, especially of the poppy, cotton, or gram.

Dhonkí, Thug. A policeman or guard.

Dhopá, Ben. (ধোপা) A washerman.

Ḍhor, Mar. Guz. (ढोर) The general name of horned cattle, or bulls, cows, and buffaloes. A man of a low caste, a worker in leather. (Another form, perhaps, of *Ḍheṛ*).

Ḍhorvero, Guz. (ઢોરવેરો) A tax on cattle.

Ḍhora, H. (ڈھورہ) An insect very destructive to the Cicer arietinum. A mound of earth raised by the side of a ditch.

Dhoṭar, Hindi (धोटर) Cultivation carried on by ploughmen from a distant village, finding their own ploughs and bullocks, and erecting a temporary residence (Puraniya).

Dhruva, S. (ध्रुव:) The north pole: thence, fixed, stationary, (in general).

Dhruva-kavulu, Tel. (ధ్రువకవులు) A permanent lease.

Dhruva-pairu, Tel. (ధ్రువపైరు) Garden produce, permanent crop. A tax levied on garden trees after a due period of their plantation.

Dhuánsa, Thug. Dry tobacco.

Ḍhuä, or **Ḍhuhá**, **Dhooa**, **Dhooha**, H. (ڈھوا, ڈھوھا) A mound of earth raised as a boundary, most usually about four feet high, and placed round the limits of each township at the distance of about 200 yards from each other.

Ḍhuh, **Ḍhooh**, H. (ڈھوہ) Elevated ground in the midst of ravines (Central Doab).

Dhúhá, **Dhoohá**, H. (ڈھوھا) A scarecrow. See also *Dhuä*.

Ḍhukli, **Ḍhooklee**, H. (ڈھکلي) A machine for raising water. See *Dhenkli*.

Dhul, Ben. (ধুল) A measure of land, a *kátá*, or the 20th of a *bíghá*.

Dhúlídhoyá, H. (ڈھولي ڈھويا) A washer of refuse or dust. (From the S. धुली, dust).

Dhuligutta, Tel. (ధులిగుత్త) A rent levied on a field before any seed is sown, a dust rent.

Dhúḷbáph, Mar. (धूळबाफ) Sowing grain in the dust, *i.e.* before the rains have begun, or immediately afterwards, before the ground is moist.

Ḍhunḍi, **Ḍhoondee**, H. (ڈھونڈي) The pod of gram, Cicer arietinum (Benares).

Dhuniá, H. (ڈھنیا) A cotton comber or carder.

Dhunká, or **Dhunrá**, H. (ڈھونکا, ڈھونرا, from ڈھون, smoke) The chimney of a sugar-cane mill.

Dhúpa, S. &c. (धूप:) Incense, the vapours of any fragrant gum or resin burnt slowly.

Dhúr, **Dhoor**, H. (ڈھور) A measure of land, the twentieth of a *biswá*.

Dhúrkí, (ڈھورکي) The twentieth part of a *dhúr*.

Dhura, **Dhoora**, H. (ڈھرہ) or **Dhúrá**, Mar. (?) A boundary, the border or limits of a village.

Dhuriyá, (?) H. A ploughman who works two days on the field of one who hires him, and one on his own (Bahar).

Dhúrkaṭ, H. (ڈھورکٹ) An advance of rent paid by the cultivators to the Zamindars in the months of Jyeshth and Áshárh (Benares).

Dhurphoṛyá, Mar. (धुरफोड्या) A quarryman, a stone-breaker by caste and occupation.

Dhus, **Dhoos**, H. (ڈھس) A kind of soil of mixed quality. Sloping ground. Sterile sandy eminences.

Dhwáṛí, Mar. (ध्वाडी) The brother's daughter of a man, the husband's brother's daughter of a woman.

Dhyán, H. (S. ध्यान) Religious meditation; meditating on a divinity so as to perceive him with his attributes mentally.

Ḍi, or **Ḍihí**, Ben. (ডি, ডিহী) A district composed of a few villages.

Ḍibandí, or *Ḍihíbandí*, Ben. (ডিবংদী, ডিহীবংদী) Settlement of the revenue of a small district.

DÍÁRÁ, or DÍWÁRÁ, corruptly, DÍRÁ, and DEWRY, H. (ديارا ,ديوارا) Alluvium, an island formed in the bed of a river, land gained by recession of a river.

DIBBA, or DIBBA-BHÚMI, Tel. (దిబ్బ, దిబ్బభూమి, from S. भूमि, land) High land, a height.

DIBBI, Ben. (দিব্বি, from S. दिव्य) An oath, an ordeal.

ḌIBÍ, Hindi (डिबी) The germ in seeds.

ḌIBIYÁ, Hindi (डिबिया) A small portion of grain given at harvest to some of the inferior village servants.

DÍCHHIT, DEECHHIT, a vernacular corruption for DÍKSHÍTA, H. (ديچهت, S. दीक्षित, initiated) A name most appropriately given to Bráhmans, and the title of one of the sixteen branches of the Kanojia Bráhmans: it is also borne by some families of Maraṭha Bráhmans; and in Ghazipur and adjacent provinces by a tribe of Rájputs. See also *Dikhit*.

DÍDAH WA DÁNISTAH, H. (P. the past part. ديده, having seen, and دانسته, having known) Wilfully, purposely: applied to committing any offence deliberately and intentionally.

DÍDÁR, H. (P. ديدار, दीदार) An overseer, an inspector, an officer formerly employed in that capacity in the Company's factories. An overseer, a person stationed by the owner of a village over the ripe crops, to see that the whole is brought to the threshing-floor: he remains in charge till the Ryots have paid their rents, or the owner is satisfied by the sale of the grain. In this latter sense it is more correctly, perhaps, *Díhdár*, q. v.

Dídár-kharch, H. (A. خرچ, expense) The charge of maintaining an overseer.

DIDHISHU, DIDHISHÚ, or DIDHÍSHU, S. &c. (दिधिषुः, -षूः, or दिधीषुः) (when a masc. noun) The husband of a woman married a second time; (when fem.) A virgin widow remarried: an elder sister unmarried, whose junior is a bride: the childless widow of a brother whom, under the old law, a surviving brother was required to marry.

DÍḌ, or DÍḌH, Mar. (दीड, दीढ, also, with the vowel short, दिड, &c., vernacular forms of H. *Ḍeṛh*, डेढ, ڈیڑه) One-and-a-half.

Diḍhíkáḍhí, Mar. (दिढीकाढी) Advance of grain by the grain-dealers to the cultivators, on condition of receiving back half as much more at the harvest.

Diḍhotará, incorrectly, *Deedotrá*, Mar. (दिढोतरा) Interest at one-and-a-half per cent. per mensem.

Diṛkí, Mar. (दिड़की) A piece of money, a *dugáni* and a half.

DIG, or DIK, also DIṢ, or DIṢÁ, incorrectly, DEESHA, H. &c. (دك, S. दिश, nom. दिक्, or दिग्) A quarter or division of the horizon, of which ten are enumerated; the cardinal and intermediate points, the zenith and nadir.

DIGAMBARA, S. (दिगम्बरः, lit. sky-clad) A mendicant going about naked. A division of the Jains, the members of which either go naked or wear coloured clothes, in opposition to the Swetámbaras, or those who wear white.

DÍGAR-RAḲM, Hindi (P. ديگر, another, A رقم, sort) Any kind of crop: a term used in leases (Puraniya).

DÍGH, Hindi (दीघ, S. दीर्घ, long) A pace, two cubits (Puraniya).

DIGHÍ, corruptly, DIGGY, H. &c. (دگهي, from the S. *dírgha*, दीर्घ, long) DÍGHÍ, DÍGÍ, Ben. (দীঘী, দীগী) A long or large tank or pond.

DIGRI, or DIKRI, Ben. Uriya (a corruption of the English word *decree*) Decision, judgment, sentence, especially that in favour of one of the parties.

DIGUMATI, Tel. (దిగుమతి) Importation, landing goods from on board ship.

DIGWÁR, corruptly, DEGWAR, and DEEGWAR, H. &c. (دگوار, from دك, a quarter) A watchman, a guard, especially one employed by the Zamindars in the Jangal Mahals: lit. a protector of the regions.

DIH, DEH, not unfrequently pronounced, and sometimes written with the hard *d*, ḌIH, P. (ده, ڈه) A village, comprehending not only the actual village, but the lands belonging to it. Mr. Elliot observes, that, in the Lower Doab and Benares, *Dih* or *Deeh* is applied to a deserted village, and the Persian *Deh* is used for an inhabited one; but Richardson and Shakespear both write the word *Dih* for a village in general.

Díh, *Deeh*, H. Land of the best quality (Bahar).

Dihát, *Dehát*, corruptly, *Deyhat*, H. (دهات, being an Arabic plural to a Persian noun) Villages collectively, as opposed to towns: any cluster of villages, especially when belonging to the same proprietors.

Díhátí, *Dehátí*, H. (دیهاتي) Belonging or relating to villages or a village.

Díhátí-jamá, H. (A. جمع) Village assessment, revenue assessed upon any number of villages forming a local division.

Diháti-istamrár, H. (from A. استمرار, continuance, perpetuity) Villages held at a fixed or permanent rent.

Dih-bandí, or *Deh-bandí*, H. (ده بندي) A detailed statement of the villages in any particular district or estate, and of the revenue assessed on each; such statements were to have been prepared by the Kanungos at the time of the decennial settlement, and deposited in the collectors' offices: also, the rate at which a Ryot holds his lands.

Dih-da, H. &c. (*Dih*, a village, and द, the letter *d*) An abbreviation used by native surveyors, implying that certain lands, passed over for the time when taking note of the measurement, lie to the south, or *dakshiṇa*, of lands actually measured. Similar abbreviations are used for the other cardinal bearings; as, *Dih-u*, for *uttara*, north; *Dih-pa*, for *paschima*, west; and *Dih-pú*, for *púrva*, east; the first syllable of each being substituted for the whole word. In Bengal the terms are *Denda*, *Denpa*, &c., q. v.

Dih-dár, H. (*Dih*, a village, and دار, who has, or the word is written *Didár*, from P. ديدن, to see, q. v.) A revenue officer, the village overseer or superintendant on the part of the landholder or the state, whose duty it is to exercise a superintendence over the village cultivation, so that the Zamindar or government may not suffer detriment by negligence or fraud; he is also to see that the lands are properly distributed, the village boundaries preserved, and to assist in effecting the collections. It is said to mean, also, a person having a prescriptive right of occupancy, who cultivates at a fixed rate (?) (Bahar).

Dih-dárí, H. The office of the village keeper or superintendant. The pay or fees of the *Dih-dár*. A special assessment (in Bhagalpur) formerly, to provide for the pay of this officer, who was more usually paid by fees from the Ryots.

Dihdár-kharch, H. Expense of the employment of a village overseer.

Dihi, H. (دهي) Village, belonging or relating to a village, a villager, village cultivator, &c.

Ḍihí, Ben. (ডিহী) A district containing a few villages, subdivision or minor portion of an estate. (Dr. Carey derives this from *Diṣ* or *Dik*, a quarter; but (?) if *Dih*, a village, is not allowable in Bengali, although not in his Dictionary, nor in that of Ram-kamal Sen, under the word village).

Ḍihí-bandí, Ben. (ডিহীবন্দী) Regulation or assessment of the revenue of a small district. See *Dih-bandí*.

Dih-jamá, H. The revenue assessment of a village.

Dih-jháda, Mar. (?) A general list of villages.

Dih-kásht, H. A resident villager. *Dih-kásht-zamin*, H. Land cultivated by a resident.

Dih-kharch, corruptly, *Deh Curch*, H. Village expenses. An assessment on a village for its quota of the charges of settlement and collection.

Dih-wál, less correctly, *Deehwal* and *Dehwal*, H. A proprietary cultivator, whether paying his revenue direct to the government, or through a landholder of greater consequence.

ḌÍHÁ, ḌEEHÁ, H. (ڈیہا) A small mound.

Ḍiha, or *Ḍihi*, Uriya (ଡିହି) Land raised for the site of a dwelling, ground on which a house is situated.

DIHÚLA, H. (دهولا) A kind of rice grown in the Benares district.

DIKHIT, or DÍKHIT, H. (دكهت, ديكهت) A tribe of Rájputs settled in some numbers from Oudh to Bundelkhand. The name is probably the same with *Díchhit* and *Díkshit*. See the former.

ḌIKRÍ, or ḌIGRÍ, H. B. (ڈکري, ডিগরী, Eng., *Decree*) Award of a judge in favour of one of the litigants.

Ḍikridár, H. (P. دار, who has) The person in whose favour sentence has been given.

DÍKSHÁ, S., and in most dialects, (दीक्षा) Religious instruction, the performance of certain ceremonies before receiving the *mantra*, or secret prayer, from a spiritual preceptor: sacrificial worship in general.

DIL, H. (دل) A small eminence, the site of an old village.

DIMMAT, Mar. (दिम्मत, from the A. ذمّة) Trust, charge, management, custody. Temporary order or agreement for a person's taking possession of property transferred before the official documents are finally granted. See *Dhimatu*.

Dimmat-dár, Mar. (from P. دار, who has) One who has charge or keeping of any thing or person.

DÍMRAÚṬ, H. (ديمروٹ) One of the twelve tribes of the Mewatis.

DINA, S., and in most dialects, sometimes vernacularly shortened to DIN, (दिनः) A day.

Dina-kúli, Karn. (ದಿನಕೂಲಿ) Daily wages or hire.

Dina-ṭhih, Uriya (ଦିନଠିକ) Total of daily measurement of land, or collection of revenue.

Dináti, Hindi (दिनाती) Time of a plough's working, usually from 10 A.M. to an hour before sunset: also, daily work of labourers (Puraniya).

DÍN, H. (A. دين) Religion, faith, especially the Mohammadan religion.

DÍṆ, H. (دين, S. अधीन, a dependant) Poor, dependent.

Dín-dayál, H. (from S. दयालु, compassionate) Benefactor of the poor, a term of respectful address from an inferior to a superior.

DÍNÁR, A. (دينار) A coin, a silver coin weighing seven, or, according to some, ten drachms: also, a gold coin, especially in the compound *Dínár-i-surkh*, or red *dínár*. In the south of India (ದೀನಾರ) Any current gold coin.

ḌÍṆḌAR, Hindi (डींडर) An earthen vessel for drawing water from a well.

ḌINGÁ, Ben. (ডিংগা) A ship, a sloop, a vessel employed in the coasting trade.

Ḍingí, Ben. (ডিংগী) A boat, a wherry, a passage boat.

DÍPA, S. and in all the dialects, also sometimes modified, as H. DÍÁ, Mar. DÍWÁ, Karn. DÍVIGE, but the M. has also *Dípa* and in Tam. and Tel. the word is pure S., or *Dípam*, (दीपं) A lamp, a lamp burning before an idol.

Dípáli, or Dípávali, S. (दीप, a lamp, and आलि, or आवली, a row or line) A festival observed by the Hindus in honour of Kártikeya, on the new moon of the month Kártik, Sept.—Oct., when lamps are lighted in honour of him. It is popularly known by the name *Díwálí*, but under that appellation is addressed to a different object, and has undergone popular modifications. See *Díwálí*.

Dípamálá, S. (from माला, a garland) A row of lights. A festival of the Sikhs, observed on the 14th of the dark half of Kártik. Also vernacularly, *Dípmál*, Mar., (दीपमाळ) A pillar in front of a temple on which lamps are suspended.

Dípárádhana, Tel. (దీపారాధన, from S. आराधनं, worshipping) Offering a lamp to an idol, worshipping an idol by waving a lighted lamp before it: also, in Mysore, setting fire to a cloth steeped in butter or oil, and suspended to the gate of a temple on the 15th night of the month Kártik.

Dípavárane, Mar. (from वारणे, to revolve) Waving a lamp before an idol, an act of worship.

Dípdán, H. (ديپدان, from S. दीप, a lamp, and दान, giving) Offering of a lamp to an idol. A particular popular ceremony, suspending a lamp to a tree for ten days after the death of a relation, in order to light the spirit on its way to Yamapuri, the city of Yama, the judge of the dead. Presenting a lamp to the Ganges, setting it afloat on the river lighted, and watching for its extinction, as ominous of good or ill luck. Also (derived from *Díp*, abbreviation of *Dwíp*, S. द्वीप, an island,) Land assigned to Bráhmans on the bank of a river, to deprecate its encroachment.

DÍRÁ, Hindi (दीरा) Fresh lands thrown up by the shifting of the courses of rivers.

DIRM, or DIRHAM, H. (A. درم, درهم) A silver coin, usually weighing from 45 to 50 grains, rather heavier than an English sixpence. As a weight, a *dirham* is considered to be equal to $3\frac{1}{2}$ *máshas*, or $46\frac{1}{2}$ grains. The *dirm* is also sometimes distinguished from the *dirham*, the latter being equal to ten of the former.

DIṬṬHWAN, H. (ڈٹھون, a vernacular corruption of S. *Devotthána*, q. v.) A Hindu festival on the eleventh lunation of the light half of Kártik, on which *Vishṇu* is awakened with music and singing from his four months' slumber, constituting the rainy season: marriages and festive rejoicings, which have been but few during the interval, are now resumed: and on this occasion the cutting of the sugar-cane is commenced by the cultivators bringing home a small quantity from a corner of the field, and spreading it out for the reception of the Sálagrám-stone, or Ammonite type of *Vishṇu*: after this only, when the fortunate hour is announced, the sugar-cane harvest commences.

DIṬṬAMÚ, Tel. (దిట్టము) Arrangement, settlement, estimated aggregate of the revenue of a village from investigation of each several holding.

DIVÁKÍRTTI, Mar. (दिवा, by day, and कीर्त्ति, repute) A barber, any one of a low caste. (A barber is not to be employed nor spoken of at night).

DIVASÁ DARWAṚÁ, Mar. (दिवसा, S., by day, and दरवडा, attack by robbers) Bare-faced extortion by the government, or officers in authority.

DIVIṬÍ-INÁM, Tel. (దివిటీఇనాము) Land granted as the portion of the village torch-bearer.

DIVYA, S. and in most dialects; vernacularly changed in some to *Dibya*, (दिव्य, divine) An oath, or, more correctly, an ordeal, various kinds of which were admitted by the Hindu law. 1. The *Tula*, or balance, in which the accused is first weighed against a weight properly adjusted, and then, after certain ceremonies, is again weighed: if he be lighter than before, he is innocent; if the same, or heavier, guilty. 2. *Agni*, or fire, in which the accused touches fire or heated metal: if his hands are burnt he is guilty. 3. *Jala*, water: the accused is to be entirely immersed while a person runs to a place to which an arrow has been shot and returns with it: if he then lives he is pronounced innocent. 4. *Visha*: the accused is acquitted on his swallowing poison with impunity. 5. *Kosha*: drinking holy water, that in which images have been bathed, and meeting with no misfortune for fourteen days afterwards. 6. *Tanḍula*: chewing grains of rice and ejecting them: if they are dry, or tinged with blood, the suspected person is pronounced guilty. 7. *Tapta-másha*: taking a *másha* weight of gold out of a vessel filled with hot butter or oil, without burning the fingers, is proof of innocence. 8. *Phála*, the ploughshare: holding with impunity a heated ploughshare, or similar blade of steel. 9. *Dharmádharma*: images or drawings of *Dharma* and *Adharma*, virtue and vice, are covered carefully with cow-dung or earth, and placed privately in a vessel: the accused draws one of them, and is declared innocent or guilty accordingly: this is also termed *Dharmárchá*, worship of *Dharma*. 10. *Tulaṣí*, holding the leaves of the Tulaṣi plant, which is sacred to *Vishṇu*, and some water, and, after repeating the form of the oath, swallowing them. Some of these forms of ordeal are still in use among native states, and that of chewing rice is occasionally employed for the detection of petty thefts by the police-officers of the British government. There are other forms also in popular use, some of which are rather modes of adjuration than ordeals, although the notions are blended; as, 1. *Kachcha ghaṭa* or *ghaṛá*, H. Mar. (from *kachcha*, raw, unbaked, and *ghaṭa*, or *ghaṛá*, a water vessel) filling an unbaked earthen vessel with water, and carrying it on the head for a certain distance without breaking it. *Bel-bhanḍára*, (q. v.) Swearing by the leaves of the *Bel*. *Gangájala*, (S. *Jala*, water) Swearing while holding a cup with the water of the Ganges, or some sacred stream. *Devála*, or *Deválaya*, swearing in a temple before an image. *Gau*, holding the tail of a cow; or *Bráhmaní*, touching the feet of a Bráhman, while pronouncing an oath. *Símá*, or *Símbá*, a boundary: in a case of contested boundaries, a person is selected by both parties, who, after performing religious ceremonies, walks over and points out the proper boundary: if no misfortune befal him or his family within a given term, his decision is considered final: or sometimes he walks the boundary with an oil-cake on his head, the falling or breaking of which vitiates his demarcation. These different modes of determining innocence or guilt, or of giving evidence, are accompanied with various forms and observances, according to the supposed sanctity, and the importance of the judgment.

DIWÁLÁ, H. (دیوالا) DIWÁLEṈ, or DÍWALÚṈ, Mar. (दिवाळें, दिवाळूं) DIWÁḶÍ, Karn. (ದಿವಾಳಿ) Bankruptcy, insolvency. *Diwaliyá*, very corruptly, *Devaleeo*, H. (دیوالیا) A bankrupt. (This and the preceding are variously derived from *dípa* or *diwá*, a lamp, because, it is said, it was formerly the practice to announce the event by placing a piece of burning cow-dung at the bankrupt's door, or because it was customary to announce insolvency at the *Diwálí* festival.

DIWÁLÍ, corruptly, DEEPOULEE, H. &c. (دیوالی) DEÚLÍ, Ben. (দেউলী) Karn. DÍWAḶIGEÏCHHA, (ದೀವಳಿಗೆಯುಚ್ಛ, from the S. *Dípáli*, or *Dípávalí*, q. v.) A popular festival of the Hindus, the feast of lights, held on the two last days of the dark half of Aṣwín and the new moon and four following days of Kártik (Sept.—Oct.). Appropriate ceremonies are allotted to each day, but on the last the night is to be spent in merry-making and festivity, and illuminations are to be made in honour of deceased ancestors. The goddess *Lakshmí*, or fortune, is also to be worshipped, and in her honour games of chance are to be played during the last night of the festival. Amongst the Maraṭhas it is the commencement of the commercial year, over which *Lakshmí* especially presides, and accounts are opened by merchants and bankers with individuals for the smallest sums—a few rupees—as ominous of success. Bankruptcies are also declared at this season. In Bengal the lower orders of the Mohammadans, in imitation of the Hindus, also offer lamps at this time to the spirits of the dead.

DÍWÁN, incorrectly, DEWAN, DEEWAN, DIVAN, H. &c. (P. دیوان): in the dialects the *i* is short, as DIBÁN, Ben. (দিবান) DIWÁṆ, Mar (दिवाण) A royal court, a council of state, a tribunal of revenue or justice. A minister, a chief officer of state. Under the Mohammadan government it was especially applied to the head financial minister, whether of the state or of a province, being charged, in the latter, with the collection of the revenue, the remittance of it to the imperial treasury, and invested with extensive judicial powers in all civil and financial causes. Under the Maraṭha government the *Díwán* was the chief minister after the *Pradhán*. The title also denoted the head officer of any revenue or financial department, as the *Díwán* of the mint, of the jewel office, and the like; in which sense it is retained under the British goverment, as the *Díwán* of the mint, of the bank, of the salt-agency, and, formerly, of a collectorate, and is even applied to the managers of Zamindárís for native proprietors, and to native servants intrusted with the management of the financial interests of a house of business, or of any responsible individual. The title of *Díwán*, or office of *Díwání*, equivalent to the right of collecting the whole revenues of Bengal, Bahar, and Orissa, was conferred upon the East-India Company by the nominal emperor of Hindustan, Shah Âálam, in 1765. The word also signifies a record or account book; and, in Mohammadan law, the bags in which the Kazi's records are kept.

Díwání, incorrectly, *Dewani*, and, corruptly, *Dewanny*, H. (A. ديواني) adj., Of or relating to a Díwán, civil, as opposed to criminal. subst., The office, jurisdiction, emoluments, &c., of a Díwán. The right to receive the collections of Bengal, Bahar, and Orissá, conferred on the East-India Company by the titular Moghul. It is used also in the early reports for the territory of which the revenue was receivable under the grant in Bengal.

Díwán-dene or *dhárá*, Mar. (from देणे, to give, or धारा, fixed rate) Any tax or assessment.

Díwán-juz, H. (جز, a little) A sub- or deputy-steward, or finance officer.

Díwán-khána, H. (from H. خانه, a house) The court or office of the *Díwán*: a court of civil or revenue jurisdiction: a hall of audience.

Diwán-khásjí, Mar. (खासजी) The chief finance minister of the Peshwa.

Díwán-kul, H. (A. كل, all) The head steward or finance officer.

Diwán-paṭṭí, Mar. (from पट्टी, a pecuniary collection) Government assessment.

Díwání-Âdálat, corruptly, *Dewanny Adawlut*, H. (from عدالت, a tribunal) The court of civil and revenue jurisdiction. See *Âdálat*.

Díwán-i-Áâlá, (from A. اعلي, most eminent) Prime minister.

Díwán-i-Âám, H. (from A. عام, all or common persons) A public court, or general audience chamber.

Díwán-i-kháṣ, H. (from A. خاص, select) Private audience chamber. A cabinet council.

Díwán-i-khálṣa, H. (A. from خالصه, pure, most eminent) The accountant-general of the royal revenue.

Díwán-i-daftar, H. (دفتر, an office) The account or record office of the Díwán.

Díwání-sanad, H. (from A. سند, a grant) A patent or grant under the authority of the Díwán. A grant of the office of Díwán. The deed of grant by which the Díwání was conferred upon the East-India Company.

Díwán-i-tan, H. (from P. تن, the body) The chief financial minister in attendance on the emperor. The officer charged with the provision of the emperor's personal expenses. (He is called, in some of the early reports, *Díwán Beutal*, which is clearly erroneous, although it may have some relation to *Byay* or *Vyay* expenditure).

Diwánu, Karn. (ದಿವಾನು) The head native officer of a *Kachcheri*.

Díwár, Deewar, H. (ديوار) The tutelary divinity of a village for whom a portion of grain is set apart at each harvest; commonly represented by a shapeless stone, although bearing various personal appellations, as, *Kateswari*, *Hanwat*, *Bhúm-sen*, *Hari-Rám*, &c.

Divelávaṇí, Mar. (दिवेलावणी) Peopling a deserted place: (lit., causing lamps to be brought).

Divelávaṇí chá kaul, Mar. (A. قول) A paper granted to settlers in deserted places, exempting them from taxes for a term.

Díyat, incorrectly, Deyit, or Deyut, H. (A. دية) The price of blood, a tax imposed for any act of offence against the person: in cases of homicide, payable to the relatives of the deceased.

Díyat-mughalaza, H. (from A. مغلظه, severe) The heaviest fine or penalty for manslaughter that can be imposed (Mohammadan law).

Do, or, as sometimes modified vernacularly, especially in composition, Du, Doo, H. (دو, from the S. द्वि, or nom. *Dual*, द्वौ, or from the Per. دو, *Dú*) Two.

Do-áb, or *Dú-áb*, H. دواب, from دو, two, and *áb*, water, by metonymy, a river) A tract of land lying between two rivers, which, after running for some distance, unite; as the country between the Ganges and Jamuna, known especially as the Doab: also the districts between the rivers of the Panjab, as the Jalandhara-Doab, between the Satlaj and the Beah, &c.

Do-anṣa, Hindi (दोअंश) A sort of soil, a light clay mixed with sand.

Dobára, or *Dúbárá*, H. (دو, and بارہ or بارا, a time) Twice, two times; also, twice as much, double.

Do-kul, or *Dú-kul*, Ben. (দোকুল, from S. कुल, a bank, or a family) Both banks of a river. Belonging to both families—of father and mother, or wife and husband.

Do-ṭarafa, H. (from طرف, a side) Applied to a suit in which both parties have been heard.

Ḍoba, Hindi (डोब) A pond (Puraniya).

Ḍobá, Ben. (ডোবা, from डूब, to sink, properly, immersed) Low and swampy or inundated land.

Ḍobá-jamí, or *-jamín*, Ben. (from P. زمين, land) Swampy or marshy ground.

Ḍobá-már, Hindi (डोबामार) Low lands which lose their moisture from sand being too near the surface.

Ḍobán, Hindi (डोबान) Land situated around and in the beds of dry ponds (Puraniya).

Dobe, Dúbe, H. (دوبي, from *do*, two, and *be*, corruption of Veda) A Bráhman who has studied or who teaches two of the four Vedas. A caste of Bráhmans so termed, generally ignorant and low persons, and by profession boxers and wrestlers.

Dobiswí, sometimes abridged vernacularly to *Dúbsi*, or *Doobsee*, H. (دوبسوي) An allowance or deduction of two *bíswas* out of a *bíghá*, or one-tenth. The right of the Zamindar in land, as the Málikána is in money. A concession sometimes made by holders of rent-free lands to the Zamindar, in acknowledgment of his superior or proprietary right; especially, according to Mr. Elliot, when they are not confident of the validity of their tenure. A per-centage, 10 per cent., allowed to farmers of the government revenue.

Docha, H. (دوچہ) The second reservoir to which water is thrown up from a pond or river for irrigation.

Dofaṣlá, H. (دوفصلا, दोफसला) Two crops raised on the same land in one year: the land so cultivated.

Dofaṣli, H. (دوفصلي, from دو, two, and فصل, harvest) Yielding two crops in a year (land).

Doḍḍadore, Karn. (ದೊಡ್ಡದೊರೆ, from ದೊಡ್ಡ, great, old, and ದೊರೆ, a master) A head-man, the chief authority in any place, the head of a mercantile firm or bank, &c.

Doḍḍappa, *Doḍḍatande*, Karn. (ದೊಡ್ಡಪ್ಪ, ದೊಡ್ಡತಂದೆ, from ದೊಡ್ಡ, great, old) A father's elder brother, the husband of a mother's elder sister.

Doḍḍi, Karn. (ದೊಡ್ಡಿ) A pound for confining cattle.

Dogar, H. (دوگر) The name of a predatory and pastoral tribe in the north-west of Hindustan. During the last century they occupied a considerable tract on the banks of the Satlaj, and made themselves formidable to the Mohammadan government of Dehli. They are Mohammadans by religion, but claim to be descended from the Chauhan Rájputs, a claim not admitted by the other converted Chauhans, who consider, apparently with reason, the Dogars to have been originally Játs and Gujars. Members of the race have latterly risen into consideration as former feudatories of Ranjit Siṇh, now acknowledged by the British as Rajas of Jamu and Kashmir.

Dogga, Thug. A pipe for smoking. An old man.

Doh, Mar. (दोह) A deep part in a river or tank.

Doháí, or Duhái, H. (دوهاي, from دو, two, or repeatedly, and هاي, alas) Dawáhi, Guz. (દવાહી) A word used as an exclamation in calling out for mercy or redress.

Doháí-tiháí-harna, To make exclamation twice and thrice, *i. e.* importunately.

Dohalí, Dohlí, or Dohrí, H. (دوهلي, دوهري, दोहली) Service land, or lands granted rent-free by Zamindars to village servants, to poor relatives, or religious mendicants. In some places it is confined to land given to Bráhmans. The terms are also applied to the perquisite of Fakirs at harvest time (Dehli).

Doháo, H. (دوهاو, perhaps from *duh*, for *dúdh*, milk, and, more correctly, *Duháo*) The Zamindar's perquisite of a certain quantity of milk from the Ryot's cows (North-west Provinces).

Dohar, H. (دوهر, from دو, two, and هر, what takes) The old bed of a river (East Oudh). Land that bears two crops in a year (Central Doab).

Ḍohár, Mar. (डोहार) A caste, or individual of it; a tanner, or worker in leather

Ḍohoḍiú, Guz. (ડોહોડીઉ) A copper pice, a quarter *ana*.

Dohrá, H. (دوهرا) A sort of ladle for taking the juice of the sugar-cane out of the boiler.

Dohur, Dohoor, H. (دوهر) A loose sandy sub-soil, which is apt to give way in sinking a well without masonry while the water from it is oily and brackish.

Ḍoíphoṛyá, Mar. (डोई, the head, and फोड्या, who breaks) The name of a class of Hindu mendicants, who knock their heads against stones to enforce compliance with their demands; hence, any importunate petitioner.

Dojíra, H. (دوجيره) A kind of rice.

Dokhí, H. (دوكهي) A raised mound, indicating the junction of two boundaries.

Ḍol, H. (ڈول) Applied locally to signify the richest black soil. (Baitul).

Ḍol, Hindi &c. (डोल, A. ڈول) A bucket, a leathern bucket used for drawing up water from a well, or for throwing up water for irrigation.

Dokaṛá, Mar. (दोकडा) A small copper coin, a half pice.

Dokaro, Guz (દોકડો) A nominal coin, one hundred of which are equal to one rupee: the decimal fraction of a rupee.

Ḍolá, or **Ḍoli**, H. &c. (ڈولا, ڈولي, S. दोला, the initial being vernacularly changed) A swing, a sort of sedan in which women are carried. A woman of inferior rank married to a man of superior rank: she takes a lower place than a wife of equal station, and is carried home privately, without any ceremonial or procession,

Doláwa, H. (دولاوہ) A well having two *Laos*, or well buckets and ropes.

Ḍolcha, H. (ڈولچہ) A small bucket.

Dol-játrá, Ben. (দোলযাত্রা, from S. यात्रा, a festival) The swing festival, held on the full moon of *Phálgun* (March—April), in honour of Krishna, when figures of him and Rádhá are swung in an ornamented swing.

Dom, or **Domrá**, fem. **Domní**, corruptly, **Dhome**, H. (دوم, دومرا, fem. دومني) The name of a low caste, apparently one of the aboriginal races. In Hindustan they are usually by avocation makers of ropes, mats, fans, and baskets. In Oudh the *Dom* is a sweeper; and in some places they perform the lowest offices, as carrying dead bodies and skeletons. The *Dom* is often a musician, and the female *Domní* is an actress and singer, who performs in the inner apartments before the women of the family. There is also a tribe of Mohammadans termed *Dom*, better known by the designation of Mír, or Mirásí.

Domaṭ, or **Dúmaṭ**, **Domut**, **Doomut**, H. (دومٹ, from دو, two and مٹي, earth, from S. मृत, दोमट्, दुमट्) A kind of soil chiefly composed of clay and sand, severally *Matiár* and *Bhúṛ*. In some places it appears to contain a proportion of about $\frac{1}{10}$th of lime. In some districts, as Farakhabad and Bareli, it is considered the first quality of soil: in others, as in Badaon, the second.

Domba, **Dombar**, or **Dombára**, Karn. **Dommara**, or **Dommari**, Tel. (ಡೊಂಬ, ಡೊಂಬರ, ಡೊಂಬಾರ, దొమ్మర) **Ḍombárí**, Mar. (डोंबारी) A tumbler, a rope-dancer, a juggler. (Probably vernacular modifications of *Dom.*)

Dombar-lingada-víra káṇiki, Karn. A tax levied on the cultivators in Mysore in lieu of smaller sums formerly distributed as presents to tumblers and mendicants.

Domṭikár, H. (دومٹكار) A division of Sarwaria Bráhmans.

Don, H. (دون) A fractional division of an estate.

Dóne, corruptly **Dony**, Tel. (దోనె) A coasting vessel, a sloop, usually with one mast.

Donga, Tel. (దొంగ) A thief, a robber.

Ḍongá, **Ḍongí**, Ben &c. (ডোঙ্গা, ডোঙ্গী) A canoe, one made of two or three sheaths of the plaintain leaves fastened together.

Ḍongar, Mar. (डोंगर) A hill, high ground.

Ḍongareṇ, Mar. (डोंगरें) A sort of coarse rice grown on the hills.

Ḍongarkoḷí, Mar. (डोंगरकोळी) A lawless tribe inhabiting the hilly country.

Ḍongarwaṭ, Mar. (डोंगरवट) Undulating, hilly.

Doní, Hindi (दोनी) Treading out the grain from the straw by bullocks (Puraniya).

Donká, Tel. (దొంకా) A path between two fields, a passage for cattle.

Ḍonwár, or **Ḍunwár**, H. (ڈونوار) A tribe of Zamindars of mixed origin, partly Bráhmans, partly Rájputs. They call themselves Thakurs, but are generally considered Bhúinhárs, Bráhman cultivators. They are numerous in the districts of Gorakhpur, Ghazipur, and Azimgarh, and were once sufficiently powerful to establish a Rajship on the Kosi, in Western Tirhut under Karnadeva.

Dopaṭṭah, H. (دوپٹہ) **Dopáṭá**, Ben. (দোপাটা, from S. पट, cloth) **Dupaṭá**, **Dupaṭṭá**, or **Dupaṭen**, Mar. (दुपटा, &c.) **Dupaṭi**, Tel. (దుపటి) A piece of cloth of two breadths, forming the principal or only garment of women of the lower orders.

Dophali, Uriya (S. फल, fruit, produce) Land bearing two crops.

Ḍoṛ, Hindi (ڈوڑ, डोड) A tribe of Rájputs, some of whom, mostly converted to Mohammadanism, are settled in the district of Aligarh, also about Banda and Sagar.

Doṛ, H. (دوڑ) Land twice ploughed.

Ḍoṛ, also **Ḍorá** and **Ḍorí**, H. &c. (ڈور, ڈورا, ڈوري) A string, a rope; also thread. *Ḍorí* is also applied to the chain or line used in land measurement; and, among the Marathas, to a land measure: a *Ḍorí* is equal to 80, or sometimes 120, *bighás*. (In Maratha the initial is the dental *d*, as दोरी. In Bengali, as in Hindi, the cerebral ডোরী).

DORA, Tel. (దొర) A master, a ruler, a prince, with the honorific affix *gáru*, *Doragáru*.

Dora-gáru, Tel. (దొరగారు) The equivalent of Mr. or Sir, applied to Europeans especially. A gentleman.

DO-RAS, DO-RUS, H. (دورس) A kind of mixed soil, consisting of the soils known as Matiár and Báluä, clay and sand, variously estimated as of first or second quality. Land yielding two crops in a year.

DO-RASTU, Tel. (దొరస్తు, from the P. رسته, grown) Land yielding a double crop. The double apportionment of the harvest. The shares of the cultivator and of the government.

DORAVU, Tel. (దొరవు) A large well.

DORWA, (?) Tel. The native head revenue officer of a district, the Mukaddam. (The word is probably a modification of *Dora* (Warangal).

ḌORIA, H. (ڈوريه) Lace. (From ڈوري, thread).

Ḍoriá, H. (ڈوريا) Striped muslin. (From the same).

Ḍorihár, H. (ڈوريهار) A pedlar selling laces and thread. A Saiva mendicant living partly by the sale of thread.

Ḍoriwálá, H. (ڈوريوالا) A ropemaker.

DORIDEṆÍ, Hindi (दोरिदेणी) Measurement of a field after the crop has grown to estimate the probable produce.

DOSÁD, or DÚSÁD, H. (دوساد) A low caste, employed as executioners, to remove dead bodies, and the like: employed also in Bengal as village watchmen and messengers.

DOSÁI, or DOSÁHI, H. (دوساي, دوساهي) Land yielding two crops a-year.

Dosari, *Dosuree*, H. (دوسري, it were more correctly *Dosíri*, from सीर, S. a plough) Ploughing land twice: the land so ploughed.

Dosál, H. (P. from دو, two, and سال, a year) Applied to lands that have been two years under cultivation.

DOSHA, vernacularly, DOSH, Ben., Uriya, Mar. &c. (S. दोष) Dos, H. (دوس) Fault, offence, crime.

Doshí, Ben. &c (S. दोषी) *Dosí*, H. (دوسي) An offender, a culprit, a criminal.

DOSHAMBA, H. (P. دوشمبه) Monday.

DOSILI, Tel. (దోసిలి) The hands joined together, so as to hold any thing: what may be so held, a handful. A small quantity of grain granted as a fee or perquisite to the village servants at the time of harvest.

ḌOSÍWÁNIO, Guz. (ડોશીવાણીઓ) A dealer in cloth, a pedlar of the Banya tribe.

DRAGOMAN, (corruption of *Tarjamán*, from A. *Tarjama*, ترجمه, translation) An interpreter.

DRÁVIḌA, S. (द्राविड) or, the *ḍ* being pronounced *ṛ*, DRÁVIṚA. The country in which the Tamil language is spoken: the Coromandel coast from Madras southward: the country below the Eastern Ghats, to Cape Komorín. An inhabitant of the country. A class of Bráhmanical tribes, called the five Dráviṛa Bráhmans, comprehending all those of the Peninsula, or *Dráviṛa*, *Karnáṭa*, *Telinga*, *Gujerata*, and *Maráṭha*.

DRAMMA, Mar. (S. द्रम्म) A piece of money equal to 16 *paṇas* of *kaunrís*, or 1280.

DRAVYA, S., adopted in most dialects, slightly modified, and met with sometimes barbarously corrupted, as in the Summary of Hindu Law and Customs, published by order of the government of Bombay, in which it is always printed DREWY, (द्रव्य) Thing, substance, wealth, property. It is distinguished as—

Stháváра, or *Sthira dravya*, Fixed or immoveable property, property in land, trees, &c.

Astháváра, *Jangama*, or *Chara dravya*, Moveable property, cattle, money, &c. It is also distinguished as *Kramágata*, descended or ancestral; *Swayamarjita*, or *Krita*, self-acquired or made; and *Ágantuka*, accidental; and again as *Sádhárana*, common, held in common; *Asádháraṇa*, that which is not common, but belongs to the holder exclusively; and *Vibhakta*, divided, partitioned among separated heirs.

DRIḌHA-BODHA, Ben. (from the S. *driḍha*, दृढ, firm, and *bodha*, बोध, understanding) Conviction, judgment. (Uriya) Presumptive evidence.

DRISHṬA, vernacularly, DRISHT, sometimes corrupted to DISHT, (S. दृष्ट) Seen, present, visible.

Drishṭádhi, or *Drishṭabandhah*, H. &c. (S. दृष्ट, with आधि, or बन्धक, a pledge) Mortgage or pledge of real substantial property, that which may be kept in view; or, also, that from which, although possession be had, no profit or benefit is derived. In the west and south of India it means mortgage or pledge, without giving up possession, except on failure of payment of the debt for which the property is pledged.

Drishṭi dosha, S. (दृष्टि, the sight, and दोषः, fault) The influence, or blight of an evil eye.

Drishṭánta, S., but used in some dialects, (दृष्टान्त) Example, proof, precedent.

DROṆA, Ben. (S. দ্রোণ) A measure of capacity, equal to $\frac{1}{16}$th of a *khári*. (In Chittagong and Sylhet) a land measure equal to 16 *kánis*.

DROṆÍ, S. &c. (द्रोणी) An oval vessel of wood or stone; a trough for watering cattle; a canoe.

DÚB, DOOB, DÚRVÁ, H. (دوب, S. दूर्वा) A kind of grass highly esteemed for fodder (Cynodon dactylon). Three sorts are described: the best, called *Paunda*, is essentially the same as Fiorin; the second, called *Khútia*, is smaller, and grows on hard ground; the third is called *White Dúb*: or it is distinguished as of two sorts, *Ghor-dúb*, horse grass, being the best fodder; and *Ban-dúb*, forest grass, of a coarser quality.

Dúb-mahál, H. (A. محال) A tax formerly levied on providers of fodder or grass cutters (Dacca).

ḌÚBÁCHAR, H. (from ڈوبا, immersed, and چر, an alluvial island) A bank or island in a river, or low alluvial lands liable to be flooded.

ḌÚBÁÍ, H. ڈوبائي, from ڈوبنا, to drown) lit., Drowning; but applied to a bribe which is given absolutely, whether the briber gain or lose his suit, in distinction to *Taraṇa*, a crossing over, *i. e.* a bribe which is to be returned if the suit is lost.

ḌÚBÁRÁ, H. (ڈوبارا, from ڈوبنا, to be immersed) An island, or land left in the channel of a river, liable to be flooded when the water rises, but cultivable in the cold weather for spring crops.

DUBARO, Guz. (દુબરો) A man of the *Bhíl* or *Kúli* tribe.

ḌUBÁRU, Ben. (ডুবারু) A caste, whose occupation is that of fishermen and divers, (from ডুবা, to plunge).

DUBÁSÍ, commonly, DUBÁSHÍ, Tel. (దుబాసి, vernacular corruption of DOBHÁSHÍ, one who speaks two languages, from S. द्वि, two, and भाषा, a language) An interpreter, a native man of business in the service of a European (Madras), but the office and the name are almost obsolete.

DUBERJÍ, Mar. (दुबेरजी) Twice brought to account, twice entered, payment, expenses, and the like; as, *Duberjí-jamá*, *Duberjí-kharch*, &c.

DÚBHÁLIS, H. (دوبهالس) Land seated in the neighbourhood of population, the soil of which is intermixed with gravel: vegetables, *jawár*, and poppy are grown in it (Behar).

DÚBRÁJ, (corruption of *Yuvarájá*, young prince) H. The heir of a Raja.

ḌUBSÍ, H. (ڈبسي, from ڈوبنا, to be immersed) Land liable to be flooded. See also *Dobiṣwí*.

DUḌḌU, Karn. (ದುಡ್ಡು) DUḌÚ, Mar. (दुडू) A copper coin, worth twenty *kás*. Mar., A fourth of a *paisa*.

DUDÉ, (?) A weight equal to the fourth part of a *maund* (Madras).

DÚDÉKULAVÁḌU, Tel. (దూదేకులవాఁడు) A cotton cleaner.

DÚDHÁ, H. (دودها) A sort of rice.

DUDHWATÍ, Hindi (दुधवती, lit., full of milk) Full of farinaceous matter, ears of corn becoming ripe.

DUDI, Tel. (దుది) Cotton after it is cleared from the seed.

ḌUGAR, H. (ڈگر) A path, a way.

DÚGARA, Tel. (దూగర) The dust of rice in the husk, bran.

DUGDHÁ, H. (دگدها) A tribe of inferior Bráhmans on the borders of Fatihpur and Allahabad.

DUGGÁṆI, Tel., Karn. (దుగ్గాణి) DUGÁṆI, Mar. (दुगाणी) A copper coin, worth about ten *kás*, or a half *pice*.

DÚGLA, H. (ڈوگلا) A sling basket of large size used for irrigation.

ḌUHÍ, H. (ڈوهي) Alluvial formations. A mark of village boundaries.

DUHITRI, S. (दुहितृ) A daughter.

Dauhitra, S. (दौहित्रः) A daughter's son. *Dauhitrí*, (दौहित्री) A daughter's daughter.

DUHOTTARA, or -TRÁ, Mar. (दुहोत्तर-त्रा) Interest at two per cent. per mensem.

DUKÁL, Mar. (दु, which in Mar. compounds is used either for दो, two, or for the S. दुर्, *dur*, bad, and काळ, time) A dearth or famine.

DUKÁN-PAṬṬÍ, Mar. (from P. *Duhán*, a shop, which occurs in most dialects, and *paṭṭi*, a cess) A tax on shops or trades.

DUKKI, Tel. (దుక్కి) Ploughing, ploughed ground, a ploughed field. Also *Dukki-polamu*.

DUKṚÁ, H. &c. (दुकडा) One-fourth of a *paisa*.

DULANDI, DOOLUNDY, (?) A Ryot cultivating land in a different village from that in which he resides.

ḌÚLI, H. (ڈولی) ḌOLÍ, Mar. (डोली) A litter, a swing cot.

Duliyá, Ben. (দুলিযা) The name of a caste, or individual of it, whose business is carrying palanquins, or other burthens.

DULLAKOṬṬUTA, Tel. (దుల్లకొట్టుత) Threshing corn.

DÚMÁ, (?) A leather case, holding about three *sérs*, in which tea was imported into Kamaon from Tibet. The tea of Kamaon itself is now exported to Tibet.

Dumálá, or **Dumálí-gáon**, incorrectly, **Doomalla**, Mar. (दुमाला, the back or tail part, from P. دنبالا, fig., reverting or turning back, and गाम्रो', a village) A reversionary village, or lands the revenues of which are granted for life or a term of years, after which they revert to the state; or lands granted for service, or through favour, subject to resumption at pleasure. Also, lands of which the revenues are not wholly alienated, but which are subject to a quit-rent. In common use it is also loosely applied to all alienated villages. (The word, in the usual sense, is more probably derived from *du*, two, and *mál*, property; the holder and the state having *both* an interest in it).

Dumbálá, Tel. (దుంబాలా) An order for giving up the government share of the produce to the cultivators.

Dumbálá-deron, (?) The issue of an order to the cultivators to reap the crops without waiting for the final adjustment of the assessment with the Zamindars. Fifth Rep., p. 644. (The second term is obviously erroneous, and the sense of the first has been, perhaps, mistaken. An absurd etymology is given in the Glossary to explain the term: as, *Dumbáleh*, P., tail of a cow, and *Dharan*, H., seizing, taking hold of the tail of a cow, to urge her along).

Dumbálą-mányam, Tel. (దుంబాలామాన్యం) Lands held free of assessment, or at a low quit-rent; under special grant, not forming part of the original assignments.

Dún, **Doon**, H. (دون) A valley.

Duná, Thug. Stocks for culprits.

Dunbi, also written **Doenbee**, (neither, perhaps, is quite correct) Mar. Split, cracked: applied to the first kind of black soil, which, although very rich, requires a copious supply of water.

Duṇḍá, H. (ڈونڈا) A bullock with one horn.

Ḍuṇḍí, or **Ḍoṇḍí**, Hindi (डुंडी) Proclamation by beat of drum.

Dundubhi, H. &c. (दुन्दुभिः) The fifty-sixth year of the cycle, the next recurrence of which will be A. D. 1862.

Dundubhi-hechchige. Karn. (ದುಂದುಭಿಹೆಚ್ಚಿಗೆ) Increase in the Mysore assessment made in a former *Dundubhi* year, 1784-85.

Ḍúnga, H. (ڈونگا) Deep; a trough, a canoe.

Ḍungaḷi, Karn. (ದುಂಗಳಿ) A measure of two-and-a-half *sérs* (South Kanara).

Dungání, H. (دنگانی) A small fractional division of an estate (Kamaon).

Ḍungar, or **Ḍongar**, H. (ڈونگر) A hill, a hilly country.

Dunr, or **Dunrí**, Thug. Cry of the victim for help.

Dupikí, Mar. (दुपिकी, from दु, two, and पिकणे, to ripen) Bearing two crops in a year (land &c.).

Duráhí, Mar. (दुराही, from S. दुर्, bad, and आह, saying, also *Dwáhí*, द्वाही) An expression used in prohibiting any thing on the part of the authorities or the Raja, implying his vengeance in case of disobedience.

Durái, Tel., Karn. (దురాయి, from the S. particle दुर्, implying deprecation or prohibition) Protest, prohibition. Citation, summons, an order of the state to bring a person to trial. (Probably a modification of the preceding).

Durakání, Mar. (दुरकानी) Drawn (as a line) through the two central columns of a sheet of country paper, leaving the first and last as margins; the form used in letters to superiors or equals.

Durbhikshá, S. &c, vernacularly, **Durbhikká**, (दुर्भिक्षा) A famine, a dearth.

Durga, S., vernacularly, **Durg**, **Doorg**, whence, erroneously, **Droog**, H. &c. (درگ, दुर्ग) A fort, a hill fort.

Durgá, S. &c. (दुर्गा) A goddess highly popular in many parts of India, especially in Bengal; the wife of Ṣiva, and, in an especial manner, the destroyer of evil beings and oppressors: her worship is permitted to the lowest castes.

Durgá-navamí, S. &c, (दुर्गानवमी) A Hindu festival, the worship of Durgá on the ninth lunation of the light half of Kártik.

Durgá-pújá, S. (दुर्गापूजा) The worship of Durgá, celebrated for ten days in the month of Aṣwin (October), with particular pomp, in Bengal.

Durgotsava, S. (from उत्सवः, a festival) The festival of Durgá, the Durgá-pújá.

Durg-bansi, H. (درگبنسی) A tribe of Rájputs in Jonpur, and Azimgarh.

Ḍuṛiá, or **Ḍoṛiá**, H. (ڈوریا) A dog-keeper. (From *Ḍorí*, or *Duṛí*, a string, with which he leads the dogs.

Durmati, S. &c. (दुर्मतिः, from दुर, bad, मति, mind) The fifty-fifth year of the cycle.

Durmukha, S. &c. (दुर्मुख, from S. दुर, bad, and मुख, aspect) The thirtieth year of the cycle.

Durvá, or **Durbá**, S. (दुर्वा) Bent grass: see **Dúb**.

Durváshtamí, S. (from अष्टमी, the eighth) The eighth lunation of the month Bhádra, on which day *Durvá* grass is used in the ceremonies observed.

Dusoṭá, Mar. (दुसोटा) Pulse, &c, sown in a field from which the regular crop has been gathered.

Dúsiga, Karn. (ದೂಸಿಗ) A cloth merchant, a tailor,

Dusáí, Hindi (دوساي, दुसाई) The second sort of sugar-cane, which is sown after the autumn crop is reaped.

Dúta, S. (दूतः) A messenger, an envoy, an ambassador.

Dwádaṣa, S. (द्वादश) Twelve, twelfth.

Dwádaṣádhika, Karn. (ದ್ವಾದಶಾಧಿಕ, S. द्वादश, and अधिक, more) Twelve fold, a rate of increase to be calculated on the produce of land.

Dwádaṣáhika, S. (from आह्निक, relating to a day, अहर्) A Bráhman householder, who keeps a store of food for twelve days' consumption.

Dwádaṣí, S. (द्वादशी) The twelfth day of a lunar fortnight.

Dwaita, S. (द्वैत, from द्वि, two) Duad. The doctrine of duality, distinguishing two principles in creation, spirit and matter, as opposed to the *Adwaita*, or monad doctrine, which acknowledges the reality of spiritual existence only.

Dwápara-yuga, S. (द्वापरयुगं) The third age of the world.

Dwár-devatá, Mar. (द्वारदेवता, S. द्वार, a door, and देवता, divinity) The attendants of a great man, who must be worshipped in order to get access to him.

Dwija, or Dwijáti, S. (द्विजः, द्विजातिः, from द्वि, two, and ज, or जाति, who is born) A twice-born man, first by his natural birth, and secondly by his spiritual birth, or investiture with the sacrificial cord. The term properly designates a man of either of the three first castes, the Bráhman, Kshatriya, and Vaiṣya, but is now generally understood of the former.

Dwípa, S. (द्वीपः) An island; also a continent surrounded by an ocean. Jambu-dwípa is that division of the world in which India lies, so named, because it is the climate of the Jambu tree: it is encircled by the sea of salt water.

Dwipadí-vyavahára, S. (द्विपदीव्यवहार) A law-suit which consists of only two of four *padas*, or steps, of a regular process. One in which the defendant admits the truth of the charge, thus limiting proceedings to the plaint and reply.

Dwipádyam, Mal. (ദ്വിപാദ്യം) A double fine or penalty.

Dwyámusháyaṇa, S. (द्व्यामुषायणः, from द्वि, two, and आमुष्य, an individual person) An adopted son, who retains his right to inherit also from his natural father. The adopted son, the *Dattaka-putra*, properly renounces all claim to direct inheritance from his natural father and paternal relations, except through any affinity which he may derive from his adoptive father; but a continuance of a double relationship may depend upon express stipulation, or where the natural father has no other son, or where certain ceremonies, as that of tonsure, have been performed prior to the adoption in his natural father's house. This sort of adoption is also sometimes distinguished as *Nitya* or *Anitya*, perpetual or temporary: the latter is the case when the tonsure has preceded adoption, and then the children of the adopted son return to the family of the natural grandfather. The term is sometimes considered applicable to the son begotten by a brother on his brother's widow; but this union is no longer regarded as legal. Among the Maraṭhas it is applied to a boy born in adultery.

Dyókáran, Mal. (ദ്യോകാരൻ) A blacksmith.

Dyúta, S. &c. (द्यूत) Gambling, playing either with animate or inanimate materials, as dice, chess, &c., or cocks, rams, and the like.

Dyúta-pratipad, or *-púrnimá*, S. (from प्रतिपद्, the first day of a lunar fortnight, and पूर्णिमा, full moon) The night of the last day of the light half and eve of the first day of the dark half of Kártik, which is to be spent in gambling in honour of *Lakshmí*, the goddess of fortune.

E

Eḍagai, or Eḍagai-Kula, less correctly, Eddagai, Karn. (ಎಡಗೈಕುಲ, from ಎಡ, left) Iḍangai, Tam. q. v. A left-hand caste. According to the Karnatic enumeration of the castes included under this head, they are nine in number:—1. *Panchála*, comprising five subdivisions; as, *Kammáranu*, blacksmith; *Bádige*, carpenter; *Kánsagár*, brazier; *Kalluruṭiga*, mason; *Akasále*, goldsmith. 2. *Bérisethí*, a class of traders. 3. *Devángada*, a class of weavers. 4. *Gáṇigár*, an oil maker. 5. *Gollur*, (?), people said to be employed to carry money; (perhaps a mistake for *Golla*, a shepherd, plur *Gollar*). 6, 7. *Paliwán* and *Palawan*, (?), two tribes of cultivators, (perhaps for *Palligavanu*, a villager, a peasant). 8. *Béḍa*, a low caste of Hindus, living by hunting and catching birds. 9. *Mádiga*, a worker in leather, a shoemaker:

the latter is generally most active in contests with the right-hand castes (Buchanan's Mysore, i. 78).

Edagai hisáb-varu, Karn. A tax levied on workers in leather and skins.

Edaru-chíṭu, Karn. (ఎదరుచీటు) A document given by the purchaser of land engaging to give it back to the seller on repayment of the purchase-money within a definite term.

Eddangalli, or **Yeddangali**, (for, in the languages of the South, and in Malayalim and Tamil especially, an initial *e* is very commonly pronounced as if preceded by an initial *y*) (?) Mal. A dry or grain measure, the measure most in use in Malabar: a cylindrical measure, $2\frac{5}{8}$in. high, $6\frac{1}{8}$in. diameter, or 85 cubic inches: it ought to contain 57,600 grains of kalama-nella, a kind of rice.

Eddu, Tel. (ఎద్దు) An ox, a bullock.

Edduvádu, Tel. (ఎద్దువాడు) A bullock-driver.

Édikóla, Tel. (ఏడికోల) The shaft of a plough.

Eduru-chíṭu, Karn. (ఎదురుచీటు) A note of hand given for another that is lost.

Égáni, Tel. (ఏగాని) A copper coin, equal to ten *kás*.

Egumati, Tel., Karn. (ఎగుమతి) Exportation.

Egumati-digumati, Tel., Karn. (ఎగుమతిదిగుమతి) Export and import.

Ekabhogam, S. **Ekabogam**, or **Yekabogam**, Tam. (एकभोग, ஏகபோகம், from *Eka*, one, and *Bhogam*, fruition) The possession or tenure of village land by one person or family without any co-sharer. The appellation is continued in some instances where other parties have been admitted to hold portions under the original tenure as long as that remains unaltered.

Ékachháya, Tel. (ఏకఛాయ) A bond signed by ten persons.

Ekádaṣí, S. (एकादशी, from एकादश, eleven) The eleventh day of a lunar fortnight.

Ekádaṣi-vrata, S. (from व्रत, a religious obligation) Fasting on the eleventh lunation.

Ekáha, S., Ben., &c. (एकाह) A single day. Fasting for a day.

Eka-játa, S. (from जात, born) Of one parentage, born of the same parents on both sides.

Eka-játi, S. (from जाति, caste) Of the same caste.

Ekámati-ekájati, Guz. (એકામતીએકાજતી, from S. एक, one, and मति, mind, with a rhyming repetition) A term used in agreements, contracts, and the like, by which the subscribers bind themselves jointly and severally to fulfil the terms specified.

Ekanháth, (?) Mar. The total sum of an account that is closed. The name of a particular mark which is drawn over the signature affixed to the account.

Ekapikí, Mar. (एकपिकी) Yielding one crop a-year—land, a field, &c.

Ekaputra, S. (from पुत्र, a son) Having one son only.

Ekariba, Thug. A single or short cry of a jackal suddenly checked—a bad omen.

Ekárṇab, Ben. (একার্ণব, from S. अर्णव, the ocean) An undistinguished multitude, a crowd of persons eating or acting together without distinction of caste.

Ekatra, or **Ekottara**, H., Mar., Ben., &c. (یکترہ, یکوترہ, S. एकत्र) Together, jointly, acting together as one. (In Bundelkhand) A sum total; also applied generally to signify interest at one per cent. per mensem.

Ekbáchhí, (یکباچھی) Distribution of any sum or cess levied upon land at an equal rate.

Ek-ba-dígari, H. (یکبدیگری) One against another (as opposite parties in a suit).

Ekbál, or **Ekwál**, Ben. (একবাল, একওাল) A total sum: a bringing together of details under one head: one of the Zamindar's accounts in which is stated the gross amount of the land in each Ryot's possession in each Mahal, with the deduction for waste, &c., and the disposition of the productive land remaining.

Ekbarda, Thug. An oil maker and vendor; a man of which employment it is considered unlucky to kill.

Ekberjí, Mar. (एकबेरजी, from S. एक, one, and P. برجی) The first entry in the books of sums disbursed or received. A sum total.

Ehberjí-daphtar, Mar. (एकबेरजीदफ्तर) An office at the seat of government, under the Peshwa, to which accounts from all departments were transmitted, and in which they were recorded, after abstracts were made of the receipts and disbursements of the year. Also, the abstracts.

Ekcheṭiyá, Ben. (একচেটিযা) Monopolized.

Ekchetiyá-byabasay, Ben. A monopoly.

Ekchháyáśríta, Ben. (একছাযাশ্রিত, from S. एक-छाया, shade, आश्रित, taking refuge) Held under one obligation (joint bondsmen or sureties).

Ekdhán, Ben. (একধান) (Land) producing one crop of rice in the year.

Ekdarrá, Hindi (एकदररा) A common rate per *bíghá*. See *Dar*.

Ehdarrá ká paṭṭá, Hindi (एकदररा का पट्टा) A lease, in

which the Ryot is to pay the same rate per *bíghá*, whatever crop he may sow.

EKE-ÁNÁ-PAṬṬÁ, Hindi (एकेआनापट्टा) Lease of a definite quantity of land, at an average rate per *bíghá*; a tenure by which Ryots hold in Puraniya.

EKERÍ-KÁRKÚN, Mar. (एकेरी, single, and कारकून, a clerk) An inferior scribe or clerk, one to whom no equipage is allowed.

EKFARDÍ, and EKFASLI, H. (يكفردي, from فرد, a kind, يكفصلي, from فصل, a crop) Land producing only one crop a-year.

EKHÁLÁ, Hindi (एकहाला) Moisture extending through the whole depth of the soil; lit., that which is in one uniform condition (Puraniya).

EKJÁI-JARÍB, Ben. (একজাইজরীব) Measurement of the whole of the lands of a village or district, with a specification of the individual holdings.

EKKAN, Mal. (എക്കൽ) Soil cast on shore by the current of a river.

ÉKKARU, Mal. (എക്കരു) Agricultural implements, apparatus for ploughing.

EKODDISHTA, S. (एकोद्दिष्ट) The *Ṣráddha*, or obsequial ceremony performed for one definite individual deceased, not including other ancestors.

EKPACHHA, H. (يكپچها, from S. एक, and पक्ष, a side) Exparte (as evidence).

EKPADIÁ, Uriya (ଏକପଦିଆ) The total rent of a village, with the proportionate charge to each Ryot.

EKPHASLÁ, Hindi (एकफसला) A single crop. Land yielding one crop a-year. Rate charged in the Ryot's lease, calculated on his rearing only one crop a-year on his land.

EKRÁ, Tel. (ఎకరా) The English word *Acre*.

EKRAKM, Mar. (from رقم, sort) In a lump, at once, the sum of different items.

EKROJO, Hindi (एकरोजो, from P. روز, a day) Authorised daily expenditure of public officers (Jodhpur).

EKSÁLA, H. (يكساله, from P. سال, a year) Annual, for one year, lasting one year, a cess levied originally for but one year.

EKṬARFA, H. (from P. طرف, a side) Ex-parte, on one side.

Ekṭarfa-mukaddama, H. An ex-parte proceeding or suit.

ÉKU, Tel. (ఏకు) A roll of cleaned cotton.

EKUN, Hindi (एकुन) Ben. (একুন) Sum total.

Ekun-beshi, Ben. (from P. بيش, more, excess) Total increase.

Ekun-jamá, Hindi (एकुनजमा) Statement of the total rent of each piece of land in the village accounts.

Ekun-jamín, Hindi (एकुनजमीन) A statement of the total land measured to each Ryot for the current year.

Ekun-kami, Ben. (from P. كم, deficient) Total remission or deficiency.

EKWÁL, Ben., Uriya (একবাল, ଏକୱାଲ, possible corruption of A. اقوال, plur. of قول, agreements) A general account of a village or estate, shewing, under the name of each cultivator, the quantity and description of the land held by him.

ELAKOḶA, or YELAKOḶA, Mal. (എലകൊള) The use of words in place of figures, in which each syllable has a numerical value, and the whole are read backwards (Malabar).

ÉLAM, Mal. (ഏലം) Auction, outcry, public sale; see *Nílám*.

ELE, Karn. (ಎಳೆ) Thread.

ELE, Karn. (ಎಲೆ) A leaf in general, betel leaf.

Elegár, Karn. (ಎಲೆಗಾರ) A betel seller.

ELLA, Tel. (ఎల్ల) ELLAI, Tam. (எல்லை) ELLÉ, Karn. ELLA, Mal. A boundary.

Ellaikal, Tam. &c. (எல்லைக்கல்) *Ellekallu*, Karn. (ಎಲ್ಲೆಕಲ್ಲು) A boundary-stone.

Ellai-takrár, Tam. (from A. تكرار) Boundary dispute.

Ellai-vyajyam, Tam. (S. व्याज) A boundary quarrel or dispute.

Ellarái, Tel. (ఎల్లరాయి) A boundary-stone.

Ellekaṭṭu, Karn. (ಎಲ್ಲೆಕಟ್ಟು) A limit, a boundary.

ELU, Thug. Any single person not a Thug.

ENDH, Thug. A woman.

ÉNDIRAM, Tam. (ஏந்திரம்) A sugar-cane press, a mill, a hand-mill.

ENGILI, Tel. (ఎంగిలి) ENJULU, Karn. (ಎಂಜಲು) ECHCHIL, Tam. Mal. (எச்சில்) Any thing that has become impure by having been in the mouth: orts, leavings, fragments, crumbs, and the like, considered as impure.

ENNAM, Mal. (എണ്ണം) Counting, an account. Charge for reaping, usually ten per cent.; or if paid in kind, one sheaf out of ten.

ENNÁṚI, Mal. (എണ്ണാഴി, from *enta*, or, in composition, *en*, eight) Eight *náṛis*, or two measures.

ENÁTÍ MÁMÚL, Mar. (एनातीमामूल, from A. *Ináyat mâmúl*, عنايت معمول) Customary presents, an additional charge on the district at the time of assessment on this account.

ENTHA, Thug. Rupees, or money of any kind.

ÉNUKÁ, or YENUKÁ, (?) Mal. A certificate given by a hereditary proprietor to the person to whom he has mortgaged or made over occupation of his lands; or a document given to the proprietor by the mortgagee, if he transfer possession (Malabar).

Énuká, or *Yenuhá muri*, (?) Mal. A similar certificate to the last, given to the person to whom the mortgage is transferred: also, a notice from the proprietor to the mortgagee that he has transferred his proprietary right and accompanying liabilities to a third party (Malabar).

Ér, or **Yér**, Tam. (ஏர்) A plough.

Éránmai, Tam. (ஏராண்மை) Tillage.

Éránar, Tam. (ஏராளர்) Husbandmen.

Érkál, Tam. (ஏர்கால்) A yoke, a plough-beam.

Érsámán, Tam. (ஏர்சாமான்) The apparatus of a plough.

Erai, pron. **Irai**, Tam. (எறை) Tax, tribute.

Erai-vari, or *Irai-vari*, Tam. All dues demandable by landholders from their tenants.

Erámáṭi, Asamese (এৰামাটি) Land that has been abandoned after cultivation.

Erápher, or **pheri**, H. (ایراپھیر, from پھرنا, to turn round: the syllable without the initial repeated) Exchange, barter.

Eravu, or **Ervu**, Karn. (ಎರವು, ಎರ್ವು) A thing lent or borrowed for temporary use.

Érí, Tam. (ஏரி) A large reservoir or piece of water, partly artificial, constructed for purposes of irrigation.

Érikarai, Tam. (ஏரிக்கரை) Bank of a reservoir.

Eṛikúdai, Tam. (எறிக்கூடை) A basket used for throwing up water. (From எறி, throwing).

Érimerai, Tam. (ஏரிமேரை) A portion of the crop set apart to meet the expense of keeping the reservoir and watercourses in repair.

Éri-páchal, Tam. (ஏரிப்பாசல்) Watered by channels conducted from a reservoir or tank (land).

Éri, Mal. (ഏരി) A row of stakes to support an embankment.

Érpádu, Tam. (ஏற்பாடு) A decision, a settlement.

Eru, Tam. (எரு) Manure.

Éru, Tel. Karn. (ఏరు) A plough with its apparatus, bullocks, &c., complete.

Erugeru, (?) Tel. Gross produce.

Eṛuku, or **Eṛukaḷa-váḍu**, Karn. (ಎಱುಕು, ಎಱುಕುಳವಾಡು) A man of a tribe living in forests and mountains, resembling gipsies in their habits: the women are famous as fortune-tellers.

Érupálu, Karn. (ಏರುಪಾಲು) The farmer's portion of the produce.

Éruváka, Tel. (ఏరువాక) The commencement of cultivation.

Eshamán, or **Yejamán**, Tam. (எசமான்) A person employing priests: vernacular form of S. *Yajamána*.

Eskar, Mar. (एसकर) A man of a low caste, a *Mahár*, one of the village servants; more usually *Yeskar*.

Étamu, or **Étámu**, Tel. (ఏతము, ఏతాము) **Éṛṛam**, pronounced **Yéttam**, Tam. (ஏற்றம்) A machine on the principle of a lever, for raising water from wells, commonly termed at Madras a *Pikota*.

Étámu-bokkena, Tel (ఏతాముబొక్కెన) The bucket by which the water is drawn.

Yéttachchál, Tam. (ஏற்றச்சால்) The bucket of the *Pikota*.

Yettakol, Tam. (ஏற்றக்கோல்) The bambu by which the bucket is suspended.

Éṛṛappuváram, pron. *Yettappuváram*, Tam. (ஏற்றப்புவாரம்) Share of the charge or tax for watering the lands.

Etu-konamuparra, (?) Mal. The rate of tax levied in Travancore; or one in eight upon the produce of garden land, and three in ten out of rice land.

Ettu, Tel. (ఎత్తు) Weight, a burden; a weight of two *vis*, or $6\frac{1}{4}$ pounds.

Ettuvaḷí, Karn. (ಎತ್ತುವಳಿ) Collecting money.

Etwár, H. (ایتوار) Sunday, abbreviation of S. *Ádítya-vára*, through, *Aïtwár*.

F

Fáâl, A. (فاعل, from فعل, to do) An agent, one who does any thing.

Faida, H. (A. فائدہ) **Pháyídá**, Tel. (ఫాయిదా) Profit, gain, interest. (In this and other Arabic words beginning with *f*, adopted into the Hindu dialects which have not the letter, *ph* is substituted for it).

Faiṣal, or, more correctly, **Faiṣala**, **Fysul**, **Fysula**, (فیصل, فیصلہ) adopted in most dialects with slight modifications, as, Ben. **Phaísálá**, (ফৈসালা) Mar. **Phaisal** and **Phaisallá**, (फैसल, फैसल्ला) Tel. **Phaisalá**, (ఫయిసలా) A decree, a judgment, a decision, adjustment of a quarrel, settlement of a debt.

Faiṣal-tírwai, H. (from the Tam. (தீர்வை) The rates settled on each field at the time of the original survey assessment (Madras).

Faisaláti, Tel. Karn. (ఫయిసలాతి) Settled, as an account especially, according to a decree or award.

Faiṣalnâma, H. &c. (فیصلنامہ) A written sentence or award.

Fak-ar-rahn, H. (A. فکّ ار رهن) Expiration or foreclosure of a mortgage, redemption of a pledge.

Fakhr ul-tujár, H. (A. فخرالتجار) The provost of the merchants: an honorific title granted by the Moghul government to any eminent banker or merchant.

Fakír, Fuqeer, H. (A. فقير, plur. **Fukrá**, فقرا, or **Fakírán**, فقيران) **Phakír**, or **Phukeer**, Mar. (फकीर) Any poor or indigent person. In law, one who possesses only a little property. The most general application is, a Mohammadan religious mendicant, who wanders about the country, and subsists upon alms. Many orders of them are known in Hindustan, named after their founder, or some peculiar practice or doctrine. They are generally divided into two classes: 1. Those who are *Básharâ*, with the law, having families, and following the precepts of the Koran; they are also known as *Sálik*, travellers or pilgrims: and 2. *Be-sharâ*, without the law, or *Majzúb*, 'abstracted,' who lead a life of celibacy and seclusion, and whose sanctity is such as to place them above the necessity of observing the rules of the Koran. The chief Hindustani *Fakírs* are, 1. The *Kádaría* or *Bánawá*, who profess to be the spiritual descendants of *Saiad Abdul-kádir Jiláni*, of Bagdad. 2. The *Chishtía*, followers of *Banda-nawáz*, whose shrine is at *Kalbarga*; they are usually Shias. 3. *Shútáría*, descendants of *Abdul-shútár-i-náh*. 4. *Tabkátía*, or *Madáría*, followers of *Sháh Madár*; many of these are jugglers, and bear or monkey leaders. 5. *Malang*, descended from *Jaman Jatí*, one of *Shah Madár's* disciples. 6. *Rafái*, or *Gurz-már*, descended from *Saiad Ahmed Kabír Rafái*, who appear to beat, cut, and wound themselves without suffering inconvenience, and who, in the belief of the faithful, can cut off their own heads, and put them on again. 7. *Jalália*, followers of *Saiad Jalál ud din Bokhárí*. 8. *Sohágia*, from *Músa Soháy*, who dress like women, wear female ornaments, play upon musical instruments, and sing and dance. 9. *Naksh-bandía*, followers of *Bahá ud din*, of *Nakshband*, distinguished by begging at night, and carrying a lighted lamp. 10. *Báwá piári ha fakírán*, who dress in white. There are other distinctions; and at the *Muharram* a number of the lower classes assume the character and garb of Fakírs, of different ridiculous personations, for the amusement of the populace, and the collection of contributions.

Fakírána, H. (فقيرانه) Appropriated to the support of Fakírs (lands, &c.).

Fakírí, H. (فقيري) *Phakírí*, or *Phakírí*, Mar. (फकिरी, फकीरी) Alms given to *Fakírs*. An item in the village accounts or charge for alms to Mohammadan mendicants. The vocation of a *Fakír*, or any thing relating to one.

Fakt, Fuqt, H. (A. فقط) lit., Only, no more; written at the end of a document, deed, petition, &c., to indicate that it is completed.

Phaktu-jaráiti, Tel. (ఫక్తుజరాయితి, from the A. فقط, and زراعت, cultivation) A richly cultivated country. Nothing but cultivation.

Falam, whence the English *Fanam*, H. (فلم, but more properly, no doubt, *Phalam*, S. (फलं) A small silver coin formerly current at Madras; $12\frac{3}{4}$ are equal to one rupee.

Falán, or **Falánah**, H. (A. فلان, فلانه) A certain person, such a one, used to designate an individual whose name is not specified.

Fáliz, H. (A. فاليز) A field of melons.

Falús, corruptly, **Feloos** and **Fluce**, H. (فلوس, plural of فلس) A small copper coin, of varying weight and value, current in Arabia and Persia, and sometimes applied to the *paisa* of Hindustan. It was also the denomination of a copper coin current at Madras: one *falus* was equal to five *kás* or *cash*.

Fará, H. (P. فرا) lit., Above, over; a term used in the Mohammadan revenue accounts for the increased revenue derived from new taxes.

Farárí, more correctly, **Firárí**, H. (فراري, from A. *Firár*, فرار, flight) Mar. (फरारी) Tel. (ఫరారి) A fugitive, especially a cultivator who has abandoned his lands and home. The head under which the names of absconded revenue defaulters are entered.

Farází, H. (فرازي, from P. *Faráz*, فراز, above) Elevation, exaltation. The name of a sect of Mohammadan reformers, who object to many of the practices of their Indian brethren, established in and about Dacca since 1828, by a man named *Sharkatullah*.

Fard, Furd, incorrectly, **Ferd**, or **Fird**, vernacularly, **Parat**, and **Pharad**, or **Phard**, H. (A. فرد) Mar. (फर्द) A single thing or individual, one out of two, a single leaf or sheet of paper, a written list or statement, a long slip of writing containing a list, a catalogue, &c.

Fard-i-hakíhat, H. (from A. حقيقة, actual state) A memorial, a statement of circumstances, a return made by the officers of government to a requisition for information, a report.

Fard-i-kásht, H. (from P. كاشت, cultivation) Statement of a Ryot's cultivation.

Fard-i-sawál, H. (from A. سوال, asking) A petition, an application. The recommendatory report of a revenue officer in former times in favour of the grant of a *Zamindárí sanad* to the person named in the application, and specifying the districts to be granted.

Fard-i-tafrík, H. (from تفريق, separation) A paper or deed of partition.

Fard-i tashkhís, H. (from تشخيص, settlement) Record of a revenue settlement.

Fariád, Furyad, H. (P. فرياد) vernacularly, Phariyád, or Phairád, Ben. (फरियाद, फैराद) Phiryád, Mar. (फिर्याद) Phiryádu, Tel. (ఫిర్యాదు) Faryádi, or Farayádi, Karn. (ಫರ್ಯಾದಿ, ಫರಯಾದಿ) Píriyádu, Tam. (பிரியாது) Cry for help, complaint, accusation, the entering of a law-suit,

Fariádi, *Furyadee*, H. (فريادي) also *Phariyádi*, *Phairádi*, *Phiryádi*, &c., as before, and corruptly, *Feriaudy*, A complainant, a plaintiff.

Faryádiyava, Karn. (ಫರ್ಯಾದಿಯವ) A plaintiff, a complainant.

Fariád-ras, H. (from P. رس, who arrives) A defender, a protector, one who listens or attends to a complaint.

Faríb, or Fareb, H. (فريب) Fraud, deception, trick, cheating.

Fárigh, H. &c. (A. فارغ) Phárík, or Pháríkh, Mar. (फारीक, -ख) Phárag, Guz. (ફારગ) Free, discharged, settled (as a debt, &c.), concluded (as a law-suit), &c.

Fárigh-khatti, or *-khuttee*, A. (فارغ خطّي, from فارغ, and خط, a writing) changed, vernacularly, to *Phárhhat*, Ben. (फारखत्) *Phárkhat*, or *Pharikhat*, Mar. (फारखत, फरिखत) *Párikhattu*, Tel. (పారిఖత్తు) and written corruptly, *Farikhut*, *Firaghkhuttee*, and *Farughuttee*, A written receipt and acquittance, a deed of release from all demands, a deed of dissolution of partnership or of parcenership, a bill of divorcement.

Fárighkhatána, H. (فارغخطانه) A fee for making out a release or discharge.

Fárkhati, or rather *Phárkhati*, Ben. (adj. फारखती) Set free, acquitted, divorced.

Faríк, H. (A. فريق, from فرق, separating) A troop, a party, a party in a law-suit.

Faríк-áwal, H. (from P. اول, first) The first party in a suit.

Faríк-dúyam, or *sání*, H. (from the P. دويم, or A. ثاني, second) The second party to a suit.

Farihain, H. (A. dual) Both parties to a suit.

Farmáish, or Furmaish, H. (P. فرمايش) Pharmáis, Ben. (फरमाइस) Pharmás, Mar. (फरमास) An order, a command, a direction, a commission to execute any work, a present to a superior.

Far-farmás, or *Phar-pharmás*, corruptly, *Fur-furmanesh*, *Phaur-phurmaish*, Mar. (फडफर्मास) Petty articles of provision formerly exacted from a village by the government or public officers: it occurs also in this sense as *Farmaish* alone. It was also applied to all sorts of produce payable to the government in kind, or at an undervaluation, as part of the government dues.

Farmán, Furman, vernacularly, Pharman, corruptly, Firman, Firmand, Phirmaun, &c., H. &c. (فرمان, फरमान) A mandate, an order, a command, a patent.

Farmán-bardár, H. (from P. بردار, who conforms to) A subject, an officer, one who obeys or executes a mandate.

Farmán-biázi, H. (from بياض) A command under the royal signature or stamp.

Farod, H. (فرود) lit., Alighting, coming down; a term used in the customs department to express the arrival and deposit of goods within certain limits.

Farokht, Furokht, vernacularly, Pharokht, H. &c. (فروخت, फरोखत) Sale, selling.

Farokht-khat, H. (فروخت خط) *Pharoht-khat*, Mar. (फरोख़ खत) A bill or deed of sale: also *Farokht-náma*.

Farosh, H. (P. فروش) Sale, selling. A seller, a dealer.

Farosh-i-namak, corruptly, *Feroosh-nemuck*, H. (P. فروش نمك) Sale of salt. Public sale of salt on account of the government. The revenue derived from the monopoly.

Farsh, H. (A. فرش, from فرش, spreading) A carpet, a mat, a floorcloth, a bed, any thing spread out.

Firásh, H. A. (فراش) A bed, a couch. A female, a wife. In law, a female slave taken to her master's bed.

Farrásh, H. (A. فرّاش, it is commonly written with one r, *Farásh*) A servant whose business it is to spread and sweep the mats, carpets, &c.

Farásh-khána, H. (P. خانه, a house) A room in which carpets, &c., are kept.

Múrda-farásh, H. (مرده فراش) A man of low caste, whose business it is to remove dead bodies when lying in the way.

Farsang, H. (فرسنگ) A Persian measure of distance—the *Parasang* of the ancients—about four miles.

Farz, H. (A. فرض, from فرض, to command) A divine or positive command or ordinance, a statute, an injunction that is not to be disobeyed, a duty not to be neglected; especially applied to the five indispensable obligations of purification, prayer, almsgiving, fasting, and pilgrimage, in contradistinction to other acts which are optional or meritorious only: also (as derivable from فرض, to divide) a definite payment or portion, inheritance, share or portion of inheritance due to an heir: also, a widow's jointure, or her share of the succession to her husband's property.

Farz-âin, A. (with عين, special, essential) An absolute obligation. See the preceding.

Farízat, A. (فريضت) A divine positive statute. A definite share.

Faráiz, H. (A. فرايض, plur. of فريض) The obligatory or divine precepts or statutes of the Mohammadan religion, those which are not to be neglected. The law of inheritance or partition of property.

Farzan, A. (فرضًا, adv.) Specially, definitely: as applied to law, conformably to the special right of inheritance.

Farzan-o-raddan, A. (from ردّ, bringing back) Conformably to direct or special claim, and also to an indirect or reversionary claim, as coming back from failure of nearer heirs.

Farz-kifáiat, A. (from فرض, and كفاية, sufficiency) The sufficiency of a religious obligation, as fulfilled by one person of a party, association, or township, on behalf of the whole.

Farz-rakât, A. (فرض ركعة) Fixed rules of performing prayer.

Farzí, H. (A. فرضي) Ben. *Farjí*, (ফর্জী) By way of proposition, supposititious, fictitious. It is applied especially to a person who is either altogether an imaginary party in a suit or purchase, or to one who, although the ostensible, is not the real principal, or to a suit or purchase conducted or effected under an assumed or fictitious name.

Farzí-mudâi, H. (فرضي مدعي) *Pharjí-bádí*, Ben. (ফর্জী বাদী) A fictitious plaintiff or prosecutor, a person put forward in that character.

Farzi-muhaddama, H. (A. مقدّمه, a law-suit) A fictitious suit or prosecution; one set on foot by other ostensible parties than those really interested.

Ism-farzí, H. (A. اسم, a name) A fictitious name; any thing done under a fictitious name.

Furuz, A. (فروض, plur. of فرض, a portion) Shares, portions, the proportions in which property is divided among those entitled to inherit.

Farzand, H. (P. فرزند, plur. فرزندان) Offspring, progeny, a son or daughter, a child, children. In Mohammadan law, lineal descendants in the male line: females and their posterity are excluded from the order of descent, except the person's own daughter. See *Báfarzandán.*

Fasád, A. (فساد) Vice, depravity, corruption. In law, any species of mental depravity not arising from defect of understanding.

Fásid, A. (فاسد) Base, vile, wicked. In law, one who, according to some authorities, may be deprived of the management of his own affairs, as unfit to be trusted with them.

Faskh, H. (A. فسخ) Breaking an agreement, dissolving a contract, breaking off or dissolving a marriage.

Fasl, **Fusl**, corruptly, **Fussul**, H. (A. فصل, from the verb فصل, to divide) A section, a chapter; but in India more commonly a section of the year, a season; thence also, a crop or harvest. There are two principal harvests in the year, spring and autumn, to which a third is sometimes added; they are—

Fasl-i-rabií, commonly, *Fusuli-rubbee*, or simply, *Rubbee*, (فصل ربع) The spring harvest, which yields dry crops, as wheat, barley, different kinds of pulse and grain that do not require irrigation or much water: the seed is sown towards the close of the periodical rains, or in September-October, and the crops are gathered about February and March.

Fasl-i-kharíf, or *-khureef*, H. (A. فصل خريف) The autumnal harvest, consisting chiefly of rice, or grains requiring irrigation. The seed is sown at the commencement of the rainy season, and the crop is usually reaped after their close, or about October-November.

Fasl-Bhádonwi, H. (فصل بهادونوي) This is an intermediate harvest of occasional cultivation, consisting of grains of quick growth, as millet and different sorts of pulse which may be sown at the beginning of the rainy season, and gathered in the month of *Bhádra*, or about September: this is, however, commonly included in the Kharíf.

Fasláná, H. (فصلانه) Relating to the harvest or the crop; a fee or perquisite derived from it, &c.

Faslí, *Fuslee*, corruptly, *Fassily*, *Fusly*, H. (فصلي) Belonging to the harvest, or season when cultivated, or lands productive of crops assessed according to the value of the crops, or frequency and abundance of the harvests. The harvest year—a mode of computing time prevailing throughout India, and one of the forms used in giving a date to all public orders and regulations. The era originated with the emperor *Akbar*, who, finding different eras current, thought to simplify the existing chronology by introducing a new mode of computing time. In fact, however, he only aggravated the confusion, by adding to the number; the old eras still continuing to be current along with the new. According to *Akbar's* directions, the year of the *Samvat*, corresponding with the *Hijra* year 963=A. D. 1555, and which was therefore *Samvat* 1612 (1555 + 57), was arbitrarily shorn of 649 years, and called the *Faslí* year 963, the same as the *Hijra*. Starting from this point, it has since gone on concurrently with the *Samvat*, or luni-solar year of the Hindus; so that by adding 649 years to the *Fasli* year, we get the *Samvat* year; and by adding 592-93, the difference of the Christian era (649 — 57=592), we obtain the Christian date. The *Fasli* year began on the 10th of the lunar month *Aswin*, corresponding to the 10th September 1555: if more than four months of the year have expired, the addition is 593. Thus, the date of Reg. i., 10th February 1833, corresponds with the 1st of *Phálgun* 1889 (1833 + 56) *Samvat*, and with the 1st of *Phálgun* 1240 (1833 — 593) *Faslí*. In the Dakhin the *Fasli* year is reckoned somewhat differently, being two years later than the same year in Hindustan, having been introduced by *Sháh Jehán*. The addition to the *Fasli* therefore, to convert it into the Christian year, is only 590; thus, the Bomb. Reg. dated *Fasli* 1239 is equivalent to A. D. (1239 + 590) 1829. The Tamil year of *Fasli*, 1257-58, corresponds with 1848 (=1258 + 590). The year is, or ought to be, sidereal; but the Madras government fixed its commencement to the 12th July. Its subdivisions are little attended to, as its sole use is its application to revenue matters; and the year only is specified, not the months.

Fasl-jástí, Tel. (ఫసలజాస్తి, from P. *ziádatí*) An extra crop, one more than usual: an extra cess imposed on land bearing more than one annual crop.

Fasl-kamí, H. (from P. كم, less) Deficiency of harvest. Deduction from the revenue on account of a scanty crop.

Fasli râiyat, H. (فصلي رعية) A cultivator paying revenue according to the crops he raises.

FÁTIHA, corruptly, FATTAHA, FATEHEH, and FATEEAH, H. (A. فاتحه, from فتح, to open) An opening, a commencement. The first *Sura* or chapter of the Koran, which, being read for the benefit of dying Mohammadans, the word has come, in India, to signify prayers offered up for defunct persons on different days after their death, accompanied by alms and distribution of food, as, *Fátiha-chahâram*, on the fourth day; *Fátiha-bístam*, on the twentieth, &c.: also, oblations and offerings to saints, and a variety of prayers and ceremonies used at marriages and funerals, including one observed by women in commemoration of Fatima, the daughter of Mohammad, called the *Fátiha-sahnak*, from *sahnak*, a dish, sweetmeats in small vessels being distributed to the female assistants.

Fátiha-buzurgwár, H. (from P. بزرگ, great) Offerings and prayers for the benefit of the souls of deceased ancestors.

FATWÁ, H. (فتوي) A judicial sentence, a judgment; but more usually applied to the written opinion of the Mohammadan law officer of a court.

Fatáwá, A. (plur. فتاوي) A collection or digest of judicial decisions, several of which are current in Hindustan, especially the Fatáwá Alemgiri, compiled by order of Aurangzeb, printed by the Bengal government (to its great credit) in six quarto volumes.

FAUJ, FOUJ, H. &c. (A. فوج, फौज) An army, a multitude. Police jurisdiction.

Faujdár, H. &c. (فوجدار, फौजदार) An officer of the Mogul government, who was invested with the charge of the police, and jurisdiction in all criminal matters. A criminal judge, a magistrate. The chief of a body of troops.

Faujdárán, H. (P. plur. of *Faujdár*) Assignments of revenue for the maintenance and remuneration of *Faujdárs*.

Faujdári, H. subst., The office of a magistrate or head of police, or criminal judge. adj., Relating to the office of *Faujdár*; criminal, as opposed to civil; levied as a tax for the support of the police, &c.

Faujdári-abwáb, H. Cesses or imposts levied for the support of the *Faujdárs*, or in commutation of the charge so incurred; or upon the *Faujdárs*, or commandants, or military chiefs on the frontiers of Bengal.

Faujdari Âdálat, H. (from A. عدالت, court of justice) The chief criminal court, more usually called in Bengal the *Nizámat Âdálat*, but this designation is in use at Madras and Bombay—Mad. Reg. vii. 1802, Bom. Reg. xiii. 1827, and subsequent Regs. See also *Âdálat*.

Fauj-jaigír, or *Fauj-saránjám*, H. (فوجسرانجام ,فوججايگير) Lands or revenue assigned for the support of troops or of police.

Fauj- or *Phauj-saranjám*, Mar. (फौजसरंजाम) Assignment of revenue for the support of troops and maintenance of forts.

Fauj-sehbandi, or *Fauj-sihbandi*, H. (سيهبندي, militia) The troops of the *Faujdár*, provincial troops or militia employed in garrisoning forts, escorting treasure, and in revenue and police duties.

Farâ-faujdári, H. (from A. فرع, a bough or branch of a tree, met., produce) In Mohammadan finance, the produce of the *Faujdári*, or criminal court, arising from fines and confiscations carried to the credit of government.

FAUTI, corruptly, FOWTEE, H. (A. فوتي, from فَوت, death) A person deceased, or one who is legally defunct, from profligacy or any legal disqualification. The property of one who dies intestate and without legal heirs, which therefore reverts to the sovereign.

Fautí-farári, H. (فوتي, and فراري, disappearance) Dead, and absconded. A list of cultivators who have died, or have deserted their homesteads.

Fauti-náma, H. (P. نامه) A document stating the death of an incumbent, and the names of his heirs.

Fautiyásámí-báhi, Karn. (ಫೌತಿಯಾಸಾಮಿಬಾಕಿ) Balance due to government from a person deceased.

FÁZIL, H. (A. فاضل) PHAJÍL, Mar. (फाजील) Much more, abundant, excessive, a surplus, excess over an estimate, receipt in excess of revenue, &c.

Fázil, H. (A. فاضل, plur. فضلا) A learned or pious man, one learned in the law.

Fázil-wasúl, H. (A. وصول, collections) Extra or additional collections.

Fazúli, H. (from A. فضله, redundance) In Mohammadan law, an unaccredited agent, one who acts for another without authority, and whose transactions are invalid unless confirmed by the principal.

Fazúli-biâ, H. (فضولي بيع) Sale of another's property without his authority: the sale may be confirmed or annulled at pleasure by the owner.

FAZÍH, H. (A. فضيح) Disgraceful, vile, infamous: mismanaging an estate or property.

Fazíhat, H. (A. فضيحة) *Phajeti*, Guz. (ફજેતી) Disgrace, infamy.

FI, H. (A. في) A particle and prefix to nouns, signifying in, with, by, with respect to; before Arabic nouns it is followed by the article ال, the initial of which merges into the final of the prefix.

Fi'l-faur, (في الفور) Now, immediately, in brief.

Fi'l-hál, H. (في الحال) Instantly, presently, actually, on the spot.

Fi'l-hakíkat, H. (في الحقيقت) In truth, in fact.

Fil-jumla, H. (في الجمله) Upon the whole.

Fil-wákiâ, H. (في الواقع) In fact, certainly, in truth.

Fi-kasi, H. (P. كس, some one, an individual) Tax per individual, poll tax.

Fi-sad, H. (from the P. صد, a hundred) Per cent.

Fi-sabíl-ullah, A. (في سبيل الله) In the way of God, or for his service: applied to alms given to persons to enable them to equip themselves for a holy warfare, or for pilgrimage.

FIDÍAT, H. (A. فدية, from فدا, ransom, sacrifice) In Mohammadan law, a redemption or redemptionary atonement for what would else be forfeited; ransom or redemptionary fine paid by a master for his slave who has committed some fault, which would make him the slave of the injured party.

FIDWÍ, H. (A. فدوي, from فدا, devoted to) Servant, slave; but only used as a term of humility in speaking of oneself, Your slave, your humble servant.

FIHRIST, H. (P. فهرست) PHIRASTU, Tel. (ఫిరస్తు) A list, a catalogue, an inventory.

Fihrist-i-dihát, H. A list of the villages of an estate or district; one of the accounts kept formerly by the Kanungos in Bengal.

FIKH, H. (A. فقه) Knowledge of religion and law. Practical jurisprudence, in which there may be difference of doctrine without involving any sectarial opinion.

FÎL, H. (A. فعل) Act, action. In A. grammar, The verb.

Fîl-shaniâ, or *Fial-i-shanía*, corruptly, *Feeal-shuneea*, H. (A. فعل شنيع) An abominable or unnatural offence.

Fîl-zámin, H. (A. فعل ضامن) *Phailjámin*, Mar. (फैलजामिन)

Phiyál-yámin, Uriya (ଫିୟାଲ୍‌ୟାମିନ୍) A surety for good or peaceable conduct.

Fil-zámini, H. (A. فعل ضامني) Security for conduct, surety for good and orderly behaviour.

FÍL, H. (A. فيل) An elephant.

Fíl-khána, (فيل خانه) Elephant stables.

FISK, H. (فسق) Iniquity, villainy.

Fásik, (A. فاسق) Wicked, abandoned, depraved; one unworthy of credit as a witness in a court of law.

FITR, H. (A. فطر) Breaking a fast. Eating at sun-set daily during the Ramazán. The ceremony of breaking the fast at the end of the month. See *Íd-ul-fitr.*

Fitrat, H. (A. فطرة) Alms given at the *Íd-ul-fitr.*

FITÚR, H. (A. فتور) PHITÚR, Mar. (फितूर) Treachery, deceit, fraud. In India it is applied more especially to traitorous or rebellious conduct; revolt, insurrection, desertion.

Fitúri, H. &c. (فتوري) A traitor, a rebel, an insurgent, a deserter, one who has changed sides.

Phitúr-phándá, Mar. (फितूरफांदा) Seditious risings and plots.

FOTAH, H. (P. فوطه) A bag, a bag of money, a purse. Tax, revenue, land-tax, annual rent of cultivated land.

Fotadár, H. (فوطهدار) *Potadár,* or *Potdár,* Ben. (পোতদার) Mar. (पोतदार) *Podár,* whence the common term *Podar,* H. (پودار) A banker, a cash-keeper, a money-changer, an officer in public establishments for weighing money and bullion, and examining and valuing coins.

Fotadárí, or *Potadárí,* H. &c. The occupation or business of a *Fotadár.*

Fota-khána, H. &c. A treasury, a banking-house, a money-changer's shop.

FURNADAYAM, (?) (perhaps from *púrṇa,* full, and *dáyam,* to be given) spelled corruptly *Fournaydyem* and *Fournydiam,* The money rent in commutation of the revenue in kind in the south of India.—App., 5th Rep. 771.

FURSAT, H. (A. فرصت) Leisure, opportunity, suspension of public business for a season.

G

GABAR, GUBUR, incorrectly, GUEBRE, H. (P. گبر) An infidel in general, but commonly applied to a *Pársi,* or fire worshipper.

GABÁSAN, Ben. (গবাসন) A skinner, a currier, a tanner.

GABBÁDU, Tel. (గబ్బాడు) Gruff goods; small articles, as treacle, cocoa-nuts, spiceries, &c., sold by hucksters.

GÁBDÍ, GÁBTI, or GÁBÍD, Mar. (गाबदी, गाबती, गाबीद) A fisherman.

GABHÁN, GUBHAN, (?) Land contiguous to a village.

GÁBHIN, H. (گابهن, S. गर्भिणी) A pregnant woman, or a cow with calf.

GABRAUṬÁ, H. (گبروٹا) A large beetle, found in old cow-dung and dunghills: also called *Gobraura* and *Gobaraunda.*

GÁCHH, Ben. (গাছ) A tree; applied to any thing fibrous, as, এক গাছ রশী, a rope of a single cord.

GACHCHU, Karn. (ಗಚ್ಚು) Mortar, plaster.

Gachchugáṇa, Karn. (ಗಚ್ಚುಗಾಣ) A lime-mill.

GACHCHHÁVAT, Ben. (? from the S. गच्छावत्, having gone, passing) The compulsory sale of articles at a higher than the market price.—2d Rep. 1772, p. 293.

GACHHÁGACHHI, Ben. (গছাগছি, from গছ, to deposit or receive in deposit) Mutually deposited or intrusted, a mutual deposit.

Gachhita, Ben. (গছিত) Deposited, a pledge.

GÁCHHÍ, H. (گاچهي) A pad for the back of a beast of burden.

GÁD, H. (گاد) Sediment of dirty water.

GAḌ, GUḌ, H. (گڈ) A boundary mark (Dehli).

GAḌ, GUḌ, Mar. (गड) also GAḌI and GAḌHI, (गडी, गढी) GAḌI, Karn. (ಗಡಿ) in Hindustani also GAḌH or GAṚH, &c., q. v. (the cerebral *ḍ* being pronounced something like *ṛ,* and in Hindustani being always aspirated) A small fort, especially a hill fort.

Gaḍkarí, Mar. (गडकरी) A soldier or peon serving in a hill fort.

Gaḍnís, Mar. (गडनीस) An officer who keeps the account of the charges of a fort.

GÁḌÁ, Mar. (गाडा) A common cart for carrying loads. See *Gáḍí.*

GAḌA, Karn. (ಗಡ) A ferry. A stipulated term for payment of a debt or sum due.

Kaigaḍa, Karn. (ಕೈಗಡ) A loan without interest.

Mungaḍa, Karn. (ಮುಂಗಡ) Advance of pay.

Tengala-gaḍa, Karn. (ತಿಂಗಳಗಡ) Monthly term of payment.

Varshada-gaḍa, Karn. (ವರುಷದಗಡ) Annual payment, or payment at the end of a year.

GADAM, GUDUM, Mar. (गदम) Watery, moist (as land), receiving and retaining water (soil).

GADAMU, Tel. (గాదము) Grass growing in fields of dry grain.

GÁDAR, also GADDAR or GUDDUR, H. (گادر) Half-ripe fruit or corn.

GÁḌAR, GAḌUR, H. (گاڑر, गाडर) A sheep.

Gadaríá, Guduria, H. (گڈریا, गडरिया) *Gádaṛiyá*, Ben. (গাড়রিযা) A shepherd, one by caste as well as occupation. There are several subdivisions of the caste in the north-west provinces, between whom no social intercourse subsists. Amongst the *Gadaríás* the younger brother marries the elder brother's widow: the elder brother has not the same privilege.

GAḌḌA, Tel. (గడ్డ) GAḌḌE, Karn. (ಗಡ್ಡೆ) A bulbous root. URLA- or URALA-GAḌḌA or GAḌḌÉ, A potatoe.

GADDA, Tel. (గద్ద) A water-course (Ganjam).

Gaddateru-inámu, (?) Rent-free grant for bringing waste land into cultivation (Madras).

GADDÁD, GUDDAD, (?) Broken uneven ground brought into cultivation by the hand. A class of landholders in the ceded districts, holding their lands at a reduced rent, on account of their having levelled and brought broken ground into cultivation. Ceded districts.—5th Rep. 794.

GADDE, corruptly, GUDDEY, Karn. (ಗದ್ದೆ) Wet or paddy land; land fit for rice cultivation, or on which rice is grown. An embankment, a bank or dike.

Gadde-bedalu, Karn. (ಗದ್ದೆಬೆದಲು) Wet and dry land, or wet and dry cultivation.

Gadde-gada, Karn. (ಗದ್ದೆಗದ) A ridge or bank dividing rice fields.

Gadde-hasi-hullu-haṇa, Karn. (ಗದ್ದೆಹಸಿಹುಲ್ಲುಹಣ) A tax formerly levied in Mysore on grass grown on the banks of the paddy fields, half of which was given by the cultivators for the horses of the Raja.

Gadde-haṭṭu, Karn. (ಗದ್ದೆಹಟ್ಟು) A bank, a dike, an embankment.

Gadde-maḍi, Karn. (ಗದ್ದೆಮಡಿ) A paddy field.

Gadde-níru-huḷi, Karn. (ಗದ್ದೆನೀರುಹುಳಿ) A tax on water supplied by government reservoirs to rent-free or pagoda lands.

Gadde-zamin, (?) Lands on which crops that depend upon the rains are grown.

GAḌḌEMU, Tel. (గడ్డెము) Force, compulsion.

GADḌHRI, H. (گڈهري) The unripe pod of the gram plant (Cicer arietinum).

GAḌḌI, Tel. (గడ్డి) Grass, straw.

Gaḍḍi-gával, Tel. (గడ్డిగావల) Waste land (Salem).

GÁDE, Tel. (గాదె) A barn.

GADI, Ben. (গদি) GÁDI, Mar. (गादी) GADDI, GUDDEE, H. (گدّي) A cushion or any padded seat, or sheet, or carpet on which a person sits. The seat of rank or royalty, a simple sheet, or mat, or carpet on the floor, with a large cushion or pillow at the head, against which the great man reclines.

Gaddi-nashín, H. (from P. نشين, who sits) A chief, a principal, a prince, one who sits upon the *gaddi*: the heir-apparent is sometimes so designated.

GADGARÁ, Hindi (गदगरा) Abounding in moisture (soil, &c.)

GADGOL, H. (گدگول) Muddy water.

GÁDHAN, Asamese (গাধন) Poll-tax.

GADHE-KÁ-HAL, H. (گدهي کا هل) An ass's plough, one drawn by asses over the ruins of a captured fort, as a mark of contempt.

Gadhe-par-charháná, H. (گدهي پرچڑهانا) To seat upon an ass, a kind of punishment or disgraceful public exposure; sometimes the culprit was seated with his face to the tail, or had his face partly blackened.

GAḌÍ, or GAṚÍ, Mar. (गडी) A person or individual of a class or caste; used in this sense in composition, as, *Bráhman-gaḍi*, an individual Bráhman, &c.

GÁḌÍ, Ben., Mar. (গাড়ী, गाडी) Tel. and Karn. (ಗಾಡಿ) A carriage, a cart, especially for the carriage of persons. In Hindustani it is written as well as pronounced *Gárí*, q. v.

Gáḍe-bagár, Mar. (गाडे बगाड) Swinging round a mast fixed in a cart which moves round the idol.

GAḌI, or GAṚI, Guz. (ગડી) A common labourer, a porter.

GAḌI, Karn. (ಗಡಿ) A district. It has a similar meaning in the Rajmahal hills, or a small division of country; also in Karn., a boundary.

Gaḍi-hallu, Karn. (ಗಡಿಕಲ್ಲು) A stone set up to mark a boundary.

GÁDÍ, Ben. (গাদী) Mar. (गादी) GAḌI, Karn. (ಗಡಿ) Half a ream, or ten quires of paper.

GÁDÍ, Mar. (गादी) An exclusive right of sale, a monopoly.

GADIÁṆUṆ, Guz. (ગદીઆણું) A goldsmith's weight, equal to 20 *vals*, 8 *máshas*, or half a *tola*, or about 52 grains troy.

GADÍCHAṬ, or GUDEECHUT, H. (گديچٹ) A sort of grass similar to Dúb, but much larger, also used as fodder.

Gádípati, Ben. (গাদীপতি, from *Gádi*, a bench) The chief of a body of religious mendicants.

Gadrá, Gudra, H. (گدرا) Unripe corn or fruit.

Gaḍuba, -bu, or **Gaḍuva**, Karn. (ಗಡುಬ, -ಬು, ಗಡುವ) **Gaḍuvu**, Tel. (గడువు) A fixed term for payment, an instalment.

Gaḍu-hundi, Karn (ಗಡುಹುಂಡಿ) A bill payable after a certain date, or by instalments.

Gael, Thug. Treasure.

Gagara, Thug. A class of Thugs so called.

Gaggari, or **-re**, Karn. (ಗಗ್ಗರಿ -ರೆ) Pieces of loose iron fastened to a stick to frighten animals and reptiles, commonly carried by post-runners.

Gágrá, H. (گاگرا) A subdivison of the Bhangi, or sweeper caste.

Gahái, H. (گہائي) The custom of treading out the sheaves of corn by bullocks.

Gáhak, H. (گاهک, from S. ग्राहक) A purchaser.

Gaham, Thug. Food.

Gahan, Guhun, H. (گہن, S. ग्रहणं) An eclipse.

Gaháṇ, corruptly, **Ghaan**, Mar. (गहाण, from S. ग्रहणं, taking) **Gahná**, H. (گہنا) A pawn, a pledge or thing in pawn, a mortgage. Land held by mortgage tenure.

Gahánkhat, Mar. (from P. خط, a writing) A mortgage-bond, a pawnbroker's ticket.

Gahán-patra, corruptly, *-putr*, Mar. (गहाणपत्र) A deed of mortgage.

Gahánwat, Mar. (गहाणवट) In pledge, by way of pledge, pledged.

Gáhan, Gáhun, H. (گاهن) A harrow with teeth for eradicating grass from ploughed land.

Gaharí, H. (گہري, गहरी) Low swampy ground, fit for rice cultivation.

Gaharwár, Guhurwar, corruptly, **Gherwál**, (گہروار) A tribe of Rájputs, extensively spread through the north-west provinces: one of the thirty-six royal races, apparently at an early period settled at Kanoj.

Gáhi, H. (گاهي) Five, a total or aggregate of five parts, a mode of reckoning; counting by *gáhis* is counting by fives.

Gahiná, Hindi (گہنا, गहिना) also read **Gáhan** and **Gahán**, (गाहन, गहान) A heavy plank or flat piece of wood on which a man stands whilst it is dragged by oxen over a ploughed field, to level the ground. See *Gáhan*.

Gahíra, Ben., Uriya (গহীর, from S. गम्भीर, deep) Land lying low, or in a hollow.

Gahloṭ, or **Gahiloṭ**, H. (گہلوت) A tribe of Rájputs, extensively spread through the north-west provinces and Rajputana. The Raja of Udaypur is a member of one of their most celebrated branches, the Sisodya.

Gahúṅ, Mar. (गहूं) Wheat. See *Gehun*.

Gahúrí, H. (گہوري) Demurrage.

Gaini, also read **Geni**, and, corruptly, **Guenie**, or **Gueny**, Karn. (ಗೈಣಿ) Rent paid to the landlord or proprietor. (The Glossary, 5th Rep., explains it incorrectly, Tenant). The word itself is rather doubtful, and does not occur in Reeve's Karnáta Dictionary. It should possibly be *Gehini*, from *Geha*, S. and Karn., a house, Relating to a house, house-rent, &c. Brown says it is the same as *Kainí*, (कैणी) A field.

Gaini-chali, or *Chali-gaini*, corruptly, *Guenie-chalie*, or *-chally*, Karn. (ಗೈಣಿಚಾಲಿ) A tenant-at-will, one whose rent is resumable.

Gaini-kár, *Gaini-gár*, or *Gaini-wálá*, Karn. A tenant, a rent-payer.

Gaini-nairmul, (?) Karn. A proprietor of land.

Gaini-shadmal, (?) Karn. A tenant at a fixed and perpetual rent.

Gaini-chiti, corruptly, *Gueny-chit*, Karn. Agreement for payment of rent, receipt or acknowledgment of rent.

Múl-gaini-gár, Karn. Original lessee or mortgagee.

Gairá, H. (گيرا, गैरा) A sheaf of corn, as much given at harvest to the lower classes of a village as will yield a *sér* and a quarter of grain.

Gairádá, Tel. (గైరాడా) Waste, uncultivated.

Gairádá-sthalamu, Tel. (from S. स्थल, soil) Waste land.

Gaita, Tel. (గైత) Name of a barbarous tribe in the Rajamahendri district.

Gaj, Guj, Ben., Mar., &c. (গজ or गज, a vernacular corruption of P. *Guz*, گز) A measure of length. See *Gaz*.

Gaj-mojaṇí, Mar. (गजमोजणी) Measuring fields by the *gaj* measuring rod.

Gájá, H. (گاجا) First sowing of rice at the foot of the hills, which takes place in the month *Baisákh*.

Gájan, Ben. (গাজন) A band or company of persons inflicting tortures on themselves in honour of *Ṣiva*, at the swing-festival. See *Charak*.

Gájar, H. (گاجر) A carrot.

Gajgír, Ben. (গজগীর) A plasterer, a terrace maker: a terrace.

Gajjar, Gujjur, H. (گجّر) Swampy ground.

GÁL, H. (گال) A kind of tobacco.

GÁLÁ, H. &c. (P. گالا, गाला) A pod of cotton, or a ball of carded cotton.

GÁLÁ, Ben. (গালা) Lac, sealing-wax.

GAḶA, Mar. (गळ) A hook, a fish-hook, the hangman's hook, that by which those who swing are suspended.

GALÁ, H. &c. (گلا, गला) The throat, the neck.

Gaḷápháṅsa, Mar. (गळाफांस) A halter, a noose for the neck.

GALÁMÁṬÍ, Hindi (गलामाटी) Rich free mould; from *galá*, rotted (Puraniya).

GAḶANTA, Mar. (गळंत) A cypher placed after the first letter of a word, or the first word of a sentence, to denote the omission of the rest.

GALÁY-DAṚI, Ben. (গলাযদড়ি, from *galay*, on the neck, and *daṛi*, a rope) Hanging, strangulation.

Galáyadaṛiyá, Ben. (গলাযদড়িযা) Deserving to be hanged.

GALÉVU, Karn. (ಗಲೇವು) A complete ploughing apparatus.

GÁLÍ, H. &c. (گالی) Abuse.

GÁLI, Tel. (గాలి) A heap of salt, equal to 15 *garces*.

GALIÁ, H. (گليا) A bullock that lies down in the midst of his work.

GAḶIGE, Karn. (ಗಳಿಗೆ) A large basket for storing corn.

GALLÁ, **GULLA**, Mar., Tel., &c. (गल्ला, గల్లా, vernacular corruption of the A. *Ghala*, غله) Grain of every kind: also *Ghalla*, q. v.

Gallá-kharídí, Mar. (गल्लाखरीदी) A cess levied on all purchases of corn by the village.

Gallá-tolapaṭṭí, Mar. (गल्लातोलपट्टी) A cess levied on a village, to cover any possible loss of weight in dividing the crop with the cultivator.

Gallekarí, Mar. (गल्लेकरी) A corn-chandler.

Galle-paṭṭi, Mar. (गल्लेपट्टी) A tax imposed upon villages under the Maraṭha government, in lieu of grain formerly exacted for the public stables. An extra money cess charged on the amount of the crop, at so much per *maund*.

GALLÍ, **GULLEE**, H. &c. (گلّی, गल्ली) A lane, an alley.

GALLU, Karn. (ಗಲ್ಲು) Hanging, as of a culprit.

Gallinahaga, Karn. (ಗಲ್ಲಿನಹಗ) A halter.

GALTANS, H. (گلتنس) Dying without issue. (From the S. *galita*, गलित, lost, and *anṣ*, अंश, portion or inheritance).

GALUÄ, Hindi (गलुआ) Soil excessively humid, in which the crops turn yellow and rot (Puraniya).

GAM, pronounced **GOM**, Ben. (গম, abbreviation of S. गोधूम) Wheat.

GÁM, corruptly, **GAUM**, H. &c. (گام, abbreviation of ग्राम) A village. See *Grám*.

Gámagánelekhkha, Karn. (ಗಾಮಗಾಣೆಲೆಖ್ಖ) Revenue account of a district containing several villages.

GAMBHÍR, Hindi, also abridged, **GAIHIR** and **GAHARÍ**, (गम्भीर, गैहिर, गहरी, from the S. गम्भीर, deep) Deep, commonly applied to soil of a rich quality, descending to a more than usual depth before reaching the sub-soil: most of the soil of Malwa is so termed.

GAMAḶLAVÁḌU, Tel. (గమళ్లవాడు) A toddy drawer; the caste following that business, said to be derived from a *Ṣúdra* father and *Kshatriya* mother.

GAMRÍ, Hindi (गमरी) The corn when swelled out with the ear not yet protruded.

GÁṆÁ, Karn. (ಗಾಣಾ) An oil-mill.

Gáṇaterige, Karn. (ಗಾಣತೆರಿಗೆ) A tax on oil-presses in Mysore.

GAṆA, S., adopted in most dialects, (गण) A troop, a flock, a multitude; an assembly of families to decide upon a domestic difference or impropriety. In Mysore it is applied apparently to the sect or society of Lingayats.

Gaṇáchár, Karn. (ಗಣಾಚಾರ, from S. आचार, usage) A fee formerly paid by the Lingayats to their priests at their marriages; subsequently included in the cesses payable to the government (in Mysore). Properly, the observance or established usage of any associated body.

Gaṇáchári, incorrectly, *Gunnacharee*, Karn. (ಗಣಾಚಾರಿ, from S. गण, and आचारी, a teacher) A censor, an inspector of morals appointed originally by the government of Bidnur, but continued under the Maraṭhas in Karnáta. His duty was especially to notice violations of caste, eating forbidden food, intercourse with impure castes, fornication and adultery, which he was empowered to punish by expulsion from the caste, and restoration to it could not be effected without his concurrence. He received fees on marriages and deaths, and fines for minor offences against caste, for which the office still subsists partially, although usually set up by the castes themselves; the individual invested with the authority being one of themselves, recognised as a chief or head.

Gaṇadravya, Karn. (from S. द्रव्य, thing) Common stock, common property.

Gaṇagoshṭhi, Ben. (গণগোষ্ঠী) A race, a family, family lineage or genealogy.

Gaṇakumáriha, Karn. (ಗಣಕುಮಾರಿಕೆ) A tax on the

income (? the marriages of the daughters) of Lingayat priests.

Gaṇapati, S. (गणपति) A name of Gaṇesa.

Gaṇárádhana, Karn. (ಗಣಾರಾಧನ) A feast given by a Jangama priest to his followers.

Gaṇeṣa, S. (गणेश) A Hindu divinity, characterized by an elephant's head, who, in his character of remover of obstacles, is worshipped especially at the commencement of an undertaking. This, and similar terms as the preceding, imply that he is lord or chief (ईश -पति, &c.) over various classes (*gaṇas*) of inferior divinities.

Gaṇeṣa-chatúrthí, S. A festival in honour of Gaṇeṣa on the 4th of the light half of Bhádra.

Gaṇiká, Hindi, &c. (S. गणिका) A prostitute.

Gaṇaka, S., adopted in most dialects, (गणकः) An astrologer, a caster of nativities, a keeper of genealogies, and negociator of marriages.

Gaṇana, S., and in many dialects, (गणन) Computing, calculating.

Gaṇauri, H. (گنَوري) A bulrush (Eastern Oudh).

Gaṇḍa, Guṇḍa, H. (گنڈه) Gaṇḍá, Ben. (গণ্ডা) A money of account, equivalent in reckoning to four *kaunris* or cowry shells, or the twentieth part of an *ana*. Twenty *gaṇḍas* make one *pan*. The value of the *gaṇḍa* in practice varies, and from four to six may be rated as a *chhadám*, but as a mode of reckoning in general it invariably implies four. To count by *gaṇḍas* is to count by fours.

Gaṇḍákiyá, Ben. (গণ্ডাকীয়া) Method of counting by four, the most usual multiple in Bengal.

Ganda, (?) Lands situated nearest to the village.

Ganda, H. (گنده) Fetid, foul smelling.

Gáṇḍá, H. (گانڈا, गांडा) Sugar-cane, or a cane when ready for cutting.

Gaṇḍá, H. (گنڈا) A knotted string round a child's neck to protect it from evil eyes. Mar. (गंडा) A string bound round the wrist or ancle, as a charm or protection against evil influences.

Gaṇḍagrám, Ben. (গণ্ডগ্রাম) A principal or respectable village.

Gándada-pommu, Karn. (ಗಂದದ-ಪೊಮ್ಮು) A fine, formerly levied from the cultivators of gardens for turning up sandal seedlings in ploughing (Mysore).

Gándal or Gándar, Gandul, Gandur, H. (گاندل, گاندر) Thatching grass, the root of which, or *khaskhas*, is used for *Tattis* (Andropogon muricatum).

Gandam, Gundum, H. (P. گندم) Wheat.

Gaṇḍapendára, Karn. (ಗಂಡಪೆಂಡಾರ) A badge of honour, a medal, &c.

Gandarwálá, Gundurwala, H. (گندروالا) Part of a sugar-mill, the receptacle of the cane before it is cut.

Gaṇḍásá, Gaṇḍási, Guṇḍasa, Guṇḍasee, H. (گنڈاسا, گنڈاسي) A sickle in general, one used for cutting down sugar-cane, *jawár* stalks, or thorny bushes. Also, in Dehli, a tax formerly levied on the number of such implements in the hands of the Ryots.

Gaṇḍeri, H. (گنڈيري) Pieces of sugar-cane.

Gandha, S. &c. (गन्धः) Smell, fragrance, any fragrant substance, sandal-wood or other odorous matter pounded for rubbing on the person or on the figures of the gods, &c. In Karn. *Ganda* or *Gandha*, (ಗಂದ, ಗಂಧ) means especially, Sandal wood.

Gandha-baṇik, Ben. (from বণিক, a trader) A druggist, a perfumer.

Gandha-biroza, H. (گندهبروزه) Frankincense, the resin of the Boswellia thurifera: also of a kind of pine (P. longifolia).

Gandhasari-nellu, Karn. (ಗಂಧಸರಿನೆಲ್ಲು) A sort of rice grown in Mysore.

Gandhel, H. (گندهيل) A fragrant grass (Andropogon calamus aromaticus), from the leaves, culms, and roots of which a sweet-smelling essential oil is distilled.

Gandhíla, H. (گندهيلا) Fetid, bad smelling. The name of a low and vagrant caste in the north-west provinces, who make mats, and exhibit feats of activity: they are also thieves.

Gandhottama, Tel. (ಗಂಧೋತ್ತಮು, S. गन्ध, and उत्तम, best) Spirituous liquor, the fermented juice of the palm, *tári* or *toddy*.

Gandha, Ben. (গংধ) Relationship, connexion, friendship.

Gandharbba, S. (गन्धर्ब्बः) A kind of inferior divinity, attendant upon Indra and Kuvera, and distinguished for musical proficiency.

Gándharbba, S. (गान्धर्ब्ब) Relating to a Gandharbba, as music, singing; a form of marriage formerly recognised as legal, depending solely upon the mutual consent of parties of the *Kshetriya*, or military order.

Gaṇḍhu, H. (گنڈهو) A branch of the Ját tribe.

Gandi, Tel. (ಗಂಡಿ) A breach in the bank of a tank made by the water, a channel cut in it to let out the water for irrigation: also a pass in the hills.

Gandrúpin, H. (گندروپن) A Hindu dancing-girl: (perhaps an abridgement of S. *Gandarbha-rúpiṇí*).

Gangá, Gunga, S. (गंगा) The river Ganges, the river Godaveri, any river. (The word occurs in all the dialects, but sometimes in composition with the final shortened or elided).

Gangála, H. (گنگالہ) Lands subject to inundations of the Ganges.

Gangá-jal, *Gunga-jul* Ben. (গংগাজল) The water of the Ganges, sometimes applied to the water of any river reputed holy. A kind of oath, swearing by the Ganges water; more correctly, *Gangá-jal-sapath*, oath by the Ganges water, or *Gangá-jal-sparṣa*, touching the water of the Ganges, which forms part of the ceremony.

Gangájali, Ben. (S. গংগাজলী) Swearing by the water of the Ganges.

Gangájaliyá, Ben. (S. গংগাজলীযা) A person who has administered, or who has taken an oath by the Ganges: used contemptuously.

Gangálábh, Ben. (S. গংগালাভ, from S. লাভ, obtaining) Being brought to the banks of the Ganges to die there. Committing a dead body to the river. Also *Gangáprápti*, (from S. प्राप्ति, obtaining) and *Gangáyátrá*, (from S. यात्रा, a going).

Gangáputra, or *Gungapootr*, S. H. (from S. पुत्र, a son) A tribe of inferior Bráhmans, who pretend to be a branch of the Kanoj Bráhmans, and who call themselves sons of Gangá, claiming a right to attend pilgrims and direct their ablutions at Benares, and other holy places on the banks of the Ganges. At Benares, where they are most numerous, they claim a hereditary right to the bank between high and low-water mark. Some follow agriculture.

Gangá-Rám, Thug. Ráma and Gangá, two divinities; but, as used by the Thugs, a hint that danger is nigh.

Gangáságara, S. (from सागर, the ocean) The place where the Bhágirathí branch of the Ganges debouches into the Bay of Bengal.

Gangá-yamuná, commonly, *Gunga-jumna*, (from गंगा, and यमुना, the river Yamuná, vulgo Jumna) A mode of adjusting an account of borrowed money, interest paid to the creditor until the whole debt is discharged, and, on the other hand, interest allowed to the debtor on all the instalments he may pay.

Gang-barár, or *-bar-ámad*, H. (گنگبرار, or گنگبرامد, from P. بر, and آمد, or آر, bringing or coming) Alluvial land recovered from a river, especially from the Ganges.

Gangodaka, S. (from उदक, water) The water of the Ganges, or any holy river.

Gang-shikast, H. (from P. شکستن, to break) Encroachments of the Ganges, or any other river.

Gangthaḍí, also *Gangátír*, Mar. (गंगथडी, गंगातीर) The country along the banks of the *Godaverí* river. (From S. स्थली, a place, or तीर, a bank).

Gángáná, Tel. (గాంగానా) By villages, settlement of revenue by villages; the same as *Mauzawár*: (vernacular corruption of *gaon*, or *gráma*, repeated).

Gangutía-bándi, Uriya (ଗଙ୍ଗୁଟିଆବାନ୍ଧି) An embankment, a dike.

Ganige, Tel. (గానిగె) An oil-mill, one worked by oxen.

Ganigár, Karn. (ಗಾಣಿಗಾರ) An oil-maker or vendor.

Ganime, Tel. (గనిమె) A ridge of earth dividing two fields.

Gaṇita, S. (गणित) Counted, computed; computation, arithmetic.

Bíja, or *Víja-gaṇita*, Algebra.

Ganj, Gunj, corruptly, Gunje, H. &c. (P. گنج) A mart, a market: in Bengal and Hindustan a village or town which is an emporium for grain and other necessaries of life: in the designation of such a place the word is commonly compounded with some other word, not unfrequently English, as, *Islám-ganj*, *Captain-ganj*, *Revel-ganj*, &c. In Maratha the word also signifies a heap or pile of grain, a rick, a stack, &c.

Ganjí, Mar. (गंजी) A small stack.

Ganjíkhána, Mar. (P. خانہ, a house) A yard with many stacks of hay, &c.: a lumber-room.

Gánja, or Gánjha, H. (گانجہ) The hemp plant (Cannabis sativa), or, according to some authorities, a different species (Cannabis indica): according to others, it is applicable to the plant only whilst young. In the north-west provinces the term also designates an intoxicating liquor, an infusion of the young flowers and leaves in water. In Bengal the same are dried and pounded, and then used in smoking. The intoxicating property depends in either case upon the resinous exudation of the plant adhering to the vegetable substance. See *Bhang*.

Gánjákhor, Ben. (গাংজাখোর) A smoker of hemp, one addicted to its use.

Gánjawálá, H. (گانجہ والا) A vendor of intoxicating preparations of hemp.

GÁNJAR, H. (گانجر) A kind of grass.

GANJELI, H. (گنجيلي) A kind of coarse sacking or canvas made from the fibres of the hemp plant.

GANJÍFA, H. &c. (P. گنجيفه, गंजीफा) Cards; the game, or the cards with which it is played. The pack consists of ninety-six cards, divided amongst eight suits.

GÁNKAR, or GÁKAR, H. (گانکر, گاکر) A kind of coarse bread, made from inferior grains or pulse, and imperfectly baked.

GANNÁ, GUNNA, H. (گنّا) Sugar-cane, a cane especially when ready for cutting.

Gankáṭa, H. (گنکاٹا) A man whose business it is to cut the cane into lengths of about six inches for feeding the mill.

GANNEL, H. (گنّيل) A species of long grass used for thatching.

GANNI, commonly, GUNNY, H. (گنّي) A name given to the coarse bags made of a sort of sacking from the fibres of the *Pát* (Corchorus capsularis): the word is a corruption of that first given to the *Pát* by Rumphius, *Gania*, which was no doubt the Maraṭha, or rather Sanskrit *Goṇa* or *Goṇi*, q. v.

GANO, Thug. A class of Thugs.

GAṆOT, Guz. (ગણોત) Ground-rent of land let by proprietors to tenants or cultivators for the purpose of cultivating and improving it.

Gaṇot-námun, or *-náon*, Guz. (ગણોતનામું) A lease of land given by the proprietor to cultivators, stating the extent, name, and site, as well as the amount of rent.

Gaṇotío, (ગણોતીઓ) A tenant, a leaseholder.

GÁNṬH, GÁNṬHÁ, or GÁNṬHÍ, H. (گانٹھ, گانٹھا, گانٹھي, S. ग्रन्थि) A knot or tie; fig., an engagement. In the north-west it is applied to the refuse of straw, comprising the knotted parts of the stalk and ear-ends, which are formed in a separate pile on the threshing-floor: the *colder* of English agriculture.

GANTHÁ, H. (گنٹھا) A fractional part, one twentieth of a *jaríb*, equal to three *gaz*. In Guz. the *Ganṭhá* (ગંઠા) is a measure of eight feet in length.

Gánṭhi-dár, H. (گانٹھي دار) An occupant of lands under a landlord at a fixed rent and by heritable tenure.

Gánṭhi-jamá, A. (گانٹھي جمع) Hereditary under-tenancy of land at a fixed and permanent rent.

Gánṭi, or *Gáṇiṭ*, Ben. (গাঁটি, গাঁইট, S. গ্রন্থি) A knot, a tie, a parcel, a bale of goods.

Ganṭhio, Guz. (ગંઠીઓ) A pickpocket, a swindler.

Gánṭi-káṭá, Ben. (গাঁটিকাটা) A cutpurse, a pickpocket: the natives usually tie their money up in a corner of their upper garment in a knot, whence the expression. Also, a plunderer or cutter open of packages.

Gánṭi-chháṛá, Ben. (গাঁটিছড়া) Tying the bride and bridegroom together, as part of the marriage ceremony: a cloth, with fruit, &c., is placed upon their hands, and one end is fastened to the borders of the dress of the woman, the other to that of the man.

GÁṆTI, Ben. (গাঁতি) Insertion of an article among others.

Gáṇti-jamá, Ben. (গাঁতিজমা) Including a small parcel of land in the general rent.

GANTRI, Ben. (S. গাঁত্রী) A car or cart drawn by oxen.

GANTU, Tel. Karn. (గంటు) Stock, capital, principal as opposed to interest: a debt.

GANU, Thug. One of the gang who on occasions shams sickness.

GANUA, Thug. Any fraud or trick of Thugs.

GÁNUGA, Tel. (గానుగ) An oil or sugar press.

GÁNW, always pronounced, and sometimes written GÁON, H. (گانو, Mar. गांव) A village. A measure of distance, four *kos*, varying from four to nine miles. (The word is a vernacular corruption of *Grám*, q. v.; also see below *Gáon*.

Ganwár, H. (گنوار, abbreviation of *Gáonwár*) Village, rude, rustic; a clown, a villager.

GÁON, corruptly, GONG, H., Mar. (گاون, the same as GÁNW, or गांव, corruption of ग्राम) A village. See *Grám*.

Gáonbaṭ, H. (گاونبٹ) A division of a Tâluk into separate villages, or of the several additional or subordinate villages attached to the one originally assessed. See *Gátábandi*.

Gáon-devatá, Mar. (गांवदेवता) The village idol.

Gáondhe, or *Gáondhegaon*, Mar. (गांवढे, गांवढेगांव) A small village, a hamlet.

Gáonganna, Mar. (गांवगन्ना) By villages; distributively, as village assessments, &c.

Gaonkar, *Gaonhur*, Mar. (गांवकर) A villager: a *Súdra* appointed in a village where there are no Bráhmans to attend upon the village idol.

Gáonkár, Karn. (ಗಾಂವ್ಕಾರ) The head-man of a village (Sonda).

Gáonkharch, H. Mar. (گاونخرچ, गांवखर्च) Village charges. See *Grámahkharch*.

Gaonkusún, Mar. (गांवकुसूं) The village wall or fence.

Gaonnemnúk, Mar. (गांवनेमनूक) Expenses of village establishments.

Gáonṣion, Mar. (गांवशींव) A general term for a village or villages.

Gáonsai, Mar. (गांवसई) Annual propitiation of the village *bhúts*, or goblins, by offerings of fruits and flowers.

Gáonṭhan, corruptly, *Gaoton*, Mar. (गांवठन, from स्थान, place) Site of a village, whether in ruins or still standing; also *Gaonṭhal* (from S. स्थल, soil).

Gaonṭá, H. (گونتا) Village expenses.

Gáonṭi, H. Mar. (گاونتي) Of or belonging to a village.

Gaonṭiá, H. (گونتيا) A small hamlet.

Gaoṭiká, H. (گوتيکا) The head manager of a village, equivalent to a *Muhaddam* elsewhere (Sohagpur). (The first term is an abbreviation of *Gáon* or *Grám*).

Gum-gáon, Mar. (गुमगांव, from P. گم, lost) A village, the site of which is unknown.

GÁPAN, Ben. (গাপন) Denial or concealment of facts, prevarication, self-contradiction.

GAPSÁ, GUPSA, H. (گپسا) Hard soil, of a whitish appearance.

GAR, or GARBHANG, Thug. A share of spoil.

GAṚÁ, GUṚA, H. (گڑا) A large sheaf; except in the Dehli district, where it denotes a small one.

Gaṛábaṭái, H. (گڑابٹاي) Division of produce without threshing, by stacking the sheaves in proportionate shares. (Rohilkhand).

GÁṚA, GAṚUH, H. (گاڑه) Low land on which water does not lie long (Upper Doab).

GÁṚA, H. (گاڑه) A class of Mohammadan cultivators in Sahâranpur.

GARÁḌÁ, Mar. (गराडा) A body (of troops, &c.) forming a cordon or investment.

GARÁḌÍ, Mar. (गराडी) A cart-rut: the groove in which the wheel moves that bruises lime and prepares it for mortar.

GARAGAḌAMU, Tel. (గరగడము) Marks made with cowdung and water upon heaps of winnowed grain to prevent depredation.

GARAGESANṆANELU, Karn. (ಗರಗೆಸಂಣನೆಲು) A sort of rice grown in Mysore.

GARAKANAṬṬU, Tel. (గరకనట్టు) A tough and deep-rooted grass, growing in some fields, and weeded only by ploughing.

GÁRA-KAṬÁ-JARÍB, Uriya (ଗାରକଟାଯରୀବ) Measured by a rod, exact measurement.

GARÁO, H. (گراو) An instrument for cutting *jawár* stalks, &c., for fodder (Central and Lower Doab).

GARAPA, Tel. (గరప) Stony, gravelly (as soil).

Garapa-bhúmi, Tel. (గరపభూమి, from S. भूमि, land) Sandy or gravelly soil.

GÁRAPAGÁR, or -GÁRI, or -GÁRYÁ, Mar. (गारपगार -री -र्या, from Mar. गार, a hailstone, and S. अपकार, who drives away) An individual supposed to have a power over hailstorms, and who is retained in some villages as part of the establishment, to prevent their injuring the crops.

GARÁRI, GURAREE, H. (گراري) The block over which the rope of a well traverses.

GARÁSÍ, H. (گراسي) An implement for cutting *jawár* stalks, thorn-bushes, &c.

GARATA, Karn. (ಗರತಿ, vernacular form of S. गृहस्थ, q. v.) A householder.

GARÁWÁ, Hindi (गरावा) A light and poor soil, in which the crops never come to perfection (Puraniya).

GARBHA, S. &c., vernacularly also, GÁBH, (गर्भ, गाभ) The embryo, the fœtus; sometimes, but less accurately, the womb. In Bengal the term is also applied to the whole space covered by the Ganges when at its utmost extent in the height of the rainy season.

Garbhádhána, S. (गर्भ, the womb, and आधान, holding) A ceremony performed on the first indications of pregnancy; one of the Sanskáras, or essential rites of the Hindus.

Garbha-gṛiha, or *Garbha-sthala*, S. (from गर्भ, the womb, and गृह, a house, or स्थल, a place) The interior of a dwelling, the inner apartments, the sanctuary of a temple, the adytum in which the idol stands.

Garbhaja, S. (गर्भज) Born of the mother, a son, whether begotten illegitimately or of a wife by another father than the husband under special appointment, when the child is legitimate.

GARDEZI, H. (گرديزي) A class of Saiyids in Muzafferpur.

GÁRDI, (English *Guard*) Native soldiers disciplined after the European mode to act as guards: (an obsolete term.)

GARDÍ, GURDEE, Mar. (गर्दी) Dustiness, confusion, disorder, tumult, rout of an army, state of public dismay and distress.

GARDOṚÁ, H. (گردوڑا) A small pit.

GAṚERAN, H. (گڑيرن) The receptacle for the sugar-cane before it is cut.

GÁRE, Karn. (ಗಾರೆ) A plaster or mortar of chunam or burnt lime, used to coat the walls of apartments.

Gárehár, Karn. (ಗಾರೆಹಾರ) A plasterer.

Vajragáre, Karn. (ವಜ್ರಗಾರೆ) A mixture of lime, plaster, and small stones, used for making floors: the *Khoa* of Bengal.

GARG, H. (گرگ, from the S. गर्गः, a celebrated Ṛishi, and founder of the Garga family) One of the sixteen subdivisions of the *Kanojia* Bráhmans.

Gargbansí, H. (گرگبنسي) A tribe of Rájputs so called, chiefly in Gorakhpur and Azimgarh.

GARGAWÁ, H. (گرگوا) A grass growing in low ground during the rains, and sometimes injurious to the rice.

GAṚH, GUṚH, H. (گڑھ) also GAḌHÍ, or GAṚHÍ, (گڈھي, گڑھي, गढी) A fort, a hill fort, a mud fort, or one the walls of which are of very thick clay, strengthened by bastions. The word occurs also in this and other dialects with the cerebral unaspirated *ḍ*, as, *Gaḍ*, *Guḍ*, (गड), but in either case the *ḍ* is pronounced much the same as *ṛ*. The word also occurs with an initial aspirate, *Ghaṛ* or *Ghaṛi*, but this is incorrect.

GAṚHÁ, H. (گڑھا, गढा) A pit, a cave, a ravine.

GAṚHAI, H. (گڑھئي) A small pond.

GARHÁL, Hindi (गरहाल) Land without moisture (Puraniya).

GÁRHAPATYA, S. (गार्हपत्य) The sacred fire of the householder, (*Gṛihapati*,) of which this is a regular derivative.

GAṚHIBAND, GURHEEBUND, H. (گڑھي بند) Tenure of land in Bundelkhand, on payment of a quit-rent much below the usual amount, arising out of the successful resistance which the possessors of the Gaṛhis, or forts, made to the Maraṭha government, who were compelled to reduce their demand to the lowest sum which the landholder would consent to pay. The holder of land on these reduced terms (Bundelkhand).

GAṚÍ, GUṚEE, Uriya (ଗଡ଼ି, from Ben. গড়ি, a wave) Undulating ground.

GÁṚÍ, or GÁḌÍ, H. &c. (گاڑي, گاڈي, गाडी) A carriage of any description, a carriage or a cart for the conveyance of persons: see *Gáḍí*.

Gáṛibán, or *Gáṛiwán*, H. &c. (گاڑيبان, گاڑيوان) A coachman, the driver of a coach or car.

Gárí, *Gálí*, Guz. (ગાડી) A cart-load, a corn measure of thirty *maunds*.

GÁṚIÁ, or GÁḌIÁ, Uriya (ଗାଡ଼ିଆ) A small tank or reservoir of water.

GARIM, (?) Tel. An apparatus for raising water from a well.

GARIṢA, corruptly, GARCE, Tel. (గరిస) GARAṢI, -ṢE, Karn. (ಗರಸಿ, -ಸೆ) A measure of grain equal to 400 *markáls*, or 185.2 cubic feet=9860 lb. avoirdupois. See *Markál*.

GARJANTAIL, Ben. (গর্জনতৈল) Wood oil, an oil that exudes from incisions in the bark of several species of Dipterocarpus.

GAṚJÁT, Uriya (ଗଡ଼ଜାତ) Estates in the hill country of Orissa.

GARKHÁ, Thug. The neck.

GARMATTU, Karn. (ಗರ್ಮಟ್ಟು) Any kind of reed, grass, or corn.

GARRI, GURREE, H. (گڑي) A haystack, a rick (Lower Doab). A large stack of wheat or barley, the produce of one field (Upper Doab). A large stack of *kharíf* produce (Rohilkhand).

GARTHA, Thug. The dead body of a victim.

GARUSU, GARASU, Karn. (గరుసు, గరసు) Gravel.

Garusu-nela, Karn. (గరుసునేల) A gravelly soil.

GARUVU, Tel. (గరువు) Gravelly soil.

GARWA, Mar. (गरवा) Ripening late; applied to particular grains which are slow of coming to maturity.

GÁSA, Karn. (ಗಾಸ, vernacular corruption of both S. *grása*, ग्रास, and H. *ghása*, घास) Subsistence, salary, pay: forage for cattle.

GASHT, H. (P. گشت) GAST, Mar. (गस्त) Tel. (గస్తు) GASTI, Karn. (ಗಸ್ತಿ) Watch, patrol going the rounds, the boundaries of a division of a town or village, a division or ward of a town, that is, the range or beat of the patrol.

Gashti, *Gushtee*, H. (گشتي, from P. گشتن, to turn round) Presents to a revenue officer, on his making the tour of his district.

Gasht-mahál, H. (گشت مهال) A toll or transit duty levied in some Zamindarís upon boats passing.

Gasht-salámi, H. (گشت سلامي) A tax or fee levied by public officers under the native governments, when making either a revenue or judicial circuit.

GÁṬA, H. (گاٹا) Yoking bullocks together to tread out grain (Dehli). A plot or piece of land, a part of a village.

Gáṭabandi, *Gaṭabundee*, H. (گاٹا بندي) Division of a village by parcels or plots of land, some of which may be scattered among the fields of several other villages. Also termed *Gátewár* (گاتيوار).

GATA-AWAJI, Ben. (গতঅবজী, from S. गत, gone, and A.

âwaz, عوض, exchange) Transfer of land or of revenue payment from one Ryot to another.

GATA-KHÁMÁR, Ben. (গতখামার, from খামার, a threshing-floor) Lapse of a Ryot's holding into the possession of the Zamindar.

GAṬHÁ, H. (گتّھا) The twentieth part of a *Jaríb*. Also *Ganṭhú*.

Gaṭhwánsí, H. (گتّھوانسي) The twentieth part of a *Gaṭhá*.

GAṬHAUND, H. (گتّھوند) A pledge or deposit tied up in a bag.

GAṬHBANDHAN, H. (گتّھبندھن, from *Gánth*, a knot) Tying a knot, especially tying the clothes of the bride and bridegroom together, as part of the marriage ceremony. See *Gánṭichhháṛá*.

GAṬHI, H. (گتّھي) A pad put on the back of a beast of burthen.

GAṬHIÁ, H. (گتّھيا) A pannier, a sack, a bundle.

GATHONI, Thug. A knot in a turban, or any piece of cloth in which money or jewels may be concealed.

GAṬHṚÍ, GUṬHṚEE, H. &c. (گتّھڑي, गठडी) A bag: money brought in payment of revenue in a bag (Benares). A bundle, a package, a parcel.

GATKUL, or GATKULÍ, H., Mar., &c., corruptly, GHUTKOOL, (गतकुल, गतकुली, from S. गत, gone, and कुल, a family) Applied to property, lands, houses, &c., the proprietors of which are extinct; unclaimed inheritance; lands of a village uncultivated, or without owners, considered in some respects as village property, so that they may be disposed of, sold, or leased by the community, but when not so disposed of they were often granted in *Inám* by the Maraṭha government.

Gatkúl, Mar. (गतकूल) An emigrated or extinct family.

GAṬṬU, Tel. (గట్టు) A bank, an embankment, a dam or dyke.

Gaṭṭu-túmu, Tel. (గట్టుతూము) One twentieth part of the gross produce collected by Zamindars from each village for the repair of tanks and embankments.

GAṬṬU, Karn. (ಗಟ್ಟು) A large trading town.

GAṬWÁRA, GUṬWÁRA, or, more correctly, GANṬHWÁRA, H. (گنتّھواره, گتّواره) A tribe of Játs in the Doab.

GÁŪ, GAO, also in the uninflected form, especially in compounds, GO, also GAÏ, or GÁY, S., but adopted in all the dialects, (गौ, गो, गाय) A cow, an ox, a bull.

Gáucharái, *Gaochuraee*, (گاوچراي) Grazing, grazing or pasture ground; a tax levied on pasture lands.

Gaudivya, Mar. (गौदिव्य) Form of oath, swearing while holding the tail of a cow.

Gáukhána, H. (گاوخانه) A cow stable or stalls.

Gaukoṣ, Mar. (गौकोश) A land measure, the distance at which the lowing of a cow may be heard.

Gáuli, *Gaolee*, (گاولي) A cowherd; a caste living by keeping cows and selling milk: different classes of them are known in the Dakhin, distinguished sufficiently by their appellations, as, *Ahír-Gáuli*, a branch of the Ahírs; *Konkani-Gáuli*, natives of the Konkan; and *Lingáyat-Gáuli*, followers of the Jangam sect.

Gáushumári, *Gaoshoomaree*, H. (گاوشماري) An enumeration or census of cattle, a tax upon cattle.

GAUCHANÁ, GOUCHUNÁ, H. (گوچنا) Land sowed with wheat and chana.

GAUḌ, pronounced GAUṚ, H. &c. (گوڑ) S. GAUḌA, (गौड, গৌড) The ancient name of Central Bengal, and that of the ruins of its former capital. A name applied to one of the two great divisions of the Bráhmans, or the Five *Gauṛas*, (see *Bráhmana*); also to one of the five, the Bráhmans of Bengal proper, who are distinguished again as *Varendriya*, *Ráṛhiya*, *Sátshati*, and *Vaidika* Bráhmans: the two first from their being settled in the several portions of *Gauṛa*, called *Varendra* and *Ráṛh*; the third as descended from 700 Bráhmanical families who were settled in Bengal before the introduction of the families from Kanoj, who are said to have been fugitives from Orissa; the fourth from their knowledge of the Vedas. The *Gauṛ* Bráhmans were also classed by *Balál Sen*, a Raja of Bengal about the eleventh century, in three divisions: 1. *Kulínas*, from *kula*, a family, the most respectable members of the community; 2. *Ṣrotriyas*, those who had passed through the established institutions, and had read part of the Vedas; and 3. *Vanṣajas*, merely born Bráhmans, possessing neither respectability nor learning. There are other divisions of Bengal Bráhmans of a still inferior description, degraded by acting as priests for the mixed castes, or by some peculiarities of a fanciful and fabulous character. The term *Gauṛ* is also applied to other castes or tribes, as specified by Mr. Elliot.

Gauṛ-Bráhman, H. (گوڑ برهمن) The Bráhman of the *Gauṛ* tribe or caste, one of the five *Gauṛs*, but located in the upper provinces throughout the Subah of Dehli to the hills. There are many subdivisions of these *Gauṛ* Bráhmans of Hindustan, who are apparently unknown in

Bengal, as, the *Ádh-Gauṛ*, *Kaithal-Gauṛ*, *Gújar-Gáuṛ*, *Sidh-Gauṛ*, &c., amounting in all to forty-two.

Gauṛ-káyath, H. (گور کایتھ) One of the twelve divisions of the Káyastha tribe, or writer caste. Although properly of Bengal, many are found in the upper provinces, where they settled under the patronage of Náṣir-ud-din, son of Balban, about six centuries ago.

Gauṛ-Rájpút, H. (گور راجپوت) One of the thirty-six royal Rájput races whose origin is doubtful. They are numerous in the north-western provinces, divided into three principal branches:—the *Bhaṭ-Gauṛ*, *Báhman-Gauṛ*, and *Chamar-Gauṛ*; names derived, Mr. Elliot supposes, from some intercourse with Bháts, Bráhmans, and Chamárs.

Gauṛ-tagá, H. (گور تگا) An important tribe of Bráhmanical descent in the north-west of India, extending through a great part of Rohilkhand, the Upper Doab, and territory of Dehli. According to the fables current among them, they were originally invited from Bengal by Raja Janamejaya, king of Hastinapur, for the purpose of exterminating the Takshakas or snakes, in concert with the Raja. Mr. Elliot considers the *Takshakas* to have been Buddhist Scythians from the north, who invaded India about 500 years B. C. The *Tagas* are so termed, it is said, from the S. *tyága*, abandoning, as they abandoned their Bráhmanical character by accepting and cultivating the lands granted to them by Janamejaya.

Gauṛ-tháhur, H. (گور تھاکر) A tribe of Rájputs, settled in the Farakhabad district.

GAUḌ, GAUṚ, or GAUḌA, also spelt GAVUḌA, corruptly, GOWDA, and GOWDOO, Karn. (ಗೌಡ, ಗವುಡ) The head man of a village in the Karnatic who superintends the cultivation and the collection of the revenue, corresponding with the *Pátíl* of the Maraṭha provinces: or one who farms the lands of a village, and lets them out to cultivators, in which case he corresponds with the Zamindar of Bengal.

Huṭṭu-gára-gauḍa, Karn. (ಹುಟ್ಟುಗಾರಗೌಡ) A head man, who is also a native of the village.

Phaṭṭe-gára-gauḍa, Karn. (ಫಟ್ಟೆಗಾರಗೌಡ) A head man, who is not a native of the village over which he presides.

Gauḍ-áya, Karn. (ಗೌಡಆಯ) Proportion of the crop formerly set apart for the head man, resumed by the Mysore government.

Gauḍa-mányam, Karn. The privilege land and fees of the head man of a village.

Gauḍa-mirás, Karn. The hereditary privilege land of the head of a village.

Gauḍa-terige, Karn. (ಗೌಡತೆರಿಗೆ) A fee formerly paid to the head man by the villagers, resumed by the government of Mysore.

GAUḌA, or GAUṚA, corruptly, GOWRA, (?) The head man of certain castes—of the potter, the shepherd, and the weaver; also, in parts of the Sahyádri hills, of the cultivator and cowherd caste. (From the locality of its use this should be a Maraṭha term, but it is not found in Molesworth).

GAUḌALU, Karn. (ಗೌಡಲು) A caste or tribe in Mysore following agriculture as labourers, or sometimes small farmers under a lease from the landholder.

GAUHÁN, H. (گوهان) A village made over by its proprietors to any person, on a permanent revenue assessment, with all the privileges of a Zamindar (Eastern Oudh).

GAUHÁNÍ, H. (گوهانی, गौहानी) Lands situated close round a village, and commonly left for pasturage: also, the entire lands of the village, or the village itself.

GAUḶIGA, Karn. (ಗೌಳಿಗ) Name of a pastoral and migratory tribe in Mysore, who rear buffaloes, and sell their milk and ghee, and accompany camps; also, a seller of buttermilk.

GAUṆA, S., Ben., &c. (गौण, from गुण, quality, property) Secondary, supplementary, special, or specific.

Gauṇa-mása, S. (from मास, a month) The lunar month, as reckoned from full moon to full moon.

Gauṇa-putra, S. (from पुत्र, a son) A subsidiary or representative son, one by adoption, &c., or any form except by birth.

GAUṆḌÍ, Mar. (गौंडी) The name of a caste, or individual of it, by calling a mason or bricklayer.—Nagpore. Jenkins, 204. (It ought to be Maraṭha).

GAÜṆI, Uriya (ଗଉଣି) A measure of rice in the husk, equal to twelve *sérs*. A basket used for measuring grain.

GAUNJÍ, Hindi (गौनजी) Fresh shoots of rice put forth after the crop has been cut and cleared.

GAURÁ, H. (گورا) A tribe of Ahírs.

GAURÁHAR, H. (گوراهر) An obscure tribe of Rájputs on the borders of Badaon and Aligerh.

GAURO, corruptly, GOWRO, (?) A person employed to estimate the crop while standing.

Gaurŭa, H. (گوروه) An inferior class of Rájputs in Agra and Mathura, and other districts west of the Jamuná.

Gautam-Rájpút, Goutum-Rájpoot, H. (گوتم راجپوت) A branch of the Chandravaṇsi, or lunar family; very numerous in the Lower Doab, and formerly very powerful.

Gautamián, H. (گوتمیان) A class of Rájputs in Azimgarh and Gorakhpur, offshoots of the preceding, but of a spurious breed.

Gauyará, or Gauyeṇḍ, Hindi, (गौयरा, गौयेंड) also written *Goyará*, or *Goïrá*, and *Goyeṇḍ*, (गोयरा, गोयेंड) Land immediately next to a village.

Gávada, Karn. (ಗಾವದ) A measure of distance, the largest, between eight and ten miles.

Gavánkár, Tel. (గవాంకారు) The head man of a village.

Gavaríga, Karn. (ಗವರಿಗ) A basketmaker.

Gavya, Tel. (గవ్వ) A kaunri shell, used as money.

Gawáh, H. (P. گواه) A witness, an evidence.

Gawáhán-chashm-dídah, H. P. (from چشم, the eye, and دیده, having seen) Eye-witnesses.

Gawáhán-samái, H. P. (from A. سمع, hearing) Hearsay witnesses, persons speaking from what they have been told.

Gawáhí, H. P. (گواهي) Evidence, testimony.

Gwáhí, Mar. (ग्वाही) Evidence: a witness; in the latter also *Gwáhídár*.

Gawaḷí, Mar. (गवळी) The caste of cowherds, or an individual of it.

Gawaḷwáḍá, Mar. (गवळवाडा) The part of a town or village inhabited by the caste of cowherds.

Gawaṇḍí, Gawaṇḍyá, Mar. (गवंडी, गवंड्या) A bricklayer.

Gawat, or Gavat, Mar. (गवत) Grass.

Gawatkaṭṭai, Mar. (गवत, grass, and कट्टाई, cutting) A cess formerly imposed on villages in lieu of grass for the government stables, or the grass so furnished; the wages of labourers employed in cutting grass for the public stables; grass-cutting in general.

Gawhalá, Mar. (गव्हळा, from गव्ह, wheat) Fitted for wheat (soil, &c.).

Gawháḷ, or *Gawháḷí*, Mar. (गव्हाळ, -ळी) Wheat grounds, fields, &c., suited for wheat crops.

Gawí, Mar. (गवी) A combination among the villagers to reject the government terms of the assessment, or to resist any orders of a public officer.

Gayál, Mar. (गयाळ) Neglected, left uncultivated, as land. Emigrated, as cultivators.

Gayáḷu, Tel. (గయాళు) Land unfit for cultivation.

Gayál, also Gayári, H. (گیال, گیاري, from *Gayá*, gone) Land of deceased shareholders unclaimed, or coming under the management of the *Mál-guzár* upon its being abandoned by the cultivator.

Gayatrí, S. (गयत्री) A form of metre, and thence applied to a verse in the Vedas, which is held to be of peculiar sanctity, and is repeated inaudibly in the daily morning worship of the Bráhmans. The sense is, "We meditate on that excellent light of the divine sun: may he enlighten our minds!" *Tat savitur-vareṇyam bhargo devasya dhímahi: dhiyo yo nah prachodayát!*

Gayáwál, or Gayálí, corruptly, Gyal, H. (गयावाल, गयाली) Gayáwaḷ, Mar. (गयावळ) A Bráhman of a class or tribe which claims the privilege of conducting the ceremonies of the pilgrimage at Gayá, and receiving fees for the same. They also officiate as collectors and conductors of pilgrims to the city of Gayá.

Gáyra, or Gaira, Mar. (from गाय, a cow) A cowherd.

Gáyrán, or *Gairán*, Mar. (गायरान्) Open pasture-ground, a common; loosely applied to all lands unsuited for cultivation.

Gaz, Guz, vernacularly, Gaj, or Guj, H. (P. گز) A measure of length, a yard. In the reign of Akbar there prevailed a great number of measures of this denomination, varying in length from 18 to 58 inches; to correct which disorder, they were all abrogated, and a standard *gaz* established in their stead, termed the *Iláhi-gaz*. The actual value of this measure was made the subject of many inquiries and experiments upon the institution of the great revenue survey of the western provinces, when it was found to be the basis of all the records of land measurements in that part of India: as no standard had been preserved, a fixed object of comparison could not be procured, and the different reports and measurements made it vary from 29 to 35 inches, and as the majority of actual measures of land made it 33 inches, that was assumed as the fixed standard value, and it constitutes the basis of the survey measurements. In trade, a greater latitude prevails, and the cloth merchant, in particular, has a *gaz* of his own, equal to two *háts*, or cubits, or an English yard.

Gázar, H. (P. گازر) A washerman by caste as well as occupation.

Gázar-mahál, H. A tax formerly levied on washermen in Bengal.

Gédáṭa, Karn. (ಗೇದಾಟ) Ploughing or tillage.

Gédára, Karn. (ಗೇದಾರ) A ploughed field.

Gehun, Gehoon, H. (P. گیہوں) Wheat, which is extensively cultivated in the upper provinces. Several kinds, but resolvable in native opinion, into two families, red and white, are grown: there is also a beardless species similarly divisible.

Geli, Tel. (గెలి) A heap of salt.

Genjá, Ben. (গেঁজা) The tops of hemp, used to make an intoxicating beverage. See *Gánja*.

Gentoo, (derived from the Portuguese *Gentio*, a Gentile or heathen,) A Hindu, a native of India.

Géṇu, Karn. (ಗೇಣು) A span from the top of the thumb to that of the little finger.

Geru, H. (گیرو) Soil of a red colour, red ochre, or ochreous clay.

Gerámáṭi, Hindi (गेरामाटी) Loam of fine clay.

Gerwá, Mar. (गेरवा, from گیرو, red clay) Blight, turning the crop of a brickdust red colour. (The word appears to be the same as the Hindustani *Girwi*, q. v., which is applied in the north-west provinces to the insect causing the disease or blight).

Gésta, Karn. (ಗೇಸ್ತ, from *Grihastha*) A householder.

Ghabáṛ, Mar. (घबाड) A lucky conjunction of the planets.

Ghabáṛmáp, Mar. (घबाडमाप) A weight or measure rather in excess of the market one.

Ġhabn-i-fáhish, A. (غبن فاحش) Shamefully fraudulent; applied, in Mohammadan law especially, to the sale of property for a price grossly inadequate to its value; also termed *Nuḳṣán-i-fáhish.* (From غبن, fraud, or نقصان, loss, and فاحش, shameful).

Ghádí, or Ghaṛí, Mar. (घाडी) A Ṣúdra attendant in a village temple.

Ghadsí, or Ghaṛsí, or Ghuṛsee, incorrectly, Gursee, Mar. (घडसी) A caste, or person belonging to it, by calling vagrant or village pipers and drummers. They are said to be descended from the aboriginal inhabitants of the great forest of the south, the Dandakáraṇya.

Ġhadír, A. (غدیر) A festival observed by the Shias of India on the 18th of Zilhaja, when three images of dough filled with honey are made to represent Abu-bakr, Omar, and Othman, which are stuck with knives, and the honey is sipped, as typical of the blood of the usurping khalifs. The festival is named from *ghadir*, a pool; Mohammad, it is said, having declared Âli his successor at a place called Ghadír-khúm, a watering-place for caravans half way between Makka and Medina.

Ghaeja, (?) Guz. The village barber and barber-surgeon.

Ġháfil, H. (A. غافل) Careless, negligent.

Ġhaflat, H. (A. غفلت) Carelessness, negligence, inattention.

Ghaī, or Ghye, H. (گهئی) Ground cleaned and raised, on which to raise a stack of straw, or pile of grain.

Ġhaib, vernacularly Gaib, (the aspirate being rejected and *g* substituted for the A. *ġh*,) H. (A. غیب, गैब) Hidden, concealed, missing, lost.

Ghaibat, or *Gaibatu*, Tel. (గైబతు) Lost, missing; extra (as collections); distant (as an outstation).

Ġhaibat-i-munḳaṭaâ, A. (غیبت منقطع) In Mohammadan law, remote distance. The absence of a husband at such a distance as renders the acts of his wife, with regard to his property, valid.

Ghains, Thug. Uproar, confusion.

Ġhair, when adopted in the Hindu dialects, Gair or Gar, H. (A. غیر) Gairah, Hindi (गैरह) Mar. (गैर) Tel. (గైర) Ben. (গৈর) Guz. (ગૈર) Different, other, without; used as a particle to imply the absence or want of a thing.

Gar-ábád, Ben. (গরাবাদ) Devoid of cultivation; land cultivable, but neglected.

Gairádá, Tel. (గైరాదా) Uncultivated, waste.

Gairádásthalamu, Tel. (గైరాదాస్థలము) Waste land.

Ġhair-band-o-bast, H. (غیر بند و بست) Unsettled; applied to lands not included in the revenue assessment.

Gair-dasta, or *-dastí*, Mar. (गैरदस्त, -दस्ती) Exempt from government imposts (fields, &c.).

Ġhair-ház̤ir, H. (غیرحاضر) *Gair-hájir*, Mar. (गैरहाजिर) Absent, not in attendance.

Ġhair-ház̤irí, H. *Gair-hájirí*, Mar. Absence, being away especially when called for, as in court.

Garjabd, Ben. (গরজব্দ, for A. غیرضبط, *ghair-z̤abṭ*) Omitted, excepted; applied to lands in Sylhet not included in any measurement, and consequently unassessed.

Ġhair-jamâ, H. (غیرجمع) Not paying revenue, rent-free.

Gairhí-kharch, Hindi (गैरहीखरच) Expenses of various kinds incurred by a village, or on account of establishments and collections.

Ġhair-ḳabúl, H. (غیرقبول) *Gar-habúl*, Ben. (গরকবুল) Denying, not admitting or confessing, not agreeing to.

Gair-kharch, Mar. (गैरखर्च) Extra or miscellaneous expenses.

Ghair-khiráj, H. (غيرخراج) Not paying tribute or revenue, rent-free lands, &c.

Ghair-mahdi, H. (غيرمهدي) A sect of Mohammadans who deny the re-appearance of the 12th *Imam*, or the Imam *Mahdi*.

Gair-marang, Hindi (गैरमरंग) Low river lands based on sand, and unable to support vegetation in the dry months (Puraniya).

Ghair-manhúla, H. (غيرمنقوله) Immoveable or real property, property other than personal; (*mankúl.*)

Ghair-mashrút, H. (غيرمشروط) Unconditional; applied to grants of land, &c., without any stipulations of service, or the like, being attached to them.

Ghair-maurúsi, H. (غيرموروثي) Not holding by hereditary descent; a tenant or farmer; not inherited; acquired.

Ghair-mazrúá, H. (A. غيرمزروعه) Uncultivated land.

Ghair-mázún, A. (غيرماذون) An absolute slave, one not allowed to do any work on his own account (Mohammadan law).

Ghair-mumkin, H. (A. غيرممكن) Barren, waste; land not capable of cultivation: (from *ghair*, not, and *mumkin*, possible).

Ghair-mustabín, A. (غيرمستبين) A totally irregular and invalid deed (Mohammadan law).

Gair-pancháhi, (?) Lands formerly held in Cuttack, which were exempt from any taxes but those specified in the deed of grant.

Ghair-sál, H. (A. غيرسال) Of a different year; applied to coins or currency, implying also their being base or adulterated.

Ghair-sanadi, corruptly, *Ghir-sundee*, H. (غيرسندي) Extra, extraordinary, contingent, not included in the *sanad* or grant.

Ghair-sarsari, H.(غيرسرسري) Regular or legal proceedings.

Ghair-silsila, H. (A. غيرسلسله) Irregular, summary; applied to judicial proceedings.

Ghair-vekenni, or, *-valáni*, corruptly, *Guire-vekenny*, or *-valauny*, (?) Resumption of an allowance of land given up to the Ryots, being the tenth of a *bigha.*—Gl. 5th Rep. (The first word is no doubt intended for *ghair*, the others must be blunders).

Gair-wáká, Mar. (गैरवाका) Misrepresentation, a false statement.

GHÁIT, Ben. (घाइत) Fault, crime, misdemeanor.

GHÁLI-PATTUTA, Tel. (ఘాలిపట్టుత) Winnowing.

GHALLA, H. (A. غله) Grain, corn; it is sometimes used to denote money.

Ghalla-farosh, H. A corn or grain seller.

Ghalla-mislat, A. (غلهمثلة) The proportion of the produce of the labour of a licensed slave which has been reserved for the master.

GHAMETA, (?) A subdivision of the Kurmi tribe in Bahar.

GHAMUS, A. (غموس) Mysterious: in law, Perjury.

GHANA, Ben. (घन) Struck, as a rupee; but applied only to rupees of native coinage.

GHAṆA, Mar. (घण) A sledge-hammer.

GHANÁ, GHUNA, H. (گهنا) A preserve for game.

GHÁNÁ, GHÁNI, H. (گهانا, گهاني) A sugar-cane press. Mar. (घाणा) An oil-mill: (see the next).

GHÁṆÁ, GHÁṆÍ, Mar. (घाणा, घाणी) The quantity of material put into a mill at once, or of cane into the sugar-mill, rice into the mortar, or of any thing to be pounded or triturated into the triturating machine. A heap of grain which, at the *Makara Sankránti*, or sun's entrance into Capricorn, the mistress of a house places on a mortar to be given to a Bráhman.

GHÁNCHI, Guz. (ઘાંચી) An oil maker, an oil dealer, one who expresses it or sells it.

GHÁNCHO, Guz. (ઘાંચો) A man of a caste whose occupation is mat-making.

GHAND, H. (گهند) A branch of the Ját tribe.

GHANGHAS, H. (گهنگهس) A branch of the Ját tribe.

GHÁNI, Ben. (घानि) An oil mill.

Ghání-gáchh, Ben. (घानिगाछ) The hollow trunk of a tree forming part of an oil mill which receives the seed, and having a hole through which the oil issues.

GHANI, A. (غني) A rich person: in law, one not poor enough to be entitled to alms.

GHAṆṬÁ, S. &c., in some dialects, GANTÁ, (घंटा) A bell, a plate of metal on which the hours are struck; an hour.

GHAR, GHUR, H., Ben., Mar., &c. (گهر, घर, घर) A house, a dwelling, a habitation: a family, the people of the house.

Gharbaiṭhá, Mar. (घरबैठा) Whilst staying at home; said of work or business done at home; without employment or service abroad.

Ghar-bandí, H. &c. (گهربندي) A slave born in the house.

Gharbár, H. (گهربار) Household concerns.

Gharbári, H. (گهرباري) A householder, the head of a house.

Ghar-báṛí, Mar. (घरवाडी) Rent of houses without owners,

levied in some towns by the former govenment. Uriya, (ଘରବାଡ଼ି) A dwelling-house. See *Gharwári.*

Ghar-bháḍá, or *-bhárá*, H. (گهربهاڑا) *Ghar-bhaḍeṇ*, Mar. (घरभाडें) House-rent.

Ghar-bharaṇí, Mar. (घरभरणी) Ceremonies observed on taking possession of a new house, house-warming.

Ghar-chár, or *Gharáchár*, Mar. (घरचार, घराचार) The rules or customs of a household or family.

Ghar-dár, Mar. (घरदार) A family, a household.

Ghar-deṇe, Mar. (घरदेणे) House tax.

Ghar-dwárí, corruptly, *Ghur-dewary*, H. (گهردواری) House tax: also an illegal cess upon shopkeepers and householders.

Gharganti, Mar. (घरगणती) Enumeration of houses in a town or village.

Ghar-jamá, (?) corruptly, *Ghur-jummah*, Mar. (घरजमा) House tax.

Gharjáwaí, Mar. (घरजावई) One who with his wife lives in the house of his father-in-law, and manages his affairs.

Gharkarí, Mar. (घरकरी) The master of a house, the head of the family.

Gharpaṭṭí, Mar. (घरपट्टी) House tax; levy or collection per house, from which Bráhman village officers were exempted.

Gharsabíl, H. (گهرسبیل) Advances to peasants to enable them to build their cottages.

Gharsárá, Mar. (घरसारा) House tax.

Gharṭí, or *Gharṭís*, Mar. (घरटी, घरटीस) Relating to each house severally, per house, as contributions, charges, taxes, &c.

Gharṭíp, Mar. (घरटीप) The numbering of the houses in a village or town; the list so taken.

Gharwaṇ, Mar. (घरवण) House tax.

Gharwáṛí, Mar. (घरवाडी) An inclosure in which is a dwelling-house. See *Gharbáṛí.*

Ghár, Gháṛ, H. (گهار, or گهاڑ, from H. گڑها, S. गर्त्त, a cavity) Clay soil in low situations where rain lies for a long time; land that has been worn away by running water; a subdivision of Matiár soil; a name given in the north-west provinces to strips of land lying along the banks of the Jamna, or, in the Agra districts, to the tract intermediate between that and the more northern portion.

Ġhár, H. (A. غار) A cave, a pit, a ravine.

Ghaṛá, H. (گهڑا, S. घट) An earthen water-pot or jar.

Ghara, Uriya (ଘର) A column (in a book or account).

Ġharáb, commonly Grab, A. (غراب) Guráb, Mar. (गुराब) A vessel of a peculiar build used on the Malabar coast and in the Arabian gulf.

Gharámí, Ben. (घरामी, from घर, a house) A man whose business it is to construct the mat houses of the poorer natives, or roof them with thatch. A thatcher.

Ghaṛaṇí, Mar. (घडणी) Document kept by the *Kulkarni* in account with the several families of a village.

Gharaṛ, H. (گهرڑ) The dry *Moth* plant, given as fodder to cattle.

Ghareṇe, Guz. (ઘરેણે) Mortgaged, pledged.

Gharenáúṇ-khat, Guz. (ઘરેણાઉંખત) A mortgage-bond, a written acknowledgment of money borrowed, or property mortgaged or pledged.

Ghareṇiá, incorrectly, *Gerania*, Guz. (ઘરેણીઆ) Lands held in mortgage or pledge.

Ghareṇiá-nakariá, Guz. (ઘરેણીઆનકરીઆ) Private lands in mortgage.

Ghareṇiá-salámiá, Guz. (ઘરેણીઆસલામીઆ) Mortgaged lands paying a quit-rent.

Ghaṛi, Ghuṛee, inaccurately, Ghurree, H. (گهڑی) Ghaṛí or Ghaṭí, Ben. (घडी, घटी) Ghaṛí and Ghaṭí, Mar. (घडी, घटी) Ghaḍi or Ghaḷige, Karn. (ಘಡಿ, ಘಳಿಗೆ) Ghaṭika, Tel. (ఘటిక) A measure of time, a term of twenty-four minutes, being one sixtieth part of a day and night: in common use it has also come to signify an English hour. Any instrument for computing and announcing time; originally the Hindu clepsydra and the brass plate or gong on which the hours were struck, but latterly the English watch or clock. The term, in its signification of an hour of twenty-four minutes, was applied also, in the Delhi district, to one mode of distributing the assessment of a village: each cultivator being charged one sixtieth of the whole for each *ghaṛi* in the day during which he had drawn water for the irrigation of his lands from the royal canal. It also denotes the subdivision of a village in the Dehli district, as, *Khandigaon*, which is divided into 144 *langris*, and each *langri* into eight *ghaṛis.* The vernacular terms are derived from the S., in which *ghaṭí* is the timepiece, and *ghaṭiká* the hour which it marks; but in use both meanings are commonly attached to the same word.

Ghaṛiál, H. &c. (گهڑیال) *Gharyal*, Mar. (घड्याल) The plate or gong on which the hours are struck with a wooden mallet.

Ghaṛiálá, or *Ghaṛialí*, H. &c. (گهڑيالا ,گهڑيالي) *Gharyál-chí*, Mar. (घड्यालची) The gong striker, the bellman.

GHÁṚÍ, GHÁḌÍ, Mar. (घाडी) A Śúdra attendant on a temple, corresponding with a *Gurav*.

ǴHARÍB, H. (A. غريب) Strange, foreign; poor, distressed, helpless.

Ǵharib-parwar, or *Ǵharib-nawáz*, H. (from P. پرور, who protects, or نواز, who is kind to) Cherisher of the poor; an expression commonly addressed to a superior, or to a European functionary, by natives of inferior rank, especially if supplicants or suitors.

ǴHÁRIM, A. (غارم) A debtor, so helpless as to be a proper object of *zikât* or alms.

ǴHARKI, ǴHURKEE, H. (A. غرقي) Overflowed, inundated.

GHARPHÁNT, also written GURPHANT, (?) H. (گهرپهانت) An arrangement made by the manager of an estate, or by the shareholders themselves, for the payment of the government revenue by each village, when more than one is included in the lease (Kamaon).

GHARṢÍ, Mar. (घडसी) A man of a particular caste, or the caste itself: the members are musicians and singers.

GHARSU BHÚMI, (?) Tel. A strong red soil (Warangal).

GHARṬÁ, or GHARṬÍ, Mar. (घरटा, घरटी) A large hand-mill.

Gharṭí-bhar-sárá, Mar. (?) A tax formerly levied by the Maratha government on millstones.

Gharṭí-khoṭí, Mar. (घरटीखोटी) A contract or farm of the exclusive privilege of grinding corn.

GHAṚWÁ, Hindi (घडवा) Gleanings from the threshing-floor fallen amidst rubbish and dirt, the perquisite of the lowest castes.

GHAS, Mar. (घस) Loss in trade, loss in drying, leakage, &c.

GHÁS, H. B. (گهاس, घास) GHÁNS, Dakh. (گهانس) also either GHÁS, or GHÁNS, Mar. (घास, घांस) Grass, meadow grass, hay, forage. In Mar. it also implies a mouthful, or a quantity equivalent, (more correctly, *Grás*, q. v.); also the quantity of grain put into a mill at once, and the grain which falls into the hollow and remains unground.

Ghás-beṛá-mahál, Ben. (ঘাসবেড়ামহাল) Land inclosed or set apart for pasturage, meadow lands.

Ghás-dáṇá, Mar. (घासदाणा) A military contribution; grass and grain for the horses, or a contribution in lieu of it.

Ghás-gaháníya, Mar. (?) corruptly, *Ghas-grenia*, A mortgage with possession, under which the produce of the land is taken instead of interest. See *Gahán*.

Ghasiárá, H. (گهسيارا) A grass-cutter. See *Ghás-kátá*, *Ghás-kar*, *-kur*, Ben. (ঘাসকর) A tax on grass or forage.

Ghás-káṭá, corruptly, *Gras-kut*, H., Ben. (گهاسكاٹا, ঘাসকাটা) A man whose business it is to cut fresh grass daily for the horses of his employer.

Ghás-káṭaní, corruptly, *Ghas-huttanee*, Mar. (घासकाटणी) Cutting grass, a fee or tax for cutting grass on government land.

Ghásuá-bhumi, Uriya (ଘାସୁଆଭୂମି) Pasture land.

ǴHASB or ǴHAZAB, ǴHUSB, ǴHUZB, A. (غصب, غضب) Violence, oppression, seizing any thing by force. In Mohammadan law, forcible or unauthorised possession and use of property belonging to another.

GHÁṬ, corruptly, GHAUT, or GAUT, H. (گهاٹ) Ben. (ঘাট) Mar. (घाट, from the S. घट्ट) which the Tel. and Karn. adhere to (ఘట్టము, ఘట్టు, ಘಟ್ಟ) A landing-place, steps on the bank of a river, a quay, a wharf where customs are commonly levied. A pass through the mountains: the mountains themselves, especially applied to the eastern and western ranges of the south of India; or, in the Maratha country, to the *Sahyádri* range, and to the *Deṣ*, or tract above.

Ghátáni, H. (گهاٹاني) A toll levied on crossing rivers or hill passes.

Ghát-bárí, H. (گهاٹباري) Lands attached to a ferry. Duty or toll levied at landing-places upon the boats that come to at them.

Ghát-bandí, Mar. (घाटबन्दी) Blocking up a pass over a hill. Toll or tax levied on passengers for keeping a pass or landing-place in repair.

Gháṭí, or *Ghátiá*, Uriya, A watchman, a police or revenue officer, especially one in charge of passes or landing-places. Mar. (घाटी) Of or belonging to the country above the *Sahyádri* range (products): when the people are meant, the term is *Ghátwaḷ* (घाटवळ).

Gháṭiyá, *Ghátyá*, H. &c. (گهاٹيا, घाटिया, घाट्या) A Bráhman who attends where pilgrims bathe, as at Benares, to take care of their clothes, and supply sandal, flowers, &c., for certain fees, which he exacts as a right, denouncing imprecations on any who resist his exactions: these people sometimes repair to a distance to escort pilgrims to their places of ablution.

Ghátmáṇjhi, H., Ben. (گهاٹمانجهي) A ferryman; applied also to a man who regulates the hire of boats, supplies boats, provides crews, and generally superintends, more by usurpation than by authority, the details of a landing-place on the river.

Ghátmárá, H., Ben. (گهاتمارا) Smuggling; a smuggler, one who evades the tolls at landing-places.

Ghátpándyá, Mar. (घाटपांड्या) An officer presiding over landing-places.

Ghát-rakhwálí, Mar. (घाटरखवाली) A guard at a pass in the hills.

Ghattí, Ben. (ঘটট্টী) A private wharf or steps to the river.

Ghattíghoshaná, Ben. (ঘটট্টীঘোষনা) Proclaiming news, making any thing public.

Ghát-ṭhíkádár, H. (گهات تهيكادار) The farmer or contractor for a ferry.

Ghátwál, or *Ghátwálá*, H. (گهاتوال, گهاتوالا) A ferryman, a person in charge of a landing-place, or a mountain pass. A member of a class of landholders in Birbhúm, holding lands under a peculiar tenure: (see the next). It is also read with the short vowel, *Ghatwár* or *Ghatwál*.

Ghátwáli, *Ghátwáli-mahál*, or *Ghátwáli-zamín*, H. (from محال, places, or زمين, land) Lands granted either rent-free or at a low rate of assessment to public ferrymen, or to officers guarding passes in the hills. In Birbhúm the lands were granted at a fixed rate of assessment in perpetuity to the holders and their descendants, as long as the revenue is paid, although apparently no longer connected with the performance of any particular duty.—Reg. xxix. 1814.

Ghatwan, (?) Ben. A man of a low caste, frequently a predial slave, in Ramgarh.

Ghaṭ, Ghuṭ, H., Ben., &c. (گهت, from the S. Ghaṭa, घट) A water-pot or jar, representing, on some occasions, the goddess Durgá.

Ghaṭapújá, S. (घटपूजा) Worship of the water-jar as Durgá. See *Ghaṭasthápana*.

Ghaṭasphoṭa, Mar. (घटस्फोट, from the S. *Sphoṭa*, a breaking) Ceremony of the ejection of a person from his caste, or of the repudiation of a wife; typically expressed by the actual breaking of a pitcher on the occasion.

Ghaṭasthápana, S. (from स्थापन, placing) The ceremony of placing a water pot as a type or receptacle of Durgá, who, after certain invocations, is supposed to be present in it, and to receive the worship addressed to her. It is one of the essential ceremonies of the Durgá-Pújá.

Ghaṭ, Ghaṭi, or Ghattí, H. (گهت, گهتي, from the v. گهتنا, to abate) Deficiency, decrease, lightness in weight, fall in price or value.

Ghát, H., Ben. (S. گهات, ঘাত) A blow, a wound, striking, killing; what is struck or hurt.

Ghátaka, H., Ben. (گهاتک, ঘাতক) A murderer, one who wounds or kills.

Gháta-chandra, *Gháta-tithí*, Mar. (from चंद्र, the moon, or तिथी, a lunar day) An inauspicious day.

Ghaṭá, Ben. (ঘটা) A crowd, a procession.

Ghaṭaka, Ben., Mar. (घटक) A person who negociates marriages between families, especially in Bengal; also, a manager, or leading man in general.

Ghaṭí, Ben. (ঘটী) A clock. The native clock is a brass plate, or *gang*, on which the hour is struck with a wooden mallet. See *Ghaṛí*.

Ghaṭiká, Ben. (S. ঘটিকা) *Ghaṭaká*, Mar. (घटका) An hour, properly of 24 minutes: the little metal vessel, by the sinking of which in water the hour is measured. See *Ghaṛí*.

Gháyí, or Ghái, Tel. (ఘాయీ) An embankment to confine water, a reservoir.

Ġházi, A. (غازي) A champion, a hero; especially one who fights against infidels.

Ġhazi-mián, H. (غازي ميان) A saint held in high repute in Hindustan, in whose honour an annual festival is celebrated in most large towns, but particularly at Barech, in the month of Jeth. It is commonly called the Shádi, or marriage of the saint, in allusion, according to one tradition, to his having suffered martyrdom on the eve of his nuptials. The origin of the festival, which is equally popular with Hindus and Mohammadans, is, however, doubtful, and much uncertainty prevails regarding the person of the saint. The most particular accounts make him a nephew of Mahmud of Ghazni, born at Ajmer, and killed in battle with the Hindus at Barech, after Mahmud's death.

Ghegará, or Gheghará, Ghegura, Gheghura, H. (گهيگرا, گهيگهرا) The unripe pod of gram. The unripe bole of cotton before it bursts.

Gheláuní, H. (گهيلوني) An addition to an article sold in favour of the purchaser. An additional per centage of an article counted, as, 110 *bambus*, or 120 *mangoes*, rated as 100 only.

Ghenai, Thug. Fetters.

Gheṇedeṇe, Mar. (घेणेदेणे, from घेणे, to take, and देणे, to

give) Borrowing and lending, dealing with, traffic, mercantile intercourse.

Ghetádetá, Mar. (घेतादेता) A regular customer, one who punctually pays what he owes.

Ghetáṇdetáṇ, Mar. (घेतांदेतां) On the conclusion of a bargain.

Ghepodepo, Mar. (घेपोदेपो) Money lending without interest, unprofitable or troublesome lending and taking back.

Ghewádewá, or *-wí*, Mar. (घेवादेवा) Traffic, dealing with, borrowing and lending, &c.

GHENṬÍ, H. (گھينٹي) The unripe pod of gram and other kinds of pulse.

GHER, or GHERÁ, H. &c. (گھير, from *Gherna*, to surround) Enclosing, surrounding; an enclosure, a fence, a boundhedge.

GHERUÄ, (?) H. A mortgagee holding land in possession as security, and in payment of the interest. See *Giro*.

GHEWÁRÍ, Mar. (घेवारी) A retail dealer, a huckster; in some places limited to one who buys and retails garden produce.

GHÍ, GHEE, H. &c. (گھي, from S. घृत) Ben. GHI, (घि) GHÍ, Mar. (घी) Clarified or oiled butter; butter boiled and then set to cool, when it remains in a semi-liquid or oily state, and is used in cooking, or is drank by the natives: (the primitive GHṚITA is also current in most dialects).

Ghí-guttá, corruptly, *Gheecottah*, or *Gheegootah*, Mar. (घीगुत्ता) The exclusive right of the renter of a village to the buying and selling of *ghí* in retail.

GHISÁṚÍ, Mar. (घिसाडी) A low caste, or individual of it, whose occupation is manufacturing common iron utensils.

GHOÍLA, Thug. Copper coin, pice.

GHOL, Ben. (ঘোল) Butter milk.

GHOḶ, Mar. (घोळ) A ring, with bits of iron attached to it, at the end of a staff, to make a noise with to frighten reptiles, birds, &c.

GHONTÁ, or GHOṬÁ, Mar. (घोंटा, घोटा) An intoxicating potion, an infusion of the leaves of the hemp.

GHONGHÍ, H. (گھونگھي) Tying the end of a blanket in a knot, and placing it on the head, so as to keep off rain. Wrapping oneself up in a blanket.

GHORÁ, H. &c. (S. گھوڑا, घोडा) A horse.

Ghoṛavíra, (?) (from *Ghoḍa*, or *Ghoṛa*, a horse) A tax paid by Rájput tribes to their chiefs in commutation of a gift of a horse.

Ghoṛchaṛha, H. (from *Ghora* and *charhná*, چڑھنا, to mount) *Ghoṛáchaṛa*, Ben. (ঘোড়াচড়া) A rider, a horseman: a subdivision of the Kurmi or Kumbi tribe, which is extensively spread throughout India, and follows principally agricultural occupations.

Ghoṛe-khád, Mar. (घोडेखाद) Grazing or pasturing of horses.

Ghoṛe-ráút, *Ghoṛe-swár*, Mar. (घोडेराऊत, घोडेस्वार) A trooper, a horse-soldier.

Ghorevâṭ, Mar. (घोडेवाट) A horse-path; especially a practicable path for horses over hilly ground.

GHOSH, corruptly, GHOSE, Ben. (ঘোষ, from S. घुष, to cry) The name of a division of the writer caste, and commonly used as their family name, as, *Chandra-ghose*: also the name of a tribe of herdsmen in Bengal. A station of cowherds.

Ghoshaṇá, Ben. (S. ঘোষণা) A proclamation.

Ghosí, *Ghosee*, H. (S. گھوسي) A herdsman, a milkman: also, in the north-west provinces, a class of milkmen, who, although said to be descended from the Ahírs, are now mostly Mohammadans.

GHOṬAKHOR, Hindi (घोटखोर, from घोट, a gulp, and P. खोर, who swallows) A diver: in some villages in the western Maraṭha states a diver forms one of the servants, and is employed in recovering articles dropped in tanks and wells.

GHOṬÍ, H. (گھوٹي) Land which has been under a rice crop.

GHUGRÍ, Mar. (घुगरी) Grain boiled in the husk. Grain presented to the head of the village, or the government officers, on the ripening of the crop: a cess formerly imposed in its stead.

ĠHULÁM, in some dialects, GULÁM, corrupted in pronouncing to GULÁP and GULÁB, H. (A. غلام) GULÁMU, Tel. (గులాము) A youth, a servant, a slave.

GHÚMÁO, GHOOMÁO, H. (گھوماو, lit., a turning round, from گھمنا, to turn round) As much land as can be ploughed in one day by a pair of bullocks.

GHUN, GHOON, H. (گھن) A weevil destructive of wood and grain.

GHUNDÍ, H. (گھندي) A herb that grows in rice fields after the crop is cut: camels are fond of it, and it is used in medicine.

GHUNGCHI, H. (گھنگچي) The seed of the Abrus precatorius; especially as a standard measure of weight: more usually *Gunja*, q. v.

GHÚNGÍ, GHOONGEE, H. (گھونگي) An insect destructive of growing gram; also *Gindar*.

GHUNGRÚ, H. &c. (گهنگرو, घुंगरू) Small bells fastened round the ancles or wrists of women, sometimes worn on the toes, especially of dancing girls.

GHÚNT, GHOONT, H. (گهونت) Rent from lands granted as endowments of religious establishments (Kamaon).

GHÚR, GHOOR, H. (گهور, घूर) The soil of the sandy ridge east of Muzaffarnagar.

GHÚRA, H. (گهورا) Soil, manure.

GHURÁB, Mar. (घुराब, A. غراب) A kind of vessel, a sloop with long projecting bows, used on the Malabar coast.

GHURAT, GHOORUT, H. (گهرت) Cattle pens (Eastern Oudh).

GHÚR-BARÁR, GHOOR-BURAR, H. (گهوربرار) Dues levied on every sharer and under-tenant, in proportion to the expenses of the village for the year: from H. GHÚRÁ, a dunghill or sweepings, all miscellaneous charges being heaped together (Bundelkhand).

GHURRAH, or GHURRAT, incorrectly, GHORRA, A. (غرة) A fine of 500 *dirms*, being the value of a male or female slave of that price, to whom also the term is applied (Mohammadan law).

GHURRAT, H. (A. غرة, whiteness, &c.) The first day of the moon's age.

GHÚS, H. (گهوس) GHUSH, Ben. (घुष) A bribe.

GHUSL, H. &c. (غسل) Bathing, ablution; especially the ablutions of the Mohammadans.

Ghassál, H. &c. (غسّال) A bather, an attendant on a bath; but applied more especially to one who washes the dead.

GHUSRÁND, H. (گهسراند) A creeping grass with a yellow flower, bearing a bitter fruit; used as a condiment for horses, but considered poisonous to men.

GIÁRWÁṈ, GÍARWÍṈ, Dakhini H. (گيارواں, گياروين, for *Igarah*) Eleventh. The eleventh of Rabi-us-ṣáni, a day dedicated to the homage of Pir-i-Dastagír, a Mohammadan saint in the south of India.

GÍCHUVALÍ, Karn. (ಗಿಚುವಳಿ) Farming, agriculture.

GÍDA, Thug. Impure, unclean; a man of a very low caste.

GIḌAGÁWAL, Tel. (గిడగావల) Taxes levied on forest produce.

GÍDARMÁR, H. (گيدرمار, lit., jackal-killer) A vagrant and thief in Upper India.

GIDDA, GIDDE, Tel. (గిద్ద, గిద్దె) The smallest measure of capacity in use, varying in different places, but calculated by Captain Jervis at 900 grains=5·837 cubic inches, the fourth of a *Sola*.

GIDDANA, Karn. (ಗಿದ್ದನ) The fourteenth part of a *maund*.

Giddáṇi, Karn. (ಗಿದ್ದಾಣಿ) The 256th fraction of a fanam, or a rupee.

GÍḌḌANGÍ, Tel. Karn (గిడ్డంగి) A shop, a storehouse, a granary, a jail.

GÍDÍA, GEEDEEA, H. (گيديا) A class of vagrants and thieves in Upper India.

GIDNA, Karn. (ಗಿದ್ನ) A measure of grain, equal to four *Solige*, q. v.

GILA, H. (گله) GILLÁ, Mar. (गिल्ला, both from the P. گله) A complaint, a remonstrance, abuse, reproach.

GILANDÁZI, H. (گلندازي, from گل, clay, earth, and اندازي, throwing) An embankment: charge for making and repairing embankments, allowed formerly in the village accounts.

GÍM, Thug. Search after Thugs: also theft.

GIMWÁ, or GIMHWÁ, Mar. (गिमवा, गिम्हवा, from गीम, or गीम्ह, vernacular of S. ग्रीष्म, the hot season) Grain raised in the hot season by irrigation.

Gimwas, Mar. (गिमवस) A field prepared for the growth of grain in the hot season by irrigating; the grain so raised.

GINDAR, H. (گندر) An insect very destructive of growing pulse: also *Ghungi*.

GINDURI, H. (گندري) A circular twist of straw or grass to support a vessel with a round bottom.

GINNA, Karn. (ಗಿಣ್ಣ) Cheese.

Ginnagaḍḍe, Karn. (ಗಿಣ್ಣಗಡ್ಡೆ) A cheese.

GINṬÍ, Karn. (ಗಿಂಟಿ) Double-thread texture.

Ginṭadavalli, Karn. (ಗಿಂಟದವಲ್ಲಿ) A single cotton cloth woven with double threads.

Ginṭadabaṭṭe, Karn. (ಗಿಂಟದಬಟ್ಟೆ) A double cloth woven with double threads.

GINTI, H. (گنتي, from S. गण, to count) Number, reckoning: the first day of the month: a specimen, a muster.

GIRÁ, Mar. (गिरा) A measure of length, a *Tasu* and a half, or one-fourteenth or one-sixteenth of a *gaz*, q. v.

GIRAKÁLU, Karn. (ಗಿರಕಾಲು) One-sixteenth of a rupee.

GIRÁN, H. (P گران) Dear: heavy.

Giráni, H. (گراني) Dearness, dearth, scarcity: weight.

GIRÁṢÍ, GIRÁSÍ, Mar. (गिराशी -सी) A caste, or individual of it, living by piracy &c.

GIRD, H. (P. گرد) Round, surrounding, a wall, an inclosure, a circle, a department.

Girdwár, or *Girdáwar*, H. (گردوار, گرداور) A patrol, a watch, a guard, a superintendant or inspector of police or customs.

Girdáwari, H. (گرداوري) Inspection, patrolling, going the rounds: looking after smugglers or contraband goods: a circular order.

GIRDA, Karn. (ಗಿರ್ದೆ) The fourth of a fanam.

Girdaṇa, Karn. (ಗಿರ್ದಣ) The fourth of a *Solige*, a dry measure.

Girdásaga, Karn. (ಗಿರ್ದಾಸಗ) The eighth of a fanam.

GIRDÍ-NAWÁYÁ, Mar. (गिरदीनवाया, from A. *Nawâh*, environs) A surrounding tract, land round any particular spot or fort. A tax levied on villages so situated, in lieu of supplies to the garrison, &c.

GIRHÁÍK, Mar. (गिऱ्हाईक, from S. ग्राहक) A purchaser, a bidder.

GIRIFT, H. (P. گرفت) Capture, apprehension.

Giriftár, H. (گرفتار) A prisoner, one seized or apprehended.

Giriftárí, H. (P. گرفتاري) Apprehension, seizure, taking up, arrest.

GIRIKE, GIRUKE, Karn. (ಗಿರಿಕೆ, ಗಿರುಕೆ) An instrument for separating cotton from the seed.

GIRO, or GIRAU, H. (P. گرو) GIRAVU, Tel. (గిరవు) A pawn, a pledge, a mortgage, a contract. (The term *Gherroas*, holders of lands on mortgage, Ben. Reg. ii. 1795, is no doubt intended to represent some derivative from this word).

Girvi, or *Girwi*, or, vernacularly, *Girbi*, H. (گروي) A pledge, a mortgage; the thing pledged or mortgaged.

Girwidár, H. (گرويدار) The holder of a pledge or mortgage.

Girwináma, H. (گروينامه) A deed of mortgage.

GIRWÍ, H. (P. گروي) An insect mischievous to standing corn: see *Gerwá*.

GO (गो, properly the crude form of the S. noun, nom. *Gau*, or *Gao*, गौः, in which form it is most commonly used), A cow: (the word *Go* is also used singly in the dialects for any animal of the cow kind, but its more common application is in forming derivatives and compounds).

Gáo, H. &c. (گاو) or *Gái*, *Gay*, Mar. (गाई, गाय) A cow, a bull.

Goálá, pronounced like *Gwálá*, Ben. (গোআলা) A cowherd, one whose business or caste it is to attend cattle and sell milk, (the word, orignally *Gopála*, is modified vernacularly as *Gonwála*, or Hindi, *Gwála*, &c. q. v.).

Goálá-párá, Ben, (গোআলাপাড়া) A village, or part of one, or of a town, inhabited by cow-keepers.

Gobaidya, Ben. (গোবৈদ্য) A cow doctor, a quack.

Gobar, *Gobur*, H. (گوبر) *Gowar*, Mar. (गोवर) Dried cow-dung, used as fuel, or for plastering floors.

Gobarát, Ben. (গোবরাট) The threshold of a door, from its being made smooth with cow-dung effused in water, forming a sort of plaster.

Gobarí, or *Gobrí*, H. (گوبري) *Gowarí*, Mar. (गोवरी) A piece or cake of dried cow-dung; paste or plaster made with it.

Gochar, *Gochará*, *Gocharáí*, H. &c., (گوچر, گوچرا, گوچراي) Pasture land, land kept free from cultivation as the grazing ground of the village.

Gocharma, Mar. (S. गोचर्म्म) A cow's hide, a measure of land as much as can be comprehended by a cow's hide.

Godandá, Uriya. (ଗୋଦାଣ୍ଡ) Pasture land.

Godána, (S. गोदान) The gift of a cow to a Bráhman, to a bridegroom, or at religious ceremonies: it is also, among the Marathas, a name of the *Sanskára* of shaving: see *Chúdá*.

Godhúl, Mar. (गोधूळ) lit. cow dust: hence, Evening twilight (from the dust raised by the cows returning from pasture). A certain division of time, thirty *palas* before and thirty after sunset: it is considered an auspicious hour for marriages.

Gográsam, Tel. (గోగ్రాసం) Fodder of a cow.

Goháí, H. (گوهاي) Treading out grain by bullocks.

Gohar, *Gohur*, H. (گوهر) A broad pathway for cattle, the preservation of which is considered as obligatory as that of a boundary.

Gohatyá, S. &c. (गोहत्या) Killing a cow—a heinous crime.

Go-ín, *Goeen*, H. (گوين) A pair of plough oxen, sometimes called *Do-gawá*, also *Gora*.

Gokallu, Karn. (ಗೋಕಲ್ಲು) Cow-stone, stones set up in Kanara for cows to rub themselves against.

Gokhadá, Uriya (ଗୋଖଦା) Damage done by stray cattle to the crops of the cultivators, for which an allowance is sometimes made.

Gokhaṭi, Uriya, (ଗୋଖଟି) Fine for stray cattle.

Gokul, H. (گوكل) A herd of cattle. The country about Brindávan, where Kṛishṇa passed his boyhood.

Gomaya, Mar. (S. गोमय) Cow-dung.

Gomedh, S. (गोमेध:) Sacrifice of a cow.

Goṇwaḷá, or *Goṇwáḷá*, Mar. (गोंवळा, गोंवाळा) A cowherd.

Gop, H. (گوپ) *Gopa*, S. (गोप:) A cowherd, a man who by caste breeds and attends on horned cattle, and sells their milk, butter, &c. fem. *Gopí*, (गोपी) a woman of the same caste; also *Gopíká*.

Gopa- or *Gopi-chandana*, S. &c. (गोपचन्दन) lit., cowherds' sandal, a sort of whitish and saponaceous clay found at Dwáraká, and valued as the most appropriate pigment with which to mark the person with the sectarial insignia of the Vaishṇava sects; also called *Gopa-máṭí*, cowherds' earth.

Gopála, H. (S. गोपालः) A cowherd by caste and occupation.

Gopandhábhúmí, Tel. (గోపంధాభూమి) Pasture land, or place where cattle go: (see the next, *Pandhá* being the same word as the S. *Panthá*).

Gopanth, Ben. (S. गोपन्थ) A road or path for cattle.

Gopáshṭamí, S. &c. (गोपाष्टमी) The eighth day of the light half of the month Kártik (Oct.-Nov.), when cattle are fed, and decorated with garlands, in commemoration of Kṛishna's passing his youth among the cow-pastures of Brindávan.

Gopmahál, H. (گوپمحال) Pasture grounds.

Gorakṣh, or *Gorakshaka*, vernacularly, *Gorakh*, H. &c. (from S. रक्ष, to preserve) A cowkeeper, a cowherd.

Goras, *Gorus*, H. &c. (from S. रस, juice) Milk, curds, &c., the fluid produce of a cow.

Gorsi, more correctly, *Gorasí*, H. (گورسي, from S. गोरस, milk) A milkpail.

Goru, *Goroo*, also Mar. *Gurú*, *Gooroo*, q. v. H. (گورو, from S. गो) A cow, an ox.

Goruá-ḍhukán, H. (گوروا ڈھکان) Twilight, time of bringing home the cows.

Goruárí-berá, H. (گوروارِي بيرا) Evening, time of bringing home cattle.

Gorukhiyá, Uriya (ଗୋରୁଖିଆ) Damage or destruction by cattle.

Goṣálá, H. (S. शाला, a hall) A cowhouse.

Goshṭha, S. &c. (गोष्ठः) A station of cowherds, a cowpen, pasture, or the like; a herd of cattle: also, vernacularly, as in Bengali, *Goṭh*, or *Goṭha* (গোঠ).

Goshtáshṭamí, H. S. The same as *Gopáshthamí*, q. v.

Gothán, H. (گوتھان, from S. स्थान, a place) Place of assembling the cattle of a village.

Gová, Hindi (गोवा) Manure, cow-dung.

Gowárí, Mar. (गोवारी) A cowherd.

Gowárí, H. (گواري) A dwelling-house, a family, a cowhouse (Dehli).

Gwál, or *Gwálá*, also read *Gual*, *Gooal*, but less correctly and more barbarously, *Gwaller*, H. (گوال, گوالا, S. गोपाल) A cowherd, one whose caste it is to tend cattle, and sell milk, butter, &c. The caste of cowherds in Orissa furnishes also palankín-bearers and domestic servants to Europeans and natives in Bengal.

Gwálin, or *Gwálaní*, H. (گوالن) A female of the cowherd caste.

Go-ÁL, H. (گوال) Unclaimed land (Dehli).

GOBBA, Thug. A circular grave.

GOBRI, H. (گوبري) A tribe in Rohilkhand, now living just under the hills.

GODA, Tel. (గోడ) Any horned cattle.

GODAGARA, or GODÁRI-VÁḌU, Tel. (గోడగర, గోడారివాడు) A shoemaker, a worker in leather, sprung from a female of the barber caste by a potter.

GODÁRÁ, H. (گودارا) A large subdivision of the Ját tribe on the borders of Hariana.

GODARÍ, H. (گودري) A circular twist of grass or twine supporting the bottom of a round vessel.

GODHAṚ, H. (گودھڑ) The weeds and grasses collected from a ploughed field by a harrow.

GÓDI, GÓDE, Karn, (ಗೋಧಿ, ಗೋಧೆ) Wheat.

GODIYÁBHUMI, Tel. (గోదియాభూమి) Stony soil.

GODNA, H. (گودنا) GOṆḌṆE, Mar (गोंदणे) Tattooing, puncturing the skin, and rubbing it with the leaves of plants, yielding a dark dye chiefly produced by women. Branding as a criminal punishment, (abolished Act. ii. 1849).

GODOWN, Ben. GUDÁM, (গুদাম) (from the Malay GADANG, گدغ) An outhouse, a warehouse, a place where household implements or goods are kept. The 'black hole' was nothing else than a Godown.

GOEND, GWEND, or GWENDÁ, H. (گوندا, گويند) A suburb, fields near a village, a homestead or neighbourhood.

GOGÁ-PIR, H, (گوگاپير) A saint held in much veneration by the agricultural population of Dehli and the Upper Doab, who, in the month Bhádon, present offerings at his shrine which is at Dudiera, 200 miles south-west of Hisar,

GOHÁNÍ, Hindi (गोहानी) Land near a village, well manured land.

GOHÁRÍ, H. (گوهاري) Rich highly-cultivated land (Ságar).

GOÏNDA, commonly, GOYINDA or GOYENDA, H. (گوينده, from P. گفتن, to speak) GOENDÁ, Ben. (গোএন্দা) An informer, a spy.

GOJAI, GOJYEE, also GOJI, and GOJARI, H. (گوجئي) Wheat and barley sown in the same field.

GOJARA H. (گوجره) Barley and chana, or chick-pea, sown together.

GOJHÁ, H. (گوجها) A species of thorny grass which springs up during the rains.

Gokhá, Uriya. (ଗୋଖା) A caste of fishermen, or a man of that caste.

Gokhru, H. (گوکھرو) A herb which springs up on *bhúr* land, bearing a fruit covered with small prickles (Tribulus lanuginosus): in seasons of dearth the poor of Hariána feed on the pounded seed: a large kind called Gokhru Dakhini bears a fruit of a triangular shape, with prickles at the angles, and hence the same name is given to the iron crows' feet thrown on the ground to check the advance of cavalry.

Gol, H. &c. (گول) A ball, a circle, any thing round, a mass of people, an associated body or society, a crowd, a troop, a brigade, a party from a different village sojourning with their cattle for pasture.

Golá, Golí, H. (گولا, گولي, from *Gol*, round) A ball, a cannon ball; a mode of trial by ordeal, in which the accused carried a heated ball of iron in his hand for a given distance, and, if his hands were unscorched, was declared innocent.

Golandáz, H. (from the P. انداز, who throws) A native artilleryman.

Golá, H. (گولا, from *Gól*, round) A granary, a storeroom, a place in which grain or salt is kept for a season. In Bengal it is usually a circular structure of mats or clay, raised two or three feet from the ground upon short pillars of wood or stone, and covered by a thatch. A grain or salt store or market; a place where it is sold wholesale. A salt or saltpetre manufactory (Agra).

Goládár, H. &c. (گولادار) *Goldár*, Ben. (গোলদার) A wholesale grain merchant or salt dealer, one who keeps a store.

Golákhati, Uriya (ଗୋଲାଖଟି) Dépôt for salt after weighing.

Golápaharu, Uriya (ଗୋଲାପହରୁ) A watchman over a salt store.

Golá, H. (گولا) Name of an inferior caste, who are employed as cleaners of rice; or of one whose business is the manufacture of salt.

Golápúrab, H. (گولاپورب) An inferior tribe of Sunadh Bráhmans, who cultivate lands in the Agra district.

Golaka, S. &c. (गोलक) A son born of a widow. Among the Marathas, the term *Golak* is considered to apply to a caste supposed to be descended from the illegitimate offspring of a woman of the Bráhman caste; distinguished as the *Kunda-golak*, (कुण्डगोलक) the adulterous progeny of a woman who has a husband, and *Randa-golak*, (रण्डगोलक) the illegitimate son of a widow. The members of this caste at Puna act as astrologers, agents, money-changers, and are held as no better than Súdras.

Golkár, Karn. (ಗೊಳ್ಕಾರ) Sons of female slaves or bondwomen.

Golla, Tel. Karn. (గొల్ల) A shepherd, a man of a caste whose duty it is to graze sheep or cattle, sometimes employed as confidential servants and assistants in public treasuries. Also *Golládu*, *Gollavádu*, plur. *Gollavándlu*, Karn *Gollar*, or *Gollaru*.

Golla-karamu, Tel. (గొల్లకరము) A tax on herdsmen and shepherds.

Golla-palli, Karn. (గొల్లపల్లి) A village of cowherds or shepherds.

Gollar-mányam, Karn. (గొల్లరమాన్యం) Taxes levied from shepherds.

Golli, Thug. Coral.

Golyá, Mar (गोल्या) A rice pounder or pestle, a man who gains a living by pounding rice.

Goma, Thug. Omen from the flight of a shrike, considered good on whichever side it is observed.

Gomájí kápasá, Mar. (गोमाजी कापशा) A fictitious name; sometimes inserted in accounts as the name of a revenue defaulter for arrears for which the head of the village, or revenue officer, is responsible: (from *Gomá*, pretended ignorance: *kápasá or kápsá* appears to be merely an unmeaning adjunct).

Goná, or **Goní**, Ben., Mar., &c. (S. গোণ, गोणी) A coarse sack made from the fibres of the *Pát*. The coarse sort of canvas of which it is made is commonly called *Gunny*: see *Ganni*.

Gonapat, or *Gonapát*, or *Gonatát*, Mar. (गोणपट, or -पाट, or -ताट) The coarse canvas or sackcloth made from the fibres of the *Pát* (Corchorus capsularis), of which sacks or bags of various sizes are fabricated.

Gona, Thug. The hand; also, amongst the Dakhini Thugs, Fine.

Gonagár-áya-jodi, Karn. (ಗೊನಗಾರಆಯಜೋಡಿ) A tax levied on those who cut betel-nuts for the village.

Gonakallu, read also **Gonikal**, (?) Karn. (ಗೊಣಕಲ್ಲು) A rough stone; stony or gravelly soil.

Gonakalluhádi, Karn. (ಗೊಣಕಲ್ಲುಹಾದಿ) A rough road.

Gonchi, Karn. (ಗೊಂಚಿ) A field, especially one rented by different tenants.

Gonchigár, Karn. (ಗೊಂಚಿಗಾರ) A proprietor or occupant of a field.

Gonchipatta, Karn. (ಗೊಂಚಿಪಟ್ಟ) A lease of fields or lands held jointly by several co-occupants.

Gonchálu, Karn. (ಗೊಂಚಾಲು) A man set to watch a field.

GOND, H. &c. (P. گوند) Gum; a solution of gum used to fasten the envelopes of letters.

Gond-dání, H. (P. دان, holding) The gum-stand.

Gond-kast, H. (P. كست, spreading) An instrument for applying the gum to envelopes.

GOND, H. (گوند) A sort of rush used in making mats and baskets.

GOND, (?) Hindi. Land immediately adjacent to a village, and, being richly manured, cultivated for vegetables and tobacco (Bundelkhand).

GOṆḌ, corruptly, GOANḌ, H. (S. گونڈ) The half barbarous inhabitants of the eastern branches of the Vindhya mountains, between Bundelkhand and Berár, and subject partly to the British government, and partly to that of Nagpore, giving its appellation to the country of Gondwána. A small portion of them is found in different tracts, bearing the title of *Ráj-gonḍ*, who are looked upon with respect by the other *Gonḍs*.

GONḌÁ, H. (گونڈا) A branch of the Ahír caste.

GONDAṆA, GONDAḶA, or GONDLI, Karn. (ಗೊಂದಣ, ಗೊಂದಳ, ಗೊಂದ್ಲಿ) GONDHALA, or GONDHAL, Mar. (गोंधळ) A tumultuous festivity in honour of the goddess Deví, celebrated, even in Mysore, chiefly by Maratha Bráhmans, it being a Maratha festival, (from the Mar. *Gondhala*, tumult, bustle,) consisting of music, and dancing, and recitation of mythological stories. The word in Kanarese, spelled with a long *ō* (ಗೋಂದಳ) is said also to mean a ceremony performed for the sick, on the birth of a child, at marriages, &c., when the tutelary household divinity is splendidly attired, and music and dancing are performed by hired musicians in the outer court. It is probably the same thing as the *Gondhal*.

Gondhalí, incorrectly *Gondali*, and *Gondli*, or *Gondlee*, corruptly *Gonedullee*, Mar. (गोंधळी) The name of a caste, or individual of it, whose business it is to sing and dance, and perform the *Gondhal*: in some places the *Gondhalí* is the village drummer; sometimes he is a vagrant musician, dancer, and tumbler, or subsists by begging.

GONEWÁR, (?) Tel. An inferior division of the Kunbi or agricultural tribe in the northern Sirkars. See *Gorinvár*.

GONGAḌI, GONGAṚI, Karn. (ಗೊಂಗಡಿ) A woollen cloth or blanket. See *Kambal*.

GONḌṚÁ, or GONṚÁ, H. (گونڈرا, گونڑا) A reservoir to which water is thrown up from a pond or pool below. The straw or reeds which are placed to protect the side of the upper reservoir. (Central and lower Doab).

GONI, Thug. A shoe.

GONIAYAT, Thug. A man who has lost his hand or nose: it is unlucky to murder him.

GONṬIÁ, H. (گونٹیا) The head man of a village, a Patel. In some places the term is restricted to a Bráhman holding that office.

GOPHNÁ, GOPHNÍ, or GOPHIÁ, H. (گوپهنا, گوپهني, گوپهيا, गोफनी, गोफया) GOPHAṆ, Mar. (गोफण) A sling, especially one used by persons stationed on a platform in a field of corn to drive away cattle, birds, &c.

GOPO, Uriya. (ଗୋପୋ) The whole household: lit., cows and children.

GOPURA, Mar, &c. (S. गोपुर) A gate, a town gate, but more especially applied in the south to the elevated and ornamented gateway or entrance tower of a Hindu temple.

GOPYA, S. (गोप्य, from गुप, to preserve) To be preserved or taken care of, as a deposit.

Gopyádhi, S. (गोप्याधिः) A pledge or deposit to be preserved, one that is not to be made any use of while in deposit: also *Gopyabandha*, &c.

GORÁ, H. (گورا) Fair, white, a European; but, when applied to cattle, red.

GOṚÁ, or GOḌÁ, Ben. (গোড়া) A foundation, a source.

Goṛagoṛi, Ben. (গোড়াগোড়ি) From the beginning, from the origin or foundation.

GORABA, GORAVA, Karn. (ಗೊರಬ, ಗೊರವ) A shepherd's priest.

GORÁÍ, Hindi (गोराई) A clan of Rájputs in the Agra district.

GORÁÍ-ZAMÍN, (? *zamín* is Persian, and *gorái* may come from *gorá*, fair, but the compound is not met with in any dictionary, nor is it confirmed by any local authority) Mixed soil of sand and fine red earth, the latter predominating, producing all kinds of grain except wheat and rice: on the best kind, sugar-cane, chilis, and tobacco may be raised.

GORANT, (?) A light soil (Bundelkhand): (probably the same as the next word).

GORAT, Guz. (ગોરાટ) A light sandy soil; one of the two principal kinds found in Guzerat: also termed *Marwá*.

Goreṭ, or **Gorai-iṭ**, corruptly, **Gorayt**, **Gorayat**, or **Ghorite**, H. (گوريت, गोरेट, गोरैइट) A watchman, a village watchman and messenger, one whose duty it is to guard the village and prevent depredations on the crops, also to carry messages for the superior village officers: he is, in most places in Upper India, one of the municipal establishment, and is especially employed under the *Patwárí* to call the villagers to the public office when required.

Gorgárí, H. (گورگاري, perhaps from P. گور, a grave) A method of deciding village boundary disputes in Chota Nagpur: two holes are dug on a spot in the contested limits, in which the watchmen of the two contending villages are severally buried up to the waist: whichever holds out longest gains the cause.

Gorhá, H. (گوڑها) Fields near a village homestead.

Gorha, or **Gorhoni**, Thug. Bread.

Gorhna, Thug. To strangle.

Goḍná, **Gorná**, H. (گوڈنا, گورنا, गोडना, गोरना) A sort of hoe used for digging up sugar-cane, and the like.

Goríwár, (?) Tel. A division of the Kunbi, or agricultural caste in the northern Sirkars: (*wár* is the vulgar form of *váḍu*, an individual).

Goṛru, Tel. (గొఱ్ఱు) A land measure, equal to 125 *kuntas*, or 45,375 square yards, or $3\frac{1}{8}$ acres: also an instrument of husbandry, used as a sort of harrow, or as a drill-plough, or sometimes for weeding after the grain is in stalk.

Gosain, H. (گوساين) A religious mendicant: see *Goswámí*.

Gosain ṭáki, H. (گوسين ٹاکي) A cess of a quarter ana per rupee on the revenue, formerly granted by a Zamindar of Bírbhúm to establishments of Gosains in the Zamindárí, and collected by them from the Ryots: as many disputes arose out of the arrangement, the right to levy the tax was finally restricted to the Zamindar, and the payment of the *Gosain-ṭáki* left to his own discretion.

Gosangiváḍu, Tel. (గొసంగివాడు) A shoemaker, a worker in leather; a low caste, whose occupation is working in skins and leather.

Gosáví, Mar. (गोसावी) A religious mendicant: see *Goswámí*.

Gosáví-paṭṭi, Mar. (गोसावीपट्टि) A cess self imposed formerly by the villagers to raise a fund for paying *Gosains*.

Gosha-nashín, H. (گوشه نشين) A Mohammadan ascetic or recluse, one who professes to have withdrawn from the world; lit., one sitting in a corner: hence, also said of a woman of rank or respectability, though the term for her is more properly *Parda-nashín*.

Goshṭa, Mar. (गोष्ट) A story, an affair, a circumstance.

Goshṭhí, Ben. (S. গোষ্ঠী) **Goshṭa** or **Goshṭí**, the unaspirated letter being substituted for the original, Mar. (गोष्ट, गोष्टी) An assembly, a meeting, especially one held for discussion or debate. Family connexions, relations, kindred.

Goshṭí-sráddh, Mar. (from S. श्राद्ध, a funeral ceremony) An obsequial ceremony performed in words only, when circumstances prevent its actual performance.

Goshwára, H. (P. گوشواره, गोशवारा) vernacularly modified as **Goṣerá**, or **Goṣwárá**, **Goshwárá**, corruptly **Gooshwarah**, Mar (गोशेरा, गोश्वारा, गोष्वारा) **Gosbárá**, or **Goswárá**, Ben. (গোসবারা) **Goshupárá**, Tel. (గోషుపారా) **Goshuáṛá**, Uriya (ଗୋଷୁଆରା) An abstract statement, giving the substance of different documents, the abstract or sum of a village or Zamindárí account, shewing the total quantity of land, and its distribution, as waste, cultivated, fallow, productive, &c., made up from the *Chiṭṭhás*, q. v. An index, a summary.

Goshwára-habulíat, H. (A. قبوليت, agreement) Counterpart or acceptance of an abstract account.

Goshwára-kul, H. (from A. كُل, all) A complete abstract or summary of the whole.

Goswámí, S. (गो, sense or passion &c., स्वामी, master, one who restrains his passions, modified vernacularly as **Gosáin**, **Goosáin**, **Gosámi**, or simply **Sámi** or **Swámi**, **Gosáí**, **Gosávi**, **Gosáyí**, &c.) A religious mendicant in general. As a special name it is applied to very different classes of persons, identified only by their professing a religious and mendicant life. The most respectable are the reputed descendants spiritually of Ṣankara Áchárya, of whom there are ten chief branches, and who are thence also called the *Daṣ-námi*, or ten-named Gosains, attaching to the ordinary Hindu appellation one of the terms, *Tírtha*, (shrine), *Ásrama*, (an order), *Vana* and *Araṇya*, (a wood), *Saraswatí*, (the goddess of eloquence). *Bhárati*, (the goddess of speech), *Puri*, (a city), *Giri* and *Parvata*, (a hill), or *Ságara*, (the ocean), as, *Ananda-giri Vidyáraṇya*, *Puran-gír*, *Rama-ásrama*. These, although they are occasionally vagrants, are usually assembled in *maths*, or conventual residences, under a superior: some of their establishments are liberally endowed, and of great reputed sanctity, particularly that of Sringeri, in the western Ghats, near the sources of the *Tungabhadrá*, said to have been founded by *Ṣankara* himself. Individuals of the three pure castes are admissible, and in some cases Ṣúdras also; but as they profess celibacy, their numbers are in part recruited by the purchase or adoption of boys at an early age. The *Daṣ-námi Gosains* worship preferentially *Ṣiva*, of whom *Ṣankara* is said to have been an *avatára*; but many have been distinguished as advocates of the Vedánta doctrines. One division of them, termed *Atíts*, differs from the more rigid *Daṇḍí-gosains*, in following secular pursuits, as traders and ministrant priests of temples: some of them even marry and settle, when they are termed *Samyogis*, or *Gharbáris*. These Gosains, although met with in Upper India, are most numerous and influential in the south. In Hindustan the name is more correctly applied to two different classes, both worshippers of Vishṇu, the *Gosains* of *Gokul*, who are descended from *Vallabha Áchárya*, and, although religious characters, are allowed to marry and follow secular pursuits, and the *Gosains* of Bengal, who are the disciples of *Chaitanya*, a native of Bengal, who instituted a new form of Vaishnava worship at the end of the fifteenth century. They also marry, and, like the *Gokulastha*, lead domestic and respectable lives. The term is also applied loosely to mere vagrants, some of whom wandered about formerly in armed gangs, and levied contributions forcibly on the villages, plundered them, or now, coming singly, or in small bodies, extort money by inflicting disgusting tortures upon themselves: these sometimes go naked.

Gosávní, Mar. (गोसावनी) A female Gosain; one who, on arriving at years of discretion, adopts a life of continence and mendicancy.

Ḍaurí-Gosávi, Mar. (डौरी गोसावी) A class of religious vagrants, said to be disciples of Gorakhnáth; in which case they are not properly Gosains, but Jogis: they sing hymns in honour of Bhairava, playing on the *ḍaura* (डौर), or a small drum shaped like an hour-glass; whence their name, *ḍaurí*, a player on the *ḍaura*.

Got, H. &c. (گوت, abbreviated from गोत्र, q. v.) A family, a race; a family of Bráhmans, bearing the common name of some Ṛishi, their supposed progenitor, or primitive spiritual head, as, *Sándilya*, *Kásyapa*, *Bháradwaja*, &c. Any branch or subdivision of a tribe or caste. A caste collectively.

Got, Thug. A large city.

Gota, Thug. Stones, especially from graves.

Gotá, Hindi (गोता) The mustard-seed crop (Puraniya).

Gotáí, Mar. (गोताई) Ceremonies observed by Ṣúdras prior to the re-admission of a man who has forfeited his caste,

Gotpat, or *-pát*, Mar. (गोतपत-पात) A caste or family collectively. Ceremonies of receiving back a man who has lost caste among Ṣúdras.

Goth, Guz. (ગોથ) Four; a private number used by merchants, &c. *Goth-padi*, fourteen.

Gótámu, Tel. (గోతము) A coarse canvas or *ganni* bag.

Goṭárá, Hindi (गोटारा) The rich lands immediately adjacent to the village (Puraniya).

Goṭbastí, Hindi (गोटबसती) The chief or first assemblage of houses erected on the settlement of a village: those subsequently built form the *thola* or *paṭṭí*.

Gotra, S. &c. (गोत्रः) Family, lineage, relationship by descent from a common ancestor of the same name. A family, a tribe, especially applied to races of Bráhmans who profess to regard some celebrated saint as their progenitor or their primitive spiritual head, and whose designation they bear; as, the *Bháradwája-gotra*, *Kásyapa-gotra*, *Sándilya-gotra*, &c. The term, at least in its vernacular form *Got*, has come to signify a subdivision of any common tribe or caste.

Gotraja, S. (गोत्रज) A kinsman of the same family and name, the '*gentile*,' in opposition to the *bandhu* or kinsman of a different family or cognate. Adoption is preferably enjoined in the same *gotra*, while marriage is prohibited.

Gotrahatyá, S. (हत्या, killing) Striking or killing a person of the same *gotra*.

Gotra-varanam, S. (from वरणं, choosing) Ceremony of repeating the genealogy of the bride and bridegroom at a marriage: (it should probably be *varṇanam*, describing, relating).

Graha, S. (ग्रह, from ग्रह, to take) A planet.

Grahapatra, S. (from पत्र, a leaf) A horoscope, a table indicating the positions and aspects of the planets at any particular moment, as at birth, marriage, &c.

Grahapújá, S. (from पूजा, worship) Worship of the planets, to render them propitious.

Grahaṇa, S., Ben., &c. (ग्रहण) An eclipse. Taking, accepting, seizing, apprehending. In the dialects more usually *Gahan*.

Grahíá, Uriya (ଗ୍ରହୀଆ) A mortgage, chiefly of lands.

Gram, English. The term current for varieties of pulse, especially for native chaná, the chick-pea (Acer arietinum).

The word is probably of Portuguese origin, from *Grao*, grain.

Grám, or Gráma, S. &c. (ग्राम), the term occurs in all the dialects, sometimes in the primitive form, but usually modified, as, Gám, Gánw, or Gáon, corruptly Gaum, (गाम, गांव, गाओं), also varied according to inflexion, as, Grámamu, Tel. (గ్రామము), or to alphabetical peculiarities, as, Kírámam, (so written though pronounced Grámam), Tam. (கிராமம்), Grámam, Mal. (ഗ്രാമം) A village, literally; but, as specifying a municipal and fiscal division, a hamlet, a township, consisting not only of the residences of the inhabitants, but of a tract of land around them within determinate boundaries, including arable and pasture lands, wood, waste, and water. The organization of such townships prevails, in principle, throughout India, but varies in practice in different parts of the country: they are, however, reducible, in the first instance, to two principal classes, one of which is so far the property of one individual that a single person is responsible for the revenue, and collects it from the cultivators as if from his tenants, exercising the right to distrain their goods, or eject them altogether, on failure of their paying their stipulated or customary share of the government demand, and claiming also a right to impose upon them occasionally cesses and charges, and, in some cases, to let the lands to temporary occupants at a stipulated rent: in the second great class the government revenue is paid direct by a number of individuals claiming proprietary rights in the village lands, paying either severally, or through a head man, who is one of their own community, representing them either by hereditary descent or election. Modifications of both these descriptions occur: thus, of the first, in Bengal generally, and in the north-west provinces occasionally, the proprietary right is vested in one individual, either by his having been in possession of such right from the earliest recorded period, or from having acquired it by purchase when lands have been sold for arrears of revenue: these are known as Zamindárí tenures. In the south of India, in the Tamil provinces, an *Ekabhogam* (sole enjoyment), or *Ijamán* (*yajamána*, or householder) *Grámam* is usually the property of a single individual, either in his own person or as head of his family: sometimes, however, the village is distributed amongst a body of hereditary proprietors, over whom the *Ijamán* has a controlling power, allotting the lands amongst them according to their shares, and apportioning and collecting the revenue: no sale of the land can be effected without his sanction. The second great class of villages, in which the proprietary right is vested in a certain number of individuals, who are responsible for the public revenue, is the most numerous class, and may once have been universal: these coparcenary tenures present many peculiarities, which it is necessary to become acquainted with for each in particular, in assessing the public revenue, but they may be chiefly distinguished as of three kinds: 1. Those in which the whole land is held and managed in common; the rents paid by the cultivators, whether they be the proprietors themselves or tenants under the proprietors, being thrown into a common stock, with all other profits from the estate, and, after deducting expenses, the balance is divided amongst the proprietors, according to old and established practice: these are called in Hindustan *Zamindárí* villages, as the occupants are termed village *Zamindars*, to distinguish them from the *Zamindárs* of Bengal, or they are termed *Bhayachara*, or brotherhood villages. In the south of India they are called *Pasung-karai* and *Pangu-vaḷi*, or by the S. terms *Samudayam* or *Samohi*. *Panguvaḷi* and *Samudayam* are especially applied to coparcenary tenures, in which the allotments are liable to revision and readjustment from time to time, on the agreement of the occupants. 2. The more general form of coparcenary villages is that termed in the north-west provinces, *Paṭṭidárí*, in which the lands are divided into *Paṭṭis*, or shares, and held in severalty by the different proprietors, or *Paṭṭidárs*, each person managing his own lands, and paying his fixed share of the government revenue; the whole being jointly responsible, in the event of any one sharer failing to fulfil his engagements: in the south these tenures are known as *Arudi-karai*, *Áchandrárkam*, *Bhaṭṭavrittí* or *Bharttvartí*, *Palabhogam*, q. v. 3. A third form is that known in the north-west provinces as the *imperfect Paṭṭídárí* village, in which part of the land is held in common and part in severalty; the profits of the land held in common being first appropriated to the government revenue and the village expenses, and the overplus being distributed, or the deficiency made good, according to a rate on the several holdings, when the proprietors are said to pay their revenue by *Dhár-báchh* or *Bighadám*, q. v. Villages may also be denominated from the mode of the distribution of the lands, as the *Bíghati* of the upper provinces, where the division of the allotments usually held in severalty is by *bíghás*, or their fractions: the *Visabadi* of the Ceded districts, where the division is by *visas*, or sixteenths, which are usually held in common: the *Nírwa* or *Bhágwár* villages of Guzerat, in which the village is distributed into *bhágas*, or portions according to the original number of sharers: these *bhágas* are subdivided by *ánas*, or sixteenths, amongst the heirs of a deceased proprietor, according to their number and respective rights, and these *ánas* may be again subdivided into fractional sixteenths, termed *ánis* and *chárwals*: *Bhágwár* villages are usually held in severalty. In some parts of Hindustan villages are primarily divided into a certain number of nominal integral parts, usually twenty, which are called *biswas*, and then again into fractions of twentieths, termed *biswánsís* and *karwánsís*: these portions are distributed amongst the representatives of the original proprietor or proprietors, constituting the proprietary shares, termed *Paṭṭís*, or sometimes *Péns*, q. v.: the *Paṭṭí* is divisible according to the number of the heirs of a *Paṭṭídár*, into smaller portions, called *thoks*, *tholas*, or *ḍheris*, and these may again be subdivided into smaller shares, termed *behrís*. *Thok* is sometimes convertible into *Paṭṭí*: see these terms severally, also the Tamil terms, *Pangu* and *Karai*. When the proprietors of a village are of different classes or religions, it is primarily divided between them according to their respective interests, and the portions in Hindustan are termed *tarafs*; so that there may be a Mohammadan and a Hindu *taraf* in one village, each being severally divisible according to the prevailing usage. Every village has an establishment of municipal officers and servants, more or less complete, according as its organization has been more or less interfered with: see under the word *Baluta*.

Grámadevatá, H. (S. ग्रामदेवता) *Grámdebta*, or *-debtá*, Ben. and Uriya (গ্রামদেবতা) *Grámdeo*, Mar. (ग्रामदेव) The tutelary divinity of a village; sometimes this is one of the ordinary pantheon, but it is more usually local, and is not uncommonly a rude block of stone: the term is also applied to lands appropriated to the expense of the village idol.

Grámádhikárí, vernacularly, *Grámadhihár*, incorrectly, *Grámádikár*, S. (from अधिकारी, one who has a right) The head of a village; either the proprietor, the head man, or the collector of the revenue on government account.

Grámádhinan, Mal. (ഗ്രാമാധീനൻ) A village carpenter.

Grámádhipati, S. (from अधिपति, master) *Grámádhipan*, Mal. (ഗ്രാമാധിപൻ) The head of a village, commonly charged also by the government with the general control of it, and the collection of the revenue.

Gráma-hissebu, Tel. (గ్రామహిస్సెబు, from the P. *Hisáb*, حساب) The general account of the collection and balance due delivered to the landlord at the time of settlement.

Gráma-kaṇakan, Tam. (கணக்கன்) S. (गणकः) *Gráma karnam*, Tel. The village accountant.

Gráma-kanthamu, Tel. (గ్రామకంఠము) A spot of ground in a village for building huts upon.

Grám, or *Gáon*, or *Gráma kharch*, H. (گرام خرچ) *Gráma kharchu*, Tel. (గ్రామఖర్చు) The private expenses of a village; the charges borne by it independently of the payments on account of revenue.

Gráma-kável, Tam. (காவல்) The village watch.

Gráma-kharch-taksím, (S. and A.) Account shewing the proportion of village charges to be borne by each Ryot. Ceded districts.

Gráma-kharch-zábita, (S. and A.) Account of the village disbursements. Ceded districts.

Grámalu-múlu, Tel. An allowance given by villages to Bráhmans of a quantity of rice in the husk at the time of harvest. Ceded districts.

Grámá mániam, Tam. (மானியம்) A certain extent of land enjoyed rent-free by a hereditary proprietor of part of the village lands, as a personal privilege attached to such a share (Ellis).

Gráma-merai, Tam. (கிராமமெறை) Allowances of a portion of the crop to the village officers and servants.

Grámamukham, Mal. (ഗ്രാമമുഖം) A market town.

Grámanattam, Tam. (கிராமநத்தம்) Ground set apart, on which the houses of a village may be built.

Gramaṇí, incorrectly, *Gramni*, S. &c. (ग्रामणी) Tam. (கிராமணி) The head man of a village. It is also a title assumed in the Tamil countries by the drawers of the *Tárí* juice. In several dialects, as, Bengali, Uriya, Tel., Karn., and Mal., it denotes also the village barber.

Grámanyan, Mal. (ഗ്രാമണ്യൻ) The head man of a village.

Gráma-otti-shettu, (?) The mortgage-deed of a village.

Gráma-purohitan, Tam. (புரோகிதன், from S. *Purohita*) The village priest and astronomer.

Gramasamishti bhumi, Tel. (గ్రామసమిష్టిభూమి) Land possessed by the villagers conjointly.

Gráma terige, Karn. (ಗ್ರಾಮತೆರಿಗೆ) A fine levied in Mysore on Ryots who have left their own villages and settled in others.

Grámattán, also, corruptly, *Graumutta* and *Graumuttan*, (கிராமத்தான்) The head man of a village (in the Tamil countries).

Grámattan-mániam, A grant of rent-free land to the head of a village, in addition to his own share of the common property paying revenue: see *Grámamániam*.

Grámattan-sutantram, (சுதந்தரம்) Fees and privileges enjoyed by the head man of a village.

Grámattár, Tam., (கிராமத்தார்) sing. An inhabitant of a village, *the* inhabitant *par excellence*, the head man: plur. The inhabitants of a village.

Grámbheṭí, Ben. (গ্রামভেটী) A present or fee to a Zamindar on the marriage of a tenant's children.

Grám, or *Gám-chálí*, Mar. (ग्रामचाली) Village usage or custom.

Grám-joshí, or *Grama-jyotishí*, Mar., S., (ग्रामजोशी, ग्रामज्योतिषी) The village astronomer, who casts nativities and calculates times and seasons.

Grám-lekhaka, Mar (S. लेखक, a writer) The village accountant.

Grámopadhyáya, S., Mar. (from S. उपाध्याय) A village priest or schoolmaster, if a Bráhman.

Grám-saranjámi„ H. (P. سرنجامي, effects) The requisite establishment or implements for the business of a village.

Grámwár, or *Grámawár*, H. By villages, as a village settlement.

Grám-, or *Gám-nisbat-inámatí*, Mar. (ग्राम-, गामनिसबत-इनामती) Rent-free lands granted to village officers or servants, on the part of, and by, the village community, usually of its own free will, but occasionally under the orders of the government.

Grámya, S. &c. (ग्राम्य) Village, rustic; any thing relating to or concerning a village, or to the practices and manners of the villagers.

Grámyadebatá, Ben. (S. গ্রাম্যদেবতা) A village or rustic deity, often represented by a rude stone placed under a large tree.

Grámyájak, or *Grámayájaka*, (S. याजकः) The village priest, who conducts the ceremonies for any or all classes. An attendant on an idol.

GRANTHA, S. (ग्रन्थ) A book in general. The book of the Sikhs, a large collection of short moral poems by Nának and others in Panjabi and Hindi.

GRANTHÍ, S. (ग्रन्थिः) A knot, a tie, a tying together.

Granthí-mochaka, S. (from मोचक, who loosens) A thief, a cut-purse, or parcel pilferer.

GRÁSA, or GRÁS, corruptly, GRASS, or GURAS, S., used in all the Hindu dialects, (ग्रासः, from ग्रस, to swallow) GHÁS, or GHÁNS, Mar. (घास, घांस) and GARÁS, pronounced GRÁS, Guz. (ગરાસ) A mouthful, or a quantity equivalent to it. Fodder for cattle. A hereditary claim to a small portion (a mouthful) of the produce of a village or villages by various Rájput chiefs, granted them by the local governments in remuneration of military service, and commuted for a pecuniary payment out of the revenue paid by the villagers. A fixed payment made to military and predatory chiefs in Guzerat and Malwa, especially in lieu of lands held by them, or in purchase of their refraining from plunder. Also lands held by Grásias in Guzerat.

Grásiá, H. (گراسيا, गरासीया) *Garásio*, Guz. (ગરાસીઓ) A military and predatory chief in Malwa, Rajputana, Guzerat, and Cutch, claiming a portion of the revenues of certain villages, either as a grant originally from the superior authority, in requital of military service, or as the price of forbearance from plunder. In Mewar the designation applies to military chiefs of mixed Rájput and Bhil descent, holding jagirs in nominal vassalage to the Rana of Udayapur, and engaging to pay a stipulated tribute. In Guzerat the term also designates a plunderer or robber.

GṚIHA, S. &c. (गृहं) A house.

Gṛihadáha, S. &c. (from दाह, burning) Arson, house burning.

Gṛihadeva, or *-devatá*, S. &c. (from देव, or देवता, a divinity) The household deity, the tutelary deity of a house, rarely bearing any specific designation, and not unusually represented by a water-pot; a rude figure; a *Sálagráma* stone or Ammonite, or the *Tulasí* plant, or sacred Basil.

Gṛihajáta, S. (from जात, born) A description of slave, one born of a female slave in the house of her master.

Gṛihapati, S. &c. (from पति, a master) A householder.

Gṛihapraveṣa, S. &c. (from प्रवेशः, entrance) The ceremonies observed upon taking possession of a new house, or upon the first reception of a bride in her husband's dwelling.

Gṛihastha, S. &c., also vernacularly, but incorrectly, *Grahasth, Girhast, Girhist, Giristh*, &c. (from गृह, a house, and स्थ, who stays or dwells in) A householder; the Hindu of the second order, who, after his course as a religious student, marries and keeps house; a respectable person; a villager or cultivator, whence, *Grahasthi*, or, vernacularly, *Girhisti*, husbandry.

Gṛihayajna, S. (from यज्ञ, worship) Domestic worship, especially the oblation of oiled butter on the household fire, a fire perpetually preserved by some classes of Bráhman householders.

Gṛihí, S. &c. (गृही) A householder.

Gṛihiṇí, S. &c. (गृहिणी) The mistress of a house, the wife of a householder.

GṚIHÍTÁ, S., also Uriya, &c. (ଗୃହୀତା, from S. ग्रह, to take, or seize) A creditor, a donor, one who claims or receives any thing.

GUÁ, GUYÁ, Ben. (गुआ, गुया, S. गुवाक) Betel-nut; also the tree that bears it (Areca catechu).

GÚḌA, or GÚṚA, Tel. (గూడ) A basket for throwing up water for irrigation.

GUḌÁKU, Karn. (గుడాకు) Prepared tobacco for smoking in a *hukka*.

GÚḌALU, Tel. (గూడలు) A basket made of woven bambu strips for drawing up water.

GUDÁM, Ben. (गुदाम) A magazine, a storeroom, a warehouse: see *Godown*.

GUDÁR, or GUDÁR-GHÁṬÁ, Ben. (गुदारघाटा, vernacular corruption of P. گزارا, GUZARA, crossing) A ferry, a landing-place.

GUDAST, Mar. (गुदस्त, vernacular corruption of P. گذشت, GUZASHT, past) Past, gone by. *Sál-gudast*, last year. See *Guzasht*.

Gudast-báki, Mar. (from A. باقي, remainder) Balance remaining of a closed account.

GÚḌAVU, Karn. (గూడవు) A small hamlet near a village.

GUDDALI, Karn. (గుద్దలి) A native spade or hoe.

Guddali-pommu, Karn. (గుద్దలిపొమ్ము) A cess levied on vegetable gardeners at so much per spade or hoe.

GUḌḌE, Tel. (గుడ్డె) High ground for dry cultivation.

Guḍḍa, Karn. (గుడ్డ) A hill, a mountain.

Guḍḍada-kóṭi, Karn. (గుడ్డదకోటె) A hill fort.

GUḌEMU, Tel. (గుడెము) A hamlet.

GÚḌEMU, Tel. (గూడెము) A small hamlet near a village.

GUḌAGÁVAL-GUTTA, Karn. (గుడగావలగుత్త) Taxes on the gatherers of wild fruits in Mysore.

GÚḌHAJA, pronounced commonly, GÚṚHAJA, S. &c. (गूढ, secret, and ज, born) The son of concealed birth, born privately of a woman whose husband is absent, the real father being unknown: also *Gúḍhotpanna*, &c.

GUḌHÁR, Mar. (गुढार) Flight of a whole people of a village from an enemy.

GUḌHI, GUṚHI, Mar. (गुढी) A pole erected on the first day of the year before the house door, and covered with cloth, mango-sprigs, &c. Flowers or grains of rice stuck on an idol consulted as an oracle: the answer is inferred from the order in which they fall off.

GÚDÍ, Ben. (गूदी) A sort of dry dock, a place made by the side of a river for repairing and caulking boats.

GUḌI, Tel. Karn. (గుడి) A temple, a pagoda.

Guḍikaṭle, Karn. (గుడికట్లె) Fixed allowance for a temple.

Guḍikaṭṭu, Tel. (గుడికట్టు) The whole extent of land attached to a temple, or a statement exhibiting it.

Guḍipárupatya, Karn. (గుడిపారుపత్య) Superintendence of a temple.

GUDIGÁR, Karn. (గుదిగార) A caste, or individual of it, at Nagar, in Mysore, carvers in sandal-wood, horn, and ivory.

GUḌISARAKU, Karn. (గుడిసరకు) A term used for the ordinary price of a pair of shoes at Nagar (Mysore).

GUḌIVARAM, Tel. (గుడివరం) The Ryot's share of the crop.

GUDRÍ, H. (گدري) A daily market.

GUDU, GOODOO, (?) A money fee payable by landholders on the Nilghari hills to the *Todas*, or native hill-men.

GÚGARI, corruptly, GÚGRÍ, GOOGREE, Karn. (గూగరి) Any fee or perquisite of the head of a village.

Gúgarí-bil, Karn. (గూగరిబిళ్) Pasture ground granted rent-free to a headman.

GUGGAL, Mar. (?) Fees leviable on Lingáyats by landholders in the Dakhin.

GUGLI, GOOGLEE, (?) Said to denote a class of Bráhmans attached to the Vaishnava objects of pilgrimage in Kattiwar.

GUJAÍ, corruptly, GOOJEY, Hindi (गुजई) A mixed crop of barley and wheat in the north-west provinces.

GÚJAR, H. (گوجر, गूजर) The name of a numerous class in the north-west provinces, chiefly engaged in agriculture, though formerly notorious for their martial and predatory character. They profess to descend from Rájput fathers by women of inferior castes. Mr. Elliot considers them as having given their appellation to the principality of Guzerat, in the west of India, and the district of the same name in the Panjáb. In the Dakhin the term is considered synonymous with *Gujaráti*, and applied to any native of Guzerat, but more especially to the traders and dealers from that country. In Bengal and Bahar one subdivision of the *Kúrmi*, or agricultural tribe, is called *Gujaráti*, having come perhaps originally from thence.

GUJAR, also GUJRÁṆ, or GUJÁRÁ, Mar. (गुजर, गुजराण, गुजारा, from P. *Guzar*, گزر, passing) Bare subsistence, mere means of livelihood.

GUJÁRÁ, Ben. (গুজারা, vernacular corruption of P. گذر) A ferry.

GUJÁRAT, Mar. (गुजारत्) Through the medium, or by the hands of; (said of money paid;) presence or act of witnessing, though without responsibility (in money transactions).

GUJÁRATI, Tel. (గుజారతి) Possession.

GUJRÍ, Tel. (గుజ్రి, from the H. گزري) A market or market-place; in Madras, the thieves' bazar. Mar. (गुजरी) The morning or evening market.

GUKHI, Thug. A person carrying the bones of his relations to some sacred stream: he is never to be assailed.

GÚL, GOOL, H. (گول) A channel cut to convey water to a field. A road, a path (Sagar). A bunch of unripe Indian corn (Dehli).

GÚL, Mar. (गूळ, from S. गुड) Coarse sugar, the juice of the sugar-cane inspissated by boiling: see *Gúṛ*.

GUL, H. &c. (گل, गुल) A ball of charcoal ground to powder and cemented with starch, put, when lighted, into a *hukka* to cause the slow combustion of the tobacco; also into the irons used for ironing linen.

GULÁL, H. &c. (گلال) The red powder thrown about at the Holi, generally the meal or flour of barley, rice, or *Singhára*, reddened with some vegetable dye, as that of the Cesalpinia sappan, or red sanders-wood.

GÚLAR, H. (گولر) Cotton pods before bursting (Rohilkhand).

GULENDÁ, H. (گليندا) The pod of the Mahwa tree: see *Gulu*.

GÚLÍ, also KÚLÍ and GUNṬÁ, (?) A measure of length; when identified with the *gunṭa*, the fortieth part of an acre, but it varies in different parts of the south; at Madras it is equal to a square of 33 feet each way, in Tanjore it is 144 square feet, at Madura 25,030 square feet.

GULI-GULI, Ben. (গুলি গুলি) Severally, individually; apportioned to each by share or lot.

GULIVINA-POMMU, Karn. (ಗುಳಿವಿನ-ಪೊಂಮು) Tax on the sock or iron of each plough (Mysore).

GULLASUNNAMU, Tel. (గుల్లసున్నము, from గుల్ల, an oyster or other shell) The best kind of *chunam* or lime-plaster, made from burnt shells.

GULÚ, GOOLOO, H. (گلو) The pod of the Mahwa tree (Bassia latifolia), which yields a useful oil, and is sometimes eaten by the lower classes.

GUMÁSHTA, vernacularly, GOMASTA or GUMASTA, incorrectly, GOMASTHA, H. (P. گماشته, गोमास्त) An agent, a steward, a confidential factor, a representative; an officer employed by Zamindars to collect their rents, by bankers to receive money, &c., by merchants to carry on their affairs in other places than where they reside, and the like: at Madras it is also the designation of a native accountant in the revenue department.

Gumáshta-kánungo, H. The agent or deputy of the Kánungo, or village registrar and accountant.

GÚMA, GOOMA, H. (گومه) A medicinal herb which grows on high ground during the rains, and in fields sown with the autumn crops (Pharnaceum mollugo).

GUMÁN, H. &c. (P. گمان) Opinion, imagination, suspicion; suspicion of crime excited by the report of a common informer.

GUMBARA, or GUMBÁRA, Karn. (ಗುಂಬರ, ಗುಂಬಾರ, vernacular corruption of *Kumbhakára*) A potter.

GUMCHÍ, H. (گمچي) A small weight, in apothecary's measure about $7\frac{1}{2}$ grains: it is also a name of the *gunja* seed, q. v.

GUMKÁ, Hindi (गुमका) The operation of causing the green ears of corn to ferment slightly, so as to make the seeds separate easily from the husk when threshed: it is done by heaping up the ears as soon as cut, and covering them with straw (Puraniya).

GUMMI, Karn. (ಗುಂಮಿ) A large basket for storing grain.

GUMNÁMA, H. &c. (گمنامه, from the P. *Gum*, گم, lost, missing) A document drawn up and duly attested, certifying the loss of any thing, as of a title-deed, &c.

GUṆA, S. &c. (गुणः) Merit, virtue; a quality, a property: metaphysically there are three *Guṇas*, the *Satya-guṇa*, or property of truth—the source of purity and wisdom; the *Rajo-guṇa*, or property of foulness—the source of passion and error; and the *Tamo-guṇa*, or property of darkness—the source of inertness and ignorance. Deity abstractedly is *Nirguṇa*, or without any of the three properties.

GUNÁH, H. (P. گناه) GUNHÁ, Mar. (गुन्हा) Fault, offence, crime.

Gunagár, H. (گنهگار) *Gunhegár*, Mar. (गुन्हेगार) An offender, a culprit, a criminal.

Gunagárí, H. &c, (گنهگاري) *Gunhegárí*, Mar. (गुन्हेगारी) Offence, crime. Fine, punishment by fine. Revenue derived from judicial fines.

Gunaká, Tel. (గునకా) Fine.

Gunnegári, Karn. (ಗುಂನೆಗಾರಿ) A fine, especially for stealing ears of corn.

GUNÁRÍ, Karn. (ಗುನಾರಿ) Servant of the head merchant of a town.

GUNCHI-PATTA, (?) A lease taken out in the name of two or more Ryots in partnership (Madras).

GUṆḌ, Hindi (गुंड) A furrow.

GUNDI, GOONDY, (?) Confederacy, association; engagement entered into by individuals, to support and stand by each other to the extent of their whole property, and even of their lives, if necessary.

GUNJ, or GUNJÁ, H. &c. (گنج, گنجا) S. GUNJÁ, (गुञ्जा) GUNJI, GUNJE, Karn. (ಗುಂಜಿ, ಗುಂಜೆ) A plant (the Abrus precatorius); also its seed, a small black-and-red seed, forming the nominal unit of Indian weights: the average weight of the seed has been stated at $1\frac{5}{16}$ grains troy, but later experiments make it a trifle more, or 1.934 grain. The jewellers' and goldsmiths' weight of the same denomination is about $2\frac{3}{16}$ grains.

GUNJÁISH, H. (P. گنجايش) GUNJÁYASHU, Tel. (గుంజాయషు) Profit, gain. In fiscal language it is applied to the capabilities of a village, particularly with reference to a proposed increase of revenue. Excess of the real over the recorded area of a Zamindárí.

Gunjáishi, H. (P. گنجايشي) Profitable.

Gunjáisu, Karn. (ಗುಂಜಾಯಿಸು) Outbidding another in a sale or contract.

GUNṬA, Tel. (గుంట) A well or pond; a field, a pit.

GUNṬA, GOONṬA, Tel. (గుంట) A square land measure, equal to 121 square yards, or the fortieth part of an acre. A measuring rod or chain, which, squared, constitutes the measure also so named, forty of which make an acre. The survey of the ceded districts directed the measurements to be made in acres, goonṭas, and anas (or sixteenths).—5th Rep. 787.

GUNṬAKA, Tel. (గుంటక) GUNṬE, GUNṬIKE, Karn. (ಗುಂಟೆ, ಗುಂಟಿಕೆ) A sort of harrow or implement for levelling ploughed ground. A sowing machine.

GUNTH, GOONTH, Uriya (ଗୁଣ୍ଠ) A land measure of sixteen *biṣwas*. (The same word most probably as *Gunṭa*, though spelled with a final aspirate).

GUNṬH, GOONṬH, H. (گونٹھ) Lands assigned rent-free for the support of a temple (Kamaon).

GUPTA, S. (गुप्त) Hidden, concealed, preserved.

Guptávadhúta, S. (गुप्तावधूत) An ascetic of a particular order, one who does not avow his profession of mendicancy, or who observes its practices in secret.

Gupt-dán, H. (گپت‌دان) lit., A hidden donation, as where a person leaves property with a Bráhman and never reclaims it; or presents him with a sealed bag; or dropping a present in the bottom of a sacred pool of water at Kurukshetra, at a solar eclipse, in which the pilgrim has bathed, leaving the officiating Bráhmans to search for it.

GUṚ, GOOṚ, H. &c. (S. گر, गुड) GUḌAMU, Tel. (గుడము) Molasses, treacle, raw sugar, the produce of the first inspissation of the juice of the cane.

GURAB, GOORUB, H. (گرب, from *Gurabná*, گربنا, to dig) Deep weeding; also, in the Upper Doab, ploughing through a field of *bájra* or *jawár* when the plant is about a foot high, to loosen the soil, but so as not to injure the plants.

GUṚARÍ, GOORUREE, H. (گڑري) A twist of rope or straw, to form a stand for a round-bottomed jar.

GUṚÁRI-GHAR, Uriya (ଗୁଡ଼ାରିଘର) Place where the salt in solution is condensed by boiling (Cuttack).

GURAV, or GURAVA, also pronounced GURAO, corruptly written GUROW, Mar. (गुरव) A caste, or individual of it, considered as a *Ṣúdra*, but who is usually employed as the servant of the village temple, sweeping it, and decking the idol: he is also the village trumpeter. See *Baluta*.

Gurav-punja, Mar. (from पुंज, S., a heap) The share of the crop allotted to the *Gurav* for his remuneration.

GURḌÁ, GOORDA, H. (گردا) A part of a sugar-mill, a scraper to prevent the sugar from resting at the bottom of the boiler.

GUṚGUṚÍ, H. &c. (گڑگڑي) A small pipe for smoking, with a straight and inflexible tube.

Gurguṛía, or *Gulgulía*, Thug. A low murmuring sound, like the bubbling of the pipe, made by a sort of owl—an unlucky omen.

GURHAUR, H. (گرهور) Stacks of cow-dung (East Oudh).

GURIKÁR, Karn. (ಗುರಿಕಾರ) The head man of a village. A head man of armed peons.

GUṚIYA, Ben. (গুড়িয়া) A confectioner, a worker in treacle.

GURKÁTI, (?) A tax or cess formerly levied on the saltmakers in the Sunderbans by the officers of government, for the privilege of cutting firewood in the Jangal.

GURKHAI, GOORKHYE, H. (گرکھئي) A kind of mortgage in Bundelkhand, in which the mortgager is responsible for three-fourths of the government revenue on the mortgaged land.

GÚRTU, (?) A land measure=$3\frac{1}{8}$ English acres (Nellur).

GURU, GOOROO, S., but adopted in all the dialects; in composition often abridged to GUR, (गुरुः) lit., Heavy, weighty, whence, metaphorically, a person of weight or respectability, as an elder or parent, and especially a spiritual teacher or guide, one who, under the primitive system, instructed the youth of the three first classes in the Vedas, but in later times one who merely communicates to him, with greater or lesser solemnity, the peculiar prayer which is considered sufficient to initiate the disciple, and make him a member of any particular sect or tribe.

Gurudev, or *-deva*, S. Ben. (गुरुदेव) A spiritual guide, a parent or elder, one who is reverenced as a divinity.

Gurudakshíná, S., vernacularly, *Gurdachhiná*, H. (गुरुदक्षिणा, گردچھنا) Present made to a *Guru* by his disciple on completing his education, or receiving his initiation. Rent-free lands originally granted to a *Guru*.

Gur-gánth, Thug. The knot or tie which the *Guru* instructs the novice to fasten.

Gurukul, S. &c. (from कुल, a family) The family of a spiritual teacher.

Gurukkul, (?) The head priest amongst the Ṣaivas of the south of India.

Gurumátá, Panjabi, A convention of the chiefs of the Sikh tribes, formerly held on all occasions of importance at Amritsar.

Gurumukhí, Panjabi (S. गुरुमुखी) The modification of the Devanagarí alphabet devised by the Sikhs: it does not differ in shape, but the powers of many of the letters are interchanged.

Gurupádáṣraya, S. (from पाद, foot, and आश्रयः, refuge) Profound reverence of the *Guru*.

Gurupújá, S. (पूजा, worship) Veneration of a *Guru*, worship offered to him; also to the planet Jupiter, who is the *Guru* of the gods.

Guruputra, S. (पुत्र, a son) The son of a *Guru*, to be held also in profound respect.

Gurpinch, Thug. The strangler who has been duly instructed by the *Guru*.

Gurutalpaga, S. (तल्प, a bed, and ग, who goes to) One who has a criminal intercourse with the wife of a *Guru*, a most heinous offence.

GURÚṆ, (the *n* very obscurely sounded, and the word in composition shortened to GUR), Mar. (गुरूं) Any animal of the Bos kind, a bull, a cow, a buffalo.

Gurakhí, or *Gurákhí*, Mar. (गुरखी, or गुराखी, an abbreviation of *Gurúṇ*, and S. *Rakhshí*, who preserves) A cow-keeper, a grazier.

Gurcharaṇ, or *Gurcharáí*, Mar. (गुरचरण, गुरचराई) Pasturage for cattle. Price paid for its hire.

GURUTU, Karn. (ಗುರುತು) A mark, as a signature, made by a person who cannot write.

GURHÁL, GUḶHÁR, Mar. (गुऱ्हाल, गुळहार) A sugar work, the place with the machinery for bruising the cane and extracting the juice.

GURZMÁR, H. (from P. گرز, a club, and S. مار, what strikes) A Mohammadan Fakir, who carries a club armed with spikes, with which he wounds himself to extort alms. The order is said to have originated with a Pir named Sayid Ahmad Kabír.

GUTÁ, GUTTÁ, or GUTKÁ, Mar. (गुता, गुत्ता, or गुतका) An exclusive right of sale, or supply of any commodity, a contract, a monopoly, farm, or rent, an income of variable amount sold or let for a fixed sum.

Gutgi-paṭṭi, Mar. A deed of agreement, of contract, or farm.

GUṬI, GUṬÍ, Ben. (গুটি, গুটী) The cocoon of the silkworm.

Guṭipoká, Ben. (গুটিপোকা) A silkworm.

GUTTA, Tel. Karn. (ಗುತ್ತ) Farm, lease, rent: (see the Mar. *Gutá*: it is no doubt the same word which is also current in Sindh as *Gutto*).

Guttagádu, Tel. (గుత్తగాడు) A renter, a farmer.

Guttige, Karn. (ಗುತ್ತಿಗೆ) Assessment, rental on land.

Guttigé-dár, Karn. (from P. دار, who has) One who rents from government the lands of a village; one who farms the revenue.

Guttigehola, Karn. (ಗುತ್ತಿಗೆಹೊಲ) A rented field.

Phalagutige, Karn. (S. फल, fruit) Assessment paid in kind.

Rokhhhada-guttige, Karn. (ರೊಖ್ಖದಗುತ್ತಿಗೆ) Assessment paid in money.

Guttinae, (?) Tuluva, The ancient term for the head of a village or *Pátil*.

Gutto-sharáb, Sindhi (from A. شراب, wine) Tax on distillers and venders of spirituous liquors.

Guṭṭe, Karn. (ಗುಟ್ಟೆ) A place where bodies are burnt. A pile and corpse when reduced to ashes.

Guṭṭu, Karn. (ಗುಟ್ಟು) Private or family affairs.

Guzar, Guzár, Guzára, H. (گذر, گذار, گذاره, these and similar words are derived from the P. *Guzashtan*, گذشتن, to pass, to pass by or over, and in other dialects occur as *Gudár, Gujár*, &c.) A ferry, a ferry station or boat, a place of transit or toll.

Guzar-bán, H. (گذربان) An officer appointed to take tolls both on the high roads and at ferries.

Guzar-gáh, H. (P. گذرگاه) A ferry, a ferry station.

Guzár, H. (گذار) One who transfers, hands over, or pays; whence—

Mál-guzár, H. (P., from *Mál*, wealth, revenue) The person who pays the government revenue, whether on his own account, or as the representative of others.

Mál-guzári, H. P., Payment of the government revenue by an individual.

Guzárish, H. (گذارش) Payment, transfer. Representation.

Guzásht, also, vernacularly, Gudast and Gujast, corruptly, Gosausth, H. (گذاشت, P. گذاشته) Mar. (गुदस्त) H. (गुजस्त) Tel. Karn. (ಗುಜಸ್ತು) Past, gone by, relinquished: deduction allowed, payment remitted, or the like: in the south it applies, as a revenue term, to the year last past only.

Guzárat, H. (گذارت) Through the medium, by the hand of (payments, &c.): see *Gujárat*.

Gujaṣtá-jamâ, Gujaṣtá-jamín, Hindi (गुजश्ता जमा -जमीन) Statements of the amount of revenue and land of the preceding year, for comparison with the increase or decrease of the current year.

Guzrán, vernacularly, *Gujrán*, H. (گذران) Living, livelihood, means or mode of subsisting.

Guzri, H., vernacularly, *Gujri*, (? گذري) A market, especially one held by the road-side in the afternoon.

Gyán, vernacular corruption of *Jnán*, (ज्ञान) Knowledge.

Gyán-krita-badh, Ben. and Uriya. Wilful homicide.

H

Ha, the letter ح, the initial of *Huzúr-navís*, Secretary of State, affixed to royal grants as a mark of attestation by the officer whose duty it is to issue them.

Habb, Hubb, H. (A. حب) A grain, a berry.

Habúb, Huboob, also *Hubúbát* or *Huboobat*, H. (حبوب, plural of حب, حبوبات, plural irregular of حبوب) Grains, &c.; but applied to cesses or imposts extra to the regular assessment: the terms seem to have been used indiscriminately with *Abwáb* (Harrington's Analysis, iii. 236, note), but they more correctly define exactions in kind, of articles for the use of the Zamindar or of persons in authority, as milk, eggs, sheep, oil, ghee, blankets, skins, and the like: they were sometimes commuted for money.

Habs, Hubs, H. (A. حبس) Imprisonment, confinement; a prison, a prisoner: a reservoir, an embankment, that in or by which water is confined.

Habshi, H. (A. حبشي) An African or Abyssinian slave under the native administration: *Habsh* being the Arabic reading of Abyss-inia.

Hadd, Hudd, or with only one final, Had, plural Hudúd, H. (A. حد, plural حُدود) Boundary, limit, term, whether of place or time. In Mohammadan penal law, statutory punishment for certain crimes, distinguished from *Kisás* or retaliation, as not being claimable by the aggrieved parties, and from *Tâzír*, as not being inflicted at the discretion of the judge, but defined by law.

Had-bandí, Hud-bundee, also *Had-bast, Hud-bust*, H. (حدبست, حدبندي) Settlement and demarcation of boundaries: as this is a constant subject of dispute, great pains have been taken in various parts of India, and particularly in the north-west provinces, to determine it by survey and record.

Haddád, A. (حدّاد) An obstruction, a doorkeeper, a blacksmith.

Haddu-patriká, Tel. (హద్దుపత్రికా) A statement of boundaries.

Had-i-janáb, H. (حد جواب) The replication or rejoinder in a legal proceeding.

Hadmahadad, Hindi (हदमहदद, vernacular corruption of the A. محدود, *Mahdúd*, bounded) A term in leases or farming-contracts which recognises the power of the farmer over all the land and crops within the limits of his farm. (Puraniya).

Hudud-arbâ, H. (A. حدوداربع) Boundaries of the four sides of an estate.

Hada, or Hadana, Karn. (ಹದ, ಹದನ) A moderate quantity of rain, so as to fit the soil for sowing. (In this and other senses these words are no doubt the Arabic *Had*, limit).

Hada-vádamare, Karn. (ಹದವಾದಮಳೆ) A heavy fall of rain, such as to saturate the soil.

Haḍap, Haḍaph, Guz. (હડપ, હડફ) A deposit in security of payment due for a toll or custom-duty.

Haḍapa, Karn. (ಹಡಪ) A barber's case, a betel pouch.

Haḍapiga, Karn. (ಹಡಪಿಗ) A barber; a king's petty cash-keeper, whose duty it is to carry betel for the prince and his visitors.

Háḍiá, or **Háṛia**, Guz. (હાડિઆ) A tenure under which land is held in Guzerat.

Hadíṣ, H. (A. حديث) The traditional sayings and doings of Mohammad, having for the most part the force of laws.

Hadíya, H. (A. هديّة) A present, especially to a superior; a present made to a teacher by the pupil who has read the Koran with him.

Háḍkí, corruptly, **Hinkee**, Mar. (हाडकी, derivative of हाड, a bone) lit., a little bone; fig., Land granted rent-free to the *Mhár*, or village sweeper, where he may deposit bones, offal, &c., but when not so used it is usually cultivated by the occupants.

Háḍolá, incorrectly, *Hudolee*, Mar. (हाडोला) Service land granted to the *Mhárs* of a village, and assessed at a low rate: the revenue from such land.

Ḥadr, incorrectly, **Hiddir**, A. (هدر) Unrequited, unavenged; in law, said of blood that may be shed, or life taken away, with impunity, as that of a criminal who dies in consequence of punishment not intended to be fatal; also, that of an apostate: no penalty or retaliation is ever to be exacted in such cases, according to some authorities.

Háfiẓ, H. (A. حافظ, from *Hafẓ*, حفظ, has preserved) A preserver, a guardian, a keeper.

Háfiẓ-i-daftar, H. (حافظدفتر) Keeper of the records; a servant or officer who has charge of the books of an office, &c.

Hafta, H. (هفته, from P. هفت, seven) A week: in the Hindu dialects *Hapta*, q. v.

Hága, Karn. (ಹಾಗ) A small coin in Mysore, a quarter gold fanam; also, a single silver fanam.

Hágada duḍḍu, Karn. (ಹಾಗದದುಡ್ಡು) The value of a silver fanam in copper, or 80 *kás*.

Háge, Hageya, Hagévu, Karn. (ಹಾಗೆ, ಹಗೆಯ, ಹಗೆವು) A grain pit, a subterranean granary.

Hayát, H. (A. حيات) Life.

Hainu, Karn. (ಹೈನು) The period between May and September—that of the heavy rains.

Hainu-gadde, Karn. (ಹೈನುಗದ್ದೆ) Wet lands, for sowing rice during the monsoon.

Hainu-pairu, Karn. (ಹೈನುಪೈರು) Corn standing in the heavy wet weather.

Hajj, usually written with one *j*, **Haj, Huj**, H. (A. حج) The pilgrimage to Mecca.

Hajj-ul-farẓ, H. (A. حجّ الفرض) The ordained or enjoined pilgrimage, which should be performed once by every Mohammadan who has the means of performing it.

Hájí, H. (A. حاجي) A Mohammadan who has performed the pilgrimage.

Hájá, Ben. (হাজা) Destruction of crops by floods or heavy rain.

Hajjám, commonly, **Hajám** or **Hujam**, corruptly, **Hejam** and **Hudjam**, H. &c. (A. حجام) A barber, a barber-surgeon, one who not only shaves but bleeds, cups, cleans the ears, pares the nails, &c.: usually included among the village establishment.

Hajámat, H. (A. حجامت) The functions of a Hajám—shaving, cupping, &c.

Hajám-áyajodi, Karn. (ಹಜಾಂಆಯಜೋಡಿ) Tax levied on the land assigned to the village barber (Mysore).

Hajám-haḍapa, Karn. (ಹಜಾಂಹಡಪ) A tax on each razor-case (Mysore).

Hajám-kasab-vari, Karn. (ಹಜಾಂಕಸಬವರಿ) Any cess or tax imposed upon barbers in Mysore.

Hájat, H. (A. حاجت) Need, want, necessity, any natural want. Confinement of persons charged with heinous offences until their trial; place where they are confined.

Hájat-i-naksha, (?) H. (حاجت نقشه) Necessity of comparing documents.

Hájat-i-siáhá, (from P. سياها, an account) Ready for or requiring entry or account (money, &c.)

Hájat-i-tajwíz, H. (from A. تجويز, investigation) Requiring or awaiting inquiry or trial.

Hajib-nukṣán, A. (حجب نقصان) In Mohammadan law, Partial exclusion with respect to inheritance, or substitution of one share for another, as in the case of a wife, who, where there are no children, has a fourth share, but where there are any, only an eighth.

Hajkul, Hindi (हजकुल) To the whole extent cultivated; (Puraniya).

Hajr, Hijr, or **Hajar**, A. (حجر) lit., Hindrance, prohibition. In law, annulment, disqualification; the invalidity of acts done by a minor, an idiot, a slave, or the like; that is, by persons incompetent to act for themselves by virtue of immature years, defective intellect, or dependent situation.

HAKK, commonly, HAK, HUK, or HUQ, barbarously, HUG, H. &c. (A. حق , हक) Truth, the true God. A true, just, legal, or prescriptive right or claim; the privilege, fee, perquisite, or grant claimable under established usage by the officers of government, village officers, &c., the power of abolishing which by the government of Bombay was affirmed by the Supreme Government Act xx. 1839. The word is used in various compounds, either with the Arabic article *al*, or the Persian sign of relation *i*; as, *Hak-al-tahsíl*, or *Hak-i-tahsíl*, &c., or occasionally without either; and in Maraṭhí it occurs with either a single or double final, as, *Hak*, *Hakk*, (हक, हक्क;) but the latter is considered more correct.

Hakk-ulláh, A. (حق الله) The right of God; or, in law, the retributive chastisement which it is the duty of the magistrate to inflict for crimes and offences, especially against morality and religion.

Hakk-ul-âbd, A. (حق العبد) The right of the slave (of God). In law, the right of an injured individual to demand redress and justice,

Hakk-un-nás, A. (حق الناس) The right of men, that is, of the public, to demand justice for any offence against the laws of society.

Hak-bhent, H. (حق بهينت) Presents made half-yearly, in general by the landholders or payers of revenue, to the government officers.

Hak-chauthái, Mar. (हकचौथाई) A fourth part of the fees annually paid to village and district officers, levied from them by the former government.

Hak-dár, *Huq-dar*, barbarously *Hug-dár*, H. &c. (دار, who holds) The holder of a right, a person vested with any property, perquisite, or privilege, the holder of a share (of the revenue or the crops), a government or village officer who claims prescriptive rights or fees, one who makes a claim or demands a right, a claimant.

Hak-dári, H. &c. Holding any right or privilege, the right of claim, privilege, or property.

Hak-i-hawáladár, H. (حق حوالدار) A portion of grain given to the officer of the Zamindar employed to collect the revenue, usually at the rate of a seer-and-a-half per maund of forty seers.

Hakíat, H. (حقيت) Right, claim, property.

Hak-i-intifâ, H. (حق انتفع) Revenue profits on payment of the government demand.

Hak-kamín-chárí, H. (حق كمين چاري) or *Hak-sián-chárí*, (سيانچاري) or *Hak-thok-dárí*, (تهوكداري) Dues and fees paid by the villagers to officers bearing the designations of *Kamín*, *Siána*, and *Thokdár*, the managers of the villages under the authority of the government in Kamáon and Garhwál.

Hahk-halál, Mar. (हक्कहलाल) Rightly and lawfully due or claimable.

Hak-krishání, Ben. (হককৃষাণী) The right of the cultivator to his share of the crop.

Hak-málikána, H. (حق مالكانه) The right of the Málik, the proprietor, or Zamindar, to a per-centage on the net revenue, or, when dispossessed of the Zamindárí, to an allowance for his support.

Hak-i-milkiat, H. (حق ملكيت) The right or due of proprietorship or mastership, the right of the Zamindar to Málikána.

Hak-i-musháhara, H. (from A. مشاهره, monthly wages) The right of receiving pay or allowances; under the Maraṭha government the term was applied to the per-centage levied upon the perquisites and allowances of the district officers, the Desmukhs and Despándyas.

Hak-ná-hak, H. (حق ناحق) *Hakknahakk*, *Hakknáhakk*, *Hakknák*, Mar. (हक्कनहक्क, हक्कनाहक्क, हक्कनाक) Right or wrong, justly or unjustly; but it usually implies wrongfully, unjustly, without regard to right or wrong, without consideration.

Hakkmál, Mar. (हक्कमाल) A rightful claim or possession.

Hak-patwári, H. (حق پتواري) The fees payable to the village accountant.

Hak-i-râaíya, H. (A. رعايا, peasantry) The right of the cultivator, his right of occupation while paying the demand of the government or Zamindar, and his right to the established share of the crop.

Hak-i-sarkar, H. (P. سركار, government) The right of the government to a share of the crop, or a money commutation.

Hak-i-sarbaráh, H. (P. سربراه, management) The right of management, as of the head of a village to conduct its affairs.

Hak-i-shufâh, or *Hak-us-shufâh* (from شفعه, pre-emption) Right of pre-emption in a person whose possessions adjoin those for sale.

Hak-i-tahsíl, or *Hak-ut-tahsil*, (from. A. تحصيل, collection) The right or due of collection, the rate or fee of the officer employed to collect the government revenue.

Haḳsái, Guz. (હકસાઈ) Fee, perquisite, brokerage commission.

Haḳúḳ, H. (pl. of حق) Rights, fees, privileges, &c.

Haḳ-us-saâi, H. (from A. سعي, labour) Reward of labour especially a present for good offices rendered by one in authority.

Haḳ-al-wáḳiâh, absurdly corrupted to *Hughly-wacca*, H. (A. حق الواقعة, Record or statement of occurences.

Hakhṭak, Mar. (हक्कटक) The dues as paid in cash to a district or village officer.

Haḳ-i-zamindár, or *Haḳ-zamindári*, H. (from P. زمين دار, landholder) The rights or dues of a Zamindar agreeably to the sanad by which he holds his lands or his engagements with the government.

HAḲÍKAT, or HAQEEQUT, corruptly HACKIKUT, H. &c. (A. حقيقت, from حق) HAKIKAT, Mar. (हकिकत) Statement, account, representation of circumstances as they are.

Haḳiḳat-i-jamâ, H. (حقيقت جمع) Particular account of the public revenue in all its branches: the accounts prepared of the revenues of Bengal and Bahar to the period of their assignment to the Company.

Haḳiḳat-i-jamâ-ṭúmári, H. (from جمع, aggregate, and طوماري, registered) Particular account of the public revenue agreeably to the recorded rates.

Haḳiḳat-náma, H. (حقيقت نامة) A written statement of particulars.

Haḳiḳat-rozinah-dári, H. (from P. روزينه دار, a daily pensioner) An account of payments made to daily pensioners, formerly kept by the Kánungo.

Haḳiḳat-taḥsil, H. (A. تحصيل) The actual state of the revenue collections.

Haḳiḳat-zamindári, The possession or condition of a Zamindar's estate and engagements.

HAKAM, A. (حكم, from the *r.* حَكَم, commanded) A judge, an arbitrator.

Hákim, H. (A. حاكم) *Hakam*, *Hákim*, Mar, (हकम, हाकीम) A ruler, a governor, the supreme administrative authority in a district; also, a judge.

Hakím, *Hukeem*, H. (A. حكيم) A sage, a physician.

Hákimi, H. (حاكمي) Belonging to the ruler or the government, as the government share of the crop, or the revenue derived from it.

Hikmat, H. (A. حكمة) Wisdom, knowledge, ingenuity, skill.

Hukámi, H. (حكامي) Applied to grants of land made by officers of government or Zamindars: (from *Hukám*, an officer or deputy).

Hukm, H. &c. (A. حكم) *Hukúm*, Mar. (हुकूम) Order, command.

Hukm-náma, H. (حكم نامة) A written order, a written award or judgment.

Hukm-náma-beríj, H. (P. بريج) The standard assessment of Mysore under Tipu.

Hukm-waẓâ, H. (A. حكم وضع) Authorised deductions.

Hukúmat, H. (plural of *Hukm*) Orders, rules, regulations.

Hakúmat, H. (A. حكومة) *Hukmat*, Mar. (हुकमत) Sovereignty, authority.

Hakúmat-al-âdl, or *Hakúmat-i-âdl*, A. (حكومت العدل) A just award, one in which the penalty is proportioned to the injury or offence, a decision by just arbitrement. Ben. Reg. iv. 1822.

HAḲERI, commonly HACKERY, (?) A native cart drawn by bullocks: (the word, although in common use, is neither Hindi nor Bengali: it may be a corruption of the Port. *carro*, or *acarretai*, to carry).

HAKKALU, Karn. (ಹಕ್ಕಲು) Gleanings of corn: rice cultivation carried on on high ground without the aid of reservoirs of water.

HÁL, H. (A. حال) State, condition, present or actual state. In revenue accounts the actual state of the collections. In Marathi and Karnáta the word commonly implies a bad state, extremity, embarrassment, distress.

Hálá, H. (حالا) An instalment of revenue, a present payment (Dehli).

Hál-ábádi, H. (حال آبادي) Under present cultivation (land), having formerly been waste.

Hál-ábádi-zamín, H. (from P. *Ábád*, cultivation, and *zamín*, land) Land under present cultivation.

Hal-ákár, H. (حل اكار) Present or actual realization of revenue.

Hálat, *Halut*, H. (A. حالت) Condition, state: the term was used also to denote a particular high duty on pepper, betel-nut, cardamoms, cassia, and sandal in Belghi and Sunda: see *Háltá*.

Hálát, H. (A. حالات, plural of حالت) Circumstances, present states or conditions.

Hál-báḳi, H. (حالباقي) Current or present balance.

Hál-baḳáiá, H. (حالبقايا) Present demand and former balance.

Hál-bhanjan, corruptly, *Hal-bunjin*, H. (from بهنجن, breaking) Anticipation of the revenue of the ensuing year.

Hál-chalani, H. (حالچلني) Present currency.

Hál-dár, H. (حالدار) A village officer next to the Paṭwárí, an assistant accountant. A name borne by some Bengal families of the trading castes, commonly *Holdar*.

Hál-dári, H. (حالداري) The office of Háldár: also, in former times, a tax upon marriages levied in Bengal.

Hál-hakíkat, H. (حالحقيقت) Statement of the actual condition of an estate, an account shewing the amount of revenue to be paid by each cultivator to government or the Zamindar, and the items of which it consists.

Hál-hásil, H. (حالحاصل) The actual produce or revenue of any tract of land.

Hál-hásilí, H. (حالحاصلي) Actually productive, land yielding revenue varying with the crops grown upon it.

Háli, H. (حالي, what is present) lit., Present, actual, new; as applied to coin, current; instalment, present payment of revenue, the government assessment (Dehli). In the west of India, a bondsman, one serving as a labourer in payment of a debt, until the debt is discharged.

Hali-dáhhal, H. and Karn. (ಹಾಲಿದಾಖಲ) Increase of the actual assessment (Mysore).

Hál-jamá, H. (حالجمع) The actual rent or revenue payable to government.

Hál-májhí, Ben. (হালমাঝী) An inferior village officer, who collects rents on the part of the Paṭwárí, and performs menial service for the superior village and Zamindari officers (Rungpore).

Hál-pariá, Uriya (ହାଲପଡ଼ିଆ) Land at present lying fallow, recently thrown out of cultivation.

Hál-puchhi-hisab, H. (from پوچهي, to ask) An abstract of current accounts kept at hand, one produced on being asked for (Northern Circars).

Hál-sál, H. (P. سال, a year) The present or current year, or of this year.

Hál-shahna, also, vernacularly, *-sahna* or *-sáhana*, H. (A. حالشحنه) An officer of the Zamindar, employed to keep the measurement of the land possessed by each cultivator, and collect the rents when due.

Hal-taujíh, H. (A. حالتوجيه) An account of revenue collections for the current period.

HAL, HUL, also HAR, HUR, q. v., H. (S. هل, هر, हल) HAL, or HÁL, Ben. (হল, হাল) A plough.

Haláitá, *Hulaeta*, or, provincially, *Haretá*, and *Halotá*, H. (هلايتا, हरेता, हलोता) The first ploughing of the season.

Halas, *Haras* or *Hanas*, *Hulus*, *Hurus*, *Hunus*, H. هلس, هرس, هنس, हलस) The beam or pole of a plough, the stick that passes obliquely between the oxen, and supports the yoke.

Hal-bandi, *Hul-bundee*, H. (هل بندي) Assessment according to ploughs; also a tenure in Bareilly, in which a few *bíghás* are assigned to each tenant who has a plough, for the cultivation of cotton and Indian corn, for which he pays one rupee per *bíghá*: for all other land he pays in kind. In Kamáon the term implies the quantity of land under cultivation by any party.

Hal-barár, *Hul-burár*, H. (هلبرار) Assessment according to the number of ploughs; collections at a certain sum per plough.

Hal-dár, H. (هل دار) The possessor of a plough.

Hal-dári-jamá, H. (هل داري جمع) Revenue assessed at a rate per plough.

Hali, sometimes *Hálee*, H. &c. (هلي, هالي, हली) A ploughman, a man employed in ploughing. In Surat, *Háli* is the denomination of a class of agricultural bondsmen, persons who have sold their labour for an advance of money, and are bound to serve, chiefly in the field, until the money is repaid: the obligation extends to their posterity: they are usually Hindus of low caste. When not employed by their master they may work for themselves, and what they earn is their own property. A *Háli* cannot be transferred to another master against his will. In Kamaon a *Háli* or *Hália* is a man of low caste, a *Dom*, who has been bought as a slave, and is chiefly employed in the labours of the field, but who cuts wood, brings in grass, carries burthens, &c., or performs domestic menial service.

Haliág, H. (هلياگ, हलयाग) The wages of ploughmen, especially when paid in kind: in some places it is said to be one-eighth of the crop.

Halsárí, *Hulsaree*, H. (هلساري) Subdivision and assessment of revenue on ploughs, assessment on each plough in a village.

Haltaḍḍi, *Hultuḍḍee*, (هلتڈي) A drill-plough.

Halvíra, *Hulveera*, Mar. (from हल, a plough) A tax on ploughs.

Halwáhá, *Hulwaha*, *Harwáhá*, H. (هلواها, هرواها, हलवाहा) A ploughman.

Halwáhí, H. (هلواهي, हलवाही) Tillage, agriculture.

HÁL, Hindi (हाल) Moisture (Puraniya).

Hálgará, Hindi (हालगरा) Land retaining moisture (*Ibid*).

Hala, Karn. (ಹಲ) A weight equal to eight Mysore *sérs*, or an Indian ounce, thirteen of which make a pound.

Ḥalák, or **Ḥalákat**, H. (A. هلاك, هلاكت) Death, destruction: in law, homicide, manslaughter.

Ḥalál, H. (A. حلال) **Hálál**, Ben. (হালাল) Lawful, allowed, in contrast to *Harám*, forbidden.

Halálkhor, H. (حلال خور, from P. خوردن, to eat) A man of the lowest caste, who performs the vilest class of functions, as a sweeper, &c.: (so termed as if considering every thing lawful food).

Haldí, **Huldee**, H. (هلدي, S. हरिद्रा) **Haḷda**, Mar. (हळद) Turmeric. The ceremony of anointing the persons of the bride and bridegroom with turmeric between the betrothment and the actual marriage among the Mohammadans. There are two ceremonies so called—the *Chor-haldí*, the private staining; and *Sáú-haldí*, the public or open staining, being performed in public, after which the married pair sit together in state.

Haldá, or **Hardá**, **Hulda**, **Hurda**, H. (هلدا, هردا) A sort of mildew affecting the cerealia, in which the plant turns yellow and withers.

Haḷepáik, Karn. (ಹಳೆಪಾಯಿಕ) The term applied in Mysore to the drawers of *tárí* who speak the Tuluva language.

Half, **Hulf**, in some dialects **Halap**, or **Hulup**, H. (A. حلف) An oath, a vow, an affidavit.

Half-darúghi, H. (from P. دروغ, a falsehood) Perjury.

Half-náma, H. (حلف نامه) A written solemn declaration by a person exempt by the Regulations from being sworn in the ordinary manner.

Hálif, H. (A. حالف) One who takes an oath, or makes an affidavit.

Hálímawálí, Mar. (हालीमवाली, plural, for A. اهالي موالي) High and low, rich and poor.

Hálímájí, Mar. (हालीमाजी, from A. حالي, present, and ماضي, past) Change of administration, removal of public functionaries, and appointment of others.

Halḳa, **Hulqa**, H. (A. حلقه, lit. a ring) A village circuit, a boundary line which includes all the lands and dwellings of a village or hamlet, a circle or estate including many villages.

Haḷḷa, Karn. (ಹಳ್ಳ) A water-course, a river bed.

Haḷḷi, Karn. (ಹಳ್ಳಿ) A small village or hamlet; added frequently to other names, and commonly written *hully*, as, *Harpan-hully*, &c.

Haḷḷigáḍu, Karn. (ಹಳ್ಳಿಗಾಡು) A country village, or one in a wood.

Haḷḷigáḍinavaru, Karn. (ಹಳ್ಳಿಗಾಡಿನವರು) Peasantry, villagers.

Haḷḷikár, Karn. (ಹಳ್ಳಿಕಾರ) A tribe of Ṣúdras in Mysore, following husbandry.

Háltá, Karn. (ಹಾಲ್ತಾ) A duty levied in Belghi and Sunda on pepper, betel-nuts, cardamoms, sandal-wood, and cassia.

Halube, or **-ve**, Karn. (ಹಲುಬೆ, -ವೆ) A sort of rake or harrow for levelling a field of corn in the blade after reaping.

Halwáí, H. (حلواي) **Háluí**, Ben. (হালুই) A confectioner, a maker of Halwá, or sweetmeats. In the Lower Doab it denotes a tribe or caste; in most other places only the maker and vender.

Hálwakkal, Karn. (ಹಾಲವಕ್ಕಲ) A tribe of agricultural Ṣúdras in Mysore.

Ḥam, **Hum**, H. (P. هم) Also, ever, like, same; much used to form compounds implying sameness or connexion; as,

Ḥam-dam, H. (هم دم) An intimate friend or associate: (from *Dam*, breath).

Ḥam-ját, H. (هم جات) Of the same caste, of the same kind.

Ḥam-jins, H. (هم جنس) Homogeneous, of the same kind or sort.

Ḥam-rái, H. (هم راي) An accomplice, a confederate; of one purpose.

Ḥam-sáia, H. (هم سايه) A neighbour.

Ḥamsái-grámamu, H. Tel. A neighbouring village.

Ḥamshahri, H. (هم شهري) A fellow-townsman.

Ḥamah, **Humeh**, H. (P. همه) All, together; used like the preceding in compounds, and vernacularly confounded.

Ḥama-bábat, H. (همه بابت) The grand total, the aggregate of the items.

Ḥama-ját, Mar. (हमजात) A promiscuous crowd, one of all castes.

Ḥama-ḳaum, H. (همه قوم) All the tribes, all classes.

Ḥamál, H. (A. حمال) A porter, a carrier: in the South, a palankin-bearer.

Hámálkhún, Ben. (হামালখুন, from A. حمل, being pregnant, and خون, blood) Causing abortion.

Hamámdastá, Mar. (हमामदस्ता) **Hámándista**, Ben. (হামানদিস্তা), (both from the P. *Hávan*, هاون, a mortar, and *Dasta*, دسته, a pestle) A mortar and pestle.

Hamí, **Hámí**, (Mar. हमी, हामी, from the A. *Hámi*, حامي, a protector) Assurance, surety, confirmation of a contract or engagement by a third party pledging himself for its execution.

Hamídár, Hámídár, Mar. (हमीदार, हामीदार) The person who affords an assurance or pledge, a security.

Hamíl, H. (A. حميل) A surety.

Hamípatra, Mar. (हमीपत्र) A security or assurance paper or bond.

HÁMISHAM, Tel. (హామిషం, corruption of S. *Anśam*, अंश) A possession, a portion.

HAMLA, H. (A. حمله) Aggression, assault.

HAṆA, Karn. (ಹಣ) Money in general: the small coin termed a fanam, whether of gold or silver.

Biḷḷí-haṇa, Karn. (ಬಿಳ್ಳಿಹಣ) A silver fanam.

Binnada-haṇa, (ಬಿನ್ನದಹಣ) A gold fanam.

Kantíráya-haṇa, Sultání-haṇa, Dotí-haṇa, Giddahantí-ráya-haṇa, Gopálí-haṇa, Bahrada-haṇa, are different kinds of gold fanams current in Mysore, each worth about four silver ones.

Haṇada-nóṭa, Karn. (ಹಣದನೋಟ) Examining and exchanging money: shroffing.

Haṇavadda, Karn. (ಹಣವಡ್ಡ) A fanam-and-a-half.

HANCHIKE, or -GE, Karn. (ಹಂಚಿಕೆ -ಗೆ) Sharing, dividing; allotment.

Hanchugoḷu, Karn. (ಹಂಚುಗೊಳು) A wooden seal used by government officers in Mysore when the farmers divide their corn on the threshing-floor.

HAṆḌÁ, or HÁṆḌÁ, H. &c. (هنڈا, هانڈا, हंडा, हांडा) A cooking pot, whether of clay or metal.

Haṇḍí, or *Háṇḍí*, H. &c. (هنڈي, هانڈي, हंडी, हांडी) A small culinary vessel or pot.

HÁNDÁ, Mar. (हांदा) The mutual assistance in labour, bullocks, &c., interchanged among husbandmen.

Hándekarí, Mar. (हांदेकरी) A labourer or a bullock lent by one cultivator to another.

HAṆE, Karn. (ಹಣೆ) A grain measure of eighty rupees weight.

HANGÁM, H. &c. (P. هنگام) Time, season, period at which any thing or business is most abundant or prevalent.

Hangám-ṣibandí, Mar. (हंगामशिबंदी) Militia or irregular troops enlisted for a time.

Hangámí, H. (هنگامي) Periodical, for a time; an extra cess imposed on the district of Jessore shortly before the permanent settlement.

HANGÁMA, H. (P. هنگامه) Tumult, disturbance.

HÁNI, Ben. (S. হানি) Loss, diminution, deficiency, injury.

Hánibá, Uriya (ହାଣିବା) Cutting and maiming.

HÁNJÁ, Mar. (हांजा) An unsettled business, an affair or transaction in suspense.

HANJÁ, Hindi (हनजा) A head of cattle.

HANKÁL-TERÍGE, Karn. (ಹಂಕಾಲತೆರಿಗೆ) A tax on the stubble on which the cattle of the Ryots were allowed to graze (Mysore).

HANSRÁJ, H. (S. هنس راج) A herb growing on brick walls in the rains, used medicinally: a kind of rice.

HÁPAR, H. (هاپر) A nursery for sugar-cane.

HAPTÁ, less correctly, HUPTEE, Mar. (हप्ता, a corruption of P. *Hafta*, a week) HAPHTO, Guz. (હપ્તો) A fixed period at which a portion of revenue, or any sum due, is to be paid; also the portion so paid, an instalment: under the former government there were four haptás in the Dakhin, or the months October, January, March, and May, when the revenue was expected to be paid.

Hapte-bandí, Mar. (हप्तेबंदी) Settlement for payments by instalments; payment of such instalments as they fall due.

HÁR, Ben. (S. হার) A rate, a common rate: in revenue language, local rate of assessment; H. (هار) A subdivision or part of an estate. In the north-west provinces, usually the land most distant from the village it belongs to, beyond the *mánjha*, or middle portion, and extending to the boundary or limits of the village lands or estate. In Ságar it means the reverse, or the cultivated space immediately round a village. In Bundelkhand it denotes a tract of land of which there may be several joint occupants: land which, from its distance, had been abandoned by the Zamindar to the cultivators, and, after a long alienation, separately assessed: also, pasture land. Again, in the district of Agra it is applied to all the different parts of a village where such divisions have been created in the course of village economy; and in Etawa it denotes the upland, or land lying above the ravines.

Hárhárí, Ben. (হারহারী) Distribution, especially of assets amongst claimants in whose favour a decree has been pronounced, proportionate to their respective claims; also, taking the whole together, a general average.

Hárí, Ben., H. (হারী, هاري) Relating or belonging to the boundary lands: occupying a part or *hár*: subject to a local rate of assessment, &c.

Hárí-raiat, Ben. A cultivator who pays his revenue in money, according to the local rate.

Hár-ḳaula, corruptly, *Her-kowla*, H. (هارقوله) Assessment fixed in money upon different portions of an estate, according to the quality of the land (in the district of Benares).

Hár, H. &c. (هار, हार) **Hár** or **Hári**, Ben. (হার, হারি) Loss, as at gaming, or of a suit at law, defeat, discomfiture.

Háribár, Uriya (ହାରିବାର) The act of losing, or of being beaten.

Ḥar, **Hur**, H. (P. هر) Every, any; used in compounds.

Ḥar-báb, Uriya (ହରବାବ, P. and A., every class) Applied to land capable of yielding any description of crops.

Ḥarbírah, Hindi (हरबीरह) Bearing the same rate of rent per *bíghá*; an estate.

Ḥar-do-hiṣṣa, H. (from هردو, each two, and حصه, a share) Both shares of the crop—the government's and the cultivator's.

Ḥar-ḥamesha, *Ḥur-ḥumesh*, H. (هرهميش, from P. هميشه, always) Words inserted sometimes in a grant, to signify one made for perpetuity, for ever and ever.

Ḥar-jins, *Ḥur-jins*, H. (P. هرجنس) Grain of sorts, any thing of various or every kind.

Harkára, *Hurkaru*, H. (هركاره, from هر, every كار, business) A messenger, a courier, an emissary, a spy.

Har, **Hur**, substituted vernacularly sometimes for **Hal**, H. (هر, S. हल) A plough.

Harái, *Haraee*, H. (هرائي) The portion of land in a field which is included within one circuit of a plough; to commence another is termed *Haraï-phándná*: beginning of the ploughing season.

Harátar, Hindi, (हरातर) Place where the ploughs are working for the day.

Haráti, Hindi, (हराती) Belonging to a plough.

Haríaunu, *Hureeaon*, H. (هرياونو) Division of a crop, in which the cultivator retains nine, and the Zamindar receives seven parts (from *har*, a plough).

Harauri, *Hurouree*, H. (هروري) The occupation of ploughing, or place where ploughing is going on. In Benares, an advance of about two rupees in money and two maunds of corn given to a ploughman when first engaged.

Harautá, *Hurouta*, H. (هروتا) Beginning of the ploughing season.

Hareta, or *Haretá*, H. (هريته, हरेता) Commencement of the plougbing season in the rains.

Harghasít, *Hurghuseet*, H. (هرگهسيت) The cultivated lands of a village (from *har*, a plough, and *ghasítna*, to draw) (Lower Doab).

Harhá, *Hurha*, H. (هرها) Unbroken and vicious bullocks, plough bullocks, (Dehli). Stray oxen.

Harhásalí, Hindi, (हरहासली) Lands bearing crops.

Hari, *Huree*, H. (هري) Compulsory contribution of assistance by Ryots in ploughing the fields of Zamindars; also sometimes voluntary mutual assistance of cultivators among one another.

Hári, Sindhi. A peasant, a cultivator (from *har*, a plough, or for *hálí*, q. v.).

Hariá, *Huryá*, H. (هريا) A ploughman.

Hariar, *Huriur*, H. (هرير) End of the sowing season. (Oudh).

Harori, Hindi, (हरोरी) Money lent by a cultivator to a person to act as ploughman, bearing no interest as long as he serves.

Harpúji, *Hurpoojee*, H. (هرپوجي) The worship of the plough on the day which closes the season of ploughing and sowing: sometimes it precedes the season, but less usually: it generally occurs in Kártik, after the autumnal sowing, but in some places it is celebrated after the spring sowing also. The plough is cleaned and decorated with garlands; and to use or lend it after this day is considered unlucky.

Harsajjá, H. (هرسجّا, S. हल, and सहायजा, companionship) Reciprocal assistance in ploughing.

Harsot, *Harsotia*, *Hursot*, *Hursotea*, H. (هرسوت from S. हल, a plough, and सूत्र, a line or thread) Ploughing a furrow, the first ploughing of the season: affording mutual assistance in ploughing: bringing home the plough after a day's work on a bullock's back, or with the share inverted (Dehli).

Harwáhá, incorrectly *Hurwa*, H. (هرواها) A ploughman, an agricultural bondsman, one who has sold his services for an advance, and is bound, together with his descendants, to serve until the advance is repaid (Allahabad).

Harwal, *Hurwul*, H. (هرول) Advances, without interest, to ploughmen (East Oudh and Benares).

Háṛá, H. (هاڑا) A branch of the Chouhán Rájputs, after whom the province of *Háráuti*, including the principalities of Kota and Bundi, is named.

Hará, H. (هرا, हरित) Green, fresh, vegetable.

Harái, H (هراي) Greenness, verdure.

Harkaṭ, *Hurkuṭ*, H. (هركٹ) Cutting rice while it is green and unripe (Rohilkhand) (from *hará*, green, and *kátná*, to cut).

Harada, Karn. (ಹರದ) A large dealer, a wholesale or maritime merchant; a lender.

Haradavattige, Karn. (ಹರದವಟ್ಟಿಗೆ) Merchandise: lending and borrowing.

Haradári, Karn. (ಹರದಾರಿ) A measure of extent, containing 2000 fathoms, or about two miles and a half, a *kos* (Mysore).

Haragalu, or Haragólu, Karn. (ಹರಗಲು, ಹರಗೋಲು) A ferry-boat, a circular boat made of bambus, and covered with leather, used for crossing rivers in Kanara.

Haragalu-kaḍa, Karn. (ಹರಗಲುಕಡ) The place of a ferry.

Haragol-gutti, Karn. (ಹರಗೋಲಗುತ್ತಿ) A tax on ferry-boats (Mysore).

Harage, Karn. (ಹರಗೆ) Partnership.

Haraj, Huruj, H. (A. هرج) Tumult, disturbance, riot.

Haraj-maraj, H. (هرج‌مرج) Confusion.

Haráj, H. (A. هراج) Auction, outcry: public proposals for the farming of the revenues of sundry villages for a short term of years (?).

Haraḷe-paṭṭaḍi, Karn. (ಹರಳೆಪಟ್ಟಡಿ, from *Haralu*, the castor-oil seed) A commutation tax paid by dealers in lamp-oil, in consideration of exemption from the visits of the officers of the *Sair* revenue (Mysore).

Haralu-paṭṭaḍi, Karn. (ಹರಲುಪಟ್ಟಡಿ) Tax on oil-dealers: see the preceding.

Haram, Hurum, H. (A. حرم) Sacred, forbidden, closed to promiscuous access; hence applied to a female connexion or relative; also to the private or women's apartments, the Harem of European writers; also to the sacred circuit round the temple at Mecca.

Harám, *Huram*, H. &c. (A. حرام) Unlawful, forbidden; applied to all things or acts which the law disallows or condemns, as prohibited food or beverage, improper actions; wicked, vicious; sacred.

Harámzáda, H. (A. حرامزاده) Base-born; a bastard, but used as a term of abuse generally, a scoundrel, a rascal.

Harím, H. (A. حريم) Prohibited, sacred; a sacred place or sanctuary; the inner apartments, or their female inhabitants; the enclosure of the temple of Mecca.

Hurmat, H. (A. حرمت) Character, reputation, honour; the seclusion of a woman of respectability; any thing held sacred or forbidden.

Hurmat-muṣáharat, A. (حرمت مصاهرة) In law, the prohibition of marriage with different women on account of their mutual affinity.

Hárampaṭṭuta, Tel. (హారంపట్టుత) Gathering ears of corn.

Haraṇbáṛí, Ben. (হরণবাড়ি) A gaol, a house of confinement for criminals.

Haraṭ, vernacular corruption of Arhat, q. v., H. (هرٹ) A Persian water-wheel.

Haratkul, H. (هرٹکل, probably for Bharat-kul, of the race of Bharata) A branch of the Gauṛ Bráhmans.

Haṛava, or Haṛuva, Karn. (ಹಾರವ, ಹಾರುವ) A Bráhman: (a term especially used by the Lingáyats),

Haráwal, corruptly, Harol and Harrewal, H. (Turk. هراول) The advanced guard of an army, the officer commanding it: a police-officer in a town or village appears to be sometimes, though not very accurately, so termed.

Harbi, H. (A. حربي, from حرب, war, battle) Martial, valiant: in law, an infidel not subject to Mohammadan rule, although at peace, such a person being an incessant object of hostilities.

Harbong ká ráj, H. (هربونگ کا راج) Civil disorders, maladministration: lit., the rule of Harbong, a Raja so named, said to have ruled at a place opposite to *Allahabad*, on the bank of the Ganges, thence termed *Harbong-pur*, and of whose silliness and unfitness for government many traditional anecdotes and proverbial phrases bear record (Elliot).

Hardá, H. (هردا) Mildew, smut in corn.

Hardaur, Hurdour, H. (هردور) A name given to oblong mounds raised in villages in Upper India, and studded with flags to avert epidemic diseases, and especially cholera; so named in honour of *Hardaul Lálá*, a Bundelkhand chief, who, the natives of Hindustan believe, visited the camp of Lord Hastings with cholera, in punishment of the profanation committed by the Europeans in having once slaughtered cows in the grove where Hardaul's ashes repose.

Hardehá, H. (هرديها) A tribe of the *Káchchis*.

Harduás, Hurdooas, H. (هردواس) A class of Rájputs, of whom a few are settled in Azimgerh and Gorakhpur.

Hari, S., but adopted in all dialects, (हरिः) A name of Vishṇu.

Háṛí, Ben. (হাড়ি) A servant of the lowest class, a sweeper, (from S. *Haḍḍa*, a bone): also *Haḍḍaka* or *Haṛṛaka*, and *Haḍika*, *Haṛika*; formerly employed also as village watchman.—Ben. Reg. xxii. 1793, s. 13. (In the Glossary of the 5th Report we have *Harees*, derived from the A. *Háris*, a defender, and explained, a petty officer of police, a guard, a sentinel; but the original word is *Háṛees*, plural of

Haree, not *Harees* in the singular, as, "All pykes, chokidars, nigahbans, Harees, and other descriptions of village watchmen."—Fifth Rep. p. 614).

HARI, (?) A third crop; one of the poorer grains raised in the hot weather between the spring and autumn crops.

HARIA, (?) Land granted to the relations of persons killed in an affray between two villages, by the authorities of that village by whose members the homicide had been perpetrated; or similar land rent-free granted to the families of Bháts who had destroyed themselves on the violation of engagements for which they had been sureties.

HARIGÓLU, Tel. (హరిగోలు) A basket boat, such as is used on the rivers of the Dakhin.

HÁRIṢA, A. (حارصة) One of the ten kinds of wounds for which compensation is claimable, a slight scratch, such as not to draw blood.

HARKAR, Hindi (हरकार) A pen for cattle (Puraniya).

HARKAT, H. &c. (A. حركت) Movement, motion, agitation, especially of an objectionable kind, as opposition, hindrance, interruption, starting difficulties, giving trouble.

HARKÍ, Mar. (हरकी, from S. *Harsha*, pronounced sometimes *Harkha*, joy) Money given by a successful litigant to the Court, in token of his gratitude: money paid to one who has brought back a lost article, or presented to the family and dependants on any occasion of rejoicing.

Harkí-viváha, corruptly, *Urkee-wiwáha*, Mar. (S. हरकीविवाह) Presents claimed at marriages by the principal Bráhmans.

HASALE, corruptly, in the plural, HUSSULLEERO, Karn. (ಹಸಲೆ) One of the supposed aboriginal tribes of Mysore, found in the hill districts of Nagar; properly woodmen, but serving as agricultural labourers.

HASARÁṆÍ, Karn. (ಹಸರಾಣಿ) A tax levied in Mysore on betel-leaf, plaintain-leaf, and other vegetable leaves.

Hásaraváṇé, Karn. (ಹಾಸರವಾಣೆ) A tax levied from the peasants, in commutation of supplies of green leaves which they were formerly obliged to furnish to the government officers.

HASARU, Karn. (ಹಸರು) Green, fresh, standing corn or pasturage: also HASURU.

HASB, H. (A. حسب) According to; used chiefly in forming compounds, as,

Hasb-ul-háṣil, or *-háṣilí*, H. (حسب الحاصل) According to the produce; land paying revenue according to the kind and value of the crops.

Hasb-ul-hukm, *Husb-ool-hookm*, corruptly, *Housbulhoohum*, H. (حسب الحكم) According to command. The initial words, and thence the title, of a document issued agreeably to royal authority, by the Vazir or other high officer of the government.

Hasb-i-ẕábiṭa, H. (حسب ضابطه) According to law, according to practice.

Hasb-ul-irṣ, A. (حسب الارث) According to inheritance, the division of an estate according to the Mohammadan laws of inheritance.

Hasb-ul-waṣúl, or *-waṣúlí*, H. (حسب الوصول) lit., According to collections or receipts; a term formerly used in revenue accounts to designate items of an uncertain value, of which no estimate can be computed, and which are entered only after their actual receipt: applied also formerly to small villages in the Monghir district paying revenue direct to government.—Fifth Rep. 240.

Hasb-ul-waṣúl-i-marocha, corrupted to *Husbulwoosoolee-marocha*, H. (A. حسب الوصول مروچه) lit., Agreeably to customary (?) realizations: an item of revenue in the early Bengal accounts, levied especially in Dinajpur and Rangpur, being an estimated amount of receipts from fees on marriages. (The word *marocha*, also met with as *maruncha*, is of doubtful accuracy; it may be a corruption of *murwaja*, مروجه, customary).

HASHM, H. &c. (A. حشم, हश्म) Train, retinue, followers of a person of rank.

Hashm-navís, or *-nís*, or *-pharnís*, or *-pharnavís*, Mar. (हश्मनवीस, -नीस, हश्मफडनीस, फडनवीस) A public officer under the Peshwa's government, who kept a muster-roll of the ordinary train of retainers attached to different chiefs, of the garrisons, of the forts, and the irregular militia.

HÁSHIA-GAWÁH, H. (حاشيه گواه) A witness to the execution of a deed (writing his name on the *háshia* or margin).

HÁSHIMA, A. (هاشمه) A fracture of the skull, inflicted by violence, and requiring legal compensation.

HASHO-MINHÁÏ, erroneously, HASHM-MINHAI, H. (حشومنهاي) Deductions from the total revenue entered on the credit side of the account with government. The term is therefore applied to rent-free and other assigned lands, also to rent-free lands exempted from resumption: (from the A. حشو, deduction on the credit side of an account). See *Báriz* and *Min-ha*, من ها, 'from it,' with ي added to form a substantive.

Hasho-wazá, H. (حشو وضع) Deduction from the total revenue credited in the government account.

HASIÁ, or HANSIÁ, H. (هسيا, هنسيا) A reaping-hook.

HASIKE, or -GE, Karn. (ಹಸಿಕೆ, -ಗೆ) Actual measurement of the crop after it is threshed, and before its partition between the tenant and landlord.

HÁSIL, H. and most dialects, (A. حاصل) HASÍL, HÁSÍL, or HÁSÍL, Mar. (हशील, हाशील, or हासील) HÁSALU, Tel. Karn. (హాసలు) Produce, profit, especially, as a revenue term, the amount derived from the government share of the produce of the soil, and from any other source of taxation, or impost; revenue, tax, duty.

Hásila, H. (حاصله) Cultivated or cropped land (Chittagong).

Hásilat, Uriya. (ହାସିଲତ) Assessed lands.

Hasil-i-bázár, or *Hásil-bázárí*, H. (حاصل بازار, حاصل بازاري) Market dues, revenue from duties on markets.

Hásil-daftar, H. (حاصل دفتر) Tax office, custom-house, custom or revenue account.

Hásil-khálárí, Ben. (হাসিলখালাড়ী) Produce of salt works, an item in the public accounts, the profit derived from the duty and the original ground-rent of the land on which the works are erected.

Hásil-i-namah, H., in Ben., Mar., &c., *nimak*, (حاصل نمك) Duty or profit or revenue derived from salt.

Hásil-zamín, H. (P. زمين) Land in cultivation and paying revenue.

Hásil-i-kalám, H. (حاصل كلام, from the A. كلام, speech) Briefly, shortly, lit., the produce or pith of speech.

HASTA, S. but used also in various dialects, as well as the vernacular form, HÁT, or HÁTH, q. v. (हस्त) The hand, a cubit from the elbow to the tip of the midle finger.

Hastákshar, Mar. (S. हस्त, the hand, and अक्षर, a letter) Sign-manual, handwriting.

Hastántarakaran, Ben. (হস্তান্তরকরণ, from S. हस्त, hand, अन्तर, different, and करण, making) Transfer of property, handing over any thing to another.

Hastántara-karan-patra, Ben. (হস্তান্তরকরণপত্র) A deed of transfer.

Hastakadi, (ಹಸ್ತಕಡಿ) Money in hand, ready money.

Hasten, Mar. (हस्तें) By, from, or into the hand of; as money paid by, or to, or through the hand of, any one.

HAST-O-BÚD, HUST-O-BOOD, also sometimes vernacularly, but incorrectly, HASTABÚD, H. (P. هست, is, and بود, was, with the conjunctive و, هست و بود) A comparative account, shewing the present and past produce of an estate: an examination of the assets or resources of a country, made before the harvest, and sometimes after measurement of the lands: a detailed statement of any lands yielding revenue: the rent roll of a village signed yearly by the Patwárí: the common form is an abstract of each Ryot's account, specifying his tenure, the amount of revenue payable by him, the quantity of land in or out of cultivation, and the amount of revenue realized or in arrear.

Hast-o-búdi, H. (هست و بودي) Designation of land which has been assessed on the basis of a comparative valuation of its produce.

Hast-o-búd-jamá, H. (هست و بود جمع) An account shewing the total amount of revenue under all heads of assessment to which any estate is liable.

Hastná-búd, H. (هست نا بود) A remission of revenue granted to Zamindars for the portion of land failing in produce (what is not as it was).

HASUGE, Karn. (ಹಸುಗೆ) Dividing, sharing, as corn, &c.

HÁT, Ben. Mar. (হাত, हात) HÁTH, or HATH, or HUTH, H. (هاته, هته) The hand, a cubit measured from the elbow to the tip of the middle finger, 18 inches; or, according to some statements, 19½: for timber, in Puraniya it was 22. (In Mar. it occurs also with the short vowel *Hat*, *Hut*.

Hátberí, Mar. (हातबेडी) Handcuff, manacle.

Hátchenchar, Ben. (হাতচেংচড়) A man who has money in hand but will not pay his debts.

Háth-chitthi, H. (هاته چتّهي, Mar. हातचिट्ठी) A letter or note written or avouched (by the hand of): a letter from a person of rank or station, either in his own hand, or signed by him, not bearing his seal only: a printed form given to the head of a village in the opium districts by the deputy collector, specifying the persons who engage to grow the poppy, and the conditions of the agreement.

Háter, Mar. (हातेर) Gratuitous labour which the Ryots of a village are bound to render in the fields to the Pátíl, revenue farmer, or other public officer.

Hatheli, H. (هتهيلي) The palm of the hand.

Hathiyár, H. (هتهيار, from هته) *Hatiyár*, Ben. (হতিযার) A tool, an implement, arms, apparatus.

Háthjorná, H. (هاته جوڙنا) *Hátjorá*, Ben. (হাতযোড়া) Joining the hands together, an attitude of supplication or humility; hence also, supplication, entreaty, reverence.

Hát-jáminí, Mar. (हातजामिनी) Security taken by the hand, an engagement taken, at first implying general responsibility, which becomes void upon the completion of more regular formalities.

Hát-karút, Ben. (হাতকরাত) A handsaw.

Hát-káṛí, Ben. (হাতকাড়ী) *Hathkaṛí*, Hindi (हथकड़ी) A handcuff.

Háthkáṭhi, Ben. (হাতকাঠি) A stick a cubit long, for measuring with.

Hatkhávaṇí, Mar. (हातखावणी) A small vegetable scraper, one that may be held in the hand.

Háth-karadu, H., Karn. (?) A rough daily account of receipts and disbursements, an off-hand account.

Hath-pher, H. (هتهہ پهير) Changing money by sleight of hand, changing good money for bad.

Háto, Guz. (હાતો) The hand given to one with whom a bargain is being made under a cloth, so that the terms may be settled by the fingers of the parties unperceived by others.

Hathoṛá, H. (هتهوڑا) A sledge hammer: *Hathoṛí*, H. (هتوڑي) A small hammer.

Hátargáṛá, Mar. (हातरगाडा) A small sugar-mill, one that may be worked by hand.

Hátrumál, Mar. (हातरुमाल, lit., a handkerchief) A small bag or budget of papers, accounts, &c.

Hát-usṇá, Mar. (हातउसणा) Lent without any acknowledgment (money), lent on hand, and for prompt payment.

HÁṬ, or HÁṬH, corruptly HAUT, H. &c. (هاٹ, هاٹهہ, or हाट, हाठ, S. HAṬṬA, हट्ट) A market, a moveable market, one held only on certain days in a week, a fair.

Háṭario, Guz. (હાટરીઓ) A banker, a shopkeeper.

Háṭ- or *Haṭṭa-chor*, Ben. (হাট-, হট্টচোর) A thief who steals in markets or fairs.

Háṭ-ká-chuṭkí, Hindi (हाटकाचुटकी) A small portion of each article brought to market taken by the renter of a village where the market is held, or of the market itself: an item in the village accounts to shew the value of what has been taken in the year.

Haṭ-tál, Hindi (हटताल) Shutting up or closing all the shops of a market as a passive resistance to exaction.

Haṭṭí, Hindi (हट्टी) A petty market or fair.

Háṭú, Hindi (हाटू) A market-man.

Haṭwá, H. (هٹوا, हटवा) A man employed as a weighman and measurer at markets.

HÁṬA, H. (حاطہ) An inclosure, a court-yard, a compound, (corruption of the Arabic *Iháṭa*, احاطہ, an inclosure).

HÁTHÍCHAK, H. (هاتهي چک) Name of a grass which grows about a foot high, and is used as fodder: a vernacular representation of the English word artichoke.

HAṬHILE, HUTHEELE, H. (هٹهيلي) A reputed saint, one of five held in veneration by the lower orders in the north-west provinces: he is buried at Barech.

HATTÁ, HUTTA, H. (هتّا) A large wooden shovel or spoon used for throwing water into fields from aqueducts.

HAṬṬÁLU, Tel. (హట్టాలు) A slave by birth.

HATTI, Karn. (ಹತ್ತಿ) Cotton in an undressed state.

Hattí-haṇe, Karn. (ಹತ್ತಿಅರಣೆ) A cotton mill for clearing it from the seeds,

Káda-hatti, Karn. (ಕಾಡಹತ್ತಿ) Wild cotton.

Karehatti, Karn. (ಕರೆಹತ್ತಿ) Black cotton plant producing very fine white cotton.

Hatti-vari, Karn. (ಹತ್ತಿವರಿ) A tax on cotton formerly levied in kind, since commuted for a money tax.

Hatti-sunka, Karn. (ಹತ್ತಿಸುಂಕ) A tax on cotton growers levied when the produce is sold.

ḤATTÍ, ḤUTTEE, Mar. (हत्ती, S. हस्ती) ḤÁTHI, H. (هاتهي) An elephant.

Ḥáthí-khána, H. (هاتهي خانہ) An elephant stable.

Ḥáthíhangám, H. (هاتهي حنگام) Remission for losses from depredations by wild elephants: (from *Ḥáthi*, an elephant). (Karnata).

Hattí-mahal, Mar. (हत्तीमहल) An elephant stall or stable, a place where he is kept.

HAṬṬÍ, HUTTEE, Karn. (ಹಟ್ಟಿ) A fold for kine, a cowpen, the residence of herdsmen, a temporary station of shepherds or graziers: it is also applied to a village or cluster of huts among the Bhils of Kandesh.

HATYÁ, S. &c. (हत्या) Killing, murder: personal injury or violence.

ḤAUDA, or ḤAUDAJ, H. (A. هودہ, هودج) A litter carried by a camel or elephant, in which females are conveyed. The former word *Hauda*, commonly written *Howdah*, is, in Hindustan, most usually applied to a kind of chair or open seat on an elephant.

HAULÁN-HAUL, A. (حولان حول) Property of which the proprietor has been in possession for a year, and which then becomes liable to the payment of *zihát*: (from حول, or حال, lasted a year). In some parts of the Dakhin, payment of revenue by the Ryots by an order on the village grain-seller who has purchased their crops in advance, subject to the share of assessment due upon them.

HAULI, H. (هولي) A liquor-shop.

HAWÁLA, corruptly, HOWALLA, H. &c. (حوالہ, हवाला) Charge,

care, custody, trust; consignment of any property, duty, or liability, to a trustworthy person; charge to pay on account of transfer of a debt or liability; security, or goods lodged for security: assignment for payments. A description of tenure in Eastern Bengal, an intermediate holding of a part of an estate, or of a farm under a Zamindar or Talukdar, to whom a stipulated portion of the rents collected from the Ryots is paid. A farm. It is said also to be applicable to a portion of an estate purchased, and therefore transferable and hereditary, the government dues being payable through the landlord; but in case of a dispute with the latter the purchaser of the farm may make his payments through another Talukdar.—Taylor's Dacca, 155. Minor divisions of these holdings are known by the name of *Ním-hawálas*, half farms. In the Maraṭha country, an order or draft for money drawn by a Ryot on the banker or grain-dealer to whom he has sold his crop, or entrusted it for sale.

Hawáladár, or *Hawáldár*, corrupted to *Havildár*, H. &c. (حوالهدار, حوالدار, हवालदार) One holding any office or trust. In the east of Bengal, a sub-renter, the occupant of a Hawála: a steward or agent for the management of a village: a native officer of the Indian army, subordinate to the Subahdar. Amongst the Maraṭhas the term was variously applied, but in all it conveyed the notion of trust, deputation, or delegated authority; as, the chief of a company of guards, guides, or messengers; a principal officer in a fort under the commandant, whose duty it was to appoint the guards, patrols, &c.: sometimes, also, the commandant himself: a subordinate revenue officer, a kind of deputy of the Mamlatdár, who was charged with the collection and remittance of the revenue of the district, and empowered to administer justice in petty complaints: an assistant of the Pátíl, or head of the village, in the collection of the revenue, and in police matters. In the Dakhin, and also at one time apparently in Hindustan, an officer appointed by the government, or the farmer of the revenue, to prevent any abstraction of the crop, or its removal from the public threshing-floor, until the revenue was paid.

Hawáldárí, corruptly, *Hawildarry*, H. (حوالداري) The office or tenure of a Hawáldár; also applied to a charge made to the villages for the expense of subordinate revenue officers sent to watch or to attach the crops.

Hawalát, or, more accurately, *Haülát*, corruptly, *Howlát*, the vernacular form of *Hawála*, Ben. (হওলাৎ) A thing given in trust, a loan for a short time, money advanced or deposited in another's hands. In treasury accounts, inefficient balances, or debts, or dependencies, unaudited advances.

Hawálat, H. (A. حوالة) Trust, charge, transfer, change. In law, the transfer of a debt from the original debtor to one who becomes responsible for it to the creditor.

Háwalhát, Hindi (हावलहाट, probable vernacular error for *Hawálat*) Balance of the village cash account in the Paṭwári's hands (Puraniya).

HAWÁLI, H. (A. حوالي) Environs, parts adjacent, round about.

Hawálishahar, H. (حوالي شهر) The suburbs or environs of a city.

Hawíli, or *Havíli*, or *Hávali*, corruptly, *Havelli*, or *Hawalie*, H. (A. حويلي, from the same root as *Hawáli*, حال, or حول, whence *Hawál*, a circle, a circuit) *Hávíli*, corruptly, *Havelie*, Tel. (హవేలి) A house, a habitation. The tract of country adjacent to a capital town, and originally annexed to it for the supply of the public establishments: it afterwards came to signify, in the Madras provinces, government lands, lands held *khás*, or under direct government management. In Bengal the term was applied to the reverse, or lands held by a Zamindár for his own benefit.

Hawíli-grámamulu, Tel. (plur. హవేలిగ్రామములు) Villages formerly retained under the management of the officers of the Nawab of the Carnatic.

HÁYAGAḌA, Karn. (ಹಾಯಗಡ) A ford, a place where a river may be forded.

HAYOBANS, HYOBUNS, H. (S. هيوبنس) A tribe of Rájputs in the province of Benares, once a dominant race on the banks of the *Narmadá*, where *Maheṣwarí* was founded by *Sahasrárjuna*, a Raja who makes a great figure in Hindu legendary tradition. The proper name of the tribe is *Haihaya*, S. (हैहयः).

HAẒÁNAT, incorrectly, HIZÁNAT, A. (حضانة) The care and bringing up of infant children according to the provisions of Mohammadan law.

ḤAZÁRI, H. (P. from هزار, a thousand) A commander of a thousand, either actually or nominally; in which latter case it was an honorary military title at the Court of the Mogul, borne by civil as well as military functionaries.

Hazárián, H. (plur. of هزاري) Regiments of one thousand men each employed in the northern Circars.

Házir, H. (A. حاضر) In the Hindu dialects *j* as usual is substituted for *z*, as, Hájir, Ben. (হাজির) Hájír, Mar. (हाजीर) the *i* is also sometimes changed to *a*, as, Hájaru, Tel. (హాజరు) Present, forthcoming, in attendance, ready. The actual state of any thing, an account shewing the assets of an estate, or tract of country.

Ghair-házir H. (A. غيرحاضر) Absent, not present.

Házir-o-názir, H. (حاضر و ناضر) Present and seeing.

Házirát, H. (A. حاضرات) lit., Presences; but applied in Hindustan to a magical rite by which absent or invisible things or persons are supposed to be made visible to a young boy or girl, who are directed to look in the flame of a lamp, in a looking-glass, in a dish of water, or on certain magic squares, &c.

Házir-báshi, H. (P. باشي, being) Regular or constant attendance.

Hájír-begárí, Mar. (हाज़ीर बेगारी) A pressed porter, but one who carries his load only to the first village on the road, where he is relieved; in opposition to one pressed for the whole of any given distance.

Háziri, corruptly, *Házri*, vernacularly, *Hájarí* or *Hájiri*, H. (حاضري, हाजरी) Presence: a muster-roll: an individual resident or present in a village. Breakfast: an offering of a breakfast, or of food, to certain Mohammadan saints, which, after being so consecrated, is distributed among their votaries or the poor.

Hájirí-bahi, Ben. (হাজিরীবহি) A muster-roll, a list of persons who should be in attendance.

Hájirí-nau-abád, Hindi (P. نو, new, and اباد, cultivation) A resident cultivator who takes up new land for the first year (Puraniya).

Hájirí-sábek, Hindi (हजिरीशाबेक, from the A. سابق, past) A resident cultivator who has held lands more than one year.

Hájír-nís, Mar. (हाजीरनीस) The muster master of the troops and establishments, one who keeps a register or roll of the troops and militia in attendance, and furnishes abstracts to the superior authorities. In Ben. *Hájirína-nís* (হাজিরানবীস) means any one who keeps a list of any persons in attendance engaged on any duty.

Házir-zámin, H. (حاضرضامن) *Hájír-jámín*, Mar. (हाजीर-जामीन्) *Hájir-jámin*, Ben. (হাজিরজামিন) A surety for the personal appearance of any one when required to attend.

Házir-zámini, or *Hájir-jámini*, H. &c. (حاضرضامن) Security, whether personal or pecuniary, for the appearance of a person charged with any debt or offence.

Hájir-jámin-dár, Karn. (ಹಾಜಿರಜಾಮಿನದಾರ) A surety or bail for a personal appearance.

Hazrat, H. (A. حضرت) Presence, dignity. A title given to a prince or person of rank, equivalent to Your Majesty, Your Highness, Your Excellency.

Húzur, *Hoozoor*, less correctly, *Hazúr*, *Huzoor*, H. &c. (A. حضور) *Hujúr*, Mar. (हुज़ूर) *Hujáru*, Tel. (హుజూరు) The presence, the royal presence, the presence of a superior authority, as of a judge or collector of revenue, and, by metonymy, the person of the prince or functionary; also the place where he presides, the hall of audience, the court; also abstractly, the state, the government.

Huzar, H. (A. plur of حضر) Attendants on the court.

Hujrá, Mar. (हुजरा) An attendant at court, a confidential servant, sometimes appointed to villages as a check upon the Pátíl.

Hujarát, Mar. (हुजरात) Troops under the immediate orders of the state, royal guards, peons attached to the station of the chief functionaries.

Hujaryá, Mar. (हुजऱ्या) A personal attendant, an attendant on court.

Huzúr-bálá, H. (P. بالا, above) The high or exalted presence, title of superior authority.

Huzúri, H. (حضوري) Relating to the chief authority, to the local or general government, as an attendant on the court, &c. Under the Mohammadan government the term was sometimes applied to such lands as paid revenue to the Diwan, or financial representative of the government, in opposition to the Nizámat lands, which paid revenue to the Názim, or viceroy. Under the British authority it applies to lands or cultivators paying revenue direct to the chief collector, not through a native collector or landholder.

Huzúri-mál-guzár, H. (from P. مال گزار, a payer of revenue) A landholder or tenant paying revenue direct to government.

Huzúri-nálish, H. (P. نالش) A complaint preferred direct to the supreme authority.

Huzúri-tâluk, H. (تعلق, a dependence, an estate) A certain district called a *Tâluk*, paying revenue direct to government, usually known as an independent *Tâluk*, that which is not held of any other proprietor or revenue payer.

Huzúr-mahál, H. (from محال) Estates paying revenue direct to government.

Hujúr-mámlá, Mar. (हुज़ूर मामला, from the A. معاملة) The

authority and jurisdiction of the state reserved over an estate or district, of which the revenues have been given in grant.

Huzúr-navís, H. (from P. نويس, a writer) A secretary of state, one who registers all royal or viceregal grants and orders.

Hujúr-págá, Mar. (हुजूरपागा) A body of horse under the immediate keeping and command of the state, the household troops.

Hujúr-sanadí, Mar. (हुजूर सनदी) Held under a grant or diploma from the government, lands &c.

Huzúr-tahsíl, H. (A. تحصيل, collection of revenue) Collection of revenue by the chief fiscal officer of the government, without the intervention of a third party. In the early days of British authority the term was applied to land paying revenue to the chief authority in a province, as distinguished from those paying it to the head of a Zilla, or subdivision of a province or collectorate, thence termed *Tahsíl-zilâ*.

Huzúr-tahsíl-i-daftar, H. (دفتر, a register) An office in Calcutta before the permanent settlement, in which revenues paid direct to government were received.

Hujúr-wár-śásan, Mar. (from S. शासन, an order) A pension or annuity formerly paid direct from the Peshwa's treasury.

Huzúr-zilâ, H. (A. ضلع) The districts which paid their revenues direct to the general treasury at Murshedabad in the early period of the British authority in Bengal.

HAZL, H. (A. هزل) lit., Jesting, applied in Mohammadan law to a contract publicly executed, as if of full force and validity, but which the parties are secretly engaged shall be of no effect: if afterwards one of them pretend that the transaction was *boná fide*, the assertion of the other to the contrary annuls the engagement.

HEBBÁRA, or HEBBÁRUVA, Karn. (ಹೆಬ್ಬಾರ, ಹೆಬ್ಬಾರುವ) A chief, a superior, the head man of the village.

Hebbáruvaru, Karn. (ಹೆಬ್ಬಾರುವರು) A class of Bráhmans in Mysore.

HECHCHU, Tel. Karn. (హెచ్చు) Increase, excess, superiority, increase of rent or taxes.

Hechchike, Karn. (ಹೆಚ್ಚಿಕೆ) Increase, excess, any thing increased.

Hechkatla, Karn. (ಹೆಚ್ಕಟ್ಲೆ) Extraordinary taxes.

HEGALAṆE, Karn. (ಹೆಗಲಣೆ) A coparcener.

HEGGAḌE, Karn. (ಹೆಗ್ಗಡೆ) The head man of a town or village, but especialy applied to one of the Jain religion. It is also used by certain castes as an affix to proper names, to intimate respectability, corresponding with Sáhib, or Mían, in Hindustan.

Kuruba-heggade, Karn. (ಕುರುಬಹೆಗ್ಗಡೆ) A head or chief among shepherds.

HEJÍB, Mar. (?) A deputy or agent appointed by the hereditary officers of the Maraṭha government to act for them.

HEL, or HELA, Mar., Guz. (हेल) The business of carrying loads; also the burthen, or the cost of conveyance.

Helkarí, Mar. (हेलकरी) A porter, a carrier of loads.

Helpáṭí, Mar. (हेलपाटी) A porter, a hired labourer (from carrying a basket, *páṭí*, on his head.)

HELA, H. (هيلا) A man of a low caste, an inferior division of the Bhangis, engaged in the lowest menial offices. The *Helas* pride themselves on eating the leavings of Hindus only.

HELE, H. (هيلي) A subdivision of the Ját tribe.

HELLAVÁR, Karn. (ಹೆಲ್ಲವಾರ) Lame beggars.

HEMANTA, S., but used in most dialects, (हेमन्तः) The cold season, the months of Agraháyana and Pausha—November-December.

Hemalamba, S. &c. (हेमलंब) The thirty-first year of the cycle; also Karn. *Hémalambi*.

HEṆḌA, Karn. (ಹೆಂಡ) Spirituous liquor, *táṛí*, the fermented sap of different kinds of the palm.

HENGÁ, H. (هينگا) A harrow.

HENNUBÁḶU, Karn. (ಹೆಣ್ಣುಬಾಳು, from *Hennu*, a woman) A woman's property or estate.

HEṚ, or HEḌ, Mar. (हेड) A drove of cattle, a flock of sheep, a troop of horses, and the like, as taken about for sale.

Heryá, Hedyá, (हेड्या) A drover or cattle-dealer.

HER, Mar. (हेर) A spy or scout.

HERÍ, HEREE, H. (هيري) A tribe of Mohammadan Rájputs, chiefly found in Jaspur, a Pargana of Moradabad.

HEṬÁ, Uriya (ହେଟା) Land granted for service.

HEṬKARÍ, Mar. (हेटकरी, from हेट, *heṭ*, signifying down, as applied to country, down the coast, to the south) A native of the country southwards from the *Sávitri* river: a native of the southern Konkan serving in the Maraṭha infantry.

HETU, vernacularly, HET, S. &c. (हेतुः) Cause, motive, reason, origin.

HEW, more correctly HIṆW, Mar. (हेव, हिंव, S. हेम) Cold, also crops that have suffered from frost.

Hewáḷá, more correctly, *Hiṇwáḷa*, Mar. (हेवाळा, हिंवाळा, from S. हिम, cold, and काल, time) The cold season.

Hewat-jamín, Mar. (?) Land ploughed up during the cold season, and left to lie fallow during the rains; also applied in the hill country to land brought into cultivation after having been left uncultivated for some years.

Hiba, or Ḥibat, incorrectly, Ḥibba, H. (A. هبة) A gift. In law, a perfect gift, one accompanied by delivery and acceptance. A gift on a death-bed is considered a bequest.

Ḥiba-bíl-âwaẓ, H. (هبه بالعوض, from عوض, return, exchange) A mutual gift; one for which a return or consideration is exchanged, as when a man gives his property to his wife in exchange for her claim of dower: it is considered analogous to a sale, and the transaction is binding before actual possession of the stipulated return.

Ḥiba-bá-sharṭ-ul-ïwaẓ, H. (from A. شرط, an agreement) A gift with stipulation for a return. In law, a gift on promise or engagement to make a requital, when the transaction is not complete until the reciprocal condition is fulfilled.

Ḥibadár, H. (P. دار, who has) The receiver of a gift, the donee.

Ḥibamushâá, A. (from مشاع, undistributed) Gift of undefined or undivided property, which is not valid until the property has been separated, and transferred to the donee.

Ḥibánáma, H. (هبانامه) A deed of gift.

Hidád, A. (حداد) Mourning. In law, the mourning of a widow for her husband, total abstinence from the use of ornaments, and of perfumes or unguents, except medicinally.

Hifẓ, Hifáẓat, H. (A. حفظ, حفاظت) Preserving, protecting, guarding, taking care of.

Ḥijra, H. (A. هجرة) lit. Departure from one's country, separation of friends or lovers; whence it gives name to the departure or flight of Mohammad from Mecca to Medina, which, in the Khalifat of Omar, was constituted the commencement of the Mohammadan era: this event took place on the night of Thursday the 15th of July, A. D. 622. The usual era therefore reckons from the dawn of the 16th of July. The Mohammadan year is strictly lunar, consisting of twelve months, each of which should count from the actual visibility of the new moon; but chronologically the months are completed at 30 and 29 days alternately, making the year consist of 354 days; but eleven times in a cycle of thirty years one day is added to the year, which makes the average length of the Mohammedan lunar year $354\frac{11}{30}$ days, or 354d. 8hrs. 48min., and the average length of the months 29d. 12hrs. 44min. The intercalary years of the cycle are the 2d, 5th, 8th, 10th, 13th, 16th, 19th, 21st, 24th, 27th, and 29th. To ascertain if any given year be an intercalary year, it is to be divided by 30, when one of the specified numbers will be the remainder; thus, A. H. 1137 divided by 30=37, leaving 27, and it will be therefore the 27th year of the cycle. The rule given by Major Jervis, from Professor Carlyle, for finding the corresponding years of the Hijra and the Christian era, is only an approximation: "Multiply the centuries of the year by 3, and add to the product for the years over the century as many times as it may be divided by 33, deduct the total from the whole number, and add to the remainder 621;" thus, Required the year of our Lord corresponding to the year H. 1396; then 13 × 3=39, to which add 2, the quotient of 96 divided by 33, making 41; then 1396 − 41=1355 + 621=A. D. 1976." That this is not correct in cases where the number in excess of the centuries, is a trifle less than 33, or a trifle more than any of its multiples is evident from a comparison with the standard tables: for instance, the year 1132 should be, according to this rule, A. D. 1720, but it begins 14th November 1719 according to the tables: so 1198 should be 1784, but in the table it begins 26th November 1783. The result, however, is near enough for general purposes, requiring correction only as to the period at which the year commences. Another rule for the same is—Multiply the Hijra year by 970203, cut off six decimals, add 622.54, and the sum will be the year of the Christian era, and decimal of the day following, in old style; thus, A. H. 1215 × 970203= 1178.796645, leaving 1178 + 622.54=1800.54. The Hijra year commences on the 25th May; so that this again is only an approximation. A more simple form, and one which also shews the day on or about which the concurrence of the Mohammadan and Christian year commences, is the following: Multiply the Hijra year by 2.977, the difference between 100 solar and as many lunar Mohammadan years; divide the product by 100, and deduct the quotient from the Hijra year; add to the result 621.569 (the decimal being the equivalent of the 15th July, *plus* 12 days for the change of the Kalendar); and the quotient will be the Christian year from the date at which the Mohammadan year begins; thus, Hij. 1269 × 2.977=37778, which divided by 100=37.778 and 1269 − 37.778=1231.222 + 621.569=1852.791, or to 9 months and 15 days, *i. e.* the 15th of October, which is the commencement of the Hij. year 1269. The reverse formula for finding the corresponding Hijra year to a given Christian year is thus laid down: Subtract 622 from the current year; multiply the result by 1.0307; cut off four decimals, and add .46; the sum will be the year, which, when it has a surplus decimal, requires the addition of 1: thus, $1852 - 622 = 1230$; $1230 \times 1.0307 = 1267.7610 + .46 = 1268.22$; add therefore 1, and we have the equivalent Hijra year 1269. Comparative tables of the Christian and Mohammadan years are to be found in "L'Art de verifier les dates," "Playfair's Chronology," "Prinsep's Useful Tables," Calcutta, and "M'Cudden's Oriental Eras," Bombay, 1846; but they are not always quite correct. The months of the Mohammadan year, and the number of days in each, are the following:—

1.	*Muharram*	days 30,
2.	*Ṣafar*	„ 29,
3.	*Rabíâ-ul-awal*	„ 30,
4.	*Rabíâ-us-ṣání*	„ 29,
5.	*Jumádi-ul-awal*	„ 30,
6.	*Jumádi-us-ṣání*	„ 29,
7.	*Rajab*	„ 30,
8.	*Shâbán*	„ 29,
9.	*Ramazán*	„ 30,
10.	*Shawál*	„ 29,
11.	*Ẓilkâda*, or *Ẓulkâda*	„ 30,
12.	*Ẓilhijja*, or *Ẓulhijja*	„ 29,

except in the intercalary years, when this last month has also 30 days. The Mohammadans in India commonly employ the Persian names of the days of the week, which are, for the first five only, the numerals prefixed to the word *Shamba*, "a day;" or sometimes the Arabic names, which are similarly composed with *Yaum*, "a day," and the numerals as far as five: the sixth and seventh have special denominations; as,

Sunday	*Ek-shamba*	*Yaum-ul-ahad*,
Monday	*Do-shamba*	— *ul-iṣnain*,
Tuesday	*Seh-shamba*	— *us-ṣaláṣa*,
Wednesday	*Chahár-shamba*	— *ul-arbâá*,
Thursday	*Panj-shamba*, or *Jumâ-rát*	— *ul-hhamis*,
Friday	*Jumâ*, (the day of assembly or prayer)	— *ul-jumâ*,
Saturday	*Shamba*, or *Hafta*, (the 7th)	— *us-sabât*, (the Sabbath).

Ḥijri, H. (هجري) Relating to the Ḥijra, or Mohammadan era.

HIJṚÁ, Mar. (हिजडा) A hermaphrodite, a person either a eunuch, or of equivocal malformation, considered as neither male nor female, but usually wearing the garb of a woman; suffered in some Maraṭha villages to claim grants of food and small coin, and exacting the claim by offensive language and menaces. The class is held in great disgust by the Ryots who contribute to their support to escape from their importunity and abuse. It is said to be a popular notion that the demands of the *Hijṛás* are countenanced by the government, on account of its levying an impost upon them; a notion of course wholly erroneous, if it have any currency.

HIKRÍ, Hindi (हिकरी) Cultivated reeds, grown on low marshy grounds.

HILÁ, Hindi (हिला) Mud, quagmire, moist ground trodden soft by cattle.

HÍLAH, H. &c. (حيله) HILLÁ, Mar. (हिल्ला) Fraud, deceit, pretence, a fraudulent or evasive pretext.

Hilláharkat, Mar. (हिल्लाहरकत) *Hillaharkattu*, Karn. (ಹಿಲ್ಲಹರಕತ್ತು) A general term for tricks and devices, as, for evading payment of a debt, or performance of a service rightfully exacted.

HIMÁLAYA, S. (हिमालयः) The range of snowy mountains bounding Hindustan to the north and north-west: (from *Hima*, snow, and *álaya*, abode).

Himad-dhán, Ben. (हिमद्धान) Rice ripening in the cold season (Nov.-Dec.).

HIMÁIAT, corruptly, HEMAYET, H. (A. حمايت) Protection, guardianship.

HÍNA, S. (हीन) in the dialects commonly *Hín*, H. (هين) Devoid of, deficient, abandoned.

Hína-játi, or *Hin-játi*, S., Ben. (from जाति, caste) Of a low caste, or rather of no caste.

Hína-paksha, S. (from पक्ष, a party) An orphan, a destitute person, one without friends or relations.

Hína-patra, S. (पत्र, a leaf) A deed of default: the title of the decision in a suit in which a nonsuit is decreed.

Hín-ráṣi, S. H. (from राशि, a heap) Seconds or soiled corn, from the lowest part of the heap.

Hína-vádi, S. *Hín-bádi*, Ben. (from वादिन्, who speaks) A person who, in a court of law, abandons his original ground of action, and asserts something different: a witness who prevaricates and contradicts himself, and whose testimony is therefore inadmissible.

Hinkas, Mar. (हिणकस) Alloyed or debased gold or silver; made of debased metal, a trinket, &c.

Hinkaul, Mar. (?) An engagement for letting out land at a reduction on the current or village rates.

HINGÁRU, Karn. (ಹಿಂಗಾರು) Latter, as applied to rain or to crops.

Hingáru-male, Karn. (ಹಿಂಗಾರುಮಳೆ) Latter rain.

Hingáru-pairu, Karn. (ಹಿಂಗಾರುಪೈರು) The latter crop.

HINJÁRA, Karn. (ಹಿಂಜಾರ) A cotton beater or dresser.

HINKKALU, Karn. (ಹಿಂಕ್ಕಲು) A small outlet for the passage of water from one garden-bed to another.

HINSÁ, S. (हिंसा) Injury, especially personal, done to any man or animal, violence, killing.

HIŎNTE, Hindi (हिओनते) A rate in a lease for crops of rice sown on low land in February, March, and April, when sown for a single crop in the year (Puraniya).

HIPPALI, Karn. (ಹಿಪ್ಪಲಿ) Long pepper.

HIRA, Uriya (ହିର) Ridge or embankment round a field.

HÍRÁNÁ, HEERANA, H. (هيرانا) Manuring a field by penning a herd of cattle or flock of sheep in it for several hours.

HIRAN-KHURI, HIRUN-KHOOREE, H. (هرن كهري) lit., Antelopes' hoof, name of a creeping herb which grows in the rainy season.

Hiraṇyagarbham, Mal. (ഹിരണ്യഗൎഭം) The ceremony of being born of, or passing through, a gold cow, performed by the Raja of Travancore: (from S. हिरण्य, gold, and गर्भ, embryo).

HIRCHAL, Mar. (?) Dry land bordering on irrigated land.

HIREKOṬṬIGE-KANDÁYAM, Karn. (ಹಿರೇಕೊಟ್ಟಿಗೆಕಂದಾಯಂ) A tax on cowhouses built outside the cottages of the cultivators.

HIRWÁ, Mar. (हिरवा) Green, raw, unripe, immature; used much as *kachcha* in Hindustani.

Hirweṉ, Mar. (हिरवें) Green herbage, tender fodder.

HIRZ, A. (حرز) Custody, safe keeping of goods or valuables: it is of two kinds in law.

Hirz-bil-háfiẕ, A. (حرز بالحافظ) Personal charge or keeping of any thing.

Hirz-bil-maḳám, A. (حرز بالمقام) Custody in place, as in a house, a shop, a warehouse: furtive abduction of any article so kept or deposed is punishable with the mutilation of a hand.

HISÁB, corruptly, HISSAUB and HISSAWB, H. (حساب) changed vernacularly to HIṢEB, Mar. (हिशेब) HISSEBU, Tel. (హిస్సెబు) An account, a reckoning: arithmetic, computation.

Hisáb-i-kharch, corruptly, *Hissawb-horcha*, H. (حساب خرچ) Account of disbursements, a particular revenue account, also termed *Ákhiri-hisáb-kharch*, q. v.

Hisáb-navís, H. (from P. نويس, who writes) An accountant.

HIṢṢA, H. (A. حصّه) HISÁ, Mar. (हिसा) A share, a part, a lot, a portion; a share of revenue or rent.

Hiṣṣadár, H. (from P. دار, who has) *Hisedár*, Mar. (हिसेदार) A shareholder, a sharer, a coparcener, one who pays his share of the revenue either to a Zamindar or the state.

Hiṣṣadárí, H. (from P. داري, having) Copartnership; applied especially to a village in which a number of sharers have a joint proprietary right in the land.

Hiṣṣa-háhimi, H. (from A. حاكم, a ruler) The share of the produce of the land or revenue to which the king or the government is entitled: a fourth or a sixth is the proportion agreeably to the institutes of the Hindus; a third was nominally taken by the Mohammadan governments, but the proportion was very variable; a third was the prevailing rate adopted by the British government, but in practice this is greatly modified, and the proportion is the subject of special determination, according to previous practice and the circumstances of the land.

Hiṣṣah-háli, H. (حصّه حالي) A ploughman's share or wages in kind, usually amounting, in the north-west provinces, to about one-eighth of the produce.

Hiṣṣait, H. (حصّيت) A shareholder.

Hiṣṣa-hashí, or *hushee*, H. (حصه كشي) Distribution and apportionment of shares agreeably to hereditary succession.

Hiṣṣa-i-málih, H. (A. مالك, a master) The share of the presumed owner or proprietor, his right to a part of the produce, or an allowance in lieu of it: see *Málikána*. The share of the government.

Hise-rásí, or *-sí*, Mar. (हिसेराशी, -सी) Making out a statement of the several shares or portions of a number of claimants.

Hiṣṣa-rasad, H. (حصّه رسد) A proportionate share or part.

Hiṣṣa-ráiti, H. (حصّه رعيتي) The proportion of the produce assigned to the Ryot.

Hissárat, Ben. (?) Portions of land formerly allowed to be held by the Zamindars of Dacca rent-free, on condition of personal service in the flotilla stationed on the Ganges to guard against the incursions of the people of Arakan.

Hiṣṣa-wárí, H. (حصّه واري) Applied to revenue settlements founded on proportionate division, either between the cultivator and the government, or according to the shares of joint owners.

Ḥíthá, H. (هيتها) A person appointed to take care of standing crops.

Hittalu, Karn. (హిత్తలు) A back yard.

Hittala-handáyum, Karn. (హిత్తలహందాయుం) A tax on back yards (in Mysore).

Hiṭṭú, Karn. (హిట్టు) Flour or meal of ground grain in general.

Hittubiṭṭi, Karn. (హిట్టుబిట్టి) Feeding government peons when passing through a town or village, and affording gratuitous services to the government in the conveyance of goods, &c.

Hiyál, A. (plur. of حيلة, fraud, deceit) Legal quirks or devices.

Hiyázat, A. (حيازت) lit., Accumulation. In law, joint acquisition by two or more persons of some article that has no owner.

Hóbaḷi, commonly, Hobli, Karn. (హోబళి) A tract of country or district comprising smaller subdivisions. In Malabar it is applied to a smaller tract or subdivision. In the Kanara province there were formerly but three *Hoblis*—*Mangalur*, *Barkur*, and *Bhágwadi.*

Hóbaḷi-shanabhog, Karn. The district accountant.

Hóbaḷi-dár, Karn. A chief of armed peons.

Hoge, Karn. (హొగె) Tobacco.

Hoge-maṇasu, Karn. (హొగెమణసు) A tax on Ryots, who formerly cultivated tobacco and chilis on corn lands, subject to division of the crop: also termed *Hoge-soppu.*

Hoge-soppina-pommu, Karn. (హొగెసొప్పిన-పొమ్ము) Tobacco contract or monopoly.

Hoge-toppu, Karn. (హొగెతొప్పు) The tobacco plant.

Hojat, Guz. (હોજત) An account settled annually between a farmer and his tenants.

Hola, Karn. (హొల) A field in general, one in which any grain is grown except rice.

Holabu, Karn. (హొలబు) A field or ground fit for cultivation: also, limit, boundary.

Holadabeḷe, Karn. (హొలదబెళె) A field of standing corn, a crop.

Holadasara, Karn. (హొలదసర) *Holagaddí vyájya*, Karn. (హొలగద్దివ్యాజ్య) Disputes about boundaries.

Holehola, Karn. (హొలెహొల) Dry land, land that cannot be easily watered by artificial means, and dependent upon rain for water, unfit therefore for rice lands.

Holár, Mar. (होलार) A man of a low or outcaste tribe, by profession a musician.

Hoḷe, Karn. (హొళె) A lake, a river.

Hoḷegekaṭṭu, Karn. (హొళెగెకట్టు) A dam, an embankment.

Holí, or Holiká, corruptly, Hooly, H. &c. (هولي, होली, होलिका) A popular festival of the Hindus, the proper season of which is the ten days preceding the full moon of Phálgun, but it is usually observed only for the last three or four days terminating with the full moon. The chief observances are sprinkling one another with red or yellow powder, addressing passers-by with coarse jokes, singing songs in praise of the juvenile Krishṇa, and lighting a bonfire, which is kept up to the close of the ceremony, when rude frolics are practised round the expiring embers. The *Holí* is chiefly observed in Hindustan, but it answers to the *Dola yátra*, or swinging festival of Bengal, and is at the same period particularly celebrated by the cowherd and shepherd castes of Orissa, one class of the palankin-bearers of Calcutta. In Maraṭhi the term means also the pile prepared for the bonfire.

Hoḷí-chí-poḷí, Mar. (होळीचीपोळी) The privilege amongst the inhabitants of a village of first placing a cake (*póli*) on the top of the pile which is kindled at the end of the *Holí* festival.

Hoḷí-che-hoḷkar, Mar. (plural होळीचेहोळकर) lit., The people that dance and sport at the *Holí*; applied also to a crowd of disorderly fellows assembled on any occasion.

Holiya, or Holeyanu, Karn. (హొలియ, హొలెయను) A Pariah, an outcaste. *Holeyaru*, corruptly, *Holleeroo* or *Holeyer*, (plural హొలెయరు) Pariahs, men of low tribes employed in the lowest offices, and considered as slaves. See below.

Holigéri, Karn. (హొలిగేరి) A street of the houses of Pariahs.

Holiya, *Holeyanu*, plural *Holeyaru*, Karn. (హొలియ, హొలెయను, plural హొలెయరు) A low man, an outcaste, commonly an agricultural labourer (from *Hola*, a field) and a slave, being saleable by the owner of the estate on which he is located, either with or without the land. The plural form, in place of the singular, is commonly employed by Europeans, who have made strange work with the name, and no little confusion with the description. The Holleeroo, Holayur, Holeyer, Hollieroo, is described as a predial slave, numerous in Kanara and Kurg: in the former he is said to be a subdivision of the Dher; in the latter, one of three principal classes of slaves called Holeyaroo, Yewaroo, and Paleroo. In both countries the Holeyaru are distinguished by various denominations prefixed, which are variously written, and the meaning of which is not explained, as Maury or Maree or Mare Holeyaroo; Byr H.; Murtha H.; Bulgi H.; Kembutta or Kimbutty H.; Badaya H.; Rookha H.: of these, the only peculiarities noted are, that the Kembatta, (?) H., is native in Kurg, the rest are natives of Karnáta. The Holeyaru generally are a more faithful class of slaves than others. Amongst the Mare H., the custom of succession through the female line to any property the man may have acquired prevails.

HOMA, S. (होमः) Burnt offering, oblations of clarified butter poured on fire; other articles may also be offered. The rite is of high antiquity, and forms part of all domestic religious observances, as marriages, adoptions, &c.

HONḌA, Karn. (ಹೊಂಡ) A public tank or pond in a village.

HOṆE, Karn. (ಹೊಣೆ) Bond, bail, surety.

Hoṇegár, Karn. (ಹೊಣೆಗಾರ) A surety, a bondsman.

HONNU, Karn. (ಹೊಂನು) Gold, money, a coin, half a pagoda.

HOR, HOL, Guz. (હોર, હોલ) A plough.

HOṚ, Hindi (होड) A wager, a bet, a bargain.

HORASAT-KÁL, Karn. (?) Lease of waste land.

HORASWASTÍ, Karn. (ಹೊರಸ್ವಸ್ತಿ) The private land held by temples in Mysore as their own property, in distinction to assignments of produce, or in money, from lands retained in the possession of the donors.

HORE, Karn. (ಹೊರೆ) A burthen, such as may be carried on the head; an allowance of grain to village servants; a load of grain: the quantity varies.

Horehullu, Karn. (ಹೊರೆಹುಲ್ಲು) A tax on cultivators who pay in kind, in lieu of straw formerly contributed to the government.

Hottehore, (ಹೊಟ್ಟೆಹೊರೆ) Living, livelihood.

HOSÁGAMA, Karn. (from ಹೊಸ, *hosa*, new) Land recently brought under cultivation.

Hosahaḷi-paṭṭa, Karn. (ಹೊಸಹಳಿಪಟ್ಟ) A fine or tax formerly imposed upon the village servants for not recovering a stray horse belonging to a head man or Paligar.

Hosahukam, Karn. (ಹೊಸಹುಕುಂ) A new regulation.

HOTÁ, or HOTRÍ. S. (होतृ, nom. होता) The priest who at sacrifices with fire invokes the deity worshipped, and pours the butter on the altar.

HOṬṬU, Karn. (ಹೊಟ್ಟು) Chaff, husk, bran.

Nellu-hoṭṭu, Karn. (ನೆಲ್ಲುಹೊಟ್ಟು) Chaff or husk of paddy.

Hoṭṭuhaṇa, Karn. (ಹೊಟ್ಟುಹಣ) A tax on the husk on the threshing-floor which is set apart for the cattle of the Ryots.

HUDA (?) H. (هدا) Statement of estates to be sold by auction.

HUDDÁ, Mar. (हुद्दा) HUDDÁ, or HUDDE, Karn. (ಹುದ್ದಾ, ಹುದ್ದೆ) HODÁ, Tel. (హోదా) A public post or office: (vernacular corruptions of A. *Áhdah*, q. v.).

Huddedár, Mar. (हुद्देदार) *Hodádáru*, Tel. (హోదాదారు) An officer, a functionary, one holding any office: see *Áhdahdar*.

HUDIGÁṚ, Karn. (ಹುದಿಗಾರ) The name of a low caste in Mysore, not much known.

HUDUVU, Karn. (ಹುದುವು) Partnership, any joint concern; property, estate.

HULAKYERI, Mar. (?) A kind of black soil in valleys, where it is less productive.

HULASWAR, Karn. (ಹುಲಸ್ವಾರ) A division of the Holeyar or Pariah tribe, often employed as peons or horsemen.

HÚLÍDDAHAṆA, Karn. (ಹೂಳಿದ್ದಹಣ, from *Húlu*, ಹುಳು, to bury) Hidden treasure.

HULI-HAṆṆU, Karn. (ಹುಳಿಹಂಣು) A tax on tamarinds gathered from the public trees (Mysore).

HULLU, Karn, (ಹುಲ್ಲು) Grass, straw, hay.

Oṇa-hullu, Karn. (ಒಣಹುಲ್ಲು) Dry grass, hay or straw.

Hullu-baṇṇi, Karn. (ಹುಲ್ಲುಬಂಣಿ) A tax on grass in the rice fields, levied from those who bring their flocks to graze in them.

Hullu-baṇṇi kuri-mányam, Karn. (ಕುರಿಮಾನ್ಯಂ) Annual tax on cowherds, and shepherds who graze their herds and flocks on government lands in Mysore.

Hullugávalu, Karn. (ಹುಲ್ಲುಗಾವಲು) An assessment on pasture lands.

Hullukelasa, Karn (ಹುಲ್ಲುಕೆಲಸ) Dealing in grass or straw: the business of treading out corn.

HULVATI-MARA, Karn. (ಹುಲವತಿಮರ) The Rottleria tinctoria, from the fruit of which a red dye is obtained.

HÚN, HOON, corruptly HOUN, H. (هون, perhaps from the Karn. *Honnu*) A gold coin, current in the south of India, a pagoda, usually about 50 grains in weight, but of different standard and value, according to the place where coined: the *Hún*, or star pagoda of the Company's currency, was intrinsically worth 7*s*. 5*d*. but was rated in the public accounts at 8*s*.

HUNBATTI, (?) Karn. Interest on money lent from the funds of temples.

HUṆḌÁ, Tel. (హుండా) Division of a province, a village, an estate (Ganjam).

HUṆḌÁ, Mar. (हुंडा) Money given at marriages by the father of the bride to the bridegroom, or by the relations of either of the contracting parties to those of the other; a practice considered disreputable, being looked on as a purchase and sale of either; also a monopoly: see the next.

HUṆḌAWÁ, less correctly **HUṆḌWÁ**, Mar. (हुंडवा) A monopoly, an exclusive privilege of selling: farming for a fixed sum any fluctuating value, as the revenue: a contract, an engagement.

Hunḍá-bhárá, Mar. (हुंडाभाडा) Contract for the transportation of goods, or the like, in which all duties and charges are included.

Hunḍekarí, Mar. (हुंडेकरी) One who contracts for a fixed sum to convey goods to a destined place clear of all charges and customs: a bridegroom who stipulates for money with his wife.

HUṆḌH, H. (هنده) Mutual assistance in tillage.

HUṆḌÍ, **HOONDEE**, corruptly, **HOONDY**, H. (هندي, Ben. হুণ্ডী, Mar. हुंडी, Tel. హుండి) A bill of exchange.

Hunḍián, H. (هنديان) Exchange, rate or commission paid for a bill of exchange, the premium or discount on a bill.

Hunḍáwan, H., Mar. (هنداون, हुंडावण) Price paid for a bill of exchange, rate of exchange, premium or discount on remittance by bill.

Hunḍi-chiṭṭhí, Mar. (हुंडीचिट्ठी) *Hunḍichiṭu*, Karn. (ಹುಂಡಿಚೀಟು) A bill of exchange.

Hunḍi-darsani, H. (هندي درسني) A bill payable at sight.

Hunḍi-mâádí, H. (هندي معادي) A bill payable after a stipulated interval.

Hunḍi-wál, H. (هندي وال) *Hunḍi-wálá*, Ben. (হুণ্ডীবালা) An exchange or bill-broker.

HUNDIGE-SUNKA, Karn. (ಹುಂಡಿಗೆಸುಂಕ) A tax paid by merchants on piece goods brought from the weavers, as an equivalent for their being stamped.

HUPPUNA-KULGA-MÁNYAM, (?) Karn. (ಹುಪ್ಪುನಕುಲಗಮಾನ್ಯಂ) Tax on people of the saltmakers' caste who use buffaloes.

HURLA, (?) Sindhi. A small water-wheel.

HÚRSÚL, (?) Mar. The rate of assessment paid by strangers resident in a village.

HURUḶI, Karn. (ಹುರುಳಿ) Horse gram (Glycine tomentosa).

Huruli-vari, Karn. (ಹುರುಳಿವರಿ) A tax on gram in Mysore, formerly levied in kind, but since commuted for a money tax.

HÚRYÁ, H. (هوريا) A small clan of Somabansi Rájputs in some parts of the province of Benares.

HUTA, S. (हुत) Offered, offered with fire, presented as an oblation.

Hutáṣana, S. (हुताशनः) Fire, especially sacrificial fire, (whose food, *Asana*, is the oblation made).

Hutáṣaní, most corruptly, *Hoothashunnee*, Mar. (S. हुताशनी) The pile collected for the bonfire at the *Holi*; any ceremony in which offerings are made with fire.

HUṬṬU-GÁRU-GAUḌA, Karn. (ಹುಟ್ಟುಗಾರುಗೌಡ) The head man of a village, who is a native of it. (This and the following are from the v. ಹುಟ್ಟು, to be born, to spring or originate from).

Huṭṭuvali, Karn. (ಹುಟ್ಟುವಳಿ) The produce of a garden or field, or of any trade; the amount of an assessment; rent, income, revenue.

Huṭṭuvali-kami, Karn. (from P. كمي, deficiency) Remission of assessment on account of deficient produce.

HUWUN, Mar. (?) An indefinite land measure signifying a whole.

HYUM, (?) A term used in Coimbatore to designate rates paid in money, either permanently fixed, or subject to small variation. (Gl. 5th Rep., a wrong interpretation of the original, in which it means only 'fixed;' and where it also is an error for *Káyam*, Karn. (ಕಾಯಂ, from A. قايم). The term is correctly *Káyam-suvarnádáya*, Fixed rent.—Fifth Rep., p. 771).

I

IÁTIḲÁD, H. (A. اعتقاد) Confidence, trust: buying an estate.

ÎBÁDAT, H. (A. عبادة) Religious worship.

IBÁHAT, H. (A. اباحة) Giving permission. In Mohammadan law, licence, authority, permission.

IBÁḲ, A. (اباق) The flight of a slave from his master.

IBBAḶA, Karn. (ಇಬ್ಬಳ) A measure equal to half a *kolaga*, (Mysore).

IBN-US-SABÍL, A. (ابن السبيل) A stranger; one who has come from a distance, and is without money or friends, and is entitled to alms, or *zukát*: lit., a son (*ibn*) of the road (*al-sabíl*).

IBRÁ, H. (A. ابراء) Remission, release, acquittance, relinquishment of claim.

Ibrá-náma, H. (ابراء نامه) A written acquittance or relinquishment of claim.

Ibra-i-zimma, H. (ابراي زمّة) Exemption from responsibility, release of trust.

IBZÁÁ, A. (ابضاع) Entering into an engagement for the disposal of goods upon commission; sending a specimen of any article for sale; sorting goods for sale.

ÍCHALU, Karn. (ಈಚಲು) A wild date tree.

Íchalunéru, Karn. (ಈಚಲುನೀರು) The fermented juice of the date or other palm, *tári*.

ÎD, or ÂÍD, commonly EID, or EED, H. (A. عيد) A festival or holy observance among the Mohammadans; but the term is especially applicable to two such occasions, the *Îdín* or *Eidein*, which are enjoined by texts of the *Koran*, and are therefore *farz*, or absolute: others are termed *sunnat*, or traditional. These two are—1. *Îd-ul-fitr*, *Îd-us-saghír*, or *Ramazán-ki-íd* (عيد الفطر ,عيد السغير, رمضان كي عيد) The festival of breaking the fast, the minor festival, or that of *Ramazán*, the occasion of which is the breaking of the fast observed throughout the month of *Ramazán*: the termination of the fast on the 1st of the month ensuing, or *Shawál*, is observed as a festival, with prayers and rejoicings, and distribution of food or other alms to the poor. 2. *Îd-uz-zahá*, *Îd-ul-kurbán*, or *Bakr-íd*, (عيد الضحا, ايد القربان, بقر عيد) The festival of the forenoon, of sacrifice, or the Bull-festival; it is observed in commemoration of Abraham's sacrifice of his son, who, according to the Mohammadans, was *Iskmaíl*, not *Isaac*: it begins on the evening of the 9th of the 12th month, *Zulkijja*, with prayers and offerings, and is continued on the morning of the 10th with public prayers, after which a sheep, an ox, or a camel is slaughtered, and the meat of the sheep and oxen eaten by the offerers, or distributed to their friends and the poor.

Îd, Mar. (ईद) Besides the preceding sense, the term denotes among the Marathas any Hindu festival occurring in the first year after a marriage, when the married pair exchange presents of coarse sugar &c.: the presents so made.

Îdí, *Eedee*, plural *Îdián*, H. (عيدني) Relating to a festival; applied also to verses given by schoolmasters to their pupils at the several festivals, for which presents are made to them: any holiday gift.

Îdiána, H. (عيديانه) Any holiday gift, or any thing relating to a festival or *Îd*.

Îd-gáh, H. (A. P. عيدگاه) A platform, sometimes screened or enclosed by a brick wall, where the Mohammadans assemble for occasional devotions, especially at the season of the *Îds* or festivals: it is usually situated on the outskirts of a town or village.

IDAI, Tam. (இடை) Weight in general, a weight of 100 Palams, equal to $2\frac{1}{2}$ *vis*, or $12\frac{1}{2}$ *sérs*.

IDAIYAN, Tam. (இடையன்) IDAM, IDAYAN, Mal. (ഇടയൻ) A shepherd, a cowherd.

Idaichcherí, Tam. (இடைச்சேரி) A village of shepherds.

IDAM, IDANKAI, IDAKKAI, Tam. (இடம், இடங்கை, எடக்கை) IDAGAI, Karn. (ಇಡಗೈ) The left side, the left-hand castes or divisions: see *Edagai*.

ÎDDAT, corruptly EDIT, A. (عدّة) The time of legal probation which a divorced woman or a widow must wait before she marries again, in order to determine whether she is pregnant.

ÍDIGA, EEDIGU, Karn. (ಈಡಿಗ) A caste, or man of a caste whose business it is to manufacture and sell the fermented juice of the palm, or toddy, or other spirituous liquors: he is also employed as a palankin-bearer.

Ídiguttige, Karn. (ಈಡಿಗುತ್ತಿಗೆ) A duty upon *tári* in Mysore.

ÍDU, Tel. (ఈడు) Pledge, pawn, mortgage, (it is also used in the same meaning amongst others in Tamil; see the next).

ÍDU, Tam. (ஈடு) Quality, applied especially to land or soil.

Kadaiyídu, (கடையீடு) Land of the lowest quality.

Talaiyídu, (தலையீடு) Land of the first quality.

Îdumupairu, Tel. (?) Land which pays rent on a crop unconditionally.

IFLÁS, A. (افلاس, lit., poverty) Becoming insolvent.

ÍHIDE, Mar. (ईहिदे, A. احد) One; used only of the Mohammadan year.

IHÁTA, H. (A. احاطه) An enclosure, a court, a compound.

IHKÁK A. (احقاق) Restoring or determining any one's *hak*, or rights.

IHLÁL, A. (احلال) Rendering any thing lawful, any act or formula by which a transaction is made legal (Mohammadan law).

IHRÁM, A. (احرام) Making or determining any thing to be unlawful; a mean dress worn by pilgrims on entering Mecca; putting on such a dress; the period of pilgrimage at Mecca; abstinence from sensual enjoyments during the month of Muharram.

IHSÁN, A. (احصان) In Mohammadan law, a person who is a free sane adult of chaste reputation, and of the Mohammadan faith, and who is therefore entitled to demand punishment for adultery committed with respect to him or her so characterized.

Ihtikár, A. (احتکار) Laying up: in Mohammadan law, monopoly, or the purchasing of grain and other necessaries of life, and keeping them with a view to enhance the price.

Iḥtimám, corruptly Eahtimam, Eahtiman, Etmaum, Itmam, Yetmaum, and Yetmannee, H. (A. اهتمام) Care, superintendence, trust, responsibility: the trust or jurisdiction of a Zamindar over certain variable divisions of a province, under the Mohammadan government of Bengal, equivalent to a Zamindárí; thus, *Burdwan*, *Rajshahi*, &c., are in early financial reports designated as *Eahtimams*. In Chittagong the term denotes a tenure similar, but subordinate to, a Taluk, and usually of small extent.

Iḥtimám-bandí, corruptly *Eahtimam*, *Etmaum-bundy*, *Yetmaum-bundy*, H. (اهتمام بندي) Revenue settlement according to the *Iḥtimám*.

Iḥtimám-dár, corruptly *Eahtimam*, *Eatihma-dar*, or *Etmaum-dár*, H. (اهتمام دار) The holder of a trust, the person charged with the realization of a stipulated revenue for a certain district under the Mohammadan government, a Zamindar; also an agent or deputy of the Zamindar, appointed by him to realize the revenue of any portion of his Zamindárí.

Iḥtimám-kachhari, corruptly *Etmaum-cutcheri*, H. (کچهري, an office) An office under the Mohammadan government for receiving the revenues from the *Iḥtimám* estates.

Ihtaṣáb, corruptly Yeteṣáb, H. (A. احتصاب) Superintendence of police, supervision of weights and measures, &c., in a market; see *Muhtaṣif*.

Ihtiṣábi, Dekh. H. (احتصابي) A supervisor or clerk of the market; the duty of a supervisor or of a superintendant of police.

Ihẓár, H. (A. احضار, from *Házir*) A summons; citing to appear.

Ijáb, corruptly *Eejab*, H. (A. اجاب) In Mohammadan law, the first proposal made by one of the contracting parties in negociating any arrangement, as a marriage-contract, sale, or the like. In Bhagalpur, balance due after settlement of accounts.

Iját-wa-ḳabúl, H. (A. اجاب و قبول) Proposal and acceptance: in the case of a negociation of marriage, the offer and assent must be declared before witnesses, and this is necessary to render the marriage valid.

Ijárá, corruptly, Ejara, Ejar, Ezara, Izara, H. (A. اجارا) Ijárá, Mar. (इजारा) Price, profit: especially employed to denote a lease or farm of land held at a defined rent or revenue, whether from government direct, or from an intermediate payer of the public revenue: a farm or lease of the revenue of a village or district, also of customs, or collections of any description, as of customary fees or allowances; any items of revenue: letting lands on farm or lease; the lands so let; a contract; a monopoly.

Ijárádár, corruptly, *Ejarahdar*, H. &c. (A. اجارادار) *Ijárdár*, Hindi and Mar. (इजारदार) A farmer of any item of public revenue, whether from land, customs, or any other source; the renter of a village or estate at a stipulated rate.

Ijárádári, or *Ijárdári*, H. &c. (اجاراداري, इजारदारी) Farming, contracting for rent or revenue; an abwáb or cess formerly levied on lands or districts let out in farm for the benefit of the farmer or contractor.

Ijára-jaghrát, Sindhi. Farm of milking cattle.

Ijára-kaul, Tel. (from the A. قول, an agreement) Renting a village of government, and subletting it, the first leaseholder being responsible for the revenue. (Warangal).

Ijára-náma, H. (اجاره نامه) A lease, any document under which a lease or farm is held; also a conditional deed of sale of a slave in Tirhut.

Ijára-paṭṭa, H. &c. (اجاره پٿّه) A deed of lease on farm.

Ijárdárí-paṭṭá, Hindi (इजारदारीपट्टा) A lease for a farm, giving authority to the holder to occupy and cultivate, or receive the rents of an estate.

Ijárpaṭ, Mar. (इजारपट) The *sanad* or public document given to a farmer or contractor; the paper given at the annual settlement of the revenue in the Maraṭha provinces to the head Pátíl, setting forth the gross amount of revenue due for that year by his village, the sum remaining to be paid after deducting remissions, and the instalments by which the balance is to be paid.

Ijázat, H. (A. اجازت) Giving leave or permission to depart, dismissal, command, sanction, or permission.

Ijázat-náma, H. (اجازت نامه) Any written order or permission; also commonly applied in Mohammadan diction to the *anumati patra* of Hindu law, or the written permission of a husband to his wife to adopt a son after his decease.

Ijlás, H. (A. اجلاس) A sitting, especially of a court of

justice, sessions; under the Mohammadan government it usually denoted an assembly of jurists or learned men for the decision of an intricate or important cause: it is also used at present for a meeting or sitting of the Supreme Council, as, *Ijlás-i-kaunsil* (اجلاس كونسل).

Ijlás-hámil, H. (from the A. كامل, perfect) A full or complete court or session.

IJMÁÂ, A. (اجماع) An assemblage, a court: a collection or sum.

Ijmáâ-i-sahábat, The concurrent authority of the companions of the prophet upon a point of Mohammadan law.

IJMÁL, H. (A. اجمال) Abstract, summary; also applied to joint occupancy or possession.

Ijmáli, H. (اجمالي) Held in common (as an estate), undivided, unpartitioned; settled with in common with two or more parties.

Ijmáli-mahal, H. (from A. محل, an estate) An undivided estate, one held in parcenership by the heirs of a common ancestor.

Ijmáyalí, Mar. (इजमायली, from the A. *Ijmál*) Summary, superficial; an account roughly prepared to answer immediate purposes.

IJRÁ, H. (A. اجرا) Giving currency or circulation to any thing, making known, carrying into effect; issue, execution.

Ijrái-dikri, H. E. (اجراي دكري) Execution of a decree of court.

IJTIḤÁD, A. (اجتهاد) Carrying on war against infidels: also care, effort; whence, in Mohammadan law, it implies the fundamental grounds or authorities in legal disquisitions, which are—*Al-kitáb*, the book or Koran; *Sunnat*, tradition, the sayings and doings of Mohammad, recorded by his successors and associates; *Ijmáâ*, the concurrent opinions of Mohammad's companions; and *Kiyás*, reasoning, the rationale of a decision not provided for by either of the preceding.

IḲÁLA, A. (اقالة) The cancelling or dissolution of a sale, on condition of furnishing an equivalent for the original price of the article; breaking a contract or engagement.

IḲBÁL, incorrectly, EKBÁL, A. (اقبال) Acceptance (of a bond, &c.).

Iḳbál dâwá, incorrectly, *Ekbál-dawee*, H. (A. اقبال, admission, and دعوا, a suit) Confession of judgment.

ÍKH, EEKH, H. (ايكه) IKHU, Ben. (ইক্ষু) also Mar. (ईख) IKSHU, S. (इक्षुः) Sugar-cane: also *Úhh.*

Ikhráj, also *Ukhráj*, H. (ايكهراج) A name given in some places in Upper India to the day on which the sugar-cane is planted, which is an occasion of festivity.

IKHRÁJ, H. (A. اخراج) Expulsion, turning out of possession: expense.

Ikhráját, H. (A. plural of اخراج) Expenses, disbursements: assignments of revenue to public servants employed in its management and collection.

Ikhráját-i-aurang, H. Expenses of the *aurang*, or commercial station. In accounts of the salt revenue the term included the expenses incurred in the manufacture, storing, and transport of the salt.

IKHTIÁR, commonly, but incorrectly, IKHTIYAR, H. (A. اختيار) Choice, option: in Hindustan, more usually pleasure, will, authority, power. *Ikhtiár-men̲-honá* is to be in one's power, or dependent upon, as a district jurisdiction; also to be according to any one's discretion, pleasure, or will, as an order, a decision, a sentence: in Mohammadan law it implies an option of divorce granted by a husband to his wife.

Ikhtiár-náma, H. A power of attorney.

Ikhtiár-i-ṣulh, A. (from صلح, agreement) An optional compromise (Mohammadan law).

Ikhtiár-i-zabha, A. (from ذبح, slaughter) Killing an animal for food according to the legal form—by cutting its throat.

IKKERI-VARAHÁ, or -HÚN, Karn. (ಇಕ್ಕೇರಿವರಹಾ) A small gold coin struck at *Ikkeri*, in Mysore, equal to thirteen gold fanams, rather less than a quarter of a Calcutta mohur.

IḲRÁH, corruptly, IKHRAH, A. (اكراه) Compulsion: in law, the constraint exercised by one person over another, to compel him to do an illegal act, or to act contrary to his own will.

IḲRÁR, H. (A. اقرار) Fixing firmly, establishing, confirming; agreement, assent, ratification. In law, the acknowledgment or admission of a right or claim, as of a debt; also of relationship, involving inheritance, &c.; also a confession or acknowledgment of guilt.

Iḳrár-i-âám, corruptly, *Ehrahaum*, A. (اقرار عام) A public acknowledgment, declaration, or confession. A will, a testament.

Iḳrár-dána-patra, H. (from S. दानपत्र) A conditional deed of gift, a deed of gift with some reservation or declaration of right in the donor.

Iḳrári, H. (اقراري) One who assents, acknowledges, or confesses.

Iḳrári-aṣámí, H. (from A. اسامي) A prisoner who confesses his guilt.

Iḳrár-náma, H. (P. نامه) A deed of assent or acknowledgment in general. In the north-west provinces it applies especially to the engagement entered into with government by the Málguzar and coparceners of a village: it is to specify the mode of paying the revenue; how the shares are to be distributed; the shares whether held in common or in severalty; the number, functions, privileges, &c., of the *Lambardárs*; the items of the Sayer; rights of irrigation; extent and appropriation of waste cultivable land; and the number, duties, and pay of the village servants: it is to be signed by all the Lambardárs and as many Paṭṭídárs as possible, to be attested by the Paṭwárí and Kanungos, and finally confirmed by the signature of the settlement officer, after being read out before him in open court in the presence of the subscribing parties.

Iḳrár-náma-ṣálaṣi, H. (from A ثالث, a third party) A deed of arbitration.

IḲṬÁÂ, incorrectly, AKTA, H. (A. اقطاع, lit., portions cut off, from *Ḳaṭâ*, قطع, to cut) Jagír lands, or lands granted in feudal tenure to the nobles of the Moghal empire, when scattered in separate allotments through different provinces.

ÎLADÁRAWÁRA, Karn. (ಇಳದಾರವಾರ) A mortgage of land with possession, sometimes for a stipulated period, the rent taking place of all interest on the loan, as well as providing for the government revenue; the land to be redeemable on payment of the debt.

ILÁḤÍ, H. (A. الهي, from *Ilah*, اله, God) Divine; the title of the era instituted by the Emperor Akbar, commencing with the first year of his reign, A. H. 963, A. D. 1556: although found on the coins of Akbar and his immediate successors, it never obtained currency, and is now obsolete.

Iláhí-gaz, H. (الهي گز) The standard *gaz*, or yard, of 41 fingers, instituted by Akbar; authoritatively fixed by the British government at 33 inches: see *Gaz*.

ÎLÁḲA, corruptly, ELAKEH, H. (A. علاقه) Dependency, connexion; a property, an estate, a district, a jurisdiction. ILÁKHÁ, Mar. (इलाखा) Claim, right, title. ILÁKHA, or ILÁKHE, Karn. (ಯಿಲಾಖೆ) A department, an office.

Îlakhé-janaru, Karn. (ಯಿಲಾಖೇಜನರು) The people under the chief officer of a district, the people of the dependency.

Îlákadár, H. (علاقه دار) The person who engages, either on his own account or as the representative of others, for the payment of the assessed revenue upon a district or village.

ÎLÁM, H. (A. اعلام, from علم, to know) Announcing, proclaiming, making known.

Ilám-náma, H. (from نامه) A summons, a citation; the first process issued against a defendant in a civil suit.

ILAMBÁDI, Tam. (இலம்பாடி) The name of the Banjara tribe in the south: also *Lambádi*.

ÎLÁN, or AÎLAN, (A. اعلان) Publishing; advertisement.

IḶANGÁḌUTARÍJU, Tam. (இளங்காடுதரிசு) Land left waste for ten years.

ILAṆJAM, Tam. (இலஞ்சம்) A bribe.

ILAṆJI, Tam. (இலஞ்சி) A tank, a large tank.

ÎLAT, H. (A. علت) Cause, motive: in the language of the Courts, the grounds of a charge or accusation, the plea of arraignment.

ILÁRÁLU, Tel. (ఇలారాలు) The thatched roofs of barns or granaries.

ILHÁḲ, corruptly, ELLAAK, (?) H. (A. الحاق) Addition; but applied to fees formerly exacted from the parties to a suit, or from the police peons: (perhaps some error from *Al-hak*, a right or perquisite).

ILKÁ-HAJAR, A. (القاء حجر) lit., Throwing a stone, a practice prohibited by the Mohammadan law, which compelled a person who threw a stone at any article exposed for sale to purchase it.

ILLAKUR, Mal. (ഇല്ലക്കൂറ) The private property of a Malabar Raja; which, on his accession to superior dignity, he assigns in some respects to his heir.

ILLARIKAM, Tel. (యిల్లరికం) Connexion of descent from a common ancestor, which is marked by bearing the same family name, commonly termed the house name, *Inṭiperu*, (ఇంటిపేరు).

ILLAṬA, Karn. (ಇಲ್ಲಟ) A bride's father having no son, and adopting his son-in-law.

ILLÁYAM, Tel. (ఇల్లాయం) House tax.

ÎLM, H. (A. علم) Wisdom, learning, knowledge.

ILTIMÁS, H. (A. التماس) Beseeching; supplication: in some places, as in Cuttack, *Iltimás*, (ଇଲତିମାସ) is used for the plaint in a suit: it is also used to denote an humble or unpretending representation.

IMÁM, corruptly EMAUM, H. (A. امام) A head or chief in religious matters, whether he be the head of all Mohammadans, as the *Khalif*, or the priest of a mosque, or the leader in the prayers of a congregation. The *Shias* recognise twelve *Imáms*, or heads of the faith, in *Âlí* and his successors, of whom the last *Imám*, *Mehdi*, is believed to be still alive. The term *Imám* is sometimes, when used singly as *the Imám,* applied especially to *Imám Sháfâi,* one of the four lawyers who founded as many schools.

Imám-bil-hak, A. (امام بالحق) A rightful *Imám,* one who posseses all the requisite qualifications.

Imámia, H. (A. امامیه) The *Shia* sect, from their recognising the twelve Imáms.

Imám-bára, or *-bári,* corruptly *Emaum-barry,* H. (from the P. باره, or H. باري, a house) A building in which the festival of the Moharram is celebrated, and service in commemoration of the deaths of Âlí, and his sons Hasan and Hasain is performed at that season; at other times their Tázias or shrines are preserved in it: sometimes it is used as the mausoleum for the family of the founder.

Imám-zámini, H. (A. from ضامني, surety) Fastening a small coin round the left arm of a person undertaking a journey, for good luck, and to secure the protection of the Imám: if in want he may spend it, not else.

IMÁRAT, H. (A. امارة) Authority, a government, the jurisdiction of an Amír.

ÎMÁRAT, H. (A. عمارة) Any public building, as a mosque, a college.

IMBISÁT, A. (انبساط) Mutual liberty: in law, a mutual right of usufruct, the right of a coparcener in common property.

IMLÁK, H. (A. املاک) Property, possession. Hindi (इमलाक) Land held rent free, which has fallen to the Zamindar for want of an owner (Puraniya).

Imlák-mankúla, A. (املاک منقوله) Personal property.

Imlák-ghair-mankúla, A. (املاک غیر منقوله) Real property.

IMMADI, Karn. (ಇಮ್ಮಡಿ) lit., Double, a double, a deputy.

IMMANU, Karn. (ಇಮ್ಮನು, from ಇಮ್ಮಿ, twice) Lands yielding two crops of rice in a year.

IMTIHÁN, H. (A. امتحان) Proof, examination.

IMTINÁÂ, H. (A. امتناع). Prohibition, restraint.

INÂÁM, H. (A. انعام) vernacularly, INÁM, corrupted to ENAM, or ENAUM, Ben. (ইনাম) Mar. (इनाम) Tel. (ఇనాము) A gift, a benefaction in general, a gift by a superior to an inferior. In India, and especially in the south, and amongst the Marathas, the term was especially applied to grants of land held rent-free, and in hereditary and perpetual occupation: the tenure came in time to be qualified by the reservation of a portion of the assessable revenue, or by the exaction of all proceeds exceeding the intended value of the original assignment; the term was also vaguely applied to grants of rent-free land, without reference to perpetuity or any specified conditions. The grants are also distinguishable by their origin from the ruling authorities, or from the village communities, and are again distinguishable by peculiar reservations, or by their being applicable to different objects. They are first classed as *Sanadi,* and as *Gáon-nisbat-Inám.*

1. *Sanadi-Inám* is a grant emanating from the ruling power of the time of the grant, free from all government exactions, in perpetuity, and validified by *Sanad,* or official deed of grant: it usually comprises land included in the village area, but which is uncultivated, or has been abandoned; and it is subject to the *Haks,* or dues of the village functionaries. It may be granted sometimes with a reservation of a half, a third, or a fourth of the government claim known as *Inám-nímai, I. tijái* and *I. chauthái.*

2. *Gáon-nisbat-Inám,* (from the A. نصبت, a portion) Lands granted rent-free by the village out of its own lands; the loss or deduction thence accruing to the government assessment being made good by the village community. Seven kinds of such grants are specified; as, 1. The *Inám* of the *Mukaddam,* or officiating head of the village, termed *Inám-passoree,* (or, perhaps more correctly, *I. páseri,* the latter meaning maintenance). This is saleable or assignable in mortgage with or without the office of *Mukaddam*; it is liable to the dues payable to the village servants on land of the like quality. 2. Land assigned to the *Mhar,* of two kinds; see *Hinki* and *Hadoli,* or *Márhi.* 3. *Devasthán,* free lands attached to temples and mosques: it is not transferable in any way, either by the village, or the persons attending on the temples, whose duty it is to sell the produce, and apply the money to the ordinary expenses of the temples. 4. *Inám-waveyley,* (? *-máwali*) Lands granted to the village artificers and servants, in place of dues upon the produce: this is more common in the *Máwal,* or hill country, than in the *Dés,* or country above the *Ghats*: the lands may be mortgaged, but not sold, and are resumable by the donors. 5. *Dharmádaya,* corruptly, *Dhermudow,* Lands assigned in charity, saleable and assignable in mortgage. 6. *Deva-tekí,* A parcel of land occasionally held by a *Muhaddam* or *Mhar,* in reward of his having established by ordeal disputed territories: it may be sold or mortgaged. 7. *Pál,* or *Sút,* A small piece of land held rent-free in connexion with land bearing revenue, to compensate for some deficiency in the produce of the latter: it

cannot be sold or mortgaged separately, but remains annexed to the larger portion.

Another classification of Maraṭha *Inám* lands arranges them under six heads, according to the objects of the donation; as, 1. *Hindu Ináms*, which are subdivided into seven classes, viz. (1) Rent-free lands assigned by the state, or by the village, to Bráhmans of reputed sanctity or learning, not engaged in secular affairs; (2) to the *Goṣávi*, or village Gosain, to enable him to keep up his *math*, or religious dwelling, and accommodate travelling mendicants of a similar character, usually a village benefaction; (3) to individuals for military services, granted by the state, or Jagírdars and great officers; (4) to *Bháts*, or bards, granted both by the state and the villages; (5) *Gaocharani badal*, revenue remitted on some of the village lands, on the plea of their being appropriated to the grazing of cattle belonging to religious persons; (6) *Jangam-inám*, land granted by villages inhabited by *Lingáits* to their priests; (7) *Yátrá-che-káthi*, lands granted by the village to persons for keeping up and conveying flags (from *káthi*, a flagstaff) to *yátrás*, or fairs held in honour of some deity. 2. The second of the major or generic classes are *Mohammadan Ináms*, consisting of rent-free grants made by opulent Mohammadans to religious persons of their own faith, and to a variety of vagrants, mendicants, tumblers, jugglers, &c. 3. *Devasthána Ináms* are lands assigned for the support of religious establishments, whether Hindu or Mohammadan, and for the keeping up of temples, shrines, mosques, &c. 4. *Dharmadáya Ináms* are lands appropriated to religious persons, as an act of charity, by the heads of the government, and by the village communities: some of these are of considerable antiquity, and are frequently confirmed by *Dána-patras*, grants inscribed on copper plates. 5. *Dehangi Ináms*, numerous but limited assignments to a variety of village artificers and servants, musicians, dancers, and the families of individuals who have lost their lives in the service of the state, or of the village. 6. *Watandári Ináms*, or assignments to the village officers and servants. Besides these classifications, which are especially applicable to the *Maraṭha* countries, a variety of terms occur in relation to the designation of *Ináms*, either of local or general applicability.

Inâámdár, or *Inámdár*, H. &c. (انعامدار, इनामदार) The holder of a rent-free grant.

Inâámat, H. (انعامت) *Inámat*, Mar. (इनामत) A gift, a benefaction, an assignment of rent-free land.

Inámatí, Mar. (इनामती) Of or belonging to an *Inám* grant; land or revenue assigned either in favour or charity, or compensation of the duties of hereditary officers.

Inâámat-i-tafrík, H. (A. انعامت تفريق) A tax levied on farmers of *Inâám* lands.

Inâám-i-altamgha, H. (انعام التمغه) A grant of rent-free land under royal seal.

Inâám-i-ikrám, H. &c. (انعام اكرام) A grant or gift in general, a grant of generosity.

Inâám-i-kánungo, H. (انعام كانونگو) An assignment of rent-free land to the village accountant.

Inám-patra, Mar. (इनामपत्र) A deed of grant, a document conveying an assignment of rent-free land.

Inám-patrak, Mar. (इनामपत्रक) An account of the lands in a village held rent-free; one of the accounts kept by the *kulkarani*, or village accountant.

Inám-paṭṭi, Mar. (इनामपट्टी) A tax upon the holders of *Inám* grants, either reserved as a quit-rent, or levied in times of emergency upon lands originally granted rent-free.

Beḍiga, or *Kaṭṭubaḍi Inámu*, Tel. (బెడిగ, కట్టుబడి, యినాము) An assignment of land at an assessment, which varies with the produce.

Bil-mahhta-inámu, Tel. (బిల్మఖ్తాయినాము) A grant of land at a fixed assessment.

Sarva-dumbálá-inámu, Tel. (సర్వదుంబాలాయినాము) A grant of land wholly rent free.

Gáon-nisbat-inám, Mar. (गावंनिसबतइनाम) A mortgage, or grant of land made by the villagers to liquidate a debt incurred by the village for public expenses: see also above.

Srotriyadínámu, Karn. (స్రోత్రియదీనాము) Grant of land at a fixed assessment.

Terige-illada-inámu, Karn. (తెరిగెయిల్లదఇనాము) An allotment of land rent-free.

Ínarásí, Tel. (ఈనరాశి) Grain of an inferior quality separated from the good by winnowing.

Înáyat, H. (A. عنايت) Favour, kindness, bounty.

Ináyat-náma, H., A deed of gift, a letter of recommendation, a written order or patent from a superior.

ÍNCH, EENCH, H. (اینچ) Security (Dehli).

INDÁRÁ, H. (S. اندارا) A large well of masonry.

IṆḌÍ, Asamese (?) (ইণ্ডী) A variety of silk, commonly known as *Eria* silk, procured in Asam, soft and of strong fibre, but difficult to reel off the cocoon.

INDARMAN, Thug. A woman.

INDRA-DWÁDAŞÍ, S. (इन्द्रद्वादशी) The twelfth day of *Bhádra*, a festival in honour of Indra, the Hindu deity of the firmament, and of Swarga.

ÍNDRAVÁḌU, Tel. (ఈంద్రవాడు) A *táṛi* drawer, a caste, or individual of it, employed to extract the juice of the palms: he is also sometimes employed as a palankin-bearer.

INDUVÁRA, S. (इन्दुवार) The day of the moon (Monday).

INFIṢÁL, H. &c. (A. انفصال) Decision, sentence, award, settlement of an affair.

INGÁR-TUPPA, Karn. (ಯಿಂಗಾರತುಪ್ಪ) A tax on the tribe called *Tálwárs* in Mysore, in lieu of a ram and a pot of ghee annually contributed by them to the *Paligars* in former times.

INGLÍS, H. (انگليس, for English) Invalid soldiers or *sipakis*, to whom allotments of land were assigned as pensions; the lands so granted. (Mr. Elliot thinks the word corrupted from invalid).

INḲISÁM, H. (A. انقسام) Division, partition.

INṢÁF, H. (A. انصاف) Justice, decision of a cause,

ÍNṬ, H. (اينٿ, ईंट, S. इष्टिका) IṬ, Ben. (ইট) IṬṬIKE, -GE, Karn. (ಇಟ್ಟಿಕೆ, -ಗೆ) A brick.

Ínṭ-gárí, H. (اينٿگاري) Brickwork.

Iṭwálá, Ben. (ইটওয়ালা) A brickmaker.

Iṭṭigeyava, Karn. (ಇಟ್ಟಿಗೆಯವ) A brickmaker.

INTIKHÁB, H. (A. انتخاب) Selection, abstract, extract of proceedings.

INTIḲÁL, H. (A. انتقال) Conveyance or removal from one place to another, from life to death, &c.

Intiḳálí, H. (A. انتقالي) A transfer of Zamindárí or other revenue property, from one person to another: the property so transferred.

Intiḳálí-bahi, H. (from بهي, an account) Register of transfers of property.

Intiḳálí-rasúm, H. (A. from رسوم) Fees for making a transfer of property in the official register.

INTIẒÁM, H. (A. انتظام) Administration, arrangement.

IPPAN ,Tam. (இப்பன்) A shepherd, a ploughman, a trader or merchant.

ÍPATDÁI, Hindi (ईपतदाइ) From the date of.

IRÁDAH, H. (اراده) A division of the page of an account book.

IṚAI, Tam. (இறை) Tax, tribute.

IṚAIPPU, Tam. (இறைப்பு) Payment of tax or tribute.

Iṛaiyumavariyum, Tam. (இறையுமவரியும்) Taxes and duty, assessment.

IRÁKKADAN, Tam. (S. இராக்கதன்) A giant, the Rakshas of Hindu mythology; a kind of marriage, the Rakshasa form or violence.

IRAKKÁRÁNMA, Mal. (ഇരക്കാരാണ്മ) Lands and tenements held by a small acknowledgment of superiority to a higher lord, fee-hold.

Irakkáránmayola, Mal. (ഇരക്കാരാണ്മയോല) Title-deeds of land held fee-hold.

ÍRAKKUCHCHAMBÁ, Tam. (ஈரக்குசசம்பா) A superior kind of the rice, called *Chambá*, or *Sambá*, which is sown in July and reaped in February: see *Sambá*.

IRAPU, Kar. (ಇರಪು) Surplus, balance, savings.

IRASAM, Tel. (ఇరసం) A measure of 24 *sérs*.

IRAṬṬU, Tam. (இரட்டு) Coarse cloth, sackcloth.

Iraṭṭuppai, Tam. (இரட்டுப்பை) A sack of coarse canvas or cloth.

IRAVAL, Tam. (இரவல்) A loan, any article lent.

ÍṚAVAN, or ÍLAVAN, Mal. (ഈഴവൻ) A caste, or individual of it, whose occupation is the extraction of *táṛi* or *toddy*, from the palm trees.

IṚAVARI, Mal. (ഇറവരി) Royal revenue, assessment, tax, impost.

IRJÍKA, Mar. (इरजीक) The practice among cultivators of giving mutual assistance, both with men and cattle.

IRKÁRU, Karn. (ಇರಕಾರು) The early and latter crop, or the two seasons of harvest.

IRṢ, H. (A. ارث) Inheritance.

IRSÁL, H. &c. (A. ارسال) Sending, despatch, a despatch of any thing; the sending of remittances from the villages to the Zamindar, or to the district treasury, and from thence to the exchequer.

Irsál-náma, H. (from نامه) A statement of money or goods remitted, an invoice.

Irsál-paṭí, Mar. (इरसालपटी) An invoice, a list of remittances of cash specifying the coins of which they consist.

IRSH, A. (ارش) A mulct or fine for bloodshed or wounds not causing loss of life: a bribe, a douceur to the judge.

IRTISHÁ, H. (A. ارتشا) Bribery, corruption.

IRTIHÁN, H. (A. ارتهان) Receiving any article as a pledge.

IRU, Tel., Tam. (ఇరు, இரு) Two, both.

Irubhágamu, Tel. (from ఇరు, two, and భాగము, S. भाग, a share) The two shares, *i. e.* of the crop, the one assignable to the government, the other to the cultivator: also read *Iru-bhogamu*, or double possession, implying the same thing.

Irubu, or *Irubogam*, Tam. (இருபு, இருபோகம்) Two crops.

Irugoru, Tel. (ఇరుగోరు) Both shares; the entire crop before the government portion is deducted.

Irumaṇabárí, Tam. (இருமணபாரீ) A soil of clay and sand.

Irunáli-páṭam, Mal. (ഇരുനാലിപാടം) lit., Two *nális* out of four; used to express an equal division of the crop between proprietor and tenant, made annually, and not very customary in Malabar.

Iru-pattu-náladi-kol, Tam. (இருபத்துநாலடிக்-கோல்) A measuring rod twenty-four feet in length.

Iruvára, Karn. (ಇರುವಾರ) Both the government's and cultivator's shares of the crop.

Iruváyam, Tel. (ఇరువాయం) The whole crop before its partition between the state and the cultivator.

IRUḶAN, Tam. (இருளன்) A man of a wild race living in the woods: from *Iruḷ*, (இருள) blackness.

ÍṢÁ, vernacularly, ISH, S. &c. (ईशा, ईश) The beam or pole of a plough.

ISANNE, Mar. (इसंने, A. اثنان) Two; applied only to the Mohammadan year in the Dakhin.

ISÁRA, or ISÁRÁ, Mar. (इसार, इसारा) Earnest money.

ÎSHÁ, H. (A. عشا) The first watch of the night, or, according to some, from the time when the sun begins to set till twilight: prayers to be said at that time.

Îshá-namáz, or *-ṣalát*, H. (from the P. نماز, or A. صلاة) Evening prayer.

ISHÁRA, or ISHÁRAT, H. (A. اشارة) A hint, a sign; in law, indicating any thing in a definite manner, in opposition to simply naming it.

ISHHÁD, H. (A. اشهاد) Evidence, testimony.

ISHṬA DEVATÁ, H. (S. from इष्ट, wished, and देवता, a divinity) A person's favourite or tutelary deity.

ISHTIHÁR, H. (A. اشتهار) adopted in various dialects, with some modifications, as, *Istihar*, Ben. (ইশ্তিহার) *Istahár*, Uriya (ଇସ୍ତାହାର) *Istiháru*, Tel. (ఇస్తిహారు) *Ishtiyára*, Tam. (இஷ்தியார) Proclamation, public announcement or notice, advertisement, an advertisement in a public place or a newspaper, notice by the collector of a sale of lands for arrears of revenue; also a paper affixed to a Ryot's cottage requiring him to renew his lease within a given term, under penalty of his being charged the highest rate levied in the village or district.

Istiharu-náma, Tel. (from نامه) A written notice or proclamation.

Ishtiyára-náma, Tam. (from نامه) A document granted by government to the purchasers of lands sold at auction for arrears of revenue, or under a decree of Court.

ISHRÁK, A. (اشراق) Rising of the sun.

Ishráh-namáz, A. P. Prayer at sunrise.

ISHTIRÁK, H. (A. اشتراك) Partnership; entering into partnership.

ISLÁM, H. (A. اسلام) The Mohammadan religion.

ISM, H. (A. اسم) A name, a noun.

Ism-farẕi, or *Ism-i-farẕi*, corruptly, *Issum-furzy*, H. (from فرضي, fictitious) A fictitious name, or the substitution of the name of one person in place of that of another, who is the real but unavowed party in a transaction, such as the purchase of lands sold at auction, and the like.

Ism-nawísi, H. (from P. نويسي, a writing) A list or roll of names, as of Zamindars in a district, witnesses in a suit, &c.; making out such a list.

Ism-wár, H. (اسموار) Attending to name; entry in public documents according to the order of the names of the individuals.

Isamuvâru-paṭṭi, Karn. (ಇಸಮುವಾರುಪಟ್ಟಿ) An individual account.

ÎṢMAT, A. (عصمة) Protection: chastity: in law, the care and defence of property by the owner, and the protection of person and property by the state or the law.

ISTÁD, Mar. (इस्ताद, A. استعداد) Goods and chattels, moveable property.

ISTAKBÍL-TÁ-GÁYAT, Mar. (इस्तकबीलतागायत, for the A. استقبال تا غايت) From a certain date to a certain date, used chiefly with respect to notes.

ISTÁWÁ, Mar. (इस्तावा, A. ISTÍWÁ, استوا, tending towards equality) The land-tax or rent levied at progressively increasing rates, until it reaches the full sum imposable on land brought into cultivation, or on villages let out to farm, &c.; the practice of so letting lands, &c.

Istáwá-ḳaul, Tel. (from A. قول, agreement) A lease or grant of waste lands at a rent progressively increasing for a term of years, when it becomes fixed.

Istáwá-chí-paṭṭí, Mar. (इस्तावाचीपट्टी) An account kept by the village accountant of lands held on progressively increasing rents.

ISTIBRÁ, A. (استبرا) Waiting for the purification of a woman, whether a slave or free, to determine whether she is pregnant before intercourse can lawfully take place.

ISTIDÂÁ, A. (استدعا) Supplication, petition.

Istidánat, A. (استدانة) Borrowing, contracting a debt, wishing to borrow, suing for a debt: in law, any transaction which the manager in a partnership, where one finds the capital and the other the management, may undertake, but for which, if not included in, or consonant to, the terms of his contract with the proprietor of the share, he alone is responsible, and the profits of which he alone is entitled to, unless his partner had given his previous sanction.

Istífá, corruptly, **Isteyafah**, H. (A. استيفا) Resigning an appointment, relinquishing a charge or possession, a deed of abandonment: settling, satisfying, paying or receiving all that is due upon an account.

Istaphá, Hindi (इस्तफा) *Istiphá*, Tel. (ఇస్తిఫా) A deed of relinquishment, such as is usually executed by Zamindars on giving up their lands.

Istífá-i-asl-zamín, H. (استيفا اصل زمين) Relinquishment of an estate held *khás*, or by the state.

Istifsár, H. (A. استفسار) Inquiry, interrogation.

Istifsári, H. (استفساري) The statement of a prosecutor, subject to investigation.

Istiftá, H. (A. استفتا) Consulting a Mohammadan lawyer, calling for the *fatwá*, or opinion of the Mohammadan law-officer of a court.

Istíghása, H. (A. استغاثة) Demanding justice, preferring a complaint.

Istihkák, H. (A. استحقاق, from حق) Demanding one's right, demanding justice: in law, a claim set up to the subject of a deed or contract by a person not a party to it.

Istihláf, H. (A. استحلاف) Causing to swear; applied especially in law to cases in which the oath of a wife is necessary for the establishment of a fact relating to her marriage.

Istihlál, A. (استحلال) lit., Making lawful: in law, the cry of a new-born child, the occurrence of which is necessary of proof in a peculiar case of inheritance, as if a man die leaving a widow pregnant, and a brother; then if proof be given that the cry of the child was heard, and should it then die, the widow, as its mother, will inherit; if no cry has been heard, the brother is heir.

Istihsán, H. (A. استحسان) Taking as a favour, approving: in law, a favourable construction or interpretation of a point of law, deviating from the strict letter of the law in kindness either to suitors or to the community.

Istikála, H. (A. استقالة) Requiring any one to cancel an agreement, or to give up a bargain.

Istikbál, less correctly, **Istakbál**, H. (A. استقبال) Ceremonious reception of a person of distinction, coming out of a town in procession to meet him.

Istiklál, H. (A. استقلال) Absolute authority, confirmation of possession, perpetuity.

Istikrár, H. (A. استقرار) Confirmation.

Istílá, A. (استيلا) Victory, power, subjection to authority by conquest, which, according to Mohammadan law, conveys a right of making the captives slaves.

Istílád, A. (استيلاد, from ولد) Claim of offspring made by a man who has a child born to him of a female slave, which he acknowledges as his own: the formal claim and acknowledgment are necessary to establish legally the paternity of the child.

Istimáá, H. (A. استماع) Hearing: in law, hearsay evidence, indirect testimony, receivable only in particular cases, and under certain restrictions.

Istimrár, or **Istamrár**, corruptly, **Istemerar**, H. &c. (A. استمرار, इस्तमरार) **Istimiráru**, Tel. (ఇస్తిమిరారు) Continuance, perpetuity: a farm or lease granted in perpetuity by government or a Zamindar, at a stipulated rent, and exempt from *abwábs*; such a lease granted in charity at a quit-rent.

Istimrári, in some dialects *Istamrári*, corruptly, *Istemerary*, H. (A. استمراري) Permanent, perpetual; applied especially to a permanent settlement of the revenue, and particularly to the settlement of the lower provinces made by the government of Lord Cornwallis.

Istimrár-dár, (from P. دار, who has) The holder of a perpetual farm or lease.

Istimrári-dihát, H. (from *dihát*, villages) Villages held on a permanent or perpetual tenure.

Istimrári-jamá, H. (from جمع, revenue) Fixed or perpetual assessment or rent.

Istimrári-jot, H. (from جوت, cultivation) A fixed or permanent tenure.

Istimirár-kirámam, Tam. (இஸ்திமிரார்கிராமம்) A village permanently settled.

Istimrári-málguzári, H. (from P. مالگزاري) Permanent or perpetual revenue.

Istimrári-pattá, H. (from پٿّا, a lease) A lease or farm granted at a permanent rent, a perpetual lease.

Istimrári-pattadár, H. (استمراري پٿّادار) Holder of a lease of lands at a perpetual rent.

ISTIRDÁD, H. (A. استرداد) Demanding or ordering restitution of any thing, whether given, pledged, or sold.

Istirdád-i-nilám, H. (from نيلام, sale by auction) Reversal of a public sale.

ISTIHSHÁD, H. (A. استشهاد) Taking evidence, summoning witnesses.

ISTISNÁÂ, A. (استصناع) Requisition to work; forced labour.

ISTRÍ, H. &c. (استري, इस्त्री, from S. स्तृ, to spread) A smoothing iron; also the act of ironing linen.

Istríwálá, H. &c. (استري والا) An ironing man, one who irons linen.

ISTUVA, or ISTUVU, Tel. (ఇస్తువ, ఇస్తువు) Property, estate.

ISUKABHÚMI, Tel. (ఇసుకభూమి) Sandy soil.

ÍSWARA, S. &c (ईश्वर) A lord, a master: a name of Siva, especially in the form of a Linga, and used in composition as *Someswara*, the *Íswara* or Linga set up originally by *Soma*: the eleventh year of the cycle.

ITAKUTI, ITAKUTIYÁN, or ITAKKORUVAN, pronounced as if the *t* were *d*, IDAKUDI &c. Mal. (ഇടകുടി, ഇടകുടിയാൻ, ഇടക്കൊഴുവൻ) An under tenant.

ÍTAKALLU, Tel. (ఈతకల్లు) The fermented juice of the date tree, *toddy*.

ÍTI, Mar. (ईति) Ben. (ঈতি) Mal. (ഈതി) A common term for seven national plagues or calamities—drought, excessive rain, rats, locusts, parrots, legal oppression, foreign invasion.

ITIKÁF, A. (اتقاف) Restraining one's senses, applied especially to a practice of pious Mohammadans who spend a great part of the month Ramazán in a mosque engaged in prayer and meditation.

ITLÁÂ, H. (A. اطلاع) ITTELÁ, Hindi (इत्तेला) Making known, information.

Itláâ, or *Ittelá-náma*, H. (from نامه) A notice, a summons, a citation: a notice served on cultivators when they fall in arrears, threatening them with an attachment if not paid by a given time.

ITLÁK, H. (A. اطلاق, lit., liberating, setting free) In Hindustan, the office and records of summonses, and fees on their delivery. Under the Mohammadan government, fees paid by suitors on the decision of their causes; also, a fee exacted from a defendant as wages for a peon stationed over him as soon as a complaint was preferred against him.

Itlákh, for *Itlák*, Mar. (इतलाख) Issued from a public treasury, payment in money or kind from such a treasury or store: it is also applied to public servants borne on one establishment and employed on another, or additional or extra servants added for a time to a public office.

Itlák-navís, H. (from P. نويس) The officer who keeps the account of the expense and fees on the issue of summonses: formerly an accountant attached to the revenue collector, who wrote orders for the payment of revenue and other purposes, and kept an account of the fees paid to the peons, the surplus of which, above their wages, went to the credit of government.

Itlákh-nemnúk, Mar. (इतलाख नेमणूक) A fixed annual payment from a public treasury or store.

ITTIHÁM, H. (A, اتّهام) Suspecting something bad: in law, a charge, an imputation.

IVEJITU-GAIÁDU, Tam. (இவெசிதுகைகாடு) Statement shewing the amount of the collections and balance in money and kind.

ÍVUMÁNÍYAM, Tam. (ஈவுமானியம்) A grant of a proportion or per-centage on any branch of land revenue which fluctuates with the improvement or deterioration of the produce.

ÎWAZ, vernacularly, IWAJ, corruptly, EBAJ and EWAJ, H. (A. عوض) Equivalent, exchange, requital.

Îwaz-náma, H. (P. نامه) A deed of exchange.

IYAVAN, Tam. (இயவன்) An outcaste, a worker in leather and skins, a drummer.

IZÁFA, or IZÁFAT, vernacularly, IJÁPHÁ or IJÁPHAT, corruptly, EZAFA, EZAFUT, EZAPUT, H. &c. (A. اضافة, इजाफत) Increase, augmentation; any increase in the amount of revenue received from a country, whether from improved or additional cultivation, or from an enhanced rate of assessment; increase of revenue from any additional sources; grant of an entire village, granted rent-free as an extra allowance to the chief hereditary village or district officer.

Izáfa-beshi, H. &c. (اضافه بيشي) General increase in the rate of assessment.

Izafat-jamâ, or, vernacularly, *Ijáphat-jamá*, Mar. (इजाफत जमा) Additional or extra receipts of various kinds, as from money realized by government from the sale of presents, or from the sequestration of estates and appropriation of the revenue; also, money received into the treasury of one district, and credited to another. Under the Peshwa's government, an assumption or appropriation of revenue by the Sirsubadárs in the southern provinces in addition to the revenue they were to pay to the state. Under the Gaikwar's government, the additional annual revenue raised from the net receipts of the districts, from arrears of unpaid charges, and from loans. In Puraniya, an item in the *Hastabúd*, the specification of the rent to be paid by the Ryots for the current year.

Ijáphat-inám-gáon, Mar. (इजाफत इनाम गांव) An entire village granted rent-free to Desmukhs and Despáṇḍyas, as an additional remuneration.

Ijápha-jamín, Hindi (इजाफाजमीन) Land relet or taken into cultivation by the Ryots for the current year, an item in the *Hastabúd*, or village rent-roll.

Izẖár, H. &c. (A. اظهار) vernacularly **Ijhár**. Making manifest, publishing: a deposition or declaration in court, an affidavit, any statement made by the parties or witnesses in a suit.

Izẖári, H. (اظهاري) Relating to a deposition, issued upon a deposition, (an order, &c) a deponent.

Izẖár-navís, H. (P. نويس) A writer of depositions, an officer of the court who takes down depositions &c.

Izẖár-salámi, H. (from سلام, a compliment) A fee paid by a person who makes a statement or deposition before a subordinate officer of police, an unauthorised charge.

Izn, A. (اذن) Leave, licence: in law, permission granted by a master to a slave to engage in business or trade.

Iztirári-zabh, A. (اضطراري ذبح) Slaughtering an animal irregularly or accidentally, or by a wound inflicted anywhere except the throat.

Îzzat, H. (A. عزّت) Honour, credit, reputation, character.

Îzzat-asár, A. (عزّت اثار) lit., Honour to the traditions; but used in some places, even by Hindus, as the heading of an official paper, in any language, without their knowing the meaning of the words.

J

Jáb, or **Jábi**, H. (جاب, جابي) The muzzle of an ox.

Jáb, Ben. (জাব) A mixture of cut straw, oil-cake, and water, for feeding cattle; earth wetted to construct a wall with.

Jábáli, Ben. (জাবালি) Rice growing, and not in ear.

Jabdi, H. (جبدي) A sort of rice cultivated in Rohilkhand.

Jábtá, Mar. (जाबता, from A. ضابطه) A law, a regulation, a statute.

Jáchá, Ben. (যাচা) Appraising, valuing, examining, (goods &c).

Jáchandár, Ben. (যাচন্দার) An appraiser, a valuer: in the time when factories for piece goods were maintained an officer for the purpose of valuing them formed part of the establishment.

Jáchandári, Ben. (যাচন্দারী) The office of an appraiser.

Jaddi, H. (A. جدّي, from *Jad*, جد, an ancestor, a grandfather) Ancestral, paternal, ancestral or hereditary estate.

Jaḍḍigamu, Tel. (జడ్డిగము) A sowing machine.

Jádi, Karn. (ಜಾಡಿ) Assessment of land, revenue, land tax.

Jadíd, H. (A. جديد) New, modern: as applied to a Ryot, one newly settled in a village.

Jádo, H. (جادو) One of the two castes in a village employed in menial offices: in some places it is equivalent to *Ṣúdra*.

Jádon, H. (جادون, from S. *yádava*, यादव, a descendant of Yadu, यदु) A tribe of Rajputs who are found in considerable numbers about Agra and Mathura, in the central Doab, and in eastern Malwa, as landholders and cultivators: the Raja of Karaoli is of this tribe: they profess to be descendants of Kṛishṇa: some of their subdivisions are held in little esteem, and are termed Bagrís by their neighbours; but they are spirited farmers and rising in wealth and consideration.

Jáḍu, Karn. (ಜಾಡು) Unripe ears of corn left to ripen after the ripe ones are cut.

Jádú, H. (P. جادو) Magic, conjuring, fortune-telling.

Jádúgar, H. (P. جادوگر) A magician, a conjuror, a fortune-teller.

Jaḍyá, Mar. (जड्या) A jeweller, a setter of gems.

Jadwal, **Judwul**, H. (A. جدول) Lines ruled in a book; a board or card with threads fastened across it, to serve as lines to write upon when the board is placed underneath the paper.

Jadwal-kashi, H. (P. كشي) Drawing lines.

Jâfari, corruptly **Jaffry**, H. (A. جعفري) Lattice-work, a sort of screen of interwoven grass or reeds.

Jág, Mar. (जाग, S. जागरण, vigil) Riotous vigils, on the tenth night after the death of a Ṣúdra dying suddenly, by his family, to compel the spirit to enter the body of his son, or some other person, and reveal any secret matter desired to be known: any bustle or stir in a house or village at festivals.

Jágá, or **Jagá**, H. (جگا, جاگا) A division of the Bháṭ tribe, also called *Jágábhát*: see *Bháṭ*.

Jaganbansi, H. (جگنبنسي) A tribe of Brahman Zamindars in the Fattehpur Zilla.

Jágalyá, Mar. (जागल्या) **Jáglá**, Guz. (જાગલા) A watchman, a village watchman, a man of the Mhár or other low tribe employed in that capacity.

Jágalyí, Mar. (जागल्यी) *Jáglí*, Guz. (जागली) The office of watchman, the fees paid him.

JAGAT, H. (S. جگت, जगत्) The world.

Jagatkarttá, H. &c. (S. جگتکرتا) The maker or creator of the world.

Jagannátha, vernacularly *Jagannáth*, corruptly *Juggernaut*, H. &c. (S. जगन्नाथ, the *t* of *Jagat* changed to *n* before the *n* of *náth*, lord) Lord of the world, a name especially applied to *Kṛishṇa* in the form in which he is worshipped at the temple of *Jagannáth* at *Puri* in Orissa.

JAGÁT, Ben., Mar. (জগাৎ, जगात, vernacular corruption of the A. *zakát*, زكاة, alms) Custom, toll, duty on goods, a contribution collected amongst the villagers for a religious celebration.

Jagát-dár, or *Jagátyá*, Mar. (जगातदार, जगात्या) A customhouse officer, a collector or farmer of custom: see *Jakát*.

JÁGAṬI, Karn. (ಜಾಗಟೆ) A gong, a circular plate of sonorous bell-metal.

Jágaṭi-dásari, Karn. (ಜಾಗಟೆದಾಸರಿ) A sort of religious mendicant in Mysore, who beats a gong as he parades the streets of a town.

JAGGERY, JAGGREE, JAGGORY, JAGORY, (a corruption of the Kanarese *Sharkare*, ಶರ್ಕರೆ, from the S. *Śarkará*, शर्करा, whence perhaps the English, Sugar) Sugar in its unrefined state, or the juice inspissated by boiling, and poured into moulds, where it is allowed to dry in the form of pyramidal balls; clayed or candied sugar: also an inferior sugar made from the inspissated juice of the date and various kinds of palms.

JÁGÍR, also, allowably, JÁIGÍR, corruptly, JAGHEER, JAGHIRE, JAEGHEER, H. (P. جاگیر, جایگیر) JÁGÍR, JÁHGÍR, JÁHÁGÍR, Mar. (जागीर, जाहगीर, जाहागीर) Karn. (ಜಾಗೀರು) lit., Taking or occupying (*gír*) a place or position (*já*, or *jái*). A tenure common under the Mohammadan government, in which the public revenues of a given tract of land were made over to a servant of the state, together with the powers requisite to enable him to collect and appropriate such revenue, and administer the general government of the district. The assignment was either conditional or unconditional; in the former case, some public service, as the levy and maintenance of troops, or other specified duty, was engaged for: the latter was left to the entire disposal of the grantee. The assignment was either for a stated term, or, more usually, for the lifetime of the holder, lapsing, on his death, to the state, although not unusually renewed to his heir, on payment of a *nazarána*, or fine, and sometimes specified to be a hereditary assignment; without which specification it was held to be a life-tenure only: Ben. Reg. xxxvii. 1793. cl. 15. A Jágír was also liable to forfeiture on failure of performance of the conditions on which it was granted, or on the holder's incurring the displeasure of the emperor. On the other hand, in the inability of the state to vindicate its rights, a Jágír was sometimes converted into a perpetual and transferable estate; and the same consequence has resulted from the recognition of sundry Jágírs as hereditary by the British government after the extinction of the native governments by which they were originally granted; so that they have now come to be considered as family properties, of which the holders could not be rightfully dispossessed, and to which their legal heirs succeed, as a matter of course, without fine or *nazarána*, such having been silently dispensed with. This is particularly the case in the Maraṭha territories, in which, when first conquered, Jágír grants were found to be numerous, reducible to three classes—1. those held by descendants of the original ministers of the Rajas, as the *Pratinidhi* and the *Pradháns*, prior to the usurpation of the Peshwa, but continued, in some instances, under his rule; 2. those held by military chiefs, on condition of service, some of whom have held their fiefs from the time of the Mohammadan monarchies; and 3. those held under grants from the Peshwas, generally Brahmans or Maraṭhas of low family: they were all allowed to retain their lands on the principle of securing their services on a moderate scale, preserving the sovereignty of the British government entire, and interference with the chiefs on extraordinary occasions only. With regard to the Jágír in general, the especial object and character of the grant was commonly specified by the designation attached to it, as in the following examples: see also Ben. Regs. xxxvii. 1793. xlii. 1795. xxxvi. 1803. xiii. 1825. Bomb. Reg. xvii. 1827. x. cl. 38. Reg. vi. 1833. The term is also in use, although with some license, to designate temporary grants, allowances, or stipends, from the government to individuals.

Jágír-i-ahshám, H. (from A. احشام, q .v.) Lands granted for the maintenance of troops.

Jáhgír-amal, Mar. (जाहगीर अमल) The share of the revenue claimed by the Moghul government for the exchequer on certain holders of Jágírs after deducting the Maratha Chauth, and another fourth, or 25 per cent., for the *Faujdár*. Under the Peshwa and the British government it denotes, in some districts, the right to the revenue which remains after deducting the *Sardes-mukhi* and *Chauth*; in others after deducting the *Muhhása* portion of the *Chauth* only.

Jágír-i-bakhshí, H. (P. بخشي, q. v.) An assessment for the support of the Paymaster General or Commander-in-chief.

Jágír-diwání, H. (P. ديواني, q. v.) The grant of the collection of the revenues of Bengal, Behar, and Orissa to the Company.

Jágír-hhidmatí, H. (from خدمت, service) Assignment of land to village servants and officers.

Jágír-mahál, H. (P. محال) A district assigned.

Jágír-mashrúṭ, or *sharṭi*, H. (A. مشروط, or شرطي, stipulated) A Jágír granted with conditions.

Jágír-ghair-mashrúṭ, or *bilá-shart*, H. (A. غيرمشروط, بلا شرط) An unconditional or absolute assignment.

Jágír-i-nawárá, H. (H. نوارا, a barge) An assignment for the expense of keeping up an establishment of boats by the Nawab of Dacca in former times.

Jágír-saranjámí, Mar. (P. سرنجام, materials, property) An assignment for a specified purpose, as *Fauj-saranjámí-Jágír*, an assignment for the equipment of troops.

Jágír-i-sar, or *sír*, H. (P. سر, H. سير) Assignment for the support of an establishment.

Jágír-siyúr-ghál, H. (P. سيورغال) An assignment exempt from any conditions, or for charitable purposes.

Jágír-i-sarhár, H. (P. سركار, chief authority) The tract originally granted to the Company by the Nawab of the Carnatic, as an assignment for the maintenance of their troops.

Jágír-i-thánaját, H. (تهانه جات, plural of تهانه) An assignment for the support, of police stations or thánas, or for that of a local militia.

Jágír-i-tan, H. (P. تن, the body) An assignment for personal support, usually unconditional, but sometimes requiring personal service.

Jágír-i-ẓát, H. (A. ذات, person) *Jágír-játi*, or *játa*, Mar. (जात, for ذات) An assignment for personal support, or sometimes requiring personal service.

Jágírdár, H. (P. دار, who holds) The holder of any assignment of revenue: for his powers in the Bombay Presidency, see Bomb. Reg. xiii. 1830, and Act xiii. 1842.

Jágírdárí, H. (P. داري, having) The possession or rights of the holder of a Jágír.

Jágír- or *Jágír-dárí-sanad*, H. (A. سند) The deed or patent under which a *Jágír* was granted under the Mohammadan government.

Jágláin, H. (جاگلاين) A tribe of Játs.

Jahannam, H. (A. جهنّم) The Mohammadan hell, of which seven divisions are enumerated, appropriated severally to wicked Mohammadans, to Christians, Jews, Sabæans, Gebrs, idolaters, and hypocrites.

Jahán-panáh, H. (P. جهان پناه) Asylum of the world; a term of respectful address to a sovereign, or to a person of rank.

Jaḥím, H. (A. جحيم) One of the seven Mohammadan hells, that destined for idolaters.

Jáhír, Mar. (जाहीर) Public, notorious, made public, proclaimed: see *Ẓáhir*.

Jahíz, Jahez, H. (P. جهيز) Woman's property, whatever she takes with her to her husband's house, as vestments, jewellery, furniture, &c.; dowry, marriage-portion. It also occurs as an Arabic noun, Jaház, or Jiház (جهاز).

Jahnu-saptamí, S. (जहुसप्तमी) The seventh of Vaisákh, when a festival is observed in honour of Jahnu, the parent of Jáhnaví, or the Ganges so called.

Ja-ï, Jye, H. (جَي) Oats, introduced by the English, but the name was before applied to a small species of barley; also, as *Jayí*, to shoots of barley reared artificially at the *Dashará* festival: see *Jay*. In some parts of the north-west provinces oats are called *Rám-jáu*—the barley of *Ráma*.

Jáidád, less correctly, Jaedad, corruptly, Jydaad, H. (P. جاي, place, position, and داد, what gives) A place, employment: assets, funds, resources, an estate, property: the means or capabilities of any district in respect of revenue: an assignment of the revenues of a tract of land for the maintenance of an establishment, or of troops, granted for life, but very commonly with permitted succession to the next-of-kin, sometimes with a rent reserved.

Jáidád-ghair-manḳúla, H. (A. غير منقوله) Immoveable property.

Jáidád-istimrárí, H. (استمراري, perpetually) An assignment of revenue in perpetuity, with a reservation of a certain amount of rent, and of other government claims.

Jáidád-manḳúla, H. (A. منقوله) Moveable property.

Jáidád-maurúṣi, H. (A. موروثي) Ancestral or hereditary property.

Jáidád-zamín, H. (A. زمين) Arable land.

JÁIFA, A. (جايفه) A wound, a stab, one of the kinds punishable by fine.

JÁÍL, H. (جايل) Twice-ploughed land (Western Rohilkhand).

JAINA, or JAIN, S. (जैन) The name of a religion differing from Hinduism, the worship of certain deified mortals, *Jinas* or *Tírthankaras*; a follower of that religion, whether clerical or secular. Jains are met with in considerable numbers, especially among the merchants and bankers in Central and Western India: they are not uncommon in Bengal, or in the Dakhin.

JÁÍS, H. (جايس) A tribe of Rájputs of the solar branch, residing principally about Mathura.

JAITÍ, JYTEE, also JAICHÍ, JYCHEE, H. (جيتي, جيچي) A species of Euphorbia which grows in the north-western provinces, and yields an excellent oil.

JAISWÁR, H. (جيسوار) A tribe of inferior *Jádobansí* Rájputs in the Central Doab.

JAISWÁRÁ, corruptly, JASAWARA and JUSWAR, H. (جيسوارا) A name given to subdivisions of low-caste tribes, from their having come originally from the town of *Jais*, in Oudh.

JAIWÁR, Hindi (जैवार) The head inhabitants of a village. (Puraniya).

JÁÍZ, H. (A. جايز) Current, passing, legal, lawful, authorized: in law, the term is applied to such contracts as may be dissolved at the pleasure of either party.

JAJMÁN, JUJMAN, corruptly, JIJMAN, H. &c. (ججمان, S. यजमानः) A person who employs and fees Bráhmans for the performance of any solemn or religious ceremony: as it is not unusual for the relation between the employer and those employed to become hereditary, the latter come to regard the former as their pupils or clients, and claim as their right or due the fees that are to be paid on such occasions, although they should not perform the ceremonies: from religious, the term passed to very miscellaneous relations, and barbers, washermen, and sweepers claim, in some parts of Hindustan, a prescriptive or hereditary right to be employed and paid by certain individuals, whom they therefore style their *Jajmáns*; and *Ghátiás* and others, who conduct parties of pilgrims to Benares or other sacred places, give the same name to all those to whom they act as guides. In the south of India, *Yajmán* or *Ijmán* commonly denotes a householder, especially one of respectability, and who is often the head man of the village, to which functionary the title is consequently also applied: see *Yajamána*.

JAKÁT, Mar. (जकात्) JAKÁTI, JAKÁYATI, Karn. (ಜಕಾತಿ, ಜಕಾಯಿತಿ) Customs, duties; land or transit duties especially, as opposed to sea customs: see also *Jagát*.

Jakátdár, Mar. (from P. دار) Collector of customs, either the government officer or a farmer.

Jakáyati-guttige, Karn. (ಜಕಾಯಿತಿಗುತ್ತಿಗೆ) A contract for custom-house duties.

JAKERI, JAKÍRI, &c., Karn. (ಜಕೆರಿ, ಜಕೀರಿ) A store, a hoard.

Jakeri-khane, Karn. (ಜಕೆರಿಖಾನೆ) A storehouse, a warehouse.

JAKERE-DHÁNYA, Karn. (ಜಕೆರಿಧಾನ್ಯ) Name of an additional cess in Mysore, imposed in place of a payment in grain.

JALA, JAL, JULU, or JUL, (adopted in all the dialects, from the S. जलं) Water.

Jala, H. (جله) A lake.

Jaladivya, S. &c. (जलदिव्यं) The oath or ordeal of water.

Jalagaḍugu, Tel. (జలగడుగు) Washing sand or soil for diamond or gold dust.

Jalagára, Karn. (ಜಲಗಾರ) A caste of persons who sweep the streets, or wash refuse, in search of lost money or valuables.

Jalagára-gutta, Karn. (ಜಲಗಾರಗುತ್ತ) A tax on persons employed in searching or washing for money or valuables.

Jalári, or *Jaladári*, Karn. (ಜಲಾರಿ, ಜಲದಾರಿ) A drain, a kennel, a gutter.

Jalása, *Julasu*, (جلاسه, from S. Áṣaya, आशय, receptacle) A pool, a reservoir, a tank.

Jalasankalpa, (जलसंकल्पः) Ratification of an agreement or a promise by pouring water upon the hand of the person with whom the agreement is made, or to whom the promise is given.

Jalchar, *Julchur*, H. &c. (جلچر, from S. चर, what moves) Any aquatic animal.

Jalchhatra, Ben. (জলছত্র) A temporary shed, where water and other refreshments are supplied gratuitously to passengers in the hot weather.

Jalganḍa, Ben. (জলগণ্ড) Land under water, a swamp, a marsh.

Jalhá, Hindi (जलहा) Inundation.

Jali, Ben. (জলি) A kind of rice.

Jalhá, or *Jelka*, (?) Ben. A long narrow boat or canoe used by river robbers.

Jalkar, Julkur, corruptly, *Jelcora,* H. (جلكر, from S. जल, water, कर, *kara,* tax or toll) Profits or rents derived from the water, lakes, ponds, or the like, upon a tract of country or an estate, with the right of fishing, and of cultivating the beds if dry.

Jalkháyá, Hindi (जलखाया) Dried up, parched, (soil, &c.); lit., the moisture of which is eaten by the sun: also *Jalgaiya,* water-gone, &c.

Jalmárg, Mar. (S. जलमार्ग) lit., The water-way, sea customs.

Jalmandir, Mar. (S. जलमन्दिर) A water-house, a summer-house in the midst of water; or subterraneous apartments constructed on the bank of a river.

Jalotsarg, H. (S. جلوتسرگ, from *Utsarga,* letting go) The typical marriage of a newly-dug well or piece of water; the bridegroom being personated by a man holding the sálagrám stone, and the bride by another holding an image: see *Banotsarga.*

Jalpad, Julpud, H. (جلپد) Land recovered from water or sea, and brought into cultivation.

Jalpáe, Uriya (ଜଲପାଏ) A water vessel: a name given in Cuttack to scattered patches of land subject to inundation.

Jalpán, Julpan, Ben. (S. জলপান, from S. पान, drinking) Drinking water, any slight or occasional refreshment, breakfast, luncheon.

Jaltarpan, Julturpun, H. &c. (جلترپن, from S. तर्पण) Presentation of water to the gods and manes, part of a Hindu's daily devotions.

Jalthal, Julthul, H. (جل تهل) Land and water, or land partly under water.

JALÁWATI, H. (جلاوتي) Emigration.

JÁL, H. &c. (S. جال) A net.

Jáli, H. (جالي) A net or bag of twisted rope for holding grass, straw, or fodder, and tied to the mouth of a bullock for his feeding while at work: a muzzle.

Jáliya, Ben. (জালিযা) A fisherman, a bird or beast catcher by nets.

JÂL, H. (A. جعل) Forgery, counterfeit.

Jâlkághaz, H. (from A. كاغذ, paper) A forged paper or document.

Jâlsáz, H. (from P. ساز, making) A forger, a counterfeiter.

Jâlsázi, H. (جعلسازي) Forging, counterfeiting.

JÁLÁ, H. &c. (S. جالا) A large water-jar.

JÁLÁ, Ben. (জালা, from S. ज्वाला) Burning, combustion, flame.

Jálan, Ben. (জালন) Kindling, lighting, as a lamp or fire: *Uriya,* (ଜାଳନ) Fuel.

Jálchauhiá, Uriya, A watch or guard over land supplying fuel for the manufacture of salt.

Jaḷít, Mar. (जळीत, corruption of Mar. and S. ज्वलित, lit., burned) Applied to money &c., extorted or lost, or not likely to be realized, as, to a fine imposed to counterbalance a gain supposed to have been made fraudulently, to a loss incurred through mismanagement, or to an oppressive and extortionary exaction; also, more literally, to injury suffered by fire, and the head under which remissions of rent or revenue are charged on account of losses by fire.

Jaḷít-bákí, Mar. (जळीतबाकी, from باقي, remainder) Money due, especially from the Ryots, given up as irrecoverable.

Jaḷít-khat, Mar. (जळीतखत) A bond or note which has been cashed, also one the amount of which is given up as never likely to be realized.

Jálpái, Uriya, (ଜାଳପାଇ) Fuel: lands assigned for the salt-boilers: allowance made to Zamindars in Orissa for the fuel cut from their lands for salt-boilers.

JÁLÁ, (?) Beds in which rice is grown before it is transplanted (Chittagong): perhaps from *Jál,* a net or lattice, from the position of the beds.

JALÁD, H. (A. جلاد) JALLÁD, Ben. (জল্লাদ) An executioner, a hangman.

JALÁLIÁ, JULÁLEÁ, H. (جلاليا) A fine species of wheat with reddish ears (Ságar).

JÁLIGUTTA, Karn. (ಜಾಲಿಗುತ್ತ) A tax on the cultivators for the leaves of the Jáli, or whitethorn tree, browsed on by the cattle (Mysore).

JALM, H. (جلم) *Jalma,* Karn. (ಜಲ್ಮ) Birthright, right in the soil (Ságar): a vernacular corruption of *Janm,* q. v.

JALÚS, H. (A. جلوس, from جلس, sitting) The accession of a sovereign to his throne, his sitting on the masnad.

Jalúsí, H. (جلوسي) The year or date reckoned from a prince's accession.

JÁM, H. &c. (P. جام) A cup, a goblet.

JAMÂ, vernacularly, JAMÁ, or JAME, corruptly, JAMMA, JUMMA, H. (A. جمع) Mar. (जमा) Ben. (জমা) Tel. (జమా) Karn. (ಜಮಾ, ಜಮೆ) Amount, aggregate, total in general, but applied especially to the debit or receipt side of an account, and to the rental of an estate; also to the total amount of rent or revenue payable by a cultivator or a Zamindar, including all cesses, as well as land-tax:

latterly it is more especially applied to the revenue assessed upon the land alone: its special application is commonly defined by the term with which it is compounded, as, *Asal-jamâ, Ain-jamâ, Bázi-jamâ, Istímrárí-jamâ*, &c., q. v.: see also Beng. Regs. i. 1793. i. ii. xxvii. 1795. xxiii. 1803. vii. 1822. &c.; Acts i. 1841. iv. 1846. &c.; Mad. Regs. xxv. 1802. ii. 1806.; Bomb. Reg. xvii. 1827. &c.

Jamâ-bandí, Jamábandí, H. &c. (جمعبندي, जमाबंदी, from *Band*, a binding) Settlement of the amount of revenue assessed upon an estate, a village, or district; a village or district rent-roll; a register of the village holdings; a statement exhibiting the particulars of the public revenue, its amount, and how assessed; annual settlement of revenue with cultivators, or Ryotwarí settlement: an annual statement, modified according to the circumstances under which the revenue is paid, whether by individuals or communities, and whether to a Zamindar or to the government. In Bengal, the Jamâ-bandí shews the name of the Ryot, his tenure, the quality of his land, its extent, the rate per *bíghá*, and the total rent formerly, inclusive of all extra cesses, paid to the Zamindar. In the north-west provinces it is a document intended to regulate the transactions between the cultivators and Lambardárs, and is the basis of the Patwárí's annual accounts; being, in the first instance, drawn up and attested by the Patwárí and Kánungos, and then signed by the settlement officer: it is a tabular statement specifying the number of the division of the village, the name of the cultivator, the names of his fields, their survey number, their extent by survey and by village measurement, any lands not included in their area, those liable to assessment, the rate of assessment per *bíghá*, rate payable in cash or in kind, the total produce, the share of the cultivators, the share of the landlord, the payment according to estimated value of the crops, shewing the kind of crops, their estimated value, and the share of the government, the fees of the Patwárí, in cash or in kind, the village charges and expenses, the total value of the produce in money or in kind, and a column for remarks. (The form is given in the original in the Appendix to the Directions for Settlement Officers, issued by the Agra government in 1844, and its translation in the Settlement Misl, or Supplement to the Directions, Agra, 1847.) Although, however, in these instances the term has a specific application, it is useable in a variety of relations to statements of revenue assessment.

Jamâ-bandí-kháṣ, H. (from A. خاص, select) Account of revenue assessment of lands in charge of an officer of the government; one of the village accounts formerly kept by the Kánungo.

Jamâ-bandí-naḳdí, H. (from A. نقد) Assessment of revenue of lands payable in money, not in produce.

Jamá-bandí-paṭṭí, Mar. (जमाबंदीपट्टी) A document formerly furnished by the collector of a district to the Páṭíl of a village, on settling the amount of revenue to be paid by the village for the ensuing year, specifying the amount, and the consent of the villagers.

Jamá-bandí-tírappu, Tam. (சமாபந்திதீரப்பு) Particulars of a revenue settlement.

Jamâ-bandí, or *-bastí-tashkhíṣ*, H. (A. تشخيص) Amount of revenue assessed upon any tract agreeably to a fixed standard.

Ásámi-wár-jamâbandí, H. (from اسامي, a cultivator) Account of revenue assessment settled with each individual cultivator: also, *Raiat-wár-jamâbandí*.

Jinswár-jamâbandí, H. (A. جنس, an article) Account of revenue assessed at certain rates, according to the produce or crops raised.

Khetwár-jamâbandí, H. (from كهيت, S. खेत, a field) Account of revenue assessed at a certain rate per field.

Ḳismwár-jamâbandí, H. (A. قسم, kind, sort) Statement of revenue assessed at certain rates, according to the kind or quality of the soil.

Jamâ-beríj, H. (P. بريج, an account) Particular statement of a revenue assessment.

Jamâ-chandína, H. (P. چندين, such, so many) Collections or revenue from miscellaneous sources.

Jamâ-dehátí, H. (P. ده, a village) Settlement of the proportion of revenue to be paid by each village severally.

Jamâí, corruptly, *Jummaee*, H. جمعي) Fiscal, financial; liable or subject to revenue, as land, &c.; a cultivator paying a fixed *jamâ*, either to the landlord or to the state, and who cannot be dispossessed as long as he pays it.

Jamâ-i-háṣil, H. (جمع حاصل) The total of the revenue collected.

Jamâ-jharṭí, H. (جمعجهرتي, from جهرنا, to flow or pass away) Receipts and disbursements of a village or estate: periodical return of either cash or grain.

Jamâ-kadím, or *Ḳadími-jamâ*, H. (جمع قديم, from A.

قديم, old) Total amount of revenue as fixed from an old date.

Jamá-hámil, or *-kamál*, H. (A. كامل, كمال, entire, perfect) Complete, final, or standard assessment. In Bengal the term usually denotes the settlement made by Akbar's financial minister, *Todar Mal*, also known as the *Jamá-kámil-ṭumári*: (see the next.) In the Madras provinces it was applied to the assessment of the revenue of the northern Sirkárs made about A. D. 1512-1570, or to one subsequently framed in the reign of *Aalamgir*, or about 1684-1687, for the whole of the Dakhin, on the principles of *Todar Mal's* assessment, and accordingly, in Kandesh it denotes the highest rate which any village had been made to pay, although not unfrequently falling short of the estimated rental, or *tanhhá*, as calculated at an earlier date. In Cuttack, the *Jamá-kamál* applied to a revision of the same, which then became the standard assessment.

Jamá-hámil-ṭumári, H. (A. طومار, a roll, an account book) The particulars of the settlement of *Todar Mal*, as modified in Bengal by *Sultan Shujá* in 1658, and *Jaffir Khan* in 1722, the latter of which was carried into operation by his successor *Shujá Khan* in 1729.

Jamá-kharch, H. (A. خرچ) Receipts and disbursements: the debit and credit sides of an account.

Patan (*puttun* ?) *-jamá-kharch*, A treasury account formerly kept, shewing the monthly receipts and disbursements.

Jamá-mahál-badraḳa, H. (A. بدرقة, an escort) Revenue, formerly levied as transit duties; an account of the same kept by the Kánungo.

Jamá-mahál-mir-behri, H. (ميربهر, harbour master) Port duties, or an account of them.

Terij-jamá-kharch, An annual treasury account of receipts and disbursements made up from the monthly statements.

Jamá-kul, H. (A. كل, all) Total amount of revenue assessment.

Jamá-mufaṣṣal, incorrectly, *-mofuṣṣil*, H. (A. مفصل, a country) The gross revenue to be collected in all the villages of a Zamindárí, as rated in the accounts, and to be paid after deducting charges to the Zamindar.

Jamá-muḥarrari, H. (A. مقرر, fixed) A fixed or permanent amount of revenue, an account formerly kept by the Kánungo of lands permanently assessed.

Jamá-munásib, (A. مناسب, proper) A fair or reasonable amount of assessment.

Jamá naḳiṣ, H. (A. ناقص, defective) Sum total of deficiencies, the amount of allowed deductions from the revenue or account of public expenses borne by the Zamindars and tenants.

Jamá-nawis, H. (P. نويس) An accountant.

Jamá-pádsháhi, or *-bádsháhi*, (P. پادشاهی) Revenue levied under royal authority, or on account of the sovereign.

Jamá-panchautra, H. (H. پنچوتره) Revenue levied as customary, or at a custom-house; an account kept of such revenue.

Jamá-parganáti, H. (P. پرگنه, a district) The revenue assessed upon a Pargana, and payable at the district treasury.

Jamá-raḥmi, H. (A. رقم, writing) An estimated or computed total, the total amount of revenue which an estate or district is estimated to yield.

Jamá-ṣadr, corruptly *ṣudder*, H. (A. صدر, chief) The revenue assessment settled with the government direct by the proprietors or contractors, in opposition to the *Jamá mufaṣṣal*.

Jamá-taḳsím, H. (A. تقسيم, division) The portions of the general rent or revenue roll belonging to different portions of territory.

Jamá-ṭúmárí, also *Jamá-ṭúmárí-hámil*, or *Jamá-ṭúmárí-tashkhís*, H. (from طومار, a roll, and تشخيص, ascertained) The settlement of the revenue according to the rent-rolls or assessments of *Todar Mal*, with the subsequent modifications made by different Subahdárs of Bengal, forming the basis on which the first financial arrangements of the English government were founded anterior to the formation of the decennial and subsequent permanent settlement.

Jamá-zamín, H. (A. زمين, land) Land, of which the assessment has been settled, or land paying revenue. As applied to an under-tenure, it means one in which the revenue has been settled at a fixed rate on the land, irrespective of cultivation (?).

Jamá-zamíndárí, H. (زميندار, a landholder) Amount of a revenue settled to be paid by a Zamindar to the government.

Jamá-wáṣil, or *-waṣúl-báḳi*, H. (A. واصل, collected, وصول, collection, and باقي, remainder) Karn. (జమావసూలుబాకీ) The amount of the collections and outstanding balances; an account shewing the particulars of the revenue to be paid, of the instalments discharged, and the arrears due: see *Akhir-i-jamá-wáṣil-báhi*.

Sadr-jamá, H. (سدر جمع) The collections or revenue of a permanently settled estate, as recognised by the government.

Siwái-jamá, H. (A. سواي, except) Revenue raised from other sources than the land-tax.

Jamâdár, Jumadár, corruptly, *Jemidár*, less usually, but allowably, *Jemátdár*, H. (جمعدار ,جمعتدار) The chief or leader of any number of persons; in military language, a native subaltern officer, second to the Subahdár; an officer of police, customs, or excise, second to the Dárogház; a head domestic servant, a sort of major-domo, but unconnected with the table department: among the Marathas, an officer appointed to protect the crops from the depredations of an army and its followers.

Jámâ-masjid, corruptly, *Jumma-musjeed*, H. (A. جامع مسجد) The principal mosque or Mohammadan place of prayer in a city.

Jamáti, Mar. (जमाती, A. جمعات, total) Additional imposts, completing the public revenue.

JAMÁDI-UL-ÁWAL, H. (A. جمادي الاول) *Jamádi* the first, the first month so named, the fifth of the Mohammadan year.

Jamádi-al-ákhir, or *-as-ṣáni*, (الثاني ,جمادي الاخر) The last or second *Jamádi*, the sixth month of the Mohammadan year.

JÁMÁI, Ben. (জামাই, S. जामातृ) JÁMÁT, Mar. (जामात) A son-in-law.

JAMÁTU, Tel. (జమాతు) The place where each manufacturer manufactures salt.

JAMBAGUTTA, Karn. (ಜಂಬಗುತ್ತ) A tax on the long grass called *jamba*, used in thatching huts and making mats.

JAMBU DWÍPA, S. (जम्बुद्वीपः) The island or circular continent of Jambu, including India.

JÁMDÁR, Mar. (जामदार) An officer in charge of the treasure, jewels, &c., of the head of the state: (probably corruption of *Jamâdár*).

Jámdár-kháná, Mar. (जामदारखाना) The public treasury.

JAMED-ÁḶU, Karn. (ಜಮೆದಾಳು) A predial slave in Kurg: (said to be from *áḷu*, an individual, and *jamâ*, lands paying revenue.

Bhúmi-jamed-áḷu, Karn. (from S. भूमि, earth) A slave attached to the soil, and only transferable with it.

Okhalu-jamed-áḷu, Karn. (from *Okhalu*, ಒಕ್ಕಲು, a cultivator) A slave attached to the person of a farmer or cultivator, and who may be either mortgaged or sold by him.

JAMI, or JAMÍN, Ben. (জমি, জমীন, from زمين) Land: see *Zamín*.

JÁMIN, Ben. (জামিন, from ضامن) JÁMÍN, Mar. (जामीन) JÁMUN, Mal. (ജാമ്യൻ) A surety: see *Zámin*.

JAMNAUṬÁ, or JAMNAUṬÍÁ, JUMNOUTA, JUMNOUTEA, H (جمنوتا ,جمنوتيا) A certain consideration given to a *zámin* or surety, generally about five per cent.

JAMOG, JUMOG, H. (جموگ) Transfer of liabilities by mutual consent, a conditional mortgage (Benares, &c.).

Jamogdár, H. (جموگدار) A person who lends a landed proprietor money, and recovers it from the Ryots.

JAMOWÁ, H. (جموا) Indigo planted before the rains, and irrigated by artificial means (Central Doab).

JAMÚAṬ, H. (جموت) Foundation of a well; the festival held on its construction.

JANALOKA, S. (जन, a man, and लोक, a world) One of the seven regions of the universe; that in which pious men or *Ṛishis* abide, after quitting the earth.

JANÁB, H. (A. جناب) Majesty; but used in Hindustan as a respectful term of address to a person of rank and office, whether native or European, Your excellency, or Your worship, or, still more respectfully, *Janáb-i-âáli*, Your high eminence.

JANÁI ṢADKA, H. (جناي صدقه) Alms given at the birth of a child.

JANÁJÁT, H. (جنا جات) Man by man, singly; applied to leases granted to each individual Ryot.

JANANÍ, H. (S. जननी) A mother, the actual mother of a child, in contradistinction to a step-mother.

JANÁZA, H. (A. جنازه) A bier, a coffin, a funeral.

JÁṆCH, H. (S. جانچ) Trial, proof, assay.

JANDÁULIÁ, JUNDOULEA, H. (جندوليا) A small clan of Rájputs in Banda.

JANDE, JANDEVU, Tel. (జంద, జందెవు) The thread worn by Bráhmans: see *Janeú*.

JANDRÁ, JUNDRU, H. (جندرا ,जंदरा) A pitchfork; also a kind of rake used in the north-west provinces to divide the fields into small beds during irrigation.

JANEO, or JANEÚ, H. (جنيو, from S. *Yajnopavíta*) JÁNWEZ, Mar. A cord or string of cotton worn over the left shoulder, crossing obliquely to the right hip: the use of it is properly restricted to the three primitive castes—the Bráhman, Kshatriya, and Vaisya, of whom the first only remains, and it should be therefore confined to the Bráhmans; but it is assumed by other castes, as by the Vaidyas, or medical caste, in Bengal, and by carpenters, blacksmiths, goldsmiths, and others, in the Dakhin.

JANGAL, JUNGUL, commonly, JUNGLE, H., and in most dialects, (جنگل, S. जंगल) A forest, a thicket; any tract overrun with bushes or trees, or suffered to be overspread with vegetation.

Jangal-buri, H. (P. بري, from بريدن, to cut) Clearing lands of jangal; also applied to a sort of tenure under under which waste or forest lands were granted in absolute property to the clearer, free of rent or revenue for a certain time, at the expiration of which such part or parts as were in cultivation were to be liable to a fixed rent and customary imposts.—Ben. Reg. viii. 1793. cl. 8.

Jangal-buri-táluḳ, H. (A. تعلقه, an estate) An estate or tract of land overrun with jangal, held on easy terms for a given term, on condition of its being cleared.

Janglá, or *Janglí*, H. (S. جنگلي, جنگلا) Wild, waste, woody, savage, any thing characterized by thicket, or living in or fit for forests.

Jangal-mahál, H. (A. محال, plural of محل) Forest tracts or estates; applied especially to the districts on the west of Bengal, between it and Berar and Cuttack.—Ben. Reg. v. 1800. xviii. 1805.

Jangal-tarí, or *-turee*, H. (P. تري, moisture) Situated in low forest land, applied to an estate so circumstanced: as designating a tract of country it denotes the lands in the north of Puraniya and Tirhut lying under the first range of hills.

Jangali, *Jangulikan*, Mal. (ജാംഗലി, ജാംഗുലികൻ) A snake catcher; one also who pretends to cure snake bites.

Jangál, Ben. (জংগাল, জাংগাল) Mal. (ജംഗാലം) A limit, a boundary, a balk in rice fields to confine the water, a dam, a dike.

Jángálbándhá, Ben. (জাংগালবাংধা) An embankment.

Jangam, or Jangama, H. &c. (جنگم, S. जङ्गम) Moveable, what has life and movement, transient, moveable (as property).

Jangam, Tel. (జంగం) A tailor.

Jangama, S. (जङ्गम, but current in the dialects, especially of the south) The priest of the Lingayit sect, who, although not a Bráhman, officiates at their religious rites: where the population of a village consists in any large proportion of his disciples he is a member of the establishment, and holds rent-free or Inám lands, thence known as *Jangama Inám*. He is sometimes domesticated in *maths*, or monasteries, and otherwise is a vagrant living on alms.

Jángaṛ, Mar. (जांगड) Goods, especially cloths, taken from a shop for inspection; memorandum of goods so taken.

Jangháŕá, Jungháŕá, H. (جنگهارا) A large and turbulent tribe of Rájputs in Rohilkhand, a branch of the Tuar clan.

Janghúlaru, Karn. (plural, ಜಂಘೂಲರು, *Śúdras* speaking Telugu, and hawking drugs for sale.

Janghá, Hindi (जंघा, in S. a leg) The post or uprights on each side of the mouth of a well.

Janghalá, Hindi (जंघला) A rate in a lease to include the inferior crops when sown (Puraniya).

Jangi, Jungee, H. (P. جنگه, *jang*, war, conflict) Warlike, quarrelsome, turbulent.

Jangi-kaṭṭubaḍi, H., Tel. (కట్టుబడి, a peon) Militiamen, feudal retainers, obliged, when called upon, to appear in arms, in consideration of which they hold rent-free or lightly-assessed lands.

Jang-zargarí, H. (P. جنگ زرگري) lit., A goldsmith's quarrel, that is, a collusive dispute between two parties in order to defraud a third.

Jangrá, Jungra, H. (جنگرا) The haulm of *kharif* or autumnal crops.

Janguḷi, Karn. (ಜಂಗುಳಿ) The cattle of the whole village.

Janguḷi-gára, Karn. (ಜಂಗುಳಿಗಾರ) One who has charge of the village cattle.

Jánibdár, H. (جانب, a side, and دار, who has) A defender.

Jánibain, H. (A. جانبين, dual of جاناب) On both sides, on behalf of both parties to a suit.

Já-nishín, H. (P. جانشين) A deputy, a substitute, a *locum-tenens*, the disciple appointed to succeed as principal of an establishment of religious mendicants.

Janikarshak, Mar. (S. जनि, birth, and कर्षक, cultivator) An old resident cultivator. (It is given also *Karshan*, but apparently incorrectly, *Karshan* meaning cultivating, not cultivator).

Janjír, Ben., Mar. (জংজীর, जंजीर, or जंजीरा, P. زنجير) A chain.

Janjír-jáminí, corruption of *Zanjir-záminí*, H. &c. (जंजीरजामिनी) Chain security, mutual or collective surety or assurance.

Janjírá, Mar. (जंजीरा, A. جزيره) A fortified rock, a fort surrounded by the sea.

Jánkar, less correctly Jákar, or Jakur, H. (جاكر, جانكر) A pledge in deposit until goods which have been taken away are finally approved of.

Janma, Junmu, commonly pronounced Janam, or Junum. or, indistinctly, Janm, Junm, vernacularly corrupted in Malwa and Mysore to Jalm, or Jalma, corruptly Jenm, Jumnum, Jummam; the more correct form, however, even in

Karnáta, is Janma, S. but in most dialects H. (جنم, S. जन्म) Ben. (জন্ম) Mar. (जन्म) Tel. (జన్మము) Karn. (ಜನ್ಮ, ಜಲ್ಮ, ಜಳ್ಮ) (?) Janmam, Tam. (சன்மம்) Mal. (ജന്മം) Uriya, (ଜନ୍ମ) Birth, also in some places, especially Malabar, birthright, the hereditary or proprietary occupancy of land, which may be sold or mortgaged in various ways, the right to which passes by descent according to law, and it can be left to strangers by will only on failure of heirs: if there be no heirs, nor disposal by bequest, it escheats to the Raja: it cannot be sold without the concurrence of the heir at law. The term is applicable to other than to individuals, as there may be the Janm lands, *i. e.* hereditary lands, of a college or temple.

Janmabhúmi, S. &c. (जन्मभूमिः) Birth-place, country of one's birth.

Janmádhikáran, Mal. (S. ജന്മാധികാരം, from S. अधिकार, right) Birthright, any claim to property or privilege derived from birth.

Janmádhikárí, Mal. (S. ജന്മാധികാരി) One who claims by right of birth.

Janmadina, S. (जन्मदिनः) Birthday.

Janma, or *Janm-dravyam*, Mal. (S. द्रव्यं, thing, substance) The price given for landed property.

Janmakáran, or *Janmkár*, Mal. (S. ജന്മകാരൻ) A landholder, a proprietor of land.

Janmakávan, Mal. (ജന്മകാവൻ) A fee given to a head man among slaves for watching rice fields.

Janmakudiyán, *Janmkudián*, Mal. (ജന്മകുടിയാൻ) A tenant or temporary occupant of a Janm, one who has acquired his property by purchase or mortgage in opposition to the old hereditary proprietor.

Janma- or *Janm-kolunavan*, Mal. A purchaser of proprietary lands.

Janmí, Mal. (S. ജന്മി) An owner of land, a proprietor, the original owner or proprietor by hereditary right.

Janmiḍosam, Mal. (S. ജന്മിദൊശം) The claim of the proprietor or landlord on mortgaged land.

Janmimáṛáttam, Mal. (ജന്മിമാറാട്ടം) Dispute about landed property.

Janma, or *Janm-ponnajam*, (?) Mal. A mortgage with posession, on which an advance on the sum lent being made the mortgager parts with any rights he might have originally reserved.

Janmaváda, Mal. (S. ജന്മവാദ) A dispute or suit about landed property.

Janma, or *Janm-panay-elluta*, Mal. (പണയ, a mortgage) A deed of mortgage, on which an additional sum being raised, the proprietor engages never to transfer the land to any other purchaser without the consent of the mortgagee: he may redeem it himself on paying the principal and interest, the latter not to exceed twice the amount of the former.

Janma-patra, or *-patriká*, S. &c. (पत्र, or पत्रिका, a leaf) A horoscope, a paper prepared at the birth of a child, foretelling his fate according to the aspects of the planets.

Janmáshṭamí, S. (अष्टमी, the eighth) The eighth lunation of *Bhádra* (Aug.-Sept.), the anniversary of the nativity of Krishṇa, observed as a solemn festival by the Vaishnavas.

Janmalagna, S. (जन्मलग्नं) The conjunction of the sun and a sign of the ecliptic at the moment of the birth of a child.

Jáṇt, H. (جانت) A wooden trough for raising water.

Jaṇtá, H. (جانتا) Jáṇteṇ, Játeṇ, Mar. (जातें, जातें) A handmill.

Jaṇtlí, Mar. (जांतली) A small handmill.

Jaṇṭe, Karn. (ಜಂಟಿ) Partnership.

Janṭebaduku, Karn. (ಜಂಟಿಬದುಕು) A joint or partnership concern.

Jantekaikágadu, Karn. (ಜಂಟೆಕೈಕಾಗದು) A paper of agreement between two persons.

Jantr, or Jantra, H. (جنتر, S. यन्त्रं) A machine of any kind, a dial, a mystical diagram.

Jantra-mantra, or *Juntr-muntr*, H. (S. यन्त्र, and मन्त्र, a charm) Conjuring, performing magical or mystical ceremonies, in which diagrams are drawn, and charms or prayers are repeated.

Jantraṇá, Uriya (ଯନ୍ତ୍ରଣା) Torture.

Jantrí, Juntree, H. &c. (جنتري, S. यन्त्री) An almanack.

Jantrí, or *Juntree-bahi*, or *-kitáb*, H. (بهي, a register, or كتاب, a book) The almanack with civil and army lists and directory, published in India, and in very general circulation. The compilation is generally known as the Gentry book.

Janukúliaru, (?) Karn. A class of slaves in Kurg (the word is in the plural).

Janútúrwa, H. (جنوتوروا) A small Rájput tribe in the district of Benares.

Janwár, Junwar, also Jinwár, H. (جنوار) A small tribe of Rájputs in Bundelkhand: (care must be taken not to reverse the quantities of the vowels, as they would not like to be called *Jánwar* or *Janwur*, a brute, an animal).

Janwariá, H. (جنوريا) A tribe of Ahírs.

Jaráitá, H. (جرايتا) A division of the Tuár clan.

Járaja, S. (जारज) A child of a woman by any other man than her husband.

Jarethá, H. (جريتها) The name of one of the clans of the Káchhís, or cultivators so termed.

Jarelá, H. (جريلا) A sort of rice grown in Rohilkhand.

Jarh, A. (جرح) Inflicting a wound, a wound, an offence against the person, in law.

Jaṛhan, or Jaḍhan, Juṛhun, Juḍhun, H. (جڈھن , جڑھن) A large species of rice reaped at the end of the rainy season.

Járí, corruptly, Jerree, H. &c. (A. جاري) lit., Flowing; met., current, going on, set a-going, issued; cultivated for a second or subsequent crop, &c. Karn. (ಜರಿ) Free from an attachment (land), exempt from revenue.

Járí-amal, Mar. (जारीअमल) Items of revenue which were once current, but are in the course of being alienated from the public revenue, as the *Sardeṣmukhí* and *Chauth*.

Járí-bhúmi, Tel. (జారీభూమి) Land cultivated by the Ryots of the state. Karn., Land, which had been sequestrated, again let or sold, and put into paying cultivation. H. (?) Land which, after yielding one crop, is again put under tillage for another.

Járí-chiṭu, Karn. (ಜಾರಿಚೀಟು) A written grant.

Járí-inámu, Tel., Karn. (జారీయినాము) A grant of land or other endowment still in force, not resumed.

Járí-inámu-háṇiki, Karn. (ರಾಣಿಕಿ) A light or quit rent on grants still in force.

Járí-rupaiá, H. (جاري روپيا) Current rupee, current coin.

Jaríb, Jureeb, H. (A. جريب) Mar., Tel. (जरीब) A measure: in its original use, a measure of capacity equal to 4 *ḳafiz*, or 384 *madd*, about 768 pounds; it then became applied to a land measure, or as much land as could be sown with a *jaríb* of seed corn; and then appears to have been loosely used as an equivalent to a *bighá*. In course of time it occurs as a measure of land of various extent, and as the chain or rope for measuring. In the north-west provinces the measurements were made by a chain, and the *jaríb* is equal to 5 chains of 11 yards each, or to 60 *gaz*, or 20 *gaṭhás* or knots. A square of one *jaríb* is a *bighá*. Before the new system of survey it was usual to measure lands paying revenue with a *jaríb* of 18 knots only, two being coiled round the measurer: rent-free lands were measured with the entire rope of 20 knots. In Sindh a *jaríb* is a measure of 150 square feet. In some dialects, as in Ben., Mar., and Tel., the term also imports land measurement or survey; in the latter, *Jaribu* (జరిబు) is applied to garden land or its produce.

Jaríbána, H. (P. جريبانه) An assessment on the cultivators for the expenses of measurement.

Jaríbí, plural, *Jaríbián*, (جريبي) A land measurer or surveyor; any thing relating to measurement, as the cost of it, &c.

Jaríb-beshi, H. (P. بيشي, excess) Increase of the land on the *Jamâ* of the current year over the past.

Jaríb-kami, H. (P. كم, less) Decrease in the year's measurement of the Ryots' land.

Jaríb-karaṇi, Mar. (जरीबकरणी) An account of the measurement of cultivated lands in a village.

Jaríb-kash, H. (P. كشيدن, to draw) A land surveyor.

Jaríb-kashí, H. (P. كشي, drawing) Survey or measurement of land.

Jaríb-kharch, H. (جريب خرچ) Expense of measuring land, paid usually by the Ryot or tenant to the landholder.

Jaríb-mauḳúfi, H. (A. موقوف, delayed) Relinquishment or postponement of an intended survey. In Jessore, an *abwáb* or cess paid by the landholders previous to the permanent settlement, as a consideration for the exemption of their lands from measurement.

Jaríb-tambáku, Mar. An extra cess on the cultivation of tobacco.

Jaríbu, Tel. (జరిబు) Small rents or farms, as of tobacco, &c.

Jot-jaríbí-ká-paṭṭá, Hindi (जोतजरीबीकापट्टा) A kind of lease, under which the cultivator pays rent only for the ground actually cultivated, the extent of which is determined by measurement.

Jarída, Jureedu, H. (A. جريده) A register, an account-book.

Jarímáná, Jureemana, corruptly, Jerumana, H. &c. (جريمانا) Tel. Jalumáná, (జలుమానా) Fine, penalty.

Jarímah, H. (A. جريمه, plural جرايم) A crime, an offence.

Jaráim-kafífa, H. (A. كفيف, light) Petty offences.

Jaráim-sangín, H. (سنگين, heavy) Heinous offences.

Jarípaṭká, Mar. (जरीपटका, from P. زري, golden, and S. पट, a cloth) The pennon of the Peshwa's standard, or his flag in general: a golden sash or girdle formerly presented by the Peshwa to general officers in his service.

Jaríṭa, Jureeṭa. H. (جريٹا) Brushwood, brambles.

JARKUL, Hindi (जरकुल) The whole extent (Puraniya).

JÁR-MULÁSIK, H. (A. جار, a neighbour, ملاسق, contiguous) A neighbour whose house is at the back of a property which is for sale, and of which he might therefore in some cases claim a right of pre-emption.

JARR, or JÁRR, incorrectly, JIRR, H. (A. جرّ, جارّ) lit., Dragging; but, in law, an authorised dragging forth of an offender, and exposing him to public contumely.

JAṚWÍ, JURWEE, H. (جڑوي, from S. *jaṛ*, जड, a root) The small shoots of the rice plant when first springing up.

JASÁWAR, or JASÁWAT, H. (جساور) A tribe of Rájputs in Mathura, not of much consideration. In Behar, a tribe of the ***Kúrmi***, or agricultural class; a man of the tribe who has sold himself, and has become classed amongst the ***Dhanuks***, q. v.

JASHN-I-WAZAN, H. (P. جشن, a royal ceremony, and A. وزن, weight) The ceremony of weighing a person of rank against money and ornaments, which were afterwards given away in presents or in charity.

JÁSTI, Tel., Karn. (జాస్తి, vernacular corruption of زيادتي) Increase, addition; also, injustice, exaction.

Jásti-paṭṭí, Tel. (జాస్తిపట్టి) An extra cess, or additional impost: the term, although not properly Maraṭhi, was known in Maraṭha finance in the same sense.

Jásti-huṭṭuvaḷi, Karn. (ಜಾಸ್ತಿಹುಟ್ಟುವಳಿ) Increase of produce.

Jásti-ságuvaḷi, Karn. (ಜಾಸ್ತಿಸಾಗುವಳಿ) Increase of assessment.

Daulujásti, Karn. (ದೌಲುಜಾಸ್ತಿ) Too high an estimate.

Wogunjásti, Karn. (ವೊಗುಂಜಾಸ್ತಿ) An unjust increase of assessment.

JÁSÚD, Mar. (जासूद, corruption of جاسوس) A messenger, a courier, a runner, a letter-carrier.

Jásúdí, Mar. (जासूदी) The business or office of a messenger.

Jásúdpaṭṭí, Mar. (पट्टी, a tax) A tax on villages for the expense of public messengers.

JÁSÚS, H. (A. جاسوس) A spy, an emissary, a messenger.

JAT, JUT, Hindi (जत) As much as; applied to the rates of a lease (Puraniya).

JÁT, H., and in most dialects; corruptly, JAUT, (جات, जात, S. जाति) Caste, clan, tribe, occupation, kind, sort.

Játbhái, or *-bháú*, H., Mar. (जातभाइ -भाऊ) A brother by caste, one of the same caste or tribe.

Játgót, Mar. (जातगोत, from S. गोत्र) A comprehensive term for one's kindred and fellows by caste.

Ját-jamát, Mar. (S. A. जातजमात) A whole caste or tribe collectively.

Játpát, Mar. (जातपात) Particulars of caste and descent: a caste collectively: dinner given to a caste by an ejected member upon his restoration.

Játwár, Mar. (जातवार) According to caste.

JÁT, or JÁTA, H., and in most dialects, (from S. जात, born, past part. of जन, to be born) Born, engendered, produced, effected; one born, a child, an individual; birth, production.

Játaka, S., H., Mar. (जातक) Horoscope, calculation or casting of nativities.

Ját, or *Játa-karma*, S. &c. (from कर्म्म, act) A religious ceremony performed at the birth of a child; one of the Sanskáras, or essential purificatory rites of the Hindus.

Játasútaká, or *Jatáṣaucha*, S. (सूतक, bringing forth, or अशौच, impurity) The uncleanness contracted by the birth of a child of a near relation.

Játavyavahára, S. (जात, become, व्यवहार, business) A youth who has attained majority, originally fifteen years, now fixed at eighteen; one who is considered competent to conduct his own affairs.

Ját-muchalká, Mar. (जातमुचल्का) A recognisance bond, a pledge for an individual.

Játsaranjám, Mar. (जातसरंजाम) Personal pay or assignment for military service.

JAṬÁ, H. &c. (S. जटा) The braided hair worn by some classes of ascetics, especially the followers of Ṣiva.

JÁTÁBÁKÍ, Karn. (ಜಾತಾಬಾಕಿ) Net revenue.

JÁTI, H., and most other dialects, (جاتي, S. जाति) Kind, sort, genus, species, caste, tribe, class.

Játigegottugára, Karn. (ಜಾತಿಗೆಗೊತ್ತುಗಾರ) The chief or head of a tribe or caste.

Játisankara, Karn. (S. संकर, mixture) Classes or castes of mixed and impure origin, the *Varṇasankara* of Bengal.

JÁṬ, also written JAUT, and, corruptly, JUT and JHUT, H. &c. (جات) The name of a very numerous race of people in the north-west and bordering provinces, also in the Panjab and Sindh, where they have become, in part at least, Sikhs and Mohammadans: they are in general industrious and enterprising cultivators, and a brave and hardy race. The Raja of *Bharatpur* is of the tribe, of which there are numerous subdivisions separated into two grand sections, the *Dhe*, or *Pachhade*, and *Hele*, or *Deswále*. The former immigrated not much more than a century since from the Panjab, but the whole refer to the far west and *Ghazni* as their original site. Although formerly enumerated amongst the thirty-six royal tribes, they are no longer regarded as *Rájputs*, nor intermarry with them, although connexions are occasionally formed. The *Jáṭs* along the *Jamuná* profess to descend from the *Yadus*, which may be the case without prejudice to their affinity with the *Getæ* and *Yue-chi* of antiquity.

JATAR, JUTUR, H. (جتر) Cultivated land (Upper Doab).

JÁṬH, H. (جاتهه) The name of a post fixed in a tank, to denote that its water has been dedicated to a deity, or married to a grove: the revolving beam or axis of a sugar-mill.

JÁTLI, H. (جاتلي) A branch of the Gujar tribe.

JÁTRÁ, H. &c. (جاترا, S. यात्रा) JATRÁ, or YÁTRÁ, Mar. (जत्रा, यात्रा) JÁTARA, Tel. (జాతర) A pilgrimage to a place of reputed sanctity: a religious festival: a place of pilgrimage attended by a fair: in the south, a festival in honour of a divinity, especially of the tutelary goddess of a village.

Játri, H. &c. (جاتري, यात्री) A pilgrim, one travelling to join a religious festival or fair.

Játri-dabbi, Karn. (ಜಾತ್ರಿದಬ್ಬಿ) A toll levied upon persons going in pilgrimage, or to a religious festival.

JATRÁNI, JUTRANEE, H. (جتراني) A tribe of Játs in Rohilkhand and Dehli.

JAṬṬI, Tel. (జట్టి) A contract for grain &c; handsel, advance.

JAṬṬI, or JEṬṬI, Karn. (ಜಟ್ಟಿ, ಜೆಟ್ಟಿ) A wrestler, a boxer.

Jaṭṭi-hiḍata, Karn. (ಜಟ್ಟಿಹಿಡತ) Wrestling.

Jaṭṭi-káḷaga, or *Jaṭṭi-kusti*, (ಜಟ್ಟಿಕಾಳಗ, ಜಟ್ಟಿಕುಸ್ತಿ) A boxing or wrestling match or combat.

Jaṭṭimuḷḷu, Karn. (ಜಟ್ಟಿಮುಳ್ಳು) Spurs fixed on the knuckles of boxers.

JATTIGE, Karn. (ಜತ್ತಿಗೆ) A sowing machine.

JÁTU, H. (جاتو) A Rájput tribe in the neighbourhood of Karnal, a branch of the Tuárs, and chiefly Mohammadans.

JÁṬÚĀ, H. (جاتوا) One of the seven branches of the Chamár tribe, located chiefly in the upper Doab.

JAŪ, JAŌ, or JOU, H. (جو, S. *yava*, यवः) Barley, a barley-corn, which is the basis of long measure: eight, measured across, are considered equal to a finger.

Jauchani, Jauchunee, H. (جوچني) A mixed crop of barley and Chana.

Jaunál, Jounal, H. (جونال) Land cultivated alternately for spring and autumn crops (Rohilkhand). Land cropped during the past season with wheat and barley (Dehli). Land in which barley is sown without its having borne an autumn crop, also termed *Jaunár* (Benares). Land on which any spring crops have been sown (Bundelkhand).

Jaunár, or *Jaunál*, H. (جونار, جونال) Land which has been ploughed and harrowed, and is ready for the first seed: (the same word no doubt as the preceding, but used in a more general sense, perhaps inaccurately).

Jaunchí, H. (جونچي) A kind of smut in barley and wheat, in which the ears are empty.

JAUHAR, plural JAWÁHIR, H. &c (A. جواهر, جوهر) JAWÁHÍR, Mar. (जवाहीर) A jewel.

Jauharí, or *Jauharíá*, H. &c. (جوهريا, جوهري) A lapidary, a jeweller.

Jawáhir-khána H. (P. خانه, a house) The treasury of gems and precious things,

JAUHAR, corruptly JOAR, H. (جوهر) The practice of some classes of Hindus, especially Rájputs, of putting their wives and children to death when unable to resist an enemy, and then sacrificing themselves.

JAUNṚÁ, H. (جونڑا) Payment of village servants in kind. (East Oudh).

JAVAḶI, corruptly, JAULIE, Tam. (சவளி) Karn. (ಜವಳಿ) Cloth, piece goods.

Javaḷi-hára, Karn. Tam. (ಜವಳಿಹಾರ) A cloth merchant.

Javaḷi-penḍi, Karn. (ಜವಳಿಪೆಂಡಿ) A tax on the trade of pedlars, and travelling traders.

JAWÁB, H. (A. جواب) vernacularly modified in some dialects, as, JABÁB, Ben. (জবাব) JABÁB, or JÁB, or JÁP, Mar. (जबाब, जाब, जाप) Karn. JARBÁBU, (ಜರಬಾಬು) An answer, a reply, whether spoken or written.

Jawáb-i-úzr, or *Jawáb-i-dáwi*, H. (جواب عذر, or دعوي) Defence, the reply to the accusation.

Jawáb-ul-jawáb, H. (جواب الجواب) Rejoinder, the refutation of the reply.

Rad-i-jawáb, H. (رد جواب) The refutation of, or reply to, the rejoinder; the last stage of the discussion; or it may also signify the third stage or rejoinder. A bill of exchange, the price of which is not discharged until notice is received of its having been cashed.

Jawábu-dárudu, Tel. *Jabábu-dáru*, Karn. (జవాబుదారుడు, ಜಬಾಬುದಾರು) A person able to answer, a responsible person.

Jawábí-hunḍí, Mar. (जवाबीहुंडी) Payment of money into the hands of a banker, as a deposit for the value of a bill, to be paid to the drawer on receiving advice that the bill has been cashed.

Jawáb-i-mújibát, or *-wajahát*, H. (from A. *mújib*, or *wajah*, reason, appeal) An answer to a petition of appeal, or to the arguments for an appeal to be filed by the respondent.

Jawáb-nawís, H. (جواب نويس) A person or clerk employed to write answers; in some places an officer of the court whose duty it is to read out reports, petitions, &c., and to draft the replies.

Jawáb-sawál, H. (جواب سوال) *Jawábsál*, or *Jáb-sál*, Mar. (जवाबसाल, जाबसाल) Altercation, conversation, question and answer.

Jawáb-sawáli, H. (جواب سوالي) *Jawábṣáli*, or *Jábsáli*, Mar. (जवाबसाली, जाबसाली) Reply, rejoinder, the answer to the question: one ready at a reply.

Jawábi-sawáli, H. (جوابي سوالي) An agent, an attorney, one ready at question and reply.

Jáb-sáli-kágad, Mar. (जाबसालीकागद, from كاغذ) Business papers, important documents and vouchers.

JAWÁLÍ, JUWALEE, corruptly, JAVULLEE, H. (جوالي) Gram mixed with barley as food for cattle, a mixture of barley and wheat.

JAWÁN, H. &c. (S. جوان) Young; a young man, an active or athletic young man, any smart and active man, a police or revenue officer, a soldier.

Jawáni, H. (جواني) A son-in-law, a daughter's husband.

JAWAN-PÚRIÁ, H. (جونپوريا) A branch of the Káchhi tribe.

JAWÁR, corruptly, JUWÁR, JOWAR, or JOAR, H. (جوار) JAWÁRÍ, Mar. (जवारी) A species of millet which grows to a height of eight to twelve feet on a reedy stem, the grain of which enters largely into the food of the peasantry in the western provinces (Holcus sorghum). There are many sorts, of which four are the most generally known: the red or *Joginia*, the *Baunia* or dwarf, the *Píria* or *Saer*, which is superior to the other two, and the *Básmati* or fragrant, which is less generally cultivated.

JAWÁR, Mar. (जवार, A. جوار, neighbourhood) The villages in the vicinity of a town.

JAWAR, H. (جوار) JUÁR, Ben. (জুআর) Mar. JOR, (जोर) Flood-tide: the last applies especially to the spring and neap tides.

JAWÁRA, or JAWÁRI, JUWARU, JUWAREE, H. (جواري، جوارہ) As much land as can be ploughed by a pair of bullocks (Central Doab); as much as may be ploughed in half a day (Dehli), also a yoke or pair of bullocks working a well. Small shoots of rice which germinate when steeped in water, and shoots of barley forced in earthen pots at the Dashará festival, and presented to friends and relations for good luck.

JAWÁSÁ, JUWÁSÁ, H. (جواسا) A kind of shrubby grass, on which cattle, and especially camels browse (Hedysarum alhagi).

JAWÁZ, JUWAZ, H. (P. جواز) A sugar or oil-mill.

JÁY, Ben. (জায) An account.

Jaybábí, Ben. (জাযবাবী) Balance of an account.

JAY, or JAYA, S. &c. (जयः) Victory; used as an exclamation, either singly or with the name or title of a person of distinction, or of a deity, *Jay-*, *Jaya-Mahárája*, *Jay-Ráma*, *Jay-Sítá*: also, gaining a cause at law.

Jayá, The name of the twenty-eighth year of the cycle.

Jayá-patra, corruptly, *Jee-potr*, S. &c. (पत्र, a leaf) A paper of victory, a written and sealed decision in favour of either party.

Jayantí, S. (जयन्ती) The eighth day of the dark half of Srávaṇa, the anniversary of Kṛishṇa's nativity, held as a festival.

JÁYÁ, S. (जाया) A wife, a married woman.

JAYÍ, S. (जयी) Blades of barley grown artificially, and presented to friends and relations at the Dashará festival.

JAZAR, H. (A. جزر) Doubling a number (in arithmetic).

JAZIA, JUZEA, more correctly, JIZIA, but most usually so written and pronounced in Hindustan, corruptly, JAZZIAH, JEZIA, JYZEYEH, H. (A. جزیہ) A capitation tax authorised by the Mohammadan law of conquest to be imposed on all subjects not of the Mohammadan religion.

JÉḌANU, Karn. (ಜೇಡನು) JÉNḌRA, Tel. (జేండ్ర) A weaver, a class of weavers.

JEHAṚ, H. (جيہڑ) A pile of water-pots placed one over the other, in which manner they are usually carried by women on their heads: to take them off the head of a woman who has separated from her husband is to imply consent to marry her: the custom prevails among the *Játs*, *Ahírs*, and *Gújars*, principally among the former.

JEJÁL, Mar. (जेजाल) JAJÁLI, JANJÁLI, Karn. (ಜಜಾಲಿ, ಜಂಜಾಲಿ) A small piece of ordnance mounted on a swivel; commonly *Ginjal*. (Molesworth derives the word from H. *Jíjál* (جيجال), but (?): it is not in Shakespeare, and it seems to be a Karnáta term).

JEL, H. (جيل) The chain of buckets in a Persian wheel; (English) A gaol, a prison.

Jelí, Hindi (जेली) A rake with wooden teeth pointing upwards, for turning over corn whilst being threshed.

Jel-khána, H. English (جيل خانه) A prison, a gaol.

Jénuguttige, Karn. (ಜೇನುಗುತ್ತಿಗೆ, from *Jénu*, honey) A tax on honey in Mysore.

Jeonár, H. (جيونار) Land that has yielded one crop, and is prepared for the sowing of a second: see *Jaunár*.

Jeoṛá, H. (جيوڑا) The perquisites of village servants.

Jeorí, H. (جيوري) The measure of land called a *Jaríb*, or the cord or chain used to measure it.

Jeṭh, H. &c. (جيٹھ, vernacular form of S. *Jyeshṭha*, ज्येष्ठ) Best, eldest, the eldest brother where there are several, a husband's elder brother: the name of a month, the second month of the Hindu year.

Jeṭhá, *Jeṭhtát*, Ben. (S. জেঠা, জেঠতাত) A father's eldest brother.

Jeṭhání, H. (جيٹھانی) The wife of a husband's elder brother.

Jeṭháns, H. (S. جيٹھانس) The share or portion of the eldest born.

Jeṭhí, Ben. (S. জেঠী) The wife of a father's eldest brother.

Jeṭh-râiat, Hindi (जेठरैयत, for S. ज्येष्ठ, *jyeshṭha*, best or oldest, and A. رعيت, a cultivator) The senior or principal cultivator; any respectable villager, but especially one who is, either by election, descent, or the appointment of a Zamindar, the manager of the affairs of the village community: if there be a distinct *Mukaddam*, the *Jeth-râiat* ranks below him, but they are often the same.

Jeṭhunḍá, Hindi (जेठुंडा) The share or right of the eldest son.

Jewá, Mar. (जेवा) A feed, a meal; subsistence which the villagers were bound to provide for the subordinate servants or *Peons* when sent to receive the collections.

Jewár, H. (جيوار) A respectable tribe of Rájputs in Bundelkhand.

Jhâbar, Jhabur, H. (جھابر) Low land on which water lies, and which is favourable for rice cultivation: when the water dries up in the cold weather, spring crops are sometimes grown upon it: also *Jhávar*, q. v.

Jhabrá, Jhubrá, H. (جھبرا) An epithet applied to the ears of animals when covered with long hair.

Jháḍ, Ben., Mar. (ঝাড, झाड, usually pronounced as if ending with a harsh *ṛ*, and in H. so written, see *Jháṛ*) A tree, a shrub, a bush.

Jháḍá, or *Jháṛá*, H. (جھاڑا, झाडा) Land which remains under water during the rains, swampy or marshy ground.

Jháḍgal, Mar. (झाडगल) A tract abounding in trees or shrubs.

Jháḍí, *Jháṛí*, Mar. (झाडी) Thick with underwood, trees, or bushes, a thicket.

Jháḍaṇ, Mar. (झाडण) also Jháṛaṇ, H., q. v. Sweeping; also, fig., Clearing or settling accounts, making a clearance of any thing (money, provisions, &c.).

Jháḍá, Mar. (झाडा) Tel. (ఝాడా) A general clearance of accounts, taking a detailed or particular account, an account particulars.

Jamínjháḍá, Mar. (जमीनझाडा) One of the chief village accounts, a statement shewing the extent, quality, cultivation, and produce in every field in a village, a village register, a rent-roll: see *Zamín-jháṛá*.

Jháḍbákí, Mar. (झाडबाकी) Complete clearance or sweeping off of a debt, &c., closing payment in discharge of a debt.

Jháḍekarí, Mar. (झाडेकरी) A searcher (as one employed by the customs).

Jháḍpaṭṭí, Mar. (झाडपट्टी) Final demand of government for house or land tax.

Jhaḍti, *Jhuḍtee*, or *Jharṭí*, corruptly, *Jhertee*, Mar. (झडती) *Jhaḍtí*, *Jhaḍiti*, Karn. (ಝಡ್ತಿ, ಝಡತಿ) *Jhaḍatá*, Tel. (ఝడతా) Examination of an account; final reckoning, clearing off, or sweeping off (of money, food, or the like). Taking an inventory of goods; the account or inventory so taken; an annual statement of the receipts and payments of a whole village; the account of the village with the revenue officers.

Jháḍú, Mar. (झाडू) A sweeper, a man of the sweeper caste, the Bhangí or Halalkhor: also a broom.

Jhagari, (?) Sowing broad-cast (Morang).

Jhajharka, or Jhajalka, H. (جھجھرکا) Early dawn, before objects are clearly discernible.

Jhákarí, Jhakuree, H. (جھاکري) A milk pail.

Jhalár, H. (جھلار) A thicket, brushwood.

Jháli, Ben. (ঝালি) An excavation at the end of a drain or water-course, for collecting water to be thrown up into higher channels for irrigation.

Jhám, H. (جھام) A large kind of hoe for excavating earth in well-sinking.

Jhamáka, H. (جھماکا) A heavy shower.

Jhamjham, or *Jhamájham*, H. (جھمجھم) Heavy continued rain.

Jhamarjhamar, (جھمرجھمر) Light rain, raining drop by drop.

Jhámp, H. (جهانپ) Ben. (ঝাঁপ) A coarse mat, used as a door or screen of a doorway. Mar. (झांप) Loppings of thorny bushes used as a fence: a branch of a tree or of the cocoa-nut palm, especially when matted to be used in roofs.

Jhámpá, Mar. (झांपा) A matted or wattled door, as of a shed or fence.

Jhámpán, Ben. (ঝাঁপান) A stage on which snake catchers and other juggling vagabonds exhibit: a kind of sedan used by travellers in the Himálaya, written Jámpaun (?).

Jhandá, or Jhandi, H. (جهنڈا, جهنڈي) Jhendá, Mar. (झेंडा) A flag or banner, a flag-staff, a flag used by surveyors.

Jhendá-patti, corruptly *Jhunder-puttey*, Mar. (झेंडापट्टी) A cess levied on the inhabitants of a village or town, and travellers and traders, to defray the expense of a new flag: a tax on the use of flags.

Jhandúlá, H. (جهنڈولا) A tree with thick foliage.

Jhángi, H. (جهانگي) Bramble and brushwood (East Oudh)

Jhánjar, Mar. (झांजड) First glimmering of dawn.

Jhanjiá, H. (جهنجيا) A subdivision of the *Mar* soil (Lower Doab).

Jhankhrá, H. (جهنکهڑا) A leafless tree.

Jhánsa, H. (جهانسه) An assessment formed without any specific ground, and only by general estimate.

Jhar, Jhur, H. (جهڑ) Heavy rain, also Jhari, (جهڑي) Continued rain, wet weather.

Jhár, H. (جهاڑ) Bushes, brambles, thicket, underwood; Dakh. A tree: see *Jhád*.

Jhárí, H. (جهاڑي) Forest, thicket.

Jhárşikrí, (झाडशिकरी) Rank weeds, old grass roots.

Jháraja, or Jhareja, Guz. (झारज) The name of the principal military tribe in Cutch, the Rao of which is of the race: they profess to trace their origin from *Jhára* or *Jharra*, a chief of the Mohammadan tribe of Summas of Sindh, whose infant son was driven from his home after his father's death, and found refuge in Cutch, where he was brought up as a Hindu, and obtained distinction and power. The *Jhárajas* pretend to be Rájputs, but their own tradition shews them to be of spurious origin, and the name should most probably be *Jára-ja*, the son of an adulterous wife. The *Jhárajas* have acquired a disgraceful notoriety as the murderers of their infant daughters.

Jháran, H. (from جهاڑنا, to sweep, to sweep away, to brush &c.) Sweeping, clearing away.

Jhárekarí, and *Járyá*, Mar. (झारेकरी, झाऱ्या) A particular caste, whose business is to wash and sweep the ashes and dust of a melting-house or goldsmith's shop, the *Nyária* of Hindustan.

Jharti-parti, Uriya (ଝଡ଼ତି ପଡ଼ତି) Sweepings of loose salt, scattered about and wasted during weighment.

Jháru, H. (جهاڑو) Ben. (ঝাড়ু) A broom: a sweeper by caste and occupation.

Jharberi, Jhurberee, H. (جهربيري) A small prickly bush bearing a kind of plum like the jujube, which is eaten by the people in the north-west provinces; the leaves are used as fodder, the briars and thorns as fences for fields, and for cattle-sheds and fuel: as the plant grows equally well in dry weather it forms an important resource in time of dearth, both for the people and their cattle.

Jhári, H. (جهاري) A pitcher with a long neck.

Jharota, H. (جهڑوتا) The close of a season.

Jharúá, H. (جهروا) A nutritious grass, the grain of which resembles Panic, and is sometimes eaten or made into bread: it ripens in the rains or the month Sáwan, and is thence called Sawán and Sawain.

Jhatiáná, or Jhutianu, H. (جهٹيانا) A small clan of Rájputs in the Upper Doab.

Jháu, Jháoo, H. (جهاو) A common shrub in the upper provinces (Tamarix diœca), much used for thatching and hedging, and as fuel.

Jhawá, *Jhowá*, H. (جهوا) A large open basket made of the twigs of the *Jháü*.

Jhávu, Karn. (ಝಾವು) A watch of three hours.

Jhávinagasti, Karn. (ಝಾವಿನಗಸ್ತಿ) A watchman.

Jháwar, H. (جهاور) Flat or low land flooded in the rains: see *Jhábar*.

Jhentuyániya, Ben. (ঝেঁটুয়ানিযা, from ঝেঁটা, a broom) A sweeper by caste and occupation.

Jhi, Ben. (ঝি) A daughter.

Jhil, or Jhíl, H. &c. (جهيل, झिल) A shallow lake or morass.

Jhinjar, H. (جهنجر) A subdivision of the Gújar tribe.

Jhirí, Jhiree, (جهري) Withered: blight.

Jhojhá, H. (جهوجها) The name of a Mohammadan tribe converted from Hinduism, considered as of base origin, but good cultivators, found in parts of the Doab and Bundelkhand.

Jhokand, H. (جهوکند) The place from which the fuel is supplied to the fire under the sugar-boiling pan.

Jholá, H. (جهولا) A cold wind which dries up the ears of wheat.

JHOḶÍ, Mar (झोळी) A four-mouth bag or wallet carried by beggars.

Jhoḷíband, Mar. (झोळीबंद) A beggar.

JHOMPṚÁ, or JHOMPṚI, H. (جهونپرا ,جهونپري). JHOMPḌÍ, Mar. (झोंपडी) JHOPRÁ, Ben. (ঝোপড়া) A cottage, a cabin, a hut.

JHOṆK- or JHOK-CHIṬṬHÍ, Mar. (झोंक, झोकचिट्ठी, from झोक, swaggering) A fraudulent note of hand or bill, one not intended to be honoured.

JHONAIÁ, H. (جهونيا) A division of the *Kúrmi* tribe.

JHONKIA, less correctly, JHOKIA, and JHUKWÁ, H. (جهونكيا) The man who keeps up the fire under the sugar-boiling pan.

JHOPÁ, or JHONPÁ, Mar. (झोपा, झोंपा) An apparatus of leafy branches fastened together, to drag over and smooth a field: a hut, a shed.

JHORÁ, H. (جهورا) The haulms or stalks of leguminous plants, ueed as fodder.

JHÚHÁ, JHOOHÁ, H. (جهوها) A large stack of Bajra (Holcus sorghum): it usually contains from 10 to 20 *bojh*, or loads.

JHÚLÁ, H. &c. (جهولا, झूला) A swing, a swinging cot or basket: a swinging or suspension bridge, common in the Himalaya, though of rude construction.

Jhulan, Ben. &c. (ঝুলন) Swinging.

Jhulan-yátrá, Ben. (ঝুলনযাত্রা) A festival in honour of Kṛishṇa in the month *Bhádra*, when images of him and *Rádhá* are swung in ornamented platforms.

JHÚLÍ, H. (جهولي) A cloth or sheet used as a fan for winnowing grain when there is no wind (Dehli).

JHÚND, H. (جهوند) A crowd, a troop, an association, a gang of wandering mendicants.

JHÚNDÍ, JHOONDEE, H. (جهوندي) A lot or parcel of land in a coparcenary village, of a determinate though varying extent, both as to the number of *bighás* it contains, and the size of the *bighá*: it is usually from five to ten *pakha bighás*: a sharer may hold several *jhúndís*. The amount of revenue assessed on each *jhúndí* in a village, payable by the holder, whether he cultivate or not (Dehli).

Jhundí-báchh, H. (باچهه) An apportionment of the revenue payment of a village coparcenership, according to their *jhúndí* shares.

JHÚNGÁ, JHOONGÁ, H. (جهونگا) Bramble, brushwood; a bullock with projecting horns.

JHUNJAR, Ben. (ঝুঁজর) Heaped measure, heaping up a measure of dry goods till it contains no more.

JHUNṬ, JHUNṬÍ, Ben. (ঝুঁট, ঝুঁটী) lit., A crest; the tuft of hair left on the top of the head at tonsure.

JHUNṬHAR, JHOONṬHUR, H. (جهونٹهر) Fields yielding a double crop.

JHÚPA, H. (جهوپا) A pile of mangoes, or other fruit.

JHÚR, Mar. (झूर) A leak or porous place in an embankment through which the water oozes; the water that so oozes: (so in Ben., ঝুর, to ooze or leak).

JHÚṬ, or JHÚṬH, JHOOṬ, JHOOṬH, H. &c. (S. جهوٹ, جهوٹه) JUṬHU, Guz. (જુઠુ) False, untrue; falsehood, lie.

Jhúṭá, *Jhúṭhá*, *Jooṭá*, *Jooṭhá*, H. &c. (جهوٹا ,جهوٹها) Uttering untruth, a liar; also left, leavings, offal.

Jhúṭhá-gawáií, Ben. (ঝুঠাগবাহী) A false witness.

Jhúṭhá-half, Ben. (ঝুঠাহলফ) A false oath, perjury.

Jhúṭa-sanak, Mar. (झूटसनक ?) A dish of leavings; a grant of land without any service attached.

Juṭhusogan, Guz. (જુઠુસોગન) A false oath, perjury.

Juṭhodastávej, Guz. (જુઠોદસતાવેજ) A forged document, a forgery.

JHÚṬHAN, H. (جهوٹهن) Land yielding a double crop.

Jhuṭháil, H. (جهوٹهيايل) Land yielding a double crop.

JHUTRÍ, Mar. (झुतरी) A dry channel or furrow, a streamlet.

JÍ, JEE, H. &c. (جي, जी) Life, soul, whence it has come to be attached to names and titles as a mark of respect: *Kṛishṇa-jí*, *Sitá-jí*, *Sáhib-jí*. It is also used singly as a respectful term of assent or as interrogatory, as, Yes; or, Your pleasure?

Jíat-bhúm, Hindi (जीअतभूम, for S. जीवद्, living, and भूमि, earth) Soil that remains moist throughout the year: also called *Jíta-jamín*.

Jídár, Hindi (जीदार) Crops in existence (Puraniya).

JIUVIYÁ, Hindi (जिउविया) Mature, come to maturity or vigour (Puraniya).

JÍD, A. (جيد) Pure money of the current or legal standard.

JIHÁD, H. (جهاد) Holy warfare, making war against infidels.

JIHÁT, H. (جهات) Duties on manufactures.

JIJHOṬIÁ, H. (ججهوٹيا) A branch of the Kanauj Rájputs.

JILÁ, Ben. (জিলা, for ضلع) A province: see *Ẕilá*.

JILÁWAṬAN, H. (A. جلاوطن) Leaving one's country, emigration.

Jiláwaṭaní, H. (A. جلاوطني) Banishment, expulsion.

JILVA, sometimes also, JALWA, H. (A. جلوه) Splendour, pomp; the first meeting of the bride and bridegroom after marriage in the presence of relations, when various ceremonies take place.

Jimma, Mar. (जिम्मा) Charge, trust; see *Zimma*.

Jin, H. (A. جن) An evil being, a genie, a goblin. **Jina**, S. (जिन) A teacher of the Jain doctrines, any one of the twenty-four deified teachers of the system, called also a *Tírthankara*: it was originally a synonym of a *Bauddha* saint, and is sometimes so used.

Jináyat, A. (جناية) In Mohammadan law, any offences or crimes against person or property, but in practice it is generally restricted to the former, attended with serious injury or death, and punishable by retaliation or by fine.

Jingar, or **Jíngar**, Mar. (जिनगर, जीनगर, from P. زين) A worker in leather, especially a saddler and harness-maker: the Maratha Jingars also make little images of Gaṇeṣa: see *Zingar*,

Jinhar, H. (جنهر) A branch of the Gújar tribe.

Jinku, (?) Tel. A base or counterfeit coin.

Jinnat, A. (جنّت) The Mohammadan paradise.

Jinpairá, Mar. (जिनपैरा) A labourer whose services are borrowed from a neighbour in agricultural operations, the like assistance being given when required.

Jins, H., and in most dialects, slightly modified, (A. جنس) **Jinís**, Ben. (जिनीस) **Jinnas**, Mar. (जिन्नस) **Jinusu**, Tel. (జినుసు) **Jinisu**, **Jinasi**, **Jinasu**, Karn. (ಜಿನಿಸು, ಜಿನಸಿ, ಜಿನಸು) Genus, species, kind, or sort; but applied, especially in the dialects, to a thing, an article, a commodity, goods, effects, &c., any objects of purchase and sale.

Jins-i-adná, H. (A. ادني, inferior) Any article of inferior quality or price; especially inferior grain for cultivation.

Jins-i-áâli, H. (A. عالي, superior) Any article of superior description; grain of the best quality.

Jins-i-kámil, H. (A. كامل, perfect) First-rate crops; the best crop that a field can bear.

Jíns-wár, H. (جنسوار) *Jinnaswár*, Mar. (जिन्नसवार) According to the article, according to the crop, as an account, a settlement, &c.

Jinswári-hisáb, H. (حساب, an account) *Jinasiwára-lekhkka*, Karn. (from ಲೆಕ್ಕ, the same) A statement or account of collections according to the articles or crops.

Jinswár-khatáüni, corruptly, *Jinswar-khutiownee*, H. (كهتاوني) An account of the portions of an estate, in which the lands are classed together according to their crops.

Jinsi, or *Jinsi-top-khána*, H., but peculiar to Maraṭhas, (from توپ, a gun, and *khánah*, a house) An arsenal, ordnance, artillery.

Jinnaskháná, Mar. (जिन्नसखाना) A store, a warehouse, a cellar, a closet.

Jinsvaratala, (?) *Jinswurtullah*, evidently corrupt. Mar. (?) perhaps (from *vartá*, वरता, over, above) The excess of a quantity of inferior grains taken in place of a lesser quantity of superior grain, when the revenue was realisable in kind.

Jins-zabti, or *Jinnis-zabṭee*, H. (جنس ضبطي) Produce or crops of a more valuable kind than ordinary, as cotton, tobacco, or sugar, paying a money rent.

Jiráhat, A. (جراحة) A wound on any part of the body except the head, punishable by fine according to its severity.

Jirásanna-nelu, Karn. (ಜಿರಾಸಂಣನೆಲು) A kind of rice grown in Mysore.

Jiráít, or **Jiráyat**, Mar. (जिराईत, जिरायत) A. **Zirâat**, q. v. **Jírát**, Hindi (जीरात) Arable land, land fit for cultivation not requiring artificial irrigation, also cultivated lands and their produce, as distinguished from garden cultivation; see *Bágáyat*; also from *Khachar*, or rice cultivation.

Jiráíti, *Jiráyati*, Mar. &c. (जिराईती, जिरायती) Pertaining or relating to fields or their crops; as tax, survey, produce, &c.: arable, as land: raised on arable land as opposed to garden produce. *Jiráíti* lands are sometimes considered the same as taxable or assessable lands, in opposition to *Inám*, or rent-free lands: and frequently also the term is applied to land not artificially irrigated, in opposition to *Tari*, wet, or rice lands.

Jaráyati-guttige, Karn. (ಜರಾಯತಿಗುತ್ತಿಗೆ) Assessment on cultivated land.

Jita, vernacularly **Jit**, (जित, past part. of जि, to conquer) Conquered, also one who has conquered or gained: often compounded with words to form proper names; as, *Runjit*, or *Runjeet*, properly *Ranajit*, the victorious (*jit*) in battle (*raṇa*).

Jítá-patr, H. (S. A. جيتا پتر) A favourable decree.

Jitáshṭamí, S. &c. (जिताष्टमी) The eighth (of victory) lunation of the dark half of Aṣwin, part of the Navarátrí festival, or Durgá Pújá.

Jíta, **Jeeta**, H. (from جينا, to live, S. जीव) Living, alive.

Jítá, **Jítera**, **Jeeta**, **Jeetera**, also **Jittá**, H. (جيتا, جيتيره, جتّا) Mutual assistance in tillage; also allowing the use of a plough and bullocks, instead of paying wages in money or kind.

Jíta, Karn. (ಜೀತ) Wages, hire.

Jítagára, Karn. (ಜೀತಗಾರ) A labourer, a person receiving wages or hire for cultivating land.

JITRAV, Mar. (जित्रव) Life-sustaining, applied especially to vegetable produce, and the animals employed in its cultivation.

Jin- or *Jín-jitrav*, Mar. (जिन, or जीनजित्रव) Standing crop of fields, growing vegetables of gardens, or fruits of plantations.

JIŪLI, Ben. (জিউলি) A fisherman.

JÍVA, S. &c. vernacularly JIO, JÍB, JÍV, (जीव) Life, the vital principle, livelihood, means of living.

Jívad-vibhága, S. (जीवद्विभागः) Apportionment of an ancestral estate by the father whilst living amongst his sons (Hindu law).

Jívagár, Tam. The designation of Buddhist teachers and ascetics, used in some parts of the south.

Jívaka, S. &c. vernacularly *Jíbaka*, (जीवक) A servant, a labourer, one who gets a livelihood.

Jivaī, *Jiwaī*, H. (?) Land granted rent free by Talukdars for services performed by them.

Jíviká, S. sometimes vernacularly *Jibiká*, and *Jíbká*, (जीविका) Livelihood, means of living. In Chittagong, *Jíbká* is applied to a portion of land excepted from assessment, being considered especially appropriated to the maintenance of the Zamindar, or landholder, and his family.

Jíva-koṭhí, corruptly, *Jewcotte*, H. (from کوٹھي, a house) A house or hospital for living creatures, or animals and reptiles, such as is maintained by the Jains at Surat.

Jívan-birt, H. (جيونبرت) A stipend allowed to the family of an old servant deceased: see *Birt*.

Jívaní-ṭíp, corruptly *Jewunee-teep*, Mar. (जीवनी, livelihood, and टीप, enumerating articles in order to tax them) A fee in grain or money to the collectors employed to assess houses for taxation.

Jívitam, Tam. (S. சீவிதம்) Subsistence, a grant of land rent-free for maintenance, or as a reward also.

Jíwantsamádh, Mar. (जीवंतसमाध) Burying oneself alive.

JÍYYARU, Tel. (జీయ్యరు) The head of the Vaishṇava Bráhmans in the south of India.

JIZIA, see JAZIA, H. (A. جزيه) Capitation tax. In Ságar a house-tax on the inhabitants of towns not engaged in tillage.

JOBRAJ, Ben. (জোবরাজ, S. युवराजा) The young Raja, the heir apparent of an estate or principality.

JOḌÁ, or JOṚÁ, H. &c. (جوڑا, जोडा) A pair or couple of things which usually go together, as a pair of shoes, a married pair, and the like.

JOḌI, or JOṚI, Tel., Karn. (ಜೋಡಿ) An easy or quit-rent, a personal tax on district officers.

Joḍí- or *Joṛi-inám*, Tel. Karn. (జోడిఇనాము) A grant of land to be held on payment of a quit-rent.

Jódige, Karn. (ಜೋಡಿಗೆ) *Jaḍigai*, Tam. (சொடிகை) A favourable or quit-rent.

JOḌKÁ, or JOṚKÁ, Mar. (जोडका) An earner, the active or earning member of a family.

Joḍhápút, Mar. (from पूत, a son) An informer in the pay of the native Maraṭha government, who furnished information on which to found a pretext for levying money by fines.

JODU, Tel., Karn. (జోడు) A pair, a couple, as of shoes, sandals, &c.: see *Joda*.

JOG, H. &c. (جوگ, S. योगः) lit., Union, junction. The practice of religious abstraction, by which it is supposed the individual may be united with the universal soul, and acquire similar supernatural powers; Hindu clairvoyance and mesmerism.

Jogí, corruptly *Jagee*, *Joghee*, *Jogie*, H. &c. (جوگي, S. योगी) A practiser of the Jog or Yog, a pretender to superhuman faculties; in general, a religious mendicant, who assumes various characters in different parts of India, as an ascetic, a conjurer, and fortune teller, a musician: a caste of Hindus who are usually weavers.

Jogar-mányam, Karn. (ಜೋಗರಮಾನ್ಯಂ) A fee levied by the Jogís of any one of their conventual dwellings in Mysore from the villagers, in a small quantity of rice and a coin of little value from each, on certain occasions: they were expected to transfer the collections to the state.

JOG, H. (جوگ) The name of the person upon whom a draft or bill of exchange is drawn.

JOHAR, H. (جوهر) A large pond or lake (Dehli); any inundated land (Central Doab), but there pronounced *Jhor*.

JOHIÁ, H. (جوهيا) A Rajput tribe, once of importance, but, of whom few remain in the vicinity of Allahabad, and of them one division is Mohammadan.

JOKH, H. (جوکھ) JONKAN, Ben. (জোঁকন) Weight, weighing; Mar. (जोख) A weight, measure, determinate size or quantity.

Jokhái, H. (جوکهاي) Weighment, weighing; the weighman's fee or perquisite.

JOKHAM, or JOKHÍM, H., Mar., Ben. (جوکهم, जोखीम, জোখম) JOKAM, Tel. (జోకం) Risk, hazard, peril; the thing hazarded, loss, deficit.

JOL, Ben. (জোল) Low marshy ground, favourable for rice plantations; a ditch, a trench, a ravine: (also *Joli*).

JONÁNGI, or ZONÁNGI, also JONAGAR and JONAKARI, Tel. (జోనాంగి) The name of a tribe on either coast of the peninsula, also called *Cholias* or *Labis*, considered to be descended from the Arabs, or, according to another tradition, from compulsory converts to Mohammadanism made by the first Mohammadan invaders. The name is supposed to be derived from the Tamil *Shonahar*, the name of a country; perhaps Sennar or Arabia.

Jonna, plural Jonnalu, Tel. (జొన్న, జొన్నలు) Jóḷa, Karn. (ಜೋಳ) Chonṇal, Tam. (சொண்ணல்) The grain termed great millet (Holcus saccharatus).

Joṛá, H. (جوڑا) lit., A joining; a fee levied upon a tenant cultivator for each plough he works with, in addition to his rent (?).

Jorάwár-bhúm, Hindi (from زور, strength) Stiff strong soil.

Joṛí, H. (جوڑی) A small pond (Dehli).

Joṛú, H. (جورو) A wife.

Joshi, H. &c. (جوشي, S. ज्योतिषी, Mar. जोशी) An astronomer, an astrologer in general; also one of a caste professing astrology and fortune-telling, and employed in casting nativities. In Upper India the name is applied to an inferior order of Bráhmans following this occupation; in the Dakhin, to a caste of Śúdras. The term, when restricted to a Bráhman conversant with astronomical science, implies considerable respectability, as is the case with the Joshis of Kamaon.

Jot, corruptly, Jote, H. (S. جوت) Tillage, cultivation; tenure of a cultivator; the rent or revenue paid by a cultivator. In the Sikhim Morang, any tract of land or estate cultivated and paying revenue to government, held by *Paṭṭa*, and hereditary, but neither to be mortgaged or sold. Mar. (जोत, S. योक्त्र) A yoke of oxen; a plough.

Jot-jamá, Hindi (जोतजमा) The land cultivated, and assessment paid by the cultivator.

Jotá, Hindi (जोता) The point of the beam of the plough on which the drag rests.

Jotá, *Jotan*, *Jotár*, *Jotíá*, H. (جوتا, جوتن, جوتار, جوتيا) A cultivator or peasant tilling his own ground.

Jot- or *Jota-dár*, (P. دار, who has) A farmer or cultivator.

Jotál, Hindi (जोताल) Land always in cultivation, never left fallow.

Jotí, Hindi (जोती) The strap that goes round the neck of the bullock to fasten the yoke.

Jotyá, Mar. (जोत्या) A ploughman.

Jowál, Mar. (जोवाल) Union of cultivators to burn and clear the ground before ploughing.

Joys, Jewellery of any kind; used commonly by Europeans at Madras and Bombay, and borrowed from the Portuguese *Jaya*, a jewel.

Juă, Jooa, H. &c. (جوا, S. द्यूत) Gambling.

Juächor, Ben. (জুআচোর) A cheat, a swindler at play, a blackleg.

Juäri, *Jooaree*, H. (جواري) A gambler.

Juá, H. (جوا) Juál, Uriya (ଯୁଆଲ) The yoke of a plough.

Juâl, corruptly, Joăl, A. (جعل) The hire or reward of labour, an extraordinary donation, extra pay or compensation, a reward for bringing back a fugitive slave (Mohammadan law).

Júgád gaur, H. (جوگادگور) A branch of the Gaur Bráhmans.

Júla, Joola, H. (جوله) A tract of land containing four *alí*, or sixteen *bísis* (Kamaon).

Jugí, Asamese (জুগী) One of a caste whose vocation is tending silkworms.

Juláhá, H. (P. جلاها) Jolá, Ben. (জোলা) A weaver; in India forming a race or tribe of weavers, who are Mohammadans.

Julí, or Jurí, Asamese (জুলী, জুৰী) A small hill stream.

Jum, Joom, (?) A Mug village, or one belonging to a forest race on the east of Chittagong; any hill or forest village in the east of Bengal.

Jumia, *Joomia*, (?) A race of people inhabiting the hills on the east of Chittagong.

Jumâh, or Jumâ, H. (A. جمعه) Friday, the day of public prayer with the Mohammadans.

Jumâ-rát, H. (رات, from S. रात्रि, night) Friday eve, *i. e.* Thursday.

Jumâgí, H. (A. جمعگي) Presents or allowances to a schoolboy, given him on Friday, and by him to his preceptor on the same day. In Hindustan, an entertainment repeated on five successive Fridays after marriage.

Jumlat, H. (A. جملة) Sum total, aggregate assemblage.

Juná, or Júṛá, Joona, Joora, H. (جونا, جوڑا) A rope of twisted grass or twine, made to support a round-bottomed jar.

Junnu, Tel., Karn. (జున్ను) Cheese.

Júṛá, H. (جوڑا, S. चूड़ा) The knot in which the Hindus tie their hair on the top of the head.

Juṛemárí, Jooremaree, H. (جوريماري) lit., Brought under the yoke; applied to land actually in possession, in distinction to what a man is entitled to by descent from a common ancestor.

Júṛí, Jooṛee, H. (جوڑي) A small bundle of sugar-cane, the tops of which are brought home on the 11th of Kártik, and are suspended from the roof of the house until the Holí, and then burnt; also a small necklace strung together from cakes of cow-dung, and cast into the Holi bonfire.

Juz, H. (A. جز) A part, a portion; a part of a book, consisting of eight leaves.

Juz-o-kul, corruptly, *Joos-oo-kool*, H. (A. جزوکل) Totally, entirely, great and small. In Bengal, a revenue account formerly kept, containing a variety of details arranged under six heads, whence it was also termed *Shash-báb-i-kaifiat*, the six-section account. Section 1 exhibited the particulars of the survey, the extent and boundaries of the land; 2, all that related to the assessment; 3, all matters connected with the rights and interests of the proprietors; 4, all that related to the rights of tenants and cultivators; 5, whatever concerned the duties and privileges of the village officers; and 6, what related to the rights and interests of village inhabitants not engaged in agriculture.

Jút, Joot, Ben. (জূত) The fibres of the bark of the Corchorus olitorius, much used for making a coarse kind of canvas, and the common *ganni* bags: it is also sometimes loosely applied to the plant.

Jútá, Júti, H. &c. (جوتا, جوتي) A shoe, a slipper.

Jutájutí, Ben. &c. (জুতাজুতী) Beating each other with slippers.

Júti-kári, H. (from کاري, doing) Beating with slippers, a disgraceful punishment.

Júti-khor, H. (from P. خور, who eats) Beaten with slippers, disgraced, abject.

Juti-már, H. (from مار, beating) Beating with slippers.

Jútá, H. (جوتا) The rope connecting the irrigating basket with the handle.

Júth, Jooth, also **Jathá**, H. (جوت, جتها, S. यूथ) **Jaṭa**, or **Júṭa**, corruptly, **Juṭha**, Mar. (जट, जूट) A gang, a troop, a company, a coparcenary, a brotherhood, a family or corporation holding lands in common. In the Dakhin, the collective designation of the members of a family, amongst whom the lands of a village were originally parcelled out; the primary *Thalkari*, the *Bhayachara* of Hindustan. It is also rather loosely applied to the land belonging to such a family, whether cultivated by themselves or let to under-tenants.

Júṭa-bháu, Mar. (जूटभाउ) A member of a proprietary family in a village or district.

Júthwár, H. (جوتهوار) Relating to common property, corporate, joint, common, belonging to proprietary families or brotherhoods; settled or assessed according to fraternities.

Juthálí, or **Jutheli**, H. (جوتهالي, جوتهيلي) also **Jutián**, (جوتيان) Land bearing two harvests in the year.

Jútiál, H. (جوتيال) A class of hereditary watchmen located in the tract under the Siwalik hills.

Jwálá-mukhí, S. (from ज्वाला, flame, and मुख, mouth or face) Any place where fire breaks from the ground, or where sulphurous gas, which may be ignited, issues from the soil, considered to be indicative of the presence of a form of Durgá, as at the town in the first range of hills so called, a place of pilgrimage of the Hindus.

Jyarum, (?) A register of lands (Carnatic).

Jyeshṭha, S. (ज्येष्ठ) Eldest, best, &c.; vernacularly, **Jeṭh**, q. v.

Jyeshṭhánsa, S. (ज्येष्ठ, and अंश, a portion) The right of primogeniture, or the right of the eldest son to a larger portion of the patrimonial property than his brothers; a right formerly recognised, but now obsolete, the partition being equal.

Jyeshṭha, or *Jyaishṭha*, S. (ज्येष्ठ, ज्यैष्ठ) The month *Jeth* or Jait (May-June).

Jyaishṭhí, S. (ज्यैष्ठी) Day of full moon in the month *Jait*.

Jyotisha, S. (ज्योतिष) Astronomy, astrology.

Jyotishí, S., vernacularly, *Josi*, *Joshi*, or *Jotishi*, (ज्योतिषी) An astronomer, an astrologer; the village priest and astronomer, who prepares the calendar, casts nativities, and announces the time propitious for any act; any astrologer or fortune-teller.

K

Kâba, A. (كعبة, from *Kâb*, كعب, a cube or square) Any square building; whence, especially, the temple at Mecca, to which pilgrimage is made by the Mohammadans.

Kábá, Mar. (काबा) A description of people to the north of the Maraṭha provinces, said to be a piratical tribe in the gulf of Kach.

Kabáḍ, Kabáṛ, or **Kábáḍ**, &c., Mar. (कबाड, काबाड) Karn. **Kabáḍa**, (ಕಬಾಡ) A bullock load of wood, grass, &c.: Guz. (કબાડ) A sort of pannier for horses.

Kabáḍi, or *Kábáḍi*, Mar. (कबाडी, काबाडी) Employed in

bringing loads, a bullock, &c.: Guz. One whose occupation is breeding horses and other animals: one who conveys articles in horse-panniers: also a wood-cutter.

Kábáḍkhot, Mar. (काबाडखोत) A monopolist of firewood.

Kábáḍkhotí, Mar. (काबाडखोती) A contract or monopoly of the supply of firewood.

Kábádára, Karn. (ರಾಬಾದಾರ) Remission of a part of the land-tax in favour of sugar cultivation, the deficiency being made good by an impost upon the produce.

KABÁLA, also KIBÁLA, or QIBALA, corruptly, CIBALEH, KUBBALEH, COBALLA, &c., H. and other dialects, (A. قبالة) Any deed of conveyance or transfer of right or property, any contract of bargain or sale signed by a judge, a bond, a bill of sale, title-deeds, and the like. In the northern Sarkárs it is said to apply especially to deeds affecting titles to houses and gardens.

Kabála-dár, H. (قبالهدار) The holder of a bond, one entitled to any right in consequence of forfeiture of a bond, or the like.

Kaṭ-ḳabála, corruptly, *Kote-cubbala*, and *Khut-kabála*, H. (كت قبالة) *Kaṭ-kobálá*, Ben. (কটকোবালা) A conditional engagement, a deed of conditional sale, as one stipulating that if the purchase-price be not returned within a given period the sale is absolute; a mortgage-deed with liability of sale if not redeemed by a stipulated time.

Khush-ḳabála, H. (خوش قبالة) Unconditional engagement, sale without stipulation: the opposite of the preceding.

KÁBÁR, Ben. (কাবার) The last day of the month.

Kábárí, Ben. (কাবারী) Relating to the last day of the month, due or payable on that day (wages, rent, &c.).

KÁBAR, KABUR, H. (كابر, काबर) Second description of the *már*, or black soil of Bundelkhand: in the north-west provinces, a mixed soil of clay and sand, suitable to any crop except rice.

KABBU, Karn. (ಕಬ್ಬು) Sugar-cane.

Kabbiná-gáṇa, Karn. (ಕಬ್ಬಿನಾಗಾಣ) A sugar-mill.

Kabbiná-lemane, Karn. (ಕಬ್ಬಿನಾಲೆಮನೆ) A sugar manufactory.

Kabbina-várada-handáya; Karn. (ಕಬ್ಬಿನವಾರದಹಂದಾಯ) Sugar-cane lands taken under the direct cultivation by the state, but subject to the land-tax formerly levied from the Ryots.

Kabbinarasa, or *-hálu*, Karn. (ಕಬ್ಬಿನರಸ, -ಹಾಲು) The juice of the sugar-cane.

ḲABÍL, A. (قبيل) A surety, bail, bond (Mohammadan law).

KÁBÍN, (P. كابين) Ratification of a marriage in presence of a Ḳaẓi; a dower, a marriage-portion.

Kábín-náma, H. (P. كابين نامه) A deed in which the dower is stated, a marriage settlement.

KÁBIRÁJ, Ben. (কাবিরাজ) A physician.

KABISO, Guz. (A. કબીસો) Intercalation, an intercalary year.

KABITA, Thug. A term for the strangler among the Jamaldehi and Lodaha clans of Mohammadan Thugs, residing chiefly on the borders of Oudh.

ḲABR, corruptly, CUBBUR, H. (A. قبر) A grave, a tomb.

Ḳabr-salámi, H. (from سلامي, a compliment) A fee to the proprietor for permission to dig a grave on ground belonging to him.

ḲABÚL, H. &c. (A. قبول) Consent; consented or agreed to.

Ḳabúliyat, corruptly, *Cabooleat*, *Kabooleat*, *Cubalot*, H. &c. (A. قبوليت) *Kabulát*, or *Kabuláyat*, Mar. (कबुलात, कबुलायत) A written agreement; especially one signifying assent, as the counterpart of a revenue lease, or the document in which a payer of revenue, whether to the government, the Zamindar, or the farmer, expresses his consent to pay the amount assessed upon his land.

Ḳabúl-jawáb, H. (P. جواب) An answer filed in a suit, acknowledging the demand.

Kabúl-karár, H., but current in Orissa, apparently in a peculiar sense, Uriya, (କବୁଲକରାର) Verbal engagement.

Kabúl-katabá, or *-katapá*, vulgarly *-kutba*, Mar. (from कतबा, or कदपा, a writing) The written assent of the Ryots to the assessment taken by the *Pátíl*, and handed over to the *Mámalat-dár*, or district collector.

Kabúla, Thug. A menial servant of Thugs, or a novice.

ḲABẒ, KUBẒ, QUBẒ, H. (A. قبض, lit., seizing) KABAJ, KUBUJ, Mar., Ben., &c. (कबज, কবজ) A receipt, an acknowledgment: in village accounts, the *Patwárí's* receipt given to the cultivator for his instalments of rent: in Maraṭhi it is also applied to seizure of property, or sequestration of income for debt, or to the property or income so sequestrated.

Ḳabz-ul-waṣúl, *Qubz-ool-wuṣool*, H. (A. وصول, acquisition) A receipt, an acknowledgment, a discharge, a document acknowledging the receipt of money or other valuables.

Kábiẓ, H. (A. قابض) A seizer, a sequestrator, an occupant, a person in possession.

KACHA, Thug. Unburied, or buried superficially (a body): a Thug informer.

Kachahrí, Kuchuhree, corruptly, Cutcherry, H. &c. (كچهري) Kacherí, Mar. (कचेरी) Kachhaharí, or Kachhárí, Ben. (কছহরী, কছারী) Kacheli, Tel. (కచెలి) A court, a hall, an office, the place where any public business is transacted: also, in Mar., the business carried on there, or the people assembled.

Kachani, Thug. One of seven principal clans.

Kachár, Kachhár, H. (كچار, كچهار, कचार, कछार) Moist land, land lying low and along the banks of rivers, so as to admit easily of irrigation or being flooded; also, alluvial formation or deposit.

Kácharai, (?) H. Rent for pasturage: (probably an error for *Gocharai*).

Kachcha, Mal. (കച്ച) Unbleached cloth; a waist belt; the end of a lower garment gathered up behind and tucked into the part that girds the waist: (from the S. कक्ष).

Kachchakkanakha, Mal. (കച്ചക്കണക്ക) An account or bill of sale of cloth given to the purchaser.

Kachchavaṭam, Mal. (കച്ചവടം) Merchandise, trade, especially in cloth.

Kachhavaṭakáran, Mal. (കച്ചവടക്കാരൻ) A merchant, a trader, a cloth merchant.

Kachchá, Kuchcha, incorrectly, Kacha, or Kucha, and, corruptly, Cutcha, Kutcha, &c., H. &c. (كچّا, कच्चा) Káncha, Ben. (কাঁচা) Káchi, Kácho, Guz. (કાચી, કાચો) Raw, unripe, immature, crude, lit. or fig.; as, a *Kachchá* house is one built of unbaked bricks or mud; a *Kachchá* person is one inexperienced, unskilful, silly: as applied to weights and measures it denotes inferiority; a *Kachcha sér* is one less than the standard *sér*: in revenue settlements it implies a direct assessment, one made with the Ryot, or Ryotwar, either where there is no recognised farmer or proprietor, or where his right of collection is suspended. In the Bombay Glossary it is also explained, when applied to a statement of any kind, to signify one minutely detailed (?).

Kachchá-ámdani, H. (P. آمدني, income) Gross income or receipts, without allowing for charges or deductions.

Kachchá-áml, Mar. (कच्चा अमल, A. عمل) An office or appointment, in the profits or loss of which the holder has no permanent interest: it is hence applied to villages and items of revenue managed by government officers for the state, in distinction to those which are farmed.

Kachchá-asámi, H. (see *Asámi*) A temporary cultivator, one having no permanent or hereditary right of occupation.

Kachchá-balani, also read *-balanny*, *-ballunny*, and *-behenny*, (?) Resumption of one-tenth of the lands held by the Ryots in Dinajpur, an item of the revenue of Bahar in 1762. (The second word is some inexplicable blunder—Fifth Rep. p. 222).

Kachchá-ḍaulu, Karn. (ಕಚ್ಚಾಡೌಲು) A rough estimate of the value of standard crops.

Kachchá-jamabandí, H. (from جمعبندي, settlement) The gross rent-roll of a village before setting off the charges and expenses, whether the balance be payable to a Zamindar or to the government.

Kachchá-khardu, Karn. (ಕಚ್ಚಾಖರ್ದು) A rough draft, a rough or sketch account, an account kept by the village accountant of money received from the cultivators.

Kachchá-mití, H. (from متي, interest) Interest from a day preceding the loan, as opposed to *Pahka-miti*, from a day after, with reference to the practice of native bankers, who, in their current account, charge interest on money advanced from the day before, but on money received, from the day following the receipt.

Kachchí-kamáviṣí, Mar. (कच्चीकमाविशी) A revenue office, of which the person holding it has no interest in the collections.

Káchimudat, Guz. (કાચીમુદત) A bill of exchange not yet due.

Kachchá-ṣeru, Karn. (ಕಚ್ಚಾಶೆರು) An inferior *sér*, one of twenty-four rupees' weight (Mysore).

Kachchá-tahṣil, H. (A. تحصيل, collection) Collection of the revenue from the cultivators direct.

Kachchá-upaj, H. (from S. उपज, produced) Gross collections.

Kachcherá, Mar. (कच्चेरा) A contractor formerly employed at Bombay to keep the market supplied with coarse rice during the rainy season.

Kachchha, S. &c. (कच्छः) A shore, a coast, a site liable to be flooded, whence the province of Cutch is so named.

Kachchaḷi, Kachchiḷi, or Kachchaḷika, Karn. (ಕಚ್ಚಳಿ, ಕಚ್ಚಿಳಿ, ಕಚ್ಚಳಿಕೆ) An honorary distinction, as a medal, for eminent services (Mysore).

Kachchí-katté, Karn. (ಕಚ್ಚಿಕಟ್ಟೆ) A sort of village hall where the respectable inhabitants assemble (Mysore).

Kachhaura, H. (كچهوره) A small clan of Rájputs, of whom a few are settled in Gorakhpur.

Káchhí, Cáchhee, H. (كاچهي) Guz. (કાછી) A tribe of cultivators found in most parts of Hindustan, of which they are the gardeners especially, being employed in market and flower gardens, and raising vegetables and flowers for sale. In Behar they are the principal growers of the poppy. Those of the north-west provinces, who are mostly industrious agriculturists, reckon seven branches, usually denominated *Kanaujia, Hardiha, Singrauria, Jamanpuria, Bamhania* or *Maghya, Jaretha,* and *Kachhwáha,* which do not eat together or intermarry. There are, however, as noticed by Mr. Elliot, other distinctions, and in the Maratha territory some of them are named from the countries whence they have come, as the *Bundela* and *Márwári Káchhis.*

Kachhiár, H. (?) Land enriched by alluvial deposit on the banks of the Chambul, commonly cultivated for market produce by *Káchhis*, whence its name.

Kachhwárá, H. (کچهوارا) Any portion of ground cultivated by *Káchhis*. Mr. Elliot derives the name of the province of Cach, corruptly Cutch, from this circumstance: it rather seems derivable from the Sanskrit *Kachchha*, any tract of low or marshy ground near to a river or the sea.

KACHHWÁ, H. (کچهوا, कछवा) Low land.

KACHHWÁHA, CUCHHWAHA, H. (کچهواها) A distinguished tribe of Rájputs professing to descend from *Kuṣa* or *Kusha*, the son of *Ráma*, and forming the ruling race in Amber of Jaypur, the Raja of which is of the clan.

KACHHWÁR, H. (کچهوار) A subdivision of the Kúrmi tribe.

KACHISA, H. (کچسا) A subdivision of the Kúrmi tribe found in Bahár.

KACHWÁNSI, H. (کچوانسي) A minute division of land measure, the twentieth of a *Tiswánsi*, of which twenty go to a *Biswánsi*, q. v.: the term is now rarely used.

KÁDÁ, Hindi (कादा) Mud, slime, alluvial deposit, mud and vegetable matter left by the waters after inundation.

Kádá-kartá, Hindi (कादाकरता) Preparing soft or muddy soil for transplanting rice.

KAḌA, or KAḌÁ, Karn. (ಕಡ, ಕಡಾ) A loan without interest.

Kaḍa-chiṭu, Karn. (ಕಡಚೀಟು) A bond, a promissory note.

Kaḍana- or *Kaḍam-patra*, Karn. (ಕಡನಪತ್ರ, ಕಡಂಪತ್ರ) A note of hand, a promissory note.

KAḌAI, Tam. (கடை) A shop, a market.

Kaḍai-káraṇ, Tam. (கடைகாரன்) A shopkeeper.

Sáráyakaḍai, Tam. (சாராயக்கடை) A spirit-shop.

KADAM, H. (A. قدم) A foot, a pace, also used as a measure; in some parts of the north-west provinces twenty *kadams* in each division make a *Kachchá bighá*, or about $\frac{1}{10}$th of an acre.

Kadam- or *Kudum-bosi*, H. (A. قدم, a foot, and P. بوسي, a kiss) Respectful salutation, paying one's respects, equivalent to kissing the feet of a superior, although not always implying even prostration.

Kadam-i-rasul, corruptly, *Kuddum-russool*, H. (A. رسول, a prophet) An allowance or deduction from the revenue granted by the native governments to the Zamindars to cover the charge of keeping up a temple in which a slab with impressions of feet, supposed to be those of the prophet, was preserved as an object of veneration.

KÁDAM, Tam. (காதம், from A. قدم, a foot or step) A measure of distance, as much as a man may walk in three hours: it varies in different places, but is never less than eight miles.

KADAMAI, Tam. (கடமை) Debt: a tax.

Kaḍan, Tam. (கடன்) Mal. (കടം) Debt, obligation: tax.

Kaḍanchiṭṭu, Tam. (கடன்சீட்டு) A bond.

Kaḍankáran, Tam. (கடன்காரன்) *Kadakáran*, Mal. (കടക്കാരൻ) A debtor, a creditor, a shopman.

Kadankoduttavan, Tam. (கடன்கொடுத்தவன்) A creditor.

KADAPÁ, Tel. (కడపా) The counter agreement executed by the tenant in exchange for his lease.

KAḌAPPU, Tam. (கடப்பு) A kind of rice that is reaped from September to November.

KÁḌÁRAMBAM, Tam., Karn. (காடாரம்பம், ಕಾಡಾರಂಬಂ) Dry land, or land which depends entirely upon rain for watering; the cultivation of such land. (This is probably the correct form of the term *Kadarnaibh-guddee*, which is said to mean land watered by rain.—Selections iv. 780.)

KAḌATAM, Karn. (ಕಡತಂ) KAḌITAMU, Tel. (కడితము) KAḌITAM, Tam. (கடித்தம்) A leaf of cloth blackened with a preparation of charcoal and gum, and used as a slate for writing on with chalk or steatite; leaves of such cloth, folded together, are commonly used as memorandum and account books in Kanara: the writing may be effaced with a wet sponge or cloth.

KAḌATTA, Mal. (കടത്ത) Ferrying over, conveying across, accompanying travellers through a dangerous place.

Kaḍattu-kadava, Mal. (കടത്തുകടവ) A landing-place, a ferry.

Kaḍattu-káran, Mal. (കടത്തുക്കാരൻ) A ferryman.

KAḌEGÁLA, Karn. (ಕಡೆಗಾಲ, from ಕಡೆ, last) The latter season.

Kaḍegálada-pairu, Karn. (ಕಡೆಗಾಲದಪೈರು) The latter crop.

Kaḍekula, Karn. (ಕಡೆಕುಲ) The lowest of the castes, as Pariah, &c.

KÁḌHÁ, Mar. (काढा) Grain stipulated to be received by way of interest or premium on money lent; the practice of so borrowing or lending.

Káḍhaṇi, Mar. (काढणी) Removal of crops from a field.

Káḍháoḍh, Mar. (काढाओढ) Borrowing from every quarter.

KADHUA, Thug. The head; peculiar to some classes.

KAḌI, Tel. (కడి) The yoke of a plough.

KAḌÍ, or KARI, Karn. (ಕಡಿ) KAṚI, Mal. (കരി) A bit, a morsel, a chip, &c.; boiled sour milk used with rice; and hence, perhaps, comes the English word *Curry*: the word, however, is apparently used similarly in Karnáta and Malabar, as in the compounds, *Majjige-kaḍi*, (ಮಜ್ಜಿಗೆಕಡಿ) A curry of rice, sour milk, spices, *chilis*, &c.

Háta-kaḍi, Karn. (ಹಾತಕಡಿ) Ready money, money in hand.

KAḌÍGAṬṬU, Tel. (కడిగట్టు) A land or boundary mark, a ridge or mound separating two fields.

ḲADÍM, or ḲADÍMÍ, H. &c. (A. قديم, lit., old, ancient) An old inhabitant of a village, one holding by hereditary descent; and, as being usually chosen from this class, applied to the head man of a village in the west of Bengal, and in some parts of the peninsula.

Kadím-al-ayám, H. (A. الايام, days) From time immemorial.

Kadim-dihwál, or *Kadím-díhvarttí*, H. (from H. *dihwál*, دهوال, or *díh-varttí*, دهورتّي, a villager) A hereditary cultivator, one professing to descend from the first settlers (Asam).

Kadímí-râiyat, H. (from A. رعيت) A cultivator of old, an occupant of land by old hereditary descent.

KADÍR, Tam. (கதிர்) An ear of corn.

Kadírmadangal, Tam. (கதிர்மடங்கல்) Close of the harvest.

KADJAN, CADJAN, A term used by Europeans for the leaves of the fan-palm, or cocoa-nut, on which the natives write with an iron style: the letters are sometimes, but not always, blackened with ink. The word is supposed to be of Portuguese origin, but this seems doubtful.

KAḌLE, or KAḌALE, Karn. (ಕಡ್ಲೆ, ಕಡಲೆ) Bengal gram (Cicer arietinum): in Karnáta, as well as in most parts of India, *Kadalí*, S. (कदली) signifies the plaintain (Musa sapientum).

KÁḌU, Tam., Karn. (காடு, ಕಾಡು) Thicket, forest; place where dead bodies are burned: in Tamil it also means high and dry land, not capable of irrigation.

Kádpáp-mányam, Karn. (ಕಾಡಪಾಪಮಾನ್ಯಂ) A fee or tax payable to a low caste of Ṣúdras, who perform the funeral obsequies (Mysore).

KAFÁAT, A. (كفائت) Resemblance; in law, similarity of condition and circumstances, such as is required between a man and woman to give legality to their marriage.

KAFÁLAT, or KIFÁLAT, A. (كفالت) Bail, security in general according to the Shias; it is limited to personal bail by the Sunnis.

Kafálat-bil-dirk, A. (بالدرك) Security against contingencies.

Kafálat-bil-mál, A. (بالمال) Surety for property.

Kafálat-bin-nafs, A. (بالنفس) Personal security.

Kafálat-náma, H. (P. نامه) A bail-bond, or written engagement of security.

Káfil, or *Kafíl*, A. (كافل, كفيل) A surety.

Mahfúl, H. (A. مكفول) Bailed, given or taken as surety for, according to the construction of the phrase; as *Makfúl-ba-hí*, the claim for which surety is given; *Makfúl-la-hu*, the person demanding bail; *Makful-an-hu*, the person or thing for whom or which surety is given.

KAFFA, H. (A. كفّه) A piece of cloth or rag steeped in the juice of the poppy, and twisted into a bundle with others; a sort of smuggling of opium.

KAFÁRA, or KAFFÁRAT, A. (كفارة) Expiation, penitence; in law, expiation for a violated vow, or the commission of any sin, by mortification, almsgiving, &c.

ḲÁFILA, H. (A. قافله) A caravan.

Ḳáfila-sálár, (P. سالار) The chief of a caravan.

KÁFIR, H. (A. كافر) An infidel, one who does not believe in the mission of Mohammad.

ḲAFÍZ, A. (قفيز) A measure containing about 64lbs., a measure of space, a square of about 124 cubits.

Ḳafíz-ṭahán, A. (قفيزطحان) Employing a miller to grind corn for the payment of a measure of flour; illustrative of illegal contracts, in which the labourer is paid with part of the produce of his labour, and which is considered as illegal.

KAGAR, or CAYGAR, (?) A tribe of Cháraus supported by the Jhárajas of Cutch (?).

KAGARA, Thug. Croaking of a large kind of crow, an omen of good or bad luck, according to circumstances.

KÁGHAZ, KAGHIZ, or KAGHID, H. (A. كاغذ, كاغد) vernacularly changed to KÁGAJ, Ben. (কাগজ) KÁGAD, Mar. (कागद) KÁKITAMU, Tel. (కాకితము) KÁGAJ, KÁGADA, Karn. (ಕಾಗಜ, ಕಾಗದ) Paper, a paper or document.

Kágada-patra, Karn. (ಪತ್ರ, S. पत्र, a leaf) A letter, a voucher, a written document.

Kághaz-bahá, H. (from P. بها, price, expense) Office allowance for stationery.

Kaghaz-i-khám, H. (from خام, rough) Rough draft of a document or account, account of gross produce.

Kawághaz-arbá, H. (A. plural of كاغذ, and اربع, four) The four written documents on which the proceedings in a suit are grounded, or the written complaint, the answer, the rejoinder and the reply.

Kághazí, H., also *Kágaji*, *Kágadí*, &c. (A. كاغذي) A paper-maker or vender, a stationer, a letter-carrier, of or relating to paper or to writings.

KÁH, H. (P. كاه) Grass, straw.

KÁHAN, or KÁHÁN, corruptly, CAHAN, CAOUN, CÁWN, KHAHOON, H., Ben. (کاهن, কাহন, काहन, S. कार्षपण) A measure of value equal to sixteen *Paṇas* of *Kauri* shells, or 1280 *Kauris*, varying, therefore, in value with the market price of the shells.

KAHÁR, H. (كهار) A tribe of Śúdras chiefly settled in Bahar, following agricultural pursuits, but employed in towns as palankín-bearers; many of them in their own provinces are slaves, and are considered impure.

KÁI, corruptly, CUY, KAY, KAYI, KYE, Tel. (కై) Karn. (ಕೈ) Tam. (கை) Mal. (കൈ) The hand: in the Dakhini languages it is extensively used in forming compound terms implying handiwork, &c.; but especially with reference to pecuniary and revenue transactions in Karnáta and Málayálim.

Kai-badalu, Karn. (ಕೈಬದಲು) A loan of money for a short time.

Kai-baraha, Karn. (ಕೈಬರಹ) Signature, hand-writing, manuscript.

Kai-chchíṭṭu, Tam. (கைச்சீட்டு) A note of band.

Kai-dastu, Karn. (ಕೈದಸ್ತು) Possession: use of public money by government officers, accounted for as a debt to the state under the former government of Mysore.

Kai-dharmam, Karn. (ಕೈಧರ್ಮಂ) Endowment payable in money to a temple by the granter direct; any small sums given as alms.

Kai-gaḍa, Karn. (ಕೈಗಡ) A loan without interest.

Kai-guruttu, Karn. (ಕೈಗುರುತ್ತು) Signature, handwriting, manuscript.

Kai-kágada, Karn. (ಕೈಕಾಗದ) A note-of-hand, a bond signed by both borrower and lender, a written statement or handwriting. Under the later government of Mysore the term *Kai-kágada*, or *Kai-kághaz*, was applied to a statement of the gross annual assessment of each collectorate, furnished by the collector, and to a similar statement required from each cultivator, shewing his whole liability, without the deductions to which it was subject.

Kai-kámil, Karn. (ಕೈಕಾಮಿಲ) Full statement, that of the maximum revenue without deductions: see the preceding.

Kai-kánam, Mal. (കൈകാണം) Property in hand, personal property.

Kai-kánam-káraṇ, Mal. (കൈകാണംകാരൻ) A tenant on an improving lease.

Kai-kánam-páttam, Mal. (കൈകാണംപാട്ടം) Tenure by labour, or by an engagement to improve the property, on condition of holding it for a stipulated period.

Kai-káran, Mal. (കൈകാരൻ) A handicraftsman, an artificer; also a person of property.

Kaikkiḷan, *Kaikkiḷavan*, corruptly, *Kykullee*, Tam. (கைக்கிளான், கைக்கிளவன்) A weaver by caste and occupation.

Kai-kóla, Tel. (కైకోల) The name of a caste, or individual of it, usually occupied in weaving.

Kai-kúli, Karn. (ಕೈಕೂಲಿ) Hire or pay at the time when work is done: Mal. (കൈക്കൂലി) A fine paid by a lessee to the proprietor on the renewal of a lease.

Kai-ole, Karn. (ಕೈಒಲೆ) A writing on an *ola*, or palm-leaf; a statement of the total assessment so written: see *Kai-kágada*.

Kai-padaru, plural, Karn. (?) A class of predial slaves in Kanara, a subdivision of the Dhers.

Kai-páda, Mal. (കൈപാട) *Kaippádu*, Tam. (கைப்பாடு) Handicraft, manual labour; in Mal. also actual possession.

Kaippanam, Mal. (കൈപ്പണം) Ready money, money in hand.

Kaippattunilam, Tam. (கைப்பற்றுநிலம்) Land in one's own possession.

Kaipporul, Mal. (കൈപ്പൊരുൾ) Possession of property, property in hand, whether personal or real.

Kaimatal, Mal. (കൈമതൽ) Personal property, money, jewels, &c.

Kaissáttu, Tam. (கைச்சாத்து) An invoice, a list; a mark in place of a signature.

Kai-tappu, Karn. (ಕೈತಪ್ಪು) A slip of the hand, a mistake in writing or in counting money.

Kai-váda, Karn. (ಕೈವಾಡ) Handicraft, manual labour.

Kai-vaḷi, Karn. (ಕೈವಳಿ) A cess formerly paid in kind for betel gardens and rice fields.

Kai-vápya, Mal. (കൈവാപ്യ) Borrowing for a short time, on a verbal promise to pay.

Kai-vasya, Karn. (ಕೈವಸ್ಯ) Actual possession.

Kai-vidu- or *Kai-vidu-oṭṭi*, corruptly, *Kyvedoothi*, Mal. (കൈവിട്ടു, കൈവിട്ടൊറ്റി) A kind of mortgage in Malabar, by which, in consideration of a sum of money, the proprietor of an estate transfers it to the lender to hold, without prejudice to his own proprietary right, but which precludes the mortgagee from disposing of the land to a third party for more than he paid, or on any other terms than those on which he acquired the occupation: if he wish to dispose of it he is bound also to give the proprietor the option of redeeming it.

Kai-vidu-otti-karanam, Mal. (from കരണം, deed) A deed of mortgage of the kind above described.

Kaiyaḍai, Tam. (கையடை) A bribe.

Kaiyeṛpu, Tam. (கையேற்பு) Allowance of grain given to village servants at harvest-time from the threshing-floor.

Idanhai, or *Idangai*, q. v. The left-hand, the left-hand castes.

Valankai, or *Valangai*, q. v. The right-hand, the right-hand castes.

KAIBARTTA, Ben. (S. কৈবর্ত্ত) A fisherman by caste and occupation; he is sometimes a domestic or predial slave, having sold himself, or been sold as a child.

ḲAID, H. (A. قيد) Confinement, bond, fetter.

Ḳaidí, H. (قيدي) A prisoner, a convict.

Kaidkhána, H. (قيدخانه) A jail, a prison.

KÁÎDA, or KÁÎDAT, plural KAWÁÎD, H. &c. (A. قاعده, قواعد) KÁYDÁ, Ben. (কাযদা) A rule a regulation, a law.

KAÍFÍYAT, KYFEEYUT, vernacularly, KAIPHÍYAT, corruptly, KYPHYUT, H. &c. (H. كيفية) Statement, description, report, account particulars. In the Jama-bandí north-west provinces a column for remarks is so headed. In the south it is applied to any authenticated document or voucher, such as a written authority from a husband to a wife to adopt a son after his demise.

Kaifíat-i-band-o-bast, H. (P. بند وبست, q. v.) Particular statement of revenue assessment, or any other settlement.

KÁÍGADḌE, Karn. (ಕಾಯಿಗಡ್ಡೆ) Pulse, any sort of leguminous vegetable.

Káiganu, Karn. (ಕಾಯಿಗನು) A seller of vegetables.

KAIL, KAILU, or KAYALU, corruptly, KYLE, Tel. (కైల, కైలు, కయలు, from the A. كيل, measure) The actual measurement of the crop after it is threshed, and before its division between the cultivator and the government.

Kail-asámiwárí-áwarjá, Tel. (see *Avárija*) A detailed statement of the produce of each Ryot's land by measurement.

Kail-dár, *Kailudáru*, &c. Tel. (P. دار, who has) A weighman or measurer, a superintendant of the measurement of the crop.

Kailí, Mar. (कैली) Relating to measure, by or of measure as opposed to weight, and prefixed in that sense to names of measures; as, *Kailí-man*, a *man* or *maund* by measure, not by weight.

Kail-pechchu, Tel. (కైల-పెచ్చు) A portion of the grain in excess of their share by measurement, granted to the cultivators.

ḲÁÍM, H. &c. (A. قايم) KÁYAM, Tel. (కాయం) Firm, lasting, erect.

Káyam-gutta, Karn. (ಕಾಯಂಗುತ್ತ) The lease or farm of a village at a fixed rent, with right of subletting the land.

Ḳáïm-maḳám, corruptly, *Kaimkan*, or *Caymacan*, H. (A. قايم مقام) A representative, a substitute, one in the place of another, a deputy, a viceroy.

Káyam-ṣibbandí, Karn. (ಕಾಯಂಶಿಬ್ಬಂದಿ) A fixed establishment.

Kaima-pen-kúru, Tam. (கைமபெண்கூறு) Portion due to a widow from her husband's estate: (from *Kaimaben*, a widow).

KAIMAḶ, Mal. (കൈമൾ) A title of rank amongst the Nairs, and used by the inferior classes when addressing them, as, My lord, and the like.

KAINI, sometimes written KHARNI, H. (?) A cultivating tenant, bound also to labour on the land retained by the landlord in his own hands, and to serve him as a porter: (probably the same word as *Gaini*, q. v.).

KAIRI, ? KAINI, Tam. An irrigated field.

KAIVERTTA, vernacularly, KAIVART, or KAIBART, S. (कैवर्त्त) A fisherman by caste and occupation: see *Kaibartta*.

KAJ, Thug. A traveller, or any man not a Thug.

Kaji, Thug. A woman, not of a Thug tribe.

KÁJÁRÍ, Mar. (काजारी) A caste, or an individual of it, whose chief occupation is making glass bracelets.

KAJJU, Tel. (కజ్జు, (?) error for కబ్జు, KABJU, for KABZ, q. v.) A receipt.

KÁKÁ, Ben. (কাকা) KAKKA, Karn. (ಕಕ್ಕ) A father's younger brother.

Káki, Ben. (কাকী) *Kakkachchi*, Karn. (ಕಕ್ಕಚ್ಚಿ) A father's younger brother's wife.

KÁKAMBI, Karn. (ಕಾಕಂಬಿ) Refined sugar, the inspissated juice of the cane.

KÁKÁPURI, Guz. (કાકાપુરી) A slave born in the house.

KAKHIÁLÍ, H. (S. کھیالی) Sheaves or bundles of corn given as the perquisite of the reapers and village servants.

KÁKPAD, Mar. (काकपद, lit., crow's-foot) A mark ˅ or ˄ indicating where something interlined should be read, a caret.

KÁKINI, Ben. (S. কাকিনী) Five *gaṇḍas* or twenty *kauris*, also a *Kauri*, q. v.

KÁKWI, Mar. (काकवी) The juice of the sugar-cane boiled to the consistence of honey.

KÁL, Tam., Mal. (கால்) The leg, the foot; in Malabar, any tree that serves as a standard for the pepper or betel-vine.

KÁLA, vernacularly KÁL, S. &c. (کال, कालः) Time in general or any particular time or season. Death, destiny; also adj., Black: see *Kálá*, and *Kálí*.

Kálakrayam, S. (कालक्रयं) Market value, price of the day.

Kálakriyápatra, Karn. (from the S. क्रिया, act, and पत्र, leaf) A deed of conveyance.

Kálapiḷḷi, Tam. (காலப்பிள்ளி) An estimate of produce taken early at the time of reaping.

Kálávadi, Tel., Karn. (కాలావధి, from S. अवधि, term) The season of cultivation, the begining of it, when arrangements are made with the Ryots: also, the close of the season, or of the year.

Káláya, Mal. (കാലായ) Land that has been reaped: the same cultivated a second time in the same year.

Kálayukti, S. &c. (कालयुक्ति) The fifty-second year of the cycle.

Káliká or *Káliká-vriddhi*, S. (कालिकावृद्धि) Periodical interest.

KALÁ, S. &c. (कला) An art, a craft, especially a fine art, as music, painting; also, a mechanical art, as carpentry and the like: also, a part, a portion.

Kaláḍiha, Uriya (କଳାଡିହ) Elevated land.

Kalásútri, Mar. (from S. सूत्र, a thread, the string that works a puppet) An exhibitor of puppet-shows; also, a rope-dancer and juggler, or an itinerant musician and dancer.

Kalávant, H. (کلاونت) A professional musician and singer.

Kalávantin, H. (کلاونتن) The female of the former, herself a singer and dancer.

KAḶA, Karn. (ಕಳ) KAḶAM, Tam. and Mal (களம்) KAḶḶAMU, or KAḶḶÁMU, Tel. (కళ్లము, కళ్లాము) A threshing-floor, a place where the grain is beaten or trodden out: see *Khala*.

Kaḷamadi, Tam. (களமதி) Estimate of the grain on the threshing-floor.

Kaḷanaḍai, Tam. (களநடை) A heap of grain unthreshed: an account of the actual produce of a field, distinguishing the shares of the government and cultivators, and the allowance to the village servants.

Kaḷappaḍi, Tam. (களப்படி) A portion of grain out of the produce of all taxable lands alloted to the labourers, whether slaves or hired servants.

Kaḷappát, Mal. (കളപ്പാട) A barn, a threshing-floor.

Kaḷappichchai, Tam. (களப்பிச்சை) Grain from the threshing-floor given in charity.

Kaḷḷatíruva, Tel. (కళ్లతీరువ) Fees on threshing grain.

Kalattuméḍu, Tam. (களத்துமேடு) A threshing-floor.

Kalavaḍi, Tam. (களவடி) Sweepings of a threshing-floor.

Kalavásam, incorrectly *Kálavásam*, and *Kallavassum*, Tam. (களவாசம்) Hire or fee given to labourers or slaves, or inferior village servants, of a portion of grain from the threshing-floor, or from the field.

KÁLÁ, H. &c. (S. کالا, काला) Black.

Kálápání, Ben. &c. (কালাপানী, from S. पानीय) Black water, the sea, applied more especially to transportation beyond sea.

KÁLÁ, Guz. (કાલા) Cotton in the pod, uncleaned cotton.

ḲALÁÍ, H. &c. (قلعی) Tin, tinning of copper utensils.

Ḳaláígar, H. (قلعیگر) A tinman, a worker in tin.

KAḶAI, Tam. (களை) Grass or weeds growing amongst corn.

KAḶAKKAR, Tam. (களக்கர்) People of a low caste, the same as the *Paleyar*, hunters and fowlers.

KALÁL, also KALÁR and KALWAR, incorrectly, KALLAL, H. &c. (کلال, کلار, کلوار, कलाल, कलार, कलवार) A distiller, a maker and vendor of spirituous liquors: (from the S. कल्यपालः).

Kalálí, *Kalárí*, Mar. &c. (कलाली, कलारी) A wineseller, a vintner, a tavern-keeper; any thing relating to spirituous liquors, a tax upon them, excise.

Kaláljamá, H. &c. (کلالجمع) Revenue from the excise or duty on spirits.

Kalálkhána, corruptly, *Kulalconna*, Mar. &c. (from P. خانة, a house) A liquor-shop, a place where spirituous liquors are sold, or where they are distilled; a distillery; a duty paid by the venders.

Ḳalam, Qulum, corruptly, Cullum and Callum, H. &c. (A. قلم, कलम) A pen, or a reed (calamus) used as one; a brush; also, sometimes, handwriting, a paragraph, an item, an article, a column of an account.

Kalambandí, Mar. (कलमबंदी) A writing under distinct heads, as, a code of instructions, articles of agreement; enrolling, enlisting. In Guz. it is used to mean attachment, sequestration; also, a document shewing the state and management of a district.

Ḳalamdán, H. &c. (قلمدان) A penholder, an inkstand, an ornamented, varnished, oblong case for holding pens and ink, and worn in the girdle as the insignia of civil office.

Ḳalamí, H. &c. (قلمي) Relating to a pen, or to writing, authentic, official, written as opposed to verbal.

Kalamkárí, Tel. (కలంకారి) Chintz, or chintz-painting or manufacture.

Kalamkucharáí, Mar. (कलमकुचराई) Bad or erroneous writing, leaving out a letter, or the like; also, fraudulent omission of an item in an account.

Kalam, corruptly, Cullum, Tam. (கலம்) A measure, equal to twelve *markáls*, q. v.

Kalama, Tel. (కలమ) A hollow formed by water that escapes from the edge of a reservoir: Tel. and Karn., Rice that ripens in December.

Kalama, Kaḷame, or Kalamige, Karn. (ಕಳಮ, ಕಳಮೆ, ಕಳಮಿಗೆ) A field of paddy, a crop of standing paddy.

Kalangam, (?) Land paying no tax except when cultivated.

Kalántar, Mar. (कलांतर) Interest on money.

Kálápáti, Ben. (কালাপাতি, Port. Calapata) Caulking a ship or boat; a caulker.

Kalappai, Tam. (கலப்பை) A ploughshare and handle.

Kaḷappu, Tam. (களப்பு) Levelling a field after removing the grass.

Kaḷar, H. (کلر, कलर) A soapy soil used by washermen, a sort of fullers' earth.

Kaḷar, Kaḷari, corruptly, Kallar, Tam. (களர், களரி) Barren soil, waste ground.

Kaḷari, Mal. (കളരി) A school where the use of arms is taught.

Kaḷarnilam, Tam. (களர்நிலம்) Barren or sandy soil.

Kaḷarmeḍu, Tam. (களர்மேடு) High land, unprofitable for cultivation.

Kalaṣí, or Kalsí, Kulsee, H. &c. (كلسي, S. कलशी) A water-jar, usually of baked clay, an ornament or knob on the top of a wall or a building.

Kalaṣípújá, S. (कलशीपूजा) Placing a water-jar in a chamber as a type of, or receptacle of, Durgá, or other divinity, and worshipping it.

Kalaṣísthápana, S. (स्थापन, placing) Setting up a water-jar as an object of worship: part of the marriage ceremony, in which offerings are made to the planets in different vessels.

Kalaṣi, Karn. (ಕಲಶಿ) A measure of grain, one third of a *mora*: in Guzerat it has the same sense, but is equal to 16 *maunds*, or 640 *sérs* or lbs.

Kalavaṛa, Mal. (കലവറ) A store, a granary.

Kalavaṛa-káran, Mal. (കലവറക്കാരൻ) A steward, a storekeeper, a treasurer.

Kaḷavi, Kaḷivi, Karn. (ಕಳವಿ, ಕಳಿವಿ) Counterfeit, forged.

Kalivi-hana, Karn. (ಕಳಿವಿಹಣ) Counterfeit coin.

Kaḷavu, Karn. (ಕಳವು) Theft, robbery.

Kaláy, Ben. (কলায) Pulse of various sorts.

Káláya, Mal. (കാലായ) Land that has been reaped and cultivated for a second crop.

Kali, or Kali-yuga, vernacularly, sometimes, Kali- or Kal-jug, corruptly, Caly-yoogum, Cal- or Kul-jogue, S., but in all the dialects, (कलि, कलियुग) The Kali age, the last and worst of the four ages that make up a great age: the present age of the world is the Kali, supposed to have begun on Friday, the 18th of February, 3102 years B.C., and it is to last altogether 432,000 years, forming a period of progressive iniquity and deterioration, and ending in the general dissolution of existing forms.

Káli, Ben. (কালি) The product of a sum in arithmetic: also, as derived from *Kálá*, black, ink.

Kálí, H. &c. (كالي) Black.

Kálí-bhúmí, or *-bhúí*, H. &c. (كالي بهومي, -بهوي, काली भूमी, from S. भुमी, earth) Black soil, a rich, vegetable, and dark-coloured mould: it forms the greater portion of the soil of western Guzerat, and spreads widely through Malwa and the valleys of the Dakhin: although less productive than another kind of soil found in Guzerat, termed *márwá*, it is highly favourable to the growth of wheat and cotton.

Káḷí, incorrectly, Kallee, Mar. (काळी, it is no doubt the same word as the Hindustani Káli, though written with a different *l*) Arable land in general, from its being usually of a dark colour: black soil or mould, cultivable land of a superior quality; the underlying ground in the Dang, receiving and retaining moisture during the cold season, and especially fit for wheat and other spring crops: the term is applied also to the crops or produce of such soil.

Káḷí-chá-paiká, or *-wasúl*, Mar. (काळीचापैका, -वसूल) Revenue from cultivated land; land-tax or revenue.

Káḷí-chunkarí, Mar. (काळीचुणकरी) Black soil upon a substratum of lime, which renders it very unproductive.

Káḷí-jamá, Mar. (काळीजमा) Revenue derived from the soil.

Dunbi-káḷí, or *Dhas-káḷí*, (?) Mar. Cracked black soil: see *Dunbi*.

Kharkal-káḷí, Mar. (खडकलकाळी) Black soil containing stones; less rich than the usual black mould, but, as more retentive of moisture, and more easily worked, it is rarely left fallow, and is very productive.

KÁLÍ, Karn. (ಠಾಲೀ) An ancient measure of weight in Mysore, equal to 40 *hánis* of 80 rupees each, or to 3200 rupees.

KÁLÍ, H. &c. (S. کالی, काली) The name of a popular goddess, the wife of Siva, so named from her black complexion; the same as *Deví* or *Durgá*.

Káḷi-chakram, Tam. (காளிசக்கிரம்) A gold coin having a figure of the goddess Kálí, formerly current in the south.

KALINGAL, Tam. (கலிங்கல்) An outlet or sluice for carrying off the surplus water of a reservoir.

KALINGU, Tam. (கலிங்கு) A dam, a stone bank or dyke, a sluice.

KALÍT, (?) Mar. An estimate of standing corn, or of fruit before gathering.

KAḶIVÁYANILAM, Tam. (களிவாயநிலம்) A clay soil.

KAḶḶA, Karn., Mal. (ಕಳ್ಳ, കള്ള) False, cheating, deceptive.

Kaḷḷa, *Kaḷḷanu*, Karn. (ಕಳ್ಳ, ಕಳ್ಳನು) A thief, a plunderer; plural *Kaḷḷaru*, (ಕಳ್ಳರು) Thieves, whence the *Colleries* of the peninsula in early English writers.

Kaḷḷachcharakka, Mal. (കള്ളച്ചരക്ക) Smuggled goods.

Kaḷḷakkammiṭṭam, Mal. (കള്ളക്കമ്മിട്ടം) Counterfeit coin.

Kaḷḷakaraṇam, Mal. (കള്ളകരണം) Forged or false title-deeds or documents.

Kaḷḷan, Mal. (കള്ളൻ) A cheat, a rogue, a liar, a swindler: (no doubt connected with the Karn. term *Kaḷḷa*, as above).

Kaḷḷapadi, Karn. (ಕಳ್ಳಪದಿ) A false measure.

Kaḷḷaruju, Karn. (ಕಳ್ಳರುಜು) A forgery, a false signature.

Kaḷḷasákkhi, Karn. (ಕಳ್ಳಸಾಕ್ಷಿ) False witness.

KAḶḶÁDI, or KAḶḶÁRI, Mal. (കള്ളാടി) A class of predial slaves in Malabar: in some lists it appears, probably incorrectly, as part of a compound term, *Kaḷḷádi-kanakan*: it is no doubt connected with the Karn. *Kaḷḷa*.

KALLAYENṬU, Tel. (కల్లయెంటు) A client; being in fact the English word.

KALLU, Thug. A thief.

Kallui, Thug. Theft.

KAḶḶI, Karn. (ಕಳ್ಳಿ) The Euphordia or milk hedge plant, very common in Mysore.

KALLI, (?) Guz. A system of assessment under which the crops are not allowed to be disposed of until the revenue is paid, or security given for its payment.

KALLU, also KALYAMU, Tel. (కల్లు, కల్యము) KAḶḶA, Mal. (കള്ള) *Táṛí*, the fermented sap of different kinds of palm trees.

KALLU, Tel., Karn. (కల్లు) KAL, plural KALLUKAḶ, Tam. (கல், கல்லுகள்) KALLA, Mal. (കല്ല) A stone.

Kallánguttu, Tam. (கல்லாங்குத்து) Hard stony ground, not worth cultivating.

Kallukuṭiga, Karn. (ಕಲ್ಲುಕುಟಿಗ) A stonecutter, a mason.

Kalluppu, Karn. (ಕಲ್ಲುಪ್ಪು) Rock-salt.

Kalkachchan, Mal. (കല്കച്ചൻ) A stonecutter, a mason.

Kallumatada-ayya, Karn. (ಕಲ್ಲುಮಠದ ಅಯ್ಯ) A Lingamite priest.

KALMAH, or KALIMAH, H. (A. کلمه) A word, a speech; the Mohammadan confession of faith, "There is but one god, and Mohammed is the apostle of God."

KALPA, S. &c. (कल्पः) A very long period of time; a day of Brahmá, or 4320 millions of years: a ceremonial or ritual precept; the ritual of the Vedas.

KALÚ, Ben. (কলু) A maker and vender of oil by caste and occupation: grinding or expressing oil from different seeds.

KAḶUBU, Karn. (ಕಳುಬು) Weeds and grass in standing corn.

KALWA, Tel. (కల్వ) A water course.

KAM, KUM, H. (P. کم) Little, less, deficient: commonly used also in compounds, as *Kam-bakht*, unfortunate, deservedly so, a scoundrel: *Kamyábi*, rarity &c.

Kamán, Ben. (কমান) Lowering the price of any thing, diminishing the rent of land.

Kamdar, Uriya (କମଦର) Land of inferior quality.

Kamdár, or *Kamdast*, Mar. (from P. دار, having, or دست, the hand) Reduced rate of assessment.

Kamí, Kumee, corruptly *Cummee,* H. (كمي) *Kammi,* Tel. (కమ్మి) Littleness, deficiency, loss: deficiency in the weight or value of coins, loss in exchange, an allowance formerly made in the public accounts to cover such losses in the collections.

Kamí-beshí-dar-fardí, H. (A. فرد, a statement, q. v.) In Bengal, an account formerly kept, shewing the diminution, (*kamí*) and increase (*beshí*) of the revenue, settled for at the commencement of the year with each cultivator.

Kami-janún, Hindi (कमिजमीन) Statement of the decrease of land in cultivation (Puraniya).

Kamín, corruptly *Kumenee,* H. (P. كمين) Base, low, inferior: applied, in the north-west provinces, to the artificers and servants of a village, who, besides allowances in grain, receive small allotments in land, and are therefore "minor" or inferior cultivators: the term is also sometimes applied to all the residents of a village, except religious mendicants, who are not cultivators: in Kamaon the term designates the superintendant of the village management.

Kamíní-báchh, H. (كميني باچه) A tax levied by the proprietors of a village on every resident who is not engaged in agriculture: a sort of ground-rent for the non-cultivator's dwelling.

Kamkásht, Hindi (कमकाश्त) Decrease in the cultivation of an individual cultivator, as compared with a preceding period (Puraniya).

Kamkholka, (?) H. Land of inferior quality, but let by the year.

Kamḳism-zamín, H. (from A. قسم, sort and زمين, land) Land of an inferior sort or quality.

Kam-o-besh, H. (P. كم وبيش) Less or more.

Kam-o-beshí, corruptly *Kumi-a-beshi,* H. (P. كم وبيشي) Less- or more-ness applied especially to disputes among the coparcenery proprietors of a village regarding the proportions of their shares.

Kám, Tel. (కాం) A revenue term implying private or own (it is no doubt a vernacular corruption of *khám,* q. v.).

Kámtekha, Tel. (కాం లెక్క) A private account usually kept by the village accountant besides his public accounts.

Kám, H. &c. (كام, काम, from the S. *Karmma,* कर्म्मः) Work, business, affair, (in composition and derivation the vowel is not unfrequently made short).

Kamáí, H. &c. (كماي, कमाई) Gain, profit, earnings: in Maraṭhí it is also applied to any complete operation or set of operations, as, in agriculture, to manuring, raking, ploughing, sowing and reaping, also to mixing up ingredients to make a single mixture, and the like.

Kamáíshi, Kamávishi, Karn. (ಕಮಾಯಿಷಿ, ಕಮಾವಿಷಿ) *Kamáishu,* Tel., Karn. (కమాయిషు) *Kamávisí, Kamavişí, Kamávis,* Mar. (कमाविसी -शी, कमावीस, from S. कर्म्म, and *vis,* विश, to enter into, or engage in) Management of affairs, whether on behalf of an individual or the estate, stewardship, superintendence: amongst the Maraṭhas it applies especially to the business of collecting the revenues, also to the collections, especially when of a miscellaneous kind: also, advantage, gain, profit.

Ain-kamávís, Mar. (ऐनकमावीस) Fixed collections in kind on various sorts of garden produce, as sugar-cane, plantains &c.

Jástí-kamávís, Mar. (जासतीकमावीस) Miscellaneous or extra collections, as of a tax on trades and professions, a discount on different sorts of rupees &c.

Kamávis-dár, or *Kamáíşí,* corruptly *Komaveesdar, Comaveesdar, Komisdar, Komashdar,* Mar., Guz. (कमावीसदार, कमाईशी) The head revenue-officer of a district, entrusted also with the police. In Kanara the *Kamáíshidár,* or *Kamávişí-dár* was also especially the collector, managing lands that were permanently or temporarily occupied by the state, the *Amín* of the upper provinces.

Kamávís-jamá, Mar. (कमावीसजमा) Revenue from miscellaneous and irregular sources, as judicial fines &c.

Kámdár, H. &c. (كامدار) A man of business, an agent, a steward, a representative, especially in revenue matters.

Kámdárí, H. &c. (كامداري) The office or duty of a manager or man of business.

Kámgár, Mar. (कामगार) A servant, a manager, a public officer, a person employed on public works.

Kámgárí, Mar. (कामगारी) Agency, deputation; also, repairs, public works.

Kámháj, H. &c. (كامكاج, कामकाज, from S. कर्म्म and कार्य्य) Work, business in general.

Kámkár, H. &c. (कामकार) Business, affairs; also, one who carries on work or business.

Kámhár-bhár, Mar. (कामकारभार, from S. भार, a burden) Public affairs, the duties of a court or of a government.

Kámkarí, Mar. (कामकरी, from S. कर, who does) A workman, a hired labourer.

Kámal or Kámil, corruptly, Kamul or Kaumil, H. &c. (A. كامل, كمال) Entire, perfect, complete: in revenue language, the whole sum raised by a village for the total of its expenses, including the government demand; also, the largest amount of revenue realized from a village or district; also, in the south of India, the fixed or standard assessment, as determined in different places by former governments.

Kamál-ákár, Mar. (कमालाकार) The total assessment of a village.

Kámil-âiár, H. (A. عيار, touch) Of perfect standard, of pure touch or assay (coin, &c.).

Kamál-beríj, *Kamál-jamâ*, H. &c. (from بيريج, جمع, &c., implying collections) The total collections or revenue of a district.

Kamál-dhárá, incorrectly, *Kumal-dhur*, Mar. (कमालधारा) The standard assessment of some of the districts of the Dakhin, as established about A.D. 1769.

KAMARḌAI, Tam. (கமர்டை) The transfer of proprietary land by a proprietor, who is unable to cultivate it himself, to another person, to hold for a given term, on condition of allowing the owner a proportion of the produce, the occupant engaging not to dispose of the land to a third party.

KAMAR-KUSHÁI, corruptly, CUMMUR-KESHAY and KUMMUR-KASHAN, H. (P. كمركشاي, from كمر, the loins, and كشادن, to open or untie) KAMAR-KHULÁÍ, Mar. (कमरखुलाई, from H. *Kholná*, to open) KOMAR-KASHÁÍ, Ben. (কোমরকষাই) lit., Undoing or opening the waistband; a fee levied by a government peon, or inferior native officer, from a person over whom he is placed in charge, for permission to perform any of the common functions of life. In Bengal it is said to mean money given to a runner or messenger on his setting out for any distance (but this is doubtful).

KÁMÁRTHÍ, H. (S. كامارتهي) A person who carries the water of the Ganges to distant places in vessels cased in basket-work.

KÁMAT, Mar. (कामत) A distinction amongst the *Senawis*, q. v., usually added to the name, as *Rám-Kámat*.

KAMATAMU, or, omitting the final, KAMATA or KAMATAM, corruptly, KUMENATAM, KAMBATAM, and COMPTUM, Tel. (కమతము) The cultivation which a cultivator carries on with his own stock, but by the labour of another: the land which a Zamindar, Jagirdar, or Inamdar keeps in his own hands, cultivating it by labourers, in distinction to that which he lets out in farm. The word occurs apparently, although not very commonly, in Upper India, as *Kámat*, (कामत), to signify lands held by a non-resident tenant, who cultivates by a hired servant, or *Kámatí*, (कामती); also, an entry in the village accounts of the land so rented, and by whom (Puraniya). In the Doab of the Dakhin, *Kámat* lands are described as either those reserved by public officers for their own use, Jagír lands cultivated by their servants, or lands not expressly Inám, but appropriated or obtained in grant by public servants or great men, and cultivated either by hired or compulsory labour.

Kamatagáḍu, Tel. (కమతగాడు) *Kamatagáranu*, Karn. (ಕಮತಗಾರನು) A person who cultivates lands belonging to another with the farming stock of the owner.

KÁMÁṬHÍ, corruptly, KAMATEE, COMPTÍE, and COMPTÍE-BANIA, Mar. (कामाठी) A caste of *Ṣúdras*, or individual of it; according to one statement, those in the Maratha districts are distinguished as Tailanga and Karnáta *Kámáthís*, from their country: at Puna they are said to be employed as rice-cleaners, grinders of corn, and cutters of sticks, tent-pitchers, and artillerymen; they also sell snuff: in Telingana they are also petty retail dealers, or chandlers: in Mysore they are chiefly employed in road-making, and in repairing public works: in general they seem to be common labourers, and are probably the same as the Ganges water-carriers of Hindustan: see *Kámárthí*.

KÁMÁṬÍ, KÁMÁṬIGANU, Karn. (ಕಾಮಾಟಿ, ಕಾಮಾಟಿಗನು) A bricklayer, Tel. (కామాటి) A pioneer, a labourer, one who works with a pickaxe or spade (no doubt the same word as the preceding Marathí term).

KAMBALA, vernacularly, KAMBAL or KUMBUL, also vernacularly modified, as KAML, KAMBALI, or KAMLI, corruptly, CUMBLY, COMLI, COMBLY, &c., S., but in all the dialects, (कम्बलः, कंबल, कमली, كنبل, كمل, كملي, &c.) A coarse woollen wrapper or shawl, a blanket: *Kamlí*, 'blanketed,' is also applied to a butcher's stall, which is usually covered with a woollen cloth.

KAMBALAI, Tam. (கம்பளை) A rice-field.

KAMBAR, Tel. (కంబర) Rope made from the fibre of the cocoa-nut tree.

KAMBÁRI, Tel. (కంబారి) A sub-tenant, an under-farmer.

KAMBÁRLU, Tel. (plural కంబార్లు) Cultivators of lands for other persons (perhaps for *Kamata-vándlu*); see *Kamata*.

KAMBAṬṬAM, Tam. (கம்பட்டம்) Coinage, fabrication of coin.

Kambaṭṭa-khúḍam, Tam. (கம்பட்டக்கூடம்) A mint.

KAMBATTAM, KAMMATTAM, Tam. (கம்பத்தம், கம்மத்தம்) Husbandry on a large scale: grant of a village for private disbursements.

KAMBU, Tel. (కంబు) A sort of millet: see *Bájra*.

Kámotsava, S. &c. (कामोत्सव) A festival in honour of Káma, the deity of love, on the 13th and 14th of Chaitra, merged, in some places, into the Holi, and so lost sight of.

Kamerá, H. (كميرا) A hired agricultural labourer in the north-west provinces, sometimes located for successive generations on the same estate, although quite free to remove.

Kamíá, H. (كميا, S. कर्म्मिकः) An agricultural labourer of some low caste: in South Bahar he is sometimes considered as a predial slave, either for a term or for ever: in the south-west provinces he is usually a bondsman or bond-slave who has sold his services for life, and may be transferred or sold himself; his children are free: one kind, the *Bandhak-kamíá*, (Bundhuk-kumeea,) is one who is a slave only until he can repay the money advanced to him for his services: see *Sevak*.

Kamishnar-ḳurḳi, H. (كمشنر قرقي) The English term Commissioner, applied to a native officer of the Collector who is charged with the enforcement of distraint, and sale by auction of property distrained and not redeemed.

Kamp, Thug. A bribe for the escape of an apprehended Thug.

Kámp, H. (كانپ, कांप) Mud thrown up and deposited by water-courses or rivers.

Kampa, Tel. (కంప) Dried brambles or thorns.

Kampakoṭṭa, Tel. (కంపకోట్ట) A hedge of dry thorns and bushes round a fort or village as a defence, a sort of abattis.

Kampú, Mar. (कम्पू, from the English 'Camp') An encampment, but especially applied to the troops of an encampment, or a body of infantry disciplined in the European fashion in the service of native princes.

Kámyakarma, S. (काम्यकर्म्म, from काम्य, agreeable, and कर्म्म, act) Any religious or other observance undertaken voluntarily in distinction to acts of necessity.

Kámyamaraṇam, S. (काम्यमरणं) Voluntary death, suicide.

Kamyaśráddha, S. (काम्यश्राद्धं) Obsequial ceremonies performed at pleasure in addition to those which are obligatory.

Kan, Kun, H. (S. كن) Appreciation, valuation, estimate, especially of the value of crops on the ground.

Kanhá H. (كنها) An officer employed to value standing crops.

Kanhái, H. (كنهاي) Valuation of standing crops.

Kankút, Kunkoot, H. (كنكوت, कंकूत, from *Kan*, valuing, or *Kan*, for *Karṇa*, an ear (of corn) and *Kút*, appraisement) Estimated valuation of standing crops by measurement of the land and inspection of the corn, or, after measuring the field, cutting a given portion of it, and weighing the grain so reaped; the object of such estimate being to assess the land at a money rate, according to the computed amount of the sale price of the grain; also an account of such appraisement kept by the village accountant.

Káṇ, Káṇam, Tam. (S. கான், கானம்) **Kánana**, Karn. (ಕಾನನ) A forest, a thicket.

Kán-kuri, Karn. (ಕಾನ್ಕುರಿ) A wild sheep.

Kánsisht, Karn. (ಕಾನ್ಸಿಷ್ತ) A tax on forest produce.

Kánavar, Tam. (கானவர்) Hill men, shepherds, hunters.

Kaṇa, vernacularly **Kan**, H. &c. (S. कण) A small particle or grain of any thing, a grain of corn.

Kaṇaja, Kaṇanja, Karn. (ಕಣಜ, ಕಣಂಜ) A granary, a store for grain.

Kangá, Mar. (कणगा) A corn bin, a large basket, a safe for grain, a granary.

Kaṇa, Karn. (ಕಣ) A threshing or treading-floor, where the grain is trodden out.

Káṇáchi, Karn. (ಕಾಣಾಚಿ) A hereditary estate; see *Káni-átchi*.

Kanágat, H. (كناگت, *Kaná*, for *Kanyá*, S. a maiden, or the sign *Virgo*) The daily celebration of obsequial rites during the dark half of *Áświn*, when the sun is in *Virgo* (September-October).

Kanakan, Kunnakan, (?) Mal. The name of a class of predial slaves in Malabar, also designated *Kanaka-charma*: according to one account they are a subdivision of the *Palayar*.

Káṇakaurí, Uriya (କାଣକଉଡ଼ି) A cracked *kauri* shell; any thing of little or no value.

Kaṇakku, Tam., Mal. (கணக்கு) Ciphering, arithmetic, accounts.

Kaṇakhan, Tam., Mal. (கணக்கன்) An accountant, a village accountant.

Kaṇakka-mániyam, Tam. (from மானியம்) A portion of land rent-free granted to the village accountant.

Kaṇakkamérai, Tam. (கணக்கமேரை) Fees in grain given to the village accountant.

Kaṇahkappíllai, corruptly, *Conicopoly* and *Konicoply*, Tam. (கணக்கப்பிள்ளை) An accountant, the village accountant.

Kaṇakkurubam, corruptly, *Kunukuroopoo*, Tam. (கணக்குருபம்) A written memorandum of an adjusted account.

Kaṇakkussuruṇai, Tam. (கணக்குச்சுருணை) A bundle of accounts on palm leaves kept by the village accountant.

Káṇam, incorrectly, **Kanom**, Mal. (കാണം) Mortgage, fee, present, reward: it applies especially to an advance or loan of money as the equivalent or consideration for a mortgage or transfer of landed property, fields, and gardens, into the occupancy of the person advancing the money, without prejudice to the proprietor's vested rights, to whom, also, the occupant is bound to pay all proceeds of the estate in excess of the interest of the money he has advanced: the term is applied also to certain fees payable at the time of executing such mortgage or transfer.

Ánandaravan-naḍu-káṇam, Mal. (ആനന്തരവൻനടു-കാണം) Fees paid to the proprietor's heir on sipping the water next noticed.

Nír-káṇam, Mal. (നീരകാണം) lit., Piece of water, a few pieces of money put into a vessel of water from the estate of the mortgager on executing the deeds.

Oppa-káṇam, Mal. (ഒപ്പുകാണം) Fees on signing the deeds of transfer.

Tushi-káṇam, Mal. (തുഷ്ഠികാണം) Fees paid to the person who draws up the deeds.

Káṇakáran, Mal. (കാണകാരൻ) The mortgagee, the lender of money on security of occupancy and usufruct of landed property.

Káṇakota, Mal. (കാണകൊട) Amount of the mortgage money; also, mortgage tenure.

Káṇapalisa, Mal. (കാണപലിശ) Interest on the money lent on mortgage.

Káṇampaṇaya-páṭṭam, Mal. (കാണംപണയപാട്ടം) A deed of mortgage.

Káṇamvaram, Mal. (കാണംവരം) A mortgagee.

Káṇappáṭṭam, Mal. (കാണപ്പാട്ടം) Mortgage tenure of lands; interest on the money advanced on mortgage.

Káṇam, Mal. (കാണം) An advance or deposit of money made to a proprietor of lands or gardens on receiving them from him at a stipulated rent, upon lease for a given term of years: the deposit bears interest, which the tenant sets off against the rent: the principal is returned when the lease expires and the occupant does not renew it. This is therefore a somewhat different application of the same term from a loan upon a mortgage where the lender holds the land as a security; here the landlord holds the deposit as a security for his rent. (Although spelt exactly in the same manner, it is possible that the two words are not identical. In Walker's report on Malabar, he says this *kánam* is from the Sanscrit word, signifying 'a little,' 'an ear of corn,' &c.; in which case the derivative, like the original (कणं), should be written with a short, not a long vowel, *Kanam* or *Kunum*, not *Kánam*, *Kanum*; the apparent identity may therefore arise from the vernacular disregard of the correct spelling).

Kánam-janm-maryáda-aranyavar, Mal. Assessors by whom the value of an estate is determined, and the proportions of the tenant and landlord adjusted.

Káṇam-kondavan, (? for *Koṛuvan*, കൊഴുവൻ) Mal. A tenant, a person who gives security by a deposit for payment of rent.

Káṇam-páṭṭam, Mal. (from പാട്ടം, rent) Leasehold tenure of lands or gardens on payment of a rent, or proportion of produce equal usually to two-thirds, or the money value of that proportion of the produce.

Kuḷi- or *Kuṛi-káṇam*, incorrectly, *Koori-hanom*, Mal. (കുഴിക്കാണം) Money paid to a tenant on his relinquishing his lease, or to a mortgagee when a mortgage is paid off, for any improvements they may have made, especially for any fruit-bearing trees, as cocoa-nuts, &c., which they may have planted: on the other hand, if the property has been depreciated by neglect, compensation is deducted from the original deposit or loan: this is also termed, according to Mr. Græme, *Náḍi-káṇam* (നാടികാണം).

Kanama, Tel. (కనమ) A breach in the bank of a tank, whether accidental or artificial; a pass between two hills.

Ḳanát, H. (A. قنات) The walls of a tent, or an external screen of canvas surrounding a tent.

Kanaujía, Canoujía, incorrectly, Kanojiya, H. (کنوجیه, कनौजीआ) A designation of various tribes in Hindustan, implying a notion of their having come originally from Kanauj, or Kanyákubja: it is especially applied to a large and influential tribe of Bráhmans, one of the five classes of Gauḍa Bráhmans: five chief subdivisions of them are reckoned, all numerous and well known—*Kanaujía proper*, *Sarwaria*, *Sanaudka*, *Jijhotia*, and *Bhuṇhár*, who are again divided into sixteen classes, named either from their reputed founders, who were celebrated sages, as *Garga*, *Gotama*, and others; or from their former acquirements, as *Dobe*, *Tewari* or *Trivedi*, *Chaube*, or as learned in two, three, or four Vedas, or from their having been teachers, as *Bhaṭṭachárj* and *Upádhyáya*; or from other circumstances, as *Páṇde*, *Díkshit*, *Bájpeyi*, &c. The *Kanaujias proper* are found principally in the central Doab, extending into Bundelkhand on the one hand, and on the other into Oudh, and are divided into six or six and a half families, thence termed *Khat-* (for *shaṭ*, six) *kul*, or, severally, *Gotes*, (from the S. *gotra*; a race), as the *Sandel-gote*, *Upamán-gote*, *Bháradwáj-gote*, *Bharadwáj-gote*, *Kátyáyana-* or *Viswámitra-gote*, *Kasyapa-gote*, and *Sakrint-gote*. These correspond in rank to the *Kulín* Brahmans of Bengal, and, although taking wives from the other tribes, allow their daughters to marry only into one of the *Khat-kul*. The *Sarwaria* class is also called *Saryu-* or *Sarju-pária*, living beyond the Sarju or Gagra river, or chiefly in Gorakhpur. The *Sanaudhas* are met with principally in Rohilkhand and the upper and central Doab, extending westwards to Gwalior. The *Jijhotias* are settled to the south-west. The *Bhoonhárs* are found with the *Sarwarias* in Oudh, and spread to the hills of Bundelkhand. The term *Kanaujia* is applied, however, to other than Brahmanical tribes, and we have *Kanaujia Kúrmis*, or agricultural castes, and even *Kanaujia Thugs*.

KÁṆAVAṬṬAM, Tam. (காணவட்டம்) A small quantity of oil daily allowed by the oilmakers to the owner or head man of the village, and to the village officers and servants.

KANCHANI, H. (S. كنچني) A dancing girl, by caste as well as profession.

KANCHARÍ, Mar. (कंचरी) KÁNCHKÁR, H. (كانچكار, from S. काच, or काच्च, glass) A glassworker, a caste working in glass and crystal.

Kanchar-katti, (? *-paṭṭi*) Mar. A tax on the makers of glass bracelets.

KANCHE, Tel. (కంచె) A hedge: waste or fallow land.

Kanchehóṭṭa, Tel. (కంచెకోట్ట) A thick hedge round a fort outside the ditch, as an additional defence.

KANCHU, Karn. (ಕಂಚು) Mixed metal, brass, bell metal.

Kanchugár, Karn. (ಕಂಚುಗಾರ) A brazier, a worker in mixed metal.

KAND, H. (A. قند) Sugar, sugar-candy: see *Khand*.

KANDÁCHÁRADAVA, or KANDÁCHÁRADAVÁLIKÁRA, Karn. ಕಂದಾಚಾರದವ, ಕಂದಾಚಾರದವಾಲಿಕಾರ, from ಕಂದಾಚಾರ, military) An armed peon, a kind of militia soldier, employed on civil duties, as well as serving in war.

Kandáchárada-baṭaváḍe, Karn. (from *baṭaváḍe*, ಬಟವಾಡೆ, pay) The pay of militia.

Kandácháravajá, Karn. (from *vajá*, ವಜಾ, deduction) Lands set apart for the pay of the militia, and therefore deducted from the revenue.

KAṆḌAM, or KAṆḌU, Tam. (கண்டம், கண்டு) Sugar, sugar-candy.

KÁṆḌÁR, or KÁṆḌÁRÍ, Ben. (কাণ্ডার, from S. कर्णधारी) A steersman, a helmsman, a pilot.

KAṆḌAVA, Karn. (ರಾಂಡವ) A class of Bráhmans.

KANDÁYA, or KANDÁYAM, Tam. (கந்தாயம்) Karn. (ಕಂದಾಯ, ಕಂದಾಯಂ) Tax, tribute, duty, land-tax, ground-rent; fixed portion of tax payable at a certain time.

KANDEṚUTTA, Mal. (കണ്ടെഴുത്ത) Survey, mensuration; measuring and estimating land.

KANDHARA, or KANDHARÁ, incorrectly, *Kundra*, Uriya (କନ୍ଧ) The class of mountaineers called *Khand*, or an individual of it, employed sometimes as village watchmen: see *Khand*.

KANDHOṚÁ, Guz. (કાંધોડા) Hiring cattle for ploughing.

KAṆḌI, Tam., Mal. (கண்டி, കണ്ടി) A measure of weight: commonly, *Kandy*, but more correctly, *Khandí*, q. v.

KANDOI, Guz. (કંદોઈ) A confectioner, a sugar-baker.

KÁṆḌOḶÍ, KÁṆḌOḶEṆ, Mar. (कांडोळी, कांडोळें) A ridge of earth in a field to detain water.

KANDRA, or KHANDRA, (?) A class of slaves in Cuttack of an impure caste.

KAṆḌU, Tam. (கண்டு) A field of corn.

Kaṇḍu-mudal, Tam. (கண்டுமுதல்) Actual produce of a field when reaped and threshed.

Kandukṛushi, Mal. (കണ്ടുകൃഷി) Government agriculture, cultivation on account of government.

KÁNDU, H. (S. كاندو) A sugar-boiler.

KAṆḌUKEṬṬA, Mal. (കണ്ടുകെട്ട) Confiscation, sequestration.

KANDÚḶI, Karn. (ಕಂದೂಳಿ) A fixed rate of assessment.

KANDÚRI, H. (كندوري) A ceremony observed in honour of some holy person, at which prayers are offered for their good, or food is prepared and distributed: when celebrated in honour of Fatima it is entrusted to women.

KAṆE, Karn. (ಕಣೆ) A roller or cylinder of a mill, whether horizontal or perpendicular.

KANGÁL, H. (كنگال) Poor, miserable, bankrupt, vagrant.

Kangálam, Mal. A class of predial slaves in Malabar.

KANGARIVERO Guz. (કાંગરીવેરો) A money-tax in commutation of grain paid by the cultivators in some places; a duty on grain.

KANGNÍ, H. (كنگني) *Kangoni*, Karn. (ಕಂಗೊಣಿ) A kind of grain much eaten by the poorer classes in many parts of India, millet (Panicum italicum).

KANGI, H. (كنگي) A granary, a store of grain.

KÁNI, corruptly, CAWNEY, Tel. (కాణి) Tam. (காணி) Karn. (ಕಾಣಿ) In numbers, an 80th fractional part, or sometimes one 64th; but the word is more generally known as the denomination of a land measure at Madras, in the Carnatic, and the south-eastern provinces of the peninsula: it varies in different places, but the standard is considered to be equal to 24 *Manais*, or 'grounds' of 2400 square feet each, being equal, therefore, to 57,600 square feet. By another computation it is made equal to the same number of square *adis*, or 57,600 native feet, each *adi* being equal to inches 10.47. By the latter measurement, the *káni* is not quite an English acre; by the former it is something more, or 1.322. In Cuttack a *káṇi* (କାଣି) is only a hand's-breadth.

KÁṆI, Tam. (காணி) Property, possession, right of possession, hereditary right.

Káṇi-káran, Tam. (காணிகாரன்) A hereditary proprietor, or a hereditary coparcener in village lands held in common.

Káṇi-mérái, Tam. (காணிமேரை) A portion of grain claimed by the Mirásidárs of the Tamil countries as a perquisite from all taxable lands.

Káṇi-peru, Tam. (காணிபெரு) The greatness or dignity of holding landed property, a term used in conveyances of Mirási rights.

Káṇi-sutantaram, Tam. (சுதந்தரம், S. स्वतन्त्वं, independence) Independent hereditary right or property: see the next.

Káṇiyáṭchi, vernacularly or corruptly, *Canachi*, *Kanáchi*, *Cainatchy*, &c. Tam. (காணியாட்சி, from *Káṇi*, and *áṭchi*, power or dominion) That which is held in free and hereditary property; hereditary right to lands, fees of office, or perquisites, held by members of village communities, or by village officers, in the Tamil countries; equivalent to the Arabic term *Mirási*, used likewise in that part of India.

Káṇiyátchi-káran, Tam. (S. காரன்) A hereditary proprietor of land or privileges.

Káṇiyátchi-máṇiyam, Tam. (மாணியம்) A portion of land held by each hereditary proprietor free of assessment.

Káṇiyáḷan, Tam. (காணியாளன்) An inheritor of land.

Kánátchi-gár, Karn. (ಕಾನಾಚ್ಚಿಗಾರ) Proprietor of a hereditary estate.

Kánátchi-gráma, Karn. (ಕಾನಾಚ್ಚಿಗ್ರಾಮ) A hereditary village. (This and the preceding, as well as *Kánátchi*, hereditary property, are provincial modifications in Mysore of the Tamil *Káṇiyáṭchi*.)

KÁṆI, Karn. (ಕಾಣಿ) A piece of inferior land not included in that which is rented.

KÁṆI BHÁGOA, Uriya (କାଣିଭାଗୋଆ) Labourers in Cuttack paid both in money and kind.

KÁṆIKE-KÁṆE, or KÁṆIKE-KAPPA, Karn. (ಕಾಣಿಕೆಕಾಣೆ, ಕಾಣಿಕೆಕಪ್ಪ) A present from an inferior to a superior, a subscription, a donation.

KANÍLÍ, Thug. Earrings; gold.

KÁNÍNA, S., and in most dialects, (कानीनः) The son of an unmarried woman.

KANJAR, H. (کنجر) KANJÁRÍ, Mar. (कंजारी) A low class of people, who live by making and selling strings of hemp and cotton, also who catch and eat snakes.

Kanjariyu, Karn. (ಕಂಜರಿಯು) Class of ropemakers.

KÁNJI, corruptly, CONJEE, CONJE, KONGY, H. (S. کانجي) Rice-water in general, although it properly denotes rice-water which has been converted into an acid beverage by acetous fermentation.

KAṄKANA, vernacularly also KANKAN, and KANGAN, or KUNGUN, S. (कङ्कण) A bracelet, a string, or riband tied round the wrist, especially at marriages, round the right wrist of the bridegroom and the left of the bride: the practice, originally Hindu, has been adopted by the Mohammadans in India, and the tying and untying of the *kangan* are important parts of their marriage ceremonies.

KAṄKÁṆAM, Tam. (கண்காணம்) Watching, inspection; a fee paid for watching the crop between the field and the stack.

Kaṇkáṇi, Tam. (கண்காணி) An inspector of crops.

KANKAR, KUNKUR, corruptly, CONKAR, H. &c. (کنکر, from S. कण, a piece) KÁNKAR, Ben. (কাঁকর) A coarse kind of limestone found in the soil in many parts of Hindustan, underlying the alluvial soil in large tabular strata, or interspersed through the superficial mould in nodules of various sizes, though usually small; also, gravel, hard sand.

Kanhaláṭ, Hindi (कंकलाट) Soil of a stiff sandy loam, as hard as *kankar* (Puraniya).

Kankari, H. (کنکري) Gravel.

Kankrelá, *Kankríli*, H. (کنکريلا, کنکريلي, कंकरीली) Stony, gravelly (as soil).

KANKÍ, or KANAKÍ, H. (کنکي, S. कणिका) Ground rice; Tel. (కంకి) Head or ear of corn.

KANNA, Karn. (ಕಂನ) KANNAM, Tam. (கன்னம்) A pit, a hole, a breach in the wall of a house.

Kannagár, *Kannadakaḷi*, Karn. (ಕಂನಗಾರ, ಕಂನದಕಳ್ಳ) A housebreaker, a burglar.

Kanna-viṭṭi-mane, Karn. (ಕಂನವಿಟ್ಟಿಮನೆ) A house broken open.

Kanna-bávulu, Tel. (?) Wells of stone masonry, where the water is some way below the surface: see *Báoli.*

Kaṇṇiváyakkál, Tam. (கண்ணிவாய்க்கால்) A small water-course for irrigation.

Kaṇṇar, Tam. (கண்ணர்) Fields on the same level, so as to be capable of irrigation from the same channel.

Kaṇṇarṟu, Tam. (கண்ணாற்று) Water-course for the supply of a rice field.

KAṆṆI, Mal. (കണ്ണി) A plot of land from eight to fourteen feet long, and five to eight broad, set apart for evaporating or manufacturing salt; a salt bed or pan.

KÁNPHÁṬA JOGÍ, H. (S. كانپهاٹا جوگي) A religious mendicant or *Jogi*, distinguished by wearing large metal ear-rings; thence named *Kán-pháṭa*, split-eared.

KÁNS, H. (S. كانس) KÁNSYA, Ben. (কাংস্য) KÁNSAMU, Tel. (కాంసము) Mixed metal, bell or queen's metal; brass, whether white or yellow.

Kansálavádu, or *Kansáli*, Tel. (కంసాలవాడు, కాంసాలి) A gold or silversmith, a worker in the precious metals, by caste as well as occupation, one of the five chief left-hand castes at Madras: the other four are the *Kanchari* or brazier; *Kammari*, blacksmith; *Vaḍlangi*, carpenter; and *Káṣi*, stonemason; these intermarry and eat together, and take the lead in all disputes with the right-hand castes: the distinction of right and left-hand castes is peculiar to the south of India, and is of modern origin, having been introduced at Conjeveram as a piece of civil policy, intended to divide the people, and diminish their power.

Kancharavita, Karn. (ಕಂಚರವಿತೆ) A mendicant belonging to the five classes of artificers.

Kánsár, or *Kásár*, Mar. (कांसार, कासार) *Kánsári*, Ben. (কাংসারী) *Kanchari*, Tel. (కంచరి) *Kánchkár*, Karn. (ಕಾಂಚಗಾರ) A man of a caste whose occupation is working in mixed metal, a brazier, a coppersmith (from the S. *Kánsya kára*).

Kasbhara, *Kusbhura*, H. (كسبهرا) The class or caste of workers in mixed metals, braziers, also melters and casters in moulds: these people, of whom there are in Hindustan various divisions, have a conventional or slang dialect peculiar to themselves.

Kásár-bangar, or *-bongar*, (?) Mar. A man of an inferior caste, whose occupation is working in brass, making pots and pans, and armlets and anklets of mixed metal.

KÁNTÁ, Thug. The braying of an ass as an omen: at setting out on an expedition it should be heard on the right; at halting, on the left: at any time in front it is unlucky.

KÁNTA, Mar. (कांत, from S. कर्तन) Shavings from a turning lathe: edge, border, coast, boundary or suburb of a village.

Kántári, Mar. (कांतारी) A caste or a member of it, whose business it is to work with a lathe in wood or ivory, a turner, a cabinet-maker.

KÁNTÁ, H. (كانٹا, S. कांटा) A pair of scales: a thorn, a fork.

Kánṭá-muharrir, H. (A. محرر) A clerk employed to note and register weighments.

Kánṭá, or *Káṭá-mornawal*, (?) Mar. A cess formerly levied upon each house in a village, imposed, it is said, by a district collector whose feet had been wounded by thorns when inspecting the village fields.

KANTÁ, KANTHÁ, H. (?) Poor soil, near the Jumna.

KAṆTHI, KAṆTHIÁ, KUNTHI, KUNTHEE, KUNTHEIYA, H. (كنٹهي, كنٹهيا, from S. कण्ठ, the throat) A necklace, any ornament worn round the neck, a string of beads worn as a necklace by the head of a religious establishment, as a mark of dignity; also one made of different kinds of wood or seeds, worn by mendicants and ascetics, and sometimes carried in the hand as a rosary.

KÁNTHAN, Thug. A knife.

KANTÍRÁÍ-VARAHÁ, Karn. (ಕಂಟೀರಾಯಿವರಹಾ) A coin of account in Mysore, equal to ten gold *fanams*, called commonly *Cantarai*, or *Cantaroy fanams*, each weighing about six grains, and of inferior quality, and worth in Madras silver currency, about Rs. 2. 14. 8.

KANTU, or KANTAKA, Karn (ಕಂತು, ಕಂತಕ) A stipulated or fixed term of payment, an instalment.

Kantágu, Karn. (ಕಂತಾಗು) A stipulated term for payment to be made in part.

Kantu-patra, Karn. (from S. पत्र, a leaf) A written agreement to pay by instalments.

KANTAWAN, Mar. (?) A tax on looms, a fee levied by the head village officers from the money-changers of the village.

KAṆUJU, Tel. (కణుజు) An artificial water course for irrigation.

ḲÁNÚN, ḲANOON, plural ḲAWÁNÍN, H. (A. قانون, قوانين) it is similarly written in most dialects, but in Maraṭha it occurs as KÁNÚ, KANOO, (कानू) A rule, a regulation, a law, a statute.

Kánúbáb, Mar. (कानूबाब) A cess formerly levied by Zamindars in the Maratha provinces.

Kánú-jábtá, Mar. (कानूजाबता, from A. ضابطه, a rule) A code, a compendium of the regulations established in any province.

Kánunbyatirikta, Uriya (from S. व्यतिरिक्तः, opposed) Contrary to law or rule, unlawful, illegal.

Kánúngo, *Kanoongo*, or *Canoongo*, corruptly, *Canongoe*, H. (from P. گو, speaking, or who speaks) lit., An expounder of the laws, but applied in Hindustan especially to village and district revenue-officers, who, under the former governments, recorded all circumstances within their sphere which concerned landed property and the realization of the revenue, keeping registers of the value, tenure, extent, and transfers of lands, assisting in the measurements and survey of the lands, reporting deaths and successions of revenue-payers, and explaining, when required, local practices and public regulations: they were paid by rent-free lands and various allowances and perquisites.

Kánúngoï, corruptly, *Canoongoey*, H. (کانونگوي) The office of Kánungo: this was abolished in Bengal at the time of the permanent settlement, but was preserved in Benares and the Ceded and conquered provinces. Beng. Reg. iv. 1808.

Kánúngoï-daftar, H. (from P. دفتر) The record or office of the Kánungo.

Kánúngo-tâlukdar, H. (from A. P. تعالقدار) A district revenue officer in Cuttack, holding certain lands rent-free in virtue of his office.

Kanwa, H. (كنوه) A measure of capacity, the sixteenth part of a *sér*.

Kanwaï, Hindi (कनवई) Clayey soil in muddy hollows, which in the dry season is formed into detached nodules by the action of underground springs: it is generally unproductive: (Puraniya).

Kanyá, S. &c. (कन्या) A maid, a virgin, a girl of nine or ten years of age.

Kanyá-dána, vernacularly, *Kanyádán*, S. &c. (दान, a gift) The presentation of the bride to the bridegroom by her parent or guardian, the giving of a girl in marriage, a gift to a girl upon her marriage, a dower.

Kanyá-páṇí-grahaṇa, S. (from *páṇí*, पाणि, the hand, and *grahaṇa*, ग्रहण, taking) The taking of the bride's hand by the bridegroom at the marriage ceremony.

Kanyá-putra, or *-suta*, S. &c. (पुत्र, or सुत, a son) The son of an unmarried girl.

Kanyá-varaṇa, S. (from वरणं, selecting) Rehearsing the genealogy of the contracting parties at marriages.

Kányá-kubja, S. (from कान्याकुब्ज, the city of Kanauj) Belonging to, originating with, &c., the city of Kanauj: see *Kanaujiya*.

Ḳanz, H. (A. قنض) Treasure.

Káp, Ben. (কাপ) The name of a subdivision of the Várendra Bráhmans of Bengal, inferior to the Kulín tribe of the same.

Kápaḍí, Guz. (કાપડી) A Hindu who has performed pilgrimages to Hinglaj; Mar. (कापडी) A religious mendicant carrying a red flag, and selling rosaries, the sacred thread, holy water, &c.

Kapale, Kapali, or Kapile, corruptly, Kumpli, Tel., Karn. (కపాలె, కపలి, కపిలె) A frame-work and pulley with a leathern bucket attached, fixed over a well, from which the water is drawn up in the bucket raised by oxen passing up and down an inclined plane from the mouth of the well; used generally in Hindustan, as well as in the Dakhin: the well from which the water is so raised.

Kápnáwal, Mar. (काप्नावल, from *Kápne*, कापणे, to cut or reap) The cost of reaping corn, hewing wood, or the like.

Kappa, or Kappam, Karn., Mal. (ಕಪ್ಪ, കപ്പം) Tribute, tax, offering.

Kappada-haṇa, Karn. (ಕಪ್ಪದಹಣ) Tribute money.

Kapparagavaru, Karn. (ಕಪ್ಪರಗವರು) An order of religious mendicants of the Lingamite sect.

Kapṛá, H. (S. كپڑا) Kápaṛ, Mar. (कापड) Cloth, clothes.

Kápsi, Thug. Any kind of corn or vegetable in the ground before harvest.

Kápu, Kapoo, Tel., Karn. (కాపు) Guarding, watching, protection.

Kápari, Tel. (కాపరి) A watchman, a watcher.

Kápu, Tel. (కాపు) A cultivator, a husbandman, a Ryot; it is also commonly applied in the Telinga provinces to the principal cultivator or head man of a village.

Kar, Kur, or Kara, H. &c. (S. کر, कर) Tribute, toll, tax, the revenue of the state, settled allowance to village officers and servants.

Karamoṛiva, Mal. (കരമൊഴിവ) Exemption from tax, granted by the sovereign.

Karachchunham, Mal. (കരച്ചുങ്കം) Land customs, transit duty.

Karagráhak, Ben. (করগ্রাহক) A collector of revenue, a tax gatherer.

Kar-sthápana, Mar. (from S. स्थापन, *Sthápana*, placing) Imposing a cess or tax.

KAR, KUR, Mar. (कर) Used in composition with the name of a town or village, to signify an inhabitant of it, as, *Holkar*, an inhabitant, originally, of the village of Hola.

KAR, KUR, Mal. Sort, quality; (but ? if it is not rather *Katta* (കട്ട), pronounced like *Kar*, a lump of earth; for no such meaning as that assigned to it in Walker's Report appears in the Dictionary).

Pasama-kar, Mal. (from പശമ, fat) The best sort of soil, a rich, greasy clay.

Rasi-pasama, Mal. (? *rasi* or *rási*, a mixture of earth and sand) Middling or mixed soil.

Rasi-kar, Mal. A poor light soil.

KÁR, H. &c. (P. کار, S. KARYA, कार्य्य, from कृ, to do) Act, affair, work, business.

Kárbár, H. (کاربار, from the P. بار, a burden) Affair, business, public business.

Kárbhár, Mar., Karn. (कारभार, ಕಾರಭಾರು, from the S. *Bhára*, भार, a burden) Affairs, business, especially affairs of state, or the business of a mercantile concern, any affairs of importance and responsibility: in Cuttack it means merely trade.

Kárbárí, or *Kárbhárí*, incorrectly, *Carbarree*, H., Mar. (کارباري, कारभारी) A person conducting affairs, a minister, a public officer, a merchant, a manager, a shopkeeper.

Kárbardár, H. (P. بردار, who bears) A man of business, a manager, a minister, &c., whence *Kárbardári*, Conduct of affairs.

Kárchob, H. (from چوب, a stick) Embroidery; an embroiderer.

Kárchobí, H. Embroidered, embroidery.

Kárdár, Sindh (P. کاردار) An agent, especially of the government.

Kárgáh, H. (P. گاہ, a place) A workshop, a factory; a weaver's loom, or weaving apparatus.

Kárgáhi, H. Any thing relating to a workshop; an impost formerly levied on weavers' looms, abolished by Reg. ii. 1795, where the word is written *Khergui*.

Kárhun, H. (from P. کن, *Kun*, making or performing) *Kárkún*, *Karkoon*, *Carcoon*, Mar. (कारकून) A clerk, a writer, a registrar; used also generally among the Marathas for an agent or manager in financial and revenue collections: an inferior revenue officer in charge of a *taraf*, or division, under the *Mámalatdár*, or district collector.

Kárkuní, Mar. (कारकुनी) The office or function of a *Kárkún*, or his fees or perquisites: a cess levied on the Ryots to pay the expense of maintaining a government *Kárkún*: an extra allowance for household expenses made to any public functionary, any thing relating to him or his services.

Kárkhána, corruptly, *Karconna*, *Karkanna*, H. &c. (کارخانه) An office or place where business is carried on; but it is in use more especially applied to places where mechanical work is performed; a workshop, a manufactory, an arsenal, also, fig., to any great fuss or bustle.

Kárhhánadár, H. &c. (P. دار) A keeper of a shop or factory, a superintendant of a manufactory.

Kárkhánánís, Mar. (कारखानानीस) A clerk or record keeper in a factory, a clerk of the works.

Kárkírd, Mar. (कारकीर्द) Reign, administration, the duration of a reign.

Káranda, incorrectly, *Kárindah*, H. (P. کارنده) An agent, a manager, an attorney, an officer.

Káraṇí, Mar. (कारणी, from S. कारण, cause) A manager, one who conducts affairs, a prime minister, a supercargo of a ship, &c.

Kárígar, *Kareegur*, H. &c. (کاریگر) Ben. *Kárikar*, (কারিকর) A workman. Mar. (कारीगर) A good workman.

Kárígarí, H. (کاریگري) Workmanship, art, the skill or employment of a workman or artisan.

Kársáz, H. (P. ساز, making) A man of business, one skilled in affairs; whence also *Kársázi*, Dexterity, adroitness, cleverness in business.

Kársází, H. (کارسازي) Management, conducting business, &c.; *Karsáji* in Hindi also has the meaning of partnership; and in Bengali, a plea or pretext, an act of fraud.

Káru, Mar. (S. कारु) A workman, an artisan, a village artist or servant, any one of the Bárá Balúte.

Kárubárí, or *-bhárí*, Karn. (ಕಾರುಬಾರಿ) A manager, a ruler, a superintendant.

Karubáru, or *-bháru*, Karn. (ಕಾರುಬಾರು, see above, *Karbár*) Rule, management, government; *Káruvágu*, Tam. (காருவாரு) Authority of revenue officers over the cultivators.

Kárya, S. (कार्य्य, what is to be done) modified in the dialects as *Káj*, *Kárj*, H. (کاج, کارج), and so pronounced in Bengali, although written correctly (কার্য), *Kariyamu*, Tel. (కారియము), *Káriya*, Karn. (ಕಾರಿಯ) *Káriyam*, corruptly, *Carram*, Tam. (காரியம்) Affair, business, transaction, any necessary act, as the marriage or funeral ceremony, a civil affair, a lawsuit, a subject of judicial investigation.

Káriyakháran, or *Káriyakurandáran*, Tam. (காரியக்காரன், காரியகுரந்தாரன்) A man of business, a manager, an agent, a conductor of affairs, whether for himself or another; the principal shareholder or Mírásidár of a village deputed to act for his coparceners.

Kárji, Tel. (కార్జి) Uriya (କାରଜି) A village officer, the head of a village, charged with revenue and judicial functions, or the accountant of a village, but sometimes filling the office of head man or manager, collecting the revenue from the villagers, and engaging for its payment to the government, in Cuttack: lit., a man of business, or one who does any thing that is to be done.

Kárj-kárí, Ben. (কার্যকারী) A man of business, an agent, a manager, any one who does what is to be done.

Káryanirṇaya, S. (निर्णय, ascertainment) Investigation of an affair, judgment, decision.

Káryarodka, S. (from रोध, impeding) Enforcing payment of a debt by preventing the debtor from following his usual occupations.

KÁR, Tam. (கார்) The ploughing season in the months of August-September; rice growing in the rainy season, and reaped in the last months of the year; the first or lesser rice crop.

KARA, Mal. (കര) KARE, Karn. (ಕರೆ) KARAI, Tam. (கரை) Bank, border, shore, edge or selvage of cloth; in *Mal.* also a small village or hamlet.

Karákár, Mal. (കരാകാര) The principal inhabitants of a village or neighbourhood.

Karaikaṭṭu, Tam. (கரைக்கட்டு) A prop or buttress for raising or strengthening a bank.

Karekaṭṭaváru, Karn. (ಕರೆಕಟ್ಟವಾರು) Persons whose occupation is working ornamental borders to blankets.

KARÁ, Mal. (കഴാ) An opening in the embankment of a field by which water may flow from one field into another.

KARA, S. &c. (करः) The twenty-fifth year of the cycle.

KÁRÁ, Már. (S. कारा) A prison: usually compounded with words signifying a house, as, *Káràgára*, *Kárágṛiha*, &c.

KARA, KURA, Mar. (?) A form of oath: a leaf of Tulasí and a cup of Ganges water, placed upon some sacred book, are held by a person on his head whilst he gives evidence: if no domestic affliction befalls him within a few days his testimony is considered conclusive (perhaps from one of the senses of *Kara*, कर, an unlucky day).

KARADÁ, or KARDÁ, Mar. (करदा) The proprietor of an estate by purchase, not by grant or inheritance.

KARAḌA, Karn. (ಕರಡ) Dry grass gathered on the hills.

Karaḍa-biṭṭí, Karn. (ಕರಡಬಿಟ್ಟಿ) A tax in lieu of hill grass formerly levied from the Ryots (Mysore).

KARAḌIGE, Karn. (ಕರಡಿಗೆ) A silver box for holding the phallus worn by the Lingáits.

KARAḌU, Tel., Karn. (కరడు) Rough, as an account, or as the draft of an official document; also, rough, coarse, as paper.

KARAGHAṬṬU, Tel. (కరఘట్టు) The dam of a river.

KARAGPAṬṬAḌI, Karn. (ಕರಗಪಟ್ಟಡಿ) A tax levied on goods manufactured in towns, or imported into them for sale.

KARÁHI, H. (S. كراهي) A shallow iron pot or vessel for cooking; whence *Karáhilená*, lit., To take the boiler, is a sort of ordeal in which the accused takes out a piece of gold which has been dropped into a vessel of boiling oil, and if he does so without being scalded he is acquitted.

KARAI, corruptly, CARAY, Tam. (கரை) A portion of land, especially a share in a Mirási, or hereditary coparcenary village, originally, in general, a determinate and entire share. (It is said sometimes to consist of four *pangs* (*pangus*) shares or subdivisions of villages held by Brahmans rent-free, but this is perhaps incorrect.—Fifth Rep. p. 826.

Karai-káran, Tam. (கரைக்காரன்) A proprietor of a determinate share in a coparcenary village.

Karai-pangu, Tam. (கரைபங்கு) A share in the village lands. (From *pangu*, a share, the word intended by *pung* in the 5th Rep., and not representing *pum* or *bkúm*, land, as proposed in the Glossary).

Karai-yáḷan, Tam. (from ஆளன், a lord or master) The proprietor of a hereditary share in a village.

Karai-yíḍu, Tam. (கரையீடு) An agreement amongst the coparceners of a village for a temporary change of their respective shares.

KÁRAK, Mar. (कारक) Customs paid by merchants.

KÁRAKÁL, Karn. (ಕಾರಕಾಲ) The rainy season.

Káragaḍḍe, Karn. (ಕಾರಗದ್ದೆ) Cultivation in the wet season.

KARAKAM, Mal. (കഴകം) Mean service in a temple.

KARAKASÁ, or KARKASÁ, Tel. (కరకసా, P. خرخشه) Quarrel, dispute, tumult.

Karakasá-bhúmí, Tel. (S. भूमी, earth) Lands of which the boundaries are in dispute.

Karaka-terige, Karn. (ಕರಕತೆರಿಗೆ) A tax formerly levied on the import of goods into Chitaldrúg.

Káráḷan, Mal. (കാരാളൻ) Possessor of freehold or private property: the agent or manager of the lands of a temple on the part of the founder or endower.

Karambu, Karambai, barbarously, Crambo, Tam. (கரம்பு, கரம்பை) Waste or uncultivated land, and which is of two kinds—*Sekal-karambu,* which is capable of cultivation, although neglected for some time; and *Anádi-karambu,* waste from time immemorial, and which cannot be cultivated with any prospect of advantage.

Kárámbi, Tam. (காராம்பி) A basket or other apparatus for throwing up water.

Ḳaran, corruptly, Kerrun, H. (A. قرن) Conjunction of the planets, an astrological period of any ten years, from 10 to 120.

Karaṇa, S. &c. (neuter करणं) Doing, act, means, instrument, an organ of sense: (masc. करणः) A doer of any thing; also, the name of a mixed caste, or an individual of it, said to have sprung from a Ṣúdra mother and Vaiṣya father, or, according to some, from a degraded Kshatriya by a pure Kshatriya female; his occupation is writing and accounts: a scribe or writer, a clerk, and, in some places, a collector of revenue, a tax-gatherer: (the word is used in all the dialects, sometimes modified as to meaning, as in the following).

Karanamu, Karaṇam or *Karnam,* corruptly, *Curnum,* Tel. (కరణము) *Karaṇika,* commonly, *Kurnik,* Karn. (ಕರಣಿಕ) A village accountant, one of the chief officers of a village: in the Telinga provinces he is usually a Brahman, in the Tamil a Ṣúdra, of the Pilli tribe.

Karaṇikam, Tel. (కరణికం) The office of a scribe or accountant.

Karnika-mirási, Tam. The hereditary fees or perquisites of the village accountant.

Karaṇika-varttana, or *Karnik-varttan,* Karn. (S. ವರ್ತನ, wages) A cess levied originally for the support of the district accountant, but consolidated with the public revenue by Tipu.

Karáni, vulgarly, *Cranny* or *Crannie,* H. (كراني, करणी) *Keráni,* Ben. (কেরানী) A clerk, a scribe, a man who by caste and occupation is a writer or accountant.

Karaṇam, Mal. (കരണം, same as the S. करणं) A deed, a title-deed, a bond, any legal writing or document: it is especially applied to the deeds by which land is transferred in Malabar, of which four are particularized, as—

Karaṇam-kayavidu-otti, Mal. The first deed executed in conveying landed property, by which two-thirds of the sum to be lent or advanced to the owner are specified.

Karaṇam-otti-kamparam, The second deed, in which a further sum of twenty per cent. on the sum specified in the preceding is engaged to be paid.

Karaṇam-kudima-nír, or *-nír-matal,* The third deed, engaging for a further advance of twenty per cent., confirmed by drinking water (*nir*) from the estate, presented to the proprietor.

Karaṇam-attipet-ola, The fourth deed, by which the purchaser engages to pay up any balance that may remain, and the Janmkár finally parts with all hold upon the property.—Report on Tenures in Malabar.

Karaṇappiṟa, Mal. (കരണപ്പിഴ) A fine for executing documents or title-deeds on an unstamped *ola* or papers, or contrary to regulation.

Káraṇam, S., and in all the dialects either as *Káran* or *Káranam,* (कारणं) Cause, origin, motive.

Káraṇavan, commonly, *Karnaven,* Mal. (കാരണവൻ) The head or origin of a family, a father, a forefather, an ancestor, a lord or master.

Kaṟancha, Mal. (കഴഞ്ചു) A weight of four kinds, as equal to ten, twelve, thirteen, or twenty-one *fanams.*

Káranjachi-bíj-gutta, Karn. (ಕಾರಂಜಚಿಬಿಜಗುತ್ತ) A tax on gathering wild cocoa-nuts (Mysore).

Karánti, H. (كرانتي) Karáti, Ben. (করাতী) A sawyer.

Ḳarár, H. (A. قرار) Fixedness, stability, confirmation: it is loosely used for a written agreement or engagement.

Karár-i-jamá-dahsála, H. (from P. ده, ten, and سال, a year) The decennial settlement; the assessment of the revenue of Bengal for ten years, preparatory to the perpetual settlement.

Karár-náma, H. &c. (P. نامه) A written contract or engagement.

Karár-sagbadi, (?) Tel. Stipulated cultivation, as compared with what has been actually executed.

Karár-vák, Tel. (from S. वाक, speech) Fixed estimate, verbal agreement.

Karar, (?) H. A class of agriculturists in the district of Mainpuri.

Karáü, Curao, H. (كراو) Marriage of a widow with the brother of a deceased husband, as practised among the Játs, Gujars, Ahírs, and other inferior tribes, in the north-west provinces, although it is looked upon as disreputable: the term is also applied to concubinage.

KARAVEPPU, Mal. (കരവെപ്പു) Plantations on high grounds.

KARAWANT, Mar. (करवंत) A particular tribe of Bráhmans, or a member of it.

KARAWO, (?) Sindhi, A man employed to watch the crops.

KÁRÁYMA, Mal. (കാരായ്മ, probablyt he same as the Tam. KARAI, q. v.) Freehold or private property.

Kárâyma-káran, Mal. (കാരായ്മകാരൻ) A proprietor of freehold land.

Kárâyma-teṭṭam, Mal. (കാരായ്മതെട്ടം) Private property obtained by purchase.

KARBÁ, Thug. Secure and complete burial (Dakh Thug).

KARBA, KARBI, Guz. (કડબ, કડબી) Stalks or straw of different grains.

Karba-paṭi, Guz. (કડબપટી) A tax on straw, originally levied in kind, afterwards commuted for money.

KARḌÁ, H. (كردا) Exchange, barter, balance of value between goods or coins.

KARDÁ, Mar. (? corruption of KARTHÁ) The denomination or heading under which the names of the actual cultivators or the fields are registered.

KARH, Thug. Search or inquiry after Thugs.

KARHU, Thug. A searcher after, or disturber of, Thugs.

KARHAÏ, Thug. A feast.

KAṚHÚÁ, H. (كرهوا) A loan, a debt, a premium on a loan, a deduction from the sum lent.

ḲARIAH, H. (A. قرية) A village.

ḲARÍB, H. (قريب, plural AKRIBÁ, اقربا) lit. Near, near to; also, near in relationship, a kinsman, a relative, a connexion by birth or marriage, excepting the relation of parent and child.

Ḳarábat, or *Ḳurbat*, H. (A. قرابت, قربت) Propinquity, relationship.

Ḳurb-jawár, H. (قربجوار) Near neighbourhood.

KÁRIKÁ, or KÁRIKA-VṚIDDHI, S. (कारिका, कारिकावृद्धिः) Stipulated interest; also *Káritávriddhi* (कारितावृद्धि).

KARIMEYAN, plural KARIMEYARU, (?) Karn. A class of slaves in Kanara, a division of the Dhers.

KARIMPATTAN, (?) A class of agricultural slaves in Malabar.

KÁRÍNÚN H. (كارينون, for *kálí*, black) Black salt, an impure preparation of a medicinal salt, or muriate of soda.

KÁRÍZ, H. (P. كاريز) A water-course, especially one constructed for irrigation underneath the surface of the ground.

KARJJA, Ben. (কর্জ্জ) A loan, a debt: (vernacular corruption of *Karẓ*, q. v.).

Karjjadár, Ben. (কর্জ্জদার) A debtor.

KARKA, (?) H. The tract that lies along the Jumna in some of the districts of the north-west provinces.

KARKACH, KURKUCH, Uriya (କର୍କଚ) Salt obtained by solar evaporation.

KARL, (?) Mar. Hard or gravelly black soil.

KARMA, S., used in all the dialects, sometimes modified, as KARM, KARAM, KARAMAM, KARUMAM, KAMMA, KÁM, (कर्म्म) Act, action, work; any act of piety or religion, as sacrifice, marriage-ceremony, funeral obsequies, duty or acts obligatory on tribe or caste; fate, as the consequence of acts.

Karmachárí, corruptly, *Kerimcharry*, Ben. (S. কর্ম্মচারী) *Karamchárí*, H. (كرمچاري) In Bengal, an officer appointed by a Zamindar, or payer of revenue, to collect the revenues, and arrange the affairs of a village; a factor, a steward.

Karmakára, S. (कर्म्मकार) *Kámár*, Ben. (কামার) *Kammari, Kammaravádu*, Tel. (కమ్మరి, కమ్మరవాడు) *Kammára, Kammáravanu*, Karn. (ಕಂಮಾರ, ಕಂಮಾರವನು) *Karmmakáran*, Mal. (കമ്മകാരൻ) An ironsmith, a blacksmith, one of the five chief castes of the left-hand castes in the south.

Kammáḷan, Tam. (கம்மாளன்) An artificer, a handicraftsman, especially one of five orders, stonemasons, carpenters, blacksmiths, brasiers, and goldsmiths.

Kammaváḍu, Tel. (కమ్మవాడు) A caste of Telinga Ṣúdras, commonly called *Kammavars*; they are numerous, and chiefly engaged in agriculture.

Kammarikamu, Tel. (కమ్మరికము) The agricultural caste called *Kammavars*.

Karamvero, Guz. (કરમવેરો) A poll-tax.

Kammiṭṭam, Mal. (കമ്മിട്ടം) Coining, making money.

Kammiṭṭapura, Mal. (കമ്മിട്ടപ്പുര) A mint.

KARṆAVEDHA, S. &c. (कर्ण, the ear, and वेध, piercing) Piercing the lobes of the ear of a child, a ceremony required to be observed previous to tonsure.

KAROḌÁ, Tel. (కరోడా) An overseer, an inspector or superintendant.

KARPÁSA, or KÁRPÁSA, vernacularly, KAPÁS, corruptly, KERPAS, KERP, COPAS, S., &c. (कर्पास, कार्पास, كپاس, कपास) Cotton, the raw or undressed produce of the Gossypium herbaceum; also, the plant.

Karraima, (?) Mal. A verbal agreement with a poorer tenant or cultivator.

Karru, Tel. (కఱ్ఱు) **Káru**, Karn. (ರಾರು) A ploughshare.

Kársaí, or **Kársáí**, Mar. (**कारसई, कारसाई**) An impost in kind, as corn, straw, &c., from a village dependent or a fort, for the use of the latter.

Karsal, Thug. The large male antelope: if he cross the road from left to right it is a lucky omen; if the reverse, unlucky.

Karsha, Karshapaṇa, S. &c. (**कर्ष, कर्षपण**) A weight of gold or silver equal to 16 *máshas*, or about 180 troy grains; in Uriya, it is written *Karisa*, and means a brass weight of four *máṛhas*.

Karsha, S. &c. (**कर्षः**) Ploughing, tillage.

Karshaka, vernacularly, *Karshak*, and *Krishak*, S. &c. (**कर्षकः**) A ploughman, a cultivator.

Kartá, Karttá, S., but adopted in all the dialects, (**कर्ता**) **Karttáva**, Mal. (കർത്താവ) An agent, a maker, one who does any thing, a husband, a proprietor, an heir, one who has inchoate rights, the active or managing member of a family.

Kaṛtá, or **Kaḍtá**, Mar. (**कडता**) An addition of $10\frac{1}{2}$ *sérs* to a *palla*, or 120 *sérs*, on various articles of consumption; this, with a further addition of $2\frac{1}{2}$ *sérs*, named *kántá*, makes up a *pakka palla* of 133 *sérs*.

Karttaní, or **Katraní**, H., Ben., &c., (كترني ,كرتّني, from S. **कृत**, to cut) lit., Chippings, cuttings; applied also formerly to unauthorised deductions from the revenue, under various pretexts, from the payments by the revenue-payers: a cess imposed in some parts of Bengal before the perpetual settlement, to compensate for such deductions.

Kárti, (?) A division of the solar year, one twenty-seventh; used for agricultural purposes, as the times of sowing, reaping, &c. (Northern Circars).

Kárttika, vernacularly, **Kártik** or **Kátik**, S. &c. (**कार्त्तिक**) The eighth month of the Hindu year (Oct.-Nov.), when the moon is full in *Krittiká*, or the Pleiades.

Kártikotsava, S. &c. (from **उत्सव**, a festival) A festival on the day of full moon, in the month *Kártik*.

Kárttika-phasal, Karn. (ರಾತ್ತಿಕ ಫಸಲ) The harvest of *Kártik*, the same as the *Kharif* crop of Hindustan, or that which is reaped between November and January.

Karttikṣáli, Ben. (**কার্ত্তিকশালী**) The rice crop of the cold season, gathered after November: the principal harvest in Bengal.

Karttik, Mar. (**कात्तिक**, perhaps from S. **कृत**, to cut) A very low caste, or member of it, whose business is that of killing animals and selling the flesh; the Hindu butcher.

Káru, Tel., Karn. (కారు) The wet season: the crop of rice sown in April, and reaped in June-July.

Kárubatta, Karn. (ರಾರುಬತ್ತ) Rice growing in the hot season, and reaped in the rains.

Kárubele, Karn. (ರಾರುಬೆಳೆ) The wet season crop.

Kárupanṭa, Tel. (కరుపంట) Rice sown in the wet season, the chief crop of the Tamil countries: it is also applied to the lesser crop, or that which is sown in spring, and reaped in the rains.

Káru, Tel., Karn. (కారు) **Karu**, Tam. (கரு) Black, dark; also, salt, saline, withered.

Kárubhúmi, Tel. (కారుభూమి) Saline soil.

Kárukáya, Tel. (కారుకాయ) Weak or blighted corn.

Karuṇkuruvai, Tam. (கருங்குறுவை) A kind of black rice of quick growth.

Karunilam, Tam. (கருநிலம்) Black and barren soil.

Kárupu, Tel. (కారుపు) Naturally produced salt, saline efflorescence.

Karuttakkadappu, Tam. (கருத்தக்கடப்பு) Black paddy, or rice in the husk.

Káru, Karn. (ರಾರು) A blacksmith.

Karumán, Tam. (கருமான்) *Karuván*, Mal. (കരുവാൻ) A blacksmith.

Kaṛú, or **Kaḍú**, Mar. (**कडू**) The offspring of a female slave, or of a woman by a second marriage.

Kaṟu, Mal. (കഴു) A stake with a sharp point, for impaling malefactors.

Karukuhun, (?) Tel. A gold pagoda, worth four rupees.

Karum, (?) Tam. The same as the *markal*, a measure of capacity holding about sixteen quarts.

Káruvái, or **Kárwai**, Tel. (కారువాయి) Estimated, as produce.

Káruvái-daul, Tel. (from H. دول, mode) Demand on each Ryot's produce, according to the estimate.

Karuvala, (?) Tel. The treasury or strong room of a temple.

Karwa, Thug. A square or oblong grave for the bodies of the murdered.

Karwánsí, H. (كروانسي) The twentieth part of a *Viṣwánsí*; a fractional portion of a joint-tenancy village.

Karwárá, H. (كروارا, **करवारा**) The vessel or bucket fastened to the rope of a lever employed to raise water.

Kᴀʀʏáᴅ, Mar. (कर्यात) A petty *mahál* or district; one comprising ten or twelve villages, some belonging to one *mahál*, some to another.

Ḳᴀʀẓ, H. (A. قرض) Kᴀʀᴊ, Mar. (कर्ज) Ben. (কর্জ) Kᴀʀᴀᴊ, Uriya, (କରଜ) Kᴀʀᴊᴜ, Tel. (కర్జు) Debt: in Mohammadan law, besides the general sense, it implies a loan to be repaid by something dissimilar, but of equal value, in distinction to *Ariyat*, the return of the identical thing borrowed: a money loan, money lent at interest for an indefinite time.

Karjádáya, Ben. (কর্জাদায) Paying a debt.

Karj-amdán, Mar. (कर्जेआमदान, from the P. آمدن, to come) The heading of that side of an account in which are to be entered future receipts, in discharge of loans.

Karjáú, Mar. (कर्जाऊ) Money lent or borrowed at interest.

Ḳarẓ- or *Karj-dár*, corruptly, *Ḳerzdar*, H. &c. (قرضدار, कर्जदार) A debtor, a borrower.

Karj-dádan, Mar. (कर्जेदादन, from P. دادن, to give) The heading of the side of an account in which are entered payments of debts to be made.

Ḳarẓí or *Karjí*, H. &c. (قرضي, कर्जी) A debtor, a borrower; any thing relating to a loan or debt.

Karjkarí, Mar. (कर्जेकरी) A borrower, a lender; an officer or servant employed to dun a debtor.

Karjkhat, Mar. (कर्जेखत) A note of acknowledgment of a debt: also, *Karj-náma*, and *Karj-rokha*.

Ḳarẓkhwáh, H. (قرضخواه) A creditor, a dun.

Ḳiráẓ, A. (قراض) Repaying, borrowing, a debt: in law, a kind of partnership in which one party advances the capital, the other the labour or skill, and the profits are divided in stipulated proportions.

Ḳiráẓi-kachherí, (قراضي كچهري) An office for the collection of outstanding revenue balances.

Kᴀʀᴊɪ-káɪ, Karn. (ಕರ್ಜಿಕಾಯಿ) A cess levied in Mysore on the heads of the Lingamite establishments in lieu of sweet cakes which they had been at one time compelled to supply the Paligárs with at the festival of Gaṇesa.

Kᴀʀᴀʏᴀ, (?) H. A hired or bond ploughman who is paid by a proportion of the nett produce of the fields he has ploughed.

Káṣᴀ, vernacularly, Káṣ, incorrectly, Káɴs, S. &c. (काश) A tall grass, growing luxuriantly in many places, especially on neglected and sandy soils, sometimes 12 or 15 feet high. (Saccharum spontaneum.)

Káṣá, Tel. (కాసా) A son by a female slave.

Kásᴀ, (?) Sindhi. A grain measure, $\frac{1}{60}$th part of a kharwar.

Kᴀsᴀʙ, H. &c. (A. كسب) Trade, business, profession, art, skill; also, in Guz., gold and silver thread used in embroidery.

Kasab-vero, Guz. (કસબવેરો) Tax on occupations and crafts.

Ḳᴀṣáʙ, Ḳᴀṣáí, H. &c. (قصاب, قصاي) A butcher.

Kasái dukán gutta, Karn. (ಕಸಾಯಿದುಕಾನಗುತ್ತ) A tax in Mysore on butchers' stalls or shops.

Kᴀsáᴅ, H. (A. كساد) Want of currency or demand, a flat or dull market.

Ḳᴀsᴀᴍ, Ḳᴀsᴍ, Ḳᴜsᴜᴍ, Ḳᴜsᴍ, H. &c. (A. قسم) An oath.

Kasam-náma, H. (P. نامه) An affidavit.

Kasámat, corruptly, *Kissimit*, H. Administration of an oath.

Ḳᴀṣᴀʀ, Ḳᴜṣᴜʀ, H. &c. (A. قصر) Defect, deficiency, diminution. In Mar. *Kasar* (कसर), as applied to accounts, signifies departure from a correct or perfect balance, whether through excess or deficiency, or the sum to be added to, or subtracted from, the totals on either side, to make them agree.

Kasaru, Karn. (ಕಸರು) Profit or loss on the exchange of coins. (It seems likely that the Hindu dialects have made some confusion between the Arabic words, *Ḳaṣar* (قصر), deficiency, and *Kaṣ̤ar*, or *Kathar* (كثر), excess, and have blended the two meanings under one term.)

Ḳaṣar, *Ḳaṣrát*, H. (قصر, قصرات) Profit and loss, a head of an account so named.

Kasarpaṭṭí, Mar. (कसरपट्टी) Excess in distributing the undivided assessment; a cess or tax imposed to make up for any deficit in the collections.

Kasarvarttálá, Mar. (कसरवर्त्ताळा) Allowance for loss or gain upon the quantity of grain brought into and received back from the public storehouses by the farmers.

Kaṣ̤rat, corruptly, *Kesraut*, H. (كثرت) Difference, properly, in excess, between the land measure established by Beng. Reg. xi. 1795, and that of preceding years.

Ḳaṣúr, or *Ḳuṣúr*, H. (A. قصور) Fault, offence, crime: deficiency, defect: allowance for difference in the value of coins, a cess formerly levied upon the cultivators to cover any difference that might occur between the value of the coins paid by them and the standard currency.

Ḳᴀsʙᴀ, H. (A. قصبه), Kᴀsᴜʙá, Tel. (కసుబా) A small town or large village, the chief or market-town of a district.

Káѕʜᴛ, Cᴀѕʜᴛ, H. &c. (كاشت, from كاشتن, to sow, as seed)

Cultivation, agriculture, tillage; a tenure by which the revenue is assessed according to the value of the crop.

Kásht-kár, H. (کاشتکار) A cultivator, a farmer.

Kásht-kár-jadíd, H. (from جدید, new) A cultivator newly settled in a village.

Kásht-kár-ḳadím, (from قدیم, old) A cultivator long established in a village, a hereditary cultivator.

Kásht-i-málikán, H. (from مالک, a master) Cultivation by the proprietors of the lands themselves.

Khúd-kásht, H. (from the P. خود, self) A resident cultivator, one cultivating his own hereditary lands, either under a Zamindar or as a coparcener in a village. In Bengal, one class of them, holding their lands at fixed rates by hereditary right, sometimes sub-let them, except the part about their dwelling, in which they continue to reside, and although ceasing to cultivate, and, engaged in trade or business, they retain their designation of *khúd-kásht*. The term is also applied in the north-western provinces to lands which the proprietor, or the payer of the Government revenue, cultivates himself.

Páhí-kásht or *Páikásht*, H. (پاهي کاشت) A non-resident cultivator, one who cultivates lands in a village in which he is not a settled or permanent resident; see *Páhí*, &c.

Kashṭa, vernacularly, Kashṭ, S. (कष्ट) Hard, painful, distressingly high, as an assessment; severe, as a punishment.

Káshṭh, or Káṭh, incorrectly, Kást, Mar. Beng. (काष्ठ, काठ, কাঠ, from the S. काष्ठ) Wood, timber.

Káṭhgaṛa, *Káṭhṛá*, Beng. (কাঠগড়া, কাঠরা) An inclosure of timber to receive offerings made at funerals and the persons who accept them; a palisade, a stockade.

Kathiara, Guz. (કઠીઆરા) A wood-cutter.

Kaṭhúya, or *Káthuriyá*, Ben. (কাঠুয়া, কাঠরিয়া) A wood-cutter and seller.

Ḳásid, corruptly, Cossid, H. (A. قاصد) A courier, a running footman or messenger, a postman.

Kasoṭí, Hindi (कशोती) An account of the revenue due by each cultivator.

Kassi, Kussee, Thug. The pickaxe used in digging graves previously consecrated by peculiar ceremonies; to swear by it is the most solemn form of oath amongst the Thugs.

Kásu, corruptly, Cash, Tel. Karn. (కాసు) A small copper coin, current at Madras, made equal, in 1832, to the Calcutta and Madras paisa and rated at 64 to the rupee: it was formerly rated at 80 to a fanam, a small silver coin: it also means, in Tamil (காசு), coin, money in general; as, *Ponahásu*, gold coin; *Vennihásu*, silver coin; *Pettalaihásu*, copper coin: it formerly denoted a coin of a certain value, supposed by Mr. Ellis to have been the same as the S. *karsha*, and equal to the double silver fanam of Madras.

Káṭ, Mal. (കാട, no doubt from the S. काष्ठ) A wood, a jangal.

Kátwáram, Mal. (കാടവാരം) A tax on lands bordering on waste or wilderness in lieu of any assessment on tracts that may be cultivated within it.

Kaṭ, Beng. (কট) A fixed term, a stipulated period; a bond.

Kaṭhana, Uriya (କଠଣା) An engagement, an agreement, a bargain.

Kat-kobálá, commonly, *Kut-habála*, or *Kut-coballa*, Beng. (কটকোবালা, vernacular corruption of the A. قبالہ, an engagement) A conditional engagement, a deed of conditional sale, stipulating that if the purchase price, or money advanced, be not repaid within a given term, the sale shall become absolute.

Káṭ, H. &c. (کاٹ, from کاٹنا, to cut, S. *karttana* कर्त्तन, cutting) Cutting, a cut, a wound, &c.; also, fig., cutting off, retrenching, &c.

Kátan, H. &c. (کاٹن) Cutting; lit. or fig., cutting off, retrenchment.

Káṭhabúl, Beng. (কাটকবুল, from قبول, consent) Obstinate refusal to confess or acknowledge a charge.

Káṭ-kuṭ, Beng. (কাটকুট) Stoppage of wages, cutting off or retrenching allowances, reducing the demand of a creditor by a counter claim. Uriya (କାଟକୁଟ) Alteration or falsification of deeds. H. (کاٹ کوٹ) Chippings, cuttings, scraps.

Katní, H. (کٹنی) Season for cutting grain, harvest-time.

Ḳaṭá, H. (A. قطع) A cutting or breaking off; a section: maiming, wounding.

Ḳatá-at-ṭárik, A. (قطع الطاریق) A highway-robber.

Kaṭaí, Mar. (कटई) A caste, or individual of it, workers in leather.

Kataíyá, H. (کٹیا, कटैया) Coarse grass growing on fields left fallow.

Kátaḷ, Mar. (कातळ) Rock stone.

Kátaḷwaṭ, Mar. (कातळवट) Rocky, stony ground.

Kátam, Mal. (കാതം) A Malabar league, consisting of four *nárigás*, or between 5 and 6 miles English.

Káṭan, Beng. (কাটন) Spinning.

Káṭaní, corruptly, *Kateenee*, Beng. (কাটনী) A female spinner: the wages of spinning.

Káṭaníyá, Beng. (কাটনীযা) A man whose business is spinning thread or cotton.

KATÁN, H. (A. كتان) Linen cloth; also, linseed.

KATBÁ, Mar. (कतबा, from كتاب, a book or writing), KATAPE, or KATABE, Karn. (ಕತೆ-ಪೆ, ಕತಬೆ) Penalty bond, recognisance, paper of agreement: a writing given to a Panchayat by the parties appealing to it asserting the truth of their statements, and agreeing to acknowledge their guilt if pronounced in the wrong.

KATGAR, Thug. A scout or spy.

KATGUTA, commonly, KUTGOOTTA, Mar. (?) Tenure of land held at a fixed rate of revenue, usually lower than the ordinary rate: the term seems to be properly Tamil; see *Kaṭṭuguttagai*.

KÁṬHÁ, Beng. (কাঠা) A measure of land, varying in different places, but usually a square of four cubits, or six feet long; see *Kattha*.

Káṭhábáṛí, Beng. (কাঠাবাড়ী) A staff or pole about six feet, used in measuring land.

Káṭhákálí, Beng. (কাঠাকালী) Working a sum in surveying, giving the result in *Káṭhás*.

KATHÁ, KUTHÁ, H. &c. (S. کتها, कथा) A story, a fable. A favourite entertainment amongst the Marhattas, or the public recitation of a narrative, insterspersed with music and singing, of the actions of the gods, or of individuals, with allusions to passing events or persons; thence, old manuscript Kathás are sometimes produced in evidence of claims to hereditary rights or property which they have alluded to.

KATHÁKU-KATHÁ, Uriya (କଥାକୁକଥା) Verbatim evidence, &c.

KÁTHAR, Thug. One of the clans of the Thugs.

KÁṬHI, Guz. (કાઠી) The name of a tribe the inhabitants of *Cattiwár*.

Káthipál, Guz. (કાઠીપાલ) A tax levied from the people by the Káthís.

KÁṬHÍ, corruptly, CUTTY, Mar. (काठी) A measure of land: as formerly used it was found to vary from five to to ten cubits: the average for the survey was taken at the valuation of five cubits and five closed fists or feet $9.11\frac{175}{1000}$ inches, making the Bíghá equal to 4383 square yards: the term also designates the measure, the rod or pole. Beng. (কাঠী) A measure of capacity, varying in different places, but usually about 10 *sérs*.

KATHAWA, Thug. The man who cuts up the bodies of the murdered before burying them, by which it is supposed that all smell is prevented and the bodies will not be thereby discovered.

KÁṬI, Karn. (ಕಾಟಿ) An obsolete grain measure in Mysore containing 40 *kánis* of 80 rupees weight, or 3200 rupees; also, a land measure used in Kanara for betel-nut gardens, containing 484 square feet.

KÁTI, commonly, CATTY, Malay (كتي) A weight in general use throughout the Archipelago, and extending to China; 100 *kátis* are equal to one *píkal* of $133\frac{1}{2}$lb. avoirdupois and each is therefore equal to $21\frac{1}{3}$ ounces or $1\frac{1}{3}$lb.; it contains 16 *Tél*, or, commonly, *Tale*: it varies in value in some of the islands.

KÁṬIKA, or KÁTIKÁI, less correctly, KÁṬKAI, Karn. (ಕಾಟಿಕೆ, ಕಾಟಿಕಾಯಿ) Plundering, pillage, marauding.

Káṭikanu, Karn. (ಕಾಟಿಕನು) A plunderer, a marauder, a fowler.

KATKHUDÁ, KADKHUDÁ, H. (P. كتخدا, كدخدا) Head of a a family; sometimes applied to the headman of a village.

KAṬKÍNA, or KAṬAKINÁ, H. &c. (كتكينه, कटकिना) A farm or lease of revenue, an under farm or lease held of a Zamindar or other proprietor: in Bengal, letting land at a rack rent.

Kaṭkínadár, H. (كتكينه‌دار) An under farmer or renter holding under the revenue payer, or Zamindar. In Bengali, the person who lets the land at a rack rent.

Kaṭkinádárí, Beng. (কটকিনাদারী) Letting land to under tenants at a rack rent; holding land under another.

KATKOLÁ, Thug. A carpenter.

ḲATL, H. (A. قتل), KATAL, Beng. (কতল), KATTAL, Mar. (कत्तल) Killing, slaughter, murder. In Mohammadan law five kinds are distinguished.

Katl-âmd, A. (قتل عمد) Wilful murder by an adult and sane person.

Ḳatl-shabah-âmd, A. (شبه عمد) Manslaughter, the death of a person caused by an injury unlikely to have caused death: lit., the semblance of murder.

Ḳatl-khaṭá, (قتل خطاء) Killing by mistake or misadventure, as killing one man for another, or a man for an animal.

Ḳatl-ḳáim-makám bá ḳhaṭá, A. (قتل قايم مقام با خطا) Killing a person by injuring him unintentionally, or through misadventure.

Katl-ba-sabab, A. (قتل بسبب) Killing unintentionally by an intermediate cause, as where a person has dug a well and not guarded against accident, and some one falls into it and perishes.

Ḳatl-mabáh, A. (قتل مباح) Justifiable homicide: this might be added to the preceding, but it is only incidentally noticed in Mohammadan law.

Kaṭli, or Kaṭle, Karn. (ಕಟ್ಲಿ, ಕಟ್ಲೆ) An order, a rule: a weight.

Kaṭlekallu or *-gallu*, Karn. (ಕಟ್ಲೆಕಲ್ಲು -ಗಲ್ಲು) Stones used as weights.

Katlai, or Kattal, Tam. (?) A single field or parcel of land amidst those of a village. Tanjore. Fifth Rep. 774.

Kaṭmáṭí, Hindi (कटमाटी) Clayey land which soon dries up on the surface.

Káṭnibandí, Hindi (काटनिबंदी) Reaping the harvest. Puraniya.

Kaṭnamu, Tel. (కట్నము) Presents made to superiors; a nazar: presents by relations to each other at the time of marriage.

Katori, Thug. Place selected for the murder, lit., a cup, but used in a phrase, *Jáo katori manjh láo*, Go and clean the cup, which implies, go and select a convenient spot for the perpetration of the murder.

Katra, (?) The small irregular rice-fields in waste tracts, which are never irrigated.

Kaṭra, Kuṭra, H. (کٹرا) A market-place, a suburb, a market-town belonging to a fort.

Kaṭrí, H. (کٹري, कटरी) Land recovered from, or left by, large rivers.

Kaṭṭa, Mal. (കട്ട) A clod of earth.

Katta regar, (?) A stiff loam. Northern Cirkars.

Katte sauda, (?) A black soil. Northern Cirkars.

Kaṭṭa-kánam, Mal. (കട്ടകാനം) A complimentary present made by a tenant or leaseholder to the proprietor of an estate.

Kaṭṭa, Tel. (కట్ట) A bank, a shore, a dam, an embankment: a custom-house station.

Kaṭṭabhatta, Karn. (ಕಟ್ಟಭತ್ತ) Parcels of grain formerly given to the village accountants by the cultivators, but afterwards appropriated by the state.

Kaṭṭaḍa, Tel. (కట్టడ) An order, a rule, a regulation.

Kaṭṭaḍaka, Karn. (ಕಟ್ಟಡಕ) A written agreement.

Káttal, Tam. (காத்தல்) Protection, preserving, watching.

Káttavaráyan, Tam. (காத்தவராயன்) A watchman, a guard.

Kaṭṭaḷai, Tam. (கட்டளை), Kaṭle, Karn. (ಕಟ್ಲೆ) An order, a command. Settled rate or price.

Kattálai, Tam. (கத்தாளை) Rice growing on high ground.

Kattanára, Mal. (കത്തനാര) The Syrian or Syro-Roman priest in Malabar.

Kaṭṭáyam, Tam. (கட்டாயம்) Force, compulsion.

Kaṭṭiyam, Tam. (கட்டியம்) A royal edict or proclamation.

Kaṭṭe, Karn. (ಕಟ್ಟೆ) A bank, a dam, a reservoir, especially one which becomes dry in the hot weather: in composition, a place where business is transacted; as,

Araḷé-kaṭṭe, Karn. (ಅರಳೇಕಟ್ಟೆ) A place where contracts for cotton are made.

Rachché-kaṭṭe, Karn. (ರಚ್ಚೇಕಟ್ಟೆ) The place where the respectable men of a village assemble.

Sunkada-kaṭṭe, Karn. A custom station, a toll-house.

Kerékaṭṭe, Karn. (ಕೆರೇಕಟ್ಟೆ) A bank or dam of masonry.

Kaṭṭhá, Kuṭṭha, corruptly, Cottah, H. (کٹّھا) A measure of land, the twentieth part of the Bengal Bíghá of 1600 square yards, containing 80 square yards, or 720 square feet. In Hindustán the term is applied also to a grain measure of five sers: see *Káṭha*: it may be doubted i these are not the same words, although differently written and explained).

Katti, also written Catty or Cattie, but apparently both are incorrect, as the word occurs in the original characters Káthi, Guz. (કાઠી) The name of a ruling tribe settled in, and giving its name to, the province of Kattiwar, who, according to one tradition, immigrated thither from the banks of the Indus some time in the eighth century; but, according to another, came originally from the Jamuna, and did not reach their present site till the fourteenth. They are divided into three principal families named Wala, or Wara, Khachar, and Khuman, of each of which there are other subdivisions. The Kattis are a tall, robust race, sometimes having light hair and blue eyes, and, until of late years, were distinguished for their turbulence and fierceness, and aversion to the pursuits of a peaceable life: latterly they have subsided into more orderly habits, and follow agriculture.

Káṭhipál, Guz. (કાઠીપાલ, from the S. *pála*, पाल, protection) Black mail paid either to the Kattis for forbearance, or to some chief for protection.

Katti, Tel. (కత్తి) A measure of land containing about fourteen acres.

Katti, Tel., Karn., and Mal. (కత్తి) A sword or knife, especially that used by the drawers of the *táṛí*.

Kattikáran, Mal. (കത്തികാരൻ) A *táṛí* or toddy drawer.

Kattippaṇam, Mal. (കത്തിപ്പണം) Tax on *táṛí* drawing.

Kattimadive, Karn. (ಕತ್ತಿಮದುವೆ) The representation of a king at his marriage by a sword as his proxy.

KAṬṬILSTHÁNAM, Mal. (കട്ടിൽസ്ഥാനം) Property given by a Nair to his wife and children.

KAṬṬU, Tel. and Karn. (కట్టు, from కట్టు, to bind) A binding, a bond, a law, a rule, an arrangement: a bunch of straw in which some of the grain is preserved for next season's sowing.

Kaṭṭubaḍi, Tel., Karn., Tam. (కట్టుబడి, from *kattu*, a bond, and *paḍi*, having fallen into, the initial changed) A revenue term usually applied to a fixed, invariable, and favourable or quit-rent, which has been assessed on lands granted to public servants.

Kaṭṭubadi-agrahâramu, Tel. (from *agrahâram*, q. v.) A village assessed at a quit rent.

Kaṭṭubadi-banṭrotulu, corruptly, *Kutpuddee Peon.* Tel. (from బంట్రోతులు, q. v.) Peons or militia paid for their services by grants of land at a quit-rent.

Kaṭṭubadi-ínámu, Tel. (see Inám) A grant of land paying a small or favourable rent.

Kaṭṭubadi-jana, Karn. (S. *jana* जन, people) Public servants holding lands at a low assessment, and who, when occasion requires, perform the duty of soldiers.

Kaṭṭubadi-khandriká, Tel. (see Khandriká) A portion of land granted at a low rate of assessment.

Kaṭṭubadi-mukhása, Tel. (See *Mukhása*) A village granted for services at a low or quit-rent.

Kaṭṭubadiyinám, Tam. (கட்டுபடியிறைம்) Land held at quit-rent.

Kaṭṭudale, Karn. (ಕಟ್ಟುದಲೆ) Agreement, settlement, rate of assessment.

Kaṭṭuguttagai, corruptly, *Kuttgoota*, *Kutgoot*, *Kuttgootee*, and *Cuttoogootaga*, Tam. (கட்டுகுத்தகை) Land held in farm at a permanently fixed money-rent, which is usually light.

Kaṭṭukálivé, Karn. (ಕಟ್ಟುಕಾಲಿವೆ) A large channel for irrigating the land and supplying reservoirs.

Kaṭṭukiḍai, Tam. (கட்டுக்கிடை) Any thing detained till it is damaged.

Kaṭṭukúli, Karn. (ಕಟ್ಟುಕೂಲಿ) Regulated hire.

Kaṭṭumara, Karn. (ಕಟ್ಟುಮರ) A cess levied in Mysore upon the owners of Areca-tree groves.

Kaṭṭutara, Karn. (ಕಟ್ಟುತರ) A paper of settlement between two disputants.

Kaṭṭúttara, Karn. (ಕಟ್ಟೂತ್ತರ) Remission of revenue on account of keeping up dams and embankments. Mysore.

Kaṭṭuttogai, Tam. (கட்டுத்தொகை) Grand total.

KAṬUBÁṆ, Mar. (कटुबाण) A grant or tenure in perpetuity of barren or fallow lands for a fixed annual sum, not liable to increase; also, the land so held.

KAṬUPPAṬṬAN, Mal. (കടുപ്പട്ടൻ) A low tribe of Nairs.

ḲAUL, KÓUL or QOUL, KOWL, H., but used in most dialects, corruptly, COWL or COWLE, (A. قول) KAUL, Beng. and Mar. (কৌল, कौल), KAVULU, Tel. (కవులు), KAVULU, KAULU, Karn. (ಕೌಲು, ಕವುಲು), KAVUL, Tam. (கவுல்) Lit., A word, a promise, an agreement or contract: the term is used in various deeds granted by superiors to inferiors, in which the engagement implies an act of grace or favour: a promise of pardon or of safe conduct to a rebel or offender to induce him to give himself up. In revenue transactions a *Kaul* usually means the document granted by the collector, proprietor, or receiver of the revenue to the subordinate payer of the revenue, or the actual cultivator, stating the terms of the agreement and the amount to be paid, and securing him against further demands: it frequently implies, also, that the contract or lease is granted on favourable conditions, as in the case of the cultivation of waste lands, for which a remission of rent is granted for a given period by a *Kaul.*

Kauláchára, Karn. (ಕೌಲಾಚಾರ) A quit-rent on land.

Kauláwaṇ, Mar. (कौलावण) The cost or fees of procuring a *kaul.*

Ḳaul-bíṛa, H. (قول بيڑہ) lit., The betel of contract: the ceremony of giving betel to the nearest male relative of a girl at the time of betrothment, to obtain his consent, practised by the Mohammadans of Hindustán.

Kaul-karár, Mar. (कौलकरार, from the A. قول and قرار) A term in written engagements, as leases, &c., to denote agreeing to the terms proposed.

Ḳaul-náma, H. (P. نامہ) The written voucher granted to the revenue-payers specifying the terms of their payments and amount: any written contract or engagement.

Kaul-patrak, Mar. (कौलपत्रक) One of the village accounts, that of lands cultivated on a reduced assessment.

Ḳaulí, H. (قولي, adj. of *Kaul*) Relating to an engagement: land held under a *kaul* or stipulated tenure. In Benares and the north-western provinces it was applied to lands in which the government made its settlement directly with the cultivators, without the intervention of a third party: it was also applied to lands of which the assessment was fixed in money not in kind. Mar. (कौली) as before: also, waste land brought into cultivation under a *kaul* from the state.

Kaulváram, Tam. (கவுல்வாரம்) A share or portion of land granted by *Kaul* in addition to his regular share, to induce the holder to cultivate.

KAUL, Thug. A village.

KAULÁ, or KAULÍÁ, H. (كولا, كوليا, from *Kaulí*, an armful) A bundle or sheaf of corn given at harvest time as a perquisite to reapers and village servants.

KAULKÍ, Thug. Liquor.

ḲAUM, KOUM, H. (A. قوم) Race, tribe, people.

KAURGA, Thug. Silver.

KAUṚÍ, KOUṚEE, corruptly, COWRIE, and COWRY, H. (كوڑی) KAṚI, Beng. (কড়ি) KOṚI, Guz. (કોડી) A small shell used as coin in the lower provinces (Cypræa moneta). In account, four *Kauṛís* are equal to one *Ganḍa*, and 80 *Kauṛís* to one *Paṇ*.

Kauṛibhágiá, Uriya (କଉଡ଼ିଭାଗିଆ) A village accountant, charged, also, with the office of collecting the rents.

Kaṛániyá, Beng. (কড়ানিয়া) Keeping accounts in *Kauṛís*.

KAULIGÉ, Karn. (ಕೌಳಿಗೆ) A registrar or accountant attached to the petty Paligars for the districts under their control, corresponding to the Karanam or Karnika of the districts under the government.

KAUSIK, H. (كوسك, कौसिक) A tribe of Rajputs, in considerable numbers in Ghazipur, Azimgerh, and Gorakhpur, claiming descent from Kusika, the father of Gádhi, the founder of Gádhi- or Ghazi-pur.

KÁVAḌI, Tel., Tam., Mal. (కావడి, காவடி, കാവടി) A pole for carrying burthens, resting on the shoulder, and having a string at each extremity by which the articles to be conveyed are slung; the *Bhangi* of the upper provinces.

Kávadi-káran, Tam. (காவடிக்காரன்) A carrier of baggage by a Kávadi, commonly accompanying a palanquin on a journey.

KÁVADAM, Tam. (காவதம்) A league, a distance of from eight to ten miles. See *Kádam*.

KAVAḶ, Mar. (कवळ) Loppings of bushes to be spread over and burnt on a field.

KÁVAL, corruptly, CAWEL, and CAWELLY, Tam. (காவல், Mal. (കാവൽ) Guarding, protecting: confinement, imprisonment: the duty of the village district watch.

Kávalan, Tam. (காவலன்) A protector, a defender, a king, a husband, a guard, a watch.

Kávaláḷi, Mal., Tam. (കാവലാളി) A watchman, a guard, a village watchman. In Tinnevelly, a prisoner, one in custody.

Kávalaithalam, Tam. (காவலைதலம்) A prison, a jail.

Kával-dés, Tam. (தேச, from S. देश, country) Watching or protection of the district: a cess levied on the cultivators to pay the expense of guarding the roads.

Kával-grámam, Tam. (கிராமம், from S. ग्राम, a village) Guarding or protecting the village, a cess levied for the purpose.

Kávalkár, or *Kávalgár*, or *Káválháran*, Tam., Mal. (காவல்க்காரன்) A protector, a guardian, a watchman: the village watchman, who also commonly acts as a messenger and guide for travellers.

Gráma-kávalkár, Tam. The village watchman.

Dés- or *Men-kávalkár*, Tam. (தேச், மென்) A powerful chief, a Pálayakár (Poligar) or protector, (from S. *pála*, protecting): the guardian or officer charged with the superintendence of a district.

Kával-anáj, Karn. (ಕಾವಲಅನಾಜ) A cess on the cultivators in kind, formerly levied in Mysore for the cost of watching.

Kávali, the Tel. form of *Kával* (కావలి) A watch or guard, custody.

Kávalikára, Tel. (కావలికాఁర) A watchman, a village watchman.

Kávali-váḍu, Tel. (కావలివాఁడు) A watchman, a village watchman.

Kával-mérai, Tam. (காவல்மேரை) Portion of grain given to the village watchman.

Kávali-rasum, Tel. (from A. رسوم) Fees or perquisites of the village watchman.

Kával-pulam, Mal. (കാവൽപുലം) Fee or tax paid for watching or protection.

Kával-talam, or *Talam-kaval*, Tam. (தலம், from S. स्थल, a place) Watch or protection of any place; fees for watching levied formerly by the petty Pálayakars.

Kával-thalam, Mal. (കാവലുലമ്പം) Share of grain given to the watchman from the threshing-floor or the field. See the last.

KAVAṚA, Mal. (കവറ) A tribe in north Malabar, who make and sell bambu mats, baskets, &c.

KAVILE, Tel. (కవిలె) An account-book of slips of palm leaves, such as is used by the village accountants in the Northern Cirkars and Tamil country, whence it is often used for the accounts themselves.

Kavilekattu, Tel. (కవిలెకట్టు) The village account kept on palm leaves.

Káya, **Káy**, or **Káï**, or, corruptly, **Koy**, Tel., Karn., Tam., Mal. (కాయ, காய்) Young or unripe fruit of plants or trees; a pod or legume.

Káyanga, Mal. (കായംഗ) The areca-nut tree.

Káyadhányamu, Tel. (కాయధాన్యము, from S. धान्य, grain) Pulse, all sorts of seeds contained in pods or legumes.

Káyatiruva, Tel. (కాయతిరువ) Duty on fruits and legumes.

Kayál, incorrectly, **Koyal**, H. (A. كيال), **Káyal**, Beng. (কাযল) A weigher, a measurer of grain, the weighman or measurer of the village, who weighed out the respective shares of the crop when the revenue was paid in kind.

Kayálí, incorrectly, *Koyali*, H. &c. (كيالي) Belonging or relating to the weighman, as his office or duty; fees or perquisites paid to the weighman, continued in some parts of Bengal as an *Abwab*, or cess, after the revenue had ceased to be paid in kind, and the office of village weighman had been abolished.

Káyal, Tam. (காயல்) A salt-pan.

Káyalpáṭam, Mal. (കായല്പാടം) Wet land.

Kayaṟu, or **Kayiṟu**, Tam. (கயறு, கயிறு) Rope, whence the term *Coir*, though that is usually applied to rope made of the fibres of the cocoa-nut alone.

Káyastha, S. also, in the dialects, **Káyasth**, **Káyath** or **Kait**, **Káyat**, corruptly, **Koit** (कायस्थ), also, **Káit**, Beng. (কাইত) A caste so termed, or a member of it, sprung from a Kshetriya father and a Vaisya mother, the occupation of which is that of the writer or accountant: it is one of the most respectable of the mixed classes. Among the Marathas the *Káyastha* is said to be distinguished from the *Káyat* by locality, the latter being peculiar to the north.

Káyat, (?) A servile caste in the countries east of Bengal, less impure than the Chandála.

Káyiká, or **Káyiká-vṛiddhi**, S. (कायिका, कायिकावृद्धि, from *káya* काय, the body) Lit., Bodily interest, or interest drawn from the use made of the bodies of animals given in pledge, as of the milk of a cow; also, according to some, interest not affecting the body or principal of a loan.

Káyittaḷavu, Tam. (காயிற்றளவு) Measurement by a rope of a heap of corn or grain in stacks.

Kayyála, Mal. (കയ്യാല) A threshing-floor; a place where corn is collected before threshing.

Kayyára, Mal. (കയ്യാറ) A water-course, a channel.

Kayyirippa, Mal. (കയ്യിരിപ്പ) Treasure or balance in hand: see *Káï*.

Ḳazf, A. (قذف) Accusing, charging, especially falsely, of unnatural crimes or adultery.

Ḳázif, A. (قاذف) A false accuser, a slanderer.

Ḳáẓí, **Qazee**, corruptly, **Cazi**, **Cauzy**, **Cauzee**, **Kazy**, (A. قاضي), in the Hindu dialects **Kájí**, Beng., Mar., &c. (কাজী, काजी) A Mohammadan judge, an officer formerly appointed by the government to administer both civil and criminal law, chiefly in towns, according to the principles of the Koran: under the British authorities the judicial functions of the Ḳáẓís in that capacity ceased, and, with the exception of their employment as the legal advisers of the courts in cases of Mohammadan law, the duties of those stationed in the cities or districts were confined to the preparation and attestation of deeds of conveyance and other legal instruments, and the general superintendence and legalization of the ceremonies of marriage, funerals, and other domestic occurrences among the Mohammadans. Beng. Reg. xxxix. 1793.

Ḳáẓí-âskar, H. (from A. عسكر, an army) A military judge or a Ḳáẓí attached to a military station.

Ḳáẓí-ul-Ḳuẓát, corruptly, *Cauzy-ul-Cauzat* or *ul-Coozat*, H. (A. plur. of *ḳaẓí*, قضات) The principal Ḳaẓi under the British government, the head Mohammadan legal officer of the Sadr Âdálats, or Courts of Appeal.

Ḳaẓá, H. (A. قضا) Judgment, administration of justice, the office of the Ḳáẓí.

Ḳaẓia, H. (A. قضية) **Kajjá**, Mar. (कज्जा) A quarrel, a dispute, a lawsuit.

Ḳazzáḳ, or **Kazáḳ**, H. (قزّاق) A robber, a freebooter; one who robs in a gang, and who sometimes plunders on horseback.

Kebra, (?) A cess levied upon the town of Salsette to cover loss upon the rice crop collected and deposited in the town until disposed of.

Kedu, Tam. (கெடு), Mal. (കെട്) Term, condition, stipulated time of payment, &c.

Keduvaḷam, Mal. (കെടുവളം) A bad soil.

Kelá, Uriya (କେଳା) A gipsy, a vagrant class of people living by catching snakes, making mats, &c.

Kelisérava, Karn. (ಕೆಲಿಸೇರವ) A barber, a hairdresser.

Kendá, Uriya (କେନ୍ଦା) *Táṛí*, the juice of the palm.

Kelasa, Karn. (ಕೆಲಸ) Work, business, employment; as, *Kallu-kelasa*, stonemasons' work.

Kembuttá, Karn. (ಕೆಂಬುತ್ತ) A kind of rice.

KEṆE, Mar. (केणे) An article of merchandise, a piece of goods, a commodity, any thing with reference to traffic: some confine it to grain, fruit, vegetables, &c.

KER, KERA, or KERÍ, Mar. (केर, केरी) Rubbish, refuse.

Kerpaṭṭí, Mar. (केरपट्टी) A tax for maintaining public sweepers and scavengers.

KERAM, Mal. (കെരം) A cocoa-nut tree, a cocoa-nut.

KERÉ, Karn. (ಕೆರೆ) An artificial lake or reservoir, a tank.

Kere banḍi, Karn. (ಕೆರೆಬಂಡಿ) A person employed to keep the embankment of a tank in repair: the employment.

Kerebanḍi-aya-joḍi, Karn. (ಕೆರೆಬಂಡಿ ಅಯ ಜೋಡಿ) A tax on the holders of small grants of land paid to the persons charged with the repairs of reservoirs.

Kere-káluve, Karn. (ಕೆರೆಕಾಲುವೆ) A channel for leading off the water of a tank.

Kere-kodi, Karn. (ಕೆರೆಕೋಡಿ) The outlet for the superfluous water of a tank.

Kere-yere, Karn. (ಕೆರೆಯೇರಿ) The bank of a reservoir.

KERIJULU, Tel. (కెరిజులు) Grain fees in general.

KESARA, Mar. Guz. (S. केशर) Saffron.

Keṣará, Mar. Guz. (केशरा) A yellow or saffron-dyed garment put on by a Rajput warrior when resolved to die or conquer.

Keṣarí, or *Keṣariá*, corruptly, KESSIRIYA, Mar. Guz. (केशरी, केशरीया) Clothed in yellow, as indicating desperate valour.

KESARAD-BHÚM, Hindi (केसरद्भूम) A soil kept always moist by natural springs near it.

KÉSU, Karn. (ಕೇಸು) Farming, agriculture.

KETÁ, Thug. Ardent spirits.

KEṬṬIÁDÁKAM, Mal. (കെട്ടിയാധാകം) Seizure of land mortgaged for a sum of money on failure of payment of the stipulated interest.

Keṭṭiádákanavan, Mal. (കെട്ടിയാധാകനവൻ) The person who takes possession of a mortgaged estate on failure of payment of interest on the mortgage loan.

KEṬṬISÁKSHI, Karn. (ಕೆಟ್ಟಸಾಕ್ಷಿ, from *ketti*, wicked, and S. *sákshya*, evidence) False witness.

KEṬṬA, Mal. (കെട്ട) Rule, regulation, bond, tie: a bank, a dam.

Keṭṭaruppa, Mal. (കെട്ടറുപ്പ) Inheritance in the paternal line (lit., cutting a knot, *i.e.* not following the order of succession by the female line, as is usual in Malabar).

Keṭṭiyirippa, Mal. (കെട്ടിയിരിപ്പ) Money in hand, property in store.

Keṭṭivarava, Mal. (കെട്ടിവരവ) Receipt in cash.

Keṭṭiveppa, Mal. (കെട്ടിവെപ്പ) Paying down money: laying up in store.

Keṭṭukeṭṭa, Mal. (കെട്ടുകെട്ട) A storekeeper, a steward, a butler.

Keṭṭuvaramba, Mal. (കെട്ടുവരമ്പ) A large bank round paddy fields to confine the water.

KETU, S. &c. (केतु) The descending node personified as the tail of the dragon, supposed to cause eclipses by seizing the moon.

KEÜT, Uriya (କେଉଟ) A fisherman, or the caste so employed.

KEVALA DATTAKA, or KEVALA DATTA PUTRA, S. (from केवल, sole, and दत्तक, or दत्तपुत्र, a son given) A son absolutely adopted, in Hindu law.

KEWAL, (?) A black loamy soil.

Kewaldas, (?) Mar. Black soil.

KEWAṬÍ, Mar. (केवटी) A huckster, a retail dealer.

KEWÍ, Mar. (केवी) A cultivator residing and cultivating lands in a village to which he does not belong.

KHABAR, KHUBUR, H. (A. خبر) News, information: care, protection.

Khabar-gír, H. (P. خبرگير) An informer, a news writer: a guardian, a protector.

KHABHA, Thug. A hamlet, a village.

KHÁBRÍ, Beng. (খাবরী) A large hemispherical vessel to receive the expressed juice of the sugar-cane or other vegetable extract.

KHÁCHAR (or (?) more correctly, KHÁNCHAR), Mar. Rice lands.

KHACHUA, Thug. A pickpocket.

KHÁD, Mar. (खाद, S. खादन, eating) Food, &c.: peculation, extortion; articles or money extorted.

KHÁD, H. (كهاد, खाद) The expense incurred by the Ryots in preparing their ploughing apparatus.

KHÁD, H. (كهاد) A hole or pit, one in which grain is kept.

KHÁDÁ, Beng. (খাদা) A large land measure, said to be equal in some places to 27,000 square yards: east of Jessore to 24 Bíghás.

KHÁḌÁ-HUNDI, Beng. (খাড়াহুণ্ডী) A bill of exchange payable at sight.

KHÁDAKA, S. (खादक) Lit., an eater; in law, a borrower, a user.

KHÁDAR, incorrectly, KHADIR, H. (كهادر, खादर) Low or alluvial lands, of easy irrigation, and especially fit for rice cultivation: rice beds, or patches of ground surrounded by low banks so as to confine the water and moisten the ground for rice cultivation; also moist alluvial ground on which, with or without irrigation, barley and wheat are grown in some places.

KHÁDÍ, H. (كهادي) A kind of coarse cloth.

KHÁEKÁR, H. (?) A cultivating tenant.

KHAFÍF, H. (A. خفيف) Light, unimportant.

Khafífa duzdi, H. (from P. دزدي) Petty theft.

Khafífa jaráim, H. (from A. جرايم) Petty offences.

Khafífa muḳaddama, (from A. مقدمه) A trivial suit or case.

KHÁG, H. (كهاگ) The horn of a rhinoceros, applied to a pillar or mound marking the boundary of a village.

KHAGHA, Thug. A hamlet, a village.

KHÁÍ, H. (كهاي, खाई) A ditch, especially as a boundary.

KHAIR, H. (A. خير) Good, well, best.

Khairát, *Khyrat*, corruptly, *Kheryaut*, H. (A. خيرات) Mar. (खैरात) Alms, charity; lands given as charitable endowments: (the term is more especially applicable to grants or alms given by, or to, Mohammadans.)

Khairát-zamín, H. (P. زمين) Land given in charity.

Khair-khwáh, H. (P. خواه) A well-wisher, a common signature to an anonymous petition or address.

KHAÍR, Hindi (खईर, S. खदिर) A sort of resin, also commonly called *Khat*: Catechu.

Khair-sál, H. Tax on collecting catechu resin. Garwhal.

KHÁJAN, Mar, (खाजण) A salt-marsh or meadow; land lying along the shore of the sea or of inlets, and exposed to be flooded; ground recovered by embankment from the sea.

KHAJÚR, H. &c. (كهجور, S. खर्जुर), KHÁJÚR, Beng. (খাজুর) A date tree (Phœnix dactylifera): its fruit. The wild date tree (Phœnix sylvestris).

Khájúrgúr, Beng. (from গুড়, molasses) Treacle or molasses made from the juice of the wild date.

Khájúr-ras, Beng. (from S. रस, juice) Juice extracted from the wild date by incisions in its bark, used to make sugar or to leaven bread.

KHÁK, H. (P. خاك) Earth, dust, ashes.

Khákí, H. (خاكي) Relating to dust or ashes: a Hindu mendicant who smears his body with the ashes of burnt cowdung: soil or land that cannot be irrigated, and depends wholly on rain.

Khákrob, H. (P. خاكروب) A sweeper, a menial servant of the lowest class; also, the sweeper of a village, acting at times as a watchman, a guide, or a police spy; one of the village establishment.

Khákistar, H. (P. خاكستر) Ashes, also calx of metals.

Kháktúda, H. (P. خاكتوده) A mark or butt of earth for shooting at.

KHAL, or KHALI, H. (S. كهل, كهلي) Oil-cake, the sediment after extracting the oil by the mill.

KHÁL, H. (خال) A maternal uncle, a mother's brother.

Khálá, (خالا) A maternal aunt, a mother's sister.

KHÁL, H. (كهال) An inlet of the sea or of a large river, a creek.

KHALA, H. (خله) A written document signed by a judge.

KHALA, Beng. (S. খল), KHALÁ, Uriya (ଖଳା), KHALLÁ, H. (كهلا), KHALEṆ, Mar. (खळें), KHALÍ, or KHALWAD, Guz. (ખળી, ખળવાડ) A threshing-floor, a place either in the field or in a shed where the grain is trodden out of the husk: see *Kala*; also, a place where the grain of any individual of the village is piled up or stacked, or where it was kept so stacked until its value had been estimated by the collector, and security for the revenue due on it given.

Khaleṇtaḷaveṇ, Mar. (खळेंतळवें) The grain that is swept up after the removal of the sheaves from the spot where they had been piled, or from the threshing-floor after threshing.

Khaḷa-punji, corruptly, *Kall-poonzee*, Mar. (खळपुंजी) Small heaps of grain taken from each larger pile at the time of measurement, and, under the Maratha government, considered as the perquisite of the state.

Khaḷavárí, Mar. (खळवाडी) An inclosed place outside a village, containing the bundles of grain to be threshed and the threshing-floors of several independent cultivators.

Khalián, also, *Khaliḥán*, H. (كهليهان, كهليان) A granary, a barn, a threshing-floor.

KHALÂ, A. (خلع) lit., Putting or turning out. In Mohammadan law, a contract for the dissolution of a marriage; the repudiation of a wife at her own desire, when she forfeits her dower: also, disinheriting a son, turning him out of doors.

KHÁLÁRÍ, corruptly, CALLARY, COLLERIE, COLLURIE, KHALLARY, &c. Beng. (খালাড়ী) A place where salt is manufactured: a salt-bed or pan; a mound of earth hollowed at the top, in which straw and other materials are placed to serve as a filter for the salt water poured upon it, and which, when freed from dirt and sand, becomes brine for boiling.

KHALÁṢ, H. (خلاص), KHÁLÁS, Beng. (খালাস) Liberation, freedom, release; liberated, enlarged, set free.

Khuláṣa, H. (A. خلاصه) Essence, abridgement, abstract.

Khaláṣi, corruptly, *Classie*, H. (خلاصي) A sailor, a tent-pitcher, a matross: a Mohammadan labourer of a superior order, employed chiefly about ships or in the army.

Kháláspatra, Beng. (S. पत्र, a leaf) An order of discharge, a deed of release.

KHALÁṬÍ, KHÁLÁṬHÍ, Mar. (खलाटी, ठी) Low rice grounds about a village.

KHÁLÁṬÍ, Mar. (खालाटी) The low country on the upper part of the Malabar coast, descending from the Sahyádri mountains to the sea.

KHÁLIHÁTH, H. (from *khali* خالي, empty, and *hath* هاتهہ, the hand) lit., Empty-handed, poor, destitute. In Mysore, a class of inferior public labourers employed as messengers, or in mending roads, carrying palankins, &c.

KHALF, H. (A. خلف) A son, an heir, a successor.

Khalífa, commonly, *Caliph*, H. (A. خليفة) The successor to sovereign power, especially applied to the successors of Mohammad, who united the characters of head of the state and of the Mohammadan religion. In India the term commonly designates a tailor, sometimes a cook, also the head boy or monitor of a class.

Khiláfat, commonly, *Caliphate*, H. (A. خلافت) Sovereignty, the office of Khalíf.

KHÁL-KHOSIA, Thug. A barber.

KHALLÍ, Thug. A Thug who hides himself from fear of creditors.

KHALÍTA. Thug. A village.

KHÁLIṢA but usually pronounced KHÁLṢA, H. &c. (خالصہ, from *khális* خالص, pure, sincere) KHÁLSÁ, or KHÁLISÁ, Mar. (खालसा, खालिसा) The exchequer, the office of government under the Mohammadan administration in which the business of the revenue department was transacted, and which was continued during the early period of British rule: as applied to lands, it means those of which the revenue remains the property of government, not being made over in *Jágír* or *Inám* to any other parties. Lands or villages held immediately of government, and of which the state is the manager or holder. It is termed in some official papers the rent-roll of the government, meaning the revenue receivable from government or *Khálsa* lands. The term has been of late familiar as the collective denomination of the Sikh government and people.

Khálsa-kachahrí, H. (see *Kachahrí*) The office of the royal exchequer.

Kháliṣa mukarrari, H. (from A. مقرّر, fixed) The designation of lands which, under the Mohammadan government, were considered as permanently paying revenue to the state.

Kháliṣa sharífa, H. (from A. شريف, noble) The royal exchequer.

KHÁLPÁ, erroneously, KALPA, Guz. (ખાલ્પા, from S. खल, skin) A low caste, or member of it, whose business is dressing skins and preparing leather: he is sometimes enumerated amongst the inferior village servants.

KHÁLSI, (?) Guz. A measure of grain equal to fourteen Guzerati maunds.

KHÁM, corruptly, KHAUM, or KAUM, H. (P. خام) Raw, unripe, crude; gross: as a revenue term it implies the gross as distinguished from the nett revenue of a village, or a settlement made with the cultivators direct, without the intervention of a third person as a farmer or Zamindar, the estate being managed, or, as is more usual, mismanaged, by the officers of government; see *Kháṣ*.

Khám-ámdani, corruptly, *Kamamdauny*, H. (from P. آمدني) Gross receipts or revenue.

Khámbhogaṭṭá, Tel. (ఖాంబోగట్టా) The gross account of a village.

Khám-chiṭhá, H. (خام چتّها) A rough statement or account.

Khám-hisabu, Tel. (from A. حساب) A general account.

Khám-jamâbandi, H. see *Jamâbandi*. Gross assessment before making deductions for charges: assessment or settlement with the cultivators direct.

Khám-lehka, Tel. (ఖాం లెక్క, from S. लेख) A rough statement or account.

Khám-navís, H. (from P. نويس) A revenue accountant under the Mohammadan government.

Khám-tahṣíl, H. (from A. تحصيل) Collection of the revenue in gross from the cultivators direct by the revenue officers of government, usually by native officers under the authority of the collector.

Khám-tadárak, H. (from A. تدارك) Imperfect inquiry or investigation.

Khám-waṣúl, corruptly, *wossool*, also, *wáṣil*, H. (from A. واصل, or وصول) Gross revenue, total collections, the gross revenue of a village or an estate before the allowed charges are deducted; a record or account of the gross revenue.

KHÁMÁR, corruptly, KHUMAR, CAMAR, COMAR. Beng. (খামার), KHAMÁR, or KHUMAR, Uriya (ଖମାର) A threshing-floor, the general threshing-ground of a village, to which all the crops are brought to be cleaned, and from which they cannot be removed till the landlord's claim is settled. Land of which the revenue was paid in kind, or of which the produce was divided in determinate shares between the cultivator and the revenue payer or Zamindar; applied also to lands originally waste, but which, having been brought into cultivation, were retained by the Zamindars in their own hands, or were let out at a grain rent: at the decennial settlement these lands, previously unassessed, were declared subject to assessment.

Khamárbhúmi, Uriya (from S. भूमि, land) Cultivated land. Land cultivated by strangers—not resident or hereditary cultivators.

Khamárchash, Uriya (from ଚଷ, husbandry) Cultivating land on one's own account.

Khamár-chhuṭṭí, Hindi (खमारछुट्टी) Releasing the grain from the threshing-ground when the rent is settled for, either in kind or money.

Khamárghar, Uriya (from S. गृह, a house) A farm-yard, a barn, a store-house.

Khamári, or *Khamároi*, Uriya (ଖମାରୀ, ଖମାରୋଇ) A bailiff, a steward.

Khamár riyât, H. (A. رعيّت) A cultivator who pays his rent in kind, or in a certain share of the produce.

Khámársál, H. (from S. शाला, a hall or room; the first word may be used as implying some analogy to a threshing-floor) A place where iron is fused after having been smelted from the ore.

Khamávishi, or Khamási, Karn. (ಖಮಾವಿಷಿ, ಖಮಾಸಿ) Land cultivated under the immediate superintendence of government.

Khamávishidár, Karn. (ಖಮಾವಿಷೀದಾರ) A person charged with the superintendence of government land.

Khamr, H. (A. خمر) Wine, the spirituous liquor made from the fermented juice of the grape, the drinking of which is positively forbidden by the Mohammadan law: the term is applied, but incorrectly, to all spirituous liquor.

Khamr-mahál, H. (from محال) Places where spirituous liquor is sold.

Khumár, H. (A. خُمار) Intoxication.

Khumár-khána, H. (from P. خانه) A tavern, a spirit-shop.

Khambá, or Khambhá, H. (S. کهنبا, کهنبها) A post, a pillar.

Khamjá, (?) H. A person whose business is the appraisement of standing crops. Upper Provinces.

Khams, H. (خمس) Five, a fifth. In law, a double tithe, or twenty per cent. levied on the owners of lands in which there are mines of metal: the fifth of booty taken in war with infidels, and set apart for orphans, the poor, and travellers.

Khán, H. (P. خان) A title borne by Mohammadan nobles, especially when of Persian or Paṭhán descent: it is also a common adjunct to Afghan or *Paṭhán* names.

Khán-hhánán, H. (P. خان‌خانان) Lord of lords, a title borne by several nobles of the court of Dehli under the Moghul government.

Khánam, H. (P. خانم) The title of a lady of rank, or of the wife of a Khán.

Khana, H. &c. (P. خانه), Kháná, Beng. and Mal. (খানা, खाना) A house, a ḍwelling, a place.

Khánabáṛí, corruptly, *Khanabarry*, H. (P. خانه, a house, and Ben. from S. বাড়ী, also a house) A house, with the grounds and outhouses attached to it: the dwelling of a Zamindar, and the ground about it, which was held free of revenue: exemption of revenue upon certain lands belonging to a Zamindar as a means of providing him with a suitable residence: a small patch of garden ground attached to a Ryot's hut, in which he grows vegetables for his own use, and for which he is usually exempt from rent by the Zamindar: the house, and ground about it, of certain classes in some parts of Cuttack, as Paiks, Súrs, and Khúshbásh Ryots, exempt from rent-charge.

Khánagí, H. (خانگي) Any thing relating to a house or household: in Kuch Bahar, the lands managed by the Raja, or officers appointed by him.

Khánajangí, H. (خانه‌جنگي) Riot, disturbance, affray: the making of disturbances: a turbulent or quarrelsome disposition.

Khángi, or *Khánagi*, H. (خانگي), *Khánkí*, Beng. (খানকী) A prostitute; also, household, domestic.

Khánákhárábí, Beng. (খানাখারাবী) Ruin of a household, or of an individual at the head of a family.

Khánashumárí, H. (from P. شماري, numbering), *Khánesumárí*, Mar. (खानेसुमारी), *Khánísumari*, Karn. (ಖಾನೀ-ಸುಮರಿ) A written statement of the number of houses in a village or town, and hence a census of the population is so termed.

Khanataláshi, H. (from P. تلاش, search) A search warrant.

Khanazád, H., *Khanájád*, Beng., Mar. (from P. زاد, born) Born in the house; *i.e.* the child of a slave girl or of any female dependant.

Khángi-zamindárí, H. (خانگي زميندارى) The household expenses of a Zamindar. In Jessore, an abwab or cess levied prior to the perpetual settlement upon the cultivators, to provide for the support of the Zamindars: it is applied also to land retained by a Zamindar in his own cultivation as a fund for his household expenses.

KHÁNCH, Mar. (खांच) A pit, a hole.

KHÁNCHÁ, H. (كهانچا, खांचा) A marsh, a quagmire, muddy or marshy soil.

KHÁNCHAR, Mar. (खांचर) A hollow, especially one worn by the rush of water.

KHÁNCHARÍ, Mar. (खांचरी) A rice field: a piece of ground banked up on all sides so as to retain water.

KHAN, H. (كهن, खनि) KHANI, or KHANÍ, Beng. (খনি, খনী) KHÁṆ, or KHÁṆÍ, Mar. (खाण, खाणी) A mine, a pit or hole, one in which rice in the husk is kept.

Khángat, Mar. (खाणगत) Revenue from mines or quarries.

KHAND, KHUND, H. &c., also written KHÁṆD, (كهند, or كهاند, S. खण्ड): it is sometimes written without the aspirate, as *Kandam*, Mal. (കണ്ടം) A piece, a portion; a district, a province, as Bundelkhand. Coarse sugar. In Marathi, KHAṆD, corruptly, KUND (खंड), also means a fine, a cess or fee levied for any licence or privilege; also a contribution levied by an enemy, a ransom; also an agreement or contract, in which sense it occurs, at least compounded with other words, in other Dakhini dialects.

Khaṇḍa patra, Karn (ಖಂಡಪತ್ರ) A paper of settlement or agreement.

Khaṇḍbachi, Mar. (खंडबची) An obligation to give one or more sheep from a flock sent to graze on a piece of land: the duty levied on a flock of sheep.

Khaṇḍbhaṭṭí, Mar. (from भट्टी, a still) A tax or excise on stills.

Khaṇḍ-daladí, Mar. (from दलदी, a fisherman) A charge for the privilege of fixing stakes in the waters of Salsette.

Khaṇḍ-dáru, Mar. (from दारू, spirituous liquor) A farm or contract for the sale of spirits.

Khaṇḍgunhegárí, Mar. (खंडगुन्हेगारी) A general term for amercements, mulcts, &c., a fine levied on the loser in a suit.

Khaṇḍkarí, Mar. (खंडकरी) A cultivator who contracts for a favourable return of produce.

Khaṇḍ-maktá, Mar. (खंडमक्ता) A contract, a monopoly: land leased at a fixed, and usually a favourable rate.

Khaṇḍmásaḷí, Mar. (मासळी, fish) Farm of the fishing at Salsette.

Khaṇḍní, *Khundnee*, Mar. (खंडनी) A fine, a mulct, an exaction on any pretext whatever: the revenue of the year after it is determined: the current assessment.

Khaṇḍní-tashríf, Mar. (from P. تشريف) A present by the head collector or farmer of the revenue to the village or district officer on determining the assessment: the salary of the *Pátíl*.

Khaṇḍnúk, Mar. (खंडणूक) A contract for work, an engagement to perform a certain work for a sum agreed upon, or the counter-agreement to receive a certain sum: a contract, a monopoly, a farm (of revenue, &c.).

Khaṇḍ-pharṣí, Mar. (खंडफरशी) A fine exacted on behalf of government.

KHANDA, Uriya (ଖଣ୍ଡ) An inclosed field.

KHANDÁ, Uriya (ଖଣ୍ଡା) Daily allowance of food.

KHANDA, Beng. (খন্দ) The season of harvest, of which three are reckoned—the *harit*, or spring, *áṣu*, or autumn, and *paush*, or winter.

KHAṆḌÁ, Uriya (ଖଣ୍ଡା) A sword, especially the national sword of Orissa.

Khaṇḍáit, also, sometimes, *Khandára*, Uriya (ଖଣ୍ଡାଇତ) The name of a class of military landholders in Orissa, residing in the hills in *kilas*, or fortified dwellings, and holding their lands at a quit-rent, on condition of acting as a feudal yeomanry or militia, and protecting the low lands from the incursions of the barbarous mountain tribes bordering on their estates: their children, especially the females, are sometimes sold in childhood, and become slaves.

Khandáiti, Uriya. The office, jurisdiction, or estate of a Khandait.

KHAṆḌAGA, Karn. (ಖಂಡಗ) A measure of grain, about three bushels.

KHANDAK, Beng. (S. খন্দক) A ditch, a moat, a land-mark, a boundary.

KHÁNDÁN, H. (P. خاندان) A family.

KHAṆḌAR, H. (S. كهندر, from S. खण्ड, a piece) The site of a ruined house, or village covered with the rubbish.

KHAṆḌÍ, incorrectly, KUNDEE, Mar. (खंडी, from S. खण्ड) A measure of weight and capacity, commonly termed *Candy* (from the Tamil spelling *Kandi*, q. v.): its value varies in different places: at Bombay it consists of twenty Bombay maunds, or, for particular substances, of only eight maunds;

at Poona it is of twenty Poona maunds, and varies, therefore, with the weight of the maund; in Malayalam it is equal to twenty-eight *Tulams*, or, corruptly, *Telongs*, or 500lb.: according to Prinsep's tables the Candy of Anjengo is called 560lb., that of Bombay also 560lb., and that of Madras 500lb.: in another statement it is said that in Malabar the Khandí is equal to 560lb. for sea customs, and 480lb. for land customs, while the country rate varies from 600lb. to 720lb.: the latest statements make the Madras Khandí of 20 maunds 500lb., the Bombay Khandí of 20 maunds 560lb., the Surat of 20 maunds 746.666lb., and the Travancore of 20 maunds 640lb. The number of maunds varies, however, and with it, of course, the value of the *Khandí*.—Note by J. W. Crawford, Esq., Accountant-General, Bombay, 1840. In Malabar there is also a *Khandí* for timber about 2 feet 4 inches square; and in the Maraṭha country there is a land measure termed, corruptly, *Cundy*, considered equal to 120 *bighás*; but it varied formerly from 15 to 45 *bighás*, and is also called 20 to 35: it also means, in Marathi, a score generally.

KHANḌÍGAR, Beng. (খণ্ডীগর, from S. खण्ड, a piece or chip) A worker in horn or ivory.

KHANḌIGUṬṬA, Tel. (ఖండిగుట్ట) A fixed rent.

KHANḌRIKÁ, incorrectly, CANDRIKA, Tel. (ఖండ్రిక, from S. खण्ड, a piece) An allotment of privileged land not exceeding four or five *Kattis*, or from 50 to 70 acres: it may be either rent-free or subject to a quit-rent.

KHANDWÁ, Mar. (खण्डवा) The part of a river bed that is dry throughout its breadth.

KHANDWADÁ, Mar. (?) Grain given in requital of the services of an ox or buffalo on a person's ground.

KHAṆI-BHÚMI, Karn. (ಖಾಣಿಭೂಮಿ) Bad land (perhaps from Khání $\frac{1}{64}$ of a fanam—land of as little worth).

KHÁNI BHÁGOÁ, Uriya (ଖାଣିଭାଗୋଆ) Labourers in Orissa paid both in money and in kind.

KHANJÁ, Uriya (ଖଞ୍ଜା) Land immediately round a house, an inclosure, a compound; assigned as a deduction from the revenue payment.

KHÁNJU, Thug. A cut purse.

KHÁNKÁH, H. (P. خانقاه) A monastery, a place where religious mendicants of the Mohammadan religion temporarily reside.

KHÁNKATI, Beng. (খাংকতি) Abatement, deficiency.

KHANKH, H. (کھنکھ, खंख) Land that requires to be left fallow for a year or two.

KHÁNSÁMÁN, corruptly, CONSUMMAH, and CONSAMMAN, H. (خانسامان, probably from *khwán*, pronounced *khan* خوان, a tray, and *sámán*, effects) A house-steward or butler.

KHAP, Mar. (खप) Sale, vent, market, the disposal or going off of goods.

KHÁPAṆÍ, corruptly, KHAMPUTTEE, Mar. (खापणी) Apportioning among the householders of a town or village an assessment, or any exaction: the share of each.

KHAPARIYÁ, H. (کھپریا, खपरिया) A heavier plough for stiff soils.

KHAPRÁ, Beng. (খপরা, S. खर्पर) A tile.

Khaprail, Beng. (খপরৈল) Tiled, a tiled house or building.

KHAR, KHUR, H, (کھر) Grass and trees.

KHÁR, H. &c. (کھار, S. क्षार), KSHÁR, Beng. (ক্ষার) KHAR, Mar. (खार) KÁRU, Tel. (కారు) Alkali, alkaline earth, soda, the lixivium of wood-ashes or the ashes of burnt leaves themselves; impure carbonate of potash or soda: saline or brackish soil: ground recovered from the sea.

Khárá, or *Khárí*, H. &c. (کھارا, کھاري) Saline, alkaline, brackish.

Khárá-páni, incorrectly, *Kárá-panee*, H. (کھاراپاني) Water impregnated with soda and alkaline earths.

Khárat, Mar. (खारट) Ground recovered from the sea.

Khári-shor, H. (کھاري شور) Very brackish and saline (as water).

Khári-zamín, or, vernacularly, *Khárá-jamin*, H. &c. (کھاري زمين) Saline soil: land impregnated with alkaline salts.

Kárubhúmi, Tel. (కారుభూమి) Brackish, a saline soil.

Khári-nimak or *-nún*, H. (from P. نمك or H. نون, S. लवण, salt) A factitious kind of salt: a kind of sulphate of soda used in medicine and for the adulteration of common salt: in Orissa it is applied to the hard saline settlement at the bottom of the salt-pans.

Khári-maṭṭi or *miṭṭi* (کھاري مٹي), *Kshâramrittiká*, S. and Beng. (क्षारमृत्तिका) Brackish or saline soil, a soil impregnated with alkaline salts, as potash or nitre, and therefore unfit for cultivation. (This word is not to be confounded with *Kharimiṭṭí*, q. v.).

Khárík, or *Khár-khánḍá*, Mar. (खारीक, खारखण्डा, the latter used contemptuously) A class, or an individual of it, employed in cultivating salt-marshes or saline soils.

Khárwá-máṭí, Hindi (खारवामाटी) Alkaline soil.

KHARA, Karn. (S. ಖರ, खर) The twenty-fifth year of the cycle.

Kharā́, Mar. (खडा) A pebble, a nodule of limestone, a lump of sugar.

Kharak, Thug. Noise made by the pickaxe in digging a grave.

Kharhak, H. (کهرهك, खरहक) A portion of grain given at the end of the harvest to the village servants.

Khaṛi, Khuṛee, also **Khaṭí, Khaṭika**, H. &c. (کهڑی, খড়ি, S. खटिका) Chalk: white clay used for plastering; also a kind of clay found in some parts of Bengal, and used in pottery; also, in Bengal, a coarse kind of grass used for thatching.

Khaṛimaṭṭí or *-miṭṭí*, *Khuṛeemuttee* or *-mittee*, H. &c. (کهڑی مٹی) Chalk, also a sort of porcelain clay. (This differs from *Khárimiṭṭí* as above, in being written with the short *a* and the hard *ḍ* or *ṛ*, instead of a long *a* and a soft *r*).

Kháṛá, Beng. (খাড়া, from the H. کهڑا), also **Khárá** (খারা) Erect; also, fig., honest, upright; payable on demand.

Kháṛá-hundí, Beng. (খাড়াহুণ্ডী) A bill of exchange payable at sight.

Kháṛá-jama, Beng. (খাড়াজমা) The entire rent or assessment.

Khaṛá-utár, Guz. (ખડાઉતાર) Payable at sight—a bill, &c.

Kharáb, H. (A. خراب) Bad, wicked, worthless, spoiled: bad, as land unfit for cultivation.

Kharába, H. (خرابه) Ruin, desolation: waste land, unproductive (as land).

Kharábáhwál, H. (خراباحوال) Ruined, wretched, either person or place.

Kharádí, H. (A. خرادی) A turner, a carpenter.

Kharaṛá, Uriya (ଖରଡ଼ା) Receipt, acquittance, receipt given to cultivators for rent.

Kharaṛá pani, Uriya (ଖରଡ଼ାପଣି) Fee for writing a receipt.

Kharaṛá patra, Uriya (from S. पत्र, a leaf) A written receipt.

Kharch, Khurch, or **Kharcha**, or, more correctly, **Kharj**, **Khurj**, of which it is the Hindustani modification, corruptly, **Khirch, Kurtch, Khurchee** (خرچ, A. خرج, pl. *Ikhráját*; from *Kharaja*, went forth): it occurs in most dialects in the first form; as, **Kharach**, Beng. (খরচ), **Kharcha**, Mar. (खर्च), **Kharchu**, Tel. (ఖర్చు) Expense, disbursement, out-goings: the authorised expenses incurred by a village or district, and set off against the revenue receipts, or a cess levied upon the cultivators to provide for expenses; the debit side of an account, the account of the disbursements or outgoings.

Kharcha-hisáb, Beng. (P. حساب, an account) A village annual account kept in Bengal, shewing the amount of the rent due on each Ryot's land in cultivation, the amount paid, and the balance outstanding.

Kharch-awarjá, Tel. (అవర్జా) An abstract account of the disbursements of a district, or of the deductions from the collections.

Kharch-i-gáon, corruptly, *Khirch-gram*, and, more usually and correctly, *Grám-kharch*, H. (خرچگاون) Village expenses, charges levied by the headmen or public officers to provide for the expenses incurred by the officers or servants of the village community.

Kharch-i-khairát, H. (خرچخیرات) A charge or allowance for charitable gifts or endowments.

Kharch-i-mufaṣṣil, H. (خرچمفصّل) Provincial charges, expenses of collection and other authorised items of expenditure deducted from the gross revenue of a province. An extra cess levied in Jessore for provincial expenses prior to the permanent settlement.

Kharch-i-nánkár, H. (خرچنانکار) Allowance or deduction from the revenue of an estate, as the subsistence money of the Zamindar.

Kharch-paṭṭí, Mar. (खर्चपट्टी) A tax for defraying occasional public charges: extra expenses in a district, as for roads, bridges, &c.: the recognised dues of the village officers and servants.

Kharch-i-pargana, H. (خرچپرگنه) Charges incurred in the management and revenue-collections of a Pargana or district.

Kharch-i-sadr, H. (خرچسدر) Charges on account of the establishment of the principal local authorities.

Kharchaṣilak, Mar. (खर्चशिलक, A. سلك) Balance after expenditure, money in hand.

Kharchu-vechcha, Karn. (ಖರ್ಚುವೆಚ್ಚ) Expenditure, disbursement.

Kad-kharch, H. (P. بد, bad) Cesses of an oppressive nature, and in excess of the stipulated rents exacted on various pretexts from the cultivators by the Zamindars. *Puraniya*.

Khaṛeband, (खडेबंद) A day-book, a journal, an account drawn out on a loose piece of paper.

Kharj, H. (A. خرج, from *kharaja* خرج, went forth) Tribute, tax, revenue.

Kharáj, or, more commonly, and equally correctly, **Khiráj**, corruptly, **Kheraj**, H. (A. خراج) Tax, tribute; applied originally in an especial manner to the tribute levied by Mohammadans upon infidels after conquest, but latterly to the revenue raised from the land, in which sense it is still employed, importing the amount claimed by the state as its rent or share of the profits of land in cultivation: hence *Lá-khiráj* (q. v.) designates lands which are exempted from any such payment.

Kharáji, or *Khiráji*, H. (خراجي) Taxable, subject to tribute or taxation.

Khiráji-bhúmi, Tel. (ఖిరాజిభూమి) Land paying revenue to government.

Kharáj or *Khiráj-guzár*, H. (from P. گزار, who passes or pays over) A payer of revenue to government, whether on his own account or as the representative of others.

Khiráji-zamín, H. (P. زمين) Land paying revenue.

Khiráj-muwazzaf, H. (A. موظف, fixed) Revenue of which the amount is fixed at a certain rate for a specific quantity of land.

Khiráj-muhásima, H. (A. مقاسمه, divided) Revenue collected at a certain rate upon the produce of land, and varying, therefore, with its quantity and value.

KHARERI, Thug. The small owl.

KHARENJA, Thug. A ravine or water-course.

KHÁRIJ, H. &c. (A. خارج, from *kharaja* خرج), KHERÍJ, Mar. (खेरीज) Excluded or separated from, extraneous to, external, additional.

Khárijálu, Tel. (ఖారిజాలు) Fees deducted from the gross produce of village lands.

Khárij-dákhil, also, *Dákhil-khárij*, q. v. (خارج داخل) Excluding and including, applied to the transfer of property, especially to lands transferred from one name to another in the collector's books.

Kháriji, or *Khárji*, H. (A. خارجي) A person who separates himself from a community or a religious faith, a seceder, a schismatic, a rebel. A member of a Mohammadan sect which excludes *Áli* from the number of Khalifs.

Khárij-jamâ, corruptly, *Kharege-jumma*, H. (A. جمع, collection) Separated or detached from the rental of the state, as lands exempt from rent, or of which the revenue has been assigned to individuals or institutions.

Kheríj-jamâ, Mar. (खेरीजजमा) Extra collections, miscellaneous items of revenue.

Kheríj-maktá, Mar. (खेरीजमक्ता) Lands let out by government direct, without the intervention of any one between it and the cultivators.

Khárij-mulk, Uriya (A. ملك, a kingdom) Transportation, banishment.

Kheríj-múșáhirá, Mar. (खेरीजमूशाहिरा) Contingent charges, extras, presents, occasional allowances.

Khárij-náma, H. (from P. نامه, a document) A deed of separation or division, a deed for the partition of a joint estate, or for the separation of an individual share, or for making a dependent *tâluķ* separate and independent, also, simply a deed of transfer.

Khárija-tâluķ, H. (from تعلق) Separation of a portion or dependency of an estate, or of a Pargana, from the general assessment, and the payment of the revenue due from it direct to the government.

KHARDÁ, or KHARDEṆ, or commonly, KHURD, Mar. (खरडा, खरडें) A rough note or memorandum, a draft, a scrawl, a waste-book. Maratha shopkeepers and bankers usually keep two such accounts; one the *Kachcha-khard*, or rough day-book; the other the *Paka-khard*, or cash-book in which the entries of the former are copied fair.

KHARÍ, Mar. (खरी) A patch of earth on a rocky substratum but cultivable for rice.

KHÁRÍ, Beng. Mar. &c. (S. खारी) A measure of grain equal to sixteen *droṇas*, or about three bushels.

Khárikam, Mal. (ഖാരികം) A field that requires, or that is sown with, a *khárí* of seed.

KHARÍD, H. (P. خريد) Bought, also the thing bought, buying.

Kharída, corruptly, *Khereeda*, (P. خريده) Bought, purchased. In Cuttack, the designation of a kind of tenure created by the district officers who sold small parcels of land which were ostensibly waste, and excluded from the rent-roll, or reported as exempt from revenue: where the purchase was without suspicion of fraud the purchasers were allowed to retain the *Kharída* lands at a quit-rent: it is also termed *Milk-kharídagí*, ownership or lordship by purchase.

Kharíd-dár, abridged vernacularly to *Kharidár*, H, &c. (خريدار) A purchaser, a holder by purchase: in Cuttack, the proprietor of purchased estates.

Kharída-muáfí, H. (A. معافي, exempt) Lands in Cuttack claiming exemption from revenue as having been bought under that condition.

Kharíd-farohht, A. (P. فروختن, to sell) Buying and selling.

Kharídí, corruptly, *Khereedy*, (خريدي) Purchasing, or relating to purchasing.

KHARÍF, KHUREEF, written vernacularly KHARIP, and

KHARIPH, corruptly, KHEREEF, H. &c. (A. خريف) The season of autumn; the autumnal harvest; the crops which are sown before the commencement of the rains, or in April-May, and reaped after their close, October-November.

KHARIPAṬÍ, Guz. (ખરીપટી) A tax collected to relieve a village from debt.

KHARÍṬA, KHUREEṬU, sometimes, vernacularly, KHALÍTA, H. &c. (A. خريطه) A bag, a purse, the envelope of a letter, especially the ornamental or silk covering of a letter addressed to, or by, a native of rank: hence, the letter itself, particularly one passing between a native prince and the governor-general.

KHARKANÍYA, Thug. Crossing of the road by a hare in front of the party, a bad omen.

KHARKHÁ, Thug. An ass.

KHARPAṚ, Mar. (खरपड) A bad year, a time of distress from failure of the crops.

KHARRÁṬ, H. (A. خرّاط) A turner's lathe, a turner (also KHARRÁṬI.

KHARTÁI, or KHARTAL, Thug. Any bad omen. Dakh. Th.

KHÁṚU, Uriya (ଖାଡ଼ୁ) Division of bullocks among cultivators.

KHÁRU, Thug. A gang of Thugs.

KHÁRŪÁ, or KHÁRWÁ, corruptly, KURWA, H. (كهاروا) A coarse kind of cotton cloth dyed red, and used in various ways, especially to wrap up books, parcels, &c.

KHARVATA, S. &c. (खर्व्वट) A country or market-town.

KHARWÁR, H. (P. خروار) A measure, said to be about 700lb., lit. an ass load: in Sindh it is called 850lb.

KHÁRWÍ, Mar. (खारवी) A caste employed in tiling houses, making plantations, &c.

KHAS, KHUS, or KHASKHAS, KHUSKHUS, H. (P. خس, خسخس) A fragrant grass (Andropogon muricatum) with the roots of which, interwoven with wicker-work, door and window-screens are made that are kept wet, and serve to cool the air as it passes through them into the room.

KHÁṢ, corruptly, KAS, KHASS, COSS, H. &c. (A. خاص) Select, eminent, noble; also private, peculiar: under the Moghul government it was applied to the chief officers of the state and the nobles of the court: as a revenue term it is applied to the management of estates and the collection of the revenue by the officers of the government, without any intermediate person between them and the cultivators, also to lands held by Zamindars and cultivated by themselves for their own benefit.

Khás-ápíl, from the English, Appeal, Uriya (ଖାସଅପିଲ) A special appeal.

Kháṣ-ajír, H. (A. خاص اجير) Private or domestic servants, whether slaves or hired.

Khásá, pl. *Khásálu*, Tel. (ఖాసా, ఖాసాలు) Own, private, applied especially, in some parts of the Northern Cirkars, to domestic servants or hereditary slaves.

Khásárambha-bhúmi, Karn. (ಖಾಸಾರಂಭಭೂಮಿ) Lands cultivated by Zamindars through their own domestic slaves.

Khás-bandí, Mar. (खासबंदी) Distribution of the lands of a village, without regard to contiguity, amongst certain families, and the assessment of each estate in the lump, without reference to measurement or rating.

Khás-bighá, Mar. (खासबीघा) The measure of land both as to quantity and quality, by which the rental of the estate of an occupant in a *Khás-bandí* village is estimated.

Kháṣ-bardár, H. (خاصبردار) An attendant carrying the arms of his lord: one armed with a firelock.

Khás-bál, Mar. (खासबाल) A mixed soil of sand and clay, yielding good crops if manured.

Khás-bátamí, Mar. (खास बातमी) Authentic or official accounts.

Kháṣ-bo, H. (from بونا, to sow) Land under the management of the Raja. Kuch Bahar.

Kháṣ-chelá, H. (from چيلا) The chief disciple and destined successor of the Mahant or head of a religious establishment of ascetics or mendicants.

Khás-dár, Mar. (खासदार) A groom, a horsekeeper: sometimes corrupted to *Kázdár*.

Khásgí, Mar. (खासगी) One's own private or personal property, in contradistinction to the revenues or concerns of the state; own, personal, peculiar.

Khásgí-paihá, Mar. (from पैका, money) One's own or private cash.

Khásgí-hárkún, Mar. (from कारकून) A private or confidential agent, clerk, or manager.

Khásgíwálá, Mar. (खासगीवाला) A title usually given to the confidential minister of the Peshwa or other Maraṭha prince, who was especially intrusted with the management of their private receipts and disbursements, or other personal interests.

Kháṣ-hál, H. (from A. حال, condition) A kind of rent-free tenure: in Sylhet, the lands cultivated by the Zamindar himself, and for his own maintenance.

Kháṣ-mahal, H. (A. محل) The female apartments.

Khás̤-mahál, H. (A. plur. of محل) Districts held in the management of the government.

Khás̤-navís, H. (P. نويس) A private secretary, a clerk or accountant of the government.

Khás̤-navísí, H. (P. نويسي) Relating to government accountants: an *abwáb*, or tax, formerly levied in Bengal from the Zamindars for the expense of the government officers of account employed in registering the annual revenue settlements.

Khás̤-o-áám, H. (A. خاص وعام) High and low, noble and vulgar; *i.e.* all classes of persons.

Khásрatah, Mar. (खासपतक) One's own private troop of horse.

Khás-ságuvaḷi, Karn. (ಖಾಸಸಾಗುವಳಿ) Cultivation of lands by the government for its own benefit, or by a Zamindar on his own account.

Kháswári, Karn. (ಖಾಸ್ವಾರಿ) A stud or troop of horses: but it is no doubt the same word as *Khás̤-sawárí*, H. (خاص سواري) said to be a respectful phrase for a person of rank, equivalent to your lordship; also a circuit made by a commanding officer: and as *Khásáswárí*, Mar. (खासास्वारी), the equipage or train of a Raja.

Khás̤-tahs̤íl, H. (A. خاص تحصيل) Collection of the revenue direct from the cultivators by the government, without the intervention of a Zamindar or farmer of the revenue.

Khás̤-tâluḳ, H. (A. خاص تعلق) A *tâluk*, or certain district under the immediate management of the state: the Nawabs of Bengal formerly selected such tracts, and occupied them for their own benefit; but the term is now applied to estates which, in consequence of the default of the occupant, or his death without heirs, are kept in the hands of the state and managed by the government officers.

Khás̤ zamín, or, vernacularly, *jamín*, H. (خاص زمين) Land of which the collection is made by the government officers immediately from the cultivators.

Khasara, or Khasárat, or Khisárat, H. (A. خسر, خسارت) Damage, injury, loss, fraud: the plea of a suit for damages: loss on a repeated sale, difference in diminution between the result of a first and second sale.

Khásia, H. (?) The designation of the people of the hill provinces.—Garhwal.

Khasrá, Khusra, H. (کهسرا, खसरा) A day-book, a journal, a field-book, especially a written record of the particulars of a rough map or plan of a village, which is called a *Shajra*, in which the fields are numbered, and their numbers are registered in the field-book, or *Khasrá*, corresponding: in this also is registered the name of the proprietor and of the cultivator of each field, whether the same or different, the name of each field, its length and breadth in *gaṭhás*, and its area in *bíghás* and *biswás*, the quality of the soil, the crop growing upon it, and any remarks that it may be thought advisable to add.

Khasrá-bahí, H. (from بهي, a book) A field-book, a book in which the *khasrá* tables or lists are entered.

Khasrá-paimáish, H. (P. پيمايش, measurement) The register or statement of a land survey or measurement.

Khástábaki, Beng. (খাস্তাবাকি, P. خواسته, what is required, and A. باقي, remainder) Balance of revenue left due after a portion has been realised by the sale of the defaulter's estate.

Khástá-nílám, Beng. (from নীলাম, sale) Balance or deficit left by a sale by auction, the proceeds of which are not equal to the demands against the property sold.

Khaṭṭ, or Khuṭṭ, H. (A. خط), Khat, Khut, Mar. (खत) A letter, a writing, an entry in a book, a written document, as a note of hand, a deed of mortgage, &c.

Khet-khaṭ, H. (کهيت خط) A deed of sale or mortgage for a field, or a portion of a coparcenary estate, conveying the land alone, without the privileges attached to it.

Khunt-khaṭ, (کهنت خط) A deed by which the rights of a coparcener in a village or estate are conveyed to another person as well as the land.

Karjkhat, Mar. (कर्जखत) A note of obligation, or promise to pay.

Gahán khat, Mar. (गहाणखत) A note of assurance that a pledge will be redeemed.

Gharenáü-khat, Guz. (ઘરેણાઉખત) A mortgage deed.

Fárigh-khat, q. v. A deed of acquittance.

Pharokht khat, Mar. (फरोक्त खत, from P. فروخت) A deed of sale.

Vechán khat, Guz. (વેચાણખત) A bill of sale, a deed of conveyance.

Khát, H. Mar. (کهات, खात) Manure, filth so applied: in H., also, *Kháḍ* and *Khúo* (کهاد, کهاو).

Khátáṛ, Mar. (खाताड) The spot outside a village where the filth is thrown.

Khát-bikrí, Mar. (खातविक्री) Sale of manure on government account.

Khátwaṛ, Mar. (खातवड) Well manured, rich, as a field or soil.

KHÁT, Thug. A bribe. Dakh. Thug.

KHÁTÁ, H. (کهاتا), Beng. (খাতা), KHÁTEN, Mar. (खातें), KHÁTU, Guz. (ખાતુ) An account-book, a day-book, a journal or ledger, also an account; account current—one kept with an individual, or of a particular concern with respect to the receipts and outlay upon it; an account of real or personal property; also, the paper or book in which such accounts are kept.

Kháte-báki, Mar. (खातेबाकी) The balance for or against a tradesman's books.

Khátá-bahí, H. (کهاتا بہی), *Khátevahí*, Mar. (खातेवही) An account-book, a day-book, or one framed from the day-book, a ledger.

Khátedár, Mar. (खातेदार) A mercantile correspondent, one with whom an account is opened.

Khátáwári, Beng. (খাতাবারি) Entries in a ledger.

Khátápotá, Guz. (ખાતાપોતા) Commercial dealings, buying and selling.

KHÁTÁ, Guz. (ખાતા) The holding of a Ryot or cultivator.

Khátâ bandi, Guz. (ખાતાબંદી) Assessment of each Ryot's holdings; a Ryotwar assessment.

KHAṬÁ, KHUṬA, H. (A. خطا) Fault, offence, crime.

KHÁṬÁ, Tel. (ఖాటా) Large scales for weighing grain in sacks.

KHATAÏ, Thug. Information of, or hostility to, a gang, or of some of its members, owing to a quarrel.

Khatiaï, Thug. Information against a gang.

Khatowa, Thug. A Thug informing against his confederates.

KHÁTAKA, Beng. (খাতক) A borrower, a debtor.

Khátakí, Beng. (খাতকী) Relating to a loan, a promissory note or bond.

KHÁṬAKA, or KHÁṬAKÍ, Mar. (खाटक, खाटकी) A caste, or an individual of it, who is by avocation a butcher.

KHÁṬAN, or KHÁṬANI, Beng. (খাটন, খাটনি) Labouring, working for hire.

Kháṭaní, Beng. (खाटनी) Wages or hire of labour, pay of a workman or labourer.

Kháṭaníyá, Beng. (খাটনীযা) A workman, a labourer.

KHATÁÜNÍ, KHUTAONEE, corruptly, KHUTEONEE, KHUTTEONI, KUTTOWNEE, KHATIOWNEE, KUTTEEANEE, KUTAMUNNEE, CUTEEAN, or CUTTEAN, H. (کهتاونی), KHATÁWANÍ, which may be pronounced KHATAÖNI, Mar. (खतावणी), KHATIYÁN, KHATIYÁNI, Beng. (খতিযান, খতিযানি), KATÁVANI, or KATÁONI, Tam. (கதாவணி) A ledger, an account-book, one in which are entered, under distinct and appropriate heads, the several items first entered in a day-book or field-book: although differently explained by different authorities, and occasionally modified as to its application, the term always denotes accounts of the nature of the ledger: thus it is said the Maraṭha Sáhukár's *khatáwani* is made up from his *kharda*, or day-book, in the order of the names of his constituents: in the government financial accounts it was a statement of all expenses and disbursements, arranged alphabetically under their several heads: in Guz. it is said to mean the act of posting items from the day and cash-books into the ledger: in Bengal, the *khatiyán* was an abstract of the *chiṭás* kept by the village accountant, shewing the whole extent of land held by each cultivator, the nature of the tenure or cultivation, as *khúd-kásht*, &c., and the species of cultivation. In the north-western provinces the *khatáoni*, or, as there also denominated, the *muntakhab*, is an account made up from the *khasrá*, in which the fields belonging to each *thok*, *paṭṭí*, and individual are brought together, and then the name of the occupant, the number of each field, its extent, with deductions for waste or the like, the rate of assessment per *bíghá*, the total rent, and the manner of its payment, are recorded.

Ásámí-wár-khatiyán, Beng. (আসামীবারখতিযান) An account kept with each individual Ásámí or cultivator, made up from the *khasrá* or field-book, specifying the fields held by him, the extent of his lands, waste or cultivated, the amount of his assessment, and the particulars of his payments.

Khátábandí, H. (کهاتابندی) The same as the preceding: an abstract account or ledger.

Jinswár-khatiyán, Beng. (A. جنس, species) An abstract account of the different crops cultivated in a village or an estate, their highest and lowest culture, and the average produce of each kind per *bíghá*.

KHAṬB, H. (A. خطب) Marrying, betrothing, contracting a marriage.

KHATI, Mar. (?) A blacksmith: in Nagpur, the village blacksmith: in Hindustán, a wheelwright.

KHATIRÍ, H. (?) A crop raised in the sand on the banks of a river by force of manure or hand watering: a nominal rent only is paid for such sowings. Agra.

KHATN, H. (A. ختن) The husband of a man's female relations with whom his own intermarriage is interdicted.

KHATN, KHATNA, KHATNAT, H. (A. ختن . ختنه , ختنت) Circumcision.

KHAṬPAURÁ, H. (کھٹپورا, खटपौरा) A kind of rake worked by two men for breaking up the soil into small beds.

KHATRÍ, corruptly, KHATRY, KHETREE, KHETERY, H. (کھتری, S. *kshatriya* क्षत्रिय) The man of the second pure tribe, the soldier and the sovereign caste. Mar. (खत्री) A caste, or individual of it, who is a silk-weaver.

KHAṬUÁ, Uriya (ଖଟୁଆ) Chief cattle-driver.

KHAUR, Thug. An army.

KHAWÁṢ, H. (A. خواص, properly, plur. of خاص) Nobles, grandees: attendants, personal servants, usually the favourite or confidential attendant on a person of rank: a boy or female servant: in the west of India the children of a female slave belonging to a Cháran or Rajput, the property of the owner of the slave, but treated as a member of the family: the word, written *Chiaus*, is the origin of the English word *Chouse.* In Puraniya the term is applied to slaves in general, whether domestic or agricultural, but the *khawáṣ* is usually originally a free person who has become a voluntary slave for protection and support, and, in some cases, has a grant of land from the Zamindar for his subsistence: another kind of *khawáṣ* is more of a client or retainer of some wealthy person than a slave, although nominally such.

KHÁWIND, or KHÁWAND, H. (P. خاوند), vernacularly, KHAMIND, Uriya, KHÁMAND, Tel. A lord, a master.

KHAZÁNA, KHUZANU, corruptly, CAJANA, or, more correctly, though less commonly, KHIZÁNA, H. (P. خزانه), vernacularly, KHAJÁNÁ, as Beng. (খজানা), also KHAJÍNÁ, Mar. (खजाना, खजीना), Tel. (ఖజానా) A treasury, the public treasury: treasure, money: the public revenue, the land-tax.

Khazánchí, or *Khuzanchee*, or, vernacularly, *Khajánchí*, corruptly, *Khajomchi*, H. &c. (خزانچی) A treasurer, a cash-keeper.

KHEDÁ, corruptly, KEDDAH and KEHDAH, H. (کهیدا) An inclosure in which wild elephants are caught: (it is derived from کهیدنا, to chase, but is probably a word of Bengali or Sanscrit origin, from Beng. খেদা, to chase cattle, S. आखेट, hunting.)

Khedá-i-afiyál, (A. افیال, plur. of *fil* فیل, an elephant) Expenses incurred in catching wild elephants, for which, under the Mohammadan government, a tax was levied upon certain districts in Bengal and Sylhet: the cess or abwáb so levied

KHÉḌ, or KHEṚ, Guz. (ખેડ) Ploughing, tillage.

Kheḍán, Guz. (ખેડાણ) Land under tillage.

Kheḍut, Guz. (ખેડુત) A cultivator, an agriculturist.

KHEḌE, Mar. (खेडे, S. खेटक) A small, and chiefly agricultural village.

KHEMKUṢAL, H. (کهیمکسل, from S. क्षेम, and कुशल) Welfare, prospering, both in personal health and worldly affairs.

KHEP, H. (کهیپ, S. क्षेप) A trip (in a boat or vessel) a cargo: a cracked or adulterated coin.

KHEPÍÁ, Guz. (ખેપીઆ) A courier, a messenger, a letter-carrier, an intelligencer, a spy.

KHEṚÁ, H. (کهیڑا) A village. See KHEḌE (it is the same word): in Bundelkhand it is the land immediately adjacent to a village.

KHESÁRÍ, Beng. (খেসারী) A sort of pulse much cultivated for food (Lathyrus sativus).

KHET, H. &c. (کهیت, खेत, S. क्षेत्र) A field, a tract of land especially fit for cultivation; a cultivated field: an agricultural division of land, in Bengal, formerly considered as equal to 60 *bíghás.*

Khet-bánṭ, H. (کهیت بانٹ), vernacularly corrupted, in Hindi, to *Khat* or *Khet-baṭ*, (کهت بٹ) Allotment of the lands of a coparcenary village, field by field, among the sharers, but in such a manner that they shall not be contiguous, or of the same quality, but so divided that each may have a due proportion of good and bad land: the term, however, has other explanations, and most correctly implies the mode in which a *Mauza*, is divided into two or more mahâls or estates; and it is commonly applied to denote the intermixture of the lands of different villages, which, although known as belonging to one village, are found lying amongst those belonging to another: in one or two instances the lands of the same *mahál* or estate are entirely scattered amongst those of others.

Khet-chiṭṭhá, H. (کهیت چٹها) Rough field-book, or notes of the fields of a tract surveyed.

Khet-dár, H. (P. دار, who has) The occupant or owner of a field.

Khet-khaṭṭ, H. (کهیت خط) Mortgage of a field: see خط.

Khetí, H. &c. (کهیتی) Relating to a field; a husbandman, a cultivator: cultivation, agriculture.

Khetíbári, H. (کهیتی باری) Agriculture, tillage.

Khetihar, H. (کهیتیهر) A cultivator.

Khetípatárí, Hindi (खेतीपतारी) Agricultural labour, field work.

Khet-jharti, Mar. (खेतझडती) Annual account of the fields of a village to be kept by the *Kulkarní*.

Khetwár, H. (كهيتوار) By fields; the assessment that is made upon each separate field according to its capability of yielding produce, and the description of the latter grown in it.

Khetwár-jamâbandí, H. (A. H. جمعبندي, q. v.) Amount of the revenue assessed upon each field.

KHEWÁ, or KHEWÁÍ, H. (كهيوا, كهيواي) Fare, ferry or passage money.

Khewat, *Khewatiá*, H. (كهيوت, كهيوتيا, खेवट) A ferry-man, a boat-man, a rower; also, *Khewak*, H. (كهيوك).

KHEWAT, (?) H. A contribution sometimes levied by the former government of Bengal on rent-free lands, when the lands assessed were unable to pay the amount, in order to compensate for any deficit in the revenue: a contribution among the coparceners of a village to the village expenses: in the north-west provinces, the record or register of the shares in which a coparcenary village is distributed: assessment with the Ryots according to their shares.—Ajmír.

Khewat-náma, H. (P. نامه) A document or statement of liabilities.

KHIÁNAT, also written KHIYANAT, (A. خيانت) Perfidy, treachery, embezzlement: in law, breach of trust, violation of an engagement.

Khaïn, H. (خين) A traitor: one who violates an engagement, or is culpable of a breach of trust.

KHIÁR, H. (خيار ? A., see the next word) Second sort of land of two species: first and second, in a classification of the lands of Dinajpur.

KHIÁR, A. (خيار) Option, selection: in Mohammadan law an optional completion or dissolution of an agreement of sale under various circumstances.

Khiár-ul-kabúl, (قبول, consent) Option of refusing to accept the terms offered before the parties separate.

Khiár-ul-majlis, (مجلس, an assembly) Option of retracting an assent before the parties separate.

Khiár-ul-ruyat, (رويت) Option of inspection, the right of a purchaser to reject what he has bought without seeing it.

Khiár-ul-âib, (عيب, fault) Option of rejecting an article bought if any defect is discovered in it.

Khiár-us-shart, (شرط, an agreement) Option of either party to annul the sale within three days, or a longer period, if agreed upon mutually.

Khiár-ut-tâyín, (تعيين) Option of the purchaser of one of several similar articles to make his own selection: other circumstances are enumerated by which sales may be optionally annulled.

KHICHRÍ, H. (كهچري), Beng. (খিচড়ি), KICHCHIDI, Karn. (ಕಿಚ್ಚಡಿ) An Indian dish of rice boiled with split pulse and spices; hence, fig., any common mixture, a confusion, hotch-potch.

Kichchidi-báchidi, Karn. (ಕಿಚ್ಚಡಿಬಾಚಿಡಿ) Turmoil, confusion, disorder.

KHIDMAT, H. (A. خدمت) Service, office.

Khidmatgár, or *Khidmat-dár*, (from H. گار, or P. دار), incorrectly, *Kidmutgar*, *Kismutgar*, and *Kitmutgar*, H. A servant, a table-servant, a personal attendant: in the Northern Cirkars usually a slave.

Khádim, H. (A. خادم) A servant, an attendant, one who is employed in the care of a shrine or mosque.

Khádim-i-dargáh, H. (خادم درگاه) An attendant on a Mohammadan tomb or mosque.

Khidmat-i-tâluhdárí or *zamindárí*, H. The service or office of a Tâlukdár or Zamindar.

KHIL, or KHÍL, Beng. (S. খিল, খীল), Mal. (ഖിലം) Waste or uncultivated land, though capable of being brought into cultivation.

Khil-jamá, Beng. (খিলজমা) Assessment of waste lands newly brought into cultivation.

Khil-jamín, Beng. (খিলজমীন) Land lying fallow or uncultivated.

Khil-patit, Beng. (from S. পতিত, fallen) Land excluded from the rent-roll in consequence of lying waste.

KHÍL, H. (كهيل) Parched grain.

KHILÁF-I-SHARÂ, H. (A. خلاف شرع) Contrary to the law, illegal.

KHILÂT, corruptly, KHELAUT, or KILLAUT, H. (A. خلعت) A dress of honour; any article of costume presented by the ruling or superior authority to an inferior as a mark of distinction: a complete *Khilât* may include arms, or a horse, or an elephant: in general it is some part of a native dress.

Khilât-bahá, H. (from P. بها, price) A cess, or abwáb, levied by the Mohammadan government to defray the cost of honorary dresses presented at court.

KHILWAT, or KHALWAT, H. (A. خلوت) Privacy, retirement.

Khilwat-khána, or *Khilwat-gáh*, H. (from P. خانه, a chamber, or گاه, a place) A private apartment, the women's apartments.

Khilwat-nashín, H. (P. نشين, who sits) A recluse, a hermit: a woman of rank; one who does not appear in public.

Khilwat-sahíh, H. (A. خلوت صحيح) Correct or lawful privacy; the retirement and cohabitation of husband and wife without natural or artificial impediment, constituting the validity of the marriage, and giving to the woman a full claim to her dower.

KHIND, Mar. (खिंड) A narrow path between two hills.

KHÍM, or KHEPNI, (?) H. Personal attendance by cultivators holding of a superior upon the chief in journeys.

KHIRMAN, H. (P. خرمن) A stack of corn, a granary, a barn.

KHIRUDU, Tel. (ఖిరుడు) Ground in cultivation.

KHISTI, Karn. (ಖಿಸ್ತಿ) Tribute; probably a vernacular form of KIST, q. v.

KHITÁB, H. (A. خطاب) A title.

KHO, or KHOÁ, corruptly, KOAR, Beng. (খো, খোআ) Coarse brick-dust or pounded bricks used in making roads, roofing houses, &c.

KHOBBA, Thug. Flesh meat: peculiar to Dakhini Thugs.

KHODÁ, Mar. (खोडा) Stocks for criminals.

KHODÁN, Guz. (ખોદાણ) Ground flooded or undermined by water.

KHODDA, Thug. An old man.

KHODELI, Thug. An eight ana piece.

KHODI, H. (كهودي) Digging, culture of land: ceremonies involving bodily labour, unremunerated except by food; Kamaon.

KHODWÁ, Mar. (खोडवा) Second crop of sugar-cane; cane sprouting from the stem of the first crop, also the latter left to bear shoots.

KHOÏ, H. (كهوي) Dry part of the sugar-cane after expressing the juice.

KHOJA, H. (خوجه), KHOJÁ, Mar. (खोजा), KHOJO, Guz. (ખોજો) A eunuch; corruption of *Khwája*, q. v. In Guz. a tribe of Indian Mohammadans.

KHOKHÁ, H. (كهوكها), KHOKÁ, or KHOKHÁ, Mar. (खोका, खोखा), KOKHUN, Guz. (ખોખું) A bill of exchange that has been paid and remains in the hands of the payer as a voucher.

KHOLÁDHAR, Guz. (ખોલાધર) A person who stands surety for a stranger demanding payment of a bill of exchange.

KHOKHÍ, Thug. Clearing the throat, a signal to prepare for action.

KHOLAMBHO, Guz. (ખોલંભો) Postponement, putting off.

KHOM, Thug. A door.

KHOMASNA, Thug. To rush at once upon travellers when there is not sufficient time for the usual forms.

KHONDAR, H. (كهوندر, खोंडर) Gleanings or leavings on the threshing-floor after the grain is removed.

KHONDU, Tel. (ఖొండు) Ripe grain.

KHONTÁ, H. (كهونٹا) Base, adulterated (as coin).

KHOPRA, H. (كهوپرا), KHOBREN, Mar. (खोबरें) The kernel of a cocoa-nut: the dried interior pulp.

Khobrel, Mar. (खोबरेल, from खोबरें, and तेल) Cocoa-nut oil.

KHORÁ, or KHORÉ, Mar. (खोरा, खोरें) A hollow or bottom between hills, a glen.

KHORÁ, Thug. Unlucky.

KHORÁÏ, Thug. Copper coin.

KHORAK, Thug. A horse; *Khorhání*, a mare.

KHORCHI, Thug. A barber.

KHORJAM, Tel. (ఖొర్జం) A bale or lot of twenty pieces, commonly called a *Corge*.

KHOSÁ, Beng. (খোসা) Husk of grain; shell of pulse; rind of fruit.

Khosán, Beng. (খোসান) Cleaning grain, separating it from the husk; shelling peas, &c.

Khosání, Beng. (খোসানী) Price of labour in husking grain, &c.

KHOSÁ, H. (كهوسا) Name of a marauding tribe in the sandy tract between Hindustan and Sindh, called the Thal.

KHOSMÁN, Thug. A Mohammadan.

KHOT, Guz. (ખોટ) A blunder: loss in trade, damages.

Khot-vadh, Guz. (ખોટવધ) Profit and loss.

KHOTA, or KHOT, Mar. (खोत) A farmer of land revenue or customs; any contractor or monopolist: in some of the Maratha provinces, an officer exercising hereditarily the office of collecting the government revenue, also one appointed to that duty.

Khot-báki, Mar. (from P. باقي) Balance of grain, &c. due from the cultivator to the landholder.

Khot-dhárá, Mar. (खोतधारा) The dues of the landlord from the cultivator or tenant.

Khotí, Mar. (खोती) The business or office of the hereditary or appointed collector, termed *khot*: contracting, farming; contracting for a crop of corn on the field.

Khotkí, or *Khotgí*, Mar. (खोतकी, खोतगी) The office of a collector, termed *khot*.

Khothharábá, Mar. (खोतखराबा) Waste lands about a village, of which the revenue is farmed and given to the farmer on his paying a fixed sum to the government.

Khotsajjá, (खोतसज्जा) Lands held of the landholder or farmer, in contradistinction to those held of government direct.

Khoṭpatra, Mar. (खोटपत्र, from खोट, false) A document acknowledging the falsehood of a claim or plea, written acknowledgment of error.

Khoṭverá, Mar. (खोटवेरा) An extra assessment to make up for some deficit in the revenue.

KHOUS, Thug. Return from an expedition.

KHOTAB, Thug. Interval between midnight and day-break.

KHUBRÍ, Beng. (খুবরী) A small hut.

KHÚD, KHOOD, H. &c. (P. خود) Self, own.

Khúdájarí páṭá, Beng. (খুদাজরী পাটা) An engagement by which, for a sum of money, a man makes himself the bondsman of another, either for a term of years or for life. (Sylhet.)

Khúd-kásht, corruptly, *Khode khasht*, P. (کاشتن, *káshtan*, to sow, as seed) Sowing or cultivating one's own ground. See *Kásht*.

Khúd-kásht râîat, H. (A. رعیت) A cultivator of his own hereditary land.

Khúd-kásht zamín, H. (A. زمین) Land cultivated by its hereditary occupant.

KHÚḌ, or KHÚṚ, H. (کهوڑ, खूड़) A furrow in a stiff soil.

KHUDA, but usually pronounced more like KHODA, and in some dialects, as in Bengali so written, H. (خُدا) Beng. (খোদা) God.

Khudá kare, H. (from کرنا, to do) Would to God! May God do!

Khudá-na-khwásta, H. (from P. خواستن, to will or wish) God forbid!

Khudáwánd, H. (P. خداوند) Master, lord, husband.

KHULÍMUDDAT, Mar. (खुलीमुद्दत, from H. *khula* کهولا, open, and A. *muddat*, مدّت, time) An undefined term or period for the performance of an engagement, payment of a debt, &c.

KHULṬÍN, A. (خلطين) A fermented liquor, infusion of dates and of raisins bottled together: it is not a prohibited liquor.

KHUḶÁ PAISÁ, Mar. (खुळापैसा) A small copper coin, current in some parts of the Dakhin: seven hundred go to a rupee.

KHÚM, KHOOM, vernacular for KAUM, q. v. Mar. (खूम), Tel. (ఖూము) People, tribe, class, caste.

Khúmwár, Mar. (खूमवार) By tribes or families, as taxes imposed on, statements of returned, or the like.

KHÚN, KHOON, H. &c. (P. خون) Blood; fig., murder.

Khún-bahá, (P. خونبها) Price of blood, mulct of retaliation.

Khúní, H. (خونی) A murderer, a shedder of blood.

Khúnrez, H. (P. خونریز) A murderer.

Khúntí, (?) Price paid to *Bhils* for protection from personal injury, black mail, price of blood.

KHÚṆ, KHOOṆ, Mar. (खूण) A mark, whence, a boundary-mark.

KHUNCHI, erroneously, KOONCHY, Beng. (খুঁচি) In dry measure, eight handfuls.

KHUṆḌÍ, Mar. (खुंडी) A sort of Jawári grown as a second crop in garden land, to serve as a green crop for cattle: the heads of the grain are also eaten.

KHÚNT, H. (کهونت) A share in the lands of a village by hereditary descent, and in all the privileges and rights which it involves.—Azimgerh.

Khúnt-bat or *-vat*, (H. वत *bat* or *vat*, implying possession) Tenure by ancestral shares in a village, as existing in Azimgerh.

Khúnt-khaṭ, H. (خونت خط) A deed of mortgage by which the mortgagee parts not only with his share of the *hhunt-vat* lands, but with all the rights and privileges attached to them.

Khúntaití, H. (خونتیتی) Payment of revenue according to the ancestral shares, without reference to the actual condition or produce of the shares.

KHUNṬÍ, Mar. (खुंटी) A peg or pin stuck in the ground, or a short stump of a tree as a land or boundary mark.

KHUNṬWÁ, Mar. (खुंटवा) A duty on vessels on coming to anchor or passing within a certain range.

KHÚRÁK, less correctly, but vernacularly, KHORÁK, H. &c. (P. خوراك) Food, daily food, allowance of food.

Khúráki, vernacularly, *Khoráki*, H. &c. (P. خوراكي) Allowance of food, or money for purchasing it; subsistence money.

Khúr-o-posh, written also, *Khor-o-posh*, H. (خوروپوش) Food and clothing, maintenance, which it is incumbent on the head of a family to provide.

Khúráhu, Tel. (ఖూరాకు) Subsistence money (see *Khuráki*) or fees paid by villagers to inferior servants employed to collect the government dues.

Khúráki-afiál, H. (A. plur. of *fíl*, an elephant) Food of elephants: a tax formerly levied in Sylhet to defray the cost of maintaining the elephants caught for government in the district.

KHÚRÁNT, H. (كهورانت) Old soil, soil trodden down by cattle with hoofs.

KHÚRD, H. (P. خورد) Little, small; used as the designation of a village or town, in opposition to *kalán*, great.

KHÚRDA, H. (P. خورده), Mar. (खुर्दा) The original implies eaten; but in vernacular use it implies, like the preceding, small, what is broken up into small parts or fragments, as small coins in exchange for large, and the like.

Khúrdagaṭá, or *Khúrdagí*, H. (خوردگي, خوردهگتّا) Changing money, giving pieces of smaller for one of larger value.

Khúrdah-farosh, H. (خورده فروش) A huckster, a dealer in petty wares.

Khúrdiá, H. (خورديا) A money-changer.

KHÚSH, H. (P. خوش) Pleased, pleasant, agreeable, &c.

Khúsh-básh, incorrectly, *Koosh-besh*, H. (P. باش, being, abiding) One who lives pleasantly or at his ease; applied variously in different places: in Sylhet, to a petty proprietor, one who possesses a small piece of ground, with a dwelling on it, for which he pays revenue; in Cuttack, to a resident in a village who pays no rent for the ground on which his dwelling stands; in Birbhúm it denoted a remission or assignment of revenue to enable the grantee to live more comfortably; in the Dakhin, and in other places, it usually means a cultivator holding land at an easy or quit-rent.

Khúsh-ḳabála or *kibála*, H. (A. قبالہ) A contract or engagement entered into willingly.

Khúsh-kharíd, H. (P. خريد) Purchase made willingly, without any constraint: what is purchased at once, without any advance or dispute.

KHUṚTAT, or KHUṚÁ, Beng. (খুড়তত, খুড়া) A father's younger brother; *Khuṛí* (খুড়ী), his wife.

KHUSHK, H. &c. (P. خشك) Dry.

Khushka, H. (P. خشكہ) Dry rice, rice boiled plain, without seasoning or other ingredients.

Khushkí, sometimes, vernacularly, *Khushi*, H. &c. (خشكي) Dryness, drought: dry land, land not artificially irrigated: by land in opposition to by water, as travelling.

Khushksál, H. (A. سال, a year) A year of drought or famine.

KHUṢÚMAT, H. (A. خصومت, from خصم, an enemy) Enmity, strife, litigation.

KHUṬBA, H. (A. خطبہ) A public prayer or discourse pronounced in the mosques at the Friday service, in which the prince is prayed for.

Khaṭíb, H. (خطيب) A preacher, a public reader or speaker.

KHWÁJA, but pronounced KHÁJA, and, corruptly, CAJA, KHOJA, H. (P. خواجہ) A rich or respectable man, a gentleman, an opulent merchant; also, vernacularly, *Khoja*, a eunuch.

Khwája-sará, H. (P. سرا, the inner apartments) A eunuch, one attached to the female apartments.

KHWÁND-KÁR, H. (P. خواندن, to read) A schoolmaster, one who teaches reading and writing.

KHYDARA, Thug. Any armed policeman, as a Barkandaz, Najíb, &c.

KIÁRI, H. (كياري) A bed in a garden; one in a field, especially for the plantation of rice in small squares, with raised borders to retain the water; a field surrounded by a high bank forming it into one large bed.

ḲIÁS, or ḲIYÁS, H. &c. (A. قياس) Reasoning, inference, logical deduction: in the absence of a positive law, judgment on the merits of a case.

Ḳiás náma, H. &c. A written judgment or decree.

ḲIBLA, H. (A. قبلہ, from قبل, what is placed before or opposite) The place to which Mohammadans look when praying, which is the direction of the temple of Mecca: any venerable person, one to whom another looks with respect.

Ḳibla-i-âálam, H. (A. قبلہ عالم) The *ḳibla* of the world, applied to a prince, His majesty, Your majesty.

Ḳibla-gáh, H. (from P. گاه, a place) The place to which the face is to be turned when praying; any august or venerable person when spoken of or to; as, a king, a father, Your majesty, Sire.

KIDAṆGU, Tam. (கிடங்கு) A tank, a pond; a store, a granary; a betel garden, a jail.

KIFÁYAT, or KIFAIAT, corruptly, KIFFUT, KEFFAYET, KEFFAYAT, H. (A. كفايت, from كفي, to be enough) Surplus, profit, advantage: profit or increase in the amount of revenue received by the government, whether by raising the rate of assessment or imposing additional taxes: in the old revenue accounts several items of increase are so denominated, as,

Kifáyat-i-hast-o-búd, H. (كفايت هست وبود) Increase of actual and past assessment founded on a revision of the value of the lands and resumption of illegal or lapsed alienations.

Kifáyat-i-Faujdárí, H. (كفايت فوجداري) Increased assessment on the frontier lands held by military governors, levied by them at first for their own benefit, but brought to the credit of the government by Kasim Ali Khan.

Kifáyat-i-sair, corruptly, *Keffyet sayer*, H. (كفايت سير) Increase of the revenue derived from miscellaneous items of taxation, whether effected by additional imposts or reduction of charges.

Kíl, A lake (?), Glossary, 5th Rep. Kíl, H. &c. (كيل), is more usually a stake, a pin, a peg.

Kilâ, H. (A. قلعه, more correctly, Ḳalâ, قلعه), vernacularly, Killá, Mar. (किल्ला), Beng. (কিল্লা) A fort, a fortress, a castle, a hill fort. In Cuttack the term applies to estates or Zamindárís in the jangal and hill tracts on the western border, some of considerable extent, paying tribute, but in some respects subject to their own Rajas : seventeen are enumerated—Ranpur, Naiaghar, Khandiapárá, Narsingpur, Báramba, Tigaria, Bánki, Áthgarh, Dekanál, Hindol, Angúl, Áthmalik, Talchír, Kyunjhar, Lera, Moharbanj, Nilghar; they are usually 200 or 300 square miles in extent, but Lera is only 20, whilst Angúl is calculated at 22,000, and Moharbanj at 15,000; they were no doubt originally named from the forts occupied by the Rajas who were held responsible for guarding the frontier against the wilder tribes to the west.

Ḳilâ, or *Killâdár*, or sometimes, vernacularly, *Killedar*, as Mar. (किल्लेदार), Karn. (ಕಿಲ್ಲೆದಾರ), H. &c. (قلعدار) The governor or commandant of a fort : in Cuttack, the holder of a fort and lands annexed on the principle of feudal service.

Ḳilla, or *Killedari*, H. &c. The office emoluments, &c., of a Killâdár.

Ḳiláját, H. (قلعجات, irr. plur. of قلعه) Forts : in Orissa the term is used collectively to designate lands chiefly in the hill country bordering on the plains, and held at a quit-rent on the tenure of military service in defending the low country from the ravages of the wild mountain tribes, for which, as well as their own safety, the Zamindars occupy numerous Kilás or forts.

Killá-vartálá, corruptly, *Kella-wurtullah*, Mar. (किल्ला वर्त्ताला) A cess imposed upon the peasantry in lieu of a reduction in the amount of the grain with which they were bound to supply the garrison of a fort.

Kilintu, Tel. (Port (?) కిలింటు) Port, clearance ; receipt for port dues paid.

Kílaka, S. &c. (कीलक) The forty-second year of the cycle.

Killari, also written Khillary, Mar. (?) The name of a tribe of migratory shepherds, feeding their flocks on all waste lands between the Taptí and Tungabhadrà, on paying a tax to the state.

Kíḻmadái, Tam. (கீழ்மடை) Land last watered, that which is most distant from the *madai*, or sluice.

Kílubhúmi, Karn. (S. ಕೀಳುಭೂಮಿ) Inferior land.

Ḳimár, H. (A. قمار) Dice, or any game of hazard.

Kimár-báz, H. (P. باز, who plays) A gambler.

Kimár-bázi, H. (P. بازي, playing) Gambling with dice or the like.

Ḳímat, Keemut, H. (A. قيمت) Price, value.

Ḳimát-i-Khisht-i-Gauṛ, H. (from P. خشت, a brick) A cess imposed by the Nawab of Bengal to defray the expense of bringing away, for public edifices, the enamelled bricks or tiles found in considerable quantities among the ruins of Gauṛ, the ancient capital of Bengal.

Ḳímatí, H. (قيمتي) Of price, precious, valuable.

Ḳimat rawáná, H. (P. روانا, going) A custom pass, in which the value of the goods that have paid duty is specified.

Kimkhwáb, corruptly, Kincob, H. (P. كمخواب), Kinkhab, Guz. (કીનખાબ) Silk stuff interwoven with gold or silver thread ; brocade.

Kiná, Beng. (কিনা) Purchase, purchasing.

Kinábiká, Uriya (କିଣାବିକା) Buying and selling.

Kinibáwálá, Uriya (କିଣିବାଓ୍ୱାଲା) A purchaser.

Kinára, H. &c. (كنارہ) Side, border, bank, shore.

Kiṇaṛu, Tam. (கிணறு) A well, a small well.

Kinḍan, Tam. (கிண்டன்) A kind of cotton cloth, commonly called gingham.

Kíníru, Tel. (?) Ground where water is found within about six feet below the surface.

Kiráḥíyat, H. (A. كراهيت) Disgust, abhorrence : in law, abominable acts, or abominations ; any infraction of moral or religious rules ; as, eating or drinking impure or prohibited articles, wearing unfitting attire, committing acts of indecency, &c.

Kírai, Tam. (கீரை) All sorts of greens and the edible leaves of trees.

Ḳirán, H. (A. قران) Conjunction of the planets : propinquity, being with or together : performing the pilgrimage to Mecca with other pilgrims.

Kiráṇá, or sometimes with jins (goods), Kiráṇá-jins, erroneously Carana-jins, Mar. (किराणा, किराणाजिंस) Groceries ; in commerce, under the head of *Kiráṇá* are included tea, sugar, spices, aromatics, almonds, raisins, cocoa and pistachio nuts, indigo, vermilion, alum, and various medicinal and dying drugs.

KIRAṚ, Mar. (?) A low tribe, whose occupation is to sell grass and exercise horses, (?) KIRÁT.

KIRÁT, S. &c. (किरात) A wild or forest tribe, barbarous races inhabiting the mountains, the Cirrhadæ of the ancients.

KIRÁYA, corruptly, KEERAY, H. &c. (A. كرايه), KERÁYÁ, Beng. (কেরাযা) Hire, rent, fare, freight; the money or rate at which any thing may be hired or rented; a small cess charged to the cultivator for the carriage of the crops to market. Karn. (ಕಿರಾಯು) Small fees in grain.

Kiráyadár, H. &c. (كرايهدار) A hirer, a renter.

Kiráyagárru, Karn. (pl. ಕಿರಾಯುಗಾರರು) Village servants paid by small fees in grain.

KÍRD, Mar. (P. कीर्द) An account or statement of receipts and disbursements: bringing lands into cultivation.

Kirdád, Karn. (ಕಿರ್ದಾದ) Tilled, fit for seed.

Kírdsár, Mar. (कीर्दसार) Arable, capable of being cultivated (land).

KIRÍCH, Beng. (কিরীচ), Uriya (କିରୀଚ) A long knife, a dirk, a dagger; perhaps the *Krís*, or *Creese* (كريس) of the Malays.

KÍRKÚḶ, or KÍRKOḶ, Mar. (कीरकूळ, कीरकोळ) Miscellaneous, petty, (as articles or goods), by retail.

Kírkolhám, Mar. (कीरकोळकाम) A job, a trifling or temporary business.

Kírkolprápti, Mar. (S. प्राप्ति, gaming) Petty profits.

KIRRÁṬ, A. (قرّات) A carat, the 24th part of an ounce.

KIRUKÓḶA, Karn. (ಕಿರುಕೋಳ) Unnecessary trouble and annoyance given to cultivators by inferior revenue officers.

KISÁN, H. &c. (S. كسان) A husbandman, a cultivator (more correctly *Kṛishán*).

ḲIṢÁṢ, corruptly, KISSAS, H. (A. قصاص) Retaliating: in law, retaliation for personal injury, claimable by the person injured, or, in the event of his death, by his next of kin.

KISHT, H. (P. كشت) A sown field.

Kishthár, H. (كشتكار) A husbandman, a cultivator.

Kishthárí, H. (كشتكاري) Cultivation, tillage.

Kisht-o-hár, H. (P. كشت وكار) Ploughing and sowing.

Kishtwár, H. (كشتوار) By fields, according to the cultivation.

Kishtzár, H. P. (كشتزار) A sown field.

KISHTÍ, H. (كشتي) A ship, a boat; an ornamented raft or float.

Kishtibán, H. (كشتيبان) A shipman, a boatman; the commander of a vessel.

ḲISM, H. (A. قسم) Kind, sort, species: partition, division; division of inheritance; equal partition of a husband's company amongst his wives.

Ḳismat, H. (A. قسمت) Share, distribution; share of prosperity, or the like, allotted to each person in life; hence by meton., fate, fortune: in law, partition of inheritance, also a separated or divided portion: applied in revenue matters to a portion of land detached from a larger division, as from a Tâluk or a Pargana, especially if subject to a different jurisdiction: a hamlet or dependent village.

Ḳismat náma, H. (from P. نامه) A deed of partition.

Ḳásim, A. (قاسم) A divider, a sharer; a public officer deputed by the Ḳáẓi to make a legal distribution of joint property.

Ḳismwár, corruptly, *Kessemwár*, H. (قسموار) According to its sort or kind: according to shares.

Ḳismwár-goshwárá, H. (قسموار گوشوارا) An abstract account of lands, classed according to their quality.

Ḳismwár jamâ bandí, H. (P. جمعبندي) An account of the assessment on the lands of a village or collectorate according to their quality.

KIṢORA, S. (किशोर) A youth, a boy, a minor, one under eighteen years of age.

ḲISṮ, H. (A. قسط), vernacularly modified, as KIST or KISTÍ, Beng. (কিস্ত, কিস্তি), KHIST, Mar. (खिस्त), KISTI, Tel. (కిస్తి), KISTI, or KISTU, Karn. (ಕಿಸ್ತಿ, ಕಿಸ್ತು) Instalstalment, portion; the amount paid as an instalment; the period fixed for its payment: as a revenue term it denotes the portion of the annual assessment to be paid at specified periods in the course of the year; such periodical payment is called a *Kist*. In Maraṭhi, *Khist* also implies various ruinous modes of borrowing money upon repayment by instalments.

Ḳisṯ- or *Ḳisṯi-bandí*, or *bundee*, H. (قسطي بندي), *Kistubandi*, Karn. (ಕಿಸ್ತುಬಂದಿ) Settlement of the instalments of the revenue both as to time and amount: a document given at the beginning of the year to the revenue payer by the collector or Zamindar, in which the time and amount of the instalments to be paid are specified: a counterpart statement of the same, kept by the receiver of the revenue, or a district account shewing the particulars of the instalments receivable: any document relating to fixed periodical payments of the revenue or of a debt.

Ḳisṯkár, H. (قسطكار) A payer of a debt or tax by instalments.

Ḳist-khiláfi, H. (from خلاف, contrary) Failure to pay the stipulated instalments.

Ḳist-munḳazi, H. (from A. منقضي, elapsed) An instalment in arrear, a past demand.

Kistuwáide, Karn. (ಕಿಸ್ತುವಾಯಿದೆ) Fixed period for paying an instalment.

KÍSWÁRÁ, Thug. A well.

ḲIṬÂ, H. (قطعه) A section, a fragment, a part. Beng. (কিতা) A share or piece of ground. KITTÁṆ, incorrectly, KEETA, Mar. (कित्तां) A word used in accounts to signify each item that is to be brought under a separate head; also for an item that is set down, but of which the particulars appear elsewhere; thus answering to miscellaneous, minor, broken, &c.

Ḳiṭâ-bandí, H. (قطعبندي, written *Khatabandí*, but ? if correctly) A mode of assessment formed upon an equal distribution among the cultivators of the good and bad soil of a village in like proportion, and holding each cultivator responsible for his share of both; also the assessment of the cultivators according to the shares of each, without advertence to the soil or the cultivation.

Kitá jaríb bandí, Hindi (किताजरीबबंदी) Specification of the dimensions of each field in a *Paṭṭa*, or lease.

Kitáwár, Beng. (কিতাবার) In portions or fragments, as a division of subordinate portions.

Ḳiṭáwári-baṭwárá, H. (بٹوارا) Partition of a joint estate in small subdivisions.

Kittábáb, Mar. (कित्ताबाब) Miscellaneous or undefined cess or charge, applied to an extra cess levied on a cultivator or village without any plea being assigned

Kittáwataní, corruptly, *wutnee*, Mar. (कित्तावतनी) A term applied to an item of local assessment, which, though actually levied, is omitted from the account, so as to reduce the apparent total, the object being to diminish the sum on which a per-centage is payable to the holders of assignments on the revenue.

KITA, Tel. (కిత, perhaps from the Arabic قطع) A heap of winnowed grain.

Kita-manikálu, and *Kita-tauvalu*, Tel. (?) Portions of winnowed grain taken from the heap and given to Brahmans and to the village servants.

KITÁB, H. &c. (A. كتاب) A book, a writing, a letter; as *the* book, it is applied to the Kuran of the Mohammadans, the Old Testament of the Jews, and the New Testament of the Christians.

Kitábat, H. (A. كتابت) A writing, a description, title of a book: in Mohammadan law, an engagement by which a slave is permitted to redeem himself, or work out his emancipation.

Kitábí, H. (A. كتابي) Relating to a book or writing; hence it is applied to the Jews and Christians by the Mohammadans, as in possession of scriptural authority, although, according to them, corrupted or superseded.

Kitáb-hukmí, H. (A. from حكم, an order) A letter from one Ḳáẓi or judge to another, containing an authenticated transcript of evidence taken in a case, the decision on which has been removed to the jurisdiction of the latter; any authoritative writing.

Kitáb-intiḳálí, H. (from A. انتقال) A book or record of transfers and other changes of property.

Kátib, H. (A. كاتب) A writer, a copyist, a scribe.

KITMITTI, Mar. (?) Applied to accounts in which interest is allowed on both debit and credit.

KIUN-KAL, (?) Tibetan. A duty of ten per cent. on the import of grain.—Kamaon.

Kiun-thal, (?) Tibetan. Tax on the profits of trade, levied in the form of transit duties.—*Ibid.*

KÍWÁḌA, Tel. (కీవాడ) The area or yard of a house: a tract of land round a village once occupied by dwellings: land fit for garden cultivation; a rich soil.

KÍWÁMÁṬÍ, Hindi (कीवामाटी) Fine, strong, and tenacious soil.

KLÍVA, S. (क्लीव) Weak, impotent, neuter: in law, an impotent man, and therefore disqualified, in many respects, as a party or an evidence.

KOBBARI, Tel. (కొబ్బరి), also KOBARI, Karn. (ಕೊಬರಿ) The white kernel of the cocoa-nut.

KOCHIÁNI, Uriya (କୋଛିଆନି) A woman who lives by selling salt in small quantities.

KODA, Tel. (కొద) Coarse rice, the third crop.

KOḌAGA, Tam. (கொடகா) Land which had been rent-free, but which has been subjected to a light or quit-rent.

KOḌAIKKÚLI, Tam. (கொடைக்கூலி) Rent, hire.

KODE, Thug. Dressed rice.—Dakhini Thugs.

KÓḌE, Karn. (ಕೋಡೆ) The season of the hot land-winds in Mysore, from May to September.

Kóḍebatta, Karn. (ಕೋಡೆಬತ್ತ) Rice grown in the hot season.

Kóḍegadde, Karn. (ಕೋಡೆಗದ್ದೆ) Land watered for the cultivation of rice in the dry season.

Kodi, Tam. (கொடி), Karn. (ಕೋಡಿ) A channel for carrying off the surplus water of a reservoir.

Kodi, Tam. (கொடி) A twining plant, a vine, especially a betel-vine.

Kodikkál, Tam. (கொடிக்கால்) A betel-vine garden.

Kodikkál-vellálan, Tam. (வெள்ளாழன்) A class of the Vellálar or agricultural tribe who cultivate betel.

Kodio, Guz. (કોડીઓ) A leper.

Kodo, H. (كودو, कोदो), also Kodram, and Mar. Kodrú, and Kodro (कोद्रू, कोद्रो, which are nearer the original S. *Kodrava* कोद्रव) A small grain eaten by the natives (Paspalum frumentaceum): in one form, which does not apparently differ from the ordinary grain, it has the property of intoxicating when made into bread; it is then called *Matáona*, from S. *mata*, inebriated.

Kodu, Tel. (కోడు) A water-course, a *nala*.

Kodu, plur. Kollu, and Kondru, whence the ordinary name Konds, Tel. (కోడు, కోళ్లు, కోంద్రు) A barbarous race of mountaineers inhabiting the hills west and north-west of Ganjam to the borders of Nagpur.

Kodukkalvángal, Tam. (கொடுக்கல்வாங்கல்), Kodukavánnal, Mal. (കൊടുക്കവൊങ്ങൽ), lit. Giving and taking; dealing mutually, buying and selling, lending and borrowing reciprocally.

Kóduvísa, Karn. (ಕೋಡುವೀಸ) Allowance of a *Vis* of grain, &c. for every bullock-load that comes into a town, paid to a person employed to check the demands of the toll-keeper (apparently from ಕೋಡು, a horn) for horned cattle.

Koerí, H. (كويري) A class of the agricultural population in Hindustan who apply themselves especially to garden cultivation, and, in Bahár, to the growth of the poppy: they are in general very respectable.

Kohar, (H. كوهر, कोहड) The frame of the mouth of a well.

Koïlu, Koeeloo, Karn. (ಕೊಯಿಲು) A measure of seed corn containing four *hanis*, or 400 rupees in weight, and reckoned to be as much as a man can sow in a proportionate space of ground in a day (from *koyya*, to cut, to reap.

Kojágara, H. (S. कोजागर) A Hindu festival on the day of full moon in the month of Aswin, in honour of Lakshmí, the goddess of fortune, who is said to have promised riches to all who should observe a vigil on the night (from *ko*, who, *jágara*, wakeful): the night is spent in festivity and in games of chance.

Kojaytí, Thug. Fetters.—Dakh. Thug.

Kokáti, Thug. Cry of the large owl, ominous of evil.—Dakh. Thugs.

Koká, H. (كوكا) A foster-brother, a nurse's child.

Kól, commonly, Cole, H. (S. كول, कोल) The name of a barbarous tribe inhabiting forest and mountain tracts in the provinces of Benares, South Bahár, and Chota-nagpur, apparently of kin to the other mountain tribes of Central India, the Gonds and Bhils, who are perhaps the aboriginal races of India.

Kól, Mal. (കോൽ), Tam. (கோல்), Kólu, Karn. (ಕೋಲು) A staff, a stick; a measuring-rod or pole; a pole, ten of which should intervene between the planting of two cocoa-nut trees.—See Jervis, 26. Kola, Tel. (కోల) Measurement, a measure of four *Gaz*.

Kolkáran, or in common use, *Kolkár*, Mal. (കോൽകാരൻ) *Kólukár*, Karn. (ಕೋಲುಕಾರ) A mace or staff-bearer: a government messenger, police or revenue peon, one employed either by public functionaries or by renters to collect duties and imposts; also as civil guards.

Kolpaimáish, Mal. (കോൽപൈമാഇഷ) Measurement of lands in Malabar by survey made in the Mal. year, 983.

Kólkurippu, Tam. (கோல்க்குறிப்பு) An abstract or summary of a land measurement.

Kola, Hindi (कोल) A piece of land closed on two or three sides by water: an offset from a field.—Puraniya.

Kola, Mar. (कोल) Property, personal or real, seized for debt or arrears of revenue.

Kola, Beng. (কোল) A class of Hindus whose principal occupation is basket and mat-making.

Kolab, (?) Sindh. A tract of inundated land.

Kolaga, or Koluga, Karn. (ಕೊಳಗ, ಕೊಳುಗ) A measure of grain, the $\frac{1}{20}$th of a *khandaga*, or 3 bushels.

Kólapíramánam, for S. Pramánam, Tam. (கோளபிரமாணம்) A statement of the whole extent and of the divisions of a village and its lands, whether cultivated or waste.

Kolbandi, Karn. (ಕೊಲಬಂದಿ) Dismantling and rebuilding.

Kolchar, Beng. (কোলচর) An addition to a sand bank; a fresh deposit or accretion.

Kole, Karn. (ಕೊಲೆ), Kolai, Tam. (கொலை) Murder, beating.

Kolaikháran, Tam. (கொலைக்காரன்) A murderer.

Kolluvana, Karn. (ಕೊಲ್ಲುವನ) A murderer.

Kolf, Mar. (?) An allowance of a few heads of grain to the village watchman.

Kolháṇṭí, Mar. (कोल्हांटी) A tumbler, a rope-dancer, one who lives by feats of activity and dexterity.

Koliït, Hindi (कोलिइत) The taking of lands on lease from one Ryot by another, or the cultivation of them by other than the party who rents them.

Kolhu, H. (کولہو) A sugar-mill, an oilman's press.

Koli, erroneously, Kollee, but also, and perhaps more correctly, Kúlí, or Koolí, Mar. (कोली) The name of a low caste, or of a member of it: their business is to bring water, in which they are sometimes part of the village establishment: they are also fishermen: the name is also that of a wild and predatory tribe in the forests and wilds of Guzerat, some of whom, however, have settled in the plains, and have become cultivators, and are collected in *bhágdár*, or joint-tenancy villages.

Koḷḷa, Mal. (കൊള്ള) Plunder, pillage (probably same as the Karn. *Kaḷḷa*, q. v.)

Koḷḷa-káran, Mal. (കൊള്ളക്കാരൻ) A plunderer, a robber.

Kollai, Tam. (கொல்லை) Dry soil, high ground not capable of artificial irrigation: a back yard, or, rather, an inclosed piece of ground belonging to one of the proprietors of a village, whether or not contiguous to his dwelling.

Kollaipayir, Tam. (கொல்லைப்பயிர்) Corn growing on high ground.

Kollam, Mal. (കൊല്ലം) The name of the æra used in Malabar, said to derive its name from a village so called, where it was first devised; but this seems to be a popular error, the current æra being the third thousand of the cycle æra of Parasuráma, the first year of which corresponds with A.D. 825.

Kollan, Tam. and Mal. (கொல்லன்) A blacksmith; also in Mal., a tanner, a worker in leather; also a turner in wood.

Koḷḷi, Karn. (ಕೊಳ್ಳಿ) Plunder, pillage.

Koḷḷigár, Karn. (ಕೊಳ್ಳಿಗಾರ) A plunderer, a robber.

Koḷḷu, Tam. (கொள்ளு) Horse gram.

Kollukai, Karn. The third crop of rice.

Kolu, H. (کولو) An oilman.

Koḻu, Tam. (கொழு), Mal. (കൊഴു) A ploughshare; also, in Mal., Ploughing, cultivation.

Koḻumídi, Tam. (கொழுமீதி) The owner's share of the produce of a field, after deducting that due to the government.

Koḻulábham, Mal. (കൊഴുലാഭം, from S. लाभ, gain) The owner's profit or portion of the produce of a field after deducting the expenses of cultivation, and the public revenue demand.

Koḻunavan, or *Koḻuvan*, corruptly, *Kolloonaven*, Mal. (കൊഴുനവൻ, കൊഴുവൻ) An occupant of land other than the original hereditary owner, holding by lease or mortgage, and, under particular circumstances, having the opportunity of converting his temporary into a permanent tenure: a tenant, a lease or mortgage-holder.

Koḻupanam, Mal. (കൊഴുപണം) lit., Price of the ploughshare: two fanams given by the tenant to the proprietor in exchange for a piece of iron, typifying the ploughshare, concurrently with a deed by which he engages to improve the produce of the estate that he temporarily occupies.

Koḷu, Karn. (ಕೊಳು) A large square reservoir with steps on each side.

Koḷweṇ, Mar. (कोळवें) A measure of capacity, $\frac{1}{8}$th of a *sér*.

Kómaram, Mal. (കൊമരം) A tribe of barbers who operate on the lower classes.

Kómaṭí, commonly, Komṭí, corruptly, Compte, Tel. (కోమటి) Mar. (कोमटी), Karn. (ಕೋಮಟಿ), Mal. (കൊമട്ടി) The name of a caste in the South, who consider themselves to be a branch of the pure Vaisya caste: they follow trade as shopkeepers and merchants, and assume the denomination of Sheth or Chitty.

Kompe, Karn. (ಕೊಂಪೆ) A house, a village.

Kompeva, *Kompeyava*, Karn. (ಕೊಂಪೆವ, ಕೊಂಪೆಯವ) A villager.

Konakan, (?) Mal. A class of predial slaves in Malabar, a subdivision of the *Vetuvar*, or forest and hunter tribe: they are employed in agriculture, also as boatmen and salt makers.

Koṇḍa, Mar. (कोंड) A circle, especially one drawn round a person to whom an oath is administered: a cluster of a few huts apart from the main village: the fields or grounds of one person.

Koṇḍa, Tel. (కొండ) A hill.

Konḍapoḍu, Tel. (కొండపోడు) A corn-field on high or hilly ground; one not capable of artificial irrigation.

Konḍra, Tel. (కొండ్ర) The space left by the plough at its first wide turn.

Kondu, Thug. The belly.

Kóníri Karn. (ಕೋನೀರ) A square reservoir with steps.

Koniyalan, (?) Mal. A class of predial slaves in Malabar.

Konjal, Thug. Cry of the Sáras or crane.

Koppah, (?) Cloth steeped in an infusion of opium: (it is

specified as one of the intoxicating articles prohibited by Regulation x. 1813, s. 17, cl. 2. but the word is not found either in Hindustani or Bengali dictionaries: it may be an error for *Kopar* or *Kopra*, Beng. cloth).

Kopudárudu, commonly, Copdar, Tel. (కొపుదారుడు) A contractor for long-cloths.

Korá, H. &c. (کورا, कोरा) properly, New, fresh: in Bengal, applied to plain undyed silk, forming one description of silk piece-goods; also, Tel. (కోరా) Unbleached, unbleached or undressed cotton cloth, whence the name *Corah* is also applied to a class of cotton piece-goods from the Northern Cirkars.

Korábandi, H. (کورابندي) A new arrangement, a list of villages or fields to be registered according to an allotment different from a preceding one.

Korá, H. (کورا) New, plain (as silk undyed), whence a sort of silk, commonly *Cora*.

Kóṛa, Mal. (കൊഴ) A bribe: tax, tribute.

Koṛá, H. &c. (کوڑا: or कोडा) Koraḍa, Karn. (ಕೊರಡ) A whip, a scourge, formerly used in the punishment of malefactors, now disused.

Koṛábardár, or *Koṛadár*, H. &c. (کوڑابردار, کوڑادار) An executioner or flogger: an officer of the criminal court employed to flog culprits.

Koracharu, also, Korcharu, Korvaru, or Korsaru, &c. corruptly, Korchoor, Karn. (ಕೊರಚರು, ಕೊರ್ಚರು, ಕೊರ್ಸರು) The name of a tribe in the Karnatic, whose business is making bambu mats and baskets, or who carry betel nuts from market to market: they live in the hills and forests.

Koṛawau, or Koḍwao, Mar. (कोडवाव, from कोडा, dry, and वावर, a field) Land unirrigated artificially: dry lands.

Koral jamin, Mar. (?) Low reddish land in a tract along the foot of the hills, capable of bearing only inferior spring crops.

Koravarava, Koramaravanu, or Koravanu, or abbrev. Koravar, Koramar, Karn. (ಕೊರವರವ, ಕೊರಮರವನು, ಕೊರವನು) The name of a low tribe in Mysore, of which there are three branches—*Kalla-koramar*, who are professed thieves; *Walaga-koramar*, who are musicians; and *Hakki-koramar*, who are a migratory race, and subsist by making baskets, catching birds, &c.: they are hill and forest tribes, and have a dialect of their own: (the name may be only a local modification of *Kola*, or *Cole*, the hill tribes of Hindustan.)

Korambu, Tam. (கொரம்பு) A dam across part of a river, leaving an opening through which the water for irrigation is to run: the place where the water issues from, or runs into, a tank.

Korewár, (?) A wild tribe inhabiting the hills about Pakhal and towards the Godaveri: (the name is *Kora*, if correctly given: *wár* is, as usual, for *vádu*, an individual.)

Koṛgu. Mar. (?) An inferior servant of a village attending on travellers.

Korharia, Thug. The Thug clan that, after their expulsion from Delhi, fixed their residence at Korhar in the Doab.

Kori, Guz. (કોરી) A small silver coin current in Cutch, equal to one-third of a rupee.

Koṛí, H. &c. (کوڑي) A score, the aggregate of twenty.

Kóriseṭṭe, Karn. (ಕೋರಿಶೆಟ್ಟಿ) The head merchant of a town.

Korrá, Thug. A low sound made by the large owl, an unlucky omen.

Kóru, Tel. (కోరు), Karn. (ಕೋರು), also, Kórúnárú, (ಕೋರೂನಾರೂ) A part, a share; as a revenue term it applies to the share of the crop which belongs to the cultivator.

Korúkam, (?) Land in Dindigal cultivated by labourers, and paid for by a usage rent as cultivated (?) 5th Rep. 765: the term is probably inaccurate, and the meaning that of the following terms—division of the crop between the owner and cultivator.

Kórukálu, and *Kórudhanya*, Karn. (ಕೋರುಕಾಳು, ಕೋರುಧಾನ್ಯ) A crop equally divided between the cultivator and the proprietor.

Kórmági, Karn. (ಕೋರ್ಮಾಗಿ) A well-tilled field, the produce of which is equally divided between the proprietor and cultivator.

Kos, commonly written Coss, H. &c. (کوس, from S. *Kroṣa* क्रोश), Kroṣ, Beng. (ক্রোশ) A measure of distance varying, in different parts of India, from one to two miles, but most usually about the latter: in Mysore the Sultání *Kos* is about four miles: the variation in Upper India depends, according to Mr. Elliot, upon the valuation of the *Gaz*; for the *Kos* consists either of 100 cords (*ṭanáb*) of 50 *gaz* each, or of 400 poles (*báns*), each of 12½ *Gaz*, making, in either case, the *Kos* = 5000 *Gaz*; and the value depends therefore on that of the *Gaz*, which at one time varied considerably, see *Gaz*: the actual measurement of the distances between the *Kos minárs* or pillars still standing in the Upper Provinces makes the *Kos* = 2 miles 4 furlongs

158 yards, at which rate the *Gaz* is = 32.8 inches, approaching the 33 inches assumed by the British Government as the standard.

KOSA, Guz. (કોસ) The large leather bucket used for drawing water from wells: a yoke of oxen working the bucket.

Kosário, Guz. (કોસારીઓ) The water-drawer, the man who works the village well: the yoke of oxen drawing the water from wells.

Koṣio, Guz. (કોશીઓ) A water-carrier, one attached to the village establishment to draw water for the villagers and their cattle and for travellers.

Kosvero, Guz. (કોસવેરો) A tax per well or per bucket.

KOSÁTAKÍ, Mal. (കൊസാതകി) Merchandise, trade.

KOSH, or KOSHA, H. &c. (S. کوش, कोष) A treasury, a repository, a magazine, a receptacle, a sheath, the cocoon of the silkworm; also, trial by ordeal, especially thrice sipping water with which an idol has been bathed whilst invoking the divinity. In Tam. *Kosham* (கோசம்) is applied to a register of village lands.

KOSHṬÁ, Beng. (কোষ্টা) A name applied to two plants, the fibres of which are used for hemp; (Corchorus capsularis and Corchorus oletorius.)

KOSHṬÍ, Mar. (कोष्टी) The name of a caste, or of an individual of it, whose occupation is spinning and weaving, or the manufacture of undyed cloths and silks, and silk threads for necklaces, &c.

KOSTUGUTTA, Tel. (కొస్తుగుత్త) The joint renting of a village by all the cultivators.

KOT, or KOṬA, written also COTE, H. &c. (کوٹ, कोट, S. कोट्ट) also KOTH, Mar. (कोठ), KOṬṬA, Beng. (কোট্ট), KOṬṬAI, Tam. (கொட்டை) A fort, a stronghold, the fortified residence of a Zamindar, the wall of a fort.

KOṬ, or KOTE, Thug. A sacrifice of goats to the goddess Deví, as a prelude to a feast, to which no Thug is admitted till he has attained the rank of strangler, unless his family have been Thugs for at least two generations.

KOT, or KOTE, H. (?) Land granted in free property to the heirs of persons killed in battle.—Garhwal.

KOTAK, Thug. A novice.

KOTÁR, Thug. A bad omen.—Dakh. Th.

KOṬÁL, Beng. (কোটাল) A watchman, a constable (probably vernacular for *Kotwál*, q. v.): in Kamaon, the village messenger.

KOṬE BIṬṬI, Karn. (ಕೋಟೆಬಿಟ್ಟಿ) A tax formerly levied in Mysore in lieu of free labour previously exacted for the repair of certain forts and carriage of stores to them.

KOTSÁL, perhaps for KOTHASÁL, (?) H. A place where the iron ore is roasted; see *Khamarsál.*

KOṬH, KOṬHA, or KOṬHÁ, H. &c. (کوٹھ, کوٹھا, S. कोष्ठ) A house built of bricks, a treasury, a granary; *Koṭh*, in Uriya (କୋଠ) has also the sense of joint, undivided.

Koṭh, or *Koṭhadár*, H. (کوٹھدار) A person in charge of a granary, a housekeeper.

Koṭharí, or *Koṭhṛi*, H. &c. (کوٹھري, कोठडी) A chamber, an apartment.

Koṭhár, Mar. (कोठार) A granary, a room or enclosure in which grain is kept.

Koṭhnís, Mar. (कोठनीस) The accountant or officer in charge of a granary, a storekeeper.

KOṬHÍ, incorrectly, KOTEE, H. &c. (کوٹھی, कोठी, S. कोष्ठ) also KUṬÍ, or KUṬHÍ, or KOṬHÍ, Beng. (কুটী, কুঠী, কোঠী), KÓTE, Karn. (ಕೋಟೆ) A spacious house, such as those inhabited by Europeans; a granary, a warehouse or storeroom; a mercantile or banking-house or firm; a government factory or establishment, as the office of the native opium agent, as well as the chief or *Sadr* factory.

Koṭhiwál or *-wála*, H. &c. (کوٹھیوالا) A banker, a merchant.

Koṭhiá, Uriya (କୋଠିଆ) A house or farm servant or slave.

Koṭh-, or *Koṭhakaraṇ*, Uriya (କୋଠକରଣ) A village accountant.

Koṭh-, or *Koṭhakhamár*, Uriya (କୋଠଖମାର) The residence of a principal farmer or Zamindar.

Koṭhi-ilákа, H. (A. علاقة, a dependency) A district under a native opium agent; one attached to his *Koṭhí* or office.

Koṭhkharida, Uriya (କୋଠଖରିଦ) Land purchased and cultivated by hired labourers.

KOṬHÁRU, Tel. (కొఠారు) A salt-pan, salt works.

KOṬI, H. &c. (کوٹی, S. कोटि) Ten millions; a hundred lakhs, or hundred thousands; commonly termed a Kror or Crore, q. v.

KOṬÍ, Hindi (कोटी) An earthern reservoir for grain.—Puraniya.

KOTIGA, KOTIGÁR, Karn. (ಕೋಟಿಗ, ಕೋಟಿಗಾರ) A stonecutter.

KOTILA, H. (?) The name of a tribe in Guzerat.

KOTKARKI, (?) H. Militia.—Kamaon.

KOTLÍ, Hindi (कोटली) A division in a granary for different sorts of grain.

KOṬṬAGÁR, Karn. (ಕೊಟ್ಟಗಾರ) A division of the Hallayar or servile tribe.

Kóṭṭai, Tam. (கோட்டை) A measure of grain, varying in different places from 21 to 24 markáls.

Kóttaḷa kóvara, Karn. (ಕೋಟ್ಟಳಕೋವರ) A man who keeps watch in the *Koṭṭala* or watch tower of a village.

Kóṭṭam, or Coṭṭam, Tam. (கோட்டம்) An ancient territorial division in the province of Tonda-mandalam, which was divided into twenty-four *Koṭṭams* (from *Koṭṭai*, a fort)

Koṭṭára, or Koṭhára, Karn. (ಕೊಟ್ಟಾರ, ಕೊಠಾರ) A pent-house, a viranda, a shed for cattle.

Kóṭṭewokal, Karn. (ಕೋಟ್ಟೆವೊಕ್ಕಲ) An agricultural tribe of a lower caste than pure Sudras.

Koṭṭiṇa, Karn. (ಕೊಟ್ಟಣ) Beating the husk from the rice.

Kottu, Tam. (கொத்து) Payment for reaping; a deduction from the gross produce on that account.

Kotwál, corruptly, Cutwal, H. &c. (P. کوتوال) The chief officer of police for a city or town, a superintendant of the markets.

Kotwálí, H. (کوتوالي) The office of a Kotwál, or any thing relating to it: an impost formerly levied on the plea of providing for his salary; a variety of town duties.

Kotwár, Mar. (कोतवार) The village watchman and messenger, attending also on the Patel—a *Dher* by caste.

Kotya, (?) Followers.—Kamaon.

Kovido, Mal. (കൊവിടൊ) A measure of distance = 6666 yards.

Kovudárudu, Tel. (కొవుదారుడు) A contractor for long cloths, commonly known as the *Copedar*.

Koyyukálu, Tel. (కొయ్యుకాలు), *Koilu*, Karn. (ಕೊಯಿಲು) Straw after the corn is reaped, stubble.

Kóvil, Tam. (கோவில்) Mal. (കൊവിൽ) A Hindu temple: also a palace: in Mal., a *Kshatriya*, and the name of a class of Nairs.

Kovilakam, corruptly, *Kovilagom*, Mal. (കൊവിലകം) A king's palace: the house of a *Kshatriya*: the ancestors or family of an individual.

Koyatá, Koyatí, corruptly, Koyt, Mar. (कोयता, कोयती) A bill-hook, a sickle.

Koyatapaṭṭí, Mar. (कोयतपट्टी) A tax levied on fields which, from their situation, cannot be ploughed, and are therefore worked by hand, according to the number of hoes or bill-hooks required for their cultivation.

Koyiki, Karn. (ಕೊಯಿಕೆ), Koyitta, Mal. (കൊയിത്ത) Reaping, mowing, cutting corn.

Koyittukál, Mal. (കൊയിത്തുകാല), *Koyekal*, Karn. (ಕೊಯೆಕಾಲ) Harvest time.

Koyittakáran, Mal. (കൊയിത്തകാരൻ) A reaper.

Koyil-maini, Mal. (കൊയിൽമൈനി) Number or succession of crops or cuttings: (the root *Koyya*, to cut, whence the above and similar forms are derived, is common, with slight variations, to all the languages of the south of India.)

Kóyil, Tam. (கோயில்) A temple, a church, a palace.

Kóyilchéri, Tam. (கோயில்சேரி) Part of a village belonging to a temple.

Kóyiṇmérai, Tam. (கோயின்மேரை) Part of the harvest set apart for a temple.

Kóviṛgrámam, Tam. (கோவிற்கிராமம்) A village belonging to a temple.

Kóviṛbaṭṭu, Tam. (கோவிற்பற்று) Lands, &c. belonging to a temple.

Krama, S., but adopted in most of the Hindu dialects (क्रमः) Order, series, succession.

Kramágata, S. &c. (from आगत, come) Descended or inherited in regular succession.

Kramágatadása, S. (दास, a slave) An inherited slave.

Kramágatadravya, S. (from द्रव्य, substance) Hereditary property.

Kramánuyáyi, S. &c. (अनु, after, and यायिन्, what goes) Succeeding or following in a direct line.

Kránti, vernacularly, *Kránt*, S., Beng., &c. (क्रान्ति) Proceeding, going in order: money of account, a third of a *kauri*, whence, in the eastern parts of Bengal, it is applied to land measure, or a similar proportionate part of an estate divided into *anas, gandhas, kaurís*, and *kránts*.

Krása, Beng. (क्रास) A complete reply, a rejoinder or refutation.

Kraya, S., also Beng., Mar., &c. (क्रय), Kirayam, Tam. (கிரயம்) Buying, purchasing, a purchase; price, value.

Krayak, S., Beng., &c. (क्रयक) A buyer, a purchaser.

Krayávikraya, S., Beng., Mar., &c. (क्रयाविक्रय) Buying and selling; trade, traffic.

Kraya chíṭu, Karn. (ಕ್ರಯಚೀಟು), Tam. (கிரயச்சீட்டு) A bill of sale.

Kraya sádhanam, S., but adopted in the dialects, as Karn. (ಕ್ರಯಸಾಧನಂ), Tam. (கிரயசாதனம்) A bill of sale.

Krétá, S., Beng., &c. (क्रेता) A buyer, a purchaser.

Kreya, S., Beng., &c. (क्रेय) A purchasable article.

Kríta, incorrectly, *Kirta*, S., Beng., &c. (क्रीत) Bought, purchased; hence, *Kríta-dása*, a purchased slave; *Kríta-putra*, a son bought.

K**ṛ**ISHI, S., adopted in all the Hindu dialects, except Tamil, but in the south pronounced KṚUSHI, KROOSHEE, (कृषि) Ploughing, tillage, agriculture.

Karsha, S., &c. (कर्ष, from कृष, to plough) Agriculture, ploughing.

Karshaka, S., &c. (कर्षक) A cultivator.

Kṛishak, and *Kṛishik*, S, Beng., &c. (कृषक, कृषिक) A peasant, a cultivator, a farmer, a husbandman.

Krishán, vernacularly, *Krisan* and *Karsán*, also *Kisán*, H. (کرشان), Beng. (कृषान) A husbandman.

Kṛishíbala or *-vala*, Beng. (कृषीवल) A husbandman, a cultivator.

Kṛushikudu, or *Kṛushivaludu*, Tel. (కృషికుడు, కృషివలుడు) A husbandman.

Krushikanu, or *Krushivalanu*, Karn. (ಕೃಷಿಕನು, ಕೃಷಿವಲನು) A husbandman, a cultivator.

Kṛushikan, *Kṛushikáran*, or *Kṛushivalan*, Mal. (കൃഷികൻ കൃഷികാരൻ, കൃഷിവലൻ) A farmer, a cultivator, a husbandman; *Kṛushikáran* is sometimes applied to the steward of an estate on the part of the owner, employed to pay the slaves and labourers, and other charges.

KṚISHṆA, adopted in all the dialects, pronounced, vernacularly, KRUSHNA, KRISHN, and KISTNA, the two last incorrectly, S. &c. (कृष्ण) Black; hence the name of the popular divinity *Kṛishṇa*, from his black complexion.

Kṛishnárpan, Beng, &c. (S. अर्पण, delivering) Grant of lands to a Brahman or temple in propitiation of Kṛishṇa.

Kṛushṇa-nílada-nellu, Karn. (ಕೃಷ್ಣನಿಲದನೆಲ್ಲು) A kind of rice grown in Mysore.

Kṛishṇa-paksha, S. &c. (कृष्णपक्ष) The fortnight of the moon's wane, the dark half of the month.

Kṛushṇa regada or *regadi* or *revaṭi nela*, or *-bhúmi*, Tel. (కృష్ణరెగడ, -రెగడి, -రేవటినేల, -రేవటిభూమి) The rich black loamy earth in the south, commonly known by the name of cotton soil, cotton being advantageously grown on it.

KṚITA, S., Beng., &c. (कृत) Done, made; as, *Kṛitadása*, a slave made; *Kṛitaputra*, a son made or adopted.

Kṛitakál, S., Mar., &c. (कृत, made, and काल, time) For a fixed term or period: applied to any agreement or contract.

Kṛitayuga, S. &c. (कृतयुग) The first of the four *yugas* or ages of the world; the golden age, extending through a period of 1,728,000 years.

Kṛitriṃa, S. &c. (कृत्रिम) Factitious, applied to one of the twelve kinds of sons formerly recognised in Hindu law, the son made; also *Kṛitrima-putra*: this kind of affiliation is still practised in Mithila.

Kṛittiká, S. &c. (कृत्तिका) The third lunar asterism, the Pleiades.

Kṛitya, S. &c. (कृत्य) What is to be, or ought to be, done; *Kṛityá*, (कृत्या) Magic, magical rites; also a female divinity to whom sacrifices are offered for destructive and magical purposes; hence applied in Maraṭhí to a virago, a scold.

Kṛiyá, S. (क्रिया) Act, action in general, or any particular act; any religious ceremony, especially such as are purificatory and essential; also obsequial rites: act of law or judicial investigation, either by witnesses, documents, or ordeal; also the last of the two acts of a process which is upheld, as when a loan and repayment are both proved the latter is called the *Kṛiyá*, the decisive act.

Kṛiyádweshí, S. (क्रियाद्वेषी) A witness whose testimony is prejudicial to the cause.

Kṛiyákarmántara, S. (क्रियाकर्मान्तर) Funeral ceremonies.

Kṛiyákarmákarma, S. (from कर्म, act, and अकर्म, non-act) Non-performance of the obsequial rites of a deceased relative, causing loss of caste.

Kṛiyálopa, S. (from लोप, omission) Neglect of essential ceremonies involving loss of caste: failure of funeral obsequies from the absence of a person competent to perform them, or any other cause.

Kṛiyápáda, S. (from पाद, a portion or stage of process) The third division of a suit at law, the counter-evidence or rejoinder, of the plaintiff.

Kṛiyapatra, S. Uriya (क्रियापत्र, କ୍ରିୟାପତ୍ର) A bill of sale.

Kṛiyavádí, S. (from वादिन्, who declares) A plaintiff in a suit.

Kṛiyávasanna, S. (from अवसन्न, finished) Nonsuited; one who has lost his cause.

KRODHANA, S. &c. (क्रोधन) The 59th year of the cycle, A.D. 1865.

KRODHÍ, S. (क्रोधी) The 38th year of the cycle, A.D. 1844.

Krodhi-hichchigi, Karn. (ಕ್ರೋಧಿಹಿಚ್ಚಿಗಿ) An increase in the assessment in Mysore, made in the year *Krodhí* of a former cycle.

KROH, or KUROH, H. (P. کروه) A measure of distance, the same as *Kos*, q. v.

KROṚ, or KAROṚ, commonly written CRORE, H. (کروڑ, کروڑ, S. कोटि) Ten millions, a hundred *lakhs* or hundred thousands.

Kroṛí, or *Karoṛí*, written also *Crori*, and, corruptly,

Croory, Crorie, and *Karoory*, H. &c. (کروری) The possessor or collector of a *Kror*, or ten millions, of any given kind of money: it was especially applied as an official designation, under the Mohammadan government, to a collector of revenue to the extent of a *kroṛ* of dams, or 250,000 rupees, who was also, at various times, invested with the general superintendence of the lands in his district, and the charge of the police: the latter was ultimately withdrawn from him, but the former continued till the downfall of the empire: the extent of the *kroṛi's* collections is that which, according to extant Regulations, should form the charge of the Tahsildár: the word is also used more generally for a tax-gatherer, an overseer, especially of a market.

KROṚAPATRA, Beng. (ক্রোড়পত্র, from ক্রোড়, the side) A supplementary page or writing, a postscript to a letter, a codicil to a will, &c.

KSHATRIYA, S. &c. (क्षत्रिय) The name of the second or military and regal caste, or a member of it; the warrior, the king.

KSHAYA, S. &c. (क्षय) Waste, loss: the sixtieth year of the cycle, A.D. 1866.

KSHEMA, S. &c., vernacularly, KHEM (क्षेम) Prosperity, welfare, conservation of acquired wealth: in law, an act of merit, as planting trees, digging tanks, erecting places of rest for travellers, and the like.

KSHETRA, vernacularly, KHETRA, and KHET, S. &c. (क्षेत्र) A field, a plain, a place of pilgrimage: metaphor., a wife: in Malabar, a temple.

Kshetraphal, S., Mar. (क्षेत्रफल) The superficial area of a field: the solid contents of a cube.

Kshetrí, S. &c. (क्षेत्री) The owner or possessor of a field; the possessor of a wife, a husband.

Kshetraja, S. &c. (क्षेत्रज) A son born of a wife duly appointed to raise issue for a husband in failure of any begotten by him; one of the twelve sons formerly recognised by Hindu law, but now repudiated.

Kshetropádhyáya, S. (क्षेत्रोपाध्यायः) A teacher, or Upádhyáya, or Brahman, engaged to conduct the ceremonies which are appropriate at a place of pilgrimage, as at *Prayága*, *Gaya*, &c.

KHETKHOLÁ, Beng. (খেতখোলা) A field.

KUCHCHHÁ, Beng. (কুচ্ছা) Slander, defamation, abuse.

Kuchchhábádí, Beng. (কুচ্ছাবাদী) A calumniator, a defamer, an accuser.

KUCHCHELA, corruptly, COCHELLA, COOCHALA, COORCHELA, Tel. (కుచ్చెల) A heap of cut corn: a land-measure in the Northern Cirkars = 8 *Goṛṛus* or 1000 *Kuntas*. See *Kunta*.

KUḌA, KUḌÁ, pron. KUṚÁ, Beng. (কুড, কুড়া) A bíghá of land.

KÚDÁ-BIGHÁ, H. (کودابیگھا, from کودنا, to jump) A bíghá peculiar to Rohilkhand, measured, as to breadth, by the rope or chain, but as to length, by a certain number of leaps taken by the measurer: the area is equal to from $2\frac{1}{2}$ to $3\frac{1}{2}$ *Kachcha-bighás*.

KÚḌAI, Tam. (கூடை) A basket.

Aḷavu-kúḍai, Tam. (அளவுகூடை) A basket for measuring rice.

KÚDÁL, sometimes pron. KODÁL, H. &c. (کودال, कुदाल) A sort of hoe or spade, the common implement used in digging, also a mattock or pickaxe. *Kúdálí* is a similar but smaller implement.

KUḌAMAN, pl. KUḌAMAR, corruptly, KOODUMMER, Mal. (കുടമൻ) A class of predial slaves in Malabar; sing., an individual of the caste.

KUḌAṆ, Mar. (कुडण) A fence, an inclosure.

KUḌAN VARIPPA, Mal. (കുടംവരിപ്പ) Rate of interest on loans of money repayable in money, not by transfer of lands.

KUḌAVA, or KUṚAVA, corruptly, COODUMBON, and KOODDUP, S., Mar., &c. (कुडव) A measure of capacity, the sixth part of a *maund*, also the fourth of a *prastha*, or a vessel four inches in diameter and as many deep, containing twelve handfuls: in pharmacy, a weight of 32 *tolas*.

KUḌAVAN, Tam. (குடவன்) A shepherd by caste and occupation.

KUDHI, KOODHEE, (?) H. A family hearth, or a place or sort of stone where food is dressed.

KUḌI, so pronounced, but written like the original Sanscrit KUṬI (कुटि), Tam. (குடி), KUḌI, KUḌÍ, Mal. (കുടി, കുടീ) A house, a village, a town: a tribe: an inhabitant, a tenant.

Kuḍia, *Koodeah*, (?) Mal. A class or caste of slaves in Coorg.

Kuḍián, more correctly, *Kuḍiyán*, also *Kuḍiyánavan*, Mal. (കുടിയാൻ, കുടിയാനവൻ) A cultivator, a Ryot, a tenant, one holding temporary occupation of lands or gardens by the tenure of lease or mortgage, not by hereditary succession.

Kuḍi-áyákaṭṭu, Tam. (குடிஆயக்கட்டு) Total of the inhabitants of a village or town.

Kuḍi-chillar, Mal. (കുടിചില്ലര) Taxes on houses, shops, huts, tools and implements, and a variety of petty articles, formerly levied in Malabar.

Kuḍichéri, Tam. (குடிசேரி) Division of a village occupied chiefly by natives of Malabar.

Kuḍi-irippa, or *Kuḍi-yirippa*, Mal. (കുടിഇരിപ്പ, കുടിയിരിപ്പ) Specification in a deed of conveyance of permission to a tenant to reside on the rented or mortgaged estate, in which case he is entitled to remuneration for any buildings he may have erected, when his tenancy ends: dwelling, habitation in general: a garden, an inclosure.

Kuḍikkáḍu, Tam. (குடிக்காடு) A village, especially one amidst cultivated ground.

Kuḍikalyáṇam, Mal. (കുടികല്യാണം) Procession of a nuptial party to the house of the bridegroom after a marriage.

Kuḍiketta, Mal. (കുടികെട്ട) Marriage of a slave.

Kuḍima, Mal. (കുടിമ) Tenancy, occupation of an estate for a season, either under lease or mortgage tenure: dwelling on the property of another.

Kuḍima-nír-karaṇam, or *Kuḍima-ola-karaṇam*, Mal. (കുടിമനീരകരണം, ഒലകരണം) One of the deeds executed in making over a proprietary estate in occupancy as security for a loan: conveying the water (*nír*) of the estate by an instrument (*karaṇam*), or by one written on a palm leaf (*ola*).

Kuḍimagan, Tam. (குடிமகன்) A village servant.

Kuḍimarammattu, corruptly, *Coodemurumut*, Tam. (குடிமராமத்து, A. مرمت) Repairs of the channels of irrigation on the borders of the fields by the cultivators themselves.

Kuḍi mirási, Tam. (குடிமிராசி) Land held in hereditary right by the village proprietors, exempt from land-tax.

Kuḍippaḍai, Tam. (குடிப்படை) Militia.

Kuḍippaka, Mal. (കുടിപ്പക) A family feud, resentment by the whole family of a wrong done to a member, or for his death.

Kuḍippaṭṭa, Mal. (കുടിപ്പാട്ട) Money taken from the people by government officers without accounting for it.

Kuḍipati, Mal. (കുടിപതി) An inhabitant, a householder.

Kuḍissika, Mal. (കുടിശ്ശിക) Arrears of rent or revenue.

Kuḍiváram, corruptly *Coodewarum*, Tam. (குடிவாரம்) The share of the produce which is the right of the inhabitants or of the cultivators.

Kuḍivarava, Mal. (കുടിവരവ) Revenue from the inhabitants: receipt: marriage procession: first occupancy of a new house.

Kuḍivila, Mal. (കുടിവില) Common country price, government price for articles of monopoly.

Kuḍiyánavan, Tam. (குடியானவன்) An inhabitant, a townsman.

Kuḍiyán-kuṛa, Mal. (കുടിയാൻകുറ) The cultivator's share of the crop

Kuḍiyiram-páṭ, Mal. (കുടിയിരമ്പാട) A deed by which the proprietor transfers any payments made by the tenant or mortgagee to a third party.

Kuḍiyiruppu-nattam, Tam. (குடியிருப்புநத்தம்) Houses and lands occupied by Mirásidárs free of revenue.

Mirásukuḍi, Tam. (மிராசுகுடி) A hereditary inhabitant.

Payirkuḍi, Tam. (பயிர்குடி) A cultivator, a husbandman.

Suhavási-kuḍi, Tam. (சுகவாசிகுடி) A settled or permanent inhabitant.

Vanatéruṇ-kuḍi, Tam. (வநதேறுங்குடி) A cultivator who has not a settled or permanent dwelling in the village.

KUDTHAL, (?) Mar. A garden ill supplied with water.

KUḌUGULU, KUḌUGÓLU, Karn. (ಕುಡುಗುಲು, ಕುಡುಗೋಲು) A sickle, or any instrument for cutting corn.

KUDUVA, Tel. (కుదువ), KUDUVU, Karn. (ಕುದುವು) A pawn, a pledge, a mortgage.

KUDURUVÁṬU, Tel., Karn. (కుదురువాటు) Management of affairs, settlement of a business.

KUGRÁM, Mar. (कुग्राम) A mean, miserable village.

KUJAO, Thug. A Thug informer, one who denounces and extorts money from them.

KUJAVAN, Tam. (குசவன்) A potter.

KUL, H. &c. (A. كل) All, total, entire.

Kulbáb, Mar. (कुलबाब) All the items of a statement or account.

Kul-band-o-bast, H. (كلبندوبست) A complete settlement, either that of a whole estate by the proprietor, or of a district by the government.

Kulcha, H. (كلچه) Capital, stock in trade.

Kulikhtyár, Tel. (కులిఖ్త్యార్) Entire or sole right.

Kuljamá, H. (كلجمع) Sum total; total realisable revenue.

Kulkallá, Mar. (कुलकल्ला, for A. كلاں, great) A minister invested with full power, a plenipotentiary.

Kulkámil, H. (كلكامل) The total or utmost amount of assessment at any time: an extinct assessment, of which the name only exists in the Northern Cirkars.

Kulkánú, Mar. (कुलकानू, for A. قانون) All laws and regulations, the whole body of the statutes: a term used in official grants.

Kulkár-bhárí, Mar. (कुलकारभारी, from S. कार, affairs, and भार, burthen) A minister or functionary invested with full authority.

Kulrakba, H. &c. (کلرقبہ) The whole area or contents of a village and its lands.

Kulupaj, Hindi (कुलुपज, from S. उपज, produced) The whole produce of a field or village.

Kulwár, *Koolwár*, H. &c. (کلوار) According to, or with, all: applied especially to the settlement of the assessment with each individual cultivator, the same as Ryotwár: (perhaps *Kul* is here the Sanscrit, not the Arabic, term; see below).

Kulwárpatti, or *Kuluvárpatti*, Karn. (ಕುಲ್ವಾರಪಟ್ಟಿ ಕುಳುವಾರಪಟ್ಟಿ) An account of the land farmed by each cultivator severally (see the last).

Kula, vernacularly, Kul, S., but in all the dialects, (कुळ), Mar. (कुल or कुळ) A family, a race, a tribe: in the revenue language of the south it appears to be applied especially to families, or individual heads of families, paying revenue, and in this sense occurs in various compounds, as hereafter specified, unless it be a different word that is so applied (see *Kula*, below.)

Kulachyuta, S., Beng. (from च्युत, fallen) Outcaste, discarded from family or caste.

Kuladevatá, S. &c. (कुलदेवता) A family or domestic deity.

Kuladharma, S. &c. (धर्म्म, duty) The peculiar duty or usage of a family or tribe: the right of a family to celebrate certain ceremonies.

Kuláchára, S. &c. (आचार, institute) Family usage or observance.

Kuláchárya, S. &c. (कुलाचार्य्यः) A family priest, one who conducts the domestic ceremonies of a family: in Bengal, a person whose occupation it is to negociate marriages, as acquainted with the pedigrees of families.

Kulajá, or *Kulji*, Beng. (कुलज) A family pedigree or genealogy.

Kulaháiha, Karn. (ಕುಲಹಾಯಿಕ) Hereditary occupation.

Kulalekhanam, S. &c. (कुललेखनं) A family writing or record, especially a horoscope of different members of a family.

Kulamaryádá, S. &c. (मर्य्यादा, duty) Family duty, usage, or observance.

Kulárg, corruptly, *Coolaruggee*, Mar. (कुळारग) By family, by families or households severally: used chiefly in composition; as, *Kulárgpattí*, a cess or tax per families: also, collectively, the proprietors or possessors of rights and properties in a village, the *watan-dárs*: it is also applied to a village occupied by families holding direct of government.

Kulárgwár, Mar. (कुळारगवार) According to, or with, families paying revenue direct, an assessment, &c.

Kulghadní, corruptly, *Koolgunnee*, Mar. (कुळघडणी) A record kept by the village accountant of the proceedings of each cultivator for the past year, shewing the extent and value of his lands, the portion actually cultivated, the revenue assessed, and all circumstances connected with his holding in connexion with the government demands: it forms the basis of the Ryotwár annual settlement.

Kulgutta, (?) Tel. Lands let to different castes at a low rent.—Ceded districts.

Kulgutta srotriyam, (?) Tel. Lands let to learned Brahmans at a low rent.—Ceded districts.

Kulkaria, (?) Karn. Chief or head of a tribe or caste.

Kulí, Mar. (कुळी) A family, a tribe, but seldom used except when speaking of the relationship of parties in marriage: if of the same *Kulí*, the marriage is allowable.

Kulika, S. &c. (कुलिक) Of a good family, the head of a tribe or family.

Kulína, S. &c. (कुलीन) Of a good family: it is applied in Bengal especially to designate a class of Brahmans who take precedence of all other Brahmans, and to whom the latter are anxious to wed their daughters, a practice leading to much profligacy and distress.

Kuljhartí, Mar. (कुलझडती) An account kept by the village accountant, of the dues and payments of each cultivator.

Kulkaran, Mar. (कुळकरण) The office of village accountant.

Kulkaraní, commonly, *Kulkarní*, corruptly, *Koolkurny*, *Kulkurny*, *Koolkurnain*, *Coolkurny*, &c. Mar. (कुळकरणी) One of the principal village functionaries under the Pátil, the village registrar and accountant, whose duty it is especially to keep accounts between the cultivators and the government, as well as those of the village expenditure: he has the keeping of all the village records and papers, and has lands and perquisites assigned him for his support.

Náda-kulkarni, or *Desa-kulkarni*, Karn. (ನಾಡಕುಲಕರ್ಣಿ, ದೇಶಕುಲಕರ್ಣಿ) The accountant of a district.

Sardesakulkarni, Karn. (ಸರದೇಶಕುಲಕರ್ಣಿ) The accountant of a province.

Kulwarg, (? an error for *Kulárg*) Mar. An account kept with each cultivator severally: the same as the *Kulghadni*.

Kula, or Kul, corruptly, Gule, Karn. (ಕುಳ) A payer

of government dues, the *Málguzár* of Hindustan: a quantity of land that may be ploughed in one day by a single plough: (the word *Kula*, a family, occurs also in Karnata, but with a different *l* (as ಕುಲ), but whether this be a radical difference is doubtful: the same difference is observable in Marathi, *Kula* (कुल), meaning family; *Kuḷa* (कुळ), more properly, a rate-payer: the diversity is probably only accidental, originating, as usual, in the want of a fixed standard for spelling in the Indian languages).

Kuḷaśisht, Karn. (ಕುಳಶಿಷ್ಟ) The system of land-revenue formerly prevailing in Mysore.

Kuḷavarttane, Karn. (ಕುಳವರ್ತ್ತನೆ) The perquisites of the village officers, receivable from the farmers and those who pay revenue to the government,

KUḶAM, corruptly, CULLUM, Tam. (குளம்) A tank, a reservoir, especially a large piece of water formed by damming up a valley or hollow between hills into which water flows and is there retained.

KULASHAJRÁ, H. (A. کلهٔشجره, from *Kulah*, a cap worn by mendicants) Succession to the property of a religious person or fakír.

KUḶAVA, KUḶVA, Mar. (कुळव) A sort of harrow for smoothing ploughed land.

ḲULBA, H. (P. قلبه) A plough: in Sylhet, a measure of land, an area of 1008 cubits in length by 144 in breadth.

KULHÁRÍ, H. (کلهاري, from کلهار, S. कुधार, an axe) A tenure by which land is held in the Northern Cirkars, or payment of rent at a rate per hatchet for the land which may be cleared by it in a given time.

KUḺI, written also, KUZHI, Tam. (குழி), KUṞI, Mal. (കുഴി) A measure of one square foot: it is also said to be a measure equal to 24 or 26 *adis*, or 22.8 feet, and is elsewhere considered the same as the *gunta* of 25,600 square feet: it is also said to be an extent of ground = 144 or 576 square feet; considerable variety thus prevailing in its valuation in different places: also, a pit, a hole in the ground, especially one in which a cocoa-nut tree is planted; whence, in Malayalam, it seems to imply planting trees.

Kuḻiveṭṭu, Tam. (குழிவெட்டு) Earth work, digging at so much per *Kuḻi*, or pit.

KÚLI, COOLEE, Tam. (கூலி), Mal. (കൂലി), Karn. (ಕೂಲಿ) Tel. (కూలి), Beng. (कूली), H. (قلي) Daily hire or wages: a day labourer, a *Cooly*: (the word is originally Tamil, whence it has spread into the other languages: in Upper India it bears only its second and apparently subsidiary meaning: it appears as *Culialu*, as the term for hired labourers, in Tulava.—Buchanan.)

Kúlichcham, Mal. (കൂലിച്ചം) Land granted rent-free, or on a low rent, on condition of service.

Kúlichchakáran, Mal. (കൂലിച്ചകാരൻ) A military retainer or servant, holding land on condition of service.

Kúlichevakam or *-sevaham*, Mal. (S. കൂലിചെവകം കൂലിശെവകം) Military service in consideration of lands rent-free, or held at a quit-rent.

Kúligár, Karn. (ಕೂಲೀಗಾರ) A labourer, a hireling.

Kúli-godám, (?) H. Personal services exacted from the peasantry.—Kamaon.

Kúlika, Karn. (ಕೂಲಿಕ)) A day labourer.

Kúlikáran, Mal. Tam. (കൂലികാരൻ) A day labourer.

Kúlivela, Mal. (കൂലിവെല) Daily labour or hire.

Kúliyál, Tam. (கூலியாள்), *Kúliyálu*, Karn. (ಕೂಲಿಯಾಳು) A workman, a labourer, a hireling.

KÚLI, KOOLEE, (?) Mar. Land held at a progressively increasing assessment.

KULUME, KOLUME, Karn. (ಕುಲುಮೆ, ಕೊಲುಮೆ) A furnace, a forge.

Kulumegutta, Karn. (ಕುಲುಮೆಗುತ್ತ) A tax on forges.

Kulumekandáyam, Karn. (ಕುಲುಮೆಕಂದಾಯಂ) A tax on blacksmiths, sometimes received in iron.

KUḶUMI, Tam. (குளுமி) A sluice.

KUMÁRA, vernacularly, KUNWAR, or KÚĀR, vulgarly, COOUR, S. &c. (कुमार) A youth, a young boy, a prince.

Kumári, vernacularly, *Kunwar*, S. &c. (कुमारी) A young girl, a princess: a name of the goddess Durgá, as a maiden, to whom a temple dedicated at the extremity of the peninsula has long given to the adjacent cape and coast the name of *Kumári*, corrupted to *Comorin*.

KUMÁRI, or KUMARI, Karn. (ಕುಮಾರಿ, ಕುಮರಿ) Cultivation of high and wooded lands after clearing them.

Kumári-maráṭṭi, Karn. (ಕುಮಾರಿಮರಾಟ್ಟಿ) A caste of Marathi origin, in Mysore, employed in clearing and cultivating high and wooded lands.

KUMBHA, S. (कुम्भः) A water-jar: the sign Aquarius: a measure of grain equal to twenty *droṇas*, or little more than three bushels and three gallons: in Guzerat it is a land measure, a square of ten *banas* or *ganthas* on each side = 3 roods 33.422 perches, or 4641 square yards.

Kumbhakára, S. (कुम्भकारः), *Kumbhár*, Mar. (कुंभार),

4 H

Kumhár, H. (کمھار) *Kumár*, Beng. (কুমার), *Kumbhár*, *Kumbár*, *Kummár*, *Kumbhahár*, Karn. (ಕುಂಭಾರ), *Kummari*, or *Kummaraváḍu*, Tel. (కుమ్మరి) A potter, a maker of earthen vessels and pottery; also, sometimes, of bricks and tiles: as one of the village servants he makes water-pots for the villagers, and brings water for travellers and for the principal village officers.

Kumbhárgaṇí, Mar. (कुंभारघणी) In some places, the refuse sugar-cane after the juice has been expressed, the perquisite of the potter of the village.

Kumbhárgundí, Karn. (ಕುಂಭಾರಗುಂಡಿ) A tax on the clay used by potters.

Kumbhár-khaṇ, Mar. (कुंभारखण) A tax on potters' clay.

Kumbhárkriyá, Mar. (S. क्रिया) The funeral rites of a Ṣúdra, properly conducted by a potter.

KUMBHUM, Guz. (કુંભું) A land measure, about a bíghá and a half of Guzerat.

KUMMÁṬṬA, Mal. (കുമ്മാട്ട) Insertion of the amount of a bond, &c., in figures, by the person who signs it.

KUṆ, KOON, (?) Mar. Tillage, agriculture: lands granted in fee for military service: (the word is of doubtful accuracy, or it might be the root of the following)—

Kuṇbí, pron. *Kumbi*, less correctly, *Coonby*, *Coombee*, H. (S. کنبي), Mar. (कुणबी), also Mar. *Kuḷambí*, (कुळंबी), *Kaṇbi*, and *Kalmi*, Guz. (કણબી, કલમી) The name of the chief agricultural caste in central, western, and southern India, whence it sometimes means a husbandman, a peasant, or cultivator in general: the Kuṇbís claim to represent the pure Ṣúdras of the Hindu system: they are for the most part an industrious and respectable race, and, amongst the Maraṭhas, reckoned the Raja of Satara, and other descendants of Sivaji, amongst their caste: they are subdivided into an infinite number of classes, many of whom do not eat together, or intermarry.

Kuṇbáú, Mar. (कुणबाऊ) Fit for, or appropriate to, a Kuṇbí, rustic, rude.

Kuṇbáwá, Mar. (कुणबावा) The business of a Kuṇbí; agricultural labour in general: land held in perpetual occupancy, under acknowledgment and payment of rent to government: also such a tenure, and the rent paid.

Kuṇbíṇ, Mar. (कुणबीण) The wife of a Kuṇbí, a woman of the agricultural caste: a female slave.

Kuṇbí-hiseb, Mar. (कुणबी हिशेब) Rustic computation, calculating by rude methods, as with pebbles, by the fingers, and the like.

KUṆAGÁ, KUṆGÁ, Mar. (कुणगा) A sum of money, or some item of common property, secreted by one of the sharers, and kept back from partition.

Kuṇagekarí, Mar. (कुणगेकरी) A shareholder of a common stock, who, upon a division, fraudulently keeps back a portion.

KÚNCH, KÚNCHA, H. (S. کونچ) The seed of the Abrus precatorius, used as a jewellers' and goldsmiths' weight: see *Gunja*.

KUNCHAMU, Tel. (కుంచము) A measure of capacity, reckoned in some places equal to a *chitánk*, or $\frac{1}{16}$th of a *sér*; in others to $3\frac{1}{4}$ *sérs*; in others to 8 and to 14 *sérs*.

KUNCHITAGÁR, Karn. (ಕುಂಚಿಟಿಗಾರ) A tribe of agriculturists in Mysore pretending to be pure Ṣúdras.

KUNḌ, or KUNṚ, Beng. (কংড) A small fen or morass, a piece of ground fit for the growth of rice.

KUNḌA, vernacularly, KUNḌ, commonly, COOND, S. &c. (कुंड) A pit, a hollow, a shallow pit or pan in which sacrificial fire is lighted, a fire-altar: a square pool or basin of water, especially if it possesses a higher temperature than the air, and has medicinal properties, when it is held sacred, as the *Sítá kunḍ*, near Monghir: the term is also applied to any natural basin in which the water that falls from surrounding heights is collected, forming the source of a river, as the *Brahmá-kunḍ*, at the head of the Brahmaputra river: also to a temporary and artificial well or reservoir for irrigation.

Kunḍurai, (?) Karn. An outlet from a reservoir, for irrigation.

Kuṛkunḍ, Hindi (कुडकुंड) A deep hole in the bed of a water-course, one in which the water remains when the bed is dry.

KUNḌA, Beng. (কুংড) The inner part of the husk of rice which adheres to the grain after the first cleaning.

KUNDA, Beng. (কুন্দ) A lathe.

Kundakar, Beng. (কুন্দকর) A turner.

KUNḌA, S. &c. (कुंडः) The child of a woman whose husband is living, by another man.

Kunḍagolak, Mar. (कुंडगोलक) The name of a caste, or of a member of it, said to be the adulterous offspring of a Brahman and Brahmaní, but it is applied to Brahmans of a low order: (properly speaking, the words *Kunḍa* and *Golaha* are distinct, the first being a bastard, the second, the child of a widow).

KUNḌI, Beng. Uriya (কুংডী) A vessel: in Cuttack it especially means a vessel in which brine is evaporated.

Kúne, Kúni, Karn. (ಕೂನೆ, ಕೂನಿ, from the P. *Gunah*, q. v.) A fault, a crime.

Kúnegar, Karn. (ಕೂನೆಗಾರ) A culprit, a criminal; the vernacular corruption of *Gunahgár*, q. v.)

Kunjrá, H. &c. (كنجرا, कंजरा) The name of a caste whose occupation is selling vegetables.

Kunr-boji, or Kunr-maṇḍlá, H. (كنربوجي, كنرمنڈلا) The day on which sowing is concluded in Benares and the Doab: the first term implies the filling of furrows (*kunr*), the second the closing of them: it is observed as a holiday, and the residue of the seed-corn is made into a cake, which is partaken of in the field, and in part distributed to Brahmans and beggars. Mr. Elliot adverts to a similar practice once observed in England.

Kunṭá, Tel. (కుంటా) A land measure, according to one statement =1089 square feet, to another to 19,600, or the 32d part of a *kaṭṭi.*

Kunṭaṇ, Mar. (कंटण) A pander, a pimp, a caste said to be sprung from a *Vaisya* father and a Brahman mother, whose office is attendance on the women's apartments, and providing dancing-girls and courtesans.

Kunṭe, Karn. (ಕುಂಟೆ) A machine for levelling ploughed land, also for weeding: the web beam of a loom.

Kunṭige, Karn. (ಕುಂಟಿಗೆ) A sowing machine, a sort of tube or funnel attached to the plough through which the seed runs.

Kunwar, vernacular corruption of Kumár, and Kumárí, q. v. H. (كنور) A youth, a prince, a princess; the deity *Kártikeya*, and thence applied to the month held sacred to him, *Kártik* (Oct.-Nov.)

Kuppa, Tel. (కుప్ప), Kuppal, Tam. (குப்பல்) A heap, a heap or stack of grain: one of filth, a dunghill.

Kuppa-anchana, Tel. (కుప్పఅంచన) Estimate of the produce of a field taken from the grain when stacked.

Kuppa-jábṭiá, Tel. (కుప్పజాబిటా) A list of grain stacks, shewing which belong to each cultivator.

Kuppa-kaṭṭu, Tel. (కుప్పకట్టు) An allowance of grain from the general heap or stack given to the village servants.

Kuppam, Tam. (குப்பம்), Tel. (కుప్పము) A small village, one occupied by low people.

Kuppaḍam, Tam. (குப்படம்) A portion of the produce of the taxable land in a village, payable to the Mirásidár after the grain is threshed.

Kuppakkáḍu, Tam. (குப்பக்காடு) A number of villages.

Kúṟ, Mal. (കൂറ) A class, a party: the people of Malabar, from the Rajas and Brahmans to the lowest races, are divided into classes, the *Chevara-kúṟ*, the fighting or ruling class, and the *Panniyur-kúṟ*, the civil and labouring class: their usages differ materially, and the distinctions are carefully preserved.

Kúṛá, H. (كوڑا, कूडा) Soil, filth, manure.

Kúṛá, Beng. (কুড়া) A bíghá, a measure of land.

Kuṛáháli, Beng. (কুড়াকালী) Working a sum in land measure and giving the result in *bighás.*

Kúragí, Kúrigí, or Kúrgí, Karn. (ಕೂರಗೀ, ಕೂರಿಗಿ) A drill plough, a sowing apparatus attached to a plough.

Ḳurâh, H. (A. قرعه) Divination by casting lots, wagers, lotteries, chance passages in books, &c.

Ḳurâh-andáz, H. (انداز, who throws) A caster or drawer of a lot.

Kúṟal, Kúṟu, Tam. (கூறல், கூறு) A public notice, a proclamation.

Kuram, (?) Mar. Grass or pasture land.

Kuramba, Karn. (ಕುರಂಬ) A shepherd by caste and occupation, he is also a weaver of coarse woollens.

Kurambu, Tam. (குரம்பு) A water-course, leading from a river, for irrigation.

Kuramuḷai, Tam. (குரமுளை) First appearance of the crop above ground.

Ḳurán, commonly, but incorrectly, Koran, and Coran, (A. قران) The sacred book of the Mohammadans, the supposed revelations made to Mohammad, and delivered by him orally, collected and committed to writing by the khalif Omar.

Ḳuráni-mullá, H. (قراني ملا) A Mohammadan officer who administers oaths taken on the Ḳurán.

Kuṛava, or Kuḍava, corruptly, Codumbon, and Koodup, S. &c. (कुडव) A measure of capacity. See *Kuḍava.*

Ḳurbán, H. (A. قربان) A sacrifice, a victim.

Íd-ul-kurbán, H. (A. عيدالقربان) A festival observed by the Mohammadans on the 10th of Zulhijja, when animals are sacrificed in commemoration of the sacrifice of Abraham.

Kurgí, Mar. (कुरगी) A measure of land, as much as may be ploughed and sown in one day with a pair of bullocks and a drill plough; the extent varies from about two to about eight acres; the average is said to be about five.

Kurh, H. (كره) A circular inclosure, in which a pile of wood was constructed, and an old woman placed in the area to be burnt alive by Brahmans in the event of any government officer attempting to put them under restraint, the consequences of the crime being supposed to devolve upon those whose oppression had driven the Brahmans to perpetrate it: the practice was prohibited by the British government, and is now never heard of.

Kurháḍ, Mar. (कुऱ्हाड) A hatchet, an axe.

Kurháḍi-jamín, Mar. (P. زمين) Land on steep acclivities which cannot be ploughed, and which is cleared and dug up with a kind of hatchet, or, rather, a sort of hoe.

Kuṛí, or Kuḍí, (?) H. A hearth, a fire-place, a tax levied on one. See *Chaubáchha.*

Kuri, Karn. (ಕುರಿ) A sheep.

Kurihánige, Karn. (ಕುರಿಹಾಣಿಗೆ) A tax on sheep.

Kuraba, Kuruba, Karn. (ಕುರಬ, ಕುರುಬ) A shepherd by caste and occupation, one who tends sheep: he is also a manufacturer of coarse woollens: also *Kuramba*, q. v.

Kuri, Tam. (குறி) A mark, a stamp.

Kuṛimósam, Tam. (குறிமோசம்) A fraudulent mark put upon a stack of grain after some has been clandestinely removed.

Kuṛi, Mal. (കുഴി) A pit, a hole, a grave: a hole in the ground for planting cocoa-nut and other garden trees, a measure of one square foot. See *Kuḷi.*

Kuṛikánam, Mal. (കുഴികാണം) Compensation allowed for the value of trees planted, or other improvements made by the tenant or mortgagee on relinquishing possession: on the other hand, a deduction from the money deposited or lent to cover injury or dilapidations: a lease or mortgage on such conditions. See *Kánam.*

Kuṛikáráyma, Mal. (കുഴിക്കാരായ്മ) Tenure of an estate or gardens, by which the tenant holds under condition of being reimbursed for improvement, and of compensating for dilapidations.

Kuṛikúr, also read *Kuyikúṛ*,(?) Mal. Tenure under which compensation for improvements and dilapidations is stipulated.

Kuṛivila, Mal. (കുഴിവില) Value of planted trees allowed for to a tenant on his giving up his lease.

Kuṛi, Mal. (കുറി) A club; an association in which a number of persons contribute monthly for a given term a certain sum or quantity of grain each; at the end of the term a lottery takes place, and the whole accumulation becomes the prize of one of the contributors: (perhaps derived from the A. *kurâh*, q. v.)

Kuṟṟi, or *Kuṭṭi*, Mal. (കുററി) The principal or manager of a club.

Kúri, (?) H. A measure of capacity for grain.—*Midnapur.*

Kuṟippa, Mal. (കുറിപ്പ) A memorandum, an item, an article of account.

Kuṟippaṭi, Mal. (കുറിപ്പടി) A written memorandum, a note.

Kuṟippaṇam, Mal. (കുറിപ്പണം) Money paid into a club or association.

Ḳurḳ, Ḳoorḳ, corruptly, Crook, H. (A. قرق), Korak, Beng. and Uriya (কোরক), Kíráku, Karn. (ಕೀರಾಕು) Sequestration, confiscation, seizure of goods, attachment, distraint for debt, or for arrears of public revenue. Beng. Reg. xvii. 1793; xlv. 1795; vii. 1799. Madras Reg. xxviii. 1802; v. 1822. Bombay Reg. xvii. 1827.

Ḳurḳ-amín, H. (قرق امين) An officer of the court employed to attach a property and realise the proceeds.

Korahdár, Beng. (কোরকদার) A bailiff, a sheriff's officer, an officer of court who attaches or distrains goods and property for debt, &c.

Ḳurḳí, H. (قرقي) Attached, sequestrated, distrained, under attachment.

Ḳurḳi-parwána, H. (P. پروانه, an order) A warrant of attachment.

Korakí, Beng. (কোরকী) Ordering or authorising an attachment.

Korak-khalás, Uriya (କୋରକଖଲାସ) Replevin, release of attachment. (*Ḳurḳ-khalás*, might be used in Hindustani for the same.)

Ḳurḳ-mahál, H. (قرق محال) An estate under attachment.

Ḳurḳ-sazáwal, H. (قرق سزاول) An officer appointed to attach and hold an estate, and realise arrears of rent or revenue, or to distrain goods for debt; a bailiff, a sheriff's officer.

Ḳurḳ-tahṣíl, H. (تحصيل) Collection of the revenue of an estate which has fallen into arrear, and from which the proprietors are nominally set aside by the native officers of the revenue: the same as *Khám-tahṣíl.*

Kurmí, Koormee, (H. كرمي, कुर्मी) The caste of agriculturists, or a member of it, in eastern and central Hindustan, being the same, essentially, as the *Kunbis* of the west and south. In Hindustan the *Kurmís* are said to have seven chief subdivisions, who do not eat together or intermarry: of these, the *Kharibind* and *Patanya* abound in the central Doab and Oudh; the *Ghorchara*, are more to the west; the *Jaiswár*, in Sagar and Bundelkhand; the *Kanaujia* in the lower tracts of the Doab; the *Kewat* to the east of Benares; and the *Jhunia* west of the upper Jumna: there are very many other branches in the west and north-west provinces, and in Bhagalpur and Bahar: they are not unfrequently found as predial slaves, having sold themselves, or been sold in their infancy, to servitude.

Kurmiat, (?) H. Tract of cultivable land of the *Bhúr* or mixed soil in the north-west provinces.

KURPHA, (?) Beng. A cultivator who rents his land from a *Khúd-kásht* Ryot. (Perhaps from *Khurpá*, a sort of hoe.)

KURSÍ, H. (A. كرسي) A chair, a throne.

Kursí-náma, H. (P. نامه, a document) A pedigree, a genealogical tree.

KURUBA, Karn. (ಕುರುಬ) A shepherd by caste and occupation, and who also makes woollen cloths or blankets.

Kurumban, Tam. (குறும்பன்) A shepherd by caste and occupation: Mal. (plur. *Kurumbar*) A class of predial slaves in Malabar.

Hála-kuruba, Karn. (ಹಾಲಕುರುಬ) One of the shepherd caste which does not make blankets.

Hánḍé-kuruba, Karn. (ಹಾಂಡೇಕುರುಬ) A shepherd of a higher order or caste.

Mésa-kuruba, Karn. (ಮೇಸಕುರುಬ) A shepherd of an inferior order or caste.

KURUMBOṚAI, Tam. (குறும்பொறை) A hill, a mountain, a forest, a village in a hilly country.

KURUṆGOL, Tam. (குறுங்கோல்) A measure of two cubits.

KURUṆI, Tel. (కురుని), Tam. (குறுணி) A measure of capacity, the same as the *Marakál*: in Tam. also a term used in computation as equal to a twelfth of a *kalam*.

KURUCHCHIYAN, or KURUMAN, Mal. (കുറിച്ചിയൻ, കുറുമൻ) A class of people inhabiting the hills in Wynád.

KÚṢA, or KÚS, Mar. (कूस) A falsity in an account, an overcharge on money expended, or undercharge of money received; any undue gain generally in managing for another.

KUṢA, usually pronounced KUSH, or KUSHA, S. &c. (कुशः) A kind of grass, esteemed holy from its being used in religious ceremonies, being strewed upon the altar or held by the Brahmans in their hands whilst repeating the formulæ (Poa cynosuroides).

Kuṣavṛitti, vernacularly, *Kuṣbritti*, S. &c. (कुशवृत्ति) lit. Maintenance by or through *Kuṣa-grass*, but in the west of Bengal, an under tenure, land granted at a quit-rent, or rent-free, for the support of a Brahman or religious person; land given: in Kamaon, the absolute gift of land to a Brahman at an eclipse, or on some solemn occasion.

KUSÍDA, S. &c. (कुसीद) Lending money at interest, usury; also a money-lender, a usurer.

KUSINI-KÁRA or VÁḌU, Tel. (కుసినికార, కుసినివాడు) A cook, a confectioner; lit., a man of the kitchen (from the Fr. *cuisine*).

KUSIVI, Karn. (ಕುಸಿವಿ) The safflower plant, also its dry leaves. See *Kusumbha*.

KUSTI, or KASTÍ, Guz. (કુસતી, કસતી) A cord or thread worn by the Parsis round the waist as a religious ornament.

KUSUMBHA, vernacularly, KUSUM, S. &c. (कुसुम्भ, कुसुम, کسم) KUSUMBÁ, Mar. (कुसुंबा) The safflower plant (Carthamus tinitorius), the dried flowers of which are used in making a red dye: also the flowers so dried, or the dye; also an infusion of hemp tops, or of opium, as an intoxicating beverage.

KÚT, KOOT, H. (كوت, कूत) Estimate, valuation, applied especially to an estimate of the proceeds of a field or farm by appraisement of the standing crop: in Garhwal, it implies the share of the produce paid in kind by the cultivator to the headman or proprietor.

KÚT, Thug. Theft amongst the Thugs themselves, pilfering some of the booty.

KÚṬA, S. (कूट) False, fraudulent.

Kuṛṛa, pron. *Kuṭṭa-nári*, Mal. (കുറ്റനാഴി) A short or fraudulent *nárí* measure.

Kúṭmahál, Beng. (কূটমহাল) Amount of revenue formerly levied in some places on vendors of spirituous liquors.

Kútsankránti, Beng. (কূটসংক্রান্তি) The entrance of the sun into a new sign on the 31st day from the preceding, a false conjunction.

KUṬI, KUṬÍ, S. &c. (कुटि, कुटी) A small house or cottage, a hut. Beng. (কুটী) Any large building, as a bank, a court-house, a European residence.

Kuṭíchara, S. (कुटीचरः) A man who makes over his property to his kindred, and devotes himself to a religious life, but continues to reside at home.

KUṬṬÁDAN, Mal. (കുട്ടാടൻ) Rice planted in the spring (Feb.-April) and ripening in the ensuing cold season.

KUṬṬAI, Tam. (குட்டை) A small tank or pond.

KUTTAKA, or KUTTATA, Mal. (കുത്തക, കുത്തത), KUTTAKAI, Tam. (குத்தகை) Farm, contract, rent, tenure.

Kuttakakáran, Mal., Tam. (കുത്തകക്കാരൻ) A farmer, a contractor, a renter.

KUTTALAÍ, Tam. (குத்தலை) Rice growing on high ground.

KUṬṬAM, Mal. (കൂട്ടം) An assembly, an assemblage: a cluster of houses, a small town or village.

Kuṭṭala, Mal. (കൂട്ടാലു, from S. आलय) Place where the property of a temple is kept, and its affairs are managed, a chapter house.

Kuṭṭárí, Mal. (കുട്ടാരി) Money subscribed to temples by the people.

KUṬṬÍ, written KUṞṞI, Mal. (കുററി) A log of timber, a tree, a post: a measure, a sort of *párah*: a cask or hogshead: a small fort: an inhabitant, &c.

Kuṭṭikánam, Mal. (കുററികാനം) A fee claimable by the owner of a plantation for every tree cut down on it by the renter or occupant: price given for a tree, to the owner before it is cut down.

Kuṭṭikanakola, Mal. (കുററികകനകൊല) A register on palm leaves of a proprietor's deeds or mortgages, a list of his tenants, amount of his rents, &c.

Kuṭṭinella, Mal. (കുററിനെല്ല) An allowance in grain made by proprietors to their tenants for keeping up the fences and inclosure of an estate.

Kuṭṭípití, Mal. (കുററിപിടി) Petty merchandise.

Kuṭṭipiṭikáran, Mal. (കുററിപിടികാരൻ) A petty dealer, one trading with borrowed capital.

Kuṭṭivásí, Mal. (കുററിവാശി) Balance or arrears of revenue due by individuals.

KÚṬṬÍRIPPA, Mal. (കൂട്ടിരിപ്പ) Living with a queen or princess as her husband.

KUTTUKAL, Tam. (குத்துகல்) A stone set-upright as a boundary mark or a buttress.

KÚṬṬUKACHCHAVAṬAM, Mal. (കൂട്ടകച്ചവടം) Joint trade, partnership.

Kúṭṭukáran, Mal. (കൂട്ടകാരൻ) A partner, an associate.

Kúṭṭukṛushi, Mal. (കൂട്ടകൃഷി) Joint agriculture, a husbandry.

KUṬUMBA, vernacularly KUṬUM, S. &c. (कुटुम्ब, कुटुम, كتم) Family, race, kindred, also a kinsman.

Kuṭumba- written, *Kuḍunba-káran*, Mal. (കുഡുമ്പകാരൻ) A householder, a kinsman by descent, a connexion by marriage.

Kuṭumbí, S. (कुटुम्बी), *Kuṭumí*, H. (كتمي) A householder, the head of a family.

Kuṭumbam, written, *Kuḍumbam*, Mal. (കുഡുമ്പം) A measure of capacity, a *nárí*, one fourth of an *edangali*.

KÚYIKÚR, (?) Mal. A deed of transfer of ancestral property (?): tenure on condition of compensation for improvements or dilapidations.

L

LABBÁ, Thug. A bullock.

LABDÁR, H. (لبدار, लबदार) Mud, thick mud formed by water flooding a stiff soil.

LABDHA, S. &c. (लब्ध) Gained, acquired.

Labdhadása, S. (from दास, a slave) A slave received as a gift or transfer.

Labdhaputra, S. (पुत्र, a son) A son gained or received, one adopted.

LÁBHA, S. &c. (लाभः) Gain, acquirement, profit.

Lábhálábha, S. &c. (लाभालाभ) Profit and loss, gain and diminution.

Lábhamu-dósili, Tel. (లాభముదోసిలి) A small portion from each heap of grain considered to be the perquisite of the cultivator (from *dósili*, two handfuls).

Lábhanasta, Karn. (S. ಲಾಭನಷ್ಟ) Profit and loss.

Lábhistu, Karn. (ಲಾಭಿಸ್ತು) Proved, verified.

Lábhwa, Guz. (લાભવા) Casting lots for dividing the produce of a field.

LABI, H. (لبي) The juice of the sugar-cane when boiling.

LABI, LUBEE, or LUBBEE, (?) A name applied at Madras to the Mapilas or descendants of the Arab colonists in Malabar. (The origin of the word seems doubtful.)

LÁ-CHÁR, H. (لاچار, from the A. neg. prefix لا, no, not, and P. *chára*, help) Helpless, destitute, without excuse or remedy.

Lácháragí, H. (لاچارگي) Helplessness, destitution.

LÁ-DAWÁ, H. (لادوا) Remediless, irremediable.

Lá-dáwá or *Lá-dáwi*, H. (A. لادعوا, لادعوي) A deed of relinquishment, a deed foregoing a claim, or admitting that there is none: the act of relinquishment.

LÁDHNÁ, Thug. To strangle.

LÁDHKÁ, Thug. Coarse sugar.

LADOHAR, Thug. Killing.

LAḌḌU, H. (لڈو, लड्डू) A sort of sweetmeat of sugar and cocoa-nut shredded, mixed up with curdled milk into large balls.

LAḌTHAḌ, or LAṚTHAṚ, Mar. (लडथड) A disputed matter, litigation concerning a subject in dispute.

LAG, H. &c. (لگ, from S. लग, to be joined to) To, near to, until, as far as; (used in various modified and derivative forms to express contiguity and connexion).

Lág, Mar. (लाग) Connexion, continuity in general,

Laggá, H. (لگا) Affection, attachment: a pole used for pushing on a boat.

Lága, Hindi (लाग) A measuring-rod for land measure. See *Lar*.

Lagán, H. (لگان) A place at which a boat may lie to or be fastened to the shore: stopping or halting a boat.

Lagan, *Lugun*, Mar. (लगन) Marriage, espousals.

Lagí, or *Laggí*, *Lugee*, *Luggee*, Beng. (লগী), H. (لگي) A pole, especially one used for punting or pushing boats along or off shore: in Mar. (लगी) A pole with a small flag, carried in processions.

Lagna, S. &c., sometimes vernacularly also *Lagan*, or *Lugun*, (लग्न, লগন, لگن) The rising of a sign of the zodiac above the horizon, a sign at the time of its rising, or the moment of the sun's entrance into a sign or division of the equator, astrologically considered as the indicator of good or evil, or as the favourable or unfavourable moment for observing ceremonies or occurrences, for holding festivals, and the like: hence it is applied to any season of rejoicing, as a marriage, a festival; and in Mar. is commonly used for marriage, matrimony, or a marriage, a wedding.

Lagnaghaṭiká, Mar. (लग्नघटिका) The hour declared to be favourable for investiture with the sacred cord or for the commencement of the marriage ceremony.

Lagna- or *Laganchiṭi*, or *chiṭhi*, Mar. (लग्नचिटी -चिठी) A paper formerly granted by the government to persons of the inferior castes permitting them to marry, a marriage licence; a paper furnished by the astrologer, declaring the time for the completion of the marriage ceremony: an invitation to a wedding.

Lagna patra, or *patriká*, Beng. Mar. (from S. पत्र, a leaf) The written announcement of the lucky moment for a marriage ceremony: among the Marathas the document is worshipped before the ceremony commences.

Lagna- or *Laganṭahá*, Mar. (लगनटका) A fee for permission to marry.

Lagnaka, Beng. (S. लग्नक) A bondsman, a surety.

Lagnakagrahaṇ, Beng. (S. লগ্নকগ্রহণ) Admitting or accepting as bail or security.

Lagán, or Lagái, H. (لگان, لگاي) The rent or revenue charged on a field or estate.

Lagaiwálá, (?) A cultivator engaging to pay direct revenue to government for a term of years on receiving an advance for the materials of husbandry, to be repaid without interest at fixed intervals of his lease.

Lagha, Thug. A grave-digger.

Laghai, Thug. The office of grave-digger.

Laghanta, Thug. Dead bodies of the victims.

Lagít, Beng. (লগীত) Location of a Ryot; appropriation of land to a tenant (Chittagong): adjacent, contiguous.

Lagiti, Tel. (లగితి) Making advances of cash to a Ryot, or supplying him with cattle, seed-corn, &c.

Lágwaḍ, Mar. (लागवड) Agricultural operations preliminary to sowing; cultivated ground: expense of bringing land into cultivation, repairing decayed houses, villages, &c.

Láglágwaḍ, Mar. (लागलागवड) Agricultural operations, inclusive of sowing.

Lágwaṇ, (लागवण) The operations of ploughing and sowing, also of planting trees; also one of the village accounts, shewing the total assessment, and by whom to be paid.

Lagtá, or Lagtí, H. (لگتا, لگتي) Assessment or stipulated rent of land.

Lagtiwár, H. (لگتيوار) An account kept by the village accountant of each cultivator's lands, rent, and produce, distinguished according to the spring and autumn crops.

Lagtá, or Lagata, Mar. (लगता) Connexion, proximity of persons, things, or places: a contiguous tract or country.

Lagtájáb, Mar. (लगताजाब) A letter of advice attached to the draft or bill, or a notice of it written within the envelope.

Lagtálákhoṭá, or *Lagatlákhoṭá*, Mar. (लगतालाखोटा, लगतलाखोटा) A letter containing advice of a bill or draft folded up and attached to the bill; a letter without an envelope, the superscription being on the same sheet.

Láguligádu, Karn. (ಲಾಗುಲಿಗಾಡು) Compensation for damages: a recompense.

Lahad, H. (A. لحد) A niche in the side of a sepulchre in which dead bodies are deposited, a place where the dead are washed, a grave.

Lahad-bharna, Finally filling up the grave of a deceased person, a ceremony performed on the 39th day after interment.

Lahaṇá, or Lahná, corruptly, Lunah, H. (لهنا) An outstanding debt or balance.

Lahaṇá báki, Uriya (ଲହଣାବାକି) Outstanding balance; excess of advance.

Lahaṇe, Mar. (लहणे) Cash or a draft sent to meet a bill drawn upon a merchant or banker who has no other funds on behalf of the drawer.

Lahaṇíhuṇḍí, Mar. (लहणीहुंडी) A bill taken up by a merchant from another who has funds in his hands to meet a bill drawn upon the former by one who has no funds in his hands, but has in the possession of the latter.

Lahariya, (?) A caste of agricultural Brahmans in the north-west provinces.

Lahárí, Mar. (लहारी) A coin equal to three anas; the value of three anas.

Láhí, Mar. (लाही) Parched rice; swollen or puffed out by slightly scorching.

LAHLHI, H. (لهلهي, लहल्ही) Mud, thick or stiff mud.

LÁHORI-NIMAK, H. (from نمك, salt) Lahore salt, rock or fossil salt, of which there are three deposits in the Panjáb.

LAHTÁR, Thug. A dagger.

LÁIK, H. &c. (A. لايق) Worthy of, fit for, suited to, &c.

Láiḳábád, H. (لايق آباد) A place or country fit for cultivation and population.

Láiḳbanjar, H. (لايق بنجر) Waste land fit for tillage.

Laiḳparia, Uriya (ଲଇକପଡ଼ିଆ) Fallow land fit for cultivation.

Láiḳ-patit, H. (لايق پتت) Fallow land capable of cultivation.

Láiḳ-zamín, H. (لايق زمين) Cultivable land.

Liáḳat, H. (A. لياقت) Fitness, ability, capability, suitableness.

LAILAT UL ḲADIR, H. (A. ليلة القدر) The night of power; the 27th night of Ramzán, when it is said the Kuṛan descended from heaven, and which is observed with much reverence by the Mohammadans of India.

Lailat ul miráj, H. (A. ليلةالمراج) The night of Mohammed's ascent to heaven.

LÁJÁ, H. &c. (لاجا) Rice parched in the husk.

LAḲAB, LUḲUB, pl. ALḲÁB, H. (A. لقب, القاب) A title, titles.

LÁKALÁM-BÁKI, H. (A. لاكلام, without a word, indisputable, and باقي, remainder) Undisputed balance of an account, or of rent or revenue.

LAKHAT, Guz. (S. લખત) A writing, a written document, a deed.

Lakhtang, Guz. (લખતાંગ) Writer, the writer, a term used in papers to denote the person who writes or addresses them.

Lakhuṇ, *Lahhupardhu*, Guz. (લખુણ, લખુપરઠુ) A writing, a document.

LÁKHIRÁJ, vernacularly, sometimes, LÁKHARAJ, corruptly, LAKERAGE, LACKIRAZ, &c. (A. لاخراج, from لا, not, and خراج, tribute) Rent-free land, applied to land exempted for some particular reason from paying any part of the produce to the state. Beng. Reg. xix. xxxvii. 1793; vii. 1822. Madras Reg. xxv. xxxi. 1802. Bom. Reg. xvii. 1827; vi. 1833.

Láhhiraj-dár, H. (P. دار, who has) A holder of rent-free lands.

Lakharaji-bhúmi, Tel. Karn. (లాఖరాజిభూమి) Land exempt from paying revenue to the state.

Laḳhiraj-zamín, H. (P. زمين, land) Alienated or revenue-exempted land.

LAKHOṬÁ, or LÁKHOṬA, Mar. (लखोटा, लाखोटा) A sealed letter, a bundle of papers sticking together. Guz. (લખોટો) The envelope of a letter, the silk bag in which it is inclosed.

LAKIR, Thug. A religious mendicant, a fakir.

LAKÍT, H. (لقيت) In Mohammadan law, a foundling: it is considered meritorious to take charge of a deserted child, and the finder becomes its guardian, but cannot make it a slave; the state is bound to provide for those foundlings of whom no charitable individual takes charge.

LAKSHA, S. (लक्ष), but current in all dialects, sometimes modified as LAK, or more commonly, LÁKH, H. (لك, لاكه), LAKSHA, or LÁKH, or in compounds, LAKH, Mar. (लक्ष, लाख) A hundred-thousand; a *Lac*, or *Láhh*, commonly, though not exclusively, applied to coin, as a *Lákh* of rupees, 100,000 rupees, or, at 2*s.* the rupee, £10,000.

LÁKSHÁ, S. (लाक्षा), commonly LAC, or LACK, vernacularly, LÁKH, H. (لاكه), Mar. (लाख), or LÁK, Karn. (ಲಾಕ್) An insect which constructs its nest in numerous small cells of a resinous substance known in common as shell-lac, and used for sealing letters, &c.: the insect itself furnishes a red dye known as Lac: (from *laksha*, 100,000, in reference to the number of insects in a nest.

LAKSHAṆA, pronounced LAKSHAN, or LAKHAN, S. &c. (लक्षण) A mark, a distinguishing or characteristic sign or token.

LAKSHMAN SINGH, Thug. Term used by the scouts to intimate the approach of danger; properly, a name of an individual.

Lakshmí, corruptly, *Lukmi*, *Lukhee*, *Luximee*, S. &c. (लक्ष्मी) The wife of *Vishṇu*, and goddess of wealth and prosperity.

Lakshmí-vár, or *bár*, S. &c. (लक्ष्मीवार) Thursday.

Lakshmí-pújá, S. &c. (लक्ष्मीपूजा) The worship of *Lakshmí*, on the full-moon of *Áṣwin* (Sept.-Oct.), by bankers and merchants especially: a ceremony in honour of the same, observed by a bride and bridegroom when the bride has been brought to the house of her husband.

LÁLÁ, corruptly, LALLA, (P. لالا) A writer, a clerk, a copyist, a schoolmaster: it is used as an address in speaking to a respectable person, not of high rank, especially with *jí*, annexed; as, *Lálá-jí*, Sir, master.

LÁḶI, Karn. (ಲಾಳಿ) A weaver's shuttle.

LAMAN, LUMUN, or LUMMUN, (?) A caste of traders who formerly brought slaves for sale to Bombay.

LAMBÁḌÍ, corruptly, LAMBALLIE, LOMBALLIE, and LOMBARDIE, Tel. (లంబాడి), also LAMBÁNI, Karn. (ಲಂಬಾಡಿ ಲಂಬಾಣಿ), LAMBÁṆ, Mar. (लंबाण), H. Dakh., LAMBÁṚÁ, (لمبارا), ILAMBAḌI, Tam. (இலம்பாடி) A migratory trader, especially in grain, better known as *Banjárá*, q. v., and travelling from place to place in more or less numerous bodies: in the south they have the character of being thieves, the men stealing cattle and the women children: a party of *Banjárás*, or *Lambáris*, on its march, or encamped.

LAMBARDÁR, LUMBURDÁR, H. (لمبردار, from the English word 'number,' and Persian *dár*, who has) The cultivator who, either on his account, or as the representative of other members of the village, pays the government dues and is registered in the collector's roll according to his number: as the representative of the rest he may hold the office by descent or by election. Beng. Reg. ix. 1824; ii. 1826. Act i. 1841.

Lambardárí, H. (لمبرداري) The office or duty of a Lambardár.

Lambari makadamá, Uriya (ଲମ୍ବରୀମକଦମା, from English *number*, and Arabic *mukadamá*, a suit) Original suit, headed according to its number on the file of causes.

LAKTÍ, H. (لكتي, लकती) The total rent of a property or an estate forming a heading of the *Khataoni*, or *Muntakhab*, of the north-west provinces; equivalent in this sense to *Jamâ-bandí*.

LÁL-JÁTRÍ, Beng. (লালযাত্রী) A pilgrim to Jagannath of the first class, paying formerly heavier fees, and entitled to peculiar privileges.

LAMBHERI, Thug. A sword.

LAMCHÁRI, Beng. (?) (লমচারী) Low land, land liable to inundation.

LÁMCHÍ, Beng. (?) (লামচি) Low, as land liable to inundation: (this and the preceding should probably be written *Namchari*, and *Namchi*, from *nam*, S. B., to bow down, to make low.)

LAMHAR, Hindi (लमहर) A tree that has sprung up of itself in a cultivated field, and which the cultivator may cut down.

LÁMKAN, Thug. The crossing of the road by a hare in front of a gang.

LAMPOCHA, Thug. Crossing of the road by a snake, an unlucky omen: the gang must stop unless they can kill it.

LÂN, or LÂNAT, H. (لعن, لعنة) Curse, imprecation: in Mohammadan law, testimony upon oath: in cases of adultery the several imprecations of the curse of God upon them by husband and wife, the former, if he accuse his wife falsely, the latter if she be not innocent: in such case, however, divorce should follow.

LÁNÁBANDÍ, H. (لانابندي, probably from *láná* لانا, to bring) An agreement formerly practised among the coparcenary proprietors of a village to contribute to the government assessment in proportion to the number of their several ploughs.

LANCHA, Karn. (ಲಂಚ), LANCHAMU, Tel. (లంచము), LÁNCH, Mar. (लांच), ILANJAM, Tam. (இலஞ்சம்), LÁNCH or NÁNCH, Uriya. A bribe, a fee: bribery.

Lánchlúch, *Lánchluchpat*, Mar. (लांचलूच, लांचलुचपत) Bribery and corruption.

Lanchagár, *Lanchahuli*, &c. Karn. (ಲಂಚಗಾರ, ಲಂಚಹುಳಿ) A receiver of bribes.

Lánchkhor, Mar. (लांचखोर), *Lanchákhor*, Karn. (ಲಂಚಾಖೋರ) One who takes a bribe, venal, corrupt.

LÁNGAL, Beng. (S. লাংগল) A plough.

Lángalá, Beng. (S. লাংগলা) Ploughing, cultivation.

Lángaliyá, Beng. (S. লাংগলিযা) A ploughman: ploughing.

LANGAR, LUNGUR, H. (لنگر) An anchor: an almshouse.

Langar khána, H. (لنگرخانه) An almshouse, a place where food and alms were distributed to the poor under the Mohammadan government, by which an assignment from the public revenue was appropriated to the maintenance of such establishments in some parts of Bengal: a similar institution, in which the poor were lodged and fed, was kept up by the Maratha government of Nagpur: in Marathi, the term means also any extensive establishment.

Langar kharch, *Lungur khurch*, H. (from خرچ) Provision or expense incurred for the poor, poor-rates.

LANGOṬ, LANGOṬÁ, LANGOṬÍ, or LUNGOṬ, &c. (لنگوٹ, لنگوٹي, لنگوٹا) A cloth passed between the thighs and tucked into a waist-belt before and behind, to conceal the privities.

LÁNJHÁ, Mar. (लांझा) An unsettled affair, a disputed claim.

LÁO, H. (لاو) The rope by which the leather bucket of a well is drawn up; whence in some places the amount of land irrigated is reckoned, or by *Láos*, instead of wells, being commonly 15 acres to a *Láo*.—Rewari.

Láo-charas, corruptly, *Lao-churrus*, H. (لاوچرس) Irrigation by water raised from wells in the leather bag or bucket called *Charas*, q. v. See also the preceding.

LAPO, Guz. (લપો) Brocade, gold or silver cloth.

LAPUA, Thug. A thief.

LAṚKÁ, H. (لڑکا) A boy.

Laṛkí, (لڑکي) A girl.

Laṛká-kol, H. (لڑکاکول) The name of a mountain tribe in *Chhattisghar*, a branch of the *Kol* tribe, q. v.

LARKIÁ, Thug. A shopkeeper.

LAR, LUR, Hindi (लर) A measuring-rod for land measure:

it varies in different places as $4\frac{1}{2}$, 6, or $6\frac{1}{2}$ cubits: 400 square *lars* is a *bighá*, 20 square *lars* a *katha.*—Puraniya.

LÁSÁ, H. (لاسا) Any viscous exudation or juice of plants, some sorts of which are used as birdlime.

LÁSH, H. &c. (P. لاش) A corpse.

LASHKAR, LUSHKUR, commonly, LASCAR, (لشکر) A native sailor, but especially applied also to tent-pitchers, inferior artillerymen, and others: (the word is properly *Lashkarí*, one attached to, or following, a *lashkar*, or army, but it has come insensibly to take the meaning and pronunciation here given).

LAṢMÁMÁṬÍ, Hindi (लशमामाटी) Adhesive-clay land.—Puraniya.

LÁṬ, or LÁṬH, H. (لاٹ, لاٹھ) A staff, a column, a pillar, especially the pillars found in various parts of Upper India, as at Allahabad, Delhi, &c., bearing inscriptions in the ancient form of the *Nágari* alphabet.

Láṭhí, corruptly, *Lattie*, and *Luttie*, sometimes short, as *Laṭh*, *Laṭhí*, H. &c. (لاٹھي, लाठी, لٹھ, لٹھي, लठी) A staff, a stick, a club, a bludgeon.

Láṭhiwálá, corrupted into, *Láṭhiwal*, and *Láṭhiyál*, or *Lutteeal*, H. (لاٹھي والا) A club-man, a man armed with a bludgeon, many of whom are retained by Zamindars, indigo planters, and others, in quarrels respecting lands and boundaries, when serious affrays sometimes take place between the opposite parties.

LAṬAN, Hindi (लटन) A name given to all the early sown cold-weather crops.—Puraniya.

LÁṬÍ, LÁṬE, Karn. (ಲಾಟಿ, ಲಾಟೆ) A wooden instrument with which parched grain is flattened: a spinning-wheel.

LATKANÍYÁ, Thug. A very small purse worn only by thieves and Thugs.

LAṬṬÁ, incorrectly, LUṬṬHA, (لٹّا, लट्ठा) A measuring-rod or pole: a *bighá* is a square of 20 *Laṭṭás*: in the survey of the north-west provinces the measuring chain is divided into 10 *Laṭṭás*, and each *Laṭṭá* into 10 links.

LAUND, H. (لوند) An intercalary month.

LAUNḌÁ, H. (لونڈا) A slave or servant-boy: *f.* LAUNḌÍ, (لونڈي) A servant or slave-girl.

LAUṢ, or LAWIṢ, H. (A. لوث) Stain, contamination: in Mohammadan law, any indication of a person or of persons being implicated in the guilt of a murder, as a cloth or sword stained with blood found in their possession, &c.

LAVA, and LAVÍ, S. &c. (लव, लवी, from लू, to cut or reap) Reaping, cutting corn.

Lavana, S. &c. (लवन) Reaping.

Lavaní, or *Launí*, H. (لوني) Wages in kind to reapers at harvest time; also, reaping, cultivation.

LAVAṆA, S. &c. (लवण), vernacularly, LAVAN, or LABAN, Beng. (লবন), LON, H. (لون), LUṆ, Guz. (લુણ) Salt.

LÁVAṆAMU, Tel. (లావణము), LÁVAṆA, Karn. (ಲಾವಣ) A list of public servants, or of soldiers: the profits of a custom-house: (it is said to be Hindi, perhaps from an obsolete causal of *Láná*, to bring).

LÁVAṆÍ, or LÁVAṆE, pronounced sometimes LAUN, or LAUNI, or LAUNE, corruptly, LOWNE, and LOWNEE, Mar. (लावणी, लावणे, from S. लू, to cut or reap), Karn. (ಲಾವಣಿ) The operation of planting, ploughing, and sowing; cultivation, agriculture.

Lavaṇí patrak, corruptly, *Lownee putruck*, Mar. (लवणीपत्रक) One of the village accounts shewing the total assessment, and by whom paid: it is also described as a general statement of the land held by each individual, with the amount of the assessment, and every other item of revenue leviable from the cultivator.

LÁVAṆYÁRJITAM, S. &c. (लावण्यार्जितं, from लावण्य, beauty, and अर्जित, acquired) Woman's property, having been presented to her by her parents and friends as a mark of respect or affection.

LAVU, or ILAVU, Tam. (இலவு) A cotton-tree producing a fine sort of cotton with thin and short fibres.

LÁWÁ, H. (لاوا) Parched grain.

LAWÁDA, Mar. (लवाद) An umpire, an arbitrator.

Lawádi, Guz. (લવાદી) Arbitration, award.

LAWÁHAḲ, H. (لواحق, plur. of *Láhak*) Servants, dependants: dependencies, appurtenances.

LÁWÁRIṢ, H. &c. (A. لا, not, and وارث, an heir) Heirless, having no heir; also, though rather laxly, having no claimant.

Láwáriṣí, H. (لاوارثي) The condition of being without a claimant or heir, as applied to property.

Láwáriṣmál, H. (from مال, wealth) Property to which there is no heir, and which therefore escheats to the state.

LÁZIM, vernacularly, LÁJIM, H. &c. (لازم) Fit or requisite for, necessarily or naturally belonging to, &c., inseparable from: in law, the term is applied to engagements which cannot be dissolved without the acquiescence of both parties.

Lawázim, or *Lawázima*, vernacularly, *Lawájima*, H. &c. corruptly, *Loazima* (لوازمه, plur. of the preceding) Necessaries, requisites, appurtenances, baggage, accommodation, perquisites or dues of office, necessary vouchers or documents. *Lawájima*, Mar. (लवाजिम) Train, retinue.

Lawázim-i-sanad, H. (لوازم سند) The particulars necessary for the grant of a patent or *sanad*: the vouchers from and to the different officers and departments requisite for the final issue of a grant of land or revenue under the Mohammadan government, and which were usually indorsed on the patent.

LEHENU, Guz. (લેહેણુ) An outstanding debt, a sum of money due from any one.

LEKHÁ, H. &c. (S. ليكها), LEKHA, Mar. (लेख), LEKHKA, Tel. (లెఖ్ఖ), LEKKA, or LEKHKHA, Karn. (ಲೆಕ್ಕ, ಲೆಖ್ಖ) A writing, an account, any written document.

Lekhak, H. &c. (S. ليكهك, लेखक), *Lekeh*, Karn. (ಲೆಕೆಹ್) A writer, a clerk, an accountant.

Lekhá-bahi, H. &c. (ليكها بهي) An account-book.

Lekhájoká, Beng. (লেখাজোকা) A set of accounts or written documents.

Lekhanihan, Mal. (ലെഖനിഹൻ) A postman, a letter-carrier: one who signs a paper by proxy, or by a mark, being unable to write.

Lekhaparhá, and *Lekhapatra*, Mar. (S. लेखपढा, लेखपत्र) A general term for official or business papers; an account, a document, a voucher, a deed; any writing.

Lekhapramána, Mar. (S. लेखप्रमाण) Written evidence or authority, a voucher, a document.

Lekhá-upare, Uriya (S. ଲେଖାଉପରେ) Indorsement; what is written above or upon a writing.

Lekhya, S. &c. (लेख्य) What may be, or is to be, written: a manuscript, a written document, a letter.

Lekhyalakshana, S. (from लक्षण, a mark) Description or definition of documentary evidence.

LENÁ-DENÁ, H. (لينادينا, a compound of the two verbs, *lená*, to take, and *dená*, to give: also abridged to LEN-DEN, and, in the aorist, LÉWE-DÉWE) Traffic, trade, barter, buying and selling: also borrowing and lending.

LENDKÍÁ, Thug. A washerman.—Dakh. Th.

LENE, Mar. (लेणे) The cave temples and their embellishments, found at Ellora, Ajunta, and other places.

LEP, H. &c. (S. ليپ, लेप) Smearing, anointing, plastering: plaster, ointment.

Lepaka, S. (लेपक) A plasterer, an anointer.

LEWÁ, Guz. (લેવા) A caste of the Kunbi tribe.

LEWÁLÍ, Thug. A blanket.

LEZAM, H. (P. ليزم) A bow with an iron chain instead of a string, used in gymnastic exercises.

LÍÁ, Hindi (लीआ) Lands which are annually flooded.

LIFÁFA, H. (A. لفافه) A wrapper, an outer cover, an envelope.

LIGÁDU, Karn, (ಲಿಗಾಡು) Compensation for damages

LIGIRÁ, Asam. (লিগিৰা) A female servant granted to officers of state, by the Asam monarch.

Lihchhau, Asam. (লিকছৌ) A male servant similarly granted.

LIHAINDÍ, H. (لهيندي, लिहैंडी) Throwing up water for irrigation from a pond or river with a kind of basket worked by two men.

LIKHÁ, H. &c. (لكها, लिखा, the same as LEKHÁ, both being derived from the S. root *likh* लिख, to draw lines, to write) A writing, a letter, &c. See *Lekhá*.

Likhan, Beng., Mar., &c. (S. लिखन) A writing, a document, a letter.

Likhita, Beng, Mar. (S. लिखित) Written, what is written, a manuscript, a document: in Mar., also, *Likhita* (लिखीत).

Likhita-sákshi, Karn. (S. ಲಿಖಿತಸಾಕ್ಷಿ) Written evidence.

LIKKHA, Dakh. Thug. A Mohammadan.

LILÁM, LILÁU (more usually, in other dialects, but less correctly, *Nílám*), Guz. (લીલામ, લીલાઉ, Port., *Leilao*) Auction sale, a public sale or auction.

LINGA, S. adopted in all the dialects, (लिङ्ग) A mark, a characteristic sign: the distinguishing mark of gender or sex; the male organ: the phallus, as the type of Śiva, and as worshipped in all parts of India: it is usually of stone or marble, and is set up in temples especially appropriated to the worship of *Śiva*, or *Mahádeva*, under this form. There were, at the time of the Mohammadan invasion, twelve principal *Śiva-lingas* in India, namely, 1. *Somanátha*, in Guzerat; 2. *Mallikárjuna*, in Telingana at Srísailam; 3. *Mahákála*, at Ujayin; 4. *Omkára*, on the Narbudda; 5. *Amareśwara*, also at Ujayin; 6. *Vaidyanáth*, at Deogerh in Bengal; 7. *Rámeswára*, at Rami-seram; 8. *Bhímaśanhara*, in Rajamahendri; 9. *Tryambaka*, at the sources of the Godávarí, 10. *Gautameśa*, where, unknown; 11. *Kedáreśa*, on the Himalaya; and 12. *Viśveśwara*, at Benares. In the south the principal *Śiva-lingas* at present worshipped are at *Kánchi* or *Conjeveram*, *Jambukeśwar* near Trichinopoly, *Tirunamale*, *Kálahastri*, and *Chidambaram*: one sect of Hindus, the *Víra-Śaivas* or *Jangamas* of the south, wear a small representation of the *linga* in a case round the neck or on one arm, whence they are called also *Lingadháris*, and *Lingavants*, as below.

Lingá-it, Mar. (लिंगाईत), *Lingadhári*, or *Lingavant*, erroneously, *Lingumut*, Karn. (ಲಿಂಗಧಾರಿ, ಲಿಂಗವಂತ) A member of the *Jangama* or *Vira-Ṣaiva* sect, or a worshipper of Ṣiva as the *Linga*, and carrying a representation of the type about his person: the sect, which is numerous in the central and southern parts of the peninsula, is of modern origin, being founded by a Brahman named Básava, residing at Kalyán in Karnata in the middle of the 12th century. The *Lingáits* differ from the Brahmanical followers of Ṣiva in denying the sanctity of the Brahmanical order, and the authority of the Vedas; in the recognition of various divinities, and in virtually abolishing the distinction of caste, and the inferiority of females. One division of them, termed *Árádhyas*, are, by birth, Brahmans; but the rest, who are more especially termed *Jangamas*, are of the *Ṣúdra* and mixed castes, and look upon the *Árádhyas* as their inferiors. The *Jangamas* are again distinguished as two-fold—*Sámánya* or ordinary, and *Visésha* or extraordinary, the latter professing greater purity of manners. There is also a lower grade of sectaries, or *Bhaktas*, who are likewise distinguished as *Sámánya bhaktas*, and *Visésha bhaktas*; the former retain their caste, but in all other respects are the same as the *Sámánya Jangamas*; the latter are entirely exempt from caste, and are bound by vow to honour the *Guru*, or spiritual teacher, the *Linga* and the *Jangama*, or brother in the faith: accounts respecting their manners vary; but as an inveterate hostility subsists between them and the Brahmans, accounts derived from the latter are not to be depended on. The *Jangamas* have a literature of their own, written mostly in the Karnata and Telugu languages, particularly the *Básava Purána* in the former. The *Árádhyas* are sometimes well versed in Sanskrit literature.—Account of the Jangams, by C. P. Brown, Madras Journal of Literature and Science.

Lingabanajigár, Karn. (ಲಿಂಗಬಣಜಿಗಾರ) A merchant or trader of the *Lingáit* sect.

Lingakáya, Tel. (లింగకాయ) The small box in which the *Linga* is kept by those who wear the emblem.

Lingí, S. &c. (लिङ्गी) One who wears the outward emblems of the order or sect to which he belongs; but it is more usually applied to signify a pretender, a hypocrite, or one who assumes the external emblems of a caste or order to which he does not belong, or of which he does not perform the duties: the bearer of a *Linga*.

Líp, or **Lípra**, Thug. Cloth in pieces, not made into garments.

Lipi, S. &c. (लिपि), in Karn. also **Liphi** (ಲಿಫಿ) Writing, a writing, a manuscript, a written document.

Liruá, Hindi (लिरुआ) Rice-straw, especially such as is suitable for fodder.

Lityá, Uriya (ଲିତ୍ୟା) A measure of time, the 60th of a *Daṇḍa*, or 24 seconds.

Lochhá, Asam. (লোছা) A land measure in Asam equal to 11½ feet square.

Lod, Thug. A bullock: among the Dakh. Thugs, blood.

Lodh, Thug. A bullock.

Lodha, Thug. A class of Mohammadan Thugs descended from, or grafted upon, the Oudh stock, and found chiefly on the borders of that kingdom, or in the Tarai bordering on Nepal.

Lodhá, **Lodhí**, H. (لودها, لودهي) The name of a caste, or a member of it, following the practice of husbandry in the north-west provinces: amongst the Maraṭhas, the foreign *Lodhí-* or *Lodhí paradésí*, from being a native of Hindustan, is employed as a thatcher and keeper of bullocks, &c.

Lógar, Karn. (ಲೋಗರ) A foreigner, a stranger.

Logili, Tel. (లోగిలి) The interior of a house, and all belonging to it.

Loha, S. &c. (लोह) Iron: any metal.

Lohár, H. &c. (لوهار, from S. *Lohakára* लोहकार) A worker in iron, a blacksmith; one of the artificers of a village.

Lohábhisára, S. &c. (लोहाभिसार) Lustration of arms: private or public worship of weapons on the ninth of the light half of Áswin: under the native rule it was a military ceremonial of much splendour observed as a preliminary to the season for military operations.

Lohá-mahál, H. (لوها محال) The iron department; revenue derived from the iron mines, and smelting and working the metal.

Lohár-khána, H. &c. (P. خانه, a house) A blacksmith's forge, a shop.

Loharbarheyá, Thug. A pair of jackals (lit. the blacksmith and carpenter) crossing the road, a bad omen, indicating arrest and confinement.

Lohoṛi, Guz. (લોહોડી, -ડી) An iron-pan or plate, a frying-pan, a plate for striking the hours on.

Loka, also, vernacularly, **Lok**, and, vulgarly, **Log**, S. &c. (लोक) Man, mankind, in ordinary use; as *Sáhib-lok*, gentry, Europeans: a world, a sphere, a region; as *Triloka*, the three worlds, heaven, earth, and hell; or earth, sky, and heaven: in mythology, fourteen spheres, exclusive of *Naraka* or *Tartarus*, are recognised, seven upper and seven lower—1. *Bhú-loka*, earth; 2. *Bhuvar-loka*, atmosphere or firmament; 3. *Swar-loka* or *Swárga*, heaven, the sphere of the inferior deities; 4. *Mahar-loka*, the region above the pole-star tenanted by saints; 5. *Jana-loka*, the sphere of the sons of Brahmá; 6. *Tapo-loka*, the region of devotion, the abode of *Ṛishis*; and 7. *Saty-loka*, or *Brahma-loka*, the region of truth, of Brahma, to which the pure are elevated. The seven regions below the earth are the habitations of the snake gods, and are named in the order of their *tala* or descent—*Atala*, *Vitala*, *Sutala*, *Rasátala*, *Talátala*, *Mahátala*, and *Pátála*: sectaries have also invented *lokas* or regions of their own, as *Vaikuṇṭha*, the sphere of *Vishṇu*; *Goloka*, the region of *Krishṇa*, &c.

Lokálaya, Beng. (S. লোকালয) The resort of men; a village, a town.

Lokáranya, Beng. (S. লোকারণ্য) A crowd, a concourse, lit., a forest of men.

Lokáyata, S. (लोकायत) A system of atheistical philosophy attributed to *Chárváka*.

Lokáyita, S. (लोकायित) A follower of *Chárváka's* doctrines.

Laukika, S. &c. (लौकिक) Worldly, popular, secular.

Lokan, Thug. A gun.

Lol, Thug. The throat.—Dakh. Th.

Lolí, or Lúlí, H. (لولي) A courtesan.

Lon, or Lún, Loon, H. &c. (لون, from S. *lavan*) Salt. See *Lavan*.

Loná, H. (لونا) Salt, saline, brackish.

Lonámáṭí, Beng. (লোনামাটী) Salt-land, land from which salt may be extracted.

Lonár, H. (لونار) A salt-pit, a place where salt is produced.

Loní or *Lúní*, H. (لوني) Saline efflorescence from walls.

Loniá, or *Lúniá*, (لونيا) Saline, brackish: a salt-maker: a class of traders.

Loṇárí, Mar. (लोणारी) A caste, or member of it, whose occupation is hewing wood, making charcoal, &c.

Londiṭeḍu, Tel. (లొండితెడు) A span measured by the thumb and forefinger.

Lopa, S. &c. (लोप) Disappearance, loss.

Lop-rahná, or *Lopná*, Thug. To lie hid or asleep.

Lopí-, *Lopi-khán*, or *Lopi-singh*, Thug. A term used by scouts to intimate the approach of danger. *Lopi-hona*, to be concealed.

Lo-paikárí, (?) An under-renter or tenant.

Loṭ, or Láṭ, H. &c. (لوت, لات) The English word 'Lot,' denoting a portion or division of property allotted for public sale.

Loṭ-bandí, H. &c. (لوت بندي, from *lot*, and *bandí*, arrangement) The schedule or list exhibiting the apportionment of an estate to be put up in lots at auction for sale or lease.

Loṭṭí, Tel. (లొట్టి) A small earthen vessel fixed on the stem of different palms to collect the *táṛí* juice.

Lóṭu, Tel. (లోటు) Loss, deficiency.

Lótu, Tel. (లోతు) Depth of water, &c.

Luchchá, H. (لچا) A libertine, a profligate; also a low abandoned fellow, who leads a dissolute life, subsisting by gambling, or by intimidating respectable persons into giving him money.

Lugaṛá, or Lugaḍá, Guz. (લુગડું) Clothes or apparel in general: in Marathi, *Lugaṛen* (लुगडें), is a long strip of coloured cloth worn as a petticoat.

Lukibidyá, Beng. (লুকিবিদ্যা) A science by which a person is supposed to have the power of rendering himself invisible.

Lukṭa, A. (لقطه) In Mohammadan law, Treasure trove, property which a person finds on the ground, and takes charge of as a trust until claimed, calling witnesses to his finding it, and announcing his intention of restoring it: if not claimed after a year he should dispose of it, if of any value, in charity, or he may keep it, but still for the owner, if the article be durable.

Luḷen, Mar. (लुळें) Mob, rabble, dregs of the people.

Luṇ, Guz. (લુણ) Salt. See *Lavana* and *Lon*.

Luṇar, Guz. (લુણાર) A place where salt is made.

Luṇo, Guz. (લુણો) Salt, or the saline efflorescence from walls.

Lung, and Lungí, H. &c. (لنگ, لنگي) A cloth passed between the thighs. Beng. (লুংগী) A petticoat: it is said also to be a large handkerchief of blue silk and cotton mixed, carried over one shoulder; used sometimes as a scarf, sometimes as a waistbelt.

Lúṭ, Looṭ, H. &c. (لوٹ) Plunder, robbery, pillage.

Lúṭáí, H. (لوٹائي) Plunder, pillage, booty.

Luṭárá, Mar. (लुटारा) A plunderer, a robber.

Luṭáú, Mar. (लुटाऊ) Acquired by plunder, booty, spoil.

Lúṭbáz, H. (لوٹ باز) A plunderer, a robber.

Lúṭí, or *Luṭiá*, H. (لوٹي, لوٹیا), Beng. *Luṭiyára* (লুটিয়ারা) or *Luṭiwálá*, (لوٹیوالا) A plunderer, a robber, a mounted robber, a Pindhárí.

Lúṭ-khúṭ, and *Lúṭ-páṭ*, H. (لوٹ کہوٹ, لوٹپاٹ) Robbing, plunder, pillage.

M.

MÁ, Tam. (மா) One-twentieth : a land measure, the twentieth of a *Veli*, more correctly, *Máú*, q. v. It is also in general use as the representative of the S. *mahá*, great, especially in compounds.

MÁ, H. &c. (ما, मा, S. माता) A mother: in Bengal, addressed to any female as an appellation of respect: when addressed by a husband to his wife it intimates his relinquishing her society in the latter character.

Másí, H. (ماسي) A mother's sister.

MÂBAR, H. (A. معبر) A ferry, a ford. MÎBAR, a ferry-boat.

MÂÁḲILAT, A. (معاقلة) In Mohammadan law, fine of atonement for bloodshed.

MÂÁSH, H. (A. معاش) Place or means of living, livelihood: the term was applied to pensions granted to various persons in Benares in 1781, and confirmed by Ben. Reg. xxxiv. 1795.

Bad-mâásh, H. (A. P. بدمعاش) A disreputable person, one living dishonestly or viciously.

MABLAḠH, H. (A. مبلغ) A sum of money, ready-money.

Mablagh-bandí, (مبلغ بندي) Specifying the sum total of an account, the adjusted balance.

MÁCHÁ, MACHÁN, H. (ماچا, مچان), MÁCHÁN, Beng. (মাচান), MANCHE, Tel. (మంచె), MANCHIGE, Karn. (ಮಂಚಿಗೆ), MÁCH, MÁCHÍ, Mar. (माची), from the S. MANCHA, (मञ्च) A raised platform, a scaffold in general, but commonly applied in Hindustan to the temporary thatched platform raised on bambus in a field where a man sits to watch the crops: in Maraṭhi, a frame supporting a stack of grass, or one on which grain is exposed to dry.

MACHH, MACHHA, or MACHHÍ, H. (مچھ, مچھي), MÁCHH, Beng. (মাছ), MACHHEMU, MATSYAMU, Tel. (మచ్ఛెము, మత్స్యము): these and other similar forms are all from MATSYA, S. (मत्स्य) A fish.

Machadiá, Uriya (ମଛଦିଆ) Rent or right of fishery.

Machalimávu, Tel. (మచలిమావు) A fishery.

Machalipannu, Tel. (మచలిపన్ను) Tax on fishing.

Máchhi, or *Máchhimár*, Guz. (માછી, માછીમાર) A fisherman, usually of the *Koli* tribe.

Máchhuyá, Beng. (মাছুয়া) A fisherman, a vender of fish.

MACHHUA, Thug. Keeper of a Saraï.

MADD, MUDD, H. (A. مدّ) Extension, prolonging: a sign denoting the commencement of a paragraph or the insertion of a new item: also a dry measure equal to a *Ratl* and a third, or, according to some, to two *Ratls*, or two pounds.

MAD, or MADA, MUD, MUDA, H. &c. (S. مد, मद) Intoxication, or any intoxicating or stupefying beverage: pride, haughtiness.

Madaka, or *Madak*, Beng. (S. মদক) Inebriating; any stupefying or intoxicating article, as toddy, opium, bhang, &c. H. (مدك) A pellet of opium or other drug for smoking.

Mada-khor, Beng. (from P. خور, who eats) A drunkard.

Madya, S. &c. (मद्य) Wine, spirituous liquor.

MÁḌA, Tel. (మాడ) A half pagoda; whence it is applied to a rate of rent, or payment of 50 per cent.: any money or coin.

MÁḌÁ, or MÁṚÁ, Beng. (মাড়া) Threshing or treading out corn.

Máḍaniyá, Beng. (মাড়নিয়া) A thresher, one who beats or treads corn.

MADAD, MUDUD, H. &c. (A. مدد) Help, assistance; allowance or provision.

Madadgár, H. &c. (مددگار) A helper, an assister, a benefactor, an ally, an assistant clerk or writer in an office.

Madad-hharch, H. &c. (P. خرچ) Charitable expenses, sums paid to help others.

Madad-mâásh, H. &c. (from A. معاش, as above) Grant of means of subsistence in general; also, assignment of revenue for the support of learned or religious Mohammadans, or of benevolent institutions, by the government.

MADAD, incorrectly, MADAT, MUDDUT, H. (مدد) An intoxicating pill or bolus formed of chopped betel leaf and opium, which may be swallowed or smoked in a pipe: the sale was originally prohibited, but was licensed, to an extent not exceeding five *tolas*, by Act. xi. 1849, s. 5.

MADAGAḌA, Karn. (ಮದಗಡ) An advance of money for carrying on cultivation, repayable at harvest time without interest.

Madagaḍadapatra, Karn. (S. *patra* पत्र, a leaf) A bond for repayment of an advance to cultivators.

MADAGU, Karn. (ಮದಗು), Tam. (மதகு) A sluice to let off water from a tank.

MAḌAI, Tam. (மடை) A sluice, a channel from a pond or the like for irrigation.

Mêl-maḍai, Tam. (மேல்மடை) Land first watered, that which is situated nearest the sluice. See *Kiḻ-maḍai*.

MAḌAKA, Tel. (మడక) A plough with oxen complete. See *Araka*.

MADÁKHIL, H. (مداخل, plur. of MADAKHAL, مدخل) Entrances, additions: income, revenue; additions to the revenue of a district, either from the annexation of other lands, or from the full assessment of lands which had been wholly, or partially, exempt from payment of revenue.

Madákhil-mahkárij, H. (مداخل ماخارج) Additions and diminutions: changes in the disposition of landed property, or in the arrangement of the shares in a village.

MADANOTSAVA, S. (मदनोत्सवः) A festival held in honour of Madana, the delighter, *i.e.* the deity of love, on the 13th and 14th of Chaitra.

MADÁR, H. (A. مدار) A place to which progress is directed, a centre, a centrical spot.

Madár-ul-mahám, H. (A. مدارالمهام) A principal manager, a prime minister: as it were, the centre of affairs.

Madárkár, H. (مداركار) A manager, a chief man of business.

MADÁRI, (مداري) A juggler.

MADÁWATNÍ, H. (مداوتني) A female match-maker: a woman employed to find a suitable match for a man.

MÁDARU (?) A low caste of people in Kurg, whose business is chiefly mat and basket making, and who are included amongst the servile classes.

Mádaruka-sabuvari, Karn. (ಮಾದರುಕಸಬುವರಿ) An annual tax on the manufacturers of baskets, mats, &c.

MADDI CHAKKA IJÁRA, Karn. (ಮದ್ದಿಚಕ್ಕೆಯಿಜಾರ) Tax levied in Mysore on the collector of the bark of the Maddi tree, from which a red dye is prepared.

MADE, Karn. (ಮಡೆ) Strong, rich, as land in the vicinity of water.

Madehola, *Madekattu*, Karn. (ಮಡೆಹೊಲ, ಮಡೆಕಟ್ಟು) Rich land.

MADEGARU, (?) Mal. A class of predial slaves in *Kurg*.

MADEPÁLU, Tel. (మడేపాలు) Share, in kind assigned to the cultivators. See *Metipálu*.

MADHAGHARÍ, Mar. (मधघडी) The second sort of paper made at *Daulatabad*, as distinguished from the best kind, termed *Bahadur-khání*.

MÁDHAVI, Karn. (S. ಮಾಧವಿ) Sugar, clayed or candied.

MADHU, S. &c. (मधु) Sweet; lit. or fig., honey, a spirituous liquor distilled from the blossoms of the Bassia latifolia: the month *Chaitra* (March-April), the season of spring.

Madhundha, Tel. (మధుంధ) Treacle produced from the fermented juice of the date and other palm-trees, commonly known in the south of India as Jagari.

Madhuparka, S., but used in most Hindu dialects, (मधुपर्कः) An offering of honey, butter, and curds, presented to a person to whom it is intended to shew particular respect on his coming to a house, as to a guest, to a bridegroom at a marriage, to a Brahman at a sacrifice, and the like; hence it is sometimes used for the occasion on which it is presented, as a marriage or other festival; also in Telugu (మధుపర్కములు, pl.) for the new cloths dyed with turmeric presented to the bride and bridegroom.

Madhur, or *Madhura*, S. &c. (मधुर) Sweet; applied also to the contrary of salt.

Madhuri, S. &c. (fem. of *madhura*, Uriya, ମଧୁରୀ) Land not within the influence of the sea and free from any saline impregnation, in contradistinction to the *Nimahi*, or salt lands, or those from which, being washed by the tide, salt is manufactured.—Cuttack.

Madhuprásana, S. (मधुप्रासनं) Putting a little honey into the mouth of a new-born male infant, one of the Sanskáras, or purificatory ceremonies of the Hindus.

MADHWA-ÁCHÁRYA, S. &c. (मध्वाचार्य्य) The founder of a sect of Vaishnavas in the south of India in the thirteenth century, hence termed *Mádhwas*, or *Madhwáchárís*.

MÁDHWÍ, S. &c. (माध्वी) A spirituous liquor distilled from the blossoms of the Bassia latifolia.

MADHYA, S. &c. (मध्य) The middle, the central, centrical: also, MADHYE (मध्ये) In the midst, in the centre. Besides the primary and correct forms which they also have, some dialects admit various modifications of these words, as *Majhár*, *Majhlá* H. (مجهار, مجهلا), *Máj*, *Májh*, *Májhe*, *Mejh*, Beng. (মাজ, মাঝ, মাঝে, মেঝ), *Máj*, *Májhárí*, Mar. (माज, माझारी), *Maddiyam*, Tam. (மத்தியம்).

Madhyadés, S. &c. (मध्य, middle, and देश, country) The middle region; in the original geography, the country bounded by the Sewalik hills on the north, the confluence of the Ganga and Yamuna on the south, the southern branch of the Himalaya on the east, and the Vindhya mountains on the west, comprising the modern provinces of Allahabad, Gorakhpur, Oudh, Delhi, Agra, and part of Bundelkhand. The term is in use among the Marathas to denote the country between the Konkan and Kandesh.

Madhya prasangá, Uriya (S. ମଧ୍ୟପ୍ରସଙ୍ଗ) Interlocutory.

Madhyastha, S. &c. (मध्य, between, and स्थ, who stands) A mediator, an umpire, a middle-man: in Malabar, the pl. *Madhyasthamár*, arbitrators, corresponds with *Panchayat* in other places.

Mádhyasthyam, corruptly, *Madesthum*, S. &c. (माध्यस्थ्यं) Arbitration, intervention, interference of a third party to secure the observance of an engagement between two others.

Madhyavarti, Tel. (మధ్యవర్తి) A mediator, an umpire, an arbitrator.

MADI, Tel. Karn. (మడి) A rice-field, a garden bed.

Madi, Tam. (மதி) Valuation, estimate; also Madipu (மதிப்பு).

Mádi, or Máṛí, Mar. (माडी) The sap of the cocoa-nut, especially when fermented; properly opposed to the sap of the *táṛ* palm, or *táṛí* (ताडी), although the latter is applied to both kinds.

Mádiga, Tel. (మాదిగ) A low caste, that of the *Chaklar*, or workers in skins and leather; the *Chamár* of Upper India.

Mádigavádu, Tel. (మాదిగవాడు) A man of the low caste of *Chaklars*.

Mádige, Tel. (మాదిగె) Of or belonging to the caste of workers in hides and leather.

Madike, Karn. (ಮಡಿಕೆ) A plough with oxen complete.

Mádiri, or Mádri, Tel. Karn. (S. మాదిరి, మాద్రి) A pattern, a specimen.

Madivaḷa, Karn. (ಮಡಿವಳ) A washerman.

Madoria, Thug. Fighting of cats, as an omen.

Madrasa, Mudrusu, corruptly, Madressah, and Madrissah, H. (A. مدرسه) A college, an academy.

Mudaris, H. (A. مدرسه) The principal or rector of a college, a teacher or professor.

Madumu, Tel. (మడుము) A stone sluice or channel by which the water flows to the fields.

Madupubídu, Tel. (మడుపుబీడు) Waste lands attached to the lands cultivated by a farmer, that he may bring them also into cultivation.

Maduve, or Madive, Karn. (ಮದುವೆ, ಮದಿವೆ) Marriage.

Maduvéprasta, Karn. (ಮದುವೇಪ್ರಸ್ತ) The marriage ceremony.

Mafḳúd, H. (A. مفقود) Missing, lost: in Mohammadan law it implies a person of whom it is not known whether he be living or dead.

Mág, Mar. (माग), Maggamu, Tel. (మగ్గము), Magga, Karn. (ಮಗ್ಗ) A loom.

Mág, Mar. (माग, S. मार्ग) A track, a channel for water to irrigate a garden or plantation.

Maga, Karn. (ಮಗ) A son.

Makkaḷu, Karn. (ಮಕ್ಕಳು) Children.

Makkaḷa-santána, or *Makkal-santán*, Karn. (ಮಕ್ಕಳಸಂತಾನ) Descendants in the male line.

Mágadha, S. (मागध) A bard or herald: one of the mixed castes, born of a Vaiṣya father and Kshatriya mother: also a native of Magadhá, or South Bahar.

Magáhi, H. (मगाहि) A tribe of agriculturists in Bahar: (probably a vernacular form of *Mágadhi*, or native of *Magadhá*).

Magamai, corruptly, Maghomy, Tam. (மகமை) Contribution formerly levied on merchants and cultivators for a temple, now given optionally: a fee or donation to which an individual or establishment may be entitled.

Mágana, Uriya (ମାଗଣ, probably for *Mángná*, q. v.) Fees exacted by Zamindars from the cultivators: a contribution raised in shares.

Mágan-khandáiti, corruptly *Mongum-khandity*, Uriya (ମାଗଣ ଖଣ୍ଡାଇତି) A tax formerly levied by the Hill Rajas of Cuttack to cover the expense of keeping up an armed police, commuted for a money payment by Government.

Máganam, corruptly, Maganny, Magaun, Mogany, Tam. (மாகாணம்), Mágani, Karn. (ಮಾಗಣಿ,-from the A. *Makán* مکان, a place, an abode) A division of a revenue district, usually consisting of six or seven villages; the subdivision of a *tahsildárí*.

Mágaṇi-paiki-grámu, Karn. (ಮಾಗಣಿಪೈಕಿಗ್ರಾಮು) A village belonging to a district.

Mágaṇi, Tel. Karn. (మాగాణి) Wet cultivation; the cultivation of low lands by artificial irrigation; lands that are so irrigated.

Mágaṇi, pron. Máháṇi, Tam. (மாகாணி) A sixteenth.

Mágáni palisa, Mal. (മാഗാണിപലിശ) A rate of interest calculated in grain, one-sixteenth of a *Yedangali*, per annum on the value of a fanam.

Magdar, Mugdur, H. (مگدر, S. *mudgara* मुद्गर) A club, a mallet; a thick heavy club used in exercise like dumb bells.

Magh, Mugh, corruptly, Mug, Mugg, (?) A name commonly applied to the natives of Arakan, particularly those bordering on Bengal, or residing near the sea; the people of Chittagong. According to Lieut. Phayre, however, the Arakanese disclaim the appellation, and restrict it to a class whom they hold in utter contempt: the descendants of the Arakanese who were settled at Chittagong and Dacca, by Bengali mothers: the origin of the word is unknown. In P. *Magh* (مغ), is a fire worshipper, also a wine-drinker or tavern-keeper.

Mágh, or Mágha, H. &c. (S. ماگھ, माघ), Mágam, Tam. (மாகம்) The month so called; the 10th of the Hindu year when the sun enters Capricorn, and when the full moon is near the asterism *Maghá* (Jan.-Feb.): on the 1st of this month, according to solar computation, or the first lunation of the moon, that is, the day of new moon, a great festival is observed in Upper India, when bathing in the sea at Ganga-Ságara, or the mouth of the Bhágírathí, is considered of peculiar efficacy.

Mágház, Hindi (माघात) Land broken up in *Mágh* for the next year's crops.

Mághát-kí-phasal, Hindi (माघात की फसल) The crops that are sown between *Múgh* and the rains.

Mámáṇgam, or, more correctly, *Mámágam*, Tam. (மாமாங்கம், மாமாகம்) A great festival held every twelve years, on the full moon of *Mágha*, at *Kumbhakonam*.

Mághí, S. &c. (माघी) Full moon of *Mágh*.

MÁGHÁRÍṆ, Mar. (माघारीण) A recently married wife, especially one who returns (from *mághárne*, to turn back) from her father-in-law's house to her own parents, or goes from them to her husband's parents.

MAGHIYA, (?) H. A division of the Dhanuk tribe.—*Bhágalpur*.

MAGRA, (?) H. A subordinate or outlying village forming part of a larger one.—Ajmer.

MAGHRAB, or MAGHRIB, H. (A. مغرب) The west, the western quarter.

Maghrabí, H. (A. مغربي) A native of the west, a North-African.

MAGHRÚR, H. (A. مغرور) In ordinary use, proud; but in Mohammadan law, a man who has married a woman under a misconception, as one within the prohibitive degrees of relationship, without being aware of it, or a slave, supposing her to be free.

MAHÁ, S. &c. (महा, from *mahat* महत्), it occurs in all the dialects without change, except in Tam., in which it is written *Maká*, or *Magá*, quasi, Μεγα (மகா), there being no *h* in the alphabet; also, as abbreviated, *Má* (மா) Great (literally or figuratively).

Mahábráhmaṇa, S. &c. (महाब्राह्मण) lit. A great Brahman, but applied contemptuously in Bengal to a low class Brahman who officiates at funeral rites, and is the first feasted after the period of mourning; also a Brahman who performs religious ceremonies for Ṣúdras and mixed castes.

Mahádeva, or *Mahadeo*, S. &c. (महादेव) The great God: usually applied to Ṣiva, especially as the *Linga*.

Mahádeví, S. &c. (महादेवी) The wife of Ṣiva: a name of Durgá.

Mahájana, or *Mahájan*, or *Muhajun*, incorrectly, *Mahajanam*, *Mehajin*, S. &c. (महाजन) lit. A great man, but applied in most parts of Hindustan and Bengal to a merchant, a dealer, a banker or money-changer; also a creditor: in Marathi, also, a particular hereditary officer in a village: in some places in the south of India it denotes the head of a trade or caste; also the head man of a village, especially where the villagers are mostly Ṣúdras and the head man is a Brahman: it is applied also to Brahmans holding lands as permanent tenants, but employing others to cultivate: it also denotes such of the villagers as hold *Mirás* or hereditary property in common. In Guzerat, *Máhájan*, pronounced, *Májan* (મહાજન), is also said to mean a public entertainment or food given to all comers.

Máhájan lagán, Guz. (?) Collections made by the merchants for charitable purposes, whether human beings or animals be the objects.

Májanangal, for *Mahájanam*, Tam. (மாசனங்கள்) An assembly of the principal inhabitants of a village: Brahmans collectively, especially when heads of villages and cultivators.

Mahákála, sometimes written, *Mákála*, S. &c. (महाकाल) A name of Ṣiva, as identified with Time: one of the great *Linga* types of him, formerly worshipped at Ujayin.

Mahákálí, S. &c. (महाकाली) One of the terrific forms of Durgá.

Mahálaya, S. &c. (महालय) A great temple or sanctuary: the obsequial ceremonies performed in the last half of the month *Bhádra*.

Mahámantrí, (महामन्त्री) A prime minister.

Mahámári, Beng. &c. (S. महामारी) Plague, pestilence, any epidemic or great mortality.

Mahánáḍu, Tam., Karn., Tel. (மகாநாடு) The great assembly: in former times it was composed of the chief landed proprietors of a *náḍu*, or district, who met to consider of agricultural interests: in some places it exists as a meeting of the tribes of the right-hand party to deliberate on questions of caste. In Karnata it is described as an assembly of the aboriginal castes, not including Brahmans and some other castes in various parts of the country: *Mantai*-(for *mantrí*, a counsellor) *mahá-náḍu*, occurs in Tamil writings as expressive of the concurrence of the government and the people, whence Mr. Ellis conceived the powers of the primitive *Mahá-náḍu* to have been analogous to those of the Saxon Witenagemote.

Mahanta, or *Mahant*, *Muhunt*, H. &c. (S. مهنت, महन्त) The head of a religious establishment of the mendicant orders of the Hindus.

Mahantí, H. (مهنتي) The office and appointment of a *Mahant*.

Máhántí, Uriya (ମାହାନ୍ତି) A man of the writer or accountant caste: the caste itself.

Mahánavamí, S. &c. (महा, and नवमी, ninth) The last day of the nine days or nights dedicated to the worship of Durgá, in Áṣwin, the last day of the Durgá púja.

Mahápáta, or *Mahapátaka*, S. &c. (महापात -पातक) A heinous crime: five acts are especially so considered, murder of a Brahman, intercourse with the wife of a Guru, stealing gold from a priest, drinking spirits, and associating with persons guilty of such offences.

Mahápraṣáda, S. &c. (महाप्रसाद) The great present of food, that is, the distribution among the persons present, of food, sweetmeats, and the like, which have been offered to an idol: it is also especially applied to such a distribution at Jagannáth.

Mahápurusha, or *-purush*, S. &c. (महा, and पुरुष, a man) A great man; but applied especially to religious ascetics, especially to such as pretend and are believed to have overcome physical infirmities, to be able to live without food, and to be impassive to external or elemental influences.

Mahárájá, S. &c. (महाराजा) A supreme or sovereign prince; applied in courtesy to every Rájá.

Mahárání, S. &c. (from राज्ञी, a queen) The principal wife of a Rájá, or a queen in her own right: applied also in courtesy to Hindu ladies of rank, although not of princely dignity.

Maháráshtra, S. (महाराष्ट्र) The Maraṭha country.

Maharshi, or *Maharishi*, S. &c. (महर्षि, महऋषि) Any very celebrated sage or saint.

Maháṣaya, pronounced, *Mahashoy*, Beng. (মহাশয, from S. *mahá*, great, and *áṣaya*, receptacle) A respectable person, one possessed of great merit: but the word is chiefly used as a term of respectful address, as, Sir, Master, Your honour.

Mahásankránti, S. (महासंक्रान्ति) The great *Sankranti*, or sun's entrance into Capricorn, the winter solstice: it also signifies the festival observed at this season in the south of India, the Pongol.

Maháshtamí, S. &c. (महाष्टमी) The great eighth, that is, the eighth day of the festival in Áṣwin in honour of Durgá, or Durgá púja.

Mahattrán, corruptly, *Mahatra*, *Mohuturan*, *Mohuteran*, *Mohaturan*, *Mahooteran*, Beng. (মহত্ত্রান, from S. महत्, great, and त्राण, protecting) Land assigned to religious persons, or for religious purposes, by Zamindars or subordinate fiscal officers; also a provision made by the state for persons of the lower castes: (the sense may vary according to the relation of the component terms, as the protection *of* great or pious persons, or of inferiors *by* great persons.

Mahávat, or *Mahávath*, commonly, *Mahout*, H. &c. (مهاوت, مهاوته, S. महामात्र) The driver of an elephant.

Maháyajna, S. &c. (महायज्ञ) A great sacrifice or act of worship; five such are recognised, 1. *Brahma-y.*, study of Brahma or the Veda; 2. *Pitṛi-y.*, offering to the manes; 3. *Deva-y.*, offerings to the gods; 4. *Bali-* or *Bhúta-y.*, worship of all existing things, also of mischievous spirits, by offerings of food scattered in the air; 5. *Nṛi-y.*, worship of man, hospitality.

Maheṣwara, S. &c. (महेश्वरः) A name of Ṣiva.

Máheṣwara, S. (माहेश्वर) A worshipper of *Maheṣwara*; a follower of Ṣiva.

MÁH, H. &c. (ماه, for S. मास्, माः), MÁHÁ, or MÁHÉ, Karn. (ಮಾಹಾ, ಮಾಹೆ) A month.

Máhewarí-lekha, Karn. (ಮಾಹೆವರೀಲೆಖ) A monthly account.

Máhiána, H. (ماهيانه) Monthly pay, wages, or salary.

Mahiná, H. (مهينا) A month; monthly pay or wages.

Máhigujasta, Tel. and P. (మాహిగుజస్త) Balance of rent, &c. due from the past month.

Máhimajkúru, Tel. A. (మాహిమజకూరు) Collections of the current month.

Mahwár, *Mahwárá*, or *Mahwári*, H. &c. (مهوار, مهوارا, مهواري) Monthly, monthly pay or wages; a deed settling the payment of the revenue by monthly instalments.

MAHAJARU, Karn. (ಮಹಜರು, from the A. محضره) Testimonial or certificate in favour of a public functionary, joined in by all present. See *Muhájara*.

MAHAL, MUHUL, pl. MAHÁL, MUHAL, H. &c. (A. محل, محال) A place, a house, an apartment, a seraglio: a station, a street, a district, a department: (in the Hindu dialects this word is written indifferently *Mahal*, or *Mahál*, as in Beng. and Mar. (মহল, মহাল, महल, महाल), confounding the sing. and plur. numbers, and using both in the sense of the singular, as in the following):

Mahál, corruptly, *Mahl*, *Mhal*, *Mâal*, *Mohaul*, *Mehaul*, *Mal*, H. &c. (محال, properly the pl. of محل, but used as a sing. noun. with a plur. of its own, or *Mahálát* محالات), *Mahál*, or *Máhál*, Guz. (મહાલ, માહાલ) A province, a district, as the *Jangal-maháls*, on the west of Bengal; a division of a *Taálluk*, or district, yielding revenue according to assessment. In the language of the Regulations a *Mahál*, or *Mehál*, is called an estate, and is defined, any parcel or parcels of land which may be separately assessed with the public revenue; the whole property of the revenue-payers in the *mehál* being held hypothecated to government for the sum assessed upon it. Beng. Reg. xlii. 1803, ch. 2, sect. 2, and xi. 1822, sec. 29. Under the Mohammadan government the term was also applied to a head or department of miscellaneous revenue derived from a tax on some particular class of things or persons, as, *Mahál-i-hágħaz*, the tax or duty on paper; *Máh-i-mahál*, the duty on fish; *Nimak-mahál*, the revenue derived from the monoply of the sale of salt; *Mahál-abkári*, the department of the excise: so in Karnata, *Mahálu* (ಮಹಾಲು) meant revenue, or sources of revenue, chiefly territorial, but comprising other objects. In Puraniya, the items of the village *Hast-o-bud*, were termed *mahál*s: the word is in fact very vaguely employed. In some places a certain right is intended, capable of being rented, as the *Mom mahál*, or right to the wax found in the forests of a given tract. In Cuttack, the plural *Mahálát* was applied to the lands which paid the full assessment to the state, in contrast to the *Kiláját*, or military estates paying a quit-rent only.

Mahaldár, Beng. (মহলদার) An officer in charge of a district; also the occupant or proprietor of an estate.

Mahálдár, Mar. (महालदार) A government officer in charge of the revenue and police of a district.

Mahál-jhadtí, or *-jhartí*, Mar. (from झडती, an account) Annual rough statement of the receipts and disbursements of a district.

Mahálkarí, Mar. Guz. (महालकरी) A revenue and police-officer in charge of a district: in the former department he was usually subordinate to the *Kamavísdár*; in the latter he was accountable to the government direct, or to its representative in the district: he has latterly been invested with the same police authority as the *Mámalatdár*. Act xx. 1835.

Mahalla, corruptly, *Mohulla*, H. (محلّه), *Mahallá*, Beng. (মহল্লা), *Mahalá*, Mar. (महला) A division of a town, a quarter, a ward.

Mahalladár, H. &c. (محلّه‌دار) An officer in charge of a particular quarter of the town, bound to give information to the Darogha of the police of any disorderly conduct, or the presence of culprits: the Regulations seem to have contemplated a female agent also in each ward, subordinate to the police, under the title of *Mohaladarin*. Beng. Reg. xxii. 1793, sec. 30.

Mahalli, H. (محلّي) A eunuch, an attendant on the female apartments.

Mahál-masrut, Beng. (মহলমশ্রুত, from the A. مشروط) An estate held on certain stipulated conditions.

Mahal-i-mujrá, H. (A. محل مجرا) Place of obeisance: settlement of accounts.

Mahál-nawárá, Beng. (মহালনওয়াড়া) Districts set apart for the payment of followers or troops.—Chittagong.

Mahál-paṭṭí, Mar. (महालपट्टी) A composition formerly levied for the farm of the sale of spirituous liquors at Bombay.

Mahál-sádir-wárid, Mar. (महाल सादिर वारिद) Contingent charges in the fiscal and police administration of a district.

Mahalsará, H. (P. محلسرا) The inner or female apartments.

Mahál-sibandí, Mar. (महालसिबंदी) Police and revenue *peons*, or armed servants attached to the magistrate and collector.

Mahálá, Maháli, Máhályá, Mar. (महाला, महाली, माहाल्या) A term of courtesy affixed to the names of barbers.

Mahár, or Mhár, corruptly, Mher, Mhao, Mow, Mar. (महार, म्हार) A man of a low caste, retained on the village establishment for the performance of the lowest menial offices, as those of a scavenger: he is also the village messenger, and is sometimes employed as watchman: also the name of the caste or tribe.

Mahárki, Mar. (महारकी) The office and rights of the *Mahár*.

Mahárki-watan, Mar. (महारकीवतन) The allowances and perquisites, in land or grain, of the *Mahár*.

Mahárpunj, Mar. (महारपुञ्ज) The portion of the crop given to the *Mahár* as his perquisite.

Mahármahárki, Mar. (महारमहारकी) An impost levied on the grants or perquisites assigned to the *Mahár*.

Mahárwará, or *-wárá*, Mar. (महारवडा, -वाडा) The ward or quarter of a village, usually outside of it, occupied by persons of the *Mahár* caste.

Máhárá, Uriya (ମାହାରା) Water-courses.

Máhári, Uriya (ମାହାରୀ) A dancing girl attached to a temple.

Máhásati, Thug. Cry of a single jackall, usually a bad omen.

Mahásh, H. (A. معاش) Goods, effects.

Maháyat, H. (A. محاياة) Partition of usufruct, as when each of two sharers enjoys a part of the thing possessed in common, or where each has the whole alternately.

Mahbas, H. (A. محبس) A prison, a place of confinement.

Mahbús, H. (A. محبوس) Confined, imprisoned, a prisoner.

Mahbús-khána, H. (A. P. محبوس کانه) A jail, a prison.

Mahbús-sanad, H. (A. محبوس سند) A warrant of committal, a mittimus.

Mahdi, H. (A. مهدي) A guide: the twelfth and last of the Imáms or successors of *Âlí*, whom the Shia Mohammadans believe to be still alive.

Máhi, Thug. The sacred pick-axe.—Dakhini Thugs.

Mahívási, or **Mewasi**, Guz. (મહીવાસી) Properly, an inhabitant of the country along the Mahí river, but applied especially to the tribes in that quarter who subsisted by lawless and predatory practices.

Máhí murátib, H. (P. A. ماهي مراتب) The dignity of the fish: the privilege of having carried before a man of rank the representative of a fish, or part of it, of metal gilt, borne upon a pole with two circular gilt balls similarly elevated; conferred formerly as a mark of distinction by the king of Delhi on individuals of the highest order only: one of the latest, or perhaps the last exercise of this favour was the grant of the privilege to Lord Lake, by Shah Âlam.

Mahíta, corruptly, **Moheeta**, H. (محيطه) Land within the supply of a well, but irrigated from it only in alternate years. See *Chak*.

Mahjúr, H. (A. محجور), incorrectly, **Mahúr**, Prohibited. In Mohammadan law, an inhibited slave; one who is incompetent to buy, sell, or transact any business on his own account, as opposed to *Mázúr*, a licensed slave.

Mahkama-aukáf, H. (محكمه اوقاف) Local agency: a court of trust, certain officers of the government charged with the superintendence of public buildings and endowments.

Mahlúf, H. (A. محلوف) Sworn, taking an oath.

Mahluf âlehí, A. (محلوف عليهي) Sworn to, the act or article respecting which an affidavit is made.

Mahr, incorrectly, **Mihr**, H. (A. مهر) Dower, marriage-gift or portion settled upon a wife before marriage: it may be either *Muâjil* (معجل), prompt, immediate, or *Muwajil* (موجل), deferred to some specified time: if no amount of dower is agreed upon at the time of marriage, the wife is entitled to a customary provision, *Mahr-i-misl*, or one suited to her condition. The written contract of dower or marriage-settlement.

Mahrána, H. (مهرانه) A fee paid to the Kázi at a wedding.

Mahr-náma, H. (مهرنامه) A deed of dower or settlement; the document in which it is specified.

Mahrús, or **Mahrúsa**, H. (A. محروس, محروسه) Guarded, protected.

Mamálik-mahrúsa, H. (A. ممالك محروسه) Well governed or protected provinces, those subject to established sovereign power: the term was applied to the territories of the Moghal.

Mahsúl, **Muhsool**, corruptly, **Mohsool**, H. &c. (A. محصول. महसूल) lit. Collected, levied: revenue duty, public income from any source, as land, customs, excise, and the like: the produce or return realized from any thing.

Mahásil, H. (A. محاصل) Produce, profit.

Mahásulu, Tel. (మహాసులు) The produce of land, the harvest, the crop.

Mahásulu-dárudu, Tel. (P. دار) An officer employed to prevent the clandestine removal of the produce of a field, before the revenue has been paid.

Mahsúldár, H. (محصولدار) Yielding, or having, a profit: a collector or receiver of taxes.

Mahsúl-i-sáir, H. (A. محصولساير) The produce of miscellaneous duties and customs: amount of miscellaneous duties or excise on salt.

Mahsúlí, H. &c. (محصولي, महसुली) Relating to revenue or taxes.

Muhassil, H. (A. محصّل), *Mahsil*, or *Mausil*, Beng. (মহসিল, মৌসিল) A native collector of revenue, a tax-gatherer, a collector of imposts, a bailiff; an officer especially deputed to realize arrears of revenue, to recover a debt, or to prevent the escape of any one. See *Mohassalu*.

Muhassilí, H. (A. محصّلي) The office of tax or custom collector.

Muhassilána, H. (A. محصّلاني) The fees or perquisites of the bailiff or tax-gatherer, &c.

Mahtá, H. (مهتا) A scribe, a clerk, an agent or man of business: (it is probably the same as the next but one below).

Mahtádi, H. (مهتادي) A head village peon: a village bailiff or constable.

Mahto, H. (مهتو, S. महत, great) The head man of a village: (in Behar), the head of a caste or trade; an agent or representative of a Zamindár, employed to collect the revenue and manage the affairs of a village.

Mahtus, (?) A cultivator of the poppy.

Mahúá, or **Mahwá**, H, (S. مهوا), **Maüá**, Beng. (মঊআ) The Bassia latifolia, a tree of which the nuts yield a substance used for butter, and the flowers a spirituous liquor by distillation.

Mahzar, H. (A. محضر, from حضر, being present), Tel. (మహాజరు) A general application or representation, a statement laid before a judge, a public attestation, or a document attested by a number of persons professing to be cognisant of the circumstances of the case, and submitted, with their signatures, to the court; also, in the Northern Sirkars, a written agreement given by the Ryots conjointly to the government for the performance of any duty.

Mahzar khána, corruptly, *Mazir khána*, H. (P. خانه, a house) A police-station or court.

Mahzar-náma, H. (P. نامه) A written collective attestation, a list or roll of persons present.

Mai, Beng. (মই) An instrument made like a ladder, used as a harrow.

Maidá, or Maira, H. (میدا , मैडा) A scaffold in a corn-field where a boy is stationed to drive away birds and beasts.

Maidán, H. (A. میدان) A plain, an open field or meadow.

Maigada, Karn. (ಮೈಗಡ) A loan without interest.

Maikádu, Karn. (?) Daily hire.

Maikaría, Thug. A barber.

Maileru, (?) plur. Karn. A class of slaves in Kanara.

Main, Hindi (मैन) A common short grass growing on rich and inundated lands, and choaking the crops.

Mainátta, Mal. (മൈനാത്ത) A washerman.

Maind, Mar. (मैंद) A machine for smoothing a ploughed and sown field. A man of a tribe who are robbers and murderers.

Mainkavilgar, Karn. (?) A head watchman.

Maisála, Karn. (ಮೈಸಾಲ) A loan without pledge or mortgage: a loan on a promissory note.

Maisáladapatra, Karn. (ಮೈಸಾಲದಪತ್ರ) A promissory note; an I O U.

Maiyat, corruptly, Mait, Mar. (मैयत, A. ميت) Blighted, blasted: extinct, dead.

Maiyat-páhaní, Mar. (मैयतपाहणी) Inspector of crops reported to be blighted.

Majara, Karn. (ಮಜರ) A small village under the superintendence of the government officers of a town.

Májará, H. (ماجرا, from A. ما, what, and جرا, has happened) Circumstances, state, condition, occurrence.

Májará, or Májrá, Mar. (माजरा) Stupefying, narcotic (as drugs and vegetables).

Májaren, or *Májren*, Mar. (माजरें) The stupefaction produced by the use of narcotic drugs.

Májá-phiryád, Mar. (माजाफिर्याद), a corruption of *Má-zu-faryád*, he who has a complaint: used as an exclamation to attract the notice of a judicial or other functionary.

Majal, Karn. (ಮಜಲ) Second sort of rice land in Mysore, producing annually one crop of rice and one of vegetables or dry grain.

Majáz, (مجاز) Lawful, admissible.

Majda, or Magda, (?) H. A mixed soil, consisting of clay and sand.—Rewari.

Majlis, H. (A. مجلس) An assembly, a court.

Majmal, H. (A. مجمل) An abstract, a compendium.

Majmúâ, Majmuâa, vernacularly, Majmu, or Mujmoo, and Majúm, or Mujoom, H. &c. (مجموع, مجموعه) Collected, brought together; an assemblage; an aggregate or total.

Majmú, Mar. (मजमू) A total, an aggregate: the particular office or duty of the *Majmúdár*, q. v.

Majmuâ-dár, H. (مجموعدار), *Majumdár*, Beng. (মজুমদার) and Tel. (మజుందారు), *Majmúdár*, or *Mujmúdár*, Mar. (मजमूदार, मुजमूदार), also, *Majmudár*, Guz. (મજમુદાર), *Mujumdár*, Tam. (முசும்தார்) A native revenue-accountant, one who keeps the account of the Jamâ, or government collections under the native governments: in Hindustan he was the revenue accountant of a district subordinate to the *Âmil* or manager, and removable at pleasure: he kept the accounts of the revenue settlements, audited those of the *kánungo*, and possessed a general power of scrutinizing the revenue accounts and assets of his district: he was also sometimes the receiver and auditor of the rents paid to the Zamindár. In Bengal the designation has become, in some cases, a hereditary appellation. In Maratha finance the *Majmúdár*, was a kind of auditor whose function it was to inscribe all writs and deeds, and to write on all accounts of receipts and disbursements, after examination and approval, the words, *Martúb súd*, a corruption of the Arabico-Persian phrase *Marattab shud*, it has been arranged. In Guzerat the title is given to the keepers of the *pargana* revenue records, who have held the office as a hereditary right since the settlement of Todar Mal, and are paid by fees charged on the villages. In the Tamil countries, a district revenue accountant.

Mâjúm, more correctly, Mâjún, H. &c. (A. معجوم, معجون) A confection, an electuary, but commonly applied to a sort of sweetmeat prepared from the larger leaves and capsules of the hemp plant, with water, ghee, sugar, and milk, boiled together: when of a sufficient consistence the mixture is poured on a slab, where it concretes into a thin cake, which is divided into small lozenge-shaped pieces: the effects of any of the preparations to the extent of one drachm, are intoxicating: there are other modes of preparing the *mâjúm* in the state of an electuary or a decoction.

MAJURÁ-DÁST, Mar. (मजुरा दास्त, from A. *mujrá*, deduction, and P. *dásht*, what has) Allowance or deduction made to the Ryots on account of grain, grass, &c., furnished by them on special requisition.

MAJÚS, H. (P. مجوس) A Magian, a Parsí or fire-worshipper, a magician.

MÁJWÍ, Mar. (माजवी) A level platform made on the slope of a hill by digging from above and banking from below.

MAKÁ, H. &c. (مکا, मका) Indian corn (Zea mays).

Makáná, Mar. (मकाणा) A single grain of maize, plur. (मकाणे) Indian-corn parched.

MÁKAL, Guz. (માકલ) Ascertaining the revenue of a field by weighing the produce in grain.

MÂḲALAT, (A. معقلة), plur. MÂÁḲIL, corruptly, MÂWAḲIL (معاقل) Fine for bloodshed: homicide for which atonement has been paid.

MAKÁN, H. &c. (P. مکان) A place, a station, an office.

Makándár, H. &c. (from دار, who has) An officer, a placeman: in the south of India it is commonly applied to a person in charge of, or having the management of, a Mohammadan mosque.

MAḲBARA, H. (A. مقبره) A burial-place, a tomb.

MAḲBÚẒÁ, H. (A. مقبوضا, from قبض, holding) Occupied, tenanted; as the lands of a village.

MAKHAMA, Tel. (మఖము) A tax or assessment for a religious purpose.

MAKHÁRIJ, corruptly, MOKHARIJE, H. (A. مخارج, plur. of *Makhraj* مخرج) Disbursements, outgoings: as a revenue term, deductions from the revenue, alienations, assignments of portions of the government claim, remissions of revenue due by the Zamindárs on account of lands dismembered or alienated.

MAKHLÁṢÍ, MAKHLÁSÍ, Mar. (मखलाशी, -सी, from the A. مخلصي, setting free, &c.) Name of the mark affixed to grants, assignments, and other documents issued by the government: grand total of an account: end of an affair, as of a law-suit, &c.

MAKHLÚṬ, corruptly, MUCKLOOT, MUHLOOT, H. (A. مخلوط) Mixed, blended; applied to lands recently annexed to an estate or district not originally part of it.

MAKHMAL, MUKHMUL, H. (A. مخمل) Velvet.

MÁKKAM, Tel. (మాక్కం) Rate of exchange of coins of different currencies.

MAHKÁR, Thug. A Rajput, of whatever calling.

MAKKI, Karn. (ಮಕ್ಕಿ) The worst kind of rice land.

MAKR, or MAKAR, H. &c. (A. مکر) Fraud, imposition.

Makár, H. (A. مکار) A cheat, a swindler, an impostor.

MAKRÚH, H. (A. مکروه) Wicked, abominable: applied in law to actions which the law condemns as wrong, but does not invalidate.

MAḲSÚM, H. (A. مقسوم) Divided, partitioned, as property: a portion, a share. See *Kism*.

MAḲṬÂ, also, MUKATTÂ, corruptly, MUGTA, MOKTA, vernacularly, MAKTÁ, and MAKHTÁ, H. (A. مقطع) Cutting, cutting off. Mar. Guz. (मक्ता) A contract, an agreement for work. Tel. (మక్తా) Rent, rate, a fixed rate or rent. See *Bílmaktá*.

Maktágutta, Mar. Tel. (मक्तागुत्ता) A contract or lease of land at a fixed stipulated rate, not liable to extra cesses; the land so held.

Maktákaulu, Tel. (మక్తాకౌలు) An agreement under which land is held at an annual quit-rent for a stipulated period.

Maktehari, *Maktedár*, or *Mahhtehari*, *Makhtedár*, Mar. (मक्तेकरी, मक्तेदार, मखतेकरी -दार) A contractor, a farmer, one holding land at a fixed rent.

Makhtá-shistu, Tel. (మఖ్తాశిస్తు) A fixed rent.

MAḲẒÚF, A. (مقذوف) Falsely accused of adultery (man or woman).

MAL, corruptly, MAUL, MHAL, MAHAL, H. &c. (مال), MÁLU, or MAHÁLU (which is a vernacular corruption), Tel. (మాలు, మహాలు) Wealth, goods, effects, property of any description: in Mohammadan law it is sometimes used for personal as opposed to real property, or for money as distinguished from goods and chattels: in India it was used for the public revenue from any source whatever, but more especially for that derived from land, to which sense, as a fiscal term, it is now restricted, or the revenue claimed by the government from the produce of cultivated lands, *the wealth of the state*.

Mál-âdálat, H. (A. مال عدالت) A revenue court in which all questions between the government and landholders, and between them and their tenants, or officers charged with the collections, and over which the collector presided, were determined: these courts were abolished by Ben. Reg. ii. 1793.

Máldár, H. (مالدار) The possessor or holder of property.

Máldhaní, H. (مال دهني, from S. धनी, wealthy) The possessor of property, especially of land.

Málen, Mar. (माळें) Pecuniary aid towards the recovery of an attached farm which the cultivator endeavours to collect by going round the neighbourhood with a small plough hung round his neck, and begging.

Mál-guzár, or *Mál-goozár*, H. (مال گذار), *Mál-gujár*, Beng. (মালগুজার), *Málugujáru*, Tel. (మాలుగుజారు) The person who pays the revenue assessed on an estate or village, whether on his own behalf, or as the representative of others, and whether he be sole or joint proprietor, or a holder under a proprietor or the state, and whether he pay the revenue to a proprietor or Zamindar, or to the officers of the government.

Huzúrí-, or *Sadr-Málguzár*, H. (حضوري , سدرمالگذار) A person who pays his revenue to the public or principal treasury, without the intervention of a proprietor or farmer, or subordinate native collector: also the one amongst a number of co-sharers through whom the revenue of the rest, or of a certain portion of them, is paid: the same as *Lambardár*.

Mazkúrí-Málguzár, H. (مذكوري مالگذار) A payer of revenue through the intervention of a subordinate native collector, or a proprietor or contractor.

Mál-guzárí, corruptly, *Malgoozarry*, H. (مالگذاري) Revenue assessment; the payment of land-revenue: also the person or land subject to such payment.

Malguzárí áima, H. (from the A. ايمه) A grant or assignment of land (see *Aima*) paying a quit-rent; an assignment of a portion of the government revenue of an estate for charitable purposes: a grant of waste land, upon a small rent, to a cultivator, who thereby acquires a proprietary right in the soil. Ben. Reg. viii. 1793, sec. ix.

Mál-guzárí-tahsíl-kul, H. (A. تحصيل, collection, and كل, whole) The entire revenue collections; the net revenue.

Málkatní, Mar. (माळकटनी) A fee for permission to cut down certain crops.

Málkhána, H. (from P. خانه) A treasury, a store-house.

Málakudáru, corruptly, *Málcoodar*, Tel. (మాలకుదారు) The proprietor of an estate, a temporary renter or farmer: (this may be a modification of *Málik*, q. v.)

Málí, H. (A. مالى) Relating to wealth or to revenue.

Málí-peshkár, H. (مالي پيشكار) A revenue accountant.

Máliat, H. (A. ماليّت) Wealth in the abstract, property, possessions; value of any thing. It is said to be also applied in Guzerat to lands producing the most valuable kinds of crops, as sugar-cane, pepper, ginger, &c.: (but perhaps, in this sense it is derived from *Málí*, a gardener, implying garden ground).

Mál-muft, H. (P. مفت, gratis) Property acquired without cost or labour, property given away without requital or benefit.

Mál-i-sáir, H. (A. ساير, rest, remainder) Revenue from customs and other sources exclusive of land.

Mál-o-matáá, H. (A. مال و متاع) Money and goods.

Málwájib, H. (A. ماجب, right) Fixed and proper revenue, which it is requisite or customary to pay.

Málugamsári-bhúmi, Tel. (మాలుగంసారిభూమి) Land paying revenue to government.

Malwujúhát, vernacularly corrupted to *Maljihát*, H. (A. وجوهات, plur. of *wajh* وجه, mode, manner), *Mahálojhá*, Tel. (మహాలోఝా) A general or collective term for the revenue received from the land.

Málzámin, vernacularly, *Máljámin*, H. &c. (مالضامن, माल-जामिन) A surety for the payment of a demand against the baillee in contradistinction to a surety for appearance.

Málzámini, or *Máljámini*, H. &c. (مالضامني, मालजामिनी) Security for payment of money.

Maál, H. (مآل) End, issue.

Maál-andeshí, H. (مآل انديشي) Consideration of the end or consequence.

Maḷa, or Malai, Mar. (मळा, मलई) A garden or plantation of edible vegetables. Rich low ground, of alluvial origin, bearing double crops, or sown with vegetables.

Máḷa, Mar. (माळ) Any extended tract of ground, a plain, a down.

Máljamín, Mar. (माळजमीन, P. *zamín*) Open country, a barren or uncultivated plain: land of inferior quality, or that which is situated on the sides of hills, or on ridges which, although they may be ploughed, cannot be irrigated, and producing only the autumnal crops.

Máḷí, Mar. (माळी) Level arable land on the acclivity of a hill.

Máḷawat, Mar. (माळवट) Abounding in open barren tracts: a district or country.

Malist, Mar. (?) A term applied in the *Ḍáng* to inferior and open land in the second year of its being brought into cultivation after lying fallow for some time.

Mála, Tel. (మాల) Of or belonging to the Paria caste.

Málavádu, Tel. (మాలవాడు) A man of the Paria caste.

Málá, H. &c. (S. मा, माला) A garland, a chaplet, a string of flowers or of beads, worn either as a necklace or a rosary, and made up of different substances according to the sect of the wearer.

Máláhár, H. &c. (مالاكار, मालाकार) A maker of garlands; a gardener. See the next.

Máli, corruptly, *Molly*, H. &c. (مالي, माली) A gardener, one who cultivates and sells vegetables, fruits, and flowers, as the occupation of his caste; also the name of the caste. In the Maratha country the *máḷí* (माळी), is distinguished by the article he chiefly cultivates; as, *Jíri-máli*, grower of cummin and other aromatic seeds; *Phúl-máḷí*, grower of flowers, &c: *Máli* (with the simple *l*) is a civil affix to the names of barbers, as, *Das-máli*, &c.

MALA, Mal. (മല), MALAI, Tam. (மலை), MALE, Karn. (ಮಲೆ) A hill.

Mala-kṛushi, Mal. (മലകൃഷി) Hill cultivation.

Malanáda, or *Malnád*, Mal. (മലനാട) A hilly country, applied to Malabar.

MALACHIA, (?) H. A class of thieves and dishonest persons in Bengal, now apparently extinct. Ben. Reg. xxii. 1793, sec. x.

MALAMÁSA, or MALAMÁS, S. &c. (मलमास, from मल, soil, dirt, and मास, a month) An intercalary month, in which no religious ceremonies should be performed.

MALAN, Beng. (মলন) Rubbing, threshing corn.

Malaniyá, Beng. (মলনিয়া) A thresher of corn.

MALANG, H. (S. ملنگ) A Mohammadan mendicant who lets his hair grow loose and uncombed.

MALANGA, Uriya (ମଲଙ୍ଗା) A place where salt is made.

Malangi, *Mulungee*, corruptly, *Molungee*, H. Beng. &c. (ملنگي, মলঙ্গী) A salt-maker, a labourer employed in manufacturing salt.

Páhi-malangi, Uriya (ପାହିମଲଙ୍ଗି) A salt-maker working at a different village from his own.

Tháni-malangi, Uriya (ଥାନିମଲଙ୍ଗି) A salt-maker working in his own village.

Malang-chará, or *-charán*, Uriya (ମଲଙ୍ଗଚରା) Land on which salt may be, or has been, made, but which may have been brought into cultivation: (in Cuttack the term occurs *Malaghna-chara*, but ? if correct).

MALAṆÍ, Mar. (मळणी) Threshing or treading out corn.

Malaṇhar, Mar. (मळणकर) A thresher.

MALAVATÍ, incorrectly, MALAVANTÍ, Tel. (మలవతి) Extra or additional assessment rated on the growing crops in proportion to their apparent richness.

MALAYAN, (?) Mal. The designation of a caste of slaves in Kanara and Malabar.

Malavāram, Mal. (മലവാരം) Hill produce, a tax on hill produce.

Malavari, Mal. (മലവരി) A pass or ghat over the mountains.

Malayaḷam, Mal. (മലയാളം) The country on the west of the Malaya mountains, the province of Malabar.

MALAY, (?) Mar. A variety of black mould liable to be flooded in the rains.

MALBÁ, H. (ملبا, lit. sweepings) Village expenses, usually liquidated in the same manner as the public assessment; the principal items in the north-western provinces are thus enumerated: feeding the members of the community when absent on public duty, or those of other villages on a visit, feeding religious mendicants, payments to subordinate police and revenue officers, allowance to village watchmen, remuneration to individuals for losses incurred in supplying cattle and carts for public service, loss on exchange on coins with which the revenue is paid, repairing tanks and wells, fines imposed for plundered property when traced within the boundary of the village, presents to dancers, singers, jugglers, and the like, for amusing the inhabitants, charitable gifts, interest on monies borrowed on account of the community, expense of religious worship, occasional ceremonies and festivals, expenses of the *Patwári* or accountant, charge for oil and lights for the place of assembly and the person in charge of it, expenses of *Panchaiats* collected on the business of the village, funeral expenses of a head man or any respectable member, marriage expenses of neighbours when passing through the village, &c.; the total varied from 10 to 12 per cent. on the public assessment.

Malba-kharch, H. (from خرچ) Village expenses.

MALBÚS, H. (A. ملبوس) Clothed, clothing.

Malbus-kháṣ, H. (A. خاص, q. v.) An annual investment of fine muslins, formerly furnished from Dacca for the royal wardrobe at Delhi.

MALAICHÁṘPU, Tam. (மலைச்சார்பு) Hilly country, land on the slope of a hill (from *Malai*, Tam. and Karn., a hill).

Malegaladanelu, Karn. (ಮಲೆಗಲಡನೆಲು) A kind of rice growing on the slope of a hill in Mysore.

Malaipunam, Tam. (மலைபுனம்) Hilly or rocky soil, not fit for cultivation.

Malevar, Karn. (ಮಲೆವಾರ) A tribe of hill men in the Nagar district of Mysore, said to be the aboriginal landholders.

Malavelan, Mal. (മലവെലൻ) A tribe of mountaineers.

MALFÚF, H. (A. ملفوف), MALPÚPU, Tel. (మలపూపు) Enclosed; an enclosure, what is sent in a bag or cover.

MÁLÍGE, Tel. (మాలిగె) A chamber or cell on the lower floor of a large or public building, opening to the street, and used as a shop or warehouse.

MALIK, MULIK, H. (A. ملك, from *mulk*, a kingdom) A king, a sovereign.

MÁLIK, H. (A. مالك, from *milk* ملك, possession, property), MÁLAK, MÁLÍK, Mar. (मालक, मालीक) A master, an owner, a proprietor: a cultivator possessing a hereditary or proprietary right in the land he cultivates, or a person having a beneficial and hereditary interest in the revenue paid by the cultivators, and responsible to the government for its share; hence considered applicable, in Bengal, to Zamindárs, and in the north-west provinces to the head man of a village, or to any member of the community who holds a part of the land in proprietary right, and is sometimes permitted to engage for the payment of the whole of the revenue assessed upon it; hence also designated as *Málik-mukaddam*, or *Málik-zamindár*.

Málikána, corruptly, *Maliconna*, H. (مالكانه) Pertaining or relating to the *Málik*, or proprietor, as his right or due; applied, especially in revenue language, to an allowance assigned to a Zamindár, or to a proprietary cultivator, who from some cause, as failure in paying his revenue, or declining to accede to the rate at which his lands are assessed, is set aside from the management of the estate, and the collection and payment of the revenue to government, which offices are either transferred to another person, or taken under the management of the government collector: in such case a sum not less than 5 per cent., and not exceeding 10 per cent., on the nett amount realized by the government was finally assigned to the dispossessed landholder. Ben. Reg. i. viii. xliii. 1793; vii. 1822. It was also applied formerly to an allowance made to the head man by the other villagers, or, when authorised to collect and pay the revenues of the village, by the state.

Málikána-khángí, H. (from خانگي, q. v.) Fees levied on cultivators by a landholder for his household expenses.

Málikána rusúm, H. (A. رسوم) Proprietary dues.

Málikhissa, H. (A. حصّه, a share) The share of the owner, or of the state.

Milk, or *Milkíat*, corruptly, *Milik*, H. (A. ملك ملكيت), *Milak*, less correctly, *Melak*, Hindi (मिलक, मेलक) Land held in absolute property, and free of rent.—Puraniya. Property, ownership, possession.

Milkdár, H. (P. دار, who has) The possessor of lands in absolute property.

Mulkí, H. (ملكي, मुलकी) lit. Of or belonging to a kingdom, or to a province: especially applied to an æra in use in some places, as in Puraniya, which is one month in advance of the Fasli year beginning with the 1st of *Srávan*.

Málikíat, H. (مالكيت) Ownership, proprietorship, the right of the *Málik*.

MÁLISH, H. (P. مالش) Rubbing; but used in the Northern Sirkars for threshing and treading-out corn.

Málishdár, H. (P. دار, having) Superintendant of the threshing-floor. See the last.

MAL-JAMÍN, (?) Mar. A variety of red or light brown soil spread thinly over rocks, stony and poor, distinguished as *Mal-murad*, and *Mal-barad* (?).

MÁLKÁNDI, Uriya (ମାଲକାଣ୍ଡି) A heap or stack of salt.

MALLA, MULLA, H. &c. (S. مل, मल्ल) A boxer, a wrestler: the name of the caste following such practices.

MALLÁ, Tel. (మల్లా) A fee in grain paid to the village potter.

MALLÁH, H. (A. ملاح) A sailor, a boatman: a maker of salt.

MALLAR, Tam. (மள்ளர்) Agricultural labourers of the *Pallar* tribe. Cultivators generally.

MALLU, Tel. (?) Beds of salt; also plur. of *Madi*, fields.

MALMARD, (?) Mar. A sort of soil, the same as *Mal-jamín*, but darker.

MALMAL, H. (ململ) Muslin.

MALMALÁ, H. (ململا) Brackish, as water.

MÁLNÁDU, Karn. (ಮಾಲನಾಡು) The woody and hilly districts of Nagar in Mysore.

MAMERÁ, H. (S. ممیرا) Relating to a maternal uncle.

Mamerá-bhái, or *-bahin*, H. (from بهاي, a brother, or بهن, a sister) A first cousin by the mother's side, the son or daughter of a mother's brother.

MAMIÁ-SÁS, H. (S. ممياساس) Husband's or wife's maternal aunt.

Mamisasur, H. (from ممسر, S. श्वशुर) Husband's or wife's maternal uncle.

MAMLÚK, H. (A. مملوك) Possessed, having as a possession or property: In Mohammadan law, a purchased slave; also a child brought up in the house of another.

MAMU, Thug. One who knows Thugs, and extorts money not to betray them.

MÁMÚ, also, but less usually, MÁMÁ, H. &c. (مامو, ماما),

Mámá, Mar. (मामा) Máman, Tam. (மாமன்), A maternal uncle, a mother's brother. Mámí, H. &c. (مامي), Mar. (मामी) A maternal uncle's wife.

Maṇ, Tam. (மண்) Earth, ground, land.

Maṇṇukkudaiyavan, Tam. (மண்ணுக்குடையவன்) A proprietor of land, a landlord.

Manmakkal, Tam. (மண்மக்கள்) Men of the fourth, or servile tribe.

Man, Mun, commonly, Maund, H. &c. (من, मन, from the A. *mann* مَنّ, Hebrew *mann*), Mahana, Uriya (ମହଣ), Manugu, Tel. (మణుగు) A measure of weight of general use in India, but varying in value in different places. Four principal varieties are specified by Mr. Prinsep; 1. the Bengal *maund*, containing 40 *sers*; 2. the *maund* of Central India, consisting of half the quantity, or 20 *sers*; 3. the *maund* of Guzerat, consisting of 40 *sers*, but of lesser value, making the Bombay *maund* 28lb. avoirdupois; and 4. the *maund* of Southern India, fixed by the Madras government at 25lb. In Bengal there were also two kinds of *maunds*, the *Bázár maund*, of the value above described, or, more correctly, 82lb., being based upon the computation of 80 sicca rupees to a *ser*, and 40 *sers* to the *maund*, the rupee weighing 179.666 Tr. grs.; and the *Factory maund*, introduced into the Company's commercial transactions in 1787, apparently for the convenience of converting it into English weight, the *Factory maund* being = 74lb. 10 oz. 10.666 drs., and three such *maunds* being almost exactly equal to 2 cwt. In 1833 the Bengal government directed the discontinuance of both in the public offices, and established a *maund* weighing 100lb. troy, or $87\frac{2}{7}$lb. avoirdupois, based upon the change of the weight of the rupee to 180 grs. troy, which made the new *maund* heavier by $\frac{2}{7}$ths of a pound. The *maund* of Akbar's time was equal to but $34\frac{3}{4}$lb.; and still, in various parts of India, great differences prevail, extending from 25lb., as at Bombay and in Mysore, to 163lb., the weight of the *maund* in some parts of the district of Ahmadnagar, in which the highest values occur: the term is used rather laxly in the west of India as the unit of land measure, one *man* being equal to four *rukas*, or 16 *payalis*, or 32 *adholis*, or 40 *chakurs*, q.v. The Hebrew *Mann*, or *Manah*, from which, through Arabic, the Indian word is derived, corresponded more nearly to the *ser*, being but 13,125 troy grains, or less than 2lb. avoirdupois.

Maniko, Guz. (મણિકો) The vessel or weight by which the *maund* is measured or weighed, or a jar holding that quantity, a stone weighing a *maund*, &c.

Mána, vernacularly, Mán, S. &c. (مان, मान) Pride, dignity, honour, respect.

Mánahání, S. &c. (मानहानि) Loss of character or reputation.

Mánahína, S. &c. (मानहीन) Disreputable, vile.

Mánkarí, corruptly, *Mancurry*, Mar. (S. मानकरी) A respectable man, a gentleman, a title borne by the descendants of those persons who held *Mansabs* under the Mohammadan princes of the Dakhin: a person entitled to certain marks of respect, and to presents at public assemblies and festivals: in the jargon of the Thugs it denotes the man who selects the spot for murdering and burying travellers.

Mánpán, Mar. (मानपान) Any honorary rights or privileges attached to respectability of station or official rank: the honours and presents due to the *Mánkarí*, the rights of the village hereditary officers, &c.

Mána, vernacularly, Mán, S. &c. (मान) Measure in general, whether of length, capacity, or weight.

Mána, Uriya (ମାଣ) A land measure equal to 25 *gunthas*.—Cuttack.

Mánapani, Uriya (ମାଣପଣି) A fee payable to Zamindárs, usually one *pan* of *kauris* per *bíghá*.

Mána, and Mánike, corruptly, Mankedu, Tel. (మానా, మానికె) A measure of capacity in the Telinga countries, in some of which eight, in others sixteen, make one *Túm*.

Mána, (?) A measure of capacity equal to about half a *ser*, or one-fourth of a *pátha*, of grain or salt; hence, also, a measure of land, as much as may be sown by a *mána* of grain.—Kamaon.

Mána-chawal, (?) A rent-free grant for life.—Kamaon.

Manâ, H. (A. منع), Maná, Beng. (মনা), Manáí, Mar. (मनाई), Prohibition, forbidding; also, in Mar., Maná (मना), Forbidden, prohibited.

Manáchiṭhí, Mar. (मनाचिठी) A written prohibition, a countermand.

Manátahsil, Uriya (ମନାତହସୀଲ) Prohibited or illegal collections.

Manai, Tam. (மனை), Mane, Karn. (ಮನೆ) A house, a dwelling; the ground on which a house stands, and that which is adjacent and attached to it, a back yard, a garden, and the like: it also denotes land held in a village; and when the word is used by itself in deeds of transfer in the Tamil provinces, it signifies ground conveyed without the rights and privileges accompanying *Mi-*

rásí holdings: as applicable to village lands, they are distinguished as *Uḷ-manai*, (உள்மனை), those within the site of the village, and *Para-manai* (பரமனை), those beyond the site. *Manai*, is also the name of a land measure equal to 2400 *kuḷis*, or square feet, or the 24th part of a *káni*: the proper form is a paralellogram of 60 feet by 40, being in fact considered as the measure of land suited to the site of a house.

Manébádige, Karn. (ಮನೇಬಾಡಿಗೆ) House-rent.

Manébesáyada-bhúmi, Karn. (ಮನೇಬೆಸಾಯದಭೂಮಿ) Land cultivated by Zamindárs through their own domestic servants or slaves.

Manaichiṭṭu, Tam. (மனைச்சீட்டு) A deed of grant or a title-deed for the site of a house.

Manéguttige, Manéterige, Manéderugi, Karn. (ಮನೇಗುತ್ತಿಗೆ &c.) House-taxes.

Manéhesaru, Karn. (ಮನೇಹೆಸರು) A house or family name: every family in Karnata has what is called a house name, taken from that of the village or occupation, and prefixed to the proper name of the individual.

Manaikkaṭṭu, or *Manaikkaṭṭu-nivésanam*, Tam. (மனைக்கட்டு, மனைக்கட்டுநிவேசனம்) The ground or site of a house.

Manai-kiraya-chiṭṭu, Tam. (மனைக்கிரயச்சீட்டு) A bill of sale of the site of a house.

Manaikolavan, Tam. (மனைக்கொலவன்) A householder: in the Tamil provinces it applies especially to Mirásidárs and other resident members of a village.

Manaimuṛi, Tam. (மனைமுறி) A bill of sale for the site of a house.

Manaivari, Tam. (மனைவரி) House-rent, ground-tax or rent.

Manaiviḍu, Tam. (மனைவீடு) A house and the ground on which it stands, including the whole area belonging to it, with the outhouses, offices, yards, and a garden, if not extensive.

Manakattai, Tam. (மணக்கத்தை) A sort of rice.

Manal, Tam. (மணல்), Manalu, Karn. (ಮಣಲು) Sand.

Manalachari, Tam. (மணலசாரி) Soil mixed with sand.

Manalaḍittarisu, Tam. (மணலடித்தரிசு) Land become waste by an accumulation of sand upon it.

Manal-taram, Tam. (மணலத்தரம்) Sandy soil.

Manamáḍu, Tel. (మనమాడు) A grandson. Manamarálu, Tel. (మనమరాలు) A granddaughter.

Mánamárí, Tam. (மானமாரி) A reservoir of water fed by the rain only.

Manatappan, Mal. (മനതപ്പൻ) A caste of cultivators originally from Coimbatore, first settled in the Pálghát province, and intermixed, and often confounded, with the Nairs.

Manautí, H. &c. (منوتي), Manotí, Guz. (મનોતી) Bail, security, a surety; especially becoming surety for payment of the revenue to the government, or to a farmer of the revenue, and receiving a heavy commission from the revenue payer; also general agency, brokerage.

Manautí-dár, or *Manotí-dár*, H. &c. (منوتي دار) A person becoming surety for a consideration, one becoming security to government for revenue payments.

Mánavári, Tam. (மானவாரி) Land of which the cultivation depends solely upon rain, not being irrigated artificially: dry cultivation.

Manavi, Karn. (ಮನವಿ) A petition or request made to a superior.

Manchu, Mal. (മഞ്ചു) A single-masted vsssel employed in the coasting-trade of Malabar of from 10 to 40 tons.

Manda, S. &c. (मन्द) Slow, dull, stupid: in Beng. &c, wicked.

Manda-ichhak, Manda-bánchak, Uriya (S. ମନ୍ଦଇଚ୍ଛକ -ବାଞ୍ଛକ) Malice prepense; malicious desire or purpose.

Máṇḍá, Beng. (মাংডা) A seed plot: a ridge of earth round the foot of a tree to keep in the water.

Máṇḍábándhá, Beng. (মাংডাবাংধা) A plot of ground surrounded by a ridge of earth, a seed-bed, a ridge round the bottom of a tree.

Manḍäi, Mar. (मंडई) A vegetable-market, one where greens and fruit are sold wholesale.

Mandái, Mar. (मंडाई) A premium or bonus to a money-lender above the stipulated interest.

Mandai, Tam. (மந்தை) A herd, a flock.

Mandai-muṛai, or *Mandai-varisai*, Tam. (மந்தைமுறை, வரிசை) The right and practice of the Mirásidárs to have in turn the cattle of the village folded on their grounds, that they may benefit by the manure.

Mandaikarai, Tam. (மந்தைக்கரை) Place to which cattle are driven for pasture.

Mandaivéli, Tam. (மந்தைவேளி) A common or open field for pasturage.

Manḍal, Munḍul, H. &c. (منڈل, मण्डल) A circle, an orbit; a district, a province, a country: in Bengal, where the term is also read Maḍal, (मडल), and corruptly, Mundle, The head man of a village, who sometimes acts as the agent of the Zamindár, letting the lands and receiving the rents of the villagers. In Puraniya it is the common title of any respectable Súdra.

Maṇḍáman-maṇí, Guz. (મંડામણામણી) Discount or premium paid to a money-lender; a bonus paid or deducted from the sum lent or advanced.

Maṇḍamu, Tel. (S. మండము) Scum, barm, froth.

Mandahárakuḍu, Tel. (మండహారకుడు) A distiller, one who extracts and prepares the juice of the palm and *tárí*, also an exciseman.

Maṇḍapa, S., but adopted in most dialects with some slight modification, as Mandap, Mándava, or Mándau, Mandwá, and in the south of India more usually Manṭapa (मण्डप), Manṭapa, Tel. Karn. (మంటపు) An open building, a pavilion or temple; a temporary structure for various festival occasions, as for receiving and sheltering idols when carried in procession, or for the performance of marriage or other festive ceremonies.

Mandasa, Tel. (మందస) A market.

Máṇḍaví, Mar. Guz. (मांडवी) A building into which goods are received from ships in sea-ports, a store, a warehouse, &c., a custom-house.

Máṇḍava-khanḍaṇí, Mar. (मांडवखंडणी) Fee paid at marriages to the priest or the astrologer.

Manḍe, Tel. (మండె) A heap of threshed ears of (Junnalu) Holcus: a pile of tobacco left to ripen: a place in general.

Mandegár, Karn. (మండెగార) A custom-house officer.

Mandeyenne, Karn. (మండెయెంణె) An annual tax levied in lieu of a maund of oil per each mill, formerly paid to the Paligars.—Mysore.

Manḍí, H. (منڈی) A market, a special market, one for any particular article: perhaps the original of the word *Mandovy*, called, the mart at Mirzapur. Reg. ix. 1810, sec. 43. Tel. (మండి) A wholesale shop.

Mandira, or Mandir, corruptly, Mandil, S. &c. (मन्दिर) A dwelling, a temple: in Bengal, usually a small temple containing a *Linga*. *Devamandira*, a temple, a pagoda. *Rájamandira*, a palace.

Manḍuá, H. (मण्डुआ) A sort of grain (Eleusine corveana).

Manḍwá, H. (منڈوا) A custom-house or station

Mane, Karn. (మనె) A tax.

Manelávádu, Tel. (మనెలావాడు) An itinerant dealer in coral and gems; commonly termed a *Manilla*-man, but probably from *Maṇi*, S. a jewel.

Mangala, vernacularly, Mangal, Mungul, S. (मङ्गल, also Mar. मंगळ) Good fortune, auspiciousness; whence it is applied to any festive ceremony or public festival, as propitious to favourable results, as to a marriage: in Marathi, uttered significantly, it implies an irregular or invalid marriage. The planet Mars.

Mangala-vára, vernacularly, *Mangal-bár*, S. (मङ्गलवार) Tuesday.

Mangaláshṭaka, S. &c. (मङ्गलाष्टक) The lucky-eight, *i.e.* eight lines of a benediction pronounced by a Brahman on a newly-wedded pair, while a piece of silk is held between them; South of India.

Mangalavádu, *Mangali*, Tel. (మంగలవాడు, మంగలి) A barber.

Mangalasútra, S. &c. (मङ्गलसूत्र) The lucky thread; a string having in the centre a piece of gold or other valuable material tied by the bridegroom round the neck of the bride, at the time of marriage, and worn by the latter as long as her husband lives: in the dialects of the south, to which the practice is peculiar, it is usually called *Táli*: in Upper India, it is a string or piece of silk tied round the wrist, and worn only during the marriage celebration.

Mangalan, *Mangali*, Tam. (மங்கலன், மங்கலி) A barber by caste and occupation, said to be sprung from a mother of the tribe of artificers and a father of the oilman caste.

Mangaḷichá, Mar. (मंगळीचा) Of an irregular marriage; the offspring; illegitimate, bastard.

Máng, Mar. (मांग) A low caste, or individual of it, employed in low and menial offices: as a member of the village, the *Máng* commonly officiates as scavenger, guide, watchman, and executioner.

Mangalia, (?) H. A woman legally married (perhaps for *Mangaliá*).

Mangi, Thug. Treasure.

Mángná, H. &c. (مانگنا), Márgaṇa, S. (मार्गण), Mángan, Hindi (मांगन), Mángan, or Mángná, Beng. (মাংগন, মাংগনা) Asking, begging, requiring; whence borrowing, asking for a loan; also a cess or impost formerly levied to defray the allowance of the public weigher of grain; also an unauthorised exaction by the native officer at landing-places and custom stations, asking a fee for themselves or the Zamindárs. In Bahar, a fee or perquisite of the headman receivable from the villagers in kind, a share of the crop.

Mángni, also *Mangni*, H. (مانگني, منگني), *Máguṇi*, or *Mágí*, Mar. (मागणी, मागी) Asking a girl in marriage previous to the betrothal; also the ceremony of betrothing: borrowing, asking for a loan; begging: a contribution solicited from the Ryots by the Zamindár on any emergency.

Mangat, or *Mangtá*, H. (منگت ,منگتا) A beggar, a borrower.

Mangetar, H. (S. منگیتر) One to whom a man or woman is betrothed.

MAṆIGA, Tel. (మణిగ) A shop.

MANIHÁR, or MANIÁR, corruptly, MUNNIAR, H. (S. منیار ,منهار) A maker of glass bracelets worn by women ; a jeweller.

MAṆIHÁMU, Tel. (మణిహాము) Trade, merchandise.

MANIKAVELI, corruptly, MUNNY CAVELLY, (?) Fees paid for the village watch (in Kanara).

MAṆIKÁRAN, Mal. (മണികാരൻ) An inferior revenue officer, a collector, see *Maniyam*: a jeweller, a lapidary.

MANIVÁR, MUNEWAR, or MUNNEEWAR, Mal. (?) The revenue accountant of a district: a superintendant of police (it is probably a corruption of *Maniyakár*).

MÁNIK, Beng. (মানিক) A measure, the eighth of a *khári*.

MANIVI, Karn. (ಮನಿವಿ) A petition, an address from an inferior to a superior.

MAṆIYAM, Tam. and Mal. (மணியம், മണിയം), MAṆIYA, Karn. (ಮಣಿಯ), MAṆIYAMU, Tel. (మణియము) Superintendence or management of affairs ; especially the superintendence of revenue to a limited amount, a subordinate office under the collector, a surveyorship of revenue : also, in Karn., a tax.

Guḍi-maniya, Karn. (ಗುಡಿಮಣಿಯ), or *Koyilmaniyam*, Tam. (கோயில்மணியம்) Superintendence of a temple.

Sunka-maniya, Karn. (ಸುಂಕಮಣಿಯ) Superintendence of a custom-house.

Úr-maniyam, Tam. (ஊர்மணியம்) Superintendence of a village.

Vaṭṭa-maniyam, Tam. (வட்டமணியம்) Superintendence of a district.

Maṇiyakáran, Tam. (மணியக்காரன்), *Maṇiyagára*, corruptly, *Monigar, Moniagar*, or *Munagar*, Karn. (ಮಣಿಯಗಾರ), *Maṇiyagáḍu*, Tel. (మణియగాడు) A superintendant in general, the head man of a village, the superintendant of a temple: in the Tamil countries it is especially applied to a subordinate native revenue officer employed in the collection and management of the revenue under the native Tahsildár, by whom he is appointed, and to whom he is responsible: he is also charged with a limited superintendence of police. The Naib *Maniyakára* is the immediate deputy of the Tahsildár, and has extensive jurisdiction under him, but the term usually implies the *Vaṭṭa maniyakár*, or collector of a small district of two or three villages: this officer is a kind of head Peon, who, in concert with the heads of villages, superintends not only the collections, but the cultivation, the reaping, and selling of the crop, when the revenue is paid in kind, and settles petty disputes.

Maṇiyaṇi, Mal. (മണിയണി) A steward or manager of an estate on behalf of the owner or Janmkár (Malabar).

MAṆJÁḌI, MAṆJÁLI, or MAṆCHÁḌI, &c. Tam. Mal. (மஞ்சாடி, மஞ்சாளி), MANJÁLI, Tel. (మంజాళి) A weight for weighing diamonds; a carat, or four grains avoirdupois. In Malabar it is said to be used for weighing gold, and *Manchaḍiyiḍ* (മഞ്ചാടിയിട) to be the name of the weight used for diamonds only.

MANJ, Thug. The fighting of cats, a good omen during the first watch of the night, but bad at any other season.

MANJÁ, H. (مانجا) Anointing the body with turmeric on festive occasions: an invitation and present accompanying it.

MAṆJANÍR, Tam. (மஞ்சணீர்) Turmeric water, the drinking of which is part of the rite of adoption, whence

Maṇjanír-chiṭṭu, Tam. (மஞ்சணீர்சசீட்டு) A writing or deed concerning adoption.

Maṇjanírppiḷḷai, Tam. (மஞ்சணீர்ப்பிள்ளை) An adopted child.

MANKI, (?) H. The head man of a village.—Chota Nagpur.

MÁNJH, or MÁNJHÁ, incorrectly, MUNJA, MUNJHA, MUNJHAR, H. (مانجه, مانجها, मांझ, from S. *madhya*, middle) The land lying between the land in the immediate proximity of a village and that on the boundaries of its lands ; it is considered the second sort of land in point of fertility.

MÁNJHI, H. (مانجهي), MÁJÍ, or MÁJHÍ, Beng. (মাজী, মাঝী) The steersman of a boat: among the Rajmahal mountaineers, a title borne by their head men: also termed MÁNHÁ.

MÁNJWÁR, Thug. A jackal.

MANKHELA, Thug. A man.

MANKAṆI, Karn. (ಮಂಕಣಿ) A basket for throwing up water from a reservoir into a channel of irrigation: a double basket for carrying four vessels, &c., on a bullock.

MANKÚLA, H. (A. منقوله) Personal or moveable, in opposition to real property.

Ghair-manḳúla, real or moveable property.

MAṆṆA, Mal. (മണ്ണ) Earth, soil.

Mannattán, Mal. (മണ്ണത്താൻ) A washerman.

MANNAM, corruptly, MUNNIM, Tel. (మన్నెం) Highlands, hill country.—Northern Sirkars.

MANNAVEḌU, also written, MUNNAVADOO, Tam. (மன்னவெடு) A village inhabited by Súdras.

MANNODDARU, Karn. (ಮಂಡೋಡ್ಡರು) A class of labourers who execute heavy work, such as heaving blocks of stone, constructing earthen walls, &c.

MANOVARTI, or MANOVARTE-INÁMU, corruptly, MUNNOVERTY, Tel. (S. మనోవర్తి) A pension, land granted for the subsistence of a pensioner.

MÁNNEVÁDU, Tel. (మాన్నెవాడు, from మన్నె, land) A proprietor, a landholder, a Zamindár.

MANNI, Tel. (మన్ని) A land measure, commonly designated a ground = (60 × 40 feet) 2400 square feet.

MANSAB, MUNSUB, H. (A. منصب) Office, dignity, a military title and rank conferred by the Moghul government of Dehli, regulated by the supposed number of horse the holder of the title could, if required, bring into the field, varying from ten to ten thousand: Jágírs were assigned for the maintenance of this force, which was in the highest and lowest grades, rather nominal than real: the first part of a *sanad*, or grant, in which the titles of the grantee were recited.

Mansabdár, H. (منصبدار) A noble holding a *mansab*, or military rank of a certain number of horse, although sometimes wholly engaged in the civil service of the state.

Mansabdárán, H. (منصبداران, plur. of the preceding) An aggregate term for the assignments of Jágírs or land revenues to the *Man abdárs*.

Mansab-zát, H. (منصبزات) The personal rank of one holding the official rank of a *mansab*.

MÁNSAJ, MANSIJ, H. (A. منسج) A weaver's shop.

MANSHÁ, H. (منشا) Provision of a law or statute.

MÁNSÚB, H. &c. (A. منصوب) Considered, determined, established.

Mansúbak, H. &c. (A. منصوبه), *Mansubá*, Mar. (मंसुबा) Determination, deliberation.

Mansubí, Mar. (A. मंसुबी) Investigation, determination of minor disputes: the office of the Pancháit.

Mansubdár, Mar. (मंसुबदार) A particular officer in a court of judicature.

MANTÍ, Hindi (मनती) Balance of rent when inconsiderable, and which the cultivator engages to pay in a few days.

MANTRA, S. &c. (मन्त्र) A prayer, a prayer of the Veda, a mystical or magical formula, the prayers or incantations of the Tantras: counsel, advice.

Mantrí, S. &c. (मन्त्री) A minister, a counsellor.

MANÚTI, Karn. (ಮನೂತಿ) An agreement: receiving interest on a sum of money for which a person has become surety. See *Manauti*.

MAN

MANWANTARA, S. &c. (मन्वन्तर) The period of the existence of a *Manu*, being equal to 71 great *yugas*, or ages of the gods, or 306,720,000 years.

MÁNYAM, corruptly, MAUNIUM, Karn. (ಮಾನ್ಯಂ), MÁNYAMU, Tel. (మాన్యము), MÁNIYAM, Tam. (மானியம்), (all three are from the S. *mánya*, respectable, respected, shewing an intention to do favour or honour) Land in the south of India, held either at a low assessment, or altogether free, in consideration of services done to the state or community, as in the case of the officers and servants of a village. These tenures are distinguished as *Tarapadi-mányam*, when it is inherited or held from an uncertain period, as an independent right; and *Dumbala-* or *Sanad-mányam*, when held by virtue of a specific grant from the ruling power. They are also distinguished as *Sarva-mányam*, (from S. *sarva*, all) when the holder is entitled not only to the revenue of the state, but the rents of the cultivators; and as *Ardhamányam* (from *ardha*, a half), where the holder has a claim only to the government revenue: the former is not frequent, except in the case of grants made to temples conjointly by the state and the cultivators: the term is also laxly applied to any free grant or perquisite held in hereditary right by members of a village community.

Gudimányamu, Tel. (గుడిమాన్యము) Land granted for the maintenance of a temple.

Máṇiyakáran, Tam. (மானியக்காரன்) The holder of rent-free land, or any hereditary right or privilege.

Káṇimániyam, Tam. (காணிமானியம்) Hereditary land exempt from all tax.

Tótimánya, Karn. (ತೋಟಿಮಾನ್ಯ) An allowance in land to a village servant.

Kuḍimakkaḷmániyam, Tam. (குடிமக்கள்மானியம்) Rent-free lands assigned to the village servants.

Méraimániyam, Tam. (மேரைமானியம்) A grant of a portion of the gross produce of cultivated lands in kind, now commuted for money.

MANZIL, H. (A. منزل), MANJIL, Beng. (মনজিল), MAJAL, Mar. (मजल), MAJILI, Tel. (మజిలి) A stage, a station, the place where the traveller suspends his march; also, in Mohammadan law, a tenement, a habitation, a place in which a family may reside.

Manázil mulázima, H. (A. plur. of *manzil*, and ملازمه, contiguous) Adjoining or contiguous tenements or apartments, such as are within the same house or building.

Manázil mutabáyina, H. (A. متباينة, distinct) Separate or distinct tenements or apartments.

MANẒÚR, vernacularly, MANJUR, or MUNJOOR, H. (A. منظور) Approved of.

MÁÖ-MAWÁSA, (?) H. A family, the several families composing a village community.—Kamaon.

MÁP, or MÁPA, H. &c. (S. ماپ, माप) Measurement of any kind, whether of weight, length, or capacity, but especially linear measure; a measure; a portion or quantity determined by measure.

Mápárí, Mar. (मापारी) An officer in large towns whose duty is to measure the grain that is brought into the market: a measure of capacity for grain, the same as a Phará, q. v.

Máp-darí, Beng. (মাপদড়ী) A measuring line.

Máp-jonk, Beng. (মাপযোংক) Measuring, a measurement.

Máp-paṭṭí, Mar. (मापपट्टी) A charge made to the cultivators for the cost of measuring the grain when the revenue is received in kind.

Máptol, H. &c. (ماپتول) A system of measures and weights.

Máptu, Guz. (માપટું) A measure, a vessel for measuring corn, wine, &c.

Mápteṇ, Mar. (मापटें) A measure of capacity, a half *ser*, whether *pakká*, or *kachchá*.

MÁPPILḶA, plur. MÁPPILLAMÁR, commonly, MOPLAH, or MOPLAY, Mal. (മാപ്പിളള) A native of Malabar, a descendant of the Arabs who first settled in Malabar, lit. the son (*pilla*) of his mother (*má*), as sprung from the intercourse of foreign colonists, who were persons unknown, with Malabar women: the term is also applied to the descendants of the Nestorian Christians, but is, in that case, usually distinguished by the prefix, *Nasráni* (നസ്രാണി), while *Jonakan* (ജൊനകൻ), from *Yavana*, is prefixed to the Mohammadan *Máppillas*: the *Máppillas* of both classes are numerous in Malabar.

MÁR, H. &c. (مار, मार, from the S. causal of मृ, to die, मारय) Beating, striking, killing.

Márámárí, H. &c. (مارامارى) Mutual beating, fighting, assault, affray.

Márana, vernacularly, *Máran*, S. &c. (मारण) Beating, killing.

Márí, Mar. &c. (मारि) Plague, destructive or epidemic disease.

Márpít, H. &c. (مارپيٹ) A beating, fighting, assault and battery, affray.

MÁR, corruptly, MAAR, H. (مار, मार) A stiff clay or loamy soil with some sand and vegetable mould: in Bundelkhand the term designates a rich black loam.

MÁR, (?) Karn. A land measure varying from 4 to 20 *kurgis*, or 16 to 80 acres.

MAṚA, Mal. (മഴ) Rain.

Maṛakálam, (മഴക്കാലം) The rainy season.

MÁRÁ, Hindi (मारा) Soil that is productive only in the rains.

MARÁÍ, Beng. (মরাই) A magazine of corn, a granary.

MARAKÁḌU, Tel. (మరకాడు) The native commander of a ship.

MARAKKÁL, commonly MARKAL, or MERCAL, Tam. (மரக்கால்) A grain measure in use at Madras, containing 8 *padis*, or *measures*, and being one-twelfth of a *kalam*: it formerly consisted of 750 cubic inches, but is now fixed at 800 cubic inches: 400 *marakkáls* = 1 *garisa*, or *garce*. A *marakkál* of rice or of salt weighs 960 rupees = 12 *sers*, or 24 lb. 6 oz. Prinsep calls the *Markal* = 27 lb. 2 oz. 2 dr. of water, or nearly $2\frac{3}{4}$ imperial gallons; but the standard, as since fixed (20th Oct. 1846), makes the *marakkál* as above, = 28 lb. 12 oz. 13 dr. 22 gr., or in measure $2\frac{9}{10}$ the imperial gallon.

MARAM, Mal. Tam. (മരം) Wood, timber.

MARAMMAT, H. &c. (A. مرمّت) Mending, repairing. *Marámat*, Mar. (मरामत) The entire operations or processes of any art, as, in agriculture, manuring, ploughing, harrowing, sowing, &c.

Marammatu-jábitá, Tel. (మరమ్మతుజాబితా) Amount particulars of the cost of repairing roads, tanks, or other public works.

MÁṚAN, Beng. (মাড়ন) Threshing or treading-out grain.

MARAPPAṆI-KÁRAN, Mal. (മരപ്പണിക്കാരൻ) A carpenter.

MARARI, Thug. A party of Thugs assembled in council.

MÁRÁṬA, Karn. (ಮಾರಾಟ) Double-dealing: selling.

MARATTALAI, Tam. (மரத்தலை) Scattered trees in a village.

Marattalai-áyakkaṭṭu, Tam. (மரத்தலை ஆயக்கட்டு) Total of plantations.

MARAVIDAÍ, Tam. (மரவிடை, from *maram* மரம், a tree) A term used in deeds of the transfer of land to convey all kinds of woods, timber, and plantations; also ground on which trees are growing.

MÁRGA, vernacularly, MÁRG, S. &c. (मार्ग) A road, a way; also, fig., a way of life or belief, a doctrine, a sect.

Aḍḍuvu-márg, Karn. (ಅಡ್ಡುವುಮಾರ್ಗ) A bye or cross road.

Bhaṛámárg, Karn. (ಭಾರಾಮಾರ್ಗ) A road for exports and imports.

Rájámárg, H. &c. (راجامارگ, राजामार्ग) A royal road, a principal or main road, or highway.

Márggakáran, Mal. (മാൎഗ്ഗക്കാരൻ) A man of a particular religious sect; applied in Malabar especially to Roman Catholics.

Márgapála, S. &c. (मार्गपाळ) A watchman, a patrol, a guardian of the road: custos-viarum.

Márgí, Hindi, &c. (मार्गी) A traveller, a follower, one who goes the road, either lit. or fig., amongst the Thugs, a pupil, a tyro.

MÁRGAḺÍ, Tam. (மார்கழி) The ninth month of the year. See the next.

Margaṣírsha, S. &c. (मार्गशीर्ष) The ninth month of the year (Nov.-Dec.), when the moon is in the asterism *Mṛiga-sírsha*, (the head of the *Mṛiga*, or deer).

MARGHAṬ, Hindi (मरघट) A place where dead bodies are burnt.

MÁṚHA, Uriya (ମାଢ) A small weight used by braziers: four make one *kariṣa*, or *karsha*.

MARHÚM, H. (A. مرحوم) Lit., one who has found mercy, *i.e.* dead, deceased.

MARHÚN, H. &c. (مرهون, from *rahan*) Pledged, mortgaged, as property.

MÁRÍ, Tam. (மாரி) Water, rain.

Márikálam, Tam. (மாரிகாலம்) The rainy season.

Marigómmu, Tel. (మరిగొమ్ము), *Marigómbu*, Karn. (ಮರಿಗೊಂಬು) An outlet by which the surplus water of a tank is carried off.

MÁṚI, or MÁṚÁḌI, Tam. (மாறி, மாறாடி) A cheat, a swindler, a thief.

MARÍCHA, S. (मरीच), MIRCH, H. (مرچ) Pepper, especially black pepper; also *Gul-mirch*, black pepper; *Lál-mirch*, red pepper from *Chillis*, or *Capsicum*.

MÂRIFAT, H. (معرفت) Knowledge, but used more adverbially to imply by means of, through or by any medium or cause.

Máraphat, Hindi (मारफत) By the hands of.

Máraphatio, Guz. (મારફતીઓ) An agent, a factor, a broker, one through whom any business is transacted.

MÁRIGA, Karn. (ಮಾರಿಗ) A man of low caste, a *Chandála*.

MARIKÁRU, Tel. (మరికారు) The second or a light crop, one of a coarse kind of rice grown between Oct. and Jan.

MARIYÁ, Khond. A human victim sacrificed on particular occasions.

MÁRKAMU, Tel. (మార్గము) Exchange, particularly of money.

MARKÁRI, Tel. (మర్కారి) A head boatman.

MAROCHA, also written, MORACA, and MORACHA, (?) Beng. A tax on marriages levied in Bengal by the Mohammadan government: a present exacted on marriages by the Zamindárs from the Ryots.

MAROT, (?) A grant of land to the heirs of a man killed in battle.—Kamaon.

MARSA, (?) H. A plant yielding a small edible grain largely consumed in the hills (Amaranthus olearaceus).

MARṢIA, H. (A. مرثيه) A dirge, an elegy; especially the verses recited at the Muharram, in lamentation for the descendants of *Âli*.

MARU, S. &c. (मरु) A dry or sandy and sterile tract, a desert.

Marubhúmi, S. &c. (मरुभूमि) Dry, sterile, or sandy land.

Marudeṣ, or *Marusthal*, H. (from S. *desa*, a country, or *sthala*, a tract) A desert country, applied especially to the sandy districts between Rájputána and the Indus.

MARÚL, (?) Mar. A kind of soil of a light black colour on the banks of rivers.

MARUMAKKAḺ, Mal. (മരുമക്കൾ) A niece: a daughter-in-law.

Marumakkan, Mal. (മരുമകൻ) A nephew: a son-in-law.

Marumakkattáyam, Mal. (മരുമക്കത്തായം) Succession to inheritance by sisters' sons, or in the female line, as observed by the Nairs, some of the Brahman and Mápilla families, and some of the servile tribes in Malabar.

MAṚUPANAYAM, Mal. (മറുപണയം, from മറു, another) A pawn pledged to another, or perhaps a counter-pledge.

Maṛupáṭṭam, incorrectly, *Marroopattom*, Mal. (മറുപാട്ടം) A copy of title-deeds kept by the seller or lessor, a counterpart lease or agreement; sometimes *Marupáttam-chit*.

MARVILIYA, (?) Tam. A messenger, a *peon*.

MÁRWÁ, Guz. (મારવા) One of the two principal sorts of soil in Guzerat, a sandy soil of a light brown colour, rapidly absorbing rain and having water at no great depth below the surface: it requires manure, but, treated properly, yields the best crops both as to quality and quantity.

MÁRWÁṚÍ, Mar. &c. (मारवाडी) A native of Central Hindustan, of *Malwa*, or, more correctly speaking, of *Márwár*, settled in other parts of India, and usually following the business of banker, broker, and merchant: some of an inferior class in the Maraṭha provinces employ themselves in trade as cornchandlers and grocers. *Márwáṛí* bankers are mostly of the Jain religion.

MARYÁDÁ, vernacularly, MARJÁDÁ, S. &c. (मर्यादा) Decorum, propriety, limit, boundary: custom, usage.

MÁSA, vernacularly, MÁS, S. &c. (मास) A month.

Másántikam, S. &c. (मासान्तिकं) Any thing relating to the end (*anta*) of a month, monthly pay, monthly accounts, &c.

Masáhará, Beng. (মসাহরা) Bargaining by the month, monthly pay: (this is probably a vernacular corruption of *Musháhara*, q. v.).

Másavṛiddhi, S. &c. (मासवृद्धि) Monthly interest; also the increase of a month, or an intercalary month.

Máskabár, corruptly, *Mashhabar*, *Maskhawar*, H. &c. (ماسکبار, from Port. *Acabar*, to end) The end of a month, a month's accounts, a monthly abstract of the cases tried in a civil court.

MÁSÁ, Hindi (मासा) A land measure, three-fourths of a *bighá*. —Kamaon.

MASÁHAT, corruptly, MUSSAUT, H. (A. مساحت) Measuring, measurement: whence *Mashátu*, Tel. (మసహాతు) Measurement of land, survey.

Máshátudáru, Tel. (మసహాతుదారు) A land measurer, a surveyor.

MASÁLAH, corruptly, MUSSALAH, H. (A. مصالح), MASÁLÁ, Beng. &c. (মসালা) Spices, condiments, seasoning: in Mar. it also applied to an exaction levied under the former government on every person summoned to answer a charge against him; also to fees payable to inferior native officers or messengers sent to collect the revenue.

MASÁN, Hindi, &c. (मसान, from the S. *smasán* श्मसान), MASÁNIHUṚÁ, Uriya (ମଶାଣିହୁଡ଼ା) A place where dead bodies are burnt, a cemetery.

MASÁRI, (?) Mar. Soil of various sorts; as, *Masab-masári*, mixed soil; *Hit-masári*, soil resembling flour; *Kemp-masári*, of a reddish colour; *Kall-masári*, stony; *Cosuck-masári*, sandy: (these are all given in the fourth volume of the 'Selections from the Records,' p. 779, but are not verifiable elsewhere, and are no doubt inaccurately printed).

MÁSH, H. &c. (S. ماش, माष), also, MÁSH-KALÁY, Beng. (মাষ, মাষকলায) Kinds of pulse very generally eaten (Phaseolus radiatus, and Dolichos pilosus).

MÁSHA, S., and in most of the dialects (माष), MÁSHA, or MÁSÁ, Mar. (माष, मासा) An elementary weight in the system of goldsmiths' and jewellers' weights throughout India, and the basis of the weight of the current silver coin: it is variously reckoned at 5, 8, or 10 *ratis*, or seeds of the Abrus precatorius, which usually weigh about 2 grains troy: the average weight of the *másha*, according to Mr. Colebrooke, was $17\frac{3}{8}$ grs.: the actual weight of several examined in England, sent from different parts of India, varied from $14\frac{7}{10}$ grs. to $18\frac{1}{2}$ grs.; the Benares *másha* weighed $17\frac{7}{10}$ grs. Mr. Prinsep, from the weight of several Akbar-shahi rupees, the standard weight of which was $11\frac{1}{4}$ *máshás*, valued the latter at $15\frac{1}{2}$ grs.: as now fixed by law, as one-twelfth of the *tola* of 180 grs., the *másha* weighs 15 grs.

MASHÁIKH, H. (A. مشايخ, plur. of *shaikh* شيخ) Elders, holy persons, heads of religious fraternities among the Mohammadans.

MASHAK, or MASHK, MUSHAK, MUSHK, H. &c. (P. مشك), MASAK, Mar. (मसक) A leather water-bag for carrying water about.

MASHAKKAT, H. (A. مشقّت), MASÁGAT, Mar. (मशागत), MASHÁKATU, Tel. (మసాకతు) Pains, labour: improvement of lands, repair of tombs, &c.: wages of labour.

Maṣágati, Mar. (मशागती) A common labourer.

MASHÂL, MUSHÂL, H. (A. مشعل) A lamp, a lanthorn, a torch.

Mashálchí, H. (مشعلچي) A torch- or lamp-bearer: as a domestic servant, he is also employed under the superior table servants to clean the plates, dishes, &c.

MASHÁṬA, H. (A. مشاطه) A waiting-woman, one who assists in dressing, and combing the hair, especially of a bride; she is also employed to negociate marriages.

MÁSHHÚR, H. (مشهور) Celebrated, notorious, well-known.

MASHÍAT, H. (A. مشيت) With pleasure: in Mohammadan law, power or will.

MASHRIK, H. (A. مشرك) The east.

MASHRÚÂ, H. (A. مشروع) Legal, conformable to, or prescribed by law: hence it is sometimes applied to a mixed stuff of silk and cotton, dressed in which it is lawful to pray; silk alone is prohibited.

MASHRÚṬ, H. (A. مشروط) Stipulated, agreed; conditional, as applied to assignments or grants of land revenue, importing that the grant was accompanied by certain stipulated conditions.

Mashrúṭ diwáṇi, H. (A. from ديوان) Conditional assignments for the remuneration of a fiscal functionary.

Mashrut-faujdári, H. (P. فوجدار) Assignments to the officers charged with the military and police establishments.

Mashrút-i-thánaját, H. (pl. of *thána* تهانا, a police station) Conditional assignments for the support of police or military stations under the Mohammadan government.

MÁSI, Tam. (மாசி) The eleventh month of the year (Feb.-March).

MASI, MUSEE, H. &c. (S. مسي, मसी), MASHI, Mal. (മഷി) Ink, also a black powder used as a collyrium.

Mashikáran, Mal. (മഷിക്കാരൻ) An ink-maker: also a conjurer, one who professes to detect theft by applying a black powder or ink to his eyes, or by rubbing it on his hand, or on a plate, and pretending to view in it the person of the thief.

MASÍNÁ, S. &c. (मसीना) Linseed (Linum utilatissimum).

MAṢLA, H. (A. مثله) An example, exemplary public punishment.

MASNÚN, H. (A. مسنون) Lawful, legalized, allowed, conformable to the sayings of Mohammad.

MASTAKÁVAGHRÁṆA, Mar. (S. मस्तक, the head, and अवघ्राण, smelling) Smelling the head, a mark of affection among the Hindus, as shewn by a parent to a child, or an elder to a junior: it is one of the ceremonials of adoption, the child being seated on the lap of the adopter, the latter smells his head.

MASTÁN, Uriya (ମସ୍ତାନ) A Brahman following the practice of agriculture.

MASTÍSA, H. (مستيسا, Port. *mestiço*) A person of mixed Indian and European descent.

MASÚR, H. &c. (S. مسور, मसूर) A kind of pulse much cultivated (Ervum or Cicer lens, or hirsutum).

MASÚLA, commonly, MUSSOOLA (of doubtful origin), A kind of boat for crossing the surf on the Madras coast: it is usually from 30 to 40 feet long by 6 broad and 8 deep, flat bottomed, and having the planks sown together with withes of straw between each plank: it has ten rowers, and can carry twenty passengers.

MASWADA, H. (مسودة), MASUDÁ, Mar., A rough draft, a foul copy, a sketch.

MASWÁḌI, or WÁRÍ, Guz. (મસવાડી) A municipal tax.

MÁT, (?) A kind of sale of land in Kamaon in which the vendor remains responsible for the public revenue: on his death its payment devolves on the purchaser: also a sale under similar circumstances, but in which the vendor reserves for himself and heirs the right to re-purchase: the word ordinarily means a pledge or mortgage.—Kamaon.

MATÁÂ, H. (A. متاع), MATÁ, Hindi (मता) Goods, chattels, furniture, merchandise.

MATA, Mal. (മട) A flood-gate, a sluice.

MATA, Beng. &c. (মত, S. मत, what is thought) A doctrine, an opinion, a form of faith, a religious sect or belief.

MAṬAKOLA, Mal. (മടക്കോല) A folded letter.

Matakolaháran, Mal. (മടക്കോലക്കാരൻ) A messenger, an ambassador.

MÁTAM, H. (A. ماتم) Mourning, especially the public mourning at the Muharram.

Mátamdár, H. (P. دار, who has) A mourner.

Mátampursi, H. (P. پرس, asking) Condolence: also funeral ceremonies.

MATAN, H. &c. (A. متن), Beng. (মতন) The text of a book: the body, middle, or text of a deed, as distinct from the attestations and endorsements: in Eastern Bengal, a deduction from the actual area of a farm allowed to the tenant for his profit, on condition of his bringing adjacent waste lands into cultivation.

MATANGI, H. (A. متنگي) What is relied on: (in a lawsuit) vouchers, documents.

MAṬHA, vernacularly, MAṬH, MUṬH, incorrectly, MUT, or MUTT, S. &c. (مٿھ, मठ) A building or set of buildings where Hindu religious mendicants reside under a superior, or *Mahant*, generally having rent-free lands in endowment, although supported in part by alms; also a small temple: or a college for Brahman students.

Maṭhadadavasa, Karn. (ಮಠದದವಸ) A tax levied in lieu of grain formerly assigned to a particular convent.

Maṭhadaiyya, Karn. (ಮಠದಯ್ಯ) A servant in a Lingáit village who supplies strangers and travellers with provisions.

Maṭha-patti-jodi, Karn. (ಮಠಪಟ್ಟಿಜೋಡಿ) A tax levied on the privileged heads of Lingáit *Maṭhs*.

MÁṬH, Beng. (মাঠ) A plain, a field, a tract of cultivable lands.

Máṭh-chiṭá, Beng. (মাঠচিটা) A rough statement or specification of the square contents of a field in surveying.

Máṭhán, Beng. (মাঠান) Lying in, or situated on, a plain.

Máṭhánjámi, Beng. (মাঠানজমি) Land lying on a plain.

MAṬHÁ- or MAṬṬHÁPATI, corruptly, MUTPUTEE, Mar. (मठापति, from *Maṭhá*, or *Maṭṭha*, butter-milk or curds) A member of a village community holding land in *inám*, rent-free, on condition of his supplying public officers and servants with butter-milk, being also paid for the same: it is said also to apply to a village servant who acted not only as purveyor to public officers but sometimes as cook for the villagers.

MÁTHÁPHOṚ, Thug. The advance of an ass braying in front of a gang, indicating they will have their heads (*máthá*) broken (*phora*) if they proceed.

MAṬHAUṬ, MUTHOUT, corruptly, MAHTOOT, MHATOOT, MAHTOOL, MATHOTE, MUTHOTE, MATHOOTY, &c. H. (متھوت, मठौट, from H. *máthá*, S. *mastaha*, the head) Capitation, poll-tax, contribution, impost; applied in Bengal to an extra or occasional cess or tax imposed upon the cultivators for some special purpose, or under some incidental pretext, either by the state or the Zamindár, or the principal revenue officer of a district: these taxes were in part abolished and in part consolidated by Ben. Reg. viii. 1793.

Fíl-khaná-mathaut, H. (from *Fíl-khana*, elephant house) A cess on the cultivators for the expense of the public elephant stables.

Zar-mathaut, H. (from P. زر, gold or money) A charge to the cultivators to cover any loss by deficiency of weight, or difference of value in the coins receivable in payment of revenue.

MATÍ, H. &c. (S. متي, मति) Mind, understanding.

MATLAB, MUTLUB, H. (A. مطلب) Object, intention: substance or purport of a document.

MÁTRI, S. &c. (मातृ) A mother, either a natural mother or a step-mother, a father's wife other than the parent: a name applied to a class of female divinities of a mystical character, the mothers of the gods, their personified *Saktis* or energies.

Mátri-bandhu, S. (मातृबंधु) A mother's cognate relation, but limited in law to the son of a maternal grandfather's sister, of a maternal grandmother's sister, and of a mother's maternal uncle.

Mátridatta, S. (मातृदत्त) Given by a mother to a bride at her marriage, constituting an item of woman's property.

MATRÚK, H. (A. متروك) Abolished, rescinded, left, abandoned.

Matrúka, H. (A. متروكه, plur. *Matruhát*, متروكات) Estate, goods, or property of a person deceased to which his heirs are legally entitled.

MATSYÁNDIKÁ, S. &c. (मत्स्याण्डिका, from *matsya*, a fish, and *anda*, an egg) Coarse sugar, the juice partially strained after the first boiling: according to some also, sugar-candy.

MATTÍ, or MITTÍ, H. &c. (مٹّي, from the S. *Mrit*, or *Mrittiká*) MÁTÍ, Beng. (মাটী), MÁTÍ, Mar. (माती), Earth, soil. MATTÍ, Karn. (ಮಟ್ಟಿ) White earth.

Máterá, Mar. (मातेरा) Dirty, mixed with earth or dirt, as grain, &c.

Mattiá, H. (مٹّيا) A well without a frame; merely excavated.

Mattiárá, *Matiyára*, *Mátiyárí*, commonly, but incorrectly, *Mutiyár*, *Mutiyára*, and, corruptly, *Mootiyáree*, H. (مٹّيارا, मटीयारा, माटीयारी) A rich clay soil, mixed with a small proportion of sand: one analysis gives one-tenth of silex, the rest alluvial mould.

Mattiár-cháhí, H. (from *cháh* چاه, a well) Rich soil irrigated by wells.

Mátikátá, Beng. (মাটীকাটা) A digger, a delver; one put to hard labour on the roads.

Mátiyál, Beng. (মাটীয়াল) Rich clay soil without sand.

MÁTTA, Mal. (മാററ) Quality, touch, or fineness, of the precious metals.

MÁTTAM, Mal. (മാററം) Change, exchange, barter, changing money.

MATTAM, Mal. (മട്ടം) A rule, a carpenter's square.

MATÚÂ, A. (متوع) In law, a person of incompetent understanding, one who can only imperfectly apprehend the nature of legal acts, as, for instance, knowing the nature of a sale, but incapable of appreciating the profit or loss attending it.

MATÚL, H. (A. متول) One to whom delay is granted in paying a debt: one who defers payment.

MÁTULA, vernacularly, MÁTUL, S. &c. (मातुल) A maternal uncle. MÁTULÁNÍ, his wife.

MATWÁLÁ, (?) Hard, as water containing saline or earthy particles (perhaps from *matti*, earth).

MAU, corruptly, MAW, MOW, Tam. (மௌ) A measure of land, the twentieth of a *Veli*, and containing 100 *Guntas* of 44 square feet. See *Má*.

MAUJÚDÁT, H. (A. موجودات, plur. of *maujúd* موجود, what exists) Assets, effects, funds, existing things or properties.

MAUKÚF, H. &c. (A. موقوف), Beng. (মৌকুফ), MAHKÚB, Mar. (महकूब) Suspended, ceased, stopped, delayed, suspended, as a decree of court; also, in Mohammadan law, bequeathed, especially for charitable endowments: used also as a substantive, cessation, arrest of judgment, bequest.

Mauhúfí, H. &c. (A. موقوفي) Stopping, suspending, arrest of judgment, suspension of proceedings.

MAULÁ, H. (A. مولا) A judge, a learned or venerable person: an assistant: a person connected with another by the relation of *wilá*, or mutual assistance, as a cause of inheritance, such as an emancipated slave, or a proselyte to whom the master or the converter bequeaths his property: a slave, especially one emancipated.

Maulá-âála, A. (مولا اعلا) A patron, one who makes, or promises, a bequest.

Maulá-asfal, A. (مولا اسفل) A client, a person in whose favour an engagement or bequest is made.

Muwálát, A. (موالات) Friendship, mutual assistance: in law, a contract of mutual amity by which each party acquires a claim to the property of the other to devolve on the survivors.

Mauláná, H. (A. مولانا) The title of a person of learning or respectability, teacher, doctor: in the Maratha countries, the usual designation of the Mohammadan village schoolmaster.

Maulaví, corruptly, *Molavi*, *Moolvy*, H. (A. مولوي) A learned man, a teacher, especially of Arabic, and expounder of Mohammadan law.

MAULI, Thug. One of the gang who carries some money for the support of the families of the party, also, a parole of rendezvous.

MAULÚD, H. (A. مولود) Verses chanted before the bier of a deceased person when carried out to be buried, a dirge, a burial service.

MAUNÍ, S. &c. (मौनी) An ascetic who has taken a vow of perpetual silence, like Paul the Silentiary; also the last day of the month *Phálgun*, when bathing in silence is to be practised.

MAUNJA, S. &c. (मौंज) Any thing relaṭing to *munjá* grass used especially to form a girdle with which a young Brahman is girt at the same time when he is invested with the sacred thread. See *Munj*.

Maunjí, S. &c. (मौंजी, fem. of the preceding) The *munja* girdle, the ceremony of putting it on, &c.

MAURHIA, Thug. A gold *mohar*.

MAURÚṢ, H. &c. (A. موروث) Hereditary, inherited, obtained by inheritance; also subst., Inheritance.

Maurúṣí, H. &c. (موروثي) Hereditary, held or holding by inheritance.

Maurusi asámi or *ráiat*, H. (اسامي, or رعيت, a cultivator) A cultivator in a village holding by hereditary descent, although not one of the propietary community: he retains his land as long as he pays the established rent, and cannot be dispossessed of it as long as that is paid: he cannot alienate his land by sale or mortgage without the consent of the parties of whom he holds.

Ghair maurusí asámí, H. (A. from *ghair* غير, contrary to) A cultivator not holding by hereditary tenure; but it denotes one holding for a stipulated term, or on lease, in distinction to the *Páhi*, or tenant at will.

Maurúṣí ijárá, H. (A. from اجارا, a farm) A hereditary farm, held either at a fixed or variable rent, according to the terms of the lease, but descending from father to son as long as the stipulated rent is paid.

Maurusi mukaddam, H. (A. from مقدّم, a preceder) The head man of a village, holding his office by hereditary descent: in some places he is looked upon as the proprietor of the village lands. See *Mukaddam*.

MAUẒÁ, H. (A. موضع), MAUJÁ, Hindi and Mar. (मौजा), MAUJI, Beng. (মৌজি), MAVUJE, or MAUJE, Tel. (మవుజె) A village, understanding by that term one or more clusters of habitations, and all the lands belonging to their proprietary inhabitants: a *Mauzá* is defined by authority to be 'a parcel or parcels of lands having a separate name in the revenue records, and of known limits.' Directions to settlement officers. The lands, however, are not always contiguous and compact, but may have outlying portions intermixed with those of other villages, but these are brought under one head with the rest in the revenue settlement of the *Mauẓá*.

Mauẓá-aṣli, H. &c. (from اصل, original) The chief village, or that originally settled: in Kamaon, the one named in the *Paṭṭa* granted to the *Padhán*.

Mauẓá-dákhilí, H. (from داخل, inclusive) All the villages and the lands which are comprised in the assessment settled with the original or principal village.

Mauẓáwár, or *Maujáwár*, H. (موضعوار) By villages: assessment of the government revenue on the lands comprised within the village limits and dependencies, settled either with the whole community of proprietary villagers or an individual representing them, distinguished therefore from a Zamindárí settlement as not recognising a single proprietor, and from a Ryotwár settlement as not formed with each cultivator separately.

Mauẓíná, H. (موضينا) A village register kept by the village accountant, shewing the extent of the lands, the average rate of rent per bíghá, the amount of cultivated and waste, and the persons paying or exempt from revenue.

MÁVA, Karn. (ಮಾವ) A father-in-law, a father-in-law's brother.

MAVASU, (?) Tam. A kind of fee or contribution payable by the cultivating tenants of fully-assessed lands to the owner.

MÁVIḌAI, or MAVADAI, Tam. (மாவிடை, மவடை) A term used in conveyances of land to express game.

Máviḍai-maravidai, Tam. (மாவிடைமரவிடை) A term used in deeds to express all kinds of plantations or timber (the combination is, however, erroneous, being expressed by the latter term alone. See *Maravidai*.)

MÁVILAN, or MUVILAN, (?) Mal. The name of a servile tribe, or individual of it, in Malabar.

MÁWAL, Mar. (मावळ) The mountain-valleys of the Sahyádrí range of mountains commencing at the western extremity, and extending about 100 miles east.

MAWÁSHÍ, H. (A. مواشي), MOWAṢÍ, Hindi (मोवाशी) Cattle, domestic agricultural cattle, as cows, buffaloes, sheep, and goats.

Mawesi, (?) Sindhi, Fee paid to government on the sale of cattle.

Mawil, Thug. A horse. Mawili, a mare.

Máy, Mar. (माय) A mother.

Máy-ájá, Mar. (माय आजा) A maternal grandfather. *Máy-ájí*, (मायआजी) A maternal grandmother.

Mayará, Beng. (मयरा) A confectioner.

Mazárât, Mazárî, Mazrúâh, H. (A. مزارعة, مزارع, مزروعة) Cultivated lands, the fields of a village in actual cultivation: a contract of cultivation in which the produce is shared between the proprietor and cultivator in stipulated proportions.

Mazrúâ, corruptly, *Muzrah*, H. (A. مزروع) Cultivated, tilled, a field with a crop upon it.

Muzárâ, or *Muzárí*, H. (A. مزارع) A husbandman, a cultivator.

Mazdúr, H. (A. مزدور), Majúr, Hindi, &c. (मजूर) A labourer, a day labourer.

Mazdúrí, H. (مزدوري), *Majúrí*, Hindi &c. (मजूरी) Wages of labour, hire, daily hire.

Mazdúr-paṭṭí, H. (مزدورپٹي) A tax on day labourers in towns not engaged in agriculture—formerly levied.

Maẕhab, H. (A. مذهب) A religion, a sect, a school of Mohammadan jurisprudence.

Máẓí, vernacularly, Májí, H. &c. (ماضي, माजी) Past, gone, former.

Májí-amaldár, Karn. (ಮಾಜೀಅಮಲದಾರ) A former collector or manager.

Maẕkúr, H. (A. مذكور), Majkúr, Mar. (मजकूर), Majkuru, Tel. (మజకురు) Before mentioned, aforesaid, stated, explained: also subst., notice, mention: contents or substance of a written statement; an account or communication of any kind, facts and circumstances related.

Maẕkúrát, *Muẕkoorat*, less correctly, *Muzcorat*, corruptly, *Muscorat*, and *Muscoorat*, H. &c. (مذكورات, plur. of مذكور) Items or particulars of deductions allowed by the Mohammadan governments to the Zamindárs on closing their revenue accounts, to cover the expenses of managing and collecting the revenue: the admitted fees and personal allowances of the Zamindárs, and petty assignments for charitable or religious purposes were also usually included under this head of remissions.

Maẕkúrí, vernacularly, *Majhúrí*, corruptly, *Muscoory*, *Mushoree*, *Mushkoree*, H. &c. (مذكوري) In old revenue accounts it was applied to small and scattered estates or Zamindárís not included in the accounts of the districts in which they were situated, and of which the assessments were paid direct to the officers of the government: subsequently it denoted a revenue payer paying through the intervention of another, except in Cuttack, where it implied the reverse, or the heads of villages paying the revenue immediately to the collector: when added to the title of an officer or servant it signifies that he is only temporarily employed: also, in the south, an inferior servant or Peon attached to a village: elsewhere, a daily messenger: allowance made to the village watchman in the Northern Sirkars.

Maẕkúri-málguzár, H. (see *Málguzár*) A subordinate payer of revenue, not paying it direct.

Maẕkúri-mahál, H. (محال, an estate) A small dependent property, the rent of which is paid through a third person.

Maẕhúri-muhaddam, H. (see *Mukaddam*) The hereditary head of a village paying the revenue of the village to government.

Maẕkúri-râiat, H. (from رعيت) A nominal or migratory cultivator, a tenant at will having no hereditary right of occupancy.

Maẕkúri-tâluḳ, (from تعالق) A dependent *tâluk* or estate of which the revenue is paid through the intervention of a Zamindár or other revenue payer.

Mazrá, vernacularly, Majrá, H. &c. (A. مزرا, मजरा) Land sown or prepared for sowing, a tilled field: in some parts of India it denotes a hamlet or cluster of houses dependent on a village, but detached from it for agricultural convenience, and managed separately: its assessment is comprised in that of the original village until officially recognized as distinct. In some places a *mazrá* is a smaller division of a *mauza*, or village.

Mâzúl, vernacularly, Majúl, corruptly, Maazaul (A. معزول) Dismissed, removed from an office or appoinement.

Mâzúlí, H. &c. (معزولي) Dismissal, disgrace.

Mâzúlí-, or *Mâzúlí-daftar*, H. (from *daftar*, a record) An office formerly kept up in Bengal for the examination and adjustment of disputed accounts and outstanding balances, especially those of public officers who had been dismissed or were charged with embezzlement, or undue exactions.

Mazún, H. (A. موزون) Weighed, measured; allowed as deductions from the revenue for petty recognised charges and expenses.

Mâẕún, A. (ماذون) Licensed; a licensed slave, one having authority from his owner to trade or to do acts to which he would be otherwise incompetent.

Mechchil, Mal. (മെച്ചിൽ) Pasture, forage.

Mechhuyá, Beng. (মেছুয়া) A fisherman.

Medá, Beng. (মেদা) A receptacle for obtaining lime from saline soil and water by filtration.

Méda, Karn. (ಮೇದ), Médara, Tel. (మేదర), Médaravan, Tam. (மேதரவன்) A caste, or a member of it, occupied in cutting and selling bambus, or making and vending bambu baskets.

Mede, Karn. (ಮೆದೆ) A stack of any kind of grain: it also implies a definite quantity = 32 Madras measures.

Medh, also written, Maindh, H. (میڈھ, मेढ, मेंढ) Gleanings, corn left on the field in small quantity.

Medhá, Mar. (मेढा) A paling, a fence, an inclosure.

Medhedái, -dáik, Mar. (मेढेदाई, मेढेदाईक) The owner of a contiguous inclosure.

Medhí, Beng. (মেধী) The post in the centre of the threshing-floor to which the cattle are fastened.

Medi, Tel. Karn. (మెడి) The part of the handle which is joined to the plough.

Megóḷu, Karn. (ಮೆಗೊಳು) Duty on goods paid in advance.

Megpanna, (?) H. Murdering poor people for the sake of kidnapping and selling their children (?).

Mehmán, or Mahimán, Mar. (मेहमान, महिमान, P. *mihman*, q.v.) A person residing in a village in which he has no hereditary rights or property.

Mehtar, or Mihtar, H. (P. مهتر) A man who follows the lowest menial offices, a sweeper, a scavenger: the term originally means a prince, and is used ironically: in Cuttack the *mehtar* is sometimes a slave.

Mehtar, or Mhetar, incorrectly, Mehtree, Mar. (मेहतर, म्हेतर) A common designation for a hereditary village officer, as the Pátil or Kulkaraní: the head of a caste or business, trade, or art, who used to exercise considerable authority over the others, and collected and paid the taxes due by them, in consideration of which he was himself exempt: (it is no doubt the same as the preceding word differently applied).

Mehto, or Meheto, Guz. (મેહતો, મેહેતો) A writer, a clerk, an accountant.

Mehuná, Mar. (मेहुणा) A wife's brother, a sister's husband.

Mehuní, (मेहुणी) A wife's sister.

Meí, or Meí-khuntí, Beng. (মেই, মেইখুঁটী) The post in the centre of the threshing-floor to which the cattle are tied.

Mej, Mar. (मेज) Measure, measuring, a measure of length or capacity.

Mejdát-dád, or *-dást*, Mar. (मेजदात, -दाद, -दास्त) Counting or numbering houses, making a list or inventory of articles, &c.

Mekhí, H. &c. (میخی), Mekí, Beng. (মেকী) Plugged, as a coin (from *mekh*, a pin or nail).

Mél, Tam. Mal. (மேல், മെൽ), Méle, Karn. (ಮೇಲೆ), Mélu, Tel. (మేలు) A particle and prefix, implying superiority in place, excess in quantity, &c.; over, above, &c.: in Tamil compounds, *Mél* may become *Men*, or *Mer*: *Mélu*, in Karn. and Tel. is also a subst., signifying superiority, excellence, profit, advantage, excess, &c.

Méladhikáram, Mal. (മെലധികാരം) Supreme power or authority.

Meláḷ, Mal. (മെലാൾ) An overseer, a superintendant, a person in charge.

Mélaṭi, Mal. (മെലടി) Rent in kind paid to the owner of fields or gardens: entrusting cattle to the charge of another.

Méléralai, Tam. (மேலேரலை) An engagement for an increased share of the crop to be relinquished to the cultivators.

Mêleṟutta, Mal. (മെലെഴുത്ത) Government registry of revenue.

Méleṟuttu-kachcheri, Mal. (മെരലഴുത്തുകച്ചേരി) Chief office of registry of lands and revenue.

Mélkanakka, Mal. (മെല്കണക്ക) Principal public accounts.

Mélkánam, Mal. (മെല്കാനം) Mortgage upon mortgage, an additional advance upon the security of occupancy paid by the occupant of an estate to the proprietor.

Mélkaram, Mal. (മെല്കരം) Additional government share of the crop: tax paid a year in advance.

Mélkoyimma, Mal. (മെല്കൊയിമ്മ) Authority, superior power or function.

Mélkoyimma-sthánam, Mal. (മെല്കൊയിമ്മസ്ഥാനം, from S. स्थानं, station) The exercise of chief authority in the affairs of a temple.

Mélmániyam, Mal. (മെല്മാണിയം) Superintendence, supervision.

Mélnoki, or *Ménoki*, (?) Mal. (മെൽനൊക്കി, മെനൊക്കി) A district accountant in some parts of Malabar.

Mélurași, Tel. (మేలురాశి) The grain in the crop threshed but not measured; a heap of winnowed corn.

Méluváram, Tel. (మేలువారం), *Mélvárum*, or *Mélwáram*, corruptly, *Malewarum*, *Mailwarum*, Tam. Mal. (மேல்வாரம்) The proportion of the crop claimed by the government.

Mélváram-tirwai, Tam. (from தீர்வை, duty) The fixed rate of the government demand on the share of the crop.

Mélvaippu, Tam. (மேல்வைப்பு) A quit-rent, or a small proportion of the crop paid by the holder of a *Mányam*.

Mélvási, Tel. Karn. (మేలవాసి) Additions, excess, addition made to the rate of the government assessment.

Mélváyippa, Mal. (മെല്വായിപ്പ) An extra loan, an additional advance.

Mélvichåram, Mal. (മെല്വിചാരം) Superintendence.

Ménavan, pronounced also, *Ménon*, corruptly, *Menewar*, Mal. (മെനവൻ) The village or district accountant in Malabar: according to some, the appropriate designation of a *Súdra*; according to others, of a Nair writer or accountant.

Ámisham Ménon, corruptly, *Umshom Ménon*, Mal. The writer who registers the estimate of the crops.

Ménkával, Tam. (மேன்க்காவல்) The superior or district watch: superintendant of police.

Ménkávalgár, Tam. (மேன்க்காவல்கார்) A petty chief in the south of India, a *Páligár*, the superior guardian or protector of the country.

MEL, H. &c. (S. ميل) Meeting, mixing, an assembly; also, fig., agreement, concord: in Guzerati, casting the balance of an account: a cash-book.

Melá, H. &c. (S. ميلا, मेला) A fair, an assemblage of people periodically at some particular spot, usually on a religious festival, but at which traffic is carried on and amusements are provided: any fair or occasional market.

MELÁDIKA, Uriya (ମେଲାଡ଼ିକ) House-land unoccupied.

MELDÁR, (?) Hindi, A village messenger sometimes acting as the watchman.—Kamaon.

MEMÁN, Guz. (મેમાન) A particular tribe of Mohammadans in the west of India.

MÉNA, Tel. (మేన) Connected through a father's sister, or mother's brother.

Ménagóḍalu, Tel. (మేనకోడలు) A female cousin, the daughter of a father's sister or mother's brother.

Ménalluḍu, Tel. (మేనల్లుడు) A male cousin through the same relationship.

Ménamáma, Tel. (మేనమామ) A maternal uncle.

Menaṭṭa, Tel. (మేనట్ట) A father's sister or mother's brother's wife.

MEṆḌ, less correctly, MEṚH, H. (ميند, मेंड) A bank to separate fields, a dam, a dyke, a boundary, the boundary of a field, the limit of the lands of a village.

Menḍhbandí, pronounced, *Meṛhbandí*, H. (from بندي, an account) A record of boundaries.

MENḌÁ, H. (? ميندا) Any village or town where a Gayawál or privileged conductor of pilgrims to Gaya has established himself.

MENDHÁ, MENDHÍ, Mar. (S. मेंढा, मेंढी) A ram, a ewe.

Mendhá-bancharái, Mar. (from *mendhá*, a sheep, *ban*, a wood, and *charái*, grazing) A tax levied on the pasturage of sheep and goats.

MENHDÍ, H. &c. (مينهدي) A plant from the leaves of which a red dye is prepared, with which the natives, women especially, stain the palms of their hands and soles of their feet and the tips of their fingers and toes (Lawsonia inermis).

MENIPÁṬAM, Mal. (മെനിപാടം) The rent of land as calculated on the average produce of different crops.

Meniviḷachchil, Mal. (മെനിവിളച്ചിൽ) The best or highest produce or crop of any parcel of land.

MEṆJOGÍ, Mar. (मेंजोगी) A class of Jogí mendicants in the Maratha country, worshippers of *Bhairava*.

MEO, (?) H. A class of cultivators in the province of Dehli.

MÉPPULAM, Mal. (മെപ്പുലം) Pasture, forage for cattle.

Méypukáran, Mal. (മെയ്പുക്കാരൻ) A shepherd, a grazier.

MÉRA, Tel. (మేర), MÉRE, Karn. (ಮೇರೆ) A limit, a boundary.

MÉRA, Tel. (మేర), MÉRE, Karn. (ಮೇರೆ), MÉRAI, Tam. (மேரை) A portion of the crop given as a perquisite to the holders of a proprietary right in the village lands, or to the hereditary village officers and servants, out of the common stock from the threshing-floor: sometimes the appropriation is made from the government share after division, but the practice and the proportion vary.

Méraidiṭṭam, Tam. (மேரைதிட்டம்) Regulation or rule for the proportionate allowances from the crops.

MERAVAṆIGE, Karn. (ಮೆರವಣಿಗೆ) A procession on a festival occasion; a religious procession; a bridal procession, in which the bride and bridegroom, with attendants according to their means, parade the streets of a town or village.

MERAKA, Tel. (మెరక) Dry land, upland, high ground. See *Metta*.

MERIA, or MERIYA, Uriya (ମେରିଆ) A human victim, usually a child or young person, kidnapped, and, after a season, sacrificed by the *Khonds*, a barbarous race in the hills west of Cuttack.

MÉRUVE, Karn. (ಮೇರುವೆ) An inclined plane or slope of earth up which blocks of stone are rolled for the upper parts of a building: a trench, a stockade.

MESHA, S. &c. (मेष) A ram, the sign Aries: in Tamil it is sometimes used for the month in which the sun enters

Aries, or April-May, corruptly or vernacularly written, *Medom*, *Medhom*.

Méṣtak, Tel. (మేస్తక్) A column, an item or head of account. Mar. (मेस्तक) A book of arithmetic, a table to facilitate calculation.

Mesari, Guz. (મેસરી) A tribe of merchants and traders in Guzerat, followers of a teacher termed *Gosâî-ji Mahárâj*.

Meṭa, Mal. (മെട) A hill, a height, high ground.

Meṭa, or Meṭ Mar. (मेट) A watchhouse or station in a village usually occupied by Mhars: a military or police out-station near a fort or walled village, or on the frontier of a district.

Méta, Tel. (మేత) Pasturage, forage.

Métarangam, Tel. (మేతరంగం) The office of a head man.

Métari, Tel. (మేతరి) A head man amongst the lower castes, as palankin-bearers, washermen, cowherds, &c. (this and the preceding are probably from H. *mehtar*, or S. *mahat*, great).

Méṭi, Tel. Karn. (మేటి) The post in a threshing-floor; also, chief, principal, the head of a body of persons, especially of inferior cultivators: an association of villagers who are partners in cultivation.

Méṭidáru, Tel. (మేటిదారు) Head man of a company or caste, a renter of a village.

Méṭigoda, Karn. (ಮೇಟೀಗೌಡ) A head farmer.

Méṭi kóru, or *Méṭi pálu*, Tel. (మేటికోరు, మేటిపాలు) The landlord's share of the crop: an agreement made amongst themselves by the cultivators with regard to what lands are to be cultivated, in which way the government revenue and other charges are to be apportioned, and how the surplus is to be divided.

Metírayat, Mar. (मेटीरयत) The head cultivator of a village.

Metí, Mal. (മെതി) Treading-out or threshing corn; the treadle of a loom.

Metrán, Mal. (മെത്രാൻ) A bishop (from the Syriac).

Meṭṭa, Tel. (మెట్ట) High and dry land, not capable of irrigation, but depending on the rain, and therefore unfit for rice.

Méṭṭaguḍḍalu, Tel. (మేట్టగుడ్డలు) High lands, fields only fit for dry cultivation.

Méṭṭajágá, Tel. (మేట్టజాగా) High ground, hills, hillocks.

Méṭṭavári, Tel. (మెట్టవరి) The crop of the dry cultivation.

Meṭṭí, Mal. (മെട്ടി) An inferior domestic servant, a term of common use in Malabar: a term of similar sound is used at Madras to signify a menial, who is usually a Pareyan, who cleans dishes, lamps, shoes, &c., commonly called a *meti-boy*; it is supposed to be derived from the nautical term *mate*, but it is perhaps the Tamil representative of the Malayalim word.

Meṭṭu, Tel. Karn. (మెట్టు) A custom-house: the stage of a journey.

Meṭṭu, Tam. (மெட்டு) A place where toll or custom is taken.

Meṭṭukáran, Tam. (மெட்டுகாரன்) A receiver of tolls, one who examines persons entering or leaving a village.

Méṭuvaṛi, Mal. (മെട്ടുവഴി) A path through a mountain, a causeway.

Mévu, Karn. (ಮೇವು) Pasturage, grazing.

Mewafarosh, H. &c. (میوه‌فروش) A fruit-seller, usually of the Máli caste; but in the Maratha country Brahmans and Kaláwants (singers) follow the business in towns: the fruit-sellers in the villages are sometimes Mohammadan gardeners.

Mewas, Guz. (મેવાસ) A tribe of *kolis* or freebooters in Guzerat.

Mewátí, H. (میواتي, मेवाती) A tribe of Rajputs inhabiting the province of *Mewat*, now known as *Macheri*, and formerly notorious for their turbulent and predatory character.

Meyaru, (?) plur. Karn. A class of slaves in Kanara, a subdivision of the *Dhers*.

Méykiṛavan, Tam. (மேய்க்கிறவன்) A shepherd.

Méyssal, Tam. (மேய்ச்சல்) Pasturage, pasture.

Mhaisá-paṭṭí, Mar. (म्हैसापट्टी) A tax on buffaloes.

Mhao, written Mhow, and Mow (?) Mar. The village messenger and watchman; probably a dialectical modification of *Mahár*, or *Mhár*, q. v.

Mhao-Mharhi, (?) Mar. A tax on the lands held by the *Mahárs*.

Miâád, H. &c. (ميعاد), Míyád, Beng. (মিযাদ) Term, limit, either of time or place.

Miâádí, H. &c. (ميعادي), *Miyádi*, Beng. (মিযাদী) Limited, terminable, conditional, also subst., limitation.

Miâádi-ijárá, H. (from اجارا, a farm) A farm or lease for a specified term, a farm for a given number of years, a terminable lease.

Mián, H. &c. (P. ميان, मीयान्) A term of respectful address to an old or respectable person, sir, master: also a mediator, an umpire, a schoolmaster.

Mián-ádmí, H. (P. ميان آدمي) A respectable man, a gentleman.

Miána, H. (ميانه) A kind of palankin, that used generally by Europeans.

Miáni, Guz. (મીઆણી) The name of a tribe of Mohammadan freebooters on the confines of Sindh and Guzerat.

MIÂRÁJ, commonly, MIRÁJ, H. (A. معراج) Ascent, whence *lailat-ul-miârâj*, means the night of Mohammad's ascent to heaven, observed as an anniversary festival by devout Mohammadans on the 15th, 16th, or 27th of the month of *Rajab*.

MÍCHAVÁRAM, corruptly, MICHAROM, Tam. (மீச்வாரம், from *Mícharam*, superior, and *varam*, share), MICHCHAVÁRAM, Mal. (മിച്ചവാരം) The landlord's share of the crop: in Malabar, the proprietor's rent, after deducting the interest of the money lent or advanced by the tenant: the surplus amount or difference between the interest of money lent on mortgage and the proceeds of the estate occupied by the mortgagee, payable to the mortgager. See the next.

Michcham, Mal. (മിച്ചം) Remainder, residue, surplus.

MIDDE, MIDDIYÁ, Tel. (మిద్దె, మిద్దియ) A house with an upper story, also one with a flat or terraced roof.

MIGIKE, MIGUTE, MIGUVIKE, Karn. (ಮಿಗಿಕೆ, ಮಿಗುತೆ, ಮಿಗುವಿಕೆ) Surplus, balance.

MIHMÁN, less correctly, MEHMAN, H. &c. (P. مهمان) A stranger, a guest.

Mihmání, H. &c. (مهماني) Hospitality, reception or charge of a guest: under the Mohammadan government, a deduction from the revenue, allowed to Zamindárs to defray the cost of their entertaining travellers, pilgrims, and strangers in general: also a cess levied in some places by the Zamindárs under pretext of providing for similar purposes.

Mihmán-dár, H. (P. مهماندار) A host, a person deputed to receive and take charge of a stranger, especially if of consequence, as an envoy from a foreign court.

Mihmán-khána, or *sará*, H. (from the P. خانه or سرا) A house where a visitor is accommodated, a place for the reception of strangers or visitors in general, sometimes found in villages and towns.

Mihmán-váram, Tam. A share of the produce of the harvest set apart for travellers and guests.

MIHNAT, H. (A. محنت) Labour, trouble, care.

Mihnatána. H. (محنتانه) Hire or wages of labour, payment for work done, compensation for the management of any affair or estate, excess over the legal rate of interest as a remuneration for the lender's trouble.

Mihnatí, H. (محنتي) Laborious, painstaking, one on whom any trouble or labour devolves.

MIHRKATTÍ, (?) H. An account kept by the village accountant in Bengal, shewing the names of the cultivators, the extent of their fields, their cultivation and crops, and the amount of their assessment.

MIJHARÍ, (?) Tax on the low caste, termed *Dóm*.—Kamaon.

MILAN, H. &c. (ملن) Mixing, association; entering into a contract or agreement with.

Milán, or *Milání*, H. &c. (ملان, ملاني) Causing a mixture or concurrence, making parties agree, adjustment, arbitration: a supplementary or subsidiary statement.

Milán-jamábandí, incorrectly, *Melan-jumabundi*, H. (ملان جمابندي, मिलान जमाबंदी) An appendix or supplement to the account of the revenues of a village, shewing the varieties that occur in the extent of land in cultivation.

MILK, MILKÍAT, corruptly, MILKEUT, and MILKYET, H. &c. (A. ملك, ملكيت) Possession, property, mastership, proprietary right; also real property, landed possessions: it is sometimes applied to the possession of rent-free lands.

Milkí, H. (ملكي) Proprietary, relating to ownership, especially in land, a proprietor, a farmer.

Milkí-lákhiráj, H. (ملكي لاخراج) Proprietorship of lands exempt from revenue payment.

Milk-kharídagí, H. (ملك خريدگي) Ownership by purchase. See *Kharída*.

Milk-kharídadár, H. (ملك خريده دار) Owner of a purchased estate (especially in Cuttack).

Milkíat-istamrárí, H. (from استمرار, q. v.) Proprietary right or possession in perpetuity.

MIM, H. &c. The letter of the Persian alphabet, *m*, م, used, under the Mogul government, as a countersign by the *Diwán* upon an imperial grant or assignment of revenue.

MÍMÁNSÁ, S. &c. (मीमांसा) Judgment, investigation: one of the Hindu schools of philosophy, the object of which is to investigate the doctrine of the Veda, and the practices enjoined.

Mímánsaka, S. &c. (मीमांसक) A judge, an umpire, a teacher of the Mímánsá philosophy.

MINHÁ, or, MINHÁI, corruptly, MINHYE, H. (A. منها, منهاي, literally, *Min* من, from, *há* ها, that,) Deduction, subtraction: as a revenue term it implies deduction from the assessed revenue of an estate or village, as on account of uncultivable tracts of wood or water, wilderness or waste, or for compensation of the Kánungos (Ben. Reg. xiii. 1825.) or for local charges: In Mohammadan law it means a usufructuary loan, or the loan of any thing which the borrower is to return, using in the mean time the produce, as of a cow, the milk of which the borrower may consume.

Minhái-dár, H. (P. دار, who has) A holder of land exempted from revenue payment, or subject to a diminished assessment.

Minhái-gí, H. (منهايگي) Deduction from the assessment on some account, as special assignment, or exemption on account of the land lying uncultivated, &c.

MINAK, or MÍNAKÍA, Thug. A religious mendicant.

MINJUMLA, H. &c. (A. منجمله) Upon the whole, generally, universally.

MINUMULU, Tel. (మినుములు) A kind of bean grown on dry lands (Phaseolus mungo).

MÍR, MEER, H. (A. مير) A chief, a head or leader; under the Mohammadans, the title of the head of a department: it is also a title borne by Sayids, or those persons who claim a descent from the family of Mohammad.

Mír-i-ădl, H. (A. ميرعدل) An officer of justice, a superintendant of the courts who revised the decisions of the Kazis and judges, passed sentence, and ordered punishment.

Mír-akhor, H. (A. ميراخور) Master of the horse.

Mír-i-átish, H. (A. P. ميرآتشت) Master of the ordnance, head of the artillery.

Mír-bahr, *H.* (A. P. ميربحر) Custom or harbour-master.

Mír-bahrí, H. (ميربحري) Port duties, fees on vessels entering or leaving port, also taxes on boat and ship-building: the term has been also applied to the fees levied from pilgrims at Allahabad.

Mír-bakhshí, H. (مربخشي) Paymaster general.

Mírdaha, H. (ميرده), Beng. *Mirdáha* (মির্দাহ), Hindi, *Mirdhá* (मिरधा) The head peon, or messenger of a Zamindár: the inspector or superintendant of a village: a native officer employed to preserve the village boundaries from encroachment: one employed to carry the measuring chain, or apply it to actual measurement in a survey: the head man of a village: In Mar. also the captain or head of spearmen, who precede great men in procession; also a head spy or messenger: (from *mír*, chief, and *deh*, ten, or a small company, or *deh*, or *dih*, a village, whence the different meanings).

Mír-i-manzil, H. (ميرمنزل) Quartermaster general.

Mír-mahallah, H. (ميرمحلّه) Head, or superintendant of a quarter of the town, inspector of police.

Mír-munshí, H. (ميرمنشي) Chief secretary.

Mír-peshkár, H. &c. (ميرپيشكار) Accountant-general.

Mír-sạmán, H. (ميرسامان) Head steward.

Mír-shikár, H. (ميرشكار) Chief huntsman.

Mír-tuzak, H. (ميرتزك) Chief marshal, an officer whose duty is to maintain order in a march or procession.

Mírán, H. (ميران) Proportion of the fees, or perquisites of the inferior officers of a department payable to the chief.

MIRÁṢ, H. &c (A. ميراث, from ورث, to inherit). Mar. (मिरास) MIRÁSI, and MIRÁSU, Tam. (மிராசி, மிராசு) MIRÁSU, Tel. (మిరాసు) MIRÁSI, Karn. (ಮಿರಾಸಿ) Inheritance, inherited property or right: the term, is used, especially in the south of India, to signify lands held by absolute hereditary proprietorship under one of three contingencies: 1. either as a joint coparcenary tenure in the lands of a village, and either cultivated in common, or allotted annually, or at some other stated period, among the proprietors; 2. As one of several parcels or lots in which the lands of the village are divided; or, 3. as a whole estate where all the lands of the village are the property of one proprietor. In some parts of the Madras provinces, especially north and south Arcot and Chinglepat, known in the native records as Tondamandalam, the term is also applied to certain hereditary privileges enjoyed by the holders of *Miráṣ* lands, consisting sometimes of a right to hold portions of their estates exempt from assessment, and, in almost all, the privilege of receiving portions of the general produce, or money compensation from the other members of the community. It also applies to the fees and perquisites receivable by the officers and servants of the community, who are not posseessed of any share of the *Mirás* land, and to hereditary succession to various offices, privileges, and emoluments, as to the post of musician to a temple or the like.—Ellis on *Mirási* right. In Sylhet it applies to Tálukas settled perpetually.

Miráṣí H. &c. (ميراثي) Hereditary, any thing relating to *Mirás*, also the same as *Miráṣ*, (and the most usual form in the south) or hereditary lands or offices, also one holding land or office in a village by hereditary descent. In the Konkan it is applied especially to the resident Mhár, or sweeper, holding his office by succession, and entitled to a share of the crop.

Miráṣdár or *Mirásidár* H. &c. (ميراثدار मिरासीदार) *Miraṣidárudu*, Tel. (మిరాశిదారుడు) *Mirásidáran*, Tam. (மிராசிதாரன்) The holder of hereditary lands, or offices in a village. In the Northern Sarkárs, especially, a hereditary village officer or servant: In Sylhet, the holder of an estate, usually of very small extent, assessed in perpetuity; a petty landholder or cultivator.

Mirási-anubhogu-dánáchá, Karn. (ಮಿರಾಶಿಅನುಬೋಗು-ದಾನಾಚಾ) Light tax or quit-rents on hereditary lands and offices.

Miraṣibábu, Karn. (ಮಿರಾಶಿಬಾಬು) Of or belonging to hereditary, or rent free land.

Miráṣi-râiat, H. &c. (A. رعيت) A hereditary cultivator, one having a right to hold his land as long as he pays the rent to the proprietor, and the government revenue.

Mirási-sutantaram, Tam. (மிராசிசுதந்தரம், from S. *swatantram* स्वतन्त्र, independent) Absolute hereditary right to lands or offices.

Miráspaṭṭi, Mar. (मिरासपट्टी) A tax levied occasionally on Mirásdárs.

Mirás-váram, Tam. (from வாரம், share) The part produce of hereditary land.

MIRDÁ, H. (ميردا) A caste of migratory shepherds in the south of India, or an individual of it.

MIRZÁ, H. (P. مرزا) When prefixed to a name, a secretary, a civilian, as *Mirza-Ibrahím*; when following it, a prince, as *Abbas Mirzá*.

MISAN, H. (مسن, मिसन) A soil mixed of clay and sand, sometimes considered as the first or best description of soil, or soil rendered highly productive by diligent tillage and plentiful manuring.

MIṢL, H. (A. مثل) Similitude; an assembly, a corporation, an assemblage of persons of the same or like station and occupations: a collection of like or similar documents forming the body of public proceedings in judicial or in revenue matters; whence the instructions to the officers employed to assess the lands in the north-west provinces are denominated the Settlement *Miṣl*: the term is also applied to a suit or proceedings at law in general.

Miṣl-diwání, H. A civil suit.

Miṣl-faujdárí, H. A criminal suit.

Miṣl-karanam, Tel. The principal or officiating village clerk or accountant.

Miṣl-reḍḍi, Tel. The farmer who is considered the head of the cultivators in a village, and represents the community.

Miṣl-mutafaraḥa ,H. (A. متفرقة) Miscellaneous proceedings.

Miṣlí, H. (A. مثلي) Like, equal: in Mohammadan law it applies to an article which, being lent or sold, is to be replaced by another of a similar description.

Misl-tirvai, Tam. (மிசல்திர்வை) An assessment on a field similar or analogous to that on the adjacent land.

MIṢKÁL, H. (A. مثقال) A measure of weight = 63½ Tr. grains.

MISKÍN, H. (A. مسكين) Poor: in law, one having no property whatever.

MISMÁR, H. (A. مسمار) Lit., destruction: applied in some places to mischief to crops committed by cattle.

MIṢR, MIṢRA, less correctly, MISHAR, H. (S. مصر, मिश्र) A name given to a Brahman of the Kanaujya tribe, and especially to the members of two of the subdivisions, *Góts*, or families belonging to it, those of the *Sandal*, and *Kátyáyana* or *Viswámitra Góts*: the term *Miṣr* was conjectured to have been connected with the ancient name of Egypt, *Miṣr*, as if some of the Brahmans had come from that country: it is more probably of affinity to *Miṣra*, mixed, indicating some mixture of race or family, the tradition of which has perished.

MIṢRÍ, H. (A. مصري), MICHHRÍ, Beng. (মিছ্রী) Sugar-candy.

MISTRÍ, H. &c. (مستري), MESTRÍ, Mar. (मेसतरी) An artificer, a mechanic, as, a mason, a carpenter, &c.: a head artificer, a chief builder, a carpenter, and the like.

MITÂT, less correctly, MATÂT, and MUTÂA, A. (متعة) Temporary cohabitation, a sort of left-handed marriage among the Mohammadans, taking a wife for a specified time; allowed by the *Shias*, but considered illegal by the *Sunis*: also a present given to a woman, upon whom no portion had been settled, on divorcing her.

Mamtuá, H. (A. ممتوع) A woman who has been temporarily a wife.

MÍṬHÁ, H. &c. (ميٹھا, S. मिष्ट), MITHÁ, Beng. and Mar. (মিঠা, मिठा) Sweet.

Miṭhái, H. &c. (ميٹھاي) Sweetmeats, confectionery.

Míṭhái-wálá, H. (ميٹھاي والا) A maker or vender of sweetmeats, a confectioner.

Miṭhánamalamchará, Beng. (মিঠানমল°চরা) Alluvial lands become sweet and fit for tillage.—Chittagong.

MÍṬHA, and in comp., MITHA, Mar. (मीठ) and Guz. (મીઠ) Salt.

Miṭhágar, Mar. (मिठागर) A salt-pan, salt-works.

Miṭhágari, Mar. and Guz. (मिठागरी) A caste, or an individual member of it, whose occupation is the manufacture of sea-salt.

Míṭhamola, Mar. (मीठमोल) A place where salt is manufactured.

Mittamoḷa-upparike, Karn. (ಮಿತ್ತಮೊಳ ಉಪ್ಪರಿಕೆ) An annual tax on each salt manufactory.

Míṭhalonári, Mar. (मीठलोणारी) A caste, or an individual of it, whose business it is to make salt, especially from inland saline deposits or marshes.

MIṬHHÁLÁ, Hindi (मिठहाला) A productive moisture inherent in the soil.—Puraniya.

MIṬHṬHE, Karn. (ಮಿಠ್ಠೆ) Land tax, assessment, rent on land.

MITHYÁ, H. &c. (S. متهيا, मिथ्या) False, falsely.

Mithyábádí, Beng. (मिथ्याबादी, from S. वादी, who speaks) One making a false assertion or charge, a calumniator.

Mithyásákhí, Beng. (साक्षी, from S. साक्षी) A false witness.

Mithyáṣapath, Beng. (from S. शपथ, an oath) Perjury.

Mithyá sukṛut, Uriya (ମିଥ୍ୟାସୁକୃତ, from S. सुकृति) Perjury.

Mithyottara, Beng. (মিথ্যোত্তর, from S. उत्तर, answer) A reply asserting the falsehood of the charge, denial of a charge (in Hindu law).

MITI, H.&c.(S. متي, मिति) Measure, limit, bounds: date: interest.

Kachchá-mití, corruptly, *Cutchameetee*, H. Interest charged by money dealers on money advanced, dated from the day before the transaction.

Pakká-miti, corruptly, *Pucka meetee*, H. Interest allowed by bankers on money received, dating from the day after the receipt.

MIṬṬÁ, Tam. (மிட்டா) Subdivision of a district, an estate forming such a division: a revenue estate created in the Madras territories under the permanent settlement.

Miṭṭádár, Tam. (P. دار, who has) The holder or proprietor of an estate forming the subdivision of a district.

MIZÁJ SHARÍF, H. (A. مزاج, temperament, شريف) A very respectful term of inquiry concerning a person's health, as if it were asked, Is your noble temperament well?

MIZÁN, H. (A. ميزان) A balance, a pair of scales: sum total.

MOBED, Guz. (મોબેદ) A priest of the Pársís.

MOCHÁ, Hindi (मोचा) Crops beat down by wind or rain.

MOCHAN, H. &c. (موچن, from S. मूष, stealing, also from S. मुच) Letting go, setting at liberty.

MOCHARÁ, Hindi (मोचरा) The crop of late-sown rice (May-June): a rate in a *Paṭṭa* for such crops when the only ones raised in the year on the same land.—Puraniya.

MOCHCHAI, Tam. (மொச்சை) A leguminous plant cultivated on dry ground: (Dolichos tetraspermus).

MOCHI, H. &c. (موچي) A worker in leather, but commonly applied to one who is by caste and occupation a shoemaker, a harness maker, or saddler. MUCHCHE, Tel. (ముచ్చె) The name of a caste in the south of India, or of a member of it, who, like the Mochi (which word is no doubt the same) of Hindustan, is a worker in leather and saddlery, but is also a cabinet or furniture-maker and a portrait painter: a *Muchche-váḍu*, or *Muchi*-man, as he is termed, is also employed in public offices, like a *daftarí* in Upper India, to make pens, ink, provide paper, seal letters, and bind books, and the like.

MOḌ, or MOṚ, Mar. (मोड, from the v. मोडणे, to break or separate) The common business hand; the broken or cursive writing used by the Marathas on ordinary occasions.

MOḌAL, or MOṚAL, Beng. (মোড়ল) The head man of a village, the *Mandal*.—Bengal.

MODALU, Tel. Karn. (మొదలు), MUDAL, Tam. (முதல்) Origin, principal, capital: first, chief. See *Mutal*.

Modaláḷu, Karn. (ಮೊದಲಾಳು) A chief or head man.

Mudalváḍai, Tam. (முதல்வாடை) A field first watered from a tank.

Modalavâru, Karn. (ಮೊದಲವಾರು) The first day of the week, Sunday.

Vaḍḍi-modalu, Tel. (వడ్డి మొదలు) Principal and interest.

Mudaláḷi, Tam. (முதலாளி) A president, a proprietor.

Mudali, *Mudalvan*, Tam. (முதலி, முதல்வன்) A title of the agricultural and some other respectable classes.

Mudaliyár, Tam. (முதலியார், plur., but used to an individual honorifically) A respectful title or address to natives in the Tamil provinces, especially those of the *Mudali* tribe, when of respectability, as Mr. or Sir: an official designation in Ceylon.

MOḌAN, or MOṬAN, corruptly MODDAM, Mal. (മൊടൻ) High land on which a particular kind of rice is cultivated.

MODÍ, H. &c. (مودي, मोदी) A shopkeeper, a steward: in Bengal, MUDÍ, or MÓDI, (মুদী, মোদী), most usually denotes the village shopkeeper, a sort of grocer or chandler and grain dealer, who sells a variety of articles of necessity to the villagers, and who are generally in his debt at a usurious rate of interest.

Modikhána, H. &c. (مودي‌خانه, मोदीखाना) A chandler's or grocer's shop: among the Marathas also, the commissaraít department, the supplies necessary for an army, the office whence they are issued, the place where they are kept, &c.

MÓDÍ, Karn. (ಮೋದಿ) The victualling department, the establishment for providing public provisions.

Módikepu, Karn. (ಮೋದಿಕೆಪ್ಪು) A herd of cattle with public provisions.

MODAK, Beng, &c. (মোদক) A confectioner, also a kind of sweetmeat.

MOGHAL, more correctly, MUGHAL, in common use, MOGHUL, H. &c. (مغل), MOGAL, Mar. (मोगल) The designation of one of the great Tartar tribes, the *Mongol*, or of a member of it: as a title it was especially applied to the sovereigns of Delhi of the house of Timur, although they were equally at least of *Turk* descent, and presented in their appearance entirely *Turkish* characteristics.

Moghlái, or *Mughlái*, vernacularly, *Mogalái*, or *Moglai*, corruptly, *Mogulae*, and *Mogullaye*, H. &c. (مغلاى, मोगलाई) Relating or belonging to the Mughals, as the period of their ascendancy in Hindustan, extended to that of the Mohammadan kings of Bijapur, Golkonda, &c. in the Dakhin; also fees paid to Moghul or Mohammadan officers: also a branch of the revenues of the Nawab of Surat, distinct from those of which the Marathas exacted the *Chauth*, q. v.

Mogalí, Mar. (मोगली) Relating to the Mohammadan rule, especially applied to such portion of the revenue payments of a village as the Marathas did not at once appropriate.

Mughal-bandí, H. (مغل بندى), *Mogal-bandi*, Uriya (ମୋଗଲବନ୍ଦି) The part of the territory of Cuttack which was formerly subject to the government of Delhi, and is now administered according to the Regulations of the British government, paying the land revenue on the same plan as that adopted in Bengal. Ben. Reg. xii. 1805.

MOGHAM, S. (मोघम्) Vain, useless, unprofitable; whence, in Marathi, it signifies indefinite, undefined, not particularized.

Mogham-báb, Mar. (मोघंबाब) A round sum given by a village in advance, or pending the collection, a payment on account, an instalment.

Mogham-bábtí, Mar. (मोघमबाबती) An undefined cess, one imposed without any specified rate, or to make up a certain sum required, without giving the exaction any name.

Mogum-jásti, Karn. (ಮೊಗುಂಜಾಸ್ತಿ, for P. *ziádatí*, increase) Outbidding, offering a higher rent for land than is likely to be realized (fruitless enhancement).

MOGHAṆ, Mar. (मोघण) A particular tube attached to a drill plough for sowing a different grain.

MOHÁSALU, MOHÁSALI, or MOHASSALU, Tel. (మొహాసలు, మొహాసలి, మొహాససలు), MOHASALU, MOHASALI, Karn. (ಮೊಹಸಲು, ಮೊಹಸಲಿ) Restraint placed upon a person to prevent his escape, or to enforce payment of a demand (derived from the A. *mahsúl*, although no such meaning is given to the latter in Hindustan).

MOHIL, Thug. A chief.

MOHTÁḌU, Tel. (మొహతాదు) A village messenger or *peon* employed on all occasions.

MOJ, Mar. (मोज) Measure, determinate quantity or measure, the quantity determined by measure.

Mojdát, Mar. (मोजदात) Counting, numbering of articles, as houses, &c.

Mojṇí, Mar. (मोजणी) Counting, numbering, a census.

Mojnídár, Mar. (मोजणीदार) A measurer, a numberer, a surveyor.

MOKALCHITHTHI, Mar. (मोकळचिट्ठि, from *mokála* मोकळा, free from, from S. *moksha*) A deed of release, or of manumission.

MOKKA, Tel. (మొక్క) A young plant.

Mokkaḍugu, Tel. (మొక్కడుగు) A second crop.

MOKSHA, S. &c. (मोक्ष), MOKASH, or MOCHH, H. (موكش, موچهه) Liberation in general, but especially liberation of the soul, and its exemption from further transmigration.

MOL, H. &c. (S. مول, मोल) Purchase, buying: price: hire, fare, wages of labour.

Molkarí, Mar. (मोलकरी) A labourer hired for a job.

Mol-tol, H. (مول تول) Fixing a price, traffic, purchasing.

MOḶA, Karn. (ಮೊಳ) A measure of length, a cubit from the elbow to the tip of the little finger.

MÓḶE, Karn. (ಮೋಳೆ) A bank, a rising ground: a leak: a salt-heap.

MÓM, H. (P. موم) Bees'-wax.

Momjáma, H. (P. موم جامه) Wax-cloth, coarse cloth steeped in melted wax and used as an outer covering for parcels.

MOMANO, Guz. (મોમનો) A Mohammadan weaver or cultivator in Cutch.

MOMAṬI, Karn. (ಮೊಮಟಿ) A sort of spade or hoe.

MONḌEMU, Tel. (మొండెము) A salt-heap, of which part has been sold.

MOPHARDU, Tel. (మొఫర్దు, from A. *mufrid*, مفرد, single, simple) An abstract account.

MÓRA, Karn. (ಮೊರ) A small fan for winnowing corn.

MORABHATTA, Karn (ಮೊರಭತ್ತ) Established fees of village servants.

MORABU, Karn. (ಮೊರಬು) Gravelly and stony soil.

MORAḌUKARAḌU, Karn. (ಮೊರಡುಕರಡು) Coarse and blotted, as a writing.

MORAMU, Tel. (మొరము) Gravel or chalk. See *Muram*.

MORANA, (?) Settlement on a wife at the time of marriage. —Chittagong.

MORAPANÉLA, Tel. (మొరపనెల) Gravelly, or calcareous soil.

MORASA, Tel. (మొరస) Gravelly, as soil.

MORAVU, Karn. (ಮೊರವು) Surplus water running from a tank.

MORÉ, MORAH, or MUDI, (?) Karn. A large measure of land: it is said to consist of 45 *Guntas*, each 33 feet square, or about $1\frac{13}{100}$th acre: it is also said to mean rent in kind.

MORHÁ, H. (موڑھا) A low stool or seat.

MORÍ, H. (P. موري) A water-course, a drain, a pipe under the surface to convey water.

MORKÁ, Thug. Extra share given to the leader of a gang.

MORKHÁÍ, Guz. (મોરખાઈ) A reward for apprehending thieves and robbers.

Morkháo, Guz. (મોરખાઓ) One who gives information of thefts or robberies, king's evidence.

MOSÁL, Guz. (મોસાલ, from A. محصل) A summons, a subpœna: a bailiff.

MOṬ, Mar. (मोट) MOṬA, MOṬU, Tel. (మొట, మొటు) The large bucket of a draw well.

Moṭasthal, Mar. (मोटस्थल) *Moṭusthal*, Tel. (మొటుస్థల) Land watered from a draw-well.

MOṬ, Beng. (মোট) MOTTAM, Tam. (மொத்தம்) Total, whole, a consolidated sum: also, in Bengal, a load or burthen.

Motámdáni, Beng. (মোটামদানী) Total receipts, total income.

Moṭámoṭi, Beng. (মোটামোটি) In the lump, in the gross, upon the whole.

Mot-hast-o-búd-jamá, Beng. (মোটহস্তোবূদজমা) Total demandable revenue.

Moṭhiá, *Moṭiá*, or *Muṭiá*, H. &c. (مٹیا, موٹیا, موٹھیا) *Motiyá*, Beng. (মোটিয়া) A porter, a labourer, a carrier of burthens.

MOṬÁDI, MOṬÁDU, Tel. (మొతాది, మొతాదు) An inferior revenue servant or *peon*, whose duty it is to look after the crops.

MOTÁḶÁ, Mar. (मोताळा) A particular tribe of Brahmans in Guzerat, or a member of it.

MOTHÁLÁ, Hindi (मोतहाला) Deficiency of moisture in soil, not enough for the seed to germinate.

MOTHIA, Thug. A class of Thugs residing cheifly in Rangpur and Dainajpur, usually following the business of weavers, said to be so termed from giving their leaders a handful (*Múthe*, or *Mothí*) of rupees from each man's share, in addition to their own.

MO-ULA, Beng. (মোউল) An advance of money for rice in the husk.—Mymensing.

MOWÁT, or MÁWÁT, (?) Mar. A class of soils of a mixed kind, and of light black colour.

MOYIṆ, Tam. (மொயின்) Any payment or contribution to a temple: any establishment. See *Muâin*.

MṚIGA, S., and in most dialects, but modified as MṚIG, MṚUG, or MÍRG (मृग) A deer, also the asterism termed likewise *Mṛigarṣirsha*, the deer's head.

Mṛigsál, Mar. (मृगसाल) The Mohammadan year.

Mirgmál, Thug. A herd of deer, ominous of a meeting with associates.

MṚITA, S. &c. (मृत) Dead.

Mṛitapatra, S. &c. (from पत्र, a leaf) A will, a testament.

Mṛitáṣaucha, S. &c. (मृताशौच) Impurity caused by the death of a relative or connexion.

Mṛitasnána, S. &c. (मृतस्नान) Bathing performed by Brahmans officiating at the burning of a dead body.

MUÂÁFÍ, corruptly, MAAFEE, MAAFIE, MAHFY, MAFFEE, MAAFFEE, MAUPHEE, H. (مُعافي), vernacularly, MÁPHÍ, Beng. (মাফী), Mar. (माफी), MÁPHI, Tel. (మాఫి), adj., Forgiven, remitted: subst., forgiving, remission or exemption from the demands of the state: a grant of land free of assessment: the word is in common use to signify exempt or free from duty or tax, as lands, goods, &c.: it also designated a particular grant formerly made by Zamindárs and the revenue officers of the government, which became hereditary and transferable, and was also applied to lands which were held free of revenue on condition of service. Ben. Reg. xi. 1795. (The vowel *u*, following *m*, in this and similar words, which are mostly the past-participles of Arabic increased radicals, is retained in Hindustani, although faintly, and almost inaudibly sounded: in the more purely Indian dialects it is either rejected or transmuted to *a* or *o*, and the Arabic *ain* ع is lost in the long *á*, as in the following examples)—

Máphái, Mar. (माफाई) Remission or abatement of the government claim for revenue.

Muâáfi, or *Máphi-chiṭṭhí*, H. &c. (معافي چٹھي, माफी चिट्ठी) An order to pass free of toll or tax, a warrant of remission: it was formerly applied especially to certain classes of pilgrims, exempting them from payment of the pilgrim tax.

Muâáfi, or *Máphi-dár*, H. &c. (معافي دار, माफीदार) One holding any thing exempt from tax, the holder of rent-free lands.

Muâáfi-istiwá, H. (from A. استوا, equal) A tenure by which waste land is held for a time rent-free, and for a further period at a quit-rent, until the given term expires.

Máphí-jamín, Mar. (माफीजमीन) Land revenue free: with the prefix *aji* (?), it is said to imply land entirely exempt, and with *apúm* (?), that which is partially so: such land is also distinguished as *chakria* (?), or exempted under certain conditions, or for certain purposes, and *ghair-sharṭi* (from A. غير, without, and شرط, condition), free from conditions;—the first, again, is distinguished as, *Prapanchártha*,

(S. प्रपञ्चार्थ) Land exempted for secular or civil objects, as in requital of the duties of a *Pátil*, or village servant, or for keeping embankments in repair, &c. and—

Dharmártha, (S. धर्म्मार्थ) Exempted in favour of religious establishments (*Devasthána*), or of individuals for performing religious functions (*Dharmadhan*, ?).

Muâáfi-mámúlí, H. (معافي مامولي) Established or customary remissions: in Benares, customary deductions from the government revenue made formerly to the native collectors and farmers on account of similar remissions made by them to their subordinates, or to the cultivators, or of charitable allowances. Ben. Reg. ii. 1795.

Muâfi-mujráí, corruptly, *Maafy-mujray*, H. (معفي مجراي) Lands exempt from tax, assigned to various individuals. See *Mujráí*.

Muâáfi-náma, H. (P. نامه, a writing) A warrant or order of exemption from duty or assessment.

Muâáfi-rawána, H. (from روانه, a pass) An order or permit for the transit of merchandise duty free; an order for the free transit of salt for the Upper Provinces. Ben. Reg. vi. 1804.

Máphí-sál, Mar. (माफीसाल) A year of exemption from assessment on some account, as bringing waste land into cultivation, &c.

Muâ-in, commonly, Mâyin, corruptly, Moven, or Moyen, H. (A. معين) Established, fixed.

Muáin-zábita, H. &c. (A. معين ضابطه) Established rule, fixed or legal charges, table or statement of wages or allowance, list of the public servants of any establishment.

Muâjjal, corruptly, Moajil, H. (A. معجل) Prompt, done without delay: in law, prompt payment of a debt, or payment within a month after it is due: also a dower or marriage settlement to be paid immediately.

Muâlim, H. (A. معلم) Málím, Mar. (मालीम) A navigator, a pilot.

Muallak, less correctly, Muwallak, A. (مُعلق) Suspended, literally: in law, any transaction not closed, as a sale in which payment of the price is deferred.

Muââmalat, H. (A. معاملت, plur. Muââmalát, معاملات, from *Muâmal* معمل) Mámlá, Mámlat, Beng. and Mar, (मामला, मामलत, मामला, मामलत), Mámlat, Uriya (ମାମଲତ) Affair, business, negociation, jurisdiction, suit, management or conduct of public affairs; civil employment under the government in the south of India, especially the collection of the revenue, and management of a district.

Mámledar, or *Mámlat-dar*, Mar. Guz. (मामलेदार मामलतदार) The head revenue and police native officer of a district, invested as a revenue officer with the duties of realising the collections, and remitting them to the treasury of the superior collector, of generally superintending the conduct and checking the accounts of the subordinate revenue officers, of investigating the payments and charges of the villages, and supervising the state of the cultivation: as civil and police officer, he exercised, under the native governments, undefined and extensive powers, which are now limited by Regulation: it sometimes denotes a farmer of the revenue.

Mámlatdárí, Mar. (मामलतदारी) The office or duty of a *Mámlatdár*, the collection or farm of the revenue, the administration of a district.

Mámláhál, Uriya (ମାମଲାହାଲ) Circumstances of an affair, particulars of a suit.

Muâtabar, H. (A. معتبر), Mátabarí, Hindi (मातबरी) Respectable, worthy of confidence, a person of credit: one who is responsible for the sufficiency of a surety, and who is liable for the amount, should both principal and surety be defaulters.

Muatak, H. (A. معتق) An emancipated slave.

Muattal, corruptly, Matíl, H. (A. مُعطّل) Idle, unoccupied, applied especially to a public officer who has been suspended or dismissed.

Mubádala, H. (A. مبادله) *Mobadalá*, or *Mobádalá*, Mar. (मोबदला, मोबादला) Exchange, interchange, transfer, hence applied, amongst the Marathas, to items which have been transferred from one head of account to another, and to balances charged to other individuals, villages, or districts, than those by which they are due; or balances carried to a different year from that in which they have occurred.

Mubah, H. (A. مباح) Allowed, indifferent: any action which incurs neither praise nor blame: any thing which may be lawfully sold: common property, that which it is lawful for any one to use.

Mubáiât, A. (مبايعت) Entering into a contract of purchase and sale.

Mubïâí, corruptly, *Mobai*, H. (A. مبيعي) Acquired by purchase or sale (any article): manufacture of salt for government by contract.—Orissa.

Mubárát, A. (مباراة) Dissolution of marriage by mutual consent, putting away a wife, dissolving partnership.

Mubarrá, H. (A. مبرّا) Released, cleared, exonerated.

Mubashir, A. (مباشر) A superintendant, an agent: in law, the doer of any thing, a culprit, a criminal.

Múbid, H. (P. موبد) A priest of the Parsis or fire-worshippers.

Múbadadalu, Karn. (మూబదదలు, from the A. مبدل, exchanged) A loan without interest: any thing lent to be returned.

Muchalka, or **Muchalká**, **Moochulka**, H. &c. (مچلکه, or مچلکا, मुचलका) **Muchchiliká**, incorrectly, **Moochilka**, Tel. (ముచ్చిలికా) A written obligation or agreement, a bond, a deed: it is commonly applied to a counterpart covenant on the part of the proprietors or cultivators of land, agreeing to the rates of assessment imposed by the government; also to an engagement under a penalty to observe the conditions of any deed or grant, or to one exacted from thieves or suspected persons engaging to desist or refrain from any illegal acts; or to one from superior police and other officers engaging to be responsible for the conduct of the subordinates appointed by themselves, or to any penal recognisance which may be required by a magistrate.

Muchalka in-dárad, H. (from the P. *in-dárad*, contains this) A phrase applicable to any agreement, signifying "the covenant contains this," but said to have been especially applied to a document taken by the *Amils* or provincial collectors from the *Desmukhs*, or *Despándyas*, stating that the collectors had exacted no more from them than appeared in the public accounts, and than they were entitled to demand.

Múdá, A. (مودع) A trustee, one to whom property is intrusted.

Mudiá, A. (مودِع) A depositor, one who leaves any thing in trust with another.

Mudabbar, or **Mudabbir**, A. (مدبّر) A slave to whom emancipation has been promised, either with or without conditions, on his owner's demise.

Mudabbir-i-tadbír, A. (مدبّرتدبير) One who makes a declaration of the purposed emancipation of his slave or slaves after his death.

Mudabbir, A. (مدبّر) A governor, a minister, a master.

Mudai, Tam. (முடை) Ground cleared of wood and prepared for tillage.

Mudaipunam, Tam. (முடைப்புனம்) Old cultivated ground.

Mudáin, H. (A. مداين) A debtor, a creditor.

Mudáinat, H. (A. مداينت) Selling on credit, giving credit.

Mudám, H. &c. (A. مدام), **Mudám**, Tel. (ముదాం), **Muddám**, Karn. (ಮುದ್ದಾಂ), **Muddám**, Mar. (मुद्दाम) Permanent, lasting, fixed, continually: in Mar., Positively absolutely: in Karn. also, Own, as *Muddám-áḷu*, (ಮುದ್ದಾಂ ಆಳು) Own servant.

Muddám begárí, Mar. (मुद्दामबेगारी) A hired porter or messenger who goes the whole distance to which a letter or parcel is to be carried, in opposition to one who is relieved on the road, or the *Hájir begárí*.

Mudám-sibandi, Tel. A militiaman or guard permanently enlisted.

Muḍava, Tel. (ముడవ) A place where platforms for stacking salt are put up: a platform of earth for piling salt upon.

Muddáá, H. &c. (A. مدّعا) Object, intention: Mar. (मुद्दा) Evidence, argument, presumption, grounds of conviction.

Muddáá-bi-há, H. (A. مدعابها) A thing or object sued for. the *chose* in action.

Muddái, or *Mudáá*, H. &c. (مدّعي, مدّعا) A plaintiff, a prosecutor, an accuser. *Muddai*, Mar. (मुद्दई) An informer, an accuser, one who traces out and furnishes grounds for proceeding against another. Tel. *Muddái*, or *Muddáidár*, (ముద్దాయి, ముద్దాయిదార) A defendant (*Dai* దాయి, from A. داعي, being used to signify plaintiff).

Muddái-ále-hi, H. &c. (A. مدّعي عليه) A defendant, the person accused, the respondent.

Muddáiat, H. (A. مدّعيت) A plaint, a charge, an accusation: a female plaintiff.

Muddáim, or *Mudáim*, Mar. (मुद्दाईम) An informer, an accuser.

Muddápattá, Mar. (मुद्दापत्ता) Evidence, proof, clue, trace.

Muddáipaná, Beng. (মুদ্দাইপনা) The office of an accuser or prosecutor.

Muddal, or **Mudal**, Mar. (मुद्दल, मुदल) Capital, principal, stock, as distinguished from interest or profits: in Mal. written *Mutal*, q. v.

Mudalámudal, Mar. (मुदलामुदल) With the capital only, without interest or profit.

Muddat, H. &c. (A. مدّت, मुद्दत) Space or length of time, interval.

Muddat-khila, Beng. (মুদ্দতখিল) Land for some time out of tillage, although not unfit for cultivation.

Muddat-patit, Beng. (মুদ্দতপতিত) Neglected or uncultivated for some time (a field).

Muddatukuyam, Tel. (ముద్దతుకుయం) Land mortgaged with option to the lender to consider it as his property if the mortgage is not redeemed within a stipulated period.

Káchi-mudat, Guz. (કાચીમુદત) Any time before a bill falls due.

Páki-mudat, Guz. (પાકીમુદત) Due date; date at which a bill becomes payable.

Muḍékamu, Tel. (ముడేకము) A coin of the value of ten *kás*.

Múdi, Muda, Morah, Moray, Múrah. See More, (?) Karn. A measure of land, 45 *guntas* of 33 square feet each, 49,005 square feet, or 1 $\frac{13}{100}$ of an acre: a certain quantity of seed-corn, sufficient for a given quantity of land, so that a field is computed by the number of *moras* or *múdes* which it requires. It is also a weight or measure of grain or rice, sometimes said to be equal to 40 *pakka sérs*. (The term Muḍi or Muṛi, usually signifies, in Karn., Tam., and Mal., a knot, a bundle, or any thing made or tied up in a bunch or bundle: its application to measurement either of length or capacity is not given in either Dictionary, and the spelling and enunciation, and possibly the proper meaning of the word, though thus repeatedly given in manuscript lists, are doubtful).

Múdigade, (?) Karn. The measure of seed which a field requires for sowing it.

Nija-múdi, *Nijja-moodee*, (?) Karn. The estimated number of *múdis* or *moras* of seed in distinction to the actual number sown in a field: sometimes they correspond, but for some lands the proportion is but half of the former to one of the latter.

Muḍi, Tam., Mal., Karn. (முடி) A knot, a tie; hair tied up in a tuft; a bundle of young rice or other plants tied in small bundles for transplanting.

Muḍippiri, Tam. (முடிப்பிரி) A receiver of rents or taxes, or any proceeds of sale; a money-changer or banker (from the cash being put up in bags).

Muḍippu, Tam. (முடிப்பு), *Muḍippa*, Mal. (മുടിപ്പ), *Muḍuvu*, Karn. (ಮುಡುವು) Money or valuables tied up in a cloth or bag, especially when intended to be presented to an idol, or to be paid in to the public treasury.

Mudrá, H. &c. (S. مدرا, मुद्रा), Mudre, Karn. (ಮುದ್ರೆ) A seal, a signet, a stamp, a badge, a brand, a stamped coin.

Mudraballa, or *-kóla*, Tel. (ముద్రబల్ల -కోల) A wooden stamp for sealing heaps of corn, &c.

Mudrehára, Karn. (ಮುದ್ರೆಹಾರ) One who applies a stamp or seal.

Mudra-káran, Mal. (മുദ്രക്കാരൻ) A peon bearing a badge.

Mudrayola, Mal. (മുദ്രയോല) A stamped *ola* or palm leaf, admitted as a voucher in the courts of the south.

Mudrádháranam, Mal. (S. മുദ്രാധാരണം) Bearing an indelible mark on some part of the body made with a hot iron, representing the insignia of some deity, as the shell of Vishnu, or the like, as a sectarial indication.

Múḍupárai, Tam. (மூடுபாறை) The top of the tunnel of a sluice.

Mufaṣṣal, corruptly, Mofussil, H. &c. (A. مفصّل) Properly separate, distinct, particular: in Hindustan, a subordinate or separate district; the country, the provinces, or the stations in the country, as opposed to the *Sadar*, or principal station or town: any other place than the ordinary place of office or residence; as a *darogha*, leaving a police station to go to a village in his jurisdiction, is said to have gone to the *Mufaṣṣal*, and the same is said of a villager who has gone from his cottage into his fields: its most usual application in Bengal, however, is to the country in general, as distinct from Calcutta. Tam. (முபசல்) Detached accounts, account particulars.

Mufaṣṣal âdálat, H. (A. عدالت) A provincial court of justice.

Mufaṣṣal diwání-âdálat, (ديواني عدالت) A provincial court of appeal whose decrees were final in certain cases before 1793: these courts were then merged into the city and Zilâ courts.

Mufaṣṣal jamâ, H. (A. جمع) The gross amount of revenue payable to the Zamindár or Málguzár by the subordinate cultivators, and, through him, to the government, which is then the *Sadar jamâ*, or state revenue.

Mufaṣṣal kharch, H. (A. خرچ) Charges of collection in the provinces.

Mufaṣṣal kánungo, H. (A. كانونگو) A district or provincial accountant and registrar.

Mufaṣṣal taâluk, H. (A. تعلق) A subordinate or dependent division of a district or estate.

Muflis, H. (A. مفلس) Poor, indigent, a pauper, a bankrupt.

Muftí, H. (A. مفتي) A Mohammadan law-officer, whose duty it was to expound the law which the *Káẓi* was to execute: the latter, in British India, usually discharges the duties of the *Muftí* also.

Múgá, Moogá, also written, Moonga, but (?) Beng. (মুগা) A kind of moth from which an inferior silk, called by the same name, is manufactured in Asam.

Múganḍuga, Karn. (ಮೂಗಂಡುಗ) A measure of capacity = to about nine bushels.

Muháb, A. (مهاب) A gift, the thing given.

Muhib, A. (مهيب) A donee, the person to whom any thing is given.

Muhábá, or Muhábát, A. (محابا, محابات, from حب, to have affection for) Properly, respect, friendship, same as *Muhabbat* : in law, an act by which a man wilfully incurs an additional charge or loss, as by adding to a stipulated dower, selling a thing under, or buying at an over valuation ; sometimes done from motives of personal regard, sometimes with a view to an ultimate advantage.

Muháfa, H. (A. محافة) A sort of palankin, especially one for women.

Muháfiz, H. (A. محافظ) Keeping, guarding ; a keeper, a guard.

Muháfiz-i-daftar, (from P. دفتر) Keeper of the records, the native officer of a court charged with the care of the public papers.

Muháḳalat, A. (محاقلة) Sale of corn in the ear, payment of revenue in kind : in law, an exchange of corn, for some which has been reaped, considered illegal.

Muhallal, A. (محلّل) Lawful, made lawful, that which was not so before ; as, in law, a woman who, having been divorced, is married to another man that he may divorce her, when she may be legally re-married to her first husband.

Muhallil, A. (محلّل) One who makes lawful that which was illegal ; a man who marries a divorced woman, that he may put her away, and so enables her to be married again to her first husband.

Muháná, corruptly, Mohana, H. (S. مهانا), Muhaná, Beng. (মুহনা) The mouth of a river, an estuary, the conflux of two rivers, the place where a branch separates from the main stream.

Muḥar, or Muḥr, corruptly, Mohur, H. (P. مهر) A seal, a seal ring, a gold coin of the value, in account, of sixteen rupees.

Muḥarhand, H. (P. مهركند) A seal engraver, a die-cutter.

Muharram, corruptly, Mohurrum, H. (A. محرّم) Sacred, unlawful, prohibited : the first month of the Mohammadan year, in which it was held unlawful to make war. Among the Shias this month is held in peculiar veneration, as being the month in which Hasan, and Hasain, the sons of Ali, were killed : their deaths are the subject of public mourning during the first ten days, when fasting and self-denial are also enjoined.

Muharrir, corruptly, Mohurrie, Moherrie, Mohrer, Mohir, &c. H. (A. محرّر) A clerk, a writer, a scribe.

Muhásabah, corruptly, Mahaseeba, H. (A. محاسبة), Mojabá, Mosabá, Mar. (मोजबा, मोसबा) Computation, calculation, settlement of an account ; an account, a statement of expenses.

Muhásib, H. (A. محاسب) An accountant, a calculator, an auditor or examiner of accounts.

Mojabedár, or *Mosabedár*, Mar. (मोसबेदार) An accountant, one who keeps or renders an acconnt.

Muházarat, H. (A. محاضرة) Appearing against : in law, suing or arraigning any one in a court of law ; also, disposing of expected property, or property in reversion, considered illegal : a deed or document signed by all parties present.

Muházir-náma, incorrectly, *Mahazer-namah*, H. (P. نامه) A document, certificate, or affidavit, signed by a number of persons, all of whom are present.

Muházir, H. (A. محاضر) Present, in attendance, in court.

Muhíl, A. (محيل) In law, one who transfers a claim made upon him to another who has consented to be responsible.

Muhkím, corruptly, Mokeem, H. (A. محكيم, from حكم) A native officer formerly employed in the cloth factories, a supervisor of the weavers.

Muhrim, A. (محرم) A prohibitor, an interdictor ; one who lays himself under certain restraints, or upon whom the season, as the month of Muharram, or his engagement as a pilgrim, imposes them ; a relative within the prohibited degree of intermarriage.

Muhsan, Muhsanat, A. (محصن, from محصنة) Chaste, continent, especially as a husband or wife : applied in law to a person, male or female, whom certain qualifications, as freedom, sanity, and mature age, entitle to exact or to undergo the punishment inflicted on adultery.

Muhtál, A. (محتال) A person who accepts the responsibility of one person for his claim upon another.

Muhtál-âlehi, A. (محتال عليه) The person who becomes responsible for a claim made upon, or a debt due by, another.

Muhtarif, A. (محترف, from *harafat* حرفة, an art, a profession) An artist.

Muhtarafa, corruptly, Mohterefa, Mohterfa, Motaherfa, Mohturpha, Mohturupa, &c. H. (A. محترفة), Motaraphá, Tel. (మొతర్ఫా), Motarappá, Tam. (மொதரப்பா), Mohtaraphá, Mhotaraphá, Mar. (मोहतरफा, म्होतरफा) A tax or taxes levied on trades and professions, on the artificers of a village or their implements, as upon the weaver's loom, upon tradesmen and their shops and stalls, and sometimes upon houses : in some places under the Madras presidency, it is properly a poll-tax upon artificers, the taxes on shops being termed

Pándari, and those on the profits of trade *Visabadi*; but the term is used in a general way to designate the several personal taxes above mentioned: the designation is in a great measure peculiar to the provinces of the presidencies of Madras and Bombay, the taxes of a similar nature formerly levied in Bengal being included in the general denomination of *Sair*.

Mohtarapha-chi-kulwár, Mar. (कुलवार, general, universal) An account kept by the village accountant of the mechanics and tradespeople of a village, and the taxes leviable on each.

MUHTAMÍM-I-BAND-O-BAST, H. (مهتمیم بندوبست) A settlement officer, an officer of government employed to make a settlement of the revenue with the different villages and divisions of a district.

MUHTASIB, corruptly, MOHTISSUB, H. (A. محتسب) A superintendant of markets and police, an officer appointed to take cognisance of improper behaviour, as of indecency, drunkenness, gambling; also of the sale of intoxicating drugs and liquors, and false weights and measures.

MUHÚRTTA, S. &c. sometimes corrupted, as in Guz., to MÚRAT (मुहूर्त) A measure of time, one-thirtieth of a day and night, or 48 minutes: it is used, though loosely, to signify a lucky hour or time for the celebration of any important or festive ceremonial.

MUJÁPHAT-JAMÁ, Mar. (मुजाफतजमा, from A. مضافات, appendages, annexations) Expenditure on account of presents by the state to public officers or to foreign powers: expenses incurred by one district on account of or to the debit of, another.

MUJÁWAR, H. (A. مجاور) A servant or sweeper of a Mohammadan temple or shrine.

MÚJIBÁT, H. (A. pl. of موجب, a motive) Grounds of appeal as set forth in the pleadings of the appellant.

MUJRÁ, or MUJARÁ, H. (A. مجرا), Tel. (ముజరా) Any authorised deduction, a pension, an allowance.

Mujrái, incorrectly, *Mujray*, H. (A. مجراي), *Mujarái*, Karn. (ముజరాయి) A pension, an allowance, any authorised deduction: applied under the Mohammadan government to an allowance to the Zamindárs of Rangpur for presents made by them to the chiefs of the hill tribes, to prevent depredations: under the British government it implies deductions from the revenue on account of allowances to cultivators or contractors, as an encouragement, or of assignments or remissions or grants of revenue for charitable purposes.

Mujarái kharchu, Karn. (ముజరాయిఖర్చు) Deductions from the public revenue for religious or charitable purposes.

Mujráiṇ, incorrectly, *Mujura-een*, Beng. (মুজরাইং) Lands assigned as an allowance, and not subject to revenue.

MUJRIM, H. (A. مجرم) A criminal, a malefactor.

MUJTAHID, H. (A. مجتهد) A jurist, a lawyer, a doctor in law, the highest authority in Mohammadan jurisprudence: a spiritual superior or director.

MUḲÁBILA, H. (A. مقابله), MOKÁBILÁ, Tel. (మొకాంబిలా) Comparing, confronting, comparison or examination of revenue accounts, or of judicial documents.

MUḲADDAM, corruptly, MOKUDDUM, MOCUDDIM, MUGADUM, H. &c. (A. مقدم), Mar. (मुकद्दम), MAKADAM, Uriya (ମକଦମ) A chief, a leader, one who goes before: in India, applied especially to the head man of a village or of a caste or corporation: in the Maratha villages the head man was usually charged with the realization of the revenue and its payment to the district collector, with the superintendence of the cultivation, the management of the affairs of the village, and the disbursements of its expenses: he was also intrusted, to a certain extent, with jurisdiction in disputes among the cultivators, and with the police: in Hindustan, the *Muḳaddam* has, in some places, become solely responsible for the public revenue, having been suffered to assume the character of a petty proprietor, and being designated as *Málik-muḳaddam*; under the former system the title was not unfrequently given to the village Zamindárs. In some places the term is applied to the hereditary occupant of an estate in a village, immovable as long as paying a fixed rate to the Zamindár or the Raja. The *Muḳaddam-biswadár* is usually a head man who holds an entire share of a village, and sometimes an entire village, but in some places he appears to have been reduced to the state of hereditary cultivator from having been part proprietor of the village, in consequence of the title having been appropriated, through fraud or violence, by some individual proprietor. In Cuttack, the *Muḳaddams* are regarded in a similar light, but are divided into two classes, the *Mazḳúri-muḳaddam*, who pays direct to government (the term *mazkúri*, q. v., having here the reverse of its usual meaning), and the *Záti*, or *Játi-muḳaddam*, who pays through an intermediate revenue payer, or *Mál-guzár*: the title is sometimes applied to a farmer of several villages. Where the *Muḳaddam* only represents the village he is sometimes allowed a portion of land, either rent-free or held at a quit-rent. Ben. Reg. ix. xii. 1805; vii. 1822. In Guz., a *Mukádam* is commonly the name of a supervisor, especially of one employed by a merchant to superintend the landing or shipment of goods, &c.

Mukaddam-karj, Mar. (करज, from قرض) A debt due by a village through its head man or representative.

Mukaddamí, *Mooqudumee*, corruptly, *Mocudmy*, *Mocuddimy*, H. (مقدمي) Relating to the office, duties, or rights of a *Mukaddam*: dues paid to him by the cultivators, or, when the revenue is collected by the state, as a money allowance to the *Mukaddam*, it denotes, in the upper provinces, a rate of from 5 to 10 per cent. on the collections: it sometimes appears as a deduction of from 3 to 4 per cent. on the gross collections. A *Mukaddamí* settlement is that made with the heads of villages as representatives of the village proprietors: a *Mukaddamí* tenure is recognised in some places as a proprietary tenure.

Mukaddama, H. &c. (A. مقدمه), Beng. *Mahaddama*, or *Muhaddamá* (मकद्दमा, मुकद्दमा), *Mukadamá*, Mar. (मुकद्दमा), Tel. (ముకద్దమా) *Mukadamo*, or *Muhardamo*, Guz. (મુકદ્દમો, મુકરદ્દમો) Business, affair, especially law affairs, a law suit.

Mukániyan, Mal. (മുക്കാണിയൻ) A Brahman of a particular tribe in Malabar, wearing the tuft of hair on the fore-part of the head.

Mukallaf, A. (مكلف) A person legally responsible or accountable for his actions.

Mukáraz, A. (مقارض) The person who, in a contract where one supplies the stock and the other the labour, is the provider of the stock.

Mukáriz, A. (مقارض) The agent or manager, the active partner in the sort of contract last named.

Mukarrar, corruptly, Mocurrer, Mocurrey, H. (A. مقرر) Fixed, established, agreed upon; exact, as a total stipulated sum.

Mukarrarí, H. (A. مقرري) Relating to what is fixed: as a revenue term it is applied to a tenure held at a fixed and permanent rate of rent when payable to a proprietor, or revenue when payable to the government. Ben. Reg. viii. 1793; i. 1815; ix. 1825; Act i. 1845.

Mukarrarí-dár, H. (P. دار) The occupant of a farm or estate paying a fixed and permanent rate of rent or revenue.

Mukarrarí-istimrári, H. (A. استمرار, q. v.) Properly, a tenure held at a fixed rate of assessment, but applied, in the upper provinces of Bengal, to tenures of which the revenue rate is permanent only for the life of the holder.

Mukarrarí-jamá, H. (A. جمع) A fixed and permanent rate of assessment.

Mukarrarí-pattá, H. (from पट्टा, a lease) A lease for a definite extent of land at a fixed sum, not liable to any extra charge.

Mukarrarí-tankhah-rakmí, H. (A. from *tankháh* تنخواه, assignment, and *rakm* رقم, a written order) The fixed assessment of the revenue in Cuttack.

Dar-mukarrarí, H. (P. در, in) An estate held under a holder of land at a permanent rate.

Mukattá, H. (A. مقطع) Fixed rate of assessment. See *Maktá*.

Mukásima, H. (A. مقاسمه) Dividing: partition of the crop between the proprietor or cultivator and the state, either in kind or value.

Mukátabat, A. (مكاتبة) Ransom or emancipation of a slave, effected by his own earnings with his owner's assent.

Mukátib, A. (مكاتب, مكاتبة) In law, a male or female slave who has been permitted to work out his or her emancipation according to a *kitábat*, or written covenant.

Mukayad, A. (مقيد) Bound, fettered, in confinement.

Mukhágni, S. &c. (मुखाग्नि) Fire put into the mouth of the dead body at the time of burning (from *mukha*, the mouth, and *agni*, fire).

Mukavan, Mal. (മുക്കവൻ) A particular tribe of fishermen in Malabar.

Mukhása, corruptly, Mocassa, Mokassa, Mocasau, H. (مخاصه, irregularly derived from A. خص, to have as one's own: see *Khás*), Mukásá, Tam. (முகாசா), Mukhásá, or Mokhásá, Tel. (ముఖాసా, మొఖాసా), Mokásá, Mar. (मोकासा) A village or land assigned to an individual either rent-free or at a low quit-rent, on condition of service; or a village held *khás* by the state, the revenue being paid to the government direct; or the share of the government in a village, or in the revenue paid by it: the term, as current among the Marathas especially, is somewhat differently explained by different authorities: according to one statement, it was applied to the remaining portion of the *chauth*, or fourth of the revenue of tributary countries after the fourth set apart for the Raja had been deducted; from this, again, a further portion, or six per cent. on the *chauth*, being set apart for certain officers of the state, the remainder, termed *Ain Mokásá*, or simple assignment, was distributed amongst the military chiefs in requital of their services. According to a different account, the *Mo-*

kásá was the remainder of the whole revenue after a fourth had been set aside; this remainder, or three-fourths of the whole, was subject to the deduction of six per cent. upon it, termed *Sahotra*, and to two per cent. termed *Nargaud*; the former of which was appropriated to the *Pant-suchiu*, the latter to the different subordinate functionaries: the several designations were preserved after the lands or villages on which the *chauth* had been levied as a tribute were incorporated with those of the Maraṭha principality: (the term, although supposed to be of Hindustani derivation, is not familiarly used in Upper India, and is chiefly current, in its vernacular forms, in the south).

Mukhása-, *Mokhasa-*, or *Mokása-dár*, Tel. &c. (from P. دار, who has) The holder of a village, or of lands, at a quit-rent, or rent-free, on condition of service: under the Maraṭha government the *Mokása-dár* had much the same powers as the *Mámlat-dár*.

Mokáṣi, or *-sí*, Mar. (मोकाशी -सी) The holder of an assignment, the farmer of a certain portion of the revenue of a village, either on the part of the state or an individual.

Kaṣar-mokása, Mar. (कशार, from A. *Kasar*, q. v.) An addition to the *Mokása*, an enhanced rate of it.

MUKHTÁR, corruptly, MOOKTAR, MUKHTEEAR, MOOKTIYÁR, H. (A. مختار), MUKHTYÁR, Mar. (मुखत्यार) An agent, a representative, an attorney: in Hindustani, the *Mukhtár*, as employed in legal affairs, is not allowed in general to plead; that is the function of the Vakíl: amongst the Maraṭhas the term is also applied to the person appointed by the co-sharers of a hereditary office to discharge its duties.

Muhhtár-, or *Mukhtyár-náma*, H. &c. (from P. نامه, a document) A deed appointing a representative or agent, a power of attorney: a deed executed by the co-sharers of a hereditary office, delegating its duties to a representative.

Mukhtarí, H., *Muhhtyárí*, Mar. Agency, representation, the office or character of a representative.

MUKHTAṢAR, corruptly, MOOKTISSUR, MUKHTESSUR, MOOKTESSOR, H. (A. مختصر) An abridgement, an abstract: in Mangalore the term is applied to a deputy, an agent or commissioner, also to the head man of a caste entitled to certain honours and privileges.

MUKHYA, S. &c. (मुख्य, from मुख, the face) Chief, principal, the head cultivator of a village, the manager of an estate, the leader or principal in any affair.

Mukhyasthan, corruptly, *Muhiasten*, Mal. (മുഖ്യസ്ഥൻ) The head man of a village: a chief, a noble.

MUḲÍM, erroneously, MOKIM, H. (A. مقيم), MUKHIMU, Tel. (ముఖిము) A broker, an appraiser: an officer whose duty it was to estimate the value of standing crops.

Muḳímí, H. (مقيمي) Brokerage, appraisement, valuation.

MUḲIRR, A. (مقر) One who admits a claim, or confesses a crime, one who pleads guilty.

Muḳirr-baḥí, A. (مقربهي) The thing or claim which is admitted, a crime confessed.

Muḳirr-lahú, A. (مقرله) The person in whose favour a claim is admitted.

MUKKÁL-PALISA, Mal. (മുക്കാലപലിശ) A rate of interest = three-fourths of ten, or $7\frac{1}{2}$ per cent. per annum.

MUKKAMPÁLU, Tel. (ముక్కంపాలు) One-third share of the gross produce of lands allowed to the cultivators.

MUKKÁVAN, Mal. (മുക്കാവൻ) A caste of fishermen, or a member or it: in Malabar he is sometimes a slave.

MUKKUSA, Tel. (ముక్కుస) A measure of capacity, three-fourths of a *Túm*.

MUKSA, Tel. (ముక్స) A measure of capacity, one-sixteenth of a *Khandí*.

MUKTASIB, H. (A. مكتسب) In law, one who makes profit, a gainer, an acquirer.

MUKTI, S. &c. (मुक्ति) Liberation, setting free in general, final liberation of the soul, and exemption from future transmigration.

MÚLA, vernacularly, MÚL, S. &c. (مول, मूल) Root, lit. or fig., the root of a tree, the origin of a family: stock or capital: the authority of a doctrine or faith.

Múladhana, or *Múldhan*, Karn. (ಮೂಲಧನ) Stock, capital, original wealth or property.

Múḷaganv, or *Múlgánw*, Mar. (मूळगांव) The original residence of the founder of a family, the original village on an estate.

Múlagár, or *Múlgár*, Karn. (ಮೂಲಗಾರ) An owner, an original proprietor, one holding an estate originally through a loan or mortgage: a lessee, a mortgagee: the original holder of a perpetual lease.

Múlagrantha, S. (from ग्रंथ, a book) A work of authority, also a book of genealogies.

Múḷapatra, Mar. (मूळपत्र) An original document, not a copy.

Múlasádhanam, Karn. (ಮೂಲಸಾಧನಂ) An acknowledgment given by the principal cultivator to the government or the landlord: a grant or assignment to an original occupant or assignee.

Múlgaini, corruptly, *Moolgueny*, *Moolghenny*, Karn. (ಮೂಲಗೇಣಿ) The tenure of an original occupant, either

4 x

of new and previously uncultivated lands, with hereditary succession, or of a hereditary farm or land at a fixed rate, corresponding with the tenure of the hereditary non-proprietary cultivator of the north-west provinces, and indefeasible as long as the stipulated rent is paid: a perpetual lease. (In the Gl. 5th Rep., *Shud-mulgueny* is said to be a tenant by simple purchase, which is no doubt erroneous; but what is intended by *Shud* is not verifiable, unless it be *Suddh*, pure, simple).

Mulgaini-chiṭi, Karn. (ಚೀಟಿ, a document) A permanent lease, the document conveying it.

Múlgaini-gár, Karn. (ಮೂಲಗೈನಿಗಾರ) A hereditary cultivator, a tenant holding a perpetual lease, not removable as long as he pays his rent.

Kraya-múlgaini, Mal. (from S. क्रय, purchase) Tenure of occupancy obtained originally by purchase at a public sale.

Múlpaṭṭa, more correctly, *Pattayam*, Mal. (മൂലപട്ടയം) A lease granted to the purchaser of an estate, constituting him original or absolute proprietor, with right of transmission to his heirs.

Múl-vargga, corruptly, *Moolivurg*, Mal. (മൂലവൎഗ്ഗ, from S. वर्ग, a class) Original proprietary right to an estate.

Múlya, S, &c. (मूल्य) Price, value, wages, hire.

Muliá, Uriya (ମୁଲିଆ) A hired labourer.

Muḷa, Mal. (മുള), Muḷai, Tam. (முளை) A shoot, a sprout, a young plant first springing from the ground.

Muláhaẕa, H. (A. ملاحظه) lit., Looking at; but used as well as *Muḳábila* (مقابله comparison), with the P. *shud* (شد, has been), as *Muláhaẕa*, or *Muḳábila shud*, Seen, examined, a phrase written by the proper native officers on public documents.

Muḷaka, Mal. (മുളക) Black pepper, pepper in general.

Muḷaha koṭi, Mal. (മുളകകൊടി) The pepper vine.

Muḷakamatissila, Mal. (മുളകമടിശ്ശില) The pepper department of the monopoly of the Raja of Travancore.

Muḻam, or Muzham, Tam. (முழம்), Muṟam, Mal. (മുഴം) A cubit measured from the elbow to the tip of the middle finger.

Muḻakol, Tam. (முழக்கோல்), *Muṟakol*, Mal. (മുഴക്കോൽ) A rod or measure of one cubit.

Mulaná, Mulána, Mar. (मुलना, मुलाना, from the A. *Maulána*) A Mohammadan lawyer, but usually applied to a Mohammadan village schoolmaster.

Muḷayan, Mal. (മുളയൻ) A servile tribe, or individual of it, the same as the *Palayan*, or the son of a *Palayan*.

Mulázamat, H. (A. ملازمت) Assiduous service or attendance: in law, continued watch over an insolvent debtor by his creditors, although he has been discharged by the *Ḳáẕi*, to discover if he possess or acquire any property that may be applied to the liquidation of his debts.

Mulḳ, Moolk, corruptly, Mooluck, H. (A. ملك), Mulúk, Beng. (মুলুক), Mulúk, Mar. (मुलूक) A kingdom, a principality, a country.

Mulḳi, H. (A. ملقي) Relating to a kingdom or a country, native, domestic, provincial: the name of an era current in Puraniya, the same as the Fasli of Bengal, except that it commences two months earlier, on the first of *Srávaṇa*, instead of the first of *Aswin*.

Mulḳi-ádálat, H. (A. عدالت) A provincial court of justice.

Mulḳi-diwani-ádálat, *Mulki-faujdárí-ádálat*, H. (from عدالت, justice) A civil and a criminal provincial court established at Benares in 1786, for administering justice to the province, exclusive of the city: these courts were abolished by Ben. Reg. vii. 1795.

Mulḳi-khazána, H. (P. خزاني) The royal or state treasury.

Mulḳgiri, H. (P. گيري, taking), Mar. *Mulúk-giri* (मुलूकगिरी) Taking possession of a country or kingdom, exercising sovereignty: periodical progress or incursion of a military force for the collection of tribute or revenue by violence or intimidation: occasional peregrination of migratory dealers or adventurers.

Mullá, H. (A. ملّا) A Mohammadan lawyer or learned man, a judge, a magistrate, the deputy of a Ḳáẕi; applied also, in some parts of India, to the village Mohammadan schoolmaster, who also has the charge of the village mosque, and sometimes acts as butcher for the Mohammadans of the village: he is more usually styled *Mulána*.

Mullá-ḳuráni, H. (from قران, the Kurán) The law officer of the courts employed to take the oaths of the Mohammadan witnesses on the Kúran.

Muḷḷa, Mal. (മുള്ള) A thorn.

Mullavallai, Mal. (മുള്ളവള്ളി) Thorn money, *i.e.* the cost of keeping up orchards or plantations.

Multaḳíṭ, A. (ملتقيط) One who finds and brings up a deserted child, one who finds a treasure.

Multánia, Thug. A class of Thugs who are all Mohammadans, and assume the character of Banjaras, trading in corn, and travelling with their families, but putting most of their female children to death: they strangle travellers with their bullock ropes: they are considered among the ancient Thugs.

MULTAVI, H. (A. ملتوي) Crooked: fraudulent: postponed, pending. MULTABI, Tel. (ముల్తబి) Fraud, trick, delay.

Multaviát, H. (plur. of ملتوي) Suits undecided or pending.

MULTAZIM, H. (A. ملتزم) A tenant or hirer; a farmer or collector of tolls or customs.

MULUMU, Tel. (ములుము) Lands which are cultivated for various kinds of millet chiefly.

MUMÁNÍ, H. (ممانی) A husband's brother's wife, an aunt.

MÚMIN, H. (A. مومن) Faithful, orthodox, a believer: in Guzerat, a convert to Mohammadanism: in the Maratha and Tamil countries a tribe of Mohammadan weavers is so styled.

Amír-ul-múminín, A. The commander of the faithful, a title adopted by the Khalif Omar, and retained by his successors in the Khalifat.

MUNÁBAZAT, A. (منابذة) lit., Throwing; a particular custom in buying and selling, by which a person to whom the vendor threw his goods was obliged to become the purchaser; considered illegal.

MUNÁDÍ, H. (A. منادي) A public crier; also the small drum which he usually beats to call attention.

MUNÁSIB, H. (A. مناصب) Proper, right, expedient, discretionary.

Munásib-jamâ, H. (A. جمع) A reasonable assessment.

MUNAFÂT, H. (A. منفعت) Gain, profit.

Munáphá, Hindi (मुनाफा) The profits of an estate, the nett rent.

MUNAJJIM, H. (A. منجّم) An astrologer, an astronomer.

MUNÂKID, H. (A. منعقد) Bound, engaged by a contract or covenant of marriage, &c.

MUNASKHA, H. (A. منسخه) A table of partition of inheritance according to Mohammadan law.

MUNDA, or, vernacularly, MÚND, H. &c. (مند, मुण्ड) The head: a head man.—Chuta Nagpur.

MUṆḌA, S. &c. (मुण्ड) Shaven, shorn, as an ascetic, or, fem., a widow.

MUṆḌA, Mal. (മുണ്ട) The cloth worn round the waist by natives of both sexes in Malabar.

MUṆḌAKAN, Mal. (മുണ്ടകൻ) Wet or irrigated lands.

MUṆḌAKAM, Mal. (മുണ്ടകം) A rice crop sown in August and ripe in January.

MUṆḌAM, Tel. (ముండం) A stump, a residue.

MUṆḌAN, H. &c. (مندن, मुण्डन) Shaving the head, a ceremony performed on the children of both Mohammadans and Hindus: the latter commonly, and sometimes the former, leave a lock of hair on the crown of the head.

MUṆḌAN, Mal. (മുണ്ടൻ) The stem of a cocoa-nut tree, from which *tárí* is extracted.

Muṇḍan-koṭṭi, Mal. (മുണ്ടൻകൊട്ടി) A gatherer of the juice of the cocoa and other palms, or *tárí*.

MUṆḌÁ-PHOṚÁ, Guz. (મુંડફોડા) A Mohammadan mendicant in the west of India, who, to extort charity, draws blood from his own head or other parts of his body.

MUṆDBANDÍ, Mar. (मुण्डबंदी) In the Dakhin, the partition of the lands of a village among the cultivators, whether proprietors or permanent tenants, agreeably to certain proportions, and subject to a collective rate of rent, at which they may be let to cultivators: it corresponds apparently with the village Zamindárí tenure of the north-west provinces.

Mundpaṭṭí, Mar. (मुण्डपट्टी) An extra rate levied on the lands of a coparcenary village (?) (it is probably the same as the preceding).

MÚNDHÁ, H. (مونڈها, मूंढा) Sugar-cane shooting from the roots of canes cut down in the previous season.

MUNIMANAMAḌU, Tel. (మునిమనమడు) A male descendant of the fourth degree, a great grandson.

Munimanamaralu, Tel. A great granddaughter.

MUNG, or MÚG, H. &c. (مونگ, मुंग, मूग, S. मुद्ग) A kind of pulse (Phaseolus mungo) much used by the natives of India as an article of food.

MUNGUTTIGE, Karn. (ముంగుత్తిగె, from *mun*, former) Rent or tax on land paid in advance.

MUNI, H. &c. (S. مني, मुनि) A holy man, an inspired sage.

MUNÍB, H. &c. (A. منيب) A master, a principal, one who employs an agent or representative, a constituent, the native superintendant of a mercantile establishment.

Muníb-gumáshta, H. (P. from گماشته) A head clerk or manager of a bank or mercantile establishment.

Muníbána, H. (منيبانه) Fee or perquisite of a manager: a redemption fee paid to the owner of a female slave, formerly, in Sylhet, upon her marriage to a stranger.

Muním, Mar. (मुनीम, corruption of *munib*) A factor, an agent, a deputy, a manager.

MUNIGUTTA, (?) Tel. (మునిగుత్త) Illegal collections or exactions, forestalled rent. (If correct, it is a vernacular corruption of the A. *manâ* منع, forbidden).

MUNJ, or MUNJÁ, S. &c. (منج, मुञ्ज) A kind of grass (Saccharum munja) of the fibres of which the girdle of a Brahman should be made: it is also loosely and incorrectly applied to the sacrificial thread worn by the Brahman over one shoulder, and to the ceremony of putting it on, or

Updnáyan: the grass grows on sandy soil in the rains, and is cut for making cord from its fibres.

Munḳaẕí, H. (A. منقضي) Past, elapsed: arrears of payment.

Munḳaẕi báḳí, H. (A. باقي) The balance of revenue of previous or past years, exclusive of that of the current year.

Munkir, H. (A. منكر) One who denies: in law, the defendant, the respondent.

Munnáman, or Munnámavan, Mal. (മുന്നാമൻ, മുന്നാമവൻ, from *munna*, three) A third or middle-man, a surety, an arbitrator.

Munnilakáran, Mal. (മുന്നിലകാരൻ) The head man of a hamlet or village, a petty officer over a village.

Munnameninellam, Mal. (മുന്നമെനിനെല്ലം) A field of rice returning three or four-fold.

Munníríppa, Mal. (മുന്നിരിപ്പു) Former balance, what was in hand,

Munshí, H. (A. منشى) A writer, a secretary; applied by Europeans usually to teachers or interpreters of Persian and Hindustani.

Munshid, A. (منشد) A person who points to the place where a thing has been lost; applied either to the loser or the finder.—Mohammadan law.

Munṣif, corruptly, Moonsiff, H. (A. منصف) Equitable, just: a decider of what is just, an arbitrator, a judge: applied, under the British government, to a native civil judge of the first or lowest rank, the limit of whose jurisdiction in Bengal was gradually raised from suits of the value of 50 rupees to that of 300. In Madras a similar extension of the authority of district *Munṣifs* took place of from 100 to 1000 rupees, the head men of the villages acting as village *Munṣifs* in suits of trifling amount. At Bombay the office of *Munṣif* was replaced by that of junior native commissioner, with a limit of jurisdiction of the value of 5000 rupees; but the title of *Munṣif* was again resumed. In some places the *Munṣif* was an officer on the part of the Zamindár, employed to superintend the measurement of the lands of a village in concert with the villagers. Ben. Reg. xxiii. 1814; ii. 1821; v. 1831. Act viii. 1836; vi. 1843; i. 1845. Mad. Reg. iv. vi. 1816; iii. 1833. Bom. Reg. ii. 1827; xxiv. 1836.

Munṣif-dár, H. (P. دار, who has) A *Munṣif* or native judge (the term is a provincial pleonasm).

Munṣif-hachhari, H. (كچهري) The *Munṣif's* court or office.

Munṣif-náma, H. (P. نامه) The decree of a native judge or arbitrator, an arbitration bond.

Munṭa, Tel. (ముంట) A grain measure containing three *sérs* and a half.

Muntakhab, H. (A. منتخب) A selection, a compendium, an abstract in general; also an abstract of the village accounts, shewing in one view the fields situated in different parts of the village owned or cultivated by the same individual. In the north-west provinces it is the detailed account of the village cultivation, and is synonymous with *Khatauni*, q. v.

Mupan, written, also, Moopen, (?) Mal. A class of agrestic slaves in Malabar.

Múppan, Tam. (மூப்பன்), Mal. (മൂപ്പൻ) An elder, a senior, the head man of a class or business, one who presides over ploughmen and shepherds: a head man among the Mohammadans.

Múppa-panam, Mal. (മൂപ്പപണം) A premium or present made to an owner or landlord by the tenant.

Múppukkaḷavu, Tam. (மூப்புக்களவு) Dues payable to the head man of a village: deduction from the revenue on that account.

Muppaṟa, Mal. (മുപ്പറ) A measure of three *paras*: a certain amount of tax on land.

Múra, Tel. (మూర) A cubit from the elbow to the tip of the middle finger.

Muṛá, or Mudá, Mar. (मुडा) A quantity of grain; at Bombay, twenty-five *maunds*; in other places, twenty eight.

Múra, Mar. (मूर) A concealed vent through which water oozes: looseness of soil.

Murábahat, A. (مرابحت) Gaining, making a profit: in law, legal profit on the sale of any article.

Murabbí, H. (A. مربّي) A patron, a guardian, a manager, a director, an advocate.

Muráhik, A. (مراهق) A youth, an adolescent, one who is nearly of years of maturity.

Muṛai, Tam. (முறை) Legality, lawfulness: turn, alternative, rotation.

Murai-nír, Tam. (முறைநீர்) Supply of water for irrigation in settled order or rotation.

Murambu, Tam. (முரம்பு) A salt-pan, a creek of the sea: a heap or hill of stones and gravel.

Muráṇ, Mar. (मुराण) Blighted corn; a field of such corn.

Murátib, H. (A. مراتب, plur. of *Martaba*, مرتبة) Dignities, honours.

Murattab, A. (مرتّب) Arranged, put in order; settled, as an account.

Murattib, A. (مرتّب) An arranger, a director.

Murda, H. (P. مرده) Dead: a dead body.

Murda-farásh, H. (مردەفراش, from P. *farásh*, a sweeper) *Murddapharás*, Beng. (मुर्द्दफरास) A man of low caste, who, amongst other unclean offices, is the remover of dead bodies: (the word occurs also, *Múrdafarosh*, from P. *farosh*, who sells).

Murdár, H. (P. مردار), Mar. (मुरदाड) Impure: a dead body: in Mohammadan law, the carcase of an animal that has died a natural death, or has not been killed in the lawful manner, and is therefore unfit for food.

Murdárkas, (?) Mar. A cess upon the village Mahars for the privilege af appropriating the skins of dead animals.

Múrddhábhishikta, corruptly, Moordawusikht, S. &c. (मूर्द्धाभिषिक्त) A mixed caste, or a member of it, sprung from a Brahman father and Kshatriya mother, and following the profession of arms.

Murheṇ, Mar. (मुऱ्हें) Mist: the hill country on the skirts of the Sahyádri range, from its being commonly in a mist.

Muṛí, or Muḍí, Beng. (মুড়ী) Parched rice.

Muṟí, corruptly, Moory, Tam. (முறி), Mal. (മുറി) A leaf, a written bond, a receipt, a bond given with the sale of a slave; any written relinquishment of property.

Muṟi-pampu, (?) Tel. Relinquishment of land or property in favour of another.

Muṟippaṭṭaiyam, *Muṟi-sádanam*, Tam. (முறிப்பட்டையம், முறிசாதநம்) A promise or agreement in writing: a bill of sale of a slave.

Muṟiyan, Tam. (முறியன்) A slave.

Muṟi, Mal. (മുറി) A division of a village.

Muṟikáran, Mal. (മുറിക്കാരൻ) A villager, one living in a division of a village.

Muríd, H. (A. مريد) A disciple, a scholar.

Múriṣ, (A. مورث) The person from whom an inheritance is derived, whether in the descending or ascending line. Múraṣ, inheritance: an heir.

Múris-âálí, A. (مورثعالي). A remote progenitor.

Murshid, H. (A. مرشد) A religious instructor, a spiritual guide.

Murtadd, A. (مرتدّ) A renegade, an apostate, one who has seceded from the Mohammadan religion, and is consequently an outlaw.

Murtaḥin, A. (مرتهن) One who takes any thing in pledge, a pawnbroker, a mortgagee.

Mus, Hindi (मुस) Land along the high banks of rivers.—Puraniya.

Múṣá, or Muwaṣṣá, A. (موصىٰ, موصي) Commanded or devised by will.

Múṣá-bahi, A. (به, with respect to *it*, the thing) A legacy, a bequest.

Múṣá-lahu, A. (له, with respect to *him*, the person) A legatee.

Múṣi, or *Muwaṣṣi*, A. (موصي) A testator.

Múṣiat, A. (موصية) A testatrix.

Musáfir, H. (مسافر) A traveller.

Musáfir khána, H. (P. خانه, a house) An inn, a *sarái*, a place for the accommodation of travellers.

Muṣáhib, H. (A. مصاحب) A companion, an associate, an aide-de-camp.

Musajjal, H. (A. مسجل) Proved, authenticated by a judge.

Musal, H. (S. موسل, मुसल) A pestle, especially a large wooden pestle used for beating grain in a mortar to free it from the husk.

Muṣálahat, H. (A. مصالحة) Compromise, reconciliation.

Musáli, Mal. (മൂശാരി) A brazier, a caster or melter of metals.

Musammát, Moosummát, corruptly, Mussomat, Mussumat, H. (مسمّات, from A. مسمّي *musammá*, the named) A title prefixed in Hindustan to the names of respectable women in public documents and judicial proceedings.

Musaṇḍá, Musáṇḍá, Mar. (मुसंडा, मुसांडा) A torrent; fig., the rush of a crowd.

Múṣar, (?) H. A tribe in Babar from whom bond-slaves are derived.

Muṣár-khor, Mar. (मुशारखोर) A hired servant.

Mushâá, A. (مشاع) Mixed as common property, so that the shares cannot be distinguished.

Musháḥara, corruptly, Mooshaira, Moshaira, Mushaira, H. (A. مشاهره), Muṣárá, Muṣáhirá, Mar. (मुशारा, मुशाहिरा) Monthly or other periodical pay or allowance; settling or hiring by the month. In Bengal, a monthly allowance granted to revenue payers and Zamindárs for collecting the revenue; also a monthly allowance paid to Zamindárs from the proceeds of their estates when deprived of the management of them on their own behalf. Amongst the Marathas, a money allowance from the state to the *Páṭil* and *Chaughala*.

Musháhara-kulkarnam, Tel. (?) An allowance granted to the village accountant in the south of India.

Mushakhaṣ, or Mushakhaṣí, H. &c. (A. مشخص, مشخصي) Musakkas, Musakkasí, Beng. (মুসক্কস, মুসক্কসী) Ascertained, stipulated: applied to lands or districts for which a settlement of the revenue has been made: it is also applied to subordinate tenures for which the holders engage to pay a fixed rent annually upon the whole lot.

Mushakhasi-jamá, H. (A. جمع) Stipulated revenue, net amount of the revenue.

MUSHÁRIK, H. (A. مشارك) A partner, an associate.

Mushárikat, H. (A. مشاركت) Partnership.

MUSHRIF, H. (A. مشرف) An examiner, an inspector, an officer of the treasury who authenticates accounts and documents.

MUSHRIḲ, H. (A. مشرق) The east.

MUSHRIK, H. (A. مشرك) An idolater, a polytheist, one who gives an associate to the one God, hence applied by the Mohammadans to Christians.

MUSHT, or MUSHṬÍ, H. &c. (مشت, مشتي), also MUṬH, and MUṬṬHÍ, (مٹھ, مٹھي, मुट्ठी, from the S. मुष्टि) The fist closed, a handful of any thing, a hand's breadth, a measure equal to four fingers.

Mushṭigár, Karn. (ಮುಷ್ಟಿಗಾರ) A man of a tribe in Mysore calling themselves *Kshatriyas*, and following agriculture, but in some respects resembling the Jettís or boxers.

Muṭhlíyá, Hindi (मुठलीया) Taking the first handful of seed to be sown.

Muṭhí, H. (मुठी) A handful, a bunch.

MUSHTARÍ, H. (A. مشتري) A buyer, a purchaser, a buyer of land sold for arrears of revenue.

MUSLIM, H. &c. (A. مسلم) A believer, applied especially to a Mohammadan: one who believes in the true faith.

Musalmán, H. (A. مسلمان, from مسلم) A believer, a Mohammadan.

MUSLIM, A. (مسلم) Advanced, paid beforehand, as the price of an article to be subsequently delivered.

Muslim-fíhi, A. (فيه, on it) The goods on which the advance is paid.

Muslim-álehi, A. (عليه, to him) The seller to whom the advance is paid in the kind of sale called *Salam*, or *Silim*.

MÚSSAT, also written MUSSAD, and MUNSAD, Mal. (മൂസ്സത) An inferior tribe of Brahmans, or a member of it, in Malabar, said to be descended from those for whom Parasuráma recovered the province from the sea.

MUSTA, vernacularly, MUTHÁ, S. &c. (मुस्त, मुथा) A kind of grass with bulbous roots growing abundantly on rich cultivated lands, and hard to be extirpated (Cyperus rotundus).

MUSTABÍN, A. (مستبين) Become evident; but used as a technical term in Mohammadan law in combination with other words, as

Mustabín-marsúm, (from A. مرسوم) A regular deed or contract, one executed in the proper legal forms.

Mustabín-ghair-marsúm, (A. غيرمرسوم) A partially irregular deed, one deficient in some formalities, and not admitted as legal evidence, but as intimation of the intention of the executer.

Ghair-mustabín, A contract or deed wholly irregular and invalid.

MUSTADÂI, H. (A. مستدعي) A petitioner, a suitor.

MUSTAGHÍṢ, H. (A. مستغيث) A complainant, a plaintiff.

MUSTÁJIR, H. (A. مستاجر), MUSTÁJARI, MUSTÁJARU, Tel. (ముస్తాజరి, ముస్తాజరు) A farmer, a renter, one who holds lands under a proprietor at a stipulated rate; also a farmer of revenue appointed to make the collections on the part of a Zamindár or proprietor, on condition of paying a fixed sum.

Mustájiri, H. (مستاجري) Renting, farming, holding in farm, settlement in farm.

MUSTAKBAL, Tel. (A. ముస్తకబల) Part of the public revenue paid before it is due (the word, which ordinarily means future, is peculiar, in this sense, to the Northern Sirkars apparently): it is said also to be used in the sense of illegal exactions.

MUSTARAD, H. (A. مسترد) lit., Returned, restored: as a law term, it signifies reversing the decision of a lower court upon an appeal.

MUSTÁMÍN, A. (مستامين) lit., One who seeks protection: applied, in law, to a stranger and person of a different religion residing in a Mohammadan state under the protection of the authorities.

MUSTAUFÍ, corruptly, MUSTOFY, H. (A. مستوفي) Paying or receiving in full (a debt): an examiner or auditor of accounts: the principal officer of the department in which, under the Mohammadan government, the accounts of ex-collectors or farmers of the revenue were examined.

Mustaufi-garí, H. (مستوفي گري) The duty of an accountant or auditor.

MUSTÂYIR, A. (مستعير) The borrower of a thing which he is to return. See *Áríyat*.

MUT, Beng. &c. (মুৎ, S. मुस्तक) A sort of grass (Cyperus rotundus): a wild leguminous plant (Phaseolus aconitifolius).

MUṬÁBIḲ, H. (A. مطابق) In conformity, or according to.

Muṭábiḳ-i-sanad, H. (A. سند) Agreeably to a grant or title.

Muṭábiḳ-i-tárikh, H. (A. تاريخ) According to the date or æra.

MUTABANNÁ, H. A. (متبنٰي) Adopted (as a son).

Mutabannagi, H. (A. P. متبنّگي) Adoption.

MUTAFARRIKÁT, H. (A. plur. of متفرّق) Separate, scattered, miscellaneous: the several items of an account: separate and scattered portions of land included in a village or estate.

MUTAFFIḲ, H. (A. متفّق) An accomplice, an associate.

MUTÂHID, corruptly, *Mutahed, Muthaahed*, H. (A. متعهد) A farmer, a contractor, one who enters into an engagement for the revenue of a tract of land.

Mutâhúd, H. (متهود) An engagement or contract for the revenue of a district.

Mutâhúd-dár, H. (P. دار) A contractor or farmer of revenue

MUTÂH, H. (A. متعة) A temporary marriage, according to *Shiâ* law.

MUTÁHIL, A. (متاهل) A married man, a man who has a wife.

MUTAḲADDIM, H. (A. متقدّم) Ancient, old: in Mohammadan law, such an interval between the commission of a crime and evidence in proof of it, as to bar the infliction of punishment.

MUTAKAFFIL, corruptly, MOOTECOPHIL, H. (A. متكفّل) Becoming surety; also the person, a bail, a surety: said also to signify an auditor of the accounts of the subordinate offices before sending them to the treasury.

MUTAKHÁṢIM, H. (A. متخاصم) An opponent, an adversary, a litigant. *Mutakhásimín* (A. du.) Plaintiff and defendant.

MUTAL, incorrectly, MUTLA, Mal. (മുതൽ) Principal, capital, stock, money, property, original estate, ancestral or landed property.

Mutalálan, Mal. (മുതലാളൻ) A proprietor of land or any other property.

Mutaláli, Mal. (മുതലാളി) A proprietor, a capitalist, a principal merchant.

Mutalavakásam, Mal. (മുതലവകാശം) Inheritance, right to property.

Mutalavakási, Mal. (മുതലവകാശി) An heir, an heiress.

Mutalchilava, Mal. (മുതൽചിലവ) Receipts and disbursements.

Mutale-duppa, Mal. (മുതലെടുപ്പ) Revenue, income, profit.

Mutalkáryyam, Mal. (മുതൽകാര്യം) Property in money, jewels, &c.

Mutalpalisa, Mal. (മുതൽപലിശ) Principal and interest.

Mutalpaṭṭa, Mal. (മുതല്പററ) Office of head man of the low caste termed *Chagon*.

Mutal paṭṭa háran, Mal. (മുതല്പററക്കരൻ) The head man of the *Chagon* tribe.

Mutal paṭṭiha, Mal. (മുതല്പട്ടിക) An account of property, stock, or principal.

Mutalpera, Mal. (മുതല്പെര) The head subordinate officer or *peon* at a police station.

Mutalpiṭṭi, Mal. (മുതൽപിട്ടി) The office of a treasurer.

Mutálpiṭṭi háran, Mal. (മുതൽപിട്ടികാരൻ) A treasurer, a cashkeeper.

MUTÂLIḲ, H. (متعلق) Dependent, connected with, dependent upon: a dependant, a servant: in Marathí (मुतालिक) it was applied, under the Peshwa's government, to the deputy of any person holding a hereditary office, acting for him in his absence, and allowed to use his seal: the deputy or agent of a *Despáṇḍya*.

Mutálahá, or *Mutálakí*, Mar. (A. मुतालका -की) Deputyship, the office of a deputy.

Mutálikán, H. (plur. of متعلق) Dependants, servants: in the Northern Sirkars, daily allowances to the families of public servants.

MUTAṢADDÍ, corruptly, MOOTSUDDY, MUTSEDDY, MUTTASEDDEE, H. (A. متصدّي) A writer, a clerk.

MUTAWALLI, corruptly, MOOTWALLEE, MOTOOWULLEE, and MUTWALLEE, H. (A. متولي) A person appointed to the care and management of a religious building and endowment.

MUTÂYIN, H. (متعين) Appointed; a deputy, an agent.

Mutâyyana, corruptly, *Mottanieh*, H. (A. متعيّنة) A station, a military or militia post, one of *Sibandi* or provincial troops.

MUṬHÁṆ, Mar. (मुठाण) A gang, a band.

MUṬH-ṬHÁ, also read MUṬṬHÁ, and, incorrectly, MÚTAH, or MOOTAH, Tel., Karn. (ముఠా) The subdivision of a district: in the Northern Sirkars, a large estate, including several villages, and corresponding with a Zamindárí in Hindustan.

Muṭhṭhadár, commonly, *Mootahdár*, corruptly, *Motahdár*, *Mutteedár*, Tel. (దార్, P. دار) The holder of a *Muṭhṭhá*, a landholder, a Zamindár: it is said to be sometimes applied to the *Pátíl*, or head man of a village.

Muṭhṭhadárí, *Muṭhadárí*, or *Mootahdárí*, Tel. The tenure or office of a *Muṭhadár*.

Muṭhṭhawárí, *Muṭṭhawárí*, or *Mootawárí*, Tel. Settlement of revenue, or assessment by *Muṭṭhás*, or subdivisions of a district.

MUṬLAḲ, H. (A. مطلق) Absolute, principal.

Muṭlaḳ-vakíl, or, more correctly, *Vakíl-i-muṭlaḳ*, H. (A. وكيل) An agent furnished with full and absolute powers.

Muṭlaḳ-vakálat-náma, H. (A. P. وكالت نامه) A full power:

a document conveying absolute authority to an agent or representative.

MUTRI, MOOTRY, MOOTEREE, (?) H. The designation of a tenure in the Benares district by which a tenant held different kinds of land, and cultivated various crops at one fixed rate of money rent to the Zamindár.

MUTTAIDE, Karn. (ಮುತ್ತೈದೆ) A woman whose husband is living.

MUTTAJJA, Karn. (ಮುತ್ತಜ್ಜ) A great grandfather.

Muttajji, Karn. A great grandmother.

MUTTIRÁCHAVÁḌU, or MUTTIRÁJU, Tel. (ముత్తిరాచవాడు) A caste, or an individual belonging to it: one of the Telugu subdivisions of the *Súdras*.

MUTTAṢIL, H. (A. متّصل) Contiguous, adjacent, bounding (as fields or villages).

MUṬṬUWAḶI, Karn. (ಮುಟ್ಟುವಳಿ) Cost, expense.

MUṬUMHÁT, Beng. (মুটুমহাত) A short cubit, one measured with the fist closed.

MUWAJJAL, corruptly, MUWAZIL, H. (A. موجّل) Deferred, as payment, applied to a dower, payment of which is deferred till after marriage: the opposite of *Muajjil*, q. v.

MUWAKKAL, H. (A. موكّل) A guardian, a trustee. MUWAKKIL, A constituent, one who appoints a deputy or representative.

MUWAḲKAT, A. (موقّت) Fixed to a stipulated or certain time.

MUWALLAD, H. (A. مولد) lit., Begotten: applied in Hindustan to an Arab born in the country, whether of whole or half blood.

MUWÁẒÂT, A. (مواضعت) A sale by which loss is incurred.

MUWAẒẒAF, H. (A. موظف) Fixed, limited, allowed: a fixed pay or pension: as a revenue term it means the rent or revenue assessed at a fixed rate on a certain quantity of land.

Muwaẓẓafa-rátiba, H. (A. راتبه, a salary) A fixed salary, pension, or contribution; fixed imposts collected by the government at stated periods.

MUYDHONḌÁ, Mar. (मुयधोंडा) A stone fixed to mark the boundary of a village.

MUZÁBANAT, A. (مزابنة) Sale of corn or fruit, &c. without weight or measure, as it stands in the field or hangs on the tree, or the like: considered illegal.

MUẒÁHARAT, A. (مظاهرة) A formula of divorce, in which a man declares his wife indifferent to him. See *Zihar*.

MUZÁHIM, H. (A. مزاحم) Hindering, obstructing, a hindrance.

Muzáhim-dár, H. (P. دار, who has) One whose rights or possessions are incidentally encroached upon.

MUZAKKÍ, A. (مزكّي) In law, a purgator of witnesses, one who testifies the credibility or competency of a witness.

MUẒÁRABAT, A. (مضاربة) A co-partnership of stock and labour, where one party finds capital, the other management, and the profits are divided between them.

Muẓárib, A. (مضارب) A factor, a manager, the partner that conducts the business as his share of the principal.

MUẒHIR, H. (A. مظهر) A claimant, a prosecutor.

Muẓhir-alehi, H. (A. مظهراليه) A defendant, one complained against.

MYÁL, Mal. (മ്യാൽ) Land on which rice plants are sown thickly for the purpose of transplanting: land watered by rain.

N.

NÁBÁLIGH, H. (P. نا, not; A. بالغ, mature) An infant, a minor.

Nábálighi, H. (نابالغي) Minority, nonage.

NÁBÚD, H. (P. نا, not, بود, was) Non-existence: in Bengal, a head of account under which remissions of revenue were formerly registered.

NABÍRA, H. (P. نبيره) A grandson, a son's son.

Nabíri, H. (P. نبيري) A granddaughter.

NÁCH, H. (ناچ, from S. नाट्य *nátya*, dancing) Dance, dancing, acting.

NACHCHI-KOṬṬU, Tel. (నచ్చికొట్టు) The drug Cocculus Indicus, also read *Nanji-koṭṭu*.

NACHCHU, Tel. (నచ్చు) Waste land overrun with knot grass.

NÁCHṆÁ, or NÁCHṆÍ, or, as commonly written, NACHENNY, NATCHENNY, NATCHENNEE, NATCHENY, &c. Mar. (नाचणा, नाचणी), NACHCHINI, Tam. (நச்சினி) A name ordinarily given by Europeans to the Eleusine corocana, or Cynosurus corocanus, which is extensively cultivated for its grain, in the south of India chiefly, although not unknown in Bengal: the plant is not known in general by this name, which seems to have originated with Rumphius, who, speaking of the introduction of its seeds from Ceylon into Amboyna, calls it *Naatsjoni*, pronounced, he says, in India, *Naachani*: the Hindustani name is *Rágí*, vulgarly, *Raggy*: it is called *Chollu* in Telugu, and, according to Van Rheede, *Jettipulugu* in Tam.

NADA, vernacularly, NAD, or NUD, S. &c. (ند, नद) A river, one of which the personification is male, as the Sindhu, or Indus.

Nadam, Tam., Mal. (S. நதம், നദം) A river, one flowing from east to west.

Nadí, corruptly, *Nuddy*, S. &c. (ندی, नदी) A river, one of which the personation is female, as Gangá, or the Ganges: in the south of India it implies also a river running from west to east.

Nadí-mátruha-pólamu, Tel. (నదిమాతృకపొలము) A field that is irrigated from a river adjacent.

Nadanírvari, Tam. (நதநீர்வரி) A tax levied in the dry districts of Trichinapali on lands watered by channels from rivers or water-courses.

Nadabhávi, Karn. (ನಡಭಾವಿ) A well with steps.

NÁDA, Beng. (নাদ) Dung of sheep or goats, a pellet of dung.

NÁḌÁ, or NÁṚÁ, Mar. (नाडा) A cord, a rope, especially the rope of a draw-well, drag-rope of carts, &c.: a coloured and twisted band worn at the Muharram, by Mohammadans, round their wrists; the tie of trowsers or petticoats, the rope or pole of rope-dancers, &c.

Náḍebahurúpí, Mar. (नाडेबहुरूपी) A rope or pole-dancer.

NÁDALÍ, H. (نادلی) A stone inscribed with words from the Kurán, and hung as a preserving amulet round children's necks.

NAḌAṆÍ, or NAḌNÍ, Mar. (नडणी) Clearing a field of grass or weeds.

NÁDÁR, H. &c. (P. نادار), Mar. (नादार), Tel. (నాదారు) Having nothing, indigent, bankrupt, insolvent.

Nádárí, H. &c. (ناداری) Poverty, insolvency.

Nádár-munásib, Karn. (from A. مناسب, fit or proper) An item of remission of revenue in Mysore, on account of the poverty of the cultivators.

NÁḌAVÁR, Karn. (ನಾಡವಾರ) An agricultural hill tribe, who pretend to be pure Sudras.—Mysore.

NAḌAVARAVA, Mal. (നടവരവ, from *naḍa*, a temple) The income of a religious establishment.

NÁDÁVÁ-SANADU, Tel. (నాదావాసనదు) A release, a discharge in full, an acquittance from all demands (from A. دعوا).

NAḌAVU, Tam. (நடவு) Planting, transplanting.

Naḍavunaṭṭérálai, Tam. (நடவுநட்டேராலை) An account particulars of transplanting.

Naḍavu-payir, Tam. (நடவுப்பயிர்) Corn in the field newly transplanted.

Naḍa-ulugu, corruptly, *Nada-woolungor*, Tam. (?) Annual account of the cultivation.

NADDÁF, H. (A. ندّاف) A cotton cleaner.

NADH, Thug. A village.

NAḌÍ, or NAṚÍ, Beng. (নড়ী) A caste, or individual of it, who make ornaments of *lák* for Mohammadan women.

NAḌICHIL, Mal. (നടിച്ചിൽ) Transplanting, a young plant to be transplanted.

Naḍíla, Mal. (നടില) Planting, transplanting.

NAḌIGA, Karn. (ನಡಿಗ) A petty chief.

NAḌIGE, Karn. (ನಡಿಗೆ) A leasehold tenure, under which half the gross produce is the landlord's share.

NÁḌU, commonly, NÁḌ, corruptly, NAAD, NAUD, or NAUR, Karn., Tel. (ನಾಡು) A province, a district, a division of a country; a country, a kingdom. (The word occurs also in Tamil and Malayalam written with the ceberal *ṭ*, though pronounced vernacularly *Náḍ*, and *Náḍu*: in their derivatives, however, the *ṭ*, single or doubled, is retained. See, therefore, *Náṭu*, *Náṭ*, &c.

Náḍina, Karn. (ನಾಡಿನ) Of or belonging to a country.

Náḍina-maryáde, Karn. (ನಾಡಿನಮರ್ಯಾದೆ) Custom of the country.

Náḍugauḍa, corruptly, *Naṭgawd*, Karn. (ನಾಡುಗೌಡ) The head man of a district, like the *Desmukh*.

Náḍu-ṣánábhoga, Karn. (ನಾಡುಶಾನಭೋಗ) The accountant of a district.

Náḍu-talavâru, Karn. (ನಾಡುತಲವಾರು) The assistant of the head of a district.

NAFÁ, H. (A. نفع), NAPHÁ, Mar. (नफा) Gain, profit, advantage.

Nafá-nukṣán, H. (A. نفع نقصان) Profit and loss.

NAFAKA, or NAFḲA, H. &c. (نفقه) Necessary means of subsistence, supply of food, clothes, and lodging, which, in law, is obligatory upon certain relations, or the support of a wife by her husband, of a child by its parent, of a needy parent by its child, and of relatives and dependants in general.

NAFL, less correctly, NUFIL, H. (A. نفل) Any voluntary religious act, one not enjoined by the law.

NAFR, H. (A. نفر), NAPHARU, Tel. (నఫరు), NAPAR, Tam. (நபர்) A man, an individual, a person; also, in Mar. (नफर) A low menial servant, a groom; and a term used in counting camels, as, *Unt naphar dáhá*, ten head of camels: in the west of Bengal, a slave who, and his offspring, are slaves for ever, and are transferable and saleable. In Puraniya, the *Nafar* is usually a domestic slave, but it also sometimes denotes an agricultural one.

Naphargatigá, Tel. (నఫరగతిగా) Individually, man by man.

Napharugatí-phaisalá, Tel. (నఫరుగతిఫయిసలా) Settlement of the revenue with individual cultivators: a Ryotwárí assessment.

Napharjamínu, Tel., *Napar-jámín*, Tam. (from A. ضامن) A security for a person, bail or surety for appearance. See *Házirzámin*.

NAFÍ, A. (نفي) lit., Prohibiting, rejecting: in law, the formal denial of his paternity to a child born of his wife by a husband: rejection or abandonment of a child.

NAFS-UL-HÁL, H. (from the A. نفس, the soul) The essence or pith of an affair, the real merits of a case.

NAG, or NUG, (?) Mar. A measure of weight for cotton = 8 *maunds* of 24 lb. each, or two and a half to a *khandi* of 480 lb.

NÂGA, vernacularly, NAG, S. &c. (S. نگ, नाग) A snake, a serpent deity, or a class of snake gods inhabiting Pátála, the regions under the earth.

Nágpanchamí, S. &c. (नागपञ्चमी) The fifth lunar day of the month *Srávaṇa* (July-August), in which the *Nágas* or serpent deities are worshipped: in the south of India offerings are made to snakes, milk, grain, and other articles being taken to the holes in which they live.

NÁGÁ, H. &c. (ناگا) A class of Hindu mendicants who go naked and carry arms, and who form sometimes mercenary bands in the service of Indian princes: a name given to various barbarous tribes inhabiting the hills along the southern borders of Asam.

NÁGAḶA, Karn. (ನಾಗಳ) A measure of grain equal to four *maraháls*, q. v.

NAGALÍ, Tel. (నగలి) A plough.

Nágalikarṟu, Tel. (నగలికఱ్ఱు) A ploughshare.

NAGAN, (?) Mar. A contribution from the most opulent inhabitants of a town or village to defray any heavy exaction either of the state or an enemy.

NAGAR, NUGUR, corruptly, NUGGUR, H. &c. (نگر, S. *Nagara* नगर) A town, a city: in compounds it is also sometimes changed barbarously to *Nagore*, as *Varáha-nagar* becomes *Barnagore*.

Nágara, vernacularly, *Nágar*, S. &c. (ناگر, नागर) Relating or belonging to, or originating with, a town; hence a dissolute or knavish person, one town bred: it is the name, also, of a tribe of Guzeratí Brahmans.

Nágarí, H. &c. (fem. of *Nágara*) Relating to a town or city: applied especially to the alphabet of the Sanskrit language, and its modifications in Hindi, Maraṭhi, &c., sometimes with *Deva*-divine prefixed, as, *Dévanágarí*.

Nágar, (?) H. A large heavy plough.—Bundelkhand. (? *Nángar*, for *Lángal*, S. a plough).

Nagar-kaul, (?) Tel. Plough tenure, land held at an assessment per plough, usually for three or four years, for dry grain cultivation only.—Northern Sirkars.

NÁGARA, Karn. (ನಾಗರ) A snake, a cobra capella.

Nágarachavuti, or *chauti*, Karn. (ನಾಗರಚವುತಿ, -ಚೌತಿ) The fourth lunar day of the ninth Hindu month, when the king of the snake gods, *Sesha*, or *Vásuki*, is worshipped.

Nágavalli, corruptly, *Nagole*, Tel., Karn. (ನಾಗವಲ್ಲಿ) The betel-vine, also the leaf, which, with the areka nut and other things rolled up in it, is presented to guests on their arrival and departure: hence it has come to mean beginning and termination: it is also applied, in the south of India, to the concluding ceremony of a marriage, which usually takes place on the fifth day, when presents of betel and other articles are interchanged between the new-married couple and their relatives and friends, and the guests are dismissed.

NÁGAURÁ, H. (ناگورا) A large and handsome breed of horned cattle, native in Guzerat.

NÁGHORÍ, Guz. (નાઘોરી) A tribe of Mohammadans in Guzerat, usually employed in driving carts and keeping cattle.

NAGHU, Thug. A body of soldiers.

NÁGSANT, H. &c. (नागसंत) The head and hood of a snake, the crest and signature of the Rájá of Chota Nagpur.—South-west frontier.

NÁGU, Tel. (నాగు) Interest paid in grain on account of grain lent.

NÁHAḲ, H. (A. ناحق) Improperly, unjustly, wrong, untrue.

NÁHÁK, Uriya (ନାହାକ) A *Náik*, see *Náyak*: a schoolmaster.

NÁHÍA, H. (A. ناحيه) A tract, a territory, a quarter, a coast.

NAHR, H. &c. (A. نهر) A stream, a water-course, a river.

NÁIB, H. &c. (A. نايب) A deputy, a representative, a lieutenant, a viceroy, a sub- or deputy-collector.

Náib-diwán, H. (A. ديوان) The deputy treasurer or accountant.

Náib-ḳází, H. (A. قاضي) The deputy of the Ḳází.

Náib-kánungo, H. &c. The deputy of the village or district accountant and registrar.

Náib-názim, H. (A. نايب ناظم) A deputy governor and administrator of justice: an officer nominally under the Nawab of Bengal, but appointed by the British authority to superintend the administration of criminal justice: the plan was adopted in 1755, but the office was abolished, and courts of circuit were substituted in 1790.

Náib-subahdár, H. The deputy governor of the Subah or province.

Nawáb, corruptly, *Nuwaub*, and *Nabob*, H. &c. (A. نواب,

plur. of *Náib*, but used honorifically in the singular) A viceroy or governor of a province under the Moghul government, whence it became a mere title of any man of high rank, upon whom it was conferred without any office being attached to it.

Niábat, H. (A. نيابت) Deputyship, vicegerency: the office of a *Náib*, or *Nawáb*.

NAIKAN, (?) A class of slaves in Karnata.

NÁJÁÍ, H. (P. ناجاي) Deficiency in produce, a tax formerly assessed in Bengal upon the cultivators present, to make up for any deficiency arising from the death or disappearance of their neighbours.

Nájái-táahud, H. (P. A. ناجاي تاحد) An extra cess or *Mahtot*, formerly levied from the Zamindárs in Bengal on the plea of providing against prospective deficiencies in the revenue by some of them, or of the farmers failing to fulfil their engagements.

Nájáil hana, Uriya (ନାକାଇଲହନା) Irrecoverable (as arrears).

NÁJÁIZ, H. (A. ناجايز) Illegal, informal, unauthentic, not current.

NAJÍB, H. (A. نجيب) Noble, either by birth or conduct, bnt the term was applied to a body of irregular infantry under the native government; some corps were retained chiefly as a kind of militia, under the British government, for a time, but the designation appears to have become obsolete.

NAJJAR, H. A. (نجّار) A carpenter.

NÁJKÁRÍ, Beng. (নাজকারী) Grain crop or cultivation, as distinguished from garden cultivation (probably a vernacular corruption of H. *anáj* اناج, grain).

NAJM, H. (A. نجم) A star, a constellation: astrology: a horoscope.

Najúmí, H. (A. نجومي) An astrologer.

NAJSH, A. (نجش) Bidding for articles on sale without intending to purchase them, for the sake of enhancing their price, held to be illegal.

NÁKÁ, H. (ناكا), NÁKÁ, or NÁKEN, Mar. (नाका, नाकें), NÁKE, Guz. (નાકે) The extremity of a road, also a point where two roads meet; hence the site of a toll or custom station, where transit duties or customs are levied; also, sometimes, the duties or customs so levied: it is sometimes applied to a subordinate police-station.

Nákábandí, H. (ناكابندي) Collections on account of land customs and transit duties; also, shutting up a road.

Nákebandí, Mar., (नाकेबन्दी) Shutting up a road or avenue.

Nákedár, Mar., Guz. (नाकेदार) A receiver of customs or transit duties, a toll-gatherer.

NÁKÁ, or NÁKÁRI, Thug. Sneezing, a bad omen at setting out.

NAḲÁRA, H. (A. نقارہ) A kettle-drum, the use of which was restricted to persons of high rank, as a mark of state.

Naḳárahhaná, corruptly, *Nákkarconnah*, H. (P. خانه, a house) The chamber where the state drums were struck from time to time, usually an open alcove over the main entrance or gateway.

NAKÁR, Mar. (नकार) Refusing, disallowing: rejection of a draft or bill, or a writing on the face of it intimating its rejection.

Nakárái, Mar. (नकाराई) The forfeit or money paid upon a bill that has been dishonoured.

NÁKÁRA, or NÁKÁRÍ, H. &c. (ناكاره, ناكاري, नाकारा, नाकारी) NÁKÁRA, Karn. (ನಾಕಾರ) Incompetent, unfit, disqualified, useless, worthless.

NAKARÍ, NAKÁRIÁ, Guz. (નકરી, નકરીઆ) Free from tax, land, &c. (from the S. *kara*, tax).

NAḲB, corruptly, NUCCUB, H. (A. نقب) An excavation, a breach: breaking or digging through a wall.

Naḳbzan, H. (P. زن, who strikes) A burglar.

Naḳbzaní, corruptly, *Nuccubzanie*, H. (P. زني, striking) Burglary, breaking, or rather digging through a wall, the native houses being very generally constructed of sun-dried clay or unburnt bricks, and therefore easily perforated.

NAḲD, NUQD, corruptly, NUCKD, H. &c. (A. نقد), in the dialects the *ḳ* is commonly changed to *g*, and a penultimate vowel inserted, as NAGAD, or NUGUD, Beng. (নগদ), Mar. (नगद), NAGADU, Tel. and Karn. (ನಗದು), NAGADA, Uriya (ନଗଦ). In Mar. it also occurs, in composition at least, as NAKTA, and NAKTÍ. Cash, money, ready money: it sometimes applies to all personal property except goods and chattels: in Bengal it implies prompt, ready, as money, &c.

Naḳdí, *Nagdí*, *Nahadí*, or *Nagadí*, corruptly, *Nuckdy*, *Nugdee*, *Nehdy*, H. &c. (نقدي, नग्दी, नगदी) Paid, or to be paid, in cash or ready money; applied especially to the land revenue which is paid in money, in contradistinction to that which is paid in kind. In Bengal, *Nagadí* (নগদী) is applied also to cash, ready money; and in Malayalim, according to Mr. Græme, *Nigadí* (നിഗതി) denotes the money revenue payable to the Mohammadan government of Mysore.

Nagadíbáb, Mar. (नगदीबाब) The heading under which items of revenue payable in money were entered in the Maraṭha accounts.

Nakdi-chhiṭṭhá, H. (چيٹھا) Cash receipt.

Nigadi-chiṭṭu, Mal. (നിഗദിചിട്ടു) A document given by a collector to each payer of revenue, stating the amount of cash demandable.—Mysore.

Nakdi-faiṣalat, H. (A. فيصلة) Settlement of cash balances.

Nakdi-gumáshta, H. (گماشتة) A cash-keeper.

Nakdi-jinsí, H. (A. جنسي, sort, kind) Money rent, calculated on the value of the produce.

Nagadi-lekhá, Tel. (నగదిలెక్క) A cash account.

Naḳdi-mazḳúrát,H.(A.نقدي مضكورات) Miscellaneous items in the revenue accounts allowed for and settled in money.

Nagad-mál, Mar. (नगदमाल) Ready property, money, or effects easily convertible into cash, as jewels, &c.; also, the prime or chosen portion of any thing.

Nagad-vikrí, Mar. (S. नगदविक्री, from S. विक्रय, sale) Ready-money sale.

Nagadu-risídi, Karn. (Eng., receipt) An account of receipts in ready money.

Nagadi-sirastá, Mar. (नगदी शिरस्ता, from P. سرشتة) A general term for various money cesses imposed by the Maraṭha government.

Nigadi-shistam, Mal. (ശിഷ്ടം, S. शिष्ट, left) A cash balance after payment of the government revenue, payable to the proprietor by the tenant or occupier, either under lease or mortgage.

Nigadi-vittu, Mal. (വിത്തു, seed) Money assessment according to the value of the seed required for a field or an estate.

Naḳd-o-jins, H. (نقدوجنس) Money and goods.

Naktabáb, or *Naktíbáb*, Mar. (नक्तबाब, नक्तीबाब) Taxes in money, not in kind.

NAKHKHÁS, vernacularly, NAKÁS, incorrectly, NIKÁS, corruptly, NUHKAS, NUKKAS, NECKAS, NEKKAS, or NEKAUSS, H. (A. نخّاس) A daily fair or market for slaves and for horses and cattle: the sale of living things: a tax formerly levied in Bengal, and still in some of the native states, upon the sale of horses and cattle.

NAKHL-BAND, H. (from A. نخل, a young tree) A gardener, a maker of artificial flowers.

NÁKHUDÁ, corruptly, NAKOUDA, NACODAH, H. (P. ناخدا) The captain or commander of a ship.

NAḲÍB, H. (A. نقيب) A servant who announces his master's approach, and repeats his titles; a kind of herald or chamberlain.

NÁKÍRD, Mar. (P. नाकीर्द), NÁKHIRUDU, Tel. (నాఖిరుదు) Lying waste or fallow (land).

Náhírdsár, Mar. (नाकीर्दसार) Land incapable of cultivation.

NÁKIṢ, H. (A. ناقص), NÁKAS, Hindi (नाकस) Defective, deficient: as applied to land, it is said to signify either land in which wells cannot be sunk without masonry, or that which is fit for the cultivation of Bájra: it is also applied to land that is unproductive and not worth cultivating.

NAKKAPANDUGA, Tel. (నక్కపండుగ) A ceremony performed at the salt-pans before the salt is brought from them.—Northern Sirkars.

NAḲL, NUQL, vernacularly, NAḲAL, or NUQUL, corruptly, NACCAL, H. &c. (نقل, नकल) A copy, a transcript, any recorded written document, a register.

Naḳl-i-paṭṭá, or *-paṭṭáját*, H. (from پتّا, a lease) A record or register of leases or revenue engagements: an account kept by the village accountant, giving, under the name of each cultivator, an abstract of his tenure, shewing the extent of his farm and amount of revenue, and the name, measurement, assessment, and revenue, of each field.

Naḳlá, *Nuqla*, corruptly, *Nuglá*, H. (A. نقلا) A smaller village dependent upon a larger, or upon an estate, forming a subordinate part of it: (included in the register, or *Naḳl*).

Náḳil, H. (A. ناقل) A reporter, a registrar.

NAḲSHA, or NAKASHÁ, H. &c. (A. نقشة, नकशा) A picture, a plan, a map, a general description, an official report.

Naḳsha-intiḳáli, Ḥ. (A. انتقالي) A deed of conveyance or transfer of landed property.

Naḳsha-i-khewat, H. The draft or transcript of the village register.

Naḳsha-juz-o-kul, H. (نقشةجزوكل) Detail of particulars, small or great: a report drawn up by the native collector or surveyor, furnishing details of cultivation, the condition of the cultivators, the quality of the lands, the mode of management, &c., so as to form a guide to the assessment.

Naḳsha-tabdíli, H. (A. تبديل, change) Record of transfer of shares in landed property.

Kisht-wár-naksha, H. (A. كشت, a field) A settlement map, a plan of fields according as they are assessed.

NAKSH-BANDIÁ, H. (نقشبنديا) A Mohammadan religious mendicant, characterised by carrying a lighted lamp in one hand and going about singing verses in honour of the Prophet,

&c.: they derive their institution and name from *Khája Bahá-ud-dín*, of *Nakshband*.

NAKSHATRA, S. (नक्षत्र) An asterism or collection of stars, which are classed in twenty-eight divisions, and serve to mark the moon's course through the ecliptic, hence called a lunar mansion: any constellation.

NAL, NUL, or NALA, NULU, H. &c. (S. نل, नल) A rod, a bambu, a reed, a measuring rod: as a standard of measure it consisted of three *Iláhi-gaz* or yards of Akbar, but the length varied in practice from 7½ to 9 feet; a larger rod was also in use varying from 26 to 33 feet; and another was known in Bengal of 400 cubits.

Naliyá, Beng. (नलिया) A bird-catcher: one who catches birds with limed rods.

NÂL, H. (A. نعل) A horse-shoe.

Nâlband, H. (نعلبند) A farrier.

Nâlbandi, H. (نعلبندي) Farriery: horse-shoe money: under the Mohammadan government, a contribution exacted from petty princes or the peasantry, on the plea of keeping up the cavalry of the state, or as the price of preventing the horsemen from devastating the country, but which was converted into a small permanent tribute: among the Maraṭhas, the equipment of cavalry for the field, or an advance to a troop when enlisted or sent on service.

Náldabá, Mar. (नालडबा) A set of horse-shoes (four): a claim of the state or public officers to a set of horse-shoes, annually, from the village blacksmith, or the money-value instead.

Nâlṣáhib, H. (نعل صاحب) A man who runs as fast as he can, carrying an artificial representation of a horse-shoe as typical of the horse of Hasain at the festival of the *Muharram*.

NÁL, (?) Hindi. A gang or body of the freebooters in Bundelkhand known as *Sanorias*, or *Utháigírs*.

NÁL, H. &c. (نال), NAḶA, Mar. (नळ) A tube, a pipe, a hollow reed or cane.

NALA, S. &c. (नल) The 50th year of the Hindu cycle.

NÁLÁ, or NÁLA, corruptly, NULLAH, H. &c. (نالا, ناله, नाला) NÁLU, NALUVÉ, Karn. (ನಾಲು, ನಾಲುವೆ) A water-course, a channel or gulley cut in the soil by rain, down which, in the rainy season, rushes a considerable body of water: a rivulet, a creek, a drain, a ravine.

Nálákandi, Uriya (ନାଲାକନ୍ଦି) An aqueduct for salt water.

NAḶA, Mar. (नळ) An aqueduct, a conduit pipe.

Naḷapaṭṭí or *Nalpaṭṭí*, Mar. (नळपट्टी) A tax on the people of a town or district to defray the cost of keeping aqueducts in repair.

NÁLÁIḲ, H. (P. نالايق) Unfit, unworthy, improper: as applied to land, barren, unproductive, incapable of cultivation.

NÁLGÓRU, NÁLKUKÓRU, Karn. (ನಾಲ್ಗೋರು, ನಾಲ್ಕುಕೋರು, from *nálhu* ನಾಲ್ಕು, four) Four shares; land which, having been untilled, is let to farmers on agreement that government shall have one share of the produce and the cultivators three.

NÁḶI, NÁṞI, or NÁẒHI, Tam. (நாழி) A measure of capacity, a *padi*, or one-eighth of a *marakál*, about 3 lbs. 6 oz.

NÁLÍ, H. &c. (S. نالي, नाली) A tube, a pipe, a hollow reed or bambu, a drill pipe, a channel, a drain: in Kamaon, a measure of space, half a *bísi*; also a measure of grain, twenty of which, of seed, are the contents of a sheep saddle-bag, and should be sown in a *bísi* of land.

NÁLISH, H. (P. نالش), NÁLIST, or NÁLISTÍ, Mar. (नालिस्त, -स्ती) Complaint, statement of wrong and prayer of redress, plaint, accusation (in a court of law).

Nálish-ghair-sarsari, or *Nálish-numberi*, H. (from P. سرسري, summary, as a suit, or the Eng. word 'number') A regular suit at law, one in which the plaint has been duly preferred and recorded according to its number.

Nálishí, H. (P. نالشي) A complainant, a plaintiff.

Nalishi-ârẓí, H. (from A. عرضي) A plaint, the representation of the complainant.

NÁLKÍ, H. (نالكي) An open litter or palankin used by persons of rank.

NALLABHÚMI, Tel. (నల్లభూమి) Black soil.

NÁLUGU, Tel. (నాలుగు) Staining the hands and feet of the bride and bridegroom yellow, part of the marriage ceremony in the Dakhin: rubbing the body with the flour of certain grains to cleanse the skin.

NALVA, Karn., Mal. (ನಲ್ವ) A furlong, a distance measured by 440 cubits.

NÁMA, also, vernacularly, NAOṆ, NAṆO, H. (ناون, نانو), and NÁO, or NAO, Mar. (नाव), vernacularly, NÁM, H. &c. (نام, नाम) Name, a name, reputation; also, in Karnataka, a sectional mark of three perpendicular lines, of which the centre is red, the other two white, made on the forehead by the worshippers of *Vishnu*: also the white clay used for the purpose.

Námdár, H. (P. نامدار) Famous, renowned.

Námávalí, Beng. (S. नामावली) A kind of cloth, or a scarf or belt stamped with the names of a deity, worn by the Hindus.

Námadárí, Tam. (நாமதாரி) A *vaishnava*, one wearing the sectarial marks.

Námkaran, or *Námakaraṇa*, H. &c. (S. نامكرن, नामकरण) Giving a name to a new-born child with appropriate ceremonies: one of the initiating rites or *Sanskáras* of the Hindus.

Námakírttana, S. &c. (नामकीर्त्तन) Repeating the names of a divinity as an exercise of devotion: in Bengal, also, the insertion of a name in a legal document or deed.

Námbarda, H. (P. نامبرده) Named, mentioned, aforesaid.

Náonisán, Mar. (नावनिशाण) Name and particulars (as country, residence, occupation, &c.).

Náonisí, Mar. (नावनिशी) A roll or list of names, also a single name borne upon it.

Náonisíwár, Mar. (नावनिशीवार) Name by name according to the roll.

Náoras, Mar. (नावरस) The name given to a child with reference to its horoscope.

NÁMA, NAMU, written, NAMAH, NAMEH, in the Hindu dialects most usually NÁMÁ, &c., H. &c. (P. نامه, नामा) A writing, a written document, a deed: its particular appropriation is indicated by the word with which it is connected, and which usually precedes it; as, *Ikrár-náma*, a deed of agreement; *Rázi-náma*, a deed of assent; *Tahsím-náma*, a deed of partition; *Tamlík-náma*, acknowledgement of ownership or property, &c.: or the terms may be transposed with the sign of connexion; as, *Náma-i-ikrár*, *Náma-i-tahsím*, but in Hindustani this is less usual.

NAMAK, or NIMAK, corruptly, NEMUK, NIMUCK, NEEMUCK, H. &c. (P. نمك), in other dialects the form is NIMAK only, as Beng. (निमक), Mar. (निमक) Salt.

Namak-, or *Nimak-chashí*, H. (P. چشي, tasting) Feeding a child for the first time when about six or seven months old, on which occasion various ceremonies are observed; also the interchange of trays of sweetmeats between the families of the bride and bridegroom at the time of betrothment.

Namak-, or *Nimak-halál*, H. (نمك حلال) Faithful, loyal.

Namak-, or *Nimak-harám*, H. (نمك حرام) Faithless, disloyal, treacherous.

Namakí, or *Nimakí*, H. (نمكي) Saline, salt: applied in Orissa to land overflowed by the tide, and where salt is manufactured.

Nimak-daláli, H. (P. دلال, a broker) A tax formerly levied in Bengal on salt-brokers or vendors.

Namak-mahál, H. (نمك محال) The salt revenue as a separate head of revenue.

Namak-, or *Nimak-sár*, H. (نمكسار) Salt-revenue, a salt-pit, saline.

Nimak-parwarda, H. (P. پرورده, cherished) A favourite and confidential servant.

NAMASKÁR, S. &c. (नमस्कार) Reverential salutation, especially to an idol or a Brahman.

NAMÁZ, H. (A. نماز), vernacularly, NAMÁJ (नमाज) Prayer, especially that prescribed by law to be recited five times a day.

Namáz-gáh, H. (from P. گاه, a place) A place of prayer, the part of a mosque where the prayers are read, or a temporary building or platform for the same purpose.

Namáz-i-janáza, H. (A. جنازه, a bier) Funeral service of the Mohammadans.

NAMBI, NAMBIYÁN, Tam. (நம்பி, நம்பியாண்), NAMBI, or NAMBADÍ, Mal. (നമ്പി, നമ്പടി), NAMBIYAVA, Karn. (ನಂಬಿಯವ) The title of a caste, or member of it, an inferior class of Brahmans, said to be sprung from a Kshatriya mother and Brahman father, and usually officiating as priest in Vaishnava temples in the south of India.

NAMBÚDIRI, commonly pronounced, and written, NAMBÚRI, or NAMBOORI, Mal. (നമ്പൂതിരി), NAMBÚRI, Tam. (நம்பூரி) A Brahman of the highest order in Malabar, also the name of the caste or tribe.

NAMBU-VETUVAR, (?) A class of slaves in Karnata.

NAMBYÁRA, Mal. (നമ്പ്യാര) A tribe of Náyars, or Nairs, in Malabar, also a member of it.

NAMUCHÍO, Guz. (નમુચીઓ) A man without mustaches, a beardless man, a term of reviling.

NAMUDÁR, H. (P. نمودار, from *namudan*, to show) A sample, a specimen.

Namudár, or *dárí*, H. (نموداري) Payment made by a cultivator upon his being exempted from actual measurement, settling his assessment by samples of the crop (?).

Namuder-besi, Beng. (नमुदेरबेशी) Increase of the rate entered on the vouchers exhibited (from P. نمود, showing).

Namuder-kamí, Beng. (नमुदेरकमी) Deficiency, or diminution of the exhibit rate. See the preceding.

Namúna, *Numoona*, H. &c. (نمونه, नमूना), *Namuná*, or *Namoná*, Mar. (नमुना, नमोना) A sample, a specimen, a pattern.

Namusúdra, corruptly, *Numoosoodr*, (?) Beng. A low caste, or an individual of it, a *Chaṇḍála*.

Náná, H. (نانا) A maternal grandfather.

Náni, H. (نانی) A maternal grandmother.

Nanad, Nanandá, Nanadí, Nanadíní, Beng. (ননদ, &c. S. ननंदृ) A husband's sister.

Náṇak, or **Náṇe**, Mar. (S. नाणक, नाणे), **Nánu**, Guz. (નાણું) Coin, a coin, any thing bearing an inscription, money.

Náṇevaṭi, or *-vaṭṭi*, Mar. Guz. (नाणेवटी -वट्टी) A money-changer.

Náṇevaṭṭam, Mar. (नाणेवट्टं), *Nánávaṭa*, Guz. (નાણાવટ) Money-changing, the business of a money-changer: the money-market, the place where the money-changers' shops are.

Náṇaya, or *Nánya*, Karn. (ನಾಣಯ, ನಾಣ್ಯ) Coin, money.

Náṇyagár, Karn. (ನಾಣ್ಯಗಾರ) A money-changer.

Nányamúbadulu, Karn. (ನಾಣ್ಯಮೂಬದುಲು) Exchanging coins.

Nányamurupaḍi, Karn. (ನಾಣ್ಯಮುರುಪಡಿ) Changing large for small money, giving change.

Nányaparkhávaṇi, Karn. (ನಾಣ್ಯಪರಖಾವಣಿ) Trying coins, determining if they are full weight and value.

Nánayavaṭṭam, Tam. (நாணயவட்டம்) Difference in exchange of coins, premium or discount.

Náṇáṛi, Mal. (നാനാഴി) A measure of quantity = four small measures.

Nánáṛikandam, Mal. (നാനാഴിക്കണ്ടം) Sown with four measures of seed (a field).

Náṇasáí, (?) Mar. A religious mendicant of a low order, who, in the west of India, extorts alms from the shop-keepers and others by importunities, abuse, and threats: (? if intended for *Nánakshâhi*, vagrant mendicants professing to be followers of *Nának Sháh*, the founder of the Sikh religion).

Nánchanebára, Uriya (ନାଞ୍ଚନେବାର) Bribery and corruption (the first term is more correctly *Lánch*, q. v., the second is probably *Lewára*, from H. *léna*, to take).

Nand, Mar. (S. नंद) A cant term amongst traders and shop-keepers, for an undue profit.

Nandana, S. &c. (नन्दन) A son; also the 26th year of the cycle.

Nandavanam, S. &c. (नन्दवनं) The grove of Indra, but used in the south of India to designate a garden, the flowers of which are appropriated to some temple.

Nandí, Nundee, S. &c. (नन्दी) The bull of Siva, a figure of whom is usually placed in front of temples dedicated to that deity.

Nándí, S. &c. (नान्दी) A benedictory verse eulogising a king or a deity.

Nándi-mukha, or *Nándi-śráddha*, S. &c. (नान्दीमुखः, -श्राद्धः) A commemorative sacrifice or offering to the manes of deceased ancestors, as preliminary to a marriage or other occasion of festivity: also, in Bengali, an ancestor.

Nandiní, H. (S. نندنی) A husband's or wife's sister.

Nandoí, Nandosí, H. (S. نندوی, نندوسی) A husband's sister's husband.

Nángar, Mar. (नांगर), **Nángal**, Beng. (না°গল, S. लाङ्गल) A plough.

Nángaraṭ, *-raṭh*, or *-raḍ*, Mar. (नांगरट -रठ -रड) Newly-ploughed ground.

Nángarṇí, Mar. (नांगरणी) Ploughing.

Nángaryá, Mar. (नांगर्या) Relating to a plough, a ploughman, a bullock, &c.

Naṉjai, or **Naṉjey**, commonly pronounced **Nanja**, or **Nunja**, corruptly, **Nunjah**, Tam. (நஞ்சை, நன்செய், from *Nal* நல், good, and *shai* சை cultivation), **Nanja**, Tel. (నంజ) Soil that is fit for the cultivation of rice, admitting of artificial irrigation, and hence commonly termed 'wet ground or soil,' in contradistinction to *Punja*, or dry.

Naṉjai mel puṉjai, or *taram puṉjai*, Tam. (நஞ்சை-மேல் -தரம்-புஞ்சை) The cultivation of grains not usually requiring irrigation on irrigated soils, but where the actual supply of water is inadequate for the growth of rice: the revenue in such a case is assessed at a medium rate between that customary on dry and on wet lands.

Nánji, Uriya (ନାଞ୍ଜି) A strip of alluvial land.

Nánkár, less correctly, **Nancar**, H. &c. (نانکار, P. نان bread, and کار, business) In Bengal finance, a term applied to an assignment of a portion of the land or revenue of an estate, made to the occupant or Zamindár as an allowance for his subsistence, usually amounting to about five, or sometimes ten per cent. on the assessment payable to the state. If removed from the management of the estate, the *Nánkár* was occasionally withdrawn, in contradistinction to the *Málikána*, which was always granted: the terms, however, are not unfrequently confounded, or used indiscriminately to signify the same thing. The term was also applied to assignments of land or revenue made as subsistence-money to fiscal and village officers. Ben. Reg. viii. 1793; xxv. xxvii. 1803; ix. 1805.

Nánkár-mujrái, H. (P. نانکارمجرای) Deductions from the revenue, or assignments from it, on account of *Nánkár*, or subsistence allowance.

Nánkár mujrái wásil báki, H. &c. (نانكار مجراي واصل باقي) An account of the revenue deducted or assigned on account of *Nánkár*: items in the general account of receipts and balances kept by the village accountants, exhibiting such deductions.

Nánkár-zamín, H. &c. (P. زمين, land) Land assigned rent-free to Zamindárs or public officers for their maintenance.

Nánparwarshi, Karn. (ನಾನಪರವರಶಿ) A pension, a grant, a salary or allowance made to a person when incapable of service.

NÁP, H. (ناپ, for *Máp* ماپ) Measuring, measure.

NÁPAT, Mar. (नापत) Want of credit or character (among mercantile people.

NÁPIT, H. &c. (S. ناپت, नापित), along with the original term the dialects have various modifications of the word, as NÁÏ, H. (ناي), NÁÍDA, NÁÍNDA, Karn. (ನಾಯಿದ, ನಾಯಿಂದ), NÁÚ, NÁHÚ, NÁHAWI, and NÁHÁWÍ, NHÁÚ, and NHÁWÍ, Mar. (नाऊ, नाहू, नाहवी, नाहावी, न्हाऊ, न्हावी) NÁPÍG, Karn. (ನಾಪಿಗ) A barber, a shaver, who usually acts also as a surgeon: the village barber, and barber-surgeon.

NAPTÁ, NAPTRÍ, S. &c. (नप्ता, नप्त्री) A grandson, a grand-daughter.

NAR, Sindhi. A large water-wheel.

NÁR, Mal. (ഞാറ) Young corn or paddy fit for transplanting.

Narrukála, Mal. (ഞാററുകാല) A bed or piece of ground from which young rice plants have been removed.

Nárrupattí, Mal. (ഞാററുപട്ടി) A bed or piece of ground in which rice plants have been sown for transplanting.

NÁRA, Tel. (నార), Mal. (നാര) The hempen fibres of various plants, whether from the stem or the bark, as the palm, the cocoa-nut, the aloe, the *San*, &c.

NÁṚÁ, or NÁḌÁ, Beng. (নাড়া) Stubble, the stubble of rice or other grain after reaping.

NARAKA, S. &c. (नरक) Hell, the place of torment for sinners: various subdivisions are enumerated.

NÁRAṬṬA, Karn. Tel. (ನಾರಟ್ಟ) Land broken by chasms and creeks.

NÁṚ-, or NÁḌ-GÍR, Mar. (नाडगीर) A revenue officer.

Nár-, or *Nád-gaund*, Mar. (नाडगौंड) The head revenue and police-officer of a district in some of the Maratha provinces, corresponding to *Desmukh* in others.

Nárgun, (?) Mar. The head of the shepherds, as holding a *watan* or claim on the revenue of a village or district: (it should be, probably, the same as the preceding).

NÁṚI, or NÁḌÍ, S. &c. (नाडी, नाडी) Any tubular pipe or vessel, a blood-vessel, the pulse.

Náríṭepá, Beng. (নাড়ীটেপা) A physician.

NÁṚÍ, or NÁṚIKÁ, S. &c. (नाडी, नाडिका), NÁḶIKAI, or NÁZHIKAI, NÁDIKÁ, Tam. (நாழிகை, நாடிகா), NÁṚIKA, or NÁṚIGA, Mal. (നാഴിക) A measure of time, an hour of twenty-four minutes, or one-sixtieth of the day and night; also, in Tam. an Indian mile, the distance a person walks in a *Náṛika*.

NÁRÍ, S. &c. (नारी) A woman.

NÁṚI, Mal. (നാഴി) A measure of capacity, the fourth part of an *Edangali*, or sometimes the same as the *Edangali*.

NARIAL, Thug. The head.—Dakhini.

NARÍHAR, Thug. Unsafe, as the place appointed for the murder.

NÁRIKELA, S. &c. (नारिकेल), sometimes modified in the dialects, as NÁRYAL, H. (ناريل), NÁRAḶ, NÁRAḶÍ, and NÁREḶ, Mar. (नारळ, नारळी, नारेळ) The cocoa-nut tree (Cocos nucifera); a cocoa-nut.

Náraḷí punav, or *paurṇimá*, Mar. (नारळीपुनव, or पौर्णिमा) Day of full moon in the month *Srávan*, when a cocoa-nut is thrown into the sea, and the monsoon is declared to be broken up.

Náraḷi utpanna, ? (from S. उत्पन्न, produced) Amount produce of the cocoa-nut trees of the state, or of the impost on private plantations.

Náraḷmár, Mar. (नारळमाड) A cocoa-nut tree kept for fruit, in distinction to the *Bandhármár* (भंडारमाड), one kept for *tári*.

Nárikela-tail, Beng. (S. নারিকেলতৈল) Cocoa-nut oil.

Nárikela-málá, Beng. (from মালা, the shell of the cocoa-nut) The internal hard shell, a cup made of it.

Náryalí, H. (ناريلي) *Tárí* from the sap of the cocoa-nut tree.

NÁRODÁ, Guz. (નારોદા) A tribe of half-caste Rájputs.

NÁRU, Karn. (ನಾರು) The fibres of plants, whether from the stem or the rind.

Undí-náru, Karn. (ಉಂಡೀನಾರು) Common hemp.

Dengina-náru, Karn. (ದೆಂಗಿನನಾರು) The fibres, or *coir*, of the cocoa-nut.

Nulináru, Karn. (ನುಲಿನಾರು) Any sort of hemp.

NÁRÚKÁRÚ, Mar. (नारूकारू) The inferior village servants, those comprised under the designation of *Aluta*, q. v.

NÁṚU, Tel., Tam. (నాఱు, நாறு) Young plants of corn fit to be transplanted.

Nárṛu, pronounced Náṭṭu, Tam. (நாற்று) Plants thickly sown, for the purpose of being transplanted.

Nárṛankál, pronounced Náṭṭaṇgál, Tam. (நாற்றங்கால்) A bed, or part of a field, kept moist, in which rice is sown for the purpose of being transplanted when it grows up.

Nárṛunadavu, or *Náṭṭunudavu*, Tam. (நாற்றுநடவு) The act of transplanting.

Náṣ, or Nás, Mar. (S. नाश, नास) Loss, injury, destruction.

Náṣwaní, Mar. (नाशवणी, from S. पाणी, water) Rain out of season spoiling the crops.

Nárta, Dakh. Thug. A soldier or policeman.

Narwá, incorrectly, Nirwa, Guz. (નરવા) An undivided village held in coparcenary, and managed by a few of the chief sharers: applied also to the assessment of the revenue by agreement with the principal shareholders.

Narwádár, Guz. (નરવાદાર) A coparcenary shareholder in a village.

Nasab, Nusub, H. (A. نسب) Family, race, lineage.

Nasab-náma, H. (P. نامه, a document) A pedigree, a genealogical table or tree.

Nisbat, H. (A. نسبت) Relationship, affinity, connexion: also used adverbially, *ba-nisbat*, with regard or respect to.

Nisbat, Mar. (निसबत, the same word as the last, but differently applied) Charge, care of, custody, control or direction of.

Nisbatdár, Mar. (निसबतदार) A person or officer having charge or control of.

Nisbatwár, Mar. (निसबतवार) Belonging to, in charge or under control of: in the order of the names of those to whose keeping things or persons are committed (a list, &c.)

Nasaḳ, Nusuḳ, H. (A. نسق) Order, arrangement: valuation of a crop by estimate (?)

Nasaḥchí, H. (P. نسقچي) An officer better known in Persia than in Hindustan, one attached to the king as chamberlain and orderly, and, on occasion, executioner.

Nasakchí báshí, H. (P. باشي) Chief chamberlain or orderly.

Nashá, H. (A. نشا) Intoxication, the effects of intoxication, a headache, &c.; intoxicating liquor.

Nashṭa, vernacularly, Nasht, or Nusht, or, sometimes, Náth, S. &c. (نشت, नष्ट) Lost, injured, destroyed: it is often used as a substantive, as,

Nashṭam, Tam. (நஷ்டம்), *Nashtamu*, or *Nashṭi*, Tel. (నష్టము, నష్టి), *Nashṭa*, Karn. (ನಷ್ಟ), *Nashṭa*, *Nashṭi*, Uṛiya (ନଷ୍ଟ, ନଷ୍ଟି) Loss, injury, damage, waste: applied especially to a deficient crop, either of corn or fruit, from temporary or permanent injury, as bad soil, scarcity of water, excess of rain, blight, tempest, lightning, &c., claiming a proportionate diminution of the assessment.

Nashṭachandra, S. &c. (नष्टचन्द्रः) The waning moon.

Nashṭavártte, Karn. (ನಷ್ಟವಾರ್ತೆ) Bad news.

Náshṭiha, S. &c. (नाष्टिक) Who or what has suffered loss, bereft of property, deprived of an owner.

Nashúṣ, A. (نشوص) In Mohammadan law, a woman who is disobedient to her husband and provokes him to maltreat her; one who abandons her husband's house in consequence of a quarrel.

Nasía, H. (A. نسيه) Delay allowed for payment, credit.

Naṣíb, H. (A. نصيب) Fortune, fate, destiny.

Nasihá, H. (نسيها, नसिहा) A light plough for ploughing light soils.

Nasíhah, or Nasíhah-daftar, corruptly, Naseha, (?) An office under the Mohammadan governments in which accounts of the revenue and revenue alienations were prepared for transmission to the supreme treasury (perhaps from *Nasíhat*, advice).

Naṣíhat, H. (A. نصيحت) Advice, counsel. Nasíhat, Mar. (नसीहत), Nasiyattu, Karn. (ನಸಿಯತ್ತು) Chastisement, punishment.

Nasl, H. (A. نسل) Lineage, race, descent.

Naslan ba naslan, H. (نسلاًبهنسلاً) In regular descent or succession.

Naṣṣ, A. (نصّ) Manifesting: in Mohammadan law, a clear and express dictum of law which cannot be set aside.

Násti, S. &c. (नास्ति) Non-existence, annihilation, what is not (it is sometimes confounded vernacularly with *Nashṭa*, and *Nashṭi*, q. v.

Nástiha, or *Nástik*, S. &c. (नास्तिक) An unbeliever, one who denies the authority of the Vedas: an atheist.

Nátá, H. (ناتا), Náteṇ. Mar. (नातें, from the S. ज्ञाति) Kindred, affinity, relationship (by blood or marriage).

Ṉáti, plur. *Ṉátiyar*, *Ṉátigal*, Tam. (S. ஞாதி, ஞாதியர், ஞாதிகள்) Relations by the same father, joint heirs.

Naṭa, Nuta, Mal. (നട) Entrance to a house: a temple.

Naṭakávan, Mal. (നടകാവൻ) A sentinel, a guard.

Naṭa, Naṭ, or Nuṭ, S. &c. (نت, नटः), Natwá, Guz. (નટવા) A dancer, an actor, a tumbler, a public performer; applied also to a tribe of vagrants who live by feats of dexterity, sleight of hand, fortune-telling, and the like, and correspond in their habits with the gypsies of Europe.

Naṭí, S. &c. (नटी) A dancing-girl, an actress.

Náṭaka, or *Náṭak*, S. &c. (नाटक) Acting, dancing, public performance : a play, a drama.

NÁṬÁÍ, Beng. (নাটাই) A reel for winding cotton.

NÁṬA, or NÁḌA, Mal. (നാട), NÁṬU, Tam. (நாடு) Country, as distinguished from town, a kingdom, a province or district: commonly pronounced *Nád*, or *Nádu*, q. v. (In the derivatives and compounds of these words the inflected forms *Náṭṭa*, and *Naṭṭu*, are substituted.

Náṭṭa, Mal. (നാട്ട) Of or belonging to the country.

Náṭṭam, Tam. (நாட்டம்) The chiefship of a district.

Náṭṭamkáran, corruptly, *Nautumkar*, Tam. (நாட்டம்க்-காரன்) The head man of a village or a district, one who directs and superintends the cultivation, and has chief authority over the village servants: the ***Pátíl*** of the Maratha provinces; also the head man of a tribe, trade, or caste, in some places.

Náṭṭán, corruptly, *Nautwán*, Tam. (நாட்டான்) The chief civil officer of a district under the native administration, whose authority is now confined to questions of caste : the post is filled by the tribe of original settlers and the *Mirásidárs*: the *Náṭṭán*, takes precedence in an assembly of various tribes.

Náṭṭánma, Mal. (നാട്ടാന്മ) Superiority of a village.

Náṭṭánma-káran, Mal. (നാട്ടാന്മകാരൻ), *Náṭṭánmai-káran*, Tam. (நாட்டாண்மைகாரன்) The chief or head man of a village or district.

Náṭṭár, or *Náḍar*, Tam. (நாட்டார், நாடர்) The people of a district or a country: the chief persons among the agriculturists.

Naṭṭukáran, Mal. (നാട്ടുകാരൻ) A rustic, a countryman.

Náṭṭukaranam, Tam. (நாட்டுக்கரணம்) The registrar or accountant of a district, a village accountant.

Náṭṭúkuṭṭam, Mal. (നാട്ടുകൂട്ടം) A general assembly of the people of a country.

Náṭṭumániyam, Tam. (நாட்டுமாணியம்) Land held rent-free as the perquisite of the head man of a village.

Náṭunaṭappa, Mal. (നാടനടപ്പ്) Custom of the country.

Náṭṭusílavu, corruptly, *Nautsellavoo*, Tam. (நாட்டுசிலவு) Charges for village expenses and the pay and allowances of village officers under the native government.

Náṭṭupuram, Tam. (நாட்டுபுரம்) A country town.

Náṭúppu, Mal. (നാട്ടുപ്പ്) Salt made in the country, in distinction to foreign or imported salt.

Nátuwári, or *Naḍuwári*, commonly, *Nadwali*, corruptly *Naurwáli*, and *Naurwai*, Mal. (നാടുവാഴി) A governor, a ruler of a district, subordinate only to the Rája, one who had command of a hundred Nayars.

Naṭṭalan, (?) The name of a class of slaves in Karnáta.

NATTAM, NUTTUM, Tam. (நத்தம்) A village, especially one inhabited by Ṣúdras, in opposition to an Agraháram, or one inhabited by Brahmans; that part of the village lands on which the houses of the *Mirásidárs* are built, the site of the dwellings of the villagers, as distinct from the lands attached to the village. (This word is written with a dental *t*, instead of the cerebral of all the preceding; it should come, therefore, from a different root, but is possibly only a vernacular variation).

Nattamakan, pl. *Nattamakhal*, and *Nattamár*, Tam. (நத்தமகன், நத்தமார், plur.) A subdivision of the Valala tribe, husbandmen, farmers.

Nattapal, Tam. (நத்தபல்) A deserted village.

NÁTAWÁN, H. (P. ناتوان, incapable) As applied to land, unproductive, yielding a scanty crop: to a person, one who is insolvent.

NÁTHA, or NÁTH, corruptly, NAUTH, NAUT, and NAUTUM, S. &c. (ناتهـ, नाथ), NÁTAN, Tam. (நாதன்) A lord, a master, a name borne by some classes of religious mendicants.

Náthwár, corruptly, *Nathtawar*, (?) Having a lord or master, said to denote certain villages superintended by head men called *Naut*, or *Nautum*, probably some error for *Nátuwáṛi*, q. v.

NATHI, NUTHEE, H. (نتهي, नथी) Aggregate of papers and proceedings relating to a law suit: a file or bundle of official papers tied up together.

Natigánthá, Beng. (নতিগাঁথা) Fastening loose papers together by a string passed through one corner (from নত, a nose-ring, and গাঁথা, a knot: this seems to be the original of the preceding, although it occurs as so modified in Behar and Bengal).

NÁTI, H. (ناتي, from S. नप्तृ, नप्त्री) A grandson, a granddaughter; the latter is also *Nátin* (ناتن), and *Natní* (نتني), or Mar. *Nátiṇ* (नातीण).

Nátú, Mar. (नातू) A grandson.

NÁTARÚ, Guz. (નાતરૂ) The second marriage of a woman whose husband is dead or is long absent, or from whom she is separated, practised by some inferior castes in the Dakhin : it is also used for the marriage of a man to a second wife.

Naṭṭu, corruptly, Nuṭh, Karn., Tel. (నట్టు) A platform of earth, a bank, a terrace: *Bent* grass (Agrestis linearis).

Naṭṭuguttige, Karn. (ನಟ್ಟುಗುತ್ತಿಗೆ) Favourable assessment on land where *Bent* grass abounds.

Naṭṭukaul, Tel. (నట్టుకౌల) Land granted on favourable terms, on condition of eradicating the *Bent* grass on the fields.

Naṭupáṭṭam, Mal. (നടുപ്പാട്ടം) Land in dispute let out to a third person.

Naṭuvan, Mal. (നടുവൻ) A mediator, an arbitrator: (this and the preceding, are from the Mal. *Naṭu*, or *Naḍu*, the middle).

Naṭukur, Mal. (നടുക്കൂറ) Allowance made by an owner to his tenant on his planting trees in the lands of the former.

Nau, H. &c. (نو, S. नव) New, young, fresh. See *Nava*.

Nau-ábád, corruptly, *Noabad*, *Nowabád*, H. (نوآباد) Recently settled or cultivated, as land: in Chittagong, lands not included in any survey or assessment, and considered to be at the disposal of the government, who may rent them to whom it pleases: one recently settled on a farm, or in a village, as a cultivator or tenant, or one who cultivates waste lands.

Nau-barár, H. (نوبرار) Land recently made subject to assessment.

Naupatti, (?) *Maháján*, H. (from مهاجن, a merchant) A banker of the highest caste.

Nau-levá, Hindi (नौलेवा) Alluvial deposit left by floods.

Nauroz, H. (P. نوروز) New-year's day, held on the sun's entrance into Aries.

Naushikast, H. (P. شکست, broken) Waste alluvial land newly cultivated.

Nausirtáláo, H. (نوسرتالاو) A newly dug tank: (although H., the phrase *Nau-sir*, new head, for new, recent, is peculiar to Madras).

Nausir-táláo-ḳaul, H. (from قول, an agreement) A grant of land on favourable terms to one who has dug a new tank or well.

Nauwaria, Thug. A tyro.

Náŭ, H. &c. (S. ناو, नौ) A boat, a vessel.

Návik, Mar. (नाविक) A steersman, a pilot.

Náwári, Mar. (नावाडी) A boatman, a steersman.

Nawára, corruptly, *Nowarrah*, H. (P. نوارہ) A large boat, a barge: under the Mohammadan government of Bengal the term was applied to a flotilla stationed at Dacca to protect the branches of the Ganges and Brahmaputra against pirates from Arakan: also to the assessments of revenue set apart for its maintenance by the state, or similar assignments to Zamindárs for keeping up a number of boats.

Nawára-âmla, H. (A. عمله) The establishment of officers for the superintendence of the flotilla: an item in the general revenue accounts of the Mohammadan government of Bengal, specifying the revenue assigned for the expenses of the boat establishment.

Nawára jágír, H. (P. جاگیر, q. v.) Assignment of revenue for the support of the flotilla, or of single boats forming part of it.

Nawára-mahál, H. &c. (محال) The boat department, the establishment of public boats; also the revenue assigned for keeping them up.

Naubat, corruptly, Nobit, H. (A. نوبت) Turn, succession: instruments of music or a band sounding at the gateway of a great man at intervals.

Naubat khána, H. (P. خانه, a house) The chamber, usually over the gateway, where a state band is stationed.

Naubat-ṭalabi, H. (P. طلب, seeking) Applying to be heard in turn in a court or suit at law.

Nauha, H. (A. نوحه) Lamentation over the dead by hired mourners.

Nauji, Tel. (నౌజి) A measure, the eighth of a *marakál*.

Naukar, corruptly, Nowker, H. (P. نوکر) A servant.

Naukarán, H. (plur. of the last) Servants: lands or revenues assigned for the maintenance of village and other public servants.

Naukarí, H. (P. نوکري) Service.

Naukari-mányamu, Tel. (నౌకరిమాన్యము) Land or revenue assigned to public servants either as pay or pension.

Nava, vernacularly, Nau, S. (नव, نو) New, also nine.

Navánna, S. &c. (नवान्न) New grain: a festival observed by the Hindus in the month of *Mágh*, upon first gathering and eating the cold-weather crop.

Naváchal, Guz. (નવાચલ) Land newly brought into cultivation, and therefore lightly taxed, or free from tax.

Navará, Mar. (नवरा) A bridegroom; *Navarí* (नवरी) A bride.

Nava-, or *Naurátri*, S. &c. (नवरात्री) The nine nights: a great Hindu festival in honour of *Durgá*, occupying the first nine days of the month of *Áswin*: the tenth day is the *Daṣahará*, q. v.

Nau-sát, H. &c. (نوسات, lit., nine and seven) A division of the crop, in some districts of Bengal, between the Zamindar and the cultivator, the former taking nine-sixteenths and leaving seven-sixteenths to the latter: also *Nau-sát-batái* (from *Baṭái*, q. v., division)

Nava-, or Nau-ṭakeṇ, Mar. (नवटकें) A measure of capacity, one-eighth of a *sér*.

Nava-, or Nau-ṭánk, or -ṭánkí, Mar., Guz. (नवटांक, also Guz. નવટાંકી) A measure of weight, one-eighth of a *sér* in weight: it appears to be used also for the measure of capacity of the like value; see the preceding, both referring to the coin known as *Tank*, q. v.

Navís, or Navísandah, incorrectly, Navishinda, H. (P. نویس, نویسنده, from *nawishtan*, to write) A writer, a clerk, a secretary, a transcriber: it is similarly used in Maraṭhí, often abbreviated to *Nís*. The first is generally used in composition; the latter is used in some places to denote a writer placed by the landlord to act as a check upon the *Patwári* in keeping an account of the measurement of the fields.

Khush-navís, A good writer, one who writes a good hand, especially a professional transcriber.

Jawáb-navís, A writer of answers to petitions.

Wásil-báḳi-navís, Writer of accounts, of receipts, and balances.

Navite, Tel. (నవితే) A measure of twelve *sérs*.—Northern Sirkárs.

Nawá-aē-thé, corruptly, Nuwa-ay-tay, H. (نواآي تهي) lit., Those who had newly come: an order of Mohammadans said to have descended from some citizens of Madina who attempted to carry off the corpse of Mohammad, and were therefore exiled and driven from city to city: the designation is peculiar to the south of India: *Kánún-i-Islám*.

Nawáib, corruptly, Nawayeeb, H. (A. نوايب) Accidents, changes of fortune: all extraordinary aids beyond the established contributions levied by the state upon the occurrence of any emergency.

Nawása, Nawásá, H. (P. نواسه, نواسا) A grandson, especially a daughter's son.

Nawási, H. (P. نواسي) A granddaughter, especially by a daughter.

Náyáḍi, corruptly, Naiades, Mal. (നായാടി) The name of an outcaste tribe, or an individual of it: they are found only in the northern parts of Cochin, and are the most degraded of all the low tribes.

Náyaka, S. &c. (नायक), also, vernacularly, Náík, as. H. (نايك), Mar. (नाईक), or Naek, Uriya (ନାଏକ), Náyakan, or Naykan, Mal. (നായകൻ, നായ്ക്കൻ), Náyakan, Tam. (நாயகன்) A leader, a chief in general; also the head of a small body of soldiers: in the Anglo-Indian army, a corporal: the head or overseer of a party of labourers: a title borne by the chiefs among several hill tribes, as the *Bhils*, *Kolis*, &c.: a military chief under the Rájas of Vijayanagar, a *Paligár* in the south of India. In Cuttack, a subordinate military leader paying tribute and service for lands held under a superior chief in the *Kilaját*: under the Marathas, an officer who assisted in making the collections in a district, and who exercised also judicial powers in trifling cases; also an overseer of government labourers, or the head of an establishment of horses, carts, &c., a job-master. In Malạbar, the chief police-officer of a district, the head of the village watch; sometimes applied to the head man of a village, sometimes (in Cuttack) to the village astrologer. Amongst the Marathas, also, an affix to the names of the Brahmans who follow the business of money-changers, as *Baloba-naik*, &c. In Kamaon it is said to imply an illegitimate child; in Sanskrit poetry and the drama, the lover, the hero.

Náyak-wáḍi, or *-wáṛi*, *Náik-wáḍi*, or *-wáṛi*, Tel., Karn. (నాయకవాడి) A *peon* stationed in a village by the collector or the landholder especially to superintend the villagers in their cultivation, and see that the produce is not misappropriated or stolen: he performs also, on occasion, the functions of village watchman and police-officer.

Náyakwáḍí, or *-waṛi*, Mar. (नायकवडी) A petty officer in forts or police-stations having authority over some ten or fifteen men.

Náikwár, H. &c. (نايكوار) Under a *Náik*, a village, a corps, &c.

Náikwárí, H. &c. (نايكواري) Any thing relating to a village, &c. under a *Náik*: (this and the preceding are essentially the same as *Náikwáḍi*, &c.).

Nayam, Tam. (நயம்) Profit.

Nayanashṭam, or *Nayanaṭṭam*, Tam. (நயநஷ்டம், நயநட்டம்) Profit and loss. See *Nashṭa*.

Náyar, commonly, Nair, or Nayr, Mal. (നായര) The name of the ruling caste in Malabar, professing to be *Śúdras*, but bearing arms and exercising sovereignty.

Návilkávali, Tam. (நாயில்காவலி) Guarding a town, or expenses incurred for its protection or security.

Náyinár, Mal. (നായിനാര) A chief, a lord, a master.

Náyinda, or **Náyída**, Karn. (ನಾಯಿಂದ, ನಾಯೀದ) A barber, the barber of the village.

Náyudu, commonly written **Naidu**, or **Naidoo**, Tel. (నాయుడు) A title added to the names of respectable persons among the low or *Súdra* castes: also, sometimes, the headman of a village.

Nazm, H. (A. نظم) Order, arrangement, administration.

Náẓim, H. (A. ناظم) An arranger, an administrator, a governor, a viceroy, the superior officer or governor of a province charged with the administration of criminal law and the police, hence applied to the *Nawáb* of *Murshidábád*.

Niẓám, H. (A. نظام) Administration; also, an administrator, a viceroy: hence applied to the viceroy of the Dakhin, who, although assuming independence, retained the title which still distinguishes his successors, the rulers of Hyderabad.

Niẓámat, H. (A. نظامت) The office of the *Niẓám*, the administration of police and criminal law: as a financial designation it was applied, under the Mohammadan government, to lands paying revenue to the *Názim*, not to the *Diwán*, or financial minister of a province, termed also *Niẓámat-mahál*.

Níẓámat-ádálat, (from عدالت, q. v.) The chief criminal court, or court of the *Niẓám*, applied at present to the chief criminal court of the British provinces, established originally at Murshidábád in 1772, but finally removed to Calcutta in 1790. Ben. Reg. ix. 1793. A second *Niẓámat-ádálat*, for the north-west provinces was established by Reg. vi. 1831.

Niẓám-ul-mulk, H. (A. نظام‌الملك) Administrator of the kingdom, the proper title of the ancestor of the rulers of Hyderabád, commonly shortened to *Niẓám*.

Naẓr, vernacularly, **Nujur**, H. &c. (A. نظر) Sight, vision, supervision.

Naẓr-andázi, H. (A.P. نظراندازي) Casting one's sight over: in revenue language, valuation of land, or estimate of the value of a crop upon inspection.

Naẓr-band, H. (from P. بند, binding) Kept in view, or under surveillance, a prisoner at large.

Naẓr-bandí, *Najar-bandí*, H. (P. بندي, binding) Surveillance, arrest, parole; also, detention, confinement.

Naẓr-díd, Sindhi (P. ديدن, to see) Inspection of crops.

Najar-páhaṇí, Mar. (नजरपाहणी) Valuation of land or of crops by inspection.

Náẓir, *Nájir*, H. (A. ناظر, नाजिर), *Nájírí*, Beng. (নাজীরী) An inspector, a supervisor: in ordinary use, the officer of the court who is charged with the serving of process, or who is sent to take depositions, and make inquiry into any breach of law or the peace.

Náẓir-jamádár, H. (ناظرجمعدار) An inspecting officer, a head *peon* or police-officer.

Náẓirkháná, H. (P. خانه) The *Názir*, or sheriff's office.

Náẓárat, H. (ناظارت) Supervision, inspection, the office of the *Náẓir*.

Naẓír, H. (A. نظير) Example, likeness, precedent.

Nazr, **Nazar**, **Najar**, H. &c. (نذر), **Najaru**, or **Nadaru**, Karn. (ನಜರು, ನದರು) A present, an offering, especially one from an inferior to a superior, to a holy man, or to a prince: a present in general: a fine or fee paid to the state, or to its representative, on succeeding to office or property: a son succeeding to a father's property was not liable to this fine among the Marathas unless he were a *Jágírdár* or other servant of government: in cases of adoption it was levied from all persons.

Najaráni, *Najaru-bandi*, *Najaruhánike*, Karn. (ನಜರಾಣಿ, ನಜರುಬಂಡಿ, ನಜರುಹಾಣಿಕೆ) An extortionate tax, a forced contribution on all the people of a village or district.

Najar-bhét, Mar. (नजरभेट) A present made to a public officer on being first introduced to his presence, lit., the present of interview: a small offering of about one rupee made to the government through its officer by each *Pátíl* on settling the assessment.

Nazr-i-dargáh, H. (P. درگاه, a shrine) An assignment of revenue under the Mohammadan government to a sacred shrine, or any religious establishment.

Nazr-i-ídain, H. (A. عيد, a festival) Presents made at the great Mohammadan *Íds*, or festivals: the *Íd-ul-fitr*, and *Bakr-íd*: presents or offerings sent to the court of Dehli on these occasions by the Subahdár of Bengal: a cess imposed to defray their cost.

Nazr-i-Imámán, H. (A. امام, a sacred person) Presents to the Imáms, an assignment or grant made to an establishment dedicated to the Imáms Hasan and Husain, the sons of *Álí*.

Nazar kaṭái, corruptly, *Nuzzur coodai*, H. (نذرقطعي) A present made to the farmer or revenue officer by the cultivators for permission to cut their corn.

Najar-najráná, Mar. (नजरनजराना) Presents to superiors, or such as are interchanged amongst persons of rank.

Najarpaṭṭi, Mar. (नजरपट्टी) A tax levied on a village or

district to raise money for a present to a public officer newly come into office, or to a prince on his accession.

Nazr-i-Ramzán, *Najar Ramjáni*, H. &c. (A. رمضان, the month so named) Presents made at the fast of the *Ramzán*: a tax or fee paid for permission to sell Ârak during the month of *Ramzán*, when all indulgences are interdicted.—Nagpur.

Nazr-i-píran, H. (P. پير, a religious man) Presents to saints: an assignment of revenue for the support of a religious person, or keeping up his tomb.

Nazr-puṇya, H. (from S. पुण्य, holy) Pious offerings, but applied to the presents exacted under the Mohammadan government by its revenue officers at the annual settlements of accounts, and carried in part to the credit of the state.

Nazr-suwárí, H. (P. سواري, horsemen) Contributions levied from the cultivators of a district as the price of the forbearance of cavalry from riding over their corn.

NAZRÁNA, corruptly, NUZZERANA, vernacularly, NAJARÁNÁ, H. (A. P. نزرانه, नजराना) A gift, a present, especially from an inferior to a superior; but the term was more particularly applied to sums received as gratuities, although in fact exacted by the state on various occasions, as fees or fines upon an assignment of revenue to an individual, or on appointment or succession to office, or to a Jágír or other possession, although hereditary; also an exaction of additional tribute from a tributary dependant, or a contribution in excess of the usual revenue payment levied upon the people of the country in professed cases of emergency.

Nazrána-i-hál, H. (A. حال, present) An actual or recent present, one recently exacted.

Nazrána-i-manṣúr-ganj, H. (from منصورگنج, a granary or dépôt so named) A tax imposed by Alivardi Khan as a gift to his grandson Suráj-ad-daula, to whom, at the same time, he granted the tolls leviable at *Mansúr-ganj*, a corn dépôt and market near the latter's residence.

Nazrána-mukarrari, H. (A. مقرر, fixed) A permanent present; a tax imposed by Shujâa Khan, governor of Bengal, ostensibly to defray the expense of the presents made by the Súbahdár to the court of Dehli, but in reality the payment of fixed presents by the Zamindárs to screen themselves from inquiries into their receipts and other pleas for extortion.

Nazrána-ṣúbahdárí, H. (A. صوبه, a province) Presents made to the court by the *Subahdárs* or governors of provinces.

NAZÚL, H. (A. نزول) lit., Descent: in revenue language, an escheat, escheated property in gardens and houses, any property that is considered to have lapsed to the state: an office for investigating lapsed claims.

NEDI, Beng. (নেদি) A cake of cow-dung dried for fuel.

NÉG, H. (نيگ) A present to relations and dependants on festive occasions: the fee of the *Patwárí* or village accountant: any fee for service.

Négí, H. (نيگي) A village servant, any public servant, or one who claims a fee or present on particular occasions.

Négí-jogí, H. (A. نيگي جوگي) Tenants and dependants, public servants, village officers.

NEGA, (?) Tibetan. A measure of weight about ten *sikha* weight.—Kamaon.

NÉGIḶU, less correctly, NEGALU, Karn. (ನೇಗಿಲು) A plough with oxen and apparatus complete: a large kind of plough used in stiff soils.

NÉIGE, Karn. (ನೇಯಿಗೆ) Weaving.

NÉKDÁRÍ, H. (P. from *nek* نيك, good, and *dárí* داري, having) The general term for the sums or portions of the crop, collected from the cultivators of a village for the village expenses and payments to the village officers and servants, as essential to the well-doing of the community.

NÉL, or NELLU, Tam. (நெல், நெல்லு), NELLA, also read NELLI, (but ?) Mal. (നെല്ല, നെല്ലി), NELLU, Karn. (ನೆಲ್ಲು) Rice in the husk, paddy, fifty-eight kinds of which are grown in Malabar; a fundamental measure, eight grains being equal to the breadth of a finger.

Nelli-kandam, Mal. (നെല്ലികണ്ടം) The space of a paddy field between the ridges or banks.

Neṛ-kadir, Tam. (நெற்கதிர்) An ear of rice.

Ner-kalaṉjiyam, Tam. (நெற்களஞ்சியம்) A granary for rice corn.

Neṛkuttakai, Tam. (நெற்குத்தகை) A grain rent.

Ner-huḻi, Tam. (நெற்குழி) A grain or rice pit.

Nellaṛ, Mal. (നെല്ലറ) A rice store or granary.

Nellari, Mal. (നെല്ലരി) Rice unhusked.

Nenmaṇi, Tam. (நென்மணி) A grain of rice corn.

Nenmá, Tam. (நென்மா) Rice flour.

Nelpalisa, Mal. (നെല്പലിശ) Lending grain at interest.

Nelpura, Mal. (നെല്പുര) A store or granary for rice.

Nellipáṭam, Mal. (നെല്ലിപ്പാട്ടം) Rent upon fields of growing rice.

NELA, Karn. (ನೆಲ) Earth, ground, soil.

Kaṭṭáni nela, Karn. (ಕಟ್ಟಾಣಿನೆಲ) A good soil.

Masubunela, Karn. (ಮಸುಬುನೆಲ) A soil between red and black.

Ken-, or *Kenpunela*, Karn. (ರೆಂ., ರೆಂಪುನೆಲ) A red soil.

Bili-nela, or *Savulu-nela*, Karn. (ಬಿಳೀನೆಲ, ಸವುಳುನೆಲ) White soil, fullers' earth.

Erenela, Kappunela, Karenela, or *Regadinela*, Karn. (ಎರೆನೆಲ, ಕಪ್ಪುನೆಲ, ಕರೆನೆಲ, ರೆಗಡಿನೆಲ) Black soil.

NELLI, Tam., Mal., and Karn. (நெல்லி, നെല്ലി, ನೆಲ್ಲಿ) The emblic myrobalan (Phyllanthus emblica).

NEMI, Thug. A call to speak gently or walk slowly.

NEMÍKHARCH, Mar. (नेमीखर्च) Fixed expenses, expenses necessarily incurred, and remaining the same.

NEMṆÚK, Mar. (नेमणूक) Salary, stipend, allowance, pension, or fixed payment in money or kind from a specified source, granted for past or present services, or as an equivalent for allowances formerly received; also, appointment to an office or duty (from S. नियम, regulation, establishment)

NENGI, Karn. (ನೆಂಗಿ) Counterfeit coin.

NENṬA, Karn. (ನೆಂಟ) A kinsman, a relation.

NEOTA, H. (S. نيوتا) An invitation, also the presents sent with the invitation, or those made by a guest.

NÉRA, Tel., Karn. (నేరు), NÉRAM, Tam. (நேரம்) A crime, a fault: fine, penalty.

Nérasta, Karn. (ನೇರಸ್ತ) A criminal.

NEṚÍ, or NEḌÍ, Beng. (নেড়ী) A female mendicant of a particular sect; a female ballad-singer, or a woman who sings at Hindu festivals.

NÉRPÁṬṬAM, Mal. (നെപ്പാട്ടം) A customary fixed rent on land.

Nérpáṭṭa-chiṭṭa, Mal. (നെപ്പാട്ടച്ചിട്ട) A rent bond, an agreement to pay a certain amount of rent, or rate of interest.

Nérpaṭṭá-yola, Mal. (നെപ്പാട്ടയൊല) A deed or bond for rent or interest.

Nérpalisa, Mal. (നെപ്പലിശ) Ten per cent. interest.

NÉSAKULA, NÉSABÍḌARU, Karn. (ನೇಸಕುಲ, ನೇಸಬೀಡರು) A particular class of bird-catchers, also employed as palankin bearers, having a broad accent, and speaking a corrupt dialect.—Karnáta.

NEṢATI, Guz. (નેસતી) A grocer.

NETUṆṆÁTI, Mal. (നെടുങ്ങാതി) A particular caste or tribe, that of the Calicut Raja.

NETTURU-KAṬṬU-INÁMU, Tel. (నెత్తురుకట్టుయినాము) Land granted as a compensation to one who has been wounded in the public service (from *Nettura*, blood).

NEY, Tam., Mal. (நெய்) Oiled butter, *ghee*.

NEYTAL, Tam. (நெய்தல்) A saltish or brackish soil, or situation near the sea.

NEYYAL, NEYTAL, Tam. (நெய்யல், நெய்தல்) Weaving.

Neyyarkáran, Tam. (நெய்யற்காரன்) A weaver.

NIÂMAT, H. (A. نعمت) Favour, bounty: an exaction from the Zamindárs by the farmer of the revenue: a douceur, a benevolence.

NIÁMAT, Thug. A traveller in the hands of Thugs.

NIÁRÁ, H. &c. (S. نيارا, apart, separate) The sweep or scoria and ashes left by the melting or refining of the precious metals, from which particles of them are to be recovered.

Niáriá, H. (نياريا) A sweep-washer, one who extracts precious metals from the dross and ashes.

NÍAT, NEEUT, H. (A. نيّت) lit., Purpose, intention; a solemn announcement at any religious ceremony of the intended repetition of a certain number of prayers; a vow or voluntary obligation to that effect.

NÍÁZ, H. (A. نياز) Petition, supplication, prayer: an offering.

Niáz-i-dargáh, H. (P. درگاه) Grant of money or land to a Mohammadan shrine or mosque.

Niáz-mand, H. (نيازمند) A petitioner, a suppliant.

Niáz-i-rasúl, H. (A. رسول) Offerings of food or alms in the name of Mohammad.

Nazr-o-niáz, H. (نذرونياز) Vows and oblations, or the engagement on a certain day to distribute food or alms in the name and honour of God or the prophet, or some celebrated saints, and the fulfilment of the self-imposed obligation.

NIBANDHA, S. (निबन्धः) In law, fixed or immoveable property; also a *corrody*, or fixed allowance granted by the Rája or person in authority, to be received from the proceeds of a manufactory, mine, or estate.

NIBARTTAN, Beng. (S. निवर्त्तन) A measure of land, the same as a *bighá*: a field, each side of which is twenty poles of ten cubits each.

NIBEDAN, H. &c. (S. نبيدن, निवेदन) A representation, a petition. *Nibedan*, Beng. (S. নিবেদন) Representation, statement, giving information respectfully.

NÍCH, H. &c. (S. نيچ, नीच) Low, base, outcaste: it is used in Maraṭhi with names of castes to signify a more degraded or inferior order, as,

Ních-nhávi, An inferior description of barber, whose office is to shave all parts of the body and apply leeches, and cupping-horns.

Ních-sonár, Low jeweller; said also to kill and eat wild animals, whether clean or unclean.

Ních-játi, Beng. &c. (S. नीचजाति) A low caste; also of a low or impure caste.

Nidán, H., Mar. (ندان, निदान, from S. *Nidána* निदानं) Used adverbially; at the last, uttermost, as price or rate, &c.

Nidán-vriddhi, Mar. (S. निदानवृद्धि) Exorbitant interest.

Nidan, or Niran, Beng. (নিড়ন) Weeding a garden or field.

Nidání, Beng. (নিড়ানী) A weeding instrument, a sort of hoe.

Nidhi, S. &c. (निधि), Nídí, Tam. (நிதி) A treasure in general: a hoard, a hidden treasure: it is used in the south of India in deeds of conveyance for treasure-trove; also *Nidhán* (निधान).

Nidhi-nikshep, Mar. (S. निधिनिक्षेप) A hoard or deposit of treasure, &c.: used in deeds and grants to imply the right of the donee to all hidden treasure on the estate. See *Nikshep*.

Nigadi, corruptly, Niggúdy, and Nigoody, Karn. (ನಿಗದಿ) Instalment: fixing a period for payment: periodical payment of the government assessment on an estate, or of a tax on property, whence applied to the government demand itself; also, but corruptly, *Negatay*, and *Negady*, the net surplus proceeds of an estate paid to the farmer or owners by the occupant (the word is probably a corruption of *Nahdi*, q. v.).

Nigáhbán, or Nigáhdár, H. &c. (P. نگاهبان, نگاهدار, from *Nigah* نگاه, watching or taking care of) A keeper, one who takes care of any thing, a guardian, a guard, a watchman, a village watchman: under the Mohammadan government of Bengal, an officer who inspected weights and measures and affixed his seal to those which were correct: in the south, *Nigávánu*, Tel. (నిగావాను) A petty revenue-officer.

Nighal, Mar. (निघळ) The grist which in grinding collects in the hollow round the pin of the mill, and which, at the close of the operation, is let through and ground.

Nihal, H. (نهل, निहल) Alluvial land recovered from water-courses.

Nij, H. (S. نج, निज) Own, peculiar: used sometimes in the sense of *Nij-jot*.

Nijcha, (?) Uriya, Land cultivated by the proprietors themselves: their own cultivation.

Nij-jot, corruptly, *Nijote*, *Neej-joot*, *Neejoot*, H. &c. (S. نج جوت, from *nij* and *jot*, cultivation) Lands cultivated by the proprietors or revenue payers by themselves, and for their own benefit; also, land allowed to be set apart for the private maintenance of a Zamindár, on which, before the decennial settlement in Bengal, no revenue was assessed.

Nij-tâluk, H. (S. A. نج تعلق) Own *tâluk* or estate: in Bengal, a portion of land of which the proprietor or rent-payer collects the rents from the cultivators direct, without any intermediate agency; also the private lands of a Zamindár, or those cultivated by himself for his own benefit.

Nij-tâlukdár, (نج تعلقدار) An independent Tâlukdár.

Nijja-mudi, or -mora, (?) Karn. The estimated number of *moras* of seed for sowing a field with, in contradistinction to the actual number.

Nikáh, H. (A. نكاح), Niká, Beng. (নিকা) Marriage, legal marriage: in Bengal the term is applied to a sort of left-handed marriage, as one contracted with a widow, or only for a given time, considered disreputable.

Nikáh mitât, H. (A. نكاح متعة) A marriage for a limited time in consideration of a present.

Nikáh muwakkat, H. (A. نكاح موقت) A temporary marriage, one for a season, but celebrated with certain forms: it is void in law, but not unfrequent in practice, at least in Bengal.

Nikáí, H. (نكاي) Weeding a field, the price paid for it.

Nikál patra, (?) Mar. Periodical returns furnished by subordinate officers, showing what has been done in executing orders or petitions referred to them: (the proper meaning of *Nikál* is putting out or forth, expulsion, &c.).

Nikaramu, Tel. (నికరము) Net balance.

Nikás, H. &c. (نكاس, from S. *nishkása*, निष्कास, putting or issuing forth) The skirts or suburbs of a town, or the outer boundary of the land belonging to it: adjustment of accounts, public or private; discharge of a debt: revenue settlement.

Nikás navís, H. (P. نويس, a writer) An accountant, a revenue accountant, one who examines and adjusts the accounts given in by the district officers.

Nikás patr, H. &c. (نكاسپتر) A statement of adjusted accounts, or of the gross produce of an estate, receivable from the cultivator.

Nikás tahsíl, H. (نكاس تحصيل) Statement of the gross produce of an estate, or the full amount receivable from the cultivators by the Zamindár or farmer.

Nikásí, H. &c. (نكاسي), *Nikású*, Mar. (निकासू) Account of the revenue assessed upon an estate: transit duties, taxes on exports, or duties levied on goods passing out of a town or district, or on goods brought from one place to another and taken away again, not having been disposed of.

Nikásí chiṭhí, H. (نکاسي چٹهي) A passport, a permit.

Nikáṣí-kágaj, Beng. (নিকাশিকাগজ) Statement furnished by a subordinate collector or revenue officer of his transactions during the year.—Jessore.

Nikásí khám, H. (نکاسي خام) Gross produce of an estate or village, receivable from the cultivators by the Zamindár, according to the accounts of the Patwárí or Gumashta.

NÍKHÁT, Beng. (S. নিখাত) A ditch, especially one dug as a boundary mark.

NIKIRÍ, Beng. (निकिरी) A class of Mohammadans in Bengal who live by selling fish.

NIKŚHEPA, or, vernacularly, NIKSHEP, pronounced sometimes NIKHEP, S. &c. (نکشیپ, निक्षेप) A pledge, a pawn, a deposit; especially one which is open, or which, if sealed, is specified as to its contents, in opposition to the *Upanidhi*, or sealed, or unknown deposit: hoarded or hidden treasure; used like *Nidhi*, or sometimes in combination with it, as *Nidhi-nikshep*, in the south of India, in deeds of conveyance or in grants, to declare the right of the new occupant to all treasures that may be found in the soil, or to treasure-trove.

Nikshep-ḳárak, or *-ḳárí*, Beng. (from S. কারক -কারী, a doer) One who makes a deposit, one who pledges an article.

NÍLA, vernacularly, NÍL, S. &c. (S. نیل) Indigo: blue.

Níl koṭhí, H. (نیل کوٹهي) An indigo-factory.

Nílárí, Mar. (नीलारी) An indigo-dyer.

Níl-wálá, H. (نیل والا) An indigo-planter.

Nílgar, (?) H. A dyer.

Nílakáran, Tam. (நீலக்காரன்) A dyer of blue.

Nílí, H. &c. (S. نیلي) The indigo-plant, also indigo.

Níligutta, Karn. (ನಿಲಿಗುತ್ತ) A tax levied on contracts for dyeing blue.

NILAIKUḌI, Tam. (நிலைக்குடி) A settled inhabitant.

NILAM, corruptly, NILLUM, Tam., Mal. (நிலம்) Soil, earth, ground; when used in contradistinction to *Bhúmi*, which is the term usually employed in treating of the rights of the sovereign, it is applicable especially to the rights of the cultivator in the soil; it also denotes a separate piece of ground or a field.

Nilattírvai, Tam. (நிலத்தீர்வை) Land assessment.

Nilavari, Tam. (நிலவரி) Ground rent, land tax.

NILÁM, H. &c. (نیلام, Port. *Leilam*) Public sale or auction.

Nilámdár, H. (P. دار, who has) Holder of an estate by purchase at public sale.

Nilámkhásta, H. (from P. خواسته, desired) Balance of revenue short realized by the public sale of lands, deficit on the sale.

NILAVA, or NILUVA, Tel. (నిలవ, నిలువ) Surplus balance.

NÍLLU, Tel. (నీళ్లు) Water.

Níllubuṭṭa, Tel. (నీళ్లుబుట్ట) A fee paid in grain at harvest time to the village potter.

NILUVU, Tel. (నిలువు) The unreaped portion of a field partly reaped.

Niluvu-anchaná, Tel. (నిలువుఅంచనా) Estimate valuation of standing crops.

NÍM, H. &c. (S. P. نیم, नीम) Half.

Ním-ána, or *Ním-ání*, (نیم آنا or آني) Half an *ána*: an extra cess levied formerly in Jessore of half an *ána* in the rupee upon the previous assessment of the revenue.

Ním-ání patwárí, (نیم آني پٹواري) Half an *ána* on the rupee given as a fee to the village accountant at the settlement of the assessment.

Nimäi, or *Nimkhái*, Mar. (निमाई, निमखाई) A half share or concern in agricultural or commercial transactions, or in other matters.

Ním-hawála, H. (نیم حواله) Half of the subdivision of an estate termed *Hawála*, q. v.

Nim-chauthái, Mar. (निमचौथाइ) lit., Half of a fourth, but applied to one-fourth of the *Batti*, q. v.

Nimkeṇ, Mar. (निमकें) Half a bullock or horse load; used especially in regard to toll or transit duties.

Nímlál, H. (نیم لال) A class of pilgrims to Jagannáth so termed.

Nímsálí, H. (from سال, a year) Half-yearly.

Nímṭáká, *Nímṭanká*, less correctly, *Nímtákí*, or *-tankí*, Beng. (নীমটাকা, -টংকা) Half a rupee: a fee of that amount per cent. upon the assessment allowed in Bengal, under the Mohammadan government, to the *Kánungo*, and included amongst the authorised deductions from the revenue to be paid by the Zamindár.

Nimtáná, Mar. (निमताना) Cutting a few handfuls of rice from different parts of the field for the purpose of estimating the whole produce by the grains contained in them; applied also, laxly, to testing the accuracy of any work done in a field by others, as the measurement, classification of soil, return of produce, amount of injury, &c.

Nímthal, Mar. (निमथल, from S. स्थल) Going shares in a

field: division of produce between the owner and cultivator: a half share of a field or its produce.

Nimtháná, Mar. (निमथाना) Valuation of a crop after it is cut, by counting the sheaves, and then selecting three from among them, apparently the fullest, poorest, and middling, and taking the average produce of the three as that of the whole number of sheaves.

NIMANDAM, incorrectly, NIMINDUM, Tam. (நிமந்தம்) Labour in general, especially laborious service in temples, as carrying images, lights, &c.

NIMAR, Hindi (निमर) Having lost its fertility, land.

NIMÁSHÁM, H. (P. نماشام) Time of evening prayer, soon after sunset.

NÍNA, (?) H. Low land capable of being flooded, and suited to rice cultivation.—Dinajpur.

NIPOṬÍ, Mar. (निपोटी, from नि, not, and पोट, the belly) Service in which the person must maintain himself out of his wages: in the Rajapur district, *Nipoṭi Rúpaye* (निपोटी रूपये) implies that daily food is allowed in addition to wages.

NIPAṆJÁ, NIPAṆJÍ, Mar. (निपणजा -जी) The grandfather or grandmother of a grandfather.

NÍṚA, Mal. (നിറ) A weight of one hundred *palams*: a weight in general; adj. in composition, full.

Niṛachaḷava, Mal. (നിറച്ചളവ) Full or heaped-up measure.

Niṛanáṛi, Mal. (നിറനാഴി) A small heaped-up measure.

Niṛapaṛa, Mal. (നിറപറ) A full measure or *paṛa*, especially one of corn, presented to the proprietor of an estate annually by the tenant.

NÍRA, S. (नीर), adopted in all the dialects, as NÍR, H. (نیر), Beng. (নীর), Mar. (नीर), Tam. (நீர், நீரம்), Mal. (നീര) NÍRU, Tel. and Karn. (నీరు) Water.

Niránikam, Tam. (நீராணிக்கம்) A village peon superintending the water-courses.

Niranilai, Tam. (நீரநிலை) Marshy ground.

Niránambam, Tam. (நீராநம்பம்) Wet lands, lands irrigated artificially for rice cultivation.

Nirattiper, Mal. (നീരട്ടിപെര) The ceremony of giving water at the time of transferring an estate, either upon mortgage or sale, by which the bargain is ratified.

Niragante, or *Nirugante*, commonly pronounced *Nirganti*, Karn. (ನೀರಗಂಟೆ, ನೀರುಗಂಟೆ) A village officer who superintends the distribution of water for irrigation.

Nirávatipairu, Karn. (ನೀರಾವತಿಪೈರು) Corn grown by irrigation.

Níróḍukál, Tam. (நீரோடுக்கால்) Low lands over which the surplus waters of a village are discharged.

Níreṛumaḍu, Tam. (நீரேற்றுமடு) High lands that cannot be irrigated.

Nírkál, Tam. (நீர்க்கால்) A water-course, a channel for irrigation.

Nírkánam, Mal. (നീർക്കാനം) Ratification of a deed of transfer of hereditary landed property by the proprietor's pouring water into the hand of the purchaser or mortgagee.

Nírmutal, incorrectly, *Neer Moodil*, Mal. (നീർമുതല) A further step in the total transfer of hereditary landed property, in which, on consideration of an additional advance from the tenant, the proprietor, with the consent of the next heir, parts with as much more of his rights as makes seven-eighths of the whole; the 'water' here is used apparently typically, the property (*mutal*) in it being made over to the new master. See *Kudima-nír*.

Nírpáychumániyam, Tam. (நீர்ப்பாய்ச்சுமானி-யம்) Rent-free land watered from a public reservoir.

Nírsávi, Tam. (நீரசாவி) Destruction of crops from deficiency of water.

Nírugatri, Karn. (ನೀರುಗತ್ರಿ) An instrument placed at the sluice of a reservoir, which cuts roots, grass, &c., that might otherwise choke the passage.

Níruvati, Karn. (ನೀರುವತಿ) Wet cultivation, as that of rice.

Nillubuṭṭa, Tel. (నీళ్లుబుట్ట, from నీళ్లు, plur. of నీరు) A basket for throwing up water from a well or pond for irrigating a field.

Aṛa-nír, Tam. (அற, without) Water allowed to flow for irrigation in greater or less abundance, according to the quantity in the reservoir, usually from the beginning of June to the end of August.

Murai-nír, Tam. (முறைநீர், from, முறை, turn) Water allowed to flow in turn, for a fixed term, to the fields of each cultivator, from about the beginning of April to the end of May.

Peru-nír, Tam. (from பெரு, plentifully) Water allowed to flow without limitation during the rainy season, or from the beginning of September to the end of March, or thereabouts.

NIRAI, Tam. (நிறை) Weight in general, a weight of 100 *palams*.

NÍRÁLI, (?) Mar. A low caste whose occupation is dyeing cloths of dark colours, or manufacturing indigo.

NIṚAN, or NIḌAN, Beng. (নিড়ন) Weeding a field or garden.

NIRANJAN, Beng. (S. निरंजन) Casting an image into the water after a festival dedicated to its worship.

Niraparádhí, Beng. (S. निरपराधी) Innocent, acquitted, (from निर, not, and अपराध, fault).

Nirbádha-bhoga, (S. निर्बाधभोग) In Hindu law, uninterrupted or undisputed possession, conferring a title to property.

Nirdhana, S. &c. (निर, not, and धन, wealth) Poor: in law, a person not entitled to hold property, as a slave, an idiot, &c.

Nirdosh, S. &c. (from निर, not, and दोष, fault) Free from blame, not guilty.

Nirgat, Mar. (S. निर, out, and गत, gone) Gone or taken out, exported: duty or custom on exports.

Nirindriya, S. (निर, not, and इन्द्रिय, an organ of sense) One who has lost or was born deficient in some one of his organs of sense, and is thereby, in law, disqualified for inheritance.

Nirindriyá, S. (fem. of the preceding) A female, or the female sex: deficient in organic vigour.

Nirjalaikádaşí, S. (निर, not, जल, water, एकादशी, eleventh) The eleventh lunar day of the dark half of *Jyeshtha*, on which so strict a fast is observed that even water is not to be sipped.

Nirkh, corruptly, Nerch, Nerk, or Nirk, H. (P. نرخ), Nirakh, Mar. (निरख), Tel. (నిరఖు) Price, rate, tariff, price-current, market rate or price: district or *pargana* rate of price, or of revenue payments, the standard rate at which the lands of a village or district are assessed: rate of exchange.

Nirkhbandí, H. (نرخ‌بندي) A document in which rates or prices are recorded, a table of rates, a price-current.

Nirkhdárogha, H. (A. داروغه) A clerk of the market, an officer who regulates the prices at which articles are sold in a public market.

Nirkhí, H. (نرخي), *Nirkhyá*, Mar. (निरख्या) An officer who fixes or records the prices of articles.

Nirkhnáma, H. (P. نامه) A tariff, a price-current, a table of prices or rates.

Níru, Tam. (நீறு) Lime slaked and reduced to powder.

Niruttara, S. &c. (निरुत्तर) Having no answer, making no defence.

Nirvanşa, S. (निर्वंश) Extinct, as a family; being without family or descendants; unclaimed, as property to which there are no heirs.

Nirvishta, S. &c. (निर्विष्ट) Profit, wages, interest; gain by usury, agriculture, or service.

Nirvedhabhoga, S. (निर्वेधभोगः) Undisturbed possession, as the ground of a title to property.

Nişáb, H. (A. نصاب) Capital, property: in law, such an amount of property, whether in money, goods, or cattle, as being capable of increase, is liable to the payment of *zikát* or legal alms.

Nişár, H. (نثار) Money thrown amongst the people at processions or at festivals.

Nişf, H. &c. (A. نصف) Half, a half, a moiety.

Nisf-jamá, H. (A. جمع, rent) Half revenue assessment, latterly levied on the holders of resumed rent-free tenures.

Nisf-khiráj, H. (A. خراج, tax) Half assessment, remission of fifty per cent. on the revenue.

Nishádа, S. &c. (निषादः) An outcaste, applied by Manu to the son of a Brahman by a Şúdra female, but generally to any degraded caste, and especially to wild and barbarous tribes inhabiting forests and mountains in various parts of India.

Nishán, H. (P. نشان) A sign, a mark, an emblem, a signet, an ensign, a flag.

Nishánbardár, H. (P. بردار) A flag-bearer.

Nishán-i-Diwán, or *Diwáni*, H. (ديوان) The official mark or stamp of the *Diwán*, or of his office: the official mark and date endorsed on a royal grant made in the *Diwán's* office upon its being registered in his records.

Nishán-i-huzúr-navís, H. (A. P. حضورنويس) The official mark with the date and attestation of registry made by the *Názim*, upon the back of a royal grant after the *Nishán-i-Diwáni* has been affixed

Nishka, S. &c. (निष्क) A weight of gold, of varying amount.

Nishkar, Beng. (S. निष्कर) Exempt from tax.

Nishkraman, H. &c. (S. نشكرمن, निष्क्रमण) Going out, taking an infant out of the house for the first time, in the fourth month, when certain ceremonies are to be performed.

Nishpattí, Beng. (S. निष्पत्ति) Accomplishment, settlement, decision, award.

Nissar, Thug. Safe, secure; as a residence, a village, a place to commit murder, &c.

Nistár, H. &c. (نستار, निस्तार) Release, acquittal; rescue: salvation.

Nişuddhi, incorrectly, Nisudi, corruptly, Neeshoody, Tel. (నిశుద్ధి, S. निशुद्धि, purification) A mutual acquittance or release; settlement of an account; relinquishment of a right or claim.

NITÁNTÁGNYÁ, Beng. (S. নিতান্তাজ্ঞা, from নিতান্ত, final, and আজ্ঞা, order) Sentence, verdict, decree.

NITAR, Hindi (निटर) Poor, worn out by over culture—land.

NÍTI, S. &c. (नीति) Polity, ethics, justice.

NÍṬU-ASARÁBHÚMI, Tel. (నీటుఅసరాభూమి, ? for నీరు, or the inflex. నీటి) A field or land dependent for irrigation upon proximity to a tank or river.—Northern Sarkárs.

Nítukáluva, Tel. (నీటుకాలువ) A water-course, a *nalla* (see the last).—Northern Sarkárs.

NITYA, S. &c. (नित्य), sometimes vernacularly, NIT, as H. (نت), Mar. (नित, but more correctly, नित्य), NITTIYA, Tam. (நித்திய) Constant, invariable, eternal: NITTIYAM (adverbially), always, eternally.

Nitya karma, or *Nitya karm*, or *Nit-karm*, S. &c.(नित्यकर्म्म) Fixed and constant duty: the observance of prescribed rites and ceremonies, daily, or at defined periods, in opposition to *Naimittika karma*, or ceremonies performed occasionally, and at the pleasure of the parties.

Nityadattaka, or *d.-putra*, S. (नित्यदत्तकपुत्रः) A son adopted in a regular and legal manner, who thereby becomes a son for ever.

Nittiyapadi moyini, Tam. (நித்தியபடிமொயினி) Daily allowance in money for ceremonies in a temple.

Nityaśráddha, S. &c. (नित्यश्राद्ध) The prescribed obsequial sacrifices to deceased progenitors, and the *manes* in general.

NIVÁḌÁ, NIVÁṚÁ, or NIWÁṚÁ, Mar. (निवाडा) Settlement, adjustment, decision, especially on a disputed point. Tel. (నివాడా) Settlement of revenue: revenue accounts: settlement of accounts with the cultivators, or determination of the proportions in which the growing crop is to be divided.

Niváṛa patra, Mar. (निवाडपत्र) A written judgment or award, or the document recording it.

NÍVÁRA, S. &c. (नीवार) Rice or other grain growing with or without cultivation; also, *Nívára-dhányam* (from *dhányam*, grain).

NIVÁRAṆ-PÁTRA, Mar. (निवारणपत्र, from S. निवारण, prohibiting) A prohibitory note to one employed to demand payment of debts.

NIVARTTAN, Mar. (S. निवर्त्तन, lit., turning back) A measure of land, 20 square *Vansas*, or 4000 square cubits.

NÍVI, Karn. (S. ನೀವಿ) Capital, stock.

NIVESANAMU, Tel. (S. నివేశనము) Ground to the extent of 2400 feet square.

NIYAMA, or NIYAM, also, vernacularly, NEM, H. (نيم), Mar. (नेम), S. &c. (नियम) Fixed institute or observance: established practice: a rule or regulation, a statute: an agreement, a contract or engagement: also, *Niyáma*, but less usually.

Niyama, or *Niyáma karttá*, S. (from कर्त्ता, maker) A lawmaker, a legislator: the legislature.

Niyamapatra, S. &c. (नियमपत्र) A deed of agreement or assent, a contract, a written engagement.

Niyati, S. &c. (नियति) Rule, regulation, fixed or established practice.

NIYOGA, S. &c. (नियोग) An appointment, a delegated duty or office.

Niyoga dharma, S. (नियोगधर्म्म) Official duty or occupation: in one sense, the appointment of a kinsman to raise up issue by the wife of a childless husband, or one deceased without leaving children.

Niyukta, S. &c. (नियुक्त) Appointed, delegated; a fnnctionary, an appointed or delegated representative.

NOḌ, Beng. (নোড) Alloy, adulteration, a debased coin.

NOḌI, or NOT, Mal., Tam. (நொடி) A small measure of time, about four seconds.

NOKICHÁRTTA, Mal. (നൊക്കിചാൎത്ത) Statement of survey or computation from inspection of the quantity of seed required for sowing a field.

NONCHA, Hindi (नोनचा) Lands abounding with saline matter.

NONḌHA, Guz. (નોંધ) A note-book, a memorandum, a bill-book in which articles are entered in the order sold.

NOR, Mar. (नोर) Passage-money for persons or goods, fare, freight.

NOTA, Karn. (ನೋಟ), NOTTAM, Mal. (നൊട്ടം) Seeing, looking at, inspection, examination; inspection and exchanging of coins, shroffage; also, conjuring, fortune-telling, or sorcery. In Tam. *Nottam*, from *Nokha*, sight, applies to the examination of coins.

Noṭagára, Karn. (ನೋಟಗಾರ) An officer who keeps the money accounts of a village; also, a money-changer: a conjuror, a fortune-teller.

Noṭṭakarippa, Mal. (നൊട്ടക്കരിപ്പ) Counterfeit coin.

Noṭṭakáran, Mal. (നൊട്ടക്കാരൻ) A money-changer.

NUAPILA-CHÁṚIBÁR, Uriya (ନୁଆପିଲାଛାଡ଼ିବାର) Abandoning a new-born infant.

NUGAM, Tam. (நுகம்) A yoke for oxen (vernacular corruption of S. *Yugam*).

NÚKA, Tel. (నూక) Grain of any kind when half ground.

NUKṢÁN, incorrectly, NOKSAN, H. (A. نقصان) Loss, injury,

deficiency: loss upon alienated lands, deficit in the revenue returns.

Nukṣán-i-fáhish, H. (A., from فاحش, shameful) Gross inadequacy of price of an article sold, which, according to some lawyers, if effected by an agent, annuls the sale.

NÚL, Tam., Mal. (நூல்), NÚLU, Tel., Karn. (నూలు) Yarn, cotton-thread.

Núláṭa, Núlhe, or *Núlike*, Karn. (ನೂಲಾಟ, ನೂಲ್ಹೆ, ನೂಲಿಕೆ) Spinning.

Núluvaráṭne, Karn. (ನೂಲುವರಾಟ್ಣೆ) A cotton-spinning wheel.

Núláké, Núluvaḷu, Karn. (ನೂಲಾಕೆ, ನೂಲುವಳು) A spinning-woman.

Nultuṇi, Mal. (നൂൽതുണി) Cotton cloth, calico.

NULI, Karn. (ನುಲಿ) Any kind of hempen or *coir* string or rope.

NUMBERDÁR, or, more commonly, LUMBERDÁR, q. v., H. (نمبر, the English word 'number,' with P. *dár*, who has) The title of the person or persons in a village who represent the community in their financial dealings with the government, and who are registered in the collectors' books by a number as well as by name.

Number-karanam, used in Tam. (நம்பர்கரணம்) A village accountant in some of the Tamil districts, who was paid by a salary, and was numbered and registered in the collectors' books when the establishment of such accountants was first formed.

Numberwár-kharaḍá, or *-kharḍá*, Mar. (नंबरवारखरडा, from *kharḍá*, a diary) A record kept by the village accountant in the Dakhin of the fields of the village he is attached to, their quality, cultivation, and other particulars of the state of the village, according to a regular system of numbering.

NÚN, or NON, H. (نون, from S. *lavaṇa*) Salt.

Núnchai, H. (نونچي, from S. चय, a heap) A factitious salt made of the ashes of burnt straw previously steeped in brine, and used to adulterate culinary salt.

Núniá, H. (نونيا) A maker of, or dealer in, salt; a salt-petre maker.

Nuner, H. (نونير, नुनेर) Saline, as soil.

NÚNE, Tel. (నూనె) Oil, as ready for use.

NÚRBÁF, H. (P. نورباف) A Mohammadan weaver, especially of fine cloth like the Dacca muslin.

NÚRU, Tel. (నూరు) Threshing or treading out grain.

NUṢAIRÍ, H. (A. نصيري) A Mohammadan who believes in the divinity of *Áli*.

NUSKHA, H. (نسخه) A copy, an example, a specimen or draught of a writing, &c.

NUZÚL, NOOZOOL, H. (A. نزول) Descent: property which falls to the state from default of heirs, an escheat.

NYÁSA, vernacularly, NYÁS, S. &c. (न्यास) A deposit, a pledge.

NYÁT, or NYÁTI, Mar. (न्यात, न्याति, corruption of S. *Jnáti* ज्ञाति) Caste, kind, sort.

NYÁYA, vernacularly, NÍÁŎ, NIÁÏ, H. (نياو, نياي), S. &c. (न्याय) Propriety, fitness, reasoning, logic: in common use it frequently also denotes justice or judgment.

Nyáyádhikára, or *adhipati*, S. &c. (न्यायाधिकार:, न्यायाधिपति) Tel. (న్యాయాధిపతి) A judge, a magistrate.

Nyáyádhíṣa, corruptly, *Niadhis, Nyaeedaish*, Mar. (S. न्यायाधीश) A magistrate, a judge.

Nyáyádhiṣí, Mar. (S. न्यायधीशी) Magistracy, the office or function of a judge.

Nyámaṛ, Hindi (न्यामड) A tree that has sprung up of itself in a cultivated field, and which the cultivator may cut down.

O.

OBBIḌI, Tel. (ఒబ్బిడి) Treading out corn, threshing by means of cattle.

ÓḌA, Karn. (ಓಡ), ÓḌAM, Tam. (ஓடம்) A boat, a ferry-boat.

Óḍagár, Karn. (ಓಡಗಾರ) A ferryman.

ÓḌAI, Tam. (ஓடை) A water-course, a tank, a ditch.

OḌAṆ, or OṚAṆ, or ONḌ, Mar. (ओडण, ओंड) Deep, sunk capable of holding water, as ground fit for rice cultivation.

ODANA, or ODAN, S. &c. (ओदन) Boiled rice.

ODAVÁRAM, more correctly, UDAVÁRAM, Tam. (ஓடவாரம்) Actual gross produce.

ODE, or ORRE, Tel. (ఒడె) A rick of corn, or a small pile just cut with the sickle.

ODEYA, ODEYAVA, or OḌIYA, or, as used honorifically in the plur., and as usually pronounced, WODEYAR, or WODIYA, Karn. (ಒಡೆಯ, ಒಡೆಯವ, ಒಡಿಯ, ಒಡೆಯರು) A lord, a chief, a ruler, a sovereign.

OḌHAṆ, Mar. (ओढण) The balance of a closed account carried forward and placed at the head of one newly opened: descent (of a belief, practice, usages, &c.) through several generations.

Oḍhanbákí, incorrectly, *Odambaki*, Mar. (A. باقي, remainder) Balance of account carried forward from year to year, especially in revenue matters, &c.: account with the cultivators.

Oḍi, pronounced Wodi, Karn. (ಒಡಿ) A division of a rice field.

Oḍiyá, Uriya (ଓଡ଼ିଆ, S. ओड्र) The people, language, &c., of Orissa.

Ogal, (?) Hindi. Buck wheat.—Kamaon.

Ogaruvumúta, Tel. (ఒగరువుమూట) An allowance of grain given to the measurers of the crop.

Ogát, Guz. (ઓગાટ) Remains of grass left by cattle on a field.

Oggá, Karn. (ಒಗ್ಗ) Seed for sowing.

Ogha, vernacularly, Ogh, S. &c. (ओघ) A torrent, a strong current or stream.

Oghal, Mar. (ओघळ) A small stream, a rill, a rivulet; also, a ravine.

Ogudu, Tel. (ఒగుడు) The straw of the great millet.

Ohdah, more correctly, Ûhdah, q. v. H. (A. عهده), Odho, Guz. (ઓધો) An office, whether civil or military.

Ohdahdár, incorrectly, *Odadár*, correctly, *Ûhdahdár*, Guz. *Odhedár*, H. (P. دار, who has) An office, a functionary, a public servant, whether civil or military.

Ojan, Beng. (ওজন, corruption of وزن, *wazan*) Weight, measure.

Ojandár, Beng. (ওজনদার) A weighman.

Ojhá, H. (اوجها, ओझा) The title of the head priest of the temple of *Vaidyanáth*, at *Deogarh* in *Birbhúm*. A conjuror, a sorcerer. Beng. (ওঝা) A snake-catcher, one who pretends to cure snake bites, and cast out evil spirits by charms. Uriya (ଓଝ) A schoolmaster: thc signature of a certain caste.

Ojja, Tel. (ఒజ్జ) A teacher, a priest.

Okatí, Mar. (ओकती) An apparatus for drawing water from a well, the transverse beam and stone weight; also the bucket.

Okil, Beng. and Uriya (ওকিল, corruption of *Vakil*) An agent, an attorney.

Okálat, Beng. and Uriya (ওকালত, corruption of *Wahálat*) Agency, representative, acting as agent or attorney.

Okkaliga, or Okkalu, pronounced Wokkaliga and Wokkalu, Vuccaloo, Karn. (ಒಕ್ಕಲಿಗ, ಒಕ್ಕಲು) A cultivator, a farmer, a tenant of the soil, an inhabitant.

Okkalatana, or *Wokhalatana*, Karn. (ಒಕ್ಕಲತನ) Husbandry, cultivation: residence, residing.

Okkalihamane, or *Wokkalihamane*, Karn. (ಒಕ್ಕಲಿಹಮನೆ) A farm-house, any occupied or inhabited house.

Okkalu-jamad-álu, corruptly, *Vuccáloo-jummed-aloo*, Karn. (ಒಕ್ಕಲುಜಮದಾಲು) A slave, especially a predial or agricultural slave, a labourer (*álu*) attached to the revenue (*jamá*) lands.—Coorg. Correctly speaking, there are two chief classes of slaves recognised in the province—*Bhúmi-jamad-álu*, and *Okhala-jamad-álu*: the first are attached to the land (*bhúmi*), and only transferable with it; the second are the personal property of their possessors, and may be sold or mortgaged at pleasure.

Okkaṇa, Tel. (ఒక్కణ), Okkane, Okkanike, Wokkane, &c. Karn. (ಒಕ್ಕಣೆ, ಒಕ್ಕಣಿಕೆ) The honorific title placed at the top of a letter or petition.

Okkula, Karn. (ಒಕ್ಕುಲ) A measure of grain containing 71 lb. 4 oz. avoirdupois.

Ol, Mar. (ओल) Moisture, damp.

Olá, Mar. (ओला) Moist, humid.

Oláchá, Mar. (ओलाचा) Cultivated, produced, &c., without irrigation or rain, from the inherent humidity of the soil.

Oládukal, or *-kál*, Mar. (ओलादुकल, -काल) A famine, the consequence of excessive rain.

Ol, H., Mar. (ओल, اول) Personal bail or security, a hostage, a surety.

Olí-ág, Mar. (ओलीआग, lit., wet fire) Any calamity occasioned by superabundant moisture, as a flood, &c.

Óla, corruptly, Ool, Olly, Mal. (ഓല), Ólai, Tam. (ஓலை), Ole, Karn. (ಓಲೆ) The leaf of any kind of palm, especially, though not exclusively, applied to the leaf as used for writing upon.

Olapura, Mal. (ഓലപ്പുര) A house thatched with leaves.

Olapeṭṭi, Mal. (ഓലപ്പെട്ടി) A box in which title deeds or other documents written on *olas*, or palm leaves, are preserved.

Olaikúḍu, Tam. (ஓலைக்கூடு) An umbrella or covering of palm leaves to keep off rain.

Paṭṭolai, Tam. (பட்டோலை) An edict or official order, any thing written upon palm leaves from dictation.

Olaga, Karn. (ಓಲಗ) An assembly, a meeting, holding a *darbár*, or levee, a meeting in a *kachhari*, for public business: in the latter sense it is also written *Oḍḍólaga* (ಒಡ್ಡೋಲಗ).

Olaṣe, Olase, Olise, Karn. (ಒಲಶೆ, ಒಲಸೆ, ಒಲಿಸೆ) Migration of the people of a district through fear of war, pestilence, &c.

Olá-utha, Beng. (ওলাউঠা) Spasmodic cholera (from *ola*, descent, and *uthá*, rising), upward and downward evacuations.

Olekára, Karn. (ఒలెకార) A servant, an armed *peon.*

Óli, Tel. (ఓలి) A marriage portion, what is given to a wife at her marriage by her relations, and consequently becomes her peculiar property.

Ólu, Karn. (ఓలు) A pledge, a hostage, a ransom.

Óḻugu, Tam. (ஒழுகு) An account kept by the village accountant of the measurement and extent of the fields composing a village.

Om, S. &c. (ओम) The mystic monosyllable to be uttered previously to any prayer, but so as not to be overheard by ears profane; supposed to consist of three letters, *a, u, m,* combined, being types of the three *Vedas,* or of the three great divinities, *Brahmá, Vishnu,* and *Siva.*

Omkara, S. &c. (ओंकार) The mystical syllable *Om*: see the last.

Ombí, Mar. (ओंबी) An ear of wheat.

Onḍá, or **Wanḍá**, corruptly, **Woonda**, Mar. (ओंडा, वंडा) A billet, a log of wood.

Onḍápaṭṭí, corruptly, *Woondapuṭṭy*, Mar. (ओंडापट्टी) A tax imposed in commutation of the labour of cutting logs for government use.

Onḍu, Karn. (ఒండు) Alluvial deposit, sediment, soil.

Ongalu, Karn. (ఒంగలు) An offering by farmers in a field before harvest.

Oppa, Mal. (ഒപ്പ), **Oppam**, Tam. (ஒப்பம்) Signature, subscription, a certificate.

Oppachāram, Tam., Karn. (ஒப்பாசாரம்) A contract, an engagement, a bond.

Oppandam, Tam. (ஒப்பந்தம்), *Oppanda*, Karn. (ఒప్పంద) A compact, an agreement, a contract.

Oppitta, Karn. (ఒప్పిత్త) Consent, agreement, signature, subscription.

Oppittaḍakágada, Karn. (ఒప్పిత్తడకాగద) A signed paper, an executed deed or bond.

Oppumoḻi, or *-mozhi*, Tam. (ஒப்புமொழி) A written agreement between two parties.

Oppukánam, also read *Opakánam*, Mal. (ഒപ്പുകാണം) Fee or present given on execution and signature of documents relating to sale or mortgage of land.

Kaiyoppam, Tam. (கையொப்பம்) Signature, certificate, the act of authenticating a document by subscription, or the document subscribed.

Oppaḍi-tugayéḍu, Tam. (ஒப்படி-துகையேடு) Abstract statement shewing receipts, disbursements, and balance in hand.

Or, H. (اور) Boundary, limit, way, direction.

Orá, **Ohará**, Mar. (ओरा, ओहरा) One of the portions of a field which are ploughed separately by concentric turns of the plough.

Orapu, Karn. (ఒరపు) Ebbing, going down: a ridge in a paddy field: a channel.

Oravi, **Oravu**, **Orave**, Karn. (ఒరవి, ఒరవు, ఒరవె) A marsh or swamp; surplus water running from a tank.

Oravinahola, Karn. (ఒరవినహొల) A swampy field.

Orre, Tel. (ఒర్రె) A heap of unthreshed grain.

Oṛuka, Mal. (ഒഴുക) An account of lands and gardens in which the boundaries are specified.

Oṛukal, Mal. (ഒഴുകൽ) Flowing or running of water.

Oṛukka, Mal. (ഒഴുക്ക) A current, a stream.

Os, Mar. (ओस) Deserted, a village; uncultivated, neglected, land.

Osá, Mar. (ओसा) A blank spot in a corn-field.

Osul, Uriya (ଓସୁଲ, corruption of *wasúl*) Payment, collection; realized as a debt or as revenue.

Oswál, Hindi (ओसवाल) The name of a tribe of Jains, chiefly merchants and bankers.

Otárí, less correctly, **Wotárí**, Mar. (ओतारी) A brazier, a caster of vessels of bell-metal, also of brass idols.

Oṭbandí, (?) Mar. Payment of a fixed amount for the use of each plough and pair of bullocks.—*Khandesh.* Beng. (ওটবন্দী) Settlement of rent to be paid for cultivating waste land. See *Utbandi.*

Oṭi, Mal. (ഒടി) A piece of rice-ground.

Ottadam, (?) Tam. A crop cultivated jointly with other crops on the same land.

Oṭṭai, Tam. (ஒட்டை) A span between the tips of the thumb and forefinger extended.

Oṭṭam, Tam. (ஒட்டம்) A conical pile of earth left by tank diggers as a measure of the depth to which they have dug.

Oṭṭan, Tam. (ஒட்டன்), Karn. *Odda*, or *Oddarava*, pronounced *Wodda* (ఒడ్డ, ఒడ్డరవ) A ditch or tank digger, a stonecutter. See the next.

Oṭṭiyam, Tam. (ஒட்டியம்) The country to the north of Madras, whence the tank diggers come, or, in fact, Orissa: the *Odhra* of Sanskrit, the *Uriya* of the current dialect, whence the people employed in this kind of labour in the south of India are said to have originally come.

Oṭṭam, Tam. (ஒட்டம்) A contract, an agreement.

Odambadike, Tel. (ఒడంబడికె) A contract, an agreement, a bond.

OTTI, corruptly, OOTTY, Tam. (ஒத்தி, ஒற்றி), Mal. (ഒററി), Karn. (ಒತ್ತಿ) A pledge, a pawn, a mortgage: in Malabar it especially designates a usufructuary mortgage, or one in which, for consideration of a sum advanced on loan, the borrower makes over the land of which he is the hereditary proprietor to a temporary occupant, who receives the rent or profits in lieu of interest on his loan, paying the difference, if his receipts exceed the interest, to the proprietor: the borrower or lender may transfer the occupancy to a third party, under certain conditions, but the latter is not at liberty to sell it, and is responsible for any damage done to the trees on the estate. The term is also sometimes used for the document of assignment or mortgage-deed. (Although written *Otti* by all the best authorities, it is also written in Tam. and Mal. *Orri*, and *Orri* (ஒற்றி, ഒററി), both, however, being always pronounced *Ottí*. In Mal. it also occurs, at least in composition, *Atti*, *Otti*, with the initial short vowel, or *o*, and cerebral *t*. See *Attiper*: (in Tam. and Karn. the *t* is dental).

Ottidravyam, Mal. (ഒട്ടിദ്രവ്യം, from S. द्रव्य, wealth) The money advanced on usufructuary mortgage.

Ottikamparam, corruptly, *Otty-koomprom*, Mal. (ഒട്ടികമ്പരം) A subsequent transaction, in which, for a further loan, the proprietor abandons finally to the mortgagee two-thirds of his hereditary rights and authority over the estate.

Ottikaranam, Mal. (ഒട്ടികരണം) The deed or instrument conveying the property to the mortgagee.

Ottikurikánam, less correctly, *Kulikánam*, Mal. (ഒട്ടിക്കുഴികാണം) A mortgage in which it is conditioned either that the occupant shall be at liberty to relinquish the estate without charge for dilapidations, ten per cent. of the principal loan being deducted to cover all injuries; or that the owner may reclaim it when he pleases; in which case he is to pay for any additional plantations or other improvements.

Ottikondavan, Mal. (ഒട്ടികൊണ്ടവൻ) A mortgagee, lit., the purchaser of a freehold.

Ottiper, or *Attiper*, Mal. (ഒട്ടിപെറ, അട്ടിപെറ) Freehold hereditary property: it is used laxly for the absolute transfer of such property.

Ottiporai-nir, (Mal. നീര, water) Ratification of an absolute and final transfer of hereditary property, by the proprietor pouring a little water into the hand of the purchaser.

Ottiperrola, and *Ottiperrola-karanam*, Mal. (*Ottiper*, or *Attiper*, as above, *ola* (ഓല), a palm leaf, and *karanam* (കരണം), a deed) The written and executed deed by which a hereditary property is absolutely sold; hence, also, the title-deeds of an estate.

OTTU, Karn. (ಒಟ್ಟು) Whole, total, aggregate amount.

Ottuchekachéri, Karn. (ಒಟ್ಟುಚೆಕಚೇರಿ) The chief post office.

Ottuguttige, Karn. (ಒಟ್ಟುಗುತ್ತಿಗೆ) The entire assessment.

Ottujameyádahana, Karn. (ಒಟ್ಟುಜಮೆಯಾದಹಣ) The total collection of the revenue of a district.

OVA, Tel. (ఒవ) Cut corn, but unthreshed.

OVANDÁ, OWANDÁ, vulgarly, WOWANDA, Mar. (ओवंडा) The holding and cultivating of lands which lie beyond the lands of the village in which the cultivator resides; also the lands so held and cultivated: hence the carrying on of any business at a distance, or part in one place and part in another.

Owandekarí, corruptly, *Wowand kurree*, Mar. (ओवंडकरी) A person living in one place and cultivating land in another.

P.

PÁ, H. &c. (پا, abbreviation of *Páda*, q. v.) A foot, a leg.

Páyáb, H. (P., from یافتن *yáftan*, to find) Fordable, a ford.

PÁCHAKA, S. &c. (पाचक) Causing to come to maturity; also, digestive, cooking, dressing; subst., a cook.

PACHÁR, (?) H. The designation of the lands and villages lying farthest from the banks of the Jamuná in the district of Etawa.

PACHBHEYA, Thug. A sect or division of the Thugs.

PACHCHADAMU, vulgarly, PATCH, Tel. (పచ్చడము) A particular kind of cotton cloth, generally twenty-four cubits long and two broad: two cloths joined together.

PACHCHÁKU, pron. PATSÁKU, vulgarly, PUTCHUCK, or PUTSAK, Tel. (పచ్చాకు) lit., A green leaf, but applied especially to an aromatic plant long cultivated in India, and thence exported by the ancients under its Sanskrit appellation, *Kushtha* (Costus indicus, or, as forming a new genus, Aucklandia costus verus).

PÁCHH, H. (پاچھ) Inoculation, inoculating.

PACHHAL, Uriya (ପଛଲ) A place where saline earth is prepared.

PACHKÍ, Mar. (पचकी) A small copper coin equivalent to a *Damri*, or fourth of a *Paisa*.

PACHPACH, Hindi (पचपच) Soft or plashy, as soil: rotten vegetable matter and mud.

PACHWÁÍ, or PACHWÍ, corruptly, PUCHWYE, H. (پچهواي, پچهوي) An intoxicating drink prepared from the fermentation of rice or other grains steeped in water.

PÁD, vulgarly, PAUD, (?) Mar. A measure of land equal to twenty *káthís*.

PAD, PADA, PÁDA, S., but occurring in all the dialects (पद्, पदः, पादः), the word also occurs, vernacularly modified in various forms, as, PÁ, PÁÍ, PÁNW, pron. PÁOṆ, H. (پانو , پاي , پا), PÁ, Beng. (পা), PÁ, PÁÚL, Mar. (पा, पाऊल) A foot, a footstep. *Pada*, &c. have other meanings also, among which *Páda*, implies a fourth, a quarter, the only sense properly attributable to its modifications, as PÁÍ, Beng., Mar. (পাই, पाई), PÁE, Uriya (ପାଏ), and PÁO, H. (پاو), but these terms are used with great laxity, and often, in their derivatives and compounds, imply also, a foot.

Páda-kánikai, Tam. (பாதகாணிக்கை) An offering to the feet, applied to a contribution paid to the *Guru*, or head of a religious establishment.

Pádárghya, vernacularly, *Padárgh*, or *Pádárgh*, corruptly, *Pudaruch*, *Pudarg*, H. &c. (S. پدارگه , پادارگه , पादार्घ्य) A respectful offering of curds, honey, &c., to a guest or Brahman; lit. an *arghya*, or offering to his feet, whence it has come to signify also an assignment of rent-free land to a Brahman, a religious person, or a religious establishment: in the north-west it is said to be a grant of rent-free land to similar objects made by a Zamindár, and for the revenue of which he continues responsible.

Padáta, *Padáti*, *Padátika*, S. &c. (पदात, पदाति, पदातिक, from *pada*, a foot) A footman, a foot-soldier, an armed retainer or messenger, whence the vernacular *Piáda*, and *Páïk*, and the English *Peon*, q. v.

Páda-vandaniká, S. (पाद and वंदन, salutation) Property given by a husband to a wife at the time of marriage in return for her humble salutation or marks of deference.

Pádodaka, S. &c. (पाद and उदक, water) Water in which the feet of a Brahman have been washed, and which it is an act of merit to drink.

Pádya, S. &c. (पाद्य) Relating to the feet, water for washing them.

PADA, S. &c. (पद) A head, title, or topic of legal or judicial proceedings, of which eighteen are enumerated by Hindu law-givers; as, 1. *Ṛinádána*, debt; 2. *Nikshepa*, deposits; 3. *Aswámi-vikraya*, sale without ownership; 4. *Sambhúya-samutthána*, concerns among partners; 5. *Dattápakarma*, resumption of gifts; 6. *Vetanádánam*, non-payment of wages or hire; 7. *Samvid-vyatikrama*, breach of engagement; 8. *Kraya-vikrayánuṣaya*, rescission of purchase and sale; 9. *Swámipála-viváda*, disputes between master and servant; 10. *Símáviváda*, boundary disputes; 11. *Daṇḍapárushya*, assault and battery; 12. *Vákpárushya*, defamation and abuse; 13. *Steya*, theft; 14. *Sáhasa*, violence; 15. *Strísangrahana*, illicit intercourse with women; 16. *Strípundharma*, obligations of husband and wife; 17. *Dáyavibhága*, partition of inheritance; 18. *Dyútamáhvayascha*, gaming and animal-fighting.

Padasankírṇa, S. (पदसंकीर्ण) A mixed plaint in a suit at law.

PÁDA, S. &c. (पादः) A quarter, as before; but as a term in Hindu law it signifies one of the four steps or stages by which a law-suit is directed to proceed, viz.

1. *Bháshápáda*, (from भाषा, speech) The declaration, the charge or plaint.

2. *Uttarapáda*, (from उत्तर, an answer) The reply or defence.

3. *Kriyápáda*, (from क्रिया, action) The essential matter, the evidence or proofs, whether oral or documentary.

4. *Sádhyasiddhi-páda*, (from साध्य, what is to be established, the fact, and सिद्धि, establishment) The judgment or decision.

PADA, S. &c. (पदः) Place, station, rank.

Padastha, S. &c. (पदस्थः), A person of rank or authority.

Padaví, vernacularly, *Padabí*, S. &c. (पदवी) A title, rank, dignity.

PAḌA, or PAṚA, Mar. (पड) Fallow land.

Paḍakara, or *Paṛkara*, Mar. (पडकर) Lying fallow, a field: being deserted or desolate, a village.

Paḍasara, or *Paḍasára*, Mar. (पडसर -सार) Uncultivated, desolate, uninhabited.

Paḍít, Mar. (पडीत) Fallow or uncultivated land.

Paḍiyá, Tel. (పడియా) Fallow, uncultivated, waste.

PÁḌÁ, or PÁṚÁ, Mar. (पाडा), PAḌÁGAI, Tam. (படாகை) A cluster of cottages situated at some distance from the village to which they belong, for the convenience of carrying on agricultural operations. See *Páṛá*.

PAḌÁ, or PAṚÁ, Uriya (ପଡ଼ା) A village; a ward of a town.

PADAKKAM, Tam. (பதக்கம்) A certain number of villages held in farm in Tanjore under the native government.

Padakatár, Tam. (பதக்கத்தார்) The renter or farmer of a number of villages.

PAḌAKATHA, vulgarly, PAR-KATH, Mar. (पडकथ) The lending of cattle and labour by one cultivator to another.

Paḍakel, vulgarly, *Paṛkel*, Mar. (पडकेल) A cultivator that helps another with labour, cattle, and the like.

PÁDAKAL, or PÁDEKAL, (?) Mal. Land exempt from revenue.

PAḌANA, Mal. (പടന) A salt pan, a salt-pit.

Padanayuppa, Mal. (പടനയുപ്പ) Manufactured salt.

PAḌAPPAM, Tam. (படப்பம்) A town surrounded by villages.

Paḍappai, Tam. (படப்பை) A yard or inclosure behind a house.

PÁDAR, Guz. (પાદર) Common land, land adjacent to a village left uncultivated.

PADARAM, (?) Mal. A fee paid to the Rája, or his representative, on a transfer of landed property.

PADÁRTHA, S. &c. (पदार्थ, from *pada*, a name, and *artha*, object) Thing, substance, a category or predicament, in logic: in Karnata, personal property, money.

PAḌASÁKSHA, or PAṚSÁKSHA, Mar. (पडसाक्ष) Corroborative evidence.

Paḍasákshí, *Paṛsákshí*, Mar. (पडसाक्षी) A witness giving corroborative testimony.

PAḌATÍ, Uriya (ପଡତି) Waste salt.

PADDU, Tel. (పద్దు) An entry in an account, an item, a memorandum.

PAḌE, Karn. (ಪಡೆ) A servant, a messenger, a *Peon*.

PAḌI, corruptly, PUDDEE, Tam. (படி), Karn. (ಪಡಿ) A measure of capacity at Madras, one-eighth of a *marakál*, being the same with the *náḷi*, or *názhi*, and containing 93.752 cubic inches, or about 3 lb. 6 oz.: in the revised scale of weights and measures it is identified with the English term 'measure,' the standard being a cylinder of 4 inches diameter and 8 inches deep, containing 100 cubic inches, or 1.44 quart, or in weight of water about 3 lb. 6 oz. avoirdupois: a *Paḍi* is also a measure of weight equal to 100 *palams*, or 125 oz. avoirdupois. In Mysore it is a measure of weight equal to half a *sér*.

Paḍihaṭṭu, Karn. (ಪಡಿಹಟ್ಟು) Weight, measure.

PAḌI, Tam., Karn. (படி) *Bhata*, additional or extra allowance to servants, troops, public functionaries, or establishments.

Paḍichára, Karn. (ಪಡಿಚಾರ) A police-officer, an armed footman.

Paḍihana, Karn. (ಪಡಿಹಣ) Extra allowance in money.

Paḍijita, Karn. (ಪಡಿಜೀತ) Pay or allowance in kind.

Paḍippanam, Tam. (படிப்பணம்) Extra allowance.

Paḍimuṛai, Tam. (படிமுறை) The fixed day or term for which extra allowance is granted.

Paḍittaram, Tam. (படித்தரம்) Allowance made to a temple.

Paḍiyáḷ, Tam. (படியாள்) A hired servant, especially one paid with grain.

PÁDÍ, vulgarly, PADDY, Malay (پادي) Rice in the husk, whether growing or cut, before threshing or before the grain is separated.

PADÍ, Beng. (পাদী) Tonnage, measurement of boats or ships for cargo.

PÁḌI, Karn. (ಪಾಡಿ) Difference of exchange in money.

PADIKÁ, Uriya (ପଡ଼ିକା) A measuring rod.

PADKÁ, (?) H. A measure of land, a subdivision of a *kaṭṭhá*.

PADMA, vernacularly, PADAM, PUDUM, S. &c. (पद्म) A lotus, a large number, a thousand millions.

PADRI, (?) Hindi. A capitation tax on artificers and traders in central India.—Malcolm.

PÁDRÍ, H. &c. (پادري, Port. *Padre*) The common term throughout India for a Missionary or a clergyman.

PÁDSHÁH, H. &c. (P. پادشاه) A king.

Pádsháhí, H. &c. (پادشاهي) Royal, imperial, made or given by a sovereign, as a grant of land, &c.

PÁḌU, Tel. (పాడు) Waste, uncultivated, fallow; also, subs. a waste, a common, a barren or uncultivated tract.

Páḍubhúmi, or *Páṭibhumi*, or *Páṭinéla*, Tel. (పాడుభూమి, పాటిభూమి, పాటినేల) A spot of ground near a village formerly inhabited, but now cultivated for tobacco.

Paḍunilam, Tam. (படுநிலம்) Barren ground.

PÁḌU, Tam. (பாடு) Deficiency on remeasurement.

PADUGAI, or PADUGAI-SATTURAM, Tam. (படுகை-, படுகைசத்துரம்) Land in the bed or on the banks of a river, especially fit for rice cultivation.

Padugar, Tam. (படுகர்) Ground fit for moist cultivation, rice-ground.

PAḌUGU, Tel. (పడుగు) The lower part of a heap of corn, or part left after the rest has been carried away. Karn. A heap of ears of corn piled in a threshing-floor, ready to be trodden out.

Paḍudáṛal, Tam. (படுதாறல்) Part of a crop decayed while standing.

PADUNU, or PADANU, Tel. (పదును, పదను) Moisture: a certain quantity of rain, sufficient to soften the earth and render it fit for ploughing: soil well moistened, miry or plashy ground.

Padunuvarshamu, Tel. (పదునువర్షము) Rain sufficient to penetrate the soil and soften it for ploughing.

Padupor, Tam. (படுபோர்) A heap of corn which has been cut, but remains unthreshed till the whole is reaped.

Paḍuvari, Tel. (పడువరి) A spontaneous crop, sprouts that have sprung up from grain left by the reapers.

PÁG, and PAGRÍ, or PUGREE, H. (پاگ , پگري) A turban: in the Delhi districts, a poll-tax formerly levied on all males above twelve years of age in villages assessed under a peculiar system. See *Chaubachha*.

PAG, PUG, H. (پگ), Mar. (पग) A foot.

Pagdanḍí, H. (پگڈنڈي) A bye-way, a foot-path.

Pagí, H. (پگي) A caste, or individual of it, who are employed to track thieves or runaways by their footmarks.

Paglá, Mar. (पगला) A village servant or officer in the west of India, whose duty it was to track fugitives and thieves by their footmarks from one village to another, which was then to take up the search: wherever the footmarks ceased the nearest village was made responsible for any property stolen.

PÁGÁ, Mar. (पागा) A body of horse under one commander, and in which the horses belong to the state: the stable or building where the horses are kept.

Págádár, Mar. (पागादार) A horseman, a trooper whose horse is provided by the state.

Págánavís, or *Págnís*, Mar. (पागानवीस, पागनीस) The writer and accountant attached to a body of horse.

PAGADI, corruptly, PUGDI, Karn. (ಪಗಡಿ), PAKUDI, or PAGUDI, Tam. (பகுதி) Toll, tribute, tax: applied also in Karnata to an extra assessment under the Mohammadan government, or to any addition to the fixed rates.

Pagudikáran, Tam. (பகுதிக்காரன்) A collector, a tax-gatherer.

PAGAI, corruptly, PUGGYE, (?) Mar. An advance made by government or the collector to cultivators at the sowing season, to be repaid at the harvest: (it is no doubt a blunder for *Tagai*. See *Takávi*).

PAGÁR, Mar. (Port. पगार) Pay, wages: also a sort of canoe carefully finished.

PÁGÁR, Beng. (পাগার) A mound, a bank, a drain, a ditch, a boundary.

PAGHÁIÁ, H. (پگهايا) A dealer in metals, cloth, &c.

PAGODA, (?). The European designation of a Hindu temple in the south of India; also the gold coin formerly coined at Madras, from its having the device of a temple on one face, but called by the natives *Hun* and *Varahá*: (the origin of this term is doubtful; it is sometimes ascribed to the Portuguese, sometimes to the Persian *But-khada*, an idol-temple, or to the name of the goddess *Bhagavatí*, who is represented on some of the coins; but neither rests upon sufficient authority).

PAGRI, (?) Land rent-free.—Central India. Malcolm.

PÁH, (?) Land which has been three years in cultivation (?).

Páh-parti, (?) Fallow land.

PÁHAL, Hindi (पाहल) The ceremony of initiation into the Sikh religion and community.

PÁHAN, Hindi (पाहन) A village officer, the head man of a village.—South-west frontier.

PAHÁṆÍ, corruptly, PAHṆY, PAHY$_N$Y, Mar. (पहाणी, from पहाणे, to inspect, to see) Inspection or supervision: in finance, a revenue survey, an inspection or numbering of lands, houses, &c.: commonly applied also to an estimate of the value of a growing crop by inspection only; more correctly termed *Najar-paháṇí* (from *Nazr*, seeing).

Paháṇa-, or *Paháṇí-dár*, Mar. (पहाण-, पहाणीदार) A revenue surveyor, an inspector and valuer of crops.

Paháṇí-kárkún, Mar. (कारकून, an agent) A surveyor or inspector of crops.

Paháṇa khardá, Mar. (from खरडा, report) A revenue survey report.

Paháṇyá, Mar. (पहाण्या) A conjuror, especially one who pretends to be able to discover lost or stolen articles.

PAHÁṚ, H. &c. (S. پهاڑ , पहाड), PÁHÁṚ, Beng. (পাহাড) A mountain, a hill.

Pahárgutta, Tel. (from గుత్త, rent) A tax or rent formerly paid for the privilege of grazing cattle on the hills.

Pahárí, or *Páhárí*, H. &c. (پهاڑي) A hill man, a mountaineer: hilly, mountainous, a tract.

PAHAR, PUHUR, H. &c. (پهر , S. प्रहर), PAHÁR, Mar. (पहार) A division of time, a watch or period of three hours, or an eighth of the day and night, four to each, whence *Dopahar*, two watches, is either mid-day or midnight.

Pahárá, Mar. (पहारा) A guard, a body of men keeping watch or guard.

Pahárekarí, Mar. (पहारेकरी) A sentinel, a guard.

Paharí or *Pahrí*, H. (پهري) A watchman, a village servant and messenger, also employed to keep watch.

PÁHÍ, H. (پاهي , पाही), Uriya (ପାହି) A non-resident cultivator, a temporary occupant of village land, a tenant at will: (the word is more commonly, but less correctly, written *Pái*, for it is derived from the Hindi *páh*, for *pás*, 'near to,' he who resides permanently, not in the village in which he cultivates, but in the vicinity or near to it.

Páhi-asámí, H. (پاهي اسامي) A non-resident cultivator, one who cultivates lands in a village in which he is not a permanent resident.

Páhi-kásht, H. (پاهي کاشت) Cultivation by non-resident cultivators or tenants at will: it is rather laxly applied also to such a cultivator.

Páhi-malangi, Uriya (ପାହିମଲଙ୍ଗି) A salt-maker in a village different from that of his permanent residence.

PAHON, (?) In the Ramgarh hills, the village priest who performs the worship of the local deities, and keeps also a record of the village boundaries, for which he receives fees in kind from the villagers.

PÁÍ, H. &c. (پاي), PÁY, Mar. (पाय) A foot.

Pái-band, H. (P. بند, binding) Fettered, bound: a fetter.

Pái-báḳí, H. (A. باقي, remainder, *quasi*, balance at the foot, *i.e.* in hand or in reserve). In Mohammadan finance, the designation of such lands as were set apart for Jagír grants, if required: also the revenue from lands so reserved not yet alienated, and of lands which, having been alienated, had been resumed and paid revenue until a fresh assignment had been made.

Pái-baki-khálisa, H. (from خالصه, the royal treasury) The revenue of resumed or lapsed but suspended alienations receivable in the public treasury.

Páidakhti, (?) A tax formerly imposed by the Zamindárs of Bengal upon the cultivators, to cover the expense of presents to the revenue-officers.

Páik, or *Páyik*, corruptly, *Pyke*, H. &c. (پايك, from S. पदातिक), *Páik*, or *Páyak*, Mar. (पाईक, पायक) A footman, an armed attendant or inferior police or revenue-officer, a messenger, a courier, a village watchman: in Cuttack the *Páiks* formerly constituted a local militia, holding land of the Zamindárs or Rájas by the tenure of military service, an arrangement not unknown in other parts of India. Ben. Reg. ii. 1797; xiii. 1805; xiv. 1816.

Páikán, H. &c. (plur. of *Páik*) Armed militia or watchmen: assignments of land for their maintenance, made formerly by the Zamindárs, of which the revenue was an admitted deduction from the total assessment.

Páimál, H. (P. پاي مال) Trodden under foot, spoiled, ruined.

Páimálí, H. (پاي مالي) Trampling under foot, laying waste, especially as crops: compensation for damage done to standing crops by the passage of troops.

PÁÍ, Beng. (পাই), Mar. (पाई) A quarter, a fourth part; in currency, the fourth part of an *ana*, but applied in Bengal to a smaller division, or one twelfth, which was formerly a money of account, but, since 1835, has been struck of copper, weighing $33\frac{1}{3}$ grains.

PÁÍ, H. (پاي, पाई) A non-resident cultivator: (the word is given both singly and in composition by unquestionable authority, but it is probably an error, or vernacular corruption of *páhí*, q. v.).

Pái-asámí, H. (پاي اسامي) A cultivator of lands in a village in which he is not a permanent resident.

Páikári, or, more correctly, *Payahári*, Tel. (పయహారి) A temporary tenant who usually receives a larger share of the crop than a resident or permanent occupant.

Páikásht, corruptly, *Pykaust*, *Pykausht*, *Paikashtee*, *Paykasht*, &c. H. (پاي کاشت) The term usually employed in Hindustan for a migratory or non-resident cultivator, one who cultivates lands in a village to which he does not belong by birth or hereditary claim, and holds his lands either for a stipulated term, or at pleasure of some member or members of the proprietary body: in some districts, probably with more accuracy, the term occurs *Páhí-kásht*.

Páikásht-râiyat, H. (A. رعيت, a cultivator) A non-resident or temporary cultivator.

Páikásht-zamín, H. (A. زمين) Land held on the tenure of temporary occupancy.

Pái-nowád, Hindi (पाईनोवाद, vernacular corruption for *nau-abád*) A non-resident cultivator who engages to cultivate for the current year.

Pái-râiyat, H. (پاي رعيت) A non-resident cultivator.

Pái-sábek, Hindi (पाईसाबेक) A non-resident cultivator who has held the lands he tills for more than a year: an item of the village rent-roll shewing the rent paid by such cultivators.

PÁÍBÁ, Uriya (ପାଇବା) A debt to be received, money due.

Paíbáwálá, Uriya (ପାଇବାୱାଲା) A creditor, one who receives or expects payment.

PAIGASTI, Tel. (పయిగస్తి, from పై *pai*, over) A superintendant, an overseer.

PAIJ, Mar. (पैज) A bargain, a compact, a wager.

PAIKÁ, Mar. (पैका), PAIKAMU, Tel. (పయికము) Money: in Tel. it also means a small coin of the value of five *kás*, also a quarter of a *dab*.

PAIKÁR, H. (پيکار) A dealer, a shopkeeper, an intermediate dealer or agent, a broker; also one who goes about with goods for sale, a hawker, a pedlar.

PAIMÁISH, vernacularly, PAYIMÁSÍ, corruptly, PYMAEESH,

and PYMÁSH, H. (P. پیمایش) Measurement, measuring, survey.

Paimáish-dár, H. (P. دار, who has) A measurer, a surveyor.

Paimáish-i-hampás, H. (کمپاس, the English word 'compass') Survey by European surveyors, a trigonometrical survey.

Kol-payimási, Mal. (കൊൽപയിമാശി) Regular survey, measurement by the *kol*, or rod.

Nok-payimási, Mal. (നൊകപയിമാശി) Measurement or survey by inspection and estimate, the most usual method under the native government of Malabar.

Paimán-kash, Sindhi (P. پیمان کش) A weighman, a measurer.

PAÏN, H. (پَیِن) A reservoir of water.

PAIN, Mar. (पैण, or पैन) A bundle of grass or hay: an impost formerly levied on cultivators in lieu of a portion of hay previously exacted from them.

PÁÍṆ, Mar. (पाइण) A small measure, a quarter of an inch: a larger land measure equal to 30 *bighás*.

PAINÁM, H. (پینام) A denomination under the Mohammadan government of the principal divisions of a *Súbah*; for instance, the *Súbah* of Bengal was divided into two chief *Painâms*, the ceded lands of 1760, and the *Diwání* lands of 1765; the latter again was subdivided into 26 *Painâms*: (the term, although given in the 5th Report, is of doubtful accuracy, and is possibly a vernacular corruption, or an error for *Paimán*, P., a measurement, a measured or definite tract of country).

PAINCHÁ, H. (پینچا) A loan: payment of a loan.

PAINṬH, Hindi (पैंठ) A duplicate bill of exchange. See *Peṭh*.

PAIRÁ, Mar. (पैरा) A day labourer, one who works by the day.

Paireṇ, Mar. (पैरें) A day's job for a woman or a boy: a woman or boy hired for the day.

PÁÍṚA, or PÁÍḌA, Mar. (पाइड) A small measure, a quarter of an inch.

PAIṚÍ, Hindi (पैड़ी) The slope or inclined plane up and down which the oxen attached to the ordinary well used for irrigation travel: in some places it seems to imply a ring or subdivision of a well, and thence the well itself.

PAIRU, Tel. (పయిరు) Growing corn. See *Payir*.

PAIRUDÁR, Karn. (ಪೈರುದಾರ) A person whose employment is carrying corn, cotton, or other articles, or oxen, from one district to another.

PAISÁ, corruptly, PYSA, PYCE, PICE, H. &c. (پیسا), Mar. (पैसा) A copper coin, which, under the native government, varied considerably in weight and value: the Company's *paisá* is fixed at the weight of 100 grains, and is rated at 4 to the *ana*, or 64 to the rupee: in common parlance it is sometimes used for money in general. In Maraṭhi, *Paisá* also signifies a land measure equal to $7\frac{1}{2}$ *bighás*.

Paisotako, Guz. (પઈસોટકો) Money in general.

PAISÁCHA, S. &c. (पैशाच, from *Pisácha*, an evil spirit) Demoniac, diabolical: one kind of marriage recognised by Hindu legislation, violation of a girl when unconscious or intoxicated.

PAISALU, Karn. (ಫೈಸಲು, for *Faisala*, q.v.) Decision, decree.

PAISÁR, Karn. (ಫೈಸಾರ) Common ground, ground left uncultivated to serve as a pasturage for the village cattle.

PAÏSHÁ, Uriya (ପଇଶା) A grain measure, four of which are equal to one *chatánk*, or the sixteenth of a *ser*.

PAITÁ, vulgarly, POITÁ, Beng. (পইতা, পৈতা) The thread or string of cotton worn by the Brahmans (from the S. *pavitra*).

PÁÍTA, Mar. (पाइत) A patch of level ground along the skirts of the hills sown with common grains (in the tract called *Dang*, q. v.)

PAIṬHÁ, corruptly, PYTHA, Beng. (পৈঠা) A district revenue account, in which the several fields of the villages, whether paying revenue or exempt, are specified under the names of their respective occupants, according to their extent, quality, and produce.

PAITṚIKA, vernacularly, PAITRIK, S. &c. (पैतृक, from *Pitṛi*, a father) Paternal, ancestral, patrimonial, hereditary.

PAIVILÁSAMU, Tel. (పైవిలాసము) Superscription, direction of a letter.

PAIWAST, or PAIBAST, Beng. (পৈবস্ত, from P. پیوسته, bound, connected) Added to, or increased, as an alluvial deposit: additional lands from any source to those held in farm.

Paiwastí, Mar. (P. पैवस्ती) Endorsement of a letter specifying the date of its receipt: also Beng., vernacularly *Paibastí*, additional, as alluvial land.

PAIYÁ, Hindi (पैया) An allowance of half an *ána* on each rupee of revenue set apart for the *Patwárí*.

PÁJÁ, Hindi (पाजा) Share or quota of grain paid to the head man and the village servants.—South-west frontier.

PÁJANÍ, Guz. (પાજણી) A brush with which a thin starch is applied to the warp, to prepare it for the loom: the warp so prepared.

Pájaní-garo, Guz. (પાજણીગરો) A man whose business

is to prepare the warp for the loom by starching the thread.

Pajáwá, H. (P. پجاوا) A brick-kiln, a brick-field.

Pákanádinavaru, Karn. (pl. ಪಾಕನಾದಿನವರು) A class of Ṣúdras practising fortune-telling from the district of *Páknád*.

Pakang, (?) H. A cow, or she buffalo, or any herd of female cattle on which a cess was levied in *Chaubáchha* villages. See *Chaubáchha*.

Pakhál, corruptly, **Puckally**, H. &c. (پکھال) A large leather bag for carrying water in, usually double, thrown over a bullock: also a leather bag used for raising water from wells, being attached to a rope passing through a pulley and drawn up by oxen passing up and down an inclined plane.

Pakhháli, corruptly, *Puchalee, Puckallee, Puckallie*, H. &c. (پکھالي) A water-carrier.

Pakhályá, Mar. (पखाल्या) Carrying a water-bag: the bullock or the driver.

Pakhela, Thug. Paper, whether written upon or not.

Pákhi, incorrectly, **Pakee**, Beng. (পাখি) A land measure nearly equivalent to a *bighá*.—East Bengal.

Páki, Karn. (ಪಾಕಿ) A small coin, the twelfth of a *Dab*. See *Dabbu*.

Pakká, **Pukka**, corruptly, **Pucka**, **Pukha**, H. &c. (پکّا, पक्का, S. पक्व) Ripe, mature, cooked, dressed: metaph., correct, complete, as a statement: substantial, solid, as a building; also, intellectually mature, intelligent, sharp, knowing: the contrast in all respects of *Kachchá*, q. v.

Pakká-ghar, H. &c. (پکّاگھر) A house built of baked bricks or stone.

Pakká-chiṭṭhá, H. &c. (پکّاچٹّھا) A revised and authentic account.

Pakká-hiṣeb, Mar. (पक्काहिशेब) A correct and carefully revised account.

Pakká-ser, H. &c. (پکّاسیر) A full or *Pakká-ser*: a measure of weight varying in different parts of India, and for different articles, but always the full or standard measure, in distinction to a smaller or less authentic, or *Kachchá-ser*: the standard, or *Pakká-ser* of Bengal is fixed at 80 *tolas*, each of 180 grains troy, and is equivalent to 2.057 lb. avoirdupois, about 2 lb. 15 drachms. In the Madras presidency the *Pakká-ser* of Arcot = 1 lb. 13 ounces, of Masulipatam = 2 lb., and this is used in dealing with persons from Hyderabad, Calcutta, &c.: the ordinary or *Kachchá-ser* of Madras was 11.4 ounces, and of Bombay 11.3$\frac{1}{5}$ ounces.

Pákka, Mal. (പാക്ക) Planting seed thickly: a bed of young plants for transplanting: betel-nut in a raw state.

Pákhanilam, Mal. (പാക്കനിലം) Land on which rice is sown for subsequent transplantation.

Pakkanam, Tam. (பக்கணம்) The residence of low and outcaste tribes.

Paksha, vernacularly, also, **Pakh**, or **Pachh**, S. &c. (पक्ष), H. (پکھ, پچھ), **Pakkam**, Tam. (பக்கம்) The half of a lunar month, or a fortnight of fifteen days: the half from the new moon to the full is termed the *Ṣukla-paksha*, the white or light fortnight, that from the full to the new moon the *kṛishṇa-pahsha*, the black or dark fortnight.

Pakuti, Mal. (പകുതി) A share, a portion.

Pál, Hindi (पाल) Crown lands kept by the ruling family in their own hands.—Kamaon.

Pál, H. &c. (پال, पाल) A dike, a dam, especially the raised earth bordering the beds in which rice is planted so as to confine the water of irrigation: also a small tent, or a cloth or blanket thrown over a transverse pole to serve as a tent.

Pál, corruptly, **Paul**, Mar. (पाळ) Exempt (from tax), remitted (as a duty or tax),

Pálnúk, Mar. (पाळनूक) Exemption from tax, remission of tax or duty.

Pálpaṭṭi, Mar. (पाळपट्टी) A tax or quit-rent imposed upon the holders of rent-free lands.

Pala, vernacularly, **Pal**, or **Pul**, corruptly, **Pull**, S. &c. (पल), H. (پل), Mar. (पल, पळ) A measure of time, the sixtieth part of a *daṇḍa*, or hour of twenty-four minutes, and consequently equivalent to twenty-four seconds. A measure of weight of gold or silver, varying in value, being equal to four *suvarnas*, to four or to eight *tolas*, or, in common use, to three *tolas* two *máshas* and eight *kattis*, or about 585 grains troy. In Cuttack, a weight for brass, &c., being the twentieth of a *bisha*, or equal to four *harshas*, or about 520 grains. In the Dakhin, a weight of twenty-eight *dabbus*, used in weighing ghee, butter, &c.: in Kamaon it is a weight of about 520 troy grains. *Pala* also occurs in Sanskrit writings as the first or lowest measure of capacity, four being equal to one *kuḍava*, a measure of 13$\frac{1}{2}$ cubic *angulas*, or fingers.

Palá, sometimes written, **Pallá**, Tel. (పలా, పల్లా) A measure of capacity equal to ten *marakáls*, or 15$\frac{1}{2}$ imperial gallons. See *Pallá*.

Pála, Uriya (ପାଲ) Land immediately in the vicinity, or on the bank of a river.

Palabhógam, corruptly, Paulbhógam, Tam. (பலபோகம், from Tam. *pala*, many, and S. *bhogam*, enjoyment, possession) The tenure by which the inhabitants of a village hold their lands in severalty under an engagement among the coparceners, each being responsible for the revenue of his own holding, and receiving the surplus for his own use: such land may be held by the same individual in more than one village: also a village or lands so held: the term is also explained to signify merely possession by more than one individual, distinguished as, *Samudayam* or where the lands are cultivated jointly and the produce is divided, and *Arudi-karai* where the lands are divided amongst the proprietors and cultivated severally: see *Arudi-karai* and *Samudayam*.

Palagaṇḍa, Karn. (ಪಲಗಂಡ) A bricklayer, a plasterer.

Palagorru, Tel. (పలగొర్రు) A kind of rake.

Pálai, Tam. (பாலை) Barren soil.

Pálaï, Beng. (পালই) A stack or rick of corn, a granary, a magazine.

Paláibá, Beng. (পলাইবা, from S. पलायन) Running away, flight, escape.

Pálaka, or Pálaka-putra, S. &c. (पालकपुत्रः) An adopted son: the vernacular equivalent *Pálak-betá*, is sometimes applied to a boy who has been bought of his parents and is considered a slave.

Palakosham, Tam. (பலகோசம்) A register of land in the occupancy of different individuals.

Pálakuṇḍa, Tel. (పాలకుండ) A certain grain-fee given to the cultivators before the grain is measured, or a portion from each measure (lit., a pot, *kuṇḍa*, of milk, *pálu*).

Palam, corruptly, Pullam, Tam. (பலம், from the S. *pala*) A measure of weight at Madras, variously rated at 546.875 and 525.75 troy grains: according to the revised table recognised by government 20th Oct. 1846, the *Palam* is equal to 1 ounce 3.75 drachms avoirdupois: it is also used in Malabar, 100 *Palams*, or *Palons*, being equal to a *tulam*, and 20 *tulams* to a *khandi*.

Palán, H. (پلان) A space of ground left for future disposal between two occupied lots.

Palaṇcheru, Tam. (பலஞ்செறு) Ploughed land prepared for transplanting.

Palapaṭṭadai, corruptly, Pullapuṭṭady, Tam. (பல-பட்டடை) A place where people of different tribes and castes reside together.

Palapaṭṭadaikuḍikal, Tam. (பலபட்டடைகுடிகள்) The inhabitants of a town where the right and left-hand castes live amicably together.

Pálsutantaram, Tam. (பால்சுதந்தரம், from S. स्वतन्त्र) Allowance in grain to village artificers.

Páláṣavidhi, corruptly, Palashweedee, Mar. (पालाशविधि) The vicarious cremation of a bundle of *Palása* leaves, in place of the body of a person who has died at a distance: in some cases widows were allowed to burn themselves with the substitute.

Palátak, Beng. (পলাতক, from S. पलायन) A fugitive, a runaway, a cultivator who abandons his lands.

Palátika, corruptly, *Platika*, Beng. (পলাতিক) Abandoned, uncultivated, land formerly cultivated, but deserted by the cultivators: a column of an account shewing the revenue formerly derived from deserted lands.

Palathí, Pulathy, (?) Damaged produce.

Paláwaṭ, Guz. (પલાવટ) A tribe of *Bhils* so named.

Páḷe, Páḷevu, Páḷeya, Karn. (ಪಾಳೆ, ಪಾಳೆವು, ಪಾಳೆಯ), Paleiyam, corruptly, Polliam, Pollam, Pollem, Pollim, Tam. (பாளையம்), Pâḷemu, Tel. (పాళెము) A tract of country subject to a petty chieftain.

Páḷegára, corruptly, Polygar, Polligar, &c. Karn. (ಪಾಳೆಗಾರ), Paḷegáḍu, Paḷeru, Tel. (పాళెగాడు, పాళెరు) Páḷegár, Mar. (पाळेगार), Pálaiyakáran, Tam. (பாளையக்காரன்) A petty chieftain: in the south of India, especially in Karnáta, the Poligar, or Polygar, of early writers, occupying chiefly tracts of hill and forest, subject to pay tribute and service to the paramount state, but seldom paying either, and more or less independent, subsisting in a great measure by plunder: on the subjugation of the country most of the Pálegars were dispossessed, some were pensioned, and a few were allowed to retain some of their villages at a quit-rent: these have now subsided into peaceable landholders.

Palaiyapádu, corruptly, *Paliaput*, *Paliput*, *Puliaput*, *Polyaput*, *Pooliaput*, Tam. (பாளையபாடு) Lands in the possession of a *Pálegar*, for which he now pays revenue to the government.

Páléru, plur. Palérlu, Paléllu, Tel. (పాలేరు, పాలేర్లు, పాలేళ్లు) A hired cultivator or labourer, one working with implements belonging to his employer: this is no doubt the same as the *Pálalu* of the northern

Cirkars, agricultural labourers considered as slaves to the Ryots, being attached hereditarily to the lands, and maintained by the cultivators during the greater part of the year; during the rest of the time they support themselves: they are transferable with the land, but are not sold separately: they may be reclaimed if they quit their employer.

PALEV, or PALEŪ, Hindi (पलेव) Land watered after ploughing.

PALÍ, Beng. (পলি) Alluvial deposit, soil left by inundation.

PÁLI, incorrectly, PALLEE, Beng. (পালি) A measure of grain, equal in some places to five, in others to eight *sers.*

PÁLIÁ, Gux. (પાલીઆ plur.) Stones marking the boundary of a field.

PÁḶIKÁPU, Tel. (పాళికాపు) An under-tenant, a cultivator.

PALIṢA, Mal. (പലിശ) Interest, usury: the following rates per 100 *fanams* per annum are specified as in practice in Malabar by Mr. Græme.

Ara-paliṣa, One-twentieth, or 5 per cent.

Arakál-paliṣa, One-eightieth, or 1 *fanam* 4 *anas* per cent.

Kál-paliṣa, One-fortieth, or 2 *fanams* 8 *anas* per cent.

Makani-paliṣa, One hundred and sixtieth, or 10 *anas* per cent.

Mukál-paliṣa, One-thirtieth and a third, or 3 *fanams* 4 *anas* seven-tenths per cent.

Ner-paliṣa, Ten per cent. per annum.

Paliṣa-madaha-olakaranam, corruptly, *Pelisha-madakom*, Mal. (പലിശമടകഒലകരണം) A deed of mortgage in which the rent of the estate transferred to the mortgagee is equal to the interest of the loan, and is so specified, which is not the case in the usual *Otti* deed.—Græme.

PÁLÍSÍ, or PÁLESÍ, Guz. (પાલીસી, પાલેસી) A *policy* of insurance.

PALÍT, (?) Beng. Offerings not fit for Purohits, or family priests, but for an inferior order of Brahmans.—Sylhet.

PÁLKÍ, H. &c. (پالکی), PALLAKKI, Karn. (పల్లక్కి) A palankeen.

Pallakki-boi, Karn. (పల్లక్కిబోయి) A palankeen bearer.

PALLÁ, Mar. (पल्ला) A measure of capacity of thirty *Payalis* = 120 *sers*, the same as the *Palá* of Madras: a measure of weight of a like amount, or 120 *sers*, for groceries, betel-nuts, oil, &c.: also the bag or sack which holds a *pallá* of grain.

PALLAMU, or PALLAM, Tel. (పల్లము) Low-lying ground.

Pallapunádu, Tel. (పల్లపునాడు) Low ground capable of being ploughed.

Pallapupanṭa, Tel. (పల్లపుపంట) A crop grown on low, moist, or irrigable lands.

PÁḶḶAN, plur. PAḶḶAR, corruptly, PUḶḶER, Tam. (பள்ளன், பள்ளர்) The name of a low and servile caste, or of an individual of that caste, most commonly the slave of the *Vellálan*, or agricultural tribe: they are much upon the same footing as the *Pareyan*, but hold themselves superior to him, as they abstain from eating the flesh of the cow.

Pallacheri, Tam. (பள்ளச்சேரி) A village of the *Pallar* tribe.

Pallarvarí, Tam. (பள்ளர்வரி) A tax upon the *Pallar* in some of the Tamil districts.

PALLE, PALLI, or PALLIYA, Tel. (పల్లె, పల్లి, పల్లియ), PALLI, Tam. (பல்லி) A village, a hamlet.

Pallehásilu, Tel. (పల్లెహాశిలు) Inland or transit duty.

Pallevádu, Tel. (పల్లెవాడు) A villager, a fisherman.

PALLI, H. (پلّی) A small village. PALLI, PALLÍ, Beng. (পল্লি, পল্লী) A hamlet, a detached portion of a village, a district.

Palligrám, Beng. (পল্লিগ্রাম) A village, a country. Tam. (பள்ளிகிராமம்) A village belonging to a temple.

PAḶḶÍ, Tam. (பள்ளி), Mal. (പള്ളി) A small town, a village: in Tam., also, a temple, a school: it is no doubt the same word as the H. and Beng. terms, but is in more general use, especially in combination, when it is corruptly written *poly*, as in *Trichinopoly*, properly *Trisirá-paḷḷi* (திரிசிர்ராப்பள்ளி) the city of the giant *Trisirá*: it is also the name of a servile tribe of Hindus in the south, similar to the *Pallar*, but who are more especially the bondsmen or slaves of the Brahman proprietors of land.

Paḷḷiyavanu, Karn. (పళ్ళియవను) A villager.

Paḷḷivásal-mániyam, Tam. (பள்ளிவாசல்மானியம்) Rent-free land attached to a temple.

PALLÍ, Beng. (পল্লী) Land of superior quality yielding crops at every harvest.

PAḶḶIṆÁYAL, Mal. (പള്ളിഞായൽ) A bed or piece of ground on which rice plants are sown for transplantation.

Paḷḷisádi, Tam. (பள்ளிசாதி) A tribe of Hindus.

Paḷḷiyaṟkáran, Mal. (from പള്ളിയറ, a bed-chamber) A chamberlain.

Paḷḷiyaṟviḷamban, Mal. (പള്ളിയറവിളമ്പൻ) Confidential or private secretary of the *Kotiote* Rája.

PALLU, or PALHU, Thug. The handkerchief with which people are strangled.

PALLU, Tel. (పల్లు) Low ground.

PALLUDÁR, H. (from پلّو, a border of a dress) A fringe maker, a worker of ornamental or gold or silver borders to dresses.

Pallut, (?) Yellow soil.—Cachar.

Pálu, Tel., Karn. (పాలు) A share, a portion, the cultivator's share of the crop, in opposition to the *Ambáramu* or government share: (in composition it also occurs, vernacularly, *Pál* and *Pálí*.

Pálinavákkalu, Karn. (పాలినవాక్కలు) A farmer who shares his crop with the government.

Pálugáranu, or *Pálgáranu*, Karn. (పాలుగారను, పాల్గారను) A sharer, a coparcener.

Pálugenichittu, (?) Karn. An agreement for a fixed term for an equal division of the crop between the proprietor and the cultivator or renter.

Paluku amarike, (?) Tel. (పాలుకుఅమరికె) Allotment of portions of land amongst the cultivators.

Pálutirugulu, Tel. (పాలుతిరుగులు) Difference of shares: it was the custom formerly, in order to deter the cultivators from neglecting the public lands for the sake of the additional portion which the holders of rent-free lands were accustomed to allow to those who worked for them, to carry the difference between the two rates to the credit of the government.

Okkala-, or *Raitara-pálu*, Karn. (ఒక్కలపాలు, రైతరపాలు) The cultivator's share of the crop.

Rájapálu, Karn. (రాజపాలు) The government share of the crop.

Paluṇ, Guz. (પલ્લું) A dower, a marriage portion given to the bride by the bridegroom or his father.

Palwár, Pulwar, H. Beng. (پلوار, পলবার) A boat of burthen, of from 15 to 20 tons, employed for carrying goods, considered as originally of Dacca build.

Palwi, Thug. A ring for the finger, nose, or ear.

Pampa, Mal. (പമ്പ) An agreement: a written order for taking an oath.

Pampakamu, Tel. (పంపకము) Sharing, dividing, share, division.

Pampalu-jábita, *Pampoola-zabita*, (?) Tel. An agreement for a division of shares amongst the contracting parties.

Pampu, Tel. (పంపు) A weight equal to five-eighths of a *ser*: a tract of land containing two or three rice-fields (?).

Pan, Pun, H. (پن), Paṇa, S. (पण), Beng. (পন) A sum of eighty *kauri* shells, equal to twenty *gaṇdas*, and of which sixteen are equal to a *káhan*; whence a *Pana* is sometimes used, as in Cuttack, for the sixteenth of any given unit, as of the amount of rent or revenue. In Sylhet four *Panas* make one *raík*: it is also a measure of land equal to a square of 3⅞ cubits: the same word becoming *Panam* in Tam. and Mal. (പണം) signifies money, also a small coin, both of silver and gold, transformed, by European pronunciation, to *Fanam*: the gold *Panam* was properly the sixteenth of a *Hun*, but the proportion varied: the silver *Panam* or *Fanam* of the Company's coinage at Madras was rated at eighty copper *kás*, at twelve *fanams* sixty *kás* to an Arcot rupee, and forty-five to a star-pagoda.

Panbahá, H. (پنبہا) Valuation, estimate.

Paṇí, Uriya (ପଣି) A sixteenth of the revenue.

Pán, corruptly, Paan, or Paun, H. &c. (پان, from S. *parṇa* पर्ण, a leaf), Beng. (পান), Mar. (पान) The aromatic leaf of the Piper betel, or, in common use, a leaf of it rolled round a few small pieces of the astringent Areka nut with a little caustic lime, a few heads of spice, and sometimes a little catechu, for the purpose of being chewed, acting as a carminative and antacid tonic: it is presented to guests and visitors, and sometimes sent to friends and relations, especially at family festivals, inclosed in gold or silver paper or leaf: it is also termed *Pán-supárí*, from *Supárí*, areka-nut, and *Biṛá* or *Biṛí*, S. *Viṭika*, whence the European word *betel*.

Pánbatta, (?) H. Distribution of *pán* on occasions of festivity.

Pándán, H. &c. (P. دان, holding) A box for containing *betel* and its accompaniments.

Pánguttá, Mar. (पानगुत्ता) Rent or farm of betel gardens.

Pánmahál, H. (پان محال) Tax on betel leaves.

Pánmaḷá, Mar. (पानमळा) A plantation, a garden of the betel-vine.

Pánpatra, H. &c. (S. पत्र, a leaf) The leaf of the Piper betel.

Pánsupárí, H., Mar. (پان سپاری, पानसुपारी) A *pán*, or the areka-nut and spices rolled up in the leaf of the Piper betel; also, in Mar., a small douceur or bribe of a few rupees to stir up or refresh the memory.

Pánubágu, Tel. (పానుబాగు, vernacular for the Hindustani *Pán ká bágh*) A betel-vine garden or plantation.

Pana, or Panna, (?) H. A large division, as a quarter or a half, of a coparcenary village and its lands under a separate head man or *Mukaddam*: in some places the lands are subject to periodical re-distribution among the members of the community.—North-west provinces.

Paṇa, vernacularly, Paṇ, S. &c. (पण) Money in general: (the same as above: see *Pan*), wages, hire, price: a bet, a wager: business: an agreement, a stipulation or clause in an agreement.

Paṇa-yellata-káran, Mal. (പണയെല്ലത്തകാരൻ) The creditor of a landed proprietor, upon an agreement that if the loan is not repaid by a stipulated period, the estate is to be assigned to the money lender.—Græme.

Paṇya, S. &c. (पण्य) Vendible, any saleable article.

Paṇyasálá, S. &c. (from शाला, a hall) A market, a market place.

Paṇyavídhi, Tel. (పాణ్యవీధి) A shop, a stall.

PANA, Tel. (పన) A sheaf of corn.

PÁṆA, Uriya (ପାଣ) A man of a low caste employed in menial offices out of the house: also the name of a wild and predatory tribe on the frontier in the south of Orissa.

PÁṆAD, PÁNAND, PÁNANDH, Mar. (पानद, पानंद, पानंध) A lane through a village, or between fields and inclosures.

PAṆAI, Tam. (பனை) A palmyra tree (Borassus flabelliformis).

PAṆAYAM, Mal. (പണയം, from S. पण *paṇa*, price) A mortgage, a pawn, a pledge.

Paṇayakkachiṭṭa, Mal. (പണയക്കച്ചിട്ട) A document given on a pledge or pawn.

Paṇayakáran, Mal. (പണയകാരൻ) A mortgagee, a mortgager, one who borrows or lends on mortgage.

Paṇaya-ola-karaṇam, Mal. (പണയഓലകരണം) An instrument or deed of mortgage written on an *ola* or palm leaf.

Paṇayappáta, Mal. (പണയപ്പാട) An article pledged or mortgaged.

Paṇayapáṭṭam, Mal. (പണയപാട്ടം) A mortgage lease, or one in which a sum of money considered as the equivalent of two-thirds of the estimated nett produce or rent, is advanced to the proprietor in consideration of his relinquishing the estate to the lender for his usufruct, in lieu of interest on his loan. See *Páttam*.

Paṇayapátta-kulihánam, Mal. (from *kulihánam* കുഴിക്കാണം: see *kánam*) A mortgage lease, under which the tenant, when it expires, has a title to compensation for any improvements he may have made.

PANCHA, PANCH, or PUNCH, also, PÁNCH, H. &c. (پنچ, پانچ, from S. *pancha* पञ्च) Five, the number five: it is also used as an abbreviation for *Pancháit*, q. v.

Panchagrámadava, Karn. (ಪಂಚಗ್ರಾಮದವ) A Brahman of a tribe of Tuluva Brahmans in the north-west of Mysore.

Pancháït, Pancháyat, less correctly, *Punchayet*, H. (پنچايت) *Pancháit*, Mar. (पंचाईत), *Pancháyati*, Tel. (పంచాయతి), *Pancháyattu*, Tam. (பஞ்சாயத்து), or the persons

Pancháyattár (பஞ்சாயத்தார்) A native court of arbitration, consisting of five or more members chosen by the parties themselves, or appointed by the civil officers of the government, for the determination of petty disputes among the people, especially in matters affecting the usages of caste or occupation: (however prized by the natives when other means of obtaining justice were unavailable, and when *Panch-parameswara*, the *Pancha* is the supreme deity, was a proverbial phrase in the south of India at least, there are now few occasions on which this sort of assembly is spontaneously had recourse to, or in which its judgments are regarded as decisive, and this notwithstanding great pains have been taken by the British government to render it effective.—Ben. Reg. xxii. 1816; iii. 1821; vi. 1832; ix. 1833. Madras Reg. Village *Pancháïts*, v. 1816; District *Pancháïts*, vii. 1816. Bombay Reg. iv. xiii. 1827.): the term also applies to the proceedings of the native court, and to the matter in dispute: also to a member of the court, an umpire, an arbitrator.

Pancháití, H. &c. (پنچايتي) A court of arbitration; the award of such a court.

Pancháit-játí, H. (from S. جاتي, caste) An arbitration by persons of the same caste as the litigant parties.

Pancháit-khánagí, H. (P. خانگي, domestic) Domestic arbitration, a settlement of family quarrels by relations and connexions.

Pancháit-náma, H. (P. نامه, a document) The written award of a court of arbitration.

Pancháit-sarkárí, H. (from سركار, the state) A court of arbitration appointed by the public authorities.

Panchaka, S. &c. (पञ्चक) Five, an aggregate of five, a tax of a fifth, a tax or cess levied formerly by the Zamindárs in addition to the regular imposts.

Panchakí, S. &c. (fem. of *Panchaka*) Cesses imposed in some of the Bengal districts formerly, in addition to the revenue and other regular imposts: lands held free of such additions were termed *ghair-panchakí*, and were considered as lightly assessed: in some places the term appears to denote lands originally rent-free, but subjected to a small quit-rent, and thence termed *Panchakí-lá-khiráj*.

Panchála, S. &c. (पञ्चाल) An aggregate of five, thence formerly applied to the *Panjab*, or country of the five rivers: in the south of India it denotes five castes collectively, or those of the goldsmith, carpenter, blacksmith, brazier, and mason, who, in Mysore, eat together and intermarry:

among the Marathas they wear the Brahmanical thread: in other places the five castes are of an inferior order, and are the carpenter, weaver, barber, washerman, and shoemaker.

Panchama, S. &c. (पञ्चम) Fifth. *Panchamí*, (fem. of पञ्चम) The fifth lunar day of each half month.

Panchaman, Tam. (S. பஞ்சமன்) An outcaste, a Pareya, a fifth caste man, not being included among the four regular castes.

Pancham-bandham, (?) Karn. Outcaste and servile tribes in Karnáta, four of whom are named, as, the *Pareya*, *Balwan*, *Chaklar*, and *Toti*, and who are the agrestic slaves of Brahman cultivators.—Buchanan.

Panchama-bánajiga, Karn. (ಪಂಚಮಬಣಜಿಗ) An outcaste, a man of the fifth order: it denotes also the *Pancham-banijigaru*, of Buchanan, traders and religious persons of the *Lingáit* sect, and the heads of the right-hand castes in Mysore.

Pancha-mahápátaka, S. &c. (पञ्चमहापातक) The five most heinous sins of the Brahmanical code: killing a Brahman, stealing gold, drinking spirits, intercourse with the wife of a spiritual preceptor, and association with a person who has perpetrated these sins: in the masc. gender, and vernacularly, a great sinner, one who is guilty of the five great sins.

Panchánga, S. &c. (पञ्चाङ्ग) An almanac, a kalendar, so named from its treating of five members (*anga*) or topics; or, 1. the *tithí*, or lunar day; 2. the *vára*, the solar day, or day of the week; 3. the *nakshatra*, or lunar asterism for each day; 4. the *yoga*, transits and conjunctions of the planets, eclipses, &c., and 5. the *karana*, or subdivisions of the lunar day: these are the five essential parts of the kalendar; but it comprises other topics, as lucky and unlucky days for undertaking any business, festival days, and the like.

Pánchánga, or *Panchángí*, S. &c. (पाञ्चाङ्ग, पञ्चाङ्गी), *Panchangan*, pronounced *Panjangam*, Tam. (பஞ்சாங்கம்) The almanac maker, the village astronomer or astrologer, who announces fit seasons for commencing to plough or reap, for celebrating marriages or festivals, or engaging in any business: in the south he is usually a Brahman, who holds his office by descent, and is paid by rent-free land, a certain portion of the crop, or other privileges and fees.

Panchánga-mániyam, Tam. (பஞ்சாங்கமானியம்) Land held rent-free by the village astrologer.

Panchánga-mirásu, Tam. (பஞ்சாங்கமிராசு) The hereditary fees and perquisites of the village astrologer.

Pancha-hrosí, vernacularly, *Panchkosí*, S. &c. (पञ्चक्रोशी) A circuit of five or six *kós*, especially that distance round a sacred city, as Benares, traversing which, and worshipping at each temple on the way, constitutes one of the principal ceremonies of the pilgrimage.

Páncharátra, Karn. (ಪಾಂಚರಾತ್ರ) The officiating priest in the temple of Vishnu in Mysore.

Panchati (?) Beng. A tax formerly levied in Dacca to defray the salaries of officers employed in examining and stamping weights and measures.

Panch-chhaták, Beng. (পঞ্চছটাক) lit., Five *chhatáks*, a fee of that quantity of grain for every rupee's worth weighed.

Panch-do, corruptly, *Puch-doo*, H. (P. دو, two) A settlement in some places in the upper provinces, in which the proprietor takes two-fifths of the produce and the cultivator three-fifths.

Panch-kosí, Mar. (पंचकोशी) A cluster of five or six contiguous villages. See also *Pancha-hrosi*.

Panch-ottara, S. &c. (पञ्चोत्तर) Five in excess or addition, five per cent., and the like: (from *pancha*, five, and *uttara*, over; but it is variously modified and corrupted by vernacular and European mis-spelling as follows):

Panchatra, (?) H. A fee of five per cent. formerly levied upon any amount in dispute from the successful litigant.

Panchattara, Beng. (পঞ্চত্তরা) A duty of five per cent. on inland traffic.

Panchotara, or *Pachotara*, H. (پچوترہ , پنچوترہ) A duty of five per cent. on the value of goods in transit: a deduction of five per cent. from the estimated gross revenue of a village: a custom or toll-house for inland traffic.

Panchotará, or *Panchotarí*, Mar. (पंचोतरा -री) Interest at five per cent. per mensem: a surplus of five thrown in with a hundred (bundles of grass or the like): a duty of five per cent. on the value of goods.

Panchotara-haifiat, H. (پنچوترہ کیفیت) Increase of revenue from reform of abuses in the inland customs: also, inland duties.

Panchótrá, corruptly, *Panchoutra*, Tel. (పంచోత్రా) A custom-house for inland or transit duties: the chief custom-station in a district.

PÁND, Mar. (पांड) A land measure, twenty square *háthís* or rods, or the twentieth of a *bíghá*; the *Bisna*, or *Visna*, of Hindustan.

PAṆḌÁ, PUṆḌA, H. (پنڈا), PÁṆḌÁ, Beng. (পাণ্ডা) The proprietary or presiding priest of a temple, usually, though not invariably, a Brahman; the office is hereditary, and in some places, as at Benares, the *Paṇḍá* officiates only on particular occasions, the duties of daily worship being performed by inferior priests or *Pujáris* in his employ: a priest who is stationary at any particular place or shrine.

PANDAL, or PANDAR, corruptly, PANDELL, Tam. (பந்தல், பந்தர்), Mal. (പന്തൽ), PANDIRI, or PANDILI, Tel. (పందిరి, పందిలి) A temporary shed or booth, a structure of cloth or basket-work supported on posts, for giving shelter to persons assembled on any festive occasion, as at a marriage: also any shed.

Paṇḍa-kával, Mal. (പണ്ടക്കാവൽ) A fee of a portion of the crop given to a slave or hired servant employed to watch it (from *pandal*, the shed in which he keeps (*kával*) watch).

Paṇḍakasála, Mal. (പണ്ടക്കശാല) A warehouse, a magazine, a store-room (vernacular for S. *bháṇḍa*, a vessel, and *sálá*, a hall).

PAṆḌALA, Mal. (പണ്ടാല) The name of a Súdra tribe in Malabar, of which the Rája of Calicut is a member.

PAṆḌAM, or BANDAM, Tam. (பண்டம், S. *bháṇḍam*) Vessels, utensils: grain: gold: any thing that should be kept safe in a store or treasury.

Paṇḍáram, Tam., Mal. (பண்டாரம், S. भाण्डार) Government: the revenue or financial department of the state: the treasury: treasure: goods and chattels.

Paṇḍára-vádai, *Paṇḍára-vádagai*, corruptly, *Puṇḍarah-vadiky*, *Puṇḍarah-vadagay*, Tam. (பண்டாரவாடை, பண்டாரவாடகை) A village or lands of which the revenue is paid direct into the public treasury, corresponding with the *Khalsa* or *Khás* collections of Mohammadan and British rule: the *Paṇḍára-vádagai* is said also to be a name given to villages in the *Paleyams* or *Paleyagar* districts of Madura and Tinnivelly, of which the inhabitants are *Ṣúdras*, and hold their lands by proprietary right.—5th Rep. p. 826.

PAṆḌÁRA, Karn. (ಪಂಡಾರ), PAṆḌÁRAM, Tam. (பண்டாரம்), PAṆḌÁRI, Mal. (പണ്ടാരി) The designation of a class of Hindu mendicants in the south of India of the *Ṣúdra* or servile caste and *Saiva* sect, often officiating as ministrant priests in the temples of *Siva*: many are very respectable individuals, and excellent Tamil scholars: (Brown (Glossary) calls them mendicant worshippers of Vishnu, in which he differs from other authorities).

Paṇḍári, Tam. (பண்டாரி) A titular name of a class of agricultural labourers: a steward, a treasurer. See *Bháṇḍárí*.

PÁṆḌAVABÍḌU, Tel. (పాండవబీడు, from S. *páṇḍava*, relating to *Páṇḍu*, or his descendants) Waste land from time immemorial, or from the heroic age or days of the *Páṇḍava* princes.

PÁṆḌE, H. (پانڈے, पाण्डे) A title of Hindustani Brahmans, but properly applicable only to a certain tribe, a branch of the *Bharadwája-gotra*, one of the chief branches of the *Kanaujia* Brahmans.

PÁNḌHARA, or PÁNḌHARÍ, corruptly, PÁNDREE, Mar. (पांढर, पांढरी) The entire village community, whether actually assembled or considered collectively: the whole extent or lands of a village or township.

Pánḍhara-paṭṭí, corruptly, *Pandraputty*, and *Panḍery-puttee*, Mar. (from पट्टी, a contribution or tax) A tax on shops, workshops, booths, stalls, &c., or upon artisans and traders, and persons not engaged in agriculture, whether levied on their persons, implements, or places of work or traffic, the same as *Muhtarafa*, q. v.

Pánḍhara-pesha, corruptly, *Panḍerpeyshe*, Mar. (पांढरपेश, from P. پیشه, practice) A term for classes considered superior to the cultivator, as the Brahman, writer, goldsmith, blacksmith, &c.

PÁṆḌI, Mal. (പാണ്ടി) A tribe of Christian fishermen in Malabar.

PAṆḌITA, vernacularly, PANDIT, or PUNDIT, S. &c. (पण्डित) A learned Brahman, one who makes some branch of Sanscrit learning his special study, and teaches it.

PÁṆḌRÁ, H. (پانڈرا, पांडरा) A kind of sugar-cane sown in *Mágh*, or *Phálgun*, and before the rains: the sugar-cane of the next or coming crop.

PAṆḌRA-POLAMU, Tel. (పండ్రపొలము) Garden ground.

Paṇḍra-vádu, Tel. (పండ్రవాడు) A seller of vegetables.

PAṆḌU, Tel. (పండు) Fruit.

PAṆḌUMU, Tel. (పండుము) A measure of capacity equal to ten *Tums*, or *Marakals*.

PÁṆḌURÍ, corruptly, PÁNDREE, Mar. (पांडुरी, from S. पाण्डुर, pale) Whitish or chalky soil.

PÁṆḌUVÁ, Hindi (पांडुवा, S. पाण्डु, pale) A light-coloured soil, a mixture of clay and sand.

PÁṆḌYÁ, Mar. (पांड्या) The writer or accountant of a village or district: an officer employed in the customs: in Madras it is sometimes applied to the head man of a district.

Páṇḍyá, Páṇḍí, S. &c. (पांड्या, पांडी) The ancient Tamil kingdom, the capital of which was Madura: it was known by the name of *Pandion* to the Romans in the time of Augustus.

Paṇejita, S. (पणेजित) A description of a slave, one who, by his own agreement, has become a slave in consequence of being overcome (*jita*) in any dispute or wager (*paṇa*).

Páng, Hindi (पांग) Mud left by inundations; alluvial soil deposited during floods.

Pangá, Uriya, (ପଙ୍ଗା) Salt prepared by boiling.

Paṇgu, corruptly, **Pung**, Tam. (பங்கு), **Panka**, or **Panga** Mal. (പങ്ക) A share, a part, a portion, a lot: a share in a coparcenary village: the share of an individual *Mirásidár*: any definite or proportionate share.

Paṇgáḷi, Tam. (பங்காளி) A sharer, a coparcener, a coheir.

Paṇgubhágam, Tam. (பாகம், S. भाग, a share) A share, a portion in village land or other divisible property.

Paṇgubádi, Tam. (பங்குபாதி) A share, a portion.

Paṇgupirindavargaḷ, Tam. (பங்குபிரிந்தவர்கள்) Joint heirs, persons who have divided amongst them patrimonial property.

Paṇgukáran, Mal. (പങ്കുകാരൻ) A sharer, a partner, a coheir.

Paṇgumáḷai, also, *Pangumálai-hanakku*, Tam. (பங்குமாலை, from *málai*, a garland, or any regular series, a list, a roll, an account; also with *hanakku* added, பங்குமாலைக்கணக்கு) A list or roll of shares in a village shewing the amount of land cultivated by each member of the community, the changes of property, the original divisions, the quality of the lands, and whether cultivated by the proprietors or by migratory cultivators.

Paṇguvídam, Tam. (பங்குவீதம்) Share and share alike; according to or *per* share.

Paṇguvikrayam, Tam. (பங்குவிக்கிரயம்) Sale of a coparcenary share.

Paṇguvikraya-chiṭṭu, Tam. (பங்குவிக்கிரயசீட்டு) A bill of sale; also compounded with the Sanskrit terms *Patra* and *Sásana* in the same sense.

Panguvaḷi, or *Panguvazhi*, Tam. (பங்குவழி) A village held in common by a certain number of coparceners, amongst whom the lands are distributed at various times, according to the votes of the majority of the sharers, and are held in severalty for a given time under such distribution.

Pangu, Thug. A river Thug of Bengal.

Pangul, (?) Mar. A class of mendicants in the Dakhin.

Paṇguni, Tam. (பங்குனி) The first month of the Tamil year (March-April).

Páṇí, H. &c. (پانی), Beng. (পানী), Mar. (पाणी), from **Pániya**, S. (पानीय, from पा, to drink, what is to be drunk, drinkable) Water (in composition and derivation it becomes *Pan*, *Pán*, *Pána*, *Páná*).

Páná, Mar. (पाना) Spoiled by rain after being cut, as grain, especially rice.

Pánáḍí, Mar. (पानाडी) A water-diviner, a man who pretends to discover water beneath the soil, and directs where to dig for it.

Páṇakyá, Mar. (पाणक्या) A water-carrier.

Pánbhar, written also, *Panboor*, (?) Mar. Land recently irrigated by sinking a new well, or such as is watered by the surplus drainage of wells or pools not situated in it: land liable to be flooded, rent of such land.

Páṇbharyá, Mar. (पाणभऱ्या) A water-carrier.

Páṇbuḍít, Mar. (पाणबुडीत) Destroyed by excessive rain—crops, &c.

Pánbúṛ, (?) Mar. Rent of land liable to be flooded.

Panchakí, H. (پنچکی). A water-mill.

Páṇḍala, Mar. (पाणदल) A place that retains water some time after the rains.

Pangáchá, Hindi (पनगाचा) Fields saturated with water and having it some inches deep on the surface.

Panhala, Mar. (पन्हल) A pipe for carrying off water, a drain, an aqueduct.

Panhará, fem. *Panharin*, H. (پنہرا, پنہرن) A man or woman carrying water-pots on the head.

Panherí, Mar. (पन्हेरी) A place by the road-side for supplying travellers with water: the act of supplying them.

Pánikar, Uriya (ପାଣିକର) Rent for irrigation.

Paniyárí, Hindi (पनियारी) Inundated.

Páṇloṭ, Mar. (पाणलोट) A slope that will carry off water: a declivity, as opposed to level ground, constituting sometimes the boundary of a tank.

Panmár, Hindi (पनमार) Soil submerged by floods so as not to be capable of cultivation.

Páṇphol, Mar. (पाणफोल) Ears of rice empty in consequence of excessive rain.

Páṇpíka, *Páṇpikaleṇ*, Mar. (पाणपीक, पाणपिकलें) Grains that must be sown at the beginning of the rainy season, such as require abundance of water.

Páṇrahâṭh, Mar. (पाणरहाट) A water-mill.

Pansál, Pansálá, H. (پنسال, پنسالا) A place where water is distributed to travellers.

Pántaka, (?) Mar. A small tax on irrigated lands.

Páṇthal, Mar. (पाणथळ, from स्थळ, soil) Watered by irrigation, soil retaining water.

Páṇwaḷ, Mar. (पाणवळ) A place or soil retaining water some time after the rains.

PAṆÍ, Tam., Mal. (பணி, S. पण) Work, workmanship, business, office, service.

Paṇikkan, Tam., Mal. (பணிக்கன்) An artisan, a workman, a head workman, a master builder, carpenter, &c.

Paṇikkal, Mal. (പണിക്കൽ) A name given to Śúdras.

Paṇikáran, Mal. (പണികാരൻ) An artisan, a workman, a servant; also an agent or officer on the part of a superior chief, superintending his dependants and administering justice in a village or district.

Paṇippura, Mal. (പണിപ്പുര) A workshop, a manufactory.

Paṇividaikáran, Tam. (பணிவிடைக்காரன்) An attendant or ministering priest in a temple.

PÁṆI, S. &c. (पाणि) The hand.

Paṇigrahaṇa, S. &c. (from ग्रहण, taking) Marriage, part of the ceremony consisting of the bridegroom's taking the hand of the bride.

Páṇigṛihítá, or *-gṛihítí*, S. &c. (पाणिगृहीता, -गृहीती) A bride, a wife, one who has been taken by the hand and legally married.

PANJ, H. (P. پنج) Five.

Panja, H. (پنجه), *Panjá*, Mar. (पंजा) The hand with the fingers extended: a representation of the same mounted on a staff and carried in procession at the Muharram, supposed to represent the hand of *Âli*.

Panjdúí, Sindhi (پنج دوي) Two-fifths of the produce levied as revenue.

Pánj-tan, or *Pánj-taní-pák*, H. (P. پنج تن, پنج تن پاك) The five persons, or the five holy persons of the *Shíás* or Muhammad, Âli, Fátima, Hasan, and Hasain.

Panj-tírthí, Uriya (from S. तीर्थ, a place of pilgrimage) A pilgrim to Jagannath of an inferior class, and who is not allowed to enter the temple.

PAṆJÁ, Mar. (पणजा) A paternal great grandfather. PAṆJÍ (पणजी) A paternal great grandmother.

PANJÁITÁ, (?) Guz. A large rake for thinning and weeding corn, drawn by bullocks.

PANJAM-ÚLÍGDÁR, (?) Mar. Any one of the chief district or or village officers to whom presents or fees (*úlíg*) are to be paid, such as the *Desái*, *Pátil*, &c.

PANJAY-TARABA, (?) Mal. A class of slaves in Kurg.

PÁNJÍ, PÁNJIKÁ, Beng. (পাঁজী, পাঁজিকা) An almanac, a kalendar. See *Panchánga*.

PAṈJU, Tam. (பஞ்சு) Cotton-cloth: cotton separated from the seeds and prepared for spinning.

Panjiṇúl, Tam. (பஞ்சிநூல்) Cotton thread.

PANJURI, Uriya (ପଞ୍ଜୁରି, from S. पंच) Five marks representing a total of five *maunds*.

PANKTI, S. &c. (पंक्ति) A row, a company, especially an assembly of Brahmans or respectable persons at some religious ceremony.

Sabhá-pankti, Karn. (S. ಸಭಾಪಂಕ್ತಿ) A company or assembly of persons of one caste, especially when assembled for discussion.

PANNACHERI, (?) Sindhi. A tax on cattle grazing on public lands.

PAṆṆAI, Tam. (பண்ணை) A field, a rice-field: cultivated ground: tillage, husbandry.

Paṇṇaikáran, Tam. (பண்ணைக்காரன்) A husbandman, the foreman of agricultural labourers, especially of the Pareya tribe, a superintendant of cultivation.

Paṇṇaissumai, Tam. (பண்ணைச்சுமை) A bundle of corn in the straw given to the labourers at harvest time.

Paṇṇai-yáḷ, Tam. (பண்ணையாள்) A ploughman, an agricultural labourer.

PANNIAH, PUNNA, PUNNAH, (?) Mal. (?) An estate or farm the property of the Rája, and cultivated by his slaves.—Kurg. (It may be a corruption of the Tam. *Paṇṇai*.

PANNIAR, (?) Mal. A class of agricultural slaves in Malabar.

PANNI-MALAYAN, (?) Mal. A servile caste in Malabar.

PANNÚ, Tam., Tel. (பண்ணூ) Tax, tribute, custom, rent.

PANOLÁ, Hindi (पनोला) Land watered after ploughing.

PÁṆSARÁ, Mar. (पाणसरा) An officer of customs, one especially employed to levy tolls or transit duties at mountain passes.

PANSÁRÍ, H. (پنساري) A druggist, a dealer in groceries, spices, herbs, &c. See *Pasári*.

Pansárhatá, H. (پنسارهتا) Dealing in groceries and drugs.

PANSERI, H. (پنسيري, for *pancha*, five, and *sér*, the measure), *Pasári*, *Pasurí*, Beng. (পসারী, পসুরী) A weight or measure of five *sérs*, used especially for grain or rice.

PÁNṢÍ, Hindi (पांशी) A net for carrying grass or straw.

PANṢÍ, Beng. (পনশী), PANSOÏ, corruptly, PAUNCHWAY,

PAUṆSWAY, H. (پنسوي) A boat for passengers or goods, varying in burthen, having a tilted roof of bambu, mats, and thatch over the aft portion, usually rowed by two or four men, but carrying a mast and two sails, the most frequent boat in use on the Calcutta river.

ANT, PUNT, Mar. (पंत), abbreviation of *Pandit*) A prefix to the titles of the eight great officers of state under the old regime, as *Pant-pratinidhi, Pant-amátya,* &c.: when it follows a name it denotes a Brahman who is not a Sanscrit scholar, but employs himself in accounts and writing: in the northern Sarkárs it denotes a Brahman employed as a writer by the government, and is usually addressed to him in the plural or *Pantulu* (Tel.)

Pantoji, Mar. (पंतोजी) The ordinary village schoolmaster.

ANTA, Tel. (పంట) Harvest, crop.

Panṭacheruvu, Tel. (పంటచెరువు) A tank for watering rice-fields.

Panṭakailu, Tel. (పంటకైలు) Measurement of the crop.

Panṭanirasam, Tel. (పంటనీరసం) Scantiness of the crops.

Panṭasála, Tel. (పంటసాల) A granary.

Pedda-panṭa, Tel. (పెద్దపంట) The first or best crop, either in time or quality: the rice or *Jawári* harvest.

NTH, PUNTH, (?) H. The name of a class of Brahmans in Kamaon.

NTHÍ, H. (پنتهي, पंथी, from S. पंथा, *panthá*, lit., a road, or, fig., a way of life, a doctrine) The follower of any particular sect or teacher, or *Aghora-panthí*, one of the *Aghora* sect; *Kabír-panthí*, a follower of Kabír.

NTHÍ, or PÁTHÍ, Mar. (पांथी, पाथी), PÁNTÍ, Guz. (પાંતી) A share in any business or property.

Pánthí-dár, Mar., *Pántídár*, Guz. (पांथीदार, पांतीदार) A sharer, a partner.

Pantiáro, Pantiálo, Guz. (પંતીઆરો-લો) A sharer, a partner, an associate.

NWÁR-SHÁDI, less correctly, PUNWAH-SHADEE, H. (P. شادي, marriage: the first term, although printed *Punwah*, should no doubt be *Pan-, Pun-wár* پنوار, from *vár*, or *wár*, in composition, according to, after the manner of, and *pan*, wages, hire) A kind of marriage in some parts of Bengal of a female slave to a nominal or vagrant husband, who, for a small payment, agrees to wed any number of such women: cohabitation rarely follows, and the object of the arrangement is to provide a putative father for any child the woman may bear, by whomsoever begotten, and which then becomes the property of the owner of the female slave.

PÁO, H. &c. (پاو) A quarter.

Páon, or *Páún*, H. (پاون, from *Pá*, for *Páo*, and S. *úna* ऊन, less, minus), Mar. (पाऊण) A quarter less: used in composition with numerals, as *Paön-e-do*, less correctly, *Paone-do*, a quarter less two; *i.e.* one and three-quarters *Paön-e-do-rúpaiya*, two rupees less a quarter; *i.e.* one rupee twelve anas, and so on.

Páo-ṭahí, barbarously, *Powtahy*, H. (پاوٹهي) A quarter of a rupee: in Chittagong, an allowance of a quarter rupee per cent., on the revenue paid to the *kánungo*.

PAONÁ, Beng. (পাওনা, S. प्रापण) Due: a debt: what is to be received or recovered.

Páoniyá, Beng. (পাওনিয়া) One who has a right to receive, a creditor, an heir.

Páotí, H. (پاوتي) Income.

PÁPA, vernacularly, PÁP, H. &c. (پاپ, पाप) Sin, crime, wickedness.

PÁPAṚ, H. (S. پاپڑ, पापड) A thin crisp cake made of the flour of any kind of pulse.

PÁPAR, Hindi (पापर) Fertile soil.

PÁPAṬAMU, Tel. (పాపటము) A harrow.

PÁR, Hindi (पार) Coarse rice stubble: lands sown with rice when measured, and so entered in the register.—Puraniya.

PÁRA, vernacularly, PÁR, S. &c. (پار, पार) The opposite bank of a river, or of any piece of water.

Párwár, properly, *Párávára*, H. (S. پاروار, पारावार) On both sides of a piece of water or river.

PÁṚA, or PÁṚ, Mar. (पाड) Rate, price-current.

PÁRA, Mar. (पार) A bank or mound round the root of a *Pípal* or *Baṛ* tree (Ficus religiosa, or F. indica), where the villagers are accustomed to assemble: hence, a village council.

PAṚA, Mar. (पड) Fallow land.

PAṚÁ, or PAḌÁ, Hindi (पडा) The boundary of a field.

PAṚA, Mal. (പറ) A measure of capacity, commonly, though incorrectly, written *Parrah*, or *Purrah*, and consequently confounded with a different measure: see *Parra*: the *Paṛa* is the common grain measure of Malabar, equal to 10 *yedangallis*, and containing 1264 cubic inches, rather more than 4 imperial gallons or 40 lb. avoirdupois: as applied to seed corn it denotes the quantity required to sow a certain extent of land so as to produce a given amount of rent by the sale-price of the crop: the land varies in extent according to its greater or lesser fertility, sometimes yielding a return of thirty times the seed, sometimes only five times: the ordinary range of extent is from about 6400 to about 9600 square feet: according to Mr. Arbuthnot (Malayalam selections), lands in Malabar are distinguished under three classes, a field of the first yielding twenty-fold, or about 40 *Paras* to two of seed, the second fifteen-fold, or thirty *paras*, and the third ten-fold, or twenty *paras*.

PARA, S. &c. (पर) Other, different, inferior, strange, foreign, &c. (it is used in composition, as is its modification *Param*, in all the dialects, in a great variety of terms having reference to one or other of its significations).

Parabattiyam, Tam. (பரபத்தியம்) Money transactions, money lent, dealings and accounts with another person.

Parabhárla, Tel. (పరభార్ల) Referred to another person for payment, assignment: placing an order for payment in the hands of another.

Paradesa, S. &c. (देश, a country) Another, or a foreign country.

Paradesí, vernacularly, *Pardesí*, S. &c. (परदेशी) A foreigner, a stranger, one from another or distant part of the same country.

Paradesavásí, Tam. (பரதேசவாசி, from S. वासी, a dweller) A foreigner, a stranger.

Paradesiga, Karn. (ಪರದೇಶಿಗ) A foreigner, a stranger.

Paradwára, Mar. (S. द्वार, a door; but this is no doubt either an error or a vernacular corruption of *dára* दार, S. a wife) Intercourse with a strange woman, especially with the wife of another man: adultery.

Paragotra, S. &c. (गोत्र, a family) Belonging to a different family, whether of the same or of a different caste.

Paraja, S. &c. (परज) Born of another father: the son of a wife appointed to raise issue to a deceased or impotent husband.

Parakudi, corruptly, *Paracoodie*, *Paracoody*, *Poorcoodie*, *Purokoodee*, *Paragoody*, *Poodoogoody*, *Pírakudi*, *Purakudi*, having been sadly distorted, Tam. (பரகுடி, from S. पर, and Tam. குடி, an inhabitant) A migratory or non-resident cultivator, one whose proper home is in another place, one not a member of the village community and having no proprietary rights, but holding and cultivating lands in the village, either for a stipulated term or at pleasure: the *Páhi-kásht* cultivator of Hindustan: see *Kudi*.

Parakudi-váram, Tam. (வாரம், a share) The share of the crop that is assigned to the cultivating tenant, the rest being the right of the *Mirásdár*, or landlord.

Ul-parakudi, corruptly, *Parakudi-ul*, more correctly, *Ulkudi*, q. v. Tam. (உள்பரகுடி) A cultivator who, although not a proprietor, has inherited the land he cultivates, and cannot be dispossessed as long as he pays the stipulated rent: (the compound, though so used, is an obvious contradiction, as the cultivator does not dwell in another place: it is either an error, or is laxly used for *Ulkudi*).

Parampara, S. &c. (परं, repeated) One after another, in succession, hereditary, traditional; fem. *Parampari*, successive arrangement, series, lineage.

Paramparágata, S. (परम्परागत) Come in succession, inherited, descended.

Parapúrvá, vernacularly, *Parapúrbá*, S. &c. (परपूर्वा) A woman re-married: one who was formerly the wife of another: seven cases of second marriage, or rather of cohabitation, are acknowledged in Hindu law, but in practice they are restricted to the *Súdra* castes: 1. when the first marriage has not been consummated; 2. when a girl has been unchaste and is married to another than the gallant; 3. when a widow is married to a kinsman to raise issue for her deceased husband: in each of these the woman is termed *Punar-bhú*, she who is (wedded) again: in the other four cases she is termed *Swairiní*, independent, uncontrolled; as, 4. when she cohabits with another man during her husband's life; 5. when she has deserted her husband for another man, but has been taken back by the former; 6. when she cohabits with a stranger after her husband's death, for her own pleasure; and 7. when she does so under the pressure of some urgent motive, as that of poverty: among the Marathas, second marriages, termed *Pat*, q. v., are not unfrequent amongst the inferior castes.

Párasava, S. &c. (पारशव) The son of a man by another's wife: the offspring of the three first classes by a *Súdra* female.

Pára-straineya, S. &c. (पारस्त्रैणेय, from *para* and *strí*, a female) The son of another man's wife, either one born of her during her husband's lifetime, when he is properly termed *kunda*, or after the husband's death, when he is termed *golaka*.

PÁRÁ, Beng. (পাড়া) A village, part of a village or town: it is commonly used in composition to form the names of villages in Bengal, as *Gokul-párá*, &c. Mar. (पाडा) A cluster of houses situated at a little distance from the village to which they belong for the convenience of carrying on cultivation.

Párágám, Beng. (পাড়াগাম) A village, a hamlet.

Parab, Guz. (પરબ, from S. प्रपा, from पा, to drink) A place where water is given to passers by.

Parabiya, Guz. (પરબીય) A person stationed at a water-shed to distribute water to passengers: one who sells water.

Parábhava, S. &c. (पराभव, from परा, implying reverse) Defeat, disgrace, nonsuit: the name of the fortieth year of the cycle, corresponding in the current cycle with A.D. 1846.

Paraiyan, commonly, but corruptly, Pariah, or Pariar, the latter from the plur. Paraivar, also, Paraiyadikiravan, Tam. (பறையன், பறையடிக்கிறவன்), Parayan, and Para, Mal. (പറയൻ, പറ) A man of a low caste, an outcaste, performing the lowest menial services: one of his duties is to beat the village drum, *Parai* (பறை), whence, no doubt, the generic appellation of the caste: the *Paraiyas*, are not known in India by that name, but they are numerous in the south, where they are usually the serfs or slaves of the *Súdra* agriculturists: they are also attached to the village communities, performing the duties of scavengers, messengers, and other low functions, for which they are paid by portions of the crops, and some small privileges, but they are not allowed to reside in the village, having a place outside assigned to them: there are said to be thirteen subdivisions, named *Valluvapparai*, *Tádaparai*, *Tangalánaparai*, *Durcháliparai*, *Kuliparai*, *Tipparai*, *Murasaparai*, *Ambuparai*, *Vadugaparai*, *Áliyaparai*, *Valiparai*, *Vettiyárparai*, *Koliyaparai*.

Paraichéri, corruptly, *Parchirry*, and *Patcherry*, Tam. (பறைச்சேரி) A *Paraiya* village, or the part outside of a village or town in which the lowest castes reside.

Parájaya, S. &c. (पराजय, from परा, reverse) Defeat, overthrow, losing a cause, nonsuit.

Parampa, or, as pronounced, Paramba, incorrectly, Parombha, Mal. (പറമ്പ) A garden, a plantation, especially of cocoa-nut and areka trees, but commonly used in a wider sense, or for an estate in general; such plantations forming very often the most valuable part of the property: also, high ground not admitting of irrigation; also land raised and drained.

Paramba-páttam, Mal. (പറമ്പപാട്ടം) Rent of plantations or of dry lands.

Parambavâram, Mal. (പറമ്പവാരം) The share of the proprietor in the produce of an estate which he has let or mortgaged.

Parambu, Tam. (பரம்பு) Extension, spreading: a board used for smoothing a ploughed field after the grain is sown.

Parambadikuradu, Tam. (பரம்படிக்குரடு) Levelling a field before ploughing.—Chtngleput.

Parambhattar, Parambhattárak, (?) Conditional sale of a slave.—Tirhut.

Paránch, or Pránch, Hindi (परांच) A vindictive practice in Central India, in which a person conceiving himself aggrieved by another attaches a notice to some outhouse or property, as a barn, an orchard, or the like, belonging to the offender, announcing that unless redress is granted, or compliance with a certain requisition promised, the property will sooner or later be demolished; a threat invariably accomplished.

Paranchá, (?) A carrier, a conductor.

Parápu, (?) Tam. A quit-rent, a cess or tax imposed by a Zamindár, or by government, upon cultivators.

Páras, or Páras-pathar, H. &c. (پارس, پارسپتهر, S. स्पर्श) The philosopher's stone.

Parasa, Parasu, vulgarly, Parsa, Parsú, Mar. (परस, परसू) An enclosure round a house, a yard, especially a back-yard.

Parasuráma, S. &c. (परशुराम, or *Rama* with the (*parasu*) axe) An avatar of *Vishnu*, to whom the recovery fiom the sea of *Kerala*, or *Malabar*, is ascribed, by casting his axe from a point of the coast, Mount Dilli, or, more accurately in Ptolemy, Purrhus-mons, or mountain of *Parasu-ráma*, to the extreme south; the sea retiring from the part over which the axe flew: he gives name to a chronological era used in Malabar, commencing 1176, B.C., and reckoned in cycles of 1000 solar years: the third, or current cycle, commenced A.D. 1825 with the sun's entrance into Virgo.

Parasuráma-srishti, S. (from सृष्टि, creation) The creation of *Parasuráma*, the Malabar coast from Gokarna to Cape Comorin.

Paratana, vulgarly, Partan, Mar. (परतन, from परतणे, to return) The extent of land that may be annually ploughed by the single going and returning of a plough, hence implying a small field or strip of land, usually about four or five *bighás*.

Paratanisá, Mar. (परतनिशा) Assurance of credit taken respecting a person for whom another has elsewhere become responsible.

Paratbhánde, Mar. (परतभांडे) Return, hire.

Párava, Mal. (പാറാവ) Confinement, imprisonment.

Páráharan, Mal. (പാറാക്കാരൻ) A guard.

Párappura, Mal. (പാറാപ്പുര) A guard-room, a place of confinement.

PARAVALKÁḌU, Tam. (பரவல்க்காடு) Brushwood.

Paravalkáḍu-punjay, Tam. (பரவல்க்காடுபுஞ்சய்) Dry cultivation amidst brushwood.

PARAVAN, Mal. (പറവൻ) A man of a low caste, or the name of the caste.

PARAVÁRÍ, vulgarly, PARWÁRI, Mar. (परवारी) The village guide and watchman, the *Mahár* who performs these duties, in which capacity this is his more respectful denomination.

PARBHÁRÁ-HAK, Mar. (परभाराहक, from परभारा, intermediately, indirectly) An incidental or occasional claim or privilege, as a share of the crop, &c., occasionally the right of a village officer or servant.

PARBHÚ, PURBHOO, commonly, but corruptly, called PURVOE, Mar. (परभू, प्रभु, a chief) The name of the writer caste in the west of the Peninsula, or of an individual of that caste: the *Parbhus* pretend to be descended from *Chandrasena*, a Rája of Malabar, and consequently to be by origin pure *Kshatriyas*; claiming, therefore, right to the purificatory ceremonies, or *Sanskáras* of the Brahminical code, to read the Vedas, and to wear the cord and other distingushing marks of the *Kshatriya*, or primary military caste; their claims are with reason denied by the Brahmans, who regard them as of menial origin, and inferior, therefore, to the pure *Śúdras*: they are divided into three classes, the *Chandraseni Parbhús*, who are principally at Puna, the *Paṭanya*, at Bombay and Surat, and the *Dhavani* (?) at Goa.

PÁRCHA, H. (P. پارچه) Cloth, clothing, a piece of cloth.

Párchái-jins, Tel. from H. (పార్చాయిజింస్) Cloth goods.

PARCHÚNÍ, H. (پرچوني) Selling flour or meal.

Parchuniá, H. (پرچونيا) A seller of flour.

PARCHURAṆ, Mar. (परचुरण) Coin of various currencies as distinguished from current coin.

PARDA, H. (P. پرده) A veil, a screen, a curtain, especially one which excludes the women of a family from the gaze of men.

Parda-nishin, *Purdah-nisheen*, H. (from P. نشين, sitting, seated) lit., Seated behind a curtain, applied to a respectable female who observes the rules of seclusion, and who is on that account excused from personal appearance in a court of justice.

PAREHA, Hindi (परेह) Land watered after ploughing, or flooded before the final ploughing and levelling of the ground.

PAREMUDAL, (?) Confiscation of smuggled goods.

PARGANA, PURGUNU, corruptly, PERGUNNAH, H. &c. (پرگنه, plur. *Parganát* پرگنات), PARGAṆÁ, Mar. (परगणा), Tel. (పంగణా) A district, a province, a tract of country comprising many villages, but of which several go to constitute a *Chakla* or *Zilá*: the actual extent varies, but the distinction is permanent.

Pargana-ḳánungo, H. (قانونگو) The record keeper of a district.

Parganát-i-jamâ, H. (A. جمع) The total amount of revenue assessed upon a province.

Panganát-i-kharch, H. (A. خرچ) The expenses and charges of a district to be deducted from the gross revenue.

Parganát-i-nirkh, H. (from نرخ, price current) The rates of the valuation of the crops and the assessment of the revenue and other items of expense and receipt which ordinarily prevail or are established in a district.

Parganawár, H. (پرگنهوار) According to district: settlement, assessment, &c.

PARI, S. &c. (परि) About, around, back, off, &c.: (used in S. and its derivatives mostly as the first member of a compound).

Parichha, corruptly, *Purcha*, Uriya (ପରିଛା) A head officer or superintendant, one of the managers of the temple of Jagannath.

Paridánam, S. &c. (परिदानं) Giving back, or in return, exchange, barter. Karn. (ಪರಿದಾನಂ) A bribe.

Paridhávi, S. &c. (परिधावी) The forty-sixth of the cycle corresponding in the current cycle with A.D. 1852.

Parigraha, S. &c. (परिग्रह) Acceptance, taking a present: adoption: a wife.

Parikhá, S. &c. (परिखा), *Pariká*, *Parikai*, Tam. (பரிகா, பரிகை) A ditch, a fosse.

Paríkshá, S., Mar., Beng. (परीक्षा), sometimes modified, as *Parakh*, *Párakh*, *Parkhái*, H. (پرکه, پارکه, پرکهاي), *Parakhái*, Tel. (పరఖాయి) Inspection, investigation, verification of measurement or assessment, assay of coins, analysis, trial, ordeal.

Paríkshaka, S. &c. (परीक्षक), *Párakh*, corruptly, *Parik*, *Párhhi*, corruptly, *Purky*, and *Párkhiá*, corruptly, *Purkea*, H. (پارکه, پارکهي, پرکهيا), *Parikh*, Guz. (પરીખ) An examiner, an investigator, a money-changer, a banker; whence it is a common cognomen for persons of that class, as in the case of *Gokul-párakh*, or *-párik*, treasurer and finance-minister of Daulat Rao Sindhia; also, in S. and the Hindu dialects, a judge: in an inferior capacity, an assayer, a tester, a guager, as the *Parkhia* of an opium factory employed to examine the quality of the opium.

Parkháüní, corruptly, *Purkavani*, H. (پرکهاوني) Examination, especially of coins, assaying.

Parkhera, H. (پرکهیرا) A money-changer, an officer whose duty it was to examine and value coins paid into the public treasury.

Pariṇáya, S. &c. (परिणय) Marriage.

Pariṇáya, *Pariṇáyya*, S. (परिणाय, परिणाय्य) Wealth received at the time of marriage, marriage ornaments, or the like, a woman's own property.

Paripálana, S. &c. (परिपालन) Protecting, cherishing, ruling over, government.

Parishkára, S. (परिष्कार) Making entire or perfect. Tel. (పరిష్కారం) Settlement of accounts in revenue matters.

Pariṣílané, Karn. (S. ಪರಿಶೀಲನೆ) Inquiry, investigation.

Parivarttanam, S. (परिवर्त्तनं), Tam. (பரிவர்த்தனம்) Exchange, barter: in the south the term is applied to the deed by which rent-free land is converted into land paying revenue, and an equivalent portion of assessed land is made exempt.

Parivitti, S. (परिवित्ति) A man whose younger brother is married before him.

Parivettá, S. (परिवेत्ता) A younger brother married before his elder.

Parivedana, S. (परिवेदन) The marriage of a younger brother before that of the elder, which is considered to be an improper act.

Parivrája, S. &c. (परिव्राज) A Hindu wandering mendicant.

Pariwálá, or *Pariya*, Hindi. A hired ploughman who is bound, by an advance which he cannot repay, to labour gratuitously during a portion of his time, for the benefit of the lender.—Gorakhpur.

Paryáya, S. (पर्य्याय) Order, succession.

Pariyáya, or *Paryáya*, Karn. (ಪರಿಯಾಯ, ಪರ್ಯಾಯ) The succession of the eight *Swámis*, or spiritual heads of the followers of *Madhwácharya*, who preside over the establishments of the sect in Karnáta in succession, and employ the intermediate period in travelling over the country, and collecting contributions.

Paṛi, or Paḍi, Uriya (ପଡ଼ି) Daily subsistence.

Paṛiá, or Paḍiá, Uriya (ପଡ଼ିଆ) Land out of cultivation, waste or fallow land.

Paṛiá-jamín, Uriya (from P. زمین, land) Waste or fallow land.

Parige, Tel. (పరిగె) Gleanings of corn.

Párína-daftar, H. (P. پارینه‌دفتر) Old records.

Paríṭ, Mar. (परीट) A washerman by caste and occupation, the village washerman.

Paríṭvárá, Mar. (परीटवाडा) The washerman's quarter, the part of the village or town where the washermen reside.

Parnála, H. (پرنالا) A drain, a conduit.

Parosí, Hindi, &c. (परोसी, S. *prati*, near, *vásí*, a dweller, प्रतिवासी) A neighbour.

Parpaiṭh, H. (پرپیٹهہ, परपैठ) The duplicate of a bill of exchange.

Parra, Tel. (పర్ర) A measure of capacity, the fortieth part of a *Túm*: it was also considered equal to five *marakáls*, or 3735.413 cubic inches or one-eightieth of a *gárisa*, = 13.836 imperial gallons: by other computations it was made to contain 3681.640, or 3744 cubic inches: the present standard *Parra* is fixed at 4000 inches: it is still rated as equal to five *marakáls*, but the *marakál* is somewhat larger: see *Paṟa*.

Parra, Tel. (పర్ర, or పఱ్ఱ) A swamp or salt-marsh.

Parra-vuppu, or *-uppu*, Tel. (పర్రవుప్పు) Swamp or spontaneous salt efflorescence.

Parre, Tel. (పర్రె) A salt-measure (perhaps the same as the Maraṭha *phara*, which, for salt, is a *man* of 64 *sers*).

Paṛṛú, or Paḍḍú, Guz. (પડુ) Suburb or branch of a village or town.

Paṟṟuchíṭṭi, pron. Paṭṭuchíṭṭi, Mal. (പറ്റുചീട്ടി) A written receipt.

Parsaí, Pursaee, (?) H. In Central India the village priest and astrologer.—Malcolm.

Pársí, Guz. (પારસી) A worshipper of fire: the name of the race settled chiefly in western India, in the Bombay presidency, who still observe the ancient Magian religion: they are distinguished as enterprising merchants, shipbuilders, and traders: their ancestors fled from Persia to India upon the conquest of the former by the Mohammadans, and settled in the latter in the eighth century: although especially applied to them as followers of a peculiar faith, the term properly signifies nothing more than a Persian (S. पारसीक), H. (پارسي).

Paṛtal, Paḍtal, Paṛtál, Guz. (પડતલ, પડતાલ) Waste or uncultivated land.

Partál, Hindi, &c. (परताल), Uriya (ପରତାଲ) Re-measurement, as a test of the accuracy of a previous measurement: revision of a former land measurement or survey:

re-weighment: (perhaps from S. *pra*, intensitive, and *tala*, surface).

Partál-jaríb, H. (from P. جريب, a certain measure of land) Re-measurement of land.

Partál-ojan, Uriya (ପରତାଲଓଜନ) Re-weighment to determine the accuracy of a previous weighment.

PARTÍ, H. (پرتي, S. पृथिवी) Waste or uncultivated land.

Partí-ḳadím, H. (A. قديم, old) Land which has long been lying uncultivated.

PÁRTHIVA, S. (पार्थिव) Earthen, relating to earth or land: the name of the nineteenth year of the cycle.

PARUGU, Tel. (పరుగు) A measure of distance, a *kos* of from two to three miles.

PARUKÍ-VARAHÁ, Karn. (ಪರುಕೀವರಹಾ) A gold coin or *Ḥun* coined by Tipu at Calicut, properly, *Fáruki*.

PÁRUPATYA, corruptly, PÁRPATYA, Karn. (S. ಪಾರುಪತ್ಯ) Management, superintendence.

Párupatyagár, Karn. (ಪಾರುಪತ್ಯಗಾರ) A manager, a superintendant, the manager of a temple under the superior, a deputy or vice-chief.

PÁRUṢHYA, S. &c. (पारुष्य) Harshness, violence: in law, two descriptions are specified; as,

Daṇḍa-párushya, S. (from दण्ड, a stick) Personal injury, assault, battery, manslaughter, homicide.

Vák-páruṣhya, S. (from वाच्, speech) Verbal injury, abuse, slander, calumny, defamation.

PARVA, PARVAN, S. &c. (पर्व्व, पर्व्वन), PARB, or PARAB, H. (پرب), PARBBA, Beng. (পর্ব্ব) lit., A joint or point of junction, but applied especially to certain junctures or periods of time, as the days of the full and change of the moon, the eighth, eleventh, and fourteenth days of the lunar half-month, the solstices, the equinoxes, the entrance of the sun into a zodiacal sign, of the moon into a lunar asterism, and the like; and as these are appropriate seasons for religious observances the word has come to signify also any sacred day, a holiday or festival.

Párvaṇa, or *Párvaṇí*, vernacularly, *Párbaṇa*, or *Párbaṇí*, corruptly, *Parbunny*, *Purbany*, *Purbony*, S. (पार्व्वण, fem. पार्व्वणी) Any thing relating to a certain *Parva* or holiday, as a ceremony then observed, especially one description of *Śráddha*, or obsequial rite; also the set of progenitors in honour of whom it is celebrated: any fee exacted for the performance of such ceremonies: an impost formerly levied on the Ryots, by the Zamindárs to defray the cost of the religious ceremonies and festivities celebrated by the latter.

Párvaṇa-śráddha, S. &c. (पार्व्वणश्राद्ध) A *śráddha*, or obsequial ceremony to be observed monthly at the *Amávásya*, or conjunction, or new moon: at this rite three balls or cakes of rice, *piṇḍas*, formerly of flesh, are presented to the manes of the father and paternal grandfather, and great-grandfather, and three to the maternal grandfather, his father and grandfather, and the crumbs or fragments of each set are presented to the remoter ancestors in each line.

PÁRVA, Karn. (ಪಾರ್ವ, probably from S. *parva*) A Brahman, one who is connected with periodical rites.

Párviti, Karn. (ಪಾರ್ವಿತಿ) A Brahman woman.

PARVATA, S. &c., vernacularly, PARVAT, or PARBAT, (पर्व्वत) A mountain.

Parvatiya, *Parbatiya*, S. &c. (पर्व्वतिय) A hill-man, a mountaineer, the hill people of Nepal.

PARWA, (?) H. Light sandy soil of a yellowish tint, capable of irrigation.—Bundelkhand.

PARWÁNA, H. &c. (P. پروانه) An order, a written precept or command, a letter from a man in power to a dependant, a custom-house permit or pass, an order for the possession of an estate or assignment of revenue; a warrant, a license, a writ; a paper of permission from a Zamindár to a cultivator to take up lands, leaving the rent to be subsequently settled.

Parwána-bázu, H. (P. بازو, the arm, ?) An order from the Moghul government to the chief financial authority of a district to relinquish the collection of an assigned amount of revenue to the person to whom it has been granted with the necessary jurisdiction.

Parwána-guẕasht, or P. *wá-guẕasht*, H. (P. from گذشت, passed) An order of the Mohammadan government to relinquish to a person to whom the revenues of specified lands have been assigned the right of collection, and all authority therewith connected.

Parwána-i-istaḳlál, H. (استقلال) An order declaratory of the right of permanent possession.

Parwána-i-ṣubahdár, H. (P. صوبهدار) An order issued by the governor of a province for an assignment of revenue, or any other right or privilege.

Parwánagí, H. &c. (پروانگي), Mar. (परवानगी) Permission, leave, license.

Parwánagí-bardár, Mar. (परवानगीबरदार) An officer stationed in the antechamber of a great man to announce arrivals and obtain permission for them to enter.

Parwánagí-chiṭhi, Mar. (चिठी, a note) A licence, a written pass or warrant.

Bâibát-parwána, H. (بيعبات پروانة, from A. بيع, sale: see *Baiâ*) An order or notice of sale, especially on the non-fulfilment of the conditions of a mortgage.

PARWAR, PURWUR, H. (P. پرور, cherishing) A patron, a protector.

Gharíb-parwar, H. (غريب, poor) Protector of the poor, a common complimentary designation addressed by an inferior or dependant to a superior or master.

Parwarda, H. (P. پرورده) Cherished, protected: a domestic slave.

Parwarish, H. (P. پرورش) Cherishing, protecting, fostering, bringing up.

Parwasti, H. (P. پروستي) Cherishing, patronising: supporting old servants or soldiers after they are past work.

PAṚWÍ, H. (پروي, पड़वी) A sort of sugar-cane sown in autumn.

PÁS, H. (P. پاس) Guarding, watching, a guard: a watch of three hours.

Pás-bán, H. (پاسبان) A watchman, a sentinel, a village watchman: also, a shepherd.

Pásí, H. (پاسي) A watchman.

PÁṢA, PÁṢÁ, PÁṢÍ, S. &c. (पाश, पाशा, पाशी) A noose, a loop, a snare, a rope, any thing wherewith to catch or tie a person or thing: in the sense of a cord or other means of strangling it occurs also *Phâns*, or *Phánsa*, q. v. *Páṣa* also means dice for gambling with.

Páṣí, H. (پاسي) A caste of people, or an individual of it, whose occupation is extracting the juice of the *Táṛí* palm, so named from their using a rope loop in climbing, passed round their bodies and round the tree: any one using a noose, or rope, or snare: a birdcatcher: also, one who plays with dice, a gambler.

PASÁËTUṆ, corruptly, PUSSAEETA, PUSSAITA, Guz. (પશાએતું) Rent-free lands allotted to the different orders of village servants in Guzerat; also assignments of the same for religious or charitable purposes.

Pasáëtawálá, Guz. (પશાએતવાલા) An inferior village-servant.

Pasáëluṇ, Guz. (પશાએલું) Land exempt from taxation in consideration of military service when required.

PASAMA, Mal. (പശമ) Soil of the best quality; also said to be designated *Pasama-kuṛ*, from *Kuṛ*, or *Kuṛi*, a pit, as it is said to be a test of this sort of soil that the hole or pit from which any quantity has been dug up will not contain it again: *Pasa* is properly 'paste' or 'glue,' referring to the adhesiveness or tenacity of the soil, which must therefore be a kind of clay.

PASÁNAM, Tam. (பசாணம்) A coarse sort of rice ripening late.

PASAR, Thug. Place or direction appointed for an expedition.

PASÁRA, PASÁRE, Karn. (ಪಸಾರ, ಪಸಾರೆ) A shop.

PASÁRÍ, PANSÁRÍ, H. &c. (پساري, پنساري) A grocer, a druggist, a vendor of drugs, herbs, spices, and groceries.

PASEṬHI, or PHASEṬHI, Uriya (ପଶେଠି, ଫଶେଠି) The head cultivator of a village.

PÁSHÁṆA, vernacularly, PÁSHÁṆ, S. &c. (पाषाण) A stone, a rock. Beng. (পাষান) A stone to weigh with. Tam. (பாசாணம்) A stone, but used in deeds of sale or grants of land to convey a right to all precious stones, minerals, or metallic ores that may be discovered in the land transferred.

Páshâṇa-chaturdaṣí, S. &c. (from चतुर्दशी, the fourteenth lunation) A festival on the fourteenth of the light half of *Márgaṣírsha*, when Durgá is to be worshipped, and cakes in the shape of stones are to be eaten.

PASHM, PUSHM, H. &c. (P. پشم, पशम) Wool, hair, fur.

Pashmina, *Pashmíná*, H. &c. (پشمينة, پشمينا, पशमीना) Woollen cloth.

PÁSÍ, Tam. (பாசி) Duck-weed.

Pásitírvái, Tam. (பாசித்தீர்வை) A tax on fish caught in ponds.

PASIKI, Tel. (పసికి), PASIKE, or PASIGE, Karn. (ಪಸಿಕೆ, ಪಸಿಗೆ) A small fee or bribe given to the government collectors of the *sair* or miscellaneous taxes.

PÁSOḌÍ, Mar. (पासोडी) Lit. A sort of shawl, applied to a small assignment of rent-free land to the *Pátil* of the village.

PASSEWA, (?) H. A semifluid sediment obtained from the capsules of the poppy after the seeds are extracted: it hardens by exposure, and is used in making up the shells of the opium cakes for export: it contains a portion of morphia.

PAṢU, corruptly, PUSHOO, S. &c. (पशु) An animal, especially a domesticated and useful animal.

Paṣupála, S. &c, (पशुपाल) A cowherd, a shepherd, a farmer, one keeping or tending cattle.

Paṣupálana, S. &c. (पशुपालन) Care of cattle, one of the especial functions of the third or *Vaiṣya* caste: the duty of cowherds, shepherds, &c.

PASUBEVALA, Karn. (ಪಸುಬೆವಳ) A merchant, a trader.

PASUGE, Karn. (ಪಸುಗೆ) A share, a portion, a part.

Pasumai, Tam. (பசுமை) Greenness, the verdure of thriving crops

Pasumpul, Tam. (பசும்புல்) Growing corn : green grass.

Pasuṇkarai, incorrectly, Pasungcaray, Tam. (பசுங்கரை) lit. Equitable distribution, the joint proprietary of the lands of a village by a number of coparceners, who may either cultivate them in common or parcel them out from time to time among the coparceners for their several cultivation, the right of each being to a definite proportion of the whole, but not to any one field or piece of land in particular : it is not in his power, therefore, to sell any actual piece of the village land, although he may, with the consent of the other coparceners, sell his share.

Pasupu, (?) Tel. A gift, a settlement or assignment of land to a daughter.

Paṭ, or Paṭa, S. &c. (पट) Cloth, coarse cloth or canvas: covered cloth or chintz : a chequered cloth on which chess or *Pachísí* may be played.

Paṭ, Mar. (पट, S. पट्ट) A roll or register, a list of names, a catalogue or written statement of particulars.

Patwár, or *Patwárí*, corruptly, *Putwarry*, Hindi and Mar. &c. (पटवार, पटवारी) A village accountant, whose duty it is to keep and to produce, when required by the government revenue officers, all accounts relating to lands, produce, cultivation, changes, and past assessment of a village: (the term is probably derived from *Paṭ*, a register, although the office is extinct, or superseded by the *Chaugala* among the Marathas; whilst, on the other hand, *Paṭ*, in the sense of a register or record, is either obsolete or lost in Hindi). The maintenance of the office of *Patwárí* in efficiency is the subject of various Regulations in Bengal: in some places he is appointed and paid by the Zamindárs; in the north-western provinces most commonly by the villagers: in Kamaon he is a government ministerial officer appointed to the charge of one or more *Paṭṭís* or subdivisions of a district, and is paid by a small monthly salary. Ben. Reg. vi. 1795; xxvii. 1803; xii. xiii. 1817; i. 1818; i. 1819.

Pát, H. &c. (پات, S. पत्र) A leaf of a plant; whence it is applied to a leaf of a book, or of paper, and thence to a written paper, a bill, a draft on a banker, a promissory note or engagement to pay a sum of money at a stipulated time.

Pát-bandí, H. (پاتبندي) A statement of the particulars of the assets and debts of an estate as agreed upon between the heirs and claimants.

Páṭ, H. &c. (پاٹ, पाट, S. पट्ट) A plank, a seat, a stool, the board on which a washerman beats clothes: a plant, of which the fibres are used as flax, and from which a coarse canvas and sackcloth are made (Corchorus olitorius and capsularis): a sack of coarse canvas, a sack of corn considered as a load: also, silk, a cocoon of silk.

Paṭwá, H. (پٹوا, पटवा) A silk-weaver, a maker of braid and fringe, a stringer of beads.

Páṭ, Mar. (पाट) A name given to a second marriage among the Marathas, whether of a girl whose betrothed husband has died, or of a widow: the celebration is acknowledged as legal among the lower castes.

Páṭdám, corruptly, *Pautdauma*, Mar. (पाटदाम) A tax formerly levied on second marriages.

Páṭkarí, Mar. (पाटकरी) The husband of a twice-married woman.

Paṭkariṇ, Mar. (पाटकरीण) A woman marrying a second time.

Páṭ, or Páṭa, Mar. (पाट) A small raised water-course for irrigating fields and gardens.

Páṭkari, corruptly, *Patcurry*, Mar. (पाटकरी) The village officer in charge of the water-courses, whose duty it is to see that they are kept in repair, and that the water is fairly distributed.

Páṭasthal, Mar. (पाटस्थल) Cultivated ground irrigated by small channels turned off from brooks or rivulets.

Páṭwar, Mar. (पाटवड) A channel to convey water for irrigation.

Paṭá, H. (پٹا, पटा) A wooden sword, a cudgel.

Patebaz, H. (پٹیباز) A cudgel-player.

Paṭá, H. (پٹا) A code or book of regulations for rent collectors.

Páṭá, Beng. (পাটা) A lease. See *Paṭṭa*.

Páṭárí, Beng. (পাটারী) An agent or factor employed by a landlord to collect his rents.

Páṭa, Uriya (ପାଟ), Páṭam, Mal. (പാടം) An open level tract, an expanse of low land or of rice-fields.

Patai, Hindi (पतै) Straw or grass strewn over a field to protect the fresh-planted roots from the sun.

Patak, Mar. (पतक) A body of horse, usually about a hundred.

Patakí, *Patakyá*, Mar. (पतकी, पतक्या) The leader of a troop of horse: a subordinate officer employed in the collection of the customs.

Pátaka, vernacularly, Pátak, S. &c. (पातक) Sin, crime. See *Mahápátaka*.

Pátakí, S. &c. (पातकी) A sinner, a criminal.

PÁṬAKÁLAGUTTA, Tel. (పాటకాలగుత్త) Rent or farm of taxes on houses and trades.

PATTAKKAN, Tam. (பத்தக்கன்) A man of a low caste, an outcaste.

PÁTAKWÁ, H. (S. پاتکوا) A messenger.

PATAM, Mal. (പതം) The portion of the crop given to the reapers in pay of their labour.

PATAMMA, PUTUMMA, (?) H. A deed of usufructuary mortgage.—Gorakpur.

PATANI, Thug. A sneeze, considered ominous.

PÁTAṚÁ, Beng. (পাতড়া) A ration of food: a waste book.

PÁTARA, Tel. (పాతర) A pit for preserving grain.

PAṬÁŪ, PAṬÁVAN, or **PAṬAŪN**, Hindi (پٹاؤ, पटाव, पटावण) Irrigation.

PÁṬAVI-KUNWAR, Guz. (પાટવીકુંવર) The eldest son of a Thákur or Raja in Guzerat.

PAṬELÁ, H. (پٹیلا) A large flat-bottomed boat used for merchandise on the Ganges.

PATH, H. &c. (پتھ, पथ, from S. पथिन) A road, a way, a *path*, fig., a doctrine, a sect.

Pathika, vernacularly, *Pathik*, H. &c. (پتھک, पथिक) A traveller.

PÁṬHA, vernacularly, **PÁṬH**, Hindi, &c. (S. पाठ) Reading, a reading, a lecture.

Páṭhak, Hindi, &c. (S. पाठक) A reader, a public reader, a Brahman who reads the epic poems and Puranas in public: the name of a class of Maraṭha Brahmans: in Orissa, a designation of mixed impure castes: (but this must be either a vernacular corruption or error for *Páṭaka*, a sinner, one fallen or degraded).

Páṭhsálá, Beng. (S. পাঠশালা) A school, a college.

PÁTHA, (?) H. A measure of seed equal to about two *sers*, whence it is applied to a measure of land or as much as may be sown with that quantity of seed: it is rated at about twenty yards by two, or 240 square feet.—Kamaon.

PAṬHÁN, H. (پٹھان) The same as *Afghan*, but chiefly used in Hindustan to designate adventurers of that nation or their descendants, who have colonised and settled in India, especially in Rohilkhand.

PATHAR, or **PÁTHAR**, H. &c. (پتھر ,پاتھر, S. प्रस्तर) A stone.

Patharilá, H. (پتھریلا) Stoney, as soil.

Páthariyá, Beng. (পাথরীয়া), *Pátharwat*, Mar. (पाथरवट) A stone-cutter or breaker by caste and occupation, a mason.

PATHORÍ, Thug. The chirping of a small owl.

PATI, H. &c. (S. پتي, पति) A husband, a protector, a master.

Patní, H. &c. (S. پتني, पत्नी) A wife.

Patníbhága, (S. पत्नीभाग) Division of property amongst a man's widows.

PÁTI, Mal. (പാതി) A half, a moiety.

Pátika, incorrectly, *Pateka*, Mal. (പാതിക) A share, a portion, especially of landed property, a half-portion.

Pátikáran, Mal. (പാതിക്കാരൻ) A partner, a sharer.

Pátiváram, Mal. (പാതിവാരം) A half-share, applied especially to a lease or tenure of land by which half the produce is to be given to the proprietor.

Pátivárachíṭṭa, Mal. (പാതിവാരച്ചീട്ട) A written engagement in a lease to pay or to receive half the produce.

PÁṬÍ, also **PAṬṬÍ**, Beng. (পাটী, পট্টী) A slip of cloth, a narrow strip of land: also the part of a market appropriated to dealers in similar articles: in some places, a village or cluster of houses detached from, though dependent on, the original village.

PÁṬÍ, Beng. (পাটী) A fine mat: a plant of which such mats are made (Cyperus inundatus).

PATIÁ, H. (پتیا, S. पत्रिका, a page) The written opinion of a *Pandit* on a question of Hindu law.

PATIÁR, Thug. The cry of the partridge.

PATIÁRA, Uriya (ପତିଆର) Trust, confidence.

PÁTICHOR, Beng. (পাতিচোর, from *páti*, a little) A petty thief.

PÁṬIDÁR, Guz. (પાટીદાર, probably vernacular corruption of *Paṭṭidár*, q. v.) A hereditary cultivator.

PÁṬÍL, corruptly, **POTEEL**, Mar. (पाटील), **PAṬEL**, corruptly, **POTAIL, POITAL**, H. &c. (پٹیل, पटेल), **PAṬÉL**, Karn. (ಪಟೇಲ) The head man of a village, who has the general control and management of the village affairs, is head of the police, and exercises, to a limited extent, the functions of a magistrate; he is also the principal agent in the realization of the revenue, and the chief medium of communication with the officers of the government: in the Maraṭha countries the office is frequently held under a government grant, in many instances that of the government of Delhi, and has certain emoluments and privileges attached to it: it is hereditary, and saleable with the consent of the government, and the actual occupant may admit a partner: the term is principally current in the countries inhabited by, or subject to, the Maraṭhas, and appears to be an essential Maraṭhi word, being used as a respectful title in addressing one of that nation, or a Ṣúdra in general: it may be derived from *Pát*, a water-course, the supply of water being fitly under the care of the chief person of the village; or from *Paṭ*, a register or roll (of the inhabitants, &c.) of the village. Bombay Reg. xii. 1827.

Páṭili, Mar. (पाटिली) The assignment of land or perquisites and allowances of the *Páṭil*.

Páṭilki, Mar. (पाटिलकी) The office of *Páṭil*.

Páṭílpatwárí, Mar. (पाटीलपटवारी) A comprehensive term for the officers of a village implied by the designation of the head man and the accountant.

PATITA, or, vernacularly, PATIT, S. &c. (पतित) Fallen: lit. or metaph., fallen from rectitude, wicked, vile, outcaste: fallen off, waste, neglected, uncultivated, fallow (as land): in Puraniya, a term for a reduced rent on lands which a Ryot is allowed by his lease to retain without cultivating them.

Patitábád, Beng. (পতিতাবাদ) The occupation or cultivation of fallow lands, or such land brought into cultivation: a tenure under which waste lands were held on favourable terms on condition of bringing them into cultivation.

Patitábádi-gird-kami, Beng. (from P. *gird* گرد, around, and کمی, deficiency; পতিতাবাদিগীরদকমি) Diminution or deficit of rent on waste lands brought into cultivation, in comparison with that levied on neighbouring lands.

Patit-kami, Beng. (পতিতকমি) Deficiency or remission of rent on account of fields left uncultivated.

PATIVA, Mal. (പതിവ) A register, a lease, a written document given to Ryots acknowleging their right to cultivate.

PAṬKÁ, H. (پٹکا) A girdle, a sash.

Zarí-paṭhá, H. (زري پٹکا) A gold sash or girdle granted by the Peshwa to his chief officers: the national Maratha standard. See *Jari-paṭhá*.

PAṬLÁ, Tel. (పట్లా) Rice-land yielding an intermediate crop between the first and second crops, being under water during the wet season.

PAṬMAÍ, H. (پٹمئي, पटमई) Sowing fresh sugar-cane after cutting the old.

PATORI, Thug. A small owl.

PATOTI, (?) H. A lease or agreement between the proprietor and cultivating occupant of land, limiting the amount of rent demandable, and leaving the tenant in possession as long as it is paid (perhaps for *Paṭṭavatí*, possession of a *Paṭṭa*).

PATPAṚ, Hindi (पतपड) Newly-formed land so situated as to receive an annual accession of alluvial deposit.

PATPAṚÍ, Hindi (पतपड़ी) Surface of soft land caked by sunshine after rain.—Puraniya.

PATRA, vernacularly, PATR, corruptly, PUTTER, &c. (पत्र), PATTIRAM, Tam. (பத்திரம்) A leaf of a plant or tree, any leaf used for writing upon, as that of the birch or palm, or a sheet of paper or metal on which grants or edicts are engraved: a written page or leaf, any written document, as a grant, a deed, a bond, an almanack.

Patriká, S. (पत्रिका), *Patrike*, Karn (ಪತ್ರಿಕೆ) A written paper, a letter, a deed, a document.

Patrudu, Tel. (పత్రుడు) A steward, a cash-keeper, a manager for another.

PÁTRA, vernacularly, PÁTR, S &c. (पात्र) A vessel; whence, fig., a fit person, a person of capacity.

PAṬRAVÁDU, Tel. (పట్రవాడు) A man of a tribe of hill people.

PAṬṬA, S. &c. (पट्ट) Silk, a band or fillet of silk, especially of old the mark of royalty; as seen on the coins of the Seleucidæ and their Indo-Bactrian successors: in Karnáta a plate of brass with magic verses worn for some days on the forehead of a Brahman to avert the conseqences of having been born under an unlucky conjunction of the stars.

Paṭṭaráṇi, S. &c. (पट्टराणी) *Pátrání*, H. (پاترانی) A queen, one who has been crowned or has had the royal fillet on her brow.

PAṬṬÁ, PUṬṬA, corruptly, POTTAH, current in most dialects, sometimes slightly modified, H. (پٹا), Mar. (पट्टा), Tel. (పట్టా), PAṬṬE, Karn. (ಪಟ್ಟೆ), PAṬṬO, Sindhi, PAṬṬA, PAṬṬÁ, Uriya (ପଟ୍ଟ, ପଟ୍ଟା): it is also read in Beng. and Uriya with a single *ṭ*, and in the former with the first vowel long, PÁṬÁ, PAṬÁ (পাটা, ପଟା), PAṬṬAYAM, PAṬṬÁ, corruptly, PATTIAM, PATTIOM, Tam. (பட்டயம், பட்டா) PAṬṬAYAM, Mal. (പട്ടയം) A deed of lease, a document given by the collector to the Zamindár, or by some other receiver of revenue, to the cultivator or under tenant, specifying the condition on which the lands are held and the value or proportion of the produce to be paid to the authority or person from whom the lands are held: the term is laxly applied to a variety of deeds securing rights or property in land, also to a deed of gift in general: also, in the south of India, to a title or appointment of office, or to the office itself, as to that of manager of a temple: *Paṭṭas* have been the subjects of frequent legislation. Ben. Reg. viii. 1793; iv. 1794; v. 1795; v. 1812; vii. 1822. Madras Reg. xxx. 1802; v. 1822.

Paṭṭá-amáni, (?) Designation of a village held under a lease by cultivators from government direct.—South of India.

Paṭṭádár, H. &c. (پٹّادار, पट्टादार) One who holds a lease or engagement for his lands.

Paṭṭá-dahsála, H. (پٹّادهساله) A lease for ten years.

Paṭṭá-janáját, H. (پٹّاجناجات, from S. जन, a man, people) Leases granted to tenants or cultivators individually.

Paṭṭákáran, Tam. (பட்டாக்காரன்) A leaseholder.

Paṭṭákattu, (?) Tam. Agreement of cultivation. See *Paṭṭukattu*.

Paṭṭámániyagár, (?) Karn. The principal or managing holder of land held by several persons under a *Paṭṭá* granted in the name of the principal.

Paṭṭámániyakáran, Tam. (பட்டாமணியக்காரன்) A principal inhabitant appointed for the collection of the revenue and management of village affairs.

Paṭátáliká, Uriya (ପଟାତାଲିକା) A list or register of leases.

Paṭṭátáluk, H. (پٹّاتعلق) A dependent *táluk*, or estate, held on lease, or *Paṭṭá*, from a Zamindár: such a tenure is generally heritable, but not transferable, and the land lapses to the Zamindár on failure of male heirs.

Paṭṭá-ṭhíká, more correctly, *Ṭhíká-paṭṭá*, barbarously, *Pattah-tucka*, 5 Rep. H. (ٹهيكاپٹّا) A contract or farming lease, a deed assigning lands in farm for stipulated conditions.

Paṭṭávirutti, Tam. (பட்டாவிருத்தி) Rent-free land held by Brahmans (from S. *viruddhi*, opposition, held without a *Paṭṭá*).

Paṭṭáwat, (?). A Rajput chief who holds land from a superior at a quit-rent, on condition of military service.

PAṬṬA, Mar. (पट्ट) A belt.

Paṭṭekarí, or *Paṭṭewálá*, Mar. (पट्टेकरी, पट्टेवाला) A messenger with a badge or belt, a *Peon*.

PATTA, (?) Hindi. A bale, a package.

PATTA, (?) Tel. A measure of land = 16 *gaz*.—Northern Sarkárs.

PAṬṬADAI, Tam. (பட்டடை) A corn-rick: a portion of the crop given as a compensation to the ploughman: a workshop.

Paṭṭadaikalaṇi, Tam. (பட்டடைக்கழனி) A cultivated field artificially irrigated.

Paṭṭadaiyár, Tam. (பட்டடையார்) Proprietor or superintendant of a manufactory.

PAṬṬAḌI, Karn. (ಪಟ್ಟಡಿ) A district.

PAṬṬAIKÁL, Tam. (பட்டைகால்) High land irrigated by water thrown up from a lower level.

PAṬṬAIYAM, Tam. (பட்டையம்) A deed of gift either on paper or copper: (see *Paṭṭayam*, under *Paṭṭa*: it is no doubt the same word with the Tamil nominal termination).

PAṬṬAKDÁR, corruptly, PUṬṬUCKDÁR, (?) An officer employed originally to collect the revenues of government in Tanjore, and who, in many cases, appropriated the estates and became identified with the *Mirásidár*—Fifth Rep. 957. (According to the Glossary, the term means lit. book-keeper, accountant, from H. *Patak* (پتک), but there is no such word in Hindustani in that sense, nor in any other dialect, as far as the dictionaries are authority).

PÁṬṬAM, commonly written, PÁTAM, and, corruptly, PATOM, Mal. (പാട്ടം) Rent, hire, contract, lease (no doubt the *Paṭṭá* of other dialects, but applied to the thing rather than to the document, as by the following): the *Pátam* of an estate in Malabar is a stipulated proportion of the produce, paid in kind in the case of grain, in money in that of plantations.

Páṭṭa-chíṭṭá, corruptly, *Patom-chit*, *Putta-chit*, Mal. (പാട്ടച്ചീട്ട) A deed of lease, the written engagement given by the landlord to the tenant, also by the tenant to the landlord, agreeing to pay a certain amount of rent.

Páṭṭa-kánam, Mal. (പാട്ടകാണം) Rent, tax: rent of a property paid to a certain extent in advance. See *Kánampátam*.

Páṭṭa-kaṇḍam, Mal. (പാട്ടക്കണ്ടം) Rented corn-fields.

Páṭṭa-káran, or *Páṭṭam-káran*, or, in current use, *Pátamkár*, (പാട്ടക്കാരൻ) A tenant, one who holds land by paying rent.

Páṭṭakudissika, Mal. (പാട്ടകുടിശ്ശിക) Arrears of rent.

Páṭṭáli, Mal. (പാട്ടാളി) One who collects the rents of a temple: a victualler at a temple.

Páṭṭanella, Mal. (പാട്ടനെല്ല) Rent paid in kind or in rice-corn.

Páṭṭapaṟa, Mal. (പാട്ടപ്പറ) A large measure, or *paṟa*, used in measuring seed-corn: the produce, and the proportion as rent.

Páṭṭaparamba, Mal. (പാട്ടപ്പറമ്പ) A garden or plantation let on lease.

Páṭṭapravritti, Mal. (പാട്ടപ്രവൃത്തി) The office of rent-gatherer to a temple: the office of a victualler.

Páṭṭayola, or *Páṭṭola*, or *Páṭṭayolakaranam*, Mal. (പാട്ടയൊല, പാട്ടൊല, പാട്ടയൊലക്കരണം, from *ola*, the palm leaf, and *karanam*, an instrument) A lease, a deed of lease or of transfer of land upon mortgage.

Maṟupáṭṭam, Mal. (മറുപാട്ടം) Counterpart covenant of lease kept by the proprietor.

Veṟum-páṭṭam, corruptly, *Veerom-paṭṭom*, Mal. (വെറും-

പാട്ടം) Rent without any advance or security, simple rent: (from *verum*, empty).

PAṬṬAM, Tam. (பட்டம், S. पट्ट) Government, authority, kingdom: a head ornament symbolical of authority: a crown.

Paṭṭaṇkaṭṭi, Tam. (பட்டங்கட்டி) A chief: a village headman of the *Paravar*, or fisherman caste.

Paṭṭólai, Tam. (பட்டோலை), *Paṭṭola*, Mal. (പട്ടോല) lit., The crown *ólai*, a royal edict: also government records, monthly abstract of the account of public receipts and disbursements.

PATTANA, S. (पत्तन), vernacularly, PATTAN, the *tt* sometimes becomes *ṭṭ*, as PAṬṬAN, or PUṬṬUN, or PATNÁ, H. (پٹن, پٹنا), Mar. (पट्टण or पत्तन), Karn. (ಪಟ್ಟಣ, ಪಟ್ಟ), Tam. (பட்டணம்) A town, a city, whence *Paṭna* in Behar, and *Puṭṭun* in Sindh, &c., as being *the* city, or one deserving the appellation: the term is said to have been also applicable to a village granted rent-free by a viceroy of a province to a Zamindár (?): in Orissa it is applied to a village without lands or township, being confined to the ground on which the houses are constructed, and paying no land revenue, though subject to *Chandína*, or miscellaneous imposts for ground-rent, &c. In Bengali, *Pattan* (পত্তন) also means the first settling of a colony, a village or town.

Paṭṭan-hami, Beng. (P. كمي, less) Remission or diminution of revenue in favour of new settlers on waste lands.

Paṭṭana-seṭṭi, Karn. (S. ಪಟ್ಟಣಶೆಟ್ಟಿ) The chief merchant of a town, the head of the traders, exercising a kind of arbitration in disputes respecting caste or usage: corruptly *Patna-chitty*, which, with another corruption wholly unverifiable, *Patna Bogami*, is said to have formerly denoted a tax on the beads of the right and left-hand castes in a town, in consideration of their being allowed to impose cesses upon the castes: under the early financial arrangements of the Madras Presidency the privilege was withdrawn from the head men, and the imposts on the castes were transferred to the government.—5th Rep. p. 766.

Paṭṭanaswámí, Tam. (பட்டணசுவாமி, from S. स्वामी, a master) A head man among some of the castes, who acts as arbitrator in disputes among themselves or one another.

Paṭṭanwár, H. (پٹنوار) A division of the Kúrmí caste in the vicinity of Nandaur.

PAṬṬAN, H. (پٹن) Act of ordering goods from a manufacturer.

Paṭṭaní, H. (پٹني) Commissioned, manufactured to order.

PAṬṬANI, or PAṬṬANÍ, incorrectly, PUṬṬANY, more usually written PATNI, or PUTNEE, Beng. (পত্তনী, पत्तनी) A tenure by which the occupant holds of a Zamindár a portion of the Zamindárí in perpetuity, with the right of hereditary succession, and of letting or selling the whole or part as long as a stipulated amount of rent is paid to the Zamindár, who retains the power of sale for arrears, and is entitled to a regulated fee or fine upon any transfer: the tenure created by an under-letting in the second degree is termed *Dar-patní* (or lease within lease); and a third under-letting is denominated *Seh-patní* (from the Persian *seh*, three): this description of sub-tenures originated in Burdwan, being created by the Rája or Zamindár: it has been extended and sanctioned by Regulation. The word *Paṭṭani*, or *Patni*, is not found in any dictionary, and is differently explained by those who use it: Mr. Harington, Analysis 3. 519, says it may be rendered 'settled or established,' which is very questionable. In the Sudder Diwání Reports 2. 99, *Puttun* is said to have been incorrectly interpreted 'dependant,' whilst it really signifies 'constituting;' but this is equally doubtful. As the term originated in Burdwan it must be Bengali, but its omission from the dictionaries leaves it uncertain whether it should be written with the cerebral or dental *t*: if with the former, it probably bears a relation to *Paṭṭa*, or *Poṭṭa*, (পট্টা) a lease; if with the latter, to *Pattana* (পত্তন), colonising: the former seems the more likely.

Pattaní-dár, or *Patni-dár*, Beng. &c. (পত্তনিদার) The holder of an under tenure.

Paṭṭani-ijárá, H. (اجارا, a farm) A farm held as an under tenure of the landholder or proprietor.

Paṭṭani-táluka, or *táluk*, Beng. &c. (P. A. تعلق, a dependency) An estate, or portion of it, underlet in perpetuity by a Zamindár at an advance on the revenue he pays to government; as long as the stipulated amount is paid, the estate is heritable and transferable, in the latter case with the concurrence of the Zamindár, on payment of a regulated fine. In the event of arrears it may be sold by public auction at the *kachchari* of the collector.

PÁṬṬAN, PÁṬṬANÁR, Tam. (பாட்டன், பாட்டனார்) A grandfather.

Páṭṭi, *Páṭṭiyár*, Tam. (பாட்டி, பாட்டியார்) A grandmother.

Kóppáṭṭan, or *Kódpáṭṭan*, Tam. (கொப்பாட்டன், கோட்பாட்டன்) A forefather, an ancestor.

PAṬṬANJAMÂ KHURD, (پٹن جمع خرد) A monthly treasury

account under the Moghul government, specifying the receipts and disbursements of each month.

PAṬṬAR, or PAṬṬARA, Mal. (പട്ടർ, പട്ടര) The name given in Malabar to foreign Brahmans who there are usually traders and money-lenders.

PAṬṬARAI, Tam. (பட்டறை) Land irrigated from wells.

PAṬṬÁRI, Karn. (ಪಟ್ಟಾರಿ) A village servant, an examiner of tax money and measurer of public grain.

PATTEMÁR, Mal. (നത്തെമാര), PHATEMÁRI, Guz. (ફતેમારી) A vessel with one mast, used on the Malabar coast, of from ten to eighty tons.

PAṬṬÍ, PUṬTEE, corruptly, PUṬṬY, H. &c. (پتّي, S. पट्टी) A part or portion, a division of a village, a division of land into separate portions or strips: in the north-west provinces, an original share in a joint or coparcenary village or estate comprising many villages: it is sometimes defined as the smaller subdivision of a *mahál* or estate, the larger being termed *Thoka*: so in Guzerat it denotes the secondary share or subdivision of a principal *bhág* or share: in Bengal it also implies the part of a market appropriated to one description of dealers: in Kamaon it is the nominal division of a Pargana.

Paṭṭidár, *Puṭṭeedár*, corruptly, *Puṭṭydár*, H. &c. (پتّيدار) The holder of a share in a coparcenary village or estate. Ben. Reg. i. 1795; xxvii. 1803. Act i. 1841.

Paṭṭidárí, *Puṭṭeedaree*, H. &c. (پتّيداري) A tenure of a coparcenary nature, but in which the lands are divided and held in severalty by the different proprietors, each person managing his own lands, and paying his fixed share of the government revenue, through an accredited representative of the whole, being jointly responsible in the event of any one sharer being unable to fulfil his engagements: this is the perfect, or *Makmil paṭṭidárí*: a modification of this tenure also exists, known as *Námakmil* (نامكمل), imperfect *Paṭṭidarí*, in which part of the land is held in common and part in severalty; the profits from the land in common being first appropriated to the payment of the government revenue and the village expenses; and the surplus being distributed, or the deficit made up by a rate, or *báchh*, on the several holdings: the principle by which the distribution of the several divisions or *Paṭṭís* is regulated is very various, and not always well defined: in some cases it has the character of ancestral or of successive partition amongst joint heirs, in others of usage only: the realisation of the government revenue, although it might be effected from each *Paṭṭidár*, is more usually, as more conveniently, received from one of their number, the *Sadr-málguzár*, or *Lumberdár*, q. v. Act i. 1841.

Paṭṭíwár, H. (پتّيوار) According to shares, assessment, &c.

PAṬṬÍ, Mar. (पट्टी) A share of a village, as above, but more usually employed to denote a general collection or contribution: it was applied especially to an addition made by a former minister of the Peshwa to the fixed assessment, thence called *the Paṭṭí*, but subsequently it came to signify any occasional or extra impost or cess, the *Abwáb* of the Mohammadans: the number and variety of these *Paṭṭís* under the Maratha administration were infinite and most vexatious: in the *Púna* collectorate alone they exceeded forty: the following are a few of the number.

Ghar-paṭṭí, (from घर, a house) House-tax.

Gosávi-paṭṭí, (from गोसावी, a religious mendicant) Collection for a band of religious mendicants on their visiting a village.

Khusál-paṭṭí, (खुसाल, for S. कुशल, prosperity) Tax on a village by a *Pátil* or other public officer on an occasion of private or public rejoicing, as a birth of a son or the like.

Kuḷwár-paṭṭí, Karn. (ಕುಳವಾರಪಟ್ಟಿ) An extra tax on the people in general; a contribution or subscription for any public purpose.

Pásoḍi-paṭṭí, (from पासोडी, a shawl) A contribution for a new shawl or a turban to the *Pátil*.

Sawárí-paṭṭí, (P. سواري, a riding) Cess to defray the expense of a visit by some person of rank or in authority.

Paṭṭíhana, Karn. (ಪಟ್ಟಿಹಣ) A money cess or contribution.

PATTI, Karn. (?) A measure of land varing with different qualities of soil: of dry lands it contains from two to twelve *kurgis*; of moist lands from one and a half to eight.

PATTI, corruptly, PUTTY, Mal. (?) A statement of a case: a petition filed in court: an account, such as that kept by the village accountant, as

Patti-wasúli, A statement of the revenue collected and remitted from a village to the district treasury: a list of accounts or vouchers.

PAṬṬI, Tam. (பட்டி) A place: a cattle pen: a small village.

Paṭṭikádu, Tam. (பட்டிக்காடு) A scattered hamlet.

Paṭṭinam, Tam. (பட்டினம்) A small village, especially one of fishermen on the sea shore.

Paṭṭinavan, Tam. (பட்டினவன்) A fisherman, one who fishes at sea.

Paṭṭi, Tel., Karn. (పట్టి) A specification of abuses or frauds charged against a public servant: it is also used in the same sense as the Marathi term for an extra cess or impost.

Pátti, Tam. (பாத்தி) A small bed or area: a small corn-field: a salt-pan: a part, a share.

Páttiyam, Tam. (பாத்தியம்) Affinity, connexion entitling to a share, inheritance: bail, security.

Paṭṭiyan, Tam. (பாட்டியன்) An heir, an administrator: a surety.

Pattige, Karn. (ಪತ್ತಿಗೆ) Share, partnership.

Pattigeyárambha, Karn. (ಪತ್ತಿಗೆಯಾರಂಭ, from S. *árambha*, undertaking) A joint farming or trading concern.

Pattina-raṇḍu, Mal. (from പത്ത, ten, and രണ്ടു, two) Two out of ten, twenty per cent. interest or profit.

Pattora, (?) One of the village accounts, an account of receipts and disbursements, made up for six or eight months, formerly kept by the *Patwárí*.

Paṭṭu, H. &c. (پٿو पट्टू) A kind of woollen cloth.

Paṭṭu, Tel. (పట్టు) Silk.

Paṭṭu, Karn. (ಪಟ್ಟು) A sum received or credited in account.

Pattukádu, corruptly, **Puttcut**, Tam. (பத்துக்காடு) A fixed assessment or rent on dry land.

Paṭṭukaṭṭu, Tel. (పట్టుకట్టు), corruptly, **Putkut**, sometimes **Pattu-kat-ráyat**, when applied to persons. A term formerly in use for the hereditary proprietor or cultivator of land in a village paying a fixed assessment to the government, considered the same as the *Mirásidár*. —5th Rep. 832, 977: lease of land held by an individual cultivator on terms rated on each field severally, the fields being so distributed as to give each occupant a fair proportion of good and bad soil: (the term occurs in this sense as *Patkat* or *Putkut* in some of the settlement reports of the north-western provinces, but its origin and correct spelling are doubtful: as well as the Telugu word, it is probably a corruption of the Tamil *Pattukádu*).

Pattuvaḷe, Karn. (ಪತ್ತುವಳೆ) Bribery, amount of frauds or embezzlement charged to a public functionary.

Patu, Uriya (ପତୁ) Alluvial deposit left by inundation.

Pátu, Tel., Karn. (పాటు) Labour, work: cultivation.

Pátunéla, Tel. (పాటునేల) High ground.

Páṭuli, Beng. (পাটুলী) A large boat used on the Ganges for carrying goods.

Pátúní, H. (پاتوني) A ferryman.

Paṭwá, H. (پٿوا) Irrigation.

Paṭwázamín, H. (پٿوازمين) Land artificially irrigated.

Páú, or **Páo**, corruptly, *Pow*, Hindi (?) A natural flood from the drainage of high upon low land in the rainy season.—Bundelkhand.

Páu, Thug. An acquaintance and accomplice.

Paudha, **Paudhelá**, Hindi (पौध, पौधेला) Ground on which plants have been sown for transplantation.

Páüli, Guz. (પાવલી) A silver coin, a quarter of a rupee.

Páunarbhava, S. &c. (पौनर्भव) The son of a twice married woman: see *Punarbhú*.

Pauní, Hindi (पौनी) A collective name for the low castes who furnish the village constables, the barber, washerman, shoemaker, and *Chandála*.

Paura, Tel. (?) A good garden soil of clay and lime.

Paurnamása, S. &c. (पौर्णमास) Relating to the *Púrnamásí*, or day of full moon, or any ceremony to be observed on that day.

Paurnamásí, S. &c. (पौर्णमासी) Day of full moon.

Pausha, vernacularly, **Paush**, or **Paus**, or **Pús**, S. &c. (पौष) The month *Pausha* (Dec.-Jan.): it is applied to the winter or cold-weather harvest.

Paushí, S. &c. (पौषी) Day of full moon in the month *Pausha*.

Pauth, (?) Hindi. A tenure of land in coparcenary villages under which the fields are subject to periodical re-distribution among the sharers.—Banda.

Pauti, (?) Beng. A measure of grain.

Páütí, Uriya (ପାଉଟି) An acknowledgment, a receipt.

Pauti-jamin, (?) Tel. A garden soil containing lime.

Pautra, fem. **Pautrí**, S. &c. (पौत्र, पौत्री) A grandson, a granddaughter, the son or daughter of a son.

Paváda, Karn. (ಪವಾಡ) The practice of Jangama priests and Vaishnava mendicants in Mysore of wounding or mutilating themselves to extort alms.

Pavera, Hindi (पवेरा) Sowing seed by hand.

Paví, Hindi (पवी) A dyke cut to let water either in or out.

Pavitra, S. &c. (पवित्र) Pure; also sub., sacred grass: the Brahmanical cord.

Pávu, or **Páü**, Tel., Karn. (పావు, from the H. *páo*) A quarter: a weight of four *sérs*.

Pakkapávu, Karn. (ಪಕ್ಕಪಾವು) A quarter of a *sér*.

Pávali, or *-le*, Karn. (ಪಾವಲಿ, -ಲೆ), *Pávalá*, *-lí*, or *Páwalá*, *-li*, Mar. (पावला -ली) A quarter of a rupee.

Pávuní, Tel. (పావుని) Division of any thing.

Páwaṛá, Hindi (پاوڙا, पावड़ा) The vessel that receives the juice of the sugar-cane as it is ground.

Payakárí, also read **Paikári**, and, corruptly, **Paycarry**

Pyacarry, and Puckaree, Tel., Karn. (పయికారి) A temporary cultivator, one who cultivates the land of another for a stipulated term and a given share of the crop: (when little was known in India of the languages, except a little Persian, this word was derived from *pai* پی, a foot, and کاریدن, to labour (it should have been, to sow), in which case the correct reading would be *Paikári*, but this is no doubt an error, and the word, although now differently spelled, should be *Payir-kári*, or *-káran*, q. v.).

Páya-kuḍi, corruptly, Pyakooḍie, more correctly, Payir-kuḍi, q. v. A temporary cultivator.

Páyalí, corruptly, Pylee, Pahaley, Puheli, Puheelee, Mar. (पायली) A measure of capacity containing four *sérs*; but the Maraṭha government, in receiving revenue payments in kind, acknowledged a *Páyali* of $3\frac{1}{2}$ *sérs*; in paying, it considered $3\frac{1}{4}$ to be its equivalent: it is used also to denote proportionate land measure, four *Páyalís* being equal to one *Ruká*, the fourth part of a *Man* or *Mun*.

Payara, or Paira, Tel. (పయర, పైర), Mal. (പയറ) Pulse, any leguminous edible vegetable.

Payarapanṭa, Tel. (పయరపంట) The last crop of the year, consisting, as that usually does, of leguminous plants.

Payaṯṯu-páṯṯam, Mal. (പയറ്റുപാട്ടം) A certain amount of rent or tax levied on dry lands.

Páychal, or Páchal, Tam. (பாயச்சல், பாச்சல்) Irrigation: share of the expense of irrigation defrayed by the villagers in common.

Payir, Tam. (பயிர்), Pairu, Tel., Karn. (పైరు) Growing corn: the Tamil term applies also to vegetables of any kind, sometimes to trees, and, by metonymy, to cultivation in general.

Payirkáran, and *Payirkudi*, corruptly, *Payakári*, *Payakoody*, *Pyakoody*, *Parakoodi*, &c. Tam. (பயிர்க்காரன், பயிர்க்குடி) A cultivator not holding any right by inheritance to the lands he cultivates: he may hold under an agreement with the *Mirásidár* or hereditary proprietor, or with the government, being placed in possession in default of the proprietor to pay his revenue, and, like the non-proprietary cultivator in Hindustan, this class of cultivator is twofold, viz.

Ulpayir-kuḍi, (உள்பயிர்க்குடி) A permanent cultivator, holding his land as long as he pays the stipulated rent or revenue, and discharges all dues rendered by the proprietor or cultivator, transmitting the land to his descendants, although not empowered to alienate it by mortgage, gift, or sale; also *Ul-kuḍi*, q. v.

Parapayir-kuḍi, or simply *Para-kuḍi*, or *Payir-kuḍi*, (பரபயிர்க்குடி) A temporary tenant, one holding his land of a proprietor, either for a stipulated term or from year to year: this tenure may be converted into the preceding, or a permanent occupancy, by agreement with the *Mirásidár*, or by possession undisturbed for several generations.—Ellis, *Mirási* Rights, p. 37, Notes.

Payir-sheykai-káran, Tam. (பயிர்செய்கைக்காரன்) A husbandman, a cultivator, a ploughman.

Payirsheymuṟáimai, Tam. (பயிர்செய்முறைமை) The business or affairs of agriculture, husbandry.

Payir-toḻil, Tam. (பயிர்தொழில்) Husbandry, farming.

Payir-vaḻi, Tam. (பயிர்வழி) Cultivated fields.

Payir-veḷi, Tam. (பயிர்வெளி) A corn-field.

Mungáru-pairu, Karn. (ముంగారుపైరు) The first crop.

Hingáru-pairu, Karn. (హింగారుపైరు) The second crop.

Kilúpairu, Karn. (కీళుపైరు) Corn.

Mélupairu, Karn. (మేలుపైరు) Fruit.

Páyposhí, Mar. (पायपोशी, from the P. پاپوشی, a slipper) A tax levied as a complimentary gift to the head of the state: slipper-money.

Pechchu, Tel., Karn. (పెచ్చు) Surplus, excess: surplus of a heap of grain or salt above the estimate: premium on exchange of coins.

Peddakápu, Tel. (పెద్దకాపు, from *pedda*, chief, elder) The head man of a village.

Peddapanṭa, Tel. (పెద్దపంట) The great or principal crop, that which is gathered in the beginning of the year.

Peddapuri, Tel. (పెద్దపురి) A superior sort of soft sugar, from its being made originally at the village of *Peddapur*, in the *Rajamahendri* district.

Peddareḍḍi, Tel. (పెద్దరెడ్డి) The chief or senior cultivator, the head of the *Reḍḍis*, or agricultural tribe of a village, the head man of a village.

Peddatandri, Tel. (పెద్దతండ్రి) A father's elder brother: the husband of a mother's elder sister.

Peddatalli, Tel. (పెద్దతల్లి) A mother's elder sister: the wife of a father's elder brother.

Peheri, -rí, Guz. (પેહેડી -ડી) A shop, a place of business, a mercantile firm.

Pejeṉ, Mar. (पेजें) One of the two products of a cow or buffalo on calving, the milk, as distinguished from the calf.

Pejeṉ-jáupeṉ, Mar. (पेजें, as before, and जावपें, a calf) The practice of placing out to be brought up a young cow or female buffalo until after her calving, when she is to be returned to the owner, the calf or milk, or both, being relinquished in requital of the cost of bringing her up.

PEN, Mal. (പെൺ) A female, a woman.

Pennál, Mal. (പെണ്ണാൾ) A female slave.

PÉN, written, but no doubt incorrectly, PANE, (?) H. A term used in the Dehli district, according to printed papers, for an original undivided share in a joint-tenancy village.

Péndár, H. (P. دار, who has) The holder of an original share in a village.

PENḌÁ, PENḌHÁ, Mar. (पेंडा, पेंढा) Rice-straw: a bundle of straw or grass.

Penḍapaṭṭí, Mar. (पेंडापट्टी) A tax upon straw, either in money or kind: a tax on the produce of fruit trees.

PENḌAI-MARAKKÁL, Tam. (பெண்டைமரக்கால்) A grain measure containing two and a half *padis* or measures.

PENḌÁRA, PENḌÁRI, Karn. (ಪೆಂಡಾರ, ಪೆಂಡಾರಿ) A marauder, see the next: of or belonging to a marauder.

PENḌHÁRA, Mar. (पेंढार) A body of marauders.

Penḍhárí, corruptly, *Pindhárí*, or *Pindárí*, Mar. (पेंढारी) A member of an organised association of mounted marauders and plunderers, who from time to time issued from their villages, and made distant excursions to commit depredations and bring home plunder: they were extinguished as a body by the measures of the Marquis of Hastings when Governor-General. (As the word is properly Maraṭhi, *Pendhára* is no douht a more correct reading than the more usual one of *Pindári*: the term also admits of a more plausible etymology than any conjectured for the latter, as it most probably, is derived from *Pendhá*, a bundle of grass, and *hara* or *hari*, who takes; for the *Pendhárís* were originally nothing more than a body of irregular horse allowed to attach themselves to the Mohammadan armies, employed especially in collecting forage, and permitted, in lieu of pay, to plunder.

PENDI, (?) Mar. Spirituous liquor distilled from grain.

PENṬA, Tel. (పెంట) Manure.

PEON, (?) The term commonly used by Europeans for the Hindustani *Piáda*, a footman, a foot-soldier, an inferior officer of police or customs, or of courts of justice, usually wearing a badge, and armed with a lance or sword and shield: in some places the term denotes a kind of local militia holding lands on condition of police or military service: it is also commonly, though laxly, used as a synonym of *Harkára*, to denote a running footman, a courier, a messenger. Ben. Reg. iv. xiv. 1793; vi. 1795; xxvi. 1814, &c.

PERA, Mar. (पेर) Corn strewed on the floor to be trodden out by oxen.

PERÁ, Mar. (पेरा) The sowing of seed.

PERAḌU, Tel. (పెరడు) The back yard of a house.

PEṚAKUḌI, Tam. (பெறக்குடி) A temporary or hired cultivator (a different reading of *Parakudi*, from *pera*, to have a price: the word also occurs, vulgarly written and pronounced *Porakuḍi* (பொரக்குடி).

PEṚÍ, H. (پیری, पेडी) A kind of sugar-cane, that which springs up from the roots of the previous year's cuttings.

PERU, Tel. &c. (పేరు) A name.

Perumátra-veppu, Mal. (പെരുമാത്രവെപ്പു, from *peru* a name, and S. *mátra*, merely) A deed by which the proprietor of an estate foregoes all claim to the lands or their produce, although he refrains from giving water as the final mark of ratification, retaining the bare title, therefore, of *Janmhár*, or hereditary owner.

PÉRU, Tam. (பேறு) A fee paid to a person who is authorised to distribute the water of irrigation.

Peru-nír, Tam. (from பெரு, great, and நீர், water) Water allowed to flow from reservoirs without limitation during the rainy months, and for some time afterwards.

PÉRUMBATTU, corruptly, PEROOMBUT, PERUMBUT, Tam. (பேரும்பத்து) Land, the proprietary right to which is in the hands of the government.

PERUNÁṚI, Mal. (പെരുനാഴി) A measure of capacity, an *Edangali*.

PERUNKÁL-TARISU, Tam. (பெருங்கால்தரிசு) Land left waste more than fifteen years.

PÉRUNIGE, Karn. (ಪೇರುನಿಗೆ) A gold or silversmith.

PERUNKOLLAN, Mal. (പെരുംകൊല്ലൻ) A blacksmith.

PERYA, (?) H. A yellow soil in which sand predominates.—Agra.

PESALU, Tel. (plur. పెసలు) A kind of pulse called commonly green gram (Phaseolus radiatus).

PESHA, H. &c. (P. پیشه) Trade, business, profession, practice, custom.

PESHÁNÍ, H. (P. پیشانی) lit., The forehead; that part of a royal grant which is left blank, and which, when the deed is folded up, forms the outer fold.

PESHGÍ, H. (پیشگی, from P. پیش *pesh*, before) Advance (of money), payment before hand or on account, money paid in deposit for rent.

Peshgi-dár, H. (P. دار, who has) A lender of money to enable a person to pay in advance.

PESHKÁR, H. &c. (پیشکار) An agent, a deputy, a manager in general for a superior or proprietor, or one exercising in revenue and custom affairs a delegated authority: in Bengal the native officer in a judge's or collector's office, next in rank to the *Sarrishtadár*. Tel., Karn. (పెష్కార) A subordinate officer, who is employed to keep the accounts: a subordinate revenue officer.

PESHKASH, PESHKUSH, or PESHCUSH, corruptly, PEISHCUSH, PESHKIST, H. &c. (P. پیشکش) Tax, tribute; lit., what is first drawn: first-fruits: fine, quit-rent: a fine or present to the ruling power on receiving an appointment or assignment of revenue, or on a renewal of a grant or the like: in Bengal, the fine paid to the Mohammadan government by a Zamindár on his investiture: in Jonpur, a quit-rent formerly paid by Mohammadan holders of otherwise rent-free grants: under the Madras presidency it was applied especially to contributions exacted from the great Zamindárs in the northern Sarkárs, and from the Paligárs of the south, as a kind of quit-rent in lieu of a fixed revenue: revenue assessed upon lands once held free of revenue, or on the tenure of military service now dispensed with: it is rather laxly applied also in some places to the government demand upon the land or the land revenue.

Peshkashi, H. (پیشکشي) Relating to land held under a tribute or quit-rent.

Peshkash-i-bázár, H. (from P. بازار, a market) Taxes levied on persons having stalls or shops in a public market.

Peshkash-i-mahájan, Sindhi (P. S.), A tax on Hindu merchants and bankers in place of the tax on infidels.

PETE, Guz. (પેટે) In part payment, on account of.

PETUṆ, Guz. (પેટું) A number of items added together.

PEṬH, or PENṬH, H. and Mar. (پیٹھ, پینٹھ, पेठ, पेंठ), PENṬ, PENṬH, Guz. (પેઠ, પેંઠ) A market, a bázár, or part of a town where shops are assembled, a trading or manufacturing town: market rate and fluctuations: a town attached to, but distinct from, a fort, the suburb or *Pettah*: a banker's letter of advice announcing his having drawn a bill or *huṇḍi*: a duplicate *huṇḍi*, or one given in lieu of another that has been lost.

Peṇṭhpáṛ, Mar. (पेंठपाड) A market rate or price.

Peṭhiá, H. (پیٹھیا) A market, a bazaar.

Parapenṭh, Mar. (परपेंठ) A triplicate bill or *huṇḍi* to supply the loss of the first and second.

PEṬISHARÍK, H. (پیتي شريك, from *pet*, the belly) A coparcener in land (?)—Tinnevelly (?).

PETTAI, commonly, PETTAH, Tam. (பேட்டை), PÉTE, Karn. (ಪೇಟೆ) A suburb, a town contiguous to a fort, but distinct from it, and usually separately fortified: a village near a town in which a fair or market is held (it is no doubt the same as the Mar. *Peṭh*, q. v.).

PETTENDAR, (?) Tel. A village officer.—Rajamahendri.

PEṬYÁL, Beng. (পেটয়াল) One included in another's office or account, a deputy, an assistant.

PEŪ- or PEWABUḌ, Mar. (पेवबुड) A fee in kind payable to a village accountant, and to the Mahárs of a village, by corn-dealers on opening their grain stores, as a compensation to the former for keeping an account of the deposit, and to the latter for storing and removing it.

PHADYÁ, Mar. (फद्या) A small copper coin, a *Paisa*.

PHÁG, H. &c. (پھاگ, फाग, S. फल्गु), PHÁGÚ, Beng. (ফাগু) PHAGU, Uriya (ଫଗୁ) The red powder thrown over one another by the Hindus at the *Holi*, whence it comes to mean also the act of throwing, or the manner of observing the festival, or the festival itself.

Phág-paṭṭí, Mar. (फागपट्टी) A cess or tax in some villages for the expense of celebrating the *Holi*.

PHALA, vernacularly, PHAL or PHUL, S., and in most dialects, (फल), H. (پھل), Beng. (ফল), Mar. (फळ), Tel. (ఫలము), Tam. (பழம்) Fruit; lit., as fruit of any kind, including cocoa-nuts, areka-nuts, &c., and fig., as result, consequence.

Phalabhoga, S. (from भोग, enjoyment) Usufruct, receiving the profit or produce of any thing.

Phalkar, *Phulkur*, H. &c. (پھلکر) Profits or produce of an estate derivable from fruit-trees growing on it.

Phalagaini, or *Phalaguttige*, Karn. (ಫಲಗೈಣಿ, ಫಲಗುತ್ತಿಗೆ) Holding a lease, or renting the produce of the areka orchards of an estate in Mysore.

PHÁL, or PHÁLÍ, H. &c. (پھال, फाल, फाली) The blade or share of a plough.

PHÁḶÁ, Mar. (फाळा) Land-tax, revenue assessed on land.

Pháḷaṇí, Mar. (फाळणी) Settling the amount of land-tax.

PHÁLGUNA, vernacularly, PHÁLGUN, or PHÁGUN, corruptly, PHAUGUN, S. &c. (फाल्गुन) The eleventh month of the Hindu year (Feb.-March).

Phálguní, (फाल्गुनी) Day of full moon in the month *Phálguna*, on which the festival of the *Holi* is.

PHALÍO, corruptly, *Phalleeyo*, Guz. (ફળીઉ) A cluster of contiguous houses, a small part of a town, a neighbourhood.

PHALPARIÁ, Uriya (ଫଳପରିଆ) Cultivable ground allowed to lie fallow for a year.

PHÁND, H. &c. (پهاند) A noose, a snare, a trap. See *Phans*.

PHÁNDÍ, H. &c. (پهاندی) A bundle of from 50 to 100 sugar-canes.

PHÁṆḌI, Beng. (ফাঁড়ি) A police-station subordinate to the principal one, a *Thanna*: the district under a subordinate station.

Phánḍidár, Beng. (ফাঁড়িদার) A police officer in charge of a subordinate or out-station.

PHANGOLA, Thug. Pearls: among the Dakhini Thugs, a cock.

PHANGOLI, Thug. Small gold coins: Dakhini, a bear.

PHANK, Thug. Any useless thing not worth keeping, especially a traveller without property.

PHÁNKARÁ, Thug. Cry of the hare when travellers are in company, an unlucky omen for the gang, as they must not then commit murder.

PHANPH, Hindi (پهنپه, फंफ) Land that requires to be left fallow for some time.

PHÁNS, PHÁNSÁ, or PHÁNSÍ, H. &c. (پهانس, پهانسا, پهانسي, फांस, फांसी, S. पाश, पाशी), also sometimes PHÁS, and PHÁSÍ, Uriya (ଫାଶ, ଫାଶି) A snare, a noose, a halter, any thing for catching hold of a person and choking or strangling him. *Phánsí* also denotes strangulation, strangling, hanging.

Phánsí-gar, or *-gár*, H. &c. (پهانسی گر, پهانسي گار), *Phansío*, Guz. (ફાંસીઓ) A strangler, a robber and murderer who strangles his victims by throwing a turban or cloth round their necks when off their guard; the same as the Thag or Thug.

Phásídebáwálá, Uriya (from *debáwálá*, ଦେବାଓାଲା, the man who gives or applies) An executioner, a hangman.

Phánsíkáṭ, Beng. (ফাঁসীকাট), or *Phásikáth*, Uriya (ଫାଶିକାଠ) A gallows (from *kát*, or *háth*, timber).

Phánsikhamba, Uriya (from ଖମ୍ବ, H. كهمبا, a post) A gallows.

Phásikhhemagya, Uriya (from ଖେମ, *khem*, S. *kshema* क्षेम, forbearance, and ଆଜ୍ଞା, S. *ájná*, आज्ञा, order) A reprieve.

PHÁNṬ, Mar. (फांट) An objection, a flaw, disagreement, discrepancy.

PHÁNT, (?) Hindi. A village register, a list of occupants and their liabilities either as sharers or cultivators.

PHÁNṬEN, or PHÁṬEN, Mar. (फांटें, फाटें) Fire-wood: an impost levied upon cultivators in lieu of provision of fuel.

PHAO, H. (پهاو) A small quantity given in addition to a quantity purchased.

PHAOṚA, H. (پهاوڑا) A sort of mattock or spade.

PHAR, Thug. Any place where the Thugs murder their victims or divide their booty.

Pharjharowa, Thug. A man left behind to clean a place where a murder has been committed, and remove all vestiges.

PHAṚ, PHUṚ, H. (پهڑ), Mar. (फड) Any place of public resort as a court of justice, an exchange, an auction, &c., a gambling-house, a place where goods are exposed for sale, or where any business is being carried on; also, in Mar., a field, a plantation, a spot where sugar-canes and other articles of agricultural produce are brought, that the quantity of the crop may be ascertained and the assessment determined. Guz. (ફડ, ફર) A distillery.

Pharḃáz, H. (پهڑباز) A gambler.

Pharḃází, H. (پهڑبازي) Gambling.

Pharıá, H. &c. (پهڑیا) A keeper of a gaming-house: a retailer of goods.

Pháṛiámí, Beng. (ফাড়িয়ামী) Retail dealing, pedlaring, hawking.

Pharḥarí, Mar. (फडकरी) One who presides over any place of public resort: a pedlar, a retailer.

Pharṇivaṣí, *Pharṇivisí*, *Phurṇivís*, also, preferably, *Pharṇiṣí*, or *Pharnísí*, or *Phurṇís*, commonly *Furnees*, and *Furnavees*, Mar. (फडनिविशी, फडनिविसी, and फडनिवीस, also फडनिशी-सी, and फडनीस, from फड, an office, and P. *nawís* نویس, a writer) A public officer of the Maratha government, the keeper of the public registers, &c., through whom all orders and grants were issued, and to whom the accounts from all the different departments of the state were transmitted: (the title is familiarly known as the designation of a celebrated personage in the latter days of the Maratha power, *Nana Farnavís*, who was many years the prime mover of the policy of the court of Poona): the term was also applied to the head *kárkún* or clerk of a district collector, who had charge of the accounts, and assisted and advised the collector.

Pharpús, Mar. (फडपूस) Public or open inquiry.

Pharpharmáṣ, or *-más*, Mar. (फडफर्माश, -मास, from P. فرمایش, command) Fruit, vegetables, &c., furnished to Rájas and high public officers upon their requisition by the villagers: remission of revenue on this account may or may not be subsequently granted by the collectors.

PHARÁ, Mar. (फरा) A measure of capacity for grain or salt, consisting of 10 or 16 *páyalís* = a *man* or *maund*: in the latest returns the *Phará* of salt is rated at $10\frac{1}{4}$ *adhalis*, that of grain at 17 *páyalís*, and is the eighth of a *khandí*; rice in the husk is reckoned by the *mora* of 25 *Pharás*.

Phari, Mar. (फारी) A half *Phará*.

PHARCHÁ, or PHARCHHÁ, H. (پهرچا, پهرچها) Decision, sentence (of a judge), settlement of a business.

PHARD-PHANT, (?) H. The register or rent-roll of a village, shewing the name of the *Padhán*, or head man, the distribution of the rent-payers amongst the *Padháns* where more than one, the revenue payable by each shareholder, the non-proprietary occupants, and names of liabilities and temporary tenants.—Kamaon.

PHARO, Guz. (ફરો) A measure of grain equal to 16 *páyalís*, or one-eighth of a *khandí*.

PHARṢÁ, Mar. (फडशा) Settlement of an affair, liquidation of a debt, and the like.

PHASKÍ, Mar. (फसकी, from A. فسيح) A handful of grain exacted from each load of grain brought to market by the superintendant or the collector; also a similar quantity presented by schoolboys to their master, by women to Siva, &c.

PHARSÍB, Guz. (ફરસીબ, Eng. precept) A writ, a capias.

PHÁṬ, H. (پهاٹ, फाट) The allotment or division of the revenue assessment among the sharers in a joint tenancy village (from S. स्फट, to break or divide).

PHÁṬAK, H. (پهاٹک, फाटक), PHATAK, Beng. (ফটক) A watchman in charge of a gate: a gate, especially a gate in a town separating it into different wards: a bar in a court of justice, where the plaintiff and defendant stand.

Phátakbandí, H. (S. پهاٹکبندي, Beng. ফটকবন্দী) Imprisonment, custody.

PHATÁKÍ, Thug. A gun.

PHATKI, Thug. A shield.

PHATYÁ, Mar. (फत्या) A stick passed at night from guard to guard, and thus kept constantly circulated: a means of keeping the watch vigilant.

PHÁUṚÁ, H. &c. (پهاوڑا, फावडा) A mattock, a hoe, a spade (from the A. فتح, opened).

PHEN, H. &c. (پهين, फेन) Foam, froth, scum, the scum which rises in boiling brine, upon the removal of which depends the whiteness of the salt.

PHERÁ, Beng. (ফেরা) A vessel of a square shape used for measuring lime, sand, and other dry substances: in the salt works a square box containing about a *maund* of dry salt and 50 to 60 *sérs* of moist salt, used to measure the daily produce of each boiler.

PHERÍDÁR, H. (پهيريدار, from پهيرنا, to wander) A vagrant, a vagabond.

PHERPHÁR, Mar. (from *pher*, H. &c. پهير, again, turn or return, and *phár*, reiterated sound: फेरफार) Difference, more or less, something over or under; (a weight or sum).

PHETANG, Tibet. A packet of gold-dust current as coin in the hills at the value of eight rupees.—Kamaon.

PHOBYNG-GAUNTHI, (?) Burman. A purchased slave, who thereby becomes the hereditary property of the purchaser's family.

PHÚL, PHOOL, H. &c. (پهول, फूल, S. फुल्ल) A flower: amongst the Mohammadans, offerings at the grave of a deceased person on the third day after the burial.

Phúlbái, (?) Uriya. A slave girl, a concubine.

Phúlí, H. &c. (پهولي) Flowered, having a flower, literally or as a mark, as a coin stamped with one.

Phúli-hún, Tel. A star pagoda.

Phúlkhárí, H. (پهول کهاري), or *Phúlkarí*, Mar. (फूलकरी) A gardener, a florist: alkaline efflorescence used to adulterate culinary salt.

Phútámal, Mar. (फूटामल, from फुट, S. स्फुट, separated, broken off, burst, and P. *amal*, office) A share of the assignments made out of the *Chauth* appropriated by the person to whom it was not originally assigned.

Phútgáon, Mar. (फूटगांव) A village of which the houses are scattered: also a detached village, one not included amongst those of the district in which it is situated, or the lands of an individual to whom the rest belong: such detached portions of villages or lands are classed together as the *Phútgaon* of the district or individual.

PHUL, Thug. Engagement to meet again when a gang is suddenly dispersed.

PHULA, Thug. The person who takes home money for the families of a party.

PHULKI, Thug. From sunrise to sunset.

Charti-phulki, From sunrise to midday.

Uttarti-phulki, Thug. From noon till sunset.

PHÚPHÁ, also PHUPHÁ, and PHÚÁ, H. (پهوپها, پهپها, پهوا) The husband of a maternal aunt.

Phúphí, H. (پهوپهي) A paternal aunt.

Phúpherá-bhái, H. (بهاي, a brother) A cousin, the son of a paternal aunt, so *Phúpherá-bahin*, (from *bahin* بهن, a sister) A female cousin, the daughter of a paternal aunt.

PHÚRKANA, Thug. A horse. *Phúrkané*, a mare.

PHURUWÁ, Tibet. A measure of capacity for grain, equal to eight handfuls.

Phús, H. (پهوس) Old and dry grass or straw.

Piáda, H. (P. پیاده), **Peadá**, Hindi (पेखदा) A footman, an armed servant, police or militia-man serving on foot: the same as *Peon*.

Peadá-mahasil, Hindi (पेखदामहसिल) A *peon* placed over defaulters to urge them to pay up arrears, and maintained by them as long as so employed.

Pichalábáki, Tel. (పిచలాబాకి, from H. *Pichhlá*, پچھلا, behind) An old balance.

Picotah, or **Pakota**, apparently Portuguese (?) A machine used in the Peninsula for raising water for irrigation.—Fifth Rep. (no such word occurs in any of the dictionaries).

Pichche, Karn. (ಪಿಚ್ಚೆ) Deficiency in measure or weight.

Pichché túka, Karn. (ಪಿಚ್ಚೇತೂಕ) Deficient or light weight.

Pichché-yalaté, Karn. (ಪಿಚ್ಚೇಯಳತೆ) Deficient measure.

Píchu, **Píju**, or **Písu**, Karn. (ಪೀಚು, ಪೀಜು, ಪೀಸು) The stringy fibres of certain plants, as that of the cocoa-nut, or *coir*.

Pichor, Hindi (पिचोर) Ground in the rear of a tank.

Píḍaran, Tam. (பிடாரன்) A snake-catcher: in some Tamil districts, one of the village servants.

Pidar-majází, H. (P. A. پدرمجازی) A representative father, an adoptive father, or one who has adopted a son.

Piḍhí, Mar. (पिढी) A generation, a single succession in genealogical descent.

Pidhíchá, Mar. (पिढीचा) Inherited, inheriting, hereditary.

Piḍhí-dar-piḍhí, Mar. (पिढीदरपिढी) From generation to generation.

Piḍhípestar, Mar. (पिढीपेस्तर, from P. پیشتر, in advance) From generation to generation.

Piḍittam, or **Piḍippu**, Tam. (பிடித்தம், பிடிப்பு) Stoppage, deduction from a payment.

Pighdár, (?) Hindi. An under tenure of a charitable nature in Ramgher.

Pih, **Peeh**, (?) H. Land in cultivation which has been cultivated for three successive years: (the word also occurs as *Puh*, but ?).

Pík, Mar. (पीक) The corn or produce of a field ripened and gathered, the crop, the harvest.

Píh-nuksán, Mar. (पीकनुकसान, P. A. نقصان) Injury of the crop.

Pík-paháṇí, Mar. (पीकपहाणी) Inspection of crops, especially with a view of ascertaining any deficiency.

Piḻár, or **Pizhár**, Tam. (பிழார்) A basket for throwing up water out of a reservoir for irrigation.

Pilháŭ, Thug. The appearance or cry on the left of the animals, from which prognostics of good and evil fortune are derived.

Piḻi, or **Pizhi**, Tam. (பிழி) The fermented sap of the palm, a kind of *táṛí*.

Piḻiyan, Tam. (பிழியன்) A vender of *táṛí*.

Píḻige, Karn. (ಪೀಳಿಗೆ) Lineage, descent.

Píḻiga, Karn. (ಪೀಳಿಗ) A descendant.

Piḻḻai, commonly, **Pilla**, Tam. (பிள்ளை) A child: a respectable adjunct to Tamil names in some of the agricultural tribes, as *Muttuswámi-pillai*.

Pilmukattáyinam, Tam. (பில்முகத்தாயிணம்) Land paying a light or quit-rent to the government.

Pílpáyá, Uriya (ପିଲପାୟା) A pillar as a land mark.

Pinatanḍri, Tel. (పినతండ్రి) A father's younger brother, the husband of a mother's younger sister.

Pinatalli, Tel. (పినతల్లి) A mother's younger sister, the wife of a father's younger brother.

Piṇḍa, vernacularly, **Piṇḍ**, erroneously, **Peend**, S. &c. (पिण्ड, پند, पिंड, &c.) A lump, a heap: a ball of rice or meat, especially that which is offered at obsequial ceremonies or *Ṣráddhas* to deceased parents and progenitors or to the manes in general.

Piṇḍa-dánam, S. (दान, gift) Presentation of the funeral cake.

Piṇḍádhikárí, S. (अधिकारी, who has a right or title) The legal presenter of a funeral cake, usually the nearest relative in the male line.

Piṇḍánwahárya, S. (पिण्डान्वाहार्य्य) A monthly offering of cakes to deceased ancestors.

Piṇḍárá, or **Piṇḍárí**, H. (پنڈارا, پنڈاري) A plunderer. See *Pendhára*.

Pingala, S. &c. (पिंगलः) The fifty-first year of the cycle.

Pinjára, Karn. (ಪಿಂಜಾರ), Guz. (પીંજારા), **Pinjiárá**, H. (پنجیارا), **Pinjárí**, Mar. (पिंजारी) A cotton cleaner, one who extracts the seeds and prepares it for spinning.

Pinjrá, H. &c. (S. پنجرا) A cage.

Pinjrápor, or *-pol*, also read *Pánjrápor*, or *-pol*, Guz. (પીંજરાપોર) An hospital for animals, kept up by the Jains of Guzerat in various places, out of small fees levied at marriages and on mercantile transactions.

Pír, **Peer**, H. (P. پیر) An old man, a holy man: among Mohammadans, a saint, a spiritual guide, the chief of a body of monks or mendicants.

Pírán, H. &c. (پیران) An assignment of land for the support of a pious man, or for keeping up the tomb of one reputed a saint.

Píratrá, or *Pírottar*, blunderingly, *Pir-burdr*, H. &c. (پيروتر , پيرترا) Grant of land for a religious man, or for his tomb.

Pírottar-ṣádir wárid, H. (from صادر وارد , incidental charge) An assignment of rent-free land to defray the contingent expenses of a mosque or Mohammadan religious establishment.

Pírpál, H. &c. (پيرپال , from S. *pál*, cherishing) A grant for the support of a Mohammadan saint, or for keeping up his tomb: and attached to a Mohammadan mosque or shrine.

Pírlapanḍuga, Tel. (పీర్లపండుగ) A name given in the south to the Moharram, when especial veneration is paid to religious Mohammadans, and the places where they are buried.

Pír-záda, H. (P. پيرزاده) A priest attached to a mosque: a Mohammadan mendicant, the son or disciple of a *Pír*.

Pirí, (?) Tel. A measure of length, one-third of a *gaz*.

Pirautí, (?) H. Land allowed to lie fallow occasionally.

Pisa, Beng. (পিসা) A father's sister's husband.

Pisás, Beng. (পিসাস, for पितृष्वसा) The name by which a man call his wife's paternal aunt, and that by which the wife calls the paternal aunt of her husband.

Pisí, Beng. (পিসী) A paternal aunt.

Pisácha, vernacularly, Pisách, S. (पिशाच) An evil spirit, one haunting the places where dead bodies are buried or burnt, and occasionally animating them, or even possessing living bodies: a devil, a ghost, a goblin.

Pisáí, H. (پساي) Price paid for grinding.

Pisán, H. (پسان) Meal, flour.

Pishánam, or Pashánam, Tam. (பிசானம், பசானம்) A coarse kind of rice ripening late: also applied to the harvest or gathering of that sort of rice.

Pisr, H. (P. پسر) A son, a boy, a child.

Pisr-ákhiáfi, H. (from A. آخيافي, by the same mother) A step-son, the son of a wife by a former husband.

Pisr-i-mutabanná, H. (پسرمتبنّا) An adopted or affiliated son.

Piṭbharí, H. (پٹ بهري , पिटभरी) An allowance of grain made by a Zamindar to the head of a village.

Píṭh, Mar. (S. पीठ) Flour, meal of any grain.

Píṭh, Guz. (પીઠ) A row or set of shops, a market, the state of a market.

Píṭha, vernacularly, Píṭh, S. (पीठ) A stool, a seat, the seat of the head of a religious society, that is, his place of abode.

Piṭipáta, Mal. (പിടിപാട) A document given to a person on being appointed to a public office: a lease or document authorising the holding of land.

Piṭipatam, Mal. (പിടിപ്പതം) A portion of the crop given to reapers.

Pitṛi, nom., Pitá, S. &c. (पितृ, पिता) A father, the designation also of forefathers deceased, the manes either of the ancestors of an individual or of mankind generally, to both classes of whom *Ṣráddhas*, or obsequial worship, is paid, and food is presented: the *Feralia* of the Romans.

Pitṛibandhu, S. (पितृबंधु) A cognate relation in the paternal line.

Pitṛidatta, S. (from दत्त, given) lit., Given by a father: one kind of woman's peculiar property.

Pitṛidroha, S. &c. (from द्रोह, who offers violence to) A parricide.

Pitṛigháta, S. &c. (from घात, killed) A parricide.

Pitṛikárya, in Bengali pronounced *Pitrikárjo*, whence, corruptly, *Pitry-kauje*, S. (from *kárya* कार्य्य, to be done) Rites to be offered to the manes or to ancestors; also (from *kṛitya* कृत्य, to be performed) *Pitṛikṛityá*.

Pitṛipaksha, S. &c. (from पक्ष, a fortnight) The half month at the end of *Bhádra* or the beginning of *Áṣwin*, according as the month is reckoned, from the new or the full moon; so termed as peculiarly appointed for the celebration of obsequial rites to the *Pitṛis* or manes: also (from *paksha*, a side) related by the father's side.

Pitámaha, S. &c. (पितामह) A paternal grandfather: fem. *Pitámahí*, a paternal grandmother.

Pitṛarjita, S. (from *pitṛi*, and *arjita* अर्जित, acquired) Derived from a father; property originally acquired by him, and therefore disposable by him at pleasure.

Pitṛiyajna, S. (from यज्ञ, a sacrifice) Obsequial offerings, worship of the manes.

Pitrya, S. &c. (पित्र्य) Paternal, ancestral, any thing relating to a father or forefathers.

Plava, S. &c. (प्लव) The 35th year of the cycle = A.D. 1841.

Plavanga, S. &c. (प्लवंग) The 41st year of the cycle = A.D. 1847.

Pod, (?) H. A land measure, a division of a *katta*—Maimansinh.

Poddár, H. (پودار) A cashkeeper, a weighman, one whose office it is to weigh and examine money: see *Fotah*.

Poḍí, or Poṛí, also written, Pauṛí, Hindi (पोडी, पोरी, पौडी) Stiff strong soil.

Poḍi, Tam. (பொடி) Dust of the earth, pollen of a flower, any thing very minute.

Podu, plur. Pollu, Tel. (పొడు, పొల్లు) Land or lands recently cleared from thicket and prepared for cultivation.

Podu, or Potu, Tam. (பொது) Commonness, common property: adj., common.

Podunilam, Tam. (பொதுநிலம்) Common ground, a common.

Podusilavu, Tam. (பொதுசிலவு) General charges in kind on the gross produce, or portions deducted from each heap of grain for fees to village servants, charges on reaping and watching, and allowances to temples, or for repairs of tanks and the like.

Pogadi, Karn. (ಪೊಗಡಿ) Tribute.

Poganda, S. &c. (पोगण्ड) A boy, one between five and fifteen.

Pohá, Hindi (پوہا, पोहा) The cattle of a village that are permitted to graze upon waste ground.

Pohonch, less correctly, Ponch, Mar. (प्रोहंच, पोंच, from H. پہونچنا, to arrive) The coming to hand of monies due: an acknowledgment, a receipt.

Poilá, Uriya (ପୋଇଲା) A slave.

Poktán, Poktání, Beng., Uriya (পোক্তান, পোক্তানী) The boiling of salt.

Pokhtánibhayá, Uriya (ପୋଖତାନିଭୟା) The writer or accountant of an *aurang* or salt manufactory.

Pokhtáni-darogá, Uriya (ପୋଖତାନିଦରୋଗା) The head officer of a salt manufactory. (*Pokhtáni*, like *Poktán*, is properly derived from the P. *pukhtan* پختن, to mature, to cook or boil).

Pol, Guz. (પોલ), Hindi (पोल) A court-yard: a quarter or ward of a town having its own gateway: a gate.

Poliá, Hindi (पोलिया) A gatekeeper, a porter.

Pola, Mar. (पोळ) A bull set at large, usually stamped with a trident or discus, as dedicated to Siva or Vishnu.

Polá, Mar. (पोळा) A festival held on the new moon of *Srávana* or *Bhádra* (July-Sept.), in which bullocks are exempt from labour, and are decorated and led in procession.

Póla, Karn. (ಪೊಲ) A field for dry cultivation.

Pola, Thug. A mark made at a place where cross roads meet, to denote the direction which the foremost of a gang have taken, as a guide to others left behind.

Polach, spelled variously, Polich, Politch, Polist, Pulich, and Pulij, Hindi (पोलच) Land constantly in cultivation, never requiring to be left fallow: [it is written as here given in the useful Hindi tract termed *Khet-karm*: the variations are from different English reports and Regulations].

Polamu, Tel. (పొలము) A field, especially one in cultivation, or the crop standing on it.

Polimera, Tel. (పొలిమేర) A boundary, a limit.

Poli, Tam. (பொலி) A heap of corn threshed, but not winnowed.

Pólihurippu, Tam. (பொலிக்குறிப்பு) A note or memorandum of the heap of corn that has been threshed.

Poleyan, or Polayan, also written Polian, and Poolian, (?) A caste of domestic or agrestic slaves, or a member of such caste, in Malabar: the husband in this caste resides with his wife, although she belong to a different master, and their children inherit the rights of the mother.

Polichcheluttu, Mal. (പൊലിച്ചെഴുത്തു) A fine or fee paid to the proprietor by the mortgagee on the periodical renewal of the mortgage: a new deed or bond.

Polichchila, Mal. (പൊലിച്ചില) Increase, augmentation.

Polichchilava, Mal. (പൊലിച്ചിലവ) Particulars of money expended.

Polikatam, Mal. (പൊലികടം) Usury: money-lending.

Polikatakáran, Mal. (പൊലികടകാരൻ) A usurer, a money-lender.

Polisa, also Palisa, Mal. (പൊലിശ) Interest, usury.

Pollái, Tel. (పొల్లాయి) Allowance of grain given to the village servants at the measuring floor.

Pollar, Tam. (பொல்லர்) The caste of shoemakers, or workers in leather, considered impure.

Pollu, Tel. (పొల్లు) Empty ears of corn: corn that has not come to maturity: chaff.

Pollupavutam, Tel. Blighted corn.

Polutikáran, Mal. (?) (പൊലുതിക്കാരൻ) The steward or manager of an estate on behalf of the proprietor.

Pombarada, Karn. (ಪೊಂಬರದ) A money-changer, a *saráf*.

Pomalo, Guz. (પોમલો) An itinerant blacksmith.

Pon, Karn. (ಪೊಂ) Gold, money: a gold coin, perhaps for *Hun*.

Ponam, Mal. (പൊനം, corruption of S. *vanam* वनं, a wood) High land overrun with underwood, but which is capable of cultivation after long intervals with particular kinds of grain sown in holes dug with a spade.

Ponakandam, corruptly, *Ponicando*, Mal. (പൊനകണ്ടം) A hill tract or fields cultivated amongst the hill *jangal*.

Ponamváram, Mal. (പൊനംവാരം) Rent or landlord's share of the produce of *jangal* cultivation.

Poṇgal, incorrectly, Pongol, Tam. (பொங்கல், from the verb *pongu-kiraku*, to boil or bubble, to boil rice) A boiling or bubbling up, the boiling of rice, whence it becomes the name of a popular festival held by the Hindus in the Madras provinces on the entrance of the sun into the sign Capricorn, or on the 12th of Jan., the beginning of the Tamil year, when rice is boiled and distributed : the festival lasts several days, but the chief celebration is confined to the three first days, which are distinguished as follows :

1. *Bhógí-panḍikai*, (போகிபண்டிகை) The festival of *enjoyment*, when good wishes and presents, new-year's compliments and gifts, are interchanged, and Indra is worshipped.
2. *Perum-poṇgal*, (பெரும்பொங்கல்) The *great* festival, when the sun is to be worshipped, and quantities of rice are boiled in milk in every family, of which a portion is given to the deities and cows, and the remainder to the guests and inmates.
3. *Máṭṭu-pongol*, (மாட்டுபொங்கல்) The *cattle* festival, when Krishṇa, the cowherd, is worshipped, and the cattle, painted and decorated with garlands, are led in procession and treated with especial veneration, and exempted from labour.

Pongali, Tel. (పొంగలి) Boiled rice, with milk and sugar, and other ingredients.

Pongaṭí-panḍaga, Tel. (పొంగటిపండగ) The festival of the *Pongal*, as above.

Pondráperallu, Tel. (పొండ్రాపెరల్లు) Dry land belonging to dealers in vegetables.—Northern Sarkárs.

Poṇe, Karn. (ಪೊಣೆ) Bail, security.

Poṇegár, Karn. (ಪೊಣೆಗಾರ) A surety, a bondsman.

Pongrhani, Burman, A bond-slave, one serving in discharge of a debt until it is paid off, or the stipulated term expires.

Ponkhálu, Tel. (పొంఖాలు, from S. पंख, mud) Stiff soil or mud.—Northern Sarkárs.

Popaḍu, Guz. (પોપડુ) Neglected or uncultivated land.

Pór, Tam. (போர்) A heap, a heap of grain or straw.

Por-hurippu, Tam. (போர்குறிப்பு) Account of the crops heaped but not threshed.

Kadírpor, Tam. (கதிர்போர்) A heap of corn not threshed.

Nerpor, Tam. (நெர்போர்) A heap of rice-grain.

Porabátu, Tel. (పొరబాటు) A mistake.

Porakula, Karn. (ಪೊರಕುಲ) An outcaste.

Porapad, Porpaad, Porpaud, (?) Mal. Net or surplus rent: balance of rent after deducting interest of advances, and the government revenue.

Poras, Hindi (पोरस) Stiff or strong soil.

Porombadom, (?) Mal. Rent of an estate in lieu of interest on mortgage (?).

Porupu, written also, Pooroopa, and Poroopu, (?) Tam. (பொருப்பு) A low or quit-rent levied from lands originally granted in *Inám*, or rent-free.—Fifth Rep. 765.

Porwál, Hindi (पोरवाल) The name of a trading or mercantile caste in Malwa, being one of the 84 *gachchas* or families of the Jains : there are also amongst the number, families denominated *Por*, and *Porwár*.

Posehoyyavadu, Karn. (ಪೊಸೆಹೊಯ್ಯುವದು) A ceremony among the cultivators in Mysore at the beginning of tillage, putting some seed in a vessel filled with earth placed on a plough, and letting it germinate.

Poshák, H. &c. (P. پوشاک, पोशाक) Clothes, vestments : in Maraṭhí especially, fine clothes.

Posháh-paṭṭi, Mar. (पोशाकपट्टी) A tax or cess on the villagers to defray the expense of a present of fine clothes to any great man or public functionary visiting the district.

Poshyaputra, S. &c. (पोष्यपुत्र, from *poshya* पोष्य, to be cherished or fostered) An adopted son.

Poshyaputratwa, S. &c. (पोष्यपुत्रत्वं) Adoption, the relationship of an adopted son.

Post, H. &c. (پوست, पोस्त) A poppy head or capsule.

Postí, H. &c. (پوستي, पोस्ती) One addicted to opium, or any dull sluggish person.

Post, Mar. (पोस्त) Money given to dependants and servants on particular occasions, as at the *Holi* festival, or for extra labour, for the purpose especially of enabling them to procure spirituous liquor : drink-money.

Pot, Hindi (पोत) Assessment on cultivated fields.

Poṭ, Mar. (पोट), Poṭṭa, Tel. (పొట్ట) The stomach, the belly, any cavity or hollow analogous to the belly.

Poṭgí, Mar. (पोटगी) Personal maintenance, allowance to village officers when they proceed on duty, or to public officers at a distance.

Poṭchak, Mar. (पोटचक) A field within a field constituting a separate property, but included in the same registered number as the larger portion.

Poṭkharábá, Mar. (पोटखराबा, P. *kharáb*, bad) Bad and untilled land lying amidst cultivated fields.

Poṭkharcha, or *-kharchí*, Mar. (पोटखर्चे, -र्ची) Personal expenses for support on a journey or a mission, forming an item in the village charges, and sometimes including the cost of public entertainments.

Potpadít, Mar. (**पोटपडीत**) A portion of cultivable land left unsown amidst land under cultivation.

Potabanik, Beng. (**পোতবনিক**, from S. **पोत**, a boat, and **वणिज**, a trader) A merchant who trades by sea, a voyaging merchant.

Potadár, commonly, Potdár, corruptly, Podár, and Pothdár, Mar. &c. (**पोतदार**: see *Fotadár*) A money-changer, a weigher and assayer of coins: he is also the village silversmith: in Karn. it is written *Pottadár*, *Pottár*, and *Pottári*, and is said to mean an inferior sort of money-changer, one in a hamlet.

Potchál, corruptly, *Potheychal*, Mar. (**पोतचाल**) The currency in which the public revenue is received.

Potdárí, Mar. &c. (**पोतदारी**) The business of a weigher or assayer of coins: money-changing, banking.

Poten, Mar. (**पोतें**, P. فوطه, *fotah*, q. v.) A bag, a money-bag, the public treasury or treasury bags, the bag of revenue, the money made up by the village and forwarded to the manager or collector.

Potnís, Mar. (**पोतनीश**) An officer of the treasury, the cash-keeper or accountant.

Potámel, Guz. (પોતામેળ) An abstract of monthly or annual accounts.

Potara, Thug. A horse: *Potari*, a mare.

Potaraiat, Thug. A man on horseback.

Potaraiati, Thug. Pulling a man off his horse and strangling him.

Pothá, Pothí, H. &c. (پوتها, پوتهي, S. **पुस्तक**) A book: especially a manuscript book, or one formed of separate leaves of paper or palmyra, connected sometimes by a string through the centre.

Pothlá, Hindi (**पोथला**) A porter's load, especially of grain. —Mherwara.

Poti, Mal. (പൊടി), Podi, Tel. (పొడి) Dust, powder, a fragment.

Potivita, Mal. (പൊടിവിത) Sowing on dry land.

Poti, incorrectly, Podi, Mal. (പൊതി) A bundle, a pack, a load, a sack for loading bullocks: a measure of grain =30 *Edangalis*, or 4 *Paras*.

Potipáta, Mal. (പൊതിപാട) An extent of land requiring a *Poti* of seed to sow it.

Potikallalu, (?) Tel. Land recovered from jangal.

Potipattu, (?) Mal. A tenth of the seed corn formerly paid to temples in some places, but merged in the general assessment on the Company's survey without any compensation.—Græme.

Potni, Thug. A waistband.

Pottal, Tam. (பொட்டல்) Barren land.

Pottaráju, or, commonly, Potráz, Tel. (పొట్టరాజు) A local deity worshipped by the agricultural classes in the Telinga provinces.

Pottu, Tel. (పొట్టు) Chaff, husk.

Potuvan, Mal. (പൊതുവൻ) A barber: one who performs funeral rites.

Potwad, Mar. (**पोतवड**) A term applied to the land situated on slopes and declivities in the hill country, or Dáng: the third and last year of its being brought into cultivation after lying fallow for some years.

Pozhakadai, or Polakattai, Tam. (பொழக்கட்டை) A small portion of ground, or a yard adjoining the dwelling of the *Mirásidár*, held rent-free, used as a kitchen-garden, or one for vegetables requiring a richer soil, as tobacco, sugar, turmerick, &c.: it is not transferable except with the entire *Mirási* property and rights.

Prabhava, S. &c. (**प्रभव**) The first year of the cycle of sixty years.

Prabhu, S. &c. (**प्रभु**) A master, a lord, a leader, a military chief.

Práchí, S. &c. (**प्राची**) The east: the country east and south-east of the Saraswatí, the country from about Dehli to Benares.

Práchyá, S. &c. (**प्राच्या**) The eastern people: the inhabitants of the Doab and adjacent provinces.

Pradhán, vernacularly, Padhán, Pudhán, and Pardhán, Purdhan, corruptly, Purdhaun, S. &c. (**प्रधान**) Chief, principal, a chief or eminent person, a minister, a prime minister: the common title of the eight chief civil and military officers of the Maratha state, as established by Sivaji: the term is also sometimes applied to the head man of a village, or to a principal farmer or cultivator: in Uriya, *Padháni* (ପଧାନି) is applied to respectable *Śúdra* cultivators or under proprietors and middlemen, differing little from Mukaddams: in Garhwal the *Padhán* is the person holding the revenue engagement (*Patta*) with the government, either in his own right or by election of the shareholders of the village lands: in communities divided into clans each elects its own chief, and all the *Padháns* are responsible, jointly and separately, for the whole revenue, unless their individual responsibility has been admitted by authority.

Hak-padhán, H. The privileges and rights of the head man, either in land or fees.—Kamaon.

Padhánchárí, H. The office and emoluments of the *Padhán*.

Paṭṭa-padhánchárí, *Padhán-khánagí*, or *Hak-padhánchárí*, H. The deed from the government district officer held by the *Padhán*, setting forth his liabilities, duties, dues, &c. —Kamaon.

Ghar-padhán, H. Privately appointed manager of a Zamindárí village, or a village with absolute proprietors.—Kamaon.

Pradáni, or, as written, *Pirdáni*, Tam. (பிர்தானி) A minister, usually applied to the third in rank, or the treasurer.

PRÁḌVIVÁKA, S. (प्राड्विवाकः) A judge, the chief justice, the representative of the Rája in the royal court.

PRÁGWÁL, Hindi (प्रागवाल) A Brahman who conducts the ceremonies of the pilgrimage at Allahabad: the ancient *Prayága*, shortened vernacularly to *Prág*.

PRAJÁ, sometimes pronounced PARJÁ, corruptly, PURJAH, S. &c. (پرجا, प्रजा) Progeny, offspring: subjects, people, tenants, dependants: in Kúch Bahar, a cultivator at will, who has half the produce of the land for himself, but is removable at the pleasure of the proprietor, to whom he is usually in debt for advances, and is more like a serf than a free agent: in Cuttack the term is applied to various low castes, as the barber, washerman, fisherman, weaver, leather-worker, *táṛí*-gatherer, &c., who sometimes sell themselves and families into slavery until they can repay the purchase-money: the children born during this period become the property of the purchaser, and, with their parents, may be bought, sold, or let out for hire until redeemed: the *Parjás* do not forfeit their caste or forego their occupations, living apart from their master, and retaining a title to their hereditary possessions.

Prajábhág, Mar. (प्रजाभाग) The share of the produce assigned to the cultivator.

Prajálí, Beng. (প্রজালী) An under-tenant.—Rangpur.

Prajápála, or *Prajápati*, S. &c. (from S. पाल, a cherisher, or पति, a lord) A king, a ruler: the fifth year of the cycle, in this series A.D. 1811-12: a name of the deity *Brahmá*.

Prájápatya, S. &c. (प्राजापत्य) Relating to *Prajápati*, the name of a form of marriage, the gift of a girl by her father to the bridegroom: a particular sacrifice performed by a man destitute of male issue before appointing a daughter to raise issue for him: a festival on the 8th of the dark half of *Pausha*, in honour of the manes: expiatory gift of cows to a Brahman.

Prajotpatti, S. &c. (प्रजोत्पत्ति) Begetting children: offspring, descendants.

Prajáwat, vernacularly, *Parjáwat*, or corruptly, *Purjote*, and *Purjosh*, H. (پرجاوت) A quit-rent, a cess levied by Zamindárs upon the Ryots on festive occasions, as at marriages: a house-tax levied by the Zamindárs upon the inhabitants of a village, not cultivators, for the ground on which their houses stand: ground-rent.

PRAKARAṆ, Mar. (प्रकरण) A department, a province, a separate business or office.

PRAKARSHIT, Beng. (S. প্রকর্ষিত, lit., drawn out) Surplus produce of a thing pledged for usufruct above the interest of the loan, which is to be repaid to the borrower.

PRAKÁṢAVIKRAYA, S. (प्रकाश, open, public, and विक्रय, sale) A public sale.

PRAKAṬANA, Tel. (S. ప్రకటన) Publishing, making known, proclamation, notification.

Prakaṭana-kágidamu, Tel. (ప్రకటనకాగిదము, from P. کاغض, paper) An advertisement.

PRAKÍRṆAKA, S. (प्रकीर्णक) A decision at law on a case not provided for by the law-books.

PRÁKRITA, S. &c. (प्राकृत) Common, natural, vulgar: not polished or refined; said either of language or of people: a man of a low caste.

PRAMÁDA, S. &c. (प्रमाद) Carelessness, negligence, stupidity.

Pramádí, S. &c. (प्रमादी) A careless or stupid fellow: the 47th year of the cycle.

PRAMÁṆA, S. &c. (प्रमाण) Authority, proof, proof in law, by ordeal or oath, by evidence oral or documentary, and by possession: proof in philosophy, by perception, inference, similarity, authoritative or scriptural assertion, presumption, and non-existence: also measure in general: in the dialects of South India, as Tel. (ప్రమాను), Tam. (பிரமாணம்), it usually implies an oath.

Pramáṇika, or, more correctly, *Prámáṇika*, S. &c. (प्रमाणिक, प्रामाणिक) Authoritative, of weight or authority established by proof, true, just, right: a person whose opinion is to be respected: a president, a principal, the chief or head of a caste or trade. *Pramániham*, Tam. (பிரமாணிக்கம்) Truth, faithfulness, honesty. *Pramánikan*, Tam., (பிரமாணிக்கன்) A trusty or upright man. Mal. (പ്രാമാണികൻ) Head of a caste or trade. In Beng. it is modified also as *Parámánik* (পরামানিক), in the sense of the head man of a tribe or trade, chief of an assembly, head of a village, and the like. An order from the supreme authority, a precept or grant summarily issued.

Pramáṇí, S. (प्रमाणी) A period or thing of authority. Mal. (പ്രമാണി) A person of weight in a village, an umpire or arbitrator in petty disputes.

PRAMÁTÁMAHA, or, f. MAHÍ, S. &c. (प्रमातामह -मही) A maternal great grandfather, or great grandmother.

PRAMÁTHÍ, S. (प्रमाथी) The 13th year of the cycle.

PRAMODA, S. &c. (प्रमोद) The 4th year of the cycle.

PRÁṆÁYÁMA, S. &c. (प्राणायाम, from *práṇa* प्राण, breath) A religious exercise with the breath, in three operations: 1. *Rechaka*, exhaling by the right nostril, whilst the left is closed by the fingers of the right hand; 2. *Púraka*, placing the thumb of the right hand on the right nostril, raising the fingers from the left and inhaling through it; and 3. *Kumbhaka*, closing both nostrils: different sects vary the succession of the operations.

PRAṆAVA, S. (प्रणव) The mystic syllable of the Hindu ritual or OM.

Ṗránnyáya, or *Pragnyáya*, also *Púrvanyáya*, S. (प्राङ्न्याय, or प्रागन्याय, and पर्व्वन्याय, from *prák*, or *púrva*, prior, and *nyáya*, judgment) In Hindu law, one who revives a suit formerly decided: also the plea of 'formerly decided' by the defendant when a charge is repeated.

PRÁNT, S. &c. (پرانت, प्रान्त) Limit, boundary: amongst the Marathas it is commonly applied to a large division of country, a province, a Zila.

PRAPANCHÁRTHÁ, Mar. (S. प्रपञ्च, the world, or worldly business, and अर्थे, for, or on account of) Land exempted from revenue attached to some secular function, as that of *Pátíl*, or any village officer, or for the purpose of keeping up useful constructions, as reservoirs or embankments, &c.

PRAPITÁ, S. &c. (प्रपिता) A paternal grandfather.

Prapitámaha, S. &c. (प्रपितामह) A paternal great grandfather.

Prapitámahi, S. &c. (प्रपितामही) A paternal great grandmother.

PRAPAUTRA, vernacularly, also, PARPUTRA, PARPOTA, &c. S. &c. (प्रपौत्र) A great grandson.

Prapautrí, (प्रपौत्री) A great granddaughter.

PRÁPTAVYAVAHÁRA, S. (प्राप्त, obtained, व्यवहार, affairs) A young man come of age, one able to conduct his own affairs and responsible for his conduct.

PRASÁDA, vernacularly, PRASÁD, S. &c. (प्रसाद) Favour, kindness: it is commonly applied to food or sweetmeats which have been offered to an idol, and which are then distributed amongst the worshippers present, or sent to the houses of the friends of the establishment, and persons of consideration, including Europeans; for all castes may partake of the *Prasád* of any image: hence the feeding in common of the pilgrims at *Jagannáth* is a practice not peculiar to that shrine, though exhibited there on a large scale: the food there distributed is termed *Maháprasád*, or, the great favour.

Prasádapatra, S. &c. (from पत्र, a leaf) A deed of gift.

PRAṢEṬHI, Uriya (ପ୍ରଶେଠି, from S. प्र, and श्रेष्ठी, chief) The head man of a village.

PRASTHA, S. &c. (प्रस्थ) A measure of capacity for grain, equal to 4 *kuḍavas* or 48 handfuls; considered by Capt. Jervis the same as the *sér*.

PRASIDDHIPATRA, Mar. (S. प्रसिद्धिपत्र, from *prasiddhi*, publicity) A paper giving publicity to any matter, a hand-bill, a notification, a proclamation.

PRAT, PRUT, Mar. (प्रत) A copy (in all its English significations): the original which is to be copied, or the copy made: a specimen: a set or class, an order or grade, a lot or parcel, an assemblage of bodies of like merit, the largest or richest of the parcels in which presents to guests are distributed on festival occasions, intended for the most distinguished persons. [In these senses it seems to be a pure Maratha word; in the sense of 'to, towards, or reverse,' &c.: it is an abbreviation of the Sanskrit prep. *prati* (प्रति)].

Pratbandhí, Mar. (प्रतबंधी) Classification: arranging by classes or lots.

Pratwár, Mar. (प्रतवार) According to classes or lots.

PRATIBHÚ, S. &c. (प्रतिभू) A surety: in Hindu law, three kinds of sureties are most usually specified, but a fourth is sometimes added.

1. *Pratyaya-pratibhú*, A surety for confidence, one who engages for the general honesty and responsibility of another.
2. *Darṣana-pratibhú*, A surety for appearance.
3. *Dána-pratibhú*, A surety for the repayment of a loan or fulfilment of an engagement.
4. *Drávyárpaṇa-pratibhú*, One who engages to give up property belonging to the debtor if he fails to pay the debt.

The two first sureties are liable for any loan or advance made upon their credit if not paid by the borrower: the responsibility of the two last, or the engagement to pay or to deliver up property extends to their sons also.

Prátibhávya, S. &c. (प्रातिभाव्य) Surety, security, the act of becoming surety.

Pratibhúgrahanam, S. (from ग्रहण, taking) Acceptance of security by the court.

PRATIDÁNA, S. &c. (प्रतिदान) Giving back, either as an equivalent or recompense, or as a refusal or repayment.

PRATIGRAHA, S. &c. (प्रतिग्रह) Acceptance of gifts, the privilege of receiving gifts, one of the peculiar rights of the Brahman: a ceremonial acceptance of a son for adoption who is resigned by his parents.

PRATIJNÁ, commonly pronounced PRATIGYÁ, S. &c. (प्रतिज्ञा) Promise, assent: a bet, a wager: in law, a plaint, more especially after it has been recorded in writing by the officers of the court.

PRATILOMA, S. &c. (प्रतिलोम) lit., Against the hair: contrary to the regular course or order, inverse, reverse.

Pratilomaja, S. (प्रतिलोमज) Born or begotten in the inverse order of the tribes, as the offspring of a Kshetriya man and Brahman woman, of a Vaisya female and a Ṣúdra father, &c.

PRATINIDHI, S. (प्रतिनिधि) A deputy, a representative, a vicegerent: a title sometimes, but incorrectly, written *Pritinidhi*, borne by a distinguished Maraṭha family, the ancestor of which first received this title from Rája Rám placing him above the eight *Pradháns*.

PRATINYÁSA, S. (प्रतिन्यास) Reciprocal deposit, interchange of deposits.

PRATIPAD, or PRATIPAT, S. &c. (प्रतिपद् -त्) The first day of a lunar fortnight, either the day of full or new moon.

PRATIPAKSHA, S. &c. (प्रतिपक्ष) An adversary, an opponent, a defendant.

PRATIPATTI, S. (प्रतिपत्ति) Acquirement, gain: in law, admission of a claim.

PRATISÁRA, S. (प्रतिसार) A wreath, a bracelet, dyed strings or threads tied round the wrists of the contracting parties at a marriage, or round the wrist of a boy at the performance of other ceremonies.

PRATISHṬHÁ, S. &c. (पतिष्ठा) Consecration or setting up of an image, or a temple: a ceremony performed on the completion of a house before it is inhabited; also, purification or re-consecration of an idol, house, or temple that has been polluted.

PRATÍTI, S. &c. (प्रतीति) Trust, confidence.

PRATIVÁDA, or vernacularly, -BÁDA, S. &c. (प्रतिवाद) Reply, rejoinder, defence.

Prativádí, or *-bádí*, S. &c. (प्रतिवादी) A respondent, a replicant, a defendant.

PRATIVÁSÍ, S. &c. (प्रतिवासी) A neighbour (from प्रति, near to, and वासिन, who abides).

PRATIVEṢÍ, S. &c. (प्रतिवेशी) A neighbour (प्रति, near to, and वेश, entering).

Prativeṣikatwam, S. (प्रतिवेशिकत्वं) Neighbourship: in law, pre-emption from vicinage, or the right of a neighbour or coparcener to purchase any property in his vicinage which is for sale, in preference to a stranger, on agreeing to give the same price.

PRATYABHIYOGA, S. (प्रत्यभियोग) A counter plaint or plea: a counter action brought against the prosecutor.

PRATYÁKALITA, S. (प्रत्याकलित) Interposed in a suit of law, the deliberation of the court upon the pleading, and the determination which party is to produce proof.

PRATYAKSHA, S. &c. (प्रत्यक्ष) Perceptible, what is before the eyes: perception, the first proof of things.

Pratyahsha-darṣi, S. &c. (दर्शी, who sees) An eye-witness.

PRATYARTHÍ, S. (प्रत्यर्थी) A defendant, an opponent.

Pratyarthí-avedana, S. (from आवेदन, information) The verbal information of the defendant in a suit which is written down by the officers of the court.

PRATYAVASKANDA, S. (प्रत्यवस्कन्दः) Special plea at law, admission of a fact, but qualifying or explaining it so as to make it no ground of accusation.

PRATYUTTARA, S. &c. (प्रत्युत्तर) A reply in general: a rejoinder or reply to a reply.

PRÁÚ, or PRAHU, commonly, PROW, or PROA, Malay (ڤرهو, ڤراو) A term for all vessels between a canoe and a square-rigged vessel.

PRAVARA, S. (प्रवरः) Subdivision of a *gotra* or family, race, lineage, descendants.

PRAVARTTAKA, PRAVARTTIKA, PRAVARTTÍ, corruptly, PARBUTTY, PARPATTI, PREVATAH, S. &c. (प्रवर्त्तक, प्रवर्त्तिक, प्रवर्त्ती, from *pra*, over, and वर्त्ती, abiding, presiding over) Any one who manages affairs, whether for himself or others: a superintendant: a judge, an arbiter: it is used, modified vernacularly, chiefly in the south, where it is applied to the head man and manager of a village, especially one held by Brahmans, also to a subordinate revenue officer: the neuter noun *Pravarttakam*, or *Pravarttikam*, is used also to signify the general or joint management of a village by the principal proprietors, or one of their number.

Párvatyam, corruptly, *Parpatya*, Mal. (പാൎവ്വത്യം), *Pár-*

battiyam, Tam. (பார்பத்தியம்) A subordinate collectorship, stewardship, superintendence.

Párvatyakáran, or *Pravṛittikáran*, corruptly, *Prowartikar*, Mal. (പാവ്ത്യക്കാരൻ, പ്രവൃത്തിക്കാരൻ), *Párbattiyakáran*, Tam. (பார்பத்தியக்காரன்) A subordinate officer in the revenue department, a native collector under the *Tahsildár*, having charge of the collections of one or more villages: it is sometimes applied to the head or manager of a village, or to a government officer appointed to conduct the affairs of a village which has no hereditary chief: also to a bailiff or manager of an estate on behalf of the proprietor.

PRAVÁSA, S. &c. (प्रवासः) Residing abroad or away from home.

Pravásásedha, S. (आसेध, restraint) In law, prohibition against removal, 'ne exeat.'

PRAVRAJYÁ, S. (प्रव्रज्या) Wandering about as a mendicant.

Pravrajyávasita, corrupted extraordinarily to *Perberjabesheet*, S. (अवसित, terminated) An apostate mendicant, also one who adopts a life of mendicancy: in either case the party forfeits his rights of inheritance.

PRÁYASCHITTA, vernacularly, PRAYASCHIT, corruptly, PRAISCHITTO, S. &c. (प्रायश्चित्त) Penance, expiation, punishment, fine.

PRAYOGA, S. &c. (प्रयोग) Principal, as distinguished from interest: a loan bearing interest.

Prayojyam, S. &c. (प्रयोज्यं) Capital, principal: a loan.

PRETA, S. &c. (प्रेत) Dead: a corpse: a ghost, an evil spirit.

Pretaṣráddha, S. (प्रेतश्राद्ध) Obsequial ceremonies to be offered to a relative during the year of his demise: fifteen are required.

PRÍTIDATTA, S. (प्रीति, affection, and दत्त, given) Property or valuables presented to a female by her relations and friends at the time of her marriage, constituting part of her peculiar property.

PÚCHI, Tel. (పూచి) Responsibility.

Hátpúchi-lekhkalu, Tel. (హాత్పూచీ లెక్కలు) Accounts necessary for current business.

PUḌÁ, or PUṚÁ, Beng. (পুড়া) A denomination of a land measure in some parts of Bengal: the same as *Bíghá* (?).

PUḌÍ, or PUṚÍ, Beng. (পুড়ী) Straw-coloured variety of sugar-cane.

PUGAIVARI, Tam. (புகைவரி) A tax on houses.

PÚGAM, S. &c. (पूगं) The betel-nut tree: a multitude: an assemblage of men of different trades.

PÚJÁ, S. &c. (पूजा) Worship, adoration: (it occurs vernacularly also with a short *u*, *Pujá*).

Pújaimichcham, Tam. (பூசைமிச்சம்) Unexpended balance of pagoda allowances.

Pújárí, H. &c. (پوجاری, पूजारी) A priest in a temple, one who conducts public worship and receives the offerings either on his own account or that of the proprietors of the temple: he is sometimes a man of low caste, and, when a Brahman, is held in disrepute: the village officiating priest.

PÚJU, Tel. (పూజు) The yoke of a plough.

PUKHTA, corruptly, POKHTA, H. (P. پخته) Baked, burnt, as bricks, whence it is applied to a brick wall or house.

PUKKACHÍṬṬA, Mal. (പുക്കചിട്ട) A receipt, a written engagement.

Pukkamuṛi, or *Pukkawáṛa*, Mal. (പുക്കമുറി, പുക്കവാറ) A receipt.

PUL, H. (P. پل) A bridge, an embankment, a causeway.

Pulbandí, H. (پلبندی) Keeping bridges or embankments in repair: the public department having that duty: a tax imposed for the purpose: in Cuttack the term is also applied to the bridge or dam.

Pulguẓár, H. (P. پلگذار) A bridge-toll.

PULÁ, Hindi (पुला) A small bundle of plants or sticks.

Púlá, or *Púlí*, H. (پولا, پولی) A bundle of grass or straw.

PULAIMAKAN, Tam. (புலைமகன்) A man of very low caste, a *Paraiya* or *Pulaya*.

PULÁKAM, Mal. (പുലാക്കം) Shrivelled grain.

PULAM, Tam. (புலம்) A field of corn.

PULAYAN, corruptly, POLAYAN, POLEYAN, POLIAN, POOLYAN, Mal. (പുലയൻ) The name of a low and servile caste, or of an individual of such caste, in Malabar: in this caste the husband resides with his wife though she may belong to a different master, and their children inherit any rights the mother may possess.

Pulachchi, *Pulakaḷḷi*, or *Pulayi*, Mal. The female *Pulayan*, or the wife of a slave so termed.

Pulakoṭṭil, or *Pulamádam*, Mal. (പുലക്കൊട്ടിൽ, പുലമാടം) A slave's hut.

Pulappaṭi, Mal. (പുലപ്പടി) A place where slaves place stones in memory of deceased relatives.

PULÁS, (?) H. Straw, fodder.

PÚLÍ, H. (پولی, पूली) A small quantity of corn given at harvest to the village officers and servants.

PÚLÍ, Tam. (?) A lease, a deed.

PULICHI, (?) Mal. The name of an outcaste tribe in Malabar residing in the woods, and not allowed to approach a respectable individual, or enter a village: they announce their wants by cries at a distance, when charitably disposed persons place food for them at the foot of a tree and withdraw: they then advance and receive the donation.

PUḶIṆAR, PUḶIṆAR, PUḶAINAR, Tam. (புளிஞர், புளிஞர், புளைஞர், plur.) An outcaste and barbarous race, the same as the *Vedar*.

PULINDA, S. (पुलिंद) A barbarian, an outcaste, one inhabiting forests and mountains.

PULINDÁ, H. &c. (پلندا) A bundle, a parcel.

PULIVAṬṬU, Karn. (ಪುಲಿವಟ್ಟು) A fund set apart for religious purposes.

PULLAR, Tam. (புல்லர், plur.) A low and servile caste employed in agriculture.

PULLAṢAN, Mal. (പുല്ലുസൻ) A man of a low servile tribe, a *Paraiyan*.

PULLIYAR, corruptly, PULIAH, POOLLEE, Tam. (புல்லியர், plur.) A low outcaste tribe classed with the *Paraiyar*: (this and similar designations are perhaps from *pulai*, and *paluvu*, flesh, the several outcaste tribes feeding upon every kind of flesh, even carrion: the word is no doubt the same as the Mal. *Pulayan*.

PULLU, Tel., Karn. (పుల్లు), PUL, Tam. (புல்) Grass.

Pullari, Tel. (పుల్లరి) A tax on pasturage.

Pulluḍinéla, Tel. (పుల్లుడినేల) Land fit only for occasional cultivation.

Pulvari, Tam. (புல்வரி) A tax on grass-land or pasturage: (the Glossary, fifth Report, gives *Pillwany*, from Tam. *pillu*, as well as *pullu*; *pil* is a common vulgarism for *pul*, grass, and *wany* is evidently a mistake for *wari*).

PUḺUDI, Tam. (புழுதி) Dry earth turned up by the plough: land prepared for dry planting.

Puḻudikáḍu, Tam. (புழுதிக்காடு) A ploughed field.

Puḻudinaṭṭu, Tam. (புழுதிநட்டு) Plants growing on dry ground.

Puḻudiviraippu, Tam. (புழுதிவிரைப்பு) Sowing seed on dry ground previously prepared.

PUḺUKKAI, Tam. (புழுக்கை) A slave.

PUMBA, H. (P. پنبه) Cotton.

PUMSTAM, (?) Tam. The office of priest in a temple.

PÚN, POON, Karn. A coin or measure of value: (possibly an error or vernacular corruption of *Hún*, or perhaps *Pon*).

PUNAKULAM, (?) Tam. Land fit for gardens or plantations.

PUNAM, Tam. (புனம்) High ground not fit for rice cultivation.

PUNARBHÚ, S. (पुनर्भू, from पुनर्, again, and भू, who is) A woman married a second time.

Punarviváha, S. (पुनर्, again, and विवाह) A second marriage.

PUNÁSA, PUNÁS, Tel. (పునాస) The first crop of the year, which consists of the smaller grains cultivable on dry soils, and

Punása-fasl, H. (A. فصل, a season) The season of the small grain crop: also the cotton harvest (?).

PUNCHA, pron. PUNJA, Mal. (പുഞ്ച) A crop sown in Nov.-Dec. and reaped in April-May.

PUNCHAKṚUSHI, Mal. (പുഞ്ചകൃഷി, for S. कृषि) Cultivation of wet land.

PUNCHANILAM, or PUNCHAPPÁTTAM, Mal. (പുഞ്ചനിലം, പുഞ്ചപ്പാടം) Wet land, or land capable of irrigation and bearing rice crops: (the analogy of *Puncha* or *Punja* to the Tamil *Punshey* or *Punjai* would suggest the sense of *dry*, not *wet*, land; but it is so explained in the dictionary).

PUṆḌA, Mar. (पुंड) A freebooter, a marauder.

Pundapál, Mar. (पुंडपाळ) The chief of a gang of robbers.

PUṆḌÁ, Beng. (পুংডা) A storehouse, a granary: a seller of vegetables.

PUNJA, S. &c. (पुंज), PUNJÁ, Mar. (पुंजा) A heap, a quantity.

PUNJAḌÁ, Guz. (પુંજડો) A class of Mohammadans in Guzerat, sellers of vegetables.

PUNJAM, commonly, but incorrectly, written and pronounced PANJAM, PUNJUM, Tel. (పుంజము) A certain number of threads, whence it has come to denote a class of cotton cloths varying in quality according to the number of threads in the woof: they were formerly very extensively exported from the Madras coast to Europe.

PÚNJÍ, H. (پونجي), PUNJÍ, Beng. Mar. (পুংজী, पुंजी) A heap, a small heap, stock, capital, a fund of any thing.

PUNSAVANA, S. &c. (पुंसवन) A ceremony observed when the first signs of conception are manifested; the first of the *Sanskáras*, or essential Hindu rites.

PUNSHEY, or PUNSEY, pronounced, PUNJAI, and written PUNJA, POONJA, PUNJAH, PUNJEE, Tam. (புன்செய், from *Pun* புன் for *Pul* புல், deficient, inferior, and *Shey* செய், cultivation) PUNJE, Karn. (ಪುಂಜೆ) Dry land or cultivation, land not admitting of complete irrigation, and therefore unfit for the growth of rice, bearing dry grains of inferior value: the converse of *Nanjai*: it is sometimes applied to a sterile soil.

Punsheykáḍu, *Punjaikáḍu*, Tam. (புன்செய்க்காடு) Cultivable dry ground.

Punsheytóṭṭam, *Punjaitottam*, Tam. (புன்செய்த்தோட்டம்) Gardens or garden land on which any dry crop is sown.

Puṇsheyvari, *Punjaivari*, Tam. (புன்செய்வரி) Tax on cultivable dry ground.

PUNYA, vernacularly, PUN, S. &c. (पुण्य) Virtue, moral merit, holiness: also, adj., pure, holy.

Punyá, corruptly, *Puneah*, vernacular corruption of *Punyáha*, q. v. H. (پنیا), Beng. (পুন্যা) In the lower provinces the day on which the revenue for the ensuing year is settled, or an annual meeting of the direct revenue payers at the office of the chief collector, or of the cultivating tenants at the court of the Zamindár, to determine the amount of the assessment; the assemblage of the rent-payers forming a kind of festival or holiday: the term is also applied to the day on which the first instalment of the annual rent or revenue is paid: in some parts of Bengal the Zamindárí accounts and receipts are ante-dated if the *Punyá* instalment has not been discharged; *i. e.* if the rent for the Bengal year 1249 had been paid before the *Punyá* of that year it would be entered as paid in 1248.

Puṇyáha, Hindi, Mar. (S. पुण्य, and अहन्, a day) A holiday, a sacred day, or one on which religious observances are enjoined; also the day on which the rent or revenue for the ensuing year is first settled, or on which the first instalment is paid.

Puṇyáhachiṭhí, Hindi, (पुण्याहचिठी) The summons from the Zamindár to his tenants fixing the day for the settlement or payment of the rents.

Puṇyáhahharch, Hindi (पुण्याहखरच्) A charge for sweetmeats given to the Ryots on settling their rent.

Puṇyáhapátra, Beng. (পুন্যাহপাত্র) The tenant who has the privilege of being the first to settle for his rent at the prescribed period.

Puṇyáhaváchaná, Mar. (पुण्याहवाचन) A preparatory or purificatory ceremony performed at marriages, or on other festive occasions.

Puṇyáhasuní, Beng. (পুন্যাহশুনী, from S. शून्य, empty) Nonpayment of rent at the customary day.

Puṇyakshetra, S. &c. (पुण्यक्षेत्र, from क्षेत्र, a field) A place of pilgrimage.

PUR, Hindi (पुर) Irrigation of fields by water drawn from wells in a large leather bag.

PURA, vernacularly, PUR, corruptly, POOR, and PORE, S. &c. (पुर) A town, a city; it is used most frequently in composition as *Srí-rám-pur*, vulgarly, *Serampore*; *Pundrapur*, vulgarly, *Punderpore*, and the like.

Purí, S. &c. (पुरी) A city, a small city.

Purseth, or *Pursethí*, Beng., Uriya (পুরশেথ, পুরশেথী, from S. पुर, and श्रेष्ठी, chief) The head man of a town, or of a ward of a town: in Cuttack, the elected head and representative of the people of a village, who was admitted to engage with government for the rent of the ground on which the village was built, and was thence sometimes considered as the Zamindár, having a title to any difference between the sum he might receive from the villagers and that which he paid to the government.

PURÁ, (?) H. A local term for a measure of land, apparently the same as a *bíghá*.—Maimansinh.

PÚRÁ, Hindi (पूरा) The grain of corn full formed in the ear.

PURÁJA, pronounced PURADZA, Tel. (పురజ. P. پرزه, an account) Daily account of the receipts and disbursements of a village: also sea-customs.

PURAJÁRÍ, Mar. (पुरजारी, from S. पुर, before, and A. جاري, current) Restoration of an *Inám*, or grant of rent-free land which had been resumed: allowing it to go on as before.

PÚRAKA, S. &c. (पूरक) Filling, completing, any terminating act, as the last presentation of the funeral cake to an individual deceased before the performance of the general *Ṣráddha* to ancestors collectively.

PÚRAKAḶAM, Tam. (புறக்களம், from S. पूर, full) An allowance of grain to the agricultural labourer after the crop has been measured.

PÚRAM, Mal. (പൂരം) A large piece of water, a lake.

PUṚAMANAI, Tam. (புறமனை, from *puṛam*, out, outside) Land lying beyond or on the outskirts of an estate or district.

PUṚAMBOKU, or PURAMPOKU, corruptly, POREMPOCO, PURRAMBOKE, Tam. (புறம்போக்கு, from புறம், out, excluded, and போக்கு, a place) Such portions of an estate or village lands liable to revenue as do not admit of cultivation, and are therefore exempted from the assessment, as sterile, or waste land, rock, water, wilderness, site of dwellings, and the like: also common land near a town: any place situated out of or beyond certain limits. PURAMBOKKA, Mal. (പുറമ്പൊക്ക) Extra expense.

PURAMKÁDAM, PORAMKADAM, (?) Mal. Final payment or loan on which the proprietary right of the owner is transferred to the lender or mortgagee.

Puráṇa, S. &c. (पुराण) lit., Old: the especial designation of a class of works of which eighteen principal are enumerated in which the ancient traditions of the Hindus, and legends and doctrines belonging to the chief sects, as Ṣaivas and Vaishnavas, are embodied.

Puṟandaṭa, Puṟavaramba, Puṟaveli, Mal. (പുറണ്ട, പുറവരമ്പ, പുറവെലി) A large internal embankment or bank.

Puránt, or Puránt-báki, Guz. (પુરાંત, પુરાંતબાકી) Balance in hand, stock.

Purat, Guz. (પુરત) A bride's portion, a dowry.

Purátanabídu, Tel. (పురాతనబీడు) Waste land, land long left fallow.

Puraṭṭási, corruptly, Pretási, Paratasi, Tam. (புரட்டாசி) The seventh Tamil month (Sept.-Oct.).

Puṟavam, Tam. (புறவம்) Hilly ground, also a wood or woodland country.

Púrdará, Hindi (पूरदरा) The highest average rate of the rent of a village.

Púrí, H. (S. پوري) A kind of cake fried in butter.

Púrián, H. (پوريان, plur. of *Purí*) The sending of fried cakes by the bride's relatives to the bridegroom a few days after the betrothment, one of the marriage customs of the Mohammadans.

Puriálam, (?) Tam. A class of *Paraiyar*.

Púrkáyath, Beng. (পূরকায়থ, from S. पूर, full, perfect, and कायस्थ) The *Patwárí*, or village accountant; also any skilful scribe or accountant.—Sylhet. It is applied also in Bengal to the Brahman who performs the ceremonies at the *Punyá*.

Púrṇábhisheka, S. (पूर्णाभिषेकः, from *Púrna*, full) Full consecration or initiation, the complete inauguration or coronation of a Rája: it is now applied to complete initiation into mysterious rites, especially those of the *Vámácháris*, or left-hand worshippers of *Ṣaktí*, the female principle, when flesh is eaten and spirits are drunk, and other impure acts are practised.

Púrṇábhishikta, (S. पूर्ण, full, and अभिषिक्त, inaugurated) An adept, one fully initiated.

Púrṇamása, S. (पूर्णमास) A religious ceremony performed on the day of full moon.

Púrṇamásí, corruptly, *Poorun Mashee*, S. &c. (पूर्णमासी) Day of full moon.

Púrṇimá, S. &c. (पूर्णिमा) Day of full moon.

Púrṇapátra, S. &c. (पूर्णपात्र) A full measure or vessel: in Mal. (പൂൎണ്ണപാത്രം) A vessel filled with clothes, ornaments, &c., to be scrambled for at a festival: a vessel full of rice, properly equal to 256 handfuls.

Puroḍása, S. (पुरोडाश) Clarified butter offered in oblations to fire, especially with cakes of ground rice which have been baked or roasted and then well steeped in it.

Purohita, vernacularly, Purohit, corruptly, Prohit, Uprohit, S. &c. (पुरोहितः), in Tam. it is spelt Purokitan, (புரோகிதன்) A family priest, one who conducts the domestic ceremonies of a tribe, a household, or family: the office is sometimes hereditary: in the south of India it is also applied to the village priest and astrologer.

Paurohityam, corruptly, *Pawrohetum*, S. &c. (पौरोहित्यं) The office of family or village priest.

Puroṇi, Tel. (పురోణి) A note, the *chit* of Bengal: a bill, a note of hand.

Purṣís, Mar. (पुरशीस or पुरसीस, P. پرسش) A questioning or interrogating as of parties or witnesses in a dispute.

Púrtta, S. &c. (पूर्त्तः) An act of pious liberality, as digging a well, planting trees, building a temple, &c.

Purusha, vernacularly, Purush, S. &c. (पुरुषः) A man, a male: embodied spirit: eternal spirit.

Purushánukrame, or *Purushkrame*, Beng. (from S. क्रम, order, succession) By or in course of succession, in the direct or male line.

Purushdhan, Beng. (S. পুরষধন) Property belonging to the man or husband in contrast to *Strídhan*, or that peculiar to the wife.

Púrva, vernacularly, Púrba, and Púrab, or Poorub, S. &c. (पूर्व्व) Before, prior, first: east, eastern, the east.

Púrvaja, S. &c. (पूर्व्व, and ज, born) First-born, the eldest son; applied especially to the son of the first married wife, although he may be born subsequently to the sons of other wives: plur. *Púrvajáh* (पूर्व्वजाः) Ancestors, progenitors.

Púrví, *Púrvíya*, or *Púrbiya*, (पूर्व्वी, पूर्व्वीय) Eastern, as a native of the eastern countries, or those lying on the east of the Ganges, beginning from Bahar: also the *bháshá*, or dialect of those districts.

Purváí, H. (پرواي, पुरवाई) The completion of the sugar-cane harvest.

Púrwa, (?) Hindi, Subdivision, or a dependency of a village: a detached cluster of houses from the principal village, for the convenience of agricultural operations.—North-west Provinces.

Purwaní, Mar. S. (पुरवणी) Fitting up or supplying a part wanting: a supplement, an appendix.

Purwani-band, Mar. (पुरवणी, and बंद, a sheet of paper) A supplementary sheet, the paper on which a supplement is written.

Purwár, Mar. (पुरवार) Substantiating by evidence.

Pús, Poos, H. (پوس) The name of a month (Dec.-Jan.): see *Pausha*.

Pushkariní, S. &c. (पुष्करिणी) A large pond or piece of water.

Pusht, H. (P. پشت) The back: ancestry, progenitors.

Pusht ba pusht, or *Pusht dar pusht*, H. (پشت بہ پشت, پشت در پشت), *Pust dar pust*, Mar. (पुस्तदरपुस्त) Generation, by or after or according to generation.

Pushta, H. (P. پشتہ), **Postá**, Beng. (পোস্তা) A bank, a buttress, an embankment, a wall or building of masonry on the bank of a river or a piece of water.

Pushtabandí, less correctly, *Pushtibandi*, H. &c. (پشتہبندی) An embankment: repairing embankments: an extra cess imposed formerly upon the revenue payers for the expense of keeping embankments in repair.

Pustaka, vernacularly, **Pustak**, S. &c. (पुस्तक), **Puttakam**, Tam, (புத்தகம்) A book, a manuscript.

Pustakpánat, Mar. (पुस्तकपानट) A general term for books and papers.

Puttakdár, correct reading of *Puttuckdár*, (?) Tam. (புத்தக்தார்) A kind of collector or Zamindár in Tanjore in charge of a district: lit., a bookkeeper.—Fifth Rep.

Puth, (?) H. Small sand hillocks commonly found at the extremity of a village where the country ceases to be level: sometimes the whole area of the village is of this description.—Agra.

Putra, S., but universally adopted, or, vernacularly, **Pút**, (पुत्रः, पूत) A son: in the old Hindu law the term was applicable to twelve objects of affiliation: 1. *Aurasa* (from *uras* उरस, the breast) A legitimate son, or one born of a wife of the same class; 2. *Kshetraja* (from क्षेत्र, a field, *i.e.* a wife, and ज, born) The son born of a wife duly appointed to raise up issue to a husband who is incompetent, or has died childless; 3. *Datta* or *Dattaha* (from दत्त, given) A son given by his parents for adoption, according to prescribed rules: a son lawfully adopted: in some cases the natural father retains a right in his son, when he is termed *Dwyámushyáyana*, or the son of two fathers, and is heir to both; 4. *Kritrima* (from कृत, made) A son made: a boy of the same class as the person adopting him, who is either an orphan, or has been deserted by his parents; 5. *Gúdhaja* (from *gúdha* गूढ, secret) Son of concealed birth: one born of the wife during the absence of a husband, or under circumstances which leave the father doubtful; 6. *Apaviddha* (अपविद्ध, lit., deserted) A foundling: one deserted by his natural parents and adopted by a stranger; 7. *Kánína* (from *kanyá* कन्या, a virgin) The son of a girl, yet unmarried, or before consummation; 8. *Sahodha* (from *saha* सह, with, and *údhá* ऊढा, a bride) The son of a pregnant bride, who, being accepted with the woman, becomes the son of the husband; 9. *Kríta* (क्रीत) The son bought, one purchased of his parents; 10. *Paunarbhava* (see *Punarbhú*) Son of a twice married woman; 11. *Swayamdatta* (from *swayam* स्वयम्, self, and *datta*, given) A son self-given, one who, being without natural parents, or being deserted by them, offers himself for adoption; 12. *Pársava* (from *para*, पर, another, and *sava* शव, a corpse) The son of a Súdra mother by a man of the three first castes. Another description of son sometimes enumerated as one of the twelve, to the exclusion of the last, is the *Putrikáputra* or son of a daughter (पुत्रिका), who, by agreement or adoption, becomes the son of her father: of these, in the present age, besides the son lawfully begotten, the son given, or adopted son, is universally recognised: the son made, or *Kritrima*, is acknowledged in some places, as in *Mithilá*: the admissibility of the son bought is disputed: the rest are universally rejected.

Putrabhága, S. &c. (पुत्रभाग) Division of inheritance amongst, or according to, sons.

Putrapratinidhi S. (प्रतिनिधि, a substitute) Any affiliated son other than the son begotten: an illegitimate son, or one who, without being legally adopted, is treated as a child.

Putreshti, S. (पुत्रेष्टि) A sacrifice performed in order to obtain male children, one performed at the time of adoption.

Putrí, or *Putriká*, S. &c. (पुत्री, पुत्रिका) A daughter.

Puttan, Mal. (പുത്തൻ) A coin current in Cochin.

Putti, Pooty, corruptly, Poottie, Poddie, Poody, Tel. (పుట్టి) A measure of capacity equal to twenty *Túms*, and containing 14941.653 cubic inches: the same as the *khandi* or *candy*: in the northern Sarkárs the *Putti* is of smaller dimensions, consisting of 3635.413 cubic inches. —Jervis: but there is also one larger termed *Malka Putti*. It is sometimes applied to a measure of land of about eight acres.

Puttidosillu, Tel. (పుట్టిదోసిల్లు) A fee of two handfuls

from each *puṭṭi* of grain paid to the village servants, prohibited at present, but frequently levied.

Puttímániké, Tel. (పుట్టిమానికె) A *mániké*, or measure so termed, or 160th part per *puṭṭi* distributed in charity.

PUTÚVAL, Mal. (പുതുവൽ, from *putú*, new) Newly inclosed or cultivated land.

Putúval-pāṭam, Mal. (പുതുവൽപാട്ടം) Rent of newly cultivated land.

R.

RÁB, corruptly, RAUB, Hindi, &c. (राब) Inspissated juice of the sugar-cane: also, in Mar., ground prepared by the burning of leaves, grass, sticks, &c., for sowing: also the crop raised on the ground so prepared.

RABA, Thug. Any trick practised on travellers.

RABÁḌI, or RABÁṚI, Guz. (રબારી) A caste of cowherds and milkmen, or an individual of the caste, who attend on and graze cattle, and sell the milk of both cows and camels, and the *ghee* made from it.

RÁBṆÍ, or RÁBṆÚK, Mar. (राबणी, राबणूक) Culture, tillage, the operations of husbandry generally.

RÁBTÁ, incorrectly, RAPTEE, Mar. (राबता, from राबणे, to labour) The practice of exacting labour on public service, or for public functionaries, from the *Mhárs* of a village: a tax in commutation of such labour: it also occurs as *Rábtá-mhár*.

Rábtyá, Mar. (राबत्या) The village *Mhár* compelled to give his labour on public work, or pay a commutation tax.

RABB, RUBB, H. (A. ربّ) A lord, a master.

Rabb-ul-ârz, H. (A. ربّ العرض) A landholder, a proprietor of land.

Rabb-ul-mál, H. (A. ربّ المال) An owner or possessor of property or capital.

Rabb-us-salam, H. (ربّ السلم) A purchaser who pays for an article in advance or anticipation.

RABIÂ, pronounced, RABÍ, commonly, but incorrectly, RUBBEE, H. (A. ربيع), Hindi, Mar. (रबी, रब्बी) The spring, the months of March-April: the spring harvest or crop sown after the rains and reaped in the first three or four months of the year ensuing: a name common to the third and fourth months of the Mohammadan year.

Rabiâ-ul-áwal, H. (A. ربيع الاول) The first of the two months termed *Rabiâ*, the third of the Mohammadan year.

Rabiâ-us-ṣáni, H. (A. ربيع الثاني) The fourth month of the Mohammadan year, the second *Rabiâ*.

RÁCH, Asam (রাচ) A loom.

RÁCHA, RÁCHAVÁḌU, pronounced, RÁTSAWÁR, corruptly, RACHEWAR, RAISWAR, ROWAR, Tel. (రాచ, రాచవాడు) probably from the S. राजा) The name of a military and ruling tribe, or of an individual of it, claiming descent from the pure Kshatriyas of the Hindus, established chiefly in the northern Sarkárs, and remarkable for their high sense of honour, and the desperate acts by which they expiate a real or imaginary insult.

RADD, or RUDD, less correctly, RAD, or RUD, H. &c. (A. ردّ) RADDU, Tel., Karn. (రద్దు) Rejection, repulsion, refutation, reply: repeal, abrogation, making null and void; sometimes, erasure: in Mohammadan law it applies especially to the return or surplus of an inheritance which remains after the legal portions have been distributed among the sharers, and which, in default of a residuary heir, returns, or is to be divided amongst the original sharers.

Rad-bátel, Guz. (રદબાતલ) Null and void: in law, abrogated, repealed.

Radd-ul-jawáb, or *Radd-i-jawáb*, H. (A. ردّ الجواب) Rejoinder, reply to a reply, refutation of a defence.

Radd-náma, H. (P. نامه, a document) A deed of rescission, one abrogating a former engagement.

Raddu-máḍida-kágada, Karn. (ರದ್ದುಮಾಡಿದಕಾಗದ) A paper or voucher on which the writing is erased.

RÁḌH, pronounced RÁṚH, Beng. (রাঢ) The part of Bengal which lies on the west of the Hugli branch of the Ganges.

Ráḍhi, *Ráḍhíya*, or *Ráṛhi*, *Ráṛhíya*, Beng. (রাঢি, রাঢীয) Belonging to the country of *Ráṛh*; applied especially to one of the two principal divisions of the Brahmans of *Gauṛ*, or Bengal, subdivided into fifty-six branches or families, of which six are considered as *Kulínas*, or Brahmans of family: their designations are *Mukhuṭí*, vulgarly *Mukharjia*, *Ganguli* or *Gangoli*, *Kanjelala*, *Ghoshála*, vulgarly *Gosaul*, *Bandhyagati*, vulgarly *Banerjia* or *Bonnarji*, and *Chaṭati*, vulgarly *Chattarji*, *Chatoji*, or *Chaturjia*: these, if correctly given, are proper names without any peculiar signification: also an armed messenger or attendant, a *Peon*, a *Barkandáz*; also the name of a low and servile caste in Cuttack.

RAFÂ, corruptly, RUFFAH, H. &c. (رفع, रफा) Settlement of an affair or dispute.

Rafânáma, H. (رفعنامه) A deed of compromise, one by which a dispute is settled.

Rafâ-dafâ, H. (رفع دفع), *Raphe-daphe*, Mar. (रफे दफे) Settlement of an affair, liquidation of a debt, deciding a dispute: sometimes used adjectively, settled, decided.

RAFIÂ, H. (A. رفيع, from رفع, elevation) High, noble; used commonly in forming titles, as, *Rafiâ-ul-darját*, the high in degree; *Rafiâ-us-shán*, the high in dignity, &c.

RÁFIẒÍ, or RAFẒÍ, H. (A. رافضي, رفضي) A heretic, commonly applied by the Suni Mohammadans to the Shías.

RAFUGAR, H. (A. P. رفوگر, from رفو, darning) A darner, one whose business is to mend or darn cloth, silk, shawls, &c.

RÁGADA, Tel. (రాగడ) Black clay soil.

RÁGÍ, vulgarly, RAGGY, Karn. (ರಾಗಿ), Mal. (റാഗി), RÁGULU, Tel. (plur. రాగులు) A kind of grain, a sort of panic commonly termed also *Nacheni*: see *Náchní*.

RAGON, Thug. An omen, good or bad.

RAGNAUTI, Thug. Taking the auspices.

RAH, RÁH, H. &c. (P. ره, راه, रह, राह), also RAHÁ, Mar. (रहा) A road, a way: (in its compounds in Hindustani it may be written with either the short or the long vowel, although, as the latter is in general more used, it is here given in that form only in the words of that language).

Ráhbar, H. (P. راهبر) A guide, a conductor; *Rahbarán*, plur., an item of deduction formerly allowed to the Zamindárs to cover the expense of providing guides for the safe conduct of travellers and traders through their estates.

Ráhdár, H. (راهدار) A collector of tolls or transit duties.

Ráhdárí, incorrectly, *Rádarree*, *Rahdarry*, and *Rahdurry*, H. &c. (راهداري, from داري, having, keeping), *Rahdárí*, or *Rahádárí*, Mar. (रहदारी, रहादारी) A passport, a custom pass or permit: transit duties, tolls and duties collected at inland stations upon grain and other articles, levied formerly by the government, or sometimes by the Zamindárs on their own authority.

Rahdárí-, or *Rahádárí-jakát*, Mar. (रहदारी -रहादारीजकात) Transit duties: in Sindh, Black mail, a fee paid to escape plunder.

Rahdárí-chíti, Tel. (రహాదారిచీటి) A custom pass specifying the duties to have been paid.

Rahdári-pullari, Tel. (పుల్లరి) A tax or fine levied formerly on cattle passing over fields.

Ráhgír, H. (راهگير) A traveller.

Ráhkharch, H. (P. راهخرچ) Way-expenses, travelling charges.

Ráhnumá, H. (P. راهنما) A guide.

Ráhzan, H. (P. راهزن) A robber, a highwayman.

Ráhzaní, H. (راهزني) Robbing on the road.

Ráhzaní-bá-khún, H. (P. خون, blood) Highway robbery with murder.

Ráhzaní-bá-zakhm, H. (A. زخم, a wound) Robbery on the road with personal injury.

RAHÁÍ, H. (P. رهاي) Liberation, escape.

RAHAṬ, or RAHÁṬ, also, vernacularly, ARHAṬ, and HARAṬH, q.v. Hindi, Mar. (रहट, रहाट) A machine for drawing water from wells, a beam connecting two wheels so employed, or the Persian water-wheel.

Rahátágar, Mar. (रहाटागर) A plantation irrigated by water-wheels.

Rahát-gáḍgeṇ, Mar. (रहाटगाडगें) A wheel with a wreath of pots round it for drawing up water from a well, the Persian water-wheel.

Raháṭi, Mar. (रहाटी) A water-wheel worked by the feet.

Raháṭwaṇí, Mar. (रहाटवणी) Water supplied by a water-wheel from a well.

RAHN, incorrectly, RAHIN, H. (A. رهن) A pledge, a pawn, property given as security for a loan, but of which the usufruct is not enjoyed by the lender, nor can it be transferred or sold.

Rahannámá, incorrectly, *Rahin-náma*, Uriya (ରହନନାମା) A deed of mortgage, a deed of pledge.

Rahan-tamassuk, Uriya (from H. تمسك) A mortgage-bond

Ráhin, H. (A. راهن) A borrower on a pledge or pawn.

Rahún, H. (A. رهون) The thing pawned or property mortgaged.

RAHNÁ, Thug. lit., 'To remain,' a temporary grave.

RAHITA, RAHITU, Karn. (ರಹಿತ, ರಹಿತು) A farmer, a cultivator (a corruption of *Raiat*).

RAHWÁ, H. (رهوا) A slave, one not purchased.

RAHWÁÍ, H. (رهواي, from *rahná*, to remain) House rent.

Rahwáiá, H. (رهوايا) An inhabitant, a householder.

RÁÍ, corruptly, ROY, H. (راي), RÁE, Hindi (राए), RÁY, Beng. (রায) A prince, being a provincialism for Raja: under the Mohammadan governments it was a title given to Hindu civil officers of high rank, whence it became a family designation, as, *Rammohun Roy*.

Ráí-ráyán, corruptly, *Roy-royan*, H. (راي رايان) A prince: lit., prince of princes, but applied as a title to Hindu civil functionaries of high rank: it was the title borne by the financial minister and treasurer of the Nawab of Bengal, and was assigned by the British government to the chief native revenue officer whom they appointed in 1772, on abolishing the office of Náib Diwán.

RÂÍ, or RÁÂI, corruptly, RYE, H. (A. راعي) Rate, the local rate of assessment, the standard rate at which the lands of a village or district are asssesed, according to their several qualities. Reg. ii. 1795.

Râí-bandí, *Rybundee*, H. (رعي بندي) A statement or table of rates, a document shewing the rates at which different descriptions of land are usually assessed in any particular district.

Râí-kankúti, H. (رعي كنكوتي) Lands of which the assessment was rated according to the value, or a fixed or customary rate, of produce per *bighá*.

Ráígar, H. (رايگر) A caste or tribe of Rajputs: in Mherwara it is applied to a low caste working in skins and leather, or employed as labourers.

Ráíj, H. (A. رايج) Customary, usual, current.

Ráíj-ul-waḳt, H. (A. رايج الوقت) The practice or custom of the time.

Ráíkat, Beng. (?) A title given in some places to the possessor of a Zamindárí, as the head of the family and rightful heir.

Râiyat, vernacularly, Ráyat, and, corruptly, Ryot, H. (A. رعيّت, plur. *Râáya*, or *Râia*, or *Râya*, رعايا, from رعي, to pasture, to feed, to protect), Hindi and Mar. (रायत), Ráiyat, Beng. (রাইযৎ), Ráyutu, Tel. (రాయుతు) A subject, but especially applied to the agricultural population, a cultivator, a farmer, a peasant.

Ráyatáwá, Mar. (रायतावा) Subjects or peasants collectively, people, peasantry.

Râiyat-azár, H. (P. ازار, who torments) Tyrannous, oppressive, an oppressor.

Râiyatí, or *Rayatí*, corruptly, *Ryotee*, H. (رعيّتي, रयती), *Ráiyatí*, Beng. (রাইযতী) Relating or belonging to a *Raiyat*: applied also in Bengal to lands of which the revenue is paid in money, in opposition to the *Khamár* lands, of which the revenue is paid in kind; also to a settlement direct with the cultivators; also, subjection, tenancy.

Râiyat-náma, H. (P. نامه, a document) An engagement given by the cultivators to the landlord or proprietor.

Râiyaṭí paṭṭá, corruptly, *Ryotee poṭṭah*, H. (رعيّتي پتّا) A lease given to a peasant or cultivator.

Râiyat-parwar, H. (P. پرور, protecting) A benevolent sovereign or landlord.

Râiyatwár, corruptly, *Ryotwar*, H. (P. رعيتوار) According to or with *Râiyats*, familiarly applied to the revenue settlement which is made by the government officers with each actual cultivator of the soil for a given term, usually a twelvemonth, at a stipulated money rent, without the intervention of a third party: it is the mode of assessment which prevails chiefly, although not exclusively, in the provinces of the Madras Presidency.

Râiyatwár-jamâ-bandí, H. (from جمعبندي) Statement of the revenue settlement made with each cultivator.

Rayání-muchchilika, Tel. (A. రయానీముచ్చిలికా) An engagement entered into by the villagers for the cultivation of the lands.

Ráj, H. (راج, S. *Rajyam* राज्यं) A kingdom, a principality.

Rájá, H. (S. راجا) A king, a prince, a title given by the native governments, and in later times by the British government, to Hindus of rank: it is also assumed by petty chiefs in various parts of Hindustan, and is not uncommonly borne by Zamindárs. (In Sanscrit compounds *Rájá* makes the final short, as *Rájadharma*, the duty of a king: and in the spoken languages this is vulgarly abridged to *Ráj*, as *Rájdharm*, *Rájdaṇḍa*, &c.: it is, of course, more correct in all cases to retain the short final vowel, but in compliance with current use some of the following terms are also given without it.

Rájabhágam, Tel. (రాజభాగం), or *Rájbhág*, Mar. (राजभाग, from S. *bhága* भाग, a share) The government share of the revenue or of the crop.

Rájakí, Mar. (राजकी, from S. राजकीय) Royal, relating to royalty; especially as vernacularly used in an evil sense, oppressive, tyrannical.

Rájahránti, or *Rájakránt*. Mar. (राजक्रांति, from S. आक्रान्ति, attack) Hostile invasion, depredation committed by an enemy, alarm attending it; also regal oppression, tyranny.

Rájabansí, *Rájbansí*, Beng. (রাজবংসী, from S. *vanṣa*, or *banṣa* वंश, a race; of royal-race) The name of a low agricultural caste in Rangpur: in its literal sense it is applicable to any of the royal or martial tribes, as the Rajputs, &c.

Rájbahá, H. (S. from بهنا, to flow) The principal or common branch of a canal.

Rájabhenṭ, H. (بهينت, a visit) A present to a great man on waiting on him, or a fee paid to a public functionary for permission to begin to reap.

Rájdaṇḍa, Beng. (রাজদণ্ড, S. दण्ड) A fine or penalty inflicted by the prince or ruler.

Rájadhání, or *Rájdhání*, H. &c. (راجدهاني, S. राजधानी) A capital city, the residence of the governing authority:

in Rangpur *Rájdhání* designates the neighbouring possessions of the Raja of Kuch Bahar.

Rájdhutí, Beng. (রাজধুতী) A piece of cloth, such as is worn round the loins, presented to a Zamindár by a tenant on receiving permission to marry.

Rájguru, or *Rájgur*, Hindi (राजगुरु) The spiritual adviser of a prince or chief; considered as belonging to a particular caste in the Dakhin: in Guzerat the Brahmans who officiate as the domestic priests of the Jharejas.

Rájík, Mar. &c. (राजीक), *Rájíkam*, Mal. (രാജീകം) Oppressive tyranny, any distress arising from bad government: also the calamities of hostile invasion.

Rájkar, Beng. (রাজকর, S. कर, a tax) The government tax or revenue.

Rájakumár, or *Rájkumár*, or *Rájakumára*, Hindi (राजकुमार, from S. कुमार, a youth, a prince) The son of a Rája, a prince: the name of a numerous and opulent caste in the north-west provinces, following agriculture, though claiming to be of the military or regal tribe: the Rájkumárs in the district of Benares were notorious for the murder of their infant daughters.

Rájaput, or *Rájput*, commonly, *Rajpoot*, H. &c. (راجپوت, राजपुत, from S. राजा, and *putra* पुत्र, a son), in some dialects, as in Guz., *Rajput*, or *Rujpoot* (રજપુત) A prince, the son of a Rája, the general designation of the races in the north and west of India, who pretend to spring from the ancient dynasties of the sun and moon, forming the *Súryavanśí* and *Chandravanśí* tribes, or from a sacred fire kindled on Mount Abu, by the saint *Agastya*, and who are thence termed *Agni-kula*, of the family of fire: from these sources thirty-six primary royal races are supposed to originate. The solar dynasties are, 1. the *Grahilote*, or *Gehlote*, of which the Rana of Udayapur is a member: it is subdivided into twenty-four *Śákhás*, or branches, of which the *Sisodhia* is the most distinguished, sometimes giving a title to the whole race; 2. *Rahtore*, said to be descended from *Ráma*, by *Kuśa*, his second son; but this is sometimes disputed: it has twenty-four branches: the Rája of *Marwar*, or *Jodhpur*, belongs to this tribe; 3. *Kachwáhá*, also said to spring from *Kuśa*, to which the Rájas of *Jaypur* belong: it comprises twelve *Kothris*, or houses. There is but one race said to spring from the moon, through *Krishṇa*, or that of *Yadu* or *Jaḍu*, comprehending eight branches, of which two are well known and powerful, the *Jháreja*, and *Bhattí*, of which the Rájas of *Cutch* and *Jaisalmer* are members. The *Tuár* tribe is of doubtful origin, although boasting of *Vikramáditya* as a member; it is usually considered a branch of the *Yadu* race. The *Agnikula* races are originally four, the *Pramára*, *Parihára*, *Chálukya*, *Chaulukya*, or *Solanki*, and *Chauhán*; the first contains thirty-five *Śákhás*, of which the best known are the *Mori*, supposed to be the same as the *Maurya*, which would include *Chandragupta*, or *Sandrocoptus*, the *Soda*, *Sanhlá*, *Khair*, *Umra*, and *Sumra* (now Mohammadans), *Vehil*, *Maipawat*, *Balhár*, *Kaba*, *Omata*, *Rehar*, *Dhundha*, *Sortiah*, and *Harir*: all these are in the west of Malwa and the desert of the Indus; 2. the *Parihára* has twelve divisions, but is little known; 3. the *Chálukya* race was once of great power in the west of India and Guzerat, as still testified by numerous inscriptions, dated in the eleventh, twelfth, and thirteenth centuries: a more ancient branch also was powerful in the *Dakhin*: sixteen branches are specified, of which the *Bhagél* tribe is the best known; 4. the *Chauhán*, or *Cháhumána*, comprised twenty-four branches, of whom the *Háras*, giving a name to the district of *Háráwatí*, and numbering amongst its ranks the Rájas of *Kota* and *Bundi*, is the most eminent. The *Khíchis* of Raghugarh, *Deoras* of Sirohi, *Sonagaras* of Jhalore, and *Pawaichas* of Pawagarh, are also distinguished branches. Besides these, the thirty-six royal races include many whose origin even fiction has not ventured to account for, as the *Chaura*, or *Cháwara*, the *Ták* or *Takshak*, the *Jit* of the Punjab, and *Ját* of the Jumna and Ganges, who, nevertheless, is never styled a Rájput, the *Hún*, the *Kátti*, the *Bátta*, the *Jhalamakwahana*, from whom *Jhálawár* is named, the *Gohil*, *Sarwaya*, or *Sariaspa*, the *Jetwa*, or *Kamari*, *Dabi*, *Gor*, *Doda*, *Gerhwál*, *Chandela*, *Bundela*, *Bir-gújar*, *Sengar*, *Sikharwál*, *Bais*, *Dahia*, *Johya*, *Mohil*, *Nikumba*, *Rájpati*, *Dahirya*, *Dahima*: the lists of these races, however, differ materially, and some of the tribes pretend also to trace their descent from the solar or lunar dynasties: of those best known almost innumerable subdivisions are to be met with in different parts of India, but especially in the Upper Provinces, extending from Bahar and Benares to the north and west of the Punjab, in Malwa, and in the region to which they give their name, *Rájasthána*, or *Rájputána*, spreading to the Indus and Sindh westward, and southward into Guzerat and Cutch.

Rájaśásanam, Mal. (S. രാജശാസനം, from S. शासनं,

an order) A royal edict or command, regal government: a royal grant, especially a grant by some prince or public officer, inscribed on plates of copper.

Rájaswa, Beng. (S. রাজস্ব, from S. স্ব, own) Tax or revenue due to the government, royal or public revenue.

Rájwár, *Rájwárá*, Beng. (S. রাজওাড, রাজওাড়া) In Rangpur, the territory of the Kuch Bahar Rája, as distinct from the Company's.

Rajwáro, Guz. (રજવાડો) The country of the Rájputs, Marwar, &c.

RAJA, Thug. The loud call of the large owl.

RAJAB, H. (A. رجب) The seventh month of the Mohammadan year, also called *Rajab-ul-murajab*, the sacred or holy year, as hostilities amongst the Arab tribes were prohibited during its continuance before Mohammadanism.

RAJÍA, (?) H. A grain-measure.—Gorakhpur.

RAJAKA, RAJAK, S. &c. (रजक) A washerman.

RAJM, A. (رجم) Stoning to death, by Mohammadan law the punishment of adultery.

RAJÂT, H. (A. رجعت) Return, return of the person divorcing to the person divorced.

RÁJI, H. A barbarous tribe in Kamaon. See *Rawat*.

RÁJÍVÁNARU, RÁJÍYAVARU, Karn. (ರಾಜೀವಾನರು, ರಾಜೀಯವರು, plur.) A class of *Śúdras* employed under the former government of Mysore as armed *peons*: a class of people in Kamaon speaking Telugu, and pretending to descend from the Kshatriya caste, practising medicine and other arts.

RÁKÁ, H. &c. (S. راکا) Full moon, also day of full moon.

RAḲAM, RAḲM, or RUKUM, H. &c. (A. رقم) A writing, a handwriting; a mark; a peculiar method of notation with the initials of Arabic names of numbers: kind, sort, manner: an item of an account; any fixed or stipulated sum; a fractional share of an undivided estate: rate of assessment: in Kamaon, rent, revenue.

Raḳam siwái, H. (رقم سواي, A. سوا, except, besides) What is over or in excess of the stipulated sum or revenue.

Raḳami, or *Raḳmi*, H. &c. (رقمي) Written, noted, registered: according to kind or sort; according to usage: estimated, computed, not exactly determined; or sometimes it means settled, fixed, permanent, especially as applied to the land tax.

Raḳam-vári, Tel. (రకంవారి) According to sort or kind, especially as to coins of different currencies.

Ráḳim, H. (A. راقم) A writer, the writer of any document.

RAKÁNÁ, Mar. (रकाना) A division or column made on a sheet of paper by folding it longitudinally.

RAKÂT, H. (A. ركعت) Repeating or reading a number of prayers of the Kuran, accompanying it with various gesticulations, as prostrations and genuflexions, which may be either commanded, or traditional, or voluntary; the orthodox attitude consists in bending the body forwards as horizontally from the hips as possible, resting the palms of the hands on the knees and fixing the eyes on the great toes. See *Rukuâ*.

RAḲBA, RUKBA, corruptly, RUCKBAH, H. &c. (A. رقبة, रकबा) Inclosure, area: the lands comprised within the boundaries of a village or township, or constituting an estate or farm paying a money-revenue: the measured or ascertained extent of such lands: (the notion may have been borrowed from the original radical *Rakaba*, meaning to put a chain or collar round the neck, whence the substantive, a collar, and thence an area): thence also, in Mohammadan law, a slave, a purchased slave.

Raḳbabandí, corruptly, *Ruckbabundee*, H. (A. رقبه‌بندي, रकबाबंदी) A statement of the area of any estate, village, or township, one of the accounts that should be kept by the village accountant, shewing the total quantity of land belonging to the community, the portions that pay or are exempt from revenue, and those which are cultivated or uncultivated, or incapable of cultivation.

Raḳbazamín, H. (from P. زمين) The ascertained whole extent of the lands of a township paying revenue.

RÁKH, H. &c. (راکھ, राख, S. राक्षा) Ashes.

Rákhrángolí, Mar. (राखरांगोळी) Total devastation of a field, country, &c., as if it was reduced to ashes.

RAKSHAṆA, S. (रक्षण), in the dialects the *s* is rejected, and the first vowel sometimes made long, as, RÁKHAN, H. (راکهن), RÁKHAN, Beng. Mar. (রাখন) Preserving, guarding, protecting, keeping: tending, as cattle and the like; sometimes, also, the hire or pay of a guard or a present or fee for protection.

Rákhṇá, Mar. (राखणा) A guard, a watch, a person set to tend cattle.

Rákhaṇdár, Mar. (राखणदार) A watch or guard over a house, field, &c.

Rakhankár, H. (رکهن‌هار) A watch, a guard.

Rákhani, Beng. (রাখনি) Hire or pay of a guard or watch.

Rákhál, Beng. (রাখাল) A shepherd, a cowherd, one who tends cattle, &c.

Rákhá, Guz. (રાખા) The purchaser of a bill of exchange, one who pays a sum of money to a banker and receives a bill of exchange for the amount.

Rakhí, H. (رکهي) Tribute paid for protection, a kind of black mail; also a protector.

Ráhhí, Hindi, &c. (राखी, S. रक्षी) A piece of thread or silk, or tinsel, bound round the wrist on particular occasions, especially on the full moon of *Śrávan*, either as an amulet and preservative against misfortune, or as a symbol of mutual dependence, or as a mark of respect: amongst the Rájputs it is sometimes sent by a lady of rank or family to a person of influence or power whose protection she is desirous of securing, and whom she thus adopts, as it were, as a male relative or brother: in Puraniya, *Rákhí* implies the portion of the lands of the village assigned as the watch or charge of each *Rakhwálá*: in Mysore the term is also applied to the actual cautery.

Rákhípúrṇimá, Hindi, &c. (राखीपूर्णिमा, from S. पूर्णिमा, day of full moon) The day of full moon in the month *Śrávan*, on which the *Rákhí* is sent to, or brought by, friends, or by Brahmans, and bound round the wrist with a suitable mantra or prayer.

Rakhopa, Guz. (રખોપ) A tax paid for protection against thieves.

Rakhopo, Guz. (રખોપો) Money paid for watching or guarding goods or houses, &c., a watchman, a guard.

Rakhwár, *Rakhwál*, or *Rakhwálá*, H. &c. (رکهوار, رکهوال, رکهوالا) A guard, a watch, a keeper of a field, one who has charge of the standing crops to prevent their being injured or plundered, a tender on cattle and the like: a protector, a guardian: in some parts the term is also applied to one who is supposed to be capable of counteracting the evil designs or practices of malevolent beings, or witchcraft, and the like.

Rakhwálí, H. (رکهوالي) The office of watching, guarding, &c., the hire of a guard or watch: money paid for protection against depredators, or for refraining from depredation, black mail.

Rakshábhogam, Mal. (S. രക്ഷാഭോഗം) Tax or fee paid by an inferior to a superior for the latter's protection.

RÁKHÁT, Hindi (राखात) Lands set apart for grazing.—Puraniya.

RÁKHLE, incorrectly RAKHILE, Mar. (राखले) A word used to denote the purchaser of a *hundi* or bill of exchange, he by whom the money has been paid, and in whose favour it is drawn.

RAKSHAS, S. vernacularly, RAKHAS (रक्षस, रखस) RÁCHHAS, H. (راچهس) An evil spirit, a demon, a goblin.

Ráhshasa, S., vernacularly, *Rákhas*, or *Ráchhas*, (राक्षस, राखस) Relating to a demon: one form of marriage anciently recognised, where a maiden has been carried off by force after her kinsmen have been subdued or slain, a fiend-like marriage: the 49th year of the cycle.

Rákhasí belá, or *Ráhshas belá*, H. &c. (راکهسيبيلا, राक्षसवेळा) Twilight, about an hour and a half before dark: time when evil spirits are abroad.

Ráchhas-biah, H. (راچهس بياه) Violent seizure and abduction of a girl.

RAKHT, H. (P. رخت) Goods, chattels, effects.

Rakht o matáá, P. A. (رخت ومتاع) Personal property exclusive of cash or bullion, or negociable stock; more properly denominated *Mál*, although *Mál*, used in a comprehensive sense, includes all personal property.

RAKT, RUKT, H. &c. (S. رکت, रक्त) Red, blood.

Raktákshí, S. &c. (रक्ताक्षी) The 58th year of the cycle: lit., the red-eyed.

Raktakoḍige, Karn. (ರಕ್ತಕೊಡಗೆ) Grant of land rent-free to the family of a servant killed in battle.

Raktamányam, Mar. (रक्तमान्यं) Free-rent lands granted for wounds or for services in war: blood-money.

Raktwán, Mar. (रक्तवान) A person whose occupation is selling ink; a servant whose duty it is to supply ink and provide and place the leaves that are used as plates at a meal.

RAMÁA, A. (رماء) Usury.

RAMÁRAMÍ, Tel. (రమారమి) An average: or, adv., upon or according to an average, more or less, according to guess.

RÁMA, vernacularly, RÁM, S. &c. (राम) A name given to three of the ten avatárs, or *Paraśuráma*, *Rámachandra*, and *Balaráma* (the latter being substituted for his brother, Krishna): the name by itself is, in current use, applied especially to the second, the prince of *Ayodhyá*: in composition it sometimes intimates excellence or superiority, as *Ráma-*, or *Rám-sálí*, a superior kind of rice.

Rámalílá, vernacularly, *Rámlílá*, H. (रामलीला, from S. लीला, sport) A dramatic epitome of the adventures of *Ráma*, performed publicly in the month of *Áświn*; in some places, as at Benares, with great splendour.

Rámanavamí, or *Rámnavamí*, H. (रामनवमी, S. नवमी, the ninth lunation) The ninth day of the light half of *Chaitra*, the birth-day of *Ráma*.

Rámawat, Hindi (रामवत) An ascetic of the Vaishnava sect, following the doctrines of *Rámánand*, and thence termed also *Rámánandí*, who taught the especial worship of *Ráma* about the end of the 13th century: his followers are collected in *maths* or monasteries, and are very numerous in the district of Benares and adjacent provinces.

Rám-báṇ, Mar. (रामबाण, from S. *vána*, an arrow) An engagement or promise that will certainly be kept (sure as the arrow of *Ráma*).

Rámbaṭái, H. (رام‌بٹائي) Division of the crop between the landlord and tenant.

Rámdave, Guz. (રામદવે) A pilfering Brahman.

Rámduhái, H. (رامدهاي) An asseveration or oath by *Ráma*.

Rám-ẓám, H.&c. (رام‌رام) An exclamation proper to be addressed to a Vaishnava ascetic: it is also used as an exclamation of astonishment or aversion: among the Maraṭhas it is the usual interchange of salutation between the common classes: in a note it answers to respects, compliments, &c.

Rámjani, H. (رامجني, from S. रमा, beautiful, and जन, a person) A dancing girl: it is applied also in Bengal, under the corruption of *Ramjohnny*, to a prostitute.

Ramási, Thug. The slang of the Thugs.

Rámiá, Guz. (plur. રામીઆ) Deep wells requiring large buckets for drawing water.

Ramnáh, or Ramná, H. (رمناه, رمنا) A park, a preserve for game: used sometimes as the general name of grass lands.

Rámosí, or Rámosí, incorrectly, Ramoosee, Mar. (रामोशी, or -सी) The name given to individuals of a low and semi-barbarous race, found chiefly in the Maratha country south of Puna, who are thieves by profession and habit, but are retained usually in the villages as watchmen: they speak a dialect of Maraṭha, in which they differ from the *Bhíls*, whom, in other respects, they resemble: they are not found farther south than Kolapur.

Rámp, Guz. (રાંપ) A plough used for clearing weeds and stubble.

Rámpri, Guz. (રાંપડી) A plough, smaller than the former, for hoeing, worked between the furrows when the grain is ripe.

Rámpi, H. (رامپي, or رانبي) A knife for scraping and cleaning skins and leather.

Ramẓán, H. (A. رمضان) The ninth Mohammadan month, during which eating, drinking, and any sensual gratification is interdicted between dawn and the appearance of the stars: the communication of the Kuran is fabled to have begun on the 27th of the month, thence termed *Lailat-ul-ḳadr*, or night of power, and prayers on that night are sure to be complied with: prayers offered on the 19th, 21st, and 23d, are also supposed to possess peculiar efficacy.

Rán, Mar. (रान) A wood or forest, a waste, wild or uncultivated land: also in compounds, wild, as,

Ránaṭ, or *Ránwaṭ*, Mar. (रानट, रानवट) Sterile, unfit for cultivation: wild, growing spontaneously.

Rándewá, blunderingly, *Rámdwá*, Mar. (रानदेवा) A fee formerly paid for leave to cut wood in the public forests.

Ránhela, Mar. A wild plantain, and the like.

Ránmárjár, Mar. (S. मार्जार, a cat) A wild cat.

Ránwá, Mar. (रानवा) Woody or waste ground, a tract left to its spontaneous produce, especially in the vicinity of a town or village.

Rána, H. (رانا, राना, probably a corruption of *Rája*) The title of Hindu princes in Central India: it is borne especially by the sovereign of Udayapur.

Rání, H. (راني, S. *Rájní* राज्ञी) A princess, the wife of a Rája.

Ráṇḍ, also Raṇḍá, H. &c. (رانڈ, رنڈا, रांड, रंडा), Raṇḍe, Karn. (ರಂಡೆ) A widow: in Maraṭha it is used contemptuously: also, a woman, a slave-girl, a courtesan.

Ráṇḍgá, and *Ráṇḍchhandí*, Mar. (रांडगा, रांडछंदी) Addicted to women, libertine.

Raṇḍá golak, Mar. (रंडागोलक) A widow's bastard; also *Golaka*, q. v.: the name of a caste among the Maraṭhas, in which the parents are both of the Brahmanical order.

Randemaga, Karn. (ರಂಡೆಮಗ) A son of a widow, a term of abuse.

Raṇḍa, Beng. (রণ্ড) A man who dies childless: a barren tree, barren.

Ráṇḍá, H. (رانڈا) Barren, applied especially to unproductive trees, as the male palm, &c.

Raṇḍká, or *Ráṇḍká*, Mar. (रंडका, रांडका) A widower.

Ráṇḍmuṇḍ, Mar. (रांडमुंड, from S. मुंड, shaven) A widow, used contemptuously: a strumpet, used as a term of abuse.

Ránd rándelí, Guz. (રાંડરાંડેલી) Devoid of ornaments, as in widowhood.

Ráṇḍwaḍá, or *Ráṇḍwalá*, Mar. (रांडवडा, रांडवला, from S आवलि, a row, a string) Pouring forth a torrent of abuse upon a woman, calling her by all sorts of opprobrious names, as, whore, strumpet, trull, &c.

Ráṇḍyá, Mar. (रांड्या) Libertine, addicted to women.

Rándhaniyá, H. (راندهنيا) A cook, a confectioner, a baker.

Raṇḍi, H. (رنڈي) A woman.

Randibáz, H. (رنڈي باز), or *Rándbáj*, Mar. (रांडबाज) A wencher, a libertine.

Randibází, H. (رنڈي بازي), *Rándbájí*, Mar. (रांडबाजी) Whoredom, fornication.

RANG, RUNG, H. &c. (S. رنگ, रंग) Colour, dye, from, kind, sport, diversion.

Rangái, or *Rangwái*, H. &c. (رنگاي, رنگواي, रंगाई, रंगवाई) Price paid for dyeing, colouring, or the like.

Rangári, Karn. (ರಂಗಾರಿ) A dyer.

Rangí, H. &c. (رنگي) A dyer: chintz of which the colours fly in washing.

Rangmahal, H. &c. (رنگمحل) An apartment fitted up for festive meetings.

Rangrez, H. (رنگريز) A dyer, a colourer, a painter.

Rangrezí, H. (رنگريزي) Dyeing, colouring, painting.

RÁNGAṚ, Hindi (रांगड) A name borne by the Rajputs in the south and west of Malwa, and in Mewar: (according to the Marathas the word is derived from *rán*, a wood, and *gaṛí* (गडी), a man, implying a semi-barbarian, or man of the woods: the Rajputs derive it from *raṇ* (रण) war, and *gaṛh* (गढ), a fort, but in that case it should be *Raṇgaṛh*, not *Rángaṛ*): in the north-west provinces the *Rángaṛs* are a class partly Hindu, partly Mohammadan, but agreeing in disorderly and dishonest habits.

Rángaṛí, Hindi (रांगडी) The dialect of the Hindi spoken along the south and west of Malwa, and in Mewar: its limits are the Indus on the west, Bundelkhand on the east, the Sátpura hills on the south, and Jaypur, Jodhpur, and Jaisalmer on the north.—Malcolm, 'Central India,' 2. 191. The name is also applied by the Marathas to all the Brahmans of Central India, except those of the south.—Ibid. 123. In Cuttack, *Rángṛi* is the name of a low servile caste.

RANGWA, Thug. A *Sipahi*, from his red coat.

RANKU, Tel. (రంకు) Adultery, fornication.

RÁNKAṚ, less correctly, RÁKAR, H. (رانكڑ, रांकड) Stony ground, or soil abounding with *Kankar* nodules.

RÁO, H. &c. (راو, राव) A Hindu title for a chief or prince: (probably derived from *Rája*, through *Rai*): amongst the Marathas it is given as a title to distinguished persons, whether military or civil, and is assumed by a caste of Śúdras pretending to be descended from the primitive *kshatriya*, or military caste.

Rao-kṛishah, Hindi (रावकृषक) The head man of a village: lit., the chief cultivator.

RAṆWATYÁ, (?) Mar. (रणवत्या) A grant of land made to a family whose progenitor has been killed in battle.

RAPAṬ, Hindi, &c. (रपट, Eng., report) An official statement or report, but commonly applied to a motion or petition to a judge in court.

RAPHTÁNIBHÁYÁ, Uriya (ରଫତାନିଭାୟା, from the P. *raftan* رفتن, to go) An officer whose business it is to superintend the despatch of salt.

RARAIN, Thug. Noise of a pack of jackalls, a good omen on the left at night, a bad one on the day of starting: on the right it is bad any time between sunrise and sunset.

RÁRÍ, Hindi (रारी) A coarse hard grass infesting poor soils.

RÁS, H. (A. راس) Head: used technically in application to cattle, as, *Ek rás gáo*, one head of cows, *i. e.* a cow; *do rás asp*, two head of horses, *i. e.* two horses.

Rás-ul-mál, A. (راس المال) In Mohammadan law, Principal, capital, fund or trading stock, the original price of an article (from *Rás*, the head, caput, or capital).

RÁS, H. (راس) Adoption, the ceremony of adoption; *Rás bithání*, or *lená*, to adopt a son, or, rather, to hold a meeting for the purpose of adopting a son.

Rás-nishín, H. (راس نشين, from P. A. نشين, who sits) An adopted son, because he sits in his adoptive father's seat.

RÁS, Mar. (रास, corrupt for *Ráśí* राशी) A heap, a pile. See *Ráśí*.

Rásmáthám, and *Rásmáthyás*, Mar. (रासमाथां, रासमाथ्यास) After harvest: after the gathering and piling of the grain.

RAS, H. (رس, रस) A kind of grass that overspreads fallow fields.

RÁS, H. (راس, रास) Corn after threshing, the grain separated from the chaff.

RÁṢ, or RÁSH, (?) Beng. The name borne by an individual when engaged in religious rites, it being the custom in some parts of Bengal for an individual to have two names, one his *Rás* name, as *Táraní-charan*, when he is engaged in religious acts, and the other his *Dák* name, as *Kesavdás*, on all other occasions.

RÁSA, vernacularly RÁS, S. &c. (रास) A circular dance, performed by cowherds and by the worshippers of *Kṛishṇa*, in imitation of one he is said to have danced with the *Gopís*: a dramatic representation, of which the subject is commonly taken from the stories of *Ráma* and *Kṛishṇa*.

Rásayátrá, vernacularly, *Rásjátrá*, S. (रासयात्रा) A festival held in *Kártika* (Oct.-Nov.) in honour of *Kṛishṇa*, when dancing and dramatic representations take place.

RASAD, H. &c. (P. رسد) A store of grain provided for, or

sent to, an army: in Bengal and Hindustan the word was early applied to a progressive increase of revenue settlement—Reg. viii. 1793, sec. 71; but it also denotes a progressive diminution, and likewise implies the amount of increase or deduction: in Maratha it denoted money paid into the public treasury by the native collectors as the amount of their collections.

Rasad-beshí, H. (رسدبيشي) An increase of revenue, a gradual increase in the amount of assessment.

Rasadí, corruptly, *Russuddee*, H. (رسدي, रसदी) Progressively increasing or decreasing, as the annual amount of revenue: Mar. (रसदी) Held on payment into the public treasury of a sum supposed to be equivalent to its revenue, a village, &c.

Rasadí-jamá, H. (رسدي جمع) A progressively increasing or diminishing total of assessment.

RAṢÁVO, Hindi (रशावो) Dressing a field, pulverising and smoothing the soil, and leaving it exposed to the air some days before sowing.

RASHAD, A. (رشد) Rectitude, direction: in law, the judicious and discreet management of property.

Rashíd, A. (رشيد) A director, a guide: in law, a person competent to the management of affairs.

RÁṢI, S. (राशि), so also Beng. (রাশি), Tel. (రాశి), and Mar. (राशि), but the latter has also RÁS (रास), which is likewise H. (راس), corruptly, RASH, RASS. A heap, a pile, a heap of grain, a heap of salt, intending thereby a definite measure in use at Bombay, and equal to 40 tons, or, with allowances for waste in shipment, 35 tons: the established rates are $10\frac{1}{4}$ *Adholís* = 1 *Phará*, 100 *Pharás* = 1 *Ana*, 16 *Anas* = 1 *Rás*: in the Konkan the proportions are somewhat differently reckoned, or 4 *Nítwás* = 1 *Adholí*, 24 *Adholís* = 1 *Phará*, 20 *Pharás* = 1 *Ana*, 16 *Anas* = 1 *Ráṣ*: as the *Nítwá* = 33.553 cubic inches, or by weight 1.08 lb. avoirdupois, the *Ana* = 6220.8 lb. and the *Ráṣ* to $44\frac{1}{2}$ tons: by another mode of reckoning, the *Ráṣ* is equal to only 10 tons.—Jervis on weights and measures, 48.

Ráṣi-aḍugu, Tel. (రాశిఅడుగు, from అడుగు, the bottom), also *Taḷaráṣi*, Karn. (ತಳರಾಶಿ) A small quantity of grain remaining after a heap has been measured, which is given to the cultivators.

Akkiráṣi, Karn. (ಅಕ್ಕಿರಾಶಿ) A heap of rice.

Bhúgara-ráṣi, Tel. (భూగరరాశి) A heap of grain before it is winnowed mixed with dirt (*bhúgara*).

Méluráṣi, Tel. (మేలురాశి) A heap of winnowed grain (from *mélu*, good).

Ubhayaráṣi, Tel. (ఉభయరాశి) A heap of grain comprising the shares of government and the cultivator (from S. *ubhaya*, both).

RÁṢI, Mal. (രാശി) Mixed soil consisting of sand and clay (from S. *Ráṣi*, a heap, the quality of the soil being tested by its again filling or being heaped in a pit or hole from which it has been dug: if light and poor it will not fill it; if heavy and solid it will more than fill it.

Ráṣi-kúṟ, Mal. (രാശിക്കൂറ) Poor light soil, consisting of loose sand chiefly.

Ráṣi-paṣama-kúṟ, Mal. (രാശിപശമക്കൂറ) Soil of an equal or middling sort, a given quantity of which will exactly fill a pit or hole from which it has been dug on being replaced in it. See *Paṣama*.

RÁSI, S. &c. (राशि) A sign of the zodiac.

Ráṣi-chakra, S. &c. (राशिचक्र) The zodiac.

RASÍD, H. (رسيد, रसीद), RASIDU, Karn. (ರಶಿದು) The English word 'receipt,' a receipt.

RASM, H. (A. رسم) Custom, usage, law.

Rasmí, H. (A. رسمي) Usual, customary.

Rasúm, or, more correctly, *Rusúm*, *Rusoom*, or *Roosoom*, corruptly, *Russoom*, and *Rushum*, H. (A. رسوم, plur. of رسم), Mar. (रसूम), Tel. (రసుము) Fees, perquisites, customary payments and gratuities, commission or allowances upon articles bought and sold made to the purchaser or the servant or agent of the buyer or seller: in Kanara, also, the allowances in a crop of grain falling to the village corporation.

Rusúm-i-chaudharí, H. (چودهري, a head man) Fees and perquisites of the head man of a trade or of a village.

Rusúm-i-gathrí, H. (گٿهري, a bundle) A fee levied under the Mohammadan government on all bales and packages passing through the custom-house of Murshedabad.

Rusúm-kánungoi, H. (كانونگو, q. v.) A small fee on the revenue collections allowed to the *Kánungo*.

Rusúm-i-khazána, H. (خزانه, a treasury) Fees charged at the public treasury on all receipts and payments.

Rusúm-i-khazánchi, H. (خزانچي, a treasurer) Fees or commission payable to a cashier or treasurer.

Rusúm-i-naẓárat, H. (نظارت) Fees payable formerly to the Náẓir or head officer in charge of remittances from the collectorates to the treasury; now, the fees payable to the Náẓir of a court on serving a process.

Rusúm-sazáwalí, H. (سزاولي) Charges formerly levied in Bengal to defray, in the first instance, the expense of *Sazáwals*, or revenue officers employed on special and temporary duty, as collecting the arrears from defaulters, but afterwards converted into a permanent charge upon the revenue-payers.

Rusúm-tihái, H. (from the Hindi تهاي, a third) A fine or quit-rent levied formerly on rent-free lands in Bundelkhand, supposed to be a third of the usual assessment.

Rusúm-zamindárí, H. (from زميندار, a landholder) The fees or perquisites allowed to the Zamindár by the Mohammadan government, or by a commission generally of 5 per cent. on the gross collections; or it sometimes designates his *Málikána*, q. v.; also fees levied by a Zamindár on his tenants, either on particular occasions, or as a fine or quit rent.

Rusúmdár, H. (from دار, who has) The holder of certain fees or perquisites.

RASHTÍ, H. (رشتي, रश्ती) An addition or bonus paid by the cultivator over his rent for permission to take into cultivation any waste or uncultivated land which he may find on the estate, and of which there is no claimant.—Puraniya.

RASSI, or RASI, RUSSEE, RUSEE, H. (رسّي, रस्सी), Beng. (রশী) A rope, a cord, a rope or line used in measuring, usually about 80 cubits long.

RASTA, RÁSTÁ, H.. &c. (P. رسته, راستا) A road, a way.

Rastabandí, H. (رسته‌بندي) Making or repairing roads.

RÁSTIJ, Hindi (रास्तिज) Provender furnished by the villagers to troops passing through the country, and deducted from their payments to the government or Zamindár.—Puraniya.

RÁSTIKANTA, Uriya (ରସ୍ତି,କଣ୍ଟା) Exact weighment (from P. *rásti*, correctness, and Beng. *hánta*, a balance).

RASÚL, H. (A. رسول) A messenger, an ambassador: the messenger (of God), Mohammad.

Rasúl-namá, Rasúl-sháhi, H. (from P. نما, showing, or شاه, a king) Classes of Mohammadan fakirs

RÁṬAṆ, RÁṬÁṆ, RÁṬAḶ, RÁṬIḶ, Karn. (ರಾಟಣ, ರಾಟಾಣ, ರಾಟಳ, ರಾಟಿಳ, corruptions, probably, of *Ráhat*) A machine for raising water, a spinning-wheel, a roundabout.

Rátáṇadabávi, Karn. (ರಾಟಾಣದಬಾವಿ) A well from which water is raised by a machine.

RÁTH, (?) H. Separate nominal division of a coparcenary proprietary; commonly, a clan.—Kamaon.

RATH, or RUTH, corruptly RUT, S. &c. (रथ) A chariot, a carriage: in common use applied to a covered carriage used chiefly by women; also to the car in which idols are conveyed.

Rathayátrá, or, vernacularly, *Rathjátrá*, S. &c. (रथयात्रा) The festival of the procession of Kṛishṇa as Jagannátha, held in the second lunation of the moon's increase in *Ásháṛh*, July-August.

Rathakára, S. &c. (रथकार) A wheelwright, a coachmaker, a man of a mixed caste sprung from a Mahishya father and Karan mother.

RÁṬHOR, or RÁṬHAUR, Hindi (राठोर, राठौर) The name of one of the principal Rájput tribes, the origin of which is doubtful: they trace their descent from *Kuṣa*, the son of *Ráma*, and should consequently be of the solar line, but they are usually classed with the lunar families: they are found in considerable numbers in Hindustan, and, at the time of the Mohammadan conquest, furnished sovereigns to *Kanoj*: at present the Rája of *Márwár* or *Jodhpur*, and most of his feudatory chiefs, belong to this tribe. (Colonel Tod writes the name *Rahtore*, which is derived, he says, from *raht*, the spine of Indra; but the word is usually written in the native characters as above: the same authority specifies twenty-four *Sákhás*, or branches, of the tribe, which are, however, different clans of *Márwár*, sprung from the Rájas *Chonda*, *Ranmál*, and *Joda*, of whom severally three, twenty-three, and ten, are still extant: the popular nomenclature of the subdivisions of the *Raṭhors* is probably different in many respects from both).

RATÍ, commonly, RUTTEE, (رتي, रति, रती), S. (रक्तिका) The seed of the Abrus precatorius, used as the basis of weights for gold, silver, and drugs: the seed varies, but from various trials appears to average about $1\frac{5}{16}$ths of a grain: the artificial weight has been found to average nearly $2\frac{1}{4}$ grains, being one-eighth of a *másha*, rated at 17.708 grains. As the *másha* in use, however, averages but about $15\frac{1}{2}$ grains, the eighth, or one *Ratí*, will weigh rather less than 2 grains, or 1.938. Jervis makes it 1.953. The term is also applied sometimes, as in Midnapur, to an estate or landed property.

RÁTIB, H. (A. راتب) Daily allowance of food to labourers or to animals, as elephants, camels, &c.

Rátiba, H. (A. راتبه) Salary, pay, allowance, pension.

Rátibakhor, H. (راتبه‌خور) A stipendiary, a pensioner.

Rawátib, H. (A. رواتب, plur. of *Rátib*) Necessaries of

life, as clothes, food, and furniture: in Mohammadan law, salaries, allowances, &c.

RÁṬIKAṬṬU-BHÚMI, Tel. (రాటికట్టుభూమి) Stony ground (from *ráï*, a stone).

RAṬL, H. (A. رطل), RATAL, Mar. (रतल) A weight, variously rated at 12 to 16 ounces, a pound: at Bombay the *Ratal* is said to be equal to thirty-six Surat rupees: in the Red Sea the *Rottolo*, as it is corruptly called, varies from 10 to 24 ounces avoirdupois.

RÁṬṬAM, Tel. (రాట్టం) A spinning-wheel.

RAUHI, Thug. A policeman, a constable, or *Chauki-dár*.

RÁÜKAR, Thug. A banker: quasi *Sáhukár*, q. v.

RÁÜḶ, corruptly, RAOUL, Mar. (राऊळ) The name of a low tribe said to be descendants from a branch of the Yogi mendicants, makers of coarse strips of cloth and of tape.

RAUL, Thug. The clamorous cry of a number of jackalls, always a good omen.

RÁÜT, Mar. (राऊत) A horse-soldier. Guz. *Ráwat* (રાવત) A horse-keeper: a title borne by some families of distinction in Kátiwar who keep studs.

RAUẒA, H. (A. روضه) A mausoleum, a shrine, the tomb of some reputed saint at which prayers are recited and offerings presented.

RÁVANIO, Guz. (રાવણીઓ) A village watchman or guard.

RAVÍSU, RAVÉSU, Tel. (రవిసు, రవేసు) Customary fees or perquisites (from P. روش).

RAVI, vernacularly, RABI, corruptly, RUBBEE, S. &c. (रवि, रबि) The sun.

Ravivára, vernacularly, *Ravi-*, or *Rabiwár*, or *-bár*, S. &c. (रविवार) Sunday.

Rabikhanda, Beng. (রবিখণ্দ) A crop ripened by the sun without rain, a cold-weather crop.

RAWÁ, H. (P, روا) Passing, going, allowable, lawful, current.

Rawádári, H. (P. داري, having) Approbation, sanction.

RAWAIAT, written also, REVAIET, H. (P. روايت) A written legal opinion by a Mohammadan law officer, a treatise on points of law, a dictum or opinion of the *Dasturs* or priests of the Parsis, a narration, a history.

RAWÁJ, H. (A. رواج), RIWÁJ, Mar. (रिवाज) Usage, custom, currency: also customary, current.

Riwáj-jásti, Tel. (రివాజజాస్తి, from P. زیاده, more) More than customary, more than the survey valuation.

Rawáj ul mulk, H. (A. رواج الملك) Custom of the country, usage, which, when clearly established, is held to be of force in the decision of law-suits, although contrary to the written law.

Rawáj-ul-waḳt, incorrectly, *Ruyaj-ool-wuqt*, H. (A. وقت) Current, customary, according to the time.

RÁWAL, H. (راول, रावल) A title borne by some Rajput princes and chiefs: a tribe of Brahmans in Central India: in Kandesh it is said to designate a tribe of Rajputs: in Kamaon, the title of the head priest of the temple of *Badarináth*, who is invariably a *Nambúri* Brahman from Malabar.

RAWALIYA, (?) A low caste of Hindus following the occupation of horse-keepers and weavers, and sometimes agriculture; they are said also to be mendicants: perhaps the same as the Maraṭhí *Ráüḷ*.

RAWÁNA, corruptly, ROWANAH, ROWANNAH, H. &c. (P. روانه, रवाना) A passport, a pass, a certificate from a collector of customs authorising goods to pass without payment of further duty.

Rawánagí, H. (روانگي) Passing, proceeding, despatching; the purport of a permit or pass, or authority to proceed. Mar. (रवानगी) A gift to a visitor on sending him away; a hint to depart: also, export.

Rawánagí-chiṭhí, Mar. (रवानगीचिठी) A pass, a passport, a port clearance.

Rawánápaṭṭí, Tel. (H. రవానాపట్టి) A passport, a permit, a port clearance.

Máppurawáná, Tam. (மாப்புரவாணா) A pass or permit for goods to pass duty free (from the A. *Muâfi*).

Mátturawáná, Tam. (மாத்துரவாணா) A pass for goods on which the duty has been paid.

Rawáná kahár, H. (رواناكهار) A low caste of Hindus, especially from the province of Behar, where they pretend to be descended from *Jarásandha*, king of *Magadhá* in the *Pauránik* times; now best known as palankin-bearers: also termed *Rawána-behárá*, either from H. *bahár*, the province, or Beng. (বেহারা) a (palankin) bearer.

RÁWAT, H. (?) The name of a tribe, considered to be the remains of the aborigines in Kamaon, leading a wandering and uncivilized life in the forests on the eastern borders of the district: it occurs also as the name of a caste in Gorakhpur.

RÁYA, Karn. (ರಾಯ), RÁYADU, Tel, (రాయడు), RÁYAN, Tam. (ராயன்) A king, a prince: *Ráya*, in Mysore, is also used as an honorific affix to the name of a Brahman.

Ráyalu, incorrectly *Rayel*, the pl. of *Ráyadu*, or *Ráya* only, was also the title of the Hindu sovereigns of *Vijayanagar* or *Bijnagar*, the last Hindu principality of importance in the south of India.

Ráyabára, Ráyabhára, or *Ráyabhárike*, Karn. (ರಾಯಬಾರ, ರಾಯಭಾರ, ರಾಯಭಾರಿಕೆ) Regal government or authority. *Ráyabáramu*, Tel. Negociation, embassy.

Ráyabháṭi, Karn. (ರಾಯಭಾಟಿ) The king's high way, a principal road.

Ráyasam, Tam. &c. (ராயசம்) The business of a secretary, especially of a secretary of state (the word occurs in all the dialects of the peninsula).

Ráyasakaran, or *Ráyasan*, Tam. (ராயசக்காரன், ராயசன்) A secretary, a secretary of state: also Mal. *Ráyaṣakáran* (രായശകാരൻ).

Ráyasadava, Karn. (ರಾಯಸದವ) A public or government secretary.

Ráyasamuváru, corruptly, *Roysum*, *Roysam*, Tel. (రాయ-సమువారు) A writer, a clerk, a secretary.

Rayuḍu, Tel. (రాయుడు) A title adopted as a surname by the Velma caste in the Northern Sarkárs.

Ráz, vernacularly, Ráj, H. &c. (P. راز, or راج, राज) A bricklayer.

Ráz, H. (P. راز) A secret, a mystery.

Rázdár, H. (P. رازدار) A confidant: in law, an accessary after the fact, one cognisant of a criminal transaction and not making it known.

Rázdárí, H. (P. رازداري) Privity to any criminal act, knowledge of it and not giving information.

Rázdárí-májará, H. (from A. ماجرا, what had happened) Cognisance of a criminal transaction, being accessory to a crime.

Rázdárí-bád-májará, H. (from A. بعدماجرا, after the event) Cognisance of a crime after perpetration, being accessory after the fact.

Rázdárí-ḳabl-i-májará, H. (from the A. قبلماجرا, before the event) Cognisance of an intended crime, being accessory before the fact.

Raẓáâ, H. (A. رضاع, from رضع, sucking, as an infant) Fosterage, which, in Mohammadan law, constitutes a bond of affinity between persons nursed by the same female, analogous to consanguinity, so that whatever is illegal by virtue of consanguinity is equally so by that of fosterage.

Raẓiâ, H. (A. رضيع) A foster-brother.

Raẓá, also vernacularly, Rajá, H. &c. (A. رضا, रजा) Assent, consent, permission, leave of absence, dissmisal from office.

Ráẓí, also vernacularly, *Ráji*, H. &c. (راضي, राज़ी) Consenting, agreeing to, contented or satisfied with: also *Ráji*, Tel. (రాజీ) Consent, agreement.

Raẓámand, H. (P. رضامند) Willing, consenting, assenting.

Raẓámandí, H. (P. رضامندي) Assent, acquiescence, being willing.

Ráẓí náma, H. (راضي نامه), in the dialects, *Ráji-námá*, Hindi, &c. (राजीनामा) A written assent, a deed of agreement or concurrence, a testimonial signed by a plaintiff at the end of a suit that he is satisfied with the decision: a deed of compromise by which the plaintiff or prosecutor acknowledges that he has been satisfied by the defendant, or a written declaration that he will be satisfied with the decision of a particular person or persons: the execution of a *Ráẓi náma* usually implies an amicable adjustment.

Rájírajáwantíne, Mar. (राजीरजावंतीने, from راضي and رضامندي) With or by the permission or assent of: used in bonds and notes, &c., commonly in connexion with *Akalhusharíne* (सकलहुशारीने), with sound mind, with free will; with full and unbiassed or unextorted consent.

Rebandí, or Raibandí, (?) Hindi (रेबन्दी, or रैबन्दी) Measuring a crop by weighing the produce and allotting the government portion.—(Mherwara).

Rebári, Guz. (?) A shepherd, or a caste of shepherds, leading a partially nomadic life, rearing camels, sheep, and goats, and subsisting chiefly by the sale of the milk and wool, not of the animals themselves.

Reḍḍi, commonly Reddy, incorrectly Rheddy, Tel. (రెడ్డి) The name of the principal caste of Telinga cultivators: a chief farmer or cultivator, especially the head man of a village in the Telinga country, who is more properly designated as the *Pedda-reḍḍi*, the senior or great *Reḍḍi* or villager.

Reḍḍiselaga, Tel. (రెడ్డిసెలగ) Fees or perquisites enjoyed by the head farmer or principal cultivator and head man of a village.

Reḍḍivaḍu, plur. *Reḍḍiváru*, vulgarly, *Reḍḍywar*, and, erroneously, *Rheddysar*, Tel. (రెడ్డివాడు) A head man of a village, a principal or respectable farmer, a man of the *Reḍḍi* caste.

Reg, H. (P. ريگ) Sand.

Régaḍa, or *Régaḍi*, vulgarly, *Régur*, Tel. (రేగడ, రేగడి) *Régaṭi*, Karn. (ರೇಗಟಿ) Rich black loam or mould, a soil in which cotton is usually planted, and thence commonly termed cotton soil.

REH, H. (ریہ, रेह) Fossile alkali, impure carbonate of soda used as soap, abounding in some soils, and rendering them unproductive: even grass will not grow where it impregnates the soil.

Rehar, H. (ریہر) Barren (as land).

REK, Beng. (রেক) A measure of a *sér* and a quarter; also a basket used to measure grain: in Sylhet, a land measure, a square of three cubits, four of which are equal to one *Jet*.

REKÁN, Hindi (रेकान) Land beyond the reach of river-water.—Puraniya.

REKHÁ, S. &c. (रेखा), also, vernacularly, REKH, H. &c. (ریکھ, रेख), REGH, Mar. (रेघ), RÉKKE, and REKHE, Karn. (ರೇಕ್ಕೆ, ರೇಖೆ) A line, a row, a furrow. IRÉKAI, Tam. (இரேகை) Amount of assessment or tax.

RÉKHÁ, incorrectly, REKÁ, Karn. (S. ರೇಖಾ), also termed *Ráya-rékhá*, from *Ráya*, the title of the *Vijayanagar* rulers: the fixed standard assessment of the lands of Karnáta according to a survey measurement and classification of the soils, and a register of the money rates of payment drawn up by order of the government of *Vijayanagar* in the reign of *Krishṇa-ráya*: the account was so arranged that the assessment of each spot of land was shewn on a separate line, whence the term, *Rékhá*, a line or row: this assessment is also termed the *Ráya-rekhá-*, or *Rekhí-már*, from *Már*, a measure of land, q. v.

Rekhá-jhaḍiti, corruptly, *Reka-jurtee*, Karn. (ರೇಖಾಝಡಿತಿ) An account prepared in *Fasli* 1210 (A.D. 1802), by order of Col. Munro, of the total of the land cultivated in Kanara, shewing the assessment rated on each individual in kind or money, the proportion due to government, and the amount of rent-free land, omitting the waste: the account was apparently made up from the record of Hyder's assessment, and not from inspection, nor was it brought down to the time of the Company.

Rája-rékhá, Karn. The standard fathom of the *Vijayaṇagar* government, equal to four cubits and a half.

Rája-rékhí-bighá, Karn. A bíghá, of which each side was measured by the standard fathom, originally 90 *háths* or cubits in length, but subsequently extended to 112 *háths*, or about 181 feet.

Ainu-rékhá-ṣistu, commonly, *Ain-reha-shist*, Karn. (ಅಯಿನುರೇಖಾಶಿಸ್ತು) The total standard assessment or revenue.

REL, or RELÁ, H. &c. (ریل, ریلا, रेल, रेला) Flood, inundation, a torrent, a stream.

RENT, Guz. (રેન્ત) A monopoly, a contract: lease or *rent* of a house, field, &c. (no doubt in this sense the English word).

RENTÍ, Karn. The common plough used in Karnáta.

RES, Guz. (રેસ) The twenty-fifth part of an *ana*, or four hundredths of a rupee.

RESHM, H. (P. ریشم) Silk.

Reshamwálo, Guz. (રેશમવાળો) A dealer in silk, or silk thread.

RET, H. S. (ریت, रेत) Sand.

Retal, or *Retar*, corruptly *Rettar*, H. (ریتل) Sand, sandy soil, containing eight-tenths silex.

Retlá, or *Retli*, or *Retilá-lí*, H. (ریتلا, ریتلي) Sandy, soil of a light description, containing a considerable proportion of sand.

Retí, H. (ریتي) Sandy, sandy soil, sands.

REUĀ, Beng. (রেউআ) The name of a tribe who live by fortune telling.—(Rangpur).

REVU, Tel. (రేవు) A ford, a beach: a division of salt-pans.

REZA, REZAGI, H. &c. (P. ریزہ, ریزگي), vernacularly, REJÁ, and REJAGÍ, (रेजा, रेजगी) A scrap, a fragment, a fractional division of a coin, as a quarter or half rupee.

Rezagi, or, vernacularly, *Rejhi*, Sindh. A tax on retail dealers.

RÎÁYAT, corruptly, REYAYAT, H. (A. رعايت, from رعي, to rule) Protecting, favouring, doing kindness to, whence it is especially applied to a remission of revenue, or an abatement of the government claim.

Ríáyati, H. (A. رعايتي) A favoured tenant or cultivator, one to whom remission or abatement has been granted.

Ríáyati-beshí, H. (P. بيشي, excess) Surplusages remitted to the cultivator.

RIÁSAT, incorrectly, RIYASAT, H. (A. رياست) Government rule, a term affected formerly by the opulent Zamindárs when speaking of their own authority.

RIBÁ, or RIBBÁ, also RIBAH, or RIBÁH, A. (ربا, ربح, رباح) Illegal excess in exchange between articles of a similar kind which may be weighed or measured: this comprises interest on money, or increase of the sum borrowed, which is considered usurious and unlawful.

ṚICH, also ṚIK, or, in composition, ṚIG, S. (ऋच) A stanza, especially of the *Veda*: the first and principal *Veda*, the *Ṛig-veda*.

RIḤÁ, also RAḤÁ, H. (P. رها) Released, set at liberty, free.

Riḥái, or, sometimes, *Raḥái*, H. (رهاي) Liberation, release.

Rijât, H. (A. رجعت) Restitution, return: in Mohammadan law, the receiving back of a divorced wife, and restoring to her her legal rights according to the circumstances of her repudiation.

Rikábi, H. (ركابي) An inferior kind of rupee current at Lucnow, but not the regular coinage: (it was probably struck on some emergency, whence its name from *Rikáb*, a plate, or a stirrup).

Rikáẕ, A. (ركاض) Treasure or precious metals or coins dug up from the ground, whether deposits found in mines, or buried treasures.—Mohammadan law.

Riḳbá, also **Raḳbá**, A. (رقبا) Expecting: in Mohammadan law, expectancy, as of a gift to take effect at the death of a donor, or to revert to him, or to be annulled, in fact, on the death of the donee: such a gift is considered invalid.

Riktha, S. (रिक्थ) Property, wealth.

Rikthagráhi, *Rikthahári*, or *Rikthí*, S. (from गृह, or हृ, to take) An heir, one who has a claim to, or succeeds to, property.

Ṛiṇa, vernacularly **Riṇ**, S. &c. (ऋण) Debt of any description.

Ṛiṇádánam, S. (from आदानं, taking) Recovery of debts by process of law, one of the titles of judicial procedure.

Ṛiṇadása, S. (from दास, a slave) One who becomes a slave to his creditor until his debt is paid.

Ṛiṇí, and *Ṛiṇíka*, S. &c. (ऋणी, ऋणीक) A debtor.

Ríni, (?) H. A measure of land, the same as a *Bisí*.—Kamaon.

Risála, H. &c. (A. رساله), **Resálá**, Beng. (রেসালা), **Rasálo**, Guz. (રસાલો) A troop of horse.

Risáladár, corruptly, *Rissaldar*, H. &c. (رسالدار) A native officer commanding a troop of irregular horse.

Ṛishi, or, as pronounced in the south, **Rushi**, S. &c. (ऋषि) An inspired sage, the author or teacher of those works which are considered sacred: in ordinary use it is applied to any Hindu ascetic of supposed superior sanctity. The name of a low caste.—Malda.

Rishta, H. (P. رشته) Relationship, connexion.

Rishtadár, H. (P. رشته‌دار) A kinsman, a relation.

Rishwat, also **Rashwat**, H. (A. رشوت) A bribe.

Rishwat-khor, H. (رشوت‌خور) One who takes bribes.

Ritáḍ, Mar. (रिताड, from रिता, S. रिक्त, empty) A body of beasts of burthen, carts, or the like, returning empty: the emptied pots on the descending side of a water-wheel.

Ríti, vernacularly, **Rít**, S. &c. (रीति) Custom, usage: practice of a family, tribe, or community.

Ṛitu, vernacularly **Rit**, S. &c. (ऋतु) A season, a period of two months, dividing the year into the six seasons of *Vasanta*, spring, *Ghríshma*, hot weather, *Varsha*, rains, *Sarat*, autumn, *Hemanta*, cold, *Śiśira*, dewy or foggy: also the season of women, whence it is applied among the Marathas to the time at which a girl, having attained maturity, is conducted to the house of her husband: any fit season, as that at which the conductor of pilgrims to Gaya should arrive at any town at which he proposes to collect them, and which extends from the beginning of the *Dasahara* festival to the full moon of *Kártiha*, an interval of 35 days; the privileges he may claim on this occasion he has no right to at any other time of the year, which is thence termed by him *Kuritu*, the bad (*ku*) season.

Rizḳ, H. (A. رزق) Food, wealth, subsistence: allowance different from pay, subistence-money, a pension.

Roä, **Roäli**, Beng. (রোঅ, রোআলি) Planted, applied especially to ground on which the young rice plants have been planted, in opposition to that on which grain has been sown.

Robin, or **Robbin**, (?) A term used in Malabar for a measure of grain: according to Mr. Græme, it is the same as the *Morah*: a different, but anonymous authority makes it a fourth of a *Khandi*, or *Candy*; in that case it may be a barbarism for the Arabic *Rabâ*, or *Arbâ*, four, a fourth.

Rogárá, Hindi (रोगारा) Crops having a healthy appearance.—Puraniya.

Rok, H. (روك), Beng. (রোক), **Rokkam**, or **Rokkamu**, Tel. (రొక్కము), **Rokka**, or **Rokhkha**, Karn. (ರೊಕ್ಕ, ರೊಖ್ಖ) Ready-money, cash, in contradistinction to goods: prompt or cash payment.

Rokaḍ, or *Rokaṛ*, H. (روكڑ), Mar. (रोकड) Money, cash, specie, jewels, or valuables readily convertible into coin. Beng. (রোকড).

Rohaḍá, Tel. (రొకడా) A purse, a bag of money.

Rohaḍyá, Mar. (रोकड्या) A person employed by bankers to carry money from one place to another.

Rokaṛiya, H. (روكڑيا), Beng. (রোকড়িয) A cash-keeper, a treasurer.

Rokaṛbahi, H. (روكڑبهي) A cash-book.

Rokádayam, incorrectly, *Rokhadayam*, Tam. (ரொக்கதாயம், from S. आदाय, taking) Ready money, collections from other sources than land, as timber, orchards, fisheries, bazár fees, and the like, some of which are now abolished: although used in some of the Tamil districts in this and similar compounds, *Roka* does not seem to be a Tamil word: it is borrowed from Telugu or Marathi.

Rokkakusagai, Tam. (ரொக்கக்குச்சகை) Ready-money, cash.

Rokkamániyam, Tam. (ரொக்கமானியம்) A grant or allowance of ready-money.

Rokh, Mar. (रोख) Consisting of money or cash (property), ready, prompt (as payment).

Rokhá, Mar. (रोखा) A written acknowledgment for money borrowed: an order from the state issued to an individual, to a village or district, to make a specified payment, or furnish certain certain supplies.

Rokhárokhí, Mar. (रोखारोखी) Ready-money transactions, trade or business carried on on the principle of receiving and paying ready-money: also doing any thing smartly, promptly.

Rokhí, Mar. (रोखी) Ready-money dealing: also cash, or coins as an article of traffic.

Rokhthok, Mar. (रोखठोक) Prompt (as payment), told down at once (money).

Rokhvikrí, Mar. (रोखविक्री) Ready-money-sale, either selling for cash, or receiving prompt payment.

ROLLDAR, H. (رولدار, from English *roll* and P. دار) One who is entered on the collector's roll or record as proprietor.

ROP, Mar. (S. रोप) A young stem, plant, or tree, intended for transplanting.

Rópar, Hindi (रोपर) Transplanted rice: a rate in a lease for crops of rice raised by transplanting.

RORA, RORÍ, H. (روري روڑ) The name of a caste of shopkeepers and traders in the north-west provinces pretending to be *kshatriyas* and commonly using the designation of *Kskatri*, or *Rora-khatri*, or *Khatri-rora*.

RORÁ, H. (روڑا) A fragment, a piece of broken brick, such as is used in making the roofs of houses or Macadamising roads.

ROSAL, or ROSALÍ, or ROSLÍ, less correctly, RAUSLI, or ROUSLEE, H. (روسل, روسلي, रोसल, रोसली) Light soil of a good quality though mixed with a considerable portion of sand: sometimes considered little inferior to the first quality, or *dákar*, and assessed at the same rate.

ROSHNÁÍ, H. (روشنائي, from P. روشن, light) Lighting, illumination; the lamps kept burning at a Mohammadan shrine or tomb.

Roshan-chaukí, H. (روشن‌چوكي, lit., light-station) A band of musical instruments playing at the residence of the chief Mohammadan authority, or, with his permission only, at the houses of opulent individuals.

RÓT, (?) H. Grant of land on the field of battle for military exploits.—Kamaon.

ROUND-GASHTÍ, or, vernacularly, -GASTÍ, H. &c. (روندگشتي, from English *round*, and P. *gashti*, passing) Patroling, going the rounds.

ROZ, H. &c. (P. روز), in the Hindu dialects, ROJ, (रोज), ROJA, or RODZU, Tel. (రోజు) A day.

Roj, Mar. (रोज) Daily hire or wages, daily pay of a messenger of government, or of a creditor sent to levy arrears, or a debt.

Roz-ádálat, H. (A. عدالت, day of justice) A court formerly held by the Nazim of Bengal every Sunday, for the administration of criminal justice.

Rozána, H. (روزانه) Daily wages or allowance.

Rojbandí, Beng. (রোজবন্দী) A daily register or diary.

Roz-, or *Rojgár*, H. &c. (روزگار, रोजगार) Fortune, the source of subsistence: service or employment as a means of subsistence.

Rozí, H. &c. (روزي, रोजी) Daily food or subsistence: daily allowance or expenses, hire or wages for a day, &c. Karn. (ರೋಜಿ) Work.

Rozína, *Rojíná*, H. &c. (روزينه, रोजीना, or रोजिना), *Rojiná*, Tel. (రోజినా) What is allowed or granted as a daily maintenance, a daily pension, a daily allowance to poor or religious persons: a deduction formerly allowed in Bengal to the Zamindárs to cover the expense of daily charitable allowances: pensions assigned by government in 1781 to various persons in the province of Benares. Ben. Reg. xxxiv. 1795; xxii. 1806.

Rozína-, or *Rojína-dár*, corruptly, *Rozendár*, H. &c. (P. دار, who holds) One receiving a daily allowance or pension: pl. *Rozínadárán*, incorrectly, *Rozindáran*, lit., holders of pensions, applied to the deduction formerly made in the revenue levied from Zamindárs in consideration of their being burthened with pensions to poor or religious persons.

Rojkírd, or *Rojkhardá*, Mar. (रोजकीर्द, रोजखरडा) Daily account of receipts and disbursements, a rough diary or day-book: one of the accounts formerly kept by the village accountant of money daily received from the Ryots and paid to the government officers.

Rozmarra, incorrectly, *Rozemera*, H. (روزمرّه, from A. مره, a turn), Hindi (रोजमरा), *Rojmará*, *-mára*, or *-murá*, Mar. (रोजमरा -मारा -मुरा), *Rojumarrá*, Tel. (రోజుమర్రా) Daily proceedings, an account of them, a diary, a journal, a day-book: also, pay, wages, daily pay or allowances.

Rojmel, Guz. (રોજમેળ) A cash-book.

Roznáma, or *námcha*, *Rojnámá*, H. &c. (روزنامه روزنامچه, रोजनामा), *Rojunámá*, Tel. (రాజునామా) A daily account-book, a diary, a journal.

Roznámakhhálá, H. (روزنامه کهالا) A ledger, an account made up from the daily accounts.

Róju, Karn. (ರೋಜು) A daily account-book.

Rójugár, Karn. (ರೋಜುಗಾರ) A servant, a workman.

Roza, H. (روزه) A fast, fasting, especially the fast observed in the month *Ramzán*.

Rozadár, H. (روزه‌دار) One who observes a fast, one who keeps *Ramzán*.

Rú, Roo, H. (P. (رو) The face.

Rú-ba-kár, H. (روبکار, from *ru*, with, *bah*, to, or towards, and *kár*, business, lit., turning the face to the affair) Engaged in, intent on, proceeding with, before the constituted authorities, as in a court of justice: plur. *Rubakárát*, causes or matters brought into court.

Rúbakárí, corruptly, *Roobicaree*, H. (P. (روبکاري) The written record of a case, stating the particulars and the grounds of the decision drawn up and authenticated by the judge in a Company's court, on passing sentence.

Rú-ba-rú, H. (P. روبرو) Face to face, in presence.

Rú-dád, or *Rúidád*, corruptly, *Roedad*, *Roidad*, H. (روداد, روي‌داد, from P. داد, giving) Narrative or record of proceedings, statement of facts or occurrences: report of a subordinate officer deputed to inquire into any affair: return to an official inquiry.

Rúposh, H. (روپوش, from P. پوشیدن, to conceal) One who is in hiding, a person who has absconded.

Rúposhí, H. (روپوشي) Hiding, absconding.

Ruá, (?) Karn. A small copper coin, three equal to a *Paisa*. —Mysore.

Ruaran, Thug. Any call of the jackall.

Rubâ, H. (A. ربع) A fourth part; the fourth part of the gross produce of the lands declared by Akbar to be the proportion due by the people as the right of the state; this was commuted for a money payment.

Rudirodgárí, S. &c. (रुधिरोद्गारी) The 57th year of the cycle.

Rudra, S. &c. (रुद्र) One of the names of Şiva.

Raudra, S. &c. (रौद्र) Relating to *Rudra*. *Raudri*, the 54th year of the cycle.

Rúí, H. (روي) Cotton, carded cotton.

Rujuâ, corruptly, Rujoo, H. (A. رجوع) Return, recourse, appeal, reference: bringing into court, as a suit: counterpart statement or engagement.

Rujuâ-min-as-shahádat, A. (رجوع‌من‌اسشهادت) Retractation of evidence, which is allowed by the Mohammadan law under certain restrictions, as before sentence; or, if after, the witnesses are liable to make good any injury done to the party against whom a cause has been decided.

Rujú, Mar. (रुजू) Ready, willing, accepted, approved, admitted: present, made or become present. Ruju, Tel., Karn. (ರುಜು) Proved, established: also subst. proof, conviction, a signature: (there can be little doubt that these words are of A. derivation, but there is an evident vernacular confounding of two radicals, *rajâ* رجع, returning, or turning to, and *razu* رضو, consenting, assenting to).

Rujúgudasta, Mar. (रुजूगुदस्त, from P. گذشته) Approved and passed in the past year (an account).

Rujúmukábalá, or *-mokábalá*, Mar. (रुजूमुकाबला -मोकाबला) Confronting or bringing together in order to investigate or compare, &c.

Rujúváta, Mar. (रुजूवात) The state of being confronted, compared, or collated, &c. (either with respect to persons, articles, documents, or the like).

Rujuvádahaṇa, Karn. (ರುಜುವಾದಹಣ) Current coin.

Rujuvu, Tel. (రుజువు) Proof, conviction: also adj., proved, established.

Rúka, Tel. (రూక) Money in general, a *fanam*, whether of gold or silver.

Ruká, incorrectly, Rookká, Mar. (रुका) The twelfth part of an *ana*: a measure of land, varying in different places from $2\frac{1}{2}$ to 10 *bighás*.

Rukâa, H. (رقعه), Róka, Rókhá, barbarously, Roggee, Karn. (ರೋಕ, ರೋಖಾ) A letter, a note, a draft, a bill.

Rukhsat, H. (A. رخصت) Permission to withdraw or depart, leave of absence.

Rukn, H. (A. رکن) A pillar, a prop: but in common use, figuratively, to form titles of Mohammadan nobles, as, *Rukn-ud-daula*, *Rukn-us-sultanat*, the pillar or prop of the state, &c.

Rukn-as-sarikat, A. (رکن‌اس‌سرقة) The prop of stealing, *i.e.* secresy in carrying off property, which, in Mohammadan law, is essential to constitute an offence of larceny.

Rukuâ, H. (A. رکوع) The proper attitude of prayer, stooping forwards and resting the hands on the knees.

Rulla, or Rull, Hindi (रुल्ल) Land that requires to be left fallow for a year or two to recover its vigour.

Rúpaniya, Thug. The cry of the hare at night on the left, a good omen.

Ruparel, Thug. The water wag-tail, as an omen.

Rúpíya, commonly, **Rupee**, H. (روپيه, from S. रूप्य, *rúpya*, silver) A silver coin, the general denomination of the silver currency of India, and the standard measure of value: the coin was first struck by Shir Shah, and was adopted by Akbar and his successors: it was of the weight of 175 grains troy, and was considered to be pure, but in the decline of the Mohammadan empire every petty chief coined his own rupee, varying in weight and value, though usually bearing the name and titles of the reigning emperor: this practice was observed to the last, and in the reign of Shah Âálam a great variety of currencies bore his name, and the years of his succession, until 1773, when they were suppressed in the territories subject to the Company, and a rupee was struck, entitled the Sicca rupee, with the following inscription on it, حامي دين محمد سايه فضل الله سكة زد بر هفت كشور شاه عالم پادشاه, *Hámí din-i-Mohammed, sáya fazl Allah, sikka zad bar haft kishwar Sháh Âálam Pádsháh.* 'The king Shah Âálam, the defender of the faith of Mohammad, the shadow of the grace of God, has struck this coin, to be current through the seven climes. Rev. ضرب مرشدآباد سنه جلوس ميمنت مانوس ١٩, struck at Murshidabad in the 19th year of the auspicious accession. The unvarying date, the 19th year of the reign, remained unaltered, in order to put a stop to a practice which the money-changers had introduced of levying an arbitrary rate of discount on rupees of previous dates, without reference to any actual diminution of weight by wear; in like manner the place of coinage remained always nominally the same, or the mint at Murshidabad, that of the Nawab of Bengal, although the rupees were coined also at Dacca, and finally only at Calcutta, for the same reason, to guard against the depreciation of the money-changers, according to the difference of place of coinage. Although the actual medium of exchange, the Company's accounts, were for a long time kept in a different valuation, or that of the *Chalani*, or current rupee, the origin of which is somewhat obscure, although it probably expressed the state of the currency at the time of its adoption, 100 Sicca rupees, supposed to be of the standard weight and value, being reckoned as equivalent to 116 current rupees. The Sicca rupee served also as the unit of weight, 80 Sicca weight being equal to one *Sér*, and 40 *Sérs* to one *Man* or *Maund.* Beside the Sicca rupee there were current under the Bengal Presidency two other coins, the Benares and Farakhabad rupee, from their being coined at those cities respectively: the Benares rupee ceased to be struck in 1819. At Madras the rupee of the Nawabs of the Carnatic, struck originally at Arcot, was the currency of the Company, and retained its name although coined at Madras or at Dacca and Calcutta, being current also in Chittagong and Dacca, between which places and the Northern Sarkárs an active traffic subsisted: its value underwent some slight modification in 1818. At Bombay the rupee of the Nawabs of Surat became the Company's coinage, and for a while it was coined concurrently with that of the Nawab; but irregularities occurring in the latter, the coinage in 1800 was restricted to Bombay, and the value of the coin was fixed, which was slightly modified in 1829. The entire inscription on the Arcot rupce was, on one face سكه مبارك بادشاه غازي عزيز الدين محمد عالمگير, the auspicious coin of the heroic monarch Âzíz-ud-din Mohammad Âálamgir (the father of Shah Âálam), and on the other ضرب اركات سنه ٢٠ جلوس ميمنت مانوس, struck at Arcot in the 20th year of the auspicious accession: that of the Bombay rupee was latterly on one face, سكه مبارك شاه عالم بادشاه غازي ١٢١٥, the auspicious coin of the heroic monarch Shah Âálam (Hij) 1215, on the other, ضرب سورت سنه ٤٦ جلوس ميمنت مانوس; struck at Surat in the 45th year of his fortunate accession: but these coins, as long as they were coined on the native plan, in common with the coins of all native mints, bear but a portion of their legends, it being the practice of the native mints in all cases to fabricate the die of twice or thrice the diameter of the coin, in striking which, consequently, only such portion of the letters as its surface could contain were impressed upon it: as, also, it was entirely accidental with which part of the die the blank coin came into contact, the portion of the legend which it received varied with every piece. In 1818 the standard of the Sicca and Farakhabad rupees was altered, but their intrinsic value was unaffected, as they continued to have the same amount of fine silver. In 1824 a slight change of the latter was made, and of the former in 1833; but in 1835 the coinage of the Company was entirely remodelled, and a coin, thenceforth termed the Company's rupee, with its proportionate subdivisions, was struck, to take the place of all the former Presidency currencies, being of the same weight and fineness throughout, and bearing inscriptions in English, or, on one face, the head and name of the reigning sovereign of Great Britain, and, on the reverse, the designation of the coin in English and Persian, with the words East-India Company in English. The weight, intrinsic purity, and value in shillings of the present British currency of these several coins are as follows:

		Weight.	Pure contents.	s.	d.
Sicca rupee, 1773,	Tr. grs.	179.666	. 175.923 =	2	2
Ditto, 1818,	„	191.916	. 175.923 =	2	2
Ditto, 1823,	„	192.000	. 176.000 =	2	2
Benares, 1806,	„	174.760	. 167.000 =	2	0¾
Farakhabad, 1803,	„	173.000	. 165.215 =	2	0½
Ditto, 1819,	„	180.234	. 165.215 =	2	0½
Ditto, 1824,	„	180.000	. 165.000 =	2	0½
Madras,	„	176.400	. 166.480 =	2	0¾
Ditto, 1818,	„	180.000	. 165.000 =	2	0½
Bombay, 1800,	„	179.000	. 164.680 =	2	0¼
Ditto, 1829,	„	180.000	. 165.000 =	2	0½
Company's, 1835,	„	180.000	. 165.000 =	2	0½

As, however, silver is subject in the London mint to a seigniorage of nearly 6 per cent., the London mint produce of the Company's rupee, if of full weight and standard value (11 dwts. fine) should be 1*s*. 11*d*.

Rupíyá-daṣkáuṛi, Beng. (রূপীযাদশকৌড়ি). A cess so denominated, or an impost of ten *kauṛis* per rupee in addition to the original assessment levied in Jessore previous to the perpetual settlement.

Rupla, (?) A tribe of slaves in Coorg so called.

Rúvu, Karn. (ರೂವು) A coin of the value of five *kás*.

S.

Ṣáâ, A. (صاع) A measure of grain about seven or eight pounds.

Sáât, H. (A. ساعت) A moment, an hour.

Sabákhia, (?) The name of a class of gang robbers in Orissa.

Sábalíá, Guz. (સાબલીઆ) The name of a low caste, or a man belonging to it, usually employed in tending cattle.

Sabárásí jaríb, Uriya (ସବାରାଶିଜରିବ) Measurement of all lands of whatever description (probably *sabá*, for *sarva*, all, *ráṣí*, a heap, and *jaríb*, measurement).

Ṣabát, or Ṣabt, H. (A. ثبات, ثبت) Firmness, stability, proof.

Ṣábit, H. (A. ثابت) Firm, proved, substantiated.

Ṣabút, H. &c. (A. ثبوت), *Ṣábúḍ*, Beng. (শাবুড), *Ṣábút*, or *Ṣábud*, Mar. (शाबूद), *Ṣábuta*, Uriya (ଷାବୁତ) Proof, evidence, conviction.

Ṣábat-bhái, Uriya (ଷାବତଭାଇ) A half-brother.

Ṣábat-bhaüni, Uriya (ଷାବତଭଉଣୀ) A half-sister.

Sabhá, S., used in all the dialects, sometimes modified, (सभा)

Sabhe, Karn. (ಸಭೆ) An assembly, an assemblage of persons of rank or respectability, or the place in which they assemble, as a hall of audience, a court of justice; also, a gaming-room or assembly.

Rája-sabhá, S. (राजसभा) A royal court, the chief court of justice, at which the king or his representative presided: other courts under the ancient Hindu system were the

Áraṇya-sabhá, (from *araṇya*, a forest) A court for deciding disputes among foresters and hermits.

Sárthika-sabhá, (from *sártha*, a company) A court for disputes amongst travellers or *káfilas*.

Sainika-sabhá, (from *sená*, an army) A court-martial.

Grámápyubhayavásí-sabhá, (from *gráma*, a village, *api*, conjunction, *ubhaya*, both, and *vásí*, a dweller) A court for deciding boundary disputes.

Ubhayánumata-sabhá, (from *ubhaya*, both, and *anumata*, assented to) A court of arbitration elected by both the contending parties.

Gráma-sabhá, (from *gráma*) A village court composed of the principal inhabitants, with the head man presiding.

Paura-sabhá, (from *pura*, a city) A court composed of citizens, a common-council court.

Gaṇa-sabhá, (from *gaṇa*, a number) An assemblage of families, tribes, or priests.

Ṣreṇí-sabhá, *ṣreṇí*, a corporation) A court of artisans and traders.

Chaturvidyá-sabhá, (from *chatur*, four, and *vidyá*, knowledge) A court of learned men versed in the four *vedas*, or in the four sciences of law, ethics, logic, and religion.

Varga-sabhá, (from *varga*, a tribe) A court composed of different classes of people.

Kula-sabhá, (from *kula*, a family) A court of the members of a family.

Kulika-sabhá, (from *kula*, as before) A court of the elders of the same lineage as the litigants.

Niyukta-sabhá, (from *niyukta*, appointed) A court held by a judge distinct from the king's court.

Nṛipati-sabhá, (from *nṛipati*, a king) A king's court held informally in the presence of a king, but without that of the judges.

Another enumeration makes the public courts but four: *Rája-sabhá*, the king's court, *Púga-sabhá*, an assembly of persons inhabiting the same place, but of different tribes and professions; *Ṣreṇí-sabhá*, a corporate court, one formed by persons of the same business, and *Kula-sabhá*, a family court.

Appeals might be made from either of these in succession, but before it reached the king's court a *Niyukta-sabhá*, or special court, was appointed to pass a judgment.

Sabhákrayasásanam, S. (सभाक्रयशासनं) A deed of corporate sale, in which the Mirasidárs of a village divest one of their number, who may be a defaulter, of his share, and divide it amongst themselves, having been made responsible for the revenue due.

Sabhanáyak, or *Sabhápati*, S. &c. (from नायक, a leader, or पति, a master) The president of an assembly, the master of the ceremonies, the keeper of a gaming-house.

Sabhásad, S. &c. (सभासद्) One who is present at an assembly, a member: an assessor in a court of justice: amongst the Marathas, a public officer whose duty it was to keep a register of petty suits, and report them to the *Mámlatdár*.

Sabhika, S. &c. (सभिकः) One who presides at an assembly, the keeper of a gaming-house or tables.

Sabhya, S. &c. (सभ्यः) Any member of an assembly: a member of a court of justice, as the *Prádviváka*, or chief judge, and the *Dharmádhyaksha*, the expounder of the law, or a Brahman so qualified, and the *Sabhásadas*, properly so termed, or assessors, who may be three, five, or seven, in number, a kind of jury; the *Purohita*, the king's family priest; a *Lekhaka*, a writer or scribe; *Sádhyapála*, the bailiff or officer appointed to enforce the decree; the *Swapurusha*, a messenger or officer who called the parties into court; and the *Aniyuktah*, unappointed persons, spectators and assistants: under the Maratha government the term was applied to an officer who kept a register of petty suits, and reported them to the *Mámlatdár*.

Sabhátámbúlam, S., but used especially in Karnata, (ಸಭಾತಾಂಬೂಲಂ) Betel distributed at a public assembly.

Ṣabi, plur. Ṣibián, H. (A. صبي, صبيان) A youth, a minor.

Sábiḳ, H. (A. سابق) Former, prior, past, as time: an old established rate of assessment.

Sábiḳán, H. (A. سابقان) Formerly, as formerly, agreeably to former or past practice.

Sabíl, H. (A. سبيل) A road: water or other drinks distributed along the streets or roads to the people at the festival of the Moharram: sheds in which such liquids are placed for distribution.

Sabníṣ, Subnees, Mar. (सबनीश, from *sab*, for *ṣubah*, or perhaps the H. *sab*, all, and the P. *nawís*, a writer) A public officer whose duty it was to pay the local militia and garrisons of forts, or the public servants of an establishment or district, and keep the records: he was one of the eight subordinate officers of districts or departments: the clerk or registrar, also styled *Daftardár*.

Sabús, corruptly, Seboos, H. (P. سبوس) Bran.

Sabzí, vernacularly, Sabjí, Subzee, or Subjee, H. &c. (P. سبزي, सबजी, from سبز, green) Greenness: vegetables, greens: the larger leaves and capsules of the hemp plant (Cannabis sativa), and more especially an intoxicating beverage prepared by washing them, afterwards drying and reducing them to powder with black pepper, cardamoms, and sometimes poppy, cucumber, and melon seeds and sugar, and then infusing the mixture either in milk and water, or cold water alone.

Sabzi-mahál, H. (سبزي محال) A tax on the sellers of vegetables: the sale of the hemp mixture was also an item of the *Ábhári*.

Ṣeo-sabjí, Mar. (शेवसबजी) Tax in kind on vegetables, levied on those brought to market.

Sach, or Sachkár, Mar. (सच, सचकार) Earnest-money.

Sáchaḳ, H. (ساچق) A ceremonial at a marriage, sending the paraphernalia of the bride to her husband's house, also the day on which this is done.

Sachiva, vernacularly, Sachio, or Sachiu, corruptly, Sucheo, and Suchew, S. (सचिव) A minister, a councillor: among the Marathas, one of the eight *Pradháns*, or chief officers of state, originally designated *Sarnís*, the general record-keeper: he was also styled *Pant-sachio*.

Ṣád, H. (صاد) The Arabic letter ص ṣ, the initial of the title of *Ṣubahdár*, affixed by him as a cypher to Zamindárí grants as their authentication.

Ṣad, H. (P. صد) A hundred.

Ṣad-wár, plur. *Ṣadwárián*, corruptly, *Sadwarain*, *Sadwanian*, *Sedwarrain*, H. (صدوار, صدواريان) An aggregate, or a company of a hundred: an item, individual, or individuals of a century: in the Northern Sarkárs, pikemen, so named from being formed in companies of a hundred, and formerly employed by the *Deṣmukhs* in revenue affairs.

Sada, Hindi (सद) A foreigner, a respectable man.

Sadá, S. &c. (सदा) Always, perpetual.

Sadáchára, S. &c. (सदाचार) Fixed and perpetual observance, the daily and regular practices of the Hindus.

Sadávartt, or *Sadávart*, corruptly, *Sadabirt*, Hindi, &c. (सदावर्त्त, from S. व्रत, a vow, or वृत्ति, maintenance) Distribution of provisions daily to passers by, mendicants, and paupers: in Kamaon, a grant of land to provide for the distribution of food at certain fixed spots to pilgrims.

SAḌÁ, or SAṚÁ, Hindi (सड़ा) Rotten, as the surface of land long under water and covered with smooth decaying vegetation.—Puraniya.

SÁDÁ, Uriya (ସାଦା) Unstamped (perhaps from Beng. (শাদা) white, blank).

SADAIKÁL, Tam. (சடைக்கால்) Land of an abandoned betel-garden.

SAḌANGÁ, SAṚANGÁ, incorrectly, SARINGA, Beng. (শাড়ংগা) A canoe, a small flat-bottomed boat.

SADARO, Guz. (સદરો) A shirt worn by the Pársís, the assumption of which is part of the ceremony of their admission to the faith.

SÁDARU, pl. Karn. (ಸಾದರು) A class of Súdra farmers.

SADD, H. (A. سدّ) Hindrance, obstruction.

Sadd-i-dáwí, H. (A. سددعوي) Bar to a claim.

Sadd-i-jawáb, H. (A. سدجواب) Reply to a reply, rejoinder: (more usually *Rad-i-jawáb*, but this form is allowable).

SADDE, Karn. (ಸಡ್ಡೆ) A sowing machine with only one aperture, used by the hand.

SÁḌE, or SÁṚE, Mar. (साडे) Certain ceremonies about the fourth day after marriage, when, after worshipping various objects, presents of clothes are made to the married couple, and the bride is given over to her husband's relations.

SÁDHANA, vernacularly SÁDHAN, S. &c. (साधन), SÁDANAM, Tam. (சாதனம்) Accomplishing, effecting, the means of accomplishment, instrument, materials: in law, also, execution, enforcing the delivery of a thing, inflicting and levying a fine; also, proving, substantiating; also means of proof, a voucher, a document, a deed, a bond: also, in Tam., a village exempt from taxation, a royal grant or patent, the same as *Sásanam*.

Sádhaní, Mar. (S. साधनी) Means of effecting, or accomplishment, means of proof, a document, a bond, or the like.

Sádhanpatra, Mar. (S. साधनपत्र) A document, a written voucher, or means of establishing any thing, a written decree or decision.

Sádana-murí, Tam. (சாதனமுறி) A promise or voucher in writing.

Sádana-patrikai, Tam. (சாதனபத்திரிகை) A bond, a deed, a will.

Sádanántaram, Tam. (சாதனாந்தரம்) An additional document or voucher, a fresh or additional count in an indictment.

Sádhansárí, incorrectly, *Sádansaree*, Beng. (S. সাধংসারী) The details of the rent-roll of a Źamindárí.—Sylhet.

Sádhya, S. &c. (साध्य) The thing or object that is to be, or may be, accomplished: in law, the matter to be proved or substantiated.

Sádhyapála, S. (साध्यपालः) The officer who executes a decree.

Sádhyasiddhi, S. (साध्यसिद्धिः) The accomplishment of what was to be done: the determination of the merits of a suit.

Sádhyasiddhipáda, S. (साध्यसिद्धिपादः) The decision, the judgment in a suit at law.

SÁDHÁRAṆA, S. &c. (साधारण) That which is common, as a common property, a specific or genuine character, possessions in common: the 44th year of the cycle, A.D. 1850.

Sádháraṇopárjana, S. (साधारणोपार्जनं) Joint earnings properly acquired by brethren living together as an undivided family.

SÁDHU, vernacularly, SÁDH, S. &c. (साधु, साध) Pious, virtuous, good, applied also to a person leading a pious or religious life, a mendicant, an ascetic; also the designation of a member of a sect of monotheistical Hindus who profess moral and personal purity: a respectable trader or merchant: in Bengali, a usurer, a money-lender.

SADHAVÁ, S. &c. (सधवा) A married woman, one whose husband (*dhava*) is living.

SADHOWA, (?) H. Stipulation or deed for payment of a balance due.

ṢADÍÁ, Uriya (ଷଡିଆ) Cultivable (as land).

SADIR, Tam. (சதிர்) Boundary, limits.

ṢADḲA, or ṢADAḲA, plur. ṢADAḲÁT, H. (A. صدقة, صدقات) Alms, properly dedicated to pious uses, voluntary alms, in distinction to those imposed by law: also, propitiatory offerings to avert sickness from a friend or relative indisposed.

Ṣadḳafarz, A. (صدقةفرض) Ordained or obligatory alms.

Ṣadḳafiṭr, H. (A. صدقةفطر) Alms bestowed upon the poor by law, at the *Íd-ul-fiṭr*, or festival which terminates the fast of Ramzán: obligatory alms.

Ṣadḳanafl, A. (صدقةنفل) Voluntary alms, not imposed by law.

ṢADR, SUDR, vernacularly, SADAR, SUDUR, corruptly, SUDDER, and SUDDUR, H. &c. (صدر, सदर) Eminence, superiority, chief, supreme: the highest or foremost of any thing: the chief seat of government, the presidency, as opposed to the provinces or *Mufassil*; but the term is most usually applied in India to denote establishments or individuals employed in the judicial and revenue administration of the state. See *Ádálat*.

Ṣadr-, or *Ṣadar-ádálat*, corruptly, *Sudder-adawlat*, H. (A. صدرعدالت) The chief court of justice, the Company's supreme court, and court of final appeal in India: the term 'Sudder Court' has latterly been made applicable to the courts of highest civil and criminal jurisdiction in all the Presidencies. Act viii. 1842. See *Âdálat.*

Ṣadr-diwáni-âdálat, H. (صدرديواني عدالت) The chief civil court.

Ṣadr-faujdári-, or *nizámat-âdálat*, H. (صدرفوجداري عدالت) The chief criminal court.

Ṣadr, or *Ṣadar Amín*, commonly, *Sudder Ameen*, H. (صدرامين) A chief commissioner or arbitrator, the title of a class of native civil judges under the British government, distinguished as *Ṣadr Amíns* and *Principal Ṣadr Amíns.* After various extensions of their jurisdiction, the *Ṣadr Amín* in Bengal was empowered to pronounce judgment in civil cases to the extent of 1000 rupees, and the *Principal Ṣadr Amín* to that of 5000, which was afterwards extended to an indefinite amount in suits referred to him by a city or Zilla judge. A limited criminal jurisdiction was also conferred upon both. Reg. xxiii. 1814; ii. iii. 1821; v. 1831; Act xxv. 1837. At Madras, *Ṣadr Amíns* have civil jurisdiction to the extent of 2500 rupees, and criminal jurisdiction in referred cases: the designation of a superior class of officers styled native judges was subsequently changed to that of *Principal Ṣadr Amíns.* Reg. iii. 1833; vii. viii. 1827; Act xxiv. 1836. At Bombay, also, the designations of Native and Principal Native Commissioner, were changed severally to those of *Principal Ṣadr Amín*, and *Ṣadr Amín*, with similar powers. Reg. xviii. 1831; Act. xxiv. 1836.

Ṣadrat-patra, H. (صدرةپتر) An assignment or grant under the authority of government, or recorded in the collector's office.

Sadarbárgír, Mar. (सदरबारगीर) A trooper stationed on guard at a court of justice.

Sadarbheṭ, Mar. (सदरभेट) Presents to government officers, forming an item of charge to every village in addition to the assessment.

Ṣadr, or *Ṣadar-jamâ*, corruptly, *Sudder-jumma*, H. (A. صدرجمع) The sum total of revenue payable to the government direct, exclusive of the charges of collection.

Ṣadr, or *Ṣadar-kachhari*, corruptly, *Sudder-cutcherry*, H (صدركچهري) The principal revenue office of a district or estate, that of the collector or Zamindár.

Ṣadr, or *Ṣadar-kharch*, H. (صدرخرچ) Expenses of the principal authority or establishment.

Ṣadr, or *Ṣadar-kánungo*, H. (صدرقانونگو) The chief native registrar or accountant of a district or collectorate.

Ṣadr, or *Ṣadar-ḳáz̤í*, H. (صدرقاضي) The chief ḳáz̤í or Mohammadan judge.

Ṣadr, *Ṣadar-ḳisṭbandí*, H. (صدرقسطبندي) The engagement for revenue instalments payable to government by the principal revenue payer, as distinguished from those entered into with him by his under payers.

Ṣadr, or *Ṣadar-málguzár*, H. (صدرمالگذار) The chief revenue payer, one who pays it either into the government treasury, or to the collector of a district, immediately, and not through any other agency: the head man or representative of a joint-tenancy village, who engages for and pays the revenue due from the community to the government.

Ṣadr, or *Ṣadar Pancháyat*, H. A supreme *Pancháyat*, one appointed to superintend other similar bodies, where there are many, and report their proceedings to the government officer.

Ṣadr, or *Ṣadar-sarrishta*, H. (صدرسرشته) The chief revenue office; in a district, that of the collector; on an estate, that of the proprietor or chief manager.

Ṣadr, or *Ṣadar-us-ṣadúr*, A. (صدرالصدور) The chief judge, the chancellor: under the Mohammadan government he was especially charged with the investigation of the cases of all those who applied to the sovereign for grants of revenue: he had also charge of *wakf* property or religious endowments, and the appointment of ḳáz̤ís and other law officers.

Ṣadárat, H. (A. صدارت) The office of chief judge or chancellor.

Sadar, Mar. (सदर) A chief court, &c., as above; but it is also used as a term in papers of accounts to signify the general heading or statement at the head of several columns of detail: also, adverbially, in the general, on the whole.

Sadar-rakam, Mar. (सदररकम) The total amount, the heading or sum of the several items of an account.

Sadara-hi, Tel. (సదరహి) Aforesaid (referring to a previous specification).

Sadarahú, Mar. (सदरहू) According to the head or specification.

ṢÁDIRWÁRID, corruptly, SADERWARED, SADURWARID, H. (A. صادروارد, from *ṣádir*, what goes, and *wárid*, what comes) A traveller, a guest: in the south of India where it is in more general use, sometimes vernacularly modified, it is differently applied, and means commonly various contingent or incidental charges borne by a village or a community, as in the following.

Sádaravárадu, Tel. (సాదరవారదు) Charge made to the

Ryots for supplying the public *kacheri* with ink, paper, oil, and the like.

Sádaravár, *Sádalavárí*, or *Sádalvárí-kharchu*, Karn. (ಸಾದರವಾರ, ಸಾದಲವಾರೀ, ಸಾದಲ್ವಾರೀಖರಚು) Contributions for a public entertainment: expenses of an annual feast in honour of *Ganésa*: *kacheri* charges for stationery, &c.

Sádirwárid, *Sádilwárid*, Mar. (सादिरवारिद, सादिलवारिद) Incidental village expenses, including periodical festivals, occasional allowances to village officers, to religious establishments, to religious mendicants, or the like, all which were defrayed by extra assessments, restricted in some places to six per cent. on the collections: in Maraṭhi the word is used in combination, as, *Sádirwárid-*, or *Sádilwár-kharch*, &c.

Sádilwárid-, or *Sádilwár-paṭṭi*, blunderingly, *Sádit-puttee*, Mar. (सादिलवारिदपट्टी, सादिलवारपट्टी) Extra assessment above the public revenue levied formerly by the revenue offices on the pretext of defraying local district charges, termed also *Mahál-sádirwárid*, not provided for otherwise by the Maraṭha government.

Sádar-kharchu, Tel. (సాదరఖరచు) Remission or allowance by the native government of a certain per centage of the revenue raised from a village for repairing tanks, alms to mendicants, and other incidental charges.—Northern Sarkárs.

Safat, Safát, Safáhat, A. (سفة ، سفاة ، سفاهت) Foolishness, folly: conduct which, according to some authorities, renders a person subject to restraint.

Safíh, A. (سفيه) A fool, a madman, one unfit to have the management of his own affairs.

Ṣafar, H. (A. صفر) The second month of the Mohammadan year.

Ṣafha, H. (A. صفحه) A page.

Saphá, Hindi (सफा) A column or page of accounts.

Ṣafi-khaṭ, corruptly, Suffie-khut, H. (A. صفي خط) A receipt, a deed of acquittance.

Ṣáfi-náma, H. (A. صافي نامه) A deed of acquittance, a deed of release or of acquiescence in the terms of a *Rázi-náma*, of which it is the counterpart; the latter, or deed of consent, being executed by the plaintiff, the *Ṣáfi-náma*, or deed of acquiescence, by the defendant.

Safína, H. (سفينه) A blank book, a common-place book. (English), Subpœna.

Ṣafḳa, A. (صفقة) Concluding a bargain, usually done by shaking hands (*ṣafḳ*).

Ság, H. &c. (ساگ, साग, from S. शाक) Greens, potherbs, edible vegetables.

Ság-pát, H. (ساگ پات) Petty dues paid in kind, lit., greens and leaves, to village officials.—Kamaon.

Sagá, H. (سگا, from S. *sagotra*), Sakkhá, Mar. (सखखा) Related by the same parents: a relative.

Sagábhái, H. (S. سگابهاي) Own brother, one by the same father and mother.

Sagái, *Sagáiwat*, H. (S. سگاي ، سگاوت) Affinity, especially by the same parents: betrothment: second marriage of a woman of low caste.

Sagam, Tel. (సగం) A half.

Ságara, vernacularly Sagar, corruptly, Saugur, S. &c. (सागर) The ocean, applied rather loosely to the low lands forming the western portion of the Delta of the Ganges, where the Hugli branch falls into the sea.

Sagaṭu, Tel. (సగటు) An average.

Ságni, or Ságnika, S. &c. (साग्नि, साग्निकः) A Brahman who preserves a perpetual household fire.

Sagotra, corruptly, Sagotr, S. &c. (सगोत्र) A kinsman, one allied by community of name and descent, a gentile relation.

Sagotra-daśántara, S. (from दश, ten, and अन्तर, within), also with the vernacular form *Daśántíl*, corruptly, *Sugotr-dushantil*, Mar. (सगोत्रदशांतील) A kinsman of the same descent within ten degrees: also such a degree of relationship.

Sagotramátra, corruptly, *Sugotrmatr*, S. &c. (from मात्र, merely) A kinsman by the same descent, but within what degree is uncertain.

Sogatrasapiṇda, S. &c. (सगोत्रसपिण्ड) A kinsman by common descent who is also connected by obsequial offerings.

Sagubaḍi, Tel. (సాగుబడి), Ságuvaḷi, corruptly, Sagoovelly, Sagwally, and Sagnally, Karn. (ಸಾಗುವಳಿ) Ságubaḍi, Tam. (சாகுபடி), also read Sakupadi. Cultivation, tillage, farming.

Ságubadi-diṭṭam, Tam. (சாகுபடித்திட்டம்) Statement of lands settled to be cultivated in the course of the year if the season permits: settlement of, or order for, cultivation.

Ságubadi-kaṇaku, Tam. (சாகுபடிக்கணக்கு) An account of the cultivation.

Ságubadi-ráji-náma, Tam. (from the A. P. راضي نامه) A deed of lease of cultivable land.

Ságusantu, Karn. (ಸಾಗುಸಂತು) Farming, cultivation.

Sáh, H. (S. ساه) A merchant, a banker, a tradesman.

Sahagamana, vernacularly, Sahagaman, S. &c. (सहगमन, from सह, with, and गमन, going) The burning of a widow with her husband's corpse : accompanying him in death.

SAHAJ, H. (سهج), Beng. (সহজ), Mar. (सहज) Easily, naturally, without effort. Uriya (ସହଜ) Slight, petty : (from S. सह, with, and ज, born).

Sahajághát, Uriya (S. ସହଜଘାତ) Slight wounding.

Sahaj-chori, Uriya (ସହଜଚୋରୀ) Petty larceny.

SAHAMARAṆA, S. &c. (सहमरण) The burning of a widow with the corpse of her husband.

ṢAHAN, H. (A. صحن) The area of a house, the ground on which it stands : a court-yard.

SAHANAK, Mar. (A. صحنك, a dish) A grant of rent-free land for subsistence.

SAHAR, H. (A. سحر) The morning, the dawn : the meal taken by the Mohammadans just before day-break in the month of Ramzán ; also *Sahargáh* and *Sahargah*.

SÁHASAN, vernacularly, SÁHAS, corruptly, SHAHESH, S. (साहसं) Violence : in law, injury of three degrees ; slight, as destruction of fruit-trees, &c. ; middle, killing of animals ; atrocious, as wounding and murder.

SAHHAT, or SIHHAT-NÁMA, H. (from A. صحة, being in health) A certificate of a person's being alive at any given date.

ṢÁHIB, H. (A. صاحب), SAHEB, Beng., Mar. (সাহেব, साहेब) A master, a lord, a companion : in Hindustani, the usual designation and address of a respectable European, like Mister, Sir, &c : when European authorities are spoken of collectively, they are sometimes termed *Sáhibán-âálishán*, most exalted gentlemen : an assistant judge or collector is termed in native patois, *Sahib-shistant*.

Ṣáhiba, H. (A. صاحبة) A lady, mistress, madam.

Ṣahábat, plur. of *Sáhib*, (صحابة) Companions, especially the companions of Mohammad, through whom his sayings have been handed down, forming a body of traditional law inferior in authority only to the Ḳurán.

Ṣáhib-i-muruwat, A. (صاحب مروة) The possessor of politeness : in law, a gentleman.

Ṣáhib-niṣáb, A. (صاحب نصاب) The possessor of so much property as renders him liable to pay Zikát, or established alms.

ṢAHÍFA, H. (A. صحيفة) A book, a leaf.

Ṣahháf, H. (A. صحّاف) A bookseller, a bookbinder, a librarian.

ṢAHÍH, H. (A. صحيح) Right, proper. SA-Í, Mar. (सई) A word attached to written documents to signify acquiescence, or uttered at the close of verbal statements with a similar import. Guz. (સહી) A term of assent ; also a signature, a written attestation.

SAḤM, pl. SAḤÁM, incorrectly, SEHAM, SUHAM, (سهم, سهام) A lot, a portion, the share of a person entitled to a part of the inheritance.

Sahm-baṭwárá, H. (بٹوارا, sharing) Division of an estate amongst the coparceners according to their several portions.

SAHOḌHA, S. (सहोढः) The son of a pregnant bride, one of the twelve sons formerly recognised by Hindu law.

SAHODAKA, S. &c. (सहोदक) Related by libations of water to deceased kinsmen.

SAHODARA, S. &c. (सहोदर) Uterine, a brother of whole blood. *Sahodarí*, a sister by the same mother.

SÁHOTRÁ, erroneously, SAHOOTRA, Mar. (साहोत्रा, from साहा, for सहा, six, and उत्तर, above) Six per cent., whether by the month or year : a fee or perquisite of six in a hundred given to a public officer : an item of the Maratha *chauth*, or six per cent. of the balance of the collections, after setting aside one-fourth to the Peshwa, assigned to the *Pant Sachiva*, or minister so termed, to whose representative the *Sáhotrá* in certain cases is still granted.

SÁHU, also SÁHUKÁR, H. &c. (ساهو, ساهوكار, साहु, साहुकार) SÁV-, or SÁÜKÁR, whence the vernacular forms, SOUCAR, SOWKAR, SAUKAR, corruptly, SHOWKAR, Mar. (सावकार, as well as साहुकार) A banker, a dealer in money and exchanges, a merchant in general : [these words are no doubt from the S. *sádhu*, good, respectable, but a facetious etymology in Maraṭhí refers *Sávahár* to *sá*, six, and *vahára*, the letter *v*, that is, to the six words beginning with *v* which characterise the opulent banker—*vastra*, dress, *vapu*, portly person, *vidyá*, knowledge, *vinaya*, decorous demeanour, *váni*, fluency of speech, and *vitta* wealth : it may be observed, that although the terms are known to most, if not all, of the dialects, they are especially in use among the Maraṭhas].

Sáühárá, or *Sáhukárá*, Mar. (सावकारा, साहुकारा) The body or corporation of bankers or monied men in a principal town : extensive money dealings.

Sáühárí, or *Sáhukárí*, Mar. (सावकारी, साहुकारी) Dealings in money and exchange : adv., relating to a banker or banking : mercantile, as business, usage, interest, &c.

Sáhúkár-ki-ṭíp, vulg., *Sowcar-teep*, H. (ساهوكاركي تيپ) A banker's bill of exchange.

SÁÏ, Hindi (साई) Earnest-money.—Chota Nagpur.

SAÏ, SAÏÁ, Hindi (सै, सैआ, from S. शती) A hundred.

Saïkṛa, or *Saïnkṛa*, H. (सैकडा, سیکڑا, सैंकडा) A hundred per cent.

SÁIBAT, A. (سايبة) A female slave or she camel set at liberty under a vow: the word is used in the formula of manumission, as *Anti-sáibat*, thou art free.

ṢAÍBA, or ṢAYIBA, A. (ثيّبة) A woman who has had intercourse with man, as opposed to a virgin, in Mohammadan law.

SAÏḌ, written also SAYÍD, and SAIYID, H. (A. سيد) A lord, a chief: a designation assumed by a number of Mohammadans who pretend to be descended from *Husain*, the son of *Âli*, and grandson of Mohammad.

Saïd-záda, H. (from A. زاده, born) The descendant of a *Saïd*, or of Mohammed.

ṢAIḲAL, H. (A. صيقل), ṢIKAL, Mar. (शिकल), ṢIKAL, Beng. (শিকল) Polishing metals, cleaning arms or tools.

Ṣaiḳal gar, H. (صیکل گر), *Sikalgar*, Beng. (শিকলগার), *Ṣikalkár*, or *-gár*, Mar. (शिकलकार, -गार) An armourer, a cleaner or polisher of arms or tools of metal.

SAIL, H. (A. سيل) A torrent or flood.

Sailáb, H. (A. P. سيلاب) A flood or torrent, an inundation.

Sailábi, Sindhi (A. P. سيلابي) Land watered by inundations.

SÁÏL, H. (A. سائل) A petitioner, one who asks or begs: one who interrogates, an examiner.

SÁIMA, pl., SAWÁÏM, H. (A. سايمه , سوايم) Herds of camels, oxen, goats, or other animals, subsisting chiefly on pasture.

SAINI, Thug. Signal for murder.

SAINDHI, (?) The fermented juice of the wild date-tree (Elate sylvestris).

SAIP, Thug. Any trick practised upon travellers; also the exerior, when respectable, of a Thug or traveller.

SÁÍR, corruptly, SAYR, SAYRE, H. (A. ساير), SÁYER, Beng. (সায়ের), SÁYAR, Mar. (सायर), SÁYARU, Tel. (సాయరు) In its original purport the word signifies moving, walking, or the whole, or the remainder: from the latter it came to denote the *remaining* or *all other* sources of revenue accruing to the government, in addition to the land-tax, from a variety of imposts, as customs, transit duties, licences, fees, house-tax, market-tax, &c., in which sense the term is current throughout India: the several imposts under this name were abolished by the British government, with the exception of government customs, duties on spirituous liquors, and other minor specified items: the privilege of imposing local taxes included in the *Sáyar*, was also taken away from private individuals, but it still applies to various items of the income from landed property not comprised in the produce of cultivation, as rent from fisheries, from timber and fruit-trees, bees'-wax, &c.: it also designates certain admitted manorial rights or prescriptive fees and cesses levied from the residents in a village, or from the cultivators by the proprietors, which have been long established, and are upon record; the former of these additions are usually taken into account, the latter not, in fixing the rate of assessment. Reg. xxvii. 1793. In A. and H. *Sáir* is also a tax on personal property, and in Maraṭhi it also signifies the place or stand where the customs are levied.

Sáir, or *Sáyar bakhsh bandar*, H. (ساير بخش بندر) Duties on markets, and customs on goods, levied at Hugli (*Bakhsh-bandar*), under the former government of Bengal.

Sáir-chalantá, H. (ساير چلنتا) Transit duties formerly levied by the Zamindárs on goods passing through their estates.

Sáir chuna cahly, (?) The title formerly given to the duties and taxes levied in and around Murshidabad: (the epithet, which is obviously an error, perhaps for *Chuna-kháli*, lime-creek or wharf, may have been taken from the site of the custom-house).

Sáir-jamâ, H. (ساير جمع) The total amount of the revenue in addition to the land-tax.

Sáir-jahát, erroneously, *Sairjât*, H. (ساير جهات) A tax on boats, an inland toll: the *Sáir* duties collectively.

Sáir-i-kharch, H. (ساير خرچ) Expenses of the collection of the *Sáir* duties.

Sáir-kharch, H. Extra or miscellaneous expenses.

Sáir-panchotara, H. (ساير پنچوتر) Five per cent. levied on the transit of goods.

Sáirwálo, Guz. (સાઇરવાલો) Collector of customs.

SÁÍS, H. (A. سايس) A groom, a horsekeeper.

SAIT, Thug. Parole of rendezvous.

SAITHÁWÁR, Hindi (सैथावार) A division of the Kúrmi or agricultural tribes in Hindustan, located chiefly in Gorakhpur and Benares.

SAJA-JAMÁ, (?) Beng. Amount of rent in kind (?).

SAJAL-STHAL, S. &c. (स, with, जल, water, and स्थल, land) A term used in deeds of transfer or sale of landed property to denote the absolute alienation of the whole.

SÁJALU, Tel. (plur. సాజలు) Labourers in salt-works.

SAJÁVÁLI, Karn. (ಸಜಾವಲಿ, probably from the A. *Sazáwali*, q. v.) Restraint on a person to enforce payment of a debt, or prevent his running away.

SAJGAṆÍ, SAJGÁṆÍ, Mar. (सजगणी, सजगाणी) A couple of

Paisas, or copper coin so termed; also, a measure of land = six *Ruhás*.

SÁJHÁ, H. (ساجها, सहायता) Partnership, association.

Sájhí, H. (ساجهي, S. सहायी) A partner, an associate, a coparcener in landed property.

SAJJÁ, Mar. (सज्जा) A continuous tract of cultivated ground.

SAJJÁDA, less correctly, SIJJÁDA, H. (A. سجّادة) A mat or carpet on which Mohammadans kneel or sit whilst praying: see *Sijda*.

Sajjáda-nishín, H. (P. نشين, sitting) The sitter on the praying carpet, usually applied to the spiritual superior of a mosque or religious endowment, as distinct from the *Mutawallí*, or secular superior and manager, although the two offices are not unfrequently united in the same person; also any religious ascetic of the Mohammadan faith.

SAJJI, SAJJI-MATI, SAJJI-NÚN, incorrectly, SOOJEE-MATEE, H. (سجي, سجيمتى, سجينون, सर्जिका) An impure carbonate of soda called *Sajji* earth, or *Sajji* salt, extracted from the soil in various parts of Hindustan, especially in the Doab.

ṢAKA, or ṢÁKA, vulgarly, SHUK, or SHUKU, S. &c. (शक, शाक) An æra in general, but the term is applied especially to that which is reckoned from the reign of a prince of the south of India named *Sáliváhana*, commencing in the 79th year of the Christian æra, and to be identified with the latter by adding $78\frac{1}{4}$: thus the current *Ṣaka* year 1772 began towards the end of March 1850.

Ṣákábda, S. (शाकाब्द), *Sagáttam*, corruptly, *Sagartham*, Tam. (சகாத்தம்) Any year of the æra of *Sáliváhana*.

SAKÁK, H. (A. سكاك) A cutler.

SAKÁM-BADH, Uriya (ସକାମବଧ, from S. *Sa-káma*, with will, and *badha*, killing) Wilful murder.

Sakám-samán-badh, Uriya (ସକାମସମାନବଧ) Culpable homicide.

SAKALÁTI, or SAKALÁTU, Tel., Karn. (సకలాతి, సకలాతు, apparently from the English 'scarlet') Woollen or broadcloth.

SAKAḶÁYA, and SAKAḶÁYA-RÁṢI, Karn. (ಸಕಳಾಯರಾಶಿ, from S. *Sakala*, all, and *ráṣi*, a heap) The whole of the crop before partition between the government and the cultivators.

SAKÁR, Mar. (सकार) Acceptance of a bill, endorsement in proof of acceptance.

Sakarái, Mar. (सकराई) The charge made by the cashier of a bill of exchange.

SAKARA, erroneously, SUKRA, H. (S. स, with, कर, tax) Subject to revenue payment, paying tax.

SÁKH, or SÁKHÍ, Mar. (साख, साखी) Mercantile credit, a good reputation in business.

ṢÁKHÁ, S., and in all the dialects, sometimes expressed SÁKH, SHÁKH, (शाखा) lit., A branch: metaphor., a division or branch of any tribe, sect, family, school, or caste, and the like

Ṣákhávalí, S. &c. (शाखावली, from *Áválí*, a row) A pedigree, a family.

SAKHÍ BHÁVA, S. &c. (सखीभाव, from *Sakhí*, a female friend) A sect of Hindus in Upper India who especially worship *Rádhá*, the mistress of *Kṛishṇa*.

SÁKIN, H. &c. (ساكن) An inhabitant, a permanent resident in any place.

SAKKÁ, H. (A. سقّا) A water-bearer, sometimes one of the village servants in Hindustan who supplies the villagers and travellers with water, and is paid by an allowance of grain at harvest.

SÁKSHÍ, S. &c. (साक्षी), SÁKHI, H. (ساكهي), it is also pronounced in other dialects, although correctly written, SÁKHÍ, A witness, an eye-witness: it is also used, less corrrectly, for witness or testimony in general, for *Sákhya*, q. v. In Mal. (സാക്ഷി) it also means a fine or forfeit of ten per cent. on the money advanced when a mortgagee wishes to give up the land he holds before his term expires.

Sákshidár, Mar. (साक्षीदार) A witness.

Sákshigár, and *Sákshiyava*, Karn. (ಸಾಕ್ಷಿಗಾರ, ಸಾಕ್ಷಿಯವ) A witness.

Sákshikkhánam, Mal. (സാക്ഷിക്കാണം) Fees paid to one who witnesses the execution of title-deeds.

Sáhshya, S. &c. (साक्ष्य), also, sometimes, *Sákhya*, and *Sákshí*. Evidence, testimony, deposition.

Sáksha-á-ṣayaru, Uriya (ସାକ୍ଷଆଶୟରୁ) Circumstantial evidence (from साक्ष्य, and the A. ساير, remainder).

ṢAKTI, S. &c. (शक्ति) Power, ability, the personified power of a divinity, a goddess.

Ṣákta, S. &c. (शाक्त) Relating to the female nature or principle: the designation of a sect who worship the female principle according to the ritual of the *Tantras*: there are two chief divisions of them, the *Dakshináchárí* and *Vámáchari*, or right and left-hand ritualists: the worship of the former is public, and no otherwise noticeable than as addressed to the goddesses, especially forms of *Durgá*, as *Bhavání*, and *Párvatí*, also to *Lakshmí* or *Mahálakshmí*, and others, commonly objects of adoration. The left-hand division worship, in preference, the *Tántrika* impersonations of *Durgá*, as *Deví*, *Kálí*, *Syámá*, &c., or a woman representing the *Ṣákti*; their worship is private and unavowed, and is celebrated with impure practices: it is said to be most numerously followed, and branches into various subdivisions.

SÁKHTU, Tel. (సాఖ్తు, P. ساخت) Manufacture, construction.

SAKULYA, S. &c. (सकुल्य) A kinsman, or, more usually, a distant kinsman, not nearer than five, seven, or ten degrees.

SÁL, H. (P. سال), SÁLU, Tel. (సాలు), SÁLE, Karn. (ಸಾಲೆ) A year.

Sálábád, Sálábádí, Mar. (सालाबाद, सालाबादी) Permanent collections or charges: used generally with the substantives, as *Sálábád-jamâ*, the permanent or perennial revenue; *Sálábád-kharch*, the permanent or fixed charges, as of a village, for establishment, charities, festivals, &c.

Sálábádu, Tel. (సాలాబాదు) Annually, year by year.

Sál-áyinda, H. (P. آينده, coming), *Sálu*, or *Sále-aindá*, Tel. (సాలు, సాలెఅయిందా) Next or ensuing year.

Sál-ba-sál, H. (سال بسال), *Sál-dar-sál*, Mar. (सालदरसाल) Year by year, annually.

Sál-bandí, Mar. (सालबंदी) A settlement for a series of years, or the papers detailing it, as affecting recurring engagements, as contracts, leases, &c.: the arrangement made by joint inheritors or proprietors for the successive enjoyment of their property.

Sálevár-kharchu, Karn. (ಸಾಲೆವಾರಖರ್ಚು) Annual disbursements.

Sálgira, H. (from گره, a knot) The anniversary of a person's nativity, when a knot is tied on a string or thread kept as a record of his age.

Sál-guẓashta, H. (from P. گذشته, past), *Sál-gudast*, Mar. (सालगुदस्त), *Sálugujastá*, Tel., Karn. (సాలుగుజస్తా) Last year.

Sáli, H. &c. (سالي, साली) Annual, relating to the year: land taken up for the year: a rate in the cultivator's lease when two or more crops are raised from the soil in the same year, that is to say, when the ground is worked throughout the year, not in one season only.

Sál-i-hál, H. (سال حال), *Sále-hálu*, Tel., Karn. (సాలెహాలు) The present or current year.

Sáliána, H. &c. (ساليانه) Annual, yearly: an annuity, a yearly salary or pension.

Sáliánadár, H. (P. دار, who has) A pensioner, an annuitant, one who receives an annual allowance, stipend, or pension.

Sáliánadárán, corruptly, *Saliandarum*, H. (pl. of the last) Annuitants: an entry in the formers tatement of the revenues of Bengal on account of annual allowances made to the Zamindárs in Sylhet.

Sáliána-háṣil, or *-tahṣíl*, H. (A. حاصل, profit, تحصيل, collections) Yearly collections from a district or estate.

Sáliná, Mar. (P. सालीना) Annually, year by year.

Sáljhaṛti-jamâ-kharch, H. (سال جهرتي جمع خرچ) A yearly account of receipts and disbursements, a debit and credit account.

Sálkarí, Mar. (सालकरी) The individual who, among a number of joint proprietors, is in possession or has the management of the common stock for a given year.

Sáltamámi-hágaja, Uriya (ସାଲତମାମିହାଗଜ, from A. تمام, entire, and كاغذ, paper) The yearly accounts.

Sálwár, H. (سالوار) By or according to the year or years.

Sálwár-waṣúl-bákí, H. (A. وصول, collection, and باقي, remainder) Accounts of the annual collections and balances for a series of years.

SÁLA, or SÁLASÚLA, Karn. (ಸಾಲ, ಸಾಲಸೂಲ) Debt.

Sálagára, or *Sáladára*, or *Sáladava*, Karn. (ಸಾಲಗಾರ, ದಾರ, or -ದವ) A creditor.

Sálagára, or *Sáladali-biddava*, Karn. (ಸಾಲಗಾರ, ಸಾಲದಲಿ-ಬಿದ್ದವ) A debtor.

Patrasála, Karn. (ಪತ್ರಸಾಲ) A debt contracted upon a bond or note.

Baḍḍisála, Karn. (ಬಡ್ಡಿಸಾಲ) A debt bearing interest

Maisála, or *Sukhasála*, Karn. (ಮೈಸಾಲ, ಸುಖಸಾಲ) Bail for a debt.

ṢÁLÁ, H. &c. (سالا, शाला, श्याल) A wife's brother, a brother-in-law: to call a stranger by such an appellation is one of the most aggravated terms of abuse in Bengal.

Ṣálí, H. &c. (سالى, शाली) A wife's sister, especially a younger sister.

Ṣálápo, Beng. (শালাপো) A wife's brother's son.

SALAF, H. (A. سلف) Ancestors, predecessors: money advanced for merchandise.

SALAGA, Karn. (ಸಲಗ) A chief or head man.

SÁLAGRÁMA, or SÁLIGRÁM, commonly SALGRAM, S. &c. (सालग्राम, सालिग्राम) A stone found in the Gandhak river, a sort of ammonite supposed to be a type of Vishnu, and worshipped by his votaries (it is derived from *sa*, with, *ala* for *ara*, a ring, and *gráma*, a multitude).

SALÁHIYAT, Hindi (सलाहियत, from the A. صلاحيت, fitness) Information sent by the village accountant or collector to the chief police authority of any criminal occurrence in the village.

SAḶAĪ, Mar. (सळई, from S. *saláki*, a pin, a stake) A sample, as a bundle of grass, a single fruit, a log of wood set aside from the mass in counting or weighing the whole, to mark the completion of the tale at each pause, and then counted to test the total: it is usually thrown into the bargain, or, when it is the tale of the crop, the bundles become the perquisite of the village accountant.

SALAKA, Tel. (సలక) A measure of capacity equal to two *Túms*.

SALAKE, Karn. (ಸಲಕೆ) Delivering over, payment, paying.

SALAKH, H. (A. سلخ) The last day of a month of thirty days: day of new moon.

SALÁKU, Tel. (సలాకు) A dent or mark on a coin denoting its goodness.

SALAM, written also SILM, and SILLIM, A. (سلم) A description of sale in which payment is immediate or in advance, and the delivery of the purchased articles may be deferred. See *Muslim*.

SALÁM, H. (A. سلام) Peace, safety: salutation (implying a wish for a person's safety and health) used as a civil term on meeting or parting, as *Sáheb-salám*; and more especially, in the Arabic exchange of compliments, *Salám-âlikum*, peace be with you; *Âli-hum-salám*, with you be peace.

Salámí, H. (A. سلامي) Relating to compliments, or a salutation, especially a complimentary present, a douceur, the first receipts of an appointment tendered to the person through whom it has been obtained: a present to a superior upon being introduced to him: a gratuity or offering on receiving a lease or settling for the revenue, or on receiving any favour real or implied: a fee or fine levied annually on the holders of rent-free tenures as a quit-rent: applied adjectively to tenures so held.

Salámi-i-khána-bárí, H. (سلامي خانه باري) A present made by the *Raiat* to a Zamindár in Bengal on his erecting a new hut, originally a free-gift, subsequently converted into an *Abwáb*, or regular impost.

SÁLAM, Hindi (सालम) Good fertile land.—Puraniya.

SÁLAN, SÁLNÁ, H. (سالن, سالنا) Meat, fish, or vegetable *curry*.

ṢALÁT, H. (A. صلات, or صلوة) Prayer, the repetition of which is directed five times a day, or, 1. at the *Subh*, between daybreak and sunrise; 2. *Ẕahr*, immediately after noon; 3. *Âṣr*, in the afternoon, shortly before sunset; 4. *Maghrib*, evening, before dusk; and 5. *Îshá*, on retiring to bed: these are the ordained seasons of prayer, but other prayers and other seasons are also recognised and recommended.

SALAVÁDI, Karn. (ಸಲವಾಡಿ) A kind of beadle or crier attached to the head of a corporation of merchants, carrying as a badge a large ladle with chain and bell on his shoulders, and whose duty it is to assemble the merchants on public occasions, &c.

ṢALAVU, Tel. (శెలవు) Leave, dismissal, permission to depart. Tel., Karn., Expense, expenditure (probably from A. صرف).

SÁLEVÁDU, corruptly, SALWA, and SARLEE, Tel. (సాలెవాండ్లు) A weaver.

SALÍ, (?) Beng. A description of land, that paying rent in kind (?)

SÁḶÍ, Mar. (साळी) A particular class of weavers in cotton and silk, or an individual of it.

ŚÁLI, S. &c. (शालि) Rice in general.

ŚALI, pron. SHULEE, Beng. (শলি) A measure for grain containing 20 *sers*: eight *Śalís* = a *Máp* (মাপ).

SÁLIK, H. (A. سالك) A class of Mohammadan devotees who observe the law, and lead a domestic life.

SALIKE, Karn. (ಸಲಿಕೆ) Payment.

ṢÁLIṢ, corruptly SALLIS, H. (A. ثالث), Beng. (শালিস) An umpire, an arbitrator (lit., a third, or one of three, from *Ṣalaṣ* ثلث, three).

Ṣáliṣ-b'il-khair, H. (ثالث به الخير) An impartial arbitrator.

Ṣáliṣi, corruptly, *Sallisee*, H. (ثالثي), Beng. (শালিসী) Arbitration, award.

Ṣáliṣ-náma, H. (ثالث نامه) A deed of arbitration, a written award.

SÁL-JAMÍN, (?) Mar. The best sort of copper-coloured or red soil.—J. Sel. 4. 556: (it is no doubt a blunder for *Lál*, red-earth.

SÁLMAL, (?) Mar. An inferior caste of Hindus said to be the descendants of a Brahman by a slave girl; whose business it is to prepare and sell *Páṇ*, or the betel-leaf and nut, &c. for mastication.

SALONO, H. (सलोनो) Day of full moon in *Srávan*, when the *Rákhi* is tied on. See *Rákhi-purnimá*.

ŚÁLOTAR, or ŚALOTARI, corruptly, SALISTRI, H. (سالوتر, from S. शालिहोत्री) A farrier, a horse-doctor: also *Sálotarí*, Farriery, veterinary practice.

SÁMÁDASKAT, Guz. (સામાદસ્કત) An account opened by a person in his creditor's book; a promissory note, a receipt.

SAMÁDHI, also, vernacularly, SAMÁDH, H. &c. (S. समाधि, समाध, سمادھ) Religious abstraction in general; that performed by Jogís, by which they pretend to be able to suspend the connexion between soul and body: the self immolation of a member of the Jogí order of mendicants, by burning or burying himself alive: the ceremony of burying, or sinking in water, the corpse of a deceased Jogí; a small and low shrine or tomb erected over the grave of a Jogí, commonly surmounted by a standing-place for a *Tulasí* plant: also a reconciling of differences, settlement of an affair.

SAMAGI, SAMAGE, Karn. (ಸಮಗಿ, ಸಮಗೆ) A person wearing a trident sectarial mark, and sometimes acting as priest to *Sudras*.

SÁMAGRÍ, H. (S. سامگری) Furniture, tools, apparatus.

SAMA-ÍK, SAMÁIK, Mar. समईक, समाईक, S. सामायिक, from समय, agreement) Held under compact or in conjunction, as lands, tenements, &c.: cultivated in common by joint proprietors or sharers, without actual division.

SAMÁJIK, Mar. (समाजिक, from S. समाज, a community) Held in common: belonging to a society or community.

SAMÁKHYÁ, Tel. (సమాఖ్య, समाख्या) A statement of facts or opinions authenticated by a number of persons, an agreement entered into by two or more individuals.

SÁMAN, or SÁMA, S. &c. (सामन्) The Sáma Veda.

SAMÁNA, vernacularly SAMÁN, S. &c. (समान, سمان) Equal, like, same.

Samánagotra, S. (from गोत्र, family) Of the same lineage, a gentile kinsman.

Samání-vriddhi, S. (समानीवृद्धि) Moderate interest.

Samánodaka, S. (from समान, and उदक, water) A kinsman connected by offerings of water to deceased ancestors; for the first seven degrees the *Samánodaka* is the same as the *Sapinda*, offering cakes and water; the former affinity extends to seven degrees further, in which water only is presented.

Samánodarya, S. (from उदर, the belly or womb) A brother of whole blood.

SÁMÁN, H. &c. (P. سامان) Furniture, goods, effects, apparatus.

SAMAN, SUMUN, incorrectly, SIMMIN, H. (A. ثمن) Price, value: in Shiâ law, gold and silver only are intended.

SÁMÁNDASKAT, Guz. (સામાંદસ્કત, H. *Sámne-dasthkhat*) An account opened by a person in his creditor's book, also a receipt, a promissory note or a writing passed by one contracting party to another.

SAMANDAR, H. (?) A small land measure.—Midnapur.

SÁMANTA, S. &c. (सामन्त) Bordering, neighbouring, a neighbouring or adjacent village or town.

SAMANVAYA, Beng. (समन्वय, S. सम्, with, and अन्वय, succession) Restoration of a person to his family or caste after expiation for the fault by which he had been degraded. This, or *Samanvayi*, is probably the correct reading of what appears in some lists of *Sámanáyi*, which has no satisfactory etymology.

SAMAN, or SUMUN, H. Beng. (سمن, সমন) The English word 'summons.'

SAMÁR, Hindi (समार) Crop-ploughing.

SAMARÁS, Mar. (समरास, from राशी, a heap) Produce of a field collected and stacked, but not divided among the sharers; undivided property in general.

SAMARPANA, vernacularly, SAMARPAN, S. &c. (समर्पण) Delivering, entrusting to: delivery, transfer.

SAMASTA-DEH-JANA, corruptly, SUMVUST-DEHIJIN, and SUMUST-DEHIJIN, Mar. (from S. समस्त, whole, दिह, a village, and जन, people) The entire village proprietary, the village community or corporation.

SAMASTÁNAM, Tam. (சமஸ்தானம், S. &c. *Sansthana*, q.v.) A metropolis, the residence of a prince or person of rank: it is used in a collective sense in the south for a family of rank and distinction, a noble house.

SAMASTHALA, S. &c. (समस्थल), SANTHAL, Mar. (संथल) Level ground, table-land.

SAMATU, vernacularly, SAMAT, Tel. (సమతు) A division of a district.

Samatudárudu, or, vernacularly, *Samatdár*, also, *Samuddárudu* or *Samuddár*, Tel. (సమతుదారుడు, సముద్దారుడు,) A revenue-officer employed by the government or by a Zamindár to superintend the tillage of a district, or of a certain number of villages, to settle disputes among the cultivators, and communicate with the district collector.

SAMÁVARTTANA, S. &c. (समावर्त्तन) The ceremony which takes place when the young Brahman has completed his course of religious study, and returns home: amongst the Marathas it is said to be a ceremony in which the *munja*, or girdle of grass, is loosened, sixteen years after it has been put on.

Samávritta, S. &c. (समावृत्तः) The religious student who has returned home after completing his studies.

SAMAYA, S. &c. (समय) Compact, agreement, engagement.

SAMAYARÁYA, Karn. (ಸಮಯರಾಯ) The high priest of the Dasari caste.

SAMBA, or SAMBANELLU, also read SHAMBÁ, and CHAMBA, Tam. (சம்பா, சம்பாநெல்லு) A superior kind of rice with white and well-flavoured grains, it is sown in July, transplanted in October, and reaped in February.

Samba, or **Shamba**, Beng. (शम्ब्र) Second ploughing of a field.

Sambala, Karn. &c. (S. ಸಂಬಳ) Pay, hire, wages: provender or stock for travelling expenses, provisions for a journey.

Sambalagár, Karn. (ಸಂಬಳಗಾರ) One who is retained or hired.

Aramané-sambala, Karn. (ಅರಮನೇಸಂಬಳ) A person in the pay of the government.

Sambal-aál, Tam. (சம்பளாளுள்) One who serves for monthly wages.

Sambandha, S. &c. (सम्बन्ध, from *sam*, together, and *bandha*, binding): it occurs unchanged in most of the dialects, but in Karn. becomes *Sammandha* (ಸಂಮಂಧ) Relationship, affinity, connexion: although not exclusive of relationship by descent, it is more correctly applicable to that by connexion, as by marriage, &c.

Sambhandí, S. &c. (सम्बन्धी), *Sammandhi*, Karn. (ಸಂಮಂಧಿ) A relation, a connexion.

Śámbarí, S. &c. (शाम्बरी) A female juggler.

Sámbhar, H. (سامبهر) Salt obtained from a lake of the same name in Ajmir.

Sambhar, Thug. Treasure.

Sambhúyasamutthánam, S. (सम्भूयसमुत्थानं) Joint performance of work, concerns among partners, partnership: a title of Hindu law.

Samdhi, also, **Samadhi**, and less correctly, **Samdi**, H. &c. (سمدهي) A father-in-law, either the father of the bridegroom or the bride, especially in regard of their mutual affinity.

Samdhin, H. &c. (سمدهن), *Samadhuni*, Uriya (ସମଧୁଣୀ) A mother-in-law. See the last.

Sámí, Hindi (सामी) Arable land.—Mherwara.

Śamí, S. &c. (शमी) A sort of tree (Acacia suma).

Śamípújá, S. &c. (शमीपूजा) Worship of the *Śamí* tree at the festival of the Dasahará.

Samjháish, H. (سمجهايش) Making to understand, explaining, warning, inducing the defendant to admit the justice of a plaint.

Samjut-patra, Mar. (संजुतपत्र, from S. *Sanyukta* संयुक्त, conjoined, and *patra*, a leaf) A paper declaratory of an amicable agreement having been come to between the litigant parties.

Samla, Hindi (समला) A crop that, after having been checked, has recovered.—Puraniya.

Sammádam, Tam. (சம்மாதம்) A compact or commutation made by merchants and traders with the customs and excise.

Sammaí, H. (سمئي, सम्मई) The pipe (a hollow bambu) of a drill plough.

Sammánam, Tam. (சம்மானம்) Lands exempt from all tax: (from S. सम् and माने, respect, a mark of respect).

Sammatapatra, vernacularly, **Sammadipatram**, corruptly, **Summadibuthrem**, S. &c. (सम्मत, assented, and पत्र, leaf) A deed of acquiescence, permission, or agreement.

Samohi, (?) In Arcot, the designation given to the villages or lands of a community held severally under periodical distribution. See *Samudayam.*

Sampádak, Mar. (संपादक, S. one who accomplishes or produces) The first person of a family who has obtained possession of lands, privileges, &c.

Sampradáyam, S. &c. (सम्प्रदायं) Custom, usage, traditional doctrine.

Samprati, corruptly, **Sumpreddy**, **Sampatee**, **Sampardy**, **Simperty**, Tel. Karn. (సంప్రతి, from the S. सम्प्रति, now, but changed in sense, or rather derived from सम, with, and प्रति, against) An assistant to a village accountant, a person employed to prepare copies of accounts, or to examine and make out check accounts.

Sampratidáru, Tel. (సంప్రతిదారు) One who keeps counter or check accounts.

Sampratipatti, S. &c. (सम्प्रतिपत्ति) Assent, acknowledgment: in law, admission by the defendant of the truth of the plaint.

Samudáyam, incorrectly, **Samadayam**, Tam. (சமுதாயம், S. समुदयं) The tenure by which the members of a village community, or Mirásidárs hold the lands in common, each occupying an assigned share, but having no permanently exclusive right to it, and holding it only for a given period until a fresh partition and distribution take place: it also designates lands not allotted to individuals, but cultivated in common: and again, it may mean a village, the produce of which is equally divided between the proprietor and the cultivators when they are distinct.

Samudáya-grámam, Tam. (சமுதாயக்கிராமம், for *gráma*, S.) A village held or cultivated in common: also one in which the produce, as before, is equally divided between the proprietors and cultivators.

Samudáyanilam, Tam. (சமுதாயநிலம்) Land held and cultivated in common.

Samúha, S. &c. (समूह) An assemblage, a multitude: an assembly formed to take cognisance of offences against caste.

Samusaram, Tam. (S. சமுசாரம், from S. संसार) Married state or condition.

Samusárakáran, Tam. (சமுசாரக்காரன்) A married man, one who has children.

Samusári, Tam. (சமுசாரி) Father or mother of a family.

Samvatsara, vernacularly also **Samvat**, **Sumvut**, or **Sambat**, **Sumbut**, S. (संवत्सर), Hindi, Mar. (संवत), Beng. (সম্বৎ) A year; but it is especially applied to the luni-solar years of the era of *Vikramáditya*, commencing with the year of the *Kali* age 3045, or 57 years B.C., which latter number is to be added to any year A.D. to find the *Samvat*; as, A.D. 1850 + 57 = 1907; and conversely to be deducted from the *Samvat* to find the A.D., as, 1907 − 57 = 1850: the *Samvat* æra is chiefly used in Telingana and Hindustan, occasionally in Bengal, rarely in the Peninsula.

Samvid, or **Samvit**, S. (संवित्) Agreement.

Samvit-patra, S. (संवित्पत्र) A deed of assent, an agreement, a deed of gift, applied in the Anglo-Indian courts to a will, a testament.

Samvid-vyatikrama, S. (from व्यतिक्रम departure) Non-performance of agreements, a breach of contract, &c.: a title of Hindu law.

San, **Sun**, H. &c. (A. سن, सन) A year: like *Samvat* it is also applied to the years of an æra, of which there are two varieties in use, the *Bengali* and the *Vilaiti*; the former current in Bengal, and very commonly quoted; the latter current more rarely in the Dakhin, but used and known as the *Amli-san* of Orissa. To convert the former into the years A.D., 593 must be added to any period within the first nine months, 594 for the other three: to convert the latter, 592 within the first four months, 593 for the other eight: thus, the Bengal *San* beginning on the first *Baisákh* 963 + 593 = A.D. 1556. The *Vilaiti San* beginning on the first of *Áṣwin* 963 + 592 = 1555. These æras were first established by the Emperor Akbar. *San* is also used in speaking of the years of a king's reign as chronicled by his coins: a rupee of the 19th *San* is one coined in the 19th year of his reign.

San-i-jalús, H. (A. جلوس) The year of the king's accession.

San-patit, Hindi (from S. पतित, fallen) Land left uncultivated or unowned for a year.

Sanwad-, or *Sanwád-bakí*, Mar. (सनवद्- सनवादबाकी) Arrears of revenue due for several years.

Sanwad-, or *Sanwád-padast*, Mar. (सनवद्-, सनवादपडसत) Waste or uncultivated for years, land, &c.

Sanwát, corruptly, *Sunat*, *Sonaut*, *Sunott*, H. (سنوات, pl. of *Sanat* سنت, a year) Years, but applied in Bengal to rupees in the third year of their currency, when their value in comparison with the money of account, or current rupee, was reduced from 16 per cent. to 11 per cent. above the latter; that is, the rupee was rated in the first year of its issue at 116 to 100 current rupees, in the second year it circulated at 113 to 100 current rupees, and in the third and ever after, at 111 to 100 current rupees, when it was termed *Sanwát*.

Ṣaṇa, vernacularly, **San**, or **Sun**, corruptly, **Sunn**, S. &c. (शण) A plant, the fibres of which are used for the manufacture of cordage, canvas, and the like: Indian hemp (Crotolaria juncea), also the flax or fibres.

Sanappan, *Shanappan*, or *Sanarpan*, Tam. (சணப்பன், சணற்பன்) A maker of hempen cloths, canvas, sacks, &c.

Sáṇá, Mar. (साणा) A person, on the part of one of the shareholders, set to watch over a joint concern to prevent fraudulent abstraction of the produce: also one set over a tenant by his landlord, from the cutting of the corn until its final disposal, that he may not be defrauded of his share (probably for the H. *Shahna*, q. v.).

Sanábhi, S. (सनाभि) A uterine brother, a brother of whole blood.

Sánabhóga, pron. **Shánabhog**, corruptly, **Ṣhanabogue**, **Shanbogue**, **Shambogue**, also **Kulkaraṇi-ṣánabhoga**, Karn. (ಶಾನಭೋಗ, ಕುಲಕರಣಿಶಾನಭೋಗ) The village clerk or accountant who keeps the accounts of the cultivation, and registers every thing connected with it: he is paid by a grant of land and portions of the crop: a writer or clerk in general.

Ṣánáya, Karn. (ಶಾನಾಯ) Allowance of grain to the village accountant.

Hajuru-sánabhog, Karn. (from A. حضور *Huzur*, q. v.) A clerk of customs.

Sanad, **Sunud**, incorrectly, or vernacularly, **Sunnud**, H. &c. (A. سند, सनद), **Sannadu**, Tel. (సన్నదు) A grant, a diploma, a charter, a patent: a document conveying to an individual emoluments, titles, privileges, offices, or the government rights to revenue from land, &c., under the seal of the ruling authority. The Mohammadan government had different forms of *Sanads* according to the nature of the grant.

Sanad-ba-dahand, H. (P. سندبدهند) Lit., Let them give a *Sanad*: the form of words inscribed by the superior authority, the *Názim*, or *Subáh-dár*, upon the *Díwán's* petition or statement, representing the particulars of a royal assignment of revenue in his district, and constituting his authority for issuing the *Sanad-mutábik*, the local patent or order to make over possession to the grantee.

Sanad-búzú, H. (P. بازو, the arm) A general term for the whole of the *Sanads* issued by the Emperor and his officers, granting and giving possession of an assignment of revenue.

Sanad-debá-wálá, Uriya (ସନଦଦେବାୱାଲା) The grantor of a patent or assignment; and *Sanad-nebá-wálá* (ନେବା-ୱାଲା) The receiver of such a grant, the grantee.

Sanad-diwáni, H. (سندديواني) A grant or assignment of land, or rather of the government revenue assessed upon it.

Sanadi, corruptly, *Sanedey*, H. &c. (سندي) Relating to a *Sanad*.

Sanad-i-khun-bahá, H. (from خون, blood, and بها, price) A grant or deed conveying property from a person or family implicated in a murder, as a retaliatory fine to the heirs of the murdered person.

Sanad-i-milkiat-i-istimrár, H. (from A. ملكيت, mastership, and استمرار, continual) The deed or document by which the British government recognised the absolute ownership of the Zamindárs of Bengal, and in some parts of the south, at a fixed assessment: the term is current chiefly in the Northern Sarkárs.

Sanad-i-zamindár, H. (P. زميندار, a landholder) A Zamindár appointed under a royal patent, on default of heirs, to succeed to another Zamindár, or on the supercession of the latter.

Sanad-mániyam, Tam. (சநத்மானியம்) Rent-free land held under government.

Sanad-mutabih, H. (A. مطابق, in conformity with) The patent or grant issued by a subordinate local officer giving effect to an assignment or grant of revenue made by his superior to any individual, and recapitulating the particulars of the original alienation.

Sanad-navisand, H. (P. نويسند, let them write) A form of words inscribed by the chief authority upon the petition or application to him for a grant of revenue, after the necessary preliminaries had been completed.

Sannadi-inámu, Tel. (సన్నదియినాము) A grant of rent-free land held under a patent or order of the Mohammadan government.

SÁNAJÁ, Uriya (ସାନଜା) Husband's younger brother's wife.

SÁNAK, Mar. (सानक) Lit., A dish; fig., a patrimony, a grant of land as subsistence, without service attached.

SÁNÁN, plur. SÁNÁR, commonly, SANNAR, SHÁNÁR, or CHANAR, Tam. (சாணன்) The name of a low caste in the south of India, whose occupation is the extraction of juice from the fruit-stalk of cocoa-palm, which, when fermented, becomes *tári* or *toddy*.

SANCHA, Thug. A grave.

SANCHÁITA, Karn. (ಸಂಚಾಯಿತೆ) The management of an estate by the collector or revenue officers of the government.

SANCHAKÁRA, Karn. (ಸಂಚಕಾರ) Earnest-money: a pledge, a deposit.

SANCHÁYAM, Tam. (சஞ்சாயம்) Daily pay of a workman: the portion of the produce of a field assigned to the cultivator.

SANCHNÍ, Mar. (संचणी) The settlement of the leases and ground-rents of a village or country.

SÁND, pronounced, SÁNR, H. (سانڈ, सांड) A bull set at liberty as an act of piety or on festival occasions, and privileged to wander about at will.

SANDAI, Tam. (சந்தை) A market, a fair, an annual fair.

SANDÁITA, Karn. (ಸಂದಾಯಿತೆ) Land, &c., not let, but farmed by the proprietor or government: an estate, or the like, in charge of the collector or government officer, in opposition to what is farmed.

Sandáita-gár, Karn. (ಸಂದಾಯಿತೆಗಾರ) One who looks after government land that has not been rented.

SÁNDAWÁ, or SÁNDÁWÁ, Mar. (सांडवा) A vent, an outlet for superfluous water from a reservoir, a sluice.

SANDÁYA, Karn. (ಸಂದಾಯ) Delivering over, making payment.

SANDÁYAM, Tam. (சந்தாயம்) Any thing held in common: daily pay, &c. See *Sanchayam*.

Sandáyanilam, Tam. (சந்தாயநிலம்) Land held in common.

SANDHI, S., Mar. (संधि), SENDH, H. (سيندھ), SINDH, Beng. (সিংধ) A hole or breach in a wall made for the purpose of entering a house to steal: also, housebreaking, burglary. (*Sandhi* properly means a holding together, union, a joint, peace, alliance, and the like: its application to a hole in a wall may have arisen from dropping in practice some such term as *bhédana*, breaking, originally connected with it, as *Sandhi-bhédanam*, a breaking of continuity).

Sandhichora, or *-chaura*, S. (from चोर, चौर, a thief), *Sendhchor*, H. (سيندھچور), *Sindhchor*, Uriya (ସିନ୍ଧଚୋର) A burglar, a housebreaker.

Sandhichaurya, S. (from चौर्य, a theft), *Sendhchori*, H. (سيندھچوري) Housebreaking, burglary.

Sendh-kántá, H. (سيندهكانٹا), *Sindh-káṭí*, Beng. (সিংধকাটী) *Sindh-haṭhi*, Uriya (ସିନ୍ଧହାଠି) An instrument for making a hole in the wall, usually an iron pin about six or eight inches long for picking out the clay or mortar in mud or brick walls.

Sindhál, Beng. (সিংধাল), Uriya (ସିନ୍ଧାଲ) Housebreaking.

Sindhuál, Uriya (ସିନ୍ଧୁଆଲ) Burglary, housebreaking.

Sindhuáli, Uriya (ସିନ୍ଧୁଆଲି) A housebreaker, a burglar.

SANDHYÁ, S. &c. (संध्या, from संधि, a joint, a juncture), vernacularly, also SANJHÁ, H. (سنجها) Either of the three principal periods of the day, sunrise, noon, sunset; also the religious worship appropriately observed at those periods, whether performed singly, as by bathing at those hours in some sacred stream, accompanied by gesticulations and prayers, or with others, either in domestic worship or in temples, by communities of Brahmans: evening, twilight, and especially the service then performed.

SANDIVÁLAM, Tel., Karn. (సందివాలం) Penalty, penal sum: money lodged or deposited: per centage, commission.

SANGA, Hindi (S. संग) A bridge used in the Himalaya formed of timbers projecting from the banks one above another until they nearly meet, when the passage is completed by a plank laid across.

SANGAMA, vernacularly, SANGAM, S. &c. (संगम) Meeting, place of meeting, the confluence of two rivers, the debouche of a river in the sea.

Sangata, vernacularly, *Sangat*, S. &c. (संगत) Met, united: subst., a place of meeting, a meeting or assembly, a place of worship, a temple, a monastery.

Sangati, S. &c. (संगति) Union, assemblage, meeting. Tel. Karn. (సంగతి) Business, affair, circumstance, contents of a writing: in one vernacular form, *Sangai*, corruptly *Senghaie*, it denotes a kind of informal, but legal marriage.

SANGÓRU, Tel. (సంగోరు) Half of the whole produce of a crop: the share of the crop assigned to the cultivator, usually considered to be half the produce, but sometimes valued at only 20 or 30 per cent.

Sangóru-pálu, Tel. (సంగోరుపాలు) A half share.

SANGSAWÁR, H. (سنگسوار) A subdivision of the Kúrmi tribe in Bahar.

ṢANI, S. &c. (शनि) The planet Saturn or its regent.

Ṣanichar, H. (سنيچر. from S. शनैश्चर, the slow mover, or Saturn) The planet Saturn, also Saturday.

Ṣanivára, vernacularly, *Sanibár*, S. &c. (शनिवार) Saturn's day, Saturday.

SÁNI, H. (ساني) Chaff or straw mixed with grain or seeds from which oil has been expressed, as food for cattle.

ṢÁNI, Karn. (ಸಾನಿ, probably from the A. ثاني, a second) A companion.

Sáni, Tel. and Karn. (సాని) A term used to designate a woman; in some cases, especially as compounded, a woman of respectability, as *Dora-sáni*, a gentlewoman, a lady: by itself it more commonly denotes a dancing-girl.

Sáni-daphtar, or *Sání-sarishta*, Karn. (from the A. دفتر, an office, P, سرشته) A colleague in a public department, especially the revenue.

ṢÁNI-NÍLÁM, H. &c. (ثاني نيلام, from A. ثاني, second) Re-sale.

ṢÁNI-TAJWÍZ, H. (ثاني تجويز), ṢÁNITAJBÍJ, Hindi (शानितजबीज) Review of judgment, second investigation.

SANJÁITA, Karn. (ಸಂಜಾಯಿತಿ) The immediate management of any branch of revenue, by the officers of government. See *Sanchâïta*.

SANJAYATHI, (?) Hindi, Undivided land of a village, whether common or held in shares.—Kamaon.

Sanjayathi-asámí, Hindi (from اسامي, a cultivator) A hereditary non-proprietary cultivator, expected, when necessary, to contribute to the payment of the government revenue.

SANKALPA, vernacularly, SANKALP, corruptly, SUNKULLOP, SUNGKULUP, SHUNKULLUP, S. &c. (संकल्प) A solemn purpose, a mental determination or a deliberate announcement of an intention to perform some pious act, or make a charitable donation, which has the force of a vow: in law, the declared wish or will of a person deceased, made known before his decease, with regard to the disposal of property, adoption of a son, or the like, made before witnesses: this is considered in some degree as equivalent to a will or testament, an act which, strictly speaking, is not recognised by Hindu law: the term is also used with considerable laxity to designate lands held under a grant or bequest.

Sanhalpadár, H. (P. دار, who has) A person holding land rent-free or at a quit-rent under a solemn declaration or vow of the grantor: one who holds lands as security for a loan to the proprietors, which the borrower has solemnly promised to repay.

Sankalpa-náma, corruptly, *Shunkullub-náma*, H. (P. نامه, a document) A deed of gift or assignment according to a previous promise.

SANKARA, S. &c. (संकर) Intermixture, confusion.

Sankarajáti, S. &c. (संकरजाति) A mixed caste or race

springing from the intermarriages of different castes; also *Varṇa-sankara.*

Ṣankara, or Ṣankaráchárya, S. &c. (शंकराचार्य्य) The name of a celebrated teacher and reformer who lived about the eighth century, and founded a dominant sect of Saiva teachers, especially in the south of India, where the heads of many *maths* or monasteries, as at the great establishment of Sringagiri, are still termed *Ṣanharácháris*, or *Ṣankaráchâryas*: the designation *Ṣankaráchári* is also laxly applied to one of the two divisions of Brahmans which prevail in some parts of Telingana.

Ṣaṇkha, vernacularly, Sankh, or Shunkh, S. &c. (शंख) The conch shell (Voluta pyrum) which, when hollowed out, is used as a lamp before idols, or, when it has one end perforated, is blown as a horn at worship: it was also used as the war-horn of the ancient Hindu heroes: it is also cut into bracelets, called *Saṇkhá*, worn by women, and is one of the articles always borne by Vishnu.

Ṣáṇkhári, Beng. (শাংখারী) A shell cutter.

Sankhol, Thug. A party of three travellers.

Sankhot, (?) H. A share in the profits of a business.

Sankhot-gumáshta, H. (گماشته) A factor or agent with a share in the concern he acts for.

Saṇkránti, vernacularly, Sankránt, and Sankrát, S. &c. (संक्रान्ति) The passage of the sun or other planetary body from one sign of the zodiac to another.

Saṇku, S. &c. (शंकुः) The pin or gnomon of a dial: also the cross used in land surveying.

Sannyásí, S. &c. (संन्यासी) The Hindu of the fourth order, who has renounced the world and lives by mendicancy: the term is now applied to a variety of religious mendicants, some of whom wander singly about the country subsisting on alms, or are occasionally collected in *maths* under a spiritual head: the *Sannyási* is most usually a worshipper of Siva.

Sanoria, (?) H. The name of a class of depredators in Bundelkhand, living together in villages, and making armed excursions in gangs to rob and plunder, but they do not kill: they are patronized by the several Rájas of the districts in which they dwell, especially those of *Tekrí*, *Dattia*, and *Bánpúr*.

Saṇsárí, vulg., Sungsaree, S. &c. (संसारी, from संसार, the world) Worldly, a man of the world, the member of a religious or mendicant order who has a wife and family.

Saṇskára, S. (संस्कार) Making, perfecting: an essential ceremony of Hindu initiation, held indispensable to constitute the perfect purification of a Hindu: these ceremonies, which are principally oblations to fire, or customary offerings to idols, are restricted to the three first castes, and are quite inappropriate to the mixed castes, but in practice they are, in part at least, observed by all castes above the lowest. The number enjoined by authority is ten, or at most twelve, but in different parts of India others are added, extending them to seventeen: 1. *Garbhádhána*, worship on the first sign of conception, sometimes on a woman's attaining maturity; 2. *Punsavana*, worship to secure the birth of a male child performed at the expiration of the third month of pregnancy, or on signs of vitality in the embryo; *Anavalobhana*, a ceremony performed among the Marathas on the third month: it is much the same as the preceding, but, as the term implies, is intended to obviate miscarriage (*an*, not, *avalobhana*, disappointment); 4. *Símantonnayana*, parting of the hair on the head of a pregnant female in the 4th, 6th, or 8th month of a woman's first pregnancy; 5. *Vishṇubali*, a sacrifice to Vishṇu on the 7th month of pregnancy, apparently peculiar to the Marathas; 6. *Játakarma*, ceremonies at birth, comprising the putting some ghee out of a golden spoon into the mouth of the infant before cutting the navel-string; 7. *Námakaranam*, naming the child on the 10th, 11th, 12th, or 101st day after birth; 8. *Nishkramanam*, taking the child out of the house when three months old, or to see the moon in the third light fortnight; 9. *Súryávilokanam*, taking the child out to see the sun when four months old: this is much the same as the preceding, and both are rarely observed; 10. *Annaprásana*, feeding the child for the first time with rice, usually in the sixth or eighth month; 11. *Karṇavedha*, boring the ears, but this is not always practised; 12. *Chúḍá-* or *Chúlá-karanam*, or simply *Chauḍá*, vernacularly, *Chauṛa*, or *Chaula*, the ceremony of tonsure, shaving the head all but one lock, which is the *Chúḍá* or crest; it should be performed in the first or third year, and not delayed beyond the fifth, although this is sometimes disregarded; 13. *Upanayana*, investiture with the sacrificial thread, which is worn over the left shoulder and under the right arm, crossing the body to the hip; this is the most important ceremony of the whole, constituting the second or spiritual birth of the three first castes, thence termed *Dwija*, twice-born: for a Brahman it should be performed in the 8th year from conception, and not be delayed after the 16th;

SAN

for the Kshatriya in the 11th year, and for the Vaiṣya in the 12th, and is not to be later than the 22d and 24th severally: in practice, however, the Brahman is the only one of the three original castes remaining, and the only one entitled to the characteristic thread, although it is assumed without due warrant by some of the mixed castes; 14. *Sávitrí-mahánámya*, the ceremony of investiture accompanied by the repetition of the *Gáyatrí* which properly it always should be, but in some places this is considered as a different ceremonial, to be performed four days after the Upanayana; 15. *Samávarttana*, the ceremony performed on the student's completion of his studies and return home; 16. *Viváha*, marriage; 17. *Swargárohana*, ascending to heaven, funeral ceremonies; of these, however, the third, ninth, eleventh, fourteenth, and fifteenth, are either local, or are mere modifications of other ceremonies, leaving them only twelve, and, by excluding the boring of the ears, and the funeral obsequies, which can scarcely be looked upon as purificatory, the number is reduced to the correcter one of ten: women have only the *Sanskára* of marriage. *Súdras* perform most of them except the *Upanayana*, *Sávitrí*, and *Samávarttanam*, but with different prayers and observances.

SAṆSRISHṬA, S. &c. (संसृष्टः) Re-united, as a family, or any member of it who, after having been separated and had his share of the property, brings it back again, and is once more a joint parcener in the family stock.

Saṇsrishṭí S. &c. (संसृष्टी) A member of a re-united family, one who continues to reside with his coheirs after partition.

SAṆSTHÁNA, S. &c. (from सम्, together, and स्थान, place, abiding) A common abode, a place where many persons dwell together, a palace, a monastery, a neighbourhood. Mar. (संस्थान), corruptly, *Sanwasthan*, *Suvusthan*, *Sowusthan*, a town, a royal town or capital, also a place supposed to be the scene of the manifestation of a deity, or sanctified by the residence of celebrated teachers or saints: a town or place made over for the especial maintenance of some deity or religious community: the site of any event considered deserving of religious commemoration. Beng. (সংস্থান) A collection of goods or money, stock, capital.

SANT, Mar. &c. (S. संत) A holy man, a religious mendicant.

SANTA, Tel. (సంత), SANTE, Karn. (ಸಂತೆ), SANTAI, Tam. (சந்தை), SÁNT, Guz. (સાંત) A market, a fair, an assemblage for the sale of goods, also in Guz., land-tax assessment.

SÁNTÁ, Hindi (सांता) Sugar-cane.—Mherwara.

SANTAK, Uriya (ସନ୍ତକ) A mark, a signature.

SANTÁN, H. (A. ستان) Circumcision.

SANTÁNA, SANTATI, S. &c. (संतान, संतति) Offspring, progeny, descendants.

SÁNṬH, Mar. (सांठ) A collection, a store.

Sánṭhwan, Mar. (सांठवण) A place or vessel in which any thing is kept, a garner, a bin, a repository.

Sánṭhwaṇí, Mar. (सांठवणी) A collection of still or stagnant water.

SANTH, Thug. A sword.

SÁNTÍ, Guz. (સાંતી) A measure of land either 60 or 90 *Wígas* or *Bighás*; each being 160 yards by 10.

ṢÁNTI, pron. vernacularly SHÁNTI, S. &c. (शान्ति) Calm, quiet, expiation, preliminary or supplementary sacrifice.

Ṣánti-jal, Beng. (শান্তিজল) Water from a sacred stream used in worship, holy water.

Ṣántikarma, S. &c. (शान्तिकर्म्म) Any purificatory or expiatory sacrifice intended to deprecate or avert calamity: a supplementary sacrifice intended to atone for any defects in the primary ceremony.

SANTOSHAPAṬṬÍ, Mar. (संतोषपट्टी) A cess levied upon the cultivators by a Rája or Zamindár, on an occasion of rejoicing, as the birth of a son, &c.

SÁNWAK, corruptly, SAWUK, SAUNK, SAUNKIA, SUNKIA, and SANKIA, Hindi (सांवक) A slave, in Chota Nagpur: there are three classes; the *Sánwak*, who is hereditary; the *Bandha Sánwah*, a slave for life, but whose children are not slaves; and the *Chúta Sánwak*, a slave for debt under a written bond. In the districts bordering on Chota Rangpur, or Ramgarh, Hazaribagh, &c., the *Sánwak* is described as one who becomes a slave for life on receiving a certain sum of money, and who cannot redeem himself by repayment of the original advance: according to other authorities he may redeem himself, but is seldom able to do so. The *Sánwaks* are generally from the low or outcaste hill tribes.

Sánwak-námá corruptly, *Saunk-námá*, Hindi (सांवकनामा) A written obligation by which a person borrowing money bound himself, and sometimes his family, to be slaves for life, or until the debt was repaid.

SANYERI, (?) Mar. Pure black soil, free from gravel.

SANYOGÍ, vernacularly, SANJOGÍ, S. &c. (संयोगी) A religious man who leads the life of a householder, or has a wife and family.

SAPATNÍ, S. &c. (सपत्नी) A fellow-wife, the wife of a man who has others, but especially any other than the one first married.

ṢAPATHA, S. &c. (शपथ) An oath, an imprecation.

Ṣapatha-patra, S. &c. (शपथपत्र) An affidavit.

ṢAPHÁI, Uriya (ଛାପ|ଇ, from A. صاف, clean) Clean salt boiled to a certain point.

SAPHARÍ, Guz. (સફરી, from the A. *safar*, a journey, also Guz. a voyage) A sailor; a ship: maritime or foreign trade from all countries beyond the Gulph of Cutch.

SAPÍNA, or sometimes SAFÍNA, H. &c. (سپینه ,سفینه) A summons, a subpœna.

SAPINḌA, S. &c. (सपिण्ड, from स, together, पिण्ड, a ball of rice or meat) A kinsman connected by offerings of balls of rice or of meat to common ancestors; the affinity extends to three individuals only in descent from the common ancestor: some authorities extend it to seven persons in both the ascending and descending line.

SAPTAPADÍ, and SAPTAPADÍ-KRAMAṆA, Mar. (S. सप्तपदी, सप्तपदीक्रमण, from सप्त, seven, पद, a foot, and क्रमण, walking) An essential part of the marriage ceremony, the bride's being led seven steps round the sacred fire.

SAR, SUR, H. &c. (P. سر, सर) The head, also, metaphorically, chief, principal: (the word is used very extensively in most of the dialects in forming compounds to intimate superiority or comprehensiveness, and has been in general very corruptly rendered by *Ser*, *Sir*, or even *Cir*, as will be seen below, but SIR is also sometimes the correct reading in the Hindu dialects, the word being derived from the S. *Ṣiras* (शिरस्) the head in general: however, the Persian derivation through the Hindustani is to be preferred.

Saranjám, *Surunjam*, corruptly, *Sarunjam*, *Serinjam*, *Surinjam*, H. &c. (P. سرانجام, सरंजाम) Apparatus, provisions, furniture, materials, what is essential to any undertaking: amongst the Maraṭhas it was applied especially to a temporary assignment of revenue from villages or lands for the support of troops or for personal military service, usually for the life of the grantee; also to grants made to persons appointed to civil offices of the state to enable them to maintain their dignity, and to grants for charitable purposes: these were neither transferable nor hereditary, and were held at the pleasure of the sovereign. They were distinguished as *Ját Saranjám* (from *ját*, individual), when personal, and *Phauj Saranjám* (from *phauj* for *fauj*, an army), when for keeping up troops.

Saranjám-dár, Mar. (P. دار, who has) The holder of an assignment for purposes specified.

Saránjámí, corruptly, *Serinjammy*, H. (سرانجامي) Relating or belonging to apparatus, materials, means of support, &c. In Bengal, under the Mohammadan government, the term was applied to allowances sometimes granted or admitted as deductions for the charges and expenses of collecting the revenue, or other incidental expenses made to the Zamindárs or farmers. Among the Maraṭhas; relating to assignments for public service, as *Saranjámí* lands and the like: a person holding such assignments.

Saranjámí-jáhgír, Mar. (जाहगीर for P. جاگير) An assignment of revenue for keeping up troops, &c.

Sar-á-pá, H. (سراپا, lit., head to foot) A complete *khilat*, or honorary dress, especially given on appointment to office by the Mogul government.

Sarásarí, H. &c. (سراسري), Tel. (సరాసరి), Tam. (சராசரி) A summary, a mean, an average, an estimate. Mar. (सरासरी) Loosely, carelessly, roughly, as a rough statement or estimate. In Hindustani the more usual form is *Sarsari*, q. v.

Sarásari-kaniku, Tam. (சராசரிக்கணக்கு) An average or rough account.

Sarásari-merai, Tam. (சராசரிமெரை) Average proportion of the crop set apart for the village officers and servants. See *Merai*.

Sar-ba-ráh, H. (P. سربراه, lit., head or means for the road, براه) Supply, means of providing for charges or expenses.

Sarbaráhkár, corruptly, *Sabracar*, *Serbarrakar*, *Surberakar*, H. (P. كار, who does) A manager, a steward, a factor, a trustee: the manager of an estate for minors, females, idiots, or disqualified proprietors, an officer appointed to such duty by the Court of Wards under the British government: the manager on behalf of unseparated coparceners. In Cuttack the title was given to the village accountant when he was the general director and manager of the revenue affairs, being paid by a per centage on the collections of his village; in some cases the office had become hereditary but without the right of alienation without the permission of the Zamindár.

Sarbaráhkárí, H. (P. كاري, agency) Management of property, stewardship, trust.

Sar-daftar, H. (P. دفتر, record) Chief record office: chief accountant and registrar.

Sar-daftar-diwáni, H. (P. ديوان, revenue minister) The chief clerk of the office of the Diwán.

Sarbaráhkár paṭṭa, H. (پټّه, a deed) A deed appointing a manager or steward.

Sardár, commonly, but incorrectly, *Sirdár*, H. &c. (سردار) A chief, a head man, a commander: the head of a set of palankin bearers.

Sardar-i-fauj, H. (P. فوج, an army) Commandant, the title of the provincial governor or collector when charged with the duties of Faujdár or commander of the troops: the title of an Amíldár under the Mohammadan government as head of the police.

Sardar-âmil, H. (A. عامل) The head *Ámil* or collector of an extensive district, invested with magisterial and military authority.

Sardární, H. (سردارني) A female head of an establishment, commonly applied to a woman who brings up girls for prostitution.

Sardeṣmukh, or *Sardeshmukh*, incorrectly, *Sirdeshmukh*, Mar. (सरदेशमुख) The head of the Maratha officers termed *Deṣmukhs* in an extensive district, and standing between them and the government: see *Deṣmukh*: in some places the title has become hereditary, and even a portion of the fees attached to the office subsist without any authority being exercised.

Sardeṣmukhí, or *Sardesmukhi*, incorrectly, *Sirdesmukhi*, Mar. (सरदेशमुखी) The office of head *Deṣmukh*. The proportion of 10 per cent. exacted by the Marathas from the revenues of the Mohammadan territories of the Dakhin, in addition to the *chauth*: it was originally claimed by *Sivají* as head *Deṣmukh*, whence the name, and was confirmed by Mohammad Shah. In some places it was an impost of 12½ per cent. in addition to the fixed assessment.

Sarhang, incorrectly, *Serang*, H. (P. سرهنك) A commander, but generally applied in India to the head man of a native crew, whether on board a ship or a boat; also to the head man of a gang of natives attached to artillery, dragging guns, or to the army in general, as tent-pitchers, and the like, or to the head of gangs of a superior order of labourers employed in public or private works, in docks, buildings, &c.

Sardeṣpánde, or *Sardeṣpándya*, incorrectly, *Sirdespandye*, Mar. (सरदेशपाण्ड्या) The head district registrar and accountant. See *Deṣpánde*.

Sarfarázi, H. (P. سرفرازي) Promotion, exaltation, notice or favour of a superior.

Sarhad, *Surhud*, corruptly, *Serkud*, *Sirhad*, *Surrud*, H. &c. (سرحد) Boundary, border, confines, limit.

Sarhad-bandí, H. &c. (بندي, a binding) Fixing a boundary by authority.

Sarhad-háṣil, (A. حاصل) Frontier duties.

Sar-kánungo, H. (P. قانونگو, a registrar) A chief *kánungo*, the provincial or district registrar and accountant: in Kandesh, a charge of one per cent. in addition to the revenue to defray the salary of a head *kánungo*.

Sarkár, more commonly, but incorrectly, *Sircar*, or *Sirkar*, H. &c. (سركار, सरकार, or सर्कार, from P. سر, the head, and كار, business), *Sarakáru*, Tel. Karn. (సరకారు) The government, the state, the supreme authority or administration: the governing authority or administrator of affairs: the ruler, the king; now generally applied to the Company's government, and to any of its civil or political officers: a landlord, a proprietor, a superintendant, a chief, a manager: in Bengal it commonly denotes a native servant who keeps the household accounts and receives and disburses money for his employer, a sort of house-steward; also any writer or accountant. The term likewise signified an extensive division of country under the Mohammadan government, a subdivision of a *Ṣúbah*, containing many parganas; a district, a province: (in this sense it has been usually, though incorrectly, written *Circar*, as in the case of the Northern Circars.)

Sarkár-âálí, H. (سركارعالي) The high court, the chief authority, the government, the viceregal establishment of the Nawab of Bengal: a Jagír or assignment to defray the expenses of the Nawab household was so termed (incorrectly *Circar Ali*).

Sarakárada-káni, Karn. (ಸರಕಾರದಹಾಣಿ) Public money, the money of the state.

Sarakarada-kacheri, Karn. (ಸರಕಾರದಕಚೇರಿ) Any government office.

Sarkárdhárá, Mar. (सर्कारधारा) Assessment or taxes imposed by the state on real property.

Sarkárí, incorrectly, *Sirkárí*, H. &c. (سركاري, सरकारी) Relating or belonging to the government, or to any superior authority.

Sarkárí-patit, Hindi (सरकारीपतित, from S. *patita*, fallen) Land left uncultivated for more than two years, and then claimable by the landlord or the government: all lands lying waste, and not included in the assessment.

Sarkári-waẓífa, H. (A. وظيفه, an allowance) Allowances or assignments or pensions granted by government.

Sarkár-kharáb, Mar. (सरकारखराब, from P. خراب, bad)

Lying fallow or uncultivated in the hands of the government, land, &c.

Sarkhaṯ, *Surkhuṯ*, corruptly, *Sirkut*, H. (A. P. سرخط) A written agreement, a receipt, a bill of sale, a deed of lease: a note of acknowledgment from the government to payers of the revenue, bearing upon it the successive instalments paid into the treasury.

Mahájani-sarkhat, H. (from महाजन, a merchant) An acknowledgment granted by a banker or merchant for money deposited.

Sarkhel, Mar. (सरखेल) A title of rank amongst the Marathas conferred by the Peshwa (from the P. *Sar-khail* سرخيل, a general).

Sarkíl, Tam. (சர்க்கீல்), *Sarikíli*, Tel. (సరికీలి) A minister, a chamberlain, a major-domo (no doubt the same as *Sarkhel*, vernacularly modified).

Sarmukh, Mar. (सरमुख) A head or principal chief, the title of the Holkar family.

Sarnáḍu-gauḍa, corruptly, *Sirna-gaur*, *Surnan-gour*, Karn. (సరనాడుగౌడ) The head farmer or principal person in an agricultural district.

Sarnáma, H. (سرنامه) Direction, address, superscription, heading.

Sarnaubat, Mar. (सरनौबत, from P. نوبت, a kettle-drum) The highest military officer under the Peshwa: also the governor of a fort, or of a part of it.

Sarnisbat, Mar. (सरनिसबत) An officer under the former government, one under the Havildár also superintending public works.

Sar-o-pá, corruptly, *Sirpao*, *Serpaw*, H. (سروپا, lit., hand and foot) A complete dress of honour.

Sarpanch, H. (سرپنچ) The president of a *Pancháit*.

Sar-pátil, Mar. (सरपाटील) The head man of a district, the chief *Pátil*: it applied also to a sort of petty Zamindár, or an officer who superintended the assessment and collection of the rents of a district, and received a per centage on their realisation.

Sar-parast, H. (P. پرست, protecting) A patron, a protector, a guardian.

Sar-rishta, more commonly, but less correctly, *Sarishta*, or *Surishtu*, corruptly, *Serishta*, *Sherista*, and *Sherishtah*, H. (سررشته, from P. سر and رشته, a line or thread, also سرشته) A record, a register, office, employment: an office of registry or record: it is sometimes, but inaccurately, used for the officer. See *Sarrishtadár*.

Sírastá, Uriya (ଶିରସ୍ତା) Establishment.

Siṛastá, or *Siristá*, Mar. (शिरस्ता, शिरिस्ता) Practice, custom (it is of course the H. *Sarrishta*).

Sarrishtadár, or *Sarishtadár*, H. (سررشته‌دار, سرشته‌دار) *Siraste-*, *Siriste-dár*, Mar. (शिरस्तेदार, शिरिस्तेदार) A registrar, a record keeper, applied especially to the head native officer of a court of justice or collector's office, who has the general superintendence of the establishment and charge of the public records and official documents and papers: it formerly denoted the head provincial or district *kánungo* or a head officer of the Ámil, exercising a superintending and controlling power over the other district registrars and accountants.

Sarrishtah-i-Amánat, H. (A. امانت, trust) In Bengal, under the Mohammadan and early British rule, an office for the examination and adjustment of disputed and outstanding accounts, particularly those of officers dismissed or charged with embezzlement or undue exactions.

Sarrishtah-diwáni, H. (P. ديوان) The office of Diwán, or collector, also the expenses of his office, including his own allowances.

Sirasta-baṭṭá, Mar. (from बट्टा, exchange) A cess levied by the Peshwa's collectors on the cultivators, to cover the risk of loss on the exchange of different currencies at the treasury at Púnah.

Sarsál, Mar. (सरसाल, from P. سال, a year) A whole year, for or during a whole year, as *Sar-sál-jamá-kharch*, the year's account of collections and charges.

Sarsálá, or *Sarsálí*, Mar. (सरसाला, -साली) Belonging or relating to a whole year, as receipts, charges, &c.

Sarsarí or *Sarásarí*, H. (P. سرسري, سراسري) Easy, loose, transacted loosely or concisely, summary.

Sarsari-ápil, H. (آپيل, Eng. 'appeal') A summary appeal.

Sarsarí-faiṣala, H. (A. فيصله) Summary decision, or nonsuit.

Sarsarí-muhaddama, H. (A. مقدّمه) A summary suit.

Sar-shikan, H. (P. سرشکن, lit., breaking of the head or capital) A grant of revenue in charity, or to village officers, made under the Mohammadan government by the Zamindárs or fiscal authorities: it was so termed because the land so appropriated was taken in small lots from different holders: the tenure was peculiar to the province of Bahár. In Tirhut it signifies a rent-free tenure: (according to Buchanan's 'Eastern India,' vol. I. p. 311, it derived its name from its being granted to the families of

Zamindárs who had lost their lives in the public service, but this seems doubtful).

Sar-shikan-mahál, H. (A. محال) A rent-free estate.—Tirhut.

Sar-shumárí, H. (from P. شماري, a counting) A census, a poll-tax.

Sarsubhedár, corruptly, *Sirsoobeedar*, Mar. (सरसुभेदार) An officer of the Maratha government superior to the *Mámlatdár*.

Sarzamín, corruptly, *Sarjamín*, H. (P. زمين, land) Boundary, limit, tract of country.

Ṣarjamín-tahkikát, Uriya (ସରଯମିନତହ୍କିକାତ) Local investigation.

SÁRÁ, corruptly, SARRA, Mar. (सारा), also with DORÁ, pleonasm, SÁRÁDORÁ, (सारादोरा) A tax on fields and enclosures, land-tax.

ṢÁRÁ, H. (سارا, from श्याल) A wife's brother, a brother in law.

ṢARAD, or ṢARAT, S. &c. (शरद् -त्) The season of Autumn, the two months following the rains, or about Sept.-Oct.

SARADAR, Uriya (ସରଧର) Land of the first quality.

SARÁÍ, H. (P. سراي) A palace, a large edifice, a building for the shelter and accommodation of travellers, usually a quadrangle surrounded by low chambers opening internally, and backed by a dead wall, the square, in the centre of which are the heavy luggage and beasts of burden, being entered by a gateway, the gate of which is closed at night: an inn, a caravanserai.

Saráï-wakfi, H. (from A. وقفي) An endowed *saráï*, the maintenance of which is provided for by an endowment, and accommodation in which is gratuitous.

SARAÏO, corruptly, SURREIYO, Guz. (સરઈઓ) A druggist, a perfumer.

SARAK, H. (سڑك) A road.

Sarak-bandí, H. (سڑكبندي) A high road or common way, as distinguished from a cross road or bye-way.

SARAḲ, or SARIḲ, SARAḲA, or SARIḲA, also read SARKA, and, incorrectly, SERKA, H. (A. سرق, سرقة) Larceny, theft, defined, in Mohammadan law, as the taking away secretly of the property of another at a time when it is, or supposed to be, in security, or under charge.

Saraḳa, or *Sariḳa*, or *Sarḳa-i-sughra*, H. (A. صغرى, small) Petty larceny, theft without violence.

Saraḳa, Sariḳa, or *Sarḳa-i-kubra*, H. (A. كبرى, great) Theft, or robbery with violence.

SARAKU, Tam. (சரக்கு), SARUKU, Tel. (సరుకు) Goods, commodities, merchandise.

SARAḶVYÁJ, Mar. (सरळव्याज) Simple interest.

ṢARAṆA, S. &c. (शरण) Asylum, refuge, shelter, protection.

Ṣaraṇágata, S. &c. (शरणागतः) A refugee, a suppliant, one who comes for protection.

ṢARÁṆÁ, Tel. (శరాణా) A fine levied upon persons stealing ears of corn, also on cattle trespassing on corn-fields.

SÁRANI, Tel. (సారణి) A sluice, a canal, a drain.

SÁRÁNS, blunderingly, SAROUCH, Mar. (सारांश, from S. सार, essence, and अंश, a share) An abstract, an epitome, a short statement of proceedings kept by the *Pancháit*, and, at the close, signed by each member.

SARÁP, H. (S. سراپ) A curse, an imprecation, an oath.

ṢARAPÁT, Uriya (ସରପାଟ) Marshy land (of a better description).

SARAS-NIRAS, H. (سرس نيرس, from S. रस, flavour, and the particles स with, and निर्, without) Good and bad: applied sometimes to distinguish the quality of a soil, or to its distribution: the good with the bad.

SÁRASWATA, vernacularly, SÁRASWAT, S. &c. (सारस्वत) The country about the *Sárasnatí* river to the north-west of Dehli: the designation of a tribe of Brahmans subdivided into ten classes, and supposed to have come originally from the north-west of India: many of the *Sáraswat* Brahmans cultivate literature, and they are in general a respectable body.

Saraswatí, S. &c. (सरस्वती) The goddess of letters and arts: the name of a river, commonly *Sarsútí* or *Sursootee*.

Saraswatí-pújá, S. &c. (from पूजा) The worship of the goddess *Saraswatí*, observed on the 5th of the light half of *Áṣwin* (Aug.-Sept.), on which occasion books and the implements of writing are held sacred and are worshipped.

SÁRATHÍ, corruptly, SARTHEE, S. &c. (सारथी) The driver of a car, a charioteer: the designation of a mixed caste said to have sprung from a Kshatriya father and Brahman mother.

SARAWÁ, or SARWÁ, Mar. (सरवा) A piece of hill ground cleared and cultivated for not longer than a year or two past: ground recently reaped.

Sarawebhát, Mar. (सरवेभात) Rice reared on recently cleared hill ground.

SÁRÁYA, Karn. (ಸಾರಾಯ), SÁRÁYAM, Tam. (சாராயம்) Any kind of spirituous liquors.

Sáráya-guttige, Karn. (ಸಾರಾಯಗುತ್ತಿಗೆ) A tax levied on spirituous liquors.

Sáráyakáran, Tam. (சாராயக்காரன்) A distiller.

SARBALAND KHÁN, Thug. A proper name uttered to direct the stranglers to be ready, also to denote the approach of danger.

SÁRBÁN, H. (P. ساربان) A camel driver.

Ṣarf, incorrectly, Ṣerf, H. &c. (A. صرف) Expenditure, exchange: in Mohammadan law, a pure sale, a sale of price for price, or one in which the articles exchanged are both representatives of price, as silver for gold, an exchange of representative values.

Ṣarf-i-sikka, H. (صرف سکّه) A charge or discount on the different currencies receivable at the public treasury: an impost or cess established at one time in Bengal to cover the loss accruing on exchange of coins.

Ṣarráf, commonly, *Saraf*, vernacularly, *Saráph*, *Sarápe*, *Sarápu*, *Sarábu*, corruptly, *Saraff*, *Sharáf*, *Shroff*, H. (صرّاف), Mar. (सराफ), Tel. (సరాఫు), Karn. (ಸರಾಫ, ಸರಾಫು, ಸರಾಬು) A money-changer, a banker, an officer employed to ascertain the value of different currencies.

Ṣarráfa, H. (A. صرافه) The place where money is exchanged, a banker's, a money-changer's shop.

Ṣarráfí, or *Saráfí*, H. (A. صرافي) The business of a money-changer: also, discount on exchange of coins, and fees paid for examining and valuing different currencies, commonly, *Shroffing*, and *Shroffage*.

Sáṛhú, H. (سارهو), Sáḍú, or Saṛú, Mar. (साडू) A wife's sister's husband.

Ṣare, Ṣere, Karn. (ಶೆರೆ, ಶೆರೆ) Imprisonment, slavery, bondage, captivity.

Ṣare-bandhána, Karn. (ಶೆರೆಬಂಧಾನ) Confinement, imprisonment.

Ṣare-mane, Karn. (ಶೆರೆಮನೆ) A jail, a prison.

Ṣare-viḍidava, Karn. (ಶೆರೆವಿಡಿದವ) A captive, a prisoner of war.

Ṣare-viḍugaḍe, Karn. (ಶೆರೆವಿಡುಗಡೆ) Liberation from prison.

Sarehá, Hindi (सरेहा) A narrow field, much longer than broad.

Sáṛhe, H. &c. (سارهي, S. *Sárddha*, from स, with, and अर्द्ध, a half), Sáḍe, and Sáṛe, Beng. (সাড়ে), Sáḍá, or Sáṛá, Mar. (साडा, pl. साडे) A half of a unit in addition to any given number above two, whether applied to number, weight, or value; as *Sáṛhe-tín*, three and a half, *Sáṛhe-panch-man*, five *mans* and a half, *Sáṛhe-panch-rupaiya*, five rupees and a half, or five rupees eight *anas*: the fraction must have reference to the unit in a decimal ratio: *Sáṛhe-nau-rupaiya* would be nine rupees eight *anas*, but *Sáṛhe-das-rupaiya* will be fifteen rupees; so *Sáṛhe-tín-sau*, will be 350, *Sáṛhe-tín-hazár*, 3500, *Sáṛhe-tín-lákh*, 350,000, the half being that of the respective unit.

Sáṛhí, or Sáṛí, corruptly, Sarrie, H. &c. (سارهي, ساري, S. शाटी), Sáḍí, or Sáṛí, Mar. (साडी) A long cloth worn by Hindu women, wrapped round the body and passed over the head, the only usual attire of the lower classes.

Sari, Tel., Karn. (సరి), Tam. (சரி) Equal, right, just, even; also, subst., equality, fitness.

Sari-bhágamu, Tel. (సరిభాగము) An equal share.

Sari-mérai, Tam. (சரிமெறை) Established, proper or just rights or privileges of individuals.

Ṣarkará, S. &c. (शर्करा) Gravel, sand, gravelly or sandy soil: clayed or candied sugar.

Sarná, Hindi (सरना) A spot of land on which trees are not to be cut (Chota Nagpur).

Sártha, S. &c. (सार्थ) A company of travellers or traders, a *kafila*, a caravan.

Sárthaváha, S. &c. (सार्थवाह) A merchant, a trader: the head of a corporation, the leader of a caravan.

Sárthi, S. &c. (सार्थी) A trader, a traveller, one of a company of traders, especially the head or leader of a caravan.

Sárú, or Sáṛhú, H. (سارهو, سارو) A wife's sister's husband.

Sarugudu, Tel. (సరుగుడు) A platform on which plants are placed ready for conveyance to the fields in which they are to be transplanted.

Saṛukai, Tam. (சறுக்கை) An outlet for the surplus water of a reservoir, a sluice or flood-gate.

Saruku, Tel., Karn. (సరుకు) Goods, commodities, merchandise. See *Sarahu*.

Sáruva, Tel. (సారువ) A small bridge over a water-course.

Saruvá, Tel. (సారువా) Low ground cultivation.

Sáruvápanṭa, Tel. (సారువాపంట) A crop in low wet ground.

Sáruvu, Tel. (సారువు) A ridge or low bank.

Sarva, S., but adopted in all the dialects, sometimes modified, as Sarba, Beng., Sarvamu, Tel., and abridged to Sab, Sub, Hindi (सर्व) All, entire, whole.

Sarvadhárí, S. &c. (सर्वधारी, lit., all-containing) The twenty-second year of the cycle.

Sarvadumbálá, Tel. (సర్వదుంబాలా) An allotment of land entirely rent-free.

Sarvágrahárammu, Tel. (సర్వాగ్రహారము) A village granted to Brahmans, entirely rent-free.

Sarva-inamu, Tel. (సర్వయినాము, from A. *Inam*, q. v.) Land held free of any charge or tax: a grant of the entire revenues of a village or tract of land.

Sarvajit, S. &c. (सर्वजित्, lit., all-victorious) The twenty-first year of the cycle, A.D. 1828—1888.

Sarvamániyam, or *Sarvamányum*, Tam. (சர்வமானி-

யம்) Land granted in free tenure, or exempt entirely from payment of revenue or rent to the grantor, whether the individual proprietor or the government.

Sarvamokhásá, Tel. (సర్వ మొఖాసా) Land free of all revenue charges.

Sarvapanṭa, Tel. (సర్వపంట) The first crop of wet land, the entire crop.

ṢÁRVARÍ, S. &c. (शार्व्वरी) The thirty-fourth year of the cycle.

SARWÁŪ, SARWÁÍŪ, Guz. (સરવાઉ, સરવાઈઉ) Monthly or yearly balance: sum total: summing up of accounts.

SÁS, or SÁSU, H. &c. (ساس, from S. श्वश्रू) A mother in law.

ṢASA, pl., ṢASALU, Tel. (శసలు) Grains of rice mixed with turmeric or other colouring ingredients, and used on auspicious occasions, as at marriages, when a basket containing the mixture is severally placed before the bride and bridegroom, and each in succession casts some over the head of the other: the ceremony of thus casting the rice.

ṢÁSANAM, S. &c. vernacularly, SÁSAN, or SHÁSAN, (शासनं) Ordering, directing, restraining, punishing, a royal order or edict, a royal grant, a patent, especially such as is commonly engraved on copper plates: a written engagement or contract, a written deed of any kind: in Cuttack, a village held by Brahmans in joint tenancy, either rent-free or at a quit-rent. Besides its usual imports, it implies in Tam. (சாசனம்) An oath; punishment.

Ṣásanavṛitti, S. &c. (शासनवृत्ति) Maintenance enjoyed under a written deed or grant.

Ṣilásásana, S. &c. (from शिला, a stone) A grant or edict inscribed on stone.

Támra-ṣásana, S. &c. (from ताम्र, copper) An edict or grant inscribed on copper plates.

Dhárásásana, Karn. (ಧಾರಾಶಾಸನ) A deed or gift of land, &c.

Krayaṣásana, Karn. (S. क्रय, sale) A deed of sale.

SÁSHTÁNGA, S. &c. (साष्टाङ्ग, from स, with, अष्ट, eight, and अंग, limb) Lit., with eight limbs: an adjunct to words signifying salutation, as *Namaskára*, *Praṇáma*, &c., reverential salutation, address, or prostration, so as to touch the ground with the eight parts of the body, the two hands, two feet, two knees, the breast, and the forehead..

SÁSTHÍ, (?) Mar. Land paying to government the maximum assessment (there is no doubt some blunder in the spelling of this word).

ṢÁSTRA, vulgarly, SHASTRA, corruptly, SHASTER, S. &c. (शास्त्रं) An order or command, a scripture, a work of authority, especially one attributed to an inspired writer: when used with a word implying the subject treated of, it may denote either a single work of the class, or the writings collectively; thus, *a Dharma-ṣástra* may imply the code of Manu, or any work of authority on the laws and the institutes of the Hindus, whilst *the Dharma-ṣástra*, means the whole science of law, and the body of the social institutions: the word is also used generally for any literary or scientific composition, or for any branch of investigation.

Ṣástrí, vulgarly, *Shastree*, S. &c. (शास्त्री) A man of learning, one who teaches any branch of Hindu learning, an expounder of Hindu law.

SASUR, or SUSAR, H. (سسر), SÁSARÁ, or SÁSUR, Mar. (सासरा, सासुर), ṢWAṢUR, Beng. (শ্বশুর), SWASURA, S. (श्वशुर) A father in law, whether of the husband or wife.

Sásre, Mar. (सास्रे) The house of a husband's father.

Sásurvás, Mar. (सासुरवास) The residence of a married girl in the house of her husband's father: the annoyance she suffers there.

Sásurvásí, or *Sásurvásin*, Mar. (सासुवाशीण) A young married woman living in the house of her husband's parents, and proverbially treated with great harshness.

ṢASYA, S. &c. (शस्यः, सस्य) Grain or corn in general, as wheat, barley, rice, &c.: also fruit.

Ṣasyakshetra, S. &c. (शस्यक्षेत्र) A corn-field.

ṢÁṢWATABERIJU, Tel., Karn. (శాశ్వత బెరిజు, from S. शाश्वत, perpetual, and P. بريج, an account) The perpetual assessment of lands, an established village assessment.

Ṣaṣwatapaṭṭi, Karn. (ಶಾಶ್ವತಪಟ್ಟಿ) A permanent grant.

SÁṬA, SÁṬI, Karn. (ಸಾಟ, ಸಾಟಿ) adj. Like, similar: subst. barter, exchange.

Sáṭáberamu, *Sátákotiberamu*, Tel. (సాటాబేరము, సాటాకోటిబేరము) Barter.

Sáṭeṇloṭeṇ, Mar. (साटेंलोटें) Traffic by exchange, barter; whence intermarrying in two families.

Sáṭíbéra, Karn. (ಸಾಟೀಬೇರ) Bartered merchandise.

Sáṭigár, Karn. (ಸಾಟಿಗಾರ) A barterer, a trader, a merchant.

Sáṭívyápára, Karn. (ಸಾಟಿವ್ಯಾಪಾರ) Bartered merchandise.

SÁTÁNI, or SATÁḶI, Tel., Karn. (సాతాని, సాతాళి) The name of a caste, or an individual belonging to it: the *Sátánis* are Ṣúdras exclusively worshipping Vishṇu, and living chiefly on alms, but practising music.

SÁTEṆ, Mar. (साटें), SÁTUṆ, Guz. (સાટું) A whole investment, the whole quantity brought to market by one person: buying up such an investment, or a bargain to purchase it.

Sáṭekhat, or *Sáṭepatra*, Mar. (**साटेखत, साटेपत्र**) The deed or writing which is executed on the purchase of a whole investment. *Sátákhát*, Guz. (સાટાખત) A written engagement to purchase goods or lands within a specified time: a written contract of sale, any written agreement.

SATHA, Thug. The first seven days of an expedition.

ṢAṬHÁNÁ, Tel. (శఠానా) A fine inflicted on persons stealing ears of corn.

SÁṬHÍ, H. (ساٹھی, S. **षष्टि**, sixty) A kind of rice ripening in the rains about sixty days after sowing.

SAṬHÍÁ, H. (سٹھیا), SÁTHÍO, Guz. (સાથીઓ) A figure made by Hindu women in place of a signature to written deeds: a kind of figured cross prefixed to account books, and also formed with flour on the ground at marriages and other festivals: a surgeon.

SATHNA, Thug. A Mohammadan.

SATHOT, Thug. The person whose office it is to strangle the victims.

SÁTHZÁT, Thug. The seven original clans of the Thugs, who were all Mohammadans.

SATÍ, corruptly, SUTTEE, S. &c. (**सती**, fem. of **सत्**, good) A virtuous wife, especially one who consummates a life of duty by burning herself on the funeral pile of her husband, either with the body, or separately if her husband have died at a distance.

Satíwár, H. (ستیوار) The place where a widow has been burned, sometimes marked by a peculiar monument.

SATIN, Beng. (সতিন) A co-wife, expressing the relationship of a man's different wives; each is said to be *Satin* to the other.

ṢATKAR, Beng. (শতকর, from শত, a hundred) Land yielding a good return for seed sown.

SATKÁRÍ, H. (S. ستکاری) One who burns the dead.

SATMÁSA, H. (ستماسا, from S. **सप्त**, seven, and **मास**, a month) A feast given in the seventh month of pregnancy: a fee paid at that period to the káẓi: the word occurs also *Satwásá* (ستواسا), and *Satwánsá* (ستوانسا), in the same sense, as also in that of a seven-month's child.

SATMÍ, Guz. (સતમી) A bill of lading.

SAṬO, Guz. (સટો) A time bargain, speculation in opium and other articles, a gambling transaction.

SATPHIRI, H. (ستپھیری) Seven turns round the sacrificial fire: the ceremonial of marriage, observed sometimes at the season of betrothal, but not held to bar subsequent union with another party.

SATRA, Mar. (S. **सत्र**), Karn. (ಸತ್ರ), SATTRAM, Tam. (சத்திரம்), SATRAMU, Tel. (సత్రము) Sacrifice, oblation: liberality, giving alms, distribution of food to Brahmans and mendicants; the place or building where it is so distributed: in Tel. and Tam. also, a *choltrí* for travellers: in Karn., also, a house, an edifice, as *Dharmasatra* (ಧರ್ಮಸತ್ರ), a court-house.

SATRAṢÁLÁ, Mar. (**सत्रशाला**, from S. **शाला**, a hall), SATRAṢÁLE, Karn. (ಸತ್ರಶಾಲೆ) A building or apartment in which food is distributed to Brahmans and mendicants: in some places, a house erected by the high road, and endowed by charitable persons for the gratuitous supply of food, and sometimes lodging, to travellers: it is usually in charge of, and managed by, a Brahman: (the building, as well as the act of distributing the food, is also termed in Mar. and Karn. *Annachhatra*, or *Annasatra*, from S. *anna*, food).

SATṢÚDRA, Mar. (**सतशूद्र**, from S. **सत्**, good) A Ṣúdra who has gone through the purificatory ceremonies of the higher castes: a common term for a cowherd or a barber, who are considered to be of a better class of the servile tribes.

SATTA, or SATHA, (?) H. An engagement to supply articles or grain, &c., on consideration of specified advances (it is perhaps the same word as the next, with a local modification of meaning).

SAṬṬÁ, Mar. (**सट्टा**) Mercantile traffic, exchange of money.

SÁTTÁTHAVAN, Tam. (சாத்தாதவன்) A *Vaishṇava* of a particular order, in the south of India; one who does not wear a lock of hair on the crown of his head, nor the Brahmanical cord: all distinctions of caste are said to be dispensed with, and the sect is accused of holding their women in common: the *Sáttáthavar* are to the *Vaishṇavas* what the *Víra Ṣaivas* are to the *Ṣaivas*; they follow chiefly the occupations of flower-sellers and minstrels, or are vagrants and mendicants.

SAṬṬU, SUṬṬOO, also SATÚÁ, H. &c. (ستّو, ستّوا, S. **सक्तु**) Grain parched and ground to flour, sometimes mixed with pease, and usually eaten made into a paste with water.

Satúá-sankránt, H. (ستواسنکرانت) The day of the sun's entrance into Aries, when a meal of parched grain is presented to Brahmans.

SAṬṬÚK, H. (A. ستّوک) Base money, money much alloyed.

SÁṬU, Karn. (ಸಾಟು) Change given to one person to pay money for another.

SATWÁRÍ, Guz. (સતવારી) A caste of Hindus employed

as gardeners and cultivators of garden produce: a man of that caste.

SATYOTTARA, S. (सत्योत्तरं) A kind of answer in a suit, admission of the truth of the charge.

SAUBHÁGYA, S. &c. (सौभाग्य) Good fortune, prosperity, happiness; vernacularly, any ornament that may be worn by a woman whose husband is living.

Saubhágyavatí, Mar. (S. सौभाग्यवती) A prosperous woman, that is, one whose husband is living.

Saubhágyavání, and *Saubhágyaváyana*, Mar. (S. सौभाग्यवाणा -वायन) An offering of articles of the toilette by married women to Brahmans and their wives, for the sake of procuring coutinued prosperity: an offering of cocoa-nuts and other articles to a Brahman and his wife at a marriage, to procure prosperity for the new-married couple.

SAUHÁGIN, or SOHÁGIN, H. (سہاگن, for सौभागिनी) A woman whose husband is living.

ṢAUCHA, S. &c. (शौच) Purity, cleanness, ceremonial purification after having been rendered unclean by any cause, as personal defilement, the death of a relative, and the like.

Ṣaucháchára, S. &c. (शौचाचारः) Rules of purification.

SAUDÁGAR, H. &c. (سوداگر, from P. سودا, trade) A merchant, a trader.

Saudágari, corruptly, *Saudagree*, H. (سوداگري) Trading, trafficking, the business of a merchant.

Saudápatra, Beng. (সৌদাপত্র) A written agreement to deliver goods to a purchaser on specified terms.

SAUDÁYIKA, S. (सौदायिक, from सु, good, and दाय, portion) Property derived from kindred as an affectionate gift: the property which a man receives with his wife: the property given to a woman, by her kindred, or her husband at the time of her marriage, becoming her exclusive right.

ṢAUDRA, S. &c. (शौद्रः) Relating or belonging to a Ṣúdra or the Ṣúdra caste, the son of a Ṣúdra woman by a man of either of the three superior castes.

SAUGAND, H. (سوگند) An oath.

SAUKÁR, vernacular corruption of SÁHUKÁR, q. v. H. (سوكار) A banker.

SAUḶU, Karn. (ಸೌಳು) Fullers' earth: adj., brackish.

Sauḷuppu, Karn. (ಸೌಳುಪ್ಪು) Earth salt.

Sauḷumannu, Karn. (ಸೌಳುಮಣ್ಣು) Earth used for making salt, also by washermen for bleaching.

SAUR, Thug. One who escapes from the attempt to strangle him.

SAUT, H. (سوت, सौत, from S. सपत्नी) A companion wife, any one married subsequently to the first.

Sautelá, H. (سوتيلا) Sprung from a different wife, as *Sautelá-bhái*, a brother by a different mother.

Sávatra, *Sautra*, Mar. (सावत्र) Sprung from, or relating to, a rival wife: used only in composition, as *Sáutra-áí* (सावत्रआई), a half-mother, *Sáutra-bháú* (सावत्रभाऊ), a half-brother, that is, by the same father but different mother.

ṢAVA, S. &c. (शव) A dead body.

Ṣavasádhana, S. &c. (from साधन, means) A magical rite performed while seated on a dead body.

SÁVADI, Tam. (சாவடி) A building for the accommodation of travellers, a *chaultrí*, a *sarái*.

SÁVARAMU, or SÁVARAM, Tel. (సావరము, from P. چاور, a certain measure of land) An allotment of land, or of the government revenue derivable from it, assigned by the Mohammadan government to the Zamindárs or other revenue officers as their personal compensation: it is also explained as that part of the Zamindárí which the Zamindár retained in his own hands.

SAVARNA, vernacularly, SABARNA, corruptly, SABURN, S. &c. (सवर्ण) Of or belonging to the same caste or clan.

SAVÁṢÁ, or SAWÁṢÁ, Mar. (सवाशा) A tribe of Brahmans, or an individual belonging to it.

SAVÁṢÍṆ, Mar. (सवाशीण, corruption of *Savasiní*) A woman whose husband is living.

SAVEDHABHOGAM, S. (सवेधभोगं) Possession or occupation that is disputed.

SÁVI, less correctly, SHÁVEE, or SHAWEE, Tam. (சாவி) Blighted corn, grain withered for want of moisture.

SAVISTAR, Hindi &c. (S. सविस्तर) Circumstantial, detailed—an account, a statement, &c.

SÁVITRÍ, S. &c. (सावित्री) The same as the Gayatrí, or most holy verse of the Veda, a short prayer addressed to Savitá, or the sun, whence its name, and the repetition of which is an essential part of the ceremony of investiture with the Brahmanical thread; hence it sometimes implies the rite of initiation.

SAVYÁJ, Mar. (सव्याज) Bearing, or united with, interest: what includes the interest accumulated with the principal; any account, a total, what bears interest, a loan, &c.

SAWÁ, (?) H. A well.—North-west provinces.

SAWÁ, H. &c. (سوا, सवा, S. स, with पाद, a quarter), Beng. (সওযা) A quarter more, with a quarter more, as *Sawá-sau*, a hundred and a quarter, or 125.

Sawái, *Sawáia*, H. &c. (سواي, سوايا, सवाई), Uriya (ସୱାଇ) A quarter more, an excess of a fourth, that which is more by a fourth: interest at a rate of 25 per cent.

SAWÁNIH-NIGÁR, or SAWÁNIHA-NIGÁR, corruptly, SAVANAGAR, SAVANNAH-NEGAR, and SEWANAHNIGAR, H. (A. P. سوانح نگار, from *Sawánih*, events, and *nigár*, who sees) A news writer, an intelligencer, also a spy.

SAWAR, or SUWÁR, H. &c. (سوار, सवार, सुवार), Beng. (সওয়ার) A rider, a horseman or person mounted, one carried by any conveyance.

Sawári, or *Suwári*, corruptly, *Sewarry*, *Sewaury*, H. &c. (سواري, सवारी, सुवारी), also *Swári*, Mar. (स्वारी) A number of persons mounted, especially on state occasions: equipage, retinue, cavalcade, a troop of horsemen: what is fit for or appropriated to riding on, as a riding-horse.

SAWÁNÁ, H. (سوانا, सवाना) Lands lying farthest from the village.

SÁWATRA, Mar. (सावत्र) Sprung from, or relating to, a different wife or mother (S. *Sapatni*), used only in composition, as

Sáwatra-áï, (सावत्रआई) A half-mother, the wife of a father, a stepmother.

Sáwatra-bháü, (सावत्रभाऊ) A half-brother, one by the same father not the same mother.

SÁYÁBANJAR, (?) (from بنجر, waste lands) Uncultivated lands divided into fields.

SÁYAGÁL-VIKRAYAM, Tam. (சாயகால்விக்கிரையம்) Inland sale.

ṢAYANAIKÁDAṢÍ, S. &c. (शयनैकादशी) The eleventh of the light half of the month *Áshárh*, or the summer solstice, when Vishnu is fabled to sleep upon the serpent *Sesha*.

SAZÁ, vernacularly, SAJÁ, H. &c. (P. سزا, सजा) Punishment, retribution, retaliation.

Sajá-ághát, Uriya (ସଜାଆଘାତ) Slight wounding.

Sazáwal, *Suzawul*, *Sajáwal*, H. &c. (سزاول, सजावल) A native collector of revenue: an officer specially appointed to take charge of and collect the revenue of an estate, from the management of which the owner or farmer has been removed: a land-steward, a bailiff, an agent appointed by a landowner or lessor to compel payment of rent by tenants or leaseholders. Ben. Reg. v. 1819.

Sazáwalí, H. (سزاولي) The office or function of a *Sazáwal*, the rights attached to it: an abwáb, or cess, imposed under the Mohammadan government upon Zamindárs to defray the cost of special native collectors of the revenue.

Sajáwalu, Tel. (సజావలు) Restraint placed upon a person to prevent his escape, or to enforce payment of a demand.

SÁZISH, H. (P. سازش, from ساز, making) Conspiracy, collusion, confederacy.

Sajulu, Tel. (సజులు, from P. ساز, making) Labourers employed in the making of salt.

ṢÉDHYA, or SHEDHYA, Karn. (ಶೇಧ್ಯ) Agriculture, farming.

Ṣédhyagár, Karn. (ಶೇಧ್ಯಗಾರ) A farmer, a cultivator.

Sedhyamu, corruptly, *Shedow*, Tel. (శేధ్యము) Land prepared for ploughing.

SEDI, (?) Beng. Presents of provisions, formerly exacted in Bengal by the Zamindár and his attendants, when travelling, from the cultivators.

SEḌIL, or CHEDIL, Tam. (செடில்) An apparatus used for suspending men, and swinging them in the air in honour of the goddess *Mariamma*. See *Charaka*.

SEGON, (?) Hindi. A soil of a reddish tint, and containing gravel, in Bundelkhand.

ṢEJÁR, SHEJÁR, Mar. (शेजार) Neighbourhood.

Ṣejári, *Shejári*, Mar. (शेजारी) A neighbour.

ṢEK, SHEK, Mar. (शेक) Hire of, or remuneration for, the use of draught cattle.

SEKÁ, H. (سيكا, सेका, from S. षिच, to sprinkle) Wheat-fields watered by wells: watering, irrigation in general.

SEKKUMUTTAI, Tam. (செக்குமுட்டை, from *sekku*, an oil-press, and *muttai*, an egg) An egg-shell filled with oil: a contribution levied by the village proprietors from each oil-press, and either distributed among them according to their respective shares, or credited to the fund for village expenses.

ṢELAGA, Tel. (శెలగ) An allowance of grain and other perquisites allotted to the hereditary village *Karanam*, or accountant, in the Northern Sarkárs: a term used by measurers of grain, who call out the numbers of the measures up to one hundred, and then, exclaiming *Ṣelaga*, begin a fresh enumeration from one.

ṢELAKYÁ, Mar. (शेलक्या) A goat-herd.

SELAVALA NILAM, Tam. (செலவலநிலம்) Red soil.

ṢELOD, Guz. (શેલોદ) An armed agent: one who levies forced contributions from the cultivators in the name of some military chief.

ṢÉMA, Karn. (ಶೇಮ) Hidden treasure.

ṢÉMÁHÍ, Uriya (ସେମାହି, from the P. *sih*, three, and *máh*, a month) Quarterly.

SEMBAKÁL, Tam. (செம்பக்கால்) A betel-garden while the vines are young.

SEN, Beng. (সেন) A family name borne in Bengal by persons usually of the medical caste, as Ram-Komol Sen, the author of the English and Bengali dictionary, and a gentleman highly esteemed by both the European and native society of Calcutta for his private worth and public spirit: he died in 1843.

Sená, S. &c. (सेना) An army.

Sená-khás-khel, Mar. (सेनाखासखेल, from *Sená-khás*, the army of the state, and *Sar-khel*, a commander, dropping the first syllable) A title conferred by the *Peshwá* upon the *Gaikwár*.

Senápati, corruptly, *Senaputtee*, S. &c. (सेनापति) A general, a commander-in-chief, one of the eight great officers of the Maraṭha state, a title conferred by the *Peshwá* upon the Rája of Berar.

Sená, H. (سینا) An officer who collects the revenue in a village.

Ṣenḍe, Mar. (शेंडे) A disease incidental to rice crops.

Ṣendí, **Shendí**, Mar. (शेंडी, from S. शिखण्ड) The tuft or lock of hair on the crown of the head left at tonsure.

Sendi, (?) Mar. The offspring of a Maraṭha Brahman by a slave girl, who becomes a Brahman in the third generation (perhaps an error for *Senwi*, q. v.)

Séndi, Tam. (சேந்தி) The sap of the palm, *táṛi*.

Ṣenwá, **Shenwa**, Mar. (शेणवा, from शेण, dung) A man of low caste employed as the village scavenger.

Ṣenwí, **Shenwi**, Mar. (शेणवी) A class of Hindus in the Maraṭha country who maintain that they are Brahmans, and wear the characteristic cord, but who are not recognised to be so by the other Brahmans, from whom they differ chiefly in eating fish.

Sepattani, incorrectly, **Sepatni**, **Seputnee**, Beng. (সেপত্তনি, from the P. *seh*, or *sih*, three) A sub-tenure or lease in the third degree.

Sepattanidár, Beng. (সেপত্তনিদার, from P. دار, who has) The holder of land in the third stage of underletting.

Ser, commonly, but incorrectly, **Seer**, corruptly, **Saer**, H. &c. (سیر, शेर, সের, from the S. शेटक, *Seṭaka*) A measure of weight, varying in different parts of India, and for different articles, but generally reckoned in Bengal at eighty *tolas*, or Sicca weight, or as one-fortieth of a *man* or *maund*: as the fortieth of the former Bázár *maund* the standard *Ser* was = avoirdupois weight 2 lb. 0 oz. 13.863 dr. and of the Factory *maund* 1 lb. 13 oz. 13.860 dr. In 1833 a slight change was made in the value of the *man*, thence known as the *Angrezi* or English *maund*, by which the proportionate value of the *Ser* became, in avoirdupois weight, 2 lb. 0 oz. 14.592 dr.: the Tamil *Sér* (சேர்) is reckoned equal to eight *palams*, while a larger or *pakhá* *sér* (பக்காசேர்) is equal to 24 *palams*. See *Palam*. On the west of India the Surat *Ser* is said to be equal to avoirdupois weight 1 lb. or 16 oz., and the Bombay *Ser* to 13 oz. only.

Serí, H. &c. (سیری, शेरी) Relating to a *Ser*: a charge or fee of one *Ser* per *man*: an allowance of one *ser* per *maund* in the division of the crop: in Marathí, a perquisite of about two *Sers* per *maund* taken by the *Kamavisdár*, or other government officer, from the grain brought by the cultivators in payment of the public revenue when receivable in kind: also the grain which the officer who supplies the public servants with their allowances deducts as his perquisites from every *maund*.

Aḍserí, Mar. (अडशेरी) Monthly grain given to a servant for his subsistence: a weight of two and a half *sers*: a measure of capacity, or half a *payali*.

Serína, H. (سیرینه) Payment of a *ser* per *man* by an hereditary cultivator in a village to the proprietary community of the village, or some individual of the community, in acknowledgment of the proprietary right: also a perquisite or deduction of a like proportion from the estimated produce of the lands claimed by the proprietors on settling for the revenue.

Ṣer, **Sher**, Mar. (शेर) Daily food, or grain, or flour, given to a messenger or labourer.

Seráweteb, Guz. (સેરાવેતેબ) A particular tenure of land.

Ṣerí, pronounced **Sheri**, corruptly, **Shairee**, **Sheyree**, Mar. (शेरी) Arable land originally excluded from the village assessment, either as fallen in consequence of neglect of cultivation or forfeiture into the hands of the government, and managed for its benefit, or such land separated under some pretext by the great officers of the state, and managed for their own advantage alone: when the *Ṣerí* lands were appropriated by the government they were sometimes rented to the Mámlatdárs at a favourable rate: latterly they were made over to the *Páṭíls* and assessed along with the other lands of the village, from which they then ceased to differ, except in retaining their original appellations.—E. I. Selections, iv. 652, 695. The same word in Telugu (శేరి) is explained in a similar manner to denote land cultivated by the Ryots on account of the state, paying usually at the rate of half the nett produce of ordinary cultivation, or one-third of that of garden cultivation: *Ṣerí* land was considered to be of two kinds, 1. land lying waste and unclaimed, and 2. land respecting which disputes not admitting of decision had prevailed—Ibid. iv. 740. *Ṣerí* is elsewhere explained to signify the same as *Baṭái*, or the partition of the produce between the state and the cultivator; and again to mean merely ploughed land, or cultivation in general.

Ṣerí-bák, Mar. (शेरीबाक) The produce of lands cultivated on account of government.

Sérígrámam, Tel. (సేరిగ్రామం) A village, the lands of which are considered to belong in proprietary right to the government.

Sérí-hissa, Tel. (from A. حصه, a share) A tenure in the Nizam's country by which irrigated or rice lands, the cultivator being the owner, pays eleven-twentieths of the produce to the government.

Ṣeríkarí, Mar. (शेरीकरी) The cultivator of lands belonging to the state.

Ṣeríjamín, Mar. (शेरीजमीन) Lands the property of the state.

ṢÉRUVE, or ṢÉRVE, Karn. (ಶೇರುವೆ, ಶೇರ್ವೆ) A company, a department.

Ṣéruvegár, Karn. (ಶೇರುವೆಗಾರ) The head of a company of artisans or workmen.

SESHA, S. &c. (शेषः) The name of the great serpent supposed to uphold the earth on one of his thousand heads, and to serve as the couch on which Vishnu sleeps during the rains: also leavings, residue, remainder.

SEṬH, H. &c. (سيٹهه), SEṬ, SEṬÍ, SEṬH, SEṬHÍ, pron. ṢHEṬ, &c., and corruptly, SETTI, SHAITEE, SHUITEE, Mar. (शेट, शेटी, शेठ, शेठी), ṢEṬÍ, or SEṬṬÍ, Tam. (செட்டி), SEṬṬI, whence the common appellation of a trader from the Coromandel coast, CHIṬṬY, Tel. (శెట్టి), SAṬṬI, or plur. honorific, SAṬṬIRU, also ṢEṬṬI, Karn. (ಶೆಟ್ಟಿ, ಶೆಟ್ಟರು, ಶೆಟ್ಟಿ) A merchant, a banker, a trader, a chief merchant: often used in connexion with the name as a respectful designation, as *Jagat-seṭh*. In some places the *Seṭh*, or *Seṭhí*, is the head of the mercantile or trading body, exercising authority over them in matters of caste and business, and, as their representative, with the government: (the different forms are all from the S. *Ṣreshṭha* (श्रेष्ठ), best, or chief, श्रेष्ठी, the chief of a corporation; also a merchant or banker).

Ṣeṭí-maháján, Mar. (शेटीमहाजन) The chief of the traders of a town, who presides over the several heads of trades.

Kómaṭi-saṭṭi, Karn. (ಕೋಮಟಿಶೆಟ್ಟಿ) A Telugu merchant.

Béri-saṭṭi, Karn. (ಬೇರಿಶೆಟ್ಟಿ) A Tamil merchant.

Seṭu, or *Cheṭu*, Tam. (செட்டு) Trade, traffic.

ṢEṬYÁ, or ṢHEṬYÁ, Mar. (शेट्या) A particular officer in a mart or commercial town, having the superintendence and regulation of the traffic; in some places the head man of each description of traders.

ṢET, pron. SHET, Mar. (शेत, corruption of S. *kshetra* क्षेत्र, Hindi *khet* खेत) A field, a piece of cultivated ground, a standing crop, agriculture, cultivation.

Ṣetáṛ, *Shetáṛ*, *Ṣetwaṛ*, or *Shetwaṛ*, Mar. (शेताड, शेतवड) The arable land around and belonging to a village.

Ṣet-, or *Shetgaṇa*, Mar. (S. गण, a class) Arable lands or fields collectively.

Ṣet-, or *Shet-bhát*, Mar. (शेतभात) A comprehensive term for arable lands, also for the business of husbandry.

Ṣetí-, or *Shetí-bhátí*, Mar. (शेतीभाती) A husbandman: agricultural operations: field business.

Ṣet-, or *Shet-jamín*, Mar. (शेतजमीन) Arable land.

Ṣet-, or *Shet-harí*, corruptly, *Shethurrie*, or *Shetcurry*, Mar. (शेतकरी) The owner of a field, a farmer: a husbandman, a cultivator, any agricultural labourer, whether working for himself or another.

Ṣet-, or *Shet-sárá*, Mar. (शेतसारा) Land-tax.

Ṣet-, or *Shet-sanadí*, less correctly, *Shetsunnudee*, and, corruptly, *Shetsundee*, *Shaitsundee*, Mar. (शेतसनदी) One holding a *sanad* or grant of lands for military service, applied especially to a local militia acting also as police and as garrisons of forts: also an assignment or grant of revenue of land for certain services; the assignment, as well as the office, may be hereditary.

SET, or SETU, H. &c. (S. سيت, सेतु) A bridge, a causeway, a mound or ridge dividing fields and serving as a path during their inundation.

SETWARI, (?) Hindi, A greenish-tinted sandy loam.—Bundelkhand.

SEÜṬÁ, (سيوٹا, सेवटा) A description of soil, a mixture of clay and sand fit for any crop except rice.

ṢEV, or SEÜ, or SHEV, or SHEU, Mar. (शेव) A portion deducted from fruit, flowers, or vegetables brought to market, as a toll or tax; also termed *Seu-mothi*, from *muṭhi*, a handful, and *Ṣeu-sabjí* (शेवसबजी). See *Sabzi*.

SEVA, or, vernacularly, SEWA, or SEBÁ, or SHEBÁ, S. &c. (सेवा) Service, domestic service; also attendance upon an idol, worship, adoration.

Sevaka, vernacularly, *Sewak*, *Sebak*, *Seük*, S. &c. (सेवकः) *Sevakuḍu*, Tel. (సేవకుడు) A servant, a slave, a worshipper: a slave of a particular class in Chota Nagpur. See *Sánwak*.

Sevakapatra, or, vernacularly, *Sewakpatra*, S. &c. (सेवकपत्र) A deed or bond by which a person binds himself to servitude either for a term or for life.

Sebáit, or *Sebáit*, corruptly, *Sebaintnámá*, Beng. (P. নামা) A deed assigning an endowment or a share of ancestral land by the owner on his demise.

Sebátí, or *Sewatí*, *Sebáit*, *Sewáit*, or, corruptly, *Shebait*, *Shewait*, *Shewayat*, Beng. (সেবাতী, সেবাইৎ) A person who has the management and superintendence of an endowed temple, persons attached to and officiating in a temple: the term also occurs as that of a person to whom a share of an ancestral estate has been assigned by the owner on his demise.

Seval, or Sheval, Tam. (செவல்) A red soil of the second class.

Séval, or Shéval, Tam. (சேவல்) Watching corn in a field.

Sévalál, *Shévalál*, Tam. (சேவலாள்) A watcher in a corn-field.

Sevváram, Tam. (செவ்வாரம்) A just division of the produce of a field between the owner and the cultivator.

Sévyamu, incorrectly, Sheviam, Tel. (సేవ్యము) Cultivation, ploughed land.

Sewala, Thug. A fox.

Sey, or Shey, also read Chey, Tam. (செய) A field of rice-corn: a certain measure of land (?).

Seykál, *Sheykál*, corruptly, *Shaigal*, Tam. (செயக்கால்) Land which is cultivated, or capable of cultivation.

Seykál-karambu, corruptly, *Shaigal-carumboo*, Tam. (செயக்கால்கரம்பு) Land lying waste though capable of cultivation.

Seykál-tarisu, barbarously, *Sey-haul-turso*, Tam. (செயக்காலதரிசு) Fallow or uncultivated land although formerly cultivated and capable of cultivation.

Punsey, or *Punshey*, Tam. (புன்செய) Dry ground, not artificially watered. See *Pun-shai*.

Shab, Shub, H. (P. شب) Night.

Shab-bedárí, H. (P. بيداري, waking) Nocturnal vigil: keeping awake at night, especially as a religious exercise.

Shab-i-barát, H. (P. A. شب‌برات) A festival observed on the night of the 14th of the month *Shâbán* in memory of deceased ancestors; it is termed the night of record (*barát*), as an angel is supposed on this occasion to inspect a register of the conduct of all living persons.

Shab-gasht, H. (P. گشت, going) The night patrol.

Shab-gashti, H. (P. گشتي, a going) Nocturnal procession, especially of a marriage: keeping vigil: night-watch.

Shab-hhun, H. (P. خون, blood) Nocturnal assault, or murder.

Shabnam, *Shubnum*, H. (P. نم, moisture) Lit., Night-dew, but applied to a very fine kind of muslin, which is not discernible when immersed in water.

Shâbán, H. (A. شعبان) The eighth month of the Mohammadan year.

Shabát, (?) Beng. (perhaps some corruption of ثبات, q. v.) A person in charge or temporary proprietorship of a temple (?).

Shább, H. (A. شاب) A young man, one under 34 years of age.

Shádí, H. (P. شادي) Gladness, rejoicing, nuptial festivity, nuptials, marriage, especially legal and respectable, in opposition to informal or temporary marriage.

Shádíát, H. (شاديات) Fees paid at marriages.

Shádíána, H. (شاديانه) Any thing relating to marriages, music and other accompaniments, fees or presents made sometimes to the Zamindár by the cultivators at marriages.

Shafá, H. (A. شفا) Healing, curing, being cured.

Shafá-khána, H. (P. خانه) An hospital.

Shafâát, H. (A. شفاعت) Intercession, mediation.

Sháfâ, H. (شافع) An intercessor, a mediator, a patron.

Sháfâi, H. (شافعي) The teacher or founder of one of the four great schools of Mohammadan law: a follower of the *Sháfâi* school.

Shaghál-khor, H. (P. شغال‌خور) Lit., A jackall eater, the designation of a class of freebooters dwelling chiefly on the Oudh frontier, but committing depredations often in the Company's territories and at some considerable distances from home: they are also found in Orissa.

Shágírd, H. (P. شاگرد) A disciple, a scholar, an apprentice.

Shágírd-pesha, H. (P. پيشه, practice) A menial servant, also retinue, attendance: a pensioner: expense of servants and dependants.

Sháh, H. (P. شاه) A king, a sovereign, a title borne by some classes of Mohammadan ascetics or mendicants: also one given to certain celebrated saints, as, *Shah Madár*, *Sháhnizam-ud-dín Aulia*, and others.

Sháh-bandar, H. (P. شاه‌بندر) A port or harbour-master, a custom master, an officer who regulates the port duties and charges: a royal harbour or maritime establishment. In the revenue accounts of the Mohammadan government of Bengal it designated especially Dacca, and the customs levied there.

Sháhí, H. (P. شاهي) Regal, relating to a king: in Chittagong, a measure of land, or an epithet of any such measure, as perhaps having been fixed by the government:

modified in Mar. as *Ṣái*, or *Shái* (शाई), and used laxly in the sense of belonging or appropriate to, as *Puna-ṣái*, belonging to Puna; *Sinde-ṣái*, belonging to *Sindhia*. *Sái-*, or *Sháiṣirastá*, Mar. (शाई शिरस्ता) Public usage or custom.

Sháh-Mohammad, Thug. An exclamation to denote that danger is near.

Sháh-nishín, H. (P. نشين, sitting) A royal seat: a miniature throne or palace carried in procession at the Muharram festival.

Sháh-raiat, (?) Beng. A temporary occupant or farmer, a middleman.

Sháh-záda, vernacularly, *Ṣháh-jáda*, H. &c. (شاهزاده, शाहजादा) A prince, the son of a king: also the son of the Mohammadan ascetic so termed.

Shaḥad, or Shaḥd, H. &c. (P. شهد) Honey.

Ṣhaḥad-guttá, Mar. (शहदगुत्ता) Farm or contract for bee-hives.

Sháhad-mom-gutta, Karn. (ಷಾಹದಮೊಂಗುತ್ತ) A tax levied on bees'-wax and honey gathered in the forests of Mysore.

Shaḥádat, H. (A. شهادت) Testimony, evidence, martyrdom, as, *roz-i-shaḥádat*, the tenth of Muharram, the day on which *Âli* was slain.

Sháḥid, plur. *Shaḥád*, H. (A. شاهد, شهاد), *Sháhíd*, Mar. (शाहीद) A witness, an evidence, a martyr.

Sháḥidí, H. (A. شاهدي), Mar. (शाहिदी) Evidence, testimony, deposition.

Ṣháḥidí-dár, Mar. (शाहिदीदार) A witness, a deponent.

Sháḥid-i-hál, H. (P. حال, present) A witness to facts.

Ṣhaháјog, Ṣháháјog, Mar. (शहाजोग, शाहाजोग, for S. योग्य, fit for) Creditable, trustworthy; applied especially to a *Hundí*, or bill of exchange marked with this word, implying that the bearer may be trusted with the money; also to coins which are manifestly good: in Guz. a promissory note, a cheque on the bank, payable to bearer.

Shahna, corruptly, Shaena, Shana, Shena, Shaina, Shiehna, H. (شحنه) A watchman, a village watchman, a person employed to watch the crops and prevent any fraudulent abstraction of the grain.

Sháhnagí, corruptly, *Shaenagee*, H. (شحنگي) The duty, pay, or perquisites of a village watchman.

Shahr, H. (P. شهر, शहर) A town, a city.

Shahr-gasht, H. (P. گشت, a going) The procession of a bridegroom through the city at a marriage festival: patrolling the city, a patrol.

Shahr-panáh, H. (P. شهرپناه), *Shaharpanhá*, Mar. (शहरपन्हा) The walls or defences of a town or city: also, fig. the police, guards, &c. appointed to protect a town.

Shahr-púrá, H. (شهرپورا) The suburbs.

Sháhu, (?) H. Name of a caste, or an individual of it, in Sylhet.

Shaï, H. (A. شي) A thing.

Shaï-mubiâ, H. (A. مبيع) A thing or article sold.

Shaï-mutanaẕir, H. (A. متنظر) A thing or property in suspense or dispute.

Shaikh, H. (A. شيخ) An old man, especially one who has authority and respect: an elder, a chief: a title given to various Mohammadan saints: the head of an Arab tribe: the term is also used to designate the descendants of *Mohammad*, of *Abubakr*, and *Omar*.

Shajara, or Shajar-náma, H. (شجره, شجرنامه) A list of saints, his predecessors, given by a religious teacher to his disciples after the manner of a genealogical tree.

Shajja, plur. Shajjáj, corruptly, Shadja, A. (شجّ, شجّاج) A wound, a personal injury short of destroying life: wounds of ten kinds are recognised by Mohammadan law as affecting the head and face in particular.

1. *Hárisat*, (حارصة) A scratch not drawing blood.
2. *Damâat*, (دمعة) A scratch which draws blood without its running down.
3. *Dámíat*, (دامية) An abrasion of skin from which blooa flows.
4. *Báẕâat*, (باضعة) A cut through the skin.
5. *Mutaláhimat*, (متلاحمة) A cut deep into the muscles.
6. *Simhák*, (سمحاق) A wound on the head reaching to the pericranium.
7. *Múẕihat*, (موضحة) A wound that lays the bone bare.
8. *Ḥáshimat*, (هاشمة) A fracture of the skull.
9. *Munakilat*, (منقلة) A fracture of the skull requiring the operation of the trepan.
10. *Ammat*, (امّة) A wound extending to the membranes of of the brain.

Of these, if wilfully inflicted, the seventh may admit of retaliation, but they may be all punished by fine accordingly as they are accidental or intentional.

Shak, H. (A. شك) Doubt, uncertainty: in law, imperfect evidence, leaving uncertainty as to the truth of the charge.

Shaḳ, H. (A. شق) A large division of a country.

Shakar, H. (P. شكر) Sugar.

Shakar-hhúri, H. (P. خوري, eating) Lit., Eating of sugar, part of the marriage ceremony among the Mohammadans: the same as the *Shukrána*, q. v.

Shakiliyan, or *Shakkili*, also pronounced *Chakkili*, and written, corruptly, *Chuckler* and *Shekliar*, Tam. (சக்கிலியன்) A man of a low caste whose business is working in hides and leather: a currier, a tanner, a shoemaker.

SHÁL, H. (شال) A shawl.

Shál-báf, H. (شالباف) A shawl-weaver.

Shálí, H. &c. (شالي) A weaver of shawls and similar articles.

SHAMBAH, H. (P. شمبه) A day, a day of the Mohammadan week: when used singly it also implies Saturday, and the following days are designated by the numerals, as, *Ek-shamba*, Sunday; *Do-shambah*, Monday; *Seh-shamba*, Tuesday; *Chahár-shamba*, Wednesday; *Panj-shamba*, Thursday; and *Shash-shamba*, Friday; but this last is also named, from its being observed as the day of meeting for prayer, *Jumâ*.

SHÁMIL, H. (A. شامل) Extending to, including, comprehending: the term, less correctly written *Shámul*, or used in the plur. as *Shámilát*, was applied in Mysore to the whole additional assessment on the land above the original standard rates made by the Mohammadan rulers Haidar and Tipu.

Shámilát, H. (شاملات, plur. of شامل) Comprehensive or coparcenary concern: lands which have never been divided, but are part and parcel of an estate held in common or in partnership by the whole proprietary body of a village: the lands of such a village, which are not let out or severally appropriated, but which are cultivated in common, and of which the produce is divided amongst the proprietors according to recorded portions.

Shámilát-banjar, H. (from بنجر) Portions of common land. —Kanara.

Shámilát-beríz, H. (from P. بريج) The entire assessment, the original, with all additions.

Shámilát-deh, H. (ده, a village) Lands included in the village lands.

Shámili-taâluh, H. (شاملي تعلق) A subordinate proprietary estate, one comprehended within a Zamindárí, and paying revenue through the Zamindár, but considered to be hereditary and independent property, and inalienable as long as the dues to the superior holder and government are paid.

SHAMSÍ, H. (from the A. شمس, the sun) Solar, as the solar year: a perquisite of the officers of government, being the difference of pay for a lunar and solar month.

SHAMSIA, Thug. The person who holds the hands and feet of the victim.

SHARÂ, corruptly, SHURRA, H. (A. شرع), SERÁ, or SHERÁ, Mar. (शेरा) *The* law; or the precepts of Mohammadanism as derived from the Kurán, sometimes classed under five heads, *Îtikádát*, articles of faith; *Îbádat*, religious worship; *Mûamalat*, social transactions, civil law; *Muzajir*, punishment, or criminal law; and *Âdáb*, good manners, moral conduct, propriety: amongst the Marathas it means also an order, a warrant, especially that which is written on the foot of a petition or representation.

Shariât, H. (A. شريعة) Law, justice, the law of the Kurán.

Sharâi, H. (A. شرعي) Conformable to the law, lawful, right.

SHARÁRAT, H. (A. شرارت) Villainy, wickedness.

SHARB, H. (A. شرب) Drinking: in Mohammadan law, the offence of drinking wine or other intoxicating liquor: also, the right to water, or to use the draw-wells or channels of irrigation, which is declared to be transferable independently of the land which is irrigated.

SHARH, H. (A. شرح), ṢERÁ, Mar. (शेरा) Explanation, a commentary, a gloss; also, pay, allowance; also, rate, rate of assessment, &c.

Sharh-bandí, H. (A. شرح بندي) A table of rates.

Sharh-i-mauza, H. (A. موضع) The rate of assessment on village lands.

Sharh-i-pargana, H. (پرگنه) The rate of assessment of a district.

Sharh-i-paṭṭa, H. (پٹّه) The rate of rent fixed by lease.

SHÁRI, or SHARREE, (?) Mar. Cultivated fields, or land enclosed (a mistake, perhaps, for *Sárá*, q. v.)

SHÁRÎ, H. (A. شارع) A highway.

SHARÍF, H. (A. شريف) Noble, exalted, a person of rank.

Sharáfat, H. (A. شرافت) Nobility, rank, eminence.

SHARÍK, H. (A. شريك) A partner.

Sharákat, *Shirkat*, H. (A. شركت , شراكت), *Sarkat*, Mar. (सरकत), *Sharákhatu*, Tel. (షరాకతు) Partnership, coparcenary, joint occupancy: in Mohammadan law partnership is distinguished as of two kinds, *Shirkat-amláh*, (شركت املاك), partnership by right of property, where the absolute right of property belongs equally to all associated, and *Shirkat-i-âkúd* (شركة عقود), partnership by contract effected by mutual consent, and in which one partner may act for the rest: partnerships of this kind are also classed under four heads, 1. *Mufáwiza* (مفاوضه), When the contracting parties agree that all their property shall be in common: a partnership not admitted by the Shiâ lawgivers. 2. *Ínán* (عنان), When the contracting parties contribute a stipulated amount either of money or goods to a common capital, to be employed for their common benefit: this is also considered to be designated by the simple term *Shirkat*, and may again be distinguished as 1. *Shirkat-al-amwál* (pl. of مال, wealth) Partnership in property, and 2. *Shirkat-ul-tijárat* (تجارت, trade) Partnership in trade or commerce; 3. *Shirkat-ul-sanáiâ* (شركت الصنايع), otherwise termed *Shirkat-ul-abdán* (pl. of بدن, the body), Association or partnership in mechanical arts or bodily labour; and 4. *Shirkat-ul-wujúh* (شركت الوجوه) Partnership of faces, when persons not having any property agree to join and obtain goods for sale upon their personal credit or assurance.

Sharik-fi-nafs-ul-mubáiât, H. (A. شريك في نفس المبايعت) A partner in the matter of buying and selling.

Sharáhat-náma, H. (P. نامه, a document) A deed of partnership

Sharákat-barádari, H. (P. برادري, fraternity) The association of brothers, or members of the same family living together on a common property.

Sarákatí, corruptly, *Shurakuttee*, Mar. (सराकती) A term applied to villages or estates, the revenues of which are shared by government with others.

Sarkatdár, Mar. (सरकातदार), *Sarihdár*, Uriya (ଶରୀହଦାର) A partner, a coparcener.

Sarkatí, or *Sarkatyá*, Mar. (सरकती, सरकत्या) A partner, a coparcener.

SHARṬ, pl. SHURÚṬ, and SHARAIAṬ, H. (A. شرط, pl. شروط, شرايط) Contract, agreement, stipulated rule or regulation.

Sharṭi, H. (A. شرطي) Conformable to rule or condition.

Be-, or *Bilá-sharṭ*, H. (A. P. بي- , بلاشرط) Absolute, unconditional, as a grant, &c.

SHASHMÁHI, H. (ششماهي, from the P. *shash*, six, and *máh*, a month) Half-yearly, the half-yearly accounts of a village.

Shash-báb-i-kaifiat, H. (P. شش, six) A Bengal revenue account arranged under six heads, also called *Juz-o-kul*, q.v.

Shashdastí, Mar. (शषदस्ती) The designation of a rod used in surveying, being a measure of six cubits, or nine feet.

SHASTAR, SHUSTER, (?) A religious temple and establishment in Asam.

Shastaría, (?) The head of a religious establishment in Asam termed a *Shastar*.

SHÁṬIR, H. (P. شاطر) A running footman.

SHATM, pl. SHUTÚM, H. (A. شتم, شتوم) Abuse, reviling not amounting to slander, and subject to punishment at the discretion of the magistrate.

SHAWÁL, H. (A. شوال) The tenth month of the Mohammadan year, the first of which, following the month of fasting and abstinence, Ramzán, is held as a festival, on which presents are made amongst friends and relatives.

SHEANQUEE, (?) A description of irregular exaction by the native officers in Bengal.—East-India Selections, i. 469.

SHIÂH, or SHIÂI, commonly, SHIA, corruptly, SHEEAH, SHYA, H. (A. شيعه, شيعي) lit., A follower, but applied especially to a follower of *Âli*, the son-in-law of Mohammad, and, in the opinion of his followers, his lawful successor in the Khalifat; the khalifs *Abubakr*, *Omar*, and *Osman*, being, in their estimation, usurpers. The Persians generally, the sovereign of Oudh, and the lower orders of Mohammadans in India, are of this sect.

SHIKAMÍ, H. (شكمي, from شكم, the belly) Subordinate, dependent, included: as a revenue term it applies to a subordinate tenure in which the holder pays his revenue, or his share of it, through some other person to the government, not direct: it applies also to the individual cultivating land on such terms; he may be a joint proprietor with the revenue payer, having equal rights, or he may be an hereditary tenant: in the former case, the superior cannot sell or mortgage any of the land without the concurrence of the *Shikamís*.

Shikamí-ásámi-, or *-râiat*, H. (اسامي, or رعيت, a cultivator) A subordinate cultivator: one who pays the revenue through a superior shareholder, and whose name is not entered in the original assessment, though it is now usually inserted in the *Muntakkab*.

Shikamí-ijárádár, H. (A. اجارادار, q. v.) A subordinate cultivator holding lands in farm.

Shikamí-káshtkár, H. (كاشتكار, a cultivator) A holder of part of the village lands as a subordinate or dependant occupant cultivating his own share, and paying his proportion of the government revenue through the representative of the community.

Shikamí-paṭṭidár, H. &c. (پتّيدار) A coparcener in a joint-tenancy village who cultivates his own lands, and pays his proportion of the government revenue through one or more of the community, whose names are recorded in the government books as undertakers for the whole.

Shikamí-sharík, or *Sharík-shikamí*, H. (A. شريك, a partner) A cosharer, a coparcener, whose revenue payments pass through an intermediate representative.

Shikamí-taâluka, H. (A. تعلقه, a dependancy) An estate

comprised within a Zamindárí, and paying the revenue through the Zamindár or other revenue contractor or Malguẕár.

Shikamí-ṯaraf, H. (طرف, q. v.) A subordinate portion of the division of land called a *ṯaraf*.

Shikár, H. (P. شكار) Hunting.

Shikár-i-máhi, Sindh (P. ماهي, a fish) Fishing: a tax on fishermen.

Shikast, or Shikasta, H. (P. شكست, شكستة) Breaking, fracture, deficiency: adj., broken, impaired, broken or carried away by inundation (land or the like): deficit in the collections, loss on the rent or farm of an estate: a broken or running handwriting.

Shikast-paiwast, H. (P. شكست پيوست, lit., broken and joined) Separation and accession of alluvial lands by alterations in the course of rivers: land so detached and deposited.

Shikastí-paiwastí, H. (شكستي پيوستي) Detached (from one estate) and attached (to another)—lands,

Shiḳḳ, H. (A. شقّ, *Shaḳḳ*, a division, a fissure) A certain tract of country forming a collectorate, or an aggregate of land from which a certain revenue is collected.

Shiḳḳdár, more usually *Shiḳdár*, H. (شقدار), *Sek-*, or *Shekdár*, corruptly, *Shaikdár*, Mar. (शेकदार), Karn. (ಶೇಕದಾರ) A revenue officer or collector appointed either by the government or a Zamindár to collect the revenue from a small tract of country, or from an estate: under the Mogul government it was sometimes applied to the chief financial officer of a province, or to the viceroy in his financial capacity: under the Maraṭhas, an officer in charge of a few villages, collecting the revenue and superintending the cultivation subordinate to the officer in charge of the larger division, called *Ṯaraf*.

Shiḳdárí, H. (شقداري), *Shekdárí*, Mar. (शेकदारी) The office of the revenue collector termed *Shiḳdár*

Shirá, H. (A. شرا) Purchase, sale, traffick: in law, purchase only.

Shírín, H. (P. شيرين) Lit., Sweet, soft, sweet as water of irrigation, irrigated by soft water, land.

Sholá, commonly Solá, H. (شولا) A plant of which the wood is light and spongy, and is used for making toys, artificial flowers, &c. (Æschynomene paludosa).

Shor, H. (شور) Salt; saline, brackish.

Shorzamín, H. (شورزمين) Saline soil.

Shora, H. (P. شوره) Saltpetre, nitre.

Shorábádi, H. (شورابادي) Saline and unproductive, as soil.

Shorakár, H. (P. كار, who makes) A manufacturer of saltpetre.

Shubḥa, H. (A. شبهه) Doubt, suspicion: in law, a legal defect, a flaw; what may be pleaded in bar of punishment: also any thing which may appear lawful but is really unlawful.

Shubḥa-i-âḳd, H. (عقد, a compact) Error of marriage, error of thinking that a right in the woman is conferred by an illegal marriage.

Shubḥa-i-milk, A. (ملك, possession) Erroneous appropriation of property.

Shubḥa-ibáhat, A. (اباحت) Doubt as to justification in the commission of a crime sufficient to prevent the infliction of the full measure of punishment.

Shubḥa-i-ḳawí, H. (A. قوي, strong) Strong presumption of guilt.

Shubḥa-i-shadíd, H. (A. شديد, strong) Strong presumption of guilt.

Shubḥa-i-ẕâífa, H. (A. ضعيف, weak) Uncertainty as to the truth or falsehood of a charge.

Shudámad, H. (P. شدن, to be, آمدن, to come) Custom, usage.

Shudámadí-ḳadím, H. (from A. قديم, old) Old established custom or practice.

Shudhár, H. (شدكار, from P. كاشتن, to sow) Ground tilled and sown: an estimate or valuation of a crop from inspection only: the designation of the temporary settlement of the revenue of the north-west provinces made in 1830 under Reg. vii. 1822: an inspector and valuer of the crop.

Shufâa, Shufâ, Shoofa, H. (A. شفعة) Any possession coveted: in Mohammadan law, the right of pre-emption vested in partners, coparceners, and neighbours, with respect to land and real or immoveable property; the right of claim is distinguished progressively, as,

1. *Ṯalab-i-muwáṣabat*, (طلب مواثبت) Immediate claim, a demand made as soon as the intended disposal of the property is known to the claimant.

2. *Ṯalab-ishhḁd*, or *Ṯalab-ishhád-wa-taḳrír*, (from اشهاد, taking to witness, and in the second form تقرير, confirming) Demand upon the person proposing to sell, made in the presence of witnesses with affirmation of the right, subsequently to the first or immediate demand, and in the event of its being inoperative.

3. *Ṯalab-i-khuṣúmat*, (from خصومت, enmity) The formal institution of a suit at law.

Shafiâ, written *Shafi* or *Shafee*, H. (A. شفيع) A person having the right of pre-emption.

Shafiâ-i-jár, incorrectly, *Shafehjar*, A. (شفيعجار) A person having right of pre-emption from occupying property in the neighbourhood of that which is for sale.

Shafiâ-i-khalít, A. (شفيعخليط) A person having right of pre-emption from occupying property in contact or intermixed with that which is for sale.

SHUHDA, H. (شهده) A profligate fellow, a vagabond, a blackguard.

SHUKKA, H. (A. شقّه) A royal letter or missive, a letter from a superior.

SHUKR, H. (A. شكر) Praise, thanks, acknowledgment.

Shukrána, H. (A. شكرانه) Praise, acknowledgment, thanks: a complimentary or grateful present: a fee or present paid by the party to a suit in whose favour it is decided: a ceremony practised at the marriages of Mohammadans in India, the sending of clothes, jewels, sweetmeats, sugar, and spices, from the relations of the bridegroom to those of the bride, of whom the nearest of kin is then required to consent formally to the marriage.

SHUMÁR, H. (P. شمار), Counting, reckoning. SUMÁR, Mar. (सुमार) Number, numerical amount: rough calculation, conjectural estimate: (it has other peculiar applications in Marathí foreign to this collection.)

Shumári, H. (P. شماري) A reckoning, a counting or enumeration, a census: in Bengal, a revenue account shewing the daily receipts of every kind, and a rough statement of the day's transactions; a day-book: also a numbering with a view to the imposition of a tax.

Shumári-hághaz, H. (from كاغص, paper) The papers or accounts of an estate collectively.

Shumar-sarrishta, H. An office or record of the number of any property, lands, fields, &c.

Gáo-shumári, H. (گاو, a cow) A census of cattle, a tax upon them.

Khána-shumári, H. (P. خانه, a house) A numbering of houses, a house-tax.

Sar-shumári, H. (P. سر, a head) A numbering of heads, a census, a poll or capitation tax.

Shumár-navis, H. (P. نويس, a writer) An accountant, a registrar.

SI, for SIH, or SEH, H. (P. سه) Three: it is also much used in different Indian dialects to form the first member of compound words, not always retaining any particular reference to its primary meaning.

Sibandí, or *Sibandi*, H. (P. سهبندي), Mar. (सिबंदी, शिबंदी) *Sibbandi*, Tel. (సిబ్బంది), corruptly, *Sebundee*, *Sebundy*, *Sibbendy*, &c. (it also occurs in Guz. as *Sarbandí* (સરબંદી) but this is probably a vernacular corruption) Irregular soldiery: a sort of militia or imperfectly disciplined troops maintained for the garrisons of forts and guards in towns and villages, and for revenue and police duties: charges in the revenue accounts for the expense of such troops.

Sibandi-fasli, H. (A. فصل, a harvest) Troops employed in revenue duties.

Mudám-sibbandi, Tel. (ముదాంసిబ్బంది, from A. مدام) Permanent establishment of militia.

Hangámá-sibbandi, Tel. (హంగామాసిబ్బంది) Temporary or occasional militia establishment.

SÍÁ, Thug. Gold.

SIÁH, or SIÁHÁ, written also SIYÁH, SIYÁHÁ, SEEAH, SEEAHÁ, incorrectly, SEHÁ, H. (P. سياه , سياها), SÍÁ, Hindi (सिया), SIHÁ, Uriya (ସିହା) An account-book, an inventory, a list: it is especially applied in Hindustan to the daily ledger or account-book of the receipts and disbursements of a village or estate, specifying all sums received, whether regular or miscellaneous, and all items of disbursement, whether customary or incidental: it begins with the day on which the *Punya* is performed, and closes with the current year: the village account is kept by the village *Patwárí*, but a similar account may be kept in the office of the collector.

Siáh-i-ámdani, corruptly, *Seeah-aûm-danny*, (P. آمدني, incoming) A treasury account of the collections received from the cultivators daily.

Siáh-bahí, H. (بهي, an account) The ledger or day-book in which daily receipts and disbursements are entered: it is sometimes applied to a journal or diary in which the orders of a court of justice are recorded.

Siáh-khazána, H. (خزانه) The day-book of the collector, or any public treasury.

Siáh-i-maujúdát, H. (A. موجودات, effects, assets) Account of daily receipts and disbursements, a cash-book, a ledger.

Siáh-navís, H. (P. نويس, An accountant, one who keeps the rough daily accounts.

SIÁNÁ, SEEANA, H. (سيانا, S. सज्ञान), SYÁNÁ, Beng. (স্যানা) Sagacious, intelligent, mature: in Hindustaní it commonly denotes a conjuror: in it is Kamaon, the designation of hereditary superintendants of several villages, or persons of respectability and authority. Uriya (ସିଆଣା) Puberty.

Siáncharí, H. (सीआनचारी) Dues levied with consent of the people by the hereditary *Siána*.—Kamaon.

Ṣiánat, H. (A. صيانت) Protection: in law, the privilege of being under the protection of the law restricted to the faithful, and withheld from aliens and infidels.

Siásat, H. (A. سياست) Government, administration of justice, punishment: discretional punishment, such as the law has not provided for, but as may be inflicted by the judge.

Siâyat, A. (سعيت) Work, labour, the labour of a slave who is partly emancipated, by which he is to work out his complete manumission.

Sidde, Tel. (సిద్దె) A leather bottle for holding oil.

Siddha, S. (सिद्धः) Effected, perfected; hence applied to a supposed magician or necromancer, an adept.

Siddhánta, S. (सिद्धान्तः) Final or established conclusion or demonstration.

Siddhártha, S. &c. (सिद्धार्थ) The fifty-third year of the cycle.

Siddháyá, Karn. (ಸಿದ್ಧಾಯಾ) Fixed assessment, especially that recorded in the *Ráya-rekhá*, q. v.—Mysore.

Siddhi, S. (सिद्धिः) Accomplishment, fulfilment, the acquirement or possession of superhuman or magical powers; such superhuman faculty.

Siddhi, H. (S. سدّهي, सिद्धि) The hemp plant (Cannabis sativa): the name is also especially applied to the larger leaves and capsules without the stalk, which are used for smoking, and in the preparation of an intoxicating drink and confection.

Sídhá, Hindi (सीधा) Land in good tilth.

Sídhá, H. (S. سيدها), Shidhá, Mar. (शिधा) Uncooked victuals, a charge made to travellers for supplies.

Ṣidorí, or *Ṣidhorí*, Mar. (शिदोरी, शिधोरी) Dressed provisions carried on a journey.

Sídi, or, more correctly, Saidi, commonly Seedee, and Siddhi, H. (سيدي), Siddhí, or Siddhí, Mar. (शिद्दी, सिद्दी) A name given to the descendants of natives of Africa in the west of India, some of whom were distinguished officers of the Mohammadan princes of the Dakhin, especially of Bijapur: they furnished the Mogul empire also with the chief naval officers on the coast of Guzerat.

Siḍi, Tel. Karn. (సిడి) A beam of wood traversing an upright post upon a pivot, to the ends of which persons are fastened to be whirled round: the suspension or swinging of a person: it is the *Charak* of Bengal, q. v.

Siḍi-kamba, Karn. (ಸಿಡಿಕಂಬ) The upright post.

Siḍi-yáṭa, Karn. (ಸಿಡಿಯಾಟ) The ceremony of swinging.

Ṣúladasiḍi, Karn. (ಶೂಲದಸಿಡಿ), *Gálapusiḍi*, Tel. (గాలపుసిడి) Swinging with hooks through the muscles of the back.

Gampasiḍi, Tel. (గంపసిడి), *Gúḍésiḍi*, Karn. (ಗೂಡೆಸಿಡಿ) Being swung seated in a basket.

Sifárish, H. (P. سفارش) Praise, commendation, recommendation.

Siftaja, A. (سَفتَجة) A transaction of exchange, depositing money with an individual on receiving from him a bill or letter of credit on another person at a place where the depositor requires assets: also a bill of exchange, a letter of credit.

Sígaun, H. (سيگون, सीगौं) A kind of soil, a mixture of clay and sand suited to any crop not requiring permanent irrigation.

Ṣígha, A. (صيغة) Marriage, a form of words used at a marriage ceremony.

Ṣighr, A. (صغر) Junior.

Ṣighr-i-sinn, A. (سِنّ, years) Tender age, minority, a minor, one who may be;—

Ṣabí, A. (صبي) A boy, a child, an infant.

Muráhiḳ, A. (مراهق) A lad, one approaching the time of puberty.

Bulúgh, A. (بلوغ) Adolescent, on the point of reaching puberty: also adolescence, majority: this is placed variously by the Mohammadan law at the beginning or end of the sixteenth year, or later; under the British government it is extended to the eighteenth year. Reg. xxvi. 1793. The Mohammadan law also recognised two modes of defining majority, especially in regard to females, the *Báligha-bil-âlámat*, (from علامة, a sign), adult by the usual signs of puberty, and *báligha-bil-sinn*, adult by age.

Sihaṣáí, Guz. (સીહાશાહી) A particular silver coin current at Baroda.

Ṣihr, A. (صهر) A relation, one by affinity within the prohibited degrees.

Síj, H. &c. (S. سيج) The milky hedge-plant, or Euphorbia, of which there are various kinds in Bengal, as *Sanka-síj* (E. tirucalli), *Nara-síj* (E. antiquorum), *Manasá-síj* (E. ligularum), &c.

Sijda, H. (A. سجدة) Adoration, prostration, an attitude in prayer: kneeling and touching the ground with the forehead, the eyes being directed to the tip of the nose.

Sijda-tahíat, H. (A. سجدة تحيت) Kneeling as before, and bowing the forehead, but placing the hands closed with the thumbs upwards on the ground, and touching the thumbs with the forehead: the other attitudes of prayer are;—

Kiám, H. (A. قيام) Standing erect with the hands hanging down and joined in front.

Ḳáúd, H. (A. قعود), or H. *Ḍo-zánu-baithná* (دوزانوبيٹهنا) Sitting, or sitting on two knees, that is, kneeling with the sole of the left foot nearly flat on the ground, that of the right perpendicular.

Rukúá, H. (A. ركوع) Bowing, inclining the body forward so as to place the palms of the hands on the knees.

SIJIL, H. (A. سجل), SIJIL, Beng. (सिजिल) A register, a record, the recorded and authenticated decision of a court of law: an attestation before a notary.

ṢIKÁ, or ṢIKYA, H. &c. (शिका, शिक्य, from S. शिक्य), ṢIKEṆ, Mar. (शिकें) A sling, a loop, the cords suspended from either end of a pole to support boxes, parcels, and the like.

SIKÁR, Guz. (સીકાર, S. स्वीकार, assent) Acceptance of a bill, endorsement.

ṢIKH, H. (سكھ, शिख, from *Sishya*, S. शिष्य) A scholar, a disciple: the name of the people in the Panjab, as the disciples or followers of Nanak Shah.

ṢIKHÁ, S. &c. (शिखा) A single lock of hair left on the crown of the head at tonsure.

Ṣikhá-vṛiddhi, S. (वृद्धि, increase) Interest at a usurious rate, calculated per day: hair-interest, growing like the lock of hair on the head.

SIKI, Beng. (सिकि) A quarter rupee.

SIKKA, Thug. The handkerchief used to strangle with (probably for *Ṣiká*, as above).

SIKKA, in some dialects SIKÁ, commonly written, SICCA, H. &c. (A. سكّه), ṢIKKÁ, or ṢIKÁ, &c. Mar. (शिक्का, शिका, सिक्का), ṢIKÁ, or ṢIKKÁ, Tel. (శికా, శిక్కా) A coining die, a stamp, a mark, a seal, a signet, a royal signet, a stamped coin, especially the designation of the silver currency of the kings of Delhi, adopted by other Indian princes, and eventually by the East-India Company.

Sikka-rupiya, H. &c. (سكّهروپيه) A Sicca rupee, a silver coin, the standard of value in Bengal under the Company's administration, until changed to the 'Company's rupee,' the silver coin now current: for the weight and value, see *Rupiya*.

Sikká-sanad, H. (from A. سند) A grant from the Crown under sign-manual, or bearing the Rájás seal.

Sikkawon, Hindi (सिक्कयोन) The difference of value between the Sikka and Sanwát rupee.

Sikke-bardár, Mar.. (शिक्केबरदार) An officer having charge of the regalia.

Ṣikke-daut, Mar. (शिक्केदौत, P. دوات, an inkstand) The vessel containing the ink for the official or royal stamp or signet.

Ṣikke-kaṭár, Mar. (शिक्केकटार, from S. कट्टार, a dagger) A comprehensive term for the insignia of royalty, the signet and the dagger (of office).

ṢIKSHÁ, S. &c. (शिक्षा) Instruction, correction, punishment.

ṢILÁ, H. (S. سلا, शिला) Gleanings of a corn-field.

Ṣiláhár, H. (سلهار शिलाहार) A gleaner.

ṢILÁ, S. &c. (शिला) A stone.

ṢÍLA, Mar. (शीळ) A stone, but especially when smooth and flat, and fit for use, as a whet-stone, a rubbing-stone, one on which to beat clothes, and the like; also a gap left in an embankment whilst in course of construction, for the passage of a small stream until the whole is filled up.

Ṣilottarapáṭíl, Mar. (शिलोत्तरपाटील) A person appointed to take charge of the gaps in embankments and keep them stopped: a name given to stones used for that purpose.

SILÁH, or SILAH, H. (A. سلاح, سلح) Arms, accoutrements: in law, any sharp-edged weapon capable of inflicting mutilation and death.

Silahbardár, H. (P. بردار, who bears) An armour-bearer.

Silahdár, H. (from دار, who has) A soldier wearing armour, vernacularly, *Ṣiledár*, corruptly, *Silladár*, Mar. (शिलेदार) A horse-soldier who provides his own horse and arms: the term is applied also to the Marathas in general, who profess arms as their employment, although engaged in other avocations, and affect to be of a higher order than the mere *kunbi*, or cultivator.

Silahkhána, H., *Silekhána*, Mar. (from H. خانه, a house) An armoury, an arsenal.

ṢILAK, Mar. (शिलक, from the A. سلك, a series), ṢILUKU, ṢILKU, Karn. (ಶಿಲುಕು, ಶಿಲ್ಕು) Balance, remainder after expenditure or consumption, of money, provisions, or the like.

Silakáwaṇ, or *Ṣilakáwaṇí*, Mar. (शिलकावण -णी) Harassing a cultivator and exacting money from him by a government messenger sent to dun him for his revenue: a fine imposed upon subordinate officers for allowing work to fall into arrear.

Ṣilakbákí, Mar. (शिलकबाकी), *Ṣilukubaki*, Karn. (ಶಿಲುಕುಬಾಕಿ) Balance of revenue outstanding for some time past, a remaining balance.

Ṣilak-band, or *-bandí*, Mar. (शिलकबंद -बंदी) A balance-sheet, an account shewing the balance of receipts and disbursements.

Ṣilakjháṛá, Mar. (शिलकझाडा) Balancing accounts, settlement, clearance.

Ṣilaksánkhalí, corruptly, *Sillikṣanklee*, Mar. (शिलकसांखली, from S. *Sṛinkhalá*, a chain) A chain of balances, balances carried on from time to time until a final adjustment: proving the correctness of a balance by counting the cash or taking stock.

Ṣilakí, Mar. (शिलकी) Left or remaining, forming part of the balance.

Ṣilakí-ḍágine, Mar. (शिलकीडागिने) Reserved as the choicest or best articles of a stock.

SÍLAKÁS, Mal. (ശിലകാശ) A small sum of *kás* or *fanams* paid as a fine or fee by the lessee of an estate to the proprietor upon the renewal of the lease (perhaps from S. *Ṣíla*, civility).

SÍLÁPPUṬṬI, Tam. (சிலாப்புட்டி) A leather bag or bucket for baling water: a man so employed.

ṢILAT, or A. (صلة) Affinity, connexion: a present, a gratuity.

Ṣilat-i-rahm, A. (صلةرحم) Intercourse with kindred: relations within the prohibited degree.

SILÍ, H. (سلي, सिली) The grain and chaff on the thressing-floor before winnowing.

SILOṬ, Guz. (સીલોટ) A head man of *Pagis*, or detectors of thieves.

SILSILA, H. (A. سلسلة) A continuous chain or series, a pedigree, a genealogy.

ṢILPA, S. &c. (शिल्पः) Any manual or mechanical art.

Ṣilpí, S. &c. (शिल्पी) A mechanic, an artisan.

Ṣilpí-nyása, S. (न्यास, deposit) Deposit of materials with an artisan to be worked up into shape.

SÍMÁ, H. &c. (سيما, S. सीमा), also, sometimes modified vernacularly as SÍM, Guz. (સીમ), SÍME, Karn. (ಸೀಮೆ), ṢÍMWA, or SÍMWA, written SEEW, Mar. (शीवं, सींवं), SÍMAI, Tam. (சீமை) A boundary, border, limit: the Karn. and Tam. term is also applied to a country, and, when without any name preceding, especially to Europe or England: *Sím*, in Guz., means also the lands or fields of a village.

Símána, or *Síwána*, H. &c. (سيمانه, سيوانه) Bordering, bounding, relating to boundaries.

Símána-, or *Síwána-dár*, H. (from P. دار, who has) A person well acquainted with the boundaries of a village or estate; one who watches that they are not trespassed or encroached upon.

Símámúl, Karn. (ಸೀಮಾಮೂಲ) The head or root of government.

Símánta-pújá, Mar. (S. सीमान्त, the end or limit of the boundary, and पूजा, worship) Honours paid at the village boundary to a person coming on any particular occasion, as of a bridegroom to take away his wife.

Símaipaṭṭu, Tam. (சீமைப்பற்று) Government jurisdiction: territory.

*Símávivád*a, S. (विवाद, dispute) Disputes about boundaries: a frequent source of litigation and of strife in all parts of India, where they have not been determined by authority.

Símollanghan, Mar. (सीमा, and S. उल्लङ्घन, crossing over) Passage of the borders of a village in procession at the festival of the *Dasahará*.

Ṣínwár, or *Ṣíwar*, Mar. (शिंवार, शिवार) Fields and meadows around and belonging to a village.

Ṣiváru, Tel. (శివారు) A hamlet, a small village attached to a town.

Ṣinwa-takrár, Mar. (P. تكرار, a quarrel) Boundary disputes.

Ṣímwasejárí, Mar. (शीवं, or सींवशेजारी) A borderer, a neighbour, one dwelling on the borders of a contiguous tract.

Ṣíme-aṣwari, or *Shími-uṣwuree*, (?) Karn. (ಶೀಮೆಅಶ್ವರಿ) Charge for village expenses consolidated by Tipu with the land revenue.—Mysore.

SÍMAL, H. &c. (سيمل, S. शाल्मली) The silk-cotton tree (Bombax heptaphyllum).

SÍMANTA, or SÍMANTONNAYANA, S. &c. (सीमंत, सीमन्तोन्नयनं) A ceremony performed during gestation: one of the *Sanskáras*, or essential rites of Hinduism: arranging the partition of the hair (*símanta* सीमन्त) as practised by women, accompanied by religious ceremonies, in the fourth, sixth, or eighth month of pregnancy: see *Sanskára*. In Telugu, according to a vulgar corruption current, the word occurs *Strímantam*.

ṢIMGÁ, Mar. (शिमगा) The *Holi* festival, the month in which it is celebrated: see *Holika*.

ṢIMPÍ, less correctly, ṢÍMPÁ, incorrectly, SEMPEE, and SEEPEE, Mar. (शिंपी, शिंपा, सिंपी) The name of a caste, or individual of it, said to have sprung from a *Súdra* by a *Dásí* or female slave: the chief occupation is sewing and making clothes, and the *Ṣimpí* is usually a tailor, in which capacity he is sometimes included amongst the village servants: individuals of the caste are also dyers and dealers in dying colours, also sellers of cloth, and they engage in other trades.

SÍNA-ZANA, H. (P. سينه, the breast, and زن, who strikes) Hired mourners, women who beat their breasts at funerals, or at the Muharram.

Sínch, or Sích, H. (S. سينچ, सींच, सीच) Watering fields, irrigation.

Sínchái, H. (سينچاي) Irrigation, price paid for irrigation.

Sínchí, H. (سينچي) Season of irrigation.

Ṣindá, or Shindá, Mar. (शिंदा) A particular tribe, or individual of it, originally sprung from female slaves.

Ṣindáporagá, Mar. (शिंदापोरगा) The son of one's female slave, living in the house as a servant.

Ṣing, H., Mar. (سنگ, शिंग, from the S. *Sringa*, शृंग) A horn.

Ṣingoṭí, and *Ṣingsingoṭi*, (शिंगोटी, शिंशिंगोटि) A general term for a horned beast, or cattle of that description, a tax upon the sale of horned cattle.

Ṣingatímahál, Uriya (ଶିଙ୍ଗଟିମହାଲ) A market for horned cattle.

Singh, H. (سنگھ, from *Sinh*, or *Sinha*, S. &c. सिंह) A lion: the sign Leo: a name borne by men of the princely or military caste and Rajaputs, and by Sikhs when fighting-men: it also denotes, in composition, any thing chief or noble, as *Sinhásana*, a lion-seat, *i.e.* a throne; *Sinhadwár*, lion-gate, principal entrance of a fort or palace.

Sinhastha, S. Mar. (सिंहस्थ:) Being in the sign Leo: the period of time during which the constellation Jupiter is in the sign Leo: the revolution indicated by the planet's returning to the sign, which is something less than twelve years: festivals are held at both periods in various parts of India, but among the Maraṭhas the period of Jupiter's conjunction with the sign is considered inauspicious, and in some places marriages are prohibited in the year in which it takes place.

Singpho, Asami, The name of a turbulent tribe in the east of Asam, between the Lohit and the mountains to the east and south-east.

Sipáh, H. (P. سپاه, also short سپه) An army, soldiers.

Sipáhí, corruptly, *Seapoy*, H. (P. سپاهي) A soldier.

Sipah-, or *Sipáh-sálár*, H. (P. سپاه سالار, سپه) A general, a commander, commander-in-chief.

Sipáí, H. (سپاي, from P. سه, three, and پاي, a foot) A tripod: a trench.

Sipurd, or Supurd, H. (سپرد) Charge, trust, consignment.

Sipurd-náma, H. (P. نامه, a document) A deed of trust, a deed of assignment, generally for an indefinite term.

Sipurdagi, H. (سپردگي) Delivery, charge: commitment by a magistrate.

Sír, Seer, H. (سير, सीर, from the S. सीर, a plough) A name applied to the lands in a village which are cultivated by the hereditary proprietors or village Zamindárs themselves as their own especial share, either by their own labourers and at their own cost, or by tenants at will, not being let in lease or farm: these lands were sometimes allowed to be held at a favourable assessment, or were unassessed so as to provide *Nánhár*, or subsistence for the proprietor: the term is also sometimes applied to lands cultivated on account of the state, or to those in which the revenue is paid by the cultivators without any intermediate agent.

Sirâb, *Seeráb*, (?) An item in the Tumar assessment of *Sáir* grants.—Gl. V. Rep.

Sírwár, H. (سيروار) According to the proprietary or privileged land, cultivated after the same manner, or on the same terms.

Sír-sájhí, H. (سيرساجهي, सीरसाझी, from *sájhi*, a partner) The Zamindár's own land, cultivated by tenants at will for a share of the produce.

Sír-i-zamindár, H. (سيرزميندار) The Zamindár's own cultivated land.

Sírimah, *Sirinath*, more probably, *Sírínah*, (?) H. The allowance paid to a proprietor of *Sír* lands when he is out of actual possession of them (some mistakes have occurred in one or both of these words).

Sírá, H. (S. سيرا) A channel of irrigation, a field flooded.

Siráyat, A. (سرايت) Contagion: in law, an incidental or additional result, as when a person intending to do one thing does something more, as designing to wound one man he unintentionally wounds another.

Ṣirf, H. (A. صرف) Purely, only, solely, merely.

Sirmá, Thug. The head.

Sirthí, (?) H. Rent paid to the proprietor by a tenant cultivator, usually in cash.—Kamaon.

Sirthan, (?) H. A tenant cultivator paying a low money-rent.—Kamaon.

Sirwa, Thug. A tradesman, a shopkeeper.

Ṣirwán, or Shirwán, Hindi (शिरवान) A person appointed by the owner of a village to superintend its affairs and enforce cultivation.—Puraniya.

Ṣirwání, Hindi (शिरवानी) A cess upon the cultivators to defray the salary of the superintendant appointed by the Zamindár.

Ṣísa, or Shísha, Hindi (शीश) An ear of corn.—Puraniya.

Si-shamba, H. (سه شنبه) The third day of the week, Tuesday.

Ṣishya, S. &c. (शिष्य, whence, vernacularly, *Sikh*) A scholar, a disciple.

Ṣiṣira, S. &c. (शिशिर) The cold or dewy season, comprising

the months of Mágha and Phálguna, or from the middle of January to that of March.

SISKÁR, Thug. A washerman.

ṢISTU, or SHISTU, commonly SIST, or SHIST, Tel. (శిస్తు), Karn. (ಶಿಸ್ತು, ಸಿಸ್ತು), S. (शिष्ट, left, remainder) Land-tax, assessment, especially revenue assessed in money: in Karnata it designates the standard assessment without additions, which was fixed originally by the Bidnur government, or that which, under the Harihar administration, applied to revenue in kind as well as money, but the word always denoted the fixed or standard rate on the land, exclusive of other imposts.

Ṣist-báḳí, Karn. (from A. باقي, remainder) Balance or arrears of revenue.

ṢIṢU, S. &c. (शिशु) The young of man or any other animal: a child under eight years of age.

Ṣaiṣava, S. (शैशव) Infancy, childhood.

Ṣiṣuhatyá, S. (from हत्या, killing) Abortion, child-murder.

SÍṬṬA, Mal. (ശീട്ട) A note, a bill (it is evidently only a vernacular form of *Chiṭṭhi*, q. v.)

SIṬṬUDÁYAM, Tam. (சிற்றுதாயம்) Fraud, embezzlement.

SITÚÁ, (?) H. An iron instrument for scraping off the exuded juice of the poppy.

SIÚNÍ, Beng. (সিউনী) A kind of basket used for throwing up water from a reservoir or river for irrigation.

ṢIVA, vernacularly pronounced SHIVA, SHIB, SHEO, SHIÚ, &c. S. &c. (शिव) The third member of the Hindu triad, the deity presiding over destruction and renovation, and ordinarily worshipped in the form of the *Linga*.

Ṣiva-bhakta, S. &c. (from भक्त, devoted to) A worshipper of Siva in preference to any other divinity: in the south of India a *Lingait*, q. v.

Ṣiválaya, corruptly, *Seivala*, *Shiwala*, *Showala*, *Shewala*, S. &c. (from आलय, an abode) A temple of Ṣiva: in Bengal, a small temple or shrine having but one chamber, in the centre of which stands a *Linga*, usually of white or black stone; occasionally twelve such temples are arranged immediately adjoining, or separated into two divisions of six each by a gateway or landing-place when on a river bank, representing the twelve great *Lingas* that were worshipped in different parts of India at the time of the first Mohammadan invasion under Mahmud of Ghazni: occasionally a larger number, or as many sometimes as 108 are found in one group.

Ṣiváḷi, Karn. (ಶಿವಾಳಿ) A caste of Brahmans, or individual of it: originally from Tuluva, common in the north-west of Mysore.

Ṣivalingí, S. &c. (शिवलिंगी) A worshipper of the *Linga*, one who carries the type on his person.

Ṣivaprít, or *Ṣivottar*, Beng. &c. (শিবপ্রীৎ, শিবোত্তর, from S. प्रीति, pleasing, or उत्तर, result) Lands granted rent-free for the maintenance of the worship of Ṣiva.

Ṣivarái, Guz. (સીવરાઈ) A copper coin current in the Dakhin, coined originally by *Sivaji*.

Ṣivarátrí, vernacularly, *Shivarát*, S. &c. (शिवरात्री) The night of Ṣiva, a popular festival in honour of Ṣiva on the fourteenth of the moon's wane in Mágha (January-February): a rigorous fast is observed during the day and night, and Ṣiva is worshipped in the form of the *Linga*.

Ṣaiva, S. &c. (शैव) A worshipper or votary of Ṣiva.

Ṣivasháhí-bighá, Mar. (शिवशाहीबीघा) The bíghá of *Sivaji's* assessment containing $3926\frac{2}{3}$ square yards.

Ṣivasháhi-káṭhi, corruptly, *Sheoshaee-katty*, Mar. (शिवशाहीकाठी) A rod used in surveying, of five *háths*, and five *múṭhis*, or nearly ten feet, named after the Maratha chief *Sivaji*. See *Káṭhi*.

Ṣivottara, corruptly, *Sheotr*, *Shewutter*, S. &c. (शिवोत्तर) Land rent-free, as originally granted in honour of *Siva*.

ṢIVÁR, Mar. (शिवार) The whole of the lands of a village.

ṢIWÁÍ, corruptly, SWAEE, H. &c. (A. سواي) Besides, except, over and above: any addition to the standard or customary revenue, whether as an increase of the amount or in the shape of a new or additional cess or impost: profits from land other than those of cultivation, as the rent of fisheries, forest produce, and the like, some of which are included in fixing the assessment: dues claimed by the proprietors of a village from non-proprietary residents for houses, shops, and temples, in some cases recognised and recorded officially.

Ṣiwái-jamá, H. (سواي جمع), *Ṣiráy-jamá*, blunderingly, *Swaee*, and *Waee-jummá*, Mar. (शिवायजमा) Extra revenue, extra or miscellaneous collections: in the south the term denotes the revenue derived from all taxes except those raised from land, and exclusive of customs and transit dues, comprising, under the native governments, a vast number of petty and vexatious imposts: in Mysore it also applied to escheats: the effects of a person dying without heirs, which descended to the government.

SIWÁÍ, or SEWÁÍ, H. (سواي, सिवाई, सेवाई) A kind of soil, a mixture of clay and sand suited for any grain except rice.

SÍYÁN, or SÍYÁR, Tam. (சீயான், சீயார்) A great great-grandfather.

SMṚITI, S. &c. (स्मृतिः) The body of the recorded or remembered law, the ceremonial and legal institutes of the Hindus.

Smártta, S. &c. (स्मार्त्तः) Relating to the *Smriti* or Hindu law: applied especially in the south of India to a numerous and influential sect of Brahmans founded by *Ṣankaráchárya*, whose expositions of the principle of unity, according to the Vedánta doctrine, they professedly follow: Ṣiva is nevertheless held by them in especial honour: their chief establishment is at Sringagiri, but they are found throughout the Dakhin, and are treated with great veneration by the people in general: they are distinguished by horizontal lines on the forehead made with the ashes of burnt cowdung.

ṢMAṢÁNA, vernacularly, also, MASÁN and SAMSHÁN, S. &c. (श्मशानं) A place set apart in which the dead are burned, a cemetery.

SNÁNA, S. &c. (स्नानं) Bathing, ablution, especially the bathing in sacred waters, considered as a daily observance or as an essential part of some particular ceremonial: the ceremony of bathing or washing an idol.

Snánayátrá, vernacularly, *Snánjátrá*, S. &c. (स्नानयात्रा) The bathing festival held on the day of full moon in *Jyeshṭha*, when images of Krishṇa as Jagannátha are carried out and bathed: this is, in Orissa, the same as the *Rathayátrá*.

ṢOBHANA, S. &c. (शोभन) Beautiful, auspicious: any festive celebration, a festival held when a wife having come of fit age is carried home to the house of her husband: the thirty-seventh year of the cycle: also, *Ṣobhakṛiti*, or, in the south, *Ṣobhakrutti*.

SOD, SOḌ, or SOṚ, or ṢOṚ, Mar. (सोड, शोड, from H. چھوڑنا, *chhorná*), SÓḌI, Karn. (ಸೊಡಿ) Letting go, remitting, remission of a debt, abatement of a charge or demand: the amount remitted or abated.

Soḍchiṭi, or *Soḍchiṭhi*, Mar. (सोडचिटी) A bill of release, a deed of acquittance or relinquishment.

SODAKA, S. &c. (सोदक, from स, with, उदक, water) A kinsman connected by offerings of water to the manes of a common ancestor.

SODARA, S. &c. (सोदर, from स, with, उदर, belly) A brother of whole blood, having the same mother as well as father.

ṢODHA, vernacularly ṢODH, S. &c. (سودھ, शोध) Correction, purification, discharge of a debt, fulfilment of an agreement, and the like.

Ṣodhana, S. &c. (शोधन) Purifying, making pure, completing, settling.

Sodhana, also *Sodhá*, Thug. Money or property concealed, search made for it.

Sódhanai, Tam. (சோதனை) Examination, search, cross questioning in a court of justice.

SODWAṆÍ, Mar. (सोडवणी) The water that runs through gardens in small temporary channels for irrigation.

SOHÁGIÁ, more correctly SAUHÁGIÁ, H. (سہاگیا) A class of Mohammadan fakírs who dress in female attire, and play and dance for hire at religious festivals.

SOHAḶÁ, SOHÁḶÁ, Mar. (सोहळा, सोहाळा) Any festive ceremony or occasion, as adoption, marriage, or the like.

SOHARWARDÍ, (?) H. The name of a class of Mohammadan religious mendicants.

SOKHÁ, Hindi (सोखा) A conjuror, a wizard.—Chota Nagpur.

SOLA, Tel. (సొల), SOLAGE, SOLIGE, Karn. (ಸೊಲಗೆ, ಸೊಲಿಗೆ) The sixty-fourth part of the measure of capacity called *Túm*, q. v.

Solage-guḍḍe, Karn. (ಸೊಲಗೆಗುಡ್ಡೆ) The fees of the village accountant.

SOLANKI, (?) The name of a Rájput tribe in the west of India and Guzerat.

SOḶULÍ, pronounced, commonly, SORULI, corruptly, SAROOLI, SOOROOLLY, Mar. (सोळुली, from सोळा, sixteen) A measure of grain containing 16 *páyalís*: the term also designates the class of villages in which the measure of 16 *páyalís* is used, in distinction from those villages which are termed *Báruli*, from their using a measure of 12 (*bára*) *páyalís*.

SOMA, vernacularly, SOM, S. &c. (सोम) The moon, also a climbing plant from which a juice is extracted by pressure, which, when fermented, is offered in libation to the gods or to fire (Sarcostema, or Asclepias viminalis).

Somavára, vernacularly, *Somvár*, *Sombár*, S. &c. (सोमवार) Monday, the day of the moon.

Somaváryáteli, Mar. (सोमवाऱ्यातेली) An oil-maker of a particular class, the members of which are worshippers of Ṣiva as *Soma*, and do no work on Monday.

Somayága, S. &c. (याग, a sacrifice) A sacrifice, a ceremony in which the juice of the *Soma* plant is presented in oblation, and drunk by the assistants when in a state of vinous fermentation: it is a Vaidik ceremonial, and has much fallen into disuse.

Somavatí, S. (सोमवती) A ceremony observed by Maratha

women; circumambulating a *Pípal* tree, and placing offerings on it when the new moon falls on a Monday.

SOMMÁḶI, Tam. (சொம்மாளி, from சொம், for स्व, own) An heir.

SOMMU, Tel. (సొమ్ము) Money, property, including jewels.

SONÁ, H. (سونا, from S. सुवर्ण), SONÁ, Beng. (সোনা), SONEṆ, Mar. (सोनें) Gold.

Sonár, Hindi, Mar. (सोनार, abridged from S. सुवर्णकार), *Sunár*, H. (سنار), *Sónagar*, Karn. (ಸೋನಗರ), *Soṇi*, Guz. (સોણી) A goldsmith, a jeweller, a worker in the precious metals and in jewellery: applied also as a name of the caste which is said to have sprung from a Brahman father and Ṣúdra mother, being in that case the Párásava of Manu: among the Marathas there are various subdivisions of the *Sonár* caste, some of whom disclaim this origin, and pretend to be Upa-Brahmanas, minor Brahmans: they wear the Brahmanical cord, and claim a right to have the Vedas performed in their families by their own priests: they are known as *Kanári*, *Pancháḷa*, and *Kokanasth Sonars*: another tribe is designated *Rathahár Sonárs*: other classes are of inferior pretensions, and are termed *Ních*, or low *Sonárs*: they eat animal food.

Sónár-áyati-dhúḷi-aya, Karn. (ಸೋನಾರಆಯತಿಧೂಳಿಅಯ) The name of the fees paid to the persons employed to measure the grain for the cultivators.

SONA, (?) Beng. Land producing *ásu* or *ouse* rice. See *Ásu.*

Sonadanga, (?) Beng. High land that cannot be irrigated.

SONṚKA, Thug. The first person murdered after setting out.

SONṬÁ, H. (سونٹا) A mace, a staff.

Sonṭebardár, H. (سونٹي بردار) A mace or staff-bearer, a servant carrying a short thick stick, usually coated with silver, attending on persons of rank.

SONTAM, Tam. (சொந்தம், from S. स्व, own) Property, own or peculiar property or possession.

Sontakáran, Tam. (சொந்தக்காரன்) A proprietor, an owner.

SONYAPHÁGAN, (?) Hindi, Present or fee to government at public festivals.—Kamaon.

SOSE, Karn. (ಸೊಸೆ) A daughter-in-law.

Sódara-sose, Karn. (ಸೋದರಸೊಸೆ) A man's sister's daughter, or a woman's brother's daughter.

SOSTÍJAMÍN, (?) Mar. Land assessed at the customary or established rate.

SOTÁ, incorrectly, SONTA, H. (سوتا, S. स्रोतस) A channel, a natural water-course or passage.

SOTAZAMIN, (?) Tel. A kind of soil, clay and lime, cultivated in the rains for rice.—Northern Sarkárs.

SOTHA, Thug. The person employed to inveigle travellers.

SOTÍ, Hindi (सोती) A ravine which in the rains or floods becomes a water-course.

SOWAḶÁ, or SONWAḶÁ, Mar. (सोवळा, सोंवळा) Pure, as a Brahman, or as articles that are free from profane contamination, that are fit for sacred offices or offerings, and liable to be defiled by impure contact.

ṢRÁDDHA, vernacularly, SRÁDH, SHRÁDH, SHRÁDDHA, S. &c. (श्राद्ध) An obsequial ceremony in which food and water are offered to the deceased ancestors of the sacrificer, or to the *Pitṛis* or manes collectively: these ceremonies are observed on occasions of rejoicing as well as of mourning, and hence various *Ṣráddhas* are enumerated.

1. *Daṣapiṇḍa Ṣráddha*, or *Preta Ṣ.* An offering of a *piṇḍa* or ball of rice to a person deceased by the next of kin, increasing the number daily for ten successive days, until they amount to ten.

2. *Ekádaṣí Ṣ.* Presentation of offerings to the deceased on the eleventh day after his decease, on which occasion Brahmans are fed, and the period of uncleanness for a Brahman terminates.

Másika, or *Anwahárya Ṣ.* Performed monthly for the first year after a person's decease, on the day of his death, accompanied also by the feeding of Brahmans.

Sapiṇḍana, or *Sapiṇḍí-karaṇa Ṣ.* Performed on the first anniversary after a person's death, in which the deceased is associated with his progenitors, and balls of food are presented to him with his father and grandfather, and water is given for four other ascending generations: sometimes the process is so far abridged that the *Sapiṇḍana* is performed on the twelfth day after a person's death. Some other supplementary *Ṣráddhas* within the twelvemonth are occasionally practised, but they are of local observance. These *Ṣráddhas* are also designated as *Ekoddishṭa*, designed (*uddishṭa*) for an individual (*eka*), being intended to secure the admission of the one person deceased into the region of the *pitṛis* or manes: as contrasted with the *Ekoddishṭa Ṣráddhas*, are the *Párvaṇa Ṣráddhas*, which are the obsequial offerings to ancestors in both the paternal and maternal lines for three generations, at the junctures or periods of the month, as the new moon: *Ṣráddhas* are also distinguished as,

1. *Nitya*, Constant, those enjoined by positive precept to

be performed, such as daily offerings to the manes in general, and those termed Ashṭakas from their being offered on the eighth lunation of certain months.

2. *Naimittika,* Occasional, such as those for a relative recently deceased, or such as are to be performed on various domestic occurrences, as the birth of a son, &c.; and

3. *Kámya,* Voluntary, performed for a special object, such as the hope of religious merit and of heaven: besides these, different authorities specify,—

Vṛiddhi, or *Abhyudayaka Ṣráddha,* Performed on occasions of increase or prosperity.

Goshṭhí Ṣ. A ceremony performed for the benefit of an assembly of learned Brahmans.

Ṣuddhi Ṣ. An expiatory or purificatory rite.

Karmáṅga Ṣ. Performed as the preparatory or subsidiary part (*anga*) of any solemn rite (*karma*).

Daiva Ṣ. In honour of the deities collectively, or *Viṣwadevas.*

Yátrá Ṣ. Performed by a person going on a journey.

Pushṭi Ṣ. Performed to obtain health and prosperity.

Nándí-mukha Ṣ. also performed for the sake of securing prosperity on occasions of domestic rejoicing.

Darṣa Ṣ., or *Amávásya Ṣ.* Performed at new moon before the moon is visible: this is the season especially appropriate to all occasional *Ṣráddhas.*

Mahálaya Ṣ. A *Ṣráddha* performed in the last half of *Bhádra,* immediately before the *Dasahará.*

The proper seasons for the worship of the manes collectively are the dark fortnight or period of the moon's wane: the day of new moon: the days called *Ashṭakas,* or the eighth lunations of the dark fortnight of the four months of the cold weather: the summer and winter solstices, the vernal and autumnal equinoxes, the sun's entrance into a new sign, certain other astronomical periods, and eclipses: the presentation of the *Piṇḍa* to the deceased and to his progenitors in both lines is the office of the nearest male relative, and is the test and title of his claim to the inheritance.

ṢRAMAṆA, S. &c. (श्रमण) A religious mendicant, especially one of the Buddhist religion.

ṢRÁVAKA, vernacularly, ṢRÁVAK, S. &c. (श्रावक) Lit., A hearer, a lay-member of the Jain religion.

ṢRÁVAṆA, vernacularly, SHRÁVAN, SÁVAN, or SÁWAN, corruptly, SAWN, S. &c. (श्रावणः) The fourth month of the Hindu year, July-August.

Ṣrávaṇí, S. &c. (श्रावणी), vernacularly, *Sávaní,* (सावनी) Day of full moon in the month *Ṣrávaṇa*: the autumn harvest.

ṢRÁVITTA-SÁKSHI, Karn. (ಶ್ರಾವಿತ್ತಸಾಕ್ಷಿ, from the S. श्रुतसाक्ष्यं) Oral testimony, or rather hearsay evidence.

ṢRAYA, pron. SHRAYA, Karn. (ಶ್ರಯ) Depreciated land, land let at a rate below its original value, to which it is expected gradually to rise again.

Ṣraya-chiṭú, or *-paṭṭé*, Karn. (ಶ್ರಯಚೀಟು, ಶ್ರಯಪಟ್ಟೆ) Lease of land let below its value.

Ṣrayaságuvaḷi, Karn. (ಶ್ರಯಸಾಗುವಳಿ) Farming land on a rent below its original value, and progressively rising to it.

ṢREṆÍ, S. &c. (श्रेणी) A row, a line: a corporation or association of persons following the same trade or occupation: a court of arbitration formed of persons in the same line of business.

ṢRÍ, S., but used in all the dialects, vulgarly, SHRÍ or SHREE, (श्री) Prosperity, fortune, wealth, also their personification as a goddess, the goddess of prosperity, and wife of *Vishṇu*: the term is used as an honorific prefix to the names of persons or divinities, and also at the beginning of manuscripts, letters, and other documents, and, when intended to be very complimentary, may be repeated, as, *Ṣrí Ṣrí Jayarám, Ṣrí Ṣrí Ṣrí Durgá*, or the repetition is indicated by a numeral, as *Ṣrí 5.* (श्री ५), means *Ṣrí* five times repeated.

Ṣrímukha, S. &c. (श्रीमुख) The seventh year of the cycle.

Ṣrípanchamí, S. &c. (श्रीपञ्चमी) A festival on the fifth of the light half of *Mágha* in honour of *Saraswatí*, the goddess of learning, when books and the implements of writing are worshipped.

Ṣrí-Ráma, or, vernacularly, *Ṣrí-Rám*, S. &c. (श्रीरामः) The demigod Ráma, whose name in this form is also used as a term of salutation between those who especially worship *Vishṇu* in this *avatára.*

Ṣrí-Ráma-navamí, S. &c. (श्रीरामनवमी) The ninth of *Chaitra*, the anniversary of the birthday of Ráma, held as a festival.

Ṣrí-vaishṇava, S. &c. (श्रीवैष्णवः) A member of the branch of votaries of *Vishṇu* who follow the teaching of *Rámánuja.*

ṢṚINKHALÁ, S. &c. (शृंखला), vernacularly, ṢANKHALÁ, Mar. (शंखला), ṢANKHOLÍ, Uriya (ଶଙ୍ଖୋଳି) A chain, fetters, a measuring chain, one measuring eleven yards (?).

Ṣṛinkhalá-jáminí, corruptly, *Sankala*, or *Saṇkali jámini*, Mar. (शृंखलाजामिनी) Joint security.

ṢROTRIYA, vernacularly, SHROTRIYA, S. &c. (श्रोत्रियः) A Brahman well read in the Vedas, who teaches and expounds them.

Ṣrotriyam, pron. Shrotriam, corruptly, Shotrium, Tel. (శ్రోత్రియము), Ṣrotriyagráma, Karn. (ಶ್ರೋತ್ರಿಯಗ್ರಾಮ), Tam. (சுரோத்திரியம்) Lands, or a village, held at a favourable rate, properly an assignment of land or revenue to a Brahman learned in the Vedas, but latterly applied generally to similar assignments to native servants of the government, civil or military, and both Hindus and Mohammadans, as a reward for past services: a *Ṣrotriyam* grant gives no right over the lands, and the grantee cannot interfere with the occupants as long as they pay the established rents.

Ṣrotriya-dár, corruptly, *Shotradár*, *Shotrium-dár*, *Shrotrium-dár*, Tel. &c. (from P. دار, who has) The holder of a village under a *Ṣrotriya* grant.

Ṣruti, S. &c. (श्रुतिः) Hearing, applied especially to the Vedas collectively, in contradistinction to the *Smṛiti*, or law.

Ṣrauta, S. &c. (श्रौत) Of or belonging to the Vedas, as a text, a ceremony, &c.

Ṣrautakarma, S. (श्रौतकर्म्म) A religious or ceremonial observance enjoined by or conformable to the Vedas.

Stambha-pújá, S. &c. (स्तम्भपूजा, from स्तम्भ, a post, and पूजा, worship) Worship of the posts of the temporary pavilions erected for marriages or other festive occasions.

Steya, S. &c. (स्तेय) Theft, robbery.

Sthala, vernacularly, Sthal, or Sthul, abbreviated to Thal, or Thul, corruptly, Stul, Stull, Stulh, S. &c. (स्थल) Spot, site, place, firm ground, whence, in some of the dialects, a field, a portion of land comprising several fields, a tract, a district, a piece of ground raised and drained: in some places a measure of land the same as the *Kurgí*, q. v. also, figuratively, station, place, appointment.

Sthala-karanam, Tel. (స్థలకరణం) The accountant of a district.

Sthalalu-jábita, Tel. (స్థలలుజాబితా) A list of fields, shewing the number cultivated and the crops raised on each.

Sthala-mányam, corruptly, *Stala-maniyem*, Karn. (ಸ್ಥಲಮಾನ್ಯಂ) Land held at a quit-rent.

Sthala-márga, Mar. (स्थलमार्ग) A road or way by land, in opposition to a *Jala-márga*, or route by water.

Sthal-bharít, Mar. (स्थलभरीत) Duty on transport of articles from a village, or on goods purchased and conveyed by land, transit duty.

Sthalwáhík, corruptly, *Sthulwayk*, Mar. (स्थलवाहीक) A cultivator who has become a proprietor by hereditary occupation of a given piece of land for a considerable period.

Sthalwár, H. (ستهلوار) According to the land or place, by or according to the fields, as an estimate of their produce, &c., also, corruptly, *Stulwár*, a village watchman; in Karnata (?).

Sthána, or Sthánam, vernacularly, Sthán, or Thán, vulgarly, Stanom, S. &c. (स्थानं) Place, site, station, an open place in a town, also the residence of a religious mendicant: also, a staying, the act or place of staying or abiding: also, continuation, and, fig., rank, dignity.

Sthánamánam, Mal. (സ്ഥാനമാനം, from S. मान, respect) The rank and emoluments of a public employment.

Sthánamkár, corruptly, *Stanomkár*, Mal. (സ്ഥാനംകാര) The head man and manager of a temple.

Sthánapati, Mal. (സ്ഥാനാപതി) An envoy, an ambassador.

Sthánikan, corruptly, *Staneehum*, *Staneegam*, *Stanahul*, Mal. (സ്ഥാനികൻ, S. स्थानिक) One who holds or belongs to a place, one who holds an office, a placeman: a governor or superintendant of a district: the director or manager of a temple, sometimes held hereditarily: a person who superintends the ceremonies or officiates in a temple, an officiating priest or Brahman.

Sthandilaṣáyí, S. &c. (स्थंडिलशायी) An ascetic who sleeps on the bare ground.

Sthapati, S. &c. (स्थपति) A carpenter, a wheelwright, a mason, a master carpenter or mason: a guard of the female apartments: a chief.

Sthávara, vernacularly, Sthávar, Sthábar, S. &c. (स्थावर) Fixed, stationary, immoveable, applied to real property, also to valuables which have long been in a family and ought not to be parted with.

Sthávara-dravya, S. (द्रव्य, thing) Immoveable property.

Sthúlamán, Mar. (स्थूलमान, S. स्थूल, gross, and मान, measure) Gross measure, measuring any thing without much regard to accuracy: a general and rough estimate or computation.

Stobhaka, (स्तोभक) An informer, one who volunteers to give secret information for the sake of profit.

Strí, S. &c. (स्त्री) A woman, a wife, a female.

Strídhana, S. &c. (स्त्रीधन) Woman's wealth: the peculiar property of a woman or wife over which, under ordinary circumstances, she has independent control, and which descends to her daughter or next of kin; her power to dispose of it during her husband's life is subject to his will, and he has a right to use it in cases of distress or necessity: the rights of both husband and wife to this description of property depend, hovever, very much upon the customs that prevail in different places. Woman's property is variously distinguished according to the sources whence it is derived, or circumstances under which it is acquired, as follows.

Adhyagni, *Adhyagnika*, or *Adhyagnyupágata*, (अध्यग्नि, अध्यग्निक, अध्यग्न्युपागत) What is given upon (*adhi*), or in the presence of, a nuptial fire, by a member of either family.

Adhyaváhanika, (अध्यवाहनिक) What is given at the nuptial procession, or when the bride is conducted to her husband's house.

Príti-datta, (प्रीतिदत्त) Given by her husband or his relations at any time, in token of affection.

Bhrátṛi-, *Mátṛi-*, or *Pitṛi-datta*, (भातृ-, मातृ-, पितृ-दत्त) What is given by her brother, mother, or father.

Yautaka, or *Yautuka*, (यौतक, यौतुक, from यु, to join) All kinds of property acquired at or by marriage.

Ayautuka, (अयौतुक) Property acquired on any other occasion than marriage.

Anvádheya, (अन्वाधेय) Whatever is to be presented (*ádheya*) to a woman after (*anu*) marriage by her husband's family.

Saudáyika, (सौदायिक) The gift (*dáya*) of affectionate (*su*) kindred.

Ádhivedanika, (आधिवेदनिक) A gift or settlement on a first wife by her husband on his contracting a second marriage.

Páriṇaya, (पारिणय) Paraphernalia, ornaments, or other property acquired by marriage.

Ṣulka, (शुल्क) Fee, tax, perquisite: properly it is the sum paid to the father of the bride as a consideration for his daughter: as applied to female property it is explained as money given to her to induce her to go to her husband's house, or pay to a woman for work done, or as a bribe to her to do something herself or induce her husband to do it.

Pádavandanika, (पादवंदनिक) A present to a bride in reward of her humbly saluting (*vandana*) her husband, or, literally, his feet (*páda*) on entering his house.

Lávaṇyárjita, (लावण्यार्जित) Property acquired (*arjita*) by a wife from her husband, given in affection or in admiration of her beauty (*lávaṇya*).

Strídharma, S. &c. (स्त्रीधर्म्मः) The duty of a wife or of a woman in general.

Stríhatyá, S. (स्त्रीहत्या) Murder or injury of a woman.

Strípumdharma, S. (स्त्रीपुंधर्म्मः) Mutual duties of husband and wife.

Strísangrahaṇa, S. (स्त्रीसंग्रहण) Adultery, unlawful or adulterous intercourse with a woman.

Strísattákaputra, S. (स्त्रीसत्ताकपुत्रः) A son obtained through the wife.

Stríyáchitaputra, S. (स्त्रीयाचितपुत्रः) A son obtained through a wife's solicitations.

SUÁL, commonly, SUWÁL, corruptly, SOWÁL, H. (A. سوال) Interrogatory questioning, a request, a petition.

Suál-i-muḳarrar, H. (A. مقرر) A petition or representation of the circumstances of a case, a representation to the ruling authority of the proceedings in respect to a grant of revenue.

ṢÚBAH, SOOBAH, H. &c. (A. صوبه), SUBHÁ, Mar. (सुभा) A province, a government: one of the larger subdivisions of the Mogul dominions, such as Oudh, Bengal, Bahar, &c.: among the Marathas it is sometimes applied to a smaller division comprising from five to eight *ṭarafs*.

Ṣúbahdár, H. &c. (صوبهدار), *Subhedár*, Mar. (सुभेदार) The governor of a province, a viceroy under the Mogul government: a native officer in the Company's army holding a rank equivalent to that of captain under the European officers.

Ṣúbahdárí, H. &c. (صوبهداري), *Subhedárí*, Mar. (सुभेदारी) The office of viceroy or governor.

Ṣúbahdárí-abwáb, H. (ابواب) Taxes imposed by the viceroy in addition to the fixed assessment. See *Abwáb*.

Ṣúbahdárí-parwána, H. (پروانه) An order issued by a Ṣúbahdár: a viceregal assignment of revenue.

ṢUBHKHEZ, H. (صبح خيز) A morning thief, one who steals before people are awake (from *ṣúbh*, morning, and *khez*, rising).

Ṣubh-namáz, or *Ṣalat*, H. (صبح نماز, صبح صلوه) Morning prayer, the prayers at day-break enjoined on all Mohammadans.

ŞUBHA, vernacularly, SUBH, or SHUBH, S. &c. (शुभ) Good, auspicious.

Ṣubhákṛiti, vernacularly, *Shubhakruti*, (शुभाकृति) The 36th year of the cycle, A.D. 1842.

ṢÚCHAKA, S. &c. (शूचक) An informer, a spy: in law, a person appointed to detect culprits, also one who volunteers to give evidence in a court of law.

SÚD, H. &c. (P. سود, सूद), SÚD, Beng. (সুদ), SUD, or SUDH, Uriya (ସୁଦ, ସୁଧ) Interest, profit, usury: an extra tax exacted from the cultivators in Bengal under the native government, and in the early period of British rule, on pretext of defraying the interest due by the Zamindárs on arrears of revenue: interest on loans subsequent to January 1793 limited to 12 per cent. per annum. Reg. xv. 1793.

Súd-al-muẓáf, H. (A. مضاف, added) The accumulation of interest so as to double the original debt.

Súd-ekottar, H. (S. एक, one, and उत्तर, additional) Interest at one per cent. per annum.

Sudhkhaibár, Uriya (ସୁଧଖାଇବାର) Usury, lending money at interest.

Sudkhor, Beng. (সুদখোর) A money-lender, a usurer.

SÚḌ, Mar. (सूड) Inquiry, investigation: an abstract village account furnished by the village to the district revenue officer at the end of the year (? the spelling of the word in the second sense).

ṢUDDHA, vernacularly, SUDH, abbreviated SU, S. &c. (शुद्ध) Pure, clean, bright: the bright half of the lunar month, or that of the moon's increase: the purificatory obsequial ceremony of a person deceased.

SUDI, H. &c. (سدي, सुदि) The bright half of a lunar month, from new to full moon.

ṢÚDRA, vulgarly, SOODER, S. &c. (शूद्र) The designation of the fourth or servile caste of the Hindus, or of a member of it: the term is now vaguely and incorrectly applied to all the mixed castes, to all who are not either Brahmans or outcastes; to all the other castes engaged in agriculture, trade, arts, and manufactures.

Sachchúdra, Beng. (সচ্ছূদ্র, from S. सत, good) A *Ṣúdra* who has gone through the initiatory ceremonies of the Brahmanical caste, a practice which, though illegal, is sometimes observed. See *Satsudra*.

SÚḌU, Tam. (சூடு) A sheaf, a bundle of rice-corn cut in the field, especially when given to the village servant: also a burning or a brand.

Súḍukol, Tam. (சூடுக்கோல்) A branding iron.

Suḍugáḍu, Karn. (ಸುಡುಗಾಡು) A place where dead bodies are burned.

Súḍugáḍusidda, Karn. (ಸುಡುಗಾಡುಸಿದ್ಧ) The keeper of a place where bodies are burned, who levies a fee from the burners: one who farms a burning or burying-place of the government.

ṢUFÍ, H. (A. صفي) Wise, a sage, the member of a particular sect of Mohammadans who have adopted a mystical pantheism and spiritual love in secret, although outwardly conforming to Mohammadanism.

SUGGI, corruptly, SOOGUY, Karn. (ಸುಗ್ಗಿ, from S. सुखी) Spring harvest, the second crop of rice.

Suggihabba, Karn. (ಸುಗ್ಗಿಹಬ್ಬ) Offering the first gatherings of the harvest to the village goddess.

Suggikál, less correctly, *Sukhikál*, Karn. (ಸುಗ್ಗಿಕಾಲ) Harvest time: a season of plenty.

SÚÍ, SÚJÍ, H. (سوي, سوجي, from S. शूचि, a needle) A tailor, the village tailor, sometimes included among the village servants.

SÚJÍ, SOOJEE, H. (سوجي) The flour ground from the heart of the wheat: the *Simola* of the Italians.

SUKAL, Guz. (સુકલ) A priest of lay Brahmans.

SUKÁLIGARU, plur. Karn. (ಸುಕಾಲಿಗರು) A class of Hindus in Karnáta leading a vagrant life, trading in wood, bambus, grain, and salt, and acting as the chief inland carriers; they have a peculiar dialect, and are considered in many respects analogous to gypsies: in other places the *Suháli* is an itinerant dealer in grain, and is considered, perhaps incorrectly, the same as the *Banjára*.

SUKARISTI, (?) Mar. An occupant of lands of which there are no proprietors, and which have become the property of the community.

SUKHA, vernacularly, SUKH, S. &c. (सुख) Happiness, ease, pleasure.

Sukhasála, Karn. (ಸುಖಸಾಲ) Bail or surety for a debt.

Sukhavási, corruptly, *Sookawasee*, *Sookwoosee*, Tam. (சுகவாசி) One who lives at his ease, or where he pleases: applied to a person who is not bound to any particular spot by the possession of houses or land, but lives comfortably by trade or industry: in Kamaon, *Sukham-básí*.

Sukhavásikuḍigan, Tam. (சுகவாசிக்குடிகள்) Persons who live by the produce of rented lands.

Sukhavásitírvai, Tam. (சுகவாசித்தீர்வை) Tribute or tax which persons living by rented lands pay to the landlords or proprietors.

Sukhavásiváram, Tam. (சுகவாசிவாரம்) The share of the produce accruing to the cultivator, as distinguished from that which goes to the Zamindár or the government.

Sukhvastí, corruptly, *Sookhwustie*, Mar. (सुखवस्ती) Residence at any place during pleasure or convenience, not being tied to it by property or office.

Sukhvastú, corruptly, *Sookwustoo*, Mar. (सुखवस्तू) A person sojourning at any place for his own pleasure or convenience.

SUKHAḌI, or SUKHARI, corruptly, SOOKREE, and SUKHIDDEE, Guz. (સુખડી) A fee, a perquisite, a bonus or reward, a douceur, a bribe.

Sukhaḍi-chándlo, Guz. (સુખડીચાંદલો) A fee, a present, a

douceur, a fee levied by the agents of the Maratha government from the villagers, for the trouble of rating the assessment.

SUKKÁN, H. (A. سکّان) A helm, a rudder.

Sukkháni, H. (A. سكّاني) A steersman, a helmsman: corrupted by Europeans commonly to *Seacunny*.

SUKKARAN, or SUKKARANKAL, Tam. (சுக்கரன், சுக்கரன்கல்) Limestone or *kankar*.

Sukkaraníru, Tam. (சுக்கரணீறு) Lime.

Sukkaranilam, Tam. (சுக்கரநிலம்) Soil mixed with limestone or nodules of *kankar*.

ṢUKLA, vernacularly, *Shukl*, S. &c. (शुक्ल) White, bright: subs., the third year of the cycle, A.D. 1809—1869.

Ṣuklpachchh, H. (سکلپچھ, for S. *Ṣuklapaksha* शुक्लपक्ष) The white or light fortnight, the half of a lunar month from new to full moon.

ṢUKRA, S. &c. (शुक्र) The planet Venus.

Ṣukravára, vernacularly, *Shukrbár*, S. &c. (शुक्रवार) Friday, dies veneris.

SUKRITA, Uriya (ସୁକୃତ, from the S. सुकृत, what is done well or properly) An oath.

SUKṚITI, S. &c. (सुकृति) Doing well, virtue, kindness.

Sukṛitibhanga, Beng. (সুকৃতিভংগ, from S. भंग, a breaking) A Brahman who has lost his character and his caste.

Sukṛiti-námá, or *-patra*, Beng. (সুকৃতিনামা, or পত্র) A written affidavit or affirmation, in which a Brahman pledges his good actions for the truth of his assertions.

SÚKSHMAMÁN, Mar. (सूक्ष्ममान, from S. सूक्ष्म, subtle, minute) Accurate or minute measurement.

ṢÚLA, vernacularly, SÚL, or SÚLÍ, S. &c. (शूल, शूली, سول, سولي) A pointed weapon, a pike or dart, a stake, a sharp stake for impaling, whence it has come to be applied to a cross, and to a gallows or gibbet.

Triṣúla, vernacularly, *Tirsúl*, S. &c. (त्रिशूल, ترسول) A weapon with three points, a trident, a weapon borne by, and a type of, *Ṣiva*.

ṢULAIYÁ, Hindi (शुलैया) Laid down, as corn by wind and rain, or rice by currents.

ṢULB, H. (A. صلب) The loins: metaph., offspring.

Ṣulbí, H. (A. صلبي) Descended, or sprung from, begotten by.

ṢULH, incorrectly, SOOLEH, corruptly, SOLA, H. (A. صلح) Reconciliation, compact, treaty: in law, composition, or a contract by which contention is put an end to or prevented, whether the subject in dispute be bodily injury or a civil engagement: a compromise, an agreement.

Ṣulh-ikhtiári, A. (from اختيار, choice) A voluntary act of composition.

Ṣulh-ḳahri, H. (from قهر, violence) Compulsory composition, made by order of the judge or other authority.

Ṣulh-náma, corruptly, *Solanama*, H. (P. نامه) A written contract of peace or agreement, a deed of compromise.

ṢULKA, S. &c. (शुल्क) Tax, toll, duty, marriage fee or dower, profits of domestic labour when considered the perquisite of the wife: in the dialects of the south this may become *Sunka*, or *Chunka*. See *Sunka*.

ṢULṢ, H. (A. ثلث) A third, a third part.

SULṬÁN, H. (A. سلطان) A sovereign prince, a king, an emperor.

Sulṭání, H. (سلطاني) Relating to the sovereign, proceeding from him or from the government.

Saláṭín, H. (A. سلاطين) Properly the plur. of *Sulṭán*, but in India designating the younger members of a royal family, especially of that of Delhi.

Sulṭanat, H. (A. سلطنت) Dominion, empire, sovereignty: an empire, a kingdom.

SÚMÚ, (?) A religious community resident in a religious establishment, in Asam termed *Shastar*.

SUN, Thug. One of the clan by birth, but who has not attained the rank of a strangler.

SÚNÁ, Mar. (सूना, S. सुना, a daughter) A daughter-in-law, also the wife of a brother's son, or of a husband's brother's son, that is, a niece-in-law.

Súnamukh, Mar. (सूनमुख) A ceremony after the consummation of a marriage, consisting of the inspection of her daughter-in-law's face by the mother of the bridegroom.

SUNBURLÍ, SOONBOORLEE, Mar. (?) Black soil mixed with lime.

SUNDARÍ, corruptly, SOONDRIE, S. &c. (सुन्दरी) A small timber tree, used chiefly as fire-wood (Heritiera minor), growing extensively in the delta of the Ganges, and giving the whole tract the name of *Sundarívana*, or forest of Sundarí trees, corrupted into Sunderbunds.

ṢUNIÁ, Uriya (ଶୁଣିଆ) New-year's day.

ṢUNIBÁ, Uriya (ଶୁଣିବା) Hearsay (from *Suna*, S., to hear).

SUNKAM, or SUNKA, Karn. Tel. (సుంకం, సుంకం), also Karn. SULKA (ಸುಲ್ಕ), CHUNKAM, Mal. (ചുങ്കം), Tam. (சுங்கம்) Duty on goods, custom, toll: (from the S. *Ṣulka*, q. v.).

Sunka-chauki, Tel. (సుంకచౌకి) Custom-house.

Sunkadachávadi, or *Sunkada-kaṭṭé*, Karn. (ಸುಂಕದಚಾವಡಿ, ಸುಂಕದಕಟ್ಟೆ) A custom-house.

Sunkadaguttige, or *-ijáre*, Karn. (ಸುಂಕದಗುತ್ತಿಗೆ, -ಇಜಾರೆ) Farm of, or contract for, government customs.

Sunkadakolkár, Karn. (ಸುಂಕದಕೊಲ್ಕಾರ) A kind of excise officer, a spy on persons passing with goods.

Sunkada-maniyagár, Karn. (ಸುಂಕದಮಣಿಯಗಾರ) A chief collector of customs.

Sunkadava, Karn. (ಸುಂಕದವ) A custom-house officer.

Sunkadaṣánabhog, Karn. (ಸುಂಕದಶಾನಭೋಗ) A clerk of customs.

Gaḍísunka, Karn. (ಗಡೀಸುಂಕ) Out-station customs.

Dárísunka, Karn. (ದಾರೀಸುಂಕ) By-way customs.

Úru-sunka, Karn. (ಊರುಸುಂಕ) Town duties.

SUNNAT, or SUNNAH, H. &c. (A. سنّت, سنّه) The traditional law of Mohammadans based upon the sayings and doings of Mohammad, and of scarcely inferior authority to the text of the Kurán in the estimation of the *Sunnis*, although not recognised by the *Shias*; also any obligatory religious ceremony, as circumcision.

Sunnat-i-rakât, H. (A. ركعت, q. v.) Ceremonial observances enjoined in prayer upon the authority of tradition: they are distinguished as *Muwakkad* (موكد), lit., confirmed or absolute, having been enjoined and practised by Mohammad, and *Ghair-muwakkad* (غيرموكد), not absolute, practised by Mohammad, but not obligatory on his followers.

Sunnat-wa-jamâât, H. (سنّتوجماعت) The followers of the traditions and of the first four khalifs.

Sunni, *Soonee*, H. (A. سنّي) A follower of the traditions: the designation of one of the two great divisions of the Mohammadans, characterized not only by the deference which the members pay to tradition, but by their affirmation of the lawful succession of the first four khalifs, *Abubakr*, *Omar*, *Othman*, and *Âli*, in opposition to the Shias, who denounce the three first as usurpers. The *Sunnis* are thence sometimes termed also *Chahár-yárís*, or votaries of the four friends. The Persians, and the lower orders of the people of India, are Shias; all the other Mohammadan nations Arabs, Turks, Afghans, and most of the educated and respectable classes of Indians, are *Sunnis*.

SÚNṚÍ, H. (سونڑي) A distiller and vender of spirituous liquors.

SUNTÁN, H. (A. سنتان) Circumcision.

SUNTI, or SUTI, Beng. (সুঁতি, সুতি) A channel between the bank of a river and a shoal or sand-bank.

SÚP, Mar. (सूप, S. शूर्प) A basket for winnowing corn: a wooden scoop suspended in a frame for throwing up water for irrigation.

SUPÁRÍ, or SUPIÁRÍ, H. &c. (سپاري, سپياري) Betel-nut, the fruit of the Areca catechu.

SUPARIYA, Thug. A gang or clan of Thugs originally from *Supar* in Sindhia's country.

SUPURD, or SIPURD, H. &c. (P. سپرد) Delivering, giving over: relinquishing, as part of an estate held on lease, from being unable to cultivate the whole.

Supurdi, H. &c. (سپردي) The article or land delivered up.

Supurdnáma, H. &c. (P. نامه, a document) A deed of delivery.

SÚR, SOOR, (?) A class of cultivators in Orissa.

SURÁ, H. &c. (S. سرا, सुरा) Wine, spirituous liquor.

Surádhwaja, S. (from ध्वज, a flag) A flag hung out as the sign of a place where liquor is sold: a brand on the forehead of a person convicted of intoxication.

SÚRA, or SÚRAT, H. (A. سوره, سورت) A chapter of the Kurán, of which there are 114.

ṢÚRAT-I-HÁL, more commonly, ṢÚRAT-HÁL, corruptly SOOROOTHAL, SORETHAL, (H. صورتحال, from A. صورت, form, fashion, and حال, condition) A representation or report of the facts and circumstances of a transaction, whether made by an individual before witnesses, or by a subordinate officer to a superior functionary: an inquest.

Ṣúrat-mahál, H. (A. محال, an estate) A list or register of estates.

Ṣúrat-náma, H. (P. نامه, a document) A written detailed account of an estate or a transaction.

SURHÍ, Hindi (सुरही) A kind of grass growing on neglected or uncultivated land.

SURKHÁ, Hindi (सुरखा) Tall lank plants, running up without a due proportion of leaf.

SURMA, H. (سرمه) Antimony or galena ground to a fine powder and applied to the eyelids to improve the brightness of the eyes.

SURNÍS, SOORNEES, Mar. (सुरनीस) One of the eight chief officers of the Maraṭha state as first organised: the general record keeper, registrar, and superintendant of correspondence, by whom all deeds and grants were examined and authenticated: (according to Molesworth the word is a corruption of the Arabic and Persian words *Shuruâ*, beginning, and *Shud*, was, or finished, with the usual corruption of *navís*, writer).

SURSANNA, vulgarly, SURSAN, corruptly, SOORSUM, Mar. (सुरसन्न, for the A. *Shahúr-san*, شهورسن, a year of months) An era, partially current in the western Maraṭha districts, adopted probably from the Mohammadans: it commences with the Hijra year 745 = A.D. 1344: to find the equivalent of any year of this era add 599: in numbering the *Sursanna* year the Arabic numerals, vernacularly modified, are employed: thus the year 1230 is expressed *Salásina-maiatín-alif.*

SÚRYA, used vernacularly, as well as SÚRJA, or, more usually, SÚRAJ, or, sometimes, SURAJ, S. &c. (सूर्य, सूरज, सुरज, سورج, سوريه) The sun.

Surajdáha, Guz. (સુરજદાહ, from S. दाह, burning) Exposure of dead bodies to the sun.

Súrajgahan, H. &c. (سورج گهن). *Súryagrahana,* S. (सूर्यग्रहण, from ग्रहण, seizing) An eclipse of the sun.

Súryavanṣa, vernacularly, sometimes, *Súrajbans,* S. &c. (सूर्यवंश, from वंश, a race) The family or race of the Sun, from whom many of the Rajput tribes pretend to derive their descent, through *Ráma,* the sovereign of Oudh, the thirty-fourth in descent from *Ikshwáku,* the son of *Vaivaswata Manu,* the son of the Sun.

Súryavanṣí, or *Súrajbanṣí,* S. &c. (सूर्यवंशी) A man of a tribe professing to descend from the sun, a Rajput of the solar race.

Súryavára, or *Súrajbár,* S. &c. (सूर्यवार) Sunday.

SUSAL, Thug. A person whose head and neck are bare and convenient for being strangled: one who is strangled without resistance: a Thug who has cleansed himself from any stain of murder.

SUSÁR, Hindi (सुसार) A dresser and seller of provisions, a cook, a provisioner.—Chota Nágpur.

SUSÁR, Beng. (সুসার, from S. सु, good, and सार, essence) Property sufficient to discharge a claim or accomplish an undertaking.

SUSAR, H. (سسر, from S. श्वसुर) A father-in-law, the father of either husband or wife.

Susrál, or *Susrár,* H. (S. سسرال, سسرار) A father-in law's house or family.

SUSIA, Thug. A class of Thugs of a low Hindu caste formerly numerous in Malwa and Rajputana.

ṢUṢRÚSHÁ, S. &c. (शुश्रूषा) Service, respectful or affectionate service, not servitude or slavery; such as the service of a Ṣúdra to a Brahman, a pupil to a teacher, a wife to a husband, and the like.

SUSTÍ, SOOSTEE, also SWASTÍ, SWASTHÍ, SOASTEE, (?) Mar. A tenure by which land is held of a proprietor by a tenant paying the full government assessment (the first word is no doubt a blunder: *Swasti,* meaning properly 'well-being,' may be right.—E. I. Selections, iv. 553, 580).

SÚṬ, Mar. (सूट, from the H. *chhúṭ* چهوٹ) Remission, abatement (of a debt or just claim), also the amount remitted: release from bondage or slavery.

Súṭyo, Mar. (सूट्यो) Liquidation or discharge of a debt.

SÚT, H. &c. (سوت, from S. सूत्र) Thread, yarn: a thread, a line.

Sutár, H. &c. (S. ستار) A carpenter, the village carpenter and wheelwright.

Sutario, Guz. (સુતારીઓ) A dealer in yarn or thread.

SUTA, S. &c. (सुत) A son. SUTÁ (सुता), a daughter.

Sútaka, S. (सूतक), vernacularly, *Sutaka,* (सुतक) Uncleanness or impurity contracted by all the members of a family on the birth of a child or a miscarriage: in current use the term is laxly extended to impurity arising from the death of a relative, the application being sometimes limited by a conjunct term, as, *Játa-sútaka,* impurity from one born (*játa*), *Mṛitasútaka,* from one dead (*mṛita*): the period of uncleanness varies according to the propinquity of the relationship and local usage.

SUTARÁ, Hindi (सुतरा) A crop which, having been checked, has recovered.—Puraniya.

SÚTRA, S. &c. (सूत्र) A thread, a line: a precept, an aphorism, a brief rule of grammar, logic, philosophy, &c., in which form the oldest Sanscrit writers usually express themselves.

SÚTRAM, written, SÚTTIRAM, Tam. (சூத்திரம்) A piece of machinery: (it has also the senses of the preceding).

Chakkar-sútram, Tam. (சக்கர்சூத்திரம்) A water-wheel.

SUVÁḶÁ, Mar. (सुवाळा) A kind of boat of from 100 to 170 *khandís* burthen.

SUVARṆA, or SWARṆA, S. &c. (सुवर्ण, स्वर्ण) Gold: a goldsmith's weight, equal to sixteen *máshas,* which, at 5 *rattís* to the *másha,* make the *suvarṇa* much the same as the *tola,* or from 175 to 180 Troy grains, according to the variations in the value of the *rattí.*

SUYÚRGHÁL, corruptly, SEYURGHAL, blunderingly, SYCURGHAL, SYKURGUL, H. (P. A. سيورغال) An assignment of land revenue for charitable purposes: a *jágír* or grant of land revenue without any stipulation of military service or other condition.

SWA, S. &c. (स्व) Own, self: in the neuter, *Swam* (स्वं), Own peculiar or independent right or property: property in general: in some of the dialects, the conjunct letter not being capable of being written although pronounced correctly, *Swa*, is represented by *Su-va*, sometimes abbreviated to *Su*, as it is in Latin *Su-us*: in Tamil, accordingly, it is written *Su* (சு), *Suva* (சுவ), and *Swam* is written *Su-vam* (சுவம்): it also occurs *Som* (சொம்).

Swachchhanda, S. (स्वच्छन्द) Independent, wilful, following one's own inclination: adv., of one's own will or accord.

Swadastúr, Mar. (स्वदस्तूर) Signature or other authentication of a letter: used also with such words as *khat*, a writing, written with one's own hand.

Swaï, Beng. (স্বই) Own right or property.

Swán, Tam. (சுவான்) A proprietor, a possessor.

Swasthán, incorrectly, *Sawusthán*, Mar. (S. स्वस्थान, from स्व, own, स्थान, place) Estate, landed property.

Swatantra, S. (स्वतंत्र, from स्व, own, तंत्र, will) One who is independent, or acts for himself: one who is legally entitled to act without control or guardianship.

Swatantram, S. (स्वतंत्रं) Own will or purpose: in Tamil, in which it is in most common use with a modified acceptation, it is pronounced in the same manner, but is variously written as *Sutantaram*, or *Sutandaram*, erroneously, *Swatantaram*, *Sotundrum*, or *Sotuntrum*, (சுதந்தரம்), also *Swatantryam* (சுவதந்திரியம்), *Swátantryam*, S. (स्वातंत्र्यं) Own or independent property, hereditary right, either to real or personal property, or to privileges, perquisites, or fees: also any fee or perquisite claimable by a proprietor from a hereditary or other cultivator of proprietary lands, either in his own right or in that of a coparcenary body of proprietors.

Swatantrakáran, Tam. (சுதந்தரக்காரன்) An owner, an heir, one who enjoys any property of his own right.

Swatantradittam, Tam. (சுதந்தரதிட்டம்) Certain fees of corn in straw before threshing, received by the *Mirásdárs* in the Tamil provinces: any fee or privilege claimable by the village servants, musicians, or the like.

Swatwa, S. (स्वत्व) Ownership, proprietary or peculiar right.

Swatwatyágapatra, S. &c. (स्वत्वत्यागपत्र) A deed of conveyance or of gift; any document conveying away proprietary or peculiar property or rights.

SWADHÁ, S. &c. (स्वधा) An exclamation used at the presentation of oblations to fire or to the manes, or at the closing term of a short prayer to them.

SWÁDHYÁYA, S. &c. (स्वाध्याय) The reading or study of the Vedas.

SWÁGATAM, S. &c. (स्वागतं, from सु, well, and आगत, come) Welcome.

SWÁMÍ, S. &c. (स्वामी), SWÁMI, or SÁMI, from the latter of which comes the common corruption in the south of India, SAWMY, Tam. (சுவாமி, சாமி) A master, an owner, a husband, a lord: a title given to idols in the south of India, and thence is often borne by individuals: it is also applied especially as a title to the head of a religious order or establishment: used sometimes honorifically in the Telugu plural *Swámulu* (స్వాములు).

Swámi-, or *Sámi-bhogam*, corruptly, *Sawmy-bogum*, Tam. (சுவாமி- சாமிபோகம், S. स्वामी, and भोगं, enjoyment) The proprietor's or landlord's right: in the Tamil country it means the share of the produce or the rent which is paid to the *Mirásidár* or hereditary proprietor by the tenant cultivator holding the land in farm for a fixed period. In Malabar and Karnata it is the fee or acknowledgment paid by the mortgagee or tenant, often no more than a peppercorn rent, to the Janmkár or birthright proprietor: it also signifies any grant or contribution for an idol.

Swámitwam, or *Swámyam*, S. &c. (स्वमित्वं, स्वाम्यं) Mastership, lordship, ownership: the rights, privileges, or authority of a superior or master: in Marathi, also the share (of the products of a contract or farm) due to him who holds it directly of the state from one who, under him, holds or manages the concern.

SWÁNUBHOGAM, Tam. (சுவானுபோகம், S. स्व, own, अनु, according to, and भोग, enjoyment) The occupation or enjoyment of an estate by the proprietor himself, or, if leased to another, an acknowledgment from the tenant that he holds the land under the proprietor.

SWÁNVAYA, S. (स्वान्वय) A person of the same lineage as the proprietor or owner.

SWARÁJ, erroneously, SEWRAJ, Mar. (स्वराज, from S. स्व, own, राज्, a ruler) The share of the revenue claimed by the Marathas from any conquered country, the same as the *Chauth*, q. v.

SWARNAM, S. &c. (स्वर्ण), Tam. (சுவர்ணம்), also SORNAM, Tam. (சொர்ணம்) Gold, money.

Swarnádáyam, or *Sornádáyam*, corruptly, *Surnadayum*, *Sonardyem*, *Saunardyem*, *Sournaydyem*, *Sournydiam*, Tam. (சுவர்ண-, or சொர்ணதாயம்) Rent or revenue receivable in money, not in kind.

SWARÚPAM, S. &c. (स्वरूपं) Natural form, inherent property or nature: it is sometimes used in the dialects for property in land or money, an estate.

Swaist, S. (स्वस्ति) A term of address or benediction often commencing a document or inscription (from सु, well, and अस्ति, it is).

Swaṣtha, S. &c. (स्वस्थ, from सु, well, and स्थ, who stays or is) Well in body and mind, healthy, prosperous, happy.

Swásthyam, S. &c. (स्वास्थ्यं) The condition of being well in all respects: in Maraṭha, also, having a comfortable subsistence, as a pension or the like. *Swástyam*, corruptly, *Swastrum*, *Swastrium*, and *Swastwam*, Tam. (சுவாஸ்திரியம்) Wealth, property, especially *Mirasí* or hereditary land and privileges possessed by Brahmans.

Swastiyamdár, corruptly, *Swastriumdar*, Tam. (P. دار, who has) The holder of hereditary property and privileges.

Swayam, S. &c. (स्वयम्) Of one's self, by one's self.

Swayamdatta, S. (from दत्त, given) Self-given, applied to a son by one form of adoption.

Swayamkṛita, S. (from कृत, made) Self-made, the same as the son self-given.

Swayamupágata, S. (उपागत, arrived) Self-come, a son in one form of adoption: see the preceding. See also *Putra*.

Swayamvara, S. (स्वयम्वर) The public selection of a husband by a princess or lady of rank from among a number of assembled suitors, a practice that prevailed in the heroic ages of the Hindus.

Swechchha, or **Swaichcha**, S. स्वेच्छ, स्वैच्छ, from स्व, own, and इच्छा, wish, *putra*, understood, or *Swechhaputra*, &c.) A son adopted by a woman of her own accord and authority, without permission from her husband.

Ṣwetámbara, S. &c. (श्वेताम्बर) A religious mendicant wearing white garments, especially applicable to one of the two great divisions of the Jains.

Swopárjita, corruptly, **Shoparjit**, S. &c. (स्व, self, उपार्जित, acquired) Acquired by a person's own exertions, property, &c.

Ṣyámá, S. &c. (श्यामा, fem. of श्याम, black) A goddess, a form of *Kálí*.

Ṣyámápújá, S. (श्यामापूजा) Worship of *Syámá*, celebrated on the last day of *Áswin*, or in the month *Kartik*.

Ṣyámaka, vernacularly, **Shámá**, and **Shyámák**, (श्यामक, H. شاما, Mar. श्यामाक) A kind of grain in general use among the poorer classes (Panicum colonum): the stalk forms good fodder for cattle.

Syáwaṛh, Hindi (स्यावढ) A name given to five handfuls or small heaps of grain set apart by Mohammadan cultivators in the north-west provinces for the poor in the name of their saints or *Pírs*.

T.

Tâaḥud, **Tâḥud**, **Tahood**, corruptly, **Toahidy**, H. (A. تعهد, from عهد *âhd*, to promise) Promise, agreement: lease, contract: a revenue lease, a farm of the revenue, an engagement with the government or its representative for the payment of the public revenue, which may be made separately, even by the coparceners in a joint estate, each becoming responsible for his own proportion.

Tâaḥud-dár, H. (P. دار, who has) One who has entered into an engagement for the public revenue due on his own share: the holder of a farm or lease.

Tâayyul, **Tayool**, corruptly, **Tyool**, **Tyyool**, H. (A. تعيّلُ, from عيل, to support) Land held in *Jágír* by a member of a royal family, an appanage: it is now applied especially to certain lands held by the king of Delhi, or members of his family in the neighbourhood of Dehli, or to some held by the king of Oudh: it formerly designated lands granted in Jágír burthened with special services, or sometimes paying a quit-rent: (this is stated with respect to, what is no doubt a typographical error, *Tycul*. 5th Rep. 639).

Tâayyul-sháhí, H. (P. شاه, a king) The royal domain; land in Delhi and the neighbourhood, the occupants of houses on which pay ground-rent to the king.

Taâlluḳ, **Taâlluḳah**, or **Taâlluḳat**, commonly, **Táluk**, **Talook**, corruptly, **Tualloog**, **Tuallooga**, H. (A. تعلّق, تعلّقة, from علق, to suspend from or depend upon), **Táluká**, Mar. (तालुका), Tel. (తాలూకా) Connexion, dependence: possession, property: a dependency, a district, a division of a province: an estate, applied to a tract of proprietary land usually smaller than a Zamindárí, although sometimes including several villages, and not unfrequently confounded with a Zamindárí, held, in Bengal at least, at a fixed amount of revenue, hereditary and transferable as long as the revenue is paid: a *Táluḳ* was sometimes granted by the Mogul government at a favourable assessment as a mark of favour, or on condition of clearing and cultivating waste lands: in the Regulations fixing the permanent settlement *Táluḳs* were considered of two kinds; 1. *Huzúrí* (from حضور, the state), of which the revenue was paid direct to the government or its officers: these were called also independent *Táluḳs*, and the holders were classed with Zamindárs, or proprietary landholders; and 2. *Mazkúri* (from مذكور, specified), of which the holders paid their revenue through the intervention of a superior, as a Zamindár or other proprietor: these were termed 'dependant *Táluks*;'

they were hereditary and transferable as long as the revenue was paid, but lapsed to the superior on failure of heirs: they were also termed *Mufassil*, or *Shámili Táluḳs.* In the north-west provinces a *Táluḳ* presents various peculiarities, but it is defined an estate, the profits of which are divided between different proprietors, or classes of proprietors, the one superior, the other inferior; the former being usually an individual who, either by a grant from the sovereign, by favour of local functionaries, or by voluntary acts of the people, has become the intermediate agent for the revenue, collecting it from the people, and paying it to the government after making such deductions to cover his risk and assure his profits as he may be entitled to by the stipulations of the grant, or by local custom: the holder of such a *Táluḳ* exercises legally no right of interference with the proprietary and hereditary rights of the cultivators, except in some cases, where, from peculiar circumstances, the inferior claimants have been absorbed in the person of a single *Táluḳdár*: many modifications of rights, many more or less obscure, are said to exist between the individual *Táluḳdár* and the inferior proprietor. Ben. Reg. i. ii. iii. viii. xliv. 1793; ii. iii. 1803; ix. xii. 1805; xix. 1814; vii. xi. 1822; v. 1831. Act viii. 1805.

Taâlluḳdár, *Táluḳdár*, H. (P. دار, who has) The holder of a *Táluḳ*: in some places a government officer; a collector of revenue from the cultivators, either on behalf of the state or of the farmer of the revenue, whose undue exactions it is his duty to prevent.

Taâlluḳdárí, *Táluḳdárí*, corruptly, *Talookdarry*, H. (P. داري, having) The tenure, office, or estate of a *Táluḳdár*.

Taâlluḳdárí-haḳ, H. (A. حق, a right) The dues or allowances payable to the *Táluḳdár* in addition to his stipulated proportion of the assessment.

Taâlluḳah-jadíd, H. (from A. جديد, new) Lit., New dependencies, a term applied to tracts annexed to the Zamindárs of Vijayanagara (*Vizianagram*), being acquired by encroachments on the bordering estates.

Taâlluḳah-ḳadím, H. &c. (A, قديم, old) Old possessions; applied especially to the portions of the Vijayanagara estate held originally by the Zamindár.

Taâlluḳah-málzáminí, corruptly, *Talookeh-mahlzaminee*, H. A. مال, and زامني, surety) Dependencies on Vijayanagara in consequence of its Zamindár being responsible for the realisation of their revenue to the government.

Taâlluḳah-zabardastí, H. (P. زبردستي, violence) Estates seized by the Zamindár of Vijayanagara from his neighbours by violence.

Ausat Táluḳ, (?) Beng. A minor or dependent *Táluḳ*: one included within another (?).

TÂÂṬÍ, A. (تعاطي, from عطي, to deliver) Giving reciprocally: in law, mutual surrender, when the vendor of an article hands it to the purchaser and he returns the price of it without either party speaking: such sale is valid according to the *Sunni* lawyers; invalid according to the *Shías*.

TABÂ, also, TÁBÎ, H. &c. (A. تبع, تابع) Following, dependent, obedient, a follower, a dependant.

Tábîdár, H. (تابعدار), *Tábedár*, Mar. (ताबेदार) Dependent, a dependant, a follower, a subject.

Tábîdárí, A. (تابعداري), *Tábedárí*, Mar. (ताबेदारी) Dependence, allegiance, subjection.

Tábîún, or *Tábâín*, A. تابعون, تابعين, plurals of تابع) Followers, especially designating the successors of the companions of Mohammad, or the contemporaries of the companions whose relations of the sayings and doings of the prophet, as they received them from the companions, form part of the *Sunna*, or traditional law.

Tabâ-i-tábîún, A. (تبع تابعون) The followers of the followers, the successors of the *Tábîún*, from whom they received traditions respecting Mohammad, which they repeated, and which, although of inferior weight, are of authority in the body of the traditional law of the Mohammadans.

TABARRAK, H. (A. تبرّك) A benediction: sacred relics: a portion of presents, or of what is left of food presented to great men, given to their attendants: commutation for an offering incumbent upon a religious mendicant holding some endowment.

TABARRÛ, A. (تبرّع) Doing any thing voluntarily, giving gratuitously.

ṬABÁSHÍR, H. (A. طباشير) Bambu manna, a siliceous deposit in the joints of the bambu.

TABDÍL, H. (A. تبديل) Change, alteration, substitution.

TABI, (?) The hot-weather crop, sown in the cold and reaped in the hot-weather season.—Northern Sarkárs.

TABKATIA, (?) H. A class of Mohammadan religious mendicants, followers of *Sháh Madár*: they dress in black, wear a chain round their ankles, and carry a small drum: they sometimes lead about monkeys and bears, and are a low and offensive race.

TABLAḲ, H. (A. تبلق) A bundle or file of papers.

TÁBÚT, H. (A. تابوت) A coffin, a bier: the representation or model of the mausoleum of Hosain carried in procession in the Moharram: under the Marathas, a tax levied on the Mohammadans for permission to carry the *Tábút*.

ṬÁCH, ṬÁNCH, Mar. (टाच, टांच, from the English 'attach') Seizure of a person's property under a decree of court; also the writ or warrant.

TACHCHAN, Mal. (തച്ചൻ) A carpenter, a stonemason, from the S. *Takshaka*, q. v.

ṬÁCHAN, ṬÁṆCHAN, Mar. (टाचण, टांचण) A memorandum, a matter noted down, the paper on which it is written.

TÁḌ, or TÁṚ, Hindi (ताड़) The palmyra tree. See *Tál*.

TADA, TADU, vulgarly, TODA, TODU, Beng. (তদ, তদু) South: north: terms used in the village register or *chitta* to designate the relative bearings of the farms or fields of cultivating occupants.

TÂDÁD, H. (A. تعداد), TAIDÁD, Beng. (তাইদাদ) Number, numbering, computation, estimate: a list, a specification or enumeration: registry of an estate in the collector's office: annual calculation or requisition of the produce of an estate.

TADÁKHAL, H. (A. تداخل) Mutual entry: a mode of apportioning inheritance. See *Tamásul*.

TÁḌANA, or TÁṚANA. S. &c. (ताडन) Corporal punishment, whipping, beating.

Tadárak, H. (A. تدارك) Reparation, redress: means of obtaining legal redress, as writings, witnesses, and the like: punishment, chastisement, infliction of fines or punishment.

TADBÍR, H. (A. تدبير) Council, deliberation, government: in law, the post-obit manumission of a slave, a promise to him that he shall be free on his owner's demise.

TÁDÍB, H. (A. تاديب) Correction, chastisement: admonition. In law, the admonition to be given by the judge to parties convicted of venial offences.

TAFRÍK, H. (A. تفريق) Separation, division: separate or individual interest or responsibility: in law, a judicial divorce, one pronounced by the *Káẕi*, as distinguished from one executed by the husband himself on his own authority. TAPHIRÍKU, Tel. (తఫరీకు) Allotment or apportionment of the contribution or assessment levied on a village: it is said to have been applied also to an extra assessment or tax imposed upon cultivators holding an undue proportion of rent-free lands, in addition to those assessed and under cultivation.

Tafríḳ-náma, H. (P. نامه, a document) A document or deed settling the shares and proportions claimed by different parties.

TAFṢÍL, H. (A. تفصيل), TAPHSÍLU, Tel. (తఫసీలు) Detail particulars—of an account, and the like.

Tafṣílwár, H. (تفصيلوار) Specifically, particularly, in detail.

TAGA, TUGGA, (?) H. A class of cultivators in the Delhi district.

TAGADDAMÁ, Tel. (తగద్దమా, from the A. تقدمه) Business, affair, matter.

TAGAPPAN, Tam. (தகப்பன்) A father.

TAGAR, (?) H. A wide tin vessel in which opium is weighed.

TAGAVU, Karn. (ತಗವು) Peremptory demand of payment of money: a dispute, a law-suit: presents given to a daughter by her parents on her marriage.

Tagavari, *Taguvari*, Tel. (తగవరి, తగువరి) A judge, an umpire, an arbitrator.

TAGHAIR, H. (A. تغير) Alteration, change; adj., changed, dismissed.

Taghíri, H. (A. تغيري) Dismission, disgrace.

TAGHRÍB, H. (A. تغريب) In law, banishment, transportation: according to some it means only imprisonment, which is a sort of banishment or separation from family and friends.

TAGULUBÁḌI, Tel. (తగులుబాడి) Charges, cost.

TAHAJJUD, A. (تهجّد) Prayers repeated at midnight by devout Mohammadans, also *Taḥajjud-namáz*, and *Taḥajjud-ṣalát*.

TAHÁLUF, A. (تحالف, from حلف, to take an oath) Conspiring, leaguing: in law, swearing both plaintiff and defendant, which is practised in some cases.

Tahlíf, A. (تحليف) Exacting an oath.

TAHÁṆ, H., Mar. (تهان, तहां) There, at that place; but in Mar. it is used only in official papers, and before official designations, as, *Taháṇ-Pátil*, the Pátil of that place; *Taháṇ-Kamavisdár*, the agent of such a district (the nasal final is very slightly sounded, but the word is incorrectly written *Tahá*).

Taháṇ-hayát or *-hayád*, Mar. (तहांहयात् -द्, *tahán*, for P. تا, until, and A. حيات, life) Until death, as long as life lasts, a phrase confined to official documents.

ṬAHÁRAT, ṬUHR, H. (A. طهارت, طهر) Purity, period of purity, ceremonial purification, washing either entirely or partially, as by *Ghasl* (غسل), bathing, or *Wazu* or *Wuẕu* (وضو), partial ablution, washing the face, mouth, hands, arms, and feet, in a particular order: when water cannot be procured for this purpose sand may be substituted, which ceremony is termed *Tayamim*, but ablution with water must be performed as soon as possible after the dry purification, or the latter is nullified.

TAHARÍ-O-PHALÍ, Hindi (तहरी ओ फली) A phrase in a lease of a mango orchard implying transfer of the ground, as well as of the fruit.—Puraniya.

TAH-BÁZÁRÍ, H. (تهبازاري, from P. ته, place on which any thing is situated, and بازار), TÁBÁJÁRÍ, Tel. (తెంబాజారి) A tax or charge levied on the sellers of articles in a bázár, either in money or kind, as the rent of the ground on which their shops or stalls are placed: this was abolished by Bengal Reg. xxvii. 1793.

TAH-KHÁNA, or TAHI-KHÁNA, corruptly, TYE-KHÁNA, H. (P. ته, underneath, and خانه, a house) An apartment under ground, or so situated as to be impervious to the sun.

TAHḲÍḲ, H. (A. تحقيق, from حق, truth) Inquiry, investigation, searching for, ascertaining the truth of a matter (the plur. *Tahḳiḳát*, is similarly used).

TAHKÍM, H. (A. تحكيم, from حكم) Placing a person in authority: in law, arbitration; also, investing a person with authority to decide a dispute.

TAHLÍL, (A. تحليل) Making any thing or act lawful (*halál*) which was not so before: dispensation under certain conditions from observance of the law. (With a different *h*) *Tahlíl* (تهليل) Repetition of the Mohammadan creed, 'There is no God but God: Mohammad is the prophet of God.'

TAHNÁMÁ, blunderingly, THANAMAR, Mar. (तहनामा, from the P. تهنامه) A treaty of peace: a bill of articles or items agreed upon by two parties.

TAHRÍR, corruptly, TUHEREER, TEREER, H. (A. تحرير) Writing, writing correctly: a written statement: a fee for writing the manumission of a slave.

Tahrír, corruptly, *Thureer*, Mar. (तहरीर) Fees paid from the money levied or set aside for village expenses paid to the *Despáṇḍyá*, for his establishment: under the Maratha government these were also payable to the *Pharnís*, and *Muzamdár*.

Taharíru, Karn. (ತಹರೀರು) A fee or per centage allowed to superintendants of public works.

TAHS̱ÍL, TUHS̱EEL, less correctly, TEHSÍL, TEHSEEL, H., but adopted in all the dialects, (A. تحصيل, from حاصل), Mar. (तहसील), TEHESÍL, Guz. (તેહેસીલ) Collection, especially of the public revenue derived from the land: the revenue collected: in the Dakhin a statement prepared and kept by the village accountant of the persons from whom the revenue is receivable, and the amount due by each.

Tahs̱íldár, H. (تحصيلدار) A native collector of revenue, a native officer collecting the revenue from a given tract under a Zamindár, or the European collector: in the Madras territories he acts also as an officer of police. Ben. Reg. ii. 1793; iii. 1794; viii. 1797; xxvii. 1803. Mad. Reg. xxvii. 1802; ii. 1803; xi. 1816.

Tahs̱íldárí, H. (تحصيلداري) The office, duty, or jurisdiction of a native collector; the district of which he collects the revenue usually consisting of one or more *Parganas*, and yielding revenue to the extent of two or three *Lakhs* of rupees: a tax levied under the Moghul government to pay the allowances of the *Tahs̱íldárs*.

Tahs̱íldár-nishándár, H. (P. نشان, a mark or emblem of office) A duly appointed and responsible native collector.

Tahs̱íl-diwání, H. (P. ديواني) Collections of revenue payable into the public treasury.

Tahs̱íl-jábitá, Tel. (తహశీలుజాబితా) Daily account of payments made by the cultivators to the collector.

Tahs̱íl-muharrir, H. (محرر, a writer) A clerk or accountant in the revenue department.

Tahs̱íl-puraja, Tel. (పురజ, q. v.) A daily cash account kept by the village accountant under the collector, of the revenue payments of the cultivators, and of the village disbursements.

Tahs̱íl-saranjámi, H. (سرنجام, effects) Charges of collection: an additional charge formerly levied to defray the expense of collection.

Tahs̱íl-was̱ílat, H. (تحصيلوصيلة) The amount realised by the collector of a district, whether on behalf of a Zamindár or the government.

Tahs̱íl-i-yád, Mar. (P. ياد, remembrance) A memorandum of daily payments of revenue by the cultivators.

Khás̱-tahs̱íl, H. (A. خاص, especial) The collection of the revenue by the government or its officers direct from the cultivators.

TÁHUT, or TÁHUD, corruptly, TAOOD, Beng. (তাহুৎ, তাহুদ, from the A. عهد) Agreement, settlement, stipulated rent, a lease, or deed of lease.

Táhud-dár, corruptly, *Taoodár*, Beng. (তাহুদদার) One holding a lease of land, &c., at a stipulated rent.

TAHVÍL, TAHWÍL, corruptly, TEVEEL, H. &c. (تحويل, तहवील) Change, transfer: charge, trust, especially cash in the keeping of a person appointed to take care of it; hence sometimes a treasury, the collector's treasury: also, funds, capital.

Tahvíldár, corruptly, *Tohweeldar*, H. (P. دار, who has) A cashier, a treasurer: in Sindh, a collector of revenue.

Tahvíldárí, H. (داري, having) The office or duty of a cash-keeper, charge of cash or collections.

Tahvíl-taṣarruf, H. (A. تصرّف, q. v.) Embezzlement.

TÁÍ, H. (تاي) A paternal uncle's wife: a father's elder brother's wife.

Táíá, H. (تايا) A father's elder brother.

Táírá-bhái, H. (تايرابهاي) A father's elder brother's son: f. *Táírá-bahin*, (بهن, a sister) A father's elder brother's daughter.

TAI, commonly, TYE, Tam. (தை) The tenth Tamil month (January-February.)

TAI, commonly, TYE, Mal. (തൈ) A young plant in general.

TÁÍ, Karn. (ತಾಯಿ) A mother.

TÁÍD, plur. TÁÍDÁT, H. &c. (A. تايد, تايدات) Aid, assistance: corroboration: an extract from a public register or other document of authority in confirmation of a claim.

Táíd-navís, H. (تايدنويس) An assistant clerk or accountant: an apprentice.

ṬÁÍFA, H. (A. طايفه) Nocturnal patrol or watch: a troop, a company, especially of dancing girls and musicians; applied commonly, as well as its plur. *Tawáif*, to any individual of the troop, especially to a female: in the Dakhin it is also applied to any class or set of persons following the same occupation, or, originally, from the same place, and taxed collectively.

TAIHJUR, Hindi (तैहजुर) Weighing.—Chota Nagpur.

TÁÍL, Thug. A company or individual who have escaped sharing the fate of a murdered party by having been left behind.

TÂÍN, plur. TÂÍNÁT, corruptly, TYNAUT, H. (A. تعين, تعينات) Appointment, deputation, engagement, business. Mar. TAINÁT (तैनात) A military charge or command: general control or management: stipend, salary.

Tâínátí, H. (تعيناتي) Object or duty of an appointment, attendance, tour of duty. *Tainátí*, Mar. (तैनाती), adj. Stipendiary: made over to, as a body of troops from one commander to another: assigned, as a town or district: in Hindustan it also sometimes designates an inferior functionary, or *Peon*, appointed by the proprietor of an estate to assist in collecting the rent or revenue from the cultivators.

Tainát-jábtá, Mar. (तैनातजाबता, from A. ضابطه, an official document) A muster-roll of pay or salaries, or of those to whom they are paid.

ṬÁÍRKHÁNA, H. (A. طاير, a bird) An aviary: a charge on the revenue, or a special tax, for the expenses of the imperial aviary at Delhi.

TÁJÁ-KALAM, Mar. (ताजाकलम, from P. تازه, fresh, and A. قلم, a pen), TÁJÁ-KALAMU, Tel. (తాజాకలము) A postscript, an appendix, a new paragraph.

TÁJIR, H. (A. تاجر) A merchant, a trader.

Tajárat, H. (A. تجارت) Trade, traffic, the business of a merchant or dealer.

TAJKARÁ, Mar. (तजकरा, from A. تذكره, a writing) A fraudulent entry or appropriation, an item of peculation.

Tajkar-nís, Mar. (तजकरनीस) An officer of the Maratha government whose office it was to detect peculation.

Tajkar-navisí, or *-nisí*, Mar. (तजकरनविसी, -निसी) The duty of checking or detecting peculation.

TAJVÍZ, or TAJWÍZ, vernacularly, TAJWÍJ, H. (A. تجويز, तजवीज) Investigation, inquiry, examining: judgment, sentence.

Tajvíz-náma, H. (P. نامه, a document) A written decree, judgment, or resolution.

ṬÁḲ, H. (P. طاق) An arch, a cupola; applied also to a mount or pillar set up as a boundary mark: hence any mark or determination of boundaries.

Ṭáḳ-bast, corruptly, *Thak-bust*, H. (P. بست, a binding) Laying down a boundary, fixing the limits of estates by a native surveyor, preparatory to a professional survey by a European officer.

ṬAKÁ, H. (S. टङ्क), Mar. (टका), TÁKÁ, Beng. (টাকা) A coin, the value of which appears to vary in different parts of India: in Hindustan it is said to be a copper coin equal to two *paisas*; in the Dakhin it is called an aggregate of four *paisas*, or one *ana*, or an aggregate of sixteen *paisas*, or in Guzerat of three: in Bengal it is synonymous with a rupee: in all the dialects it is laxly used for money in general.

ṬAKÁ, also, but ? if correctly, TÁK, corruptly, TUKKA, Mar. (टका) A land measure, varying in different places: it is sometimes considered equal to a *Chávar* = 24 *Rukas*, or 120 square *bighás*: according to a different statement it is a seventy-second part of a *Chávar*, and to another it is any division of a *Chávar* into equal parts, as a half, a fourth, a twentieth, &c.: others make it 4 *bighás*, others again 48 *bighás*: in Kamaon it is half a *bísi*.

Ṭahábándí, Mar. (टकाबंदी) Fixing the land-tax at so much

6 M

per *Ṭaká*: settled or estimated according to the *Ṭakás* it contains (land): keeping an account in *Ṭakás* (the copper coin so named).

TAKABBAẒ, A. (تقبّض) Mutual surrender or silent exchange of an article and its cost. See *Tâati.*

TAKẠDUM, A. (تقادم, from قدم, going before) Being ancient or prior: in law, such an interval between the commission of a crime and the giving of evidence respecting it, as operates in bar of punishment.

TAKAFFAL, A. (تكفّل) Taking security: becoming security for another: bail.

TÁKAṬṬU, Tel., Karn. (తాకట్టు, from the A. طاقت, power) Charge: pawn, pledge, mortgage.

TAKÁVÍ, corruptly, TUCKAVY, TUCCAVY, TUCKAY, TUCKAIR, TAGAKEY, H. (تقاوي, from قوي, giving strength to, or assisting), Tel., Karn. (తకావి), TAGÁÍ, TAGÁYÍ, Mar. (तगाई, तगायी) Advances of money made by the government to the cultivators at the time of sowing, especially in the south of India, where the Ryotwárí settlement prevails, to be repaid when the crop is gathered: similar advances are made in bad seasons, and the like, or sometimes made to the cultivators to enable them to extend their cultivation. Ben. Reg. ii. xiv. 1793. Mad. Reg. xxvii. 1802; i. 1803.

Takávi-haikágada, Karn. (ತಕಾವಿಹೈಕಾಗದ) A bond or note of hand given by the cultivators in acknowledgement of advances received.

Taḥávi-patramu, Tel. (from S. पत्र) A written acknowledgement for advances given by the cultivators to the collector.

TAKÁẒÁ, H. &c. (A. تقاضا), TAGÁDÁ, Mar. (तगादा), Tel. (తగాదా), TAGÁDÍ, TAGÁDE, Karn. (ತಗಾದಿ, ತಗಾದೆ), also TAGAVU, q. v. Importunity in urging the settlement of a claim or payment of a debt, dunning: in the south of India, formerly, enforcing payment by various modes of annoyance, as by stationing persons at the house of a debtor from morning to night at his expense for their daily hire; obstructing the conveyance of water into the debtor's dwelling, or cooking in it: the creditor sometimes took his station himself at his debtor's door, threatening to do himself personal injury (this process is the same as the S. *Dharaṇa* (धरण) and H. *Dharná* (دهرنا), or *Dharná-baiṭhná* (دهرنابيٹهنا) to sit in *dharná* for the sake of extorting compliance with any demand, a practice now prohibited): also suing a creditor in a court of law, whence it comes to signify any suit at law, or the prosecution of any claim by legal means.

Tagádá-dár, or *Tagádá-gír*, Mar. (तगादादार, -गीर) An officer under the Maratha government appointed to enforce the demands of the state against defaulting cultivators: in Hindustan a *Takáẓá-*, or *Takáẓ-gír*, implies a person appointed by a capitalist to collect debts due to him.

Tagád-dár, *Tagádí-khór*, Karn. (ತಗಾದ್ದಾರ, ತಗಾದಿಖೋರ) A dun, a creditor who is urgent for payment.

TAKBÍR, H. (A. تكبير) Repetition of the Mohammadan belief in God, or *Allah-u-akbar*, God most great: in Hindustan it is multiplied by various repetitions to the same effect: it is also considered as the especial war-cry of the Mohammadans.

TAḲDIMA, H. (A. تقدمه) Final adjustment or audit of an account.

TAKHALLUF-I-YAUMIA, H. (A. تخلف يوميه) Fraud in payment of a pension (?).

TAKHÁRUJ, (A. تخارج) In law, a composition entered into by joint heirs to property, by which some relinquish their shares for a specific payment: partition of an estate amongst themselves by the lawful heirs.

TAKHFÍF-I-JAMÂ, H. (A. تخفيف, abatement) Abatement or remission of revenue.

TAKHLIA, A. (تخليه) Vacating: in law, extinguishment, tacit or declared, of all right by the seller in an article which he has sold: manumission of a slave: divorce of a wife.

TAKHMÍNAN, H. (A. تخميناً) By estimate, conjecture, or appraisement, about, more or less.

Tagmina, or *Takmina*, (? a vernacular form of the preceding) H. A general survey statement of village lands, the same as the *Khasra*, q. v.

TAKHṢÍṢ, corruptly, TUCKSEES, TUKKSHEESH, H. (A. تخصيص) Appropriation, appropriating, particularizing.

Takhṣíṣí, H. (A. تخصيصي) Special, appropriate, not liable to division.

Takhṣíṣí-táâluḳ, H. (تخصيصي تعلق) An undivided *táluk*, one held entire by an individual.

Takhṣíṣ-jamâ-bandí, H. (تخصيص جمع بندي) A particular statement of the assessment concluded with the revenue-payers under the Mohammadan governments: also the standard assessment of *Toral Mal*, as corrected by *Jâfir-âli-khan* in 1772: see *Tashkhíṣ*.

TAKHT, H. (P. تخت) A throne, a chair of state: also, as an abbreviation of *Takhta*, a plank, a platform.

Takht-nishín, H. (تخت نشين) The reigning sovereign.

Takht-posh, H. (تخت پوش) A covered stage or platform.

Taḥht-rawán, H. (from P. روان, going) A litter, especially for females or persons of rank.

TAKHTA, H. (تختہ), TAKTÁ, Mar. (तक्ता) A plank, a platform: also, in Mar., a tabular statement, the heading of such a statement.

Takhta-, or *Takht-rawán*, H. (تختہروان), *Takt-rāṇwa*, Mar. (तक्तरांवा) A plank or platform on which public performers, singers, and dancers, are carried on men's heads in festival and religious processions: (this seems to be erroneously identified with the compounds of *Taḥht.*),

TÁKHT-TÁRÁJ, H. (P. تاخت, and تاراج, both meaning devastating) Depredation, laying waste (a country): havoc.

TÁKHYÍR, A. (تاخير) In law, giving an option or choice.

TAKI, (?) Beng. (apparently an error or local corruption of *Ṭáká*, q. v.) A rupee: a fee, a perquisite of one rupee: interest on sight at the rate of one rupee per cent.

TAKÍÄ, H. (P. تكيه) A pillow: the stand or seat of a *Faḳír*: the spot where he usually abides, whether it be open or enclosed.

Takíä-dár, H. (P. دار, who has) A Mohammadan religious mendicant, a *Faḳír*.

TÁKÍD, H. (A. تاكيد), Mar. (ताकीद), Tel., Karn. (తాకీదు) Injunction, warning, direction, an order from a superior.

Tákíd-chiṭhí, Mar. (ताकीदचिठी) A letter of injunction, a written mandate or direction.

Takíddár, Mar. (ताकीददार) A person sent to give injunction or warning: a sentinel stationed to keep back stragglers or camp-followers from a field or village.

Tákídi-kágada, Karn. (ತಾಕೀದಿಕಾಗದ) A written order or injunction.

TAKÍNA, (?) H. A cess paid in lieu of proportion of fodder, or the fodder itself: rents of a number of houses collected by an agent.

TAKÍT, H. (A. تكيت) A monied man in a village appointed to collect the shares of the assessment from the villagers and pay them to the principal revenue-payer, or *Málguzár*.

ṬAKO, Guz. (ટકો) Interest of one per cent. per mensem: a copper coin varying in value from two to four *Paisas*. See *Ṭaká*.

TAKRÁḶ, Mar. (तकराळ, from the A. تكرار; see the next) Discrepancy, inconsistency (in a narration), a fabrication, a story invented to deceive.

TAKRÁR, H. (A. تكرار), Mar. (तकरार) Dispute, contention, quarrel, a quarrel or dispute: in Mar. also, a statement in disproof or disallowal (as by litigants).

Takrár-khafíf, H. (A. خفيف, petty) A petty quarrel or disturbance.

TAKRI, (?) Tel. A weight for metals equal to five *kachchá sers.*—Northern Sarkárs.

TAKSHAKA, vernacularly, TAKSHAK, and TAKHKAK, S. &c. (तक्षक) A carpenter, a stonemason.

TAḲSÍM, TUḲSEEM, corruptly, TUCKSEEM, H. (A. تقسيم) Division, dividing, partition, sharing, distribution of the assessment of the revenue upon the several subdivisions of an estate or district, the same as *Taḳsím-jamâ*, Mar. (तकशीम) A portion, a share. *Takkisamu*, Tel. (తక్కిసము) Contributions raised amongst the inhabitants of a village to defray the village expenses.

Taḳsím-dár, Mar. (तकशीमदार) A sharer, the holder of a share, either of land perquisites or privileges: one who receives a portion at a division of property.

Taḳsími, H. (تقسيمي) Divisible, portionable, liable to partition, according to allotment, &c.

Taḳsím-jamâ, H. (A. تقسيم جمع) In Mohammadan finance, the distribution of the whole standard assessment among the different territorial subdivisions, whether large or small, a province, a Zamindárí or a village: also, the apportionments of the revenue payable by a village or estate amongst joint proprietors.

Taḳsím-náma, H. (P. نامه, a document) A deed of partition amongst joint proprietors when ceasing to hold their estate in common.

Taḳsím-pargana-wár, H. (پرگنهوار, according to *pargana*) Subdivision of the whole assessment under the Moghul government, according to the district divisions termed *parganas*: accounts of the standard assessment of each *pargana*, extracted from the general rent-roll of the empire.

Taḳsím-i-taâlluḳ, or *Taḳsím-bandi-taâlluḳ*, H. (see تعلّق) A *Táluḳ* which was separately registered in the original rent-roll, or *Tumár-jamâ*, of the land revenue of Hindustan, and of which, under the British administration of Bengal, the lands and assessment are unalterable: also a *Táluḳ* held in shares.

TAḲṢÍR, H. (A. تقصير) Fault, offence, crime.

TAKÚB, Mar. (तकूब, from A. *tawaḳḳuf*, توقّف, delaying, stopping) Suspension, stoppage: in a state of suspension, as a public work, collection of revenue, &c.: the head under which outstanding balances of revenue are entered pending the decision of the superior authorities as to their realization or remission.

Takúbchiṭhí, Mar. (तकूबचिठी) An order of suspension of revenue collections granted by the government, exempting persons for a time from the demands of the collector.

TÁKUBAḌI, Karn. (ಠಾಕುಬಡಿ) Extra expense.

TAKWET-KAUL, or TAKWET-CHIṬHÍ, Mar. (तकवेतकौल -चिठी, from the A. *Taḳviat* تقويت, confirmation) A temporary deed of assurance: a paper or token granted by the state to a payer of revenue, or a contractor, to be held until a formal and regular agreement can be prepared.

TÁL, H. (تال) A pond, a pool, a piece of water.

TÁLA, vernacularly, TÁL, TÁṚ, TÁḶÍ, S. &c. (تال, تاڑ, ताल, ताली), TÁḶI, TÁḶIPPANAI, Tam. (தாளி, தாளிப்பனை) The palm tree, especially the Corypha (Corypha talliera): it is also very generally applied to the Palmyra (Borassus flabelliformis), and laxly to many other trees of the same class, as the cocoa-nut, date, and others.

Táḷipatra, vernacularly, *Tálpatra*, or *Tálpát*, corruptly, *Tálipot*, and *Tállipot*, S. &c. (तालपत्र, तालपात) The leaf of the Corypha palm tree, especially when dried and used to form umbrellas or parasols, or when split into oblong pieces and used for writing upon: also the tree itself.

TÁLA, or TÁL, S. &c. (ताल) Time in music, beating time, tune: also, in Mar., a mound or bank raised in a field to detain or turn off water.

TÁḶ, Tam. (தாள்) Stubble or stem of corn, of flowers, and the like.

Táladi, Tam. (தாளடி) A second cultivation on the same ground.

Táladippór, Tam. (தாளடிப்போர்) A stack of grain that has been winnowed by hand, but not yet trodden out by cattle.

TALA, vernacularly, TAL, S. &c. (तल), TALA, TAḶA, Mar., (तल, तळ) Surface, bottom, level or low ground.

Tal, plur. *Taláon*, H. (تل, تلاوں) Low grounds: in Mar., also the site of an encampment, a camp.

Talchuä, Hindi (तलचुआ) Light land above clay, which soon becomes soft and spongy in wet weather.—Puraniya.

Taljhárá, Mar. (तल, the bottom, and झाडा, a sweeping) A thorough clearing or sweeping out: fig., a thorough search or investigation.

Talpaṭ, Mar. (तळपट) Rain, desolation, devastation of a country. Hindi (तलपट) Destruction of crops by the trampling of cattle.

TÁḶÁ, Mar. (S. ताळा) Agreement, correspondence, conformity as of different accounts, statements, measures, &c.

Táḷeband, commonly, *Tálaband*, corruptly, *Tullabund*, *Tallibund*, Mar. (ताळेबंद) A treasury account shewing the correspondence between the balance in hand and that which should be left on a comparison of receipts and disbursements: an abstract of the ledger or general account-book: as a financial account, the monthly *Táḷeband* forwarded by the district revenue officers to the government exhibits the receipts and disbursements of the preceding month, and the balance at its close: the similar account furnished at the end of the year contains a complete detail of the actual receipts and disbursements of the year, as well as of the outstanding balances at its beginning and at its close.

Táḷeband-báḳí, Mar. (A. باقي, remainder) The balance of revenue as shewn in the account at the end of the year.

Táḷeband-goshwára, Mar. (from the H. *goshwára*, q. v.) An abstract of the *Táḷeband* account.

Táḷeband-jamá, Mar. (जमा, from the A. جمع) The heading under which the items of revenue are entered, which are realised subsequently and in addition to the assessment derived from concealed cultivation detected, or from land taken into cultivation after the settlement of the assessment.

ṬÁLÁ, Hindi (टाला) Quagmire, decayed vegetable matter or stagnant water.—Puraniya.

ṮALAB, ṮULUB, corruptly, TULLUB, H. &c. (طلب) Pay, wages, salary: request, demand, petition: calling or sending for, summons: demand of arrears of revenue.

Ṯalabána, corruptly, *Tallubana*, *Tulbanna*, H. (A. طلبانه) Daily pay or fees to a subordinate officer of the court charged with serving process, issuing summonses or writs, payable by the parties on whom they are served. Ben. Reg. xxvi. 1814. See xiv.

Ṯalab-báḳí, H. (باقي) An account shewing the amount due from each payer of the revenue, the sums realised and balance due.

Ṯalab-chhiṭṭhí, H. (چهتهي, a note) A warrant, a summons, a writ, a written demand for arrears of revenue.

Ṯalab-dastak, H. (P. دستك, a note) A summons, a writ, a demand for payment of revenue.

Ṯalab-ishhád, H. (اشهاد, testimony) Claim made in the presence of witnesses, especially by a claimant of the right of pre-emption. See *Shafá*.

Ṯalab-náma, H. (P. نامه, a document) A warrant, a writ, a notice or summons.

TALAI, Tam. (தலை), TALA, Mal. (തല) The head.

Talachchennaval, Mal. (തലച്ചെന്നവർ) The principal native collector of the revenue.

Talai-kaṭṭu-vari, Tam. (தலைக்கட்டுவரி) A tax on houses.

Talai-kával, Tam. (தலைக்காவல்), *Tala-kával*, Mal. (തലകാവൽ) The main or principal guard: the town or village watch.

Talaimúṭṭai-káran, Tam. (தலைமூட்டைக்காரன்) A porter, one who carries a load on his head.

Talappanam, Mal. (തലപ്പണം) Head-money, poll-tax.

Talappáṭṭam, Mal. (തലപ്പാട്ടം) Poll-tax, head-money.

Talaivan, Tam. (தலைவன்), *Talavan*, Mal. (തലവൻ) A head person, prefect, governor, director, a king, a priest, an elder, an elder brother.

Talaivari, Tam. (தலைவரி), *Talavari*, Mal. (തലവരി) Poll-tax.

Talaivetti, Tam. (தலைவெட்டி) An executioner: a villain.

Talavila, Mal. (തലവില) First selling price of grain or other produce after harvest.

Talaiyadi, Tam. (தலையடி) The first corn reaped and threshed.

Talaiyána, Tam. (தலையான) Principal, chief.

Talaiyána-attáṭchi, Tam. (தலையானவத்தாட்சி) The principal evidence.

Talayáṛi, corruptly, *Taliar*, Mal. (തലയാറി) A head man, a chief.

TAḶAI, Tam. (தளை) A division in rice-fields, or a rice-field divided into many beds.

ṬALÁḲ, H. (A. طلاق) Divorce, dissolution of marriage, whether reversible or irreversible, besides a divorce justified by bodily or mental diseases or defects: various kinds are recognised by Mohammadan law, as the following:—

Ṭaláḳ-i-ahsán, A. (احسان, most excellent), also *Ṭaláḳ-i-báin*, A. (بائن, separated) The most reputable kind of divorce, in which the husband pronounces, 'I have divorced you' once before the *Iddat* or time of the woman's probation has expired: this is reversible.

Ṭaláḳ-i-rajâî, (from رجع, return) The form of divorce in which the declaration of the husband to that effect is twice repeated: also reversible.

Ṭaláḳ-i-husn (حسن, goodness), or *Ṭaláḳ-i-mutallaha* (from مطلّقه, a divorced woman, perhaps from مطلق, absolute) The form in which the husband pronounces three different sentences of divorcement in as many months: this is irreversible, and the wife cannot be taken back until she has been married and divorced by another man: (some strange perversion has changed this in Cuttack to *Taláḳ-túka*): these three forms are classified as,

Ṭaláḳ-i-sunna, Divorce, legal according to traditional law, as opposed to the next;—

Ṭaláḳ-i-bidât, (بدعت, innovation, heresy) Heterodox divorce, in which the husband makes the usual declaration three times in one month: this is deemed irreversible: other modifications are—

Ṭaláḳ-kináiat, (كناية, metaphor) A divorce in which the terms used, although not expressly declaring a divorce, are legally sufficient.

Ṭaláḳ-muajjal, (موجّل) Divorce which is to take place at a specified time; also applicable to divorces under various specified conditions.

Ṭaláḳ-ṣaríh, (صريح, clear) Divorce in which the declaration is explicit: the following terms are also applied to divorces:—

Aila, q. v. Divorce consequent upon abstinence from cohabitation for a given period.

Istiṣná, (استثنا, excepting) Divorce declared with a reservation which may render the declaration null.

Khalâ, (خلع, drawing out) Dissolution of marriage at the suit of the wife, in which she agrees to make her husband compensation for her loss by relinquishing to him an adequate portion of her peculiar property, and by foregoing claim of dower.

Lân, (لعن, imprecation) Divorce upon accusation of adultery by the husband, to be confirmed by him by his imprecating upon her the curse of God, whereupon separation takes place.

Mubárát, (مبارات) Separation by mutual consent.

Yamín, (يمين, a vow) A conditional divorce contingent upon some future possible occurrence.

Ẓihár, (ظهار, assisting) Divorce consequent upon a man's comparing his wife to some female relative with whom marriage is prohibited: a separation must take place until proper expiation has been made.

Tafwíẓ-ul-ṭaláḳ, (تفويض, referring to another) Divorce by delegation: giving to a wife the option or liberty of being separated, or to a third person authority to pronounce a separation between husband and wife.

TALÁḲÍ, A. (تلاقي, a meeting) In law, forestalling the market by meeting a *Káfila* and buying up the goods.

TALAM, Tam. (தலம், for the S. स्थल) A place, a site: a town, a village: a temple: also, in the sense of place, TALAI.

Talam-kával, corruptly, *Talam-cavel*, *Tallum-carwell*, Tam.

(தலம்க்காவல்) A guard, the main guard, village or town guard or watch (it is more correctly *Talai-kával*, q. v.)

Talári, corruptly, *Tallary*, *Tullary*, Tel. Karn. (తలారి), *Talaiyárí*, corruptly, *Talliar*, *Tolli*, *Tolliar*, Tam. (தலையாரி) The village watchman, one of the subordinate officers of a village.

Talattár, Tam. (pl. தலத்தார்) The principal town's-people.

TALAMBRÁLU, Tel. (తలంబ్రాలు) Throwing rice over the head of the bride and bridegroom at a marriage, for luck: the rice so thrown.

TALÁSH, H. &c. (A. تلاش) Search, inquiry.

Taláshi, H. &c. (تلاشي) An inquirer, a searcher: an officer who examines goods at a custom-house: also search, seeking: fees formerly levied at Benares on persons leaving the town, and liable to be searched.

TALÁṬÍ, corruptly, TALLATY, Guz. (તલાટી) The village accountant, usually in the employ of the government.

TAḶÁṬÍ, TAḶÁṬHÍ, Mar. (तळाटी, तळाठी) Collection of revenue from the cultivators: the officer collecting it.

Talátdár, *Taláṭhdár*, Mar. (तळाटदार, तळाठदार) An officer whose dnty it is to collect the sums due by the cultivators to the government.

TALAVÁRA, Karn. (ತಳವಾರ) A village watchman paid for his services by a grant of land at a quit-rent.

TÁLI, (?) H. A fee paid to the *Patwári* out of the government share on his taking an account of the crop.

TAḶÍ, corruptly, THULLEE, Mar. (तळी) A term for plunder, arson, and murder, publicly perpetrated by the people of one village upon those of another in satisfaction of the exactions of a government officer, or of the claims of the perpetrators: it has various other meanings, as, a platter in which contributions are collected for presentation to an idol, the slab of a hand mill, articles sent by a newly-married boy to his young bride at her mother's house, &c.

TÁLÍ, corruptly, TALLY, Tam. (தாலி) A piece of gold, forming either the centre or the sole ornament of a necklace, which is tied on the neck of the bride by the bridegroom at the time of marriage: the term and practice are common to all the people of the peninsula.

Táli-boṭṭu, Tel. (తాళిబొట్టు) The piece of gold which is tied round the neck at marriage.

TÁLÍḲA, TÂLÍḲA, H. (A. تاليقة, تعليقة) An inventory, a list of articles.

TÁLÍMUNDÁ, Uriya (ତାଳିମୁଣ୍ଡା) Land for sowing rice in seed upon.

TALJÍAT, A. (تلجية) Forcing the will: in law, the interpretation of a contract or engagement in a different sense from that which the terms properly denote.

Baiá-i-taljíah, (بيع تلجية) A nominal sale, one in which no sale has been effected, although by a belief in its reality some object is attained by the seller: in law such sale is of no effect, although the purchaser may declare it to have been a bona-fide transaction.

TALḲÍN, H. (A. تلقين) Informing, instructing: the ceremony of admitting a person into any order or society and initiating him in its institutions.

TAḶḶA, Mal. (തള്ള), TALLI, Tel. (తల్లి) A mother.

Taḷḷakuṟa, Mal. (തള്ളകുറ) Inheritance, by the mother's side: the mother's inheritance or portion.

Taḷḷavari, Mal. (തള്ളവരി) The mother's line.

TAḶḶUPADIPATRAM, Tam. (தள்ளுபடிப்பத்திரம்) An invalid or rejected bond or voucher.

TAḶḶUTAL, Tam. (தள்ளுதல்) Putting away or divorcing a wife.

Taḷḷutalin-chiṭṭu, Tam. (தள்ளுதலின்சீட்டு) A bill or writing of divorce.

TÁLMADAṈGAL, Tam. (தாளமடங்கல்) Close of the wet-crop harvest.

TALPAT, (?) Guz. Land paying full rent or assessment, or a half or other proportion of produce to the government, as distinguished from lands held as private property, or at a quit-rent, or rent-free.

TAMÁDÍ, H. (A. تمادي, from مدي, what has lasted) A long time, limitation of time, rules of limitation which bar a civil prosecution.

TAMÁKU, TAMÁKHU, H. (تماكو, تماكهو, तमाकू, तमाखू) Tobacco, the plant or leaf: three kinds are distinguished, *Tamáku-kábulí*, *Tamâku-lokrá*, and *Tamáku-mákú*: the last is considered the best.

TÁMALÍ, Beng. (তামলী) An inferior caste of Hindus in Bengal, usually petty retail dealers and shopkeepers.

TAMÁSHÁ, H. &c. (A. تماشا) Show, spectacle, a show, any thing attracting and amusing spectators.

TAMÁṢUL, H. (A. تماثل) Equality: in Mohammadan law, the division of an inheritance among the legal sharers when their number and that of the shares is the same; as for instance, where there are four sharers having equal rights severally to four shares, such numbers are termed *Mutamáṣul*: other terms describe various modifications of the principle of allotment as follow:—

Tadákhul, (تداخل) Concordance, when the number of shares may be divided without remainder by the number of sharers, as where there are nine shares and three sharers: the numbers are termed *Mutadákhul*.

Tawáfuk (توافق) Commensurability, the division of the shares and sharers by a common divisor, as where there are eight sharers and twenty shares, both divisible by four, termed *Mutawáfuk*.

Tabáyun, (تباين) Incommensurability, when no third number will equally divide the numbers of shares and sharers, as when they are severally nine and ten: the numbers are termed *Mutabáyun*.

TAMASSUK, corruptly, TUMMASOOK, TUMUSSOOK, TUMSOOK, TOMSOOK, H. &c. (تمسّك) A bond, a note of hand, a written acknowledgment or engagement.

Tamassuk-i-házir-zámini, H. (see *Hazir-zámini*) A bond or recognisance as a security for personal appearance: a bond formerly given by Zamindárs to the revenue officers of the government on receiving the grant of a Zamindárí as a surety for their personal appearance whenever required by the government or its officers.

Tamassuk-jáidádi, H. (P. جايداد, q. v.) A bond hypothecating property.

TÁMB, TÁMBARÁ, TÁMBÁRÁ, Mar. (तांब, तांबरा, तांबारा) Blight attacking a field of wheat.

TAMBALAVÁḌU, Tel. (తంబళవాడు) A man of a mixed caste, the offspring of a female Brahman by adulterous intercourse with a Brahman: he is commonly a priest in a temple of *Śiva*.

TAMBÁN, Mal. (തമ്പാൻ) A prince, a member of a royal family.

Tambáṭṭí, Mal. (തമ്പാട്ടി) A princess, a female of royal descent.

Tambi, Mal. (തമ്പി) A younger brother: the title of the Raja of Travankur.

TAMBÍH, H. (A. تنبيه) Correction, admonition: in law, admonition to be given by the judge to parties guilty of venial offences.

TÁMBÚLA, TÁMBÚLÍ, S., but adopted in all the dialects, sometimes slightly modified, as TÁMÚLÍ, TAMBOLI, TAMBLI, &c. (तांबूल -ली) Piper betel; also the pungent leaf of it rolled up for mastication with small pieces of areka-nut and spices, with sometimes a small quantity of catechu and caustic lime. See *Pán*.

Tambolí, H. (S. تمبولي), *Támbolí*, Mar. (तांबोली), *Tamolí*, Guz. (તમોલી) A caste, or member of it, whose occupation is selling betel leaves.

Tambolin, H. (S. تنبولن), *Támbolíṇ*, Mar. (तांबोलीण), *Tamolin*, Guz. (તમોલીણ) A woman who makes up and sells the leaf of the Piper betel prepared for mastication.

Támbúl-srávaṇí, Mar. (तांबूलश्रावणी) A present made by a man newly married to the member of the village community who is charged with the superintendence of public ceremonies in honour of the tutelary deity of the village.

TAMBURÁN, Mal. (തമ്പുരാൻ) A prince, a Rája, a lord, a master, the title of the Cochin Rája.

Tamburaṭṭi, Mal. (തമ്പുരാട്ടി) A queen, a princess, a lady, a mistress.

TAMGHÁ, H. (T. تمغا) A royal seal or stamp, a royal grant. See *Altamghá*.

TAMIḺ, or TAMIZH, Tam. (தமிழ்) The Tamil language, that of the people subject to the Madras Presidency, from Madras to Cape Komorin.

TÂMÍR, H. (A. تعمير) Restoring, repairing: in law, rendering a house habitable by putting it in repair, or a field productive by judicious cultivation.

TAMLÍK, H. (A. تمليك, from ملك) Possessorship, property.

Tamlík-náma, H. (P. نامه, a document) A deed of transfer, whether of gift or conveyance.

Tamlík-wa-tauliat-náma, H. (A. P. تمليكوتوليةنامه) A deed of gift and trusteeship which assigns property in trust to a particular person, with the proceeds of which he is to defray the expenses of a religious establishment, and, if there be any surplus, he may apply it to his private use.

TÁMRÁ, vernacularly, TÁMÁ, TÁMBÁ, TÁMBEṈ, S. &c. ताम्रा, تاما, تانبا: तांबा, तांबें) Copper.

Támbaṭ, Mar. (तांबट) A brazier, a coppersmith by caste and occupation.

Támbrí, Mar. (तांबरी) Copper-coloured, a sort of soil of a reddish or coppery hue: it is a stiff clay mixed with sand in various proportions, and not in general very productive.

Támrapatra, S. (ताम्रपत्र), *Támrapaṭ*, Mar. (ताम्रपट) A copper plate, especially one on which grants to temples or individuals are inscribed, such plates are found in all parts of India, but are especially numerous in the south of India.

TÁNÁ, H. &c. (S. تانا, ताना), Mar. (ताणा) The warp, the threads lengthwise on the loom.

Tání, H. &c. (تاني, तानी) The warp of cloth: the price paid for weaving.

ṬANÁB, incorrectly, TENAB, H. (طناب) A tent rope: a measure for measuring land: it was originally of rope, but in the time of Akbar it was ordered to be made of bambus joined by iron rings.

TANÁḲAẒ, A. (تناقض) Contradiction: in law, bringing forward two opposing and incompatible claims to the same property which are considered to invalidate each other.

TANÁKHORÍ, Mar. (तनाखोरी) Embezzlement, fraudulent appropriation of money or of goods received for expenditure, or in trust.

TÁNAKIRI, Mal. (താനകിരി) A small bag of money as an offering to an idol.

ṬÁNḌ, H. (ٹانڈ, टांड) A scaffold in a field of corn on which a man or boy keeps watch to drive away beasts and birds when the grain is about to ripen.

ṬÁNḌ, Hindi (टांड) High and poor soil.—Chota Nagpur.

TANḌA, Mal. (തണ്ട) An open palankin, used in Malabar, commonly called *Manjil.*

TANḌÁ, Tel., Karn. (తండా) A troop of travelling traders, Lambádis or Banjáras: any assemblage of people, a crowd, a mob.

TAN-DAFTAR, H. (P. تن, the body, or an individual, دفتر, record) An office, under the Mohammadan government, in which assignments of revenue to individuals were registered.

TANDÁÏ, (?) Tel. An inferior native revenue-officer or collector under the head farmer.

TANDAL, Tam. (தண்டல்) Collection, demand.

TANDAL, Thug. One of the seven primitive clans.

TANDE, Karn. (ತಂದೆ) A father.

TANḌELU, vulgarly, TINDAL, Tel. (తండేలు), TÁNḌEL, Mar. (तांडेल) The head or commander of a body of men: in ordinary use, a petty native officer employed on board ship, or in the ordinance and tent departments on shore: also in buildings and public works: the head of a gang of labourers.

TANḌRI, Tel. (తండ్రి) A father.

Tandrisaidóḍu, Tel. (తండ్రిసైదోడు) A father's brother or sister.

ṬANGÁ, Hindi (टंगा) A large reedy kind of grass, growing on high ground (Saccharum procerum).

TANIKI, Tel., Karn. (తనికీ, from the A. تنقيح) Ascertainment: used as a revenue term to signify the examination or comparison of a statement or account; ascertaining its correctness.

Tanikídár, Tel. (తనికీదారు) An inspector, an auditor, an examiner, an overseer.

TÁNIO, Guz. (તાનીઓ) A wire.

TANJÁLI, Tel. (తంజాలి) A seller of betel leaves.

ṬANKA, S. (टंक) A weight of silver equal to four *máshas*: among the Marathas the *Ṭank*, or *Ṭánk* (टंक, टांक) is variously rated at four or nine *máshas*, or as the same with a *tola*, or the seventy-second part of a *pakka sér*: a coin, a stamped coin in general; whence it came to be applied, sometimes slightly modified, to specific coins in different metals.

Ṭanká, Tanká, Beng. (টঙ্কা, তঙ্কা) Money in general: a rupee: see *Taka.* Uriya (ଟଙ୍କା) A measure of money value = ten *káhans* of *kauris.*

Ṭankam, Tel. (టంకం) A coin formerly current, but now used only in account, = to four silver single fanams: there was also a gold *Ṭankam*, and a copper coin similarly named, both obsolete: the latter, however, may be preserved at Goa, in the copper coin there called, vulgarly, *Tong*, = to 16 Goa *paisas*, or one-twelfth of a Goa rupee, being a large and clumsy piece of copper.

Tankam, Mal. (തങ്കം), *Tangam*, Tam. (தங்கம்) Fine gold.

Tankakása, Mal. (തങ്കകാശ) A gold ducat.

Ṭankaṣálá, vernacularly, *Ṭaksál*, or *Ṭáksál*, corruptly, *Tacksal, Tankasarlee, Tunkisal, Tanksall*, S. (टंकशाला) H. (ٹکسال), Mar. (टंकशाळ, टांकशाळ) A mint.

Ṭaksálí, Ṭaksáliá, H. (ٹکسالي , ٹکساليا), *Ṭánk-*, or *Ṭaksályá*, Mar. (टांकशाल्या) An officer or master of the mint: a caste, or member of it, whose occupation is coining.

Tankavelakáran, Mal. (തങ്കവേലക്കാരൻ) A goldsmith.

ṬÁNKA, ṬÁNKAN, ṬÁNKANI, Beng. (টাঁকা, টাঁকন, টাঁকনি) Appraising goods, fixing a value or price.

ṬÁNKEṆ, or ṬÁKEN, Mar. (टांकें, टाके), ṬÁNKH, (ٹانکھ, said to be Guzerathi) A reservoir of water, an artificial pond, commonly known to Europeans in India as a *Tank.*

Ṭánki, Guz. (ટાંકી) A reservoir of water: a small well.

Tángal, Tam. (தாங்கல்) A small natural pond or reservoir.

TANKACHCHI, pron. TANGACHI, Mal. (തങ്കച്ചി) The wife of the Rája of Travankur: a female of the same family or class.

Tangai, or *Tangaichi*, Tam. (தங்கை, தங்கைசி) A younger sister: (it is no doubt the same word as the preceding).

TANKAR, (?) A tax on looms.—Kamaon.

ṬANKÁRÁ, Guz. (ટંકારા), ṬANKÁRÍ, or ṬAKÁRÍ, Mar. (S. (टंकारी, टकारी) A stonecutter, a quarrier, a miner.

TANKHWÁH, pronounced TANKHÁ, corruptly, TANKA, TUNKA, TUNKWAH, TUNCAW, H. &c. (تنخواه), TANKHÁ, Mar. (तंखा) An order or draft for money, a bill of exchange, an assignment by the ruling authority upon the revenue of any particular locality in payment of wages, pay, gratuity, or pension, or in repayment of advances, or any specified head of charge: in the Dakhin, the standard rent-roll of a village or district; also the oldest revenue assessment, or that fixed by the *Âdil-Sháhí* princes of Bijapur, and re-settled by *Toral-Mal*, in the reign of Akbar, for the same tract of country: also, under the Moghul government, an assignment of revenue to maintain vessels of war at Surat to convoy pilgrims going to Mekka by sea.

Tankhwah-dahand, H. (P. دهند, let them give) The form of words inscribed by the Vazír upon a written application for an assignment of revenue when complied with: if the sum exceeded 90,000 *dáms* the emperor's signature was necessary.

Tankhá-rakamí, Uriya (ଟଙ୍ଖାରକମୀ) The title given in Cuttack to the assessment of the land revenue by *Toral-Mal*.

TANKÍH, H. (A. تنقيح), TANIKÍ, Tel. (తనికీ) Investigation, search, inquiry, especially examination and verification of accounts or revenue payments.

TANKÍ, (?) Uriya. A light or quit-rent.

Tankí-dár, (?) Uriya. The holder of land at a quit-rent.

Tanki-jamín, (?) Uriya. Land held at a low or quit-rent.

TANKSÚKU, Karn. (ಠಂಕಸೂಕು) An extorted assessment.

TANNÍRKÁL, Tam. (தண்ணீர்க்கால்) A water-course.

Tannír-pandal, Tam. (தண்ணீர்ப்பந்தல்) A shed where water is distributed to passers by.

TANSIF, H. (A. تنصيف) Dividing in half: settling a disputed claim by taking the medium of the value in litigation.

TÁNT, H. &c. (S. تانت, तांत, तंत्र), Beng. (তাঁত) A loom, a weaving apparatus: also thread, fibre, sinew, the string or wire of a musical instrument.

Tántabáya, Beng. (তাঁতবায, S. तंत्रवाय) A weaver.

Tánt-gárá, Beng. (তাঁতগাড়া) A hole sunk in the floor in which the treddles of a loom play.

Tántí, H. &c. (S. تانتي, तांती) A weaver by caste and occupation: in Cuttack the weaver caste is considered one of the impure and servile castes: in Guzerat the word, modified as *Táï*, is applied to a low caste of Mohammadan weavers.

Tántikallaru, corruptly, *Culleroo*, (?), see *Kalla*, Thug., Said to be applied to a clan of Thugs in Karnata who employ a noose of wire or gut for strangulation.

Tántichipa, Uriya (ତାନ୍ତିଚିପା) Strangulation.

Tánt-har, vernacularly, *Tandkar*, H. (from S. कर, a tax) A tax on looms in Kamaon.

TANTA, Mal. (തന്ത) A father.

Tantakúra, Mal. (തന്തക്കൂറ) Inheritance by the father's side.

Tantavari, Mal. (തന്തവഴി) The father's line, or inheritance through the father.

TANTÁ, TANTE, Karn. (ತಂಟಾ, ತಂಟೆ) Debt, deceit, knavery: slander: dispute, quarrel: any unpleasánt matter, or one of difficult adjustment.

Tantekhor, Karn. (ತಂಟೆಖೋರ) A knave, a cheat, one in debt, a troublesome person.

ṬANṬAN, vulgarly, TOM-TOM, Beng. (টনটন) A small drum, especially one beaten to bespeak notice to a public proclamation: it is laxly applied to any kind of drum.

TÁNTRIKA, vernacularly, TÁNTRIK, S. &c. (तांत्रिक) A follower of the doctrines of the Tantras, a set of works inculcating mystical and impure rites in honour of different forms of *Siva* and *Durgá*, constituting the principal authority for the worship practised in many places, and influencing Hindu opinions and observances in the present day more than either the *Vedas* or *Puránas*.

TÁP, Thug. Bread.

TAPA, TAPÚ, vulgarly, TOPO, TOPU, Beng. (তপ, তপূ) West, east; technical terms so used in the village register to indicate the relative position of different fields or properties.

ṬAPÁ, Hindi (टपा) An island in a river.

ṬAPAKCHI, H. (P. تپكچي) A head accountant under the Mohammadan administration, a chief revenue accountant attached to the *Âmil*, or provincial collector's establishment.

TAPARIHÁÚ, Hindi (تپرهاو, तपरिहाऊ) Land cultivated in small patches, interspersed amongst the uncultivated portions of an estate.

TAPAS, S. &c. (तपस्) Penance, ascetic, devotion, the infliction of personal self-denial or torture.

Tapaswí, vernacularly, *Tapasí*, or *Tapassí*, S. &c. (तपस्वी, تپسي) A devotee, an ascetic a penitent. *Tapaswiní*, or *Tapasiní*, a female ascetic.

Tapasyá, S. &c. (तपस्या) Austere or ascetic devotion.

Tapodhana, S. &c. (तपस्, and धन, wealth) Rich in devotion, an ascetic, one who leads a life of penance: in Guz. the servant and minister of a temple.

TAPÁSNÍS, corruptly, TAPPOSNUVEES, TUPUSNEESE, Mar. (तपासनीस, from *Tapás* तपास, inquiry), TAPÁSNÁR, Guz. (તપાસનાર) An officer under the Maratha government whose duty it was to inquire into, and report upon, robberies and other crimes committed in his district: he was also authorised to apprehend offenders, or to compel the village authorities to apprehend them, and, upon their failure, to impose upon the village a fine in proportion to the value of any property stolen: a sort of inspector of police.

TAPPÁ, TUPPÁ, H. &c. (ٹپّا, तप्पा) A small tract or division of country, smaller than a pargana, but comprising one or more villages: a division of country for the revenue of which only one engagement is entered into with the government: a small estate: in some parts of the north-west provinces a *Tappá* denotes a tract in which there is one principal town, or a large village, with lands and villages dependent upon them; or a cluster of villages acknowledging the supremacy of one amongst them, and forming a sort of corporate body, although not otherwise identical.

Tappádári-mauza, H. (ٹپّاداري موضع) The principal village of a *Tappá*, usually giving its name to the whole *Tappá*.

ṬAPPÁ, Tel. (టప్పా), Mar. (टप्पा), ṬAPPÁ, ṬAPPÁLU, ṬAPPE, Karn. (ಟಪ್ಪಾ, ಟಪ್ಪಾಲು, ಟಪ್ಪೆ), ṬAPO, pronounced ṬAPPO, Guz. (ટપો) A stage, a halting place, a place where relays of letter-carriers or palankin bearers are posted, also the relay itself; also, in Tel. and Karn., the post: more usually *Tappál*, see the next.

Ṭappálu, Tel. Karn. (టప్పాలు), *Ṭappál*, Mar. (टप्पाल), *Ṭapál*, Guz. (ટપાલ) The post: the carriage and delivery of letters, &c.

Ṭappákágada, Karn. (ಟಪ್ಪಾಕಾಗದ) A letter sent by post.

Ṭappálu-khané, Karn. (ಟಪ್ಪಾಲುಖಾನೆ) Post-office.

Ṭappálu-vádu, Tel. (టప్పాలువాడు) A postman.

Ṭappi, Tel. (టప్పి) An express.

TAPPAL, TAPPOWAL, Thug. A bye-path, one out of the highway into which travellers are decoyed.

TAPPALU, Tel. (pl. తప్పలు) Corn of which the ears are empty from blight or dearth.

TAPTI, (?) Tel. A wooden stamp for marking patches of earth put upon piles or stacks of corn.

ṬÁPÚ, H. (ٹاپو, टापू) An island.

TAPU, Beng. (তপু, abbreviation of S. तत्, that, and पूर्व, before) A term used in accounts, especially in measurement or land surveying, equivalent to aforesaid, as before, already.

TAR, Hindi (तर, for S. तल) Bottom, underneath, under-surface.

Tarsiddha, Hindi (तरसिद्ध) The under-surface (of land or of a field) broken up and prepared for sowing, although the upper surface is covered with grass.—Puraniya.

Tar-upar, Hindi (S. उपरि, upper) Breaking up the upper surface of land slightly so as to remove the grass and weeds.—Puraniya.

TAR, H. (P. تر) Moist, wet, fresh, green, &c.

Tara, H. (P. تره) Garden herbs, vegetables, greens.

Tarái, H. (ترائي) Marsh, meadow, marshy ground: it is applied especially to the moist and jangli tract running along the foot of the first range of the Himalaya for several hundred miles, varying in breadth from two to fifteen: low, moist land lying along the banks of rivers.

Tarí, corruptly, *Turree*, H. (تري) Moisture. Mar. (तरी) Wet or rice-lands. Uriya (ତରି) Alluvial deposit.

Tarṣuä, Hindi (तरशुआ) Water or moisture exuding from underneath the soil.

TÁṚ, H. &c. (S. ٹاڑ, ताड़) A palm tree: it is applied to both the Palmyra or Borassus flabelliformis, and the Corypha talliera, and loosely to various other kinds of palms: it is most appropriate to the Palmyra, from the stem of which the juice is extracted which becomes *táṛí*, or, vulgarly, *toddy*: the Corypha does not yield the same, but its leaves are used for writing upon: the letters are cut with an iron style, and then smeared over with a preparation of lamp-black serving as ink, which is wiped off from the surface of the leaf.

Táṛ-ban, erroneously, *Tarbund*, H. (from S. *bana*, or *vana* वन, a wood) A plantation of palm trees.

Táṛí, *Táḍí*, vulgarly, *Toddy*, H. (ٹاڑي, ताडी) The juice or sap of the Palmyra tree and of the cocoa-nut, which is drawn off by incisions made in the bark, and the exudation is received by small earthen vessels fastened over the wounds in the bark: when first drawn the juice is sweet, somewhat insipid, and harmless, but when allowed to stand for a day or more it undergoes spontaneous fermentation, and becomes a fiery and highly intoxicating spirit.

Táṛípatra, S. &c. (पत्र, a leaf) The leaf of the Corypha palm, especially when used for writing upon: any document written on palm leaves. See *Tálapatra*.

Táṛíwálá, H. &c. (ٹاڑي والا, ताडीवाला) A man who climbs the palm trees and extracts the sap for the making of *táṛí*.

Tarwaro, Guz. (તરવારો) A man who extracts *táṛí* from palm trees.

TÁR, H. (P. تار) A wire, a thread, the string of a musical instrument.

Tárkash, H. (P. تاركش) A drawer of gold or silver wire.

TARA, Mal. (തറ) A town, a village, a district.

TARADDUD, H. (A. تردّد), TARADDÚDU, Tel. (తరద్దూడు) Active exertion, especially labour in agriculture, whence it comes to signify cultivation in general.

Taraddudi-jamín, less correctly, *Taruddudi-zamín*, H. (تردديزمين तरद्दुदी, or तरद्दुदी जमीन) Cultivated land, especially land that is always in cultivation, never requiring to lie fallow.

Taraddúdu-jábitá, Tel. (తరద్దూడుజాబితా), *Taraddúdina-paṭṭi*, Karn. (ತರದ್ದೂದಿನಪಟ್ಟಿ) An account shewing the species and quantity of seed sown, the extent of land under cultivation, and the portion left fallow.

ṬARAF, ṬURUF, vernacularly, TARAPH, corruptly, TEREF, TURRUF, blunderingly, TURNEFF, H. &c. (طرف, तरफ) Lit. Side, part: also a tract of country, a subdivision of a *pargana*, including several villages: in some places it merely designates the lands or estate belonging to an individual which is named after him, as, *Ṭaraf Jaynáráyan Ghosál*: in Mar. it signifies also a portion of village lands.

Taraph-bandí, *Turuph-bundee*, Mar. (तरफबंदी) A system of assessment and tenure in which the lands of a village are divided into large parcels, each of which is held of government by an entire family, not a branch of it, the individual members of the family making an arrangement amongst themselves for the cultivation of the several portions, but being answerable collectively for the whole assessment.

Ṭaraf-bánṭ, H. (طرف بانٹ) The holding of several separate divisions of village lands by different branches of the community, the coparceners of one *Ṭaraf* having no interest in another, although included under the same village: the division may sometimes originate in difference of caste or religion, so that a village may have a Mohammadan and a Hindu *Ṭaraf*.

Ṭaraf-dár, H. &c. (P. دار, who has) An officer of government in charge of a *Ṭaraf*, collecting the revenue and exercising chief revenue and police authority in his district: the holder of a *Ṭaraf*, or portion of village lands: also, generally, one who takes a side or part, an assistant, an ally, a partisan.

Ṭarafain, H. &c. (A. *du*, طرفين) Both sides, both parties in a law-suit.

Taraphaian, Guz. (તરફૈઅન) A drill-plough (having a drill tube on each side of the handle).

Ṭaraf-ṣání, H. (A. ثاني, second) An adversary, an opponent, the defendant in a suit.

TARAGU, Tam. (தரகு), TARAGA, or TARAKA, Mal. (തരക), TARAGU, TARUGU, Tel. (తఱుగు, తఱుగు) Brokerage, commission, a small deduction from the price of the articles purchased claimed by the agent of the purchaser, the *dastúrí* of Hindustan, q. v.: a balance, a measure: a grant of land, or the like; also, in Tel., wastage, deficiency.

Tarakan, pronounceable, *Taragan*, Mal. (തരകൻ) A broker, an agent: the name of a caste of Súdras, or of an individual of the caste.

TARÁḶ, Mar. (तराळ) A man of a low caste attached sometimes to the village establishment, who acts as a porter, carrying burthens for government or travellers as far as the nearest village; he officiates also as a sort of beadle: the term is derived from the office, as the duty is discharged and the fees are received for a given time by each of the village Mahárs in rotation.

TARAM, corruptly, TERRIM, Tam. &c. (தரம், from the A. طرح, sort), TARAMU, Tel. (తరము) Sort, kind, class: it is especially applied in the south of India to designate the different classes of village lands, and the heads under which they are arranged in the village accounts.

Taram-chiṭhṭhá, corruptly, *Turm-chitta*, Tel. (తరంచిఠ్ఠా) A rough valuation or classification of land.

Taramdárudu, or *Taramdár*, corruptly, *Terrimdár*, Tel. (తరందారుడు) An assessor, a surveyor and classifier of land: in Mar. *Taram*, incorrectly, *Turrum* (तरम्), is used also, but rather laxly, in this sense, being the appellation of any officer who, in former revenue surveys, determined the classification and assessment of the lands, but who, in the present day, has only to class them according to selected specimens of the different sorts of soil.

Ṭaram-mutaṣaddi, corruptly, *Terrim-mutaseddi*, Tam (from the A. متصدّي) An assessor of land.

Tarappurattu, Tam. (தரப்புரட்டு) Fraud in classifying the lands of a village.

Tarappadi, Tam. (தரப்படி) Statement of the extent of a village as arranged in different classes.

Tarappadi-kanakku, Tam. (கணக்கு, an account) The portion of the village register which records the extent and description of the several sorts of the village lands.

Tarappadi-mányam, Tam. (மானியம், a free grant) Those portions of the village lands which are particularised in the village register as held rent-free hereditarily, either by ownership or by office.

TÁRAṆA, S. &c. (तारण) The 18th year of the cycle.

TARATAKA, (?) Mar. A fee on marriages, or rather on the awnings erected in front of the houses at the celebration of a marriage.

TAṞAWÁṬA, or TAṞAWAḌA, vulgarly, TARWÁD, TARWAUD, Mal. (തറവാട) A house, a family, especially a united family whose affairs are managed by one or more of the chief members; the union may be broken up altogether or subdivided by mutual consent; the family are bound by the acts of the recognised manager: the institution appears to be in some respects peculiar to Malabar, and to present some singular provisions, as where the property is considered as restricted to the females of the *Tarwád*, and the males have no power of alienating it.—Madras Decisions, Calicut, May 1852.

Taṟawáṭṭa-janma, Mal. (തറവാട്ടജന്മ) Family hereditary property.

Taṟawáṭṭukáran, Mal. (തറവാട്ടുക്കാരൻ) A householder, a man of family, the managing member of a united family: formerly these heads of families were looked upon as authorities and arbitrators in disputes amongst the people of a district, especially in regard to matters concerning caste, marriages, obsequial rites, and religious ceremonies.

Tarawáṭṭu-mutal, Mal. (തറവാട്ടുമുതൽ) Family property.

TARÁWI, H. (A. تراوي) Certain prayers to be read by an *Imám* or *Háfiz* in the presence of a congregation daily after evening prayer during the fast of *Ramzán* for twenty or thirty days: also a daily supererogatory prayer which may be read at eight A.M.

TARÁZU, H. (P. ترازو) A balance, a pair of scales: in Sindh, a money tax on all articles of food sold in the báẓár.

TAṚÍ, Tam. (தறி) A weaver's loom.

Taṛikadamai, and *Taṛivari*, Tam. (தறிக்கடமை, தறி-வரி) A duty or tax levied upon weavers, especially on those settled in villages, payable in money to the proprietors of land, and carried to the credit of the general fund for village expenses.

TARIÁ, Thug. A gold mohur.

TÂRÍF, H. &c. (A. تعريف, from عرف, to know), TÁRIPH, Hindi (तारीफ), ṬARIPHU, Tel. (టరీఫు) Determination, ascertainment, a table of rates of export and import duties, in which sense the word has been adopted in English and other European languages: (probably through the Spanish from the Arabic).

TARÍKA, or TARAKAH, incorrectly, TARKA, H. (A. تركه, تريكه, from ترك, to be left) Property of every description left by a person deceased: inheritance of such property, whether by succession or bequest.

TÁRÍKH, H. &c. (A. تاريخ) Date, era, epoch.

Táríkh-wár, H. &c. (تاريخوار) According to the date.

TARIPÁR, Guz. (S. તરીપાર, from *tarí*, a crossing over, and *pára*, the opposite bank) Transportation beyond sea.

TARISU, corruptly, TERSEE, TEERSEY, TERSEY, Tam. (தரிசு) Waste or uncultivated land, whether so from time immemorial or only for a season, fallow: any uncultivated field: the boundaries of a village.

Tarisa, Mal. (തരിശ) adj., Fallow, uncultivated.

Tarisunilam, Mal. (തരിശുനിലം) Waste or fallow land.

TÂRÍẒ, vernacularly, TÁRÍJ, H. &c. (A. تعريض, exchange) Statement of particulars of landed property deposited in the collector's office.

Táríj, Guz. (A. તારીજ) Abstract recapitulation, a number of items set down without detailed specification, for the purpose of adding them together and getting a total.

TARJAMA, TARJAMÁ, H. &c. (A. ترجمه, ترجما), TARJAMÁ, TARJUMÁ, Mar. (तरजमा, तरजुमा) Translation, interpretation: in Mar., also, an abstract statement, a report of proceedings; an abstract framed from the *ek-berjí* papers of the total receipts, expenses, and balances of the government on all accounts for the year: in Bengal it is also applied to the English abstract which accompanies native documents transmitted to the superior authorities.

Tarjamán, *Tarjumán*, H. &c. (A. ترجمان, तरजमान, तरजुमान) A translator, an interpreter, whence the European corruption, *Dragoman*.

TARKÁRÍ, H. &c. (تركاري, तरकारी) Esculent vegetables: a tax imposed on gardens or ground on which vegetables are grown, especially those of most value, as ginger, turmeric, tobacco, and the like, on which a higher rate of assessment is usually levied.

TARPANA, vernacularly, TARPAN, S. &c. (तर्पण) Lit. Satisfying, but applied especially to the daily presentation of water from the palm of the hand to the *manes* at the time of bathing.

ṬARRÁR, H. (A. طرّار) A cheat, an impostor, a swindler, a pickpocket.

TARU, Tam. (S. தரு) A tree, as in Sanskrit, but it is a term inserted in deeds of sale or gift of land, to indicate the conveyance of all the vegetable products of the lands transferred.

TARUGÁRA, (?) Karn. A village officer in Karnata whose

business it is to keep the cultivators to their work, and watch that they do not remove any of the crop before the government share has been taken (perhaps a mistake for *Talavára*, q. v.).

TARUMBU, Tam. (தறும்பு) A dam to stop a stream and turn it into a different direction.

TÁS, Thug. The blue jay: on the right, or crossing from left to right, a good omen: the contrary indicates neither good nor ill.

TAṢADAḲ, H. (A. تصدق) Alms, giving alms.

Tasadíku, or *Tastíku*, Karn. (ತಸದಿಕು, ತಸ್ತೀಕು) Allowance by the government to a temple or religious establishment.

TASAR, less correctly, TUSSUR, H. (تسر, S. त्रसर) An inferior sort of silk, the produce of a worm found wild in many parts of India (Bombyx paphia).

TASAR, Mar. (तसर) A sum compounded for with the cultivators by the government in lieu of payment in kind.

TAṢARRUF, H. &c. (A. تصرّف) Possession, property, ownership, holding any thing at one's own disposal: in law, any act of ownership, the rights of a proprietor over his property, as sale, lease, mortgage, &c.

Taṣarruf-ẕámin, H. (A. ضامن, a surety) A surety for possession: see the next.

Taṣarruf-ẕáminí, H. (A. ضامني, security) Security for possession: security given by the party in the possession of litigated property that no loss shall be sustained by the opposite party or claimant in the event of its being decreed to him.

TASBÍH, H. (A. تسبيح) Praying to God: also a rosary, which should consist of a hundred beads of different seeds, woods, or precious stones, which are turned over as the prayers are repeated: the term is commonly prefixed to writings, and is used frequently in speech.

TAṢDÍḲ, H. (A. تصديق) Verifying, attestation: a countermark attached to documents passing through the hands of government officers or clerks, especially on petitions to the Mohammadan government for assignment of revenue: specification of establishment and expenses: fixed amount or scale of expenditure for any special purpose.

TAṢ-HÍHA, corruptly, TESHIHA, H. (A. تصحيحه) Muster, especially under the Mohammadan government, of the horses belonging to the state, for the purpose of being stamped. See *Dágh-i-taṣhiha*.

Taṣ-hiha Dároghaï, H. (P. داروغه) The office of the Dárogha or superintendant of the examining and stamping of the horses of the state: assignment of revenue or allowances to the officers in charge of the department.

TASHḤÍR, H. (A. تشهير) In Mohammadan law, public exposure, as by carrying the delinquent through the town on an ass with his face blackened, formerly the especial punishment of perjury. Ben. Reg. ii. 1807, abolished by Act ii. 1849.

TASHKHÍṢ, strangely corrupted as TESHKEES, TESKEES, TUCKSEES, H. (A. تشخيص) Distinguishing, ascertainment, valuation, assessment: corrected assessment: net standard revenue, or the actual or absolute amount of realisable revenue: particular account of such revenue, or the available funds which it constitutes: (the term is used with some laxity, but it always implies a determinate or determinable amount of revenue assessment): Ben. Reg. ii. 1795.

Tashkhíṣ-jamâ-bandí, corruptly, *Teshkees-*, *Teshees-*, or *Tuchsees-jumma-bundy*, H. (جمعبندي, annual assessment) The net amount of revenue engaged for at the perpetual settlement in Bengal; the total amount of revenue to be collected under the terms of that settlement: an account shewing these particulars: a statement of the net annual settlement previously concluded with Zamindárs, Tálukdárs, and others.

Tashkhíṣ-muḳarrari, H. (A. مقرّر, fixed) A fixed assessment: assessment of the lands in Cuttack made by the *Subahdárs* of Bengal when Orissa was also under their authority.

Tashkhíṣ-i-Bhunsla, (?) The assessment of the lands in Cuttack made by the government of Nagpur when the province was subject to the *Bhunsla* or Rája of Nagpur.

Tashkhíṣ-i-taâluḳa, H. (A. تعلقه) A dependent or subordinate property held of a superior upon payment of the revenue according to the current rate of the district.

Tashkhíṣ-i-ṭumár-jamâ, H. (A. طمارجمع, account of the revenue) The revised assessment of the revenue of Bengal by Jaffir Âli Khan in 1722, in modification of that originally fixed by *Todar Mal*.

Tasgisu, Tel. (తసగీసు, vernacular corruption of *Tashkhiṣ*) Account of the government share of the crop, valued according to the current rates.

TASHRÍF, H. (A. تشريف), TASRÍPH, Mar. (तसरीफ) Honouring, conferring honour upon any one, as by paying him a visit, presenting a dress of honour, or any complimentary donation: the present or honorarium so paid: in the south of India, complimentary presents made by the cultivators to the native revenue officers at the time of fixing the annual assessment.

TAṢIVAM, Tel. (తశివం) Balance of revenue due by the native collectors.

TASLÍM, H. (A. تسليم) Salutation, the performance of *Salám.* Tel. (but ?) Peculation, collections withheld.

TASMA-BÁZÍ, H. (تسمهبازي, P. تسمه, a strap, and بازي, playing) A low gambling game played with a leather strap and a stick: (a favourite game with the lower orders of natives in the north-west provinces, for a knowledge of which they are indebted to a European soldier.

TASÚ, TASÚṆ, Mar. तसू, तसूं) A measure of length, the 20th or 24th part of a *gaz*, q. v.: it is known in the north-west provinces as the subdivision of a *gira.*

TÁTA, Tel. (తాత) A grandfather.

Tátamma, Tel. (తాతమ్మ) A grandmother, a paternal grandmother.

ṬÁṬ, H. &c. (ٹاٹ, टाट), TÁṬ, Mar. (ताट) Canvas, sackcloth.

Ṭáṭí, more usually, *Ṭaṭṭí*, H. &c. (ٹاٹي ٹٹّي, टाटी, टट्टी), *Táṭí*, Mar. (ताटी) A matted screen, a frame of wicker-work filled with the roots of the fragrant Andropogon grass and placed before the open doors and windows of a house, where it is kept constantly sprinkled with water, by the evaporation of which the air that passes through into the interior of the house is kept much below the temperature of the external air: also, from its being inclosed with mats, a privy.

TÂṬÍL, H. (A. تعطيل) Holiday, vacation.

TATIMMA, H. (A. تتمّه) Appendix, supplement: a supplemental pleading or petition.

Tatimma-ârẓí, Tatimma-sawál, H. (from عرضي, a representation, or سوال, a request) A supplemental or amended plaint or petition.

Tatimma-tafríḳ, H. (A. تفريق, separation) A supplementary record of separate interests or shares.

TÁTPARYAM, vernacularly, TÁTPARJ, H. &c. (S. तात्पर्य्य) Purport, object, intention, meaning.

ṬAṬṬU, H. &c. (ٹٹّو, टट्टु), TAṬṬU, Tel. (తట్టు) A pony: the undersized horse that is the prevailing breed in Bengal and most parts of India proper.

TÁTTUDÁRI, corruptly, TATOODARRY, (?) A land tenure in the Northern Sarkárs held at a low unalterable rent.—Gl. 5th Rep.

TAU, Thug. A party, either of travellers or Thugs.

TAUFÍR, vulgarly TOWFEER, H. (A. توفير) Increase: applied in revenue language to an augmentation of the revenue, either from extended cultivation or the lapse or resumption of alienated assignments: excess above an intended amount of assignment, which, when realised in a Jágír, was considered to be the right of the state, although rarely acknowledged or paid. Kásim Âli Khan, in order to cover the loss arising from concealment of surplus, assumed its realisation universally, and imposed an *Abwáb*, or cess, upon assigned lands in its stead, which was thence also called *Taufír*: the term is applied also to the surplus on a Jágír or an assignment of rent-free land which is discovered on either being resumed.

Taufír-i-Jágírdárán, H. (P. جاگير, q. v.) Increase or surplus revenue on the resumed assignments of the holders of *Jágírs.*

Taufír-kámil, or *Taufír-kamál*, H. (كامل, or كمال, complete) The highest rate of assessment imposed: the standard revenue assessment: (it is current in this sense especially in the Dakhin).

Taufír-mauẓâ, H. (A. موضع, a village) A village not originally included in the assessment: a village in excess.

Taufír-zamín, H. (P. زمين, land) Lands in addition to, or excess of, an original grant or measurement.

TAUHAD, Hindi (तौहद) Renting.—South-west provinces.

TAUJÍH, incorrectly, TOUZEH, TOUZIH, H. (A. توجيه) Explaining: adjustment of accounts: assessment: a revenue account shewing, under the name of each payer of revenue, the total amount as it falls due by monthly instalments, the portion actually paid, and the balance outstanding: it is usually a village account, and is kept by the village accountant: also a register of the estates of a collectorate kept in the collector's office. Act i. 1845.

Taujíh-mahál, H. (A. محال, an estate) An estate that pays an assessed revenue.

Taujíh-nawís, H. (P. نويس, who writes) An accountant who keeps the account termed *Taujíh.*

TAULÁ, H. (تولا, तौला) An intoxicating liquor made from the flowers of the Mahwa tree steeped in water until fermentation takes place.—Oudh.

TAULÍAT, H. (توليت, from ولي) Trusteeship or superintendence of a religious foundation: the management of the funds appropriated to its support: appointing a person to such an office, transferring property to him for such a trust: the term is principally used in these senses in India: in Mohammadan law, it also signifies a sale in which the owner disposes of the article sold at the price which he originally paid for it.

Tauliat-náma, H. (P. نامه, a document) Deed of trusteeship, one appointing a person to the management of a religious endowment.

Tauliat-mâ-al-wasiat, H. (A. معالوصيت, with a will) A deed of endowment or trusteeship, executed as a bequest or will to take effect only after the death of the devisor.

TÁUNARI, Thug. A pretext or trick to beguile travellers.

TÁÜT-DÁR, (?) Beng. Manager or factor of an estate : a collector of rents, retaining a portion as his compensation: (an error for *Táhuddár* : see *Táhut*).

Dar-táüt-dár, Beng. A sub-collector or contractor for the rents of an estate : (see the last).

TAVANAI, Tam. (தவணை) A term, a fixed term, as for payment, &c.

Tavanai-kraya-patram, Tam. (தவணைக்கிரயபத்திரம்) A deed of sale, after a term; by which land is transferred on mortgage liable to redemption within a stipulated term, but becoming the absolute property of the mortgagee if not redeemed within the time.

Tavanakka-chițța, Mal. (തവണക്കച്ചിട്ട) An agreement to pay a loan by instalments.

Tavanamudakkam, Mal. (തവണമുടക്കം) Lapse of term fixed for an instalment; failure to pay at the stipulated time.

Tavanappanam, Mal. (തവണപ്പണം) An instalment, a stipulated periodical money payment.

TAWÁFUK, H. (A. توافق, from وفق) Divisibility by a common number, as in the case of an inheritance where the number of shares and sharers is so divisible, as where there are twenty shares and eight sharers, either is divisible by four or by two.

TAWAHAM, A. (توهم, from وهم, imagination) Doubt, suspicion : in law, a doubt expressed by a witness that he may not have given full or accurate testimony through forgetfulness or embarassment, which doubt does not invalidate his testimony if he be a person of good repute.

TAWAJJE, corruptly, TAWAJEE, Karn. (ತವಜ್ಜೆ, from the A. توجه, attention to) An allowance made to landholders.

TÁWÁN, H. (A. تاوان) Fine, retaliation, compensation, damages: in law, the fine for *díat*, or bloodshed, as opposed to *kisás*, or retaliation: among the Marathas *Táwan* (तावण), implying fine, is understood to signify one especially imposed on unfounded suspicion of peculation, or on any unjust grounds.

TÂWÍZ, H. (A. تعويذ), TÁBIJ, Beng. (তাবীজ) An amulet, a charm, especially a verse of the Kurán engraved on a stone or a piece of metal, inclosed in a case and strung on a thread worn round the neck : a platform or slab of stone placed over a grave.

TAYAMMUM, H. (A. تيمّم) Purifying the hands, face, or other parts of the body, by rubbing them with sand or dust where water is not to be had for the purpose of purificatory ablution.

TÁYAVÁYKKÁL, Tam. (தாயவாய்க்கால்) A large water-course.

TÁZÍ, H. (P. تازي) Arab, Arabian : an Arab horse.

Tází-khána, H. (P. خانه, a house) A dog-kennel.

TÂZÍA, H. (A. تعزيه) A representation or model of the tomb of Hasan and Hasain, at Karbala, carried in procession at the Muharram by the Indian Shías: it is usually made of a light framework of bambu slips covered with paper, painted and ornamented with mica and glass, and artificial flowers, and illuminated within and without; it is sometimes of considerable size and elaborate execution, and, according to the wealth and piety of the owner, may be constructed of more costly materials, as glass, ivory, sandalwood, or silver: the common ones are usually thrown away or destroyed at the end of the solemnization, the more valuable ones are preserved.

Tâzía-dár, H. (P. دار, who has) A person who sets up a *Tâzía* at the Muharram.

Tâzía-khána, H. (P. خانه, a house) The place where the model tombs of Âli and his sons are kept when too costly to be thrown away: this is usually the *Imám-bára*, q. v. or a place adjoining it.

TÁZIÁNA, H. (تازيانه) A whip, a scourge, an instrument formerly used in the Company's courts for the punishment of delinquents, but the use of which has been abolished.

Táziána-bardár, H. (P. بردار, bearer) The functionary who was formerly charged with the duty of flogging culprits condemned to be whipped.

TÂZÍL, H. (A. تعزيل) Removing or dismissing from office.

TÂZÍR, H. (A. تعزير) Punishment, correction : in law, punishment inflicted at the discretion of the judge with a view to public justice; that is, in cases where, from some impediment or collusion, the legal penalties might be escaped or evaded, these discretional penalties are to be imposed: they may extend from simple reproof to mutilation, and even to death.

Tâzír-ânif, *Tâzír-shadíd*, H. (عنيف, or شديد, severe)

Severe or rigorous punishment inflicted at the discretion of the judge.

TAZKÍAT, H. (A. تزكيت) Sanctifying, purifying : that part of a man's wealth which is dedicated to pious uses : in law, the evidence given by a number of persons in favour of the credibility or competence of other persons to give their testimony : expurgation of evidence : the purgators are termed *Muzakkí* (مزكي).

TAZWÍJ, H. (A. تزويج) Joining, association : in law, marriage, contracting in marriage.

TADAL-PUNJAI, corruptly, TEDDUL-POONJA, (?) Tam. (ததல்புன்செய) High land incapable of irrigation.

Tadal-punja-tírvai, Tam. (ததல்புன்சதீர்வை) Assessment of high unirrigated land.

TEDI, Tel. (తెది) A day of the solar month (? a corruption of *Tithi*, q. v.).

TEDVATÍ, (?) Mal. Designation of a bond in which, for money advanced, land is assigned to the lender until the loan is paid (perhaps it should be *Tadvatí*, S. the like of, such as).

TEGUBADI, Tel. (తెగుబడి) Ploughing.

TEGUḶA, Karn. (ತೆಗುಳ) The general designation of the people who speak Tamil.

ṬEHRÁ, H. (تهرا) A village.

ṬEKÁḌ, Mar. (टेकाड) A mound, a hillock.

TÉKKA, Mal. (തെക്ക), TÉKKU, Tam. (தேக்கு) The Teak tree (Tectona grandis).

ṬEKRO, Guz. (ટેકરો) A mound, a hillock.

TEL, H. &c. (تيل, तेल, from S. तैल, *tail*, derivative of *til* तिल, sesamum) Oil in general, especially oil extracted from sesamum seeds.

Telcharháná, H. (تيل چرهانا) Smearing the head, shoulders, hands, and feet of the bride and bridegroom with oil taken from the jar provided for the occasion.

Teldirvali, (?) A contribution levied in kind upon the oilmen of a village by the *Pátíl*.

Telghaṛá, H. (تيل گهرا) A jar or pitcher of oil painted and used at marriage ceremonies.

Telgháṇá, Mar. (तेलघाणा) An oil-mill : certain ceremonies performed at the marriage of a Súdra.

Telí, H. &c. (تيلي, तेली), *Telío*, Guz. (તેલીઓ) An oilman, one whose caste and occupation is expressing oil by mills from different sorts of seeds, and selling it, considered as a low and impure caste.

Teliá, Teliyá, H. (تيليا, तेलीया) Oily, applied in the north-west to a sort of water of an unctuous appearance, and the use of which cakes and hardens the soil and is unfavourable to cultivation.

Teligutta, Tel. (తెలిగుత్త) A tax on oil mills.

Telí-khúrt, (?) A tax imposed on oilmen at so much per mill.

Telitambolí, Mar. (तेलीतंबोली) An oilman and betel seller, a comprehensive term for persons of these and other low castes.

Telphal, Mar. (तेलफल) Marriage presents, consisting of cocoa-nuts, oil, &c., sent by the bridegroom to the bride shortly before his own coming to celebrate the marriage.

TELINGA, TILANG, or, more correctly, TELINGÁNÁ, H. &c. (تيلنگ , تلنگ , تيلنگانا) TELANGAṆ, Mar. (तेलंगण) The country so named by the Mohammadans, the modern Carnatic : according to Campbell (Introd. Telugu Gr.) the word is derived from *Trilingam*, three celebrated Lingas constituting the boundaries of the province : the proper Sanscrit name is *Andhra*.

Tilangá, H. (تلنگا), *Telangá*, Mar. (तेलंगा) A native of Tilang, from whom the first native soldiers, dressed and disciplined after the European fashion, having been raised, it came to denote a soldier, a *Sipáhí*.

Telugu, or *Tenugu*, Tel. (తెలుగు) The language of Telinga (from which word Campbell derives it).

TENḌÁ, Tel. (తెండా) A *Pakota*, a lever for raising water.

TENDAL, Mal. (തെണ്ടൽ) Begging.

Tendalkáran, Mal. (തെണ്ടൽകാരൻ) A beggar : a collector of taxes.

TEṆṆA, Mal. (തെങ്ങ), TEṆGU, Tam. (தெங்கு) A cocoa-nut-tree (Cocos nucifera).

Teṇgaṇkáy, Teṇkáy, Tam. (தெங்கங்காய், தெங்காய்) The cocoa-nut.

Tengu, Karn. (ತೆಂಗು) The cocoa-nut.

Tenginamara, Tenginagiḍa, Karn. (ತೆಂಗಿನಮರ, ತೆಂಗಿನಗಿಡ) A cocoa-nut tree.

Teninginanáru, Karn. (ತೆಂಗಿನನಾರು), *Téṇgáynár*, Tam. (தேங்காய்நார்) The fibres of the cocoa-nut shell and of the stem of the tree used to make rope, mats, &c., commonly termed *Coir*.

TENGALAY, (?) The name of a religious sect in the south of India.—Kombakonam.

TENPI, Tel. (తెంపి) A widow.

ṬENṬÁRÍ, Beng. (টেঁটারী) A brazier.

ṬEP, Mar. (टेप) A mound or hillock.

ṬEP, Guz. (ટેપ) Sentence of imprisonment or transportation for a given term, civil or military decision of a judge.

Teppa, Tel. (తెప్ప) A float or raft of timber on which the natives go out to fish at sea; also the float attending the embarkment boats at Madras, commonly called *Kattamaran.*

Terah-tezí, H. (تیرہ تیزی, from H. تیرہ, thirteen, and P. تیزی, sharpness, applied in India to a lunar day in the month *Ṣafar*) The first thirteen days of the month *Ṣafar,* which are considered very unlucky, as Mohammad was seriously unwell on those days: on the 13th *tezí* (or day of the lunar month), which, according to one reckoning may be the 12th, or to another the 13th day of the month; good Mohammadans are to bathe and distribute food and alms.

Teravu, Karn. (ತೆರವು) Price paid to the friends of a female child about to be betrothed.

Terbulige, (?) Karn. Giving back.

Térgaḍe, and **Terugaḍe**, Karn. (ತೇರ್ಗಡೆ, ತೆರುಗಡೆ) Settlement of an account, acquittance.

Terike, Terige, Tenge, Karn. (ತೆರಿಕೆ, ತೆರಿಗೆ, ತೆಂಗೆ) Taxes.

Terigékágada, Karn. (ತೆರಿಗೇಕಾಗದ) A written lease, or a paper containing an account of the periods when instalments of the taxes are to be paid.

Terigé-kuḷa, Terigé-yokkalu, Karn. (ತೆರಿಗೇಕುಳ, ತೆರಿಗೇಯೊಕ್ಕಲು) One who pays taxes, a tenant of the soil.

Tetta, Karn. (ತೆತ್ತ) Paid, as taxes.

Tetta-kásu, Tetta-gánike, Karn. (ತೆತ್ತಕಾಸು, ತೆತ್ತಗಾಣಿಕೆ) Tax money.

Tettakuḷa, &c. Karn. (ತೆತ್ತಕುಳ) A person who pays taxes, a tenant of the soil.

Ṭhag, Ṭhug, H. &c. (ٹھگ, ठग), **Ṭhak, Ṭhag**, Mar. (ठक, ठग) A cheat, a knave, an impostor; latterly applied to a robber and assassin of a peculiar class, who, sallying forth in a gang of smaller or larger numbers, and in the character of wayfarers, either on business or pilgrimage, fall in with other travellers on the road, and, having gained their confidence, take a favourable opportunity of strangling them by throwing their turbans or handkerchiefs round their necks, and then plundering them and burying their bodies: it has also been applied to child-stealing and robbery not amounting to *Dakaiti.* Act iii. 1848: the more correct appellation is *Phánsigár,* q. v.).

Ṭhagí, Ṭhugí, corruptly, *Tuggee, Thuggee,* H. &c. (ٹھگی, ठगी) The practice of strangling and robbing, the practice of child-stealing. Act xviii. 1837; xviii. 1839; iii. 1848.

Ṭhákur, Ṭhakoor, H. &c. (ٹھاکر, ठाकुर, S. ठक्कुर), Beng. (ঠাকুর), *Ṭhákúr,* Mar. (ठाकूर) An idol, a deity: any individual entitled to reverence or respect, whence it is generally applied to persons of rank and authority in different parts of India, as a lord, a chief, a master, a spiritual guide, the *Bhát* or genealogist, the head of a tribe, the head of a village, and the like: in the west it is commonly given to the great feudal nobles of *Rájputána,* as *Bhím Sing Ṭhákur,* &c., and is the usual title of a *Rájput* or *Grásia* chieftain elsewhere: in the Dakhin it is borne by the head men of the *Bhíls* and other wild races, and is there said to signify also a particular tribe inhabiting the forests: in Upper India it frequently denotes the individual members of village communities of Brahmanical or Rajput descent, who are notorious for irregular and turbulent conduct: it also means a barber. In Bengal it is equivalent, as a term of address, to Sir, Master, Your worship; and is a family name indicating respectable and Brahmanical origin: the *Ṭhákurs,* of whom *Dwárakánáth Ṭhákur* deserves especial notice as a man of liberal opinions and enterprising character, who died in London in 1846, constitute a family of Brahmans well-known and much respected in Calcutta.

Ṭhákurái, H. (ٹھاکرائی, ठाकुराई) The rank or office of a chief or *Ṭhákur.*

Ṭhákuráni, or *Ṭhahuráin,* H. &c. (ٹھاکرانی, ٹھاکراین, ठाकुराणी) A goddess, a lady, a mistress, the wife of a spiritual preceptor, the wife of a Rajput chief, and the like: in addressing a female it is equivalent to Madam, Your ladyship.

Ṭhákuráït, H. (ٹھاکرایت) The holding, or tenure, or rank of a *Ṭháhur.*

Ṭhákur-báp, Beng. (ঠাকুরবাপ) A grandfather; lit., a venerable father, &c.

Ṭháhur-má, A grandmother, &c.

Ṭhákur-báṭi, or *-báṛí,* Beng. (ঠাকুরবাটী, -বাড়ী) A temple, an idol-house.

Ṭhákur-dwárá, H. &c. (S. द्वार, a door) A temple, a building in which the village idols are kept.

Thahuríyá, Asam (ঠাকুরীযা) The title of a subordinate revenue officer charged with the collections of a subdivision of a *pargana* comprising two or three villages.

Ṭhákurjhí, Beng. (ঠাকুরঝী, from ঝী, a daughter) A wife's sister, a husband's sister; that is to say, the husband calls his wife's sisters by the name: the daughter of a spiritual preceptor.

Ṭhákur-khuṛá, Beng. (from খুড়া, an uncle) A paternal uncle

Ṭhákur-sevá, H. (S. सेवा, service) lit., The service of an idol, applied to a grant of revenue for maintaining the worship of an idol.

THAKUR, Thug. The loud cry of the large owl.

THAL, THUL, H. &c. (تهل, थल, from the S. स्थल) Firm ground, place, spot, site, a sand-hill, a sand-bank, the sandy tract interposed between the west of Rajputana and the Indus: in Maraṭhí, the share (of the lessor or lessee) in the produce of a field; also, a portion of land consisting of several fields; also, inspection and estimate of the crop at harvest: with the peculiar *ḷ*, THAḶ (थळ), the word has the general import of place, spot, in a restricted sense: it also means a sugar-cane plantation.

Thalbarít, Thulbureet, Mar. (?) Customs levied on articles despatched from the village or town in which they are produced.

Thalkarí, Mar. (थलकरी) A landed proprietor, the owner of the land, whether he cultivate or let it; the reverse of the *Uparí*, or tenant cultivator.

Thaljháṛá, Mar. (थलझाडा) The record of the fields belonging to a village.

Thalmod, Mar. (थलमोड) Customs levied on articles brought into a town or village for sale.

Thalwáik, also written *Thalwáhik*, Mar. (थलवाईक, थलवाहिक) A landed proprietor, the owner of a piece of land.

Thaḷwáik, Mar. (थळवाईक) The possessor of sugar plantations.

THÁL, Tibet. Tax, duty.—Kamaon.

THALA, (?) H. A sort of soil, the same, in some parts of the north-west provinces, as *Bhúr*, q. v.

THALYÁT, Beng. (थल्यात्, from थली, a bag) A receiver of stolen goods.

THAMDI, (?) Tel. The name of an agricultural and proprietary caste in the Nizam's country.

THAMUKADU, (?) A proclamation, a public notice.—Kumbakonam.

THAMUNI, Thug. Bribery.

THÁN, H. (تهان, S. स्थान) A piece of cloth, or of coin, as, *ek-thán-ashrafí*, a gold mohar.

THÁNÁ, or THÁNAH, corruptly, TANNAH, H. &c. (تهانا, تهانه, थाना, from S. स्थान, a place), ṬHÁṆE, Mar. (ठाणे) A station, a military post, a police-station: under the native governments it was a military post or garrison, a place, sometimes with a small fort, where a petty officer, with a small irregular force, was posted to protect the country, preserve the peace, and to aid in making the collections: under the present system it properly applies, in Bengal, to the police jurisdictions into which the Zilas were divided, each *Tháná* averaging about twenty miles square, under a *dárogha* and establishment: in the Upper Provinces the site of a *Tháná* is regulated by considerations of area and population, and generally corresponds with the divisions of a *Pargana* (Ben. Reg. 1792, No. xlix., and Reg. xxii. 1793): its common use denotes any police-station, whether under a *dárogha* or a subordinate officer; also, a village or station assigned to invalid Sipahís. Ben. Reg. xliii. 1793. Tel. *Ṭháṇá*, (ఠాణా) The head station of a district.

Thánádár, H. &c. (تهانادار), *Ṭháṇedár*, Mar. and Guz. (ठाणेदार) An officer in charge of a *Tháná*, formerly, an officer under the Faujdár, employed, with a small irregular force, in protecting the country and enforcing payment of the revenue: a petty police-officer subordinate to a *dárogha*. Ben. Reg. vii. 1799; xxviii. 1803.

Thánádárí, H. (داري, having) The office or jurisdiction of a *Thánádár*.

Thánádárí-abwáb, H. (ابواب, q. v.) A cess for the purpose of paying the establishment of the *Thánádár*.

Thánaját, or *Thánahát*, H. (تهانجات, تهانهات, plur. of تهانه) Police-stations: a cess for defraying the expense of their establishment.

THANA, Tibet. A grain measure, a skin = equal 60 *kalis*.—Kamaon.

THÁNÍ, H. (تهاني) Stationary, resident: a permanent cultivator, a proprietor.

Tháni-malangi, Uriya (ଥାନିମଲଙ୍ଗି) A salt manufacturer working at his own village.

Tháni-ráyet, Uriya (ଥାନିରାୟେତ) A resident cultivator, one who has a proprietary interest in the soil.

THANḌÁ, Hindi (ठंडा) Lit., Cool, cold: free from weeds, soil.

THÁNG, H. (تهانگ) A den of thieves.

Thángí, or *Thángídár*, H. (تهانگي, تهانگيدار) A receiver of stolen goods.

Thángídárí, H. (تهانگيداري) Receiving stolen goods.

THÁNKHANJÁ, Uriya (ଥାନଖଞ୍ଜା) A detailed list or muster-roll of the *Malangis* or other workmen.

THÁP, or THÁPÁ, Thug. Place of encampment where the gang pass the night, usually outside the village: hence, also, a river, the banks being a frequent halting-place.

THÁPÁ, H. (تهاپا, थापा) Gleanings, corn left on the field after harvest.

Ṭhapá, H. (تهپا, ठपा) A stamp, a die.

Ṭhápaṭí, Mar. (थापटी) A cake of dried cow-dung: a stamp or mark set by authority upon an article, prohibiting its being used or removed: the prohibition so indicated.

Ṭhapká, Mar. (ठपका) A stigma, a slur, imputation of crime.

Thaptiá, Thug. A potter.

Ṭharáo, H. Mar. (تهراو, ठराव) Settlement, determination, fixing or determining.

Ṭharáo-band, Mar. (ठरावबंद) A paper of instructions furnished to a native revenue officer on his going to take charge of a district: a document specifying the terms of a settlement or decree, or conveying instructions for their being carried into effect.

Ṭharáo-beríj, corruptly, *Ṭharow-beriz*, (ठरावबेरीज) Fixed rent or rate of assessment.

Tháru, (?) H. The designation of the people occupying villages in the *Tarái* on the borders of Rohilkhand.

Thát, (?) H. Property in the soil derived from royal grant, immemorial occupation, or purchase.—Kamaon.

Thátwán, (?) H. A proprietor of the soil.—Ibid.

Thátha, (?) H. Channel for carrying off surplus rainwater.

Ṭhaṭherá, H. (تهتهيرا, ठठेरा) A brazier, a worker in tin and copper.

Thatthar, (?) H. An account kept in the upper parts of Bengal, shewing, under each name, the quantity of land held, the amount of revenue payable, and charges, payments, remissions, and balances.

Thaṭṭí, Mar. (थट्टी) The cattle department, the public establishment of draft bullocks, their drivers and attendants.

Ṭhek, H. (تهيك, ठेक) A portable granary: a dispute, disputed lands or boundaries.

Theki, corruptly, Theckee, (?) Mar. A land measure in use in some parts of the Dakhin, of an indefinite value; it may be one or twenty *bíghás*.

Thekyi, (?) H. A lot or parcel of land in a coparcenary village, divided into 37 such shares, assessed severally.—Dehli.

Thenga, Thug. A sword.

Ṭhenga, Uriya (ଠେଙ୍ଗା) Rising ground.

Ṭhep, Mar. (ठेप) Limit, boundary, an appointed or assigned term or time.

Ṭhev, or Ṭheo, Ṭhevá, Ṭhevaṇí, Mar. (ठेव, ठेवा, ठेवणी) A hoard or hidden treasure, a deposit: also *Ṭhévaṇí*.

Ṭhevanáṭi, corruptly, Tevantee, Karn. Deposit of money as security, especially by contractors or renters of taxes, instead of personal surety: putting money in a treasury or bank: advance of cash.

Thibao, Thug. An omen on the right hand.

Ṭhík, Ṭheek, H. &c. (تهيك, ठीक) Exact, exactness, sum.

Ṭhiká, corruptly, *Ticca*, *Tucka*, *Teecka*, H. &c. (تهيكا, ठीका) Hire, fare, fixed price, contract for work; a farm of revenue, a contract by which a person engages to pay a fixed amount of revenue on an estate or district, on being allowed to collect the revenue payable to the proprietor or the state; a farm of cultivation, a lease, the contractor paying a money rent for the lands he cultivates: a farm of salt works, paying either in money or a given return of salt: the revenue accruing from such leases or farms: also a mortgage in which the person who advances money on landed security occupies the land, and sets off the produce against the amount of interest.

Ṭhikábandí, corruptly, *Teekabundee*, H. &c. (تهيكابندي) A settlement by farm or contract, a farm or lease, the farm held on lease: in the Dakhin, a stipulated rent on each field, without reference to its extent.

Ṭhíka-bhet, H. (تهيكابهيت) Extra imposts, personal service, presents or gratuities of money.—Kamaon.

Ṭhíká-dár, corruptly, *Teechadar*, *Tuckadar*, H. &c. (P. دار, who has) A farmer, a leaseholder, a middleman, one who receives the rents from the cultivators and pays a stipulated amount to the proprietor: one who farms a licence for the sale of spirituous liquors, or the like.

Ṭhíká-otbandi, Beng. (ওটবন্দী, q. v.) Lease of land at a low or estimated rate.

Ṭhíká-paṭṭá, corruptly, *Teekapottah*, *Tikaputtah*, *Tuchapottah*, H. پٿا, पट्टा, q. v.) A document conveying a lease or farm.

Ṭhíká-peshgí, H. (P. پيشگي) Lease or farm of which the rent is paid in advance.

Ṭhikáṇ, Ṭhikáṇá, corruptly, Tikan, Mar. (ठिकाण, ठिकाणा) A residence: a definite spot or plot of land belonging to a given individual.

Ṭhikáná, H. (تهكانا, ठिकाना) Determining, concluding, certainty: boundary, limit: residence, place of dwelling or abiding.

Ṭhíkar, or Ṭhíkrá, H. (تهيكر, from تهيكرا, a potsherd) The duty of keeping the village watch, taken in succession by the villagers in the Rohtak district: the order is determined by lot, the names being inscribed on bits of broken pots or tiles, and put into a vessel, from which they are drawn daily to the extent required, by the *Patwárí*.

Ṭhike, incorrectly, Tika, Mar. (ठिके) A parcel or lot of ground.

Ṭhikebandí, Mar. (ठिकेबंदी) Assessment of a field or piece of ground.

Ṭhikewár, Mar. (ठिकेवार) By lots or parcels, assessments.

Ṭhikí, Mar. (ठिकी) A stack, a rick (restricted to corn): a quantity of any kind of grain piled up in store.

Thob, (?) H. Revenue payments suspended.

Thok, incorrectly, Thoke, and Toke, H. (تهوك, थोक) A share, a portion, a secondary or inferior share of the lands of a coparcenary village: authorities differ as to its relative value, and it probably varies in different places: according to some it is smaller than a *Paṭṭí*, which contains, it is said, a variable number of *Thoks*, and each *Thok* a varying number of *Behris*.—East-India Selection, iii. 167: on the other hand the directions for settlement officers makes the *Thok* the larger division of the village lands, sometimes containing a number of *Paṭṭís*; again, a *Thok* is sometimes said to denote a class of villages; and at others to be the same as the *Paṭṭí*: in Kamaon, it is defined the local division of a village specified in the measurement books.

Thok-bandí, H. (P. بندي, a binding) A written engagement specifying the distribution of the shares of a coparcenary village.

Thok-bast, H. (P. بست, bound) A classification of *Paṭṭís* or other subdivisions of a village into *Thoks*.

Thok-dár, H. (P. دار, who has) The holder of a *Thok*, or sometimes the principal of the holders amongst whom the lands or fields of a *Thok* may be shared, and their representative in settling and realizing the assessment: the *Thokdár* and *Paṭṭídár* are sometimes confounded in this capacity of Lumberdár or Málguzár or payer of the revenue: the term sometimes, also, is said to imply a wholesale dealer: in Kamaon, the *Thokdár* is a ministerial officer, usually by inheritance, confirmed, or sometimes appointed by the ruling authority to exercise a general superintendence over the villagers, and to conduct police and purveyance duties in a varying number of villages, of one or more of which he is ordinarily, though not necessarily, the *Padhán* (q. v.).

Thok-dárí, H. (P. داري, having) Property, office, or duty of a *Thokdár*.

Thok-dárí-paṭṭá, H. (from پٿا, a lease or grant) The official title-deed given to the *Thohdár* in Kamaon by the government, specifying the villages under his authority, and the fees he is entitled to.

Haḳ-, or *Dastúr-Thokdárí*, H. (from A. حق, right, or دستور, custom) Fees payable to the *Thokdár* by the other *Padháns*.—Kamaon.

Thok-paṭṭí, H. (from پٿي, a share) A division of a *Thok* into *Paṭṭís*, with the rate of assessment on each: a share-record, or register.

Ṭhok, Mar. (ठोक) Lump, mass, whole: in or by the lump.

Ṭhoktálá, Mar. (ठोकताळा) A rough estimate or valuation, a valuation in the gross or lump.

Ṭhokebandí, Mar. (ठोकेबंदी) Assessment or agreement by the lump.

Ṭhoká, Mar. (ठोका) Letting out fields for a portion of the produce.

Thoka, (?) H. A point where three or more boundary lines meet.—North-west Provinces.

Thoka, or Toka, (?) Beng. (perhaps from थोक, a lot, a heap) A term applied to documents shewing a title to a certain amount of land (?).

Thoki, Thug. Ejection of saliva by the leader, a hint to suspend operations.

Thola, corruptly, Toleh, (?) H. A secondary subdivision of village lands: in the Delhi district, a variable fractional part of a *Pana* or *Pan*, and itself divisible into smaller portions.

Tholadár, H. (P. دار, who has) The holder or occupant of a *Thola*.

Thola, Thug. A police-station or guard.

Thora, (?) Mal. The unit of land measure: in Malabar the breadth of the seed of a *Yevam*, which is said to be a species of opium or aniseed; (but ? if it is not the S. *yavam*, or barleycorn): it is called $\frac{1}{8}$th of a *veral*, or $1\frac{1}{7}$th of an inch (Walker, Report on Malabar; but according to Bailey, Mal. Dict., there is no word in *Malayalam* beginning with *th*).

Thú, (?) Tibet. A cloth measure, a cubit.

Thumbá, H. (تهونبا, थूंबा) A lump of earth put on the loose end of the lever used for raising water from wells to balance the bucket suspended to the end that is over the well.

Thúni, Thooni, (?) Mal. A weight of grain or dry measure =86,400 grains of rice: (see remark on *Thora*).

Ṭi-áne, Hindi (टीआने) A charge of a small per centage on

the revenue, made by the proprietor to Ryots cultivating on *Jot-jaríbí* tenure.

Tídal, Tam. (திடல்) High ground surrounded by water or rice fields.

Tidar, Tam. (திடர்) A low hill or rising ground: an open barren space.

Tidar-paraiyar, Tam. (பறையர்) The Paraiya or Pariah slaves, who do not reside in the suburb set apart for them, but are scattered over the barren spots of the village lands: in deeds conveying *Mirásí* right this phrase is inserted to imply conveyance of a right to a participation in the labour of all the agrestic slaves of the village, in proportion to the share of proprietary right conveyed to the land.

Tigaḷara-játi, Karn. (ತಿಗಳರಜಾತಿ) A class of people of Karnata, speaking a corrupt Kanarese, cultivating land and dealing in greengrocery, lime, &c.

Tighani, Thug. The eye.

Tihaï, Uriya (ତିହାଇ) Collection of rent thrice a year (S. त्रि and हायन, a year).

Tíhaiät, H. (تيهايت) An aggregate or assemblage of three: a court of arbitration of three or more persons: a third person, an umpire.

Tihotrá, Mar. (तिहोत्रा) Interest at the rate of three per cent. per *mensem*.

Tíj, H. (تيج, तीज, S. तृतीया) The third day of a lunar fortnight.

Tíjá, H. (تيجا) The third day after a Mohammadan's decease, when offerings are made: the offerings made on the occasion.

Ṭíká, H. &c. (ٹيکا, टीका, S. तिलक) A round painted spot, or a patch of gold or metal placed on the centre of the forehead as an ornament, a sectarial distinction, or a mark of high rank: conferring the *ṭíká* upon a subordinate or feudatory chief is the privilege and indication of supremacy: it is exercised especially by Rajput princes, as by the Rana of Udayapur, and Raja of Jaypur; also by the hill chiefs, as the Raja of *Bilåspur*: some chiefs retain the privilege from their ancestral dignity rather than any political pre-eminence, as the Raja of *Badáwar*, near Agra.

Tikala, Thug. Any suspicious article taken from a victim which it is dangerous to have about the person as likely to lead to detection.

Ṭíkar, H. &c. (ٹيکر, टीकर) High lands of indifferent quality.

Tikár, Hindi (S. त्रिकार) Three ploughings.

Ṭíkarí, Hindi (टीकरी) A small field of inferior land.—South-west Provinces.

Ṭikarí, or Ṭikrí, H. (ٹکري, टिकरी) Soil which is irretentive of moisture, and that soon dries.

Ṭikaribastí, Beng. (টিকরিবসতি, from টিকর, rounded) A site fit for a village or a dwelling, being raised above the inundations.

Tikka, (?) Mar. (perhaps an error for Thíka) A division of a district: a village named separately, and particularized by its contents in *bighás*, portions held by proprietors or unoccupied, cultivated and waste lands, rate of assessment per *bighá*, total assessment and description of cultivators.

Tíkuṛhá, Uriya (ତିକୁଢା) A division of produce into three parts, two of which go to the cultivating occupant and one to the landlord or proprietor.

Til, corruptly, Teel, H. &c. (S. تل, तिल) The seed of the Sesamum, extensively used in the making of oil, and as an ingredient in offerings to idols: the term is also applied in Bengal to a small division of land measure, one-twelfth of a *krânt*, or, in account, to one-eightieth of a *kauri*: see *Tel*.

Tíl, Thug. A person found watching the gang.

Ṭílá, Ṭílhá, H. &c. (ٹيلا, ٹيلها, टीला, टील्हा) A low hill, a rising ground.

Tilaka, vernacularly, Tilak, S. &c. (तिलक, تلك) A coloured spot on the forehead worn as an ornament, a sectarial mark, or mark of distinction: see *Ṭíká*: it occurs also in Mar. *Ṭilá*, *Ṭilak*, (टिला, टिलक), as well as *Tilah* (तिलक), and designates any coloured sectarial spots or lines on the face or person. In some places, as in Bahár, the term is applied to certain presents or dues in money or goods at the time of a betrothal made to the intended bridegroom by the father of the bride.

Timáshí, H. A silver coin of the value of two to three *anas*.—Kamaon.

Tingoti, (?) Mar. A tax on the sale of cattle in some parts of the Maratha territories.

Tinna, Tinmuä, Thug. A boy.

Tiṇṇaḷ-panam, Mal. (തിങ്ങൾപണം, from തിങ്ങൾ, a month) General monthly levy of contributions from all classes by the Rájas of Malabar.

Tiṇṇalkhoppa, Mal. (തിങ്ങൾക്കൊപ്പ്) Monthly provisions for a temple or victualling house.

Ṭíp, H. &c. (ٹيپ, टीप) A note of hand, a promissory note or bill, a bond, a cheque; besides these meanings, which are common to all the dialects, it has special applications in some, as in Mar. (टीप), taking a list of the number of houses, trees, cattle, &c., preparatory to a tax upon them. Guz. (ટીપ), A list, an inventory, a catalogue, a roll or register. *Ṭípu*, Tel. (టీపు) A grant or assignment of revenue to a capitalist who has advanced money to the government.

Ṭípkár, *Ṭip-*, or *Ṭípnís*, Mar. (**टीपकार, टिप- टीपनीस**) The officer who numbers the houses, &c., of a village, in order to tax them.

Ṭípá-moharir, Uriya (ଟୀପାମୋହୁରିର) A clerk who notes the amount of the weighment of salt at the salt-office.

Ṭípaṇ, Mar. (**टिपण**) A note, a memorandum: also a memorandum paper.

TÍP, Thug. A fire kindled for evil purposes.

ṬIPAṚÍ, Guz. (ટીપરી, ટીપડી) A grain measure = half a *ser*.

TIPPAṚÍ, Mal. (തിപ്പടി) A grain measure, the same as a *nála*, or one-fourth of an *Edangali*, q. v.

TÍR, H. (P. تير) An arrow.

Tirkaranár, (?) Mar. A low caste, formerly extant, whose occupation was making arrows.

TÍRA, vernacularly, TÍR, S. &c. (تير, **तीर**) A bank, the bank of a river, a shore, a belt of sand along a river's bank, sometimes admitting of a scanty cultivation, alluvial soil along a river.

Tír, or *Tírmadhya*, Beng. (**তীর, তীরমধ্য**) The space or land included within 150 cubits beyond the highest reach of the inundations of a river on the 14th of the moon's wane in *Bhádra* (Aug.-Sept.).

TÍRA, commonly TÍR, TEER, Mal. (തീര) A written receipt or acknowledgment: a deed of assignment of land for value received.

Tírmma, Mal. (തീൎമ്മ) Discharge, acquittal, settlement.

Tírmmuṟi, corruptly, *Teermoorie*, Mal. (തീൎമ്മുറി) A written receipt.

TÍṞA, Mal. (തീറ) Tribute, tax.

TIRÁÍT, TIRHÁÍT, corruptly, TIRAYUT, Mal. (**तिराईत, तिऱ्हाईत**) An umpire, an arbitrator, any third person, a stranger, a *panchâyat* collectively.

TIRANAISUVAR, Tam. (திரணைசுவர்) Parapet wall of a sluice.

TIRDHAL, Mar. (**तिरधल**) A third of the produce of a field, especially as payable by the occupant tenant to the landlord.

Tirdhalí, Mar. (**तिरधली**) A cultivating tenant who pays a third of the produce of his fields to the proprietor.

TÍRGÚḶ, Mar. (**तीरगूळ**) A particular tribe of Brahmans, or an individual of it, whose occupation is cultivating the Piper betel: the name of a low caste, formerly extant, employed in making arrows.

TIRHIA, Thug. A bag or knapsack.

TÍRIJ, or TÍRAJ, corruptly, TÍRJ, TURJ, TAREJE, TARIJ, TAREEJ, TERIDGE, TEYRIJ, H. &c. (تيرج, **तीरज**), TÉRÍJU, Tel., Karn. (తేరీజు), TERÍJ, Mar. (**तेरीज**) An abstract account completed from other detailed accounts: an item in a number of items to be added together, a paper or list of items to be added together.

Tírij asámíwár, H. (اساميوار, according to cultivators) One of the village accounts under the former system, and recognised in the settlement of the north-west provinces as one of the documents constituting the settlement *Misl*: it is the abstract of the *Khateoní Asámíwár*, specifying the number of each *Thok* or subdivision of the village lands, the name of its occupant, the number of *bighás* occupied, without particularising the fields, and the amount assessed upon the whole land.—Directions for settlement officers, App. xi.

Tírij-goshwára-jinswár-asámíwár, H. (see *Goshwára*, &c.) A tabular abstract statement of each kind of produce (*jins*) of the fields of a village, with the name of the occupant.

Tírij-jinswár-asámíwár, H. (A. جنس, genus, thing) A specification of the fields in the occupation of each person cultivating on his own account.

Tírij-jamâbandí, H. (جمبندي, rent-roll) Account, particulars of the annual revenue and charges of an estate.

Tírij-jamâ-kharch, H. (A. جمع, income, خرچ, expense) A summary account of the receipts and disbursements of a village, made up at the end of the year.

TIRKIA, Thug. A goldsmith.

TÍRPPU, Tam. (தீர்ப்பு), Tel. (తీర్పు), TÍRPPA, Mal. (തീൎപ്പ) A decree, an award, a decision: an agreement, a settlement, a final arrangement.

TÍRTHA, vernacularly, TÍRTH, and TÍRATH, S. &c. (**तीर्थ**) A holy place, especially one that derives its sanctity from the confluence of two rivers held sacred, as the Ganges and Jamna, also various places along the banks of rivers esteemed holy, and, more laxly, any holy place or place of pilgrimage: water brought from a sacred stream, or that has been consecrated by pouring over an idol: also, fig., any venerable person, as a father or a spiritual preceptor: in the south of India it is also applied to a hereditary office in a temple.

Tírthakára, S. (**तीर्थकार**) A holy personage, one privileged to drink the sacred water and partake of the food that has been offered to idols: *Tírthakára*, or *Tírthankara*, is also the generic title of the persons held sacred by the Jains.

TIRU, Tam. (திரு), Mal. (തിരു), Karn. (ತಿರು) A word used chiefly as a prefix in the sense of the Sanscrit *Srí*, implying auspicious, venerable, sacred, and the like; it enters into the names of many places in the south of India, corrupted by English mispronunciation to *Tri*, as *Trivatoor*, for *Tiru-vatúr*; *Tripetty*, for *Tiru-patí*, &c.

Tiruka, Karn. (ತಿರುಕ) A mendicant, a beggar, a vagrant.

Tirukkuḷam, Tam. (திருக்குளம்) A tank with stone steps.

Tiruman, Tam. (திருமண்), *Tirumani*, Karn. (ತಿರುಮಣಿ) Sacred earth, a kind of white clay with which the Vaishnavas especially draw perpendicular lines on their foreheads or on other parts of the face or body: the marks or streaks so made.

Tirumul-kárya, Mal. (തിരുമുൽക്കാഴ്ച) A complementary present to superiors on visiting them: an annual acknowledgment paid to the prince for a grant of rent-free land.

Tirunál, Tam. (திருநாள்) A holy day, a festival.

Tirupaṇi, Tam. (திருப்பணி) A fund for the repairs of temples, created by a trifling deduction from each heap of grain at the time of harvest.

Tirupati, corruptly, *Tripety*, Tam. (திருப்பதி) A temple dedicated to some form of Vishṇu, and hence the name of a town famous for the temples dedicated to various personations of Vishnu.

Tirupe, Karn. (ತಿರುಪೆ) Alms: begging.

Tiruvana, Mal. (തിരുവാണ) An oath, swearing: a citation on the part of the Rája, or any public functionary.

Tiruvásal, Tam. (திருவாசல்) The gateway of a temple: a building for the accommodation of travellers.

TIRUKÁ, Mar. (तिरुका) A piece of money, the fourth of an *ana*.

TIRUMALA, Karn. (ತಿರುಮಲ) A name common to Súdras.

TIRUMURU, Karn. (ತಿರುಮುರು) Exchange.

TÍRUVA, Tel. (తీరువ) Duty, customs.

TÍRUVE, Karn. (ತಿರುವೆ) Settlement, adjustment, of duties and the like.

TÍRVAI, or TÍRWAI, corruptly, TEERVA, TEERWA, TEERWAH, Tam. (தீர்வை, probably from the S. *sthira* (स्थिर), what is fixed or determined), TÍRVA, Mal. (തീൎവ്വ) Tax, duty, custom, a cess or impost, a money assessment of revenue on land, or on its produce: rate of assessment according to the quality of land: money-rent: also a decision, a sentence.

Tírvai-diṭṭam, Tam. (தீர்வைதிட்டம்) Rate of assessment.

Tírvai-jásti, (?) Tam. An additional assessment on inferior land when made to produce crops, usually limited to land of superior quality, as garden crops, or those raised from wet or irrigated land.

Tírvaipat, or *Tirvaipaṭṭu*, corruptly, *Teervapett*, also with *Nilam*, land, added, *Tírvaipaṭṭanilam*, Tam. (தீர்வைப்பட்டு, தீர்வைப்பட்டநிலம்) Land paying a fixed money assessment.

TÍRVE, TÍRVIKE, Karn. (ತೀರ್ವೆ, ತೀರ್ವಿಕೆ) Settlement, adjustment. See *Tiruve*.

TÍRVILA, Mal. (തീൎവ്വില) A bargain.

Tírvilayola, Mal. (തീൎവ്വിലയോല) A bill of sale.

TISÁLÁ, Mar. (तिसाला, from S. त्रि, three, and A. سال, a year) Of or for three successive years, as an account, &c.

TISWÁNSÍ, H. (تسوانسي) A smaller division of a *bighá*, the twentieth of a *bíswánsi*.

TIṬṬA, Mal. (തിട്ട) A shoal, a bank, an island of alluvial formation, or one from which the water has recently retired.

TÍVU, (తీవు) Money deposited as security.

TÍWÁRÍ, Hindi (तिवारी, corruption of *Trivédí*) The name of a caste or tribe of Brahmans, originally men learned in the three Vedas, but now agriculturists, soldiers, and cudgel players or boxers.

TIYAN, plur. TIYAR, Mal. (തിയ്യൻ) A caste, or a member of it, in Malabar, whose occupations are agriculture and *tári*-drawing: they are numerous, and enjoy some consideration.

Tiyatti, Mal. (തിയ്യത്തി) A woman of the *Tiyan* caste: they are distinguished by wearing no covering above the waist.

TOḌA, or TOṚA, Mar. (तोड), Guz. (તોડ, તોર) Compromise, composition, adjustment, settlement of conflicting claims.

Toḍagrás, or *Toṛagrás*, Guz. (તોડગરાસ, તોરગરાસ) Cash composition levied by the Grasiyas from villages in lieu of other claims, or of plunder.

TOḌA, TODAWAR, written also TODAR, THODA, THODAWUR, (?) The name of a pastoral people inhabiting the *Nilgiri* mountains, and claiming to be the original occupants and proprietors of the whole of the hilly country.

TOḌAI, Tam. (தொடை) A term in the Ceylon pearl-fishery: a dive, that is, the produce of a diving, two of which are given daily to the owner of the boat.

TOḌAR, Tam. (தொடர்) A chain, a fetter: pursuit, lit. or fig.

Toḍarmuṛi, Tam. (தொடர்முறி) A deed or promise in writing not to pursue a person further at law.

Toḍu, Tam. (தொடு) A garden, ground fit for rice cultivation. See *Toṭṭam*.

Toḍuppu, Tam. (தொடுப்பு) Implements of ploughing, plough gear.

Toḍuvaḻakku, Tam. (தொடுவழக்கு) A continuous quarrel or law-suit.

Togri, Thug. A turban.

Ṭoká, Mar. (टोका) A sort of weevil infesting grain: rice in the husk, paddy.

Toka, (?) Beng. A receipt.—Sylhet.

Ṭoká-paṭṭá, Hindi (टोकापट्टा) A permanent *paṭṭa* or lease. Puraniya.

Tokkam, Tam. (தொக்கம்) A law-suit.

Ṭokrá, **Ṭokrí**, corruptly, **Toghra**, H. &c. (توكرا, توكري) A basket, large or small: in the Dakhin *Tokrá* also means a sort of ferry-boat, or one made of basket-work, covered with leather: in Puraniya it is said to mean also extirpated weeds.

Tol, **Tola**, H. &c. (تول, तोल) Weight, weighing, a weight.

Tola, H. &c. (تولا, तोला) A certain weight, especially of silver, containing, under the old want of system, a varying number of *Máshas*, but usually regarded as equivalent to the weight of the Sikka rupee, or 179.666 troy grains. By Beng. Reg. vii. 1833, the weight of the *Tola*, taken as the unit of the new system of weights, was fixed at 180 troy grains: the scale is, 4 *Dháns* = 1 *Ratí*; 8 *Ratís* = 1 *Másha*; 12 *Máshas* = 1 *Tolá*; 5 *Tolás* = 1 *Chitánk*; 16 *Chitánks* = 1 *Ser*; 40 *Sers* = 1 *Man* or *Maund*, which is thus exactly equal to 100 troy pounds.

Toládár, H. (P. دار, who has) A weighman, one who weighs coins or goods in a market.

Tolah, (?) Beng. A money payment or fee for goods, formerly paid by the retailers of wares in the Calcutta markets to the government.

Tól, Tam. (தோல்), Mal. (തൊൽ) Skin, bark, leather.

Tol-hollan, Mal. (തൊൽകൊല്ലൻ) A worker in leather or skins, a currier, a shoemaker.

Tóṭṭunnar, Tam. (தோற்றுன்னர், plur.) Workers in leather and skins, shoemakers, curriers.

Ṭol, Beng. (টোল) A school, a college, an establishment for instruction, especially in Sanskrit and some branch of Sanskrit learning, as grammar, law, logic, &c., kept by a *Pandit* or Brahman teacher, at which lodging and instruction are gratuitously provided for the students by the teacher, the former gaining their subsistince by alms from the neighbouring shopkeepers, the latter deriving his compensation from the repute he enjoys and presents made to him at Hindu festivals by opulent Zamindárs.

Ṭolá, **Ṭolí**, Beng. (টোলা, টোলি) The suburb of a town or village, the part of a town by persons of any particular occupation, as *Kaṣái-tola*, butchers' town: a supplementary hamlet, or huts outlying from the chief village: it is said to mean also uncultivated ground.

Toḻil, Tam. (தொழில்) Work, occupation, business.

Toḻilálan, Tam. (தொழிலாளன்) A workman, an artisan, a labourer.

Toḻuvan, Tam. (தொழுவன்) A workman, an artisan, a cultivator, a husbandman.

Toḻiláli mányam, Tam. (தொழிலாளிமானியம்) Rent-free land assigned to the village servants in requital of their labour.

Tollik, Tel. (తొల్లిక) A sort of hoe.

Tolúkari, Tel. (తొలుకరి) The first rainy season.

Toḻumbu, Tam. (தொழும்பு) Slavery.

Toḻumban, Tam. (தொழும்பன்) A slave.

Toḻuttai, Tam. (தொழுத்தை) A female slave, a dancing girl.

Tóm, Thug. Any peculiarly valuable article of booty, such as may be set apart to be presented to the patron of the gang.

Ṭomṇí, Mar. (टोमणी) lit., A very small dish: fig. a small grant of land to the village *Mahár*.

Ṭoná, H. &c. (ٹونا, टोना) Witchcraft, magic. Thug. A trick, a deception.

Toṇḍai maṇḍalam, sometimes read **Toṇḍu maṇḍalam**, Tam. (தொண்டைமண்டலம், from S. मण्डल, a tract, a country) An ancient division of the Peninsula comprehending the modern districts of north and south Arcot and Chinglipat. Mr. Ellis supposes it to have derived its appellation from *Tondamán*, a prince so named, who conquered the country probably before the era of Christianity, and granted peculiar privileges to the first settlers: *Tondamán* meaning, properly, a chief, a lord, in general; became, latterly, the designation of a petty chief in the vicinity of Trichinapali, whose country is known to early English writers as *Tondiman's* land.

Tondiváram, Tam. (தொந்திவாரம்) The share of the cultivators in the division of the crop: (perhaps an error for *Tunduváram*, q. v.).

Toṇḍu, **Tottu**, Tam. (தொண்டு, தொத்து) A slave, slavery.

Tongar, Thug. A Marátha.

Toní, vulgarly, **Dhoney**, Mal. (തൊണി) A long boat or

coasting sloop: also applied to a smaller vessel used for crossing rivers: a ferry-boat.

TONKAL, Thug. A party of travellers too strong to be attacked.

TO-O, incorrectly, TOYO, Guz. (ટોઓ) A person stationed to watch the crop and scare the birds.

TOP, H. &c. (Turk. توپ) A gun, a cannon, a piece of ordnance.

Topchi, H. (T. توپچي) A conductor of ordnance, an artillery officer.

Topkhána, H. (T. توپخانه) An arsenal, an artillery park, a foundry for cannon, a place where military stores are kept.

ṬOPÍ, H. &c. (توپي, ? from Port. *Topo*), ṬOPÍ, ṬÚPI, Beng. (টোপি, টুপি), TOPPI, Mal. (തൊപ്പി) A hat, a cap, a skull-cap.

Topas, (Port. *Topaz*, perhaps from the H. *Topí*, a hat) A native Christian sprung from a Portuguese father and Indian mother in the south of India: in the early history of the Company these people were extensively enlisted as soldiers; hence the term came to be applied to the Company's native soldiery generally in the Peninsula: it is now obsolete.

Topiwálá, H. (توپي والا) A hat-wearer, a European.

Toppi-kuḍa, Mal. (തൊപ്പിക്കുട) A hat-umbrella, a hat with a projecting brim on the crown, worn by fishermen and other castes in Malabar: the term seems to be of old, and to precede the Portuguese.

TOPKA, Thug. Cloth of any kind.

TOPPALU, Karn. (ತೊಪ್ಪಲು) Tobacco.

TÓPU, Tel., Karn. (తోపు, ತೋಪು), Tam. (தோப்பு) A grove of trees, properly of those that bear fruit, as mango, tamarind, cocoa-nut, &c.; commonly termed *Tóp* or *Tópe*: in Tam. it is also extended to woodlands of every description (the term seems to have been introduced from the south to Hindustan, where it is in common use, although not found in Shakespear or Carey.

TOṚ, H. (تور, from تورنا, to break) Irrigation effected by breaking down the ridges of water-courses, and letting the water flood the garden or field.

TOṚÁ, H. (تورا) A purse, a bag of money, when sealed supposed to contain 1000 rupees.

TORAṆA, vernacularly, TORAN, S. &c. (तोरण) An ornamental doorway or arch, a temporary arch hung with drapery or festoons of flowers and leaves.

TORMI, Thug. A thief, a robber, a Thug.

TORO, Guz. (તોરો) A chief, a man of rank and dignity.

TORTANKAR, Thug. Search after, or apprehension of, Thugs.

TOṚU, TOṚUVU, Tam. (தொறு, தொறுவு) Slavery.

TOSHA, H. (P. توشه) Provisions, especially for a journey; also food carried at funerals as provision for the deceased's journey to the next world: any article of curiosity or value kept in store.

Toshakhána, H. &c. (P. توشه‌خانه) A storeroom, a wardrobe: chambers in which objects of curiosity or value, not in daily request, are kept: less correctly *Toshak-khána*.

TOSSÁ, (?) Tel. A cultivator, a Ryot.

TÓṬI, Karn. (ತೋಟಿ) A tax.

Tóṭiyakáḷu, Karn. (ತೋಟಿಯಕಾಳು) Taxed corn.

Tóṭiyarokhka, Karn. (ತೋಟಿಯರೊಖ್ಖ) Tax-money.

TOṬṬAM, Tam., Mal. (தோட்டம்), TOṬA, Tel., Karn. (తోట) Uriya (ତୋଟା) A garden, an orchard.

Toṭṭakál, corruptly, *Totacul*, *Totical*, *Tottykal*, *Totycaul*, Tam. (தோட்டக்கால்) Land appropriated to the cultivation of garden produce, as various kinds of fruit, betel, edible vegetables, and other articles of value, and therefore subject to a higher rate of assessment.

Tótavádu, *Tótiḍu*, Tel. (తోటవాడు, తోటిడు) A gardener, a grower of garden produce.

Toṭṭamániyam, Tel. (தோட்டமானியம்) A garden, or garden ground, free of assessment.

TÓṬṬI, Tam. (தோட்டி), TÓṬI, and TÓṬIGA, Karn. (ತೋಟಿ, ತೋಟಿಗ) A village servant, a man of a low caste who waits upon the villagers generally, discharges the offices of police, is set to watch the crops, and assists in measuring them, &c.: he appears, however, to be different from the menial domestic servant who bears the same name, or *Tóṭṭi*, and does the dirtiest work of the house.

TOṬṬIYAR, plur. Tam. (தொட்டியர்) People originally from the north, settled in Coimbatur.

TOYYIL, Tam. (தொய்யில்) Cultivated moist land.

TRAGA, (?) The shedding of blood, either his own or of a connexion, by a *Bhát*, in order to enforce the fulfilment of an engagement for which he has pledged his personal surety; punishable by law. Bombay Reg. xiv. 1827.

TRETÁ, S. &c. (त्रेता) The second of the four ages.

TRETÁGNI, S. &c. (त्रेताग्नि) The three sacred fires of the Hindus.

TRIBHÁGAMU, Tel. (త్రిభాగము, from S. त्रि, three, and भाग, a share) A third of the annual crop payable to the government.

Tribhágamu-mukhásá, Tel. (ముఖాసా) A village held on condition of paying a third of the crop to government.

TRIDAṆḌÍ, S. &c. (त्रिदण्डी) A Saiva mendicant carrying three slender staves (*daṇḍa*) as typical of his command over his thoughts, words, and actions.

TRIKA, Tel. (S. త్రిక) A triangular frame or bar over the mouth of a well, over which the rope of the bucket travels: a frame at the top or bottom of a well to support the sides.

TRIPUṆḌRA, S. &c. (त्रिपुण्ड्र) The three horizontal lines made on the forehead with ashes of burnt cowdung or sandal paste, &c., by the worshippers of *Śiva* especially.

TRIVEDÍ, S. &c. (त्रिवेदी) A Brahman who professes to have read the three Vedas, or to have descended from such a Brahman, whose title has thence become a family designation.

TRIŚÚLA, S. &c., but usually, in the dialects, *Tirsúl* (त्रिशूल) A trident, a three-pronged lance, the weapon peculiarly of *Śiva*.

TUḌAGADANA, Karn. (ತುಡಗದನ) Stray cattle.

ṬUGHRÁ, H. (A. طغرا) The imperial signature, the sign-manual on a royal grant of revenue: the royal titles usually prefixed to a public document, written in an ornamental character also called *Tughrá*.

ṬUK, H. (S. (تك, टुक) A little, a small piece, a fragment. Mar. (तूक) A weight $=2\frac{1}{2}$ *máshas.*

TUKA, Mal. (തുക) An amount, sum total.

TUKHM, H. &c. (P. تخم) Seed.

Tukhm-rezí, H. (P. from ريزي, scattering) Sowing seed; an account of the seed sown kept by the village accountant.

Tukhm-sokht, H. (from P. سوخت, burnt) Land in which seed has been sown, but, from want of rain or other cause, has not germinated.

Tukum, Tel. (తుకుం) An advance of seed.

ṬÚKI, Karn. (ಟೂಕಿ) A guess, a conjecture: abstract of the contents of a letter.

Ṭúkilekhkha, Karn. (ಟೂಕಿಲೆಖ್ಖ) A guess account, a calculation by the head.

TUKKAḌI, Tam. (துக்கடி) A district, a division.

TÚKKÁRAN, Mal. (തൂക്കാരൻ) A man who swings at the swing festival; see *Charak*: a hangman, an executioner: a weigher.

TÚKKIRI, Tam. (தூக்கிரி) A head watchman or overseer of a village.

Túkkiri-merai, Tam. (தூக்கிரிமேரை) The quantity of corn given from the threshing-floor to the watchman.

ṬUKRÁ, ṬUKRÍ, H. &c. (تكرا, تكري, टूकरा -री, or टुकडा -डी) A piece, a fragment: in Mysore, a troop of soldiers, a division of an army.

Ṭukrídár, Dakh. (تكريدار) An officer commanding a detachment of the Mysore Silahdár horse.

TUL, Hindi (तुल) The breadth of a field.—Puraniya.

TULÁ, S. &c. (تلا, तुला) A balance, a pair of scales, the sign Libra, the month when the sun enters Libra, measure by weight: a various reading of *Tolá*, q. v.: in the south of India, the balance-lever used for raising water.

Tulábháram, Mal. (തുലാഭാരം) An equal weight of gold or other articles intended for distribution with the weight of the donor.

Tuládána, S. &c. (तुलादानं) Gift to Brahmans of gold, silver, rice, or other articles, equal in weight to the person of the donor, who is weighed against them.

Tulam, Mal. (തുലാം) The month when the sun enters Libra, Sept.-Oct.

Tulám, corruptly, *Toolom*, Tam., Mal. (துலாம், തുലാം) A measure by weight of 100, or sometimes 200 *palas* = 145 or 190 ounces troy: the lever of the apparatus used for drawing water.

Tulamu, Tel. (తులము) The weight of one rupee, or thirty *Kántirái* fanams.

Tulaparíkshá, S. &c. (परीक्षा, trial) Ordeal by the balance; the accused person having been accurately weighed in a pair of scales, is removed, and, after the performance of certain ceremonies, is again weighed; if he is lighter than he was at first he is innocent; if equal, or heavier, guilty: he is also guilty if, without obvious cause, any part of the balance be damaged.

TULA, Tel. (తుల, from the A. طول, length) The measured length of a heap of grain, or the measurement round it: the length of any thing.

Tulárjulu, Tel. (తులార్జులు, from the A. طول and عرض, width) Measurement of the length and breadth of the heaps of grain prepared to be measured on the threshing-floor.

TULAŚÍ, S. &c. (तुलसी) The *Ocymum sanctum*, or sacred Basil, venerated by the Hindus as a type of Vishnu, said, in modern legend, to have been a nymph beloved by him in the character of Krishna: it was used in the administration of oaths to Hindus, a few leaves with some holy water being held in the hollow of the hand of the deponent while the oath was repeated, and afterwards swallowed by him.

TULU, Mal., TUḶUVAM, Tam. (துளுவம்) The northernmost division of the Malayalam country, or, in more modern times, the country of Viziapur between Kanara and the Konkan: the language of the province.

Ṭúmár, H. (A. طومار) A roll, a record, a register, an account: also same as the next.

Ṭúmár-jamá, H. (A. جمع, total) The sum total of the land revenue according to register: the recorded standard assessment of the land revenue of the provinces of the Mogul empire in the reign of Akbar, as settled by his minister, Toral Mal, and subsequently revised at different periods down to the time of the grant of the Diwani to the East-India Company.

Ṭúmár-jamá-nakdi, H. (A. نقد, ready money) The standard assessment as settled in money.

Túmaram, Mal. (തൂമരം) A measure of timber, one-fourth of a *khaṇḍi*, or 144 square inches.

Tumbamari, Mal. (തുമ്പമറി) Certificate given by a proprietor to the holder of his land on lease or mortgage, that he has sold his right to another, or one which the holder gives to the owner, if he transfers his occupancy to another tenant. See *Yenuka*.

Túmiá, H. (تومیا) Thread made of carded cotton.

Túmu, Tel. (తూము) A sluice, a flood-gate, a drain, a water-course: a measure of capacity, a *Túm* or *Toom*, varying in value, but always the twentieth of a *khaṇḍi*.

Tuṇḍam, or Tuṇḍu, Tam., Mal. (துண்டம், துண்டு) A piece, a fragment, a piece cut off, a little.

Tuṇḍáyam, Tam. (துண்டாயம்) A gold *fanam*.

Tuṇḍírsal, Tam. (துண்டிர்சால்) A small remittance, one made frequently.

Tuṇḍuchiṭṭu, Tam. (துண்டுசீட்டு) A small note.

Tuṇḍupíḷḷí, Tam. (துண்டுப்பிள்ளி) The estimate of the grain produce of a small part of the village.

Tunduváram, corruptly, *Tondoowarum*, Tam. (துண்டுவாரம்) The share of the landlord from all lands cultivated by temporary cultivators.

Túp, Mar. (तूप), Tuppa, Karn. (ತುಪ್ಪ) Ghee, or clarified butter; a certain quantity paid as a cess or fee by vendors of milk and butter.

Túppaṭṭí, Mar. (तूपपट्टी) A tax on ghee, or a quantity set apart for the village officers.

Túpsisht, Mar. (तूपशिष्ट) A contribution to government, or to the village functionaries, of a certain amount of ghee from each village, or a money payment in lieu.

Tupháne, Karn. (ತುಫಾನೆ) A calumny, a false accusation.

Tuppadáṭí, Karn. (ತುಪ್ಪದಾಟಿ) A contract of marriage: an entertainment given by the father of the bride to the bride-groom's friends on signing the contract.

Turavu, Tam. (துரவு) A large well, but one that is not considered public property, and is specified in deeds of transfer as belonging to an individual.

Turhadi, Karn. (?) A species of mortgage in Kanara in which the mortgagee only receives a quantity of rice equal in value to the interest due on his loan: (the word is from the 5th Rep., but is not found elsewhere, and there is probably some blunder in the spelling).

Túrika, Karn. (ತೂರಿಕೆ) Winnowing.

Túrpára-pattadam, Tel. (?) The act of winnowing grain.

Turumbu, Tam. (துரும்பு) A straw, a rush, a straw given to a wife as a token of divorce.

Turumbudan-ambáram, Tam. (See *Ambáram*) A heap of corn not cleansed, not freed from the straw.

Turwathen, Mar. (तुरवठें) A terraced and cultivated patch of ground on a hill side or rocky elevation.

Tús, (?) The fundamental long measure in the Northern Sarkárs, varying from 1½ to 2¼ inches.

Tusaḷ, Mar. (तुसळ) Chaff remaining in husked rice: rice with chaff remaining in it after cleaning.

Tusár, corruptly, Teesur, Toosorr, Mar. (?) Crops that ripen after the rains are over, or in the cold season, having been sown at the commencement of the rains: the early crop, on the near ripening of which an estimate of the value was loosely made, and an equal portion of the revenue collected: (in general, *Tushár*, or *Tusár*, in Mar., as well as in S., means Dew, mist, thin rain; but the following confirms the meanings given in the Selections, 4.744).

Tusárpaṭṭí, Mar. (तुसारपट्टी) The land-tax, of which payment was required from the cultivators immediately on the appearance of the grain in the ear.

Tusha, S. &c., vernacularly, Tush, (तुष) Husk, chaff, the integument of rice or other grain.

Tushágni, *Tushánala*, S. &c. (from अग्नि, or अनल, fire) Capital punishment by twisting straw round the limbs of a criminal and covering him with chaff and setting it on fire.

Tuṣí, pronounced Tushí, Mal. (തുശി) The iron style used in writing: the fee paid to the writer who draws up the mortgage-deed; also, in this sense, more correctly *Tuṣí-kánam*.

Túsí, (?) Harvest reaped in the rainy season.

Túṭ, Mar. (तूट) Deficiency, loss: difference in the quantity of grain by the beards being rubbed off in the carriage (same as the H. توت, توتا, from S. त्रुटि, fracture, diminution).

Túṭ, H. (?) Loss or deficiency to landholders in payment of revenue.—Kamaon.

TÚT, H. &c. (توت, तूत) The mulberry tree (Morus indica).

TUṬAM, Mal. (തുടം) A liquid measure containing about one-tenth of an *Edangali*.

TUVARI, Tel. &c. (తువరి) A kind of pea, commonly Dhál, the seed of the Cytisus cajan.

TUVAṬA, Mal. (തുവട) A measure of timber, one-sixth of a *Tumaram*, or 24 square inches.

TYACUT, (?) Land, in the Dindigal district, 5th Rep. (some mistake, perhaps, for *Tyahta*, q. v.).

TYÁGA, S. &c., vernacularly, TYÁG, (त्यागः) Leaving, relinquishing: parting with, as money, whence it comes to signify liberality, munificence.

Tyágí, S. &c. (त्यागी) One who has abandoned the world, a mendicant, a liberal man.

Tyágpatra, Beng. (ত্যাগপত্র) A bill of abandonment, or of divorce.

Tyakta, S. &c., vernacularly, *Tyakt*, (त्यक्त) Left, deserted: given away, bestowed.

TYARGAÍN, (?) H. A temporary cultivator.—Kamaon.

U.

UBÁR, Mar. (उबार) In papers of account, applied to the balance in hand brought forward from the last account closed, and placed at the head of the new account opened; also, surplus, supernumerary.

UBHÁ, Mar. (उभा) Erect, standing, not cut down (as crops).

UBHARÁ, vulgarly, UBHRÁ, Hindi (उभरा) Unladen, as a cart or boat.

Úbharan, Beng. (উভরন) Unloading a boat or cart.

UBHAYA, S. &c. (उभय) Both.

Ubhayamárga, Mar. (उभय, both, and मार्ग, a road) Transit duties.

Ubhayánumata sákshí, S. (उभय, with, अनुमत, assented to, and साक्षी, a witness) A witness consented to by both parties (the term is known colloquially in Mysore).

Ubhayaráśi, Karn. (ಉಭಯರಾಶಿ, S. उभय, and राशि, a heap), *Ubhíráṣ*, corruptly, *Ooberas*, Mar. (उभीराश) The heap of corn gathered and stacked, but not yet apportioned between the sharers, especially when they are the government and the cultivators: in Mar. it hence comes to have the sense of unportioned or undivided property in general, the enjoyment of which is suspended.

UBHAYAM, Mal. (ഉഭയം) Interest on money given in mortgage: land: fruit, or produce of trees.

UBḶAK, Mar. (उबळक) Not brought finally to account: not finally concluded (as an agreement): not settled or determined (as price)

Ublakh, Mar. (उबलख) Unspecified; in the gross, in the lump (this and the preceding are evidently corruptions of the A. *Mablagh*, q. v.).

ÚCHA, or UTSA, Tel. (ఊచ) Stalk of the great millet.

Úchabeyyamu, Tel. (ఊచ బెయ్యము) Unripe grains of the great millet.

UCHALAN, Beng. (উচলন) Winnowing, tossing corn or other light things in a sieve to get rid of the lighter particles.

UCHÁPAT, H., Mar. (اچاپت, उचापत) Taking up goods on credit, the articles so taken, money borrowed, &c.

UCHAKÁ, Mar. (उचका) Swindling, shoplifting, pocket-picking, getting money or property by fraudulent means or dishonest practices.

Uchakyá, *Uchalyá*, Mar. (उचक्या, उचल्या) A cheat, a swindler, a pickpocket.

UCHAL, Mar. (उचल) A portion of land given at the partition of an estate in exchange for some other portion to a different sharer.

UCHCHA, S. &c. (उच्च), also, in most dialects, UNCH, UNCHÁ, H. (اونچا, اونچ), Mar. (उंच) High, lofty, lit. or fig.

Uchchapada, Beng. (উচ্চপদ) A high office.

Unchán, *Unchái*, H. (اونچان, اونچائی) Height, eminence.

Uncháḍ, *Unchawaṭá*, Mar. (उंचाड, उंचवटा) High ground, a mound, an eminence.

Unchaṭ, *Unchawaṭ*, Mar. (उंचट, उंचवट) Rising, ascending (as ground).

UCHCHÁPATI, Karn. (ಉಚ್ಚಾಪತಿ) Taking and giving goods on credit.

Uchchápati lekhkha, Karn. (ಉಚ್ಚಾಪತಿಲೆಕ್ಕ) A running account, a shop bill.

UCHCHHISHṬA, vernacularly, UCHCHISHT, S. &c. (उच्छिष्ट) Rejected, left, the leavings of a meal.

Uchchishtabhojana, S. (उच्छिष्टभोजन) An inferior, a menial, one who eats another's leavings: an attendant on an idol, eating the food offered to it.

UCHHIKUṆ, UCHHINUṆ, Guz. (ઉછીકું, ઉછીનું) Borrowed, received on loan or on credit.

UCHITA, vernacularly, UCHIT, S. &c. (उचित) Fit, right, appropriate, suited to.

UḌAIKUḶAM, Tam. (உடைகுளம்) A tank or reservoir which has burst its bank.

Uḍaippu, Tam. (உடைப்பு) A channel formed by the bursting of a dam or tank.

Uḍaippu kaṭṭu, Tam. (உடைப்புக்கட்டு) Repair of a breach in a dam or the bank of a reservoir.

UḌAÍVÁRAM, Tam. (உடைவாரம்) The whole produce.

UḌAIYÁR, commonly written WODEIYAR, Tam. (உடையார்) A title borne by some Hindu tribes: it is that of the Rájas of Kurg.

UḌAIYAVAN, UḌAITTÁNAVAN, Tam. (உடையவன், உடைத்தானவன், from உடை, of or belonging to), UḌAYÁKARAN, Mal. (ഉടയക്കാരൻ) A possessor, an owner, a proprietor.

Ástikuḍaiyavan, Tam. (ஆஸ்திக்குடையவன்) An heir.

Ástiyuḍaiyavan, Tam. (ஆஸ்தியுடையவன்) A proprietor. See *Ásti*.

UDAKAKRIYÁ, S. (उदक, water, and क्रिया, rite) The ceremony of offering libations of water to deceased ancestors as far as the fourteenth in affinity.

UDAMÍ, Mar. (उदमी) A trader, a dealer.

UḌANPAḌIKAI, UḌANPAḌUGAI, UḌANPÁḌU, incorrectly, ODUMBADIGAI, UTTANBADIKAI, UTTAPADI, Tam. (உடன்படிக்கை, உடன்படுகை, உடன்பாடு, from உடன், together with), UḌAMBAḌI, Mal. (ഉടമ്പടി) A contract, a covenant, an agreement, a settlement, a lease.

Uḍan paṭṭavan, Tam. (உடன்பட்டவன்) A person bound by a stipulation or agreement.

Uḍanpankáli, Tam. (உடன்பங்காளி) The right of a brother's sons to share in the family property.

Uḍanpiṛappu, Tam. (உடன்பிறப்பு) Children of the same father and mother.

Uḍappiṛanavan, Mal. (ഉടപ്പിറന്നവൻ) A brother.

Uḍappiṛanavaḷ, (ഉടപ്പിറന്നവൾ) A sister.

UDÁS, H. (S. उदास) Indifferent, stoical: as applied to agriculture, a sickly crop.—Puraniya.

Udásí, S. &c. (उदासी) A religious mendicant, one affecting indifference to worldly feelings and interests: a religious order among the Sikhs.

Udásína, vernacularly, *Udásin*, S. &c. (उदासीन) An indifferent person, one neither a friend nor a foe: an umpire, an arbiter: it is sometimes confounded with the preceding.

UḌAVÁRAM, Tam. (உடவாரம்) The whole of the divisible produce of the land, or the entire crop before partition.

UDAYA, S. &c. (उदय) The rising of a planet, especially of the sun.

Udayakála, S. &c. (उदयकालः) Time of sunrise.

UDDARUVU, Tel. (ఉద్దరువు) The pawning or mortgaging of grain or similar perishable articles.

UDDARÍ, UDDARE, Karn. (ಉದ್ದರಿ, ಉದ್ದರೆ) Credit.

UDHÁN, Guz. (ઉધાન) The name of a private number used by Hindu brokers: the number three.

UDHAṚ, OODHUR, Mar. (उधड) In the gross, in the lump.

Udhaṛjamábandí, Mar. (उधडजमाबंदी) Assessment in the lump: assessing the total revenue of a village upon the chief proprietor, and leaving it to him to distribute the proportions.

Udkaṛ-salámi, Mar. (?) Rent collected in the gross on private land, without reference to any details.

UDDHÁRA, vernacularly, UDDHÁR, or, less correctly, UDHÁR, S. &c. (उद्धार, properly, extracting, lifting up or out) A deduction, a portion deducted: the first division of an estate: portion of the paternal estate assigned to the eldest son in excess over the shares of the others: a debt, a loan, especially one not bearing interest. Guz. subs. Buying or selling upon trust: adv. on trust or credit.

UDDI, Tel. (ఉద్ది) A low ridge in a field for retaining the water of irrigation: a bank raised above the level of a reservoir, with a channel in it into which the water of the reservoir is thrown for conveyance to fields of a higher level.

UDÍCHÍ, S. (उदीची) The north.

ÚDIGAMU, Tel. (ఊడిగము) Slavery, domestic service.

Úḍigavuváḍu, Tel. (ఊడిగవువాడు) A slave: a domestic servant.

UDÍM, OODEEM, Mar. &c. (उदीम, S. उद्यम, industry), UDIMA, UDUMU, UDUME, Karn. (ಉದಿಮ, ಉದುಮು, ಉದುಮೆ) Traffic, dealing, shopkeeping.

Udími, incorrectly, *Udmí*, Mar. (उदीमी), *Uddami*, &c., Karn. (ಉದ್ದಮಿ) A shopkeeper, a dealer.

Udímpaṭṭi, Mar. (उदीमपट्टी) A cess or tax on shopkeepers and traders.

UḌKIDAI, Tam. (உட்கிடை) A hamlet, an associated or subordinate village or market: also *Ulkadai*, q. v.

ÚḌU, Karn. (ಊಡು) The pole or shaft of a plough.

ÚḌUPU, Tel. (ఊడుపు) Transplanting.

Úḍupumaḍi, Tel. (ఊడుపుమడి) A plot or field in which grain has been transplanted.

UḌUVU, Tel. (ఉడువు) Clothes belonging to another person borrowed for wear from the washerman.

UDVÁHA, S. &c. (उद्वाह) Marriage.

UDYÁPANA, vernacularly, UDYÁPAN, S. &c. (उद्यापन) Closing ceremonies, the observance that winds up and completes any religious rite, or the dedication of a temple, tank, &c. to religious or benevolent purposes.

UDYOGA, vernacularly, UDYOG, or UDJOG, S. &c. (उद्योग) Exertion, business, occupation. *Udyogamu*, Tel. (ఉద్యోగము) Situation, employment.

UGÁDI, Tel. Karn. (ఉగాది) The first day of the Telugu sol-lunar year.

UGÁL, Thug. Old clothes.

UGÁLÁ, H. (اوگالا, उगाला) Land always saturated with moisture.

UGHADÍ, Mar. (उघडी) A flood-gate, a sluice.

UGHÁI, Hindi (اوگهاهي, उघाई) Revenue payable by the cultivator to the government (Khet Karm, 39), less correctly, *Aogáhi*, q.v.

UGHRÁT, Guz. (ઉઘરાત) Collection of revenue.

Ughrátdár, Guz. (ઉઘરાતદાર) A collector, a tax gatherer.

UGRA, S. (उग्र), UGRUḌU, Tel. (ఉగ్రుడు) A man of a mixed caste, sprung from a Kshatriya father and Súdra mother: their business is killing animals living in holes: some are bards, and some have charge of treasure or hill forts.

UGRÁNAMU, Tel. &c. (ఉగ్రాణము), UGRÁNA, Karn. (ఉగ్రాణ) UGRÁNAM, Mal. (ഉഗ്രാണം) A storehouse, a treasury, a pantry.

Ugráṇi, or *Ugráṇapuváḍu*, Tel. (ఉగ్రాణి, ఉగ్రాణపువాడు), *Ugráṇih*, *Ugráṇadava*, Karn. (ಉಗ್ರಾಣಿಕ, ಉಗ್ರಾಣದವ) A storekeeper, a steward, a butler, a treasurer, a collector of revenue.

UGWANI, UGWÍL, UGÁWÁ, UGRÁNÍ, Mar. (उगवणी, उगवील, उगावा, उग्राणी), UGHRANÍ, Guz. (ઉઘરાણી) The gathering in or realising of money due: the collection of the revenue: the amount collected.

ÛHDAH, commonly pronounced, OHDA, or AHDAH, q. v., corruptly, HUDDA, and WOODA, H. (A. عهده) An agreement, an engagement, a contract, an obligation: a commission, a trust, an office or function, civil or military.

Ûhdahbandí, H. (عهده‌بندي) Fixing a period for discharge of a debt, wholly or in part: an instalment bond.

Ûhdahbarái, H. (عهده‌براي) Fulfilment of an engagement, discharge of a debt, &c.

Ûhdahdár, commonly, *Ohdahdár*, q. v., corruptly, *Woodedár*, &c. H. (عهده‌دار) An officer, a servant of the government, filling either a civil or military appointment: under the Mohammadan government the name was also applied to the farmer or contractor of revenue; also to a salt-contractor.

UJÁN, Beng. (উজান) The upper country, the part from which the rivers flow.

UJÁR, UJÁḌ, H. &c. (اوجار, اوجاڑ, उजाड) Desolate, desert, uninhabited, uncultivated, waste: the reverse of *Ábád*. Beng. (উজাড) A wilderness, a deserted place.

Ujúhát, Beng. (উজুহাত, ? from A. وجوه, reasons) Pleadings on the different points of a case in writing, objections urged in writing. See *Wujúhát*.

UJÁR, Hindi (उजार) Grazing down a standing crop.—Puraniya.

UJURI-JAMÁ, Hindi (उजुरीजमा, from the A. عزر) An entry in the annual account shewing remissions of the rents of the Ryots.

Ujuri-jamín, Hindi (उजुरीजमीन) Account of land struck off from the previous year's assessment as overcharged.

UKÁḌÁ, or UKÁṚÁ, Mar. (उकाडा) The practice of taking in regularly a certain quantity or articles, as milk, &c., and making periodical payment; running up a score; also such quantity regularly taken.

UKAḶÍT, Mar. (उकळीत) Gathering in of sums due, collecting alms or contributions: collections of their dues, especially in kind, by village officers and servants, from the cultivators direct: fees in kind collected by the village officers as their dues from persons exposing articles for sale in the village bazárs.

UKH, H. &c. (اوکھ, ऊख, S. इक्षु) Sugar-cane (Saccharum officinarum).

Uhhári, H. (اوکھاري, उखारी) Sugar-cane: in the eastern districts *Ukhári* (ऊखारी) A field of sugar-cane.

ÚKHAL, H. (اوکھل, ऊखल) Land recently brought into cultivation.

UKHAL, UKHALI, or UKHLI, Hindi, &c. (उखल, उखली, S. उलूखल) A mortar of wood or stone, large or small, for pounding rice in or freeing grain of its husk, by bruising with a wooden pestle.

UKHAḶ, Mar. (उखळ) The first ploughing of a field: the turning up of the ground; also a mortar: see H. *Ukhal*.

UKHAR, Guz. (ઉખર) Fallow land ploughed and prepared for cultivation next year: uncultivated land.

UKHAR, Mar. (उखर) Shallow, capable of containing little depth of water (used of rice-grounds on a slope or with low banks).

UKKI, UKKE, Karn. (ಉಕ್ಕಿ, ಉಕ್ಕೆ) Ploughing.

Ukkéhola, Karn. (ಉಕ್ಕೆಹೊಲ) A ploughed field.

ÛKR, A. (عقر) A woman's dower, or the money paid as her portion; also a sum of money which is paid by a man to a woman, with whom he has had illicit intercourse, by way of dower.

UKTA, S. &c. (उक्त) Said, spoken: it is used in documents, sometimes for, aforesaid.

UKTÁ, or UKTE, incorrectly, UKTI, OOKTEE, Mar. (उक्ता, उक्ते)

In the gross, in the lump, in the mass, said of goods purchased, land assessed, &c.

Uktejamín, Mar. (उक्तेजमीन) Land assessed in the gross at a round sum, instead of certain rates per *bighá* or plough: also lands assessed at reduced rates, which have, for a temporary purpose, been fixed in a rough manner, and which are less than the land can bear.

Ukti, Mar. (उक्ति) The sum total of the assessment imposed upon a village, and at which it is leased for a given term of years, with the assent of the cultivators.

ÛKÚBAT, H. (A. عقوبت) Punishment, chastisement: in law, punishment inflicted by the magistrate at his discretion.

Ûkúbat-shadíd, H. (A. شديد, severe) Severe punishment, extending to death, inflicted at the discretion of the magistrate.

UKUNBÁṚÍ, Beng. (উকুনবাড়ি) A pole of bambu used by the cultivators in Bengal for separating short straws and other refuse from the corn after threshing.

ULAÍ, Hindi. Lands on a lower level easily irrigated and therefore more productive.—Kuch Bahar.

ULANGU, more correctly, OḶUNGU, Tam. (ஒழுங்கு, arrangement) A standard rate for assessment, or for the price of grain, &c.: a detailed account of the lands of a village.

UḶAVU, UḶAVUTTOḶIL, Tam. (உழவு, உழவுத்தொழில), URAVA, Mal. (ഉഴവ) Ploughing, agriculture, tillage.

Uḷupadai, Tam. (உழுபடை) A plough.

Ulada, Karn. (ಉಳದ) Unploughed, waste.

Uḷudakáḍu, Tam. (உழுதகாடு) Ploughed high land.

Uḷudal, Tam. (உழுதல) Ploughing.

Uḷudanilam, Tam. (உழுதநிலம்) Ploughed land.

Uḷukai, Tam. (உழுகை) Agriculture.

Uḷuke, Uḷike, Ulavika, &c. Karn. (ಉಳುಕೆ, ಉಳಿಕೆ, ಉಳವಿಕೆ) Ploughing.

Uḷunar, Tam. (உழுநர், plur.) Husbandmen, ploughmen.

Uṛavukáran, Mal. (ഉഴവുകാരൻ) A ploughman, a cultivator.

Uḷavár, Uḷavór, Tam. (உழவார், உழவோர்) Ploughmen, cultivators.

Uḷavadai, Tam. (உழவடை) The act or right of ploughing, the right to cultivate the lands: as this right is originally inherent in the holders of *Kániátchi* tenures, it is sometimes used in the same sense.

Uḷavadai-kániátchi-sásanam, Tam. (உழவடைகாணியாட்சிசாசனம்) A deed by which a proprietor transfers his right of cultivation to a *Payirhâran*, or tenant, as far as allowable by the custom of the villages, after which he cannot remove him, or substitute another in his place.

Uḷavadai-ulkuḍi, Tam. (உழவடைஉள்க்குடி) A cultivator who, although not an original sharer in the village lands, has acquired the right of hereditary succession and continuous occupation. See *Ulkudi*.

Uḷavuḍai-váram, Tam. (உழவுடைவாரம்) The cultivator's share of the crop.

UḶAVAN, Tam. (உளவன்) A spy, a scout.

ULGÍDA, Mar. (?) Public servants, those of a village.

ÚḶIGA, Karn. (ಊಳಿಗ) Service, work.

Úligadavanu, Úliganu, Karn. (ಊಳಿಗದವನು, ಊಳಿಗನು) A servant, a police *peon*.

ÚḶIGA, Karn. (ಊಳಿಗ) Items of different accounts put down indiscriminately, not under their proper heads.

Úligavarga, Karn. (ಊಳಿಗವರ್ಗ) Items of account under their proper heads.

UḶKAḌAI, Tam. (உள்கடை) A hamlet, an associated or incorporated village or market: same as *Udkiḍai*.

UḶKUḌI, OOLKOODY, Tam. (உள்குடி, from உள, in, within (the village), and குடி, an inhabitant), also UḶ-KUḌI-PAYIRKÁRAN, corruptly, OOLCOODY-PAYACARNY, also, UḶ-PAYIRKUḌI, and UḶ-PARAKUḌI, corruptly, OOL-PYAKOODY, OOL-PARACOODY, see *Payir-kuḍi*, Tam. (உள்குடிபயிர்க்காரன், உள்பயிர்க்குடி, உள்பரக்குடி) A permanent cultivating tenant, one who, by himself or his forefathers, has been settled in a village and carried on cultivation in it for a considerable time, although not one of the original coparceners: he cannot be dispossessed as long as he pays the stipulated rent to the proprietor or proprietors, usually a quit-rent, and his proportion of the government assessment: he has the right of hereditary succession and independent cultivation, but cannot mortgage or sell the land, and is not entitled to the emoluments and privileges considered as the right of the *Mirásidárs*: he corresponds in all respects with the *Khúd-kásht* of Hindustan.

ULLÁKU, Tel. (ఉల్లాకు) A written memorandum left with goods or grain, specifying the quantity and the owner.

ULLAṆA, Karn. (ಉಲ್ಲಣ) A grass-cutter, a grass-carrier.

UḶLAVAN, Tam. (உள்ளவன்) A proprietor, a rich man.

UḶLIṬṬÁR, also occurring ULLUTÁR, or OOLLOOTAR, corruptly, OOLLOOTORE, Tam. (உள்ளிட்டார்) Partners, all concerned in the same bargain or business, coparceners in land: it is sometimes restricted to descendants of the original holder or grantee, but this seems questionable: it is also sometimes extended to heirs generally.

Uḷliya, or Uḷliyamániyam, corruptly, Wooliah, Woolija, and Wooliga, Tam. (உள்ளிய, உள்ளியமானி-யம்) Rent-free lands granted for services, especially as militia or police.

Uḷmanai, Tam. (உள்மனை) An inhabited house.

Uḷpaṭṭi, Mal. (ഉൾപ്പട്ടി) Rice-lands.

Ultá-, or Ulthájamín, Mar. (उलटा-, उलथाजमीन, from उलथा, turning over) Land left to rest for a certain period, either by being uncultivated, or sown with crops of a less exhausting nature than those previously raised upon it.

Ulu, Beng. (S. উলু) A coarse kind of grass used in thatching (Saccharum cylindricum).

Uḷuku, Tam. (உளுகு) An account kept by the village accountant of the lands of the village, their extent and capability.

Uḷume, Karn. (ಉಳುಮೆ) Salary paid in kind to government servants.

Uluphá, corruptly, Wulfa, Tel. (ఉలుఫా), Uluphi, Karn. (ಉಲುಫಿ) Uluppai, Tam. (உலுப்பை) Supplies furnished gratuitously to great persons on a journey by the villages on their route (from the A. *Âlf*, *Âlúfa* علف, علوفي, subsistence, &c.).

Uluva, Tel. (ఉలువ) A crop of a coarse kind of pulse or grain (Glycine tomentosa).

Uḷváram, Tam. (உள்வாரம்) The owner's share of the produce of his land.

Uḷvaṭṭam, Tam. (உள்வட்டம்) Premium or difference in favour of a coin exchanged for one of less value.

Uḷváykál, Tam. (உள்வாய்க்கால்) Water-course or channel within a village.

Umbaḷi, vulgarly, Umbli, Karn. (ಉಂಬಳಿ) Subsistence, a grant to an individual for his subsistence. See the next.

Umbaḷige, Ummaḷi, Ummaḷige, Ummuḷi, Ummuḷige, Karn. (ಉಂಬಳಿಗೆ, ಉಂಮಳಿ, ಉಂಮಳಿಗೆ, ಉಂಮುಳಿ, ಉಂಮುಳಿಗೆ), Umbilikai, Tam. (உம்பிளிக்கை) Land granted by government rent-free, as a reward for, or in consideration of, public services.

Ummaḷigráma, Karn. (ಉಂಮಳಿಗ್ರಾಮ), *Umbali-grámam*, Tam. (உம்பிளிக்கிராமம்) A village granted rent-free in reward for, or on condition of, public services.

Ummaḷigár, or *-dár*, Karn. (ಉಂಮಳಿಗಾರ, -ದಾರ) The holder of lands, or a village, rent-free.

Umbaḷi-uttár, Karn. (ಉಂಬಳಿಉತ್ತಾರ) Grant of rent-free land for subsistence. See *Umbaḷi* and *Uttár*.

Umbará, Mar. (उंबरा) A quantitity of dwellings.

Umbar-paṭṭí, or *Umbar-sárá*, Mar. (उंबरपट्टी-सारा) House-tax.

Umed, H. (A. اميد) Hope, expectation.

Umedwár, H. (اميدوار) An expectant, a candidate for employment, one who awaits a favourable answer to some representation or request.

Umed-usul, Uriya (ଉମେଦଉସୁଲ, from A. وصول) Recoverable revenue.

Úmí, Hindi (ऊमी) An ear of corn half ripe.

Umi, Mal. (ഉമി) The husk of rice or other grain, chaff, bran.

Umm, H. (A. اُمّ) A mother.

Umm-al-walad, A. (امّ الولد) In Mohammadan law, a female slave who has borne a child to her master, and is consequently free at his death.

Umúmat, A. (امومة) Being a mother, maternity.

Ûmra, H. (A. عمره) Visiting a wife while in the house of her parents.

Ûmudain, A. (du. of عمود, a pillar) In Mohammadan law, the pillars or supporters of a family, designation of the children of a kinsman, however distant, and whether in the ascending or descending line: ancestors or descendants in the direct line.

Umuka, Tel. (ఉముక) The husk of rice.

Ún, H. (اون, S. ऊर्ण) Wool, coarse hair that may be woven.

Úna, S. &c. (ऊन), Uṇá, Mar. (उणा) Less, deficient; used chiefly in composition, shortened to *Ún*, with numerals to denote one less, as *Ún-hattar*, one less seventy, *i. e.* sixty-nine.

Unálo, Guz. (ઉનાળો, S. उष्ण, heat) The hot season.

Unchko, Guz. (ઉંચકો) A contract or stipulation to do any thing at a fixed rate by a given time, the profit or loss to be borne by the contractor: different articles sold in the lump; the bargain for them collectively.

Undarati, or Undariti, or Uṇdara paṭṭam, Mal. (?) Walker has *Undardi*, from *Undoir*, to eat, *Ariti*, clear: A form of mortgage in which the mortgagee occupies the estate at a fixed stipulated rent, out of which he pays himself the amount of the interest on his loan, and such proportion of the principal as shall liquidate the principal in a specified number of years: if the holder throws up the property before the stipulated time expires, he has to allow to the proprietor a further deduction from the principal of 20 per eent. as *Sahshi*, and 3 per cent. for *Tushi*, or drawing up the deeds: it is a disputed question whether in such case the mortgagee is entitled to claim any allowance on the profits of cultivation: Mr. Walker says not, Mr. Græme states that he is, entitled to them.

Uṇḍi, Uṇḍikai, Tam. (உண்டி, உண்டிகை), **Uṇḍiku-kulasam**, Mal. (ഉണ്ടികകുലശം) A treasury-box in which duty or custom-money is deposited, a money-box, an alms-box.

Uṇḍikappaṇam, Mal. (ഉണ്ടികപ്പണം) Money or treasure received at custom-houses, &c: money deposited as alms in the treasury of a temple.

Uṇḍige, Uṇḍigi, Karn. (ಉಂಡಿಗೆ, ಉಂಡಿಗಿ) A custom-house stamp.

Uṇḍige-chíṭu, Karn. (ಉಂಡಿಗೆಚೀಟು) A custom-house permit: a formal written dismissal of an officer for bad conduct.

Uṇḍika, Mal. (ഉണ്ടിക) A bill of exchange, a cheque, a draft, a stamp, a passport (the Hind. *Hundi*, q. v.).

Uṇḍichchiṭṭu, or *Uṇḍikaichiṭṭu*, Tam. (உண்டிச்சீட்டு, உண்டிகைச்சீட்டு) A bill of exchange, a cheque, a draft, a *Hundi*.

Ungidi, Tel. (ఉంగిడి) A disease of cattle from their grazing on sprouts of millet, or leaves of the castor-oil plant.

Undurkhád, Mar. (S. उंदुरखाद) Damage done by rats devouring the grain.

Unhálá, Mar. (उन्हाळा, from the S. उष्ण, hot, and काल, time) The hot season, the dry season, or the eight months as distinguished from the four *monsoon* months.

Unjarí, H. (اونجری, उंजरी) A small heap of corn set apart at harvest time by the Mohammadans in the name of some saint.

Unkuva, Tel. (ఉంకువ) A marriage portion properly given to a woman at her marriage by her relatives: an item of woman's wealth.

Únviṟpór, Tam. (ஊன்விற்போர்) Sellers of flesh.

Upabhoga, corruptly, **Oop-bhog**, S. &c. (उपभोग) Usufruct, temporary occupation or enjoyment.

Upádhi, S. &c. (उपाधि) Fraud, artifice: lawful deceit, as recovery of a debt by some deception or device.

Upádhyáya, corruptly, **Oopadhyaya**, S. &c. (उपाध्याय) A teacher, an instructor; originally, a teacher of the Vêda, but now used in a general sense.

Upádhyá, Mar. (उपाध्या, vernacular corruption of the preceding) A priest who conducts the ceremonies of a family in a village.

Upagráma, S. &c. (उपग्राम) A secondary or subordinate village: in the south, a tract of cultivated and inhabited land of specified extent, but wanting some of the incidents of a village, as a separate municipal body, &c.

Upaj, H. (اپج, S. उप and ज, born) Produce.

Upjao, H. (S. اپجاو) Fertile, productive.

Upajíviká, S. &c. (उपजीविका) Livelihood, means of livelihood, trade, business, &c.

Upaḷ, Mar. (उपळ) The state of ground, saturated, as after heavy rains, and emitting rills of water in different parts.

Upaḷ, or *Upaḷí*, Mar. (उपळ, उपळी) A rill, a streamlet trickling down hills or breaking from the ground after rain.

Upalaga, Guz. (ઉપલગા) Supernumerary, not entered in accounts: balance in hand, surplus.

Upaláṇa, Guz. (ઉપલાણ) High land in villages.

Upaláṇ-nicháṇ, Guz. (ઉપલાણનીચાણ) The high and low lands of a village in relation to each other.

Upanám, Beng. (S. উপনাম) A surname.

Upanchakí, Beng. (উপচকী) Land held in perpetuity at fixed rents; it is the same as an *Istimrárí* tenure, but the term is in general use only in Rangpur and Kuch Bahar, and is probably a vernacular corruption of *Panchaki*, q. v.

Upanchakidár, Beng. (P. দার) A holder of land in perpetuity, paying a fixed rate to the Zamindár or government.

Upandam, Dakh. (اپندم ?) An obligation, written or verbal, entered into by the cultivator for a sum of ready money, while the crop is on the ground, to sell it, when cut, to the person making the advance at a price below the actual market rate: (it should be a Telugu word, but is not given in the dictionary).

Upanaya, Upanayana, corruptly, **Upiniany**, S. &c. (उपनय, उपनयन) The solemn investiture of youths of the three first tribes, Brahman, Kshatriya, and Vaiṣya, with a peculiar thread or cord worn over the left shoulder, by which they are considered as regenerated and admitted to all the privileges of their original birth: as the Brahman is the only one of the three original tribes remaining, the ceremony is properly confined to the youth of that caste, and should be performed not earlier than eight, nor later than sixteen years of age: in various parts of India, however, different Ṣúdra and mixed castes assume the right of wearing the Brahmanical cord.

Upanidhi, S. &c. (उपनिधि) A pledge, a deposit: in law, one that is sealed or covered, so that the contents are unknown: hidden treasure.

Upanikshepa, S. &c. (उपनिक्षेप) A sealed or inclosed deposit or pledge.

Upapátaka, S. &c. (उपपातक) A heinous offence, as killing a cow, selling a daughter, atheism, or any crime only less atrocious than the *Mahápátaka*, q. v.

Upapátaki, S. (उपपातकी) A sinner in the second degree.

Upar, Oopur, H. (اوپر, S. उपरि), Upari, Hindi, Mar., Beng. (उपरि) Over, upper, on, upon, above.

Upará, Uparáhár, H. (اوپرا, اوپراهار) Upper or high land not admitting of artificial irrigation.

Uparáḷá, Mar. (उपराळा) Surplus stock, goods in reserve, excess of weight: calumnious or false accusation.

Uparí, vulgarly Upri, H. (S. اوپري) Upper, over; stranger, exotic, foreign: also, extra, surplus, in excess, over and above.

Uparí, vulgarly, *Upri, Oopuree, Oopree*, Mar. (S. उपरी) A cultivator not belonging originally to a village, but residing and occupying land in it, either upon a lease for a stipulated term of years, or at the pleasure of the proprietor: a tenant, a temporary occupant, a tenant at will: it may be also applied, as in distinction to the *Thalkarí* or proprietor, to tenants whose ancestors have held the lands for many generations, but who are not considered to have a proprietary right in the soil: also an officer employed to supervise the crops when brought to the threshing-floor when the government dues are not paid in kind: an overseer, a superintendant.

Uparí-kharch, Beng. (উপরিখরচ) Extra expenses.

Uparwár, H. (اوپروار) Over, upper (as land, relatively to lower).

Uparwáriá, Guz. (pl. ઉપરવાડીઆ) Cultivators not belonging to the village the lands of which they cultivate.

Upaṣalya, Karn. (S. ಉಪಶಲ್ಯ) Space near a village, suburbs of a village where the outcastes reside.

Upaṭyá, Mar. (उपट्या) A sharper, a thief, a swindler.

Upavartana, Karn. (S. ಉಪವರ್ತನ) A country, a district.

Upavása, S. &c. (उपवास), also, vernacularly, Upás, H. (اپاس, اپواس) Fasting, a fast.

Upavasatha, Karn. (S. ಉಪವಸಥ) A village.

Upavíta, S. &c. (उपवीत) The cord properly worn by the three pure castes only, though assumed by some others: for the Brahman it should be of cotton, of flax for a Kshatriya, and of wool for the Vaisya: it is worn ordinarily over the left shoulder, hanging diagonally across the body down to the right hip.

Upekshá, S. &c. (उपेक्षा) Neglect, disregard: in law, laches, silent neglect of a right, which is held to constitute or amount to its forfeiture.

Uphtá, Hindi (उफता) The low part of the banks of a river over which the water flows upon the fields when the river rises.—Puraniya.

Uppari, Upparaváḍu, Tel. (ఉప్పరి, ఉప్పరవాడు) A man of the caste of tank diggers, whose business is to dig tanks and wells, repair water-channels, and raise embankments; they are said to be descended from a Ṣudra father and mother, the latter having been forcibly violated: the woman of the caste is termed *Upparadhi*.

Uppu, Tel., Karn., Tam. (ఉప్పు, உப்பு), Uppa, Mal. (ഉപ്പ) Salt. (In derivatives and compounds *Uppu* often becomes *Uppa* and the Malayalim *Uppa* appears as *Uppu*.

Uppudibbe, or *Uppukaṭṭé*, Karn. (ಉಪ್ಪುದಿಬ್ಬೆ, ಉಪ್ಪುಕಟ್ಟೆ) A square lump or block of salt.

Uppaguṇi, Karn. (ಉಪ್ಪುಗುಣಿ) A salt-pan.

Uppaḷam, Mal. (ഉപ്പളം) A salt marsh. Tam. (உப்பளம்) A salt-pan. Tel. (ఉప్పలము) Ground fit for the manufacture of salt by solar evaporation, same as *Uppunela*: also, in Tel., *Uṭṭu* (ఉట్టు).

Uppaḷavan, Tam. (உப்பளவன்), *Uppalavuváḍu*, Tel. (ఉప్పలవువాడు) A salt manufacturer.

Uppuleru, Tel. (ఉప్పు ఏరు) A salt-water river.

Uppumaḍi, Tel. (ఉప్పుమడి) A salt-pan.

Uppaḷam, Tam. (உப்பளம்) A salt-pan, a salt-marsh.

Uppamaippór, Tam. (உப்பமைப்போர்) A salt manufacturer.

Uppunela, Tel., Karn. (ఉప్పు నెల), *Uppunilam*, Mal. (ഉപ്പുനിലം) Salt-ground, soil impregnated with salt, earth on which salt is manufactured, water having been let in from the sea upon soil previously prepared or adapted for the purpose is suffered to evaporate, and the salt left is collected in crystals.

Uppinakuṇi, Karn. (ಉಪ್ಪಿನಕುಣಿ) A salt-pan.

Uppinarévu, Karn. (ಉಪ್ಪಿನರೇವು), *Uppurevulu*, Tel. (ఉప్పు-రేవులు) The bank of a back water communicating with the sea, from which salt-pans are supplied.

Uppuparra, Tel. (ఉప్పుపఱ్ఱ) A salt-marsh.

Uppupaṭanna, Mal. (ഉപ്പുപടന്ന) A salt-marsh, a bed in which salt is made by solar evaporation.

Uppáramányam, Karn. (ಉಪ್ಪಾರಮಾನ್ಯಂ) Taxes levied from the second class of salt-makers in Mysore.

Uppáranu, Uppáraravanu, Karn. (ಉಪ್ಪಾರನು, ಉಪ್ಪಾ-ರರವನು) A salt-maker; also, a tank digger, a bricklayer or plasterer.

Upparavoḷe, Uppáravoḷi, Uppiravoḷe, Karn. (ಉಪ್ಪರವೊಳೆ, ಉಪ್ಪಾರವೊಳಿ, ಉಪ್ಪಿರವೊಳೆ) A salt-marsh, the soil that is prepared to produce salt by evaporation.

Upputaṇṭa, pron. *Uppuḍaṇḍa*, Mal. (ഉപ്പുതണ്ട) A cake or block of salt.

Upputtarai, Tam. (உப்புத்தரை) Soil impregnated with salt.

Uppuváḍi, Tam. (உப்புவாடி) A platform for piling salt upon.

Uppuvánikar, Tam. (உப்புவாணிகர்) Salt merchants; also *Umanar* (உமணர்).

Uppuviṭṭiḍu magaḷír, Tam. (உப்புவிற்றிடுமகளிர்) Women who sell salt.

Gajuppu, Karn. (ಗಾಜುಪ್ಪು) A mineral, a medicinal salt.

Kalluppu, Karn. (ಕಲ್ಲುಪ್ಪು) Sea or rock salt.

Karuttavuppu, Tam. (கருத்தவுப்பு) Black salt produced from the ashes of certain plants.

Kaṛiyuppu, Tam. (கறியுப்பு) Kitchen-salt.

Peṭlupu, Tel., Karn. (పెట్లుప్పు), *Vettiyuppu*, Tam. (வெட்டியுப்பு) Saltpetre.

Parravuppu, Tel. (పర్రవుప్పు) Swamp or spontaneous salt.

ÚR, OOR, Tam. (ஊர்), ÚRU, Tel., Karn. (ఊరు, ಊರು) ÚRA, Mal. (ഊര) A village, a town, a country: (this word has undergone the same change which the bad ear and articulation of our countrymen have inflicted upon the Sanscrit *Pur* in Hindustan, and has been universally changed to *ore* in the numerous names in which it occurs in the Peninsula, as *Vellore* for *Vellúr*, *Nellore* for *Nellúr*, *Coimbatore* for *Kayambatúr*, *Tanjore* for *Tanja-úr*, &c.

Uṛaiyuḷ, Tam. (உறையுள்) A village, a town.

Úrán, Tam. (ஊரான்) The head person in a town or village.

Úrár, Tam. (ஊரார்) Townsmen, citizens.

Úrdaḷavara, Karn. (ಊರ್ದಳವಾರ) A village servant; also *Úradalavára*.

Úrgaṇika, Karn. (ಊರ್ಗಣಿಕ) A village astrologer.

Úrkaraṇiga, Karn. (ಊರ್ಕರಣಿಗ) A village accountant.

Úrkávaliga, Karn. (ಊರ್ಕಾವಲಿಗ) A town or village watchman: also *Urukáyava*, &c.

Úrkelasiga, Karn. (ಊರ್ಕೆಲಸಿಗ) A village barber.

Úrkoḷa, Karn. (ಊರ್ಕೊಳ) A public tank.

Úrmániyam, Tam. (ஊர்மானியம்) Village free lands, generally used to signify lands exempted from revenue assigned by government for the performance of village duties, as distinguished from *Kániátchi Mányam*.

Úrvalam, Tam. (ஊர்வலம்) A procession, state, marriage, or religious, through a town, &c., when the party begins to move to the right.

Úrubéli, Karn. (ಊರುಬೇಲಿ) A hedge round a village, as a defence.

Úrubhápi, or *Úrabhávi*, Karn. (ಊರುಭಾಪಿ, ಊರಭಾವಿ) A public tank.

Úrucheruvu, Tel. (ఊరుచెరువు) A village reservoir, a public tank.

Úrugavuḍa, or *-gauḍa*, Karn. (ಊರುಗವುಡ) The head man of a village.

Úruguttige, Karn. (ಊರುಗುತ್ತಿಗೆ) Assessment of a village.

Úruholabu, Karn. (ಊರುಹೊಲಬು) The limits or boundary of a village.

Úrukaṭṭé, Karn. (ಊರುಕಟ್ಟೆ) A village tank or pond: a raised seat round a tree in front of a village where the villagers are accustomed to assemble.

Úrukáyuva, &c. Karn. (ಊರುಕಾಯುವ) A town or village watchman.

Úrumbaḷi, *Úrummaḷi*, &c. Karn. (ಊರುಂಬಳಿ, ಊರುಂಮಳಿ) A village granted free of assessment.

Úrumeravaṇi, Karn. (ಊರುಮೆರವಣಿ) Procession of a town or village with idols, or at marriages, and the like.

Úruni, Tam. (ஊருணி) A public tank.

Úrupálu, Karn. (ಊರುಪಾಲು) Portion of the crop which falls to the share of the cultivators of a village.

Úrupallelu, Tel. (ఊరుపల్లెలు) Villages, great and small.

Úratalavára, Karn. (ಊರತಲವಾರ) A village servant.

Úruterige, Karn. (ಊರುತೆರಿಗೆ) Assessment of a village.

UṚA, Mal. (ഉറ) A measure of quantity = 20 *Paṛas*.

URA, (?) H. A land or boundary mark.

URADI, URATI, URATU, (?) Mal. A class of predial slaves in Malabar (probably errors for the next).

ÚRÁḶI, Mal. (ഊരാളി) A man of a low or servile caste, a *Ṣúdra*: a low outcaste tribe inhabiting chiefly the forests.

ÚRÁNMA, Mal. (ഊരാണ്മ) Proprietorship of a temple or place of worship.

Úránmakáran, Mal. (ഊരാണ്മക്കാരൻ) The proprietor of a temple.

Úráḷan, Mal. (ഊരാളൻ) Guardian or manager of a temple, whether singly or in partnership with others.

Úráyáma-sthánam, (?) Mal. The management of the affairs of a temple (the first is perhaps an error for *Úránma*).

UṚÁṬIYÁ, Beng. (উড়াটিয়া) Land unfit for cultivation.

UṚÁVÁMAṬÍ, Hindi (उड़ावामाटी) A free loose mould.—Puraniya.

UṚAVU, Tam. (உறவு) Relationship, consanguinity.

Uṛavan, Tam. (உறவன்) A relation, a kinsman.

ÚRDDHABÁHU, S. &c. (ऊर्द्धबाहु) An ascetic who holds up one or both of his arms until they become rigid and remain fixed in that position (from *Úrddha*, up, and *báhu*, the arm).

Úrddhapundra, S. &c. (ऊर्द्धपुण्ड्र) A perpendicular line, usually red, but also white or yellow, down the centre of the forehead, indicating a worshipper of Vishṇu.

Urdú, H. (اردو) A camp, a royal encampment: applied more commonly to the Hindustani language as spoken at the Courts of Dehli and Lucknow, and by the Mohammadans of India generally, being formed by a copious though not preponderating influx of Arabic, Persian, and Turkish words upon a basis of Hindi and Sanscrit, and following the grammatical inflexion of the former occasionally slightly modified.

Ûrf, Oorf, H. &c. (عرف, ऊर्फ़) Known (by the name of), commonly so called: it corresponds in use with 'alias.'

Uri, Ure, Karn. (ಉರಿ, ಉರೆ) A loop or sling fastened to the end of a pole for carrying burthens: a net or knotted strings for suspending articles in a house.

Uṛí, Beng. (উড়ী) Wild, applied especially to wild rice growing sometimes abundantly on borders of lakes or swamps.

Uṛídhán, Beng. (উড়ীধান) Wild rice.

Uri, Tam. (உரி) The half of a measure commonly termed *Arai-paddi.*

Urimai, Tam. (உரிமை) Property, possession.

Urittánavan, Tam. (உரித்தானவன்) A proprietor, a possessor: an heir.

Uríyár, *Uríyór*, Tam. (உரியான், உரியோர்) Relations, connexions, ancestors, forefathers.

Uríyavan, Tam. (உரியவன்) A proprietor, an heir.

Urlu, Karn. (ಉರುಳು) A noose, a snare, a halter.

Urlugambha, Karn. (ಉರುಳುಗಂಭ) A gibbet, a gallows.

Urs, H. (A. عرس) Offerings of food, incense, or lamps, made by Mohammadans on various occasions at the shrines of reputed saints, and especially on the 12th of *Rabî-ul awal*, the anniversary of the death of Mohammad: also nuptials, marriage, a marriage feast.

Urtu, H. (ارتو) Crimping or plaiting of linen.

Urtugár, H. (ارتوگار) A plaiter or crimper of linen.

Uru, corruptly, Ooroo, Mal. (ഉരു) A part, a piece, a portion of a field.

Urvara, Mal. (ഉർവര) Fertile soil yielding every kind of crop: land in general.

Ús, Úns, Mar. (ऊस, ऊंस) Sugar-cane.

Úschaḍh, or *Úscharh*, Mar. (ऊसचढ) A progressively increasing tax on sugar-cane plantations.

Usaná, Mar. (उसना) Borrowed, lent, as money without interest, or articles to be returned or repaid in kind.

Usanavaṭ, *Usanavárí*, Mar. (उसनवट, उसनवारी) Loan, the state of being borrowed or lent.

Úshara, vernacularly, Ushar, or, in some dialects, Usar, S. &c. (ऊषर) Saline, as soil: land impregnated with alkaline particles, and unfit for cultivation.

Úsara-bhúmi, Tel. (ఊసరభూమి) Saline soil.

Ûshr, H. (A. عشر) A tenth part, a tithe. See *Âshr.*

Ûshr-ut-tijárat, A. (عشرالتجارت) Duty on merchandise, customs, a tenth of the value.

Ushtá, Mar. (उष्टा, abbrev. of S. उच्छिष्ट) Left, of a meal, leavings.

Ushṭával, Mar. (उष्टावळ) Fragments, scraps, leavings of a meal.

Uṣír, S. &c. (उशीर) The root of a fragrant grass (Andropagon muricatum) which is woven into screens placed before doors and windows, and kept constantly wet to cool the air admitted through them into the house.

Ustád, H. (A. استاد), Wastád, Mar. (वस्ताद) A master, a teacher, one skilled in any art or science.

Ustawárí, Mar. (उस्तवारी, P. استواري, strong) Repairing, restoring, re-peopling (ruined houses, villages, &c.).

Uṣúl, Beng. (উশুল, from وصول, q. v.) Collections, revenue.

Ut, or Aút, H. (اوت, abbrev. of S. अपुत्र) One who dies without issue, an unmarried man.

Uṭakkárá, Beng. (উটক্কারা) Foreign, unknown, vagrant.

Uṭama, Mal. (ഉടമ) Wages, payment.

Uṭana, Uṭaná, Beng. (উটন, উটনা) Taking goods on credit.

Uṭangaḷa, Mar. (उटंगळ) A hillock, a mound: uneven, as ground.

Utár, H. &c. (اتار, उतार) Descent, decline, lit. or fig.: deduction, abatement, remission of revenue, scale of decrease in the rate of revenue levied from different qualities of soil: also a ford or ferry, charge for ferrying: ebb tide, low water.

Utaraṇ, *Utarwáṇ*, Mar. (उतरण, उतरवण) A declivity, a slope.

Utárí, *Utárú*, Mar. (उतारी, उतारू) A passenger, a traveller, especially by ship or boat.

Utárpenṭh, Mar. (उतारपेंठ) A commercial city, a mart, an emporium.

Utárta, *Utarwaṭ*, Mar. (उतरता, उतरवट) Declivious, sloping.

Utáryá, Mar. (उताऱ्या) A ferryman.

Utávali, (?) Mal. Surplus profit or rent of an estate held on mortgage, after defraying the government demand and interest of the loan: (an error, or local corruption for *Huttuvali*, q. v.).

Utbandi, also written Otbundee, Outhbundee, (?) Beng. A settlement of revenue with reference to the quality of the land, the description of produce, and customary rate of assessment (perhaps connected with *Aüt-bandi*, q. v.).

Utbandi-jamá, (?) Beng. A settlement in some parts of Bengal where the cultivator pays rent only for the land actually cultivated in each year.

UTEṆ, Mar. (उतें) Rice raised from seed on land that has not been previously prepared by burning.

UṬHÁN, Mar. &c. (उठान) An area in the interior of a house, a court, a yard: also lifting up, raising: (but this is more correctly, *Utthán*.

Uṭhánghát, Beng. (উঠানঘাট) A landing-place, a wharf, a quay: (wrong spelling for *Utthán*),

UTKOCHA, vernacularly, UTKOCH, S. &c. (उत्कोच) A bribe, any thing given as an illegal or unavowed consideration: a reward for the detection of crime.

UTKSHEPA, S. &c. (उत्क्षेप) A throwing away: also for *Uthshepaka* (उत्क्षेपक, a thrower away) A pilferer, a pickpocket, one who robs a person by craft or sleight of hand so that he is not aware of it.

UTOTI, (?) Mar. Sloping land close to a *Dáng* village in which young rice-plants intended for transplanting are raised from seed; they are then steeped in water and sweated by the aid of blankets until the rootlets are thrown out, when they are transferred to the field prepared for their reception.

UTPANNA, Mar. (S. उत्पन्न) Produced, born; also, subst., Produce, profit, proceeds, realised rent of a village, produce of the harvest.

UTSARGA, UTSARJANA, S. &c. (उत्सर्ग, उत्सर्जन) Letting go, abandoning: gift, donation: turning a bull loose and leaving him to wander about at will, on the occasion of some festive or religious celebration.

UTSAVA, S. &c. (उत्सव) A festival, a holiday, a religious festival.

Utsava-móyíní, Tam. (உச்சவமோயினி) Money allowed for the expense of public festivals.

UTTAMARṆA, S. &c. (उत्तमर्ण) A creditor.

UTTAMASÁHASA, S. (उत्तमसाहस) Severe or capital punishment, of which five kinds are reckoned, mutilation, branding, confiscation, exile, and death.

UTTARA, vernacularly, UTTAR, corruptly, OTTAR, S. &c. (उत्तर) An answer, a reply, rejoinder, defence: also, north: and adj. subsequent, posterior: it is in general use also as the second member of a compound, implying lands granted or belonging to; as, *Devottar*, granted to a god; *Brahmottar*, granted to a Brahman.

Uttarábhása, S. &c. (from आभास, what seems like) An evasive or prevaricating reply, the semblance, not the soundness, of an answer.

Uttarádhikára, S. &c. (उत्तराधिकार) Succession, inheritance.

Uttarádhikári, S. &c. (उत्तराधिकारी) A successor, an heir.

Uttarakarttá, S. &c. (उत्तरकर्त्ता) An answerer, a respondent, one who makes a reply.

Uttarakriyá, S. &c. (उत्तरक्रिया) Funeral ceremonies.

Uttaralakshaṇa, S. &c. (from लक्षण, a mark or sign) The characteristics of a reply, namely, that it be applicable to the whole charge, that it be maintainable by law, that it be not equivocal or evasive, that it be consistent with itself, and that it be perspicuously expressed.

Uttarántar, Beng. (S. উত্তরান্তর) A reply which is irrelevant to the charge, an evasive reply.

Uttara-páda, S. (उत्तरपाद) The defence or reply in judicial proceedings.

Uttara-phiryádu-dárudu, Tel. (ఉత్తరఫిర్యాదుదారుడు) An appellant: lit. a defendant who complains.

Uttarasákshí, S. (उत्तरसाक्षी) A witness for the defendant.

Uttaravádí, S. &c. (उत्तरवादी) A defendant, a respondent: in Karn. also, a bondsman, a security.

Uttarayáṇa, S. &c. (उत्तरायण) The sun's northern declination, or his passage from the southern to the northern limit of the ecliptic, the winter solstice.

Uttarottara, S. &c. (उत्तर, repeated) Rejoinder, reply to a reply.

Uttar-pratyuttar, Beng. (S. উত্তরপ্রত্যুত্তর), *Uttara-pratyuttara*, S. (उत्तरप्रत्युत्तर) Defence and rejoinder, or, generally, pleadings in a suit at law.

UTTÁRA, corruptly, OOTHUR, Karn. (ಉತ್ತಾರ), S. UDDHÁRA, (उद्धार) Deduction, remission: land given by government to an individual as a reward for services at a quit-rent or rent-free: land given to a temple.

Joḍiyuttára, Karn. (ಜೋಡಿಯುತ್ತಾರ) Assignment or grant of land at a favourable rent.

Púrvaduttára, Karn. (ಪೂರ್ವದುತ್ತಾರ) A grant of land rent-free.

UTTHÁNA, S. &c. (उत्थान) Rising, getting up: raising, lifting up.

Utthánaikádaṣí, S. &c. (उत्थानैकादशी) The eleventh lunar day, which sometimes falls in *Kártik*, sometimes in *Agraháyana*, when Vishṇu is supposed to arise from four months' sleep, being the close of the rainy season.

Utthit-patit, Beng. (S. উত্থিৎ, risen, পতিৎ, fallen) Land that cannot bear a crop every year, and is therefore left fallow occasionally.

UṬṬU, Tel. (ఉట్టు) Ground fit for the preparation of salt

whose brackish water is let in from the sea upon a soil charged with saline particles, the evaporation of which leaves the surface coated with salt.

Úṭṭu, written Urru, Tam. (ஊற்று) A spring.

Uwár, Hindi (उवार) Ploughing up a standing crop.—Puraniya.

Ûzr, H.&c. (A. عذر) Excuse, apology: claim, pretension: objection.

Ûzrdár, H. (عذردار) A claimant, an objector.

Ûzrdárí, H. (عذرداری) Claiming, petitioning, submitting an objection to a claim or statement.

V.

Vách, nom. Vák, S. &c. (वाच्, वाक्) Speech.

Vágdána, S. &c. (वाग्दान) A gift in words, a promise: betrothment.

Vágdatta, S. &c. (वाग्दत्त) Promised: affianced, betrothed.

Vágnişchaya, or *Váṅnişchaya*, S. &c. (वाग्निश्चय, वाङ्निश्चय) Assurance, averment: betrothment, affiance.

Váj-, or *Váng-múlamu*, Tel. (వాఙ్మూలము, వాంగ్మూలము, from S. वाच and मूलम, root) A declaration, a deposition.

Vákdána, more correctly, *Vágdána*, as above, S. &c. (वाक्दान) A verbal or promised gift: affiance, betrothal, promise to give a boy in adoption or a daughter in marriage.

Váhku-múlam, Tam. (வாக்குமூலம்) A deposition before a judge or *Panchayat*.

Vákpárushya, S. &c. (वाक् and पारुष्य, harshness) Abuse, defamation, scandal, calumny punishable by law.

Vachana, S. &c., vernacularly, Vachan, or Bachan, (वचन) A sentence, a dictum in law, a text from a work of authority.

Vad, Vadi, Guz. (વદ, વદી) The dark half of a lunar month. See *Badi*.

Váda, vernacularly, Vád, Wád, Bád, S. &c. (वाद) Speech, discourse: argument, dispute: pleading in court, a law suit.

Vádaprativáda, vernacularly, *Vádprativád*, S. &c. (वादप्रतिवाद) Charge and defence, plaint and reply, pleadings in a suit.

Vádí, Bádí, Wádí, S. &c. (वादी) A speaker a disputant, a complainant, a plaintiff in a suit.

Váḍa, vernacularly, Váḍ, Váṛ, Báṛ, S. &c. (वाड) An inclosure, a fence, an inclosed space.

Váḍá, Wárá, Mar. (वाडा), *Vádo, Váṛo*, Guz. (વાડો) A quarter of a town, a ward, a part inhabited by persons of the same caste or occupation, as, *Bráhmana-wárá*, the Brahman's quarter; *Kasái-wáṛo*, the butcher's quarter: also, in Mar., a public building, as *Rájwáṛá*, a palace *Sarkár-wáṛá*, any government building.

Váḍí, Wáḍí, Wáṛí, Mar. (वाडी) An inclosed piece of ground, especially of meadow or arable ground: a cluster of huts at a little distance from the main village, a hamlet or dependent village: a separate quarter of a village: in Guz. also, a garden, an orchard, a plantation: in Tel. a street.

Váḍkar, Wáḍhar, Mar. (वाडकर) The proprietor of an inclosed piece of ground.

Váḍagai, Tam. (வாடகை) Hire, rent.

Vadagaly, (?) Tam. A sect of Hindus.

Vadai, Tam. (வதை, S. वध) Murder.

Vadaikáran, Tam. (வதைக்காரன்) A murderer.

Váḍai, Tam. (வாடை) A village, a small village or street, especially of herdsmen, shepherds, or foresters.

Váḍaiváyakál, Tam. (வாடைவாயக்கால்) A channel for carrying off surplus water from a village.

Váḍavattu, (?) Tel. A village held free from assessment.

Vaḍḍeváḍu, see *Oṭṭan*, Tel. (వడ్డెవాఁడు) A caste, or individual of it, whose occupation is working in quarries, tank digging, and the like.

Vádhkápio, Vadhkutio, Guz. (વાધકાપીઓ, વાધકુટીઓ) A surgeon, one who dresses wounds and performs operations (from વાધ, a wound).

Váḍike, Karn. (ವಾಡಿಕೆ) Customary, usual; also, subst., custom, usage: experience.

Vádio, Vádhio, Guz. (વાદીઓ, વાધીઓ, S. वर्द्धकी) A carpenter, a builder, a shipwright.

Vadukan, plur. Vadukar, Tam. (வடுகன்) A native of Telinga.

Vaga, Waga, Tel. (వగ) A minor division of a village: it is used in Guzerati for a subdivision of the lands of a village.

Vagairaguṭṭa, Tel. (వగైరగుట్ట) Rent of a village engaged for by several persons (from the A. and H. *Wa-ghaira*, and others).

Vághari, Waghrí, corruptly Vagree, Wagree, Mar. Guz. (वाघरी, from वाघर, S. वागुरा, a net) A caste, or an individual of it, whose occupation is snaring and catching wild beasts.

Váhánnavaṭí, or Vahannaṭi, Guz. (વાહાણવટી, from S. वाहन, a vessel) A sailor, a shipowner

Váídá, Wáídá, Tel. (వాయిదా, A. وعده) A fixed term for payment of money, an instalment.

Vaidéha, Vaidéhaka, Karn. (ವೈದೇಹ, ವೈದೇಹಕ) A trader by caste and occupation, said to have sprung from a Vaişya father and Brahman mother: in S. the latter origin and the same name are applied to an individual whose business it was to attend on the female apartments.

VAIDIKA, vernacularly, VAIDIK, S. (वैदिक) Relating to the *Vêdas*: a Brahman conversant with the text of the *Vêdas*.

VAIDYA, VAID, or BAID, S. &c. (वैद्य) A physician, a man of the medical caste and profession.

VAIKÁSI, corruptly, VYAUSEE, VYASSAI, Tam. (வைகாசி) The second month of the Tamil year (May-June).

VAIKUNTHA, S. &c. (वैकुंठ) Vishnu's heaven: applied ironically by the Mohammadans of Bengal to pits filled with all sorts of impurities, in which, under the government of *Jâfar-khan*, farmers of revenue, Zamindárs, and others, who were defaulters were plunged, in order to compel payment or a revelation of their resources: it is said to have been devised by *Jâfar-khan* himself, but to have been rather held out in terrorem than to have been carried into execution. See *Baikunth*.

VAIPPUMÁNIYAM, Tam. (வைப்புமானியம்) A grant of a portion of the government revenue claimable from the estate of an individual.

VAIRÁGA, S. (वैराग) Suppression of worldly passions, whether of affection or aversion.

Vairágí, or *Bairágí*, q. v. S. &c. (वैरागी) A religious mendicant professing to have subdued all worldly emotions, leading a vagrant life and subsisting upon alms; properly a worshipper of *Vishṇu*, especially in the form of *Ráma*, and, in relation to him, of *Sitá* and *Hanumán*: there are various distinctions and orders, some of whom are collected in *maths*, conventual establishments under, a superior: the greater number profess a life of continence, and, if becoming *Vairágís* after being householders, separate from their families: some of those who have been excluded from their order marry and engage in trade, and are said to be known in the Dakhin as *Bhat* (?) *Vairágís*.

VAIṢÁKHA, S. &c., vernacularly, VAISÁKH, or BAISÁKH, (वैशाख) The first month of the Hindu solar year (April-May), the second of the luni-solar.

Vaisákham, (?), corruptly, *Wysaghum*. Crops reaped in the month of *Vaiṣákh*.

VAISHṆAVA, S. &c. (वैष्णव) A worshipper of *Vishṇu* in especial, under one or other of his forms: in Hindustan it also designates a respectable body of Hindus who are bankers and merchants, and are followers of Vishnu.

VAÍṢYA, S. &c., vernacularly, VAIS, or BAIS (वैश्य) The name of the third primitive caste of the Hindus, whose means of subsistence, according to Manu, are agriculture, trade, and the keeping of cattle.

VAITA, (?) Guz. Land of a superior quality and most highly assessed.

VAJÁ, Tel. (వజా, from the A. وضع) Deduction, subtraction.

VAKA, or WAKA, Mal. (വക) A part, a portion: capital, stock: goods, estate.

Vaka- or *Waka-káran*, Mal. (വകക്കാരൻ) A kinsman, a co-heir: a partner.

Vaka- or *Waka-chil*, Mal. (വകച്ചിൽ) The Raja's share of the produce of lands, or one-fifth in kind in the northern districts of Malabar, prior to the establishment of a money rate by Haidar after his conquest.

VÁKAṆAI, Tam. (வாகணை) An embankment for carrying off water.

VAKARO, or WAKARO, Guz. (વકરો) Money collected from the sale of goods: the proceeds of sales of merchandise: the sale of goods: stock, cash: the cash-box.

VAKKA, VAKKANÁRA, or WAKKA, WAKKANÁRA, Mal. (വക്ക, വക്കനാര) Hemp.

VAḶADHARMA, Karn. (ವಳಧರ್ಮ) Produce of lands assigned to a temple.

VALAGÁNIO, Guz. (વલગાણિઓ) A man of a low caste, a worker in skins and leather, the *máng* of the Marathas.

VALAIYAN, Tam. (வலையன்) A fisherman by caste and occupation.

VAḶAKKU, or VAZHAKKU, Tam. (வழக்கு) A quarrel, a law-suit.

Vaḷakkan, Tam. (வழக்கன்) A plaintiff, a complainant.

Vaḷakkáḷigal, Tam. (வழக்காளிகள்) The parties in a law-suit.

Edirvaḷakkan, Tam. (எதிர்வழக்கன்) A defendant.

Orudalai-vaḷakkan, Tam. (ஒருதலைவழக்கன்) An *ex-parte* statement.

VALAṄ-KAI, Tam. (வலங்கை), BALAGAIYYÍ, Karn. (ಬಲಗೈಯ್ಯಿ) The right hand: applied also to those mixed castes which constitute what are termed the right-hand castes in the south of India, in contrast to those constituting the left-hand castes, with whom there are frequent disputes, and sometimes affrays, regarding claims and privileges usually of a trifling character: for the left-hand castes, as known in Karnáta, see *Edagai*: according to the same authority the right-hand castes are eighteen: 1. the *Bánijaga*, or trader; 2. the *Okhaliga*, cultivator; 3. *Jotiphana*, (?) oil-maker employing but one bullock in the mill; 4. *Rangajiva*, calico printer and dyer ; 5. *Láḍaru*, Mohammadan traders and artificers (?); 6. *Gujerati*, merchant of Guzerat; 7. *Komati*, trader and merchant; 8. *Jaina*, a follower of the Jain religion; 9. *Kuruba*, a class of shepherds and workers in wool; 10. *Kumbára*, a potter; 11. *Agaṣa*, a washerman; 12. *Besta*, a fisherman, also employed as a palankin bearer; 13. *Padma shalaysa*, (?) a kind of weaver; 14. *Náindu*, a barber; 15. *Uppáranu*, a tank digger; 16. *Chitragára*, a painter; 17. *Golla*, a cowherd; 18. *Wallia* (?), or *Páreyan*, commonly, *Paria*, who, like the *Madigar* or *Sakali* of the left-hand caste, is the especial champion of the whole. The principal members of both the right and left-hand castes are the same throughout the Peninsula, but there are variations both of caste and of nomenclature in several of the subordinate divisions; and some of those specified in the above list are too general to be included with propriety, such as *Guzerati* merchants and *Jains*: some few of the names also are not verifiable, as indicated by the mark of interrogation attached.

VALAṆGAIYAN, plur. -YÁR, Tam. (வலங்கையன், -யார்) One of the right-hand tribe, or the right-hand men or tribes.

VÁLARÁ, Guz. (વાલરા) Land on which the weeds have been burnt previous to ploughing.

VALARTTÁḶ, Tam. (வளர்த்தாள்) A foster-mother.

Válarttapiḷḷai, Tam. (வளர்த்தப்பிள்ளை) A foster-child.

VALASA, vulgarly, WULSA, Tel. (వలస), VALASE, Karn. (ವಲಸೆ) Flight of people in a body from a village or town through fear of some public calamity or exaction.

VALAT-DÁNÍÁ, or -DHARANÍÁ, corruptly, VULLET-DANEEA, VULT-DÁN, Guz. (વલતદાણીઆ -ધરાણીઆ) A particular kind of mortgage; money borrowed by mortgaging the produce of land or other property: any fund pledged to repay the amount of a loan.

VÁLE, Karn. (ವಾಲೆ) Leaf of the palm, as used for writing on.

Válekár, Karn. (ವಾಲೆಕಾರ) A messenger, a courier, a peon.

VALI, (?) Tam. A measure of land in Tanjore: probably the same as *Veli*, q. v.

VAḶI, VAZHI, Tam. (வழி), VAṚÍ, or VALI, Mal. (വഴി) A road, a way.

Vaṛi-háran, Mal. (വഴിക്കാരൻ) A traveller, a wayfarer.

Vaḷippaṛi, Tam. (வழிப்பறி) Robbery on the highway.

Vaḷiselavu, Tam. (வழிச்செலவு) A journey: money for the expenses of a journey.

Variyútta, Mal. (വഴിയൂട്ട) Food given to travelling Brahmans.

VALLA, S. (वल्ल), VÁLA, Mar. (वाल) A weight equal to three seeds of the Abrus precatorius, or, popularly, to one-fortieth of a *tolá*.

VALLAM, Mal. (വല്ലം) A large basket for storing grain: a dam: a place for watering fields or letting out water.

VAḶḶAM, Tam. (வள்ளம்) A grain measure containing four *padis*, or about a peck.

VALLAVA, (?) Mal. One of the three divisions of the servile caste, the Palayar.

VALLAVAN, Tam. (வல்லவன்) A herdsman.

VALLI, Mal. (വല്ലി) Wages paid to the servile classes, or Palayars.

Valliyál, Mal. (വല്ലിയാൾ) A Palayar slave.

VAḶḶIKÁNAM, Mal. (വള്ളിക്കാണം) Earnest money.

VALLIYAM, Tam. (வல்லியம்) A village of shepherds or herdsmen.

VAḶḶUVA, VAḶḶUVÁDU, Tel. (వల్లువ, వల్లువాడు), VAḶḶUVAN, Tam. (வள்ளுவன்) A man of a class of Parias, considered to be of a somewhat superior description, and held by the caste in the light of a family priest.

VANA, vernacularly, VAN, WAN, and BAN, q. v., S. &c. (वन) A wood, a grove, a forest.

Vánaprastha, S. (वानप्रस्थ) The man of the three first castes who, after the term of his householdership has expired, has entered the third *Áṣrama* or order, and has proceeded (*prastha*) to a life in the woods (*vána*), the *Hyllobios* of the Greek writers.

Vancharái, or *Wancharái*, Mar. (वनचराई) Price paid for the grazing of cattle in forests or on waste lands.

Vanegávili, Karn. (ವನೆಗಾವಲಿ) Farm of wood and timber: a tax upon them levied by the former government of Mysore.

VANA, Guz. (વણ) The cotton-plant.

Vankár, Guz. (વણકાર) A weaver.

Vánvaḷá, *Wanwaḷá*, or, vulgarly, *Wanoḷa*, Mar. (वानवळा, from वान and ओल *ola*, green) A cess levied upon various kinds of grain, vegetables, and fruits, when they first come to maturity: a similar claim or fee on behalf of the village servants.

VANCHIBHRAMI, VANCHIKSHMÁ, Mal. (വഞ്ചിഭൂമി) The country of Travancore (from *vanchi*, a boat, boat-land).

Vanchi-virutti, Mal. (വഞ്ചിവിരുത്തി) Land granted rent-free in Malabar, on condition of providing boats for the state when required.

VÁNDHO, Guz. (વાંધો) An unsettled transaction, an affair involved in dispute (in trade).

VANDIGRÁHA, S. (वन्दिग्राह) A thief, a housebreaker, especially one who breaks into a place where something precious or sacred is kept, as into an armoury or temple, or chamber where the sacred fire is burning.

VANḌIL, or VANḌI, vulgarly, BANḌY, Tam. (வண்டில், வண்டி), Mal. (വണ്ടി) A two-wheeled chaise, the ordinary European vehicle in Madras and the other presidencies; also a cart, a wain, or waggon.

VANDRA, Tel. (వంద్ర) Land granted at an easy rate of assessment.

VANḌUBHÚMI, Tel. (వండుభూమి) Land on the banks of a river.

VANGAḶAMAR, Tam. (plur. வண்களமர்) Men of the servile tribe, agriculturists, originally landholders, now following other avocations.

VANṆÁN, Tam. (வண்ணான்) A washerman.

VÁNNIO, Guz. (વાણીઓ) The name of a caste, or of an individual of it, who are numerous in Guzerat; the *Banya* or *Banian* of other dialects, and of European writers: in Guzerat they are distinguished into two great classes, as *Vaishnavas*, or *Jains*, both of whom follow various lines of business, as shopkeepers, retailers, merchants, and bankers. see *Banya*: in Mar. the term is modified as *Váṇi* or *Wáṇi* (वाणी): it is no doubt derived from the S. *Vanij* or *Vanik*.

VANṢA, WANṢA, BANṢA, S. &c. (वंश) A race, a family, also a bambu: see *Banṣa*.

Vanṣávali, S. &c. (वंशावली) A genealogy, a list of persons of one family or race.

Vánsphoṛo, Guz. (વાંસફોરો) A caste, or member of it, who works in bambus, making mats, baskets, &c.: see *Bansphoṛ*.

VANTA, VUNTA, or WUNTA, Mar. (वंत), VANTU, Tel. (వంతు) A share, a part, a portion (of an estate, of a contribution, of a mercantile concern, &c.)

Vanta- or *Wantá-dáṛ*, Mar. (वंतदार) The holder or contributor of a share.

Vantni, or *Wantni-patra*, Mar. (?) A document specifying the proportions in which any property is to be divided.

VÁRA, or, vernacularly, VÁR, WÁR, or BÁR, S. &c. (वार) A day, used in composition as *Soma-vára*, day of the moon, Monday; *Mangala-vára*, day of Mars, Tuesday; *Buddha-vára*, day of Mercury, Wednesday; *Vrihaspati-vára*, day of Jupiter, Thursday; *Ṣukra-vára*, day of Venus, Friday; *Ṣani-vára*, day of Saturn, Saturday; *Rabi-*, or *Áditya-vára*, day of the Sun, Sunday: see *Bár*.

VÁRA, Karn. (ವಾರ), VÁRAM, or WÁRAM, corruptly, WAREM, Tam., Mal. (வாரம், വാരം) A share of the crop or of the produce of a field: in Kanara, whether it be that of the cultivator or of the government as landlord; in Malabar it usually designates the rent or landlord's share of the produce, and in some districts is limited to the landlord's share of the produce of fields bearing hill-paddy and sesamum only, or to fields of the wet cultivation: in Tamil it is distinguished as

Uḍai-váram, (உடைவாரம்) The whole produce of all the cultivated lands of a village subject to partition between the cultivator and landlord, or the state.

Kuḍi-váram, (குடிவாரம்) The share of the produce assigned to the cultivator.

Mélváram, (மேல்வாரம்) The share of the produce due to the landlord or the state.

Váradiṭṭam, Tam. (வாரத்திட்டம்) Adjustment of the shares of the produce belonging to each party interested: a register kept by the village accountant of the respective shares of the produce assignable to the cultivator and proprietor, or the state.

Várada-davasa, Karn (ವಾರದದವಸ) The crops divided between the tenant and landlord.

Várana-bhumi, Karn. (ವಾರದಭೂಮಿ) Land of which the rent or assessment is paid by a portion of the crop.

Váraḍai-olai, Tam. (வாரடைஓலை) A deed of lease.

Várapaṭṭu, vulgarly, *Várapat*, Tam. (வாரப்பற்று) Subject to share, held in shares, an estate, &c.: it is applied also to lands, a share of the produce of which is receivable by the government in kind, as distinguished from *Tirvai-paṭṭu* lands, or those paying a money assessment, and *Mányam*, those held rent-free: *Várapat* lands may be either in wet or dry cultivation.

Várapaṭṭu-nilam, Tam. (நிலம்) Land, the produce of which is divided in shares.

Várapirivu, Tam. (வாரப்பிரிவு) Division of shares.

Várasaṭṭam, Tam. (வாரச்சட்டம்) A table or register of the cultivator's share of the crop.

Váratundu, Tam. (வாரத்துண்டு) A deduction from the share of the cultivator added to the government share.

Várávári, Karn. (ವಾರಾವಾರಿ) Settlement, assessment, adjustment of shares.

VARA, vernacularly, BAR, BUR, S. &c. (वर) A bridegroom.

Varadakshine, Karn. (S. ವರದಕ್ಷಿಣೆ) Present made by the bride's father to the bridegroom on the consummation of the marriage.

Varadhárá, *Vardhárá*, Mar. (वरधावा, वर्धावा) The brother

of the bride, or some person representing him, going in procession to bring the bridegroom.

Varaghoḍá, Mar. (वरघोडा) The marriage procession of a bride and bridegroom; also of a boy on his way to be invested with the characteristic cord.

Varaṇa, Mar. (S. वरण) Choosing or accepting in marriage, betrothal.

Varáta, or *Varát*, in H. *Barát*, Mar. (वरात) A marriage procession, the friends and attendants escorting the married pair to their home.

VARÁḌÁ, Karn. (ವರಾಡಾ) A subscription among the villagers to defray the village expenses.

VARADÁ CHATÚRTHÍ, S. &c. (वरदाचतुर्थी) A festival in honour of Durgá as the giver (*dá*) of blessings (*vara*) on the fourth of *Mágha*.

VARADI, Karn. (ವರದಿ) News, report.

Ukkadadavaradi, Karn. (ಉಕ್ಕಡದವರದಿ) A patrol or police report.

VARAGU, Tam. (வரகு) A kind of grain (Paspalum frumentaceum): it is also applied to other kinds of millet, as *Pulvaragu* (புல்வரகு) (Panicum colonum).

VARAHÁ, Tel. (వరహా), VARÁHAN, Tam. (வராகன்) A gold coin, so named from its originally bearing the figure of a boar (*varáha*), or of *Vishṇu* in the boar *avatár*, the signet of the Rajás of Vijayanagar: it was subsequently more usually termed by the Mohammadans *Hun*, or by Europeans *Pagoda*, the latter from its having on one face a Hindu temple.

VÁRAKAMU, less correctly, WARAKUM, Tel. (వారకము) VÁRAKKAM, Tam. (வாரக்கம்) Advance made to cultivators to enable them to carry on cultivation; more usually designated *Takávi*, q. v.

VAṚAKKA, or WAṚAKKA, Mal. (വഴക്ക) A plaint, a claim, a lawsuit.

Vaṛakku-káran, Mal. (വഴക്കുകാരൻ) A plaintiff, a complainant.

VÁRÁNILAM, Mal. (വാരാനിലം) Barren or waste land.

VARAPU, VARUPU, Tel. (వరపు, వరుపు) Drought, dry weather.

VARAPPU, VARAMBU, Tam. (வரப்பு, வரம்பு) A limit, a border, a boundary, a low ridge or bank to retain water in fields for irrigation.

VARAṢI VÁRI BÁKÍ, Tel. (వరశివారిబాకీ) Total balance.

VARÁTA, Karn. (ವರಾತೆ) An assignment on the revenue, an order for payment: see *Barát*.

Jóru-varáta, Karn. (ಜೋರುವರಾತೆ) A compulsory demand of payments.

VARÁṬAKA, S. &c. (वराटक) The small *kaunri* shell used as money.

VARAṬHÁ, VARṬHÁ, vulgarly, WARTHA, Mar. (वरठा) A washerman.

VARAVA, Tel. (వరవ) A channel for conveying water to a reservoir.

VARAVU, Tel. (వరవు) Income, profit.

VARAVUḌU, Tel. (వరవుడు) A servant.

VÁRDDHUSHIKA, S. &c. (वार्द्धुषिक) A money-lender, a usurer, one lending money at interest.

VÁRENDRA, S. (वारेन्द्र) A native of Varendra, part of Bengal north of the Ganges, designating especially one great division of the Brahmans of Bengal.

VARGA, vernacularly VARG, vulgarly, WURG, S. &c. (वर्ग) A class, a tribe, a multitude of similar persons or things: in *Karnata*, an ancestral hereditary estate.

Vargadár, vulgarly, *Wurgdár*, Karn. (ವರ್ಗದಾರ) The proprietor of a hereditary estate, and in that capacity sometimes the representative of a whole village, collecting and paying the assessment of the whole, although others may have portions of the village lands as separate property: the title is also, though laxly, assigned to lessees under the original proprietor, who are known as *Sub-wurg-dárs*.

Múlavarga, corruptly, *Mooly-wurg*, and *Wurg-mooly*, Karn. (S. मूल, root) Original proprietary right in land.

Múlavargadár, corruptly, *Moolwurgdár*, Karn. (P. دار, who has) The proprietor of an ancestral hereditary estate.

Vargawár, Karn. (ವರ್ಗವಾರ) According to estates, assessments, &c.

VARI, Tam. (வரி), Karn. (ವರಿ) Tax in general, toll, tribute, cess, impost, assessment.

Manaivari, Tam. (மனைவரி) House-tax.

Pulvari, Tam. (புல்வரி) A tax on pasturage.

Talaivari, Tam. (தலைவரி) Poll-tax.

Varikáran, Tam. (வரிக்காரன்), *Varigára*, Karn. (ವರಿಗಾರ) A tax-gatherer, a collector of duties or taxes.

Varisai, Tam. (வரிசை) Fixed rate of assessment.

VÁRI, Mal. (വാഴി) A ruler, a governor.

VARI, vulgarly, WUREE, Tel. (వరి) Rice in the stalk, *paddy*.

VAṚI, Mal. (വഴി), VAḶI, VAZHI, Tam. (வழி) A road, a way.

Vaṛikáran, Mal. (വഴിക്കാരൻ) A traveller, a wayfarer.

Vaṛikari, Mal. (വഴിക്കരി) Provender for a journey.

Variyutta, Mal. (വഴിയൂട്ടു) Food given to travelling Brahmans by the state.

VÁRI, S. &c. (वारि) Water.

Váripuram, Mal. (വാരിപ്പൂരം) A flood, an inundation.

VÁRI, also, VÁRINÁMA, (?) Mal. An agreement, a contract, a written engagement.

VÁRIYAN, Mal. (വാരിയൻ) A man of a particular class, a servant in a temple.

VARṆA, vernacularly, VARAN, BARNA, or BARAN, S. &c. (वर्ण) A tribe, a class, a caste.

Varṇasankara, barbarously, *Burrunshunkur*, S. &c. (वर्णसंकर) A mixture of castes: a mixed caste, or one of a mixed caste, one sprung originally from parents of different castes, either in successive or inverted order, as from a Brahman father and Ṣúdra mother, or from a Ṣúdra father and Brahman mother, constituting in the present day the entire body of the Hindus exclusive of the Brahmans; the pretensions of some of these castes to represent the genuine unmixed Kshatriya, Vaisya, or Ṣúdra, being in the highest degree questionable.

VÁRO, Guz. (વારો) A small spot of land assigned to each of the principal inhabitants of a *Koli* village.

VARSHA, also, vernacularly, VARAS, and VARKHA, S. &c. (वर्ष) Rain, the rainy season: also a year.

Várshka, S. &c. (वार्ष) Annual, celebrated annually, relating to a year: also relating or belonging to the rainy season.

Várshagánth, Mar. (वर्षगांठ) A birthday, or the ceremonies observed upon it; lit. the year knot, the age being recorded by a knot tied annually on a string kept for the purpose.

Varshala, Mar. (वर्षल) The year of possession by one of a number of proprietors of an estate who occupy it for a year in turn.

Varshásan, vulgarly, *Wurshasun*, Mar. (वर्षासन), *Varkhásan*, *Varkhásuṇ*, *Varsán*, Guz. (વરખાસણ, વરખાસું, વરસાણ) An annual allowance, a salary, a pension paid either by the public treasury or by assignment on the revenues of a village or district, and entered upon the village expenses: also an assignment or a charge on an estate made by the proprietor in favour of another person.

Varshásandár, Mar. (वर्षासनदार) The holder of an annual allowance, either in pay or in assignments.

Várshika, S. &c. (वार्षिक) Relating to the rainy season, produced in it, &c.: annual, occuring or celebrated yearly.

VARTTANA, vernacularly, VARTAN, S. &c. (वर्त्तन) Means of subsistence, occupation, income, profit. In Tel. and Karn. *Vartana*, *Vartane*, (వర్తన, వర్తనె) *Vartanai*, Tam. (வர்த்தனை) Fees, perquisites, especially of grain, paid to the public servants of a village or town for their support.

Varttaka, S. &c. (वर्त्तक), Tel. Karn. (వర్త్తక) One who possesses or earns a maintenance, a trader, a merchant.

Vartakamu, *Vartaka*, Tel., Karn. (వర్తకము, వర్తక) *Varttakam*, Tam. (வர்த்தகம்) Trade, traffic: also, Karn. a trader, a merchant.

Vartakudu, Tel. (వర్తకుడు), A merchant: also, *Vartaka*, or *Wartaka*, Mar. (वर्त्तक) A particular officer of a town or village, a sort of bailiff.

VARTTÁḶÁ, or WARTTÁLÁ, Mar. (वर्त्ताळा) Surplusage or gain on exchanging coins of different currency, excess of grain as measured in a particular way: balance over or in hand (in squaring accounts).

VARTANÍO, or VARATANÍO, or BARTANIO, corruptly, BHURTUNEEA, Guz. (વરતનીઓ) A village guard or watchman, the village *Chaukídar* of Hindustan: he is commonly a man of low caste, or a *Bhíl*, and is paid by an allowance of land rent-free.

VARTTANÚKA, WARTTANÚKA, or WARTTANÚK, Mar. (वर्त्तणूक) Conduct, behaviour; subsistence.

Varttanúka-jáminí, or *Wurtunook-zámin*, Mar. (वर्त्तणूकजामिनी) Security given by friends of the parties litigating before a *Panchayat* that they will respectfully obey the award.

VÁRUṆÍ, S. &c. (वारुणी) A festival on the thirteenth of the latter half of *Chaitra*, in honour of Varuṇa, the deity of the waters; if it fall on a Saturday it is of especial sanctity, and is termed *Mahá-váruní*.

VAṢA, Mal. (വശ) A husband's sister; a wife.

VÁSA, S. &c. (वास) A dwelling, a habitation: dwelling, abiding.

Vásí, S. &c. (वासी) A dweller, a native.

VASÁ, or WASÁ, corruptly, WUSSA, Guz. (વસા) A square measure of land, twenty of which are equal to one *bíghá*: in Guzerat it contains $142\frac{2}{9}$ square yards.

Vis-vasá, corruptly, *Wis-wussa*, Guz. (વીસવસા) The twentieth part of a *Vasá*.

VÁSÁ-BANTRAVUTU, or pron. -BANṬRATO, Tel. (వాసాబంట్రవుతు) A watchman or guard appointed to superintend cultivation.

VASANTA, vernacularly, VASANT, or BASANT, S. &c. (वसन्त) Spring, the season of spring, the two months *Phálgun* and *Chaitra*.

Vásanta, Vásantí, also *Vasantotsava,* S. &c. (वासन्तः -ती, वसन्तोत्सव) A festival, or series of festivals, celebrated in spring.

Vasati, Tel. (S. వసతి) A dwelling: an allowance, subsistence money, or land granted rent-free for that purpose: also, Guz. Population, inhabitants.

Vasati-dára, Tel. (వసతిదార) A holder of an allowance, or rent-free land, for his support.

Vasati-patrak, Guz. (વસતીપતરક) A census, a statistical return of population.

Vasaváiá, incorrectly, Wasswáya, Wuswaieea, Guz. (વસવાઈઆ) The village establishment of artisans and servants: the land assigned them for their services.

Vasaváiá kamál, Wuswaya kumal, Guz. (A. كمال, total) The whole amount or value of fees paid to the village servants.

Vaselá, Guz. (વસેલા) Fallow (as land left for a year uncultivated).

Vastu, S. &c. (वस्तु) Thing, substance.

Vastuvaka, Mal. (വസ്തുവക) Property, real or personal: estate, goods, chattels.

Vástavika, vernacularly, *Vástavik,* S. &c. (वास्तविक) Substantial, real, actual, genuine, correct.

Vástavika-vṛiddhi, S. (from वृद्धि, increase) Just or legal interest of money.

Vástu, S. &c. (वास्तु) The site or foundation of a house: also a house.

Vástupújá, S. &c. (वास्तुपूजा) Ceremonies observed on laying the foundations of a dwelling.

Vásudeva, corruptly, Wasoodeo, Mar. (वासुदेव) A class of mendicants in the Dakhin who beg early in the morning to wake up the residents, so named from *Vásudeva,* a name of Krishna, the son of Vasudeva.

Váṭa, vernacularly, Váṭ, or Wáṭ, S. &c. (वाट) A road, a path, a way.

Váṭ-máryá, Mar. (वाटमाऱ्या) A footpad, a highwayman.

Vaṭáu, Guz. (વટાવ) Exchange, balance of different currencies: discount or premium: see *Baṭṭa.*

Vaṭṭam, or Wattam, corruptly, Wuthum, Tam. (வட்டம், S. वृत्त) A circle, or any thing of a circular form, as a well, a pond, &c.: applied also, in Tanjore, to a small tract or district comprising three or four villages under one head man.

Vaṭṭamániyakáran, corruptly, *Wuthum monigár,* Tam. (வட்டமாணியக்காரன்) The head man of a district exercising undefined authority in revenue and judicial matters, under the order of an officer of government in charge of a district.

Vaṭṭakainilam, Tam. (வட்டகைநிலம்) An enclosed field.

Vaṭṭa, Karn. (ವಟ್ಟ), Vaṭṭamu, Tel. (వట్టము), Vaṭṭam, Tam. (வட்டம்) The rate of exchange between currencies of different values, either premium or discount: the *Baṭṭa* of Upper India.

Vaṭṭachchíṭṭu, corruptly, *Vaṭṭachít,* Tam. (வட்டச்சீட்டு) A bond with premium granted for goods exchanged or money lent on interest.

Vaṭṭasochcham, Tam. (வட்டச்சொச்சம்) Interest, balance, or premium.

Vaṭṭakkáran, Tam. (வட்டக்காரன்) A money-changer.

Vaṭṭi, Tam. (வட்டி, S. वृद्धि) Interest on money.

Anyáya-vaṭṭi, Tam. (அநியாயவட்டி, from S. अन्याय, improper) Usury, unlawful interest.

Darma-vaṭṭi, Tam. (தர்மவட்டி, from S. धर्म्म, law) Lawful interest.

Vaṭukan, Mal. (വടുകൻ) A bondsman, a servant, a man of a certain tribe considered as originally from Telingana.

Váv, or Váü, Guz. (વાવ, S. वापी) A large oblong well with steps to the water's edge.

Vávaḍi, or *Vávari,* the H. *Baori,* or *Baoli,* q. v. Guz. (વાવડી, વાવરી) A small well into which people descend to get water.

Vávaní, Guz. (વાવણી) The act of sowing seed.

Vávanio, Guz. (વાવણીઓ) A drill-plough, a sowing machine.

Vávar, or Wáwar, Mar. (वावर) The cultivated or cultivable land in a village.

Vávvá, Guz. (વાવવા) Planting, as trees: sowing seeds.

Vayal, Tam., Mal. (வயல்) A rice-field: ground fit for rice cultivation: any open field or plain.

Vayalkkarai, Tam. (வயல்க்கரை) A rice-corn field.

Vayalpáṭṭam, Mal. (വയൽപാട്ടം) Rent of rice-fields.

Váyippa, Mal. (വായിപ്പ) A loan, a debt.

Váykál, Tam. (வாய்க்கால்) A water-channel.

Váyola, Mal. (വായൊല) A written agreement on palm-leaf, making over land, &c. to another: a deed of transfer or conveyance: a written voucher deposited in a heap of grain specifying its quantity.

Vechala, (?) Karn. A small additional contribution or fee in grain from the Mániyam or privilege land claimed from the holders by the original proprietor.

VECHÁN, Guz. (S. વેચાણ) Sale, the act of selling (H. *Bechna*, to sell).

Vecháníá, Guz. (વેચાણીઆ) Saleable, applied to lands properly belonging to the state, but which have been sold by the *Patéls* and have been excluded from the assessment. Bom. Reg. x. 1831.

Vechánkhat, Guz. (વેચાણખત) A deed of sale, a conveyance.

Vechán nakariá, Guz (વેચાણનકરીઆ) Lands exempt from tax or rent.

Vechánsabhámíá, Guz. (વેચાણસભામીઆ) Land subject to a quit-rent.

VEDA, S. &c. (वेद) The general name of the chief scriptural authorities of the Hindus: it is most correctly applied to the four canonical works entitled severally the *Ṛig-Veda*, *Yajur-Veda*, *Sáma-Veda*, and *Atharva-Veda*, but it is extended to other works of supposed inspired origin, in the sense of science or system, as *Áyur-Veda*, the science of life, *i.e.* medicine; *Dhanur-Veda*, the science of the bow, or military science; *Gándharba-Veda*, the science of music, so named from the heavenly musicians or *Gándharbas*.

Veda-kriyá, or *-karma*, S. &c. (वेदक्रिया -कर्म्म) Any ceremonial regulated by the texts of the Vedas, as are all the essential observances or Sanskáras of the Hindus.

VEDÁNTA, S. &c. (वेदान्त) A system of pantheistic philosophy or psychology inferred from scattered texts of the Vedas, and thence named their 'end' or substance.

VEDA, Tel. (వెద) Sowing seed.

VÉDAN, plur. VÉDAR, corruptly, VAIDUN, VEDDAH, also BEDAN, or WEDEN, Tam. (வேடன், plur. வேடர்), Mal. (വെടൻ) A hunter, a fowler, a name given to a wild tribe, or to an individual of it, inhabiting the hills and forests in the south of India, almost in a state of nature, and gaining a wretched subsistence by killing birds and beasts with bows and arrows; possibly the aboriginal race of the peninsula: in Malabar they are included amongst the prædial slaves, and are employed in cutting timber, constructing fences, and watching crops, but are not permitted to take any part in agricultural labour: they are described as very wild and miserable, but timid, and flying from the approach of other tribes to the woods: the name is also written *Vedu* and *Veduvan*, but incorrectly: the first meaning hunting, and the second being properly *Véttuvan*, q. v.

VEDEṆPÍK, or WEDEPEEK, Mar. (वेडंपीक, from वेडा, mad) A mad crop, one that is excessively exuberant or that wholly fails.

VÉLAI, Tam. (வேலை) Work, labour.

Vélaikáran, *Vélaiyán*, Tam. (வேலைக்காரன், வேலையான்) A servant, a workman.

VELAMA DORA, Tel. (from దొర, a master, a chief) A name given to a military tribe, formerly retained by government for service in the northern Sarkárs.

VELAMA, incorrectly, VELMA, Tel. (వెలమ) The name of a principal tribe of Telugu Súdras, or of a member of it; they claim descent from the Rájas of *Waranhal*.

VEḶI, erroneously, VELLAI, Tam. (வெளி) An open place or field.

Manadai-veli, Tam. (மந்தைவெளி) A public place for cattle outside a village.

Meyssalaveli, Tam. (மெய்ச்சலவெளி) A pasture ground.

Vayalveli, Tam. (வயல்வெளி) A rice-corn field.

VÉLI, corruptly VALEE, VALIE, VALY, VAILY, WELI, Tam. (வேலி) A measure of land containing five *hánis* or six acres and six-tenths: a field of that extent.

VELIVÁḌA, Tel. (వెలివాడ) The outer part of the village tenanted by *Pareyar*.

VELLAM, Tam. (வெள்ளம்) Flood, inundation, irrigation.

Vellahádu, Tam. (வெள்ளக்காடு) Total inundation of a place or field.

Vellapáḷ, Tam. (வெள்ளப்பாழ்) Corn destroyed by inundation.

Vellavári, Tam. (வெள்ளவாரி) A channel for supplying water to a tank.

VEḶḶÁMAI, Tam. (வெள்ளாமை) Agriculture, husbandry, as depending especially upon irrigation.

Veḷḷáḷan, or *Vellázhan*, or *Velláḷan*, Tam. (வெள்ளாழன், வெள்ளாளன்) A man of the agricultural caste, which constitutes a numerous body of the cultivators of southern India: during the native Tamil government no other classes were permitted to hold landed property in *Tondamandalam*.

Vellánhuḍi, Tam. (வெள்ளாங்குடி) A village of farmers.

Vellánseṭṭi, Tam. (வெள்ளாஞசெட்டி) A merchant of the tribe of agriculturists.

Vellavarsi, (perhaps for வெள்ளவரிசை, which last word is used for order, rank) Tam. (?) A class of cultivators in Dindigal and Coimbatur, resident in the villages, and cultivating the lands for themselves, but not having a hereditary or proprietary right to them: (there is some mistake most probably in the name: 5th Rep. p. 832, and in another place, p. 977, the *Velláḷar* are substituted for them).

VENATÍ, (?) Mar. House-tax, or tax on trades; apparently the same as *Muhtarafa*, q. v.

VENNILAI, Tam. (வெண்ணிலை) Any thing given without a pledge or mortgage.

Vennilai-patram, Tam. (வெண்ணிலைபத்திரம்) A note of hand, or bond, without a mortgage.

VENNU, Tel. (వెన్ను) An ear of corn.

VEPPA, or VEPPU, (?) Mal. Mortgage-bond (?).

VÉRI, Tam. (வேரி) The unfermented sap of the palm tree.

VERO, incorrectly, VEERA, VEYRAH, Guz. (વેરો) Tax, impost, duty, any tax or cess levied in addition to that on land, as upon trades, professions, goods, and the like: a particular tax levied upon the land, or upon ploughs, in addition to the standard assessment; also a tax levied on the Grásia tenures paying no other revenue to the state.

VÉRU, Tel. (వేఱు) Separation, division, especially of families which had been previously living together in common.

VERUMPÁṬṬAM, corruptly, VEEROMPAṬṬOM, Mal. (വെറുംപാട്ടം) Rent of land or gardens without any advance or loan. See *Páṭṭam*.

Verumpáṭṭachiṭṭa, Mal. (വെറുംപാട്ടച്ചിട്ട) Lease of lands or gardens, agreement to pay a stipulated rent.

VES, or WES, Mar. (वेस) The gate of a village, hence the payment of the government revenue which was formerly enforced by shutting the gates of the village and allowing no one to leave it until all demands had been realised.

Veskar, *Weskar*, Mar. (वेसकर) The porter or gatekeeper of a village, usually a *Máng*, and employed in other menial offices for the village.

VESANGIPANṬA, Tel. (వెసంగిపంట) A crop that is cut in the hot season.

VETA, (?) Mar. Excess of rate of assessment upon one portion of an estate in consideration of another being under assessed. Bom. Reg. xvii. 1827.

VEṬAN, pronounced commonly, VEDAN, or WEDAN, q. v. Tam. Mal. (வேடன்) The name of a wild forest tribe

Vetuvan, Mal. (വെട്ടുവൻ) One of a tribe of wild people.

VETANA, vernacularly, VETAN, or WETAN, S. &c. (वेतन) Wages, hire: in Marathí it especially applies to the stipends of public officers.

Vetanádánam, S. (वेतनादानं) Non-payment of wages, a branch of judicial proceedings.

Vetaní, or *Wetanee*, Mar. (वेतनी) Stipendiary, receiving pay or wages, given in lieu of wages (land, &c.): relating to pay or wages in any respect.

VEṬH, or WETH, Mar. Guz. (वेठ) Labour or service exacted by government, or a person in power, without paying for it: a load carried by a person or animal impressed: also, but superfluously, *Veth-begár*. See *Begár*.

Veṭhió, Guz. (વેઠીઓ) A person pressed to carry wood, or to perform any labour without recompense.

VET-KÁNAM, (?) Mal. A mortgage-lease engaging to reimburse the mortgagee for any improvements he may make on the lands he holds, in lieu of interest.

VÉṬṬAI, VÉṬṬAM, Tam. (வேட்டை, வேட்டம்) Hunting, the chase.

Véṭṭuvan, Tam. (வேட்டுவன்) A hunter, especially a man of a wild and forest tribe whose chief subsistence is from the chase. See *Vedan*: they are considered as prædial slaves in Malabar.

VEṬṬÁN, Tam. (வெட்டான்) A married woman.

VEṬṬI, Tam. (வெட்டி) A road, a way. Tel. (వెట్టి) Performance of the lowest offices in a village, as those of a labourer or porter, grain watcher, scavenger, &c.

Veṭṭimai, Tam. (வெட்டிமை) The office of an inferior village servant; see the next.

Veṭṭiyán, Tam. (வெட்டியான்) A village servant who discharges the lowest offices, sweeping the *chaultri*, keeping the threshing-floor clean, measuring the grain, and, according to some authorities, employed to burn dead bodies: he is also the messenger of the *Pátíl*, and acts as a guide to public officers and travellers (from *Veṭṭi*, a way, which is from *Veṭṭa-kiradu*, to cut or dig, as a road or way).

Veṭṭiváḍu, Tel. (వెట్టివాడు) A *Veṭṭí*-man, a village servant who acts as messenger, scavenger, &c.

Veṭṭubaḍi, Tel. (వెట్టుబడి) An advance on goods or merchandise.

VEVÁ, VEHAVÁ, Guz. (વેવા, વેહવા, from the S. विवाह) Marriage.

VEVILIPOLAMU, Tel. (వేవిలిపొలము) A field ploughed last year but left fallow this year.

VIBAKÁRAM, and VIVAHÁRAM, Tam. (விபகாரம், விவகாரம்) Law-suit, legal proceedings. See *Vyavahára*.

VIBHÁGA, S. &c., vernacularly, VIBHÁG, and BIBHÁG (विभाग) Part, portion, division, especially portion of inheritance or partition of property: according to law, either the simple apportionment of the property of a deceased person amongst his heirs, who may nevertheless hold the whole in common, or, as more usually employed, the several distribution of the shares amongst the sharers, and their mutual separation.

Jívad-vibhága, S. (from जीवत्, living) Partition made during the life of a father.

Ajívad-vibhága, S. (अजीवत्, not living) Partition after a father's decease.

Prahása-vibhága, S. (from प्रकाश, manifest) A public partition made in the presence of witnesses.

Rahasya-vibhága, S. (from रहस्य, secret) Partition made privately in the presence of a few friends only.

Anyonya-vibhága, S. (from अन्योन्य, one with another) Mutual partition made by the sharers without the presence of any other persons.

Sama-vibhága, S. (सम, equal) Division of the property amongst the sons in equal shares.

Vibhága-bhák, S. (भाक्, who shares) One who shares in property already distributed, as a son born subsequently to the partition of the paternal inheritance.

Vibhága-patriká, S. (पत्रिका, a leaf) A deed of partition, the deed drawn up at the time of partition which should specify whether the property is ancestral or acquired, the particulars of its acquisition, the names of the sharers with their respective shares: it should be signed by the parties, witnessed and dated.

Vibhakta, S. &c. (विभक्त, past part. of विभज, to divide) Divided, separated; either the property, or, as applied to persons, the sharer who has separated from his coheirs and holds his portion in severalty.

Vishama-vibhága, S. (विषम, unequal) Division of the property by the father in his lifetime amongst his sons in different proportions, which may take place with property self-acquired, not with ancestral property: after the father's death the sons divide equally, although under the ancient law the eldest son was entitled to a larger portion, or to a preferential choice of certain articles, and the practice prevails in some places, or in some families, especially in the Dakhin, where also various modifications of the law of partition are admitted in different castes and with reference to different hereditary rights and possessions.

VIBHAVA, S. (विभव) The second year of the Hindu cycle, A.D. 1808 in the current cycle.

VICHÁRA, S. &c. vernacularly, VICHÁR (विचार) Investigation, judgment.

Vichárane, erroneously, *Vecharanai*, Karn. (ವಿಚಾರಣೆ) Superintendence, management.

Vicharanekarta, Karn. (ವಿಚಾರಣೆಕರ್ತ) A superintendant, a manager.

Vijárippu, Tam. (விசாரிப்பு) Management, superintendence: a district or village, &c. under any one's charge.

Vijárippukáran, Tam. (விசாரிப்புக்காரன்) An administrator, a manager.

VIDAI, Tam. (விதை) Seed of plants: also *Virai*, q. v.

Vidaittal, Tam. (விதைத்தல்) Sowing.

Vidaippunam, Tam. (விதைப்புனம்) A spot of ground newly cultivated.

VIDEṢA, S. &c. (विदेश) A foreign country.

Videṣastha, S. &c. (विदेशस्थ) One living abroad.

Videṣí, S. &c. (विदेशी) Foreign, foreigner.

VIDHA, Tel. (S. విధ) Hire, wages.

VIDHAVÁ, S. &c., vernacularly VIDHWÁ (विधवा) A widow (*vi*, without, *dhava*, a husband).

VIDHI, S. &c. (विधि) A rule, a precept, especially one enjoining some particular act or observance in law or religion, any act, or rite, or ceremony, so enjoined.

VÍDU, Tam. (வீடு) A house.

Viṭṭukkuḍaiyavan, Tam. (வீட்டுக்குடையவன்) The master or owner of a house, a landlord.

Viṭṭuppaḍiyán, Tam. (வீட்டுப்படியான்) A field or outdoor servant who receives his daily hire in rice-corn.

VIDYÁ, S. &c. (विद्या) Knowledge of any kind, learning, science, art, &c.

Vidyádhana, S. &c. (धन, wealth) Money acquired by teaching.

VIDYAMÁNA, S. &c., vernacularly, VIDYAMÁN, corruptly, VIDYMÁN, WEEDYMAN, Mar. (विद्यमान) Being present: applied in Mar. to the presence of a third person as a witness in money transactions.

VÍJA, S. &c. vernacularly, VÍJ, or BÍJ (वीज) Seed, lit. or fig.

Víjí, S. (वीजी) A sower: a progenitor: the kinsman appointed by a childless man to raise up issue by his wife: the father of a son legally begotten on another's wife.

VIJAYA, S. &c. (विजय) Victory: the twenty-seventh year of the cycle.

VIJAYÁ, S. &c. (विजया) Hemp: also a name given to the 3d, 8th, and 12th days of the lunar fortnight: see also the next.

Vijayádaṣamí, (विजयादशमी) The tenth lunation of the light half of *Áswin* (Sept.-Oct.) on which the image of Durgá, on the termination of the festival in her honour, is cast into the water.

VIKÁRÍ, S. &c. (विकारी) The twenty-third year of the cycle = A.D. 1839-40.

VIKRAMA, S. &c. (विक्रम) The fourteenth year of the cycle.

Vikraya, S. &c. (**विक्रय**) Sale, selling.

Vikrayánusaya, S. (**विक्रयानुशय**) Rescission of sale.

Vikrayí, S. (**विक्रयी**) A vendor, a seller.

Vikríta, S. &c. (**विक्रीत**) Sold.

Vikrítaputra, S. &c. (**विक्रीतपुत्र**) A son sold by his natural parents and bought to be adopted as a son.

Vikríyásampradánam. S. (**विक्रीय**, having sold, **असंप्रदानं**, non-delivery) Non-delivery of an article sold, recission of sale.

Vikṛita, S. &c. (**विकृत**) The twenty-fourth year of the cycle.

Vila, or **Wila**, Mal. (വില), **Vilai**, Tam. (விலை) Price, value.

Vilacharakka, Mal. (വിലച്ചരക്ക) Goods exposed for sale, merchandise, a valuable article.

Vilatírva, Mal. (വിലതീര്) A bill of sale transferring property without any reservation of future claim.

Vilattaram, Mal. (വിലത്തരം) Price or value of corn levied as tax or rent.

Villangamu. Tel. (విల్లంగము) A claim or dispute.

Sarvavillangasuddhigá, Tel. (సర్వవిల్లంగశుద్ధిగా) Without any reservation or claim, a phrase used in bills of sale and transfer.

Vilai, Tam. (விலை) Price, value.

Vilaidundu, Tam. (விலைதுண்டு) A charge on the gross produce of a village, deducted from the share of the villagers and added to that of the government, on account of the difference between the price at which the cultivators had sold their grain and the exported retail prices at the place of sale.

Viḷai, Tam. (விளை) High ground not supplied with water.

Viḷaichchal, Tam. (விளைச்சல்) Ripe corn in the field ready for reaping.

Viḷaiṇar, Tam. (விளைஞர்) Husbandmen, ploughmen.

Viḷai-nilam, Tam. (விளைநிலம்) A field, fertile or arable ground.

Viḷaivu, Tam. (விளைவு) Growing of corn in a field.

Viḷaivupalan, Tam. (விளைவுபலன்) The corn or crop in a field.

Viḷaiyuḷ, Tam. (விளையுள்) A field.

Vilambin, S. &c. (**विलंबिन्**, lit. delaying) The thirty-second year of the cycle = A.D. 1838.

Vílu, Tel. (వీలు) Estimated revenue of a village or district, an arrangement or settlement.

Vílujábitá, Tel. (వీలుజాబితా) An account according to estimate.

Vimarṣa, S. &c. (**विमर्श**) Investigation, trial.

Vímo, Guz. (વીમો) Insurance, a contract of idemnity, by which one party engages for a stipulated payment to make good to another any loss that may arise from accidents: the premium paid to the insurer (this is a corruption of the H. *Bíma*, q. v.).

Vimáni-chiṭhi, Guz. (વીમાનીચીઠી) A policy of insurance.

Vimukkádu, Tam. (விமுக்காடு) Rate.

Viṇai, Tam. (வினை) Work, action.

Viṇaiseyvor, Tam. (வினைசெய்வோர்) Servants, labourers.

Viṇaiṇar, Tam. (வினைஞர்) Artificers, ploughmen, men of the servile or labouring classes.

Vináyakuḍu, Tel. (వినాయకుడు) The vernacular form of **Vináyaka**, S., a name of Ganesa, but as a revenue term it signifies a certain quantity of grain offered to that deity at the time of measuring.

Vinnapam, Tel. (విన్నపం, S **विज्ञापनं**) Respectful representation, petition.

Vipala, vernacularly, **Wipal**, or **Bipal**. S. &c. (**विपल**) An instant, the sixteenth part of a *pal*. See *Pala*.

Virá, (?) Mar. A local tax or cess on persons possessing rent-free lands. Bom. Reg. xvii. 1827.

Vírasaivar, Tam. (வீரசைவர்) A name given to the followers of *Basava*, or the Jangamas, the worshippers and wearers of the Linga, a type of Siva.

Virai, Tam. (விரை) Seed of plants.

Viraigal, Tam. (விரைகால்) Land fit for sowing.

Viraippadu, Tam. (விரப்பாடு) Sowing a field.

Viraippu, Tam. (விரைப்பு) Land on which seed is sown.

Virálamu, Tel. (విరాళము) A tax or impost.

Virāttam, pron. **Vrattam**, Tam. (விராத்தம்) Collection of tribute or rent.

Viráttakkáran, Tam. (விராத்தக்காரன்) A collector, a tax-gatherer.

Virodhakṛit, S. &c. (**विरोधकृत**, making obstruction) The forty-fifth year of the cycle, A.D. 1851

Virodhí, S. &c. (**विरोधी**, obstructing) The twenty-third year of the cycle.

Viruddhasambandha, S. (**विरुद्ध**, opposed, **संबन्ध**, connexion) Degree of consanguinity or relationship, within which marriage is prohibited, extending to seven degrees, or all connected by offerings of the funeral cake or *Sapindas*.

Virutti, Mal. (വിരുത്തി) Land, &c. granted by the government free of tax or assessment on condition of performing any public service when required without pay.

Viruttikáran, Mal. (വിരുത്തിക്കാരൻ) A person holding land free of rent or tax on condition of public service.

VÍSA, Karn. (ವೀಸ), VÍSAMU, or VÍSAM, corruptly, VISSUM, VEESUM, Tel. (వీసము), VÍSAM, Tam. (வீசம்) The sixteenth part or fraction of any thing: a weight of gold equal to one grain of rice-corn: a measure of land equal nearly to two acres: a share, a portion.

Vísabaḍi, or *Vísubaḍi*, corruptly, *Veesabuddy*, *Vissabady*, *Veespaddi*, Tel. (వీసబడి, వీసుబడి) In the ceded districts, and Telingana, under the Madras Presidency, a coparcenary village, of which the lands or profits are allotted by sixteenths and fractions of sixteenths, among the hereditary proprietors: the revenues of such a village being engaged for by some of the principal sharers, the proportions are allotted in the same way as the lands, so that a distinct portion of the gross revenue is fixed upon every field or lot of land: a *Vísabaḍi*, settlement is therefore identified with the settlement by fields or their individual cultivators, and is the same as a Ryotwar settlement: also a tax on the profits of trade levied in periodically settled proportions upon the merchants, traders, shopkeepers, retail dealers, mercantile agents, and all the inhabitants of a village or town engaged in trade.—Madras Reg. iv. 1818.

VÍSAI, Tam. (வீசை), VÍSE, Tel., Karn. (వీసె) A weight in use at Madras, commonly called *Viss*, one-eighth of a Madras *maund*, or 3lb. 2oz. avoirdupois.

VÍSÁLU, Tel. (వీసాలు) An elementary weight, equal to one grain of rice.

VISÁRA, or VISÁRÁ, WISÁRA, &c. Mar. (विसार, विसारा) Earnest money.

VISARJANA, S. &c. (विसर्जन) Gift, donation, dismissal: setting a bull at liberty on particular occasions: throwing images of divinities into the water at the close of festivals in their honour.

VISHA, S. &c., vernacularly, VISH, or BISH, (विष) Poison, any poisonous substance, animal, vegetable, or mineral: in Hindustan it especially indicates the root or juice of the Aconitum ferox.

Vishpadárth, Mar. (S. पदार्थ, a substance) Poisonous substances and drugs collectively, especially those specified in Bombay Reg. xiv. xxi. 1827.

VISHṆU, S. &c. (विष्णु) The second of the three principal deities of the Hindus, the preserving power personified.

Vishṇubhakta, S. (विष्णुभक्त) A worshipper of Vishṇu in one or other of his manifestations, especially as Rámachandra or as Krishṇa.

Vishṇupríti, S. (विष्णुप्रीति) Land granted rent-free to Brahmans in honour of Vishṇu, or to maintain his worship.

Vishṇúttara, S. &c. (विष्णूत्तर) A grant of rent-free land for the worship of Vishṇu.

VISHṬI, S. &c. (विष्टि) Labour, especially enforced and unpaid labour: also, wages, hire.

VIṢHU, Mar. &c. (विषु, S. equal) The equinox, either vernal or autumnal; also the fifteenth year of the cycle.

Vishuva, S. (विषुव) The sun's entrance into Aries and Libra: the vernal or autumnal equinox.

VISVÁSÍ, corruptly, WISWUSSA, Guz. (વીસવાસી) A land-measure, one-twentieth of a *Vasá*, q. v., $\frac{1}{400}$th of a *bighá*: a nominal coin of the lowest value, $\frac{1}{1000}$th of a rupee.

VIṢWÁVASU, S. &c. (विश्वावसु) The thirty-ninth year of the cycle.

VÍṬ, WEET, Mar. (वीट) Blight, mildew.

VÍTAM, Tam. (வீதம்) A share, a portion; a rate.

VITASTI, S. &c. (वितस्ति) A long span measured by the thumb and little finger extended, considered equal to 12 fingers.

VÍṬIKÁ, S. &c. (वीटिका) A preparation of pieces of Areka nut with spices and a small quantity of caustic lime, rolled up in a leaf of the Piper Betel and used for mastication. See *Pán*.

VITTA, S. &c. vernacularly, VIT, or WIT, (वित्त) Wealth, substance.

Vittavishaya, or *Vittvishay*, barbarously, *Weetweesaye*, Mar. (वित्तविषय) Riches, possessions.

VIṬṬAL, Tam. (விற்றல்) Selling, sale.

VITTU, Tam. Tel. (வித்து, విత్తు), VITTA, Mal. (വിത്ത), VITTANAMU, Tel. (విత్తనము) Seed of plants.

Vittara, Mal. (വിത്തര) A certain rent paid by a cultivator or renter to the proprietor, or as a tax to the government, amounting to half the quantity of seed sown.

Vittanalu-jábitá, Tel. (from A. ضابطه) A statement of the description and quantity of seed sown by each Ryot.

Vittukál, Mal. (വിത്തുകാൽ) Rent or tax equal to a fourth of the seed sown.

Vittumáṯṯam, Mal. (വിത്തുമാററം) Harrowing, after sowing.

Vittupáṭa, Mal. (വിത്തുപാട) The quantity of ground sown.

Vittupáti, Mal. (വിത്തുപാതി) An agreement between the cultivator and proprietor, by which the latter allows the former half the seed, and receives half the produce.

Vittupáṭṭam, Mal. (വിത്തുപാട്ടം) Rent or tax equal to the whole amount of the seed sown.

Vittuvali, incorrectly, *Vettoovally*, Mal. (വിത്തുവലി) Seed and labour.

VIṬṬUMUDAL, Tam. (விற்றுமுதல்) Proceeds of sale.

VIVÁDA, S. &c. (**विवाद**) Dispute, discussion, a legal dispute. a law-suit.

VIVÁHA, S. &c. (**विवाह**), VEVÁ, VEVÁHA, VEHEVÁ, Guz. (વેવા, વેવાહ, વેહેવા) Marriage, of which eight forms are enumerated by Manu: 1. *Bráhma*, the gift of a daughter to a Brahman bridegroom learned in the Vedas, voluntarily invited: Tam. *Aranilai*. 2. *Daiva*, the gift of a daughter to the officiating priest at a sacrifice. 3. *Ársha* or that of the *Ṛishis*, in which the father of the bride receives from the bridegroom one or two pair of kine: Tam. *Porul-kol* and *Áridam*. 4. *Prájapatya*, that of the *Prajápatis*, or patriarchs, in which the father gives away his daughter with due reverence: Tam. *Oppu*, meaning consent. 5. *Ásura*, that of the *Asuras*, in which the bridegroom makes valuable gifts to the father and relations of the bride: Tam. *Arumponi-vinai*. 6. *Gándharba*, that of the *Gandharbas*, in which the mutual agreement or inclination of the parties is alone necessary: this is considered to comprehend the *Swayambara*, in which a princess chose her husband publicly from a number of suitors assembled for the occasion: Tam. *Yáḻor-kúttam*. 7. *Ráhshasa*, that of the *Rahshasas*, or evil spirits, the violent abduction of a maiden after defeating or slaying her relations: Tam. *Irákkadam* (the *i* being prefixed for euphony). 8. *Paisácha*, that of the *Pisáchas* or goblins, the violation of a girl when asleep or in liquor, or of weak intellect: Tam. *Péy-nilai*. Some of these forms are considered to be illegal, and the one more commonly in use is the *Ásura*, in which presents are made to the father.

Viváhaswámí, S. (from **स्वामी**, a lord, a husband) A husband, but especially a first husband, second marriages being allowed amongst some of the inferior castes in the Dakhin.

VIVÁSA, S. (**वि**, separate, **वास**, dwelling) Banishment, expulsion from house and home.

VIYOGÍ, vernacularly, BIJOGI, corruptly, BEYJOGEE, S. &c. (**वियोगी**) One who is separated from society, applied especially to a religious mendicant who is unmarried and has no family: the reverse of *Sanyogí*.

VIYYAMU, Tel. (వియ్యము) Connexion by affinity or marriage.

Viyyanhuḍu, Tel. (వియ్యంకుడు) The mutual connexion of fathers-in-law.

Viyyapurálu, Tel. (వియ్యపురాలు) The mutual affinity of mothers-in-law.

VONDRA, or ONDRA, Tel. (ఒంద్ర) A favourable assessment.—Kondavír.

VOHORO, or WOHORO, also, OHORO, Guz. everywhere else called BOHRA (વોહોરો, ઓહોરો) An individual of a a class of Mohammadan Indians found chiefly in Western India, following various occupations and trades, as pedlars, packers, glaziers, lantern makers, haberdashers, &c.: the more respectable are bankers and merchants: they are divided into two principal tribes denominated *Sulimáni* and *Dáüdi*.

VOWS, Mar. (?) Race, lineage, family (it is either some corruption of, or some blunder for, *Vans* or *Wans*, q. v.)

VRATA, S. &c. (**व्रत**) Any devout or ceremonial observance, as fasting, offering sacrifice, or the like, voluntarily imposed upon one's self: gifts under a self-imposed obligation to Brahmans.

VRÁTYA, S. &c. (**व्रात्य**) A man of either of the three first castes for whom the ceremony of investiture with the characteristic cord had not been performed within the prescribed ages, and who therefore becomes an outcaste: in Tam. *Vrátyan*, (விராத்தியன்) is said to mean a man who is born of a father of low rank by a mother of a higher caste: also one who has relinquished the duty of his tribe.

Vrátyastoma, S. (**व्रात्यस्तोम**) A sacrifice performed by persons who have lost their caste through not receiving investiture, for the purpose of being again allowed to receive it.

VRIDDHA, S. &c. (**वृद्ध**) Old, ancient, an old man, one above seventy.

Vṛuddhapadíyá, Tel. (వృద్ధపడియా) Land uncultivated from time immemorial.

VṚIDDHI, S. &c. (**वृद्धि**), in the dialects of the south, VṚUDDHI (*ṛi* being pronouneed *ṛu*), it also occurs as VAḌḌI, and VAḌḌÍ, Tel. (వడ్డి, వడ్డీ), VṚUDDHI, and BAḌḌI, Karn. (ವೃದ್ಧಿ, ಬಡ್ಡಿ), and VAḌḌI, and VIRUTTÍ, Tam. (விருத்தி) VAḌḌÍ, or VAṬṬÍ, Mal. (വട്ടി) Increase, especially the increase of money, interest: various kinds of interest are recognised by Hindu lawyers, as, 1. *Káyik-vṛiddhi* (from S. *Káya*, body) Bodily interest, explained as either the advantage arising from the body of an animal pledged as security for a loan, or as interest paid repeatedly without reducing the body or principal: Karn., interest on money paid at stated periods; 2. *Káliká-vṛiddhi*, (from *Kála*, time) Periodical, payable weekly, monthly, annually, &c.:

it is most usual in practice to compute interest by the month: in Karnata this term is explained, the usual interest on money left to accumulate (apparently the meanings of this and the preceding being interchanged); 3. *Chahra-vṛiddhi*, (from *Chahra*, a wheel) Compound interest, interest upon interest; 4. *Káritá*, or *Káriká vṛiddhi* (from *Kára*, act) Stipulated interest, interest at a stipulated rate higher than the usual rate, or without regard to the legal rate; 5. *Sikhá-vṛiddhi* (from *Sikhá*, a lock of hair, as growing continually), Interest at a usurious rate, payable daily; 6. *Bhogalábha* (from *bhoga*, use, and *lábha*, getting), Advantage accruing to a creditor from the use of any article handed over to him as security, as the usufruct of land, gardens, beasts, &c.: other terms occur more or less adopted in the dialects, as, *Dharma-vṛiddhi*, Lawful interest; *Anyáya-vṛiddhi*, Improper or usurious interest; *Nidána-vṛiddhi*, Moderate interest; *Parama-vṛiddhi*, or *Pará-vṛiddhi*, Interest at the highest legal rate; *Samáni-vṛiddhi*, Interest at the usual or a moderate rate; *Vástavá*, or *Vástaviká-vṛiddhi*, Established, just, or customary interest.

Vṛiddhi-sṛáddha, S. (वृद्धिश्राद्ध) An offering to the manes celebrated on any joyful occasion, as at the birth of a son, or the like.

VṚIHASPATÍ, S. (वृहस्पति) The planet Jupiter and its regent, the preceptor of the gods.

Vṛihaspati-vára, S. &c. (from वार, a day) Thursday, *dies Jovis*.

VṚINDÁ, S. (वृन्दा) The Tulasí plant, the holy Basil (Ocymum sanctum), personified also as a nymph beloved by Kṛishṇa: a creation of very modern times.

Vṛindávana, vernacularly, *Vrindavan*, and, vulgarly, *Bindraban*, S. (वृन्दावन) A town near Mathurá, fabulously the site of a forest in which *Kṛishna*, as *Gopála*, or the cowherd, passed his youth, associating with the cowboys and milkmaids attached to the cattle grazing in the forest: at present there are but few trees and no pasturage, and probably they never were there: a raised platform or altar of earth in a house in which the followers of *Kṛishṇa* plant and preserve the *Tulasí* or *Vṛindá*.

VṚISHOTSARGA, S. &c. (वृष, a bull, and उत्सर्ग, letting go) Letting a bull go loose at certain ceremonies, as at marriages, obsequies, &c.: the bull is considered sacred, and wanders about unmolested and unappropriated.

VṚITHÁDÁNA, S. &c. (वृथादान) An improper gift, and one that may be annulled, or, if only promised, not performed, as gifts to courtesans, wrestlers, panegyrists, or money lost at play, &c.

VṚITTI, S. &c., in the south, VṚUTTI, in Hindustan changed to BIRT, q. v. (वृत्ति) Maintenance, means of livelihood profession: the proper means of subsistence for a Brahman are 1. *Ṛita* (true), Lawful gleaning; 2. *Amṛita* (immortal), Unsolicited alms; 3. *Mṛita* (deadly), Solicited alms, begging: in time of distress he may have recourse to 4. *Pramṛita* (very deadly) Agriculture; 5. *Satyánṛita* (true and false), Trade, traffic; the last kind, 6. *Śwavṛitti*, or dog-maintenance, that is, servitude, should never be engaged in: the term means, also, a customary allowance, fee, or perquisite, a grant of revenue from a small tract of land made by Zamindárs to indigent Brahmans: lands assigned to Zamindárs, or appropriated by them for their personal support: a particular tenure in Gorakhpur and Benares of the nature of a dependent *táâluk*, granted by a great revenue proprietor to the head man of a village: in the Tamil countries it is applied to the portion of land held in joint proprietary or *Mirási* right by Brahmans.

Vṛittichhed, Mar. (वृत्तिछेद, from S. छेद, cutting off) Confiscation of a patrimony, deprivation of a hereditary office, any taking away of the means of subsistence.

Vṛitti-ijárá, or *Birt-ijárá*, Beng. (P. اجاره) A grant of land in perpetual farm made by a Zamindár to some person for his maintenance at a stipulated amount of revenue payment.

Vritti, or *Britti-mahábráhmaní*, Hindi, &c. (वृत्तिमहाब्राह्मणी) Fees and presents received by a Brahman who conducts funeral obsequies: fees received as of hereditary right by a body of Brahmans at Gaya, where the performance of the *Sráddha*, or obsequial rites is of especial efficacy.

VURTTÍ, VOORTY, (?) Tel. A measure of land.

VYABHICHÁRA, S. &c. (व्यभिचार) Going astray, doing wrong, profligacy, adultery.

Vyabhichárịṇí, S. &c. (व्यभिचारिणी) A loose woman, an adultress.

VYÁHÍ, Mar. (व्याही) The father-in-law of one's son or daughter: the two fathers are so termed respectively to one another, and to their child's mother-in-law (S. *viváhí*, connected by marriage).

VYÁJA, vernacularly, VYAJ, BIAJ, or VIÁJ, S. &c. (व्याज) Interest, usury.

Vyajáú, *Vyájú*, *Vyají*, Mar. (व्याजाऊ, व्याजू, व्याजी) Bearing interest, a loan, a debt.

Vyájkatáwaṇi, or *Vyájphailáwaní*, Mar. (व्याजकटावणी,

व्याजफेलावणी) Making out an interest account, calculating the interest at different periods on sums on either side of the account, and drawing out the balance.

Vyájbaṭá, or *-baṭṭá*, Mar. (व्याजबटा -ट्टा) A general term for the items of the business of a banker or money-lender.

Vyájbharí, Mar. (व्याजभरी) One deeply in debt, whose whole resources are absorbed in the payment of interest.

Viáju, Guz. (વીઆજુ) Lent or borrowed at interest.

Viájhhor, Guz. (વીઆજખોર) A usurer, a money lender.

VYÁJYAMU, Tel. (వ్యాజ్యము) A dispute, a law-suit.

Vyájyarthadu, Tel. (వ్యాజ్యర్థుడు) A suitor, a litigant.

VYÁPÁRA, vernacularly BYÁPÁRA, S. &c. (व्यापार) Business, affairs, trade, occupation, profession.

Vyápárí, vernacularly, *Byápári*, &c. S. (व्यापारी) A trader, a dealer, a man of business.

VYÁSA, S. &c. (व्यास) A celebrated sage, the reputed arranger of the Vedas in their present form.

Vyásanthole, (?) The model of a hand said to be carried in procession by the *Lingaits*, in commemoration of the alleged amputation of the hand of Vyása.

Vyásokta, S. (व्यास, and उक्त, said) A class of Brahmans in Bengal said to have been constituted Brahmans by the appointment of Vyása.

VYASANA, S. &c. (व्यसन) Vice, dissipation, profligacy.

VYAVAHÁRA, vernacularly, BYOHÁR, BYOUHAR, H. q. v., S. &c. (व्यवहार), VEVEHÁR, WEWEHÁR, Guz. (વેવેહાર) Affairs, business, worldly occupation, as trade, profession, &c.: but especially judicial procedure, practice of the courts of law, administration of justice, both civil and criminal: law-suit.

Vyavahára-vishaya, S. (व्यवहारविषय) Object or title of legal procedure: according to Manu the titles or subjects are 18: 1. *Ṛinádána*, Contraction of debt; 2. *Nikshepa*, Deposit, bailment; 3. *Asvámivikraya*, Sale without ownership or authority; 4. *Sambhúya samutthána*, Concerns amongst partners; 5. *Dattápradániha*, Resumption of gift; 6. *Vetanádana*, Non-payment of wages; 7. *Samvid vyatikrama*, Breach of agreement; 8. *Krayavikrayá nuṣaya*, Rescission of sale and purchase; 9. *Swámipálayor viváda*, Disputes between master and dependant; 10. *Símá viváda*, Boundary disputes; 11. *Váhpárushya*, Defamation, abuse; 12. *Daṇḍa párushya*, Assault; 13. *Steya*, Theft; 14. *Sáhasa*, Violent seizure of property, robbery; 15. *Strísangraha*, Adultery; 16. *Strípumdharma*, Duties of man and wife; 17. *Dáyabhága*, Partition of inheritance; 18. *Dyúta*, Gambling: these titles are sometimes differently classed, and a few are added, as *Vyavahára mátrika*, Legal process in general; *Sákshya*, Oral evidence; *Lekhya*, Written testimony; *Divya*, Ordeal; *Abhyupetya susrúshá*, Contracted service; and *Prakírnaka*, Miscellaneous.

Vyavahárí, *Vyavaháriká*, S. &c. (व्यवहारी, व्यवहारिक) Relating to law or judicial procedure: a suitor, a litigant: an adult, one who is of age to manage his own affairs, one who is engaged in the active occupations of life.

Vyavahári Jyotishí, barbarously, *Wywharee josee*, Mar. (S. व्यवहारी ज्योतिषी) A Brahman who, besides the duties of daily worship, conducts the ceremonies of initiation, marriages, and, in some places, funerals, and keeps the kalendar; he is entitled to certain fees and perquisites which he may dispose of to others: in some cases he also discharges the duties of the *Dharmádhikárí*, having authority to investigate alleged infractions of caste, to prescribe penance, impose fines, and sentence loss of caste.

VYAVASÁYA, S. &c. (व्यवसाय) Labour, effort, active occupation. VEVASAYA, or WEWASAY, Mar. (वेवसाय) Buying and selling, trade, traffic. VYAVASÁYAMU, Tel. (వ్యవసాయము) Agriculture, cultivation.

VYAVASTHÁ, corruptly, BYWUSTAH, BYWUSTER, barbarously, WYWAUST, S. &c. (व्यवस्था), VIVASTHÁ, or VEVASTHÁ, or WIWASTHÁ, &c. Mar. (विवस्था) Separating, setting apart: settlement, arrangement: a written opinion on points of law, with citation of the original texts on which it is based, given by Hindu law Pandits.

Vyavasthá patra, S, (पत्र, a leaf) The written dictum or opinion of a Hindu lawyer.

VYAYA, S. (व्यय) Expense, outgoing: the twentieth year of the cycle = A.D. 1826.

W.

WÁBASTAH, H. (P. وابسته) Bound to, connected with, dependant upon: a dependant, a relation, an adherent.

Wábastagí, H. (وابستگي) Dependence, connexion, adherence.

WÂDA, H. (A. وعده), WÁYADÁ, Mar. (वायदा) A promise, an agreement, an engagement, especially with a fixed term, a farm, a contract.

Wâdabandí, H. (وعدهبندي) An agreement, especially for the payment of money at a stipulated period.

Wâdadár, H. (وعدہدار) One who is bound by an engagement, a contractor, a government officer responsible for the collections of a Zamíndárí, a farmer of the revenue.

Wâdadári, H. (وعدہداري) Farm of the revenue of a district, making a contract or engagement.

Wâdahkhiláfi, H. (A. خلاف, contrary to) Breach of promise or engagement.

Wáyade-chiṭṭhí, or *-rokhá*, Mar. (वायदेचिट्ठी, -रोखा) A written engagement, especially with a specified term for its fulfilment.

WADÂ, or WIDÂ, H. (A. ودع) Depositing or entrusting any thing to another.

Wadiât, H. (A. وديعت) A deposit, a trust, any article or property given in charge or trust to another.

WAḌÁRA, WAḌÁRÍ, Mar. (वडार, वडारी) A low caste, or a member of it, whose chief occupation is killing rats and vermin.

WAḌÍL, Mar. (वडील) An ancestor.

Waḍlopárjita, Mar. (वडलोपार्जित, from S. उपार्जित, acquired) Amassed or acquired by one's ancestors, property, &c.

Waḍlo, *Waḍliṉ*, Mar. (वडलो, वडलीं) By or through ancestors.

WAFÁ, H. (A. وفا) Faith, fidelity, keeping a promise or engagement, a conditional or security sale: see *Baia-bil-wafá*.

WÁGUZÁSHTA, H. (P. واگذاشته) Released from attachment or distraint, relieved from assessment, remitted.

WAHÁBI, H. (A. وحابي) A follower of the doctrines of an Arabian reformer of Mohammadanism, *Shaikh-ul-Wahâb*, who attempted to reform many of the abuses that had crept into the religion, especially the practices of the Shías: in India it has become a term of abuse equivalent to infidel or unbeliever

WAHÍ, corruptly, WYHEE, Mar. (वही) A stitched book for accounts, of which several are kept by bankers and merchants, as the *Kachcha-wahí*, rough cash or day-book; *Pakka-wahí*, daily cash-book or journal, shewing receipts and disbursements; *Nakl-wahí*, a register of *hundís* or bills drawn, accepted, and paid; *Jarígar-wahí*, in which an account is kept of goods given to a broker for sale; *Chiṭhṭha-wahí*, a letter-book; *Vyáj*, or *Wajuk-wahí*, interest account-book, &c.: it is the *Bahi* of Bengal, q. v.

WÁHIB, H. (A. واهب) A giver, a donor: in law, one who executes a deed of gift.

WÁHÍL, WÁHEL, Mar. (वाहील, वाहेल) Tillage, cultivation.

Wáhíl, Mar. (वाहील) Cultivated, not waste.

WAHIWÁṬ, Mar. (वहिवाट) Administration, management.

Wahiwáṭdár, Mar. (वहिवाटदार) An officer entrusted with the conduct of any important business, as the government of a province or collection of the revenue: the representative or manager of the affairs of an individual, especially in his absence.

WAHM, H. (A. وهم) Opinion, imagination: in law, suspicion, doubt, notion of the improbability of a charge, or doubt of the evidence.

WAIRÁN, WIRÁN, H. (A. ويران) Desolate, depopulated, waste: a village under the head man of a different village.

Wairána, H. (ويرانه) A deserted or desolate place.

Wairán-kheṛá, H. (كهيڑا, from S. खेट) Deserted site of a village.

WÁJÁ, (?) Name of a military and agricultural tribe in *Kattiwár*,

WAJAB, H. (P. وجب) A space of nine inches.

WAJH, H. (A. وجه) Cause, motive: face, appearance: also P. and H., wages, hire, salary.

Wajáhat, *Wajuh*, H. (A. وجاهت, وجوه) In law, personal respectability, credit.

Wajhá, H. (وجها) Salary, pension.

Wajh-i-hál, H. (وجهحال) Mode of living, state of circumstances.

Wajh-i-kiraia, H. (وجه كرايه) Ground-rent, charges for lodging.

Wujúh, *Wujúhát*, corruptly, *Ojoohat*, H. (وجوهات, وجوه, pl.) Salaries, allowances, wages: extra collections by Zamíndárs for personal expenses: in law, pleas, reasons, or grounds of appeal; also the summing up of the judge, with the grounds of his decision.

Wujúhát-i-kháṣ-navísi, H. (خاص نويس, government writer) A former cess on account of the salaries of government clerks.

WÁJIB, H. (واجب) Right, proper, necessary.

Wájib-ul-ârz, H. (A. واجب العرض) Lit. Fit for, or worthy of representation: a petition, a written statement or representation, a written agreement: in the north-west provinces it designates what is considered to be the most important of the documents relating to the village administration, describing the established mode of paying the government revenue, the actual shares or holdings, whether held in severalty or in common, and how separation or re-allotment takes place, the powers and privileges of the Lambardárs, and how elected, what extra items of collection are recognised, the rules regarding fruit and timber trees on the estate, and how irrigation is maintained; the appropriation of waste lands, the village servants and their fees, and the pay of the village watchmen: it should be, in fact, a complete view of the organization of the village, and is to be attested by the signatures of all the Lambardárs and as many of the shareholders as choose to sign, and by the signatures of the Patwárí and Kánungo: it should be read aloud in open court in the hearing of the subscribing parties and the settlement officer, and be approved and signed also by him: the term seems to have been superseded of late years by *Khewaṭ*.

Wájib-ul-ḳatl, H. (A. واجب القتل) Deserving death, capital, as an offence.

Wájab-miti, Mar. (वाजबमिती) The true time: the actual date of an occurrence set down in a bond or other document, either before or after its happening.

WAJJHÁ, Mar. (वज्झा) A man following the double occupation of blacksmith and carpenter.

WAḲF, H. (وقف) A bequest for religious or charitable purposes, an endowment, an appropriation of property by will or by gift to the service of God in such a way that it may be beneficial to men, the donor or testator having the power of designating the persons to be so benefited.

Waḳf-náma, H. (P. نامه, a document) A written deed of endowment.

WAKHÁR, Mar. (वखार) A warehouse, a store-room.

Wakhárdár, Mar. (वखारदार) A store-keeper.

WÁḲÎ H. (A. واقع) Happening, occurring.

Wáḳîa, H. (A. واقعه) Event, occurrence: news, intelligence.

Waḳáiâ, H. (A. وقايع, plur. of *Waḳûa* وقعه) Events, occurrences, news.

Waḳáiâ-navís, or *-nigár*, corruptly, *Waḳeh-negar*, *Wakenegar*, H. (وقايعنويس -نگار, from P. *navís*, a writer, or *nigár*, an inspector) A remembrancer, a recorder of events: an officer on the royal establishment under the Moguls, who kept a record of the various orders issued by, and transactions connected with, the sovereign, in the revenue department: an officer of this denomination was also attached to the *Názim* or provincial governor, who reported to the principal remembrancer at the court the particular revenue transactions of the province: any communicator of official intelligence.

Wákanivís, or *-nís*, vernacular form of the preceding, Mar. (वाकनिवीस -नीस) An officer on a great man's establishment, the manager of the household and chief caterer, a sort of major-domo: under *Sivají* the *Wákanís* was one of the eight principal ministers whose duty it was to keep the private journal, records, and letters, and to superintend the household troops and establishment: any news-writer or intelligencer (but little known in this sense).

Fil-wáḳîa, H. (A. في الواقعه) In fact, truly, actually.

WAKÍL, WUKEEL, often read VAKÍL, VUKEEL, VAGÍL, corruptly, VAQUEEL, H. &c. (A. وكيل) A person invested with authority to act for another, an ambassador, a representative, an agent, an attorney: in India, an authorised public pleader in a court of justice. Ben. Reg. xxvii. 1814. Act xiii. 1838. Mad. Act vii. 1843: amongst the Maraṭhas also the hereditary assistant of the *Deṣmukh*: a cess imposed to meet the expense of entertaining a *Wakíl*.

Wakálat, or *Vakálat*, corruptly, *Vaqualut*, H. (A. وكالت) Representation, agency, attorneyship, the office of a *Wakíl*.

Wakálat-mufridát, H. (A. from مفرد, single, simple) Special agency limited to some particular transaction.

Wakálat-náma, *Vakálat-náma*, H. (P, نامه, a document) Credentials, letter of authority, power of attorney.

Wakíl-muṭlaḳ, H. (وكيل مطلق) A plenipotentiary, a representative with absolute powers.

WAKLA, WUKLA, (?) Mar. A bullock-load of grain.

WÁL, or WÁLÁ, H. (A. وال, والا) Used only in composition it denotes a person who does any act, is possessed of any property, is charged with any duty, &c., as, *rakh-wálá*, a guard or guardian; *gáo-wálá*, or *gwálá*, a cowkeeper; *ghar-wálá*, the master of the house; *Dilli-wálá*, a man or inhabitant of Dehli, &c.: (its origin is uncertain, but it is probably from the S. adjunct *ván*, in the sense of having, possessing, as *dhana-ván*, having wealth, wealthy: in Telugu it becomes *váḍu*, or *wáḍu*.

WALÁ, also WILÁ, A. (ولا, lit., proximity, kin, friendship) In Mohammadan law, a peculiar relation voluntarily established, and conferring a right of inheritance on one or both of the parties so connected: it is of two kinds.

Walá-âtáḳat, or *-niâmat*, (from عتاقة, manumission, or نعمت, favour) Relationship between a master and a manumitted slave in which the former inherits any property the latter may acquire after emancipation.

Walá-muwálát, A. (from موالات, related persons) The connexion arising out of mutual friendship, especially between a Mohammadan and a convert. See *Maulá*.

WÁLÁJÁH, or WÁLÁSHÁN, (والاجاه, والاشان, from P. والا, superior) High in rank, noble, of great dignity.

WALA, (?) A Rajput tribe forming the ruling tribe in Kátiwar.

WALAD, WULUD, H. (A. ولد) A son.

Walad-maghrúr, A. (ولدمغرور) In law, the son of a person who has mistaken the condition of the mother, as begotten on a female within the prohibited degrees of relationship without his being aware of it, or on a female slave supposing her to be a free woman: in the latter, the child is the property of the master of the slave, but the father may redeem it.

Wálid, H. (A. والد) A father. *Wálida*, (والدة) A mother.

Walagbeth, (?) Dues claimed by the *Padhán*, or head man of a village.—Kamaon.

Wáland, Guz. (વાલંદ) A barber, a village barber.

Wali, H. (A. ولي) A master, a friend, a prince, a saint: in law the term indicates the relation, natural or legal, in which one person stands to another, as a guardian, a trustee, protector, or the like; also, the person entitled to exact retaliation for personal injury or murder committed upon a kinsman or connexion.

Waliâhad, H. (A. ولي عهد) An heir, especially to a sovereignty, the heir apparent, a vicegerent, a deputy.

Wali-bâíd, H. (A. بعيد, remote) A legal guardian of a more remote degree than father, brother, or uncle.

Wali-jabír, or *-majbír*, A. (ولي جبير،-مجبير) An authoritative guardian recognised by the law.

Wali-jináyat, A. (ولي جناية) The next of kin, or other person entitled to exact retaliation for offences against the person of a relative, or of one under his charge.

Waliniamat, H. (A. ولي نعمت) A title of respect designating a father, a patron, a benefactor.

Wali-ud-dam, A. (ولي الدم) A person entitled to exact retaliation, or the price of blood.

Wálít, Mar. (वाळीत) Ejected or turned out of a caste: outcaste; also, sub., the expulsion of one from his caste.

Walras, (?) Guz. A spot of land in a jangal prepared for tillage by burning the bushes and brushwood and leaving the ashes as manure.

Walsari, (?) Mar. A sandy soil, a variety of the Támri, copper or red soil.

Waluvan, (?) Mal. A class of agrestic slaves in Malabar.

Wám, H. (P. وام) Debt, either lending or borrowing, a loan.

Wámdár, H. (وامدار) A debtor, a creditor.

Wámkhwáh, H (P. وام خواه) A creditor.

Wángí, Mar. (वानगी) A sample, a specimen, a portion of grain or goods exacted by the hereditary officers of a village, portion of produce presented by the lessee to the lessor of a garden, plantation, &c., a portion of an article given to the officers of the customs, over and above the duty, as a perquisite: a tax on grain, &c., brought to a market, originally granted to the person opening it, but reverting to government.

Wáṇí, Mar. (वाणी, S. वणिज) A particular caste, or member of it, usually a retail dealer: a grocer or corn-chandler, the *Banya* of Bengal.

Wanjárá, or Wanjárí, Mar. Guz. (वंजारा -री) A particular caste, or a member of it, carriers of grain: see *Banjára*: the same caste, but following a different occupation, makers of coarse hempen cloths and bags.

Wanjár, Mar. (वंजार) A camp or company of *Banjáras*.

Wánṭá, or Wáṭá, corruptly, Waunta, Mar. (वांटा, वाटा, the H. *Bát, Batái*, S. *Vata, Vanta*) Share, part, portion, division: also *Vanta*, q. v.: in Guzerat it denotes lands either exempt from assessment or held at a quit-rent, chiefly by Rajputs, although sometimes by *Kolis* and Mohammadans: the tenure is prescription of remote antiquity without any deeds or grants.

Wánṭedár, Wánṭekarí, Wánṭelí, &c. Mar. (वांटेदार, वांटेकरी, वांटेली, &c.) A sharer, a divider, a partaker.

Wánṭaṇí, or *Wánṭṇí*, Mar. (वांटणी) Distributing, apportioning: a share, a portion.

Wánṭṇi-báb, Mar. (from बाब, an item) Items of shares of assessment to be divided among the cultivators.

Wánṭṇipatra, Mar. (S. पत्र, a leaf) A writing or document exhibiting the proportions in which patrimonial or other property is to be distributed.

Wáṛ, Wári, also Vátí, and Báti, or Baṛí, (H. واڑ, واري, from S. वाटी) An inclosure, a garden, a house, a dwelling: see *Váda*.

Wáṛkuṛe, Mar. (वाडकुडे) A yard round a house.

Wara, (?) Guz. A portion of land assigned to each member of a *Koli* village at a quit-rent.

Wáraṇ, or Váran, Guz. (વારણ, from the English 'warrant') A writ, an order for the apprehension of a criminal.

Warát, Mar. (वरात) A marriage procession, an assignment on the revenues. See *Barát*.

Wáṛhí, or Wáḍhí, Mar. (वाढी) Surplus (of grain, &c.) given by way of compensation in returning a quantity borrowed.

Wáṛhí-diṛhi, Mar. (वाढीदिढी) The practice of borrowing or lending grain, &c., on condition of receiving back half as much again, more or less.

Wárid, H. (A. وارد) Coming, approaching.

Wáridát, H. (واردات, plur. of وارد) Events, occurrences, circumstances.

Wárid-ṣádir, H. (A. وارد صادر) A guest, a traveller.

WAṚÍL, or WAḌÍL, Mar. (वडील) One from whom a person descends, an ancestor, an elder, a superior, the head of a family.

Waṛílpana, Mar. (वडीलपण, from वडील, best, and पण, affix, implying the abstract, as 'hood,' &c. in English) The rights and privileges of the eldest member or head of a family; also those of the eldest son, primogeniture (the first word is only a various reading of the preceding, substituting *r* for *ṛ*).

Waṛílparampará, Mar. (वडीलपरंपरा) Line or succession of ancestors.

WÁRIṢ, H: &c. (A. وارث), VARASU, Tel. (వరసు) An heir any one having right of heritage.

Warṣa, or *Wirṣa*, H. &c. (A. ورثه), *Wárasá*, Mar. (वारसा) *Várasu*, Tel., Karn. (వారసు) Heritage, an inheritance, a property acquired by inheritance or bequest, any claim or title to property.

Warṣa, or *Wirṣa-dár*, H. (ورثه‌دار), *Wárisdár*, or *Wársedár*, Mar. (वारिसदार, वारसेदार), *Várasudár*, Tel. Karn. (వారసుదారు) An heir, a proprietor by hereditary right.

Warṣanáma, or *Wáriṣnámá*, H. &c. (ورثنامه, वारिसनामा) A document setting forth a claim to inheritance.

Waráṣat-náma, or *Varásat-náma*, incorrectly, *Verasut-nama*, H. (P. نامه) A deed or document, either in proof of the distribution of an inherited property, or of being legal heir of the deceased.

Wiráṣat, H. (A. وراثت) Heritage, hereditary right, receiving by inheritance, the condition of being heir.

WÁRKAR, (?) Mar. A sort of money-lender amongst the Maraṭhas, frequenting the weekly markets and lending small sums of money for short periods at a high rate of interest (from *wára*, or *vára*, a day).

Wárkari, (?) Mar. A cess or tax levied on the preceding class or money-lenders.

WARKAS, Mar. (वरकस) Common denomination for the inferior grains, for all except rice and the kinds of pulse: it is also applied to the dry cultivation, and to the lands on which it is carried on.

Warkas-jamín, Mar. (from P. زمين) Land suited to the cultivation alone of the inferior grains.

WARRU, (?) The name of a tribe in Katiwar.

WAS, Mar. (वस, also *Os* ओस, q. v.) Desolate, forsaken, as a village: uncultivated, as land.

WAS, Guz. (વસ) Division of a *Koli* village under its own head man.

WAṢÍ, corruptly, WUSSEE, H. (A. وصي) A testator, one who commands, recommends, or bequeaths any thing: an executor, an administrator, a guardian, meaning one appointed by will, in distinction from the *Wali*, or natural guardian.

Waṣáia, *Waṣiat*, H. (A. وصايه, وصية) A precept, a command: in law, a will or testament defined to be the endowment of any thing or person with his property by an individual, after his demise: a will can convey away only one-third of the testator's property, except with the consent of the lawful heirs, and in the order of discharge, legacies come after liquidation of debts, before the claims of inheritance.

Waṣiat-náma, corruptly, *Waṣayout-námu*, H. (P. نامه a document) A written will or testament: the will.

WAṢÍKAT, A. (وثيقة) A compact, an agreement, a bond, a written obligation.

WÁṢIL, H. &c (واصل, from وصل) Joined, connected, attached, realized: as a revenue term it implies the amount of revenue collected: it formerly denoted, in Bengal, the amount of all collections from additional sources, as from the annexation of territory, assessment of lands previously rent-free, or resumption of assignment: in Bombay, the total amount of revenue received in the last or a recent year from any portion of land.

Wáṣilát, H. &c. (واصلات, plur. of واصل), *Wásalát*, Mar. (वासलात) Collections of revenue from every head of receipt, the proceeds of an estate, mesne profits of land: in Mar., also, the line having part of the letter *w* at the head, drawn across the paper containing revenue accounts, as the designation of papers on that subject.

Wáṣilát-patra, Uriya (ଓ୍ୱାସିଲାତପତ୍ର) Account of revenues collected.

Wáṣil-báḳí, H. &c. (واصل باقي) Collections and balance, an account shewing the amount of revenue realized, and the remainder outstanding.

Wáṣil-báḳí-kharch, H. (A. خرچ, expense) An account formerly kept shewing the amount of revenue assessed, the portion realized, the balance outstanding, with the deductions for charges of collection: it was drawn up at the close of the year at the settlement of the revenue accounts.

Wuṣúl, H. &c. (وصول), *Wasúl*, Mar. (वसूल) Collections, revenue, rent, &c.: money annually realized by government, proprietors, or bankers.

Wasúlbákí, Mar. (वसूलबाकी) Collection and application or administration of the revenues.

Wasúldár, Mar. (वसूलदार) A collector of revenue.

Wasúlí, Mar. (वसूली) Yielding a good revenue; also an inferior officer employed in the collection of the revenue, likewise *Wasúlyá* (वसूल्या).

Wasúlwásúl, Mar. (वसूलवासूल) Revenue, rent (comprehensively), the collection, appropriation, and management of it.

WASÍLA, H. (A. وسيله) Prop, support, means, mediation, intervention.

Wasiladár, H. (وسيلهدار) A client, a dependant.

WASÍL-BIL-NIKÁH, (?) H. (وسيل به ال نكاه) An agent or negociator in effecting a marriage (? if the first term should not be *Wakíl*, or *Wásit*).

WÁSITA, incorrectly, WÁSTA, WASTAH, H. &c. (A. واسطه) Any thing or person intervening, as an agent, a broker, a middle-man, one who contracts with a dealer to supply him with goods manufactured by others, also *Wasitagár*, and *Wastáni*, and *Wasitadár*, corruptly, *Wastahdár*.

Wásitatâluh, H. (A. واسطهتعلق) A dependent *taâluk*, one subordinate, not to a Zamindár, but to a superior *Taâluhdár*.

WASK, A. (وسق) A load of corn, a horse or camel load.

WÁT, Mar. (वाट) A road, a way. See *Bát*, and *Vát*.

Wátádí, *Wátádyá*, Mar. (वाटाडी -ड्या) A guide, one who accompanies to shew the road.

Wátmárgí, Mar. (वाटमार्गी) A traveller, a wayfarer.

Wátmáryá, Mar. (वाटमाऱ्या) A robber. a highwayman; also *Watpádú*, and *Wátpádyá* (वाटपाडू, वाटपाड्या). See *Bátpár*.

WATAN, WUTUN, incorrectly, WUTTUN, H. &c. (وطن, वतन) Country, native country, place of residence, home: amongst the Marathas it has come to import any hereditary estate, office, privilege, property, or means of subsistence, a patrimony.

Watanbandhu, or *Watanbháú*, Mar. (वतनबंधु, वतनभाऊ) A co-heir, a joint inheritor, also a fellow hereditary officer, one who holds an office jointly with another, a brother *Desmuhh*, a fellow *Pátíl*, &c.; many of the district and village offices, with their emoluments, being held conjointly by more than one individual.

Watandár, Mar. (वतनदार) The holder of a hereditary right, property, or office, with the privileges and emoluments attached to it.

Watanjaptí, Mar. (वतनजप्ती, from A. *zabtí* ضبطي, seizure) Produce of rent-free lands or other emoluments of hereditary officers sequestrated by the government.

Watanpatra, Mar. (S. पत्र, a leaf) Title-deed of hereditary property.

Wataní, Mar. (वतनी) Pertaining to a property or *Watan*, privileges, emoluments, deeds, &c., obtained by inheritance or purchase, held in one's own right.

Watanwárí, Mar. (वतंवाडी) A patrimonial estate, patrimonial lands and tenements.

WAVEYLEY, (?) Guz. The privilege lands granted to village servants and officers.

Waveyleekára, (?) Guz. Village servants and artisans holding rent-free lands.

WAZÍÂ, WAZIÂT, (A. وضيع, وضيعة) Trust, deposit: a deposit: a deduction: in the revenue accounts of the Mohammadan government it designated the authorised deductions from the gross revenue on account of dismembered territory and legal allowances to the Zamindárs. See *Mukhárij* and *Mazkurát*.

WAZÍFA, H. (A. وظيفه, plur. *Wazáif* وظايف) A pension a stipend, a grant of land rent-free, or at a quit-rent, to pious persons, or for past services: revenue collected at a stipulated or fixed rate for a certain quantity of land.

Wazífa-dár, H. (وظيفهدار) The holder of a pension, or of a rent-free grant of land.

WAZN, or WAZAN, H. &c., in the Hindu dialects, WAJAN, or OJAN, (A. وزن, वजन, or, Beng. *Ojan* ওজন) Weight, weighing.

Wazndár, H. &c. (وزندار) A weighman.

Waznkash, H. (وزنكش) A weighman, one who weighs the grain of the village: it appears to be used sometimes laxly for cash-keeper or money-weigher.

Waznkashí, corruptly, *Wozunkushee*, H. (وزنكشي) The office dues or perquisites of the village weighman.

WAZÍR, WUZEER, sometimes VAZÍR, incorrectly, VIZIR, VIZIER, H. &c. (A. وزير, वजीर) The principal minister in a Mohammadan sovereignty.

Wazárat, H. &c. (A. وزارت) The office of prime minister.

WÍGU, or WÍGHU, less correctly, WÍGA, or VÍGA, Guz. (વીગુ, વીઘુ, no doubt a vernacular corruption of *Bíghá*) A land measure in Katiwar, the sixtieth part of a *Santí*, said to measure 160 yards by 10: the Gujarathi *Bíghá* is equal to $284\frac{2}{9}$ square yards.

WILÁYAT, H. &c. (ولايت, विलायत) An inhabited country, a foreign country; applied by the natives of India to England especially, sometimes to Europe generally, and to Persia and Turkey.

Wiláyati, or *Viláyati*, H. (ولايتي) Foreign, European: the name of an æra current in Orissa commencing A.D. $592\frac{3}{4}$.

WINDÁRI, or VINDÁRI, Mar. (विंदारी, from S. विदारण, splitting) The name of a caste, or a member of it, said to be sprung from a Kshatriya mother and Vaiṣya father, whose occupation is drilling beads and pearls, and polishing shells, &c.

WODÁLA, WUDDALA, (?) A class of Mohammadans on the coasts of Gujarat and Kach, manning either trading or pirate boats.

WOLLA-DHARMA, (?) Mal. A private gift to a temple or religious establishment.

WORABAT, (?) H. Inheritance.—Shahabad.

WORRAH, (?) Tel. A well lined with cylinders of coarse earthenware.—Northern Sarkárs.

WOṢÁON, Hindi (वोशाओन) The winnowing of grain.

WOUSH, (?) Mar. Race, family, generation (a blunder, no doubt, for *Vans* or *Wans*).

WOWANḌKARÍ, or OWANḌKARÍ, Mar. (वोवंडकरी, ओवंडकरी) A person cultivating land in a village, but residing in, and belonging to, another.

WUḌIAWÁR, WOODERAWAR, (?) probably for UḌIYA, or UṚIYA-VÁḌU, Tel. A man of the *Udia* or *Orissa* country, considered as of a low caste, and employed especially in cutting stones and digging wells and tanks in the Northern Sarkárs.

Y.

YÁ, pron. JÁ, Beng. (যা) A husband's brother's wife.

YÁD, H. &c. (P. یاد) Remembrance. Mar. (याद) A memorandum, a scrap, a little account, a note addressed to an equal on official subjects.

Yád-dásht, H. &c. (یادداشت, from P. داشتن, to have) *Yádástu*, Tel. (యాదాస్తు) A note, a memorandum, a memorial, a petition, a certificate.

YÁCHITA, S. (याचित, lit. asked) A particular form of deposit, in Hindu law, in which the holder of the deposit may have the use of it.

Yáchitaka, S. (याचितक) An article deposited or lent for use.

YADṚICHCHHIKA-PUTRA, S. (यदृच्छिक-पुत्रः, from यदृच्छा, of one's own accord or will) A son who offers himself for adoption.

YADU, S. &c. (यदु) An ancient Hindu sovereign, eldest son of Yayáti, and founder of the race of *Yadus* or *Yádavas*

Yaduvanṣa, S. &c. (यदुवंश) The race of *Yadu*, a name borne by several Rajput tribes who pretend to trace their descent from this prince.

YÁFT, H. &c. (یافت, from P. یافتن, to find) Profit, gain fees, perquisites, as,

Yáft-i-Ṣúbahdár, the income or revenue of a *Ṣúbahdár*, or *Nawáb*.

Yáft-i-khidmat, corruptly, *Yáft-kedmat*, H. (from خدمت, service) Attainment of office or employment, fees or presents paid on the grant of an office or jurisdiction, as of a Zamindárí.

YÁGA, S. &c. (याग) A sacrifice, an offering, an oblation.

YAINÍR, or AINÍR, Karn. (ಯೆನೀರ) Rice used for the first crop: the first crop of rice.

YAJAMÁNA, S., and in most dialects modified as YAJMÁN, vernacularly, AJMAN, IJMÁN, corruptly, YIJMAN, EEJIMAN, EJHAMAN, or YEJAMAN, (यजमान) A person who employs a priest or priests to perform for him either fixed or occasional religious ceremonies: as he is usually a householder, it has come to signify also the head of a family or household, a chief, a head man, a master, the head of a caste, tribe, or trade: it is sometimes applied to one of several associated in the employment and payment of priests for a sacrifice; the office of family priest is sometimes hereditary, and the *Yajamána* has no power to change him as long as he performs his functions efficiently: in some parts of the Tamil countries the *Yajamán*, or *Ijaman*, as head of the community, has peculiar powers and rights: he distributes the lands when held in common according to fixed rules among the cultivators, and holds a parcel of land rent-free, as well as appropriates the *Mirásidárs'* grain fees; no sales can be made, nor strangers allowed to settle, without his sanction, sometimes singly, sometimes in conjunction with other head villagers; his land and emoluments are hereditary privileges, not grants from the state, and are transferable by sale, gift, and the like.

Yajamán, or *Ejamán-grámam*, Tam. (யஜமான், கிராமம்) A village where the lands are cultivated in common, but under a distribution made by the head man: also a village which is the property of a single individual. See *Ekabhogam*.

Yajamán-mániyam, Tam. A grant of rent-free land to a respectable householder.

Yajamána-kṛityá, S. &c. (यजमानकृत्या) What is to be done in the family of the patron or master of a ministering priest, astrologer, or the like.

Yajamání, Mar. (S. यजमानी) The principal or presiding person at a marriage feast or other entertainment amongst Ṣúdras.

Yajana, S. &c. (यजन) Sacrificing, offering sacrifices, either personally or by competent ministers, on one's own account: the duty of the three first classes.

Yájana, S. &c. (याजन) Conducting sacrifices or ministering for others: the exclusive office of the Brahman.

Yajna, S. &c. (यज्ञ) A sacrifice, performance of a sacrifice, offering of libations of Soma juice, or oblations of butter.

Yajna paṣu, S. &c. (यज्ञपशु) A victim, an animal offered in sacrifice.

Yajnopavíta, S. (यज्ञोपवीत) The cord originally worn by the three first classes, but now of right only by Brahmans: the ceremony of investiture.

YAJUSH, S. &c. (यजुष्, in composition *Yajur*, as *Yajur-veda*) The second of the four scriptural authorities of the Hindus.

YAK, (?) The *chaunri*-tailed ox of Tibet (Bos or Poëphagus, grúnniens).

YAK, H. (P. يك) One: more usually EK, q. v.

YAKSHA, S. &c. (यक्ष) A sort of demigod, especially attendant on *Kuvera*, the god of riches.

Yakshiṇí, S. &c. (यक्षिणी) A female *Yaksha*, attendant on Kuvera and Durgá, but often holding intercourse with mortals.

YALÁM, or YÁLAM, incorrectly, YALIUM, (?) Public sale, auction, a lottery (a corruption, apparently, of *Nilám*).

YÁḺAVALLOR-KUṬṬAM, Tam. (யாழவல்லொர்க்குட்டம்) The *Gándharba* form of marriage, union by mutual consent.

YAMA, S. &c. (यम) The Hindu ruler and judge of the dead.

Yamadanshtrá, Mar. (S. यमदंष्ट्राः, lit. *Yama's* teeth) The last eight days of the month *Áṣwin*, and the whole of *Kártik*, considered as a period of general sickness.

Yamadwitíyá, S. (यम, and द्वितीया, second) The second of the light half of *Kártika*, when brothers and sisters exchange gifts and honours (in allusion to the attachment of *Yama* and his sister *Yami*).

YÁMA, corruptly, JAMAM, and ZAMUM, S. &c. (याम) A watch, an eighth part of the day, or period of three hours.

YAMÍN, H. &c. (A. يمين) An oath, a vow, an adjuration by the name of God, or by such of the divine attributes or other terms ordinarily employed for the purpose.

Yamín-ghamúṣ, A. (غموص, perjury) A false oath, wilful perjury concerning an affair past.

Yamín lagho, (لغو, inconsiderate) A rash or inconsiderate oath relating to past events, one the swearer hastily believes to be true although in fact false.

Yamín munáḳid, or *máḳúd*, A. (from منعقد, or معقود, bound, from عقد) An oath or vow concerning some future matter which should be kept unless sinful, in which case it may be broken, subject to expiation.

Yamín-faur, or *Yamín-fúr*, A. (from فور, haste) A sudden oath or vow, one made upon an emergency.

YANTRA, S., in all the dialects, sometimes pronounced JANTRA (यंत्र) A machine, an instrument, an engine, any mechanical contrivance.

Yantrakáran, *Yantrikan*. Mal. (യന്ത്രക്കാരൻ, യന്ത്രിക്കൻ) An engineer, an artificer, a mechanic.

YÁR, H. (A. يار) A friend.

Cháryárí, H. (P. چارياري, from چهار, four) A sect of Mohammadans who venerate equally the four successors of Mohammad: a silver coin or rupee having the names of the first four *khalifs* on the margin.

YÁRA, H. (P. يارة) Toll, tax, revenue.

YARA, Karn. (ಯರ) A loan.

YÁRAKALAPA, Tel. (యారకలప) Implements of husbandry.

YARAPU, also ERAPU, Karn. (ಯರಪು) A loan without interest.

YÁRDÍ, Mar. (याद्दी) The hereditary assistant of the *Despándyá*: in general *Yárka*, and *Yárdá*, are applied to men and animals of little value or estimation.

YARGHAMÁL, corruptly, ERUGMAL, H. (P. يرغمال) A hostage

YARLAN, read also YERLUN, YERLINALOO, (?) Mal. The name of a class of agrestic slaves in Malabar.

YASÁWAL, H. (P. يساول) An officer of parade, one carrying a gold or silver staff, a state messenger.

YÁTA, YÁTAMU, Karn. Tel. (ಯಾತ, యాతము) An engine on the principle of a lever for raising water for fields or gardens.

Kaiyáta, Karn. (ಕೈಯಾತ) An irrigating machine worked by hand.

Kágadayáta, Karn. (ಕಾಗದಯಾತ) A paper-mill.

YATHÁRTHA, S. &c. (यथार्थ) Truly, rightly, correctly, according to the sense or object.

YATHÁYOGYAM, S. &c. (यथायोग्यं) Suitably, fitly, as it is proper or right.

Yatheshṭha, S. &c. (यथेष्ट) According to desire, as it is wished or commanded.

YATÍ, or also, vernacularly, JATÍ, S. &c. (यति) An ascetic, the member of the fourth order of the Hindus: in common use applied especially to a religious teacher of the Jains.

YATÍM, H. (A. يتيم) An orphan, a ward: it is applied in

Mohammadan law to a child whose father dies before he or she arrives at maturity, although the mother be living.

YÁTRÁ, S. &c., also, vernacularly, JÁTRÁ (यात्रा) Going about, travelling, but especially travelling to places of reputed holiness, pilgrimage: a periodical festival in honour of some idol to which its worshippers resort: a company of pilgrims: in Bengal, a dramatic representation.

Yátraḍabí, Mar. (यात्रडबी) Proceeds of the votive offerings by pilgrims in a temple.

Yátrakaru, *Yátrekarí*, or *Yátrekarú*, Mar. (यात्रकरू, यात्रेकरी, यात्रेकरू) A pilgrim.

Yátrí, or *Játri*, S. &c. (यात्री) A pilgrim.

Yátrotpanna, corruptly, *Yatra ootpun*, S. (यात्रोत्पन्न) Fees paid for the privilege of erecting stalls at places of pilgrimage.

YAUTAKA, or YAUTUKA, S. (यौतक, यौतुक), YATUKA, Beng. (यतुक) A nuptial gift, presents made to a woman at her marriage, becoming her property; a marriage dower or portion; also, a gift to a youth or child at any of the initiatory ceremonies or *Sanskáras*.

YAUM, H. &c. (A. يوم) A day.

Yaum-al-fiṭr, H. (A. يوم الفطر) The day of breaking fast, after the fast of *Ramazán*.

Yaum-al-inkiṭáâ, A. (يوم الانقطاع) The day of cessation, the day on which any thing terminates: in law, the last day on which any one who has become possessed of property illegally may restore it, or make compensation to the owner.

Yaum-ul-ḳarr, H. (A. يوم القر) The day of rest, the day after the sacrifice of the tenth of *Zilhijjah*, when people repose from their labours.

Yaum-un-nahr, H. (A. يوم النحر) The day of sacrifice, that is, the tenth of the month *Zilhijjah*, or the festival of the *Bakr-íd*.

Yaumiá, corruptly, *Yeomiah*, *Yeomea*, H. &c. (يوميا) A daily allowance to pensioners of any kind.

Yaumiadár, H. &c. (P. دار, who has) A daily pensioner or grantee.

YAVA, S. &c., vernacularly, YAU, or JAU, (यव) Barley, a barley-corn, especially as a rudimental measure of length.

YAVANA, S. &c., vernacularly, YAVAN, or JABAN, (यवन) A foreigner, applied originally by the Hindus to the Ionians or Greeks, but in later times to Arabs and Europeans: in Tam. the plur. *Yavanar* (யவனர்) implies all kinds of artificers, also the lowest class of Mohammadans.

YAVANNA, or YAWANNA, (?) Tam. A fee in money paid to the collector or manager of the revenue.—Tinnivelly.

YEDARU-CHÍṬU, corruptly, YÉDROONOODY-CHIṬ, Karn. (ಯೆದರುಚೀಟು) A counterpart agreement, an engagement given by the tenant of an estate held under lease or mortgage to pay a consideration annually for its occupancy: also a writing given by the purchaser of land to the proprietor, engaging to give it back on receiving his money again within a stipulated period. See *Edaru-chíṭu*.

YEDURU-GAṬṬU, Tel. (యెదురుగట్టు) Throwing a dam across a canal or river: also *Eduru-gaṭṭu*.

Yeduru-baḍisanadu, Tel. (యెదురుబడిసనదు) A *sanad* or agreement passed by one to another in discharge of the original *sanad* or grant: more properly, *Eḍuru*, &c., q. v.

YELLAVÁḌU, more correctly, ELLAVÁḌU, corruptly, YELLAWAR, Tel. (ఎల్లవాడు) lit. The boundary man, a village servant, usually of a low caste, who looks after the village boundaries, distributes water, and acts as guide to travellers.

YELMI, (?) Tel. A class of cultivators in the northern Sarkárs, who are often soldiers, and affect to be regarded as Rájputs.

YENUKA, also, YENUKA-CHIṬ, more correctly, ENUKÁ, corruptly, YENNUCK, YENNEK, YENKE, YENNUCK-CHIṬ, ENNACK, (?) Mal. A document of various application, but connected with the transfer of landed property; as, a certificate or acknowledgment from the owner to a lessee or mortgagee that he has let or mortgaged his estate; authority to such lessee or mortgagee to transfer his interest to another; or in the event of sale or mortgage to a third party by the owner, a deed of notice or apprisal of the sale, and directions to the occupant to receive the amount of his claims from the purchaser: also, a counter document given by the occupant to the proprietor announcing his having transferred his interests in the property.

YERÍ, (?) Mar. Black soil.

YERKULLEVAR, (?) Tel., probably for ERUKUVÁḌU, plur. ERUKUVÁNḌLU, and the same as those corruptly termed YERKELWANLOO, YERA-KEDI, YERAKELLOO (ఎఱుకువాడు) The designation of a wild migratory tribe who subsist on game and all sorts of flesh: they make and sell baskets and mats, and are considered as outcastes: both men and women pretend to be fortune-tellers and conjurors: they are also said to be called *Koorshe-wanloo*, *Yerkel-wanloo* (*wánlu*, or, more correctly, *vánḍlu*, being only the plur. of *váḍu*), *Yera-kedi*, and *Yerakelloo*, but to be known amongst themselves as *Kuṛṛu*: they are possibly the same who appear among the prædial slaves in Kúrg under the name of *Yerrwanroo*, i. e. *Erra-vánḍlu*, ? red men, or *Yevaru*, q. v.

or *Yerlan*, or *Erehlen*, (?) also specified amongst the servile races of Kúrg.

YEṚṚACHAKKU, more correctly, EṚṚACHAKKU, Tel. (ఎఱ్ఱచెక్కు, from ఎఱ్ఱ, red) A red sort of soil containing a small quantity of lime.

YERRAH-WALLEROO, (?) Tel. A division of the shepherd or Dhangar tribe in the northern Sarkárs.

YERWADDY, (?) A Ryot who cultivates land in a village in which he does not reside. 5th Rep. 832: (corruption of some derivative of *Ér*, (Tam.) a plough, as *Érálar*, ploughmen.

YES, Mar. (येस) The gate of a village (preferably *Wes*, or *Ves*, वेस).

Yeskar, Mar. (येसकर) A village servant, the porter or gatekeeper, who performs also other duties, and is usually a Mhar (preferably *Veskar*).

YÉTUBATTE, Tel. (ఏటుబట్టె) A canal cut from a river: (from *Eṛu*, q. v).

YEVARU, or more correctly, EVARU, (?) Mal. The designation of a tribe of prædial slaves in Kúrg, of whom several subdivisions are specified, as *Panay-Yevaru*, *Punjay-Yevaru*, &c.

YOGA, S. &c. (योग) Abstract devotion, by means of which superhuman faculties are supposed to be acquired: it is one of the schools of Hindu philosophy, but, in common use, is the practice of magic or supposed magical rites: in law, collusion, fraud: wealth, or its acquisition: an assembly or court of Brahmans, which took cognisance of religious matters.

Yogí, S. &c., in various dialects *Jogí* (योगी) A follower of the *Yoga* philosophy, a practiser of ascetic devotion, in common use, a religious mendicant, and reputed conjuror or magician: there are various orders or sects of *Yogís*: the name of a Hindu caste, usually weavers.

Yogahshema, S. &c. (योगक्षेम, from योग, gaining, and क्षेम, preserving) Property, possessions: having property, being well off: in law, especially property assigned for the performance of religious ceremonies and accomplishment of benevolent objects, as constructing temples, reservoirs, &c.: also, transport or custody of goods, and charges on that account.

Yoginí, S. &c. (योगिनी) A female devotee: a female fiend or divinity of an inferior order, often associating with human beings, and usually working mischief.

YUDDHAPRÁPTA-DÁSA, S. (युद्ध, war, प्राप्त, obtained, and दास, a slave) A slave by reason of having been taken in battle.

YUGA, S. &c. (युगः) An age, especially a subdivision of a great age, or aggregate of four *Yugas*, which are severally the *Kṛita*, or *Satya-yuga*, the *Dwápara-yuga*, the *Treta-yuga*, and the *Kali-yuga*, the duration of which is severally computed at years 1,728,000, 1,296,000, 864,000, and 432,000, making a *Mahá-yuga* of 4,320,000 years: the world is now (1854) in the year of the *Kali* age 4955.

YUKTI, S. (युक्ति) Union, connexion, fitness: in law, the reason of a thing or argument, consistency given to a passage of law by the determination of its sense or purpose: also usage, custom.

YUVARÁJÁ, corruptly, JOB-RAJ, S. &c. (युवराजा) The young Rájá, properly the eldest son of a Rájá who succeeds to the Raj by the right of primogeniture; but it is also applied to a young prince associated with his father in the government before his death.

Z.

ZABARDASTÍ, H. (P. زبردستي) Violence, force, oppression.

ẒÁBIṬA, in the Indian dialects, JÁBITÁ, or JÁBATÁ, H. &c. (ضابطة, जाबिता, जाबता) A rule, a statute, a law: established practice, usage. Tel. (జాబితా) A list, a roll.

ẒABH, H. (A. ذبح) Killing an animal, either for sacrifice or food, according to the prescribed manner, by cutting the vessels of the throat so as to exhaust the blood, and invoking the name of God: where circumstances render this impossible, as in killing wild animals or game by shooting, the eating may be allowed.

Ẓabíh, H. (A. ذبيح) Sacrificed, a sacrifice.

Ẓábih, H. (A. ذابح) A sacrificer, a butcher.

ẒABṬ, ẒUBṬ, also ẒABṬÍ, ẒUBṬEE, vernacularly, JUBT, JUBTEE, JUPTEE, JUPHT, H. &c. (ضبط, ضبطي, जबत, जप्ती) Occupation, seizure: in law, attachment, distraint, sequestration, taking lands under the management of the government officers: land which had been held free but has been subjected to a money-assessment.

Ẓabṭí, vernacularly, *Zapti*, *Zafti*, *Jabtí*, *Jaftí*, *Japtí*, corruptly, *Zebty*, H. (ضبطي, जबती, जप्ती) Sequestrated, attached, applied to lands taken possession of by the government officers, or to rent-free lands which have been subjected to assessment: in Bengal lands were so designated which had been resumed from *Jágír* grants by *Jaffar Khan*: in the north-west provinces the term is applied to the assessment in money on lands in which the more valuable products are raised, as sugar-cane, tobacco, cotton, esculent vegetables, and the like.

Zaft, or *Japht-amínu*, Tel. (జప్తుఅమీను) An officer sent to sequestrate estates.

Zafti, or *Japhti-paṭṭa*, Karn. (from H. پٹا) A document conveying a title to land or houses sold under distraint to the purchaser; and *Watan-zabti*, or *-japtí*, Mar. (see *Watan*) Produce of lands sequestrated by the state, an item of revenue: in Guz. the lands once exempt, now subject to assessment.

Japtídár, Mar. (जप्तीदार) A bailiff, an officer employed to execute an attachment.

Zád, H. (زاد) Food, provisions, especially such as are taken with him by a traveller setting out on a journey.

Zádah, H. (P. زاده) Born, a child, used chiefly in composition as *Sháh-zádah*, a prince, a king's son; *Sháh-zádí*, a princess: *Ḥaram-zádah*, of illegitimate birth: used as a term of abuse, rascal, scoundrel.

Ẓahr, H. (A. ظهر) Mid-day.

Ẓahr-namáz, H. (A. نماز, prayer) Mid-day prayer.

Ẓáíâ, H. (A. ضايع) Lost, destroyed. Jáyá, Tel. (జాయా) Loss, damage.

Zaif, A. (زيف) Light or clipt money, current but not receivable at the public treasuries.

Zail, H. (A. ذيل) Appendix, supplement to a letter or book, the margin of a book with annotations: the lower margin of a Zamindárí grant, in which the names of the lands granted are recapitulated: any supplementary detail of particulars.

Zakát, vernacularly, Jakát, H. (A. زكات) Alms, contributions of a portion of property, obligatory on every Mohammadan possessed of capital: it is received by the *Imám* and is payable by him to the poor and needy: the proportion is properly a tenth, but it may be increased to any amount, according to the piety of the individual: the term literally signifying purification, is applied to the *Zakát*; because the alms, &c. given, sanctify the use of the remainder.

Ẓamán, or Ẓamn, A. (ضمن, ضمان) Surety, bail, security in general, answering or being surety for another, either for person or property: according to the Shias the term is restricted to security for property, whilst *Kafálat* is that applied to personal bail.

Ẓamánat-náma, H. (P. نامه, a document) A deed of surety by which a person makes himself answerable for the debts of another.

Ẓamán-ba-úhdat-us-ṣamaní, A. (ضمان به عهدت الثمني) Security for the fulfilment of a bargain of sales on the part of the vendor.

Ẓamán-b'il-dark, A. (ضمان بالدرك) Bail for accidents, for any contingency, or for any undefined amount.

Ẓámin, vernacularly, *Jámin*, H. &c. (ضامن), *Jámín*, Mar. (जामीन) A surety, a security.

Ẓáminí, vernacularly, *Jámini*, or *Jamíni*, H. &c (A. ضامني) Suretyship, becoming responsible for another, either for person or property, distinguished as

Fíl-ẓáminí, H. (A. فعل, act) Security for good conduct, or for a person's refraining from any proscribed offence or misdemeanor.

Háẓir-ẓáminí, H. (from حاضر, present) Being surety for a person's appearance.

Mál-ẓáminí, H. (from مال, wealth) Being surety for property, as for the payment of any pecuniary obligation.

Zar-ẓáminí, H. (P. زر, gold) Surety for money payment.

Zanjír-ẓáminí, H. (from P. زنجير, a chain), *Jámin-sánkhalí*, Mar. (from सांखळी, S. शृंखला, a chain) Chain security, a number of persons binding themselves severally or jointly for each other, joint responsibility of the cultivators of a village or district for the whole revenue, or for money borrowed of a banker.

Janjarbandí-jáminu, Karn. (ಜಂಜರಬಂದೀಜಾಮಿನು) Bond or bail for a prisoner: (Reeve, but *quere* if not the same meaning as the preceding).

Varttaṇúh-zámín, Mar. (from वर्त्तणूक, conduct) A surety for a person's submitting to the decision of a *Pancháyat*, though it should be against him.

Jámín-katabá, or *-kadabá*, Mar. (जामीनकतबा -कदबा, from A. كتاب, a book) A security bond.

Jámínkí, Mar. (जामीनकी) Suretyship, security.

Jámíndár, Mar. (जामीनदार) A surety.

Zamín, Zumeen, vernacularly, Jamín, Jamí, H. &c. (P. زمين, जमीन् जमी) Earth, the earth, land, ground, soil, &c.

Zamín-báb, H. (A. باب, an item) Relating to land.

Zamíndár, *Zumeendár*, vernacularly, *Jamíndár*, *Jamídár*, *Jamidár*, corruptly, *Zemindár*, H. &c. (زمين, land, and دار, who has or possesses, जमीनदार, जमीदार, జమిదార) An occupant of land, a landholder: the rights of the *Zamíndár* have been the subject of much controversy with reference

ZAM

to his character as hereditary owner of the land he occupies, or as the responsible collector only of the revenues on behalf of the government. Under the Mohammadan administration the latter was the capacity in which the Zamíndár was ordinarily considered, and the chief authorities never hesitated to exercise the power, when they possessed it, of turning out a Zamíndár and placing another in the Zamindárí, whence the one in possession was termed *Sanadi*, or *Akkámi*, the Zamíndár by patent or command. Whilst managing the lands and realising the revenue the Zamíndár was allowed a fee or commission of ten per cent. upon the total collections, and a portion of the land was exempted from the revenue assessment to the extent of five per cent. on the collections, under the denomination of *Nánkár*, being intended for the personal support of the Zamíndár and his family: further deductions from the stipulated amount of revenue, termed *Maṭhaut*, were also allowed, to cover various charges borne by the Zamíndár: on the other hand, he was empowered to levy internal duties and customs on articles of trade passing through his district, and to impose petty taxes, or *Abwábs*, on the cultivators, in addition to the portion of the public revenue demandable from them individually: on his relinquishing the management of the Zamíndárí, or being removed from it without cause of grave offence, it was customary to assign him, as *Málikána*, ten per cent. on the *Sadr* collections, or the same rate on the nett collections when held *khás*, or managed by the government officers direct. But although in these respects the Zamíndár appears to be a representative of the state, employed to realise and transfer to the public treasure nine-tenths of the revenue, and to be nominated or removed at pleasure; yet the practice of hereditary succession, and the right to mortgage and sell, partook more of the tenure of ownership, and extensive tracts came to be held by successive generations of the same family, through more or less protracted periods, in some instances apparently from a date anterior to the fiscal regulations of the Mohammadan governments: in the decline of the latter, also, many Zamíndárís which were held originally under a special grant were converted into hereditary proprietaries, and the Zamíndárs, appropriating by fraud or force very extensive districts, assumed the state of chiefs and princes, and were sometimes powerful enough to resist the authority and withhold the revenues of the state. The question of right was, however, set at rest in Bengal, Bahar, and Orissa, in 1793, by the terms of the perpetual settlement, which recognised Zamíndárs and independent Taluḳdárs as "actual proprietors," enjoying their estates in absolute ownership as long as they paid the government revenue, or nine-tenths of the fixed nett proceeds of the lands, and liable to dispossession in case of failure, by the sale of their lands at public auction. Ben. Reg. viii. 1793; iii. 1794; v. 1795; ii. xxvii. 1803. The same measure was subsequently adopted at Madras, and Zamíndárs were designated as proprietors of land, along with other classes with whose rights and recognition, as was afterwards explained, it was not intended to interfere. Mad. Reg. xxv. 1802; ii. 1806; iv. 1822. In the Upper Provinces, Zamíndárís sometimes occur which are held by an individual in absolute proprietary right, the most common instances of such tenure being where the right has been acquired by purchase, and especially where this has been effected at public sale for arrears of revenue; but the more usual form of Zamíndárí tenure is where the lands are held by a number of coparceners, thence termed Mufassal or village Zamíndárs, who hold and manage the village lands in common: the rents paid by the cultivators, whether those cultivators be the proprietors themselves or tenants holding under them, together with all other profits from the estate, are thrown into a common stock, and, after deduction of the government demand, and other expenses, the balance is divided amongst the proprietors according to a fixed law. Ben. Reg. ii. 1795, &c. From the circumstance of one of the number of such coparceners representing the whole, as responsible for the government revenue, the designation has been given to him especially of Zamíndár, or *Málik-zamíndár*, but he is a Zamíndár only by virtue of the share or shares he holds in the joint proprietary: the designation of *Sadr* or *Pargana-zamíndár*, denotes merely a *Zamíndár*, or *Taluḳdár*, in the sense of an individual proprietor. In the Maraṭha provinces the term Zamíndár was applied indiscriminately to the local hereditary revenue officers, whether of the districts, as *Deṣmukh*, *Despaṇḍe*, and others, or of the villages, as the *Patíl*, *Chaughala*, and *Kulkarani*.

Zamín-dárán, H. (plur. of *Zamíndár*) Feudal tenures of the nature of conditional Jágírs conferred on certain of the frontier Zamíndárs of Bengal by the Mohammadan government.

Zamíndárána, H. (زميندارانه) The pay of a Zamíndár, the allowance made to him when set aside.

Zamíndárí, vernacularly, *Jamíndárí*, corruptly, *Zemindarry*, H. (زميندارى) The office and rights of a Zamíndár: the tenure of a Zamíndárí, whether individual or coparcenary: the tract of land constituting the possessions of a Zamíndár or of coparcenary Zamíndárs: it more usually designates the former.

Zamíndár-hazúr-tahṣíl, H. (A. حضور, the state, and تحصيل, collections) A Zamíndár in the ceded Provinces formerly paying his revenue instalments to the collector of the Zilâ, and charged with the superintendence of the police in his Zamíndárí. Ben. Reg. xxv. 1803.

Zamíndárí-hiṣṣadárí, H. (A. حصّه, a share, P. دارى, having) A Zamíndárí held in shares, described as a village or estate in which the sharers cultivate separately, and raise the government revenue by a *báchh*: the lands are not divided amongst the sharers in proportion to their shares and interests in the village, and no sharer can have his share separated except by decree in a civil suit: the term is regarded, however, as somewhat ambiguous.

Zamíndárí-paṭṭa, H. (پتّه, a lease) A document granted by government in recognition of the possessions of a Zamíndár.

Zamíndárí-sanad, H. (A. سند) Deed or patent granting a Zamíndárí.

Zamíndárí-rasum, H. (A. رسوم, fees) Cesses or fees levied by a Zamíndár.

Zamíndárí-jamâ, H. (A. جمع) The amount of revenue which the holder of a Zamíndárí engages to pay to the government.

Zamíndárí-chaukí, H. (چوكى, a station) A post at which the officers of the Zamíndár formerly collected tolls and customs on goods passing through his estate.

Zamíndárí-daftar, H. (دفتر, a record) An office established by the British government in Bengal in 1772, in which all grants of Zamíndárís, Táluḳs, &c., were prepared and registered, as were mortgages and transfers of the same: the record and accounts of a Zamíndárí.

Zamíndárí-muchalka, H. (A. مچلكه, an agreement) An obligation entered into by a Zamíndár on receiving the grant of a Zamíndárí, engaging for the due observance of its conditions.

Zamíndár-jamâdár, H. (زميندار جمعدار) An officer charged with the preservation of the peace and administration of justice in the town of Chandranagar, upon its capture from the French.

Zamín-ḳábil-zarâiat, H. (A. قابل, fit, زرعيت, cultivation) Cultivable land.

Zamín-khirájí, H. (A. خراج, tribute) Land paying tribute.

Zamín-mazruâ, H. (A. مزروع, cultivated) Tilled land.

Zamín-navísí, H. (P. نويسى, writing) An office for the registry of estates and transfers and mortgages of land.

Zamín-uftáda, H. (P. افتاده, fallen) Waste land, land left uncultivated.

Jamín-jumlá, Mar. (जमीनजुमला, from A. جمله) Lands and tenements, a whole estate.

Jamínjhaṛá, blunderingly, *Zumeen-ihara*, Mar. (जमीनझाडा) A descriptive paper or roll of towns, villages, lands, &c.: one of the village accounts shewing the extent and distribution of the lands.

Jamín-mojaṇí, Mar. (जमीनमोजणी) Survey of land.

Jamín-navís, or *-nís*, Mar. (जमीननवीस -नीस) The officer that inspects the soil, crops, &c., and fixes the assessment.

Jamín-ṣirastá, Mar. (जमीनशिरस्ता) Rate of land, the rate of assessment established after survey.

Jamínujhaḍiti, *Jamínujháḍi*, Karn. (ಜಮೀನುಝಡತಿ, ಜಮೀನುಝಾಡಿ) A particular account of the produce of a Zamíndárí or of the qualities of lands belonging to a village.

Zamín-sang-jamâ-wáṣil-báḳí, H. (S. سنگ, together with) An account of the lands of a village, of the revenue assessed, and the state of its realization; one of the village accounts.

Zanána, vernacularly, Janána, incorrectly, Zenana, H. (زنانه, from P. زن, a woman) The female apartments, used sometimes for their inhabitants: the females of a family.

Zanáni-zubán, H. (P. زبان, the tongue, speech) The style or language of the women, differing in some terms and phrases from ordinary Hindustani, and considered improper for men to use.

Zanjír-zámíní, less correctly, Zanjira, vernacularly, Janjir-jaminí, or Janjira, H. (P. زنجير زامنى) lit., Chain-security, persons becoming mutually sureties for each other: in some provinces it applies especially to the different payers of revenue in a village; if one is in default the others are expected to make the deficit good.

Ẓann, A. (ظن) Opinion, suspicion: in law, presumption that a charge is well founded although the evidence is inconclusive.

Zann-i-ghálib, or *Ghálib-oos-ẓaná*, A. (غالب, strong) Strong presumption of the truth of a charge, although the evidence does not amount to conviction.

Zannár, vernacularly, Janar, incorrectly, Zennar, H. (A.

زنار, जनार) A belt, a *zone*: the thread worn by the Brahmans, and sometimes assumed by other castes.

Zannár-dár, H. (P. دار, who has) The wearer of the characteristic thread or cord, especially a Brahman.

Zar, Zur, incorrectly, Zer, H. (P. زر) Gold, money, a money-payment, the land revenue in money.

Zar-andúd, H. (P. اندود, smeared) Gilt.

Zar-báft, H. (P. بافت, woven) Brocade, cloth of gold.

Zar-doz, H. (P. دوز, sewing) Embroidered with gold: an embroiderer.

Zar-gar, H. (P. زرگر) A goldsmith.

Zar-kharíd-Taâlluḳ, H. (P. زرخريد, bought with cash) In Bengal, a purchased Táluḳ, one bought of a Zamíndár: it implies generally a dependent Táluḳ held hereditarily under a Zamíndár, and reverting to him on failure of heirs.

Zar-mathaut, H. (زرمتهوت) A series of cesses imposed by the Mohammadan government of Bengal, consisting of four items: 1. *Naẓr-i-punya*, Presents exacted from the Zamíndárs, at the time of the *Punya* or annual settlement; 2. *Bahái-i-khilât*, A charge to defray the expense of honorary dresses presented to individuals by the government; 3. *Pushta-bandí*, Charge for keeping in repair the banks of the *Bhágirathí*, in the vicinity of *Murshidabad*; 4. *Rasúm-i-Naẓárat*, A fee paid to the Nazir or officer commanding the escort of the collections from the interior to the public treasury. In the first fiscal arrangements of the British government through native functionaries these charges were added to the standard collections, and carried to the credit of the government, amounting to about one and a half per cent. on the total assessment, and realizing a lac and a half of rupees: (the word is written *Zermathote*, (زيرمتهوت), and, corruptly, *Zyr-mathote*, in the fifth Report, and is explained in the Glossary as derived from the P. *Zer* (زير), under, below, but it is called in the text, p. 278, a *money-contribution*, which makes it most probable that *Zer* is intended for *Zar* or *Zur*, money).

Zar-parjouti, (?) H. Revenue, principal and interest.

Zar-i-peshgí, or *Zarpeshgí*, H. (P. پيشگي, advance) Payment in advance, a deposit or engagement to advance money, a bonus or premium on a lease, an advance of money upon the farm of the revenue: money lent upon a usufructuary mortgage.

Zar-i-peshgí-dár, H. (P. دار, who has) One who has advanced money.

Zar-i-surkh, H. (P. سرخ, red) Red, *i.e.* pure gold, gold in general.

Zar-i-samán, H. (S. سمان, like, equal to) Purchase-money of an estate bought at public auction.

Zar-i-taufír-nilám, H. (A. توفير, increase, and نيلام, auction) Surplus of sale proceeds, balance realised over the amount of defalcation, for which the lands are sold, payable to the defaulter.

Ẓarb, H. (A. ضرب) A blow, striking: a stamp, an impression, stamping coin: stamped, struck, as coin; as *Ẓarb-i-Murshidabad*, *Ẓarb-i-Arkát*, struck at those cities, part of the inscription on the Sikka and Arcot rupees.

Ẓarúriát, H. (P. ضروريات, P. ضرور, necessary) Necessaries, requisites.

Ẓát, H. (A. ذات) Possessed of, master, owner: person; essence: (S. जाति) Sort, kind, tribe, caste, race, lineage, family, birth. See *Ját*, *Játi*, &c.

Ẓáti, H. (A. ذاتي) Essential, natural, personal.

Ját- (for *Ẓáti*) *jágír*, or *Saranjám*, incorrectly, *Zat-suranzam*, Mar. (जातजागीर, जातसरंजाम) A grant of the revenues of lands alienated from the government revenue in favour of individuals, either as a personal favour, or on the condition of personal service; a personal grant.

Játká, Mar. (जात्का) Personal, as a grant of revenue, either as a personal favour or for personal service.

Ját-saranjám-Jágír, Mar. (जातसरंजाम-जागीर) Grant of lands, or their revenue, on condition of personal service.

Ẓáti-, vernacularly, *Játi-muḳaddam*, H. (ذاتي مقدّم) In Cuttack, a class of head men who, although collecting the government revenue from the villagers, act in this respect either as the agents of the *Málguzár* or person who is responsible for the payment to the officers of the government, or as the representatives of the inhabitants of the village, having no substantive right of their own to pay the whole revenue.

Zátmiráṣ, (?) Fees in grain allowed by the cultivators out of the gross produce to the servile class.

Zawájir, H. (A. زواجر, plur. of زجر) Prohibitions, forbidden things. *Zawájir-i-sharâí*, Prohibited by law.

Ẓawí-ul-Arhám, A. (ذوي الارحام, from ذو, possessed of, and رحم, the womb) Uterine relations, kindred between whose affinity a female intervenes; they are considered as distant kindred in Mohammadan law, because under the rules of inheritance a share rarely comes to them.

Zer-zamíní, H. (زيرزميني) A subterraneous chamber, one

under (*zer*) ground (*zamín*), intended as a retreat in the hot weather.

ZEVETUM, Karn. (?) corruption for JÍVITAM, S. (जीवितं), Means of living, subsistence.

ZIÁD, ZIÁDA, ZIÁDAT, commonly, ZIYÁD, ZIYÁDA, &c. H. (A. زیاد, زیاده, زیادة) Increase, surplus, more.

ZIÁN, H. (A. زیان), Loss, damage.

Zián-wa-nafâ, H. (A. زیان ونفع) Loss and profit.

ẒIÁFAT, H. (A. ضیافت) A feast, an entertainment, an invitation.

ZIÁRAT, H. (A. زیارت) Pilgrimage, going on pilgrimage to any holy shrine among the Mohammadans: in Hindustan, also, repairing to the grave of a deceased person on the third day after the burial, when the Ḳurán is read and prayers are recited, and offerings made in expiation of the sins of the defunct; also called *Tijá* (S. *tritíyá*) Third, the third (day), and *Phul-charháná*, Scattering flowers, flowers being the chief offerings.

Ziáratgáh, H. (P. گاه, a place) A place of pilgrimage, a holy spot or shrine.

Ẓ*I-HAIÁT*, H. (A. ذي حيات) Living, possessed of life: during life, a life-tenure.

ẒI-HAḲ, H. (ذي حق) lit. Possessed of right: applied to a class of pensions payable under treaty through the *Nawab* of Farakhabad.

ẒIHÁR, H. (A. ظهار) A formula of divorce, such as saying to a wife "You are my mother," *i.e.* our marriage is within the prohibited degrees, and is therefore dissolved.

ẒI-HIJJA, or ẒI-L-HIJJA, H. (A. ذي حجّه, ذي الحجه) The last month of the Mohammadan year.

ẒILÂ, corruptly, ZILLAH, ZELAH, plur. ẒILÂJÁT, H. (A. ضلع, plur. ضلعجات) Side, part, a division, a district: under the British administration, a province, a tract of country constituting the jurisdiction of a commissioner or circuit Judge, and the extent of a chief collectorate. The Ẓilâ Courts in Bengal and Bahar were established by Reg. iii. 1793; those of Benares, &c. by Reg. vii. 1795; those of the ceded provinces by Reg. viii. 1805; but various modifications have been since made from time to time, some having been abolished, some created, and the limits of others having been altered. Act xxi. 1826. Mad. Act vii. 1843. The Ẓilâ Courts are at present as follows, according to their usual but corrupt designations, and to those which are probably more correct—

I. BENGAL.—1. Backergunge (*Bákhirganj*); 2. Beerbhoom (*Bírbhúm*); 3. Behar (*Bahár*); 4. Bhaugulpoor (*Bhágalpur*); 5. & 6. East and West Burdwan (*Bardmán*); 7. Chittagong (*Shatgáon*); 8. Cuttack (*Kaṭak*); 9. Dacca (*Dháka*); 10. Dinagepore (*Dinájpur*); 11. Hooghly (*Huglí*); 12. Jessore (*Jaísúr*); 13. Midnapore (*Medinipur*); 14. Mymensing (*Maimansinh*); 15. Moorshedabad (*Murshidábád*); 16. Nuddea (*Nadiya*); 17. Patna (*Pattana*); 18. Purneah (*Puraníya*); 19. Twenty-four Parganas; 20. Rajashahye (*Rájasháhí*); 21. Rungpore (*Rangpur*); 22. Sarun (*Sáran*); 23. Shahabad (*Sháhábád*), 24. Sylhet (*Silhat*); 25. Tipperah (*Tripara*); 26. Tirhoot (*Tirhút*). Recently the Commissionerships of Asam, Arakan, Kachár, Házáribágh, and Tenaserim, have been included among the Ẓilâs of the Lower Provinces.

II. NORTH-WEST PROVINCES.—1. Agra; 2. Allahabad; 3. Allyghur (*Alighar*); 4. Azimgurh (*Azimghar*); 5. Benares (*Banáras*); 6. Bareilly (*Báreli*); 7. Bundlecund (*Bundelkhand*); 8. Cawnpore (*Khánpur*); 9. Delhi; 10. Furruckabad (*Farakhábád*); 11. Futtepoor (*Fatihpur*); 12. Ghazeepoor (*Gházipur*); 13. Goruckpoor (*Gorakhpur*); 14. Jounpoor (*Jonpur*): 15. Mynpoor (*Mayinpur*); 16. Meerut (*Merath*); 17. Mirzapoor (*Mirzapur*); 18. Moradabad; 19. Saharunpore (*Sahāranpur*). To which are to be added the Courts of the Commissioners of the Narmadá districts and Kamaon.

III. MADRAS.—1. Bellary (*Belári*); 2. Calicut (*Kálikat*); 3. Chikakol (*Śríkákol*); 4. Chingleput (?); 5. Chittoor (*Chitúr*); 6. Combaconum (*Kumbhakonam*); 7. Coimbatore (*Koyimbatúr*); 8. Cuddalore (?); 9. Cuddapah (*Kadapah*); 10. Gantoor (*Gantúr*); 11. Honore (*Honáwar*); 12. Madura (*Madhurá*); 13. Mangalore (*Mangalúr*); 14. Masulipatam (*Machlípattan*); 15. Nellore (*Nelur*); 16. Rajamundry (*Rájamahendrí*); 17. Salem(?); 18. Tellicherry (*Telícherí*); 19. Tinnavelly (*Tinavallí*); 20. Trichinopoly (*Trisirapallí*). There are also Agency Courts at Ganjam and Vizagapatam.

IV. BOMBAY.—1. Thana, comprising Ratnagiri; 2. Surat, including Baroch; 3. Ahmadábád; 4. Ahmadnagar; 5. Candeish (*Khandes*?); 6. Dhárwár; 7. Poonah (*Púna*); 8. Sholapore (*Solapur*).

Ẓilâ-tahṣíl, H. (تحصیل, collection) Collection of the revenue by an officer in charge of a Ẓilâ or district, in opposition to the collections received by the chief European officer, the *Hazúr-tahṣíl*.

Ẓilâ-ádálat, H. (A. عدالت) The chief civil and criminal court of a Ẓilâ.

Ẕilâdár, H. (P. دار, who has) The officer in charge of a Ẕilâ, a provincial governor, sometimes applied to the European collector or judge, whose authority extends over the Ẕilâ: in the Delhi territory the title was also given to the head of a village, who was chosen to superintend the revenue affairs of several adjacent villages, united under him for the convenience of revenue arrangement: in the Maratha country, a petty revenue officer, having jurisdiction over several villages, comprising a *taraf*, or other small division of country subordinate to the officer in charge of a *Pargana*.

Ẕilâdárí, H. (P. ضيلعداري) The office or jurisdiction of a *Ẕilâdár*.

Ẕilâ-kharch, H. District expenses, said, in Tirhut, to include the cost of weeding indigo fields, and other incidental expenses of the factory.

ẔIMÁN, A. (ضمان) Recompence, compensation.

Ẕimán-i-âták, A. (عتاق, manumission) Extra labour performed by a slave as a compensation for his manumission.

Ẕimán-i-fasád, or *Ziman-ul-ifsad*, A. (فساد, injury) Compensation for personal injury or damage.

Ẕimán-i-janáiat, A. (جناية, a wound) Compensation for any act of violence against the person, as for wounds and the like.

Ẕimán-i-tamalluk, A. (تملّك, taking possession of) Compensation for appropriation of property: the indemnification which a man who possesses only a share in a slave pays to his partners on setting the slave at liberty.

ẔIMÁR, A. (ضمار) In law, any thing uncertain, as disputed debts, treasure-trove, fugitive slaves, and the like: any property of which the possession or recovery is doubtful.

ẔIMMA, or ẔIMMAT, H. (A. ذمّة) A deed of protection, an authorised assurance of immunity in life and property, such as may be granted to infidels under a Mohammadan government: also the corresponding obligation of subjection, fidelity, obedience; also, trust, charge, custody: a tenure in trust, but which, by possession, came to signify a tenure in right in some places, in others an under tenure or a subdivision of an estate, in which the holder is entitled to levy the revenue due by the cultivators, and pay it either to the Zamíndár, or sometimes direct to the government: a sub-tenure, part of a *Hawála*.

Ẕimmadár, H. (ذمّهدار) A trustee, a person in charge: in Eastern Bengal it is applied especially to the holder of an under tenure or portion of a Zamíndárí, paying revenue either to government direct, or to a Zamíndár: it also applies to a Zamíndár who is authorised to collect, on behalf of government, the payments of properties in the vicinity of his own: these dependent *Táluks*, or estates, are designated his *Ẕimma*, in distinction from his own, or *Nij*.

Ẕimma-náma, H. (ذمّهنامه) A deed of trust, authority to have charge and make the collections of an estate.

Ẕimmawár, H. (ذمّهوار) A person placed by government in charge of an estate in arrear of revenue until it is sold.

Ẕimma-náma, H. (زمّهنامه) A deed of trust, authority to have charge and make the collections of an estate.

Ẕimmí, H. (A. ذمّي) One living under protection, a client, a dependant, especially applied to a subject of a Mohammadan government of a different religion, as a Christian, a Jew, &c., who is allowed to live without molestation on paying tribute.

ẔIMN, corruptly, ZIMIN, ZIMMUM, ZYMN, H. (A. ضمن) The endorsement of a grant, giving an abstract of its contents: an abstract statement or account, a cover, an envelope, a clause in a legal regulation: also, suretyship, obligation. See *Zaman*.

Ẕimn-navísand, H. (P. نويسند, let them write) A form of words, 'let them write the abstract,' formerly inscribed upon a *sanad* granting an assignment of revenue or Zamíndárí, which served as authority for the subordinate officers to make out the particulars of the assignment or grant.

ZIMNOTA, (?) Consideration usually received by a surety.

ZÍN, H. (P. زين) A saddle, a horse's trappings.

Zíngar, H. (P. زينگر) A saddler.

ZINÁ, H. (A. زنا) Fornication, adultery, any illicit intercourse of the sexes, whether the parties be married or single.

Zání, H. (A. زاني) A whoremonger, a fornicator, an adulterer.

ZINDAGÍ, or ZINDAGÁNÍ, vernacularly, JINDAGÍ, JINDAGÁNÍ, H. (P. زندگاني, زندگي) Life, means of living or subsistence.

Jindagi, *Jindagáni*, Karn. (ಜಿಂದಗಿ, ಜಿಂದಗಾನಿ) Treasure, money.

Jíndige, Karn. (ಜಿಂದಿಗೆ) An estate, a domain.

ZINDÁN, H. (P. زندان) A prison, a gaol.

ZIRÁÂ, also pronounced, DIRÁA, corruptly, DIRRAH, DIREH, H. (A. ذراع) A measure of length, a cubit, a yard: in the Regulations it is considered synonymous with *Gaz*, q. v.

ZIRÁÂT, H. &c. (A. زراعت), vernacularly also JIRÁÍT, and JIRÁYAT, q.v., corruptly, ZARAYET, ZEROYET. Agriculture, cultivation, farming: a cultivated farm or field: sometimes lands not artificially irrigated; also, Karn., a pension.

Ziráâti, vernacularly, *Jiraiti*, corruptly, *Zeroytee*, H. &c. (زراعتي) Cultivable arable lands; also, sometimes, assessable lands, subject to assessment.

Zor-ṯalab, H. (P. زور, force, and A. طلب, seeking) A compulsory exaction, enforced augmentation of amount of revenue.

Ẓu, H. (A. ذو) A lord, a master, used chiefly in composition to imply possessed of, as *Ẓu-al-karnín*, Possessed of two horns, *i.e.* of the east and west, a sovereign: applied especially to Alexander the Great.

Ẓu-al-yad, A. (ذواليد, having in hand) The actual occupant or possessor of property.

Ẓuát-ul-Imṣál, A. (ذوات الامثال) Things possessed of equivalency, in respect of weight or measure, receivable as the price of an article sold, as grain and the like.

Ẓuát-al-ḳím, A. (ذوات القيم) Things possessed of price, *i.e.* of money value, as the equivalents of an article sold, goods, chattels, &c.

Zubán-bandí, H. (P. زبان, the tongue, and بندي, binding) Deposition, affidavit, a written record of the questions put to a witness, and his answers.

Zubání, H. (زباني), *Jabáni*, Mar. (जबानी) A deposition, a declaration, a written as well as a *viva voce* statement of a claim.

Zulfaḳárí, H. (A. ذوالفقاري) The current silver coin of Hyderabad (from its bearing the impression of a sword, that of Mohammad, and afterwards of Âli, named *Zu-al-faḳár*).

Ẓulm, H. (A. ظلم) Tyranny, oppression, extortion, a heavier assessment than the people can bear.

Ẓálim, H. (A. ظالم) An oppressor, an extortioner.

ADDITIONS AND CORRECTIONS.

A.

Ábchah, H. (آبچك) A water-way, a drain.

Ábádí, H. (آبادي) The part of the village lands on which the dwellings are erected.

Ábád-kárí, H. (آبادكاري) Right derived from first clearing away and occupying land: also, adj., improving, as an estate, increasing, as rent.

Abhimána-putra, S. &c. (अभिमानपुत्र) A foster son.

Áchandrárkam, corruptly, Auchendrarkum.

Áḍam, Tam. (ஆடம்) A measure used for oil=20 *padis*.

Áḍepáḍe, Mar. (आडेपाडे) Portion of grain taken by the *Pátil* from each cultivator's heap as his due.

Adhiár, corruptly, *Adyar*, H. A cultivator who assists in cultivating land on condition of receiving half the crop.

Adhihár, vernacularly, *Adhiár*, corruptly, *Adyar*.

Adhikári, corruptly also *Adigary*, *Odhecaree*: in Bengal the term is sometimes used as a family name or title, as *Jabalkiswar Adhihári*: it usually implies a Brahman descent.

Áḍhak, Áṛhak, also Áṛhá, Áṛhi, corruptly Ara, Arra, Aree, Arree, Ben. (আঢক, আঢা, আঢী). In Bengal the *Áṛhí* is a grain measure containing two *maunds*: in some places it also denotes a measure of land, apparently much the same as a *Bighá* subdivided into *Kaṭṭhás*.

Adholí, corruptly, Adolee, Adoly, Mar. (अधोली) A measure of capacity, properly equal to half a *Páhali*, or two *Sers*, but varying in different places.

Áḍi, corruptly, Audy, Tam. (ஆடி) The fourth month of the Tamil year (July-August).

Aḍima-janm. The mortgage so designated is said sometimes to imply perpetual immunity from servitude when granted to a person of a servile caste.

Ág, corruptly, Aug, Hindi (आग) Rate levied as a share of government revenue on the cattle of a coparcenary village; rate of grazing charge for cattle, that on a buffalo being called an *Ág*, that on a cow half an *Ág*, and that on a calf a quarter *Ág*.—Delhi.

Ágario, Guz. (આગરીઓ) A salt-maker.

Agradána, corruptly, Ugurdanee: the same Brahman is also termed *Agraṣráddhí*, corruptly, *Ugursradee*.

Áhar; also any piece of water. *Áhari*, vulgarly, *Áhrí*, a small reservoir.

Áhitágni, corruptly, Auhaetagee.

Ahl-i-kár, in the sing., less correctly *Ahil-kár*, is also the title of the chief native judge, whether criminal or civil, in Kuch Bahár.

Ail bater, (?) A narrow pathway sufficient for cattle, especially on the top of a boundary ridge or mound, whence it denotes a boundary of such a description: a cow-road (perhaps from A. *Ail* ايل, a goat or stag, and H. بات, *bát*, a road).

Aima, erroneously, Ima.

Aima-kharáj, H. A grant of land bearing a quit-rent.

Âin, corruptly, Iyen.

Ainat, or *Ainath* (?) H. Rate of assessment.

AIYAṆ, corruptly, IEAYER: also the head of a religious community.

Ájná-patra, corruptly, *Agian-putr*.

ÂL, incorrectly, AIL, ALL: also a boundary mark. See *Ail-bater*

Alavagulu, also read *Alavoloogoo* and *Oolagoo*.

ALAVI: also, an instalment.

Alavi-patra, corruptly, *Alvyputra*, Karn. An instalment bond.

ALI is sometimes said to be a measure of $2\frac{1}{2}$ *Bisis*.—Kamaon.

Aliya santána, corruptly, *Alyasantan*.

AMADA, (?) Tel. A distance of eight or ten miles.

Amdáni, Guz. (અમદાની) also, duty on imports.

ÂM, H. (A. عم) An uncle, a father's brother.

Âm zâda, H. (عمزاده) An uncle's son, a cousin.

Anamat-patti, (?) Tel. A separate account.

ANGAN: in the S. more usually ANKANAM, corruptly, ANKAUNUM.

ÁNI, more correctly, ÁṆI (ஆனி) The third month of the Tamil year (June-July).

ANKAṆAM, corruptly, ANCUNNA, Tel. (అంకణం) A measure of land, a definite quantity of ground: a division of a house, which is commonly described as consisting of so many *Ankaṇams*, from three or four to between thirty and forty: it also applies to ground unoccupied adjacent to the house: according to Brown, it means an apartment, or the space between two beams or pillars, which latter is also Campbell's interpretation: the former appears to be its ordinary meaning.

ANKHRA, ANKRA, (?) Guz. The total assessment of an estate, without reference to the items of which it consists: (no doubt from *Ánkhu* આંખુ, whole).

ANṢ, also a land measure = 1 *Bísi*.—Kamaon.

ANṢAM, corruptly, AMSHOM, Mal. (S. അംശം) A part, a share, a subdivision of a province, a territorial division.

ANUBHAVAM, corruptly, ANUBHOM.

ANUMATI, corruptly, ANOOMATY, S. (अनुमति) Assent, consent, permission.

Anumati-patra, corruptly, *Oonamuttee-putter*, *Unamuttee-pottah*, *Unamuttee-puttur*.

ÁPAS-NÁMA, H. (آپس, self, selves) A voluntary deed of adjustment between parties.

ARAVÁR, vulgarly, ARWÁR: it is said also to designate a usufructuary mortgage for a stipulated period.

Áriyat-náma, H. An engagement to return any article or property which has been given on loan or in trust.

ARKÁTÍ, H. (اركاتي) A pilot.

ARKATIA, URKUTTEEA, (?) H. A difference of $2\frac{1}{2}$ *Biswas* per *Bighá* between local and government measurement.—Ghazipur.

ARPAN-NÁMA, H. (from S. अर्पण, delivering) A deed of gift, especially to a temple or idol.

AṚPASÍ, corruptly, ALPESEE, Tam. (ஐப்பசி) The seventh month of the Tamil year (Oct.-Nov.).

ARRA, ARRAR, (?) Beng. A fishery, a hole in the bed of a river in which fish are caught.

ARTHI, corruptly, ARUTEAH.

Árzi musanná, H. (عرضي مثني) A petition or plaint in duplicate.

ÂṢBIAT, H. (A. عصبيت) Affinity entitling to a share of inheritance: according to some authorities, to a sixth.

ÁSIN, sometimes AṢWAJA.

ASTÁCHI, (?) Tam. A writing, a deed, an agreement.

ATVETH, (?) Mar. Personal service exacted from the cultivators by the revenue contractor or government officers.

Auḳát guzárí, (اوقات گذاري, plur. of *Waḳt*, time) Subsistence, allowance, means of passing one's life.

AUSAT, corruptly, OSUT, OSHUT, OSIT, USIT, (? perhaps from A. وسط *wasṭ*, middle, included) Beng. Subordinate, under, dependent, as a tenure of land, or part of an estate held of a superior: the term is peculiar to East Bengal, and is much the same as the *Pattani*, or *Patni* of the west.

Ausat-hawála, Beng. A subordinate holding termed *Hawála*, q. v.

Ausat-táluḳ, Beng. A portion of a *Táluḳ* held in subordination to the entire *Táluḳ*.

Ním-ausat-táluḳ, Beng. (P. نيم, a half) A subdivision of the preceding.

Áútki, Mar, (आउतकी) A portion of grain per plough levied at harvest as the perquisite of the *Pátil*.

ÂVAṆÍ, vulgarly, AUVANY, AUNY, Tam. (ஆவணி) The fifth Tamil month (Aug.-Sept.).

AVÍRÁ, barbarously, OBEERA.

ÁWAN: it is also elsewhere called the field into which the rice has been transplanted.

Ayakattu-alavogulu, (?) Karn. An account of the lands of a village, and of their distribution amongst the cultivators and proprietors.

Ayamera, corruptly, *Ayameera*, Karn. Portions of the crop assigned at harvest-time to the village servants and officers.

AZMÁISH, vernacularly, AJMAISH, corruptly, AJMASH.

Ajmaishi-patti, or *-patta*, corruptly, *Ajmaishy-putty*, (?) Survey statement.

B.

BABRIA, (?) Guz. The name of a tribe of Hindu cultivators in Kattiwár, after whom the district of Babriawar is named: seventy-two divisions of them are enumerated, of whom the *Kotila*, *Dhánkra*, and *Wara* clans are the principal.

BADARRO, corruptly, BUDUROW, H. (P. بدررو) A drain, a sewer.

BÁDIGA, incorrectly, BADEGA.

BÁDIKARI, (?) Mar. A non-resident cultivator in a *Khot* village engaging for a share of the crop.

BAGALO, commonly, BUGGALAH, Guz. (બગલો) A trading vessel navigating along the Malabar coast and in the Persian Gulf.

BÁHÁ, erroneously, BHAHA.

BAHÁDUR, H. &c. (P. بهادر) A hero, a warrior: under the Mohammadan government, a title of honour given to the nobles of the Court, usually associated with some others, as *Khán-bahádur*, *Raja-bahádur*: in more recent times it is given to persons of inferior, although respectable station, and to some of the government native officers.

BAHÍ, corruptly, BHAI, BHYE.

Bahí-dán, H. (P. دان, who knows) An auditor, an accountant, a person appointed to examine an account-book or books.

Bahí-sultáni, H. (from سلطان, a prince) A public or government register.

Bahí-yád-dásht, H. (P. یادداشت) A memorandum or note-book: a diary of proceedings kept by an *Amín*, or *Sadr-amín*.

BAHLÍ, H. (بهلي , बहली) A two-wheeled carriage for riding in.

Baí-baiáána, corruptly, *Bye-beanah*, H. (بيع بيعانه) A contract of sale, with acknowledgment of advance on account of the purchase-money.

Baí-kámil, H. (كامل, perfect) Final or absolute sale.

Baí-muáámla, H. (معامله, affair) A fictitious sale.

Baí-mukása: add; or sale of property in favour of a wife in lieu of her relinquishment of dower: in some cases it is a fraudulent transfer of property to a wife as an equivalent for a dower, but which she sells: it is also laxly used for a deed of sale for a settlement, and for a deed of sale to a widow by the heirs of her husband.

Baí-náma, corruptly, *Bayana-náma*.

BAILU, corruptly, BHYLE.

BAIRAK, BAIRAKH, H. (بيرك , بيركھ) A flag, especially one set up on taking possession of new or unoccupied land, whence it has come to signify the act of taking possession of such land, or official authority to do so: this, however, is more correctly expressed by *Bairak-ábádi*, corruptly, *Byruch-abadee*.

BAISHNAV, very corruptly, BUSTUM and BOSHTOM, which seem to be, however, vernacular corruptions.

Baishnavottar, corruptly, *Bushtomoottur*, *Boshtomoottur*.

BAITHÁN, corruptly, BYTAN, H. (بيتهان) A homestead, a farm, the residence of the farmer, and ground adjacent.

BÁJANTARI, corruptly, BIRJUNTRY.

Bájriá, Guz. (બાજરીઆ) Producing millet or other inferior grains: a village or class of villages.

BAKÁ, Tib. A cloth measure = 2 breadths.—Kamaon.

BAKHAR, incorrectly, BUKKAR.

BAKHRÁ, incorrectly, BUKRA.

BÁKI, barbarously, BUCKOY.

BÁKÍ-JÁI: add, or any balance.

BAKLA, (?) Beng. A small square of timber used in ship or boat-building.

BAKRA, (?) Uriya. A measure of land, apparently the same as a *Bighá*.—Cuttack.

BALAL, BALLAL, (?) Karn. A title in some parts of Karnata (perhaps the same as *Vallálan*, q. v.).

BAND: this is sometimes employed, though laxly, to designate the piece of water confined by an embankment.

BANDAR: when not a sea-port it especially applies to a mart on the banks of a river like *Kalna* or *Patna*.

Bandara, (?) A stone dam or dyke, an embankment of masonry.

Bandhak, corruptly, *Bandok*: the word is also laxly used for a piece of water confined by a dyke or embankment.

Ghair-band-o-basti, H. (غير, other) Unsettled, as an estate unassessed or with the revenue not determined.

Band-phánta, blunderingly, *Bund-phatuk*.

Bandhwára, H. (بندهواره) Specification of boundaries.

BÁNÍKÁRÍ, Beng. (বানীকারী) An abetter and aider in an offence: (but, properly, the term denotes only one who joins in disseminating language (*báni*) which may be calumnious or libellous).

BÁNS: also the standard measuring-rod in Guzerat, equal in some *parganas* to 20 feet $5\frac{1}{4}$ inches, in others to no more than 7 feet $5\frac{6}{10}$ inches.

Bantoï, (?) H. Coparcenary proprietor.—Kamaon.

Bhái-bánṭ, H. (بهاي بانت) Hereditary family share, applicable only occasionally to all the shares of a coparcenary village.

Anbánṭ, H. (انبانت) Undivided, unseparated: paying the revenue collectively through a representative, a village, &c.

BANYA, corruptly also BUNNEEA.

BÁR; add, a piece of forest land.

BAR, (?) Guz. Weight by which cotton is weighed, equal to 20 *Dharis* of 48 *Sers* each, or to 960 *Sers*.

BARÁR, incorrectly, BERAR.

BARDÁSHT: add, Furnishing porters and provisions to government officers and troops, and European travellers.—Kamaon.

BARGUNI, (?) Asam. Police tax.

BÁRHÍ, (?) H. Garden lands belonging to the government.—Kamaon.

Barhtí-baṭṭa, H. (برهتي بتّه) Commission, charge for agency.

BÁRI, Asam. Village lands.

BAROṬHÁ, Hindi (बरोठा) A washerman: a vestibule, a portico.

Bas-o-bás, (?) H. A local rate or cess payable by resident cultivators in addition to the land revenue, calculated at one rupee eight anas per plough: held to be illegal.

BÁSTU, vernacularly, BÁST.

BATER, BATÚR, (?) H. Raised boundary of a field: see *Ail-bater*, it occurs also *Gur-batur* ? for *Ghar-bater*.

BAṬ: also a small land measure.—Ghazipur.

Batwárá, is now most generally in use to imply a separation of coparcenary holdings at the desire of some or of all the coparceners, or the detachment of the share of an individual so as to constitute his share an entirely distinct property, made with the sanction of the revenue authorities: it is also, though laxly, applied to the deed or document under which the partition is made.

Sambatwárá, H. (from S. सम, all) The entire division into severalties of a coparcenary estate.

BATELÁ, corruptly, BOTILLA: it is a single-masted vessel of the burthen of from 30 to 85 tons, employed in the coasting trade of the Malabar coast.

BÁṬÍ, corruptly, BATTEE, page 67, 2d col. 38th line.

BAULI, more correctly, BHAULI, q. v., should be BHAOLI, q. v.

BAÜRI: add, A land measure.—Bahar.

Bayána-patra, Beng. (S. पत्र, a leaf) Acknowledgement of an advance.

BAYENGI, (?) H. The wool of the hill or Tibetan sheep.

Báz-dâwá-náma, H. (بازدعوي نامه) A deed of relinquishment.

Be-wáriṣ: also, used laxly, without an owner.

BEHRÍ: also a large division of a village including many *Paṭṭis*.—Bundelkhand.

Berij-paṭṭa, Mal. A grant of land by the government at a stipulated rent.

BESAR, BESARÍ, (?) Guz. A mixed sort of soil partaking of the properties of black and light soil.

BETH, (?) H. Occasional personal services of the villagers to the head man or proprietor, especially in cultivation (it is most probably an error for *Bheṭ*, q. v.)—Kamaon.

BETT: also, waste land.

BEWARTTA, (?) Uriya. An officer or agent under a Rája or Zamíndár of the *hilaját* estates, who manages the affairs of a district more or less extensive.

Bhadonwí, also, corruptly, *Bhudwee*, *Bhudduee*, *Bhuddye*, *Bhodaee*.

Bhága-vivaram, corruptly, *Vibaram*, Tam. (பாகவிவரம்) Separation or separate account of shares.

Bhágzát, (?) Beng. An agreement to divide a property under specified conditions.

Dori-bhág, (?) Guz. A principal share.

Bhaihar, (?) H. Petty rent in kind paid to the owner, a quit-rent.—Kamaon.

BHAINS, H. (بهينس) A buffalo. See *Bhyns*.

Bhainslet, H. (from ليتنا, to roll) A puddle, a pool (where buffaloes might roll).

BHÁRÁ, (?) H. A land measure $= 2\frac{1}{2}$ *Bisís*.—Kamaon.

BHARANA, corruptly, BHURRUN, BURRA.

BHARARI, (?) Alluvial land.

BHARAT: also Responsibility of an individual as *Lumberdar*.

BHÁRATÍ, corruptly, BHARTHEE, Hindi (भारती) Name of one of the ten orders of *Das-námi* ascetics.

BHARÍ, corruptly also BHERREE, it also denoted a rupee, the Company's Arcot rupee coined in Calcutta, in value $3\frac{1}{2}$ per cent. less than the Sikka rupee.

BHARNÁ, corruptly, BURNA, BURHNA: also, a pledge: a terminable mortgage, or one redeemable by the application of the surplus proceeds of an estate held as security.

Bharnádár, H. (P. دار, who has) A mortgagee, one who has occupation of an estate, the rent of which is retained until it liquidate the principal and interest of the debt.

Tamassuh-bharná, H. (تمسك, a bond) A bond with property pledged or land transferred, the proceeds of which are to be set off against the principal and interest of the loan.

Bharte, H. (بهرتي) lit. A filling: an accretion of land from alluvial deposit.

Bhata, (?) Guz. Light sandy soil, but productive: also a tract in which such soil prevails.—Guzerat.

Bháti, (?) H. A grant of land made originally for the support of the grantee.

Bhátijamá, H. Revenue derived from *Bháti* land.

Bháṭu, also read **Bháṭá**, Guz. (ભાઠુ) Land subject to inundation, or deposited by returning floods: alluvial soil.

Bhaüṅriá, corruptly, **Bhoureah**, **Bhowreah**.

Bhavantí: also a tiled house.

Bháwar, (?) H. Another name for the *Tarái* or low lands along the foot of the Himalaya.

Bhed-bahi, (?) Beng. A waste-book.

Bheja, Guz. (ભેજ) Moisture oozing from the surface of the soil, also damp exuding from walls, &c.

Bheli, corruptly, **Bhailee**.

Bhenṭ-náma, H. (بهينت نامه) A deed of gift.

Bhera, (?) H. Cess on wild-bees' nests.—Kamaon.

Bhet, also, in Kamaon, personal service exacted by the Zamíndár or *Padhán* from the cultivators.

Bhítar-báṛí, corruptly, *Beetur-báree*, H. (بهيتر, inner, باڑي, a house) The ground on which a house stands, and the land immediately adjacent or inclosed round it.

Bhiṭí-báṛí, H. (بهٹي باڑي) A homestead, the site of a house and the land adjoining to and dependent upon it.

Bhogyádhi, corruptly, *Bogueady*.

Bholáṇ, Guz. (ભોલાણ) Flood, inundation: adj. swampy, marshy.

Bhúndari, also corruptly, *Boondah*.

Bhúra, (?) Beng. A given quantity of sand; a boat load.

Bí, **Bee**, (?) H. A measure of grain, a subdivision of a *Pauti*.—Dinajpur.

Bíd, (?) Karn. A temple.

Bíghá, also, corruptly, **Biggah**.

Bíjáwari, also, corruptly, *Bejawary*, *Beejevary*.

Bilká, (?) H. A sheaf of corn, used in Kamaon as a means of measuring land, the number of *Bilkás* being computed as corresponding with that of the *nalis* of seed sown in a *Bísí*.

Bimbati, (?) Asam. Wet land.

Bindast, Mar. (S. P. बिनदस्त) Exempt from revenue, land, &c.

Biral, *Birral*, *Beral*, (?) A kind of hook for holding planks together in ship building.—Chittagong.

Binwánsí, H. (بنوانسي) A subdivision of a *Tíswánsí*. See *Bíswánsí*.

Birádar, H. (S. برادر) A brother.

Birádar-âm-záda, H. A first cousin, an uncle's son.

Birt, also of various kinds; as,

Birt-jajmán, or *-jajmání*, H. (from S. यजमान) The right to the performance of the domestic ceremonies of a householder, and the fees payable thereupon.

Birt-khairát, H. (A. خيرات, alms) A small gratuity to religious persons on various occasions.

Birt-patra, H. (S. پتر, a leaf) A title-deed, or rather a voucher for any holding of land or property as *Birt*, or subsistence.

Birt-purohití, corruptly, *Birt-prohitai*, H. (S. पुरोहित) Dues claimed by the hereditary family priest.

Bekh-birt, (?) H. A kind of tenure, land held on a quit-rent.—Saran.

Kús-birt, (?) The hereditary right of certain Brahmans to perform the domestic ceremonies of the better orders of the *Kúrmi* class of cultivators.—Bahár.

Mitiya-birt, (?) H. The hereditary right of certain Brahmans to perform the domestic ceremonies of the lower orders of the *Kúrmi* class of cultivators.—Bahar.

Nahdí-birt, H. (A. نقد, ready money) A money allowance or pension.

Bís, Beng. (बीस) A large measure of grain = 40 *mans*.

Bísa, (?) H. A measure of land equal to four *Bísís*.—Kamaon.

Bisaya, (?) Asam. A native officer who collects the revenue from the cultivators (perhaps the *Bisoi* of Orissa).

Bishní, (?) H. A denomination of lands held under a peculiar local tenure.—Shahabad.

Bísí: the measure of land in Kamaon is also said to be as much as should be sown with twenty *nális* of seed.

Biswánsí: the subdivisions of this are differently enumerated, and the proportions nowhere defined, although they are possibly twentieths: one statement makes them *Tíswánsí*, *Kachwánsí*, *Anwánsí*; another *Kachwánsí*, *Nanwánsí*, *Tíswánsí*; and a third, *Tíswánsí*, *Kachwánsí*, *Anwánsí*, *Nanwánsí*.

Bogsa, Name of a tribe inhabiting the low *Tarái* adjoining Rohilkhand.

Bohuda, (?) H. Rent-free land granted by village communities to religious societies.—Doab.

Bohra, in Guzerat a considerable portion of the *Bohras* are agriculturists.

Boládár, less correctly, *Bolehdar*, H. (بولادار) A tenant under a verbal agreement: in some parts of the north-west provinces there are two descriptions of such cultivators, viz.

Boládár-band-sharâ, the cultivator of land, amount not specified, at a fixed rate during the term of the present settlement of the district.

Boládár-bil-muhta, the cultivator of a specified amount of land during the same term at a quit-rent: both tenures are hereditary during the stipulated term.

Borá, also H. (بورا): also a canvas sack for holding grain or salt, and sometimes considered as a measure of a definite quantity of two or three *maunds*.

Bosí, (?) Sindh. Cultivation depending on river inundation.

Brahmottara: other corruptions are *Burmetter*, *Burmitter*, *Burmutteear*, *Bilmootter*.

Brita, (?) H. Tenure of land held by Brahmans (probably corruption of *Birt* or *Brit*).—Kamaon.

Kuṣa-brita, H. (S. कुश, sacred grass) Absolute grant of land to a Brahman at an eclipse, or on some other solemn occasion, the grant being affirmed by the presentation of a tuft of *kuṣa* grass.—Kamaon.

Buddali, Buddili, Karn. A leather vessel for holding oil, opium, &c. (? from the English 'bottle').

Bukka, (?) Karn. A hollow bambu tube attached to the plough of cotton-fields, serving as a drill.—Karnáta.

Búṛhá, H. (بوڑها) lit. An old man: in Kamaon, the senior or head man of a village.

Búrhálí, H. (بورهالي) Land or privileges attached to the headship of a village: the same as *Padhánchári*.—Kamaon.

C.

Chak-basta, H. (P. بسته, bound) A definite portion of land.

Chak-basta-dár, H. (P. دار, who has) A renter of a definite portion of an estate.

Chak-náma: A register or specification, &c.

Chakránkam, S. &c. (चक्रांकं) The mark of the discus of *Vishṇu*, stamped with a hot iron on the persons of his worshippers.

Chakránkadam, Tel. (from S. द, who or what gives) Stamping the followers of Vishṇu with his *chakra* or discus.

Chalán, also, *Chelan*, *Chillun*: also, a memorandum of money received and invested.

Chaltá, Guz. (ચલતા) Entire, perfect, as a share in a village.

Chamár, corruptly, Chumhar, Chumbar.

Chamárin, H. (چمارن) The wife of a *Chamár* or female of the caste, who commonly officiates as the village midwife.

Chándni-ráyat, Beng. A shopkeeper or artificer owning the ground on which his shop or dwelling stands in a bazár.

Chándlá: also a present sent to a man in whose family a marriage is about to take place.

Chara, (?) Beng. Land on which plants are reared for transplanting.—Sylhet.

Charáï: also a tax on pasturage levied in the *Taraï*.—Kamaon.

Charaṇdás, Hindi (चरण, the foot, दास, the slave) The name of a founder of a sect of Vaishnavas in the middle of the eighteenth century.

Charaṇdásí, Hindi (चरणदासी) A follower of the sect of *Charaṇdás*: the peculiar observances and doctrines of the sect.

Charkh, Charkhá, Sindh (P. چرخ) A water-wheel: cultivation dependent on water supplied by a wheel.

Charkhábi, Sindh (P. from اب, water) Irrigated by means of water-wheels, land, &c.

Charhhshumárí, Sindh (P. شماري, a numbering) Tax on water-wheels.

Chás, also a ploughed furrow.—Guzerat.

Chásio, Guz. (ચાસીઓ) Grown in furrows, applied especially to the best sort of wheat.

Chattiram, inaccurately, Chutrum, also a temple.

Chaubáchha: in some villages the specification is *Kuṛi*, *Pág*, *Ág*, cattle, and *Dhartí*, land.

Chaudhari: also, in Asam, the hereditary native collector.

Chauhadda: also a boundary statement, a boundary map or plan.

Chautheli, Mar. (चौथेली) The fourth part of the produce of a farm or field.

Cháwal: this share is said to be equal to a sixteenth of an *ana*, or subdivision of a *bhág* or share: it should properly be a sixteenth, but this is not always the case; six *bhágs* of a certain village being reported as containing ninety *anas*: (but this may be an error for ninety-six.)

Chawar, (?) Guz. A drill plough.

Cherukánam, (?) Mal. A sub-mortgage lease.

Chháṛ, also Chháṛ-chitthi, incorrectly, Char, H. (چهاڑ, چهاڑ چٿّهي) A deed of remission of rent or revenue granted by the proprietor or by the collector on the part of government.

Chháṛ sanad, incorrectly, *Char sunnud*, H. A revised and confirmed *sanad* or grant.

Chihnit, corruptly *Chinnut*: also a division of an estate.

Chílla: also a place or house in which a temporary shrine of a Mohammadan saint may be set up.

Chinká, (?) H. (S. *kshanika*, temporary) An apparatus for crossing rivers in the Himalaya, a cable fastened across a stream to trees or posts, along which a basket in which the passenger places himself travels, suspended by a wooden ring and drawn across by ropes.

Chirághí: also, in Eastern Bengal, a tenure of land apparently rent-free.

Chitpaṭṭa, H. (چت پٿّا) A memorandum of a lease.

Chittarai, Tam. (சித்திரை, S. चैत्र) The first month of the Tamil year (April-May).

Chiṭṭhá, also, corruptly, **Chitta**: also a banker's acknowledgment of accountability for money deposited.

Chok, (?) A subdivision of an estate.

Chopri, also **Choprá**, Guz.: also a field-book containing a specification of the lands of a village.

Chorakharch, Guz. (ચોરખરચ) Private expenses, secret service money, the contingent expenses of a village for entertaining travellers, &c., not entered in the regular accounts of disbursements.

Chotela, (?) H. A measure of land, a *Bísí* and a quarter. —Kamaon.

Chukání: also, in Asam, land cultivated by tenants on the tenure of an equal division of the crop with the landlord.

Chukti: also annual rent.

Chulavero, Guz. (વેરો, a tax) A tax on hearths or cooking places.

Chúrú, (?) Asam. Hearth tax.

D.

Ḍáb, also **Ḍháb**.

Ḍába, also **Ḍáb**: also an abstract of a list or register, a statement of shares.

Ḍábar: also a hollow.

Dada, **Dudah**, (?) A list of the cultivators of a village.

Daf, H. (P. دف) A small flat drum or tambourine.

Dafálí, H. (دفالي) A drummer, a player on the *Daf*, one whose especial business it is to play on the instrument.

Daïn-mahr, corruptly, *Deyn-mohur*, *Dine-mohur*, *Denmeher*, H. (دين مهر) A dower, the amount due as a dower. See *Mahr*.

Daïn-mahr-muâjil, corruptly, *Den-meher-moujjul*, H. (A. معجل) Dower paid at the time of marriage. See *Mahr*.

Daka, Sindh. A water-wheel for irrigation, the cultivation depending on it.

Dákhil-hár, corruptly, *Duhl-har*.

Dákhilá, corruptly, *Dahhilla*, *Dhakhilla*.

Dal, **Dul**, Beng. (দল) A sort of aquatic grass (Panicum stagninum).

Dalbehera, corruptly, *Dulbera*.

Dal, (?) Determination of the value of a crop by selecting and threshing portions from different parts of a field.

Daladok, (?) H. Village dues, usually in kind.

Dálán, H. (دالان) An apartment: a vaulted building: used laxly for any building.

Dalhi, (?) Mar. Arable land on acclivities inaccessible to the plough.

Dám: also, in Kamaon, the maximum weight of metals, &c. equal to about 100 Farakhabad rupees weight.

Damdatt, ? **Dándatt**, H. Gift upon gift of land.—Kamaon.

Damola, (?) Half a *kánch* or *tola* of gold dust.—Kamaon.

Dánpaṭṭi, H. (دان پٿّي) A deed of gift.

Dánságar, H. (S. सागर, the ocean) A ceremony, as a *Ṣráddha* or the like, at which the full amount of usual gifts is distributed.

Dandakavila (?) Tel. Specification of the shares of a divided property.

Ḍángá: also used laxly for land in general or any particular spot, as,

Kalai-dángá, inferior land; *Gochar-dángá*, pasture land or common.—Bírbhúm.

Dar-ijára-dár, H. (P. دار, who has) The holder of a sublease or farm.

Dar-o-bast-hakúk, H. (A. حق, a right) All right and title whatever.

Darail, **Daryle**, (?) H. A ridge of land forming a boundary.

Dariábádí, H. (from دريا, the sea, ?) Land recovered from the Sunderbans in Eastern Bengal.

Dariche, (?) Mar. Land prepared for sowing by previous burning.

Darkhást, corruptly, also, **Durgast**, and **Dirgast**: it is also sometimes applied to the document issued by the revenue officer acceding to the terms offered for land.

Darhást-dár, Mar. (दरखास्तदार) The offerer of a tender of rent or purchase of land.

Dar-shikamí, H. (from شكم, the belly) Subordinate, as a tenure or sharer under a *shikami* holding or holder.

Dasabandam, incorrectly, *Dusabundum*: also, land held at a reduced rent.

Daṣabhágam, S. &c. (दशभाग) A tenth part, tithe: the tenth of the produce of a field irrigated from a reservoir, applied to keeping it in repair.

Dásanu, vulgarly, *Dasen*, Karn. (ದಾಸನು, S. दास) A slave: a hereditary mendicant.

Dastáwez, also, corruptly, *Dustavees, Dustiwuj.*

Dastaiwaj-yádí, Mar. (दस्तऐवजयादी) A bond, an acknowledgment of a loan.

Dastbandhah, corruptly, *Dushtbunduch*, H. A simple mortgage.

Dast-gardán, Dast-garda, H. (? the latter): also, a loan on verbal acknowledgment: any purchase or loan on a verbal promise to pay: it is also applied laxly to a note of hand promising payment of a settled sum or value.—Tirhut.

Dastúr-i-khándán, H. (P. خاندان) Family usage.

ḌAUL: also a counterpart lease.—Tirhut.

Ḍaul-darṣaní, corruptly, *Dool-dursanee*, (?) H. A roll or register of landed proprietors kept in the north-west provinces under the native government.

DAURA, (?) Beng. A canal, a water-course.

Dáyáda, corruptly, *Diadee, Diadi, Diadul.*

Dáyará, corruptly, *Daierah*, Hindi (दायरा) Inheritance, hereditary property.

DE, Tibet. A measure of capacity, one-twelfth of a *Dobu.*—Kamaon.

DEAKE, (?) Asam. The deputy or vice-president of a religious conference or assembly.

DEBBA, (?) Marshy land.—Chittagong.

Debsebá, Beng. (S. দেবসেবা) lit. Service of a deity: any religious purpose or endowment.

DEGREE-JÁRI, Beng. (দেগরীজারী, from the English 'degree') Proceeding or recovering, as a loan, gradually, or by degrees; a sentence of court to that effect.

ḌEORHI: it is also applied to an inclosure containing a lesser or greater number of buildings.

Devasét, Mar. (देव, and शेत, a field) Land granted free to a person who has been successful in an appeal to divine agency, as in an ordeal on behalf of the village community.

Devaṣevá, vulgarly, *Debsheva*, H. (S. सेवा, service) Doing the duty or managing the affairs of a temple; also a religious grant or endowment.

Devasom, (?) Mal. A temple (perhaps an error or corruption of *Devasthán*, or *Devaswam.*

DEVALA, H. (S. देवल) A bankrupt.

Devottara, also corruptly, *Dewutter, Daooter, Debater.*

ḌHÁLBOL, also DHÁLI-BOLI: also, foreclosure of a mortgage.

DHALKAZAMÍN, Sindh. Land paying money-rent, as growing articles more valuable than grain, as cotton, tobacco, &c.

Dhána-bandí: also, in Sindh, settlement of division of the crop between the cultivator and the government according to previous agreement.

Dhán-maḍi, corruptly, *Danmoodie.*

DHANGARIA, DANGUREEA, (?) Guz. Villages or lands producing rice crops.

Dhanu, Mal. (S. ധനു) The fourth Malabar month, December, the sun being in *Sagittarius.*

DHARA, (?) H. A subdivision of a village.—Kamaon.

DHÁRÁ: a right to a portion of a village, varying in extent and value from many fields to a single tree, held at a fixed rate of assessment.

DHÁRO, incorrectly, DARA, Guz. (ધારો) Rule for government dues and collections.

Dhárekarí, incorrectly, *Darehuree*, Mar. (धारेकरी) The holder of land lightly assessed: laxly, the land so held.

DHARI, corruptly, DURREE: in Guzerat it is also applied to a measure of cotton = to 48 *sers.*

Dharmásanam, vulgarly, *Durmasanom*, Tam. (S. धर्मासनं) Land or villages granted to Brahmans either rent-free or at a quit-rent.

Dhármasádhana, S. &c. (from साधन, a means) A deed of gift.

DHARTA, corruptly, DURTA: also, bonus, premium.

DHARTÍ: also, proportion of government revenue in some of the villages of the north-west provinces payable by each coparcener according to the extent of his share.

DHEKURÍ, (?) Guz. An apparatus for raising water from a river by bullocks, similar to that used for wells, practicable only when the river runs under a nearly perpendicular bank.

ḌHON, (?) H. A grain measure = 16 *Pathas*, or one-twentieth of a *Khárí* (? if it should not be *Dron.* See *Khárí*).—Garhwal.

DHOTAR, (?) Karn. A coarse cotton-cloth manufacture in Dharwar.

DHUNGRA, (?) Guz. Name of people who gather the cotton pods from the field.

DÍÁRÁ, also corruptly, DEARAH, DEEHARA.

Digrí-járí, Beng. (দিগরীজারী) The written sentence or decree of a court.

Dehbandí, incorrectly, *Dehabundee.*

Díhwárí-muntakhab, H. (A. منتخب) An abstract account of an estate, according to the villages in it.

Dikári, Asam. The head of a religious assembly or conference (probably an abbreviation of *Adhikárí*).

Díkshá, corruptly, Theetcha.

Dínár: also, a gold coin variously valued at $2\frac{1}{2}$ or 5 rupees, being said to be of the weight of 20 *Kiráts*, each *Kirát* being equal to 5 *Jaus* (seed of barley or millet): a *Dínár*, therefore, is equal to 100 *Jaus*, or 10 *Chinams*, which, at 15 rupees per *tola*, is equal to 5 rupees.—Masulipatam.

Diwan-bo, (?) H. Revenue from newly-cultivated waste land.—Kuch-Bahar.

Ḍoba, incorrectly, Dhoba, a pond.

Dobhal, (?) H. The name of one of the principal Brahman tribes in Garhwal.

Dobu (?) Tibet. A measure of capacity equal to a *Kachchá man* of 20 *Sers*: in some places it is said to be equal to 18 *De*, in others to 12.

Doko, (?) Beng. A fishery in marshy land.

Doja, (?) Tibet. An ingot of silver stamped at Lhassa, current in the hills for something less than 20 Farakhabad rupees.

Dokaṭṭhi, corruptly, *Docutty*, H. (P. دو, two) A feudal claim by the lord paramount of the produce of two *Kaṭṭhas* per *Bíghá*, now obsolete—Bhágalpur.

Don, (?) Beng. Partly dry bed of a river.

Drishtabandhak, vernacularly, *Dishtbandhak*, corruptly, *Distbunduk*.

Drona, commonly, Droon, sometimes Doon, A land measure in Sylhet, &c.

Dru-payir, Tam. (from S. द्रु, a tree) Produce of trees, as cocoa-nuts and the like.

Dugalamu, Dugulamu, Tel. (దుగలము, దుగులము) The sixteenth part of a pagoda.

Dulhá, Hindi (दुल्हा) A bridegroom.

Dulhan, *Dulhin*, corruptly, *Dholohn*, H. (दुल्हन, दुल्हिन) A bride.

Dumálá-jhárá, Mar. (from झाडा, a sweeping away) An official scrutiny of titles to alienated lands.

Durah-jár, (?) H. A comprehensive term for lands within the limits of a known portion of an estate (some blunder perhaps for *Dar-ijárá*).

Dwár, or Doar, Asam. A frontier district (perhaps from *Dwár*, a door).

E.

Eddangali, corruptly, Dungalie, Dungally: sometimes said to be equivalent to a Madras *Ser*.

Eḍḍavam, less correctly, Edavam, Mal. (ഇടവം) The ninth (? the eighth) month of the Malayalam year (May-June).

Edurunuḍi, or *Yedurunuḍi*, Karn. (ಎದುರುನುಡಿ) A counterpart agreement.

Ekjái, H. (from P. جا, place) In one lump, in one total: in the same place.

Elebale, (?) Leaf of the Piper betel.

Elangal-tottakál, (?) Tam. Land lately prepared for garden cultivation.

Errayat-náma, (?) Tam. A document issued by a collector confirming and authenticating a compromise between parties in a litigation concerning land.—Tiniveli.

F.

Faisala, corruptly, Fysalla.

Faiṣalnáma-ṣáliṣi, H. (A. ثالث, third) An arbitration award.

Fard: also, a statement or account.

Fard-paṭṭidárí, H. (فردپٿيداري) A list or schedule of the shares of a joint estate.

Do-fardí, H. (دو, two) A double account, shewing the amount of land held, and rent paid by each Ryot.

Hisáb-i-fard, H. (حسابي فرد) A detailed account, an account particulars.

Fárigh-khattí, also, corruptly, *Farghuttee*, *Farkuttee*, *Parekut*.

Faringatí, (?) Asam. Dry or unirrigated land.

Farmáish: also, a requisition on a village for small articles of consumption, as grass, firewood, &c.; formerly levied for the use of the district officers.

Faṣl-chár, H. (فصل چار) An acquittance granted by the collector for the harvest produce of land exempted from revenue.

Faṣl-jástí, barbarously, *Fuzzle-jaste*: also used laxly for any enhanced assessment on land.

Faṣl-náma, corruptly, *Fusul-namah*, H. (P. نامه, a document) An agreement entered into by a number of the members of a village community (perhaps it should be *Faiṣal-náma*.

Foras, (Port. *fora*, without) A term applied in Bombay to waste land adjacent to cultivated land, and granted to the cultivators of the latter at a quit-rent: it occurs in old grants of the local government especially in the phrase *foras* and *pertenças*, the latter also Port., dependencies, appurtenances.

G.

GABHÁN : also, Guz., land on which to erect a house, or that on which the houses of a village are erected.

Gadi, also, in Bengal, often denotes a house of business, a banking-house ; also, the headship of a religious establishment.

GÁDÍ, or GADDI, (?) H. A class of cultivators in the Delhi district.

Gaini-eduruvali, (?) Karn. A written agreement to pay a stipulated rent, given by the renter to the proprietor.

Chal-gaini, (?) Mal. (S. चल, to go) The tenure of a temporary occupant, a terminable lease.

Kraya-gaini, (?) Karn. (S. क्रय, purchase) Purchase of the property and rights of an original proprietor.

Múl-gaini, (?) Karn. (S. मूल, root) Original and unvarying rent, a perpetual lease.

GAIRÁN, Mar. (गैरान, from the A. غير, other) Lands in a village other than those regularly assessed.

GAMETI, (?) Guz. Designation of proprietary villages held by Rajputs paying revenue.—Guzerat.

GANḌA : it is also in constant use to denote a proportionate quantity of land.

Gándharba : the practice still exists among the hill Rájas, and gives to the woman a station above that of a concubine, although below that of a wife married according to the *Vaidik* ritual.

GANOT, less correctly, GUNWUT : also, any lease of land.

Ganotiá, incorrectly, *Gunwuteea*, Guz. (ગણોતીઆ) Paying rent or revenue per *bíghá*, according to agreement with each cultivator separately—a village or estate.

Chálu-ganot, Guz. (ચાલુ, inactive) A permanent rent.

Phirta-ganot, Guz. (from H. پهرنا, to go about) Varying rent.

GANṬHÁ : or rather 7 feet $5\frac{6}{10}$ inches : in some places the *Ganṭhá* is the same as the *Báns* or standard rod = 20 feet $5\frac{1}{4}$ inches.

Dar-gánṭhí-dár, H. (P. در, prefixed) A sub-tenant holding of the *Gánṭhi-dár*.

Gánṭhi-jama, corruptly, *Gatee-jumma*.

Gánwín, corruptly, *Gaeen*, Hindi (गांवीं) Village expenses.

Gáonkar, sometimes *Gámkar* : also, the head man of a village.

Gáonkarí, Mar. (गावंकरी) A villager, but especially one having a right to share in the village lands or crops.

Gaon-ká-goti, (?) Asam. A village accountant under the native collector.

Gáon-ki-watan, Mar. (see *watan*) Hereditary and indefeasible right to a share in the lands of a village not effaced by even long absence.

Gáonkhátá-zamín, (?) Guz. Land let on account of the village community ; such as they may be able to dispose of, from a lapsed *bhág* or share, through want of heirs.

Gáon-nisbat-mirás, Mar. (मिरास, hereditary property) Land of which the proprietary right resides in the community collectively.

Gáonsárí-chalán, or *-dáh*, H. Passing on letters, goods, prisoners, treasure, &c., on public service, from village to village without charge.—Kamaon.

GARASI, or GARSI, (?) Tel. A frame-work of sticks lining a temporary shallow well dug in a loose soil.

Garasi-bávi, Tel. A shallow well in a loose soil.

GARBHOTTAR, corruptly, GARBUTTER, Beng. (গর্ভোত্তর) A ravine forming in the rains a water-course leading to a *Nala*.

GÁṚH, H. (گاڑہ) A weaver's seat, the place in which his loom is erected.

Garjan-khola, (?) A plantation of Garjan trees (Dipterocarpus).

GAUDA, (?) Karn. A large granary or grain store.

GAUL, (?) H. A water-course.—Kamaon.

GAUN, (?) Beng. A land measure larger than a *Dún*.

Gawik, (?) Mar. The fourth part of the lands of a village held by a *Khot*, and managed by himself.

GAYÁL, corruptly, GYALLEE.

GAZ : in Guzerat the *gaz* is $27\frac{1}{4}$ inches.

Reshmi-gaz, (?) Mar. A measure under the former government = 18 or 19 *tasus*.

GEHUN, incorrectly, GHOON.

Gehun-chásia, Guz. (from ચાસ, a furrow) Wheat grown without irrigation.

Ghardhan, H. (घरधन) lit., house-wealth : in Asam, poll-tax.

Gharenia, also, corruptly, *Girrania*, *Gurranea* : also, lands alienated on mortgage by village communities, and on that account withdrawn from assessment, an unauthorised alienation of public revenue.

Ghaṛidár, H. (P. دار, who has) The clock or bell striker.

Ghaṛ-padhán : also, the oldest *Asámí* appointed in a coparcenary Zamíndárí to manage the estate. See *Pradhán*.

Ghas-dána: it was originally imposed for the use of the cavalry employed in the *Mulkgiri* collection of the revenue, but was continued after the practice had ceased.

Ghátí, H. (گھاتي) An out-station of police.

Ghatwar, (?) H. An open space between the houses of a village and the land where cultivation commences: it is also termed the homestead or land in which a house stands, with the ground adjacent.

Ghuï-kar, H. (from S. کر, a tax) Pasturage tax formerly levied: a small present of milk, curds, and one pie per head, given to the village shareholders by other persons permitted to pasture their cattle on the village grass lands.—Kamaon.

GIRA, H. (گرہ) A division of a *Gaz*, three finger breadths.

Girá, Mar. (गिरा) A fourteenth or sixteenth of a *Gaz*, a *tasu* and a half.

GOLA-DÍP, H. (from S. *divya*) A kind of ordeal, carrying a red hot ball or bar of iron, not long since in use in Kamaon.

Góna, Tel. (గోణ) A sack, considered also as a measure = 10 *mans*.

GORÁḌU, GORÁṚU, Guz. (ગોરાડુ) A light coloured soil; one of the principal soils of Guzerat, varying from almost mere sand to a soil of the richest quality, a mixture of sand and clay.

Goráṛu-kuwetar, Guz. (કુવેતર, watered from wells) The soil called *Goráṛu* when irrigated by water supplied especially by wells.

Goráṛu-ubhaṛiá, Guz. (ઉભડીઆ, dry land) *Goráṛu* soil not irrigated.

Goráṛu-pandhar, (?) Guz. *Goráṛu* soil unirrigated and of the poorest sort.

Gorát: this contains more mould than *Goráṛu*.

GORMA, Tib. A silver coin current in Kamaon, rated at four *Jyus*, five of which are exchangeable for a Farakhabad rupee.

GOSHA, H. (P. گوشہ) A corner, a secluded spot, a detached field or piece of ground.

Gum-náma, H. (P. گم, lost) A written declaration of the loss of vouchers or documents.

GUNJÁISH, corruptly, GONZEASH.

GUNT, (?) H. The hill or Tartar pony.

Gunth: it is the twenty-fifth part of a *mána* or *bighá*: in Guzerat it is a measure of five *háths*, or cubits, or eight feet, and is one-twentieth of the side of a *bighá*.

GÚṚ, Mar. (गूड) Corn in the sheaf, especially in the portion of the crop assigned to the village servants before removal from the field.

Gurighar, (?) A cottage, a bangala.

Guzásht: it also denotes in some places land rented of proprietors and sub-let or *passed on* to cultivators: it may apparently be held hereditarily by both parties.—Shahábad.

Guzáshta-jamâ, corruptly, *Goozeeshta-jumma*, H. (جمع, revenue or rent) Past rent, or rent in arrear.

GWÁL, or GWÁLÁ, H. (گوال, گوالا) A cowherd.

Gwálin, corruptly, *Gywallin*, H. (گوالن) A woman of the cowherd caste, the wife of a cowherd.

H.

Had-bandi, also plur. *Hudud-bandí*.

HAFTAGÁNA, commonly, HAFTGANA, H. (هفتگانه) A register or diary of revenue claims and payments kept in the collector's office.

Haftnahksha, (?) H. A set of papers of village accounts kept by the *Patwárí*.

Hak-ájiri, (?) H. Proprietor's right, or rather the claim of the proprietor to the hire or rent of property let by him on lease.—Bahar.

Hak-murâfik, H. (A. مرافق, a companion) Actual or associated rights.

Hakím, H. In the Jangal Mahâls a title sometimes given to the second son of a Rája.

HAL: a plough; also, a measure of land in Sylhet: it is also used in the Mírath Zilâ as a nominal division of village lands equivalent to the division by *biswas*.

Hál-ábádí: also, the assessment imposed on newly-cultivated land.

Hál-i-dahhl, H. (دخل, entry) Actual possession.

Bahál-i-dahhl, H. (بحال, upheld) Upheld or confirmed in possession.

Hál-sákin, H. (P. ساکن, dwelling) Personal residence.

Hál-shana, (?) H. (perhaps from *Hal-siána*, plough-elder) A village officer or servant.—Birbhúm.

Halfan, barbarously, *Hul Fun*, H. (A. حلفاً) By or according to oath.

Halligádde, corruptly, *Hulligaday*, Karn. (ಹಳ್ಳಿಗದ್ದೆ) The wet or rice-lands of a village.

HAMṬÂÁM, corruptly, HUMTAUM, H. (A. طعام, food) One who eats or messes with another or with a family.

HANE, corruptly, HUNNAY.

Harsála, H. (سال, a year) Perennial, perpetual, as a lease.

HARAJ: also, a nuisance.

Haraj-áyanda, corruptly, *Hureejaindeh*, H. (P. آينده, coming) Prospective injury or loss.

HARIA, corruptly, HURREEA, Guz.

Hasbána, corruptly, *Husubana*, H. (حسبانه) According to custom, customary: applied to fees and perquisites claimed by village officers.

HASARNÁMA, (?) H. An agreement to abide by the award of an arbitrator.

Háthchitá, incorrectly, *Haut-chitta*, Beng. (হাথচিটা) A note of hand, any acknowledgment in a person's own handwriting, or bearing his signature.

Hath-khátá, corruptly, *Hat-kattur*, Beng. (হাথখাতা) A banker's book or account.—Rájsháhí.

HÁṬA, incorrectly, HATHA, HATTA.

HAWÁÏ, (?) Salvage on goods recovered from a wreck.—Sindh.

HAWÁLA: a farm at a fixed rent, unless otherwise stipulated: also, the deed by which such farm or holding is leased.

Hawálat, Beng.: also, a place of security, a temporary prison.

Hawálat-patra, Beng. A note of hand; acknowledgment of a temporary loan or obligation.

Hawili-grámamulu: and subsequently by the British government, being cultivated for its benefit, and constituting what were termed the 'Home-farms.'

HEGGAḌE, corruptly, HEGADAY.

HIBA, corruptly, HEBAH.

Hiba-mutlaḳ, H. (A. مطلق) An absolute and unconditional gift.

Hiba-náma, corruptly, *Ebah-náma*.

Hiba-tamlik, incorrectly, *Hibbeh-tumleek*, H. (A. تمليك, property) A deed of gift, a gift of property.

HÍR, (?) H. A piece of water.—Birbhúm.

Hissa-i-hákim, incorrectly, *Hissa-hukeem*, The share or right of the proprietor.

HOSÁGAMA, corruptly, HOSSOGAMY.

HOTHA, (?) H. A land measure = 1600 square paces.—Kamaon.

HUDA, (?) Beng. An estate, one comprising a number of villages.

HUJJAT, H. (A. حجّت) Proof, argument, a written voucher or acknowledgment.

HURḌÁ, Mar. (हुरडा) A portion of *Jawári* or holcus in the ear or sheaf, the perquisite of the village servants at the harvest.

Hurmat-bahá, H. (P. بها, price) Damages, compensation for calumny or libel.

HURO, Tib. Transit duty.

Huṭṭuwaḷi, corruptly, *Hootwaly*, *Hootoovully*.

Hajir-huṭṭuwaḷi, Karn. Actual or present produce.

Rawáj-huṭṭuwaḷi, corruptly, *Rivaz-hootvully*, Karn. (from H. رواج, current) Customary or average produce.

I.

Idumupairu: also the crop which is raised towards the end of the revenue year, the tax on which is brought to account before it is stacked.

Iḥtimámi, corruptly, *Itmamee*, H. (اهتمامي) Held in trust, held as an under tenure or part of a *táluḳ*, land, &c.

IJÁZAT, vernacularly, IJAJAT.

Ijázat-náma: also, a deed of authorisation.

Ijmáli-gumáshta, H. (P. گماشته, a factor) An agent or factor for persons holding property conjointly, or the manager of property so held.

Ijmáyali, corruptly, *Ijmuilee*.

IKBÁL: also, acquiescence, assent.

Ikbálí, H. In the way of or according to, assent or agreement.

Ikbal-dáwá, also, corruptly, *Ikbal-dawee*.

Ikrár-náma-ṣálaṣí: also, an agreement to abide by an award of arbitration.

Ikrár-náma-sipurdagí, H. (P. سپردگي, giving up, or over) A deed of hypothecation, by which property is assigned over as security for a loan.

Iladárawára, corruptly, *Illadarwar*, *Illdarwar*.

Illahur, less correctly, *Illumhoora*.

ILLAM, vulgarly, ILLOM, Mal. (ഇല്ലം) A house, a dwelling: but it is also used for a household, or the members of a family collectively.

ILLÁM-NÁMA, (?) H. A summons.—Midnapur.

IMLA, (?) Mar. A house, a building.

Inám-ṃániyam, corruptly, *Enam-moneyem*, Karn. Land granted in endowment rent-free: (a superfluous repetition of synonyms, one Arabic, one Sanskrit).

INDI: also written ENDI.

IṚA, Mal. (ഇറ) Feehold tenure of land.

ITANA, (?) Guz. Light but fertile soil.

Itláá-náma, corruptly, *Itila-namah*: also, a notice served on cultivators, announcing an enhancement of rent, as a condition of continued occupancy: it has been ruled that this is the only legal form or purpose of an *Itláá-náma* under Ben. Reg. v. 1812, cl. 9, 10.

Itláâ-yábí, corruptly, *Itilah-yabee*, H. (P. يابي, a finding) Return to a summons or citation, the finding of the person to whom it is addressed, serving a writ.

ÎWAZ, also, corruptly, EOSIE, EUZ, EWUZ.

IZN: it is also laxly used for bequest or distribution of property.

Izn-náma, H. (P. نامه, a document) A will, a distribution of property by a testator, whether Mohammadan or Hindu.

J.

Jád-bandhahi-ijárá, (?) Beng. A mortgage in which the usufruct or rent of land is transferred to the mortgagee in lieu of interest.

Jágir-páïkán, H. (see *Páïk*) Land granted to military retainers and militia in Cuttack on the tenure of military service.

Jagúlí, (?) H. A small money-rent paid by an occupant cultivator to the proprietor.—Kamaon.

JAHÍZ, corruptly, JAIHEZ.

JÁÍ, corruptly, JAIEE, also EK-JÁÍ, (?) H. An agreement.—Bahar.

Jáibandi, (?) H. An agreement, a written engagement or undertaking.

JÁIDÁD: also, an acknowledgment of revenue payable: a specification of land held, given by the holder and deposited with the collector: a receipt: a final acknowledgment of the transfer of landed property.

JAJAN-JÁJAN, JUJUN-JAJUN, vernacular forms of YAJANA-YÁJANA, S. &c. (यजन याजन) Offering sacrifices or reciting the appointed mantras or prayers on one's own account or on behalf of others, the office of a religious Brahman.

JALKAR: also used laxly for a fishery or right of fishing.

Jamá-parti, (?) H. A favourable and fixed rate of assessment.

Jamá-pautí, (?) Uriya. An acknowledgment of money received for the purpose of paying it over on account of the person first transferring it.

Jamá-raiyati, H. Rent paid by a tenant cultivator.

JAMLOGÍ, JUMLOGEE, (?) H. A class of Brahmans in Kamaon.

JAMOG, incorrectly, JUMOK.

Jamog-náma, H. (جموگنامه) A deed of transfer of liabilities, as in the case of a loan contracted by a landholder, for which he transfers to the lender the rents of his tenants.

Janma-koshṭhí, barbarously, *Joonmoo-koostee*, Beng. (জন্ম কোষ্ঠী) A horoscope, a nativity.

Janma-koru, (?) Karn. A permanent hereditary lease.

Janmi, frequently, but absurdly, *Jemmy*.

JARÍB: there were under the former system two kinds in use, the *Âalam-gírí* and the *Bádsháhí-jaríb*, of which the former was a trifle the larger.

Jaríb-bhaunría, Uriya (see *Bhaunría*) Statement of the measurement or survey of the lands of a village.

Jaríb-chiṭṭhá, H. (جريب چتّها) A paper or record of the measurement of land.

Jaríb-khardá, corruptly, *Jereef-khurda*, Mar. (जरीबखरदा) Record of annual field measurement.

JÁSÁ, or JÁṆSÁ, Guz. (જાંસા) A threat or commission of violence against an individual by one who considers himself aggrieved, prohibited by law.—Bom. Reg. 1827.

JÁÜ: in some places it also denotes a small land measure, as *ana*, *pie*, *krant*, *jáü*.—Fatihpur.

Jawáb-dâwá, H. (دعوى, a plaint) An answer to a complaint.

JAWAR, (?) Beng. A subdivision of a *táluḳ*.

Jetháns, corruptly, *Jutunsee*.

Jethundá, corruptly, *Jetoonda*: it also denotes the land held by a hereditary *Padhán*.—Kamaon.

JHÁḌÁ, also JHÁṚÁ.

JHÚLÁ: also, a measure of land.—Garhwal.

Jiráiti: in some places in the northern Sarkárs if *Jiráiti* land is left waste the title of the occupant is considered to have lapsed, and it may be leased by the government to another person.

Jiváï: also, land assigned as subsistence to relations and dependants.

Jíviká, also, corruptly, *Jebeka*, and *Jeebha*.

Jívátam corruptly, *Jeevatam*.

JNÁTÍ, commonly pronounced GYÁTI, and corruptly written GNATI, GATI, GUYATEE, S. &c. (ज्ञाति) A kinsman, a relation, especially a distant kinsman, one who does not participate in offerings of food or water to common ancestors.

Jodi-, or *Jodige-mányam*, Karn. A grant of land at an easy or quit-rent.

Jodî-rázi-náma, (?) Karn. An engagement to give up a lease of land.

Mahál-jodi, (?) Tel. A quit-rent paid by district officers for their own estates.

JOHAR: also, any reservoir or pond.

JOT, also, corruptly, JHOTE: also, land held of a superior on the terms of a tenant cultivator, enjoying no proprietary rights, although sometimes holding at a fixed rate and sometimes hereditarily.

Jot-jamá: it is sometimes rent derived from land leased to a cultivator.

JOTÁ, (?) H. A partition wall.

JUMI, (?) Land that may be cultivated by the hoe without needing a plough, and which is therefore occupied by a class of *Magh* cultivators, thence termed *Jumias.*—Chittagong.

JUN, JOON, (?) Land cultivated by the mountaineers of Tipra.

Jyeshthánsa, also, *Jyeshthottara*, corruptly, *Jeshtootter.*

JYU, Tibet. A coin or weight of silver = 3 *máshas*, fabricated at Ladakh: five are equal to one Farakhabad rupee.

K.

KABÁLA, also, corruptly, COBOLA, KUWALLA, KOALA, KOBALA, KOOBALA, KAWALLA.

Kabála-nilámí, H. (نيلام, sale) Deed of sale.

Kat-kabála-be-miâdi, H. A conditional agreement as to terms, but not as to time.

Kabín-náma, incorrectly, *Kavín-náma.*

Kabuliyat, also, corruptly, *Quobooleut*, *Coobooleat*, *Kubooleeat*, *Caboolyat*, *Kaboolet.*

Kabul-jamâ, H. Stipulated rent or revenue, that which is assented to or agreed upon.

Kabul-khat, corruptly, *Kirbool-khut*: a written assent or agreement.

Ḳábiz-hál, H. (A. حال, now) A person in actual possession.

Ḳabẕwár, H. (A. قبضوار) In the way of seizure or distraint.

Ḳabẕwárpaimáish, H. (P. پيمايش) Measurement of an estate to determine the extent of sequestration.

Kachchat (?), incorrectly, *Cuchat*, and *Kutchat*, Mal. A bill of sale or note of goods delivered, and payment received: a palmyra leaf stamped; with the collector's acknowledgment of the instalments received from the cultivator, and a note of the lands he holds: also, any rough account of money received.

KÁDÁ, or KÁNDÁ, (?) Guz. Bed to detain water for rice cultivation, whence it is applied to rice soil in general.

Kafal-kár, erroneously, *Kafeel-kár*, H. A responsible agent.

KÁG, (?) Beng. A small division of money of account less than a *ganḍa* of *Kauris.*

KÁHAN: also, a measure of grain or straw.—Burdwan.

KAHRÁKÁT, (?) Guz. Grass land, pasture ground (?).

Kaichiṭṭu, commonly, *Kaichit*: also, any note, any written memorandum.

Kaikánam-páṭṭam, also, laxly, *Kaikánam*, corruptly, *Kaykanom*, *Koyeekanom.*

Kainiwala, H., as applied to land, land cultivated by *Kaini* or vassal tenants.—Kamaon.

Kaippanam, corruptly, *Kaypanum*: also, a portion brought by a wife.

Kaipaṭṭu, vulgarly, *Kyput.*

KAJIAR, (?) H. A sub-tenant, an actual cultivator (perhaps for *Káryakár*).

Kála-banjar, H. (from كال, time, and بنجر, barren) Land left fallow for a considerable time after cultivation.

KALÁÍ, corruptly, KULLYE, H. &c. (S. كلاى, कलाई) The name of various kinds of pulse generally cultivated.

KAḶA, KALAM, also, corruptly, KALLOM.

Kalasandi-kattali, (?) Tam. A particular ceremonial in the temple of *Kumbhiṣwara*, at *Kumbhakonam*, for which lands are assigned.

Kalaṣí-vero, Guz. (વેરો, a tax) A tax on grain at so much the *Kalaṣí* measure.

KALATRÍ, or KALLATRÍ, Sindh. The head man of a caste or trade, who collects the duties levied on the rest.

KAḶAR, corruptly, KULLUR: also, barren soil.

Kálí-báṛí, Beng. (বাড়ী, a house) A temple of the goddess *Kálí.*

KALINGAL: also, a stone facing or embankment for keeping the water of a reservoir at a uniform level.

KALLAPURA, (?) Mal. A small cottage.

KALTAR, Guz. (કલતર) Estimated produce of a crop.

Kanekan-kaltar, Guz. (from S. कण, a particle) Exaction of the revenue on the full estimated amount of the crop.

Ubhá-kaltar, Guz. (ઉભા, standing) Estimate of a standing crop.

Dohoṛa-kaltar, incorrectly, *Dhora*, Guz. (દોહોડકલતર) Allowance in favour of the cultivator of one half of the estimated amount of the crop.

Savá-kaltar, Guz. (સવાકલતર) Allowance of a fourth of the estimate of the crop to the cultivator.

KALWÁR, H. (كلوار) A distiller and vender of spirituous liquors.

KAMIN: also, a landholder to whom the office of collecting the government revenue of a village or estate is delegated.

KAMUL, (?) Mal. Head of a family (?).

KAN, KUN, Mar. (S. कण) A particle: a share, a part: a definite portion of an inheritance.

Kanbaṭái, incorrectly, *Khunbattai*, H. (كنبتائي) Apportionment of the crops amongst the coparceners of a village: equal division of the crop.

Kanakkappillai, also, corruptly, *Conocopilly*: also, any clerk or accountant.

Kanahkkurúbam: also, a promissory acknowledgment of a balance with collateral security for its liquidation: also, a settlement of accounts.

KANARA, (?) A class of herdsmen and cattle dealers—Khandesh.

Kánch, (?) H. A weight of gold dust = to a *tolá*.—Kamaon.

KAṆD, Guz. (કાંડ) An oblong unburnt brick used in constructing wells: a well made of such bricks.

KANDAVÁRAM, (?) Mal. Future rent by estimate.

KANDÁYA: money-rent.

KANDEGAH, (?) A separate division of village lands.—Chinglepat.

KANDUR, (?) H. A ravine.

KÁNÍ: also, a land measure in Chittagong, being one-tenth of a *drún*; but there are two kinds according to *Sháhí* or to *Maghi* measurement, the *Sháhí-káni* being, according to some, four times, and to others, eight times the extent of the *Maghi*, the latter of which is ordinarily measured by a rod of eight *háths*, and consisting of 24 such rods long by 20 broad; sometimes it is of half that extent, or 12 rods by 10: it is also used in Chittagong for a rice measure.

KANKARA, (?) Guz. Salt in crystallized lumps.

KANKOTRÍ, Guz. (કંકોતરી) A note of invitation from an individual, or from one village to another, to a wedding.

KANNI, corruptly, KANI, KHANI, KANY, Mal. (കന്നി, from S. कन्या, a virgin) The Malayalam month in which the sun is in *Virgo* (Aug.-Sept.): the crop sown at that time gathered in the spring.

KÁNṢ, Guz. (કાંસ) A canal for drainage or irrigation.

Kanthí-mahantái, H. A necklace put on the neck of a newly-elected *Mahant*, or head of a religious establishment, as a mark of his election.

KANTÍ, (?) Beng. Indigo stubble.

KANWA: also, an outlet in a dam to let off any excess of water.

KANYA, less correctly, KANIA, Mal. (കന്യ, S. कन्या) A gold coin of the value of about five rupees, the Venetian *sequin*, from having the figure of the virgin on one face.

Kanyádánam, corruptly, *Cunnikadhanum*, *Kunnitcadanum*.

Kanyápátrí, Hindi (S. कन्यापात्री) A girl married by the *Gándharba* form, or simple mutual consent.

Kanyáṣulkam, corruptly, *Cunnikasoolkum*, *Cunniasolahen*, Karn. (S. शुल्क, a dower) Money paid by the bridegroom, to the father of the bride, intended as a dower for her benefit.

KARA: tax.

Akara, incorrectly, *Ukra*, H. (S. अ neg., कर, tax) Exempt from tax, revenue-free.

Sakara, incorrectly, *Sukra*, H. (स with, कर, tax) Bearing tax, subject to revenue payment.

Akaría-máfidár, H. A holder of land not paying tax or revenue.

KARA, corruptly, KORRAH, (?) Beng. A money of account, a subdivision of a *gaṇḍa*.

Kárkún-daftar, Mar. The office of a revenue accountant.

Kárnavati, fem. of *Kárnavan*: a female manager or representative.

Kárpardáz, H. (P. پرداز, who transacts) An agent, a representative, a manager.

Kársází: also, a forgery, a fabrication.

Káriyakáran: also, *Kariyagár*, corruptly, *Cáriagar*, Karn. (ಕಾರಿಯಗಾರ).

Kárya ráyakam, vulgarly, *Karayom rayagom*, (?) Mal. Permanent service in a temple.

Káryasthan, corruptly, *Karyustun*, *Karisten*, Mal. (കാര്യസ്ഥൻ) An agent, a manager, a man of business, an attorney, an advocate.

KAṚÁHÍ, also, corruptly, KURHAEE, KURHAO: also, a cauldron, a large iron sugar-boiler.

Kaṛáhi, also, *Karáhí-divya*, vernacularly, *Karáhí-díp*.

Karai-olai, or *Karaiyolai*, less correctly, *Karai-ola*, Tam. (கரையோலை) A written specification of the limits of an estate: a deed transferring a share of a village.

Karaiyídu, corruptly, *Coryeedoo*, *Karayeed*.

KARAL, KARRAL, (?) Tel. Hard, compact, black soil on the plains of the Krishṇa, requiring copious rains to be worked.

Karamkár, for *Karmmakár*, Beng. (করমকার) An agent, a broker.

Karamvero, Guz.: rather, a tax on trades.

Káranavan: also, the head of a united family, authorised to manage all its affairs, although not invariably so doing.

Karárí, H. (کراری) What is firm: as applied to land it means that of which the title is unquestionable: also, that which was the original extent.

Karáü: also, it is sometimes maintained that among the Játs the connection entitles the woman to the rights of a wife.

Karát-marát, corruptly, *Kurrat-murrat*, H. (A. کرات مرات) Repeatedly, over and over.

Karayma-kánam, (?) Mal. A tenure of the nature of a mortgage, but perpetual (?).

KARB, (?) Guz. A small plough for cleansing the ground before sowing.

KAṚBA, otherwise KAḌBA, KAḌBÍ.

ḲARBÁRÍ, (?) Guz. A kind of hoe for clearing away the weeds between rows of corn or cotton.

KARBICH, (?) Tib. A sheep's saddle-bag as a measure of capacity for grain, salt, &c., varying from four to sixty *nálís.*

KARDA, (?) Guz. A detailed register of the lands in each of the government villages.

KARDE, (?) Mar. A cultivator holding land under a *Khot,* q. v., and paying him a varying rate of assessment.

KARGAH, H. (P. كرگاه) A weaver's loom.

Kargahí, incorrectly, *Khargeha,* H. (كرگهي) A tax upon looms.

KARHOR, (?) H. Thatching grass.

Karikatana, (?) Asam. House tax.

KARIRAPATRA, (?) Uriya. A running receipt.

Kapásiá, Guz. (કપાસીઆ) Cotton seed.

KARSA (perhaps for *Karsha*) A farm, an estate (?), a kind of tenure (?).

Kartá-putra, or *-putrí,* H. (كرتاپتر, -پتري) Any son or daughter who performs a father's obsequies, and is therefore considered entitled to the inheritance: (although the claim is sometimes set up it is of doubtful validity).

KÁRÚ, Mar. (कारू) An artificer.

Kárúnárú, Mar. (कारूनारू) The artisans of a village, as the carpenter, blacksmith, potter, &c.

KARWA-KUNBÍ: a division of the Kunbí tribe.—Guzerat.

KÁS, Mar. (कास) An estate, the lands belonging to a village or an association of villages.

Kásbandí, Mar. (कासबंदी) Assessment of a village in portions, according to the quality of the land, as determined by the *Pátíls.*

Kasbáti, Guz. (કસબાતી) An inhabitant of a Kasba, or town, usually a Mohammadan convert: also, a designation of a class of villages in Guzerat held by Mohammadans of the principal Kasba or town.

Kasbí, Kasbín, H. (كسبي) A woman of the town, a prostitute.

Kásavargam, Kasavargamdár, (?) Tam. Traders and makers of canvas sacks, residing in a village and claiming certain fees and perquisites, having a proprietary right to their houses, but not to the ground on which they stand.

KÁSHT: also, a tract of cultivated land, a farm.

KAT: sometimes used for *Kat-kabála,* but laxly, also in the sense of a mortgage.

Katala-nimak, (?) H. Rock salt.

Káthi-jangal, H. Thicket reserved for firewood.

KATAR, KUTTUR, (?) (perhaps for *Khata*) A book or shop account.

KATBÁ: also, an application to arrest a sale of property. Bombay Reg. iv. 1827, cl. 67.

KATHOR, (?) Guz. General term for all kinds of pulse.

KAṬHWO, less correctly, KUNTWA, Guz. (કઠવો) A wooden frame for supporting the sides of unbuilt wells.

Kaṭki-ijárádár, (?) H. An under-renter or farmer: (the first is perhaps an error for *Kaṭkina*).

Kaṭkinadár, corruptly, *Kothinadar*: also, in some places, an under-renter in the third degree.

Katnamu: also, a fee paid to musicians, and the like.

Kaṭṭalai: also, expenses of an idol or temple: an endowment: worship, service.

KATTI, (?) Beng. An excavation in a rice-field, for catchlng fish.

Kaṭṭuguttigai, also, blunderingly, *Cuttoocolegay, Cutguddy.*

Kaul-náma: also, written rules on the subject of rent.

Kaul-patram, Mar. (पत्रं, a leaf) A deed of agreement.

KAURDA, (?) Guz. Rice-land, land suited for rice cultivation: also, a salt-pan at the works on the borders of the *Raṇ.*

KEORI, (?) H. The name of a caste, or of an individual belonging to it, in the north-west provinces, whose chief occupation is garden cultivation, and that of the poppy, sugar-cane, and other valuable products.

KEṬU, Mal. (കെട്ടു) A term, a condition, a stipulated term for payments.

Keṭuhánam, Kerkanom, (?) Mal. Foreclosure of a mortgage.

Khabar-rasán, H. (P. رسان, causing to arrive) A courier, a messenger: in Bundelkhand the village messenger.

KHÁËKAR, Hindi (खाएकर) Old occupant, non-proprietary cultivator, not unfrequently the descendant of a *Thátwán,* or proprietor, who had been superseded by a new grantee (from *Khána,* to eat, and *Kar,* the revenue, probably the more correct form of *Kháekár*).—Kamaon.

KHAIR, (?) Beng. Land of an inferior quality.

Khairat, also, corruptly, *Kherat.*

KHAJA, (?) H. Quit-rent paid in kind.—Kamaon.

KHAK, or KHAGAM, (?) Tibet. Measure of cloth; the breadth.

KHALA, also, corruptly, KULLY.

Khalian, also, corruptly, *Kullean.*

Khalífa: also, the superintendant of a mosque.

KHÁM: also, the revenue of a village before any deductions are made for cost of cultivation, charges of collection, village disbursements, &c.: also, in the north-west provinces, it is used sometimes in the sense of *Kachchá*, as a *Khám bighá*, and the like.

KHÁMÁR, also, incorrectly, KAMAR: also, a farm, a farm-yard.

Khangi-khámár, Beng. Land held by an individual under *Khámár* tenure.

Khás, or *Khálsa-khámár*, barbarously, *Koss-komar*, Beng. Private land, land uncultivated by the proprietor.—Birbhúm.

Mál-khámár, Beng. Paying the revenue to government in money, but realising the amount in kind from the cultivators by the landlord.

KHAN, (?) Mar. A part: a division of a house (perhaps an error for *Kaṇ*).

Khána-kiráya, H. (كرايه, rent) House-rent: ground-rent.

Khánagi-dakhl, H. (P. دخل, entrance) Occupation or possession of a village: taking up a residence in it.

Khandhár, or *Kandhar*, (?) H. Included, as a portion of an estate, land, fields, &c.

Khanḍ-sál, H. (خنڈ سال, from S. शाला) A sugar-boiling house.

Khanḍ-sárí, H. (خنڈساري) A sugar-boiler or manufacturer.

KHANDAGA, corruptly, CUNDAGUM.

KHANDELA, (?) H. Rent-free land granted to servile cultivators, termed *Hálís*, by their masters.—Kamaon.

KHANDI, (?) Beng. A portion of the lands of an estate, as *Upar-khandi*, upper-land; *Ních-khandi*, low-land (it is probably only a modification of *khand*, a part or portion in general).

KHANDÚRÍ, (?) H. The name of a principal tribe of Brahmans in Garhwal.

KHÁR: also, the name of a plant the ashes of which yield soda (Coronylon Griffithii).

KHARÁR, Sindh. A grain measure, usually rated at 60 *Kásas* of two *daris*, each *dari* = to 7 *Patoïs*, and 1 *Patoï* = 4 *Chuntáis*.

Khárájí: hence also considered equivalent to being had or possessed, land, an estate.

Kharijí-jamá, also sometimes read *Kharij-jamá-aima*, q. v.

Khárij-paṭṭa, corruptly, *Kharjee-pottah*, H. (from پٹه, a lease) A lease of a detached or separated portion of an estate.

Kharíd-khat, Mar. (खरीदखत) A deed of sale: a fee to the village accountant for drawing it up.

KHÁS, (?) H. A granary, a place where grain is stored.

Kháṣ-dakhl, H. (P. دخل, entrance) Taking actual possession.

Kháṣ-patit, H. (خاص پتت, S. पतित, fallen) Government land left uncultivated.

Khás-paṭṭi-char, Beng. (from चर, a sand-bank) An alluvial accession to an estate taken possession of by the government.

Khasra-taksim, H. (A. تكسيم, division) A register of shares or divisions, a register of persons in a village subject to ground-rent for the sites of their houses.

KHÁT, Asam. Land recovered from the wilderness and the hereditary property of the clearer.

Khátá-bahi, corruptly, *Khatboe*, *Khatabye*.

KHÁTÁ, Guz., also applied to the holding of a *Pátidár*, or to any estate of definite extent: it is sometimes calculated by the number of ploughs required for its cultivation.

Khatáüni, also *Goshwára-khataüni*, H. An account of the total village lands and particulars of their distribution.

Khewaṭ-khataüni, H. An account of the village management, the distribution of the lands, and names and rights of the occupants.

KHATELÍ, (?) Mar. A cultivator paying revenue direct to the government.

Khatpatr, Beng. (S. पत्र, a leaf) A written promise or engagement.

KHATTÁ, KHATTÍ, Hindi (खत्ता, खत्ती) A grain pit, a hollow in which grain is preserved.

KHEL, (?) Asam. A tribe, a clan.

KHELA, (?) Beng. Waste land (perhaps a mistake for *Khil*, q.v.)

Khetbat, also, corruptly, *Khitbut*.

KHETTAN, (?) Beng. Land held at a fixed rate.

KHEWAṬ, corruptly, KHEEWUT, H. (كهيوت) also, a record of the particulars of the administration of a village, specifying the names of the occupants and all circumstances connected with their occupancy: the term is of comparatively recent introduction in the north-west provinces, being much the same as the *Wájib-ul-arz*, q. v.: it also occurs in the sense of rent, of settlement or assessment, and of a share in a coparcenary village: it seems to be very laxly used, and is nowhere precisely defined.

Khewaṭ-dár, H. (P. دار, who has) The holder of a share in a coparcenary village.

Khichṛí, corruptly, *Keecheree*: also, miscellaneous charges or taxes.

KHIDMAT, also, corruptly, KISMUT, KHIZMUT.

Khádim: also, one who has charge of a religious bequest or endowment.

Khádima, H. A concubine.

KHOJ, H. (کهوج) Tracking any thing lost or escaped.

KHON, (?) Hindi. A grain pit.

KHOND, (?) The name of the barbarous people occupying the hilly and jangli country on the west and north-west of Orissa: their more correct appellation is *Kuï*.

KHOR, (?) Guz. An allowance in favour of the cultivator of ten or twenty per cent. upon the estimated crop.

KHORJAM: also, a grain measure.—Malabar.

KHOTA, or KHOT: also, in the Konkan, the *Khot* by virtue of an original grant from the state or by employment, as hereditary revenue officer, has come to hold the position of a Zamindár, and to claim hereditary and proprietary right in the land, exacting from the cultivators annually as large a proportion of the crop as he can enforce.

Khotpatra, Mar. (खोतपत्र) A deed of contract for the sale of a crop, a fee to the village accountant for drawing it up.

Khotwár, Mar. (खोतवार) Settlement of a village through a farmer or *Khot*.

Khuntaiti, corruptly, *Khootaitee*.

Khur-o-posh: also, allowances for personal expenses.

Khurish-poshish, H. (خورش پوشش) Allowance for personal expenses.

Khush-bash, also, corruptly, *Koosh-bash*, *Khoos-bas*: also, in Tippera, especially if the occupant be a relative or dependant of the Zamíndár: in the Haiderabad country, it usually denotes the inhabitant of a village who is lightly assessed, or wholly exempt, on account of his character or services, as a Brahman, a schoolmaster, a dancing girl, a Jangam, or a servant of the community.

Khush-báshí-jamâ, H. An easy or quit-rent.

Kikánam, *Keekanom*, (?) Mal. (perhaps for *Kaihánam*) A sub-mortgage.

KILAMAI, KIZHAMAI, Tam. (கிழமை) A day of the week, the names of the Tamil days are, with two exceptions, peculiar; although, as in the rest of the Hindu kalendars, they are named after the planets, as *Náyiru* (ஞாயிறு) the sun; *Tíngal* (திங்கள்), the moon; *Sevváy* (செவ்வாய்), Mars; *Buden* (புதன்), Mercury; *Viyálam* (வியாழம்), Jupiter; *Velli* (வெள்ளி); *Sani* (சனி), Saturn.

Kiráya-náma, H. (P. نامه, a document) A document engaging to pay certain hire or rent, and endorsed with the periodical payments.

Kirdí-nagdí, Mar. (कीर्दी नगदी) Cash account, account of money received.

Kisán-kadím, H. An ancient cultivator: in some places the same as the *Maurúsi*, or hereditary cultivator, and having the right of sale and mortgage of their lands, and many of the privileges of proprietorship except those of electing the *Lambardár*.

KIST, also, corruptly, CIST.

KITÂ, also, corruptly, KITTEH: also, a parcel of land, a portion of village lands.

KODAMBAN, (?) Karn. Head of a village of *Pallar*, or outcastes.

KÓL: also, a carpenter's rod, =2 feet 4 inches.

KOLHU, incorrectly, KOLOO.

KOLLUKÁNAM, (?) Mal. Fine on renewal of a lease.

KORADU, (?) Karn. A raised flooring of brick work.

KOSHṬHÍ, corruptly, KOOSHTEE, Beng. (কোষ্ঠী) A horoscope.

Kothi-báns, H. (بانس) A grove or clump of bambus.

Kothá: also, a house or hut in general.

Kothá-khám, H. (خام, unbaked) A house of clay or unburnt bricks.

KOTHÁRU: or more correctly the platform on which salt is heaped and stored after it is brought from the pans.

KOṬṬÁRAM, Mal. (കൊട്ടാരം) A palace, a temple, a place where the property of a temple is kept, and its affairs managed: a branch or subdivision of a *Kovilakam* or section of a Rája's family in Malabar.

Kovilakam, also, corruptly, *Kolgum*: also, a political subdivision of Malabar governed by a separate Rája.

KOYAMA, (?) Mal. Principal of a temple (perhaps for *Koyimma*, authority).

Kranti, also, corruptly, *Kuranth*: also, in Cuttack, a division of a *pie*, one-twentieth, (?).

Kraya-náma, H. (P. نامه, a voucher) A bill of sale.

Avadhi-kraya, corruptly, *Avidy-kraya*, Karn. (S. अवधि, a limit) A sale for a term, a conditional sale, becoming absolute if the purchase-money is not repaid before the term expires.

Krishnárpan, corruptly, *Kishnarpun*, *Kisnarpun*.

KUDALI, Tel. (కుడలి) The contiguity or meeting of boundaries: a boundary: a boundary mark.

Kudihattu, (?) Mal. A union of several villages.

Kudima, also, corruptly, *Kodima*.

Kudima-janmam, Mal. Holding land on a quit-rent.

Kuditara, (?) Tam. Village accounts, shewing the quantity and description of land belonging to each proprietor.

Kudiyirippu, (?) Tam. Land in a village on which houses are or may be built.

Kudiyulavu, (?) Tam. Right of cultivation.

KUḌUMBAM, KUḌUMBU, Tam. (குடும்பம், குடும்பு, S. *Kutumba,* q. v.) A family, a race.

Kudumbu-kániyátchi, Tam. (see *Kániyátchi*) Family hereditary property.

Kuláchára: also, corruptly, *Kolachar,*

Kulbáb-kul-kánún, Mar. (कुलबाब कुल कानून) A phrase used in grants or *sanads* to imply the unreservedness and absoluteness of the grant, with all rights and privileges attaching to the land.

Kulárg: add, who are sometimes considered the same as *Dhárákarís,* q. v.: the term is also applied to cultivators paying a fixed rent, either to government direct or through the head man, which rent cannot be increased except upon a new survey and assessment.

Kuḷárgí, Mar. (कुळारगी) A tenure by individuals or families holding land at fixed rates, alterable only upon a new survey and assessment.

KULBA: its subdivisions are termed *kiár, páo, jet, neg, pon, ganḍa. kauri.*

KULI, or KUZHI, also, corruptly, COOYIE.

Kúli-gudám, (?) H. Furnishing supplies of fodder and food to government officers, troops, and travellers.—Kamaon.

Kúli-kánam, corruptly, *Kooyeekanom, Kooykanom.*

Kunbi: the caste in Guzerat is divided into two principal classes termed *Karwa-kunbi,* and *Lewa-kunbi*: in some places there is a third distinction, that of *Anjra-kunbi,* which partakes more of the Rajput character.

KUNCHAMU: also, a measure of land.

KUNḌÁ, H. (كنڈا) A shallow pan, a small earthen dish, an earthen vessel in which molasses and the like are carried.

KUNKUMA, or KUNUMA, (?) Tel. Gift of land or property to a daughter or sister.

KÚRA, (?) Mal. Right, property.

Illam-kúra, (?) Mal. Private property.

Swarúpa-kúra, (?) Mal. Rank or dignity.

KURA, KOORRAH, (?) H. Apportionment of different shares in an estate (perhaps for the A. *Kurâh,* casting lots).

Kura-taksím, (?) H. A specification of the apportionment or distribution of the shares of an estate.

KURÁṆ, Mar. (कुराण) Grass land.

KURFA, KURPHA, KOORFAH, (?) Beng. A sub-tenure in western Bengal, in which the occupant holds of a *Khúd-kásht* cultivator, and is not recognised by the Zamíndár: the lease sometimes makes over the whole of the rights of the lessor, but it is more usually for a specified term, or at pleasure.

Kurfadár: A sub-tenant.

KURHAL, (?) Mar. Low underlying land in *Khandes,* of a reddish tint, capable of bearing spring crops.

KÚRI: it is larger than a *Man,* smaller than an *Áṛka.*

KURPHA is probably wrongly explained: see *Kurfa.*

KURRU, COORROO, (?) Tel. The name of a migratory race in the ceded districts.

KURUKAM, vulgarly, KURKAM, (?) Tam. A land measure.

KÚṬ: also, a cess, a tax, a rate.

Kuyuvarkam-panayam, (?) Mal. A lease on mortgage tenure.

KUYIKUR, corruptly, KOOYKOOR.

L.

LÁBÚDÍ, H. (P. لابودي) Personal expenses.

LÁG, LÁGAT, (?) H. Expenses incurred in cultivation, irrigation, &c., whether on account of any one cultivator or of the village: an account of them in either case kept by the *Patwárí.*

Lagání-jamâ, H. (لگاني جمع) A rate of rent fixed in perpetuity.—Maimansinh.

LÁGÍ: also, a measuring rod or pole.

LAGIT, incorrectly, LUGGIT, H. (لگت) Account of rent for the year, including balances of former years kept by the *Patwárí.*

Lagit-kásht, H. (لگت کاشت) Rent of land according to a stipulated rate: an account kept of such rent.

LÁGUJÁRI, Karn. (ಲಾಗುಜಾರಿ) Rent-free land.

LÁKHIRÁJ, also, corruptly, LACKERAGE, LACKERAJ, LEEAKEERAZEE.

Lákkiráj-abwáb-jamâ, H. (see *Abwab* and *Jamâ*) Land held at a quit-rent.

Lákhiráj-bást, H. (باست, S. वास्तु) Ground on which a house is built held rent-free.

Lakota, Tibet. A silver ingot stamped at Lhasa, current in the hills.

LANKA, Tel. (లంక, from S. लंका, the island of Ceylon) An islet in a river yielding grass, timber, &c.: land left dry by the recession of a river, whilst the water remains round it, forming a small island.

LAṬṬÁ, also, incorrectly, LOTTA.

Lawad-náma, Mar., Guz. Deed of arbitration, written award.

Lawázima: also, village papers especially.

LEWÁ, Hindi (लेवा) Paste used in forming the shells of opium cakes.

LIKSU, Asam. A *páïk* or armed peasant assigned as a labourer or slave to a great officer of state.

Likhan: also, a note of acknowldgement.

LOBHA, vernacularly, LOBH, S. &c. (लोभ) Covetousness, greedy desire, and, by inference, corruptibility, venality.

Lobhí, S. &c. (लोभी) Covetous, greedy; whence, venal, corrupt: also, subst., bribery, corruption.

LODIKHÁNA, or LUDÍKHÁNA, (?) H. A sort of measurement formerly in use in Bahar.

Lot-bandi: also, notice or advertisement of the sale of an estate.

LÚBHÍ, more correctly, LOBHÍ, H. (لوبهي, S. लोभी) Covetous, greedy, insatiable; whence, by inference, it has been ruled rather laxly to signify venal, corrupt, open to bribery.

M.

Mablagh-bandi: also, sum total.

MAFKÚD, also occurs as *Mafkúd-ul-khabar*.

MÁGAR, (?) Karn. A gift promised to a bride at marriage.

Maghrabí: also, a small gold coin current on the Malabar coast, a Venetian sequin or Dutch ducat.

Mahattrán, also, corruptly, *Mohoteran*, *Mohatrawn*, *Mohuthran*.

Mahál-miláni, H. (from ملانا, to cause to find) A record kept in the collector's office of the several shares of an estate.

MAHR: *muâjil*, corruptly, *moujjul*: *muwajil*, corruptly, *moujjul*.

Mahrána, corruptly, *Mohurranna*: also, a present made or promised to the bride by the bridegroom at the time of marriage, by way of dower.

Majmuâdár: also, in Asam, a registrar or secretary, especially of a religious conference.

MAJMÚN, Guz. (મજમુન, from A. *Mazmúm* مضموم, additional) Additional land not included in the shared lands of a *Narwa* village, sometimes cultivated by the shareholders, sometimes let to strangers.

MAKARAM, vulgarly, MAGAROM, Mal. (S. मकर) The sign Capricornus: the month in which the sun enters it (Nov.-Dec.): the crop sown in the cold-weather season.

MAKHAL, (?) Guz. Division of the government and cultivator's share of the crop by weight, taken on the threshing-floor.

MAKKATTÁYAM, Mal. (മക്കത്തായം) Inheritance by the male line.

Mál-japti, for *Mál-zabti*, Guz. An officer appointed by the state, but paid by the village to prevent the removal of any of the crop from the threshing-floor till authorised by the collector.

MAḶÁÍ, Mar. (मळई) Rich or alluvial ground along the banks of rivers: a field of garden or meadow land.

MALHAḲ, H. (A. ملحق) Joining, contiguous, adjacent.

MALIK, also, corruptly, MALLEK: also, a Mohammadan cultivator in Guzerat.

Málik-mukarraridár, H. A possessor of an estate or farm on a perpetual fixed rate of rent or revenue, apparently not the original proprietor, but one who by long possession claims to be considered as *Málik* or proprietor.

Málikána: it is also applied in some places, as in Tirhut, to land occupied rent-free, instead of rent for the whole estate: also to an annual allowance levied from the cultivators in the character of a *Málik* or original proprietor or under his authority, or as purchased from him: in the north-west provinces the *Málikána* is sometimes rated higher than the regulation rate.

MAMTÚÂ, H. (A. ممتوع) A concubine, a temporary wife.

MÁMÚL, MÁMÚLÍ, Beng. (मामूल, मामूली, A. معمول) Established, customary, usual.

Mámúli-báṭṭá, Beng. (मामूली बाट्टा) Customary premium or discount; usual difference of exchange. See *Báṭṭá*.

Manaikaṭṭu, corruptly, *Manicut*.

MANDAPA, corruptly, MUNDUB.

MANDHAN, (?) Guz. Assessment on each cultivator, agreeably to a stipulated rate for a certain number of ploughs, whether actually used or not.

MANDI, MANDOOY, also, MUNDWEE.

MÁNI, (?) H. A grain measure.—Gorakhpur.

MANKÚHA, H. (A. منكوحة) Married, a legally married wife. See *Nikáh*.

MANNEVÁḌU: also, a title assumed by the great Zamíndárs in the northern Sarkárs.

Mannaváda-hávali, Tel. (హవలి) The duty of preserving the public peace entrusted to the Zamíndárs: revenue of certain lands set apart for the maintenance of a police, and expenses of preserving the public peace.

MANNÍPAM, MANNÍPU, incorrectly, MANIPAM, Tam. (மணி-

ணீபம், மணணீபு) Exemption from revenue, remission of government demand, rent-free tenure.

MANTÁ, (?) Tam. A grain measure, subdivision of a *Túm*.

Manzúr : it is sometimes written across a paper or bond to authenticate it, and confirm its acceptance.

MÁP : also, a measure of grain in the husk.

Mápá, Guz. (માપા) A fee of two per cent. on the sale of grain paid to the village *Banya*.

Mápárkí, Mar. (मापारकी) A portion of grain out of each measure of the crop, the perquisite of the *Pátil*, also of the *Mhár*.

MARAKKAL : the term is also applied in Madura to a measure of land : perhaps as much as requires such a quantity of seed.

MARAMMAT, also, corruptly, MURHUMMUT : it is also applied in law language to an amended plaint or plea : also, *Marammat-sawál*.

Maravarttana, (?) Tel. Fees and perquisites of the hereditary village accountant (?).

MARHALA, H. (A. مرحله) A stage, a station, a police-station on the great roads at certain distances.

MARKÁ, (?) H. Platform in a field for watching crops.

MARWAL, (?) H. Rent-free land granted to the heirs of a person deceased.

MARYÁDÁ, corruptly, MURIADY : also, any customary compliment or privilege, as the right of being the first invited, the first presented with *betel*, and the like.

MASÁLÍA-BAND-O-BAST, (?) A voluntary settlement or assessment.—Chittagong.

MAṬHA, also, MAṬHAM, corruptly, MADUM.

Maṭhádhi-patí, corruptly, *Madathí-putty*, Karn. (S. मधिपति, chief) Head of a religious establishment.

MAṬṬIÁL, H. (متّیال) A hollow, a pit.

MAULA, Guz. A measuring rod of the length of 20 feet $5\frac{1}{4}$ inches.

Maurúsi : *Ghair-maurusí*, other than hereditary : it is sometimes used, though laxly, to signify a tenant at will.

Maurúsí-aima, H. Hereditary rent-free tenure. See *Aima*.

Mauziná, corruptly, *Mauzzina*, *Moaznah*, *Mowazna*.

MAWÁJIB, corruptly, MOWAJIB, H. (A. مواجب) Salaries, pensions : applied in Cuttack to a grant of rent-free land for services, and held by actual cultivators.

MAWÁR, (?) Guz. Light sandy soil.

MÁẒÍ : in marriage contracts it is sometimes considered essential to their validity that this word *maẓi*, done, or past and gone, should be pronounced by the contracting parties before witnesses.

MEHER-GIL-ANDÁZI, (?) H. The enclosure of an embankment.

Mel-sádhanam, Karn. A conditional deed of mortgage, the pledge being forfeited if the loan is not repaid by a given term.

Melvára-ijárá-kaul, corruptly, *Melwarem-ezara-cowle*, Tam. (from the A. *ijárá*, farm, and *kaul*, assent) A deed of lease of the proprietor's share of the produce.

Melváram : it is used sometimes, rather laxly, for the share claimed by a proprietor or landlord from a tenant, especially in the case of rent-free land where there is no government claim.

Melváram-tirwái : also, the claim of the landlord upon his tenant.

Melvaippu, corruptly, *Melvappu*.

Melváyippa, corruptly, *Melveppu*.

Menḍ, also, *Menḍh*, (मेंढ).

MEO : the word is an abbreviation of *Mewáti*.

Meṭṭukáran : also, a revenue *peon*.

MEWÁSI, corruptly, MEHEWASSEE, Guz. (મવાસી) Held by the *Mewás* tribe, a village, &c., paying tribute to the government in lieu of assessment.

MIGIKE, also, corruptly, MIGTE : also, nett produce.

Mihnatana, corruptly, *Mihuntanu*.

MÍNÁR, H. (A. مینار) A turret, the tower of a mosque or minaret : a post as a boundary mark or measure of distance, a mile-stone.

MINHÁ, also, corruptly, MENAH : it is also laxly used for rent-free in general.

MIRÁS-PAṬṬÁ, Beng. (মিরাসপাট্টা) A lease with right of succession.

MISL, corruptly, MISSIL.

Misl-karanam : or when the office is held by several individuals jointly.

Misl-reddi : or rather one who represents several farmers or proprietors and is responsible for the revenue.

Misl-tirwái : add, not having been fixed at the time of the survey.

MITI, (?) H. A piece of water, a pond.

Modafat, (?) Late, lately deceased. See *Muzafat*.

Mudali, corruptly, *Moodelly*.

MOḌAN : also, dry cultivation.

MOHAMAI, (?) Tam. A cess, a fee.

MOKA, (?) Sindh. Cultivation dependent on irrigation by canals.

Mol-islam, (?) Guz. A Rajput converted to Mohammadanism.

Morana: local corruption of *Mahrána*, q. v.

Mot, corruptly, **Mohot**.

Mṛigsál, corruptly, *Murgsal*, or *Mirgsal*: as a revenue term it is used for the commencement of the revenue year: it is also the cultivator's or husbandman's year, commencing with the end of *Vaisákh* or beginning of *Jyeshṭh* (May-June), when the grain is sown: hence it is applied to both the *Sursan* and *Faṣli* years of the Marathas.

Muâáfi-nazránadár, H. (from *Nazrána*, q. v.) A property exempt from revenue, but paying a fine or quit-rent.

Aji-máphi, (?) Mar. Absolute and entire exemption from revenue payment.

Apúrṇ-máphi, Mar. (S. अपूर्ण, incomplete) Partial exemption from revenue payments.

Muâlem, corruptly, **Maloom**.

Muchalka, corruptly, **Mutchelka**.

Muhafiz: also, a registrar, a record-keeper.

Muharrir, corruptly, **Mohorer**.

Sthita-muharrir, Beng. (S. स्थित, stayed) A permanent or regular clerk.

Utpanna-muharrir, Beng. (S. उत्पन्न, produced) An occasional or extra clerk.

Muháṣil, H. (A. محاصل) Produce, profit, proceeds of an estate, interest of money, &c.

Muhaṣṣil, corruptly, *Mussullee*, H. (A. محصّل) A bailiff, a collector, a tax-gatherer.

Muhaṣṣilí, H. (A. محصلي) The office of a collector of rent or taxes.

Muházir-khána, corruptly, *Mazir-khanu*, H. (P. خانه, a house) A station-house, a place in a village where persons apprehended are first secured.

Muhtarafa, also, incorrectly, *Muhtarifa*.

Mújibát, corruptly, *Mojibat*.

Mujmal, H. (A. مجمل) An abstract, a compendium.

Mujmalan, incorrectly, *Mujmilan*, H. (A. مجملاً) Compendiously, summarily.

Mukhbir, H. (A. مخبر) An attesting witness to a deed.

Muhhtyár-námaját-i-âám, H. (A. عام, people) General or universal power of attorney.

Múlaṣásanam, S. &c. (मूलशासन) Primary deeds or documents, original title-deeds.

Múla-vigraha, S. &c. (विग्रह, body) The chief idol of a temple.

Múlazim, H. (A. ملازم) A servant, an attendant, a person employed to watch a debtor.

Mumin, incorrectly, **Momun**.

Munafâ, corruptly, *Monofah*: also, the surplus proceeds or nett profits of an estate.

Mundwáhik, Mar. (मुख़्दवाहिक) A cultivator of a parcel of village land at a stipulated rent.

Muníb, corruptly, **Moneeb**.

Munim, corruptly, *Moneem*.

Muráfâa, H. (A. مرافعه) A law-suit, an action.

Muráfi, H. (A. مرافع) A plaintiff.

Muṟi: also, relinquishment of rent or profit in favour of another party.

Muriṣááli, corruptly, *Moorisullah*.

Musaedat, (?) H. An embankment, a reservoir (?).

Musavi, corruptly, **Mosavi**, H. An embankment, a reservoir (?).

Mushahhaṣ; corruptly, *Moshuksy*. *Mushakhaṣi jot*, H. A farm or lands held at a stipulated rent.

Mushakhasidár, H. (P. دار, who has) A landholder with whom a settlement has been made.

Musht: *Ek-musht*, Hindi. Ready-money payment, prompt payment.

Mushtaraka, or **Mushtarika**, H. (A. مشتركه) Held in common or partnership, land, &c.

Muṣíbat, H. (A. مصيبت) Any urgent necessity or misfortune, such as might justify alienation of trust property: any unavoidable expense.

Mustaufi, corruptly, **Mustaphi**: also, an officer deputed to get information on the spot where any transaction has occured.

Mutanázâ, H. (A. متنازع) Disputed, contested: in law, under dispute or litigation.

Mutawalli, also, corruptly, **Mutowolee**.

Muwáro, Guz. (મુવારો) A dependent, an outlying village, a hamlet.

Muẕáfat, plur. **Muẕáfát**, corruptly, **Modafat**, H. (A. مضافه, مضافات) Annexed, added, resumed, as lands: recent, late, as a person deceased: subst., annexations, additions, exemptions.

Muzáhim, corruptly, **Mozahim**: also, one who brings a cross action, or interferes in a suit, especially in order to obstruct proceedings.

Muzáhimí, H. (مزاحمي) Action in bar of proceeding, a cross suit.

Muzáhimí-nathí, corruptly, *Mozhahimee-nuthee*, (see *Nuthi*)

Papers relating to a cross suit, or suit in hindrance of proceedings.

Muẕẕin, corruptly, Muzin, H. (A. مُؤَذِّن) The crier of a mosque, who summons the people to prayer.

N.

Nagaurá: it is also applied to a superior breed of buffaloes from *Nawanagar*.

Namúna, also, erroneously, *Mumoona*: also, in Guz., government register of assessment rates.

Nánkár: also, a rent-free grant of land for service in lieu of pay.—Kamaon.

Nárukáru: or rather the artisans of the village, as the carpenter, &c.

Narwá: also, a share of a coparcenary village.

Narwá-santhela, (?) Guz. (said to be from *sant*, an annuity) An allowance payable to an original shareholder in a coparcenary village, whose share has from some cause been taken from him or transferred to another, an allowance equivalent to *Málikána* or *Nánkár* in other parts of India.

Nashíb, H. (A. نشيب) A declivity, uneven and low ground.

Násí, (?) Beng. A drain.

Náṭṭam-káran, also, corruptly, *Natamagár*, *Nátamaigar*.

Nathí, corruptly, Nuttee.

Jári-nathí, H. (A. جاري, current) Papers or written orders issued by a Court.

Nattangal, (?) Tam. Land in which young plants of rice are grown before transplanting: see *Nadavu*.

Navisht, *Nawisht*, H. (P. نوشت) What is written, a writing.

Navisht-o-khwán, H. (P. نوشت وخوان) A writing and reading, the execution of a legal deed or document, signing and delivering or accepting.

Navutu, (?) Tel. A measure of grain = 4 *hunchams*.

Nizámat: it is still applied in some places to land paying a fixed revenue in perpetuity to the state.

Nazarát, *Nazurat*, (?) H. Subject to a fine: held under such a fine, but otherwise rent-free: also, land granted to a Mohammadan tomb or religious establishment.

Nerra, (?) H. A reservoir of water.

Nigar, (?) H. A water-course.

Nigar-bahá, (?) H. A sluice, a cut from a reservoir that may be opened and shut: or the terms may be used separately, *Nigar* being a channel or drain for carrying off the waste water of a village; *bahá*, one carrying off the surplus water of a reservoir or river.

Nijári, (?) H. Land bearing grain.

Nikás: also, an account current.

Nikásí, also termed *Nikásí-jamá-bandi*: also, an account shewing the value of the produce of an estate, the revenue payment, and the nett profit: also, an account of the village lands kept by the *Patwárí*.

Nilam: as opposed to *Páramba* it means land fit for any other cultivation than that of garden or orchard.

Nimbúr, Mar. (निंबूर) Portion of corn, especially of *Bájra*, in the ear or sheaf, assigned to the village servants.

Nishast-jamá, corruptly, *Nishisht-jumma*, H. (P. نشست, a sitting or occupancy) Adjustment of rent with a tenant.

Nivesanamu, *Niveshanam*: also, such an extent as is fit for a house: hence, also, building ground.

Núlachάram, (?) Mal. A divorce granted to a wife.

O.

Oḍhá, Mar. (ओढा) A perquisite of the village scribe, as much corn from each heap as he can grasp with both arms.

Oglá, (?) Guz. Made up into sheaves or bundles—corn.

Ol, or Wol, Guz. (ઓલ, વોલ) Payment made to predatory chiefs to induce them to abstain from pillage: black mail.

Oḷ, Mar. (ओळ) A row, a line: a class.

Olá, it is also laxly used for any deed or document written on the palm leaf.

Olia, (?) Guz. A land measure in the northern part of the Ahmadabad collectorate, 50 double paces in length by 100 in breadth, or 125,000 square feet.

Ombyá, Mar. ओंब्या) A portion of wheat in the ear or sheaf, the perquisite of the village servants.

Oppandam, also sometimes defined a verbal contract.

Osrá, (?) H. Keeping watch in a village by turns, each inhabitant taking the duty in succession.

Otbandí: also, an estimate of the probable outturn at some future period.

Oḍambadike, also, *Uḍanbaḍikai*, Tam. (உடன்படிக்கை).

Otapadi, corruptly, Othapudy, (?) Karn. A final account, settlement of accounts.

Otti-anubhogam, Mal. A mortgage with usufruct.

Otti-miras, Tam. Occupation under mortgage tenure but comprising *Mirásí* rights and privileges.

P.

Padaví, Padon, (?) Mar. A verandah.

Páïk: also, a subordinate collector of rents.

Paidá, H. (P. پیدا) Born, produced, created.

Paidáwár, *Paidáwárí*, H. Produce of a field or an estate.

Jamâ-paidáwár, H. The total amount of the produce of an estate.

Paigar, (?) H. A ditch, a boundary.

Paiyad, Pyud, (?) A sluice, an embankment: a channel for carrying off the surplus water of a reservoir: a channel for letting in water on a large scale.

Pákhar, H. (پاکھر) A canvas covering or tarpaulin.

Pakli, (?) H. A net for holding straw for cattle to feed upon.

Pallá, H. (پلا) A bag used as a definite measure, especially for sugar.

Pán-bahá, (?) H. Distribution of betel to persons present at an assembly as a mark of respect: money expected as an equivalent of such compliment.

Pana: it is sometimes considered synonymous with *Paṭṭí*.

Panaya-pátta-kuḷi-kánam: it occurs apparently, though very corruptly, as *Kooyavarakam-ponium*, *Kooywarkom-paunayom*.

Panchakí-jamá, Beng. (পঞ্চকীজমা) Rent payable on land otherwise rent-free, a sort of quit-rent.

Panchakí-mahattrán, Beng. (মহত্ত্রান) Land granted at a quit-rent to religious persons or Brahmans.

Panchakí-maujá, Beng. (মৌজা) A village held at a quit-rent.

Karárí-panchakí-jamá, Beng. (A. করারী) A perpetual quit-rent.

Pandára-katlai, (?) Tam. A parcel of land in a village paying revenue direct to the government.

Paún-ser, corruptly, *Paosher*, H. &c. A *ser*, minus a quarter: the term is applied also to any definite measure of land minus one-fourth.

Parakuḍi, also, corruptly, *Pooracoody*.

Páṛá: also, an outlying village or hamlet.

Parajúwá, (?) Guz. A land measure equal to three *Olias*, q. v.

Párásam, (?) Tam. A nuptial gift.

Parbharu-bábtí, less correctly, *Purbaree-babtee*, Guz. (પર-ભારું, બાબતી) A cess formerly levied on the villagers, by the Tálukdárs on various pretexts.

Parchit, (?) Beng. A walled inclosure.

Parela, (?) Guz. Lapsed, abandoned, as a share of a village.

Parichárak, H. (S. परिचारक) Superintendant of a temple.

Párína-daftar: or rather the office where they are kept: *Párína* papers appear in some places to be memoranda from which the *Pargana* register is framed, to be filed by the Kánungo.

Partá, (?) H. A favourable or quit-rent.

Partál, less correctly, Partár: also, land now waste, but formerly cultivated.

Partan, Mar. (परतन) lit. Turning: fig., a field, one in which a plough may conveniently turn.

Partí-jadíd, H. (A. جدید, new) Land recently left waste.

Páṭ, incorrectly, Path.

Patgheri, (?) Asam. A native collector of revenue.

Patawat, (?) Guz. A feudal chief.

Páṭí, Pánṭí, Guz. (પાતી, પાંતી) A share in some common property or business.

Pántidár, Guz. (પાંતીદાર) A partner, a shareholder.

Path-ail, Beng. (পথআইল) A bank with a pathway above it, especially when raised as a boundary.

Pátidar, also read *Páṭidar*, but (?) Guz. (પાતીદાર) also, a coparcener, the holder of a proprietary share of village lands.

Paṭṭádárí, H. (پٹّاداري) Leasehold tenure: it is also applied to a particular settlement made with the Ryots of the twenty-four *Parganas* in 1783.

Paṭṭásalámi, (پٹّاسلامي) A fine, fee, or complimentary present of money on receiving a lease.

Pattakán, (?) H. A bank serving as a boundary.—Kamaon.

Pattálí, (?) Mal. Head or manager of the affairs of a temple.

Pattakdár: or the term designated *Mirásidárs* who had got the management of the whole country into their own hands, and who, when their illegal authority was suppressed became again mere *Mirásidárs*.

Pattana: it also applies in Orissa to a tract of land or estate of cultivable ground comprising two or more *Chaks*, formerly held rent-free, but latterly subject to a quit-rent.

Patti, Mal.: also, any written voucher or document, and especially one not strictly legal or formal.

Paṭṭí, Karn.: it also designated an addition of as much again to the amount of the assessment.

Páṭṭiyam: also the right of village proprietors to all descriptions of land within the limits of their villages.

Paṭṭukaṭṭu, or Putkut: also, the usual holding of a Ryot.

Penmúl, less correctly, Penemool, Mal. (പെണ്മുല) Settlement or assignment of property to a female.

Peṛ, H. (پیڑ) A tree.

Peṛí, H. (پیڑی) Relating to trees: a cess or tax on trees

Peshgídár: also, a person who has paid in advance.

PETTAI: in some places in the south, it also denotes a *Sarái* or inclosed space, and buildings for the accommodation of travelling traders of the caste of the owner.

PHALA: also, in Guzerat, the proportion or quota of the assessment paid by each shareholder of village lands.

Phántadár, (?) H. A cultivator originally a member of the village and enjoying certain privileges.

PHÁR, (?) Uriya A fishing ground (perhaps for *Phánd*, a snare).

Phaṭ-bandi, H. An agreement to pay a demand in separate proportions.

PHATECHÁS, incorrectly, FATACHAS, Guz. (ફતેચાસ) Assessment levied on the lands of a village, without any distinction of the class of soil.

PHAURÍ, (?) A land measure.

Phúṭ-gáon, corruptly, *Foot-gaon*: also, a village assessed and managed separately.

PHÚṬÁ, H. (S. پھوٹا) Broken, divided, levied on the cultivators severally, as rent or revenue.

PIAL, PYAL, (?) Tel. The verandah or portico of a house.

PÍR, (?) Uriyá. A village or district occupied by the Larka-kol tribes bordering on the north-west of Orissa.

PÍRU, (?) Tel. Money of account, one-sixteenth of an *ána*.

PITALGOLA, (?) Beng. Small and divided patches: lands of an estate so scattered.

PODIPÁD, (?) Tam. A portion of land.

PON: a coin of less value, 1 *Pon* being equal to 1 rupee 8 anas 10 pie.

POROMKÁDOM: also, an additional loan or advance to that made upon landed property held in usufruct: a deed fixing he amount of surplus profit to be set off against the interest of a loan, and the balance to be paid (?).

POWALA, (?) Guz. A grain measure = five-eighths of an Ahmadabad *ser*: 4 *Powalas* = 1 *Pali*, 4 *Palis* = 1 *Manu*, 4 *Manus* = 1 *Man* or 40 *Sers*.

POTÍ, (?) H. A measure of grain.

Prajáwat, also sometimes termed *Bhúprajáwat*, incorrectly, *Bho-purjote*.

Pramánika, also, corruptly, *Paramanick*.

PRASÁDA: also, in some cases, the distribution to certain religious mendicants was made daily, and had become a prescriptive right, until it was commuted to a money payment.

PUCHHAVERO, Guz. (પુછ્છવેરો, from S. पुच्छ, a tail) A tax on milch buffaloes.

Púli-tírvái, (?) Tam. Account of assessments paid on a leasehold estate (?).

PURA, Guz. (પુર) A dependent or outlying village subordinate to the principal.

PURÁ: it is also used in Asam, where it is about $1\frac{1}{4}$ statute acre.

PURI, (?) Karn. A small granary or grain store.

PUROHITA, also, corruptly, PROITH.

Kritapurohita, corruptly, *Kirtuprohit*, H. (S. कृत, done) A priest who performs or conducts certain ceremonies.

Kulapurohita, corruptly, *Kool-uprohit*, H. (S. कुल, a family) A hereditary family priest

PUSHKARINÍ, vernacularly, POKHARÍ, corruptly, POKREE.

Putraputrádi, more correctly, perhaps *Putrapautrádi*, H. (S. पुत्रपौत्रादि) lit. Son, grandson, &c.: when used in a deed of conveyance it restricts the succession to the direct heirs of the person to whom the transfer is made.

Putreshti, incorrectly, in Bengali, *Putroishto-jág*.

R.

Rahan-dár, H. (رهن‌دار) The holder of a mortgage, a mortgagee.

Rahandárí, H. (P. داري) Holding a mortgage: the rights it conveys.

RÁÍ, H. (A. راي) Opinion, judgment, decision of a native judicial officer.

RAÍS, corruptly, REIZ, A. (رئيس) A prince, a chief: used in some parts of Bengal for the manager or occupant of a religious endowment.

Riásat, corruptly, *Reazut*, H. (A. رياست) Headship, clerkship, authority.

Raiyati-baiṭha-bárí, Beng. (বাড়ী, a house) A homestead in a village.

Rákhá-jángal, Beng. (রাখাজাংগল) Forest land preserved uncleared for the sake of the timber.

RÁSTÍ, Guz. (રાસતી, P. راستي, rightness) Held immediately and entirely by government, an estate, a village.

RAULIA, (?) H. Head man of a village.—Kamaon.

RAWAJA, or RAWOZA, (?) The head man of a *Magh* village. —Chittagong.

Rawaliya: in Guzerat they are thread and tape makers.

Rawánagí: also, export duties.

Rázináma: it is sometimes said that this differs from a *Ṣulh-náma*, inasmuch as it imports a determination to be satisfied with the decree that is still to be passed, the latter implies the entire cessation of proceedings: in the Dakhin it also denotes a petition from a cultivating occupant of land to be permitted to give up his holding, to be drawn up by the *Kulkaraní* and duly signed and witnessed.

Reddivádu, also, plur. *Reddivándlu*, whence, corruptly, *Reddlawar*: also a title given to the great Zamíndárs of the northern Sarkárs.

Regada: several varieties are enumerated though not defined, as *Achcha-regar*, *Katta-regar*, *Chauka-regar*, &c.

RISHWAT, corruptly. ROOSHWUTH.

Rítimoṭé, Beng. (রীতিমোটে) According to custom.

ROKBA, (?) H. An engagement dependent for fulfilment on an uncertain contingency.

RU, RUÏ, Guz. (રૂ, રૂઈ) Cotton.

Rudrabhúmí, S. (रुद्रभूमि) A place where dead bodies are burned.—Kumbhakonam.

Rujúâ-navís, vulgarly, *Roojoo-nuwees*, H. (رجوع نويس) A clerk appointed to keep a check or counterpart account.

Rukâa: also, a note or acknowledgment of money borrowed at interest: a receipt: a summons, a notice to pay.

RÚPÍT, Asam. Lands assigned rent-free to a local militia.

S.

SADHOWA: also, a deed of assignment of land in usufruct, the rent being set off against the principal and interest of a loan until paid off.—Sáran.

SÁGCHIT, (?) Karn. (perhaps from *ságu*, to cultivate) A deed under which land is held: a lease, especially one for a stipulated term, and conditioning relinquishment at the end of it.

SAHAJOG, or SAHAYOG, Beng. (সহজোগ) Joint execution of a deed or engagement.

Sáïl-síúm, H. (P. سيوم, third) A third party to a suit.

Sáïr-mahál, H. (ساير محال) An extra head of impost, especially one still allowed in some places, such as rents of stalls or standings in a bazár, imposed by the owner of the ground.

SAJJI: also, the alkaline produce of a plant (Coroxylon Griffithii) obtained from its ashes when burnt: three qualities are distinguished, *Choa-sajji*, the purest; *Hátha-sajji*, the next; and *Khára-sajji*, the most impure: all three are varieties of the barilla or soda of commerce.

Ṣákhá-ki-ṣákhá, H. Branch after branch, a genealogical descent of a family conveying hereditary claims.

Ṣaláhíyat-bahí, corruptly, *Ṣulahut-buhee*, H. (A. صلاحيت بهي) A memorandum-book or diary kept by a native officer of police or revenue.

Sál-mahájani, H. (from مهاجن, a merchant) The mercantile year: a mode of reckoning peculiar to merchants and traders in Bengal, concurrent with the *Samvat* year, but commencing seven months earlier.

SAMBA should be SAMBÁ, incorrectly, SUMBAH: it is also applied to any rice-crop reaped between January and July.

Samudayam: also occurs to mean the office of superintendant of a temple.

SANGALI, (?) Tam. A land measure.

SANGIRAV, vulgarly, SANGIRO, Guz. (સંગીરવ) A pledge for a loan, which may be left in the hands of the borrower and is only surrendered in case of his failure to pay the principal and interest of the loan.

SÁNT, incorrectly, SATHEE, Guz. (સાંત) A plough.

SANTÁL, vulgarly, SANTAL, SONTHÁL, (?) H. The name of a race of semi-barbarous people, settled as cultivators on the skirts of the Rájmahal hills.

SANTHELA, (?) Guz. Land resumed, but on which an allowance is charged in favour of the dispossessed holder.

Saranjám-paṭ, Mar. (पट, a register) A general account of all *Saranjám* grants under the Peshwa's government.

SARINGA, (?) Beng. A canoe made out of a single block of wood.

ṢÁSANAM: *Múla-ṣásanam*, Karn. (S. मूल, root) Primary or principal deeds: title deeds.

Sáswata ságubaḍi, corruptly, *Saswitha sagoopudee*, Tel. (శాశ్వత సాగుబడి) Right of perpetual cultivation, with exemption from the landlord's rent but liability to the government revenue.

SÁTHÍ, A coarse kind of rice.

SATTA: also, a contract or engagement to grow and supply indigo.

Satta-bahi, (?) H. A deed of transfer.

Saudápatra, corruptly, *Soudaputro*, *Sowdaputtur*: also, a bill of sale.

SAWÁDIU, (?) Guz. A tax levied upon irregularly alienated lands equivalent to one-third of the full assessment.

Sazáwal, also, corruptly, *Suzawool*, *Suzaool*, *Suzwal*.

SEGA, (?) Beng. Resumed rent-free land.—Sylhet.

SEJA, SENJA, Guz. (સેજ, સેંજ) Held in common, not in shares, land or a village.

SERA, SEERA, (?) H. Low land capable of being irrigated.

SETH : also, corruptly, *Shetee* : also, sometimes, the head man of a particular trade.

Sebáït : also, an assignment for religious purposes especially.

Sebátí : also, management of the lands attached to a temple or assigned in trust for religious purposes.

Sháhí : also termed *Khara-sháhí*, one *háni* of which is said to equal eight ordinary *hánis.*—Chittagong.

Sháhí-nal, Beng. The royal rod or measure, four or eight times the length of the ordinary measure.—Chittagong.

Shámilát-banjar : also, portions of a field within its area left uncultivated, chiefly where the field is very large.

Shámilát-dasabandham, Karn. A tenure in which a portion of the assessment on irrigated land is remitted in favour of the person by whom the reservoir whence the water is drawn was constructed.

Shara-barida, (?) H. Customary or stipulated rate.

Sharh-náma, H. (P. نامه) A statement of rates at which the cultivators agree to hold their lands.

Sharti-rukâa, H. (A. رقعة) A paper of agreement or acquittance.

SHEMERAYA, (?) Mal. Agent or representative of the religious teacher of the lower orders.

Shikami, *Dar-shikami*, H. Subordinate, as a tenure, or as a sharer under a *Shikami* tenure or sharer.

Shikami-sharík, H. (A. شريك, a partner) A partner who does not take an active share in the conduct of a joint concern, a sleeping partner.

Shikdár, *Sikdár*, Beng. (শিকদার) In Bengal the term has become a family designation, as *Rádhá-náth-Sikdár*.

SISTU, corruptly, CIST.

Sodhapatra, corruptly, *Sodahputtroh*, (শোধপত্র, from S. शुद्ध) A written agreement or acknowledgment, a receipt, a deed of acquittance.

SONA : or SUNA, SOONA.

SRÁDDHA, also, corruptly, ASRAD, SHRÁD.

STHALA, also, STALUM, STULLA.

Sthánika, *Sthánika*, *Sthánigár*, corruptly, *Stanegar*, Karn. (స్థానిక, స్థానీక, స్థానిగార) The head man or manager of a temple or other public establishment.

Sthánikam, corruptly, *Stanegum*, Karn. (స్థానికం) The office of superintendant or manager of a temple.

STHITA, vernacularly, STHIT, vulgarly, STEETH, H. (S. स्थित, lit. stood, stayed) An account of the regular receipts and disbursements of an estate.

Sthita-chauhaddi, H. Permanent or fixed boundary.

Strídhana, vulgarly, *Streedhun*.

Sukhavásí, also, corruptly, *Succawaskee*, *Soogavasi*, *Sukkahavasi.*

Sukhlambari, corruptly, *Sookhlumbree*, H. (from *Sukh*, and Eng. *lambar* for number) Granted rent-free to invalid native soldiers by the government—land, a village.

SÚKSAM-BANJAR, Tel: (for S. सूक्ष्म *súkshma*, small) A spot of inferior ground in a large field, left purposely uncultivated in order to obtain an abatement of rent or assessment of the field.

Swatantram : also, the share of each individual proprietor in the rent paid by tenant cultivators.

Swarnádáyam : also, in some places applied especially to the rent of garden or orchard land.

Swásthyam : also, the share in a village of which the government revenuc has been made over, either wholly or in part, to Brahmans.

T.

T'AHUT, see *Tâahud* : also, a subdivision of a village.

Táhud-jamá, Beng. Admitted or stipulated amount of rent or revenue.

ṬÁL, H. (ٹال, टाल) A stack of straw : a store or quantity of straw collected for sale.

Túladi also, sometimes land, the crop of which has been reaped.

Talab-brahmottara, corruptly, *Tullub-birmooter*, H. Land granted at a quit-rent for religious or charitable purposes.

TANGAL, Mal. (തങ്ങൾ) A Mohammadan or Mapilla priest.

Tannír-kárí, Tam. (தண்ணீர்க்காரி) A water-carrier, a female who brings water.

Tari-bágháyat, H. Garden or orchard ground irrigated from tanks, as opposed to *Khushhi-bágháyat*, or similar land watered from wells.

Taramdár, also sometimes styled *Sar-taramdár*.

Tarappadi, corruptly, *Tarapaddy*, *Turrabuddy* : it is also supposed to be the original account of the village lands, distinguishing the varieties of soil, produce, and tenure, and the ancient dues and perquisites of the village officers and servants.

ṬARÍKA-TAHSÍL, H. (from A. طريقة, a way) Statement of arrangements for the collection of the revenue in a village or estate, and its general financial result.

TARKÍB-DIHI, H. (تركيب دهي, from *tarkíb*, fashion, and

dihí, giving) A cunning or knowing trick, an artful contrivance or evasion.

TARWÁ, (?) H. A small drain.

Tas̤arruf: it sometimes implies unlawful appropriation, as, *Tahwíl-tas̤arruf*, embezzlement of cash balances.

Tas̤arrufát, corruptly, *Tusrufat*, H. (تصرفات) Mesne profits.

Tas̤ríh-paṭṭidárí, H. (تصريح پٹيداري) A record or statement of the shares of a village and the rights of the sharers.

Taufír: also, to any addition to the originally recorded lands of an estate.

Taújih-náma, H. A deed of record or registry of occupation of land granted either by the collector or by the Zamíndár to the occupants.

TADAL-PUNJAI: or a patch of land above the level of the surrounding rice fields, but capable of bearing a similar crop.

TEṈ, Tam. (தென்) Southerly.

Terku, Tam. (தெற்கு) The south.

Terkattiyán, Tam. (தெற்கத்தியான்) A native of the south.

Teṉgalai, Tam. (தெங்கலை) A branch of the Vaishnavas, the southern, as distinct from the northern branch, or *Vadagalai*: the two are irreconcileably hostile, although separated by no material difference of worship or doctrine.

Thiká: also, an assignment, an order upon a renter or farmer to pay his rent, wholly or in part, to a third person.

Thíká-peshgí: or rather, a lease or farm upon which a sum of money has been paid in advance to be afterwards set off against the rent.

ṬHEVANÁTÍ, or ṬHEVANI, (తేవణాటి, తేవణి).

TÍÄ, TEEAH, (?) H. A boundary mark.

Tíä-bandí, H. Settling a boundary.

TÍRIJ, also TERIJ: also, a register of official documents in the collector's office.

TÍRTHA: and laxly extended to the person performing the office: an officiating prieet; one receiving the offerings made to the idol.

Tírtham, corruptly, *Teerthum*, Karn. An officiating priest in a temple, under the head man or manager.

Tirthaprásáda, S. Food or water from a holy stream offered to an idol.

Ṭolah: also, a petty tax on articles exposed for sale in a *háth* or temporary market, levied by the proprietor of the ground.

TOND, (?) H. A measure of land, less than a *Jáü*.

TRIKÚT, corruptly, TIKUT, TEEKOOT, Hindi (त्रिकूत) A third share of the crop.

Tulárjulu: also, survey, measurement.

TUNTA, (?) Tel. An apartment, a division of a house: the same as *Ankanam*.

U.

UDAVÁRAM, corruptly, WOODAWARUM: it also applies to a fixed, estimated, or average amount of gross grain produce.

UDIKI, vulgarly, WUDIKI, (?) Karn. Marrying a widow, as allowed in some of the inferior castes.

Uḻuku, also, *Uḻugu*, vulgarly, *Ooloogoo*.

UPANAYANA, also, barbarously, OOBONOYANUM.

URÁNMÁ: it occurs most frequently URAIMÁ, or OORAIMAH.

UYI-MURI, (?) Mal. A deed of relinquishment: see *Muri*.

V.

VAḌA, Tam. (வட) North, northern.

Vaḍakku, Tam. (வடக்கு) The north, the north country.

Vaḍakkattiyán, Tam. (வடக்கத்தியான்) An inhabitant of the north.

Vadagaly, properly, *Vadagalai*, Tam. The northern Vaishnavas, a sect opposed to the *Tengalai*, or Vaishnavas of the south, q. v.

Váratundu: or the deduction may be added to the share of the proprietor.

Vellavási, (?) Tam. Rate of assessment according to the market price of grain.

VET-KÁNAM, more correctly, VETTU-KÁNAM: also, a lease on favourable terms on condition of clearing and bringing waste land into cultivation.

Vishu-sankramanam, or *Vishu-sankránti*, S. &c. (संक्रमण, संक्रान्ति, arriving at) The sun's entrance into either of the equinoctial signs.

W.

WOLI, Tel. A marriage present, a dower: see *Oli*.

Wujuhát-parwána, H. (پروانه, an order) An order or authority from a Zamíndár to his Ryots to pay their rents, or other collections, to his agent or representative.

Z.

ZAIL, corruptly, ZEYL: it was especially applied to a specification of the different rates in which the rent was to be paid, whether in money or in kind, by the Ryot, annexed to the *Paṭṭa* granted by the Zamíndár.

Zamin-karsa, (?) Beng. Land held under a particular tenure. —Bakhargang.

INDEX.

B.

C

D

G

I

J

K.

L.

N.

S.

T.

V.